HOW MARRIAGE BECAME ONE OF THE SACRAMENTS

Among the contributions of the medieval church to western culture was the idea that marriage was one of the seven sacraments, which defined the role of married folk in the church. Although the idea had ancient roots, this new way of regarding marriage raised many problems, to which scholastic theologians applied all their ingenuity. By the late Middle Ages, the doctrine was fully established in Christian thought and practice but not yet as dogma. In the sixteenth century, with the entire Catholic teaching on marriage and celibacy and its associated law and jurisdiction under attack by the Protestant reformers, the Council of Trent defined the doctrine as a dogma of faith for the first time but made major changes to it. Rather than focusing on a particular aspect of these intellectual and institutional developments, this book examines them in depth and in detail from their ancient precedents to the Council of Trent.

PHILIP L. REYNOLDS has taught at Emory University, Atlanta since 1992, where he is Aquinas Professor of Historical Theology. He is also a senior fellow of Emory's Center for the Study of Law and Religion, and he directed CSLR's five-year project on The Pursuit of Happiness (2006–2011).

CAMBRIDGE STUDIES IN LAW AND CHRISTIANITY

The Law and Christianity series publishes cutting-edge work on Catholic, Protestant, and Orthodox Christian contributions to public, private, penal, and procedural law and legal theory. The series aims to promote deep Christian reflection by leading scholars on the fundamentals of law and politics, to build further ecumenical legal understanding across Christian denominations, and to link and amplify the diverse and sometimes isolated Christian legal voices and visions at work in the academy. Works collected by the series include groundbreaking monographs, historical and thematic anthologies, and translations by leading scholars around the globe.

Volumes in the Series:

How Marriage Became One of the Sacraments

THE SACRAMENTAL THEOLOGY OF MARRIAGE FROM ITS MEDIEVAL ORIGINS TO THE COUNCIL OF TRENT

PHILIP L. REYNOLDS

CAMBRIDGE
UNIVERSITY PRESS

CAMBRIDGE
UNIVERSITY PRESS

University Printing House, Cambridge CB2 8BS, United Kingdom

Cambridge University Press is part of the University of Cambridge.

It furthers the University's mission by disseminating knowledge in the pursuit of
education, learning and research at the highest international levels of excellence.

www.cambridge.org
Information on this title: www.cambridge.org/9781107146150

© Philip L. Reynolds 2016

First published 2016

A catalogue record for this publication is available from the British Library

Library of Congress Cataloguing in Publication data
Reynolds, Philip Lyndon, 1950–
How marriage became one of the sacraments : the sacramental theology of marriage from
its medieval origins to the Council of Trent / by Philip L. Reynolds.
pages cm
Includes bibliographical references and index.
ISBN 978-1-107-14615-0 (Hardback : alk. paper)
1. Marriage–History of doctrines–Middle Ages, 600-1500.   2. Sacraments–History of
doctrines–Middle Ages, 600-1500.   3. Council of Trent (1545–1563 : Trento, Italy)   I. Title.
BT706.R49 2015
234'.16509–dc23   2015032527

ISBN 978-1-107-14615-0 Hardback

Contents

12.2.3 The ontology of marriage   495

12.2.4 Marriage and nature   503

     12.2.4.1 William of Auxerre on monogamy in the Natural Law   504

     12.2.4.2 William of Auvergne: Marriage as the natural convergence of the sexes   506

     12.2.4.3 Marriage as a divinely instituted union   511

13 Scholastic sexual ethics   515

13.1 The basis in Augustine   516

13.2 The ends of sexual intercourse   520

13.3 The pleasure problem   531

     13.3.1 Historical background to the problem   531

     13.3.2 Robert Courson's moral particles   534

     13.3.3 William of Auxerre's divided-self theory   536

     13.3.4 William of Auvergne's moral exchange theory   540

     13.3.5 Sexual pleasure in Eden   543

13.4 *Excusatio coitus*   545

14 Marriage as a sacrament   556

14.1 The theological task   556

14.2 Marriage as a sacred sign   559

14.3 The privilege of religion   561

     14.3.1 The double analogy rationale   562

     14.3.2 The spiritual death rationale   569

     14.3.3 Formal explanations   572

14.4 The sacrament of marriage and the good of sacrament   574

14.5 Institutions and sacred history   578

14.6 Marriage as one of the seven sacraments   588

     14.6.1 The parsing of marriage   588

         14.6.1.1 Form and matter   588

         14.6.1.2 Tripartite analysis   589

     14.6.2 Objections and solutions   592

14.7 Clandestine marriage   599

14.8 Voices of dissent: Olivi and Durandus   605

     14.8.1 Univocity, equivocity, and semantic zones   605

     14.8.2 Peter John Olivi   608

     14.8.3 Durandus of Saint-Pourçain   617

     14.8.4 Paludanus's refutation of Durandus   621

15 The question of grace   623

15.1 The preventive model   623

15.2 The discourse on sacramental efficacy   628

Plates

Abbreviations

abbr.	abbreviation, or abbreviated as
arg. 1c [etc.]	The first of the contrary arguments in a scholastic article. (Contrary arguments are those which appear in the second place, after the arguments for the initial thesis, regardless of which set represents the position that the author defends in his response.)
ASD	*Opera Omnia Desiderii Erasmi*. Amsterdam edition. Leiden, 1969–.
ADHLMA	*Archives d'histoire doctrinale et littéraire du moyen âge*
BA	Bibliothèque Augustinienne, Oeuvres de Saint Augustin. Paris, 1949–
BMCL	*Bulletin of Medieval Canon Law*
BGPh(Th)MA	*Beiträge zur Geschichte der Philosophie (und Theologie) des Mittelalters*
Brev.	*Breviarium Alaricanum*, = *Lex Romana Visigothorum*, ed. Hänel (1848)
CCL	*Corpus Christianorum. Series latina*
CCM	*Corpus Christianorum. Continuatio medievalis*
CIC	*Corpus Iuris Canonici*, ed. E. Friedberg, 2 vols (Leipzig, 1881)
CJ	*Codex Iustinianus* [2nd ed. 534]
1 *Comp.* (etc.)	*Compilatio prima* (etc.), in *Quinque compilationes antiquae*, ed. E. Friedberg.
CSEL	*Corpus Scriptorum Ecclesiasticorum Latinorum*
CT	*Concilium Tridentinum: Diariorum, actorum, epistularum, tractatuum nova collectio*, edidit Societas Goerresiana Promovendis inter Germanos Catholicos Litterarum Studiis (Friburgi Brisgoviae 1901–2001)
CTh	*Codex Theodosianus*
DDC	*Dictionnaire de droit canonique*

Dig.	*Digesta Iustiniani*
DS	Denzinger-Schönmetzer, *Enchiridion Symbolurum, Definitionum et Declarationum*
ed.	"edited by," "edition," or "editor," as appropriate in context.
Esmein-	A. Esmein, *Le mariage en droit canonique,* 2nd edition, ed.
Genestal	R. Génestal and J. Dauvillier, 2 vols (Paris, 1929, 1935)
Gaius, *Instit.*	*Gai Institutiones iuris civilis comentarii quatuor*
Inst.	*Iustiniani Institutiones*
IPH 1 [etc.]	Patristic sentences of the *In primis hominibus,* as enumerated by Matecki
JL	Refers to the numeration of decretals in Jaffé-Loewenfeld, *Regesta pontificum romanorum ab condita ecclesia ad annum post Christum natum MCXCVIII.*
LB	*Desiderii Erasmi Roterodami Opera omnia,* ed. J. Leclerc (Leyden, 1703–1706)
Le Bras, "Mariage"	G. Le Bras, "Mariage. La doctrine du mariage chez les théologiens et les canonistes depuis l'an mille," DDC 9.2, 2123–2317.
Lottin, PsM V	O. Lottin, *Psychologie et morale aux XIIe et XIIIe siècles,* vol. 5
LP 1 [etc.]	*Sententiae* of the *Liber Pancrisis* enumerated according to MS British Library, Harley 3098. See Giraud, *Per verba magistri,* 503–51.
MGH	*Monumenta Germaniae Historica*
MWCh	Philip L. Reynolds, *Marriage in the Western Church* (Leiden, 1994)
Nov.	*Novellae Iustiniani*
Mansi	J.-D. Mansi (ed.), *Sacrorum Conciliorum Nova et Amplissima Collectio*
NE	*Nicomachean Ethics* (Aristotle)
NF 1 [etc.]	The enumeration of *sententiae* in Lottin, "Nouveaux fragments théologiques," RThAM 11–14 (1939–1947)
Paulus, *Sent.*	*Sententiae Pauli*
PG	*Patrologia Graeca,* ed. J.-P. Migne
PL	*Patrologia Latina,* ed. J.-P. Migne
PM 1 [etc.]	The enumeration of *sententiae* in Lottin, PsM V
RDC	*Revue de droit canonique*
repr.	Reprinted, or reproduced
RThAM	*Recherches de théologie ancienne et medieval*
RThPhM	*Recherches de théologie et philosophie médiévales*
s.c.	*sed contra*
SC	Sources Chrétiennes. Les Éditions du Cerf, Paris

SMA 1 [etc.]	*Sententiae Magistri A.: De matrimonio,* as enumerated in Reinhardt's edition
Tanner-Alberigo	*Decrees of the Ecumenical Councils* (London, 1990)
THTH	Philip L. Reynolds and John Witte, Jr. (eds), *To Have and to Hold* (Cambridge University Press, 2007)
un.	*unicus* (as in *articulus unicus, quaestio unica,* etc.)
WA	*D. Martin Luthers Werke: kritische Gesammtausgabe* [Weimarer Ausgabe], *Schriften.* Weimar, 1883–1948.
WH	Refers to the numeration of decretals in the *Walther-Holtzmann-Kartei* index.
X	*Liber extra,* = *Decretales Gregorii IX.* In Friedberg, *Corpus Iuris Canonici,* vol. 2
Citations	3:3/3 = vol. 3, p. 3 (or col. 3), line 3. Lines are enumerated from the top of the text on each page unless the edition provides its own enumeration.

Preface and acknowledgments

This book is my contribution to a project on Sex, Marriage, and Family and the Religions of the Book, organized by the Center for the Study of Law and Religion (CSLR) at Emory University in Atlanta. The project ran from 2001 through 2007, with regular meetings among the senior fellows through 2003. I am very grateful to the late Don S. Browning and to John Witte, Jr., who co-directed the project, as well as to The Pew Charitable Trusts, which funded it.

I have endeavored to explain herein how marriage came to be regarded as one of the seven sacraments. It is well known that this doctrine, like the universities and much of due process in our courts of law, was one of the medieval church's contributions to western culture. It is equally well known that the doctrine was first defined as a dogma of faith at the Council of Trent in 1563, which defended it against the Protestant reformers. Its origins were in the early twelfth century, and the core of the doctrine was complete by the middle of the thirteenth. This history is well documented, although until now a minimal reading list covering it adequately would have to include literature of varying quality in several languages, most of it now showing its age. But this literature would tell us only who said what and when, what were the arguments and counterarguments, the rival theories, and so forth.

I realized even before I started writing the book in 2003 that it would have to be very long. I would have to revisit all the ground that had already been covered in the extensive secondary literature on the topic, amplifying, updating, and adding to it. But I wanted to do more than that: to take a broader, more distanced, and more searching view. I try to explain what was new when the doctrine emerged, and to distinguish that from what was received and traditional. I try to show *why* theologians, canonists, and other clerics argued as they did, for they often used forms of argument that would convince few if any today. What were their presuppositions? What difference did the doctrine make? Why did it matter? What was at stake?

Moreover, the doctrine was largely the work of scholastic theologians, no two of whom agreed about this or any other subject at every point. Their arguments and counterarguments about marriage as a sacrament were extremely intricate. Only a small part of any theologian's treatment of marriage in a commentary on Peter Lombard's *Sentences* or in a *summa* of theology was devoted to the sacramentality of marriage, but the topic elicited enormous invention and ingenuity, partly because marriage did not fit the sacramental paradigm easily. In several salient respects, marriage did not *look* like a sacrament. Furthermore, scholastic theologians were intellectuals who thoroughly enjoyed their work and relished problems in need of solution. That a certain master had said one thing was often sufficient reason for another to say something different, especially when no established dogma was at stake and there was no risk of heresy. For example, the schoolmen assumed that each sacrament had an essence composed of form and matter. In the case of baptism, the form was the formula of blessing spoken by the minister, whereas the matter was the ritual ablution with water. But what were the matter and the form of marriage? The question was not dangerous. Any professional theologian could come up with plausible candidates and defend them adequately. There was no need to fear that marriage would be shown not to be a sacrament because it did not have an essence composed of form and matter. But extending the hylomorphic analysis from paradigmatic sacraments such as baptism and eucharist to marriage was a stretch. Theologians delighted in coming up with their own personal solutions to such problems.

The dimensions of the project expanded as I worked on it, largely because the chronological scope of project extended both backwards and forwards. I had originally planned to begin in the early twelfth century, when the doctrine originated, and to finish with Thomas Aquinas, in whose work it arguably reached its full development. But the origination of the doctrine involved a new reception of Augustine. Theologians during the early twelfth century gathered hitherto little used material from Augustine on marriage from florilegia, sometimes assembling it in ways that he could not have anticipated. I had intended to refer readers in this book to what I had written on marriage in Augustine in an earlier book,[1] but I found that I was not entirely satisfied with the earlier treatment, and I decided to make a fresh start. This book includes, therefore, three preliminary chapters on Augustine (Chapters 2–4), in which I try to establish what Augustine himself meant by what he said about marriage, as distinct from what twelfth-century theologians creatively made out of his statements and opinions on the topic. Again, the origins of the sacramental doctrine presupposed conceptions of marrying that differed from those prevailing in the early Middle Ages, and one needs to construe that emergence as part of an effort on the part of bishops and clerics to take control over how people married; to enforce the rules and regulations. Both of these considerations require attention to traditional structures and presuppositions: the nuptial process, marital consent, and consummation. Here, too, I had planned to refer to my earlier book but decided on reflection to make a fresh start, recounting the historical background of marital

---

[1] *Marriage in the Western Church* (Leiden, 1994).

consent and consummation, the ambiguities that these traditions presented to churchmen, and the competing solutions to such ambiguities that evolved during the late eleventh and the twelfth centuries (Chapters 5–7).

The study also extended forward to the sixteenth century. I could not find a natural boundary during the central Middle Ages. The theology of marriage continued to evolve through the fourteenth century. It is true that some famous theologians of that era, working in the ingenious but crabbed spirit of late-medieval scholasticism, were so preoccupied with narrowly philosophical and epistemological problems that they chose to ignore marriage and the other sacraments. At the same time, many four-teenth-century theologians ceased to cover the canonical rules and regulations of marriage, partly because there was little there that was problematic or controversial, and partly because the disciplines of theology and canon law had grown apart. Nevertheless, a few major theologians continued to provide new solutions to old problems in the sacramental theology of marriage. In particular, the objections of Durandus of Pourçain (d. 1334) to the sacramentality of marriage elicited new solutions and counterarguments (Section 14.8). Each new contribution sheds fresh light today on the preceding treatments. Although not much happened in the theology of marriage during the fifteenth century, I could not find any medieval end point that would have seemed more than arbitrary. Eventually, I realized that the first natural boundary was the Council of Trent. That, too, sheds new light on marriage in medieval scholastic theology and canon law during the previous centur-ies. To treat Trent adequately, however, I had to examine Protestant critique, the Catholic response to that critique during the first half of the sixteenth century, and the proceedings on marriage not only at Trent in 1563 but also at Bologna in 1547, where the council's deliberations on marriage began. The last four chapters of the book (Chapters 17–20) are devoted to these sixteenth-century developments.

There was another reason for the project's growth. Thoroughness breeds thor-oughness. Subjects that I might have mentioned only *en passant* in a succinct study called for a full discussion in a study on this scale. For example, Vacarius's theory of marrying as a form of *traditio* (Section 7.5), while interesting from the perspective of legal theory, contributed little to the story of how marriage became a sacrament. In a brief study of that topic, therefore, I might have mentioned Vacarius's theory only in passing, as a historical curiosity. But that omission would have been inappropriate and even unforgivable when I cover much else extensively.

Realizing that I could not expect many interested readers to read a book com-posed on this scale sequentially from cover to cover, I endeavored to make it as accessible and as useful as possible by dividing and subdividing each chapter into numbered sections, which are identified in the table of contents. I include cross-references to these sections parenthetically in the main text.

Because the table of contents reveals the scope and organization of the book fully and clearly, an introductory chapter-by-chapter synopsis would have been redun-dant. Instead, the first chapter is an essay that provides the reader with an overview of the entire study. I do not claim to have said everything worth saying on my subject – far from it – but I believe that I have provided a treatment that will serve as a point of reference for other related or more detailed studies, whether they are historical or theological.

A note on my policies of translation: English translations of patristic and medieval Latin texts are my own unless otherwise stated. I provide the Latin original for a passage that I have translated only if its wording is remarkable, problematic, or discussed in the main text, or if the source is not readily available in a printed edition. Many early printed editions of scholastic works that were virtually inaccessible twenty years ago are now readily available through online services such as Google Books and Hathi Trust Digital Library.

I have based English quotations of the Bible sometimes on the Douai-Rheims version but more often on the King James Bible. The former was a faithful, rather literal translation of the Vulgate. Although the translators and editors of the King James Bible consulted the Hebrew and Greek sources available to them, this was in effect a revised version of the Douai-Rheims, incorporating many of its idiomatic solutions (a debt that is rarely acknowledged). As a result, the King James Version remains remarkably close to the Vulgate. Moreover, like the works of William Shakespeare, it still has the advantage of cultural familiarity among English-speaking readers, for the influence of its phrases and idioms on our usage is pervasive. When quoting from the Douai-Rheims or King James version, however, I have sometimes modernized obsolete idioms that would have been pointlessly obscure or distracting to the modern reader. Moreover, I have modified these sources without notice to convey as closely as possible the sense of the Vulgate *as it was understood and interpreted by the authors whom I am discussing.* Quotations of the same verses of the Bible in English, therefore, are not always consistent throughout the book.

The section on Pedro Guerrero's treatise on clandestine marriage in Chapter 20 has been published (with minor variations) in Troy L. Harris, *Studies in Canon Law and Common Law in Honor of R. H. Helmholz*, copyright 2015 by the Regents of the University of California, The Robbins Religious and Civil Law Collection, School of Law, University of California at Berkeley.

I am deeply grateful to Dr Line Cecilie Engh, who convened a workshop on medieval marriage symbolism at the Norwegian Institute in Rome in June, 2014, and summoned me to it. The meeting caused me to rethink and revise my treatment of marriage as sacred signifier in the first chapter. After working in the field for some thirty years, I still find the logic, argument, and semiotics of signs in the medieval theology of marriage both baffling and fascinating. The work of the Rome project that Line inaugurated is still unfolding.

I have received practical help and advice from many established scholars, graduate students, librarians, and archivists in the course of writing this book. They are too numerous to name, and a short list might offend those whom I failed to mention. I shall limit myself, therefore, to a few words of special thanks to three colleagues who were personally involved in the project. I am very grateful to Severin Kitanov, who is now a professor of philosophy at Salem State University, and to Sarah Bogue. Severin, whom I first met while teaching in Helsinki, helped me with bibliographical research at an early stage of the project, when he was a visiting doctoral student at Emory University. Sarah, who is currently writing her dissertation on Hrostvit of Gandersheim at Emory, read all of the chapters in draft, alerting me to corrigenda and pointing out places where the sense was unclear. Finally, I must acknowledge a huge debt to my colleague John Witte, Jr., director of Emory's Center for the Study of Law and Religion, of which I am privileged to be a senior fellow. John not only encouraged me to write the book but also discouraged me from abandoning the project at moments when I was becoming daunted by its emerging scope. I am grateful to John, too, for his work as an intellectual leader at Emory University, where the CSLR under his direction fosters free and diverse but disciplined and informed inquiry into law and religion.

1

Marriage as a sacrament

How did marriage come to be regarded as one of the sacraments? The doctrine was not defined as a dogma of faith until 1563, when the Council of Trent declared that marriage was properly one of the seven sacraments of the New Law and spelled out the implications of the dogma. Criticism of the doctrine by Luther and others had made it seem an indispensible pillar of Catholic teaching. Any narrative that follows the development of something over a long duration presupposes an end point – although the historian must try to regard each stage as if nothing came next, since at that time the future did not yet exist – and the end point for this monograph is the Council of Trent.

When did the doctrine emerge? By the sixteenth century, it was already well established in Catholic theology and practice. Tracing the development of the doctrine retrospectively, one reaches its origins during the first half of the twelfth century, and the trail peters out around 1100. The emergence involved two surges of constructive theology: one during the first half of the twelfth century, and another during the first half of the thirteenth. But belief that marriage was a holy estate, a Christian vocation, and a way of participating in the life of the church was ancient. What was new was the decision on the part of churchmen to account for that holiness by construing marriage as one of the sacraments of the New Law. This decision was not a sudden event but a complicated development of thought, practice, and imagination that took place over a period of more than a century.

Two major shifts in perspective resulted from that decision. First, marriage as a sacrament was primarily the transient act of marrying rather than the enduring condition of being married. Hitherto, theologians and moralists had focused on the married estate. But now, just as the sacrament of baptism was the rite that took place at the church font and not the resulting baptismal character, so the sacrament of marriage was the couple's exchange of mutual consent, which ideally took place in a church. Second, the doctrine entailed a new use of Scripture.

The "great sacrament" of Ephesians 5:32 became identified with marriage, which theologians now characterized as the "sacrament of Christ and the church." Exegetes from the patristic period until the late eleventh century, on the contrary, had identified St Paul's *sacramentum magnum* either with the union between Christ and the church or with Genesis 2:24, construed as a prophecy. St Paul's discourse on marriage in Ephesians (Eph 5:22–33) became the chief biblical authority on the holiness of marriage in theology – albeit not in the nuptial liturgy, which remained untouched by theological developments for several more centuries. Use of this discourse to illuminate marriage was rare before 1100, as was the notion that literal, human marriage – the institution in reality rather than figurative marriage – should be interpreted as representing Christ's union with the church. A handful of patristic and early-medieval texts comparing marriage to Christ's union with the church and alluding obliquely to Ephesians 5:32 became crucial in theology and canon law during the central Middle Ages, when they were frequently quoted, misquoted, and analyzed. That use has tended to disguise the rarity of the comparison before 1100, when churchmen often regarded the church as the bride of Christ but rarely regarded literal, mundane marriage in that light.

1.1 THE DEVELOPMENT IN RETROSPECT

On March 3, 1547, at Session VII, the Council of Trent declared that there were seven sacraments of the New Law: baptism, confirmation, eucharist, penance, extreme unction, orders, and marriage (Section 18.2.1). The first of the canons on the sacraments in general anathematizes anyone who says that these were not all instituted by Jesus Christ, or that there are more or less than seven, or that any of them is not "truly and properly" (*vere et proprie*) a sacrament.[1] These sacraments are collectively necessary for salvation, for "faith in the divine promise" does not suffice. Each sacrament contains a grace that it signifies, conferring it *ex opere operato* on any recipient who puts no obstacle in its way.[2] The seven sacraments differ fundamentally from the sacraments of the Old Law, therefore, and not only in respect of ceremonies and external rituals.[3] Marriage was no exception.

The general dogma implied that the seven sacraments constituted a closed genus, of which each member was a species. Unlike good things, for example, or sacred signs, the sacraments were countable, and each member was fully

---

[1] Session VII (March 3, 1547), *Canones de sacramentis in genere*, canon 1 (Tanner-Alberigo 684).
[2] Ibid., canons 4, 6, 8 (684, 685). To say that a sacrament confers grace *ex opere operato* was to say that the recipient would receive the grace by virtue of receiving the sacrament (rather than as a result of any personal work or effort or pre-existing grace), provided that he or she did not present an obstacle to grace, such as a wrong intention in receiving the sacrament or a mortal sin.
[3] Ibid., canons 5 and 2.

individuated. Their number was fixed and rather small, like that of the primary colors. The historical category of sacraments of the New Law was coextensive with the ontological category of sacraments properly so called, or sacraments in the strictest sense. These shared a common essence, which could be predicated univocally of all seven sacraments. The common definition defined the genus, whereas each sacrament had its specific differences and other salient properties. Any theologically literate reader would have understood what that generic essence was. These were by definition sacred signs that conferred graces that they signified. In other words, they were efficacious sacred signs, or saving signs. Each sacrament conferred its own specific and unique grace, and all the sacramental graces flowed or ramified from the Passion of Jesus Christ (Plate 2). Together, they made up a complete system, providing all the sacramental graces that were necessary for salvation.

The council went on to publish specific doctrines on each of the seven sacraments in turn, treating them in the standard order (as listed earlier) and coming at last to marriage.[4] The decrees on the sacrament of marriage were published on November 11, 1563, at Session XXIV (Section 18.5). The first of several dogmatic canons on marriage confirmed the particular implications of the dogma of the sacraments in general. Marriage is not something "invented in the church by human beings," as Luther claimed. Rather, it is "truly and properly [*vere et proprie*] one of the seven sacraments of the evangelical law," it was instituted by Jesus Christ, and it confers grace.[5]

The preface to Trent's decrees on marriage explains the role of this sacrament in the economy and history of salvation. Adam, inspired by the Holy Spirit, said: "This is now bone of my bones, and flesh of my flesh. For this reason a man shall leave his father and mother and shall cleave unto his wife, and they shall be two in one flesh" (Gen 2:23–24). Adam implied that marriage was an indissoluble bond. Jesus Christ was referring to Adam's dictum when he said, "they are no longer two but one flesh," adding: "What God has joined, therefore, let not man separate" (Matt 19:4–6, Mark 10:6–9). But marriage is also a sacrament of the New Law. Jesus Christ, who instituted and perfected the seven sacraments, merited through his Passion a grace that would perfect the natural love in marriage, confirm the indissolubility of the union, and sanctify the spouses (see Plates 2–3). St Paul implied all this when he said that husbands should love their wives as Christ loved the church (Eph 5:25), and that marriage was a great sacrament in Christ and the church (Eph 5:32). Through this grace, Christ raised

[4] Baptism and confirmation: Session VII (March 3, 1547). Eucharist: Session XIII (Oct. 11, 1551). Penance and extreme unction: Session XIV (Nov. 25, 1551). Orders: Session XXIII (July 15, 1563).

[5] Canon 1 (Tanner-Alberigo 754/25–27): "Si quis dixerit, matrimonium non esse vere et proprie unum ex septem legis evangelicae sacramentis, a Christo domino institutum, sed ab hominibus in ecclesia inventum, neque gratiam conferre: a[nathema] s[it]."

marriage above what it had been under the Old Law, so that it was henceforth one of the sacraments of the New Law, as "our holy fathers, the councils, and the universal tradition of the church have always taught." But recently, the decree continues, diabolical errors have beset the church. The Protestant heretics have rejected the church's teaching on this and other sacraments. "Introducing the freedom of the flesh under the pretext of the Gospel as is their wont," the Protestants have "asserted in writing and in speech many things that are alien to the mind of the Catholic church and to custom proven since apostolic times, and not without doing great damage to Christ's faithful."[6] This last admonition alluded to the Protestant attack on priestly and institutionalized celibacy, but in the eyes of the prelates at Trent, as well as of the Protestants, the sacramentality of marriage and the superiority of celibacy went hand in hand and were aspects of a single ideology.

The canons did not identify the specific grace that the seventh sacrament conferred, but anyone familiar with Catholic theology of the period or with the proceedings at the council would have recognized this grace in the reference to Ephesians 5:25. Marriage chiefly signified the union between Christ and the church (Eph 5:32). In an obvious sense, the marriage of any couple was not the cause of that union. Nevertheless, the love between husband and wife could not sufficiently emulate the love between Christ and the church, as Ephesians 5:25 required, without grace. The dual citation of Ephesians 5:25 with 5:32 was an answer to the criticisms of Erasmus and Luther, who had pointed out that Ephesians 5:32 by itself was not proof that marriage was one of the sacraments. The prelates at Trent, like most sixteenth-century theologians, identified the sacramental grace of marriage with a supernatural, God-given enhancement of conjugal love that enabled the spouses to remain together until parted by death. This was the grace that "perfects that natural love" between the spouses. Christian spouses could not justly claim, therefore, that as mere human beings they were not strong enough to remain married for life.

The preface to Trent's canons on marriage seemed to imply that orthodox Christians had always recognized marriage to be "truly and properly" one of the seven sacraments of the New Law, but everyone knew that that was not the case. Most of the prelates conceded that in Peter Lombard's opinion marriage did *not* confer grace; and, according to the Lombard's own premises, that denial implied in turn that marriage was not properly one of the sacraments of the New Law. Even from the perspective of sixteenth-century observers, therefore, whose sense of history was much weaker than ours, the doctrine was less than four centuries old. If the doctrine indeed went back to the apostolic era, it must have existed then only implicitly and obscurely, beyond the awareness of councils, clerics, and theologians. No general council or pope before Trent had declared as a matter

---

[6] Tanner-Alberigo 753–54.

of dogma that there were "truly and properly" seven grace-conferring sacraments or that marriage was a sacrament in that sense, although the prelates at Trent could cite a series of official statements that seemed to confirm the dogma.

Regarded in retrospect, Peter Lombard's treatment of marriage was a definitive moment or milestone on the way to the doctrine defined at Trent (Section 11.4). One may look forwards from that vantage point to marriage in scholastic theology and eventually to marriage at the Council of Trent, and backwards to the Lombard's sources and to the origins of the idea. Writing in the 1150s, the Lombard began the last of his four books of *Sentences* by explaining what the sacraments were in general and distinguishing the sacraments of the New Law from those of the Old. The sacraments of the New Law were "baptism, confirmation, the bread of bene-diction (that is, eucharist), penance, extreme unction, orders, and marriage."[7] The Lombard did not say that these were the *only* sacraments of the New Law, but the composition of his treatise on the sacraments and its apparently comprehensive scope implied that there were no others. The list was still fairly new, for its first extant appearances date from the 1140s (Section 11.2). The Lombard listed the seven sacraments in what would become the standard order, and he went on to devote a treatise to each of the seven in turn. He took his material on marriage mainly from a few favorite sources written during the previous quarter of a century, chiefly Gratian, Walter of Mortagne, and Hugh of Saint-Victor. They had in turn drawn liberally on earlier twelfth-century sources, including florilegia. The Lombard harvested and compiled the results of an extraordinarily vibrant and creative period in sacramental theology, collecting and sorting his material on marriage in his usual manner, which was pedestrian but practical, serviceable, and astute: a marvelous tabulation of current thought.

The Lombard's division of theological topics as well as what he said about them would become fundamental after his *Sentences* became the standard textbook of theology in the 1220s. The master who pioneered of this use of the work was Alexander of Hales, an English member of the theology faculty in Paris (Section 15.3.1). The textbook became the subject of countless commentaries.[8] Masters of theology were free to disagree with Peter Lombard – the Parisian masters published lists of his mistakes during the thirteenth century – but his *Sentences* established the agenda for theological studies until the sixteenth century. From the 1220s until the sixteenth century, therefore, discussion of the sacrament of marriage would always be located within the framework that Peter Lombard had established: a setting that raised as many questions as it solved.

Peter Lombard wrote more about marriage than about any of the other six sacraments. The number of *distinctiones* devoted to each sacrament in Book IV suffices as a rough guide, although these units are not equal in length, and the

---

[7] Peter Lombard, *Sent.* IV, 2.1.1 (239).

[8] P. W. Rosemann, *The Story of a Great Medieval Book* (Peterborough, Ontario, 2007).

division was the work not of Peter Lombard but, again, of Alexander of Hales.[9]
Here is a conspectus of the treatment of the sacraments in Book IV, with the number
of distinctions devoted to each sacrament in parentheses:

Baptism: distinctions 2–6 (4.5)
Confirmation: distinction 7 (1)
Eucharist: distinctions 8–13 (6)
Penance: distinctions 14–22 (9)
Extreme unction: distinction 23 (1)
Orders: distinctions 24–25 (2)
Marriage: distinctions 26–42 (17)

This distribution does not mean that the Lombard found marriage to be more
important or more interesting than the other sacraments, or that he considered it to
be the most worthy, sacred, or sanctifying. Like most medieval theologians, he
considered marriage to be the least of the sacraments in intrinsic worth albeit
the greatest in what it signified. Marriage required so much space because of
all the rules and regulations that it entailed, such as those regarding the impediments.
Most of the Lombard's contributions to the sacramental theology of marriage occur
in the first two distinctions on the topic, whereas the remaining distinctions are
largely devoted to the canonical rules. Likewise, most of what medieval theologians
wrote about marriage in commentaries on the *Sentences* and in *summas* of theology
was devoted to the same rules and regulations. Discussion of them was largely
independent of properly theological premises, such as those regarding the saving
work of Christ. Following Peter Lombard's agenda, which had evolved during the
first half of the twelfth century, most scholastic theologians from the thirteenth
century throughout the Middle Ages treated marriage as the last of the seven
sacraments, beginning their treatment with an account of its definition, purpose,
sacred history, and sacramentality before proceeding to the canonical aspects.

Having listed the seven sacraments of the New Law, Peter Lombard divided them
into three sorts: those which "fortify us with grace and virtue," such as eucharist and
orders; those which "offer a remedy against sin and confer helping grace," such as
baptism; and those which work *only* as remedy, such as marriage.[10] But he had
already established that saving efficacy was what distinguished the sacraments of
the New Law from those of the Old. A sacrament in the proper sense of the term was
"a sign of the grace of God, and the appearance of an invisible grace, in such a way
that it bears its image and is its cause."[11] The sacrifices, offerings, and other rituals of

---

[9] Peter Lombard divided each book into a continuous series of chapters. Alexander of Hales
     seems to have been responsible for inserting the level of distinctions between books and
     chapters as an aid to teaching and commentary.
[10] *Sent.* IV, 2.1.1 (239–40).
[11] *Sent.* IV, 1.4.2 (233): "Sacramentum enim proprie dicitur, quod ita signum est gratiae Dei et
     invisibilis gratiae forma, ut ipsius imaginem gerat et causa exsistat."

the Old Law were sacraments in a broader sense of the term, but they were not sacraments in the proper sense because they had no supernatural efficacy. They promised and signified the future advent of Jesus Christ and its graces, but they did not confer grace.[12]

Peter Lombard's assumption that marriage, unlike the other six sacraments of the New Law, was merely remedial and conferred no gift of grace was conventional and remained virtually unquestioned until around 1220. Until then, theologians accepted what I call the "preventive model" (Sections 11.5.3 and 15.1). They assumed that marriage obviated sin without bestowing any positive gift. Whereas the other sacraments reformed the soul, bestowing grace and virtue and cleansing the soul from guilt, marriage only prevented the subject from committing sexual sins, chiefly by providing a licit setting in which to satisfy compulsive sexual desire. Theologians were not concerned about the apparent inconsistency. Those who noticed it solved it by pointing out that marriage had not been *instituted* under the New Law but in Eden. Institution implied innovation. Jesus Christ did not institute marriage but rather gave his approval (*approbatio*) to it.[13] In what sense, then, was marriage one of the seven sacraments of the New Law? Not in the sense that it was a member of a physical or ontological genus, sharing the salient features of the common essence. But marriage was at least analogous to the other six sacraments in certain respects, and, above all, it belonged among them in a *functional* sense: as a member of a collection of things that fulfilled a certain instrumental role in the life of the church, and that together constituted a system.

For reasons that are not obvious, theologians moved away from the preventive model after around 1220, and by the middle of the thirteenth century the consensus of the profession was that marriage conferred sanctifying grace *ex opere operato* (Section 15.3). Alexander of Hales was a pivotal figure at the beginning of this development. Canonists hardly noticed the development and continued to rehearse the old assumptions until well into the fourteenth century. The theologians' contention that marriage conferred its own specific sanctifying grace *ex opere operato* was part of a broad effort to assimilate marriage to the sacramental paradigm by showing that it exemplified all the essential and salient features of the genus. As Trent would later put it, marriage was "truly and properly" one of the sacraments of the New Law.

For many years after the formation of that theological consensus – at least a century – questions about the full sacramentality of marriage and about whether marriage conferred grace *ex opere operato* remained technical matters that were of concern only to professional theologians. Canonists, bishops who had no formal training in theology (always the majority), and parish priests considered marriage to be a sacrament of the church without taking that premise to its logical conclusions or trying to defend it against objections. Pious lay folk presumably regarded marriage

[12] *Sent.* IV, 1.6 (235–36). [13] For example, Peter of Poitiers, *Sent.* V, c. 14 (PL 211:1257D).

in the same light, for no one was instructing them differently. What mattered was that everyone understood the place of marriage in sacred history, in the hierarchical structure of the church, and in personal salvation, and that lay folk followed the rules and regulations of marrying. Bonaventure discussed the question of conjugal grace carefully in his commentary on Peter Lombard's *Sentences*,[14] composed in the 1250s (Section 15.3.4), but he did not raise it in the chapter on marriage in his *Breviloquium* (c. 1256), a compendium of theology that he wrote for his Franciscan students in Paris after completing his commentary.[15] Indeed, Bonaventure said nothing in the latter work about marriage that that could not have been written a century earlier, and nothing to show that marriage was a sacrament in the proper sense. Similarly, Guido of Monte Rochen said nothing about the sacramentality of marriage or about marriage as a means of sacramental grace in his handbook for parish clergy, composed in the 1330s. Guido explains at length how to marry, who can marry whom, and the impediments, but his explanation of the nature of marriage and its place in the Christian life is limited to a commonplace summary of the circumstances and reasons for its institution, the proper motives for marrying, and Augustine's three conjugal goods: faith, offspring, and indissolubility.[16]

There are early signs of change in the reaction against Peter John Olivi, O.F.M. (d. 1298). Olivi conceded that marriage was a sacrament in some sense, but he denied that it had full univocity (*plena univocatio*) with the other six sacraments, and he questioned whether marriage conferred sacramental grace. In 1283, a committee of Franciscan theologians commissioned by their Minister General to examine Olivi's orthodoxy found numerous serious errors in his work. Although his position on marriage was not among the issues that motivated this inquiry, it was the only one of his errors that the commission found to be potentially heretical. "Marriage is a sacrament of the New Law that confers grace," they countered. "To affirm the contrary is erroneous; to sustain the contrary is heretical; to doubt it is entirely forbidden" (Section 14.8.2). Nevertheless, another contrarian friar, Durandus of Pourçain, O.P. (d. 1334), could still claim with good reason that whether marriage conferred sanctifying grace was an open question, and not a settled dogma. Like Olivi, Durandus conceded that marriage was a sacrament in some sense while denying that it had full univocity with the sacraments of the New Law (Section 14.8.3). He cautiously declined to say whether or not marriage conferred grace, but he noted that the jurists held one position, and the theologians another (Section 15.3.8). Almost all "modern theologians" held that marriage conferred sanctifying grace *ex opere operato*, he conceded, but the jurists took the opposite position, which he tacitly favored:

> The jurists — who know the text of the decrees and decretals by which the position of the Roman church is expressed, and who have expounded and glossed the

---

[14] Bonaventure, *II Sent.* 26.2.2 (4:667–69). [15] Bonaventure, *Breviloquium* VI.13 (5:279–80).
[16] Guido of Monte Rochen, *Manipulus curatorum* 1.7.2 (Paris: 1501, fols 59r–72r).

canons and decretals, and some of whom have belonged to the College of
Cardinals of the Holy Roman Church — hold that grace is not conferred in the
sacrament of matrimony.[17]

Durandus was factually correct, but he erred if he implied that the jurists defended
their negative position in the same way as the theologians defended their own
affirmative position. The question of conjugal grace was still the preserve of professional theologians, and the canonists were still content to repeat what their predecessors had said about the matter during the twelfth and thirteenth centuries.

   The question of conjugal grace appeared in a very different light in the sixteenth
century, when Luther and his followers attacked the system of the seven sacraments
and the entire medieval doctrine and canon law of marriage, along with the
elaborate impediments and the preference for celibacy. In the minds of the prelates
at Trent, therefore, the univocity of the seven sacraments and the full sacramentality
of marriage were indispensible articles of faith. The critiques of Luther and
Erasmus prompted them, as they had been prompting Catholic theologians since
the 1520s, to propose new arguments and to revisit the basis of the doctrine in
Scripture.

   Sixteenth-century Catholic clerics and theologians insisted that the Bible had to
be interpreted in light of tradition, especially of the official pronouncements of
councils and popes. In their view, Luther's purported reliance on Scripture alone
was arrogant and foolhardy. Thus, they appealed not only to the work of the most
authoritative "scholastic doctors" of the central Middle Ages to defend the sacramentality of marriage, but also to a series of official declarations on the sacraments,
especially to Pope Lucius III's *Ad abolendam* (1184), to the profession of faith that
Pope Innocent III sent to the bishops of the Vaudois in 1208, to the *Profession of
Faith of Michael Palaeologus* from the Second Council of Lyon, convened by
Gregory X (1274), and, above all, to Pope Eugenius IV's *Bull of Union with
the Armenians*, from the Council of Florence (1439). But none of these declarations
about the sacraments in general and about marriage as a sacrament in particular
amounted to a formal definition of a dogma, and none of them affirmed or
even implied that marriage was a sacrament in the proper sense of the term.
Ad abolendam anathematized heretics who held opinions "other than what the
sacrosanct Roman church preaches and observes" regarding eucharist, baptism,
penance, marriage, and "the other ecclesiastical sacraments."[18] The profession of
faith that Pope Innocent III sent to the bishops of the Vaudois in 1208 was a standard
of orthodoxy for the Waldensians. As well as emphasizing the insolubility of
marriage and the right of widows to remarry, it required acceptance of the sacraments of baptism, confirmation, eucharist, penance, the anointing of the sick, and

---

[17] Durandus of Saint-Pourçain, *IV Sent.* 26.3, §6 (367v). Durandus describes the consensus
among theologians at ibid., §8.
[18] X 5.7.9, *Ad abolendam* (CIC 2:780–82).

marriage. (Priesthood, which was still not always counted among the sacraments at this time, is mentioned as a prerequisite for eucharist.)[19] *The Profession of Faith of Michael Palaeologus* (1274) was part of a summary of the Roman faith that Pope Clement IV had sent to Michael VIII, the emperor of Byzantium, in an effort to reunite the Roman and Byzantine branches of the church. It affirmed that "the Holy Roman church holds and teaches that there are seven ecclesiastical sacraments," namely, baptism, confirmation, penance, eucharist, orders, marriage, and extreme unction (in that order).[20] This was the first formal enumeration of the seven sacraments in an official declaration. Pope Eugenius' IV's *Bull of Union with the Armenians*, issued at the Council of Florence in 1439, incorporated a summary of the doctrine of the sacraments adapted from an exposition of the articles of faith and the sacraments by Thomas Aquinas.[21] The summary followed the plan established by Peter Lombard, beginning with an account of the sacraments in general before expounding each of the seven in turn. It is remarkable that this bull presented the doctrine of the seven sacraments as something that the Armenians would have to accept if they wanted to belong to the Roman church, but the bull said nothing specific about the sacramentality of marriage in the section on this sacrament in particular. What would later be cited as proof that marriage was a sacrament in the proper sense was in the bull's preliminary account of the sacraments in general. This affirms that whereas the sacraments of the Old Law only prefigured the grace that would be given through the Passion of Jesus Christ, the sacraments of the New Law not only signify but also contain and cause this grace, conferring it on those who receive the sacraments worthily. Furthermore, these sacraments result from the coming together of "things" (*res*), which serve as matter, and of words, which constitute the form, with "the person of a minister, who confers the sacrament with the intention of doing what the church does." No sacrament is complete, the bull adds, unless all three components are present: word, element, and minister.[22] But this affirmation proved to be problematic. Because virtually all theologians conceded that the priestly blessing was not essential to marriage, they had to explain how in this respect the bull did not imply what it seemed to imply.

If one traces the development further back beyond Peter Lombard, one comes first to his immediate sources, especially Hugh of Saint-Victor (Chapter 10), Walter of Mortagne (Section 11.3), and Gratian (Section 6.4), and thence to the anonymous treatises composed of "sentences" (*sententiae*) during the first quarter of the twelfth century (Chapters 8 and 9). For want of a better term, I refer to the authors of this

---

[19] DS 794.   [20] *Profession of Faith of Michael Palaeologus*, DS 860.
[21] *Bulla unionis Armenorum*, Tanner-Alberigo 534–59. Thomas Aquinas, *De articulis fidei et ecclesiae sacramentis*, in *Opera omnia*, Leonine edition 42:245–57.
[22] Tanner-Alberigo 542/1–8: "Haec omnia sacramenta tribus perficiuntur, videlicet rebus tanquam materia, verbis tanquam forma, et persona ministri conferentis sacramentum cum intentione faciendi, quod facit ecclesia. Quorum si aliquod desit, non perficitur sacramentum."

sentential literature, following the preamble to the *Liber Pancrisis*, as the *magistri moderni*. These largely anonymous scholars pursued theology by collecting and assembling florilegia of patristic and contemporaneous sentences, by making comparable statements of their own, and by composing treatises built up from such material. The *sententiae* ("judgments," "theses") were brief, notable, and more or less authoritative statements on specific topics, or answers to specific questions (Chapters 8 and 9). The *magistri moderni* not only assembled the rules and regulations of marriage into handy compendia but also prefaced this canonical material with theological reflections on the role of marriage in the life of the church and in God's saving plan, and on merits of married life in comparison with their own, superior vocation of celibacy.

Most of the fresh material from which the *magistri moderni* constructed their theological accounts of marriage had come originally from Augustine, although they apparently gathered it not from Augustine's own writings but from florilegia. The flowers that they picked were not fresh but already cut and dried. Among the chief remote sources were Augustine's *De bono coniugali*, *De nuptiis et concupiscentia*, and *De Genesi ad litteram* (Chapter 8). Collections of Augustine's writings on marriage and celibacy copied in monastic *scriptoria* during the Middle Ages and held in monastic libraries, presumably as resources on the morality of these estates (Section 2.3), but there had been no attempt to use Augustine's work on marriage constructively and systematically in theological writing since the Carolingian period, and no attempt to do so extensively and systematically since Augustine had left this world. Because Augustine's writings, sayings, opinions, and ideas were fundamental to the medieval theology of marriage, I shall devote the following three chapters to them (Chapters 2–4).

Working in a period when speculation about the sacraments was flourishing, the *magistri moderni* applied the concepts, distinctions, and terminology of current sacramental theology to marriage. Unfettered by the larger context of what Augustine said about marriage, they used this material freely to meet current speculative and pastoral exigencies. The most seminal of the sentential treatises on marriage, known from its incipit as *Cum omnia sacramenta*, begins with a statement that would be repeated again and again throughout the twelfth and thirteenth centuries:

> Whereas all the sacraments were instituted after sin and because of sin, marriage alone was also instituted before sin occurred, and not as remedy, like the others, but as a duty.[23]

The distinction between marrying in order to fulfill the duty to "increase and multiply" (*ad officium*) and marrying to receive remedial benefits of marriage (*ad remedium*) came from Augustine (Section 3.2). The statement presupposes

---

[23] *Cum omnia sacramenta* I, ed. F. P. Bliemetzrieder, *Anselms von Laon systematische Sentenzen*, BGPhMA 18.2–3 (Münster, 1919), 129/24–27: "Cum omnia sacramenta post peccatum et propter peccatum sumpserunt exordium, solum coniugii sacramentum ante peccatum etiam legitur institutum, non ad remedium, sicut cetera, sed ad officium."

that the sacraments are numerable, so that one might name and count them, but the role of marriage among them is anomalous. As medicines of the spiritual life, the sacraments were instituted after sin had entered into the world. Marriage, too, is a remedy in that sense. But this sacrament was *also* instituted in the earthly Paradise, even before the first sin. Was it already a sacrament then? If so, in what sense?

1.2 HOLY MATRIMONY BEFORE 1100

Theologically informed discussions of marriage as a Christian institution are rare between Augustine and 1100. To understand how clerics regarded marriage during this long period, one has to rely largely on fragmentary and incidental evidence, such as the *ordines* of nuptial liturgies and the theological preambles to ostentatious dotal charters. The major exception to this long silence is the *De institutione laicali* by Jonas of Orléans (d. 841/842), bishop of Orléans from 818. Jonas wrote this work on the life and morals of the laity at the request of Matfrid, Count of Orléans. The chapters on marriage (II.1–16) are designed to show how married folk can live righteously and avoid the many pitfalls and dangers of their chosen estate, especially sins of impurity. Jonas establishes some theological foundations at the beginning of this section. In the early twelfth century, the author of the *Cum omnia sacramenta* (mentioned earlier) appropriates much of the material from this introduction to marriage.

When God created the world, Jonas begins, God saw that everything he had created was good (Gen 1:21). Jonas cites texts from the Old and the New Testaments to show that marriage was among the countless good things that God had created: Genesis 2:24, on the primordial union ("Therefore shall a man leave his father and his mother, and shall cleave unto his wife, and they shall be one flesh"); Matthew 19:4–6, on Jesus' confirmation of the primordial union ("What God has joined together, let not man separate"); Genesis 1:27–28, on the primordial blessing and the precept of fecundity ("be fruitful and multiply"); Proverbs 19:14 ("a prudent wife is from the Lord"); 1 Corinthians 7:28 ("if a virgin marry, she has not sinned"); and Hebrews 13:4 (on the *thorus immaculatus*: the "bed undefiled"). But human beings are inclined to abuse the good things with which God has provided them, Jonas observes. The proper reason for marrying is to beget and raise children, whereas many men marry chiefly to satisfy their lust. Jonas provides a dossier of quotations from Augustine's *De bono coniugali* and *De nuptiis et concupiscentia* – works that were rarely cited before the twelfth century – to corroborate and elaborate this point.

Augustine also said in a sermon, Jonas notes, that married life (*vita coniugalis*), as well as the celibate vocations, has its proper place in the body of Christ.[24] Jonas takes this to mean that marriage is one of the orders from which the church is

---

[24] Augustine, *Serm.* 354.4 (PL 39:1564–65).

constituted. Citing Ezekiel and Bede, he argues that there are "three orders and divisions of the faithful in the church": the order of prelates (*ordo praepositorum*) or teachers (*doctorum*), the order of ascetics (*ordo abstinentium*), and the order of married folk (*ordo coniugatorum*). The three men who would be saved at the end according to Ezekiel's prophecy – Noah, Daniel, and Job (Ezek 14:13–14, 19–20) – represent the three orders:

> Through Noah the order of prelates [*praepositi*] is signified, through Daniel that of ascetics [*abstinentes*], and through Job the life of good married folk. Married folk, therefore, assisted by divine grace, should imitate according to their abilities the life and actions of this man of such probity, praised by the Lord for his holy virtues with so many and such great paeans, so that they may justly deserve to be admitted into his company [*collegium*]. For a *triclinium* is described as being in the house of the wedding [at Cana], which is the church of Christ, because there are undoubtedly three orders of the faithful in the church: that of teachers [*doctores*], that of ascetics, and that of married folk. The same three orders are distinguished elsewhere in the Gospel, where the life of ascetics [*continentes*] is signified by the two in bed, that of prelates by the two in the field, and that of married folk by the two at the mill.[25]

Jonas alludes here to the wedding at Cana (John 2:1–11), where Jesus performed the first of his miracles. John refers to the feast-master or chief steward as the *architriclinus* (John 2:8–9), and Jonas deduces from this detail that the feast took place in or at a *triclinium*. The term originally denoted the benches or couches that were arranged around three sides of a dining table, with the fourth side left open for the servers, although by extension it could denote the table or even the dining room. All that matters here is the prefix, *tri-*. There were three companies at the wedding feast, for these represent three orders in the church, which is the bride and the body of Christ.

Several divisions of the church into three orders circulated during the early Middle Ages, and scholars sometimes combined or conflated different versions. Patristic authors divided the faithful by their chosen sexual practices into consecrated virgins, consecrated widows, and married folk, in descending order of dignity and holiness.[26] Jerome interpreted the thirtyfold, sixtyfold, and hundredfold fruit in the parable of the sower (Matt 13:23, Mark 4:20) as the eternal rewards of marriage, consecrated widowhood, and consecrated virginity respectively.[27] Medieval theologians developed this theme of the three yields (*fructus*) to show that a single virtue, sometimes identified as chastity, was the basis all three vocations, which differed not in kind but only in degree (Section 14.8.2).

[25] Jonas of Orléans, *De institutione laicali* II.1 (SC 549:326/132–146).
[26] For example, Ambrose, *De viduis* 4.13 (PL 16:241D–242A).
[27] Jerome, *Adv. Iovinianum* I.3; II.19 (PL 23:212B–214A; 313C–314C). See also Jerome's commentary on Matt 13:23 (CCL 77:105–06). Cf. Augustine, *De sancta virg.* 44(45); 45(46) (CSEL 41:289/11–14; 290/8–291/15). Augustine is cautious about this particular interpretation of the three yields. On medieval uses of the allegorical division, see M. Bernards, *Speculum Virginum* (Cologne, 1955), 40–51.

Jonas's interpretation of Ezekiel belongs to a tradition to which both Augustine and Bede contributed. According to Augustine, the three classes of Christians are continents (*continentes*), ministers (*rectores, praepositi*), and married folk (*coniugati*). The continents here are the celibates, or contemplatives. This version was based on Ezekiel's apocalyptic vision (Ezek 14:14–16), which Augustine interpreted in the light of an apocalyptic parable (Luke 17:34–36 and Matt 24:40–41). Daniel, Noah, and Job respectively typify the three classes of Christians, for these men are the only ones who will be saved in Ezekiel's vision. Noah's ark represents the church. Job's trials represent the mundane preoccupations of married folk. Augustine discovered a parallel typology, to which Jonas also alludes, in Matthew 24:40–41 and Luke 17:34–35. When the Son of Man returns, there will be two men working in a field, two persons asleep in bed, and two women grinding flour at a mill. From each pair, one will be saved and the other left behind. The persons asleep in bed stand for the contemplatives, according to Augustine; the men who cultivate the field for the ministers of the church; and the women at the mill for married folk. The women's subordinate gender shows that they represent the laity, and the grinding of the mill wheel represents the unending cycle of mundane preoccupations.[28] Augustine says that he cannot think of any other classes of Christians in the church besides these three.[29]

Bede's version, which Jonas also mentions, is an allegorical exegesis of the Temple of Solomon. The temple has three floors, with the narrowest at the top and the broadest at the bottom (1 Kgs 6:6). The arrangement of floors represents the hierarchical ordering of the church, according to Bede, and the breadth of each floor indicates both the character of the corresponding way of life and the relative number of those who follow it. At the top is the constrained life of the virgins (the religious), who have renounced marriage and worldly things to devote themselves to prayer, vigils, and psalmody. They anticipate the next life, where the blessed will neither marry nor be given in marriage but will be like the angels (Matt 22:30, Luke 20:35–36). At the middle level of the temple are the continents (*continentes*). At the ground level are the married folk. Their way of life is the broadest, for Christ does not ask them to sell their possessions and to give everything to the poor (Matt 19:21) but only to obey the commandments (Matt 19:17–20).[30]

---

[28] G. Folliet, "Les trois catégories de chrétiens: Étude de ce thème augustinien," in *Augustinus Magister* (Paris, 1954–1955) 2:631–44. Idem, "Les trois catégories de chrétiens. Survie d'un thème augustinien," *L'année théologique augustinienne* 14 (1954): 82–96. See also B. Kress, "Noah, Daniel and Job – The Three Righteous Men of Ezekiel 14.14 in Medieval Art," *Journal of the Warburg and Courthauld Institutes* 67 (2004): 259–67. On the variety of divisions, see G. Constable, "The Orders of Society," in *Three Studies in Medieval Religious and Social Thought* (Cambridge, 1955), 249–360; on the tripartite divisions in particular, see ibid., 305–23.

[29] Augustine, *Quaest. Evang.* II.44.2 (CCL 44B:106/37–38).

[30] Bede, *De templo* I, 7.5 (CCL 119A:163). On Bede's allegorical exegesis of Solomon's temple, see T. J. Furry, *Allegorizing History* (Eugene, 1913), 47–50.

Bede's architectural image appealed to the Carolingian moralists, who liked to imagine the church as a great building, such as a palace or a cathedral.[31]

The identity of the two upper orders varied and was often unclear or only vaguely characterized in the Middle Ages, but married folk always populated the lowest of the three levels. Although they remained in the world rather than devoting their lives wholly to Christ or to the church, their order was integral to the whole. The edifice could not stand without them. Moreover, the model showed that marriage was the *only* way in which the laity could expect safely to achieve salvation. Belonging to one of the three classes was no guarantee of salvation, but there were no other orders from which some would be chosen at the end. Ivo of Chartres invoked the typology of Daniel, Noah, and Job in a letter to Louis VI, in which he commended the king for becoming betrothed to Adélaïde de Maurienne. Ivo was keen to see Louis safely married. Having seen a previous betrothal break down, Ivo feared that a breakup of this betrothal would divide both the nation and the church, for "every kingdom divided against itself is brought to desolation, and every city or house divided against itself shall not stand" (Matt 12:25). There are only three vocations (*professiones*) among those who "live well," Ivo explains: the ascetics (*continentes*), represented by Daniel; the ministers of the church, represented by Noah; and the married folk, represented by Job. "Whoever shall not be found in one of these vocations," Ivo warns, "will be judged an outlaw by the eternal tribunal and will not have his eternal inheritance."[32]

The *Enarrationes in Matthaeum*, a work sometimes ascribed to Anselm of Laon,[33] follows Augustine when commenting on Matthew 24:40–41, which the author correlates with the apocalyptic parable of Luke 17:34–36. The two persons in bed represent the *continentes* (i.e., the contemplatives, or ascetics), typified by Daniel; the two men cultivating the field represent the ministers of the church, typified by Noah; and the two women at the mill represent the married folk, typified by Job.[34] Commenting on the parable of the sower and the three yields, the author divides the church into contemplatives and actives and then subdivides actives into continents and married folk.[35]

As already noted, authors writing on marriage before 1100 rarely invoked the discourse on marriage from Ephesians (5:22–33) or noted that marriage signified

---

[31] Candidus of Fulda, *Opusculum de passione Domini* 18, PL 106:95B–96A. Christian of Stavelot, *Expositio in Matthaeum evangelistam* 42, PL 106:1414C–D. Smaragdus, *In collectiones epistolarum et evangeliorum de tempore et de sanctis, Dominica II post theophania, in Ioannem,* cap. 2, PL 102:88D–89A.

[32] Ivo of Chartres, *Epist.* 239 (PL 162:246C–247C). Ivo had opposed an earlier prospect in *Epist.* 209 (PL 162:214A–C). On the political background to *Epist.* 239, see J. Dufour, "Louis VI, Roi de France (1108–1137), à la lumière des actes royaux et des sources narratives," in *Académie des Inscriptions et Belles-Lettres. Comptes rendus des séances, April–June 1990* (Paris, 1990), 456–82, at 465.

[33] See A. M. Landgraf, *Introduction à l'histoire de la littérature théologique de la scolastique naissante,* ed. A.-M. Landry (Montréal, 1973), 71–72.

[34] *Enarrationes in Matthaeum* 24 (PL 162:1455C–1456C). [35] Ibid., 13 (1370A–B).

the union between Christ and the church. The absence is not easy to explain. The passage would seem to be an obvious source at least for pastoral counsel on marriage, if not for theological reflection. Needless to say, rarely is not the same as never. There are a few notable exceptions, some of which became crucial in medieval debates about marriage. Jonas cited Ephesians 5:25 and 5:28–29 with Proverbs 5:18–19, Ecclesiastes 9:9, and 1 Peter 3:7 to show how husbands ought to love and cherish their wives as the "weaker vessel,"[36] but this was his only reference to the discourse. Moreover, he made no reference to the discourse in his theological introduction to holy matrimony (II.1), and he did not cite Ephesians 5:32 anywhere in the *De institutione laicali*. When authors prior to 1100 did invoke or allude to Ephesians 5:32 with reference to marriage, they assumed, as Augustine had done, that the "great sacrament" to which Paul referred was either the union between Christ and the church or Adam's prophetic utterance (Gen 2:24).

To show that marriage was holy and divinely instituted, authors before 1100 turned chiefly to the creation of Adam and Eve and the primordial marriage, to Genesis 2:24, and to Jesus' gloss on Genesis 2:24 in Matthew 19:6: "What God has joined together, let not man separate." Weddings prompted churchmen to reflect not only on Eve's formation from Adam's rib but also on the creation of everything, as if the world began again ritually whenever spouses plighted their troth. Jonas of Orléans was typical in this respect. One finds the same emphasis in nuptial liturgies and other early-medieval texts witnessing or commemorating marriages. The association of the holiness of marriage with the primordial union endured throughout the Middle Ages. Protestants and Catholics during the sixteenth century were equally attached to it. It appealed more than Paul's discourse on marriage in Ephesians did to the imagination of prelates and clerics who lacked formal education in theology.

The Book of Tobit was an ancillary resource. Not only is its treatment of marriage the most extensive in the Jewish scriptures, but it is unique in its emphasis on the importance of righteous observance, of prayer, and of the involvement of the Deity in marrying.[37] An archangel, Raphael, is the go-between who helps Tobias to marry his chosen bride, Sarah. Jerome's Vulgate version of the book includes four prayers for nuptial blessings. The first is the prayer that Raguel recites when gives his daughter in marriage to Tobias. It contains the first known reference to the joining of right hands (*dextrarum iunctio*) as a wedding rite:

> And taking the right hand of his daughter, he gave it into the right hand of Tobias, saying: The God of Abraham, and the God of Isaac, and the God of Jacob be with you, and may he join you together, and fulfill his blessing in you. (Tob 7:15)

---

[36] Jonas of Orléans, *De institutione laicali* II.5 (SC 549:362).

[37] K. Stevenson, *The Nuptial Blessing* (New York, 1983), 5–7. M. Searle and K. W. Stevenson, *Documents of the Marriage Liturgy* (Collegeville, 1992), 21–24. On marriage in the pre-Vulgate versions of Tobit, see G. D. Miller, *Marriage in the Book of Tobit* (Berlin, 2011). On the peculiarities of Jerome's (Vulgate) version, see C. E. Moore's commentary in *Tobit*, Anchor Bible (1996), 61–63.

The second prayer for blessing is said by Tobias on their wedding night to exorcize the demon that had killed her previous husbands. It weaves together a blessing, a commemoration of the primordial marriage (Gen 2:18–24), and a petition, in which Tobias affirms that his motivation is not lustful but pure and asks God to let them grow old together:

> So they both arose, and both prayed earnestly together that health might be given them. And Tobias said: Lord God of our fathers, may the heavens and the earth, and the sea, and the fountains, and the rivers, and all thy creatures that are in them, bless thee. You made Adam of the slime of the earth and gave him Eve for a helper. And now, Lord, you know that not for fleshly lust do I take my sister to wife but only for the love of posterity, in which your name may be blessed for ever and ever. Sarah also said: Have mercy on us, O Lord, have mercy on us, and let us grow old both together in health. (Tob 8:6–9)

Another blessing is said by Raguel when he finds the spouses sleeping safely together (Tob 8:17–19) during the wedding night, and another by Gabelus at the wedding feast (9:9–11). These prayers, especially the first two, were sources of nuptial blessings in medieval nuptial liturgies, although the book was rarely cited to support the doctrine of marriage as a sacrament until the sixteenth century.

Most of the biblical quotations and allusions in nuptial *ordines* surviving from the sixth through eleventh centuries were from the Old Testament. There is little in the wording of these rites that would have seemed alien to Jewish couples. They refer to the creation of the world, the formation of Eve from Adam, and the primordial marriage; to the married patriarchs, especially Abraham, Isaac, and Jacob; to exemplary Old Testament women, especially Rachel, Rebecca, and Sarah; to some of the Psalms, especially Psalm 127 (128 in the Hebrew enumeration); and to the marriage of Tobias and Sarah. References to the conjugal debt of 1 Corinthians 7:3 and to the wedding at Cana (John 1:1–11) begin to appear in the eleventh century, the former to remind spouses of their duties, the latter because it was the perennial defense against anti-matrimonial heresies. References or allusions to the discourse on marriage in Ephesians 5 were rare in nuptial liturgies throughout the Middle Ages, as were lectionary readings from this source in the nuptial mass.[38]

The only reference to marriage as a sign of Christ and the church in the extant nuptial *ordines* of the early Middle Ages that I am aware of occurs in the *Hadrianum*, also known as the *Gregorian Sacramentary*, which Pope Hadrian I gave to Charlemagne in the late eighth century. Here, too, the setting is a commemoration of the primordial marriage. The minister beseeches God as the one who created the world, who made Adam in his own image, and who made Eve as his helper. What it pleased God to make into a single thing should never be divided into two. The minister

[38] J.-B. Molin and P. Mutembe, *Le rituel du mariage en France du XIIe au XVIe siècle* (Paris, 1974), 276–78. On the lectionary readings, see Molin and Mutembe, *Le rituel du mariage*, 212–13, and Searle and Stevenson, *Documents of the Marriage Liturgy*, 273.

addresses God as the one who "consecrated conjugal union with such an excellent mystery that you prefigured the sacrament of Christ and the church in the compact of marriage."[39] These words allude to Ephesians 5:32. Marriage is a mystery: it is significant, or pregnant with allegorical meaning. But here the "sacrament of Christ and the church" is not the couple's marriage but Christ's union with the church, as in Augustine's interpretation.

The same themes populate the theological preambles to some ostentatious Frankish dotal charters. These charters belong to an enduring tradition stretching from Merovingian and Carolingian Gaul to eleventh-century France. Their primary function was to settle and to record the dowry that would pass from the suitor to his bride-to-be when they became man and wife,[40] but the charters were also a written record of the preceding betrothal and of the intention to conclude the marriage in due course, when the spouses would come together. Eleven of the dotal charters in Karl Zeumer's collection of formulas,[41] ranging from the ninth through eleventh centuries, have a theological preamble, which expounds the place of marriage in God's plan and the moral responsibilities and proper intentions of the spouses. Some of the sacred preambles are brief and formulaic, but others are complex, inventive, and learned. I have analyzed this material in detail elsewhere, and it suffices here to summarize some of my findings.[42]

As in the nuptial liturgies, references to the Old Testament predominate. Most of the sacred preambles begin with the creation of the world and the primordial marriage. Several recall that human procreation was the means to fill the places in Heaven left vacant by the fallen angels. They do not posit a new institution of marriage as a remedy against sin or as a sacrament of the New Law. Instead, they construe the forthcoming marriage as a seamless continuation of the primordial institution. Some of them cite Jesus' confirmation that marriage, as recorded in Genesis, is the union of two in one flesh (Matt 19:5–6, Mark 10:7–9). They include counsel about morals and duties, some of it drawn from 1 Corinthians 7. The signifying of Christ and the church appears only in one of the later, more elaborate examples, which cites Ephesians 5:25 for its pastoral message: "Husbands, love your wives as Christ loves the Church."[43] Ephesians 5:32 does not appear in any of these preambles.

The theological preamble to the splendid marriage charter that Holy Roman Emperor Otto II gave to his bride, Theophanu, in 972 develops similar reflections. This preamble may be divided into three sections, respectively on the creation of the world and the primordial marriage, on marriage in the Gospel, and on conjugal

---

[39] K. Ritzer, *Le mariage dans les églises chrétiennes du Ier au XIe siècle* (Paris, 1970), 427–28.
[40] In Latin, a *dos* – but the modern convention is to refer to a *dos ex marito* as a dower, to distinguish it from the dowry that a bride brought to a marriage from her parents.
[41] *Formulae Merowingici et Karolini Aevi*, MGH Legum V, *Formulae* (Hanover, 1886).
[42] P. L. Reynolds, "Dotal Charters in the Frankish Tradition," THTH 114–64.
[43] *Extrav.* I 9, in Zeumer, *Formulae*, p. 538, trans. in THTH 159.

ethics. The primordial discourse invokes God as the creator of all things and then recounts the creation of human beings as God's image and likeness, with dominion over all creatures (Gen 1:26). It explains that sexual procreation was God's way to fill the places left by the vainglorious fallen angels, and it recounts the forming of woman from Adam's side as man's helpmeet in procreation (Gen 2:18). The Gospel discourse recounts Christ's birth from the "immaculate womb of the virgin," it alludes to Christ's marriage to the church, it recalls the wedding at Cana, and it affirms Jesus' commandment (a gloss on Gen 2:24): "What therefore God has joined together, let not man separate" (Matt 19:6, Mark 10:9). The moral discourse commends the "undefiled bed" (*thorus immaculatus*) of Hebrews 13:4, it reminds the spouses that procreation rather than any base motives is the proper purpose of marriage, and it commends insoluble conjugal affection (*mutua et indissolubilis dilectio*). Only a theologian would recognize that the motif of the church as Christ's bride was dependent on Paul's discourse on marriage in Ephesians 5, for the author does not invoke Ephesians 5:32 or refer to marriage as a *sacramentum* or a *mysterium*:

> To the same end, he, the Lord Jesus Christ himself, the author of both testaments, the mediator between God and human beings, arriving in human flesh, having come forth "like a bridegroom who has come forth from his bedchamber" [Ps 18:6] from the immaculate womb of the Virgin to join himself to the church, his bride — he chose to attend a marriage in order to sanctify it, to gladden it with the first of the miracles of his greatness when he turned water into wine, and to show that a marriage celebrated in accordance with the lawful norms is good and holy, and that he is its author. Moreover, he said in the Gospel, showing by his own edict that God made marriage, "What God has joined together, let not man separate."[44]

The allusion to Psalm 18:6 – "He has set his tabernacle in the sun, and he as a bridegroom coming out of his bride chamber has rejoiced as a strong man to run the way"[45] – echoes a gloss on this text by Augustine, who identifies the bridegroom with God and the bride with human nature, to which the Son of God united himself by coming forth.[46] The author might have found Augustine's gloss in any one of numerous Carolingian commentaries.

---

[44] In H. K. Schulze, *Die Heiratsurkunde der Kaiserin Theophanu* (Hannover, 2007), 90: "Ad hoc ipse utriusque testamenti institutor, mediator dei et hominum dominus Iesus Christus in humana carne adveniens, ipse ex inmaculato virginis utero tamquam sponsus egressus de thalamo ad coniungendam sibi sponsam aeclesiam, ut ostenderet bonas et sanctas esse nuptias legitima institutione celebratas seque auctorem esse earum, ad eas venire et primo maiestatis suae miraculo eas laetificare, dum aquam vertit in vinum, voluit et sanctificare. Edicto denique proprio a deo factas esse nuptias ostendens in evangelio dicit: quod deus coniunxit, homo non separet." I am grateful to Prof. Eliza Garrison for bringing this charter to my attention.

[45] "Soli posuit tabernaculum in eis et ipse quasi sponsus procedens de thalamo suo exultavit ut fortis ad currendam viam."

[46] Cf. Augustine, *Enarr. in Ps.* 18.1.6 (CCL 38:102/5–8): "'et ipse tamquam sponsus procedens de thalamo suo'. et ipse procedens de utero uirginali, ubi deus naturae humanae tamquam sponsus sponsae copulatus est." The use of this source accounts for the odd duplication of

The same traits are apparent in the preambles to three dotal charters from northern Aquitaine on which Philippe Depreux has commented, which date from the late tenth through mid-eleventh century. All begin by invoking God as the almighty creator and go on to describe the primordial marriage. One (c. 975) notes how Jesus referred to the primordial marriage, saying, "What God has joined together, let man not separate" (Matt 19:6, Mark 10:9). Another (c. 990) recalls how God blessed the first couple, telling them to be fruitful and multiply (Gen 1:28), and how God commanded the man to leave his father and mother and cleave unto his wife (Gen 2:24). By the grace of the Holy Spirit, this text continues, "the prophets and patriarchs and perfect faithful men of the holy Church" have continued to fulfill that ancient commandment to this day. The latest of these examples, dated February 4, 1083, adds that Jesus confirmed the goodness of marriage at Cana, where he performed the first of his miracles (John 2:11).[47] Some preambles to dotal charters from the tenth and eleventh centuries – two for dukes of Normandy, the others preserved at Cluny – follow a similar pattern, weaving together texts from Scripture to recall creation, the primordial marriage, and the role of marriage in God's plan.[48]

Clerics before 1100, then, to prove that marriage was a holy estate, looked first to the primordial marriage. Then, for confirmation, they looked to the marriage at Cana, where Jesus confirmed the holiness of marriage by performing the first of his miracles. They did not posit a new institution of marriage under the New Law or the Gospel. Instead, they considered Holy Matrimony to be primordial and perennial. They rarely invoked the discourse on marriage in Ephesians 5. Even after the doctrine of marriage as a sacrament had become established, clerics with no formal training in theology looked to the primordial marriage as their chief resource, appealing to it even as evidence that marriage was a sacrament, as Chaucer's parson did:

> This, as seith the book, is a ful greet sacrament. God maked it, as I have seyd, in paradys, and wolde hymself be born in mariage. And for to halwen mariage he was at a weddynge, where as he turned water into wyn; which was the firste miracle that he wroghte in erthe biforn his disciples.[49]

It was easy for the Protestant reformers to set aside the relatively newfangled sacramental theology of marriage, with its dependence on Ephesians 5:22–33, and to revert to the old themes, which had been a mainstay of popular preaching and instruction for centuries.

the word *ipse* in the cited passage. See also Augustine, *Serm.* 192.3 (PL 38:1013) and *Serm.* 361.17 (PL 39:1608–09), where Augustine returns to the theme.

47 P. Depreux "La dotation de l'épouse en Aquitaine septentrionale du IXe au XIIe siècle," in F. Bougard et al., *Dots et douaires dans le haut moyen âge* (Rome, 2002), 219–44, at 241, 242, and 243 (nos 1, 2, and 4).

48 L. Morelle, "Marriage and Diplomatics: Five Dower Charters from the Regions of Laons and Soissons, 1163–1181," THTH 165–214, at 175–76.

49 Chaucer, *The Parson's Tale*, X.917.

1.3 THE SEVEN SACRAMENTS

Theologians before 1100 used the word *sacramentum* in several interrelated senses.[50] In the sense most pertinent to the development of twelfth-century sacramental theology, the sacraments were the ritual "mysteries," or rites, of the church. Each rite involved some material stuff (*elementum*) that was humble in itself but pregnant with significance: water, oil or chrism, and bread and wine. Augustine had said that a sacrament resulted from the application of a *verbum* to an *elementum*.[51] The stuff became a sacrament when a priest invoked a prescribed verbal formula over it. These sacramental rites were associated with initiation into a cult. They were either means of initiation, such as baptism, or they were rites reserved for initiates, such as eucharist. Eucharist and baptism were the sacraments *par excellence*, therefore, but the model could be extended to ancillary features of those rites and even to independent rites *mutatis mutandis*. Isidore of Seville said the that sacraments were "baptism and chrism, body and blood." Following Augustine, Isidore explains that a sacrament involves a ritual (*caelebratio*) in which the action (*res gesta*) signifies something that ought to be received in a holy way.[52] Isidore derived the word *sacramentum* both from *secretum* ("secret," "hidden") and from *sacer* ("sacred"), for "under the covering of corporeal things a divine power very secretly brings about the saving effect [*salus*]."[53] Isidore's phrase "baptism and chrism" probably denoted two aspects of baptism rather than baptism and confirmation as separate sacraments (compare "body and blood"), but one cannot be sure. There would have been no point in insisting on a number.

The model outlined earlier, emphasizing ritual performance, verbal formulas, and material substances, endured throughout the Middle Ages. Theologians some-times emphasized the stuff itself (e.g., water), which was said to contain grace, and sometimes the ritual action performed with the stuff (e.g., ablution with water). Twelfth-century theologians generally emphasized the stuff rather than ritual action, and thirteenth-century theologians generally emphasized the ritual action rather

---

[50] On the early development of sacramental theology and terminology, see J. de Ghellinck, "Un chapitre dans l'histoire de la définition des sacrements au XIIe siècle," in *Mélanges Mandonnet* (Paris, 1930), 2:79–96; D. Van den Eynde, *Les définitions des sacrements pendant la première période de la théologie scolastique (1050–1240)* (Rome, 1950); and B. Stock, *The Implications of Literacy* (Princeton, 1983), 254–59. For a succinct but detailed history of seven sacraments, see A. Lagarde, *The Latin Church in the Middle Ages* (New York, 1915), 32–82: not faultless, but still a superior account, notwithstanding more recent advances in the field.

[51] Augustine, *In Iohannis evangelium tractatus* 80.3 (CCL 36:529/4–7): "detrahe uerbum, et quid est aqua nisi aqua? accedit uerbum ad elementum, et fit sacramentum, etiam ipsum tamquam uisibile uerbum."

[52] Cf. Augustine, *Epist.* 55, 2 (CSEL 34.2:170/11–13): "sacramentum est autem in aliqua celebra-tione, cum rei gestae commemoratio ita fit, ut aliquid etiam significare intellegatur, quod sancte accipiendum est."

[53] Isidore, *Etymologies* VI.39–40.

than the stuff, but such emphasis was never exclusive. The inclusion of penance and marriage among the sacraments stretched the paradigm and raised difficult questions. These questions were the focus of much discussion and debate from around 1225, as theologians began to work out the implications of treating the seven as a univocal genus.

One should distinguish between *listing* and *enumerating*. Peter Lombard *listed* the sacraments, tacitly implying that the list was complete, closed, and countable, but he did not explicitly enumerate them. He did not say that there were seven or identify them by their ordinal numbers. The explicit enumeration of seven, with emphasis on the number, developed later, as the idea of the list as a matter of settled doctrine and practice took root.

It is misleading to ask how many sacraments were recognized in earlier periods, for no one was counting. Encyclopedias continue to tell us that Peter Damian (d. 1072) posited twelve sacraments, but the source is a treatise or sermon on the sacraments long known to have been the work of Nicholas of Clairvaux, Bernard's secretary, which was published under the name of Peter Damian in Migne's *Patrologia Latina*. Nicholas entered the community at Clairvaux around 1145, left it around 1152, and died after 1176. Writing in a florid, inflated style that verges on parody, Nicholas enumerates twelve sacraments: baptism, confirmation, the anointing of the sick, the consecration of a bishop, the anointing of a king, the dedication of a church, confession, the sacrament of canons, the sacrament of monks, the sacrament of hermits, the sacrament of nuns, and marriage. Nicholas explains that these correspond to the twelve crosses inscribed or placed around the walls of a church. They fall into two equal sets, for whereas the first six involve the "oil of unction," the rest do not. Eucharist is not among the twelve. Unlike Peter Lombard, Nicholas enumerates his sacraments. He insists the number, which he treats as significant, and he introduces each sacrament with its ordinal number: "The first is the sacrament of baptism," and so forth.[54] Some say that Cardinal Humbert of Silva-Candida (d. 1061) was the first to enumerate seven sacraments,[55] but this claim is misleading. Humbert refers to confirmation as the "seventh of the sacraments of regeneration." He does not name the seven, but they are not the sacraments of the New Law. Instead, they constitute a sequence

---

[54] PL 144:897C–902B. The text is identified here as Peter Damian, *Sermo LXIX, In dedicatione ecclesiae*. On the work's authorship, see J. J. Ryan, "Saint Peter Damiani and the Sermons of Nicholas of Clairvaux: A Clarification," *Mediaeval Studies* 9 (1947): 151–61; and J. Leclercq, *Recueil d'études sur saint Bernard et ses écrits*, vol. 1 (Rome, 1962), 47–82.

[55] H. Chadwick, "Ego Berengarius," *Journal of Theological Studies* 40.2 (1989): 414–45, at 422, says that Humbert "is the first to speak of seven sacraments." M. M. Adams, *Some Later Medieval Theories of the Eucharist* (Oxford, 2010), 46, citing Chadwick, says that Humbert "was the first to insist that the number of new-law sacraments is seven — baptism, confirmation, penance, eucharist, ordination, matrimony, and extreme unction." Humbert did not say what his seven sacraments of regeneration were, but he was probably referring to tasting consecrated salt, exsufflation, daubing the ears and nostrils with saliva, anointing the breast with holy oil, ablution with holy water, chrismation, and confirmation.

that begins with the pre-baptismal rite of the tasting of consecrated salt and terminates in confirmation. Humbert assumed that there were seven of them because the gift of the Holy Spirit, which was associated especially with confirmation, was also sevenfold.[56]

Peter Lombard relied chiefly on two sources for his sacramental theology: Hugh of Saint-Victor's *De sacramentis christianae fidei* (1130–1137) and the *Summa sententiarum* (1138–1141). The latter source, which was written by a certain Odo (probably Odo of Lucca), incorporates ideas and material from Hugh and used to be ascribed to him. Hugh neither lists nor enumerates the sacraments. It would be pointless to count them on his behalf, for his extraordinarily rich sacramental theology is fluid and many-layered (Section 10.2). His *De sacramentis* encompasses salvation history from beginning to end, in which sacraments of various sorts have cardinal roles. Hugh divides the sacraments diachronically into those of the natural law, of the written law, and of the age of grace. He also divides them synchronically into three functional classes: major sacraments, such as baptism and eucharist, which are necessary for salvation; minor sacraments, such as sprinkling with water and the distribution of ashes, which help to sanctify the soul but are not necessary for salvation; and preparatory sacraments, such as priestly vestments. Having mapped out the terrain that the sacraments inhabit, Hugh leaves the reader to decide to which class any given sacrament belongs. Hugh discusses the sacramentality of marriage at length, but this is a sacrament only in an exceptional, *sui generis* manner. Hugh does not try to integrate his theology of marriage as a sacrament into his general theory of the sacraments. Moreover, he posits *two* sacraments in marriage, that is, two respects in which marriage signifies holy things, only one of which presupposes sexual union (Sections 10.4 and 10.5). The section on the sacraments in Odo's *Summa sententiarum* begins with a discussion of the sacraments in general as well as of the sacraments and precepts of the Old Law. Odo then treats five sacraments of the New Law individually: baptism, confirmation, eucharist ("the sacrament of the altar"), penance, and the anointing of the sick. But Odo neither lists nor enumerates the sacraments.[57] There is no treatise on orders in the *Summa sententiarum*, although the author mentions the "sacrament of ordination" in passing.[58] Nor is there a treatise on the sacrament of marriage. To fill the latter gap, someone soon attached Walter of Mortagne's treatise on marriage (Section 11.3) to the *Summa sententiarum* as its final tractate. Walter's treatise is one of Peter Lombard's chief sources of material on marriage, especially regarding the rules and regulations and the ethical aspects.

---

[56] Humbert of Silva-Candida, *Adversus simoniacos* II.20, MGH *Libelli de Lite*, 1:163/32–36: "isti [symoniaci] catecismum, baptismum et perfectae christianitatis sigillum vendunt, scilicet a primo pabulo sacrati salis usque ad confirmationem per episcopum, quae est septima sacramentorum regenerationis secundum eundem septemplicem Spiritum ad remissionem omnium peccatorum."

[57] *Summa sententiarum* 4–6 (PL 176:117A ff.).   [58] Ibid., 4.15 (PL 176:145A).

The earliest authentic references to seven sacraments are in writings associated with a certain Master Simon, which date from the 1140s (Section 11.2). Unlike Peter Lombard, these authors did not present a list of sacraments as the basis of a systematic, sequential exposition of the entire system. They posited the seven in order to distinguish between two sorts of sacraments: common sacraments, which were received by all Christians and were individually necessary for salvation; and special sacraments, which were exclusive to a particular group were not individually necessary for salvation. The five common sacraments were baptism, confirmation, penance, eucharist, and extreme unction. The two special sacraments were marriage and orders. The authors tried to show that the five common sacraments comprised a complete system, in which each performed a necessary therapeutic or developmental function in the spiritual journey of life. Thirteenth-century theologians used the same technique with all seven, identifying each sacrament with a species of medication or with a phase in the spiritual life.[59]

There is no entirely satisfactory historical explanation as to why theologians settled on these seven. That there were *seven* of them seems to have been incidental, for Peter Lombard did not enumerate them, and there is no reason to attribute the choice of seven to numerological considerations. It is an odd list, and it generated many problems. The sacrament of ordination conferred a ministerial power that thirteenth-century theologians classified as *gratia gratis data*, not sanctifying grace. Neither penance nor marriage involved any material stuff. Nor did marriage require any prescribed verbal formula. Contrariwise, if marriage and penance could be accommodated, why were the solemn vows or consecration of religious not included? This anomaly vexed Peter John Olivi (Section 14.8.2).

The success of Peter Lombard's *Sentences* and the fact that it became the basis of systematic theology from around 1220 must have entrenched the list of seven, causing it to become routine and habitual. Indeed, André Lagarde attributed the success of the seven sacraments to this "fortuitous circumstance."[60] But to attribute a doctrine that was so enduring and successful to happenstance is an explanation of last resort. The list begins to make sense if one construes the sacraments as the remedies dispensed by the clergy as Christ's mediators to the laity. The sacraments were the chief therapeutic means in the clergy's care and cure of souls (*cura animarum*), as distinct from the duty of preaching and instruction.

The listing of seven sacraments went hand in hand with new emphasis on clerical authority and *cura animarum*, which was a sequel to the Gregorian Reform of the

---

[59] On the medical model, see Guy of Orchelles, *Tractatus de sacramentis* 1.2.3 (pp. 5–6); William of Auxerre, *Summa aurea* IV.4 (pp. 62–63); Bonaventure, *IV Sent.* 2.1.3 (4:53) and *Breviloquium* 6.3 (5:267b–268a). Thomas Aquinas, *Summa theologiae* III.55.1, resp. (2847), derives the sevenfold system from the premise, "Vita enim spiritualis conformitatem aliquam habet ad vitam corporalem."

[60] A. Lagarde, *The Latin Church in the Middle Ages* (New York, 1915), 34. Lagarde provides an excellent summary of the evolution of the seven sacraments.

eleventh century.[61] Social and political historians usually focus on the papal monarchy when they write about this social and institutional revolution, but the political advancement of the papacy was one of several convergent developments, which cannot be convincingly attributed to common cause. Nor can they be reduced to a single program of reform. Nevertheless, the broad movement fits the paradigm of church reform, although the term *reformare* with its cognates does not occur frequently or prominently in the writings of the period.[62] A reform, in this sense, presupposed that the church had become lax and corrupt by falling away from standards that it purportedly used to meet. The aim of reform was to restore the original order by radical, structural means, such as through changes in governance. Needless to say, the historian can recognize the salient characteristics of reform without sharing the ideology of its agents, advocates, and polemicists.

One aspect of this broad movement of reform was the segregation of the clergy as members of a distinct caste, who were distinguished from the laity most conspicuously by celibacy, and who were identified less as citizens of their local communities than as members of a universal, hierarchically organized corporation. Reforming churchmen and enthusiastic laypersons regarded simony (the marketing of *spiritualia*) and nicolaitism (marriage or concubinage among men in holy orders) as contaminating and enfeebling. Whatever the motives or advantages of this clericalism may have been, its success depended on the widespread but theologically questionable conviction among the laity that the mediation of the priesthood (*sacerdotium*) was vital for salvation, and that priests needed to be both pure and manly to perform this vital work.[63]

---

[61] The modern literature on the Gregorian Reform is vast, and even the term "Gregorian Reform" used to be hotly debated. For a broad but detailed account, see C. Morris, *The Papal Monarchy* (Oxford, 1989).

[62] W. L. North, J. Rubenstein, and J. D. Cotts, "The Experience of Reform: Three Perspectives," in S. Murillo (ed.), *Haskins Society Journal* 10 (Woodbridge, 2002), 113–61. See also C. M. Bellitto, *Renewing Christianity* (New York, 2001), 48–63, on the Gregorian Reform precisely as reform.

[63] K. G. Cushing, *Reform and the Papacy in the Eleventh Century* (Manchester, 2005), 121–38, esp. 116. On Nicolaitism and clerical celibacy in the Gregorian Reform, see H. L. Parish, *Clerical Celibacy in the West* (Farnham, 2009), 87–122. On the ideology of clerical celibacy, see E. Dachowski, "*Tertius est optimus*: Marriage, Continence and Virginity in the Politics of Late Tenth- and Early Eleventh-Century Francia," in M. Frassetto, *Medieval Purity and Piety* (New York, 1998), 117–29; H. E. J. Cowdrey, "Pope Gregory VII and the Chastity of the Clergy," in Frassetto, *Medieval Purity and Piety*, 269–302; M. C. Miller, "Masculinity, Reform, and Clerical Culture: Narratives of Episcopal Holiness in the Gregorian Era," *Church History* 72.1 (2003): 25–52; D. Elliott, "The Priest's Wife: Female Erasure in the Gregorian Reform," in Elliott, *Fallen Bodies* (Philadelphia, 1999), 81–106; and M. McLaughlin, *Sex, Gender, and Episcopal Authority in an Age of Reform, 1000–1122* (Cambridge, 2010), 31–36. On how the reform seemed to married clergy, see C. N. L. Brooke, "Gregorian Reform in Action: Clerical Marriage in England, 1050–1200," *Cambridge Historical Journal* 12.1 (1956): 1–21; and J. D. Thibodeaux, "The Defense of Clerical Marriage: Religious Identity and Masculinity in the Writings of Anglo-Norman Clerics," in P. H. Cullum and K. J. Lewis, *Religious Men and Masculine Identity in the Middle Ages* (Rochester, NY, 2013), 46–63.

Among the sequels to the reform was a new emphasis on the pastoral ministry of the clergy and on their duty of care toward the laity.[64] The dominant ecclesiology of the early Middle Ages presupposed a cultic model of Christian discipleship. Priests, monks, and nuns contributed to the community at large as the professional praying persons (*oratores*). The work that justified their existence was prayer and other good works, from the merits of which everyone would benefit, including those who were too entangled in their worldly status and obligations (the *bellatores*) or too busy working (the *labores*) to devote themselves to prayer. This model survived throughout the Middle Ages – monastic foundations would have been impossible without it – but clerics during the central Middle Ages began to emphasize in addition their pastoral role. They turned their faces, as it were, from the altar to the people. The emphasis on the pastoral ministry of the clergy to the laity is evident in the series of early Lateran Councils, which culminated on the Fourth Lateran Council of 1215 under Innocent III. The new emphasis also inspired the mendicant orders, especially the Dominicans and Franciscans. The *cura animarum*, which had originated in the culture of the early desert ascetics, appeared in this new pastoral setting as a professional duty of care.[65]

Peter Lombard introduced his treatise on the sacraments in Book IV of the *Sentences* by invoking the parable of the Good Samaritan, who is moved with compassion when he finds a wounded man abandoned by the roadside. Jesus says that the Samaritan, "going up to him, bound up his wounds, pouring on oil and wine" (Luke 10:34). The bandages, according to the Lombard, represent the sacraments:

> For the Samaritan, going up to the wounded man, applied the sacraments as bandages [*sacramentorum alligamenta*] to care for him, because God instituted the sacraments as remedies against the wounds of original and actual sin (Luke 10:30–37).[66]

Four chief questions arise regarding these "remedies," the Lombard continues: what a sacrament is, why each was instituted, what its composition is, and what the difference is between the sacraments of the Old Law and those of the New Law.[67]

---

[64] A. Vauchez, "Le tournant pastoral de l'Église en occident," in *Histoire du christianisme des origines à nos jours*, t. V: *Apogée de la papauté et expansion de la Chrétienté* (1054–1274) (Paris, 1993), 737–66.

[65] N. Tanner, "Pastoral Care: The Fourth Lateran Council of 1215," in G. R. Evans, *A History of Pastoral Care* (London, 2000), 112–25. L. E. Boyle, "St Thomas Aquinas and the Third Millennium," in A. Duggan et al., *Omnia Disce* (Aldershot, 2005), 294–307.

[66] Peter Lombard, *Sent.* IV, 1.1.1 (231): "Samaritanus enim, vulnerato approprians, curationi eius sacramentorum alligamenta adhibuit; quia contra peccati originalis et actualis vulnera sacramentorum remedia Deus instituit."

[67] Ibid., 1.1.2. This opening passage is an expansion of *Summa sententiarum* IV.1 (PL 176:117A): "Contra peccata tam originalia quam actualia, de quibus jam diximus, inventa sunt sacramentorum remedia, de quibus haec tria consideranda sunt: quid sit sacramentum, quare institutum, et in quibus consistat."

Peter Lombard was expanding a text that he found in the *Summa sententiarum*. Having discussed original and actual sin, the *Summa sententiarum* turns to the sacraments, which are the remedies to sin:

> The sacraments were introduced as remedies against both original and actual sins, of which we have already spoken. Three things must be considered about these: What a sacrament is, why it was instituted, and in what it consists.[68]

Readers familiar with Augustine's allegorical interpretation of the parable would not miss the Lombard's allusion to the Good Samaritan, who used bandages to care for or to cure the wounded man (*curationi eius*).[69] The wounded man is Adam with all his descendants; the thugs who beat and rob him are Satan and his followers; and the Samaritan is Christ. The Lombard took the phrase *sacramentorum alligamenta* from his own gloss on Psalm 146:3, where the Psalmist praises God as the one who "heals the broken in heart and binds up their wounds." Peter Lombard explains in this commentary, following Augustine, that the "bandages of God" are the sacraments, with which God consoles us until we shall be restored to perfect health (*perfecta sanitas*). Only then will God remove them, just as physician removes the bandages once a broken limb has fully healed.[70]

The clergy took upon themselves this duty of care. Hugh of Saint-Victor likened the sacraments to phials of medicine, which priests as emissaries of the Great Physician conveyed to their sick patients (Section 10.2.2). The simile suited Hugh's notion of the sacraments as ritual applications of consecrated stuffs (*elementa*). Peter Lombard shifts attention to the minister, or *dispensator*, of the sacraments. Although penance did not fit the ancient paradigm easily because it involved no *elementum*, it was the priestly remedy *par excellence* in this new *cura animarum*. In no other respect was the laity as dependent on the priesthood for their salvation. The Fourth Lateran Council required the faithful of both sexes to receive eucharist and to confess at least once a year. The decree likens penance to a consultation with a professional physician:

> Let the priest be discerning and cautious, so that in the manner of an expert physician he may pour wine and oil [Luke 10:34] over the wounds of the injured one, diligently inquiring into the circumstances of the sinner as well as of the sin, so that through

---

[68] *Summa sententiarum* 4.1 (PL 176:117A): "Contra peccata tam originalia quam actualia, de quibus jam diximus, inventa sunt sacramentorum remedia, de quibus haec tria consideranda sunt: quid sit sacramentum, quare institutum, et in quibus consistat." Peter Lombard used material from Hugh of Saint-Victor, *De sacramentis* I.9.1 (PL 176:317B) and I.11.4 (PL 176:345A) to expand this agenda.

[69] See R. J. Teske, "The Good Samaritan (Lk 10:29–37) in Augustine's Exegesis," in F. Van Fleteren and J. C. Schnaubelt, *Augustine: Biblical Exegete* (New York, 2001), 347–57, esp. 351–54.

[70] Peter Lombard on Ps. 146:3 (PL 191:1274D). This gloss is from Augustine, *Enarr. in Ps.* 146 (CCL 40:2127/6–9).

these he may understand prudently what counsel he ought to give him and what remedies to apply, using diverse treatments [*experimenta*] to heal the sick person.[71]

The confessor envisaged here was less a stern judge than a benign physician, who applied tangible remedies as well as giving advice. All the intended readers would have understood the allusion to the Good Samaritan in the reference to wine and oil, and theologically literate readers would have been reminded of Peter Lombard's preamble to the sacraments. The next canon concerns physicians of the body (*medici corporum*), who when called upon to treat persons with bodily ailments should advise them first to consult physicians of the soul (*medici animarum*). Bodily infirmities sometimes arise from sin and guilt, and patients may be cured more easily after their spiritual health (*salus spiritualis*) has been restored.[72]

1.4 MARRIAGE AS ONE OF THE SACRAMENTS

The western church, in contrast to the eastern church,[73] did not treat marriage as an essentially ritual event, administered by a priest. Those who held the church in contempt by marrying without the blessing of a priest were sinful and impious, but their marriages were valid. No priest was needed to join the spouses together insolubly in matrimony. Instead, the spouses joined themselves. Most medieval theologians accepted this principle and tried to accommodate it in their accounts of how marriage was a sacrament.

In what sense, then, was marriage one of the sacraments? Albertus Magnus suggested that the church's legal control over marriage fulfilled the role of sacramental ministry.[74] The proposal would seem far-fetched if one regarded the sacraments primarily as rituals or consecrated stuffs (*elementa*), but it makes sense if one regards them primarily as church-dispensed therapy. Medieval theologians regarded marriage as a remedy to lust, and the essentials of marriage were wholly subject to ecclesiastical jurisdiction. In the marriage treatises of the early twelfth century, in Peter Lombard's *Sentences*, in commentaries on the *Sentences*, and in numerous other theological works that follow the ground plan of the

---

[71] *Concilium Lateranense IV*, canon 21 (Tanner-Alberigo 245/13–17). On how thirteenth-century theologians and pastors understood this duty of care, see N. Bériou, "La confession dans les écrits théologiques et pastoraux du XIIIe siècle: médication de l'âme ou démarche judiciaire?" in *L'aveu* (Rome, 1986), 261–82.

[72] Canon 22 (Tanner-Alberigo 245/25–32).

[73] On the Byzantine tradition's gradual adoption of the nuptial blessing "first as a desirable, then an obligatory, factor in legalizing marriage," see J. Meyendorff, "Christian Marriage in Byzantium," *Dumbarton Oaks Papers* 44 (1990): 99–107, at 104–06. *Novel 89* (893) by Emperor Leo VI (886–912) was crucial, for it required nuptial blessing by a priest as a necessary condition of a valid marriage among free persons. Priests both joined and separated (i.e., divorced) couples in the Byzantine tradition, whereas spouses joined themselves inseparably in the Roman tradition.

[74] Albertus Magnus, *De matrimonio* 1.2, ad 3 (Cologne edition, 26:156b): "ideo necesse est, quod quantum ad efficientia [matrimonium] dependeat a contrahentibus. Nihilominus instituta, secundum quae fit contractus, dependent a ministris ecclesiae."

Sentences, discussion of marriage as a sacrament is a prelude to the much longer treatment of the rules and regulations of marriage, which churchmen both codified and enforced.

The process by which marriage became one the sacraments during the first half of the twelfth century seems natural and effortless and not at all forced when one reads the literature of the period. The theologians were probably not aware that they were innovating. The easiness of the transition was partly a result of vocabulary. Augustine had characterized the indissolubility of marriage as the "good of sacrament" (*bonum sacramenti*), and early twelfth-century theologians did not distinguish clearly between the good of the sacrament and the sacrament of marriage. (Early thirteenth-century theologians, on the contrary, noticed the distinction, regarding it as problematic, and discussed it extensively: see Section 14.4.) Moreover, the term *sacramentum* could denote any sacred oath, including the marriage vows. Ivo of Chartres had referred to marrying as a sacrament in that sense (Section 5.4.1, final paragraph). Marriage was also a sign of the union between Christ and the church, and the term "sacrament" in a very broad sense included any "sacred sign" (*sacrum signum*), or "sign of a sacred thing" (*signum sacrae rei*). Much of the talk of marriage as a sacrament during the first half of the twelfth century pertained to the signification of marriage and especially of consummation. Equally important was the place of marriage in salvation history, which in early twelfth-century theology was sacramental history. Positing any sacrament in the earthly Paradise was anomalous, but historical theology followed a narrative of Paradise, fall, atonement, and eternal bliss, and marriage belonged as naturally in that setting as any sacrament did. Augustine had traced the changing nature and function of marriage in relation to Paradise and fall, to the life of God's people under the Old Law, and to the Gospel of Jesus Christ. Theologians during the first quarter of the twelfth century were familiar with use of the word *sacramentum* in the context of marriage, therefore, and they extended it by applying current notions of sacramentality to marriage. But they did so in an *ad hoc* manner to answer particular questions, without implying or presupposing any developed theory of marriage as one of the sacraments. That development began in the schools of Paris during the late twelfth century.

Insofar as medieval treatises on the sacrament of marriage had anything to say about the day-to-day task of being married, this was only at a very generalized, abstract level. These treatises do not provide pastoral illumination of the sort that a student in a modern seminary would expect to receive from a course entitled, "The Theology of Marriage." One might argue that medieval theologians were too committed to vocational celibacy to pass beyond the threshold of the married estate, for marriage was the only one of the seven sacraments in which they did not directly participate as beneficiaries. But neither do treatises on the sacrament of baptism offer much pastoral counsel on the task of being a Christian. Two relevant points are worth making here, both regarding modes of discourse. First, the Middle Ages left no theologically informed accounts of married life: nothing comparable to the theologically informed accounts of monastic life, such as William of Saint-Thierry's *Golden Epistle*. Second, the literatures related to confession and to preaching contain a rich hoard of material on the day-to-day task of married life, but these reflections were not informed by the theology of marriage as a sacrament, and they rarely invoked Scripture to illuminate marriage. Rüdiger Schnell has pointed out that there were in effect two "discourses" on marriage and gender in the Middle Ages: one in the *summas* and commentaries on the *Sentences*, and the other in sermons, *exempla*, and manuals for confessors. In the former discourse, man and woman are related as ruler and ruled, and their relationship is idealized and polarized. Such is the depiction of husband and wife in Ephesians 5 and in Augustine's theological writings on marriage. In the latter discourse, men and women compete and negotiate, and each sex sometimes masters the other. Wives are sometimes nagging and disobedient, but they may also use their wiles to mollify their husbands and to make them unwittingly into better, more righteous men.[75] Thomas of Chobham, who had studied arts and theology in Paris in the early thirteenth century before becoming subdeacon of Salisbury, advised confessors that women should "always be encouraged during penance to be preachers to their husbands, for no priest is as able to soften the heart of a man as his wife is."[76] There was nothing analogous in the church's relationship with Christ. Discussions of marriage as a sacrament of Christ and the church, therefore, belonged to the former discourse, which idealized gender and was detached from the complexities of everyday life.

If the point of the theology of marriage as a sacrament was not to provide the basis of pastoral counsel for married couples, what was its point? Three things above all, it seems to me. First, the abstract, idealized level on which theologians regarded the relationship of husband and wife was not negligible. Baptisms and weddings remain moving, meaningful events today even to observers who cannot articulate what these rites mean, and theologians have the task of giving shape to such intuitions. Second, the fact that marriage was a sacrament provided a rationale for the church's exclusive jurisdiction over the essentials of marriage. Third, the theology located marriage in salvation history, in the Christian life, and above all in the constitution of the church. Being married placed one squarely among secular Christians, for celibacy was the distinguishing trait of the spiritual elite, but marriage was more than a

---

75 R. Schnell, "The Discourse on Marriage in the Middle Ages," *Speculum* 73 (1998): 771–86. On the construal of gender in confessional and homiletic literature, see also S. Farmer, "Persuasive Voices: Clerical Images of Medieval Wives," *Speculum* 61 (1986): 517–43; and R. M. Karras, "Gendered Sin and Misogyny in John of Bromyard's *Summa predicantium*," *Traditio* 47 (1992): 233–57. The following studies focus on sermons that emphasize the ideal conjugal relationship: N. Bériou and D. L. d'Avray, "The Image of the Ideal Husband in Thirteenth-Century France," in Bériou and d'Avray, *Modern Questions about Medieval Sermons* (Spoleto, 1994), 31–69; and D. L. d'Avray and M. Tausche, "Marriage Sermons in *Ad status* Collections of the Central Middle Ages," ibid., 77–134.
76 Thomas of Chobham, *Summa confessorum*, ed. Broomfield, 375/3–6.

secular vocation. As already noted, it was an order: a mode of participating in the life of the church.[77] It was inferior to the celibate and religious vocations, yet only in degree and not in kind. Inasmuch as one could distinguish between what was due to God and what was due to Caesar, marriage as a sacrament was something that one ought to "render unto God" (Matt 22:21). The inclusion of marriage among the seven sacraments was arguably not the only way in which those ends could have been achieved, but it was the most secure way, and it was the way most congruent with the new emphasis on the pastoral ministry of the clergy. It also excluded anti-matrimonial heresy, which had troubled mainstream clerics since the early centuries of Christianity and was the subject of special concern during the twelfth and thirteenth centuries.

As already noted, to regard marriage as one of the sacraments was to regard it in the first place not as an estate or as a way of life but as the transient event of marrying. This is perhaps today the least appreciated and most misunderstood feature of the medieval doctrine of marriage as a sacrament. Sacraments were typically *caelebrationes*: ritual performances or enactments. When theologians spoke of the sacrament of baptism, for example, they were referring primarily to a rite conducted at the font, and only indirectly to the enduring character or to membership of the church.[78] Again, the sacrament of penance was the act of confessing and receiving absolution, not the subsequent acts of penance. Insofar as marriage was construed as one of the sacraments, therefore, it was not the estate of marriage but the act of marrying. The only major medieval theologian who regarded marriage chiefly as an estate was Peter John Olivi, O. F. M. (d. 1298), and he doubted whether marriage was properly one of the seven sacraments. Martin Luther, too, preferred to regard marriage as an estate, and he utterly rejected the sacramental doctrine.

This particular implication of the doctrine was not clear at first, during the first half of the twelfth century. It was becoming clear in Peter Lombard, although he was still inconsistent. It was fully settled by 1200. Duns Scotus explained that whereas both the sacrament and the contract of marriage were things that existed only in the act of coming into being (*in fieri*), the marriage bond (*vinculum*) that resulted had enduring being (*esse permanens*).[79] Theologians who argued that sinful or false intentions would prevent the reception of marital grace were referring not to failings in the spouses' married life, but to their intentions in marrying, on their wedding day.

---

[77] Cf. N. Bériou and D. L. d'Avray, "Henry of Provins, O.P.'s Comparison of the Dominican and Franciscan Orders with the 'Order' of Matrimony," in Bériou and d'Avray, *Modern Questions about Medieval Sermons*, 71–75.

[78] Technically, the act at the font is the *sacramentum tantum*, whereas the enduring character is the *sacramentum et res*.

[79] Duns Scotus, *Reportatio Parisiensis, IV Sent.* 28.un. (*Opera omnia*, Vivès 24:383). See Section 14.1.

Some complications should be noted. First, scholastic theologians after 1250 identified marriage as *coniunctio* ("joining," or "union") with the continuing condition of being married, whereas they identified the sacrament of marriage chiefly with the event of getting married (Section 12.2.1.2). The term *coniunctio* was the basis of some classical definitions of marriage, and theologians recognized that what the classical jurists had defined was the married estate. Whereas the exchange of mutual consent was the efficient cause of marriage as union (*coniunctio*), therefore, it was the formal cause of the sacrament. (According to the schoolmen, efficient causes were extrinsic, whereas formal causes were intrinsic.) Second, theologians were never entirely consistent even about the temporal identity of the sacrament. Their vocabulary permitted ambiguity, for both *matrimonium* and *coniugium* could denote either the event or the state. (These two terms were coextensive and interchangeable during the Middle Ages, although they had different connotations. The former emphasized lawfulness and validity and invoked ideas of motherhood, whereas the latter emphasized the partnership of two persons who became in certain respects a single social unit.) The term *nuptiae* primarily denoted marrying or the wedding, but it was also used by extension to denote the state of being married. Thus, although theologians assumed by default that the sacrament of matrimony was the transient event of marrying, they attended instead to the state of being married when the context demanded it. Their identification of the sacrament with marrying broke down, for example, when they considered the Pauline Privilege (1 Cor 7:10–15), for in that case an existing but non-sacramental marriage between unbelievers automatically became a sacrament when one of them converted to Christianity and was baptized, without any new ceremony or plighting of troth. When theologians remarked on the correspondences between marriage and Christ's union with the church, they were sometimes referring to features of marrying and sometimes to features of the married estate. Nevertheless, Robert Bellarmine (d. 1621) was the first major theologian to argue that the estate of marriage might itself be construed as the sacrament. From the premise that a sacrament was an outward sign of an inward mystery or grace, Bellarmine deduced that both the visible act of getting married and the visible condition of being married (rather than the interior bond, which was invisible) were aspects of the same sacrament.[80]

Although the focus on the act of marrying rather than on the estate of marriage determined the theological agenda, medieval theologians did not ignore married life entirely. The purpose of performing or receiving the sacrament of marriage was in its enduring effects, just as the purpose of being baptized was to be liberated from original sin and to be incorporated into the mystical body of Christ. But perhaps medieval theologians would have reflected more extensively and

---

[80] Robert Bellarmine, *Controversiarum de sacramento matrimonii liber*, contr. 2, c. 6 (*Opera omnia*, 5:57–59).

in greater depth on the theology of married life if they had been less preoccupied with the transient act of marrying.

1.5 ECCLESIASTICAL JURISDICTION

Inasmuch as marriage was a sacrament, it was necessarily subject exclusively to canon law and to the jurisdiction of ecclesiastical courts. Marriage became one of the sacraments during a period when the church was taking control of marriage. Kenneth Stevenson famously spoke of the church's "taking over" marriage during this period.[81] He was referring chiefly to new liturgical practices, but these were aspects of a wider development that was above all about law and jurisdiction. The phrase "taking control" is more apt than "taking over," however, for the church was not wresting control from a competing authority.

What was taking control? The church – but the term "church" is equivocal. Modern social and political historians often use the term "church" to denote a corporation populated by bishops, clergy, and religious. The church in this sense was separate by definition from the laity, and the two parts of medieval society are sometimes regarded today antagonistically, as if the church ruled through a form of oligarchy. In the minds of medieval theologians, on the contrary, the church was above all the mystical body of Christ, which included all Christians but was hierarchically organized. This holistic model has virtue even from a non-confessional, purely historical perspective, for the medieval church could not have existed without aristocratic patrons and popular piety. Medieval clerics and religious used the term *ecclesia* also in senses that fall somewhere between the two outlined earlier. For example, they regarded the church both as the bride of Christ and as a mother who cares for her young.[82] By an extension of those metaphors, clerics regarded the bishop as the *amicus sponsi* (cf. John 3:29), as an attendant of the bride (*paranymphus*), and even as the bridegroom of his diocese. Eleventh-century English clerics regarded the parish priest as the church's spouse.[83] Construed rather as Christ's bride than as his body, the church was a pastoral organization providing spiritual counsel and sacramental therapy to the laity.

There is something to be said for avoiding the equivocal word "church" in historical accounts of medieval religion and referring instead to bishops, to religious, to clergy, and so forth: terms that are more specific as well as more concrete. But the specificity comes with problems of its own, and I shall continue to use the term "church" sparingly in what follows, trusting that the context will resolve any ambiguities. The church that was taking control of marriage around the beginning

---

[81] Stevenson, *Nuptial Blessing*, 67. P. Biller, *The Measure of Multitude* (Oxford, 2000), 21–23, develops the wider implications of Stevenson's insight.

[82] McLaughlin, *Sex, Gender, and Episcopal Authority*, 123–59.

[83] M. McLaughlin, "The Church as Bride in Late Anglo-Saxon and Norman England," in M. Aurell, *Les stratégies matrimoniales (IXe–XIIIe siècle)* (Turnout, 2013), 257–66.

of the twelfth century was above all a legally constituted authority: an *oberkeit*. For the church was also a legally constituted authority. Today, we use the term "state" to refer to an authority of that sort, which includes all of us in principle yet embodies powers that only a few exercise, by virtue of their office.

The new regime is apparent in liturgical developments, especially in northern Europe. Marrying had been a largely secular or domestic affair even among the nobility during the post-Carolingian period. Although the evidence is sparse and its meaning disputable, it seems that the clergy's role in solemnizing marriages had been limited to the *benedictio in thalamo*: the blessing of the bedchamber, of the bed, or of the newlyweds in the bedchamber.[84] A new way of marrying before the church (*in facie ecclesiae*) developed quickly in northern France and Anglo-Norman England during the early twelfth century.[85] This involved a preliminary, prenuptial betrothal rite conducted in the presence of the parish priest at the door or in the porch of a church. There, in the presence of the couple's parents, family members, kinsfolk, and friends, the priest would interrogate the partners to ascertain that there were no impediments and that they freely consented to their union. The extant *ordines* for this pre-nuptial rite include features traditionally associated with betrothal contracts, such as the gift of a ring. After the partners had plighted their troth, the party would proceed into the sanctuary, where the priest would bless the now-married couple in a nuptial mass. Clerics encouraged couples to prepare for such weddings with prayers and vigils and by receiving eucharist. The earliest extant example of the new procedure is in a manuscript written at Bury St Edmunds between 1125 and 1135, by which time the procedure was probably already well established.[86]

Legal competence, or the power of law, embraces both legislative and jurisdictional authority. Legislative competence is the power to make laws. Jurisdiction is essentially the power to adjudicate (to judge cases), although it presupposes jurisprudence (the interpretation of laws), legal process, and enforcement. Medieval canon law did not formally recognize precedent, or case law (the binding consequences of adjudication), although legislation and jurisdiction merged in decretal law (the *ius novum*), since the pope was both supreme judge and supreme legislator. Modern historians tracing the development of the church's legal competence over marriage and other matters regard jurisdiction as primary and legislation as a necessary support. Medieval theologians, preoccupied with the relation of human law to natural and divine law and with questions of teleology, well-being, and epistemology, regarded legislation as primary and mentioned enforcement only incidentally.

---

[84]　Molin and Mutembe, *Le rituel de mariage*, 254–70, on the *benedictio in thalamo*.

[85]　Molin and Mutembe, *Le rituel de mariage*, 30–47. Ritzer, *Le mariage*, 393–95. Stevenson, *Nuptial Blessing*, 68–71. C. N. L. Brooke, *The Medieval Idea of Marriage* (Oxford, 1989), 248–57.

[86]　Molin and Mutembe, *Le rituel de mariage*, Ordo V, 289–91. Searle and Stevenson, *Documents of the Marriage Liturgy*, 148–55.

Most aspects of marriage that were subject to legal control fell into three categories: (1) essential matters pertaining to the formation and validity of marriage, to divorce, and to the intrinsic obligations of the bond of marriage; (2) consequent matters regarding property and wealth; and (3) sexual conduct that was not contained by lawful marriage, including simple fornication, adultery, rape, sodomy, and bestiality.[87] When historians attribute exclusive competence over marriage to the church during the central Middle Ages, they are referring chiefly to the first of those three categories. This embraces the validity and legitimacy of marriages, diriment impediments, prior contract (*impedimentum ligationis alteri*), clandestinity, the conjugal debt, the mutual obligations of cohabitation and marital affection, and divorce – including the dissolution of invalid marriages, the dissolution of valid but unconsummated marriages under special circumstances, and legal separation without the option of remarriage. In theory, church courts had exclusive competence over the validity of marriage, whereas secular courts had exclusive competence over the material consequences, but the demarcation was not always so clear in practice. In areas such as bastardy (the illegitimacy of offspring) and dowry (*dos*), ecclesiastical and secular jurisdictions did not always adjudicate according to the same rules, and there was nothing to prevent secular courts from applying their own criteria of legitimacy.[88] Moreover, church courts reserved the right to handle the property consequences of nullity and separation suits.[89] According to Tancred, "judgment regarding the dowry belongs to the ecclesiastical judge ... because when a matrimonial case is initiated, the case of the dowry as an accessory to it is understood to have been initiated as well."[90] Competence regarding the third category – contravention of conjugal and sexual norms – was blurred and mixed. The convergent interests of ecclesiastical and secular authorities in sexual crimes was especially important during the late-medieval and Reformation periods, when citizens, local communities, and their rulers throughout Europe were increasingly preoccupied with norms of sexual behavior, and when sexual license and deviance seemed to threaten the civic order and even to invite the wrath of God.[91]

---

[87] J. F. Harrington, *Reordering Marriage and Society in Reformation Germany* (Cambridge, 1995), 101–7. Harrington's characterization of the first category as "validity disputes" is potentially misleading, for church courts could and did prosecute both instance cases (disputes brought to the court by the parties) and office cases (initiated by the court). Sometimes an office case originated in an instance case.

[88] See N. Adams and C. Donahue, *Select Cases from the Ecclesiastical Courts of the Province of Canterbury c.1200–1301* (London, 1981), introduction, 84, regarding English law.

[89] J. A. Brundage, *Law, Sex, and Christian Society in Medieval Europe* (Chicago, 1987), 479–80.

[90] Tancred, *Summa de matrimonio*, title 39 (ed. Wunderlich, p. 108). Raymond of Penyafort, *Summa de matrimonio*, title 25 (Rome, 1603, p. 581).

[91] Brundage, *Law, Sex, and Christian Society*, 319, 545–46. Harrington, *Reordering Marriage*, 27–38. Harrington, ibid., 114–18, 122–24, 139–40, and 153–73, shows how *causae mixtae* and the preoccupation with sexual crimes in sixteenth-century Germany resulted in mixed but essentially civic tribunals such as the lay synods, in which regional clerics and leading laymen collaborated.

The inclusion of marriage among the sacraments presupposed that the church had exclusive legal competence as regards both legislation and jurisdiction over the essential matters of marriage. The church alone could determine whether or not a marriage was valid, even though everyone agreed that the Christian sacrament presupposed an essentially civil compact that was fundamental to political life everywhere.

Exclusive competence was also inclusive, for it extended to marriage as a secular, civic partnership. The church's competence to determine who was validly married and to regulate the marriage bond was as much a civil matter as it was a spiritual one. The church regulated marriage *in the political community*, or *in civil society*. The church had exclusive competence over marriage to the extent that it had the power to determine whether or not a marriage was valid even as regards its secular consequences, for marriage was in the first place a civic institution. Regardless of what penalties the church might use to enforce a judgment that a marriage was invalid, even including excommunication, the church had exclusive jurisdiction only to the extent that its judgment had civil consequences and was recognized by the secular authorities. Absent that recognition, ecclesiastical judgment was merely private and disciplinary. Jurisdictional competence was complex during the central Middle Ages, and the boundaries between ecclesiastical and secular legal competence were often unclear, but it is safe to say that by the twelfth century the church in northern Europe had something approximating to exclusive jurisdiction over the essentials of marriage in the manner outlined earlier, notwithstanding some exceptions regarding the secular consequences. If the medieval church declared that a couple's marriage was invalid, they were not married at all.

It had not always been so. Bishops and theologians during the patristic period had insisted on the difference between God's law and the secular law of marriage, which included the laws of the Christian emperors. The remarriage of divorcees was a crux. Augustine noted that Christians alone observed the *bonum sacramenti*, whereby persons who had divorced and remarried were committing adultery. Mosaic law and the law of the Gentiles (i.e., Roman civil law), on the contrary, permitted divorce and remarriage (Section 4.3).[92] Augustine remarked in a sermon that such forbidden remarriages were adulterous in the heavenly tribunal (*ius coeli*) but valid in the secular tribunal (*ius fori*).[93] Similarly, Jerome contrasted the laws of the Caesars regarding such marriages with the laws of Christ, and the jurisprudence of Papinian with that of "our Paul" (i.e., St Paul in contradistinction to the Roman jurist of the same name).[94] Ambrose said that such marriages were permitted inasmuch as human law (*lex humana*) did not prohibit them, but that divine law (*lex divina*)

---

[92] See especially Augustine, *De nupt. et conc.* I.10(11) (CSEL 42:222–23), where Augustine contrasts the *lex huius saeculi* and the Mosaic law with the *lex evangelii* (223/9–17).

[93] Augustine, *Epist.* 392.2 (PL 39:1710): "Adulterina sunt ista conjugia, non jure fori, sed jure coeli."

[94] Jerome, *Epist.* 77 (Ad Oceanum), 3 (CSEL 55:39).

did prohibit them.[95] Gregory the Great made the same distinction when discussing whether a spouse had the unilateral right to enter the religious life, leaving the other in the world. Human law permitted such separation, Gregory argued, but divine law did not. The human law to which he referred was that of the emperor Justinian.[96] That said, although evidence regarding how bishops or synods attempted to enforce their ecclesiastical prohibitions during the patristic period is sparse, they presumably handled infractions by excommunication and reconciliation. Their actions would not have affected the status of the marriages in secular law.

The schema that Adhémar Esmein proposed in 1891 to describe the rise and fall of the church's exclusive jurisdiction over marriage is still widely accepted and cited by historians today, although it was based on a very narrow selection of evidence. Tracing the development of legal competence from Constantine through Carolingian Francia and medieval Europe to the Reformation and the early-modern period, Esmein posited three main periods.[97] During the first period, which extended from Constantine through the Carolingian era, secular authorities had exclusive competence over marriage, although they adopted features of church teaching in their own legislation. Churchmen insisted on the distinction between divine law and secular law, but their rule was "disciplinary" rather than legal, and excommunication was the strongest measure available to them. Esmein argues that the relation of secular to ecclesiastical power was essentially the same under the Carolingians as it had been under Constantine, although secular rulers and bishops collaborated even more closely. Esmein points out that even the pseudo-Isidorian forgeries and the false decretals of Benedict the Deacon, which make extreme claims for the power of bishops, never attributed general jurisdiction over marriage cases to the church.[98] During the second phase, the church enjoyed exclusive jurisdiction over the essentials of marriage. While conceding that it is difficult to determine when this regime arrived,[99] Esmein argues that it had become established in France and Italy by the middle of the tenth century. He attributes the development to the weak and fragmented authority of secular rulers. Finally, according to Esmein, the order reverted to something akin to that of the first phase during the Reformation and early-modern periods.

George Hayward Joyce presented a fuller and more satisfying account in *Christian Marriage* (first published in 1933), acknowledging his debt to Esmein.[100]

---

[95] Ambrose, *in Luc.* VIII, 5, on Luke 16:18 (PL 15:1767A): "Dimittis ergo uxorem quasi jure, sine crimine; et putas id tibi licere, quia lex humana non prohibet; sed divina prohibet. Qui hominibus obsequeris, Deum verere. Audi legem Domini, cui obsequuntur etiam qui leges ferunt: Quae Deus conjunxit, homo non separet."

[96] MWCh 138–41.   [97] Esmein-Genestal, 1:1–66.   [98] Ibid., 25.   [99] Ibid., 27.

[100] G. H. Joyce, *Christian Marriage*, 2nd edition (London, 1948), 215–31. Joyce (216–17) is rightly cautious about the scope of the bishop's court (*iudicium episcopale*, known in Justinian's *Code* as the *episcopalis audientia*) that emerged under Constantine as a means for Christians to settle their disputes within the community (cf. 1 Cor 6:1–7). It was largely (perhaps entirely) limited

During the Carolingian period, a litigant in a matrimonial case could opt to have the case "tried before the secular or the ecclesiastical court," Joyce points out, and he or she was then bound by that choice.[101] The ecclesiastical courts in this setting were usually synods. Joyce questions whether the civil officials were always bound to enforce the decisions of ecclesiastical courts, but he argues that the secular courts grew weaker and the ecclesiastical courts stronger during the second half of the ninth century. By the end of the ninth century, the church in France and Germany "had acquired exclusive cognizance of matrimonial cases, and the secular power recognized the obligation of enforcing the sentence given in the bishop's court."[102] Joyce tacitly implies that the bishops were applying ecclesiastical law, but the capitularies of the Carolingian rulers generally complied with that law in any case. The two branches collaborated in enforcing a code that included the prohibition of remarriage after divorce, the prohibition of marriage to a woman already betrothed to another, and the impediments of consanguinity, affinity, and religious vows.[103]

Pierre Daudet proposed a less linear model of the development in two influential studies of ecclesiastical jurisdiction: one, which was his doctoral dissertation, on Carolingian France and Germany (1933), and the other on France from the tenth through twelfth centuries (1941).[104] Reforms and developments in canon law during the Carolingian period established that the church was more competent to adjudicate matrimonial cases than the state, but this advance was more theoretical than practical, Daudet argues. Carolingian church courts could adjudicate some matrimonial cases by the end of the ninth century, but secular courts still adjudicated most of them. In the tenth century, neither the secular nor the ecclesiastical authorities made much effort to control marriage and divorce among the nobility. Popes and bishops during the eleventh century pursued a determined and vigorous campaign to enforce the church's rules on marriage and divorce, with little competition from secular authorities.[105]

The church had acquired effective and virtually unchallenged legal control over marriage by the beginning of the twelfth century. James Brundage argues that church courts "enjoyed their greatest success in securing exclusive jurisdiction ...

to binding arbitration, and there is no reason to think that it applied a distinctive church law. The institution was an important milestone in the development of episcopal adjudication, since a single bishop rather than a synod acted as judge, but it had little if any role in the evolution of ecclesiastical competence over marriage. See MWCh 145–47; R. M. Frakes, *Contra Potentium Iniurias* (Munich, 2001), 195–229; and A. J. B. Sirks, "The episcopalis audientia in Late Antiquity," *Droit et cultures* 65 (2013): 79–88.
[101] Joyce, *Christian Marriage*, 220.   [102] Ibid., 223.
[103] See K. Heidecker, *The Divorce of Lothar II* (Ithaca, 2010), 11–35, on the Carolingian reforms. Heidecker maintains that the "priestly blessing of the nuptials was made compulsory" (34), but in this respect he arguably exaggerates the realism of the *Pseudo-Isidorian* literature.
[104] P. Daudet, *Les origines carolingiennes de la compétence exclusive de l'église* (Paris, 1933). Daudet, *L'établissement de la compétence le l'église en matière de divorce et de consanguinité (France Xème–XIIème siècles)* (Paris, 1941).
[105] Daudet, *Les origines*, 172.

over marriage legislation" around 1100, when "even kings and great nobles ordinarily brought questions concerning the validity of their marriages to ecclesiastical authorities and were often prepared, however reluctantly, to abide by their decisions."[106] This chronology inevitably highlights the work of Ivo, who was bishop of Chartres from 1090 until his death in 1116. He was the foremost authority on canon law of his day. Ivo's letters show him using his hoard of canonical material creatively but impartially to solve the matrimonial cases and conundrums referred to him by laypersons as well as by fellow bishops (Section 5.4).

Many historians have construed the church's achievement of exclusive competence over marriage during the central Middle Ages as the waxing of one ideology and the waning of another. George Duby famously proposed that a battle was played out between the proponents of two models of marriage, respectively ecclesiastical and aristocratic.[107] The aristocratic model favored insolubility and endogamy and was tolerant of concubinage, whereas the ecclesiastical model favored insolubility, exogamy, and monogamy. Duby's approach has been fruitful and productive, but many historians have resisted it, and with good reason. David Herlihy and Christopher Brooke are representative of early criticisms. Herlihy complains that Duby uses the term "model" equivocally. The church's model was prescriptive, a "set of rules or recommendations," whereas the lay model was descriptive: a "generalized portrayal of actual behavior." By treating the two models as comparable, Herlihy argues, Duby "clouds his analysis."[108] Herlihy's criticism would not be fatal if the noblemen were consistently pursuing an ideology, even if it remained implicit, but it would be fatal if the noblemen were only opportunistically pursuing their own self-interest, as seems to have been the case. Christopher Brooke objects that the notion of two dueling groups is unrealistic. If the two had fundamentally different ideologies of marriage, Brooke asks, how can one explain why "the lay aristocracy of Europe allowed the Church to take over almost completely the jurisdiction of the law of marriage"?[109] The trend in recent scholarship on medieval marriage has been to construe the waxing of ecclesiastical jurisdiction over marriage not as the victory of one model or one social group over another, but rather as the result of a complicated interplay of shared convictions, self-advancement, and opportunism.[110]

By the end of the eleventh century, the church's competence over marriage was also beginning to extend to a broader spectrum of the laity. The population of the

---

[106] Brundage, *Law, Sex, and Christian Society*, 223.

[107] G. Duby, *Medieval Marriage: Two Models from Twelfth-Century France* (Baltimore, 1978). Duby pursued his two-model theory in *Le chevalier, la femme et le prêtre* (Paris, 1981) and other writings.

[108] D. Herlihy, "The Family and Religious Ideologies in Medieval Europe," *Journal of Family History* 12 (1987): 3–17, at 7.

[109] Brooke, *Medieval Idea of Marriage*, 126.

[110] S. McDougall, "The Making of Marriage in Medieval France," *Journal of Family History* 38.2 (2013): 103–21, rejects *all* explanations that posit conflicts and negotiations between clergy and aristocracy, including Duby's. That may be going too far, but she makes an interesting case.

middle social strata – minor landowners, merchants, elite artisans, and so forth – was also growing. Some of the laypersons who feature in Ivo's letters on matrimonial cases were from the nobility, but many were middling folk. Pope Hadrian IV ruled in his decretal *Dignum est*, issued in 1155, that unfree persons (*servi*) were free to marry without the consent of their lords, both because there was neither bond nor free in Jesus Christ (Gal 3:28) and because marriage was one of the sacraments, for no one had the right to prevent any Christian from having access to a sacrament (Section 11.6). How much access poor and unfree persons had to marriage litigation and to the protections of church law and jurisdiction during this period is debatable, but Hadrian's decretal presupposed that the legal implications of counting marriage among the sacraments extended to everyone in reality, and not only in theory. According to Michael Sheehan, the "essential elements of the ideal of marriage had been rather successfully applied among the lower levels of society" by the end of the fourteenth century. Sheehan concludes that "the marital ideals and institutions, which were developed during the twelfth and early thirteenth centuries, were intended to assure that the new theory and practice would become the model for the populace at large."[111]

The inclusion of marriage among the seven sacraments was not a necessary condition for the church's exclusive jurisdiction, although it was a sufficient one. Canon law extended to many temporal matters. Nor is there any evidence that churchmen insisted on the sacramental doctrine as a way to assure their legal competence, as if they were staking their claim to a territory. G. H. Joyce argues that the church during the eleventh century "exercised jurisdiction ... as an inherent prerogative consequent on her divinely-given authority over the sacraments," but the flow of ideas was if anything in the opposite direction, at least when regarded from a merely historical perspective. The inclusion of marriage among the sacraments was fitting *because* marriage was subject in its essentials exclusively to canon law and to ecclesiastical jurisdiction. Nevertheless, the doctrine must have confirmed the church's competence, putting it beyond debate.

1.6 CONCOMITANTS OF THE SACRAMENTAL DOCTRINE

The doctrine of marriage as a sacrament presupposed three other doctrines: that marriage was indissoluble; that the mutual consent of the spouses was by itself sufficient to establish a valid marriage; and that the diriment impediments of relationship extended far beyond naturally abhorrent, incestuous unions. The relationship of these doctrines to the sacramental theology of marriage is difficult to determine, but the four doctrines were inseparable aspects of a single ecclesiastical view or model of marriage.

---

[111] M. M. Sheehan, "Theory and Practice: Marriage of the Unfree and the Poor in Medieval Society," in Sheehan, *Marriage, Family, and Law* (Toronto, 1996), 211–46, at 246.

1.6.1 *Indissolubility*

The doctrine of absolute indissolubility, precluding all possibility of valid remarriage, separated the western church from Roman law and jurisprudence, from Judaism and Islam, and even from Byzantine Christianity.[112] The doctrine gave rise in western canon law to the possibility of legal separation, or "divorce from board and bed" (*divortium a mensa et thoro*), for which there are few if any parallels in other legal systems.[113] Nevertheless, it was the least examined of all major, consequential Christian doctrines during the Middle Ages, perhaps in part because it fell somewhere between a conviction of reason and an article of faith. Scholastic theologians debated for the sake of argument whether Christ should have become incarnate and even whether God existed, but few of them debated or questioned whether Christian marriage was absolutely indissoluble. The doctrine was often a premise of arguments about marriage, but it was rarely a conclusion.

The principle of indissolubility imposed extraordinary pressure on the regulation of validity during the central Middle Ages. In marrying, couples embarked on a union from which they could escape only by dying. Because the church alone, in the guise of episcopal tribunals, could determine whether a marriage was valid and whether a prior union would or would not invalidate a subsequent one, rules and procedures for deciding such matters in litigation were vital, and until the twelfth century tradition and precedent were often unclear or inconsistent.

The medieval understanding of indissolubility was derived from Augustine's. The manner in which Jesus condemned divorce in the synoptic gospels seemed to imply that spouses who had separated, even if one had divorced the other on permitted grounds, would commit adultery if they remarried. Augustine's friendly debate with Pollentius showed him that his exegetical reasoning was faulty, but he never relinquished the premise (Section 2.2.3). This premise in turn implied, Augustine reasoned, that spouses who had separated or divorced were in some sense still married to each other. In what sense, he was unable to explain. He considered the matter to be a mystery that surpassed human understanding, although he noted that there were analogous bonds in baptism and ordination. Baptism established an insoluble "sacrament of faith," indelibly marking the subject as a member of the church, and apostasy did not destroy that sacrament of faith. Instead, the sacrament remained and made the infidelity more sinful. In an analogous way, "something conjugal" remained in the spouse who divorced, causing a re-marriage to be adulterous (Section 4.3.1).

---

[112] On reformist attitudes to divorce-remarriage during the central Middle Ages, see McLaughlin, *Sex, Gender, and Episcopal Authority*, 43–47.

[113] J. Kamas, *The Separation of the Spouses with the Bond Remaining* (Rome, 1997), 31–118. G. Marchetto, *Il divorzio imperfetto. I giuristi medievali e la separazione dei coniugi* (Bologna, 2008), 21–231.

Spouses were normally bound to cohabit, to support each other, and to observe the conjugal debt until parted by death, therefore, but something of the bond remained and prevented them from remarrying even if they divorced or separated on valid grounds. Augustine called this feature of marriage the "good of sacrament" (*bonum sacramenti*). It was the third of three goods in which the value of marriage chiefly lay, the others being the goods of offspring (*bonum prolis*) and of faith (*bonum fidei*). The good of offspring was the begetting, nurturing, and educating of children, ideally as Christians who would worship the true God. The good of faith was primarily observance of the conjugal debt (1 Cor 7:3), although it also entailed fidelity in the modern sense. In Augustine's view, the observance of the third good, insolubility, was what chiefly distinguished marriage among Christians from marriage under both Mosaic and Roman law. Only the church fully observed the *bonum sacramenti* and refused to permit remarriage after divorce as long as both spouses survived.

That said, what indissolubility meant in practical terms during Augustine's day remains unclear. Christian bishops were not in a position then to determine that a marriage was invalid. The most severe penalty at their disposal was excommunication. One would expect bishops like Augustine to have refused to reconcile remarried divorcees with the church unless they agreed to separate or at least to practice continence, but there is little evidence that marginalized communities of legally remarried but permanently excommunicated divorcees troubled western dioceses during late antiquity.[114]

Medieval theologians and canonists inherited Augustine's association of indissolubility with sanctity and with faith in Christ. Early twelfth-century theologians saw in the Pauline Privilege, by which an unbeliever who converts to Christianity may under certain circumstances divorce and to remarry within the faith, evidence that marriages between unbelievers were soluble, or at least less than fully insoluble (Section 9.5.2). But medieval theologians increasingly resisted that notion. It seemed to them that the law of indissolubility began not in the Gospel but when God joined the first couple as two in one flesh (Gen 2:24), for Jesus had reminded his hearers of that primordial law when he condemned divorce (Matt 19:4–6, Mark 10:6–9). Jesus did not imply that he was instituting anything new. Moses recognized divorce only to prevent worse things from happening, scholars reasoned, but it remained unlawful

---

[114] On divorce in early Christianity, see H. Crouzel, *L'Église primitive face au divorce du premier au cinquième siècle* (Paris, 1970); Crouzel, "Les Pères de l'Église ont-ils permis le remariage après séparation?" *Bulletin de littérature ecclésiastique* 70 (1969): 3–43; J. T. Noonan, "Novel 22," in W. M. Bassett, *The Bond of Marriage* (Notre Dame, 1968), 41–90; J. Meyendorff, "Christian Marriage in Byzantium," *Dumbarton Oaks Papers* 44 (1990): 99–107, at 101–2; and P. Blažek, "Divorce. Greek and Latin Patristics, and Orthodox Churches," in *Encyclopedia of the Bible and its Reception* (Berlin, 1913), 6:1006–8. On the doctrinal history of indissolubility from the early church to Trent, see Joyce, *Christian Marriage*, 304–99; and A. Bevilacqua, "The History of the Indissolubility of Marriage," *Proceedings of the Catholic Theological Society of America* 22 (1967): 253–308;

even then under divine law. Theologians noted that marriage according to the Roman jurist Modestinus was a "partnership for the entire life" (*consortium omnis vitae*).[115] Marriage was insoluble in principle, therefore, even under Roman law. Some theologians reasoned that marriage was insoluble or at least lifelong under the natural law because a permanent union was necessary to support parents' responsibilities toward their offspring, although the force of this argument is unclear.[116]

Many theologians, nevertheless, reasoned that although marriage was an intrinsically lifelong and even insoluble union, Jesus had confirmed, strengthened, or fully realized that insolubility by raising marriage to the level of a sacrament of the New Law. This position seems to presuppose the difficult notion that indissolubility is capable of degrees. Some authors seem to have meant that conjugal grace made lifelong marriage endurable, removing the excuse of human fallibility, but this rationale was not well developed. Alexander of Hales was among the few theologians who developed a theological, even ontological rationale for indissolubility. In his view, the permanence of Christian marriage was based on the firm foundation of the baptismal character, which was in turn causally dependent on the Passion of Jesus Christ (Section 16.1).

1.6.2 Solus consensus

The principle that the consent of the spouses alone (*solus consensus*) was sufficient to establish a valid and indissoluble marriage emerged with the doctrine of marriage as a sacrament. The two ideas went together and seemed inseparable until the sixteenth century, when the Council of Trent severed them in the decree *Tametsi*. Modern scholars associate the *solus consensus* principle chiefly with Pope Alexander III (r. 1159–1181),[117] who insisted on its implications in his decretals, but early twelfth-century theologians already took the principle for granted and strove to accommodate it despite the judicial problems that it generated. They considered marriage to be a *coniunctio animorum*: a union of wills or intentions. The mutual consent of the spouses was constitutive of this union, and not only a necessary precondition, for only the spouses' mutual consent could constitute a union of their wills.

The principle that consent alone was sufficient excluded several other things that could plausibly be and sometimes had been considered necessary for a valid marriage. For convenience, one may divide these excluded items into four overlapping categories: the consent of other parties, such as parents; contractual formalities, such as betrothal gifts, dowries, and documentation; publicity, witnesses, and

---

[115] *Dig.* 23.2.1

[116] L. Ryan, "The Indissolubility of Marriage in Natural Law: A Disputed Point in the Teaching of St. Thomas Aquinas," *Irish Theological Quarterly* 30 (1963): 293–310, and 31 (1964): 62–77.

[117] C. Donahue, Jr., "The Policy of Alexander the Third's Consent Theory of Marriage," *Monumenta Iuris Canonici*, series C: Subsidia, vol. 5 (Vatican City, 1976), = *Proceedings of the Fourth International Congress of Canon Law*, ed. Stephan Kuttner, 251–81.

community involvement; and religious rites, such as the nuptial blessing and the priestly joining of right hands. Any or all of these things might be considered important, pious, fitting, or honorable, but according to the principle of *solus consensus* none was strictly necessary for a valid marriage. Nor could a marriage be annulled on the grounds that any such condition had not been satisfied. The principle of *solus consensus* was especially important in cases of prior contract. For example, if a man married one woman privately but then married a second woman publicly in a church ceremony, the second marriage was invalid because the man was already married. A church court would annul the second marriage if there was sufficient evidence that the first had taken place.

Discussion of *solus consensus* in medieval theology and canon law turned on a few endlessly repeated authorities. Some of these affirmed the principle, whereas others seemed to contradict it and required conciliation or solution. The most frequently cited contradictory authority during the Middle Ages and at the Council of Trent was a decretal that was ascribed to Pope Evaristus (d. c. 107), although in fact it was the work of a Carolingian forger. It existed in two versions: a longer version found among the church laws supposedly collected by Isidorus Mercator (Isidore the Merchant), and a truncated version included among the capitularies supposedly collected by Benedictus Levita (Benedict the Deacon). These collections belonged to a corpus of partly forged and partly authentic but spuriously elaborated legal texts produced in the archdiocese of Reims and completed by 837. The texts supported a conservative movement of reform, with emphasis especially on the authority of bishops.[118]

In the following translation of the text, the passage in italics is missing from Benedictus Levita's version,[119] but the two versions are otherwise the same:

> ... we have maintained as something preserved and handed down that a wife should be lawfully [*legitime*] joined to her husband, for, according to what we have received from the fathers and have found passed down by the holy apostles and their successors, a marriage is not lawful [*legitimum*] unless the wife is asked for from those who are deemed to have authority over her and custody of her, and she has been endowed and betrothed by her parents and kinsfolk and given away in accordance with the laws, and when her time has come she has been blessed, as is customary, by a priest with prayers and offerings in a priestly manner, and then, at the appropriate time, having been asked for in accordance with the laws, she is given away by her kinsfolk and solemnly taken, watched over and accompanied by

---

[118] On the pseudo-Isidorian corpus, see H. Fuhrmann, "The Pseudo-Isidorian Forgeries," in D. Jasper and H. Fuhrmann, *Papal Letters in the Early Middle Ages* (Washington D.C., 2001), 137–95; K. Zechiel-Eckes, "Auf Pseudoisidors Spur, oder: Versuch einen dichten Schleier zu lüften," in Wilfried Hartmann and Gerhard Schmitz, *Fortschritt durch Fälschungen?* (Hannover, 2001), 1–28; and E. Knibbs, "The Interpolated Hispana and the Origins of Pseudo-Isidore," *Zeitschrift der Savigny-Stiftung für Rechtsgeschichte: Kanonistische Abteilung* 99.1 (2013): 1–71.

[119] Benedictus Levita III.463 (PL 97:859C–D).

her paranymphs, and [the spouses] preserve their chastity and devote themselves to prayer for two or three days, so that good children may be generated from them and their conduct may be pleasing to the Lord, for in that way they will please the Lord and generate children that are not spurious but legitimate and capable of inheriting. *Accordingly, my dearest and deservedly illustrious sons, know that a marriage contracted thus, supported by the catholic faith, is lawful, whereas one presumptuously contracted in a different manner is not marriage but undoubtedly is rather adultery or cohabitation or promiscuity or fornication than lawful marriage, unless it is founded on their own will and supported by lawful vows.*[120]

The decretal requires the three chief formalities of marrying current among the landed elites during the early Middle Ages: the petition, whereby the suitor formally asked the woman's father, parents, or guardian for her hand in marriage; the dowry (*dos*), which came from the husband's side during this period, and which would normally involve a written contract completed before the wedding; and solemnization by a priest in a church ritual, with the blessing of the couple or of the bride alone. Whether the decretal implied that a marriage without these formalities was invalid is unclear, and this point was much debated during the Middle Ages. Much depends on how one interprets the term "lawful" (*legitimum*), for a marriage contracted in a manner that contravened the laws was not *ipso facto* invalid. It seems unlikely that anyone would have considered the presence of paranymphs (attendants of the bride) and observance of the Tobias Nights (Tob 8:1–3) to be conditions of validity. The final passage, which is missing from Benedict Levita's version, seems to insist that a marriage without the above formalities is invalid, but one might construe that as hyperbole. Moreover, the exceptive clause at the end – "unless it is founded on their own will and supported by lawful vows" – seems to undermine the preceding admonition and to reestablish the principle of *solus consensus*.

Most of the authorities and maxims that medieval scholars cited to defend the principle of *solus consensus* during the Middle Ages came directly or indirectly from a remarkable letter that Pope Nicholas I sent to Boris, the Khan of Bulgaria in 866

[120] PL 130:81B–C (or P. Hinschius, *Decretales Pseudo-Isidorianae et capitula Angilramni* [Leipzig, 1863], 87–88): "Similiter custoditum et traditum habemus, ut uxor legitime viro jungatur. Aliter enim legitimum, ut a Patribus accepimus, et a sanctis apostolis, eorumque successoribus traditum, invenimus, non fit conjugium, nisi ab his qui super ipsam feminam dominationem videntur habere, et a quibus custoditur, uxor petatur, et a parentibus aut propinquioribus sponsetur, et legibus detur, et suo tempore sacerdotaliter, ut mos est, cum precibus et oblationibus a sacerdote benedicatur, et a paranymphis, ut consuetudo docet, custodita et sociata a proximis tempore congruo petita legibus detur, et solemniter accipiatur, et biduo vel triduo orationibus vacent et castitatem custodiant, ut bonae soboles generentur, et Domino in actibus suis placeant. Taliter enim et Domino placebunt, et filios non spurios, sed legitimos, atque haereditabiles generabunt. *Quapropter, filii charissimi, et merito illustres fide catholica suffragante, ita peracta legitima scitote esse conjugia. Aliter vero praesumpta non conjugia, sed aut adulteria, aut contubernia, aut stupra, vel fornicationes potius quam legitima conjugia esse non dubitate, nisi voluntas propria suffragata fuerit et vota succurrerint legitima.*"

(Section 5.3). Nicholas described for Boris the nuptial process and the solemnities customarily observed in the west, but he noted that no solemnization was strictly necessary, as it was in the east, because formal weddings were expensive and many could not afford them. Consent alone was necessary. But Nicholas assumed, as the Roman jurists had done, that marriage required the consent not only of the spouses themselves but also of "those in whose power they are." Sons and daughters who were still in the power of their fathers, parents, or legal guardians could not validly marry without their consent.

Marrying among the landed elites during the early Middle Ages was typically what I call "traditional marriage" (Sections 5.1, 5.3.1, and 5.3.2). The contract was between men from both sides, typically the suitor and his future father-in-law. The bride was rather an object of the contract than a party to it. Agnes Arnórsdóttir shows that the transition from traditional to canonical marriage, in which the union of the spouses' will or intentions constituted their marriage, occurred rather quickly in Iceland during the fourteenth and early fifteenth centuries. The clasping or joining of hands took on a new function in Iceland under the influence of European canon law and ecclesiastical traditions. Formerly, the woman's male guardian and her future husband or his father concluded the marriage contract by joining hands. This gesture of *handaband* was a common way of clinching property agreements in Iceland and elsewhere throughout the Middle Ages. But now the bride and bride-groom joined hands to confirm their contract, and the notion of *hjónaband* (the bond between husband and wife) appeared alongside that of *handaband* in the documents and tended to supplant it. At the same time, written property contracts recorded the agreement of the partners alone, whereas "earlier contracts had given equal weight to the consent of the parents and of the partners."[121]

The role of consummation in the formation of a marriage was the subject of much inquiry and debate during the twelfth century. The canonical texts cited to establish the principle of *solus consensus* seemed to imply that a marriage was insoluble as soon as the spouses plighted their troth. Nevertheless, secular laws and customs, ecclesiastical precedents, hagiography, and commonsensical intuitions conspired to suggest that a marriage was not fixed (*ratum*) until it had been consummated in sexual intercourse. Clerics generally accepted that a newly married person could validly abandon his or her betrothed to enter the religious life before the union was consummated, leaving the other free to remarry, for the union with God trumped the union with another human being. (I refer to this right as the Privilege of Religion.) But that means of escape was no longer available after the marriage had been consummated. How did consummation affect cases of prior contract? Would a prior but unconsummated marriage to one person render a subsequent marriage to another null and void, even if the second marriage was consummated?

---

[121] A. A. Arnórsdóttir, "Marriage Contracts in Medieval Iceland," THTH 360–89, at 375–80. The quotation is from p. 379.

Two solutions emerged during the first half of the twelfth century, one in the schools of northern France, and the other in Gratian and in the writings of Bolognese legal scholars who based their new discipline of canon law on Gratian's work. According to the French theory, a marriage was *ratum* and the spouses were insolubly united as soon as they exchanged mutual consent, but only if they agreed about the present (*de praesenti*), or in the present tense (Sections 5.5 and 7.3). An agreement to marry in the future (*de futuro*) was only a promise to marry, and a promise to do something could not be the same as actually doing it. A betrothal promise was binding, but if someone who had promised to marry one person with *de futuro* consent married a second person with *de praesenti* consent, the second contract trumped the first. According to the Bolognese theory, a betrothal (plighting of troth) created only an initiate marriage (*matrimonium initiatum*), which was incomplete and not yet fixed (*ratum*). Marriage was perfected (*consummatum*) in sexual intercourse (Sections 6.4 and 7.2). The tense of the contract was immaterial. But Gratian upheld the principle of *solus consensus* in his own way, for he regarded consummation as the means by which the spouses sealed their own mutual consent. No one else's consent, in his view, was necessary. Sexual intercourse by itself, without the preceding mutual consent of the spouses to marry, established relationships and impediments of affinity, but it did not establish a marriage.

The Bolognese model was more congruent with the prevailing view among medieval people that marrying was a process involving several stages (Section 7.3.3). In principle, the French theory implied that a *de praesenti* contract established a marriage all at once. As the *Summa Parisiensis* put it: "We say that marriage is at once initiated, consummated, and established [*ratum*] as soon as consent is expressed in words of the present tense."[122] But the notion that marrying evolved in stages, or what is sometimes known as processual marriage, was too deeply entrenched in custom to be eradicated.

By the end of the twelfth century, a hybrid doctrine had become established as the universal law of the church (Section 7.6). This doctrine incorporated the distinction between *de futuro* and *de praesenti* betrothals, but it recognized the role of sexual consummation in two ways. First, a *de futuro* betrothal automatically became a fixed, fully established marriage if the partners subsequently had sexual intercourse. This rule presumed that the subsequent act of coitus expressed *de praesenti* consent, although most theologians recognized that this was *only* a presumption and, indeed, little more than a legal fiction. Second, the Privilege of Religion automatically dissolved an unconsummated, *de praesenti* contract, whereas only the death of either spouse could separate a consummated marriage. In the ideal course of events, therefore, there would be at least three phases in the contracting of a marriage:

---

[122] *Summa Parisiensis* on C. 32 q. 5 c. 16 (ed. McLaughlin, p. 246): "Sed nos dicimus statim matrimonium esse initiatum consummatum et ratum ex quo fit consensus expressus per verba praesentis temporis si contrahentes in contrahendo legitimae fuerint personae."

matrimonium initiatum (the *de futuro* betrothal), *matrimonium ratum* (the *de prae-senti* betrothal), and *matrimonium ratum et consummatum*.[123]

The clergy's efforts to take control of marriage during the central Middle Ages presupposed that clerics would oversee the process, verify the contract, and make sure that there was no impediment. To the same end, it was important that spouses married publicly, and preferably before the church. One of the earliest canonical statements regarding publicity and solemnization is in the *Decretum* by Burchard of Worms, composed soon after 1000. It occurs in Book XIX, a penitential manual known as the *Corrector sive medicus*, which includes a series of "interrogations" that confessors should put to penitents, with the appropriate prescriptions. One interrogation concerns marriage. The priest should ask men whether they have married covertly, or without the ministry of a priest:

> Have you taken a wife and have not performed the nuptials publicly, and you and your wife have not come to church and have not received the blessing from a priest, as it is written in the canons, and you have not endowed her with a dowry of whatever kind you are capable, whether it be land or moveable goods or gold or silver or serfs or animals, or whatever is within your means, so that she has been endowed at least with a shilling [*denarius*] or with something with the value of a shilling or with the value of a penny [*obolus*]? If you have not done so, you ought to do penance for three *quadragesimas* during ordinary days.[124]

Burchard requires formalities of three sorts here: publicity, solemnization in church (with the priestly blessing), and dotation. The canon presupposes that all these formalities went together, indicating that there were two recognized tracks to marriage: a formal track that was largely the preserve of the landed elite; and an informal track followed by everyone else, especially the poor. The description of the dowry is pro-forma, but Burchard goes out of his way to embrace persons of all means and classes. If the man cannot endow his bride with the wealth and real estate that were expected among the landed elite, he should at least give her some cash or something equivalent as a betrothal gift. If he cannot afford a shilling, he should give her a penny. But Burchard does not suggest that these requirements were necessary for validity.

As already noted, a new way of marrying before the church (*in facie ecclesiae*) emerged in northern France and Anglo-Norman England during the early twelfth century.[125] This involved a prenuptial rite conducted in the presence of the parish priest at the door or in the porch of a church, and it preceded the nuptial celebration in the sanctuary. It was in effect an ecclesiastically supervised betrothal, incorporating some of the elements and traditions that featured in betrothal

---

[123] On consummation and indissolubility in medieval thought, see J. A. Coriden, *The Indissolubility Added to Christian Marriage by Consummation* (Rome, 1961).

[124] Burchard of Worms, *Decretum* 19.5 (PL 140:958B–C).

[125] Molin and Mutembe, *Le rituel de mariage*, 30–47. Ritzer, *Le mariage*, 393–95. Stevenson, *Nuptial Blessing*, 68–71. Brooke, *Medieval Idea of Marriage*, 248–57.

contracts. It provided the parish priest with an opportunity to ascertain that the partners knew what they were doing, that they consented, and that no one present knew of any lawful impediment. There was still nothing to prevent a couple from marrying informally and privately, although they might need witnesses if the marriage became the subject of litigation.

The principle of *solus consensus* imposed a severe check on what bishops and clerics were trying to achieve in the regulation of marriage during the twelfth century. Hugh of Saint-Victor wrote the first extended account of the perils of clandestine marriage in the 1130s. Hugh noted that the problem could be solved if church weddings were required for validity, but he conceded (perhaps reluctantly or grudgingly) that the consensus of ecclesiastical opinion was against requiring solemnization (Section 10.6.1). Why clerics insisted on the principle of *solus consensus* and considered it to be indisputable remains a matter for speculation. Perhaps they were constrained by secular norms and expectations as well as by ecclesiastical precedents and traditions. Or perhaps people were so used to marrying in domestic settings, without the presence of a priest, that requiring solemnization would have greatly increased the number of couples living out of wedlock. Or perhaps by permitting couples to marry covertly, without their parents' consent, clerics were disrupting the traditional control of families and parents over their children's choice of partner, so that *solus consensus* was a wedge that helped the clergy to take control. Or perhaps by not requiring any formalities, the church was extending the reach of its control over marriage to everyone, even to the masses of anonymous poor and the unfree.

The Fourth Lateran Council of 1215 prohibited clandestine marriages, recognizing the problems associated with them (Section 12.1.2). Henceforth, parish priests were to observe the "special custom of certain places" whereby they announced the date of a forthcoming marriage in church, inviting anyone who knew of any lawful impediment to come forward meanwhile. This "special custom" was the reading of the banns, or *denunciationes*, which had emerged in Anglo-Norman parishes during the first half of the twelfth century. An "appropriate penance" would henceforth be imposed on persons who married clandestinely. Parish priests who participated in or were present at such unions or declined to forbid them were to be suspended from office for at least three years (Section 14.7).[126] But this law still did not render clandestine marriages null and void. The principle of *solus consensus* remained in force throughout the Middle Ages, and few theologians or canonists seriously questioned it. In their view, it was an unassailable matter of principle.

To understand what clandestinity entailed, one should keep in mind, again, that medieval people continued to regard marrying more as a process than as an event. There was nothing at all to prevent a couple from plighting their troth in the present tense in private or in a domestic setting but later having the banns read and their

---

[126] *Concilium Lateranense IV*, canon 51 (Tanner-Alberigo, 258). = X 4.3.3 (CIC 2:679–80).

union solemnized in church. Their marriage became indissoluble as soon as they plighted their troth. The delay was not in itself irregular or reprehensible, provided that they intended to solemnize their union in due course.[127]

The Council of Trent revisited the issue (Chapters 19–20). A substantive minority of the prelates maintained that the church ought not to overturn a principle that had been well established for centuries. Many opponents questioned whether the church could render clandestine marriages null and void without altering the essence of the sacrament, which almost all agreed was impossible. Nevertheless, the council finally ruled in the decree *Tametsi* at Session XXIV in 1563, despite the resolute objections of many prelates, that marriages not contracted in the presence of the parish priest and at least two other witnesses would in future be invalid. The council also required priests to solemnize and to bless marriages, joining the partners together, but not as a condition of validity (Sections 20.8 and 20.9).

It is difficult for the modern reader to grasp the attitude of theologians and other clerics during the central Middle Ages to solemnization and the priestly blessing. The minimum required for a valid marriage was not the same as what the spouses ought to do when they married. From a legal point of view, solemnization was not necessary to establish a valid and indissoluble marriage, and a prior unsolemnized union rendered a subsequent solemnized union invalid. Most theologians after Alexander of Hales agreed with him that the priestly blessing was a sacramental and not an integral part of the sacrament. Thomas Aquinas distinguished between the essence and the solemnities of marriage, maintaining that only the spouses' mutual consent was essential. But the essence of eucharist could have been performed in less than a minute in a barn. That was far less than a sacred mass, however, and to perform the bare essence alone would have been an act of impiety, even of sacrilege. Several major theologians, including Bonaventure, Albertus Magnus, and Thomas Aquinas, thought that a marriage enacted without the ministry and blessing of a priest did not fully realize its identity as a sacrament of the church. An unsolemnized trothplight in the present tense contained the essence of the sacrament, but it was morally incomplete. To fail to solemnize one's marriage, holding the church in contempt, was an act of gross impiety. It was a serious sin that might prevent the reception of conjugal grace. In the sixteenth century, Melchor Cano argued that a marriage contracted without the priestly blessing was merely contractual, and not a sacrament (Section 16.7.3). A dozen prelates at Trent held similar positions. But most theologians did not go as far as that, and a majority

---

[127] The contested marriage of Robert Middleton to Elizabeth Frothyngham, 1351, recorded in the York Cause Papers (CP E 79), is an excellent case in point. Having married in her family's private chapel with the assistance of a chaplain, they had the banns read for three successive Sundays before marrying publicly in the parish church of Frysmersk (a village on the Humber estuary that was subsequently inundated). The marriage came to court because of a claim against the husband of prior contract. See F. Pedersen, "Marriage Contracts and the Church Courts of Fourteenth-Century England," THTH 287–331, at 309–12 (analysis) and 320–31 (text).

of prelates at Trent resisted the theory. Nevertheless, many churchmen felt its attraction, and most regarded solemnization in church as the proper setting of the sacrament. Solemnization with the priestly blessing was not necessary in a causal sense, therefore, but it was required in a moral and practical sense, for that rite alone fully expressed the identity of marriage as one of the sacraments of the church. The priestly joining of right hands of the later Middle Ages had the same role in popular understanding. It was not canonically or theologically necessary, but without it how would one manifest the fact that God himself joined the spouses together in matrimony?

1.6.3 *The impediments of relationship*

The medieval church enforced impediments that extended far beyond the Leviticus code, although couples were sometimes dispensed from the more remote impediments.[128] As well as the impediments of consanguinity (blood relationship), there were those of affinity (acquired through coitus or marriage), of spiritual cognation (acquired through sponsoring a person's baptism), and of legal cognation (acquired through adoption). The basic aim of the systems of impediments was to keep relationships separate, so that no one could can both be mother and sister of the same child, for example, or father and godfather of the same child.[129]

Until Lateran IV (1215), the impediment of consanguinity extended as far as the sixth degree, although dispensation from the impediment was possible from the fourth and subsequent degrees to avoid scandal.[130] There was no need to limit the range of consanguinity in the direct line, for few parents lived long enough even to see their great-grandchildren. It was necessary to limit the scope of lateral consanguinity, however, because all medieval persons had at least two ancestors in common, namely, Adam and Eve. The rule that consanguinity petered out at the sixth or seventh degree came originally from Roman law, although in that context it limited only rights of inheritance and not the capacity to marry.[131] Medieval scholars were familiar with Isidore's numerological explanation: that just as there are six ages of the world and six ages in the human life span, so consanguinity perishes after the sixth degree.[132]

[128] F. X. Wahl, *The Matrimonial Impediments of Consanguinity and Affinity* (Washington, D.C., 1934). S. Worby, *Law and Kinship in Thirteenth-Century England* (Woodbridge, 2010), 9–38.

[129] See S. Gudeman's studies of godparenthood and copaternity in Latin America: "Spiritual Relationships and Selecting a Godparent," *Man*, n.s. 10 (1975): 221–37; and Gudeman, "The *Compadrazgo* as a Reflection of the Natural and Spiritual Person," *Proceedings of the Royal Anthropological Institute of Great Britain and Ireland* 1971: 45–71.

[130] *Cum omnia sacramenta I*, BGPhMA 18.2–3 (Münster, 1919), 148/21–23: "Causa tamen commoditatis ecclesie solet fieri dispensatio his qui sunt a quarto gradu supra."

[131] *Inst.* 3.5.5.

[132] Isidore, *Etymologies* IX.6.29. Ivo, *Decretum* IX.7 (= *Panormia* VII.74). SMA 213 (p. 235). *Cum omnia sacramenta I*, BGPhMA 18.2–3, 143/12–14. *Cum omnia sacramenta II*, ed. Bliemetzrieder, 282/174–175.

The method by which degrees of consanguinity were measured was even more restrictive than the number of degrees, for church courts used the ecclesiastical method of computation (*computatio canonica*). According to the measure used in Roman civil law (*computatio legalis*), the degree of relationship was equal to the number of intervening acts of begetting (*generationes*). For example, brother and sister were related in the second degree because two acts of generation separated them. But churchmen by the eleventh century were applying the so-called canonical computation, whereby one counted the successive generations of lateral kin. By this measurement, brother and sister were related only in the first degree.[133] These norms are traceable in church law to the ninth century. Their prominence in the eleventh century, such as in the work of Peter Damian, may plausibly be attributed not only to the advance of ecclesiastical jurisdiction over the essentials of marriage but also to the general mood of reform and to a new preoccupation with conjugal purity, which was a side effect of the preoccupation with clerical celibacy.

The purpose of this extraordinarily restrictive regime remains debatable. Jack Goody speculated that the aim was encourage the alienation of wealth to the church, for exogamy made it more difficult for kinsfolk to retain wealth within their group or their line,[134] but there is no evidence that medieval scholars and clerics saw the policy in that light. Duby's notion of competing "models" of marriage, respectively ecclesiastical and aristocratic, may seem promising, but it does not explain *why* churchmen wanted to extend the impediments of consanguinity so far. Moreover, members of the nobility seem to have been as keen on exogamy as bishops and scholars were, most of whom came from the upper social strata. As suggested earlier, Duby probably exaggerated the extent to which the two estates pursued opposing goals or were engaged in a "battle."[135]

Medieval theologians maintained that the reason for exogamy was to enhance peace by preventing interfamilial strife and extending the scope of familial charity (*caritas*). That rationale was apparently consistent with the practical sentiments of

---

[133] C. Rolker, "Two Models of Incest," in Andersen et al., *Law and Marriage in Medieval and Early Modern Times*, 139–59. Thomas Aquinas explains the difference between *computatio canonica* and *computatio legalis* succinctly in *IV Sent.* 40.1.2, resp. (Vivès 11:235): "Sed tamen diversa est ratio computandi gradus in diversis lineis" etc.

[134] J. Goody, *The Development of the Family and Marriage in Europe* (Cambridge, 1983). D. d'Avray, "Peter Damian, Consanguinity and Church Property," in L. Smith and B. Ward, *Intellectual Life in the Middle Ages* (London, 1992), 71–81, at 75–79. For critical retrospective reviews of Goody's theory, see J. Martin, "Zur Anthropologie von Heiratsregeln und Besitzübertragung. 10 Jahre nach den Goody-Thesen," *Historische Anthropologie* 1 (1993): 149–62; and M. Mitterauer, "Christianity and Endogamy," *Continuity and Change* 6.3 (1991): 293–333.

[135] C. B. Bouchard, "Consanguinity and Noble Marriages in the Tenth and Eleventh Centuries," *Speculum* 56.2 (1981): 268–87. Bouchard, *Those of My Blood: Creating Noble Families in Medieval Francia* (Philadelphia, 2001), 40–44. D'Avray "Peter Damian, Consanguinity, and Church Property," at 79–80. S. McDougall, "The Making of Marriage in Medieval France," *Journal of Family History* 38.2 (2013): 103–21.

the nobility. Churchmen found the basis of the rationale in Augustine.[136] Theologians and canonists did not assume that there was anything naturally problematic or abhorrent in unions that the Leviticus code did not prohibit. On the contrary, they attributed the more remote impediments entirely to positive law, celebrating the power of the church to make such laws. Exercising the same power, the Fourth Lateran Council of 1215 reduced the impediments of consanguinity to the fourth degree, explaining that the remote impediments had become counter-productive and noting that there was nothing wrong with altering human laws when circumstances changed.[137]

1.7 MARRIAGE AS THE SACRAMENT OF CHRIST AND THE CHURCH

Peter Lombard asks in one of his rubrics, "Of what thing [*res*] is marriage a sacrament." Inasmuch as marriage is a sacrament, he replies, "it is both a sacred sign and a sign of a sacred thing, namely, of the union [*coniunctio*] of Christ and the church." For proof, he cites Ephesians 5:31–32.[138] These claims were commonplace, and no medieval theologian questioned them even for the sake of argument. The notion that marriage was in the first place a sacrament of Christ and church depended on Paul's discourse on marriage in Ephesians, and it became associated especially with Ephesians 5:32. Conversely, theologians identified the union (*coniunctio*) between Christ and the church as the *res* of this sacrament. Theologians posited other divine–human relationships as *res* of the sacrament as well. Some were particular aspects of the union between Christ and the church, such as the charity that brought and held them together. Others were separate but kindred unions or relationships, such as the personal union between the two natures of Christ, or the union of charity between God and a faithful soul. Sometimes theologians conceded that marriage *only* signified and did not cause the union between Christ and the church, distinguishing between that and the *res* that this sacrament both signified and caused. But the notion that marriage was a sacrament of Christ and church was the historical point of departure for the doctrine of marriage as a sacrament, and it was always fundamental.

What was the *sacramentum–res* relationship in general, and how was it instantiated in marriage? What relationship does the genitive idiom signify in phrases such as "sacrament of Christ and the church"? Clearly, this is not a possessive genitive,

---

[136] D'Avray "Peter Damian, Consanguinity, and Church Property," at 71–75. M. H. Gelting. "Marriage, Peace and the Canonical Incest Prohibitions," in M. Korpiola, *Nordic Perspectives on Medieval Canon Law* (Helsinki, 1999), 93–124. Rolker, "Two Models of Incest," 143–45. Augustine, *De civitate Dei* XV.16 (CCL 48:476–79). Jonas of Orléans, *De institutione laicali* II.13 (SC 549:422–24).

[137] *Concilium Lateranense IV*, canon 50 (Tanner-Alberigo 1:257–58).

[138] Peter Lombard, *Sent.* IV, 26.5.6 (419): "Cuius rei sacramentum sit coniugium." The rubrics were apparently original. See I. Brady, "The Rubrics of Peter Lombard's Sentences." *Pier Lombardo* 6 (1962): 5–25.

as in the phrase "sacrament of the church." The schoolmen had a ready answer to the question, for a sacrament was by definition a sign of sacred thing (*signum sacrae rei*). The genitive idiom "sacrament of" denoted signification or, more specifically, figuration. Marriage was a sign or a figure of Christ and the church. But that answer was at best incomplete, as a careful reading of the ways in which the schoolmen invoked the *sacrament–res* relationship in discourse about marriage reveals. Like other features of the sacramental paradigm, the notion that sacraments were signs of sacred things or signs that caused what they signified did not fit marriage easily.

A sacrament was by definition a sacred sign (*sacrum signum*), or a sign of a sacred thing (*signum sacrae rei*). Augustine had proposed *sacrum signum* as a gloss or etymology of the word *sacramentum*, but twelfth-century theologians preferred their expanded version. Moreover, a sacrament in the proper sense conferred what it signified. But no couple's marriage caused Christ to be united with the church, and the relationships that medieval theologians envisaged between this sacrament and its *res* were more than figurative. Whereas baptism was a figurative washing, and eucharist a figurative meal, the sacrament of marriage really was a marriage. Durandus of Saint-Pourçain focused on the last difference when he criticized the theologians' doctrine of marriage as a sacrament (Section 14.8.3).

1.7.1 *Sacrament, sign, and figure*

Medieval scholars used the terms *signum* and *figura* to characterize the special relationship between marriage and Christ's union with the church. Both terms had specific senses and connotations in medieval thought. Medieval scholars spoke of what a sign signified or what a figure figured as its *res*. I shall translate the word *res* here sometimes as "thing" and sometimes as "reality," according to the context. To every sign there was a *res*, also known as its signified (*significatum*). But in some contexts the term *res* also denoted the referent as real rather than figurative. The link between the noun *res* and the adjective *realis* was obvious to anyone familiar with Latin, but it is impossible to capture in modern English.

Medieval scholars appropriated the theory of signs that Augustine had outlined in his *De doctrina Christiana*. A sign, according to Augustine, is a thing (*res*) that conveys an impression to the mind as well as presenting its own appearance to the senses.[139] All signs are also things, therefore, but not all things are signs.[140] The sensory impression is a vehicle conveying something to the mind that is not apparent to the senses. For example, visible smoke is a sign of unseen fire. The notion of appearance may be extended to include things that are manifest in some other easily accessible, quasi-tangible manner even if they are not literally

---

[139] Augustine, *De doctrina christiana* II.1(1) (CCL 32:32/5–7): "signum est enim res praeter speciem, quam ingerit sensibus, aliud aliquid ex se faciens in cogitationem uenire."
[140] Augustine, *De doctrina christiana* I.2(2) (CCL 32:7/12–14).

accessible to the senses. Again, although animals do not have minds, they respond to things in comparable ways. Augustine distinguishes in the *De doctrina Christiana* between natural signs (*signa naturalia*) and given signs (*signa data*).[141] Smoke is a natural sign of fire, for example, whereas spoken words are given signs of the thoughts that they express. Most interpreters and translators assume that Augustine's *signa data* are conventional signs, but what he says about them is not consistent with that assumption. The crux is the role of will or intention. A natural sign conveys knowledge of its source unintentionally. Fire, for example, does not emit smoke to communicate its presence. The *signa data*, on the contrary, are intentional, expressive signs: signs that a voluntary agent (or something analogous or comparable) puts forth to signify something. What distinguishes given from natural signs, according to Augustine, is a "will to signify" (*voluntas significandi*).[142] A smoke signal, for example, is a given sign, not a natural sign.

Peter Lombard introduces Augustine's distinction between *res* and *signum* at the beginning of the *Sentences*, for it provides him with a rough division of theological topics.[143] Augustine divided *res* into those which ought to be enjoyed (i.e., loved for their own sake), and those which ought to be used (i.e., sought for the sake of something else). Only God is the proper object of enjoyment, whereas all creatures should be used (in this technical sense) as means to that end. Sacred doctrine, therefore, treats God, created things, and sacraments, in that order: things that should be enjoyed (God), things that should be used (non-rational creatures) or that use things (rational creatures), and sacred signs. Among sacraments, the Lombard explains, some are only signs, whereas other are signs that justify and sanctify as well as signify:

> Among these, some are used entirely to signify and not to justify, i.e., those which we use only for the sake of signifying something, such as some of the sacraments of the Old Law [*sacramenta legalia*], whereas there are others which not only signify but also confer something that helps inwardly, as do the sacraments of the New Law [*evangelica sacramenta*].[144]

Having discussed God and created things and the relations between them, therefore, the Lombard comes at last in Book IV to the "doctrine of signs." Sacraments are given signs (*signa data*), at least insofar as they have been instituted to signify something. Moreover, a sacrament is a sign that "bears a likeness of the thing [*res*] of which it is sign." In other words, sacraments signify through resemblance. Contrariwise, if there is no resemblance, as Augustine says, there is no sacrament in the proper sense of the term. Finally, a sacrament properly so called also causes what it signifies, for these sacraments "were instituted for the sake not only of

---

[141] Ibid., II.1(2) (32–33).
[142] G. Manetti, *Theories of the Sign in Classical Antiquity* (Bloomington, 1993), 166.
[143] Peter Lombard, *Sent.* I, 1 (55–61).   [144] *Sent.* I, 1.1.1 (55/12–15).

signifying but also of sanctifying."[145] Through its divine institution, the sacrament not only resembles its *res* but also is a given sign of it.

Theologians also characterized the sacraments as figures (*figurae*). Sacraments in the proper sense caused the things of which they were figures, as Thomas Aquinas noted:

> ... the sacraments of the New Law are at once cause and signs. Hence, as is often said, they "effect what they figure" [*efficiunt quod figurant*]. From this is it clear that they satisfy the conditions of sacrament completely inasmuch as they are ordained to something sacred not only signs of it but also as causes of it.[146]

A *figura* by definition represents through resemblance. The term had three special connotations that conditioned how theologians used it in particular settings. First, it was term of art in exegesis and rhetoric. To say that X was a figure of Y was to that X might be posited as a simile of Y, or said metaphorically of Y, or interpreted allegorically as Y. Marriage was a figure of Christ and the church in this sense, for the church was the bride of Christ (*sponsa Christi*). Marriage could be used as a simile to illustrate that union, the union could be spoken of figuratively as a marriage, and a marriage in Scripture could be interpreted allegorically as Christ's union with the church. A figure of Y was not *really* Y, but it could be predicated of Y metaphorically. It was a shadow of the reality (*res*), an outward appearance of it, a way of imagining it. For example, the ablution that one observes in baptism is only a figure of the spiritual cleansing that is the point of the action. It is not even a real ablution. Second, the term *figura* meant "shape." In this sense, *figura* was one of the four species of quality in Aristotle's division of the categories. By extension, the term *figura* could denote a pattern, an arrangement, or a particular ordering of things. Both of these connotations converged on the idea of analogy: a comparison or equivalence of relations, such that A is to B as C is to D.[147] Third, the notion of figures and figuration belonged in the first place to the interpretation of Scripture. In patristic writing, the verb *figurare* usually meant "to prefigure." The sacrifice of the Paschal Lamb (Exod 12), the bronze serpent (Num 21:8–9), and the rock that Moses struck (Exod 17:1–7), for example, were all said to "figure" the lifesaving Crucifixion of Jesus Christ.

Medieval theologians generally assumed that a sacrament was significant not only because of an analogy but also because it had been *instituted* to signify something sacred. Hugh of Saint-Victor captured this feature by distinguishing between

---

[145] *Sent.* IV, 1.4.1–2 (233).   [146] Thomas Aquinas, *Summa theologiae* III.62.1, ad 1 (2822a).

[147] I use the term "analogy" here in the sense that Aristotle used it. For reasons that are not obvious, the scholastics used the term *analogia* chiefly to denote modes of name-sharing akin to Aristotle's *pros hen* equivocation, although they recognized the older sense. Boethius coined the term *proportionalitas* to denote Aristotelian *analogia*. On *analogia* in Aristotle, see M. D. Philippe, "*Analogon* and *analogia* in the Philosophy of Aristotle," *The Thomist* 33 (1969): 1–74. On the origins of the scholastic analogy, see P. L. Reynolds, "Analogy of Names in Bonaventure," *Mediaeval Studies* 65 (2003): 117–62, at 121–36.

representation and signification (Section 10.2.2).[148] Representation, according to Hugh, was a natural resemblance, such as that between the cleansing of dirt from the flesh with water and the cleansing of sin from the soul with the grace of baptism. Washing is to literal dirt on the skin as baptism is to the figurative dirt of sin on the soul. Hugh assumed that such representations were part of the created order of things. But signification required in addition an act of institution. For example, Jesus Christ had instituted baptism *as* a sign of spiritual cleansing. Later theologians were less explicit and less consistent on this point than Hugh was, but they generally assumed that God had instituted marriage as a sign of Christ and the church, and that the natural law alone could account for that signification.

1.7.2 *Figurative marriage*

Medieval exegetes were used to interpreting Scripture both literally and spiritually, both historically and mystically. Spiritual interpretation arose from the conviction that the incarnation of Jesus Christ fulfilled ancient prophecies and mysteries, from the effort to reconcile the Old and New Testaments, from meditative reflection on Scripture, and from the application of Scripture to daily life in preaching. Exegetes during the central Middle Ages assumed that the non-literal senses inhered primarily not in the text but in the historical events that the text described. For example, Scripture records that Moses struck a rock, causing water to gush and refresh God's people (Exod 17:1–7, Num 20:2–13). Following St Paul, medieval exegetes interpreted this narrative as an allegory of Christ on the Cross (1 Cor 10:4). In their view, the event itself, rather than the text in which it was recorded, was the primary vehicle of meaning. Moses' historical striking of the rock prefigured Christ on the Cross.

The scholastics adopted John Cassian's fourfold division of the senses of Scripture: the historical (or literal), the allegorical, the moral (or tropological), and the analogical. The allegorical sense referred to Christ and the church, the moral sense provided lessons about the Christian life that people should apply to themselves as individuals, and the anagogical sense referred to the next life. This fourfold division was important as a demonstration of a range of possibilities, but it remained largely theoretical, for exegetes rarely applied it systematically in biblical commentary or preaching. For most practical purposes, the twofold distinction between historical and spiritual interpretations sufficed.

The theory of the four senses of Scripture gave rise to the topos of the four species or kinds of marriage, although these species did not always correspond to the standard four senses. The topos seems to have originated in Cistercian monastic preaching during the twelfth century, the authors of which used the non-literal senses of marriage to illuminate the contemplative life of the monk. One of the four species is usually the literal, "carnal" marriage between a man and a woman, but the

---

[148] Hugh of Saint-Victor, *De sacramentis* I.9.2 (PL 176:317B–D).

identity of the other three species varies. Authors and preachers could freely construct and adapt the division to meet their particular ends and to show off their exegetical skills and their inventiveness.

Aelred of Rievaulx (d. 1167) used the topos in a sermon for the feast of the purification of the Blessed Virgin Mary. Although the topic of his sermon is love, Aelred explains, and although he has already spoken about marriage in an earlier sermon, he will first speak of marriage again, for love and marriage belong naturally together. Among men and women, love is the beginning, the middle, and the end of marrying (*nuptiae*). (Note that Aelred is referring here to the act of marrying, and not to the estate of marriage.) At first, their love is aroused through affection. Then their love is extended and drawn out through desire. They become betrothed, and their desire increases more and more in the expectation and the celebration of their marriage. Finally, love achieves its fruition through mutual consent, when they have plighted their troth and can enjoy each other's bodies by rendering the conjugal debt.[149] Turning "from carnal things to spiritual things," Aelred finds the same pattern in spiritual love. To that end, he posits "three kinds of marriage" (*tria genera nuptiarum*): one in which human nature has been married to the Word in Christ incarnate; another in which the church as bride has been married to Christ as her bridegroom; and another in which the perfected soul of the monk is married to the Word every day. In marriage of the first kind, the two natures of Christ, divine and human, come together in Mary's womb to be united in one Person. In marriage of the second kind, Christ figuratively "leaves his father and his mother and cleaves unto his wife so that they become two in one flesh" (Gen 2:24), for this dictum refers allegorically to Christ's incarnation and to his union with the church (Eph 5:32). In marriage of the third kind, "the rational creature, having contemned all things, cleaves unto his creator so that they are two in one spirit." The first marriage occurred in the Nativity, when "the Word was made flesh and dwelt among us" (John 1:14); the second occurred with the visit of the Magi and the Epiphany; the third occurs whenever "the soul, loving and ardent, comes at last to the embraces and kisses of the Savior." Spiritual love is "aroused through affection and drawn out through desire so that through consent it may deserve to enjoy [God]." In spiritual as well as in carnal life, therefore, love progresses from affection to desire to wholehearted enjoyment.[150]

Another Cistercian author, Isaac of Stella (d. c. 1169), developed the topos in a sermon for the first Sunday after the octave of Epiphany, when the gospel reading was John 2:1, on the wedding at Cana. Initially, Isaac posits three species of marriage, which comprise a temporal sequence of human development: the exterior union between male and female, from which a child is begotten; the interior union of

---

[149] The comparison is ironic. No medieval monk or cleric would have described the secular nuptial process so frankly in a sermon preached to laypersons. Instead, he would have admonished his hearers not to marry in order to satisfy lust.

[150] Aelred of Rievaulx, *Sermo 5 (In ypapanti Domini)*, 2–3 (CCM 2B:40–47, at 40–41).

body and soul in the one who is begotten; and the intimate, transcendent union between this human being and God. The first is a union of flesh and flesh, the second of flesh and spirit, and the third of spirit and spirit. But there is fourth species of marriage: the union between the Word and human nature, or between Christ and the church. This was the last of the unions to emerge historically, but it is what enables the individual to progress from the natural union of flesh and spirit to the supernatural union of spirit and spirit. There are in total four species of marriage, therefore: the union of flesh and flesh (literal marriage), the union of spirit and flesh (the anthropological union of soul and body), the personal union of the Word with human nature or with human kind, and the union between God and the human mind. Isaac correlates these species of union with the four senses of Scripture, albeit for reasons that are not entirely obvious. The first species is historical, the second moral, the third allegorical, and the last anagogical. Jesus partook only in the three non-literal species of marriage, for he never married literally. Nevertheless, he attended a carnal marriage at Cana, where he performed the first of his miracles. He confirmed by his presence there that carnal marriage is a special sign of the unions between God and human nature and between God and the human mind.[151]

Innocent III (r. 1198–1216) used the topos in a treatise on the four species of marrying.[152] He must have written this treatise either before he became pope or during the following year, for he refers to it in a sermon that he prepared for the first anniversary of his pontificate. Whereas Aelred and Isaac used the topos to illuminate monastic love, Innocent uses it to illuminate the Christian life in general and the church. The first species is the historical, carnal marriage between man and woman: the union of two in one flesh (Gen 2:24, Mark 10:8). The second species is the allegorical, sacramental marriage between Christ and the church: the union of two in one body (Rom 12:5). The third species is the tropological, spiritual marriage between God and the justified soul: the union of two in one spirit (1 Cor 6:17, 1 John 4:16). And the fourth species is the anagogical marriage between the Word and human nature: the union of two in one Person (John 1:14).[153]

Innocent expounds and elaborates the mystical marriages, especially the personal marriage between the Word and human nature, by exploring their parallels with literal marriage. To that end, he finds correspondences for every aspect of the nuptial process, from the preliminary negotiations and the impediments to the three conjugal goods, supporting each correspondence with quotations from Scripture. Some of these biblical texts already refer to marriage and must be interpreted allegorically or figuratively before they have the meaning that Innocent perceives in them. Among the features of carnal marriage for which Innocent finds

---

[151] Isaac of Stella, *Sermon 9*, 1–14 (SC 130:205–221, at 205–16).
[152] Innocent III, *De quadripartita specie nuptiarum*. I have used the working edition by C. M. Munk, *A Study of Pope Innocent III's Treatise, De quadripartita specie nuptiarum* (dissertation, University of Kansas, 1975), which is based on PL 217:921–68 and two manuscripts.
[153] II.1, pp. 4–6.

correspondences in the personal union of the Word and human nature are the betrothal (Heb 2:16, Gen 22:18, Gal 3:1), the betrothal oath (Ps 131:11, Luke 1:32, Isa 9:97), the bride's family (Rev 19:16, Ps 44:2), the man's betrothal gift, the bride's beauty, the fullness of time, the *paranymphus* (who is the angel Gabriel), the witnesses, the bedchamber (the Virgin's womb: see Ps 18:6), the ring (Exod 8:9, Luke 11:20, Isa 11:2–3), the bride's finery, the crown, the kiss (Song 1:1), the *traditio*, and the wedding feast.[154] Innocent shows that the ring represents the gift of the Holy Spirit, whereas the finger on which the ring is placed represents the Holy Spirit himself.[155] Although the bride's father gives her to the groom in carnal marriage, here the *traditio* occurs when the Word hands over human nature into the right hand of the Father, at which he sits (Heb 1:4).[156] In a few instances, the absence of any correspondence is significant. For example, there is nothing in the personal marriage between the Word and human nature corresponding to the dowry that a bride receives from her parents, since human effort and merit contribute nothing to this gracious union.[157]

Following Hugh of Saint-Victor and Peter Lombard, Innocent posits two unions in carnal marriage: the union of wills (*consensus animorum*) and the union of bodies (*commixtio corporum*). The latter is a great sacrament of Ephesians 5:32, but the former is a greater sacrament, for "it is the spirit that vivifies, whereas the flesh profits nothing" (John 6:64). These unions signify respectively the spiritual marriage between God and the justified soul and the sacramental marriage between Christ and the church.[158] Just as a man leaves his father and mother to be joined to his wife in carnal marriage (Gen 2:23–24), so God the Son took upon himself the form of a human servant (Phil 2:6–7), leaving the Father to become flesh and dwelling among us (John 1:14).[159] The mother whom Christ left in order to cleave unto the church was the Synagogue.[160] Just as a man first becomes betrothed to a woman and later takes her in marriage, an event known as the *traductio*, so Christ was first betrothed to the church through faith and later appeared in the flesh.[161] Just as literal marriage is soluble before consummation but insoluble after consummation, so the spiritual union between God and the soul is soluble, whereas the sacramental union between Christ and the church is insoluble.[162] Innocent proposed this double analogy in a letter to King Philip II of France regarding his contested marriage to Ingeborg (Section 14.3.1).

Innocent emphasizes that even the mystical marriages are not clandestine. The sacramental marriage between Christ and the church is not clandestine but solemnized and manifest to all believers (Ps 18:5–6, Ps 97:2, Matt 10:27, Matt 10:32, Mark 4:21, Mark 16:15, 16:20, Rom 10:10, Luke 9:26). Four witnesses were present at the

---

[154] II.4–24, pp. 7–15.   [155] II.17, p. 12.   [156] II.22, p. 14.
[157] II.8, p. 9. Nor is there a dowry in the unions between Christ and the church and between God and the soul: see II.53, pp. 38–39.
[158] II.30, pp. 20–21.   [159] II.34, pp. 23–24.   [160] II.35, p. 24.
[161] II.66, pp. 52–53.   [162] II.43, p. 30.

personal marriage between the Word and human nature: God the father, the Virgin Mary, the Holy Spirit, and the angel Gabriel. These correspond respectively to father, mother, priest, and *paranymphus* in literal marriage. Two of them were outwardly and visibly present, and two were inwardly and invisibly present. It is true that the spiritual marriage between God and the justified soul is contracted secretly (*in occulto*) inasmuch as "God justifies man without man" (John 3:8, 1 Cor 2:11), but even so there are three witnesses: Father, Son, and Holy Spirit.[163]

In the anniversary sermon, Innocent summarizes the fourfold division of marriage that he expounded in the treatise on the four species, situating himself as the friend of the bridegroom (*amicus sponsi*) in the sacramental marriage between Christ and the church (John 3:29). But because an ancient tradition regarded bishop and diocese as figuratively married to each other,[164] Innocent introduces a fifth species: the marriage between the pope and the universal church. Unlike the earlier treatise, the sermon is an exercise in political theology. Pursuing a partly allegorical, partly legal argument, Innocent derives the chief constitutional features of the papacy from the premise that the pope is the bridegroom of his church.[165]

In Florence during the thirteenth through sixteenth centuries, the ceremonies by which a newly appointed bishop took possession of his see included his marriage to the abbess of the city's oldest Benedictine convent. This ritual, which like all Florentine weddings among the well-to-do was fully notarized, included a betrothal ceremony with a ring, the giving of a dowry and antenuptial gifts, and a wedding feast. The bishop slept overnight in the convent in a nuptial bed prepared by the nuns. The ritual would have been meaningless without the themes of mystical marriage in the background, but its meaning was more political than spiritual. It was a way to recognize and negotiate relationships of power and property.[166] Needless to say, this was a merely figurative wedding. The bishop did not really marry the abbess.

David d'Avray has edited and analyzed six sermons for the first Sunday after the octave of Epiphany by thirteenth-century Dominican and Franciscan preachers. Although written in Latin, these sermons on John 2:1 (the wedding at Cana) circulated in manuals used for preaching to the laity. Since Advent was among the forbidden seasons, d'Avray points out, when no one was permitted to marry, the friars would have preached these sermons when "marriage would be on many people's mind while the backlog was being cleared, and a more attentive audience

[163] II.65, pp. 51–52. [164] McLaughlin, *Sex, Gender, and Episcopal Authority*, 56–61.
[165] For an introduction and summary, see *Pope Innocent III: Between God and Man*, trans. C. J. Vause and F. C. Gardiner (Washington, D.C., 2004), 28–32. See also J. Doran, "Innocent III and the Uses of Spiritual Marriage," in F. Andrews et al., *Pope, Church and City* (Leiden, 2004), 101–14.
[166] S. T. Strocchia, "When the Bishop Married the Abbess," *Gender and History* 19.2 (2007): 346–68. M. M. Miller, "Why the Bishop of Florence Had to Get Married," *Speculum* 81.4 (2006): 1055–91. The practice is documented from 1286 to 1583.

might be expected than for many sermons."[167] That being so, the amount of attention that the friars paid to the several species of mystical marriage is remarkable. The preachers expound the marriages of the two natures in the incarnation, of Christ with the church, and of Christ or God with the penitent soul or the convert to the religious life. Three of the sermons in d'Avray's collection explicitly use the topos of the four species of marriage.[168] The preachers discuss literal marriage chiefly as a prelude to their expositions of mystical marriage. They affirm that literal marriage is good, they expound its benefits, and they highlight its pitfalls, but this moral counsel is conventional and unoriginal, whereas their treatment of the mystical species of marriage is ingenious and inventive. Moreover, the preachers do not apply their reflections on the mystical marriages to illuminate the qualities, norms, or regulations of literal marriage. It seems that their thinking about the literal marriage and their thinking about the mystical marriages, even that between Christ and the church, were disconnected and proceeded along independent lines, although at some level of consciousness the two themes must have been rooted in the same analogical imagination.

Figuration is not the same as exemplarity. Preachers and exegetes who used the topos of the four species of marriage focused on the figurative relationship. They posited the special resemblance between marriage and the divine–human relationships that it signified or figured chiefly to illuminate the latter. They did not do so to persuade their listeners and readers, except perhaps subliminally, that Christian marriage in reality, as a mundane human relationship among members of the church, had certain attributes because or inasmuch as it signified the divine–human relationships. The laity must have sensed intuitively that all these spiritual parallels dignified their own marriages and made them sacred, but the preachers rarely encouraged them to do so or showed them how to make the comparison or to draw its lessons.

1.7.3 *Ephesians 5:22–33 and its reception*

Theologians found their biblical support for the doctrine of marriage as a sacrament chiefly in the discourse on marriage in St Paul's letter to the Ephesians (Eph 5:22–33).

1.7.3.1 *Paul's argument*

Ephesians 5:22–33 is the first part of a threefold household code, which runs from Ephesians 5:21 to 6:4.[169] Beginning with the premise that all members of the church

---

[167] D. d'Avray, *Medieval Marriage Sermons* (Oxford, 2001), 2.

[168] That is, those of Pierre de Saint-Benoît, O.F.M., Gérard de Mailly, O.P., and Guibert de Tournai, O.F.M.

[169] The following exposition of the text is very limited and designed only to fit the task in hand. I have tried to keep in mind medieval reception of the text without regarding it

should be "subject to one to another, in reverence of Christ," Paul works out the implications of that premise for the relationships of wives toward their husbands and husbands toward their wives (Eph 5:22–33), of children toward their parents and parents toward their children (Eph 6:1–4), and finally of slaves toward their masters and masters toward their slaves (Eph 6:4–9). The closest biblical parallel is the household code of Colossians 3:18–4:1, which describes the same sequence of relationships.[170] What distinguishes the Ephesians code is its premise. Without trying to unsettle or to undermine the inequality in each pair of reciprocal relationships, Paul uses the principle that all Christians are subject to each other in Christ to mitigate the dominant relationship of ruler to ruled.

Paul pursues the implications of the premise further in his treatment of marriage than he does in the treatment of the other two relationships. He holds up the union between Christ and the church, which is both Christ's bride and his body, as the model that Christian spouses should strive to emulate:

> (22) Let women be subject to their husbands, as to the Lord, (23) because the husband is the head of the wife, as Christ is the head of the church. He is the savior of his body. (24) Therefore, as the church is subject to Christ, so also let the wives be to their husbands in all things. (25) Husbands, love your wives, as Christ also loved the church and delivered himself up for it, (26) that he might sanctify it, cleansing it by the laver of water in the word of life; (27) that he might present it to himself, a glorious church, not having spot or wrinkle or any such thing; but that it should be holy and without blemish. (28) So also ought men to love their wives as their own bodies. He that loves his wife loves himself. (28) That he might present it to himself, a glorious church, not having spot or wrinkle or any such thing; but that it should be holy and without blemish. (29) For no man ever hated his own flesh, but nourishes and cherishes it, as also Christ does the church: (30) Because we are members of his body, of his flesh and of his bones. (31) For this cause shall a man leave his father and mother, and shall cleave unto his wife, and they shall be two in one flesh [Gen 2:24]. (32) This is a great sacrament — but I am saying this in Christ and in the church. (33) Nevertheless, let every one of you in particular love his wife as himself, and let the wife revere her husband.[171]

That wives ought to obey their husbands was too obvious in Paul's context to need any explanation, and Paul does not dwell on it or shed any new light on it. Instead, he focuses on how husbands ought to regard their wives. Although the husband is the dominant partner, he should cherish his wife as Christ cherished the church. Paul mingles counsel on married life with figurative images of betrothals and nuptials (Eph 5:26–27). "Husbands, love your wives, as Christ also loved the church

---

anachronistically. For detailed analysis informed by the discipline of biblical studies, see P. J. Sampley, *"And the Two Shall Become One Flesh": A Study of Traditions in Ephesians 5:21–33* (Cambridge, 1971); and G. W. Dawes, *The Body in Question: Metaphor and Meaning in the Interpretation of Ephesians 5:21–33* (Leiden, 1998).
[170] See also Tit 2:1–10 and 1 Pet 2:18–3:7. [171] Douai-Rheims version, slightly modified.

and delivered himself up for it" (Eph 5:25). Husbands should care for their wives and love them as if they were their own bodies, for the church is the body of Christ. To show how husband and wife are joined so closely that a man's wife is like his own body, Paul cites Genesis 2:24: "For this cause shall a man leave his father and mother, and shall cleave to his wife, and they shall be two in one flesh" (Eph 5:31): the same primordial text that Jesus cited when he condemned the Jewish law on divorce and remarriage (Matt 19:5, Mark 10:7).

Genesis 2:24 reminds Paul of a different but closely related topic, and the thought prompts a brief digression. The quoted dictum was a "mystery" predicting Christ and the church: "This is a great sacrament — but I am saying this in Christ and in the church" (Eph 5:32). In the original Greek, Paul spoke of a great mystery: a veiled prefiguration of Jesus Christ that remained hidden during the time of the Old Law but become revealed with the advent of Christ (Eph 3:3). The term *mystērion* had apocalyptic connotations. Paul used it to refer to an unfolding of hidden things as the end approached.[172] Latin translators of the New Testament sometimes translated *mystērion* as *sacramentum* and sometimes transliterated it as *mysterium*. The choice was apparently arbitrary. In this case, as it happens, the usual choice was *sacramentum*, although Latin patristic authors sometimes used *mysterium* when alluding to the verse.

Finally, Paul returns from the great mystical marriage between Christ and the church to his main theme: the unions between individual men and women in the church: "Nevertheless, let every one of you in particular love his wife as himself, and let the wife revere her husband" (Eph 5:33).

The brief digression complicates the argument, but the discourse as whole presents Christ's union with the church as the exemplar that Christian spouses should emulate in their own marriages. With the possible exception of a contested passage in Malachi,[173] the argument is unique in Scripture. The Jewish scriptures (the Christian Old Testament) often referred to God's relationship or covenant with his people figuratively as a marriage.[174] In the same spirit, Paul tells the Corinthians that he has betrothed them to Christ, intending to present them to him as a chaste virgin (2 Cor 11:2). But in Ephesians 5:22–33, Paul reverses the import of the simile, using the mystical marriage morally to illuminate literal marriage. At the same time,

---

[172] B. Gladd, *Revealing the Mysterion: The Use of Mystery in Daniel and Second Temple Judaism with Its Bearing on First Corinthians* (Berlin, 2008).

[173] Mal 2:13–16 presupposes that God's covenant with Israel may be likened to a marriage but uses that analogy as a pretext to complain about the prevalence of divorce and miscegenation, which are symptoms of Israel's failure to live up to the covenant. Several English translations have God saying, "I hate divorce" in Mal 2:16, but this reading was unknown before the sixteenth century, and it requires a conjectural emendation of the problematic Masoretic text. Most scholars today reject it.

[174] The covenant between God and his people is explicitly compared to a marriage in Ezek 16:8, Ezek 59–62, Ezek 16:60, Jer 31:32, and Hos 2:18. Other passages in which marriage is a figure of God's relationship to his people include Jer 3:14, Jer 2:1–2, Hos 2, Isa 50:1, Isa 54:5, Isa 62:4–5.

the images of bride and groom and of betrothal and marrying supersede the Old Testament image of an already established albeit often fraught marriage, for Paul believes that he is living in the end times. "The time is short" (1 Cor 7:29), and "the fashion of this world passes away" (1 Cor 7:31).

Paul presents the union between Christ and his church as the normative exemplar, paradigm, or model to which the analogous human relationship ought to conform. It is normative in the sense that it establishes a moral obligation that can be fulfilled to a greater or lesser degree, ranging from abject failure to perfection, albeit a perfection to which fallen human beings can hardly aspire. No doubt those who succeed can do so only with the help of the indwelling Christ. Paul complicates that argument by embedding within it a brief reflection on Genesis 2:24 as a prophecy of Christ and the church. Because that text, whatever else it might mean, records the original institution of marriage, Ephesians 5:32 implies that marriage can be used figuratively as a way to understand Christ's union with the church. But Paul assumes in the discourse as a whole that Christ's union with the church is the normative exemplar that Christians ought to emulate in their marriages.

There is no general principle from which it follows that if F may be used figuratively to characterize R (figuration), then R is the exemplar of F (exemplarity). Figurative use includes metaphor, simile, and allegory. Thus, Christ's union with the church may be spoken of as a marriage (metaphor), likened to a marriage (simile), or discovered through mystical interpretation of a biblical text about a marriage (allegory). Why did Paul assume that the relationship was also exemplary? A biblical scholar might seek Paul's reasons in his notion of *mystērion*, or in his use of non-literal interpretation and *allegoria* (cf. Gal 4:24, 1 Cor 9:8–11, 1 Cor 10:4), or in the "somatic" dimension of his theology (e.g., 1 Cor 12:27). But the apparent reversal will seem intuitively right to someone for whom the figure is already more than figurative. In some sense, the church really was Christ's body, in Paul's view, and it really was his bride. This "non-metaphorical understanding of metaphors"[175] is among the most elusive and intractable features of Paul's thought for the modern reader. Even medieval theologians did not fully share his sensibility, for they emphasized the distance between *figura* and *res* where Paul conflated them.

1.7.3.2 *Patristic reception*

In the minds of patristic theologians and exegetes, the most consequential feature of Paul's discourse on marriage in Ephesians was the Christological digression (Eph

---

[175] I am alluding to Joseph Kitagawa's phrase, "nonsymbolic understanding of symbols," by which he characterized the inadequacy of the notion of symbols in the prevailing *Religionsgeschichte* of the mid-twentieth century, especially in the work of Eliade, to capture the function of symbols in the "monistic" worldview of traditional Japanese religion. See J. M. Kitagawa, *On Understanding Japanese Religion* (Princeton, 1987), 45–48.

5:31–32), which required them to construe Genesis 2:24 as a prophetic utterance. Paul showed that when Adam awoke from his "deep sleep" (*sopor*) and saw the first woman, he spoke not only literally, referring to marriage, but also figuratively and prophetically, referring to Christ and the church. Although the Hebrew word used here for Adam's sleep, *tardemah*, could denote a prophetic trance, Jewish exegetes had no reason to regard it as anything more than a profound sleep. But the word was translated as *exstasis* in the Septuagint and in some Old Latin variants (e.g., in Tertullian), a term that did suggest a prophetic trance, and Paul's interpretation of the text in Ephesians 5:31–32 confirmed that interpretation. Jesus must have attributed Adam's deep sleep to the creator because God was speaking through Adam, as Augustine explains:

> Scripture itself bears witness that these were the words [Gen 2:23–24] of the first man, yet our Lord in the gospel declares that God said them [Matt 19:4–5].... so that we should understand from this that because of the ecstasy that he had just undergone, Adam was able to speak under divine inspiration as a prophet.[176]

Patristic exegetes, including John Chrysostom and Augustine, confirmed that construal by interpreting the manner in which Eve was formed from Adam's side as an allegory of Christ and the church. Just as Adam fell into a deep sleep, and his wife was made from his own flesh and blood, so Christ died on the cross, and water and blood – tokens of baptism and eucharist – flowed from his side, completing the mystical marriage between Christ and the church, and prolonging the saving efficacy of the mystical marriage through the sacraments.[177]

Patristic exegetes did not equate the great sacrament (*sacramentum magnum*) of Ephesians 5:32 with Christian marriage, as western theologians will do after 1100. Instead, they assumed that Paul's great sacrament was either Adam's dictum in Genesis 2:24, construed as a figurative, prophetic description of the union between Christ and the church, or the union itself. Both interpretations occur in Augustine.[178] According to the latter interpretation, the marriage of any Christian couple was a *sacramentum minimum* (Eph 5:33): a figure of the great sacrament between Christ and the church. "Therefore, what is great in Christ and in the church," Augustine explains, "is very small in each and every husband and wife, and yet it is a sacrament [i.e., a sacred sign] of an inseparable union."[179]

Although Augustine never cited Ephesians 5:32 to illuminate Christian marriage, the verse probably had some influence on his use of the term *sacramentum* in

---

[176] Augustine, *De genesi ad litteram* IX.19 (CSEL 28.1:294/12–19).   [177] MWCh 284.

[178] See MWCh xxv–xxvi, 282–97. Tertullian identified the great sacrament with Adam's prophetic dictum. His interpretation depended on a textual variant in the *Vetus Latina*: *in Christum et ecclesiam* (in + accusative), rather than *in Christo et in ecclesia* (in + ablative), as in Augustine and the Vulgate. I now think that I exaggerated the importance of Eph 5:32 for Augustine's view of marriage in MWCh. It was not so much that particular verse that influenced his thinking as the discourse as a whole (Eph 5:22–33) and Eph 5:25 in particular.

[179] Augustine, *De nupt. et conc.* I.21(23) (CSEL 42:236/22–24). Cf. Eph 5:33.

relation to marriage. Explaining why God permitted polygyny under the Old Law, even though it contravened the original institution of marriage as a union of two in one flesh, Augustine suggests that Old Testament polygyny was a sacrament of the union between Christ and the church in the present age, whereas the strict monogamy of the New Law is a sacrament of that union in the life to come. For whereas Christ is now gathering his followers from all the races, they will all be united with him in the life to come.[180] Augustine uses the term *sacramentum* here not to refer to the indissolubility or the insoluble bond of marriage, as he usually does, but to denote a prefiguration: a mystery in Paul's sense of the term.

Augustine cites Ephesians 5:25, not Ephesians 5:32, to prove that marriage is indissoluble, appropriating what Paul had presented as a normative exemplar but presenting it as a prescriptive exemplar. To propose an exemplar prescriptively is to use it to establish a rule distinguishing in a binary fashion between what is licit and what is illicit, with no continuum of compliance and no room for aspiration. This may be either a rule of behavior that can either be complied with or broken, or a rule determining whether or not a contract or institution is valid. Explaining in the *De nuptiis et concupiscentia* how marriage possesses the three benefits (*bona*) of marriage, faith, offspring, and sacrament, he finds the likely reason for the *bonum sacramenti* in the analogy between marriage and Christ's union with the church (Section 4.3). The term *sacramentum* in this context denotes the permanence of marriage, which Augustine considered to be the chief indicator of the special holiness of marriage "in the city of our God, in his holy mountain" (Ps 47:2). Whereas the Mosaic law and Roman civil law permit remarriage after divorce, Augustine observes, the church prohibits it. To corroborate his explanation, Augustine cites Ephesians 5:25: "Husbands, love your wives as Christ also loved the church." Christ loves the church in such as way that he will never permit himself to be separated from it. Just as there is never any divorce between Christ and the church, Augustine argues, so also must Christian spouses remain married for life, regardless of their circumstances.[181] Augustine was probably referring to the same analogy when he speculated in the earlier *De bono coniugali* that God established the *sacramentum* in order to make out of a merely human, fallible relationship "a sacrament of some greater reality [*res*]."[182] Whereas Paul was referring to the quality of conjugal love, Augustine applies his argument to indissolubility. One should remember that Augustine associated the *bonum sacramenti* with a special, highly spiritual form of conjugal love, which can survive despite infertility and even celibacy (Sections 4.1 and 4.2). Nevertheless, the absence of such love does not release a couple from their marriage. Augustine's use of the analogy, therefore, is more legalistic than Paul's, for he proposes the union between Christ the church more as a prescriptive than as a normative exemplar. For the most part,

---

[180] Augustine, *De b. coniug.* 18(21) (CSEL 41:214–15).
[181] Augustine, *De nupt. et conc.* I.10(11), 222–23.   [182] Augustine *De b. coniug.* 7(7), 197/6–16.

medieval theologians followed Augustine, emphasizing the prescriptive implications of Paul's comparison and largely overlooking its normative implications.

1.7.3.3 *Reception after 1100*

Theologians of the central Middle Ages assumed that marriage was a sacrament inasmuch as it was a sign or a figure of Christ's union with the church. As Chaucer's parson put it, "This sacrement bitokneth the knyttynge togidre of Crist and of hooly chirche."[183] Medieval theologians discussing marriage focused on Ephesians 5:32, paying only cursory attention to its setting and identifying the *magnum sacramentum* with Christian marriage. They largely ignored Ephesians 5:33, therefore, which had become redundant. Augustine's sacrament *in* (i.e., between) Christ and the church became the medieval sacrament *of* (i.e., signifying) Christ and the church, and the verse became a convenient proof text for the sacramental doctrine.

Medieval scholars undoubtedly misinterpreted and wrongly applied the verse, as Erasmus rightly pointed out. Nevertheless, the notion that the entire sacramental doctrine resulted from a faulty interpretation of Ephesians 5:32 is absurd. Historically, the doctrine preceded and resulted in the interpretation. Moreover, theologians did not base their defense of the doctrine on this verse. In scholastic articles, they cited it as proof only in the preliminary dialectical arguments of an article or in a *sed contra*, and not in the corpus, or response, where the master expounded his own position. Through a form of metonymy, the verse came to stand for a complex web of arguments and associations. Erasmus understood this usage and continued to cite Ephesians 5:32 with reference to Christian marriage. Luther, moved by righteous indignation and polemical zeal, was blind to it.

Scholars of the central and late Middle Ages invoked Ephesians 5:32 in ways that narrowed and slanted and arguably distorted Paul's argument in two ways. First, whereas Paul had invoked the union of two in one flesh to explain how the husband should cherish his wife, medieval theologians identified the union narrowly with sexual consummation, construed as the means of clinching the indissoluble contract. In their minds, the union of two in one flesh was chiefly a legal entity, to be observed in litigation. Second, whereas Paul proposed the exemplar of Christ's union with the church normatively, to show how husband and wife should regard and treat each other, medieval scholars proposed it mainly in a prescriptive manner: not to show spouses what they should strive to achieve with Christ's help, but to show them what they could not escape from, however far from its exemplar their married life had strayed.

---

[183] Chaucer, *The Parson's Tale*, X.842.

1.7.4 *The* sacramentum–res *relation in argument*

Medieval scholars assumed that marriage was holy because it was a sign of some-thing holy. To be sure, the values of *sacramentum* and *res* were not proportional. Alexander of Hales remarked that if the seven sacraments were ranked in order of the dignity of what they signified, marriage would come first. Marriage was always listed last, according to Alexander, because it was the least of the seven in sanctifying power (Sections 14.5 and 15.3.1.1).[184] Nevertheless, the signification gave value to the sign. Because marriage was a "sign of a sacred thing" (*signum sacrae rei*), it was *ipso facto* holy. Bruno the Carthusian (d. 1101) made this point in a gloss on Ephesians 5:32, although he did not equate the *sacramentum magnum* with marriage. (Nor did he consider marriage to be one of the sacraments. These were later developments.) According to Bruno, the sacrament to which Paul referred is Adam's dictum in Genesis 2:24: "Wherefore a man shall leave father and mother, and shall cleave to his wife: and they shall be two in one flesh." Christ figuratively left his father and mother to be united with his wife, Bruno explains, "to whom he betrothed himself with the ring of faith." The father in this simile was God the Father, whom Christ left through taking on human nature, his mother was the Synagogue, and his new wife was the church:

> Accordingly, "this," i.e., that "a man shall leave his father," etc., is "a great sacrament," i.e., a sacrament of a great reality [*res*]. For the statement, "a man shall leave his father," signifies that the Son of God left the Father when he who was invisible in his divine nature, like the Father, presented himself as visible under the appearance of slave [Phil 2:7]. He also left the mother who had nurtured him, i.e., the Synagogue, and cleaved unto his wife, i.e., the church, whom he betrothed to himself with the ring of faith [*annulus fidei*]. Now this, "I am saying," is a sacrament. "But I am saying" that the reality of this sacrament exists "in Christ and in the church," as has been said. Even if there were nothing else to recommend it, marriage would still deserve to be celebrated if only because of the dignity of the reality [*res*] of which it is a figure. But although the reality [*res*] of this sacrament is only "in Christ and the church" [Eph 5:32], and not in a man and a woman, "nevertheless, let every one of you in particular love his own wife" and not his neighbor's wife "as himself, and let the wife" not only love but also "revere her husband" [Eph 5:33].[185]

Marriage is worthy of reverence, according to Bruno, *because* it is a sign of Christ and the church. All theologians after 1100 shared this conviction, even though they did not assume that the value of marriage was proportional to what it signified.

---

[184] Alexander of Hales, *Glossa in IV Sent.* 26.2a (445–46). See also Petrus Paludanus, *IV Sent.* 26.4.2 (141rb–va), discussed in Chapter 14, Section 14.8.4.
[185] Bruno, *Expositio in epistolas sancti Pauli*, in Eph 5:32 (PL 153:346D).

Theologians and canonists of the central Middle Ages used the premise that marriage was a sacrament of Christ and the church chiefly to explain why marriage was indissoluble and to account for or to illuminate the effect of sexual consummation on the marriage bond. The two topics were closely related. Because medieval people regarded marriage not as an all-or-nothing event but as a process, canonists asked at what point in that process the union became fixed (*ratum*), irrevocable, and immune to dissolution. According to one view, popular during the twelfth century, the first act of coitus after the plighting of troth confirmed the bond, making it irrevocable and putting it beyond exceptions.

One should distinguish here between proof and rationale. An *a priori* proof is also an explanation (what the scholastics called a *demonstratio propter quid*), but explanations are not always proofs. Theologians used the premise that marriage was a sacrament of Christ and the church not only to prove that this sacrament possessed a certain feature or property, but also to provide a rationale for attributes already established on other grounds. The two uses are often conflated in the modern literature on medieval marriage, and, to be fair, they are not always easy to distinguish in the medieval literature. The explicit, formal purpose of a posterior rationale was to explain why a certain feature belonged to marriage, or to show that it was fitting, or to shed light on it, or to corroborate it, but not to prove that marriage had a certain property. For example, when Augustine proposed that God had made marriage indissoluble so that it would be a figure of "some greater thing," he did not posit this correspondence to establish that marriage was indissoluble but only to explain why God had caused marriage to be indissoluble. His only proof of the rule was the authority of Scripture: the fact that Jesus condemned remarriage after divorce as adultery. Although it is not always clear to which of the two categories an argument or explanation belongs, use of the premise to provide a posterior rationale for an already established thesis was much more common than its use as formal proof during the central and late Middle Ages.

Nevertheless, Thomas Aquinas used the premise in the *Summa contra Gentiles* to prove that marriage was monogamous and that it had the goods of faith (*bonum fidei*) and of sacrament (*bonum sacramenti*) (Section 16.6.1). In order to show that the Roman church's doctrines on marriage were reasonable, Thomas arrived at them deductively, although some of his arguments are obviously less than demonstrative. Marriage as a sacrament *of the church*, Thomas argues, is a sacrament *of Christ and the church*.[186] Now, "a figure must correspond to what is signified."[187] The signified is a "union of one [masculine] to one [female]" (*coniunctio unius ad unam*), for "One is my dove, my perfect one" (Song 6:8). Moreover, the two are united indivisibly. Christ himself said, "Lo, I am with you always, even unto the end

---

[186] Notice the two different uses of the genitive, respectively possessive and signifying.

[187] *Summa contra gentiles* IV.78 (Leonine 15:246/13–15): "Quia igitur per coniunctionem maris et feminae Christi et Ecclesiae coniunctio designatur, oportet quod figura significato respondet."

of the world" (Matt 28:20), and Paul said, "so shall we always be with the Lord" (1 Thess 4:17). Marriage, too, must a *coniunctio unius ad unam*, therefore: a union of one male to one female, and the spouses must be united indivisibly. It follows that marriage is monogamous and that it has the goods of faith and sacrament, Thomas argues. The indivisibility or inseparability of marriage is called *sacramentum* because it signifies the inseparability of Christ's union with the church, for a sacrament by definition is a sign of something sacred.

Thomas uses signification and correspondence here to prove that marriage as a sacrament has certain features. He assumes that the salient features of the signifier correspond to the salient feature of the signified, as if one thing were a map of the other. This way of thinking was rooted in habits of biblical interpretation.

The logical core of Thomas's argument is an analogical syllogism. Note that this logic *per se* does not commit Thomas to holding that marriage is indissoluble *because* it signifies Christ's union with the church, or that marriage would be soluble if it were not a figure of that union. Analogical syllogisms have the following form:

A is to B as C is to D.
But the relation of C to D is R1.
Therefore, the relation to A to B is R2
(where the relations R1 and R2 are the same or at least equivalent).

Such syllogisms are common in medieval theology. Here are some typical examples: William of Auxerre uses an analogical syllogism to pose an objection to the Privilege of Religion, which entitles either spouse unilaterally to dissolve an unconsummated marriage by entering the religious life:

Again, marriage signifies the union of Christ and the church. But the union of Christ and the church is inseparable, for the Lord says in Matthew: "Lo, I am with you always, even unto the end of the world" (Matt 28:20). Therefore, marriage is indissoluble. Therefore, a marriage is not dissolved if one of the partners enters the religious life.[188]

Similarly, Bonaventure proposes the following argument to show that the soul is entirely present everywhere in the body, without any spatial distribution:

Augustine says that just as God is in the macrocosm, so the soul is in the microcosm. But God is in the macrocosm in such a manner that he is entire in any and every part of it. Therefore, the soul is present in that manner in the microcosm, that is, in the body.[189]

---

[188] William of Auxerre, *Summa aurea* IV.17.2.2 (387/69–73). This is an objection to a position that William upholds.
[189] Bonaventure, *IV Sent.* 8.2.un.3, arg. 1 (1:170a). Bonaventure is referring to the twelfth-century compilation *De spiritu et anima* (18, PL 40), which he ascribed to Augustine. The original source was Claudianus Mamertus. The is an argument for a position that Bonaventure upholds.

Again, Thomas Aquinas proposes the following argument to show that the intellect cannot exercise actual cognition without using phantasms (imaginary images):

> ... the Philosopher says in *De anima* III that phantasms are related to the intellect as colors are to vision. But corporeal vision cannot see anything without color. Therefore, our intellect cannot understand anything without a phantasm.[190]

As far as I am aware, no medieval logician codified the rules and constraints of such arguments, although they presuppose assumptions as to which features are salient, and they require tacit adjustments *mutatis mutandis*. For example, no schoolman would take the following argument seriously:

> The soul is present in the microcosm as God is present in the macrocosm. But God is present in the macrocosm as its creator. Therefore, the soul is present in the body as its creator.

But the schoolmen rarely relied on analogical syllogisms to establish what they needed to prove. In a scholastic article, the form is more likely occur in the preliminary arguments than in the body of the article (i.e., in the corpus, or response). This is the case with the three examples cited earlier.

From a merely logical point of point of view, Thomas's syllogism in the *Summa contra gentiles* could have gone either way. On the basis of the same analogy, one might begin with the premise that Christ's union with the church has certain properties and conclude that marriage has the equivalent properties, or one might begin with the premise that marriage has certain properties and conclude that Christ's union with the church has the equivalent properties. In reality, though, the argument is bound to proceed from the signified to the signifier – from the union between Christ and the church to marriage – even though the signifier is better known and more apparent than the signifier. The reason is that Christ's union with the church, as St Paul made clear in Ephesians 5:25, is the exemplar that marriage is required to emulate.

Many, perhaps most, of the earliest references to marriage as a sacrament of Christ and the church pertain to the role of consummation in marriage (Sections 6.3 and 6.4). The topic was much debated during the first half of the twelfth century, partly for canonical and partly for moral and ideological reasons. Since marriage was a lifelong union, clerics exercising and expanding their control over the essentials of marriage had to know when a marriage became fixed (*ratum*), or fully established. For example, would a prior but unconsummated marriage render a subsequent consummated marriage invalid? Or would the second union trump the former? Most of the pertinent canonical texts implied that the spouses became indissolubly united as soon as they exchanged mutual consent, but customs, precedents,

---

[190] Thomas Aquinas, *I Sent.* 3.1.1, arg. 5 (ed. Mandonnet, 1:90). Thomas uses this argument to establish the premise of the main argument. Thomas accepts the premise, but the main argument is an objection to a position that he upholds: that created intellects can know God.

hagiography, deep-seated intuitions, and such secular traditions as the morning gift, seemed to imply that a marriage was incomplete or not fully formed until it was consummated in sexual intercourse (Section 6.1).

On a moral or ideological level, some twelfth-century theologians perceived a tension between the claim that marriage was holy and sacramental and the assumption that sexual intercourse was in some sense integral to it. All agreed that the Virgin Mary's betrothal never been consummated, but some, following Augustine, reasoned that Mary's union with Joseph was the most perfect marriage of all, and that Jesus was their legitimate child. Many theologians accepted Augustine's exegetical argument that Mary had taken a solemn but private vow of perpetual virginity even before she plighted her troth to Joseph. This way of thinking flourished with the rise of the cult of Blessed Virgin during the first half of the twelfth century.

A new dossier of texts purporting to show that marriage was not fully fixed (*ratum*) until it was consummated first appeared in the sentential literature during the first quarter of the twelfth century (Section 6.2). These proof texts provided French theologians, who were inclined to play down the role of sexual intercourse in marrying, with a convenient foil, for they could cite them dialectically to contradict the standard consensual proof texts.

The coital texts were ascribed to Pope Leo I and Augustine, but they were partly misquoted and partly spurious. The original source of the dossier was Pope Leo I's decretal, *Non omnis mulier*, which he addressed to Rusticus, the bishop of Narbonne (Section 6.2.1). Leo advised that a certain Christian man who had been cohabiting with a servile woman and had begotten children with her was free to marry another, free woman. (In the original source, the man was a cleric, but this incidental but inconvenient detail was lost in the canonical tradition.) The partnership between the free man and a servile woman, according to Leo, would not amount to marriage unless the man first emancipated her and married her publicly. Leo noted that his position was congruent with Roman law, but he based his argument on Paul's allegorical exegesis of Hagar and Sarah as types of the old covenant of servitude and the new covenant of freedom respectively (Gal 4:21–31). A Christian marriage should be understood on two levels, Leo argued. Besides the union of the sexes (*praeter sexuum coniunctionem*), it contained a sacrament of Christ and the church. Consequently, "there is no doubt that a woman in whom it is shown that there has been no nuptial mystery does not pertain to marriage." The words *sacramentum* and *mysterium* in Leo's argument allude to Ephesians 5:32.

Hincmar of Reims adapted Leo's argument to his own ends in 860, when he advised two archbishops how to conduct a tribunal on the scandalous case of Stephen, an Aquitainian nobleman (Section 6.2.2). Stephen had gone through the formalities of marrying but had refused to consummate his marriage, claiming that he had had sexual intercourse with a near relation of his bride before they married. As a result, intercourse with his wife would be incestuous. The girl's father referred the matter to a church council at Tusey. Hincmar adapted Leo's logic to shed light on the role of sexual union in the formation of a marriage. According to Leo, "a woman in whom it is shown that there has been no nuptial mystery does not pertain to marriage." In the same way, Hincmar argued, there was no "nuptial mystery" in a marriage that could not be consummated without incest, for it could never adequately represent Christ's union with the church.

Hincmar's letter was in turn the source of the early twelfth-century coital proof texts (Section 6.2.3), which supported the theory that marriage was not fully established (*ratum*) until it had been consummated through coitus. Leo is quoted as saying that without sexual intercourse (*praeter commixtionem sexuum*) marriage does *not* have in itself a sacrament of Christ and the church. (The insertion of the word *non* altered the meaning of *praeter*.) And Augustine is quoted as saying, "Marriage does not have in itself a sacrament of Christ and the church if sexual intercourse does not follow it."

Hugh of Saint-Victor, writing in the 1130s, introduced another strand into the argument by proposing that sexual union altered the signification of a marriage. Hugh was chiefly interested in the moral and ideological aspects of the matter, and especially in the virginal marriage of Mary and Joseph, which he considered ideal. Hugh was appalled by the suggestion that Mary consented to have coitus with Joseph by marrying him, or even to observe the conjugal debt if Joseph demanded it. To show that Mary was a virgin mentally as well as carnally, Hugh argued that marriage *per se* was an essentially non-carnal union, which would have thrived in Mary's case. The sexual dimension of marriage was a secondary, optional matter. Spouses could validly consent to marriage without consenting to sexual intercourse, as Mary must have done.

Hugh conceded that marriage could not be the "great sacrament" of Christ and the church without sexual union, for the spouses would not become two in one flesh (Eph 5:32). Nevertheless, he argued, the affective, essentially non-carnal union of marriage was a *greater* sacrament of the loving union between God and the soul (Sections 10.4 and 10.5):

> Rightly, therefore, it is said: "a man shall leave father and mother, and shall cleave to his wife, and they shall be two in one flesh," for in the fact that he cleaves to his wife there is a sacrament of the invisible partnership that is to be made in the spirit between God and the soul, whereas in the fact that the two are in one flesh there is a sacrament of the visible partnership that was made in the flesh between Christ and the church. That they "shall be two in one flesh" is a great sacrament in Christ and the church. But that they shall be two in one heart, in one love, is a greater sacrament in God and the soul.[191]

Note that Hugh still identifies the great sacrament of Ephesians 5:32 with Adam's dictum (Gen 2:24), although he applies this significance to the marriages of Christians in his own day. But what makes one of these sacraments greater than

[191] Hugh of Saint-Victor, *De beatae Mariae virginitate*, ed. Sicard, 208/354–62.

the other cannot be the relative values of the things that are signified. Hugh cannot have thought that the union between Christ and the church was less worthy of admiration than the loving union between God and an individual soul. He may have meant that the former made the latter possible. Chiefly, though, Hugh reasoned that the non-carnal union of affection between man and wife was intrinsically far greater and more valuable than sexual union. Moreover, the resemblances between the two human unions and the corresponding divine things are not of the same kind or of the same order. The manner in which sexual union resembles Christ's union with the church cannot be the same as the manner in which conjugal affection resembles God's loving union with the soul. Christ's union with the church is not sexual union, although sexual union represents it figuratively. But the love that Hugh envisages between husband and wife and the love that he posits between God and the soul are qualitatively alike. Moreover, the former depends on the latter for its existence, for sublime conjugal love, as Hugh imagines it, is a manifestation of divine love.

Gratian of Bologna returned to the canonical question in his *Decretum*, first published around 1140 (Section 6.4). Gratian used the coital proof texts with other resources to show that a marriage was incomplete and, therefore, soluble at least in certain circumstances before it was consummated in sexual intercourse, for until then it was not in the fullest sense a sacrament of Christ and the church. Among the circumstances that dissolved an unconsummated union was a second, consummated marriage to another partner.

Peter Lombard rejected Gratian's argument and appropriated Hugh's theory, adapting it meets his own needs. The *res* that marriage signifies is Christ's union with the church, according to the Lombard, but Christ is united to the church in two ways: spiritually, through charity; and corporeally, through "conformity of nature" (i.e., by sharing human nature through the incarnation). Likewise, there is a sign (*figura*) of each of the divine unions in marriage. The spouses' mutual consent signifies the spiritual union (*copula spiritualis*) between Christ and the church, which results from charity. Subsequent sexual intercourse (*commixtio sexuum*) signifies another union between Christ and the church, which results from conformity in human nature:

> **Of what thing is marriage a sacrament?** Since, therefore, marriage is a sacrament, it is both a sacred sign and a sign of a sacred thing, namely, of the union between Christ and the church, as the Apostle says. For it is written, he says, "a man shall leave his father and mother, and shall cleave unto his wife, and they shall be two in one flesh [Gen 2:24]. This is a great sacrament — but I am saying this in Christ and in the church" (Eph 5:31–32). For just as the union between spouses exists both as regards the consent of their wills and as regards the mixing together of their bodies, so the church is joined to Christ by will and by nature, because she wills the same as he does, and he took his outward form from human nature. The bride [the church] is joined to the bridegroom [Christ], therefore, both spiritually and corporeally, i.e.,

in charity and in the conformity of nature. There is a figure of both unions in marriage, for the consent of the spouses signifies the spiritual union of Christ and the church, which results from charity, whereas the mixing together of the sexes signifies the union that results from conformity of nature.[192]

Note that the two signifiers, consent and sexual intercourse, are aspects of marrying, and not of the state of being married, whereas the two signifieds are aspects of Christ's enduring union with the church. That said, twelfth-century theologians considered the church to be the bride of Christ rather than his wife, for the union was still emerging and would not be fully realized until the *eschaton*.

Canonists during the second half of the twelfth century adapted Hugh's theory to show why a valid but unconsummated marriage was soluble under certain circumstances, as Gratian had held, whereas a valid and consummated marriage could not be dissolved under any circumstances. They proposed that marriage signified a soluble union before consummation, and an insoluble union after consummation. Rufinus (fl. 1150–1191) used this rationale to explain the effects of consummation in Gratian's theory, and Huguccio (d. 1328) adapted it to accommodate the hybrid doctrine that had become established by the end of the twelfth century, which incorporated the distinction between *de futuro* and *de praesenti* betrothals (Section 11.6.3).

Pope Innocent III used this rationale, as already noted, to explain the effect of consummation in a letter that he sent to Philip II of France in 1208 regarding the king's contested marriage to Ingeborg:

> ... just as sexual intercourse signifies the union between the Word and human nature, because "the Word became flesh and dwelt among us" [John 1:14], so also the consent of wills may signify the charity between God and the just soul, since the person who cleaves to God is one spirit with him. Therefore, just as the bond of union between the Word and human nature cannot be separated, so also the conjugal bond between man and wife after they have been made one flesh through sexual intercourse cannot be separated as long as they are alive, whereas just as the tie of charity between God and the soul is often dissolved, so also can the conjugal connection be separated when the consent of their wills is all that exists between the spouses, because of what the Apostle says when he expounds the dictum of the first-created one, "they shall be two in one flesh" (Gen 2:24): "This, however, I say is a great sacrament in Christ and in the church" (Eph 5:32).[193]

But Innocent proposes this argument not as a proof but as a rationale. The only reason for allowing the Privilege of Religion, Innocent argues, is that "the examples of the saints and the statutes of the fathers" provide sufficient precedent. It would be

---

[192] Peter Lombard, *Sent.* IV, 26.1.1 (420).
[193] Pope Innocent III, *Regestum XI, Epist.* 177 (182), in *Die Register Innocenz' III*, vol. 11, ed. R. Bösel and H. Fillitz (Vienna, 2010), 286–93, at 287/24–288/2.

presumptuous, he concedes, to claim that the right could be established on the basis of Scripture alone.

Theologians had adopted this double analogy argument or rationale by 1200 (Section 14.3.1), and they continued to use it throughout the Middle Ages, but its popularity waned considerably during the thirteenth century. Ambrosius Catharinus refuted it in the sixteenth century (Section 18.3.1). The argument was circular, for the chief reason for maintaining that unconsummated marriage signified a soluble union and that consummated marriage signified an insoluble union was that unconsummated marriage was soluble, whereas consummated marriage was insoluble.

If the sacraments "effected what they figured," did a couple's marriage cause Christ's union with church? Even before the causal paradigm became explicit, the *Cum omnia sacramenta* had argued that by marrying a couple entered into the order of *coniugati*, adopting one of the three chief ways of being members of the church:

> The reality [*res*] of this sacrament is to become a member of Christ, for those who live legitimately in a legitimate marriage serve God through their marriage as well, and they are his members. Just as virgins through their virginity, and continents [*continentes*] through their continence, so good married persons [*coniugati*], through their legitimate union, are made members of Christ. Virgins occupy a certain supreme degree, continents a middle one, and married persons the lowest. These are the three men who alone, Scripture says, will be saved, namely, Daniel, Noah, and Job, that is, virgins, continents, and married persons.[194]

During the second quarter of the thirteenth century, on the contrary, theologians treated the special relationship between marriage and Christ's union with the church as a problem, for no couple by marrying could cause Christ and the church to become united. The sacraments of the New Law effected what they signified; but marriage signified the union between Christ and church, which it did not cause; therefore, marriage was not a sacrament of the New Law. Albertus Magnus solved this objection by distinguishing between the contained and uncontained signifieds of the sacrament (*res contenta, res non contenta*). From the principle that the sacraments of the new law "effect what they figure," Albert pointed out, it did not follow that these sacraments conferred *everything* that they signified. Conjugal grace was the *res contenta*, which the sacrament both signified and conferred, whereas the union between Christ and the church was a *res non contenta*. (One should keep in mind that the sacrament to which Albert referred was the transient act of marrying, not the state of being married.)

Most thirteenth- and fourteenth-century theologians adopted Albert's solution to the objection. Although it separated the sacramentality of marriage from its foundation in the discourse on marriage in Ephesians 5:22–33, most theologians recognized that the grace of marriage had some special kinship with the union between Christ

---

[194] *Cum omnia sacramenta* I, 134/24–135/5. Cf. Jonas of Orléans, *De institutione laicali* II.1, ed. Dubreucq, SC 549, 326–30 (PL 106:169C–170C).

and the church. Thomas Aquinas restored this special relationship in the *Summa contra Gentiles*. From the premise that marriage signifies Christ's union with the church, Thomas deduces that marriage confers grace:

> And just as in the other sacraments something spiritual is signified through the things done outwardly, so too in this sacrament the union of Christ and the church is signified through the union of male and female, as the Apostle says: "This is a great sacrament, but I speak in Christ and in the church" (Eph 5:32). And because the sacraments "effect what they figure," one must believe that a grace is conferred through this sacrament on those who are marrying: a grace through which they may belong to the union of Christ and the Church. And this is especially needful for them, so that they may strive not to be disjoined from Christ and the church by carnal and earthly things.[195]

Because theologians always considered Christ's union with the church to be a figurative marriage or betrothal, and because all the graces were implicated in that union, they were bound to associate the grace of marriage with the union between Christ and the church. If there was a serious problem, it was that this feature did not sufficiently distinguish conjugal grace from the graces of the other sacraments.

Sixteenth-century theologians interpreted the premise somewhat differently, partly because they explicitly identified the grace of marriage with conjugal love, and partly because they broadened the biblical basis of the doctrine in response to the criticisms of Erasmus and Luther. Erasmus was able to regard the New Testament as a historical document, unencumbered by the accumulated traditions of interpretation. Although he accepted that marriage was one of the sacraments, therefore, he realized that one could not validly cite Ephesians 5:32 as proof. Erasmus suggested that the mistake might not have occurred if *mystērion* in Ephesians 5:32 had been translated as *mysterium* and not as *sacramentum*, but that point was incidental. His chief objection was that Paul nowhere else used the term *mystērion* , whether translated as *sacramentum* or as *mysterium*, to denote one of the sacraments (Section 17.2.4). Luther adopted and polemicized Erasmus's critique in his *Babylonian Captivity* (1520), but he went further (Section 17.3). Insisting on his own definition of sacrament, Luther contended that marriage was not a sacrament, and that including it among the sacraments of the New Law only invited confusion. Luther did not deny that marriage was an apt figure of Christ and the church, but he argued that the same could be said of things that no one would count among the sacraments. Marriage was not a sacrament, therefore, although it was a "real allegory," that is, a real thing that could be interpreted as a figure of Christ and the church:

> Christ and the Church, therefore, are a mystery, i.e., a thing that is hidden and great [*res secreta* ... *et magna*], which, indeed, could and ought to have been

---

[195] *Summa contra Gentiles* IV.78 (Leonine 15:246b).

figured through marriage as if by a real allegory [*reali quadam allegoria*], but marriage ought not to have been called a sacrament for that reason. The heavens to which Psalm 18 refers are a figure of the apostles [Ps 18:2], and the sun of Christ, and the waters of the peoples, but these are not for that reason called sacraments.[196]

Luther's argument was not entirely new. Peter John Olivi had suggested in a rash moment that marriage might be a sacrament in the same sense as the bronze serpent (Num 21:8–9), the Tabernacle, and the ark of Moses were sacraments, although he later retracted the statement (Section 14.8.2). The chief weakness of Luther argument, as the prelates at Trent will point out, was that he failed to perceive that Paul had presented the divine union as the exemplar of Christian marriage. Luther may have been right in arguing that marriage was not a sacrament in the way that baptism and eucharist were sacraments – not only Olivi and Durandus but every theologian before 1100 would have agreed with him – but he was wrong to propose that marriage, according to Paul, was no more than a figure or a "real allegory" of Christ and the church. To this extent at least, it seems to me, the prelates and theologians at Trent had Scripture and logic on their side.

Responding to Erasmus and Luther, Catholic theologians in the sixteenth century were reluctant to concede that the *magnum sacramentum* was not marriage, but they did concede that Ephesians 5:32, considered in itself, was not a proof that marriage was a sacrament in the proper sense. They appealed to other biblical texts to support the doctrine, therefore, broadening its biblical basis, and they revised their interpretation of Ephesians 5, arguing that what God required of couples in marriage was not humanly impossible without grace. Henry VIII pursued this line of argument is his refutation of Luther's Babylonian Captivity (1521) (Section 17.4), and it appeared frequently during the proceedings at Trent. Without grace, for example, the "undefiled bed" (*thorus immaculatus*) of Hebrews 13:14 would not be humanly possible. Again, without grace, no man could love his wife as Christ loved the church. Ephesians 5:25, which had rarely appeared in medieval accounts of the sacramentality of marriage, came back into focus. In Trent's preface on marriage, as we have seen, Ephesians 5:25 appeared alongside Ephesians 5:32. The two verses *taken together*, according to the preface, proved that marriage was a sacrament of the New Law. This theology recovered something of the normative dimension of Paul's discourse on marriage in Ephesians 5:22–33.

Ambrosius Catharinus, O.P. – an amateur but remarkably astute theologian – developed this new line of argument in the treatise on marriage that he addressed to the general council in 1551, the year in which the council was reconvened in Trent.

---

[196] Luther, *De captivitate Babylonica*, WA 6:552/14–18. Steinhaeuser translates Luther's *realis allegoria* as "outward allegory" (*Works of Martin Luther*, vol. 2 [Philadelphia 1915], p. 260; reprinted in *Luther's Works*, vol. 36: *Word and Sacrament II*, §6.7), whence the phrase appears in countless English-language accounts of Luther on the sacraments and on marriage. Luther understood the distinction between *figura* and *res*.

Catharinus had been present at the council as the bishop of Minori during its sojourn at Bologna in 1547. The council at Bologna was inconclusive and published no substantive decrees, but the prelates had begun to discuss the sacramental theology and the reform of marriage. It had already become clear that the topic of clandestine marriage would pose intractable problems.

Catharinus analyzes the peculiar relationship between the sacrament of marriage and its *res* (Section 18.3). Defending the Catholic doctrine that marriage is a sacrament in the proper sense of the term, Catharinus replies to the stock objection that these sacraments by definition cause what they signify, whereas marriage does not cause the union between Christ and the church. He replies that marriage does not signify Christ's union with the church simply (*simpliciter*), but as an exemplar that the spouses should emulate in their married life. Moreover, God enables the spouses to emulate the exemplar by bestowing grace *ex opere operato* on spouses who do not present an obstacle to it when they marry:

> ... the bond of marriage signifies the union of Christ and the church, and in signifying that union it also signifies what God brings about in the spouses through the sacrament of marriage. For it does not signify Christ's bond with the church simply, but rather as the exemplar to which carnal marriage should be assimilated, as the Apostle himself declares if he is correctly interpreted. For in the same way as the union of Christ and church was meant to generate children in the spirit for God, and just as Christ, the bridegroom, so loved the church, his bride, through that union that he "delivered himself up" unto death for her salvation (Eph 5:25), so also ought a man to love his own wife, and so she conversely ought to serve and honor her husband lovingly and reverently. The bond of marriage should signify all of this, therefore, with an oblique motion,[197] for inasmuch as marriage signifies the mystery of Christ and the church as its own type and exemplar, that [mystery?] surely signifies what it effects. Thus, when marriage is celebrated in a Christian way, in the fear of God and with the good intention of begetting offspring for God, God does not cheat the spouses of their holy desire but rather invisibly blesses their marriage and commends it. Many really experience this, but only if they join themselves together in Christian modesty, for too many Christians err gravely and disgracefully in this sacrament as in others by posing an obstacle that prevents them from receiving grace.[198]

Marrying clandestinely was likely to prevent the reception of conjugal grace *ex opere operato* in married life, since for Catharinus the sacrament *per se* was the transient event of marrying. Catharinus held that God alone was the minister who joined the

---

[197] I.e., with a motion composed of two specifically different motions. The edition reads *"cum reflexo modo."* This might perhaps be translated as "in a reflexive way," but the preposition seems wrong. I assume that it should be *"cum reflexo motu."* The *motus reflexus*, also known as *motus obliquus*, is the species of locomotions that result from the combination of two motions, e.g., helical motion is a *motus reflexus* resulting from the combination of the rectilinear and circular motions.

[198] Ambrosius Catharinus, *De matrimonio*, Q. 1, 229/12–39.

spouses in marriage, and he doubted whether God joined clandestine unions (Section 18.3.2). He also doubted, therefore, whether clandestinely contracted marriages were valid in the eyes of God, although he conceded that they were valid in canon law (Section 19.9.2).

1.7.5 *Conclusions and suggestions*

Medieval theologians never fully explained how marriage was a sacrament of Christ and the church. Instead, they posited the *sacramentum–res* relationship in an *ad hoc* manner to solve particular problems about marriage or to explain particular features of the sacrament, without pausing to analyze the relationship in depth. Theologians noticed no reason to explain what they were doing because they were drawing on ingrained habits of mind that were second nature to them: habits that had as much to do with biblical exegesis as with sacramental theology.

Use of the terms "symbol" and "symbolism" to characterize features of medieval religious thought and practice is unexceptionable as a provisional topic indicator, and I shall occasionally use the terminology in this book. Nevertheless, I doubt whether any of the specific notions of symbolism available today can shed much light on the medieval theology of marriage, partly because talk of symbolism tends to conflate figurative and sacramental uses of the comparisons, but chiefly because there was no term or phrase in their vocabulary that corresponds to "symbol" as we understand that term today. Medieval scholars used the term *symbolum* in something like the modern sense only rarely,[199] and then almost always when they were referring or alluding to the pseudo-Dionysius. Instead, they spoke of signs and figures: terms that had their own specific associations and theoretical underpinnings in medieval scholarly discourse. Modern notions of symbols and symbolism might be appropriate in an anthropological study of medieval practice, if such a thing is possible in the absence of field work, but they have limited use in intellectual history, where the aim is to interpret and to shed light on medieval discourse.

Moreover, the disadvantages as well as the advantages of the modern talk of "symbols" pertain to its use in comparative religious studies and *Religionsgeschichte*, which presupposes that one can isolate features common to many or even to all religions. It has proved hard to steer a course between an imposing, preconceived essentialism, which overrides the particularities and contexts of different religions and different periods, and an obtuse nominalism, which pretends that the religions have nothing in common. This difficulty accounts for the decline of comparative religious studies as a systematic academic discipline. Mircea Eliade's notion of symbols, in particular, has come in for much reasonable criticism among historians and observers of religions over the last twenty or thirty years, for Eliade imposed an overly rich and imaginative model of symbols in an essentialist dogmatic manner on

---

[199] I set aside its usual medieval sense, whereby it meant "creed."

diverse religions without attending sufficiently to their particularities.[200] Whether a modern notion of symbolism such as that of Eliade, Paul Tillich, or Paul Ricoeur can shed light on medieval talk of signs, figures, and sacraments is certainly a matter worthy of reflection and inquiry, but we should not *presuppose* that the modern notions capture the thought of our medieval authors, and I shall not pursue the inquiry here.

Medieval theologians characterized the essential relation between the sacrament of marriage as its *res* chiefly as that of a sign to what it signified. But signs reveal and instruct. They make the invisible manifest in the visible, the intelligible in the sensible, the interior in the exterior, the spiritual in the material, the eternal in the temporal, and the sublimely intangible in the commonplace. Figurative marriage was certainly a sign in that sense, as was rite of marrying, especially when performed in a liturgical setting, just as baptism was a sign of redemption from sin. But medieval theologians rarely construed real marriages – the mundane unions of Christian couples – as material signs revealing spiritual truths.

I suggest that the relationship in medieval theology between marriage as a sacrament and Christ's union with the church as its *res* had less to do with signification in Augustine's sense than with exemplary conformity. Theologians assumed that the union between Christ and the church was the exemplar that marriage was supposed to emulate, even to embody. Such was Paul's argument in Ephesians 5:22–33, which medieval theologians appropriated in their own way. Perhaps they conflated the relation of *res* and *signum* with that of exemplar and *exemplatum*. I take it that Chaucer's parson was referring to the exemplary aspect of the relation when he argued that marriage was monogamous because "it is figured bitwixe Crist and holy chirche."[201] He did not say that marriage figured the union between Christ and holy church, although that would have been true. Erasmus (Sections 17.2.3 and 17.2.4) and Ambrosius Catharinus (as quoted earlier) recognized that in marriage the signified was the exemplar that the sign ought to emulate.

This relation of exemplarity presupposed that marriage was holy or sacred *because* or *inasmuch as* it represented Christ and the church. The signifier shared the value of the signified. There is no reason why figures in general have to share the value or any other qualities of what they signify. For example, Christians have never regarded thieves as holy because the Bible says that Christ will return as a thief (1 Thess 5:2, Rev 16:15). With Cistercian commentaries and sermons on the Song of Songs in mind, and especially the sermons by Bernard of Clairvaux, Jean Leclercq claims that

---

[200] For a critical review of symbolism in the study of religions, see N. K. Frankenberry, "Religion as a 'Mobile Army of Metaphors'," in N. K. Frankenberry (ed.), *Radical Interpretation in Religion* (Cambridge, 2002), 171–87. For a cautious theological reflection on symbolism and myth in revelation, see A. Dulles, "Symbol, Myth, and the Biblical Revelation," *Theological Studies* 27.1 (1966): 1–26.

[201] Chaucer, *Parson's Tale*, X.920–21: "and it was ordeyned that o man sholde have but o womman, and o womman but o man, as seith Seint Augustyn, by manye resouns. First, for mariage is figured bitwixe Crist and holy chirche."

"monastic authors must have considered marriage as being great and beautiful since they saw it as the symbol of the most sublime mysteries."[202] But this argument is arguably a non sequitur. The likeness between figure and figured does not necessarily include correspondence in value or even of qualities that can be evaluated.

Consider, for example, how Guigo II (d c. 1188), the ninth prior of La Grande Chartreuse, used the sexual climax to illustrate the highest rung of the ladder of *lectio divina*:

> Just as the soul is so conquered by carnal concupiscence in certain bodily functions that it loses all use of reason and the human being seems to be entirely flesh, so conversely in this sublime contemplation the fleshly motions are so overcome and absorbed by the soul that the flesh does not contradict the spirit in any way, and the human being seems to become entirely spiritual.[203]

It was a commonplace of medieval sexual ethics that the entire human being (*totus homo*) became flesh in the moment of sexual climax (Section 13.1).[204] No one considered this loss of reason to be a good thing in itself. It was a sign of the fallen human condition. But Guigo uses the loss of rationality in the orgasm as an analogy to illustrate conversely (*econtra*) the highest, contemplative stage of *lectio divina*, in which affective rapture supersedes reasoned meditation on Scripture and petitionary prayer.

Marriage as a sacrament is much more than figurative marriage. An obvious difference between figurative marriage and the sacrament of marriage is that figures exist primarily in texts and in the imagination, whereas sacraments exist in the real world. But there is less to this difference than meets the eye. The medieval practice of spiritual interpretation was historically and culturally rooted in texts and exegesis, but medieval scholars assumed that the non-literal senses of Scripture inhered chiefly in the historical events narrated in Scripture. For example, when exegetes interpreted Rachel and Leah figuratively as the contemplative and active lives respectively, they assumed that they were interpreting two real women in sacred history, and not only a biblical narrative (Gen 29:16–30). Nevertheless, they did not suppose that Rachel was in reality a contemplative. The interpretation was merely

---

[202] J. Leclercq, *Monks on Marriage* (New York, 1982), 86. For an illuminating study of Bernard's work in this field, see Line C. Engh, *Gendered Identities in Bernard of Clairvaux's "Sermons on the Song of Songs": Performing the Bride* (Brepols, 2014).

[203] Guigo II, *Scala claustralium (Epistola de vita contemplativa)* 7, SC 163:96/168–174: "Et sicut in quibusdam carnalibus officiis anima adeo vincitur carnali concupiscentia quod omnem usum rationis amittit et fit homo quasi totus carnalis, ita econverso in hac superna contemplatione ita superantur et absorbantur carnales motus ab anima ut in nullo caro spiritui contradicat, et fit homo quasi totus spiritualis."

[204] The dictum came from a sermon fragment in which Augustine discusses how to interpret 1 Cor 6:18. See *Serm.* 162, PL 885–89 (or CSEL 9.1:1026–29). The fragment is preserved in Eugippius, *Excerpta ex operibus s. Augustini* (CSEL 9.1:1024–32). Cf. Peter Lombard, on 1 Cor 7:18–20, PL 191:1584B: "Sic enim totus homo absorbetur a carne, ut jam dici non possit, ipse animus suus est, sed simul totus homo dici possit caro."

figurative, although it was an interpretation of real women. The kinship that theologians envisaged between the sacrament of marriage and Christ's union with the church was much more than Luther's "real allegory."

Was the resemblance between the sacrament of marriage and its *res* only analogical, or was it also qualitative or participatory? It seems to me that medieval theologians envisaged a resemblance that was *more than* analogy, notwithstanding their use of the analogical syllogism. Aristotle showed that analogy is the basis of metaphors, and it is also the basis of figures and similes. But analogical resemblance is indifferent to distance. The ratio 1:2 equals that of 150:300 and that of 12 million to 24 million. Again, analogical resemblance does not necessarily entail similarities of quality or value. Two thirteenth-century Franciscan theologians, Jean de la Rochelle and Bonaventure, perceptively argued that the analogies between the human being and God, such as the Augustinian correspondences between the three faculties of the mind and the Trinity, were value-neutral and did not make the human being pleasing to God. Bonaventure characterized the Trinitarian analogies as the sharing of a common *figura*. What did make the soul pleasing to God, they argued, was sanctifying grace, which entailed a resemblance that was not analogical but purely qualitative, with no correspondence between structures.[205]

The qualitative and evaluative aspects of the resemblance between the sacrament of marriage and Christ's union with the church are clear in sixteenth-century theology, where the sacramental grace of marriage is identified with conjugal affection. Counter-Reformation theologians, defending the Catholic doctrine against the Lutherans, restored something of Paul's argument in Ephesians 5:22–33. They held that Christian spouses ought to emulate in their own small way, with the help of grace, the love that united Christ and the church. Ambrosius Catharinus explicitly recognized, as noted earlier, that the special relationship between the sacrament of marriage and Christ's union with the church was both figural and exemplary.

1.8 THE SACRAMENT OF MARRIAGE IN IMAGINATION

I have included two depictions of the sacrament. One is a woodcut depicting the sacrament of marriage and its primordial exemplar from *L'Art de bien vivre and et de bien mourir*, first published in Paris by Antoine Vérard in 1492 (Plate 1).[206]

---

[205] P. L. Reynolds, "Bonaventure's Theory of Resemblance," *Traditio* 58 (2003): 219–55.

[206] The woodcut reproduced here is from the English (more precisely, Scots-English) edition, *The book Intytulyd The art of good lywyng and good deyng*, printed by Vérard in Paris, 1503. On this edition, see F. Stubbings, *The Art of Good Living* (STC 791), *Transactions of the Cambridge Bibliographical Society* 10.4 (1994): 535–38. On Vérard's work as a publisher, see M. B. Winn, *Anthoine Vérard, Parisian Publisher, 1485–1512* (Geneva, 1997). E. Hall, *The Arnolfini Betrothal* (Berkeley, 1994), plate 5, reproduces a beautiful colored exemplar of the illustration on vellum.

PLATE 1: The Sacrament of Marriage: Woodcut from *The book intytuled The art of good lywyng [and] good deyng*, published by Antoine Vérard in Paris, 1503, from a copy held by the British Library. Image produced by ProQuest as part of *Early English Books Online*. www.proquest.com

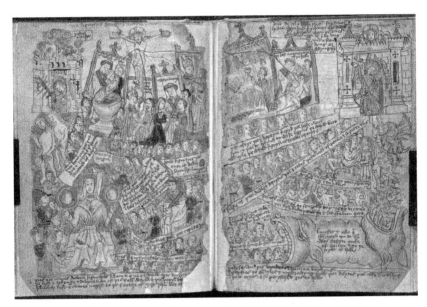

PLATE 2: Diagram of the Spiritual Journey of Life: British Library Additional Manuscript 37049, ff. 72v–73r.

The other is a double-page diagram of the spiritual journey of life from British Library Additional Manuscript 37049, which is described in the library's catalogue as "a Carthusian miscellany of poems, chronicles, and treatises in a northern-English dialect" (Plate 2). The former is one of the seven illustrations comprising a seven-sacrament cycle. The latter is a diagram or flow chart of the spiritual life, with the system of seven sacraments displayed prominently. These images show far more fully and vividly than words could ever do how people of faith – bishops, parish priests, and pious lay folk – imagined the sacrament of marriage during the late Middle Ages.

1.8.1 *Seven-sacrament cycles*

Depictions of the seven sacraments became popular in French, Flemish, and English church art during the fifteenth century.[207] Typically, each scene depicts a priest going about his allotted task, often in a church or sanctuary, although the sacrament of extreme unction usually occurs in a layman's bedchamber. The most famous example is the *Seven Sacraments Altarpiece* (1443–1455) painted by or under the direction of the Flemish artist Rogier van der Weyden. It was probably

[207] G. McN. Rushforth, "Seven Sacraments Compositions in English Medieval Art," *Antiquaries Journal* 9.2 (1929): 83–100. A. E. Nichols, *Seeable Signs: The Iconography of the Seven Sacraments, 1350–1544* (Woodbridge, 1994).

commissioned by Jean Chevrot, bishop of Tournai. Most seven-sacrament cycles, including Rogier van der Weyden's, arrange the sacraments around the crucified Christ, emphasizing the Christological as well as the ecclesiological aspects of the sacrament. This arrangement emphasizes the homogeneity of the sacramental system, for all seven sacraments are instruments of Christ's saving work. The subject also celebrates the role of the church's ministers in the daily life of the laity. It must have functioned, too, as a didactic instrument, even as sacramental propaganda. The cycles teach that laypersons cannot be saved without the sacraments of the church and the ministry of priests.

In some of the Christ-centered depictions, blood flows from the wound in Christ's side to each of the seven sacraments, demonstrating the dependence of sacramental efficacy on the grace and merits of Christ. Eljenholm Nichols characterizes these versions of the subject as "vulneral."[208] The stream that reaches the spouses as they plight their troth runs to their heads, to their hearts, or (as in BL Additional MS 37049) to their joined hands (Plate 3). Albertus Magnus argued that the grace of marriage flowed "from the betrothal of human nature with the divine nature in the person of Christ," a betrothal that was fully realized on the Cross.[209] Albert cited Exodus 4:25 as proof: "A bloody bridegroom art thou to me."[210] Thomas Aquinas considered the objection that marriage could not be one of the sacraments of the New Law because it lacked the required "conformity" with the Passion. The Passion was painful, whereas marrying is associated with pleasure. In reply, Thomas points out that Christ suffered on the Cross out of love and in order to unite the church with himself as his betrothed. Marriage as a sacrament is conformed not to the pain of the Passion, Thomas argues, but to the underlying love.[211]

1.8.2 *The Vérard woodcut*

This is the final illustration in a cycle depicting the seven sacraments.[212] Each illustration depicts one of the sacraments taking place in the present day, but with a vignette depicting an Old Testament prefiguration set in a canopy above, which is cleverly integrated into the architecture. Above baptism, for example, Naaman is being cured of leprosy in the Jordan while Elisha holds his clothes (2 Kings 5); above eucharist, the high priest Melchisedek offers bread and wine to Abram, who is returning from battle (Gen 14:14–20); and above extreme unction (a death-bed scene), the prophet Samuel anoints David as king (1 Sam 16:13). The marriage

---

[208] Nichols, *Seeable Signs*, 9–18.　　[209] *IV Sent.* 26.5, resp. (103b); ad q. 3 (123b). Cf. Plate 3.
[210] Albertus Magnus, *IV Sent.* 1.2, resp. (Borgnet 29:9a).
[211] Thomas Aquinas, *IV Sent.* 26.2.1, arg. 3; ad 3 (71b, 72a). *IV Sent.* 26.2.3, ad 1 (74a). Likewise, Adrian Florensz, *Quaestiones de sacramentis in Quartum Sententiarum librum*, 5: *De matrimonio*, Q. 1, ad 2 (Rome, 1522: 189vb).
[212] The publication consists of a sequence of four parts or monographs, which were sometimes issued separately. The seven-sacrament cycle is part of the fourth part, entitled *Le bien vivre*.

PLATE 3: BL Add. MS 37049, detail.

scene depicts the rite of *dextrarum iunctio* (joining of right hands). In the main
scene, a priest joins the right hands of the spouses in a church. In the scene inset
above, God the Father joins the right hands of Adam and Eve in the earthly Paradise
(Gen 2:22–24). The liturgical action is exactly the same in the two weddings, but the
circumstances are very different. In one, the spouses stand naked in the Garden of
Eden, with God the Father as their minister and sole witness. In the other, the bride
and groom are richly dressed in a church, surrounded by their family, kinsfolk, and
friends, who witness their union as the priest solemnizes it.

This pairing of present-day sacraments and Old Testament prefigurations is
unusual, but it occurs also in a seven-sacrament tapestry made in the Southern
Netherlands around 1435–1450. Here, the images are arranged in two parallel strips,
with the prefigurations in the upper strip, and the sacraments of the church in the

lower strip. Captions set in scrolls between the two strips explain the function of each sacrament.[213] The scroll between the primordial and present-day weddings explains that in forming Eve from Adam's side as his companion, God revealed the sacrament of marriage and its purpose:

> Le sacrement de mariage, dont multiplie humain lignage, moustra dieus quand adam crea, et de sa coste eve fourma, qui fu des femmes la premiere, et a adam amie chiere.[214]

Adam and Eve are shown bare-footed and clothed in simple smocks, in contrast both to God the Father's regal robe in the primordial scene, and to the modern couple's richly embroidered garments in the present-day scene. A striking feature of these depictions of nuptials is the exact correspondence between the two weddings, respectively primordial and present-day. The primordial precedent is more than a prefiguration. The different circumstances only emphasize that the rite of joining itself is exactly the same.

1.8.3 Dextrarum iunctio

Depictions of marriage as one of the sacraments of the church are rare before 1300, but they become common in northern Europe during the fourteenth century. From that time forward, they almost always show a priest joining the partners' right hands, usually in a church and in the presence of the couple's *propinqui et amici*.[215] The ritual of *dextrarum iunctio* must have already been widespread and familiar, but there are only a few traces of its use in art before 1200. The emergence and rise of the image in art coincides with that of the doctrine of marriage as a sacrament.

The origins and history of the rite remain obscure. Roman spouses are depicted with their right hands joined together from the second century AD on sarcophagi and in other funerary art, and even on coins. Concordia, the goddess of marriage

---

[213] A. S. Cavallo, *Medieval Tapestries in the Metropolitan Museum of Art* (New York 1993), 156–73. The tapestry was in the collection of Isabel la Católica in 1503, who gave it to the Capilla Real in Granada in 1504, where it remained until 1871. Eight separate pieces of the tapestry are extant, of which five are in the Metropolitan Museum, New York (07.57.1–5), two in the Burrell Collection, Glasgow, and one in the Victoria and Albert Museum, London (T.131–1931). Together, these depict five of the seven sacraments. Two documents, one regarding a tapestry that Jean Chevrot, bishop of Tournai, bequeathed in 1458 to the church of St Hippolytus in Poligny, Burgundy, and the other regarding a tapestry that Pasqual Grenier of Tournai and his wife gave to the church of Saint Quentin in Tournai c. 1475, seem to refer to different artifacts made to the same design.

[214] Cavallo, *Medieval Tapestries*, 164. Translation: "God revealed the sacrament of marriage, from which the human race multiplied, when he created Adam and from his side formed Eve, who was the first among women and a dear companion to Adam."

[215] Sometimes one or both of the partners uses the left hand. A few of these depictions seem to indicate that something improper was going on, such as a clandestine marriage, but most examples may safely be attributed to ineptitude on the part of the artist. I am grateful to Prudence Hardi for alerting me to the significance and importance of this iconography.

and civic harmony, sometimes stands behind them with her hands on their shoulders.[216] But classical scholars today generally agree that this image did not depict a betrothal or a wedding, as formerly supposed, but rather represented the married state, although the hand-joining gesture had a long history with many meanings and was often associated with oaths and agreements in classical Rome and elsewhere.[217] Nevertheless, similar configurations appear in depictions of marrying or betrothal in Christian art during the fourth through fifth centuries.[218] In a mosaic depicting the marriage of Moses and Sephora in Sancta Maria Maggiore, Rome (432–440), for example, Sephora's father occupies the position of Concordia as he brings the spouses together, albeit without joining their hands.[219] And two identical gold medallions on a Syrian marriage belt of the late sixth or early seventh century, now at Dumbarton Oaks, show Christ joining the spouses' right hands, with the caption, "From God, concord."[220] It is likely that these examples are remnants of a Christian hand-joining rite performed in betrothals or weddings, but, if so, the practice must have soon died out. Images of nuptial hand joining do not appear again in the west until the central Middle Ages.

The earliest witness to the rite of *dextrarum iunctio* in a betrothal or a wedding is the Vulgate version of Tobit. Raguel, "taking the right hand of his daughter, gave it into the right hand of Tobias, saying: The God of Abraham and the God of Isaac and the God of Jacob be with you, and may he himself [*ipse*] join you together, and fulfill his blessing in you" (Tob 7:15).[221] The book was composed c. 200 BC in a Semitic language, probably Aramaic, but Raguel's blessing occurs only in Jerome's somewhat eccentric recension. Some biblical scholars suspect that Jerome made up the passages that do not occur in other witnesses, but it is hardly likely that he invented the hand-joining rite. Perhaps the passage reflects a practice of the fourth century AD with which Jerome was familiar.

---

[216] See L. Larsson Lovén, "*Coniugal Concordia*: Marriage and Marital Ideals on Roman Funerary Monuments," in L. Larsson Lovén and A. Strömberg, *Ancient Marriage in Myth and Reality* (Newcastle upon Tyne, 2010), 204–20.

[217] G. Davies, "The Significance of the Handshake Motif in Classical Funerary Art," *American Journal of Archaeology* 89 (1985): 627–40.

[218] C. Breuer, *Reliefs und Epigramme griechischer Privatgrabmäler. Zeugnisse bürgerlichen Selbstverständnisses vom 4. bis 2. Jahrhundert v. Chr* (Cologne, 1995), 15–39. Hall, *Arnolfini Betrothal*, pp. 19–20 and figs. 6–8.

[219] Hall, *Arnolfini Betrothal*, pp. 20–21 (with fig. 9 on p. 21). G. Bovini, "Le scene della dextrarum iunctio nell'arte cristiana," *Bullettino della commissione archeologica communale di Roma* 72 (1946–1948): 103–17.

[220] Hall, *Arnolfini Betrothal*, pp. 21–22 (with fig. 10 on p. 22). A. Heimann, "Die Hochzeit von Adam und Eva im Paradies nebst einigen andern Hochzeitsbildern," *Wallraf-Richartz Jahrbuch* 37 (1975): 11–40, at 25. L. Reekmans, "La *dextrarum iunctio* dans l'iconographie romaine et paléochrétienne," *Bulletin de l'Institut Historique Belge de Rome* 31 (1958): 29–95, at 88.

[221] Tob 7:15, Vulgate: "et adprehendens dexteram filae suae dexterae Tobiae tradidit dicens, Deus Abraham et Deus Isaac et Deus Iacob sit vobiscum, et ipse coniungat vos impleatque benedictionem suam in vobis."

The Raguel prayer (quoted earlier) became a common feature of medieval nuptial liturgies. Its first extant uses are in nuptial *ordines* from the eleventh century: in the Spanish *Liber ordinum*, and in the French *Benedictional of Archbishop Robert*, which probably came from Rouen. In both texts, the prayer occurs in a ceremony of blessing that follows the nuptial mass. These *ordines* do not say that the minister should join the spouses' hands, although that might have been tacitly understood.

The work of Adelheid Heimann and Edwin Hall has amply demonstrated how the ritual of *dextrarum iunctio* reemerged in medieval depictions of marrying. A summary of their findings will suffice here. The two earliest explicit depictions of nuptial hand joining are in portrayals of the marriage of Mary and Joseph in illustrated gospel books from Reichenau, which date from the first half of the eleventh century. A man who is probably a priest stands between the spouses and presents Mary to Joseph, as if he were her father, while the spouses themselves join *both* their hands together.[222] Depictions with a minister joining the spouses' *right* hands appear rather suddenly toward the end of the thirteenth century, and this gesture becomes the norm in art during the fourteenth century.[223] Hall proposes that the rite in which a priest joined the spouses' right hands replaced an earlier *traditio* ceremony, traceable in art to the tenth century, in which the bride's father gave her away to the groom by joining their hands.[224]

Depictions of the primordial marriage follow a parallel development. Genesis records only that God the Father, having formed Eve from Adam's side, "brought her to Adam" ("*adduxit ea ad Adam*," Gen 2:22). Before 1300, depictions of this scene follow the text literally, without presenting the scene explicitly as a wedding. In some examples, one of the partners stretches out a hand to greet the other. God the Father usually stands behind Eve as the partners meet, having brought her to Adam. This image occurs, for example, in the frontispiece to Genesis in the Moutier-Granval Bible from Tours, from around 830–840. Here, the narrative from the creation of Adam to the expulsion and travails of the first couple are depicted in four parallel strips, with two scenes on each strip. God brings Eve to Adam in the first scene of second strip.[225] A panel of the famous bronze doors that Bernward, bishop of Hildesheim, commissioned for his cathedral c. 1012 depicts the same scene. Here, there are sixteen panels, arranged in eight facing pairs, with the narrative sequence running continuously from top to bottom on the left and then from bottom to top on the right. God brings Eve

---

[222] These are: (i) The Gospels of Otto III, Reichenau, ca. 1000, MS Munich, Bayerische Staatsbibliotek, Clm 4453, fol. 28r (Hall, *Arnolfini Betrothal*, p. 38, fig. 14). (ii) Bernulfus Gospels, Reichenau, ca. 1040/1050, MS Utrecht, Rijksmuseum Het Catharijneconvent, ABM ms. 3, fol. 7v (Hall, *Arnolfini Betrothal*, plate 4).

[223] Hall, *Arnolfini Betrothal*, pp. 22, 36–37, and 145–48 with n. 65.   [224] Ibid., 33–34.

[225] London, British Library, MS Addit. 10546, f. 5v. Reproduced in John Beckwith, *Early Medieval Art* (London, 1964), plate 46.

to Adam in the second panel from the top on the left. The partners approach each other with outstretched arms (with Eve on the viewer's left), with their hands still not quite touching. God the Father stands behind Eve with his hands on her shoulders, gently pushing her toward Adam from the viewer's left to right.[226] In the facing panel on the right, the women approach Christ's empty tomb from right to left, and the angel addresses them from the tomb (Matt 28:2). The pairing of images on left and right may have been happenstance, but if so the artist made the most of it.

By the thirteenth century, artists depicted the primordial wedding with God the Father joining the spouses' hands, usually but not always with Adam on his right (the viewer's left).[227] God takes both hands of each partner in one of his own in the earliest examples, whereas God joins their right hands from around 1300.

The artists must have depicted the primordial wedding with *dextrarum iunctio* because that rite was customary and familiar from contemporaneous church weddings. The meaning of the two images, however, runs in the opposite direction. The joining of hands was a non-verbal representation of Jesus' dictum that no man should separate what God has joined together (Matt 19:6, Mark 10:9), which was in turn a gloss on Genesis 2:24. The Vérard image tells the observer that marriage today reenacts the primordial wedding. Who, then, joins the spouses in the present day: God himself, or the minister?

The first extant use of Jesus' dictum in a nuptial setting is in the *ordo* that Hincmar of Reims composed for the wedding and coronation of Judith, daughter of Charles the Bald, in 856. Here, the formula accompanies the betrothal:

> Accept this ring, a sign of fidelity and love and a bond of conjugal union, so that no man may separate those whom God joins. Who lives and reigns forever and ever.[228]

Hincmar changed the *quod* ("what") of the original verse to *quos* ("those whom"). With *quod*, the statement seemed to posit a law that God had enacted in the beginning. The *quos* form suggested that God himself joined the spouses in the present day, just as he had joined Adam and Eve in Eden. To make this implication explicit, Hincmar also changed the tense from past to present, saying not "what God has joined," but "those whom God joins."

---

[226] H. Stahl, Harvey, "Eve's Reach: A Note on the Dramatic Elements in the Hildesheim Doors," in E. Sears and T. K. Thomas (eds.), *Reading Medieval Images*, 163–75.

[227] Heimann, "Die Hochzeit von Adam und Eva," 13–17. MS Bodleian 270b, fol. 6r (ca.1239). Codex Vindobonensis (Vienna Codex), MS Vienna, Österreichische Nationabibliotek, cod. 2554 (c.1220–1225). MS British Library, Add. 18719, fol. 7v. (ca.1300). A. Wilson and J. Lancaster Wilson. *A Medieval Mirror: Speculum humanae salvationis, 1324–1500* (Berkeley, 1984), 30–31, 35, 143–44.

[228] In R. A. Jackson (ed.), *Ordines Coronationis Franciae*, Ordo V.4, 1:77: "Accipe anulum, fidei et dilectionis signum, atque coniugalis coniunctionis vinculum, ut non separet homo quos coniungit Deus. Qui vivit et regnat in omnia secula saeculorum."

The *quos* form occurs in theological writing as well in the nuptial liturgy. Tertullian quoted the dictum in the *quos* form in his *De monogamia*, presumably because it was what he read in his Old Latin source.[229] So does Vacarius in his *De monogamia*, written in the 1160s. Vacarius argues that a marriage between infidels is not established or insoluble, since, according to Augustine, "a marriage that is without God is not *ratum*."[230] Divine law, unlike human law, prohibits "those whom God has joined" from divorcing, Vacarius explains.[231] Again, Thomas Aquinas quotes the verse in the *quos* form in his commentary on the *Sentences* (c. 1256). Since no man may separate "those whom [*quos*] God has joined together," one might object the church has no power to introduce or to alter the impediments of relationship. Thomas replies that just as God does not join a couple when their union is contrary to a divine precept, so God does not join a couple whose union is contrary to the church's precepts.[232] But it is God who joins them, not the church. During the proceedings of the Council of Trent, the bishop of Namur, according to the secretary's record, attributed to Thomas the maxim, "Those whom the church does not join, God does not join."[233]

After Hincmar, six centuries pass before the next extant appearance Jesus' dictum in the nuptial liturgy. In an *ordo* from Lyon, c. 1498, the priest says the formula in its *quod* form during the pre-nuptial rite performed at the entrance to the church, while the partners stand before him with joined hands.[234] Use of this formula, usually in the *quod* form, had become common by the middle of the sixteenth century, and it remains common today. During the same period, Matthew 19:3–6 or its parallel, Mark 10:1–9, became a frequent choice as the gospel reading during the nuptial mass.[235]

1.8.4 *Diagram of the spiritual journey of life (BL Additional MS 37049)*

This extraordinary miscellany dates from the last quarter of the fifteenth century.[236] The vernacular English of the text places it in Yorkshire or perhaps Lincolnshire,

---

[229] Tertullian, *De monogamia* 5.2, SC 343:148/9-10: "ideoque, quos Deus ab initio coniunxit in unam carnem, hodie homo non separabit"; ibid., 9.1, 168/5–6; ibid., 9.2, 170/11: "quos Deus coniunxit, homo non separabit;" ibid., 10.6, 178/47–48: "[vita aeterna] in qua magis non separabit quos coniunxit Deus."

[230] In fact, the source was Ambrosiaster, *Ad Corinthos prima* 7:15, CSEL 81:77. Vacarius had found the text in Gratian, C. 28 q. 1 *dictum ante* c. 1 (1078–79).

[231] Vacarius, *Summa de matrimonio*, in F. W. Maitland, "Vacarius on Marriage (Text)," *Law Quarterly Review* 13 (1887): 270–87, at 286: "Quamuis ergo lege fori diuertere poterant, tamen lege poli non debeant *quos deus coniunxit*. et ideo ratum est eorum matrimonium."

[232] Thomas Aquinas, *IV Sent.* 40.un.4, ad 1 (Vivès 11:239).

[233] Namurcensis, CT 9:670/4: "Item allegavit S. Thomam dicentem: Quos ecclesia non iungit, Deus non iungit."

[234] Molin and Mutembe, *Le rituel de mariage*, Ordo XVIII, p. 315. See also 115n112.

[235] Ibid., 120, 128.

[236] J. Hogg, *An Illustrated Yorkshire Carthusian Religious Miscellany British Library London Additional MS. 37049*, vol. 3: *The Illustrations* (Salzburg, 1981), reproduces all the pages with visual content and provides brief summaries of the content.

and internal references indicate that the codex was the work of Carthusians. It may have come from Mount Grace, a charterhouse that was especially active in the manufacture and illustration of books. The codex is profusely illustrated. Whereas text and illustration in medieval manuscripts are usually separate enterprises, here the two media are integrated as means to the same end, and the depictive technique is an extension of penmanship, with no pretensions to skill or ornamental beauty. Modern scholars used to approach the textual and visual elements in the miscellany separately and found both to be disappointing and crude, but more recent work regards the collection holistically and more sympathetically, observing that text and image are integral parts of a single discourse.[237] The construction and design of the illustrated pages is clever and thoughtful. Much of the material is didactic and seems to have been designed either to instruct laypersons or to help parish priest instruct them, but the purpose of the material remains a matter for speculation. Although Carthusian monks were contemplative solitaries, the day-to-day functioning of their communities depended on lay brothers (*conversi*). Some have suggested, therefore, that the material of this miscellany was designed for the instruction of the lay brothers, but much of it seems overly complicated for that purpose. Because commercial book production was a major part of the monks' manual labor in the English charterhouses, it is possible that the pages were sketches for books to be published in due course. Or they may have been the work of theologians who preferred this combination of image and text as their medium of reflection and inquiry.

The double-page illustration reproduced here depicts the entire Christian economy, in which the sacramental system is prominently situated.[238] The whole design is graphical. Text is limited to explanatory or narrative captions, and it is enclosed in banners that serve to divide the various classes of people as they proceed to their allotted ends. The diagram is organized around two axes. The course of life follows the horizontal axis from left to right, whereas good occupies the top half of the illustration, and evil the bottom half. The earthly Paradise is situated within ramparts at the top left. A cherub with a sword has cast out Adam and Eve from the gate, and they proceed downwards (Gen 3:24). Opposite, at the top right, there is a corresponding image of the celestial Paradise, where an angel at the gate with a long sword is forcing demons down into the jaws of Hell. The heads of Jesus and the blessed are visible above the parapet. The Great Whore (Rev 17:5), labeled in Latin (*Meretrix Magna*), is seated at the lower left, holding up twin mirrors of vanity. Hell with two sets of gaping jaws is at the lower right.

---

[237] H. Mellick, "In Defence of a Fifteenth-Century Manuscript." *Parergon* 8 (1974): 20–24. D. Gray, "London, British Library, Additional MS 37049 – A Spiritual Encyclopedia," in H. Barr, Helen and A. M. Hutchinson (eds.), *Text and Commentary from Wyclif to Bale* (Turnhout, 2005), 99–116. J. Brantley, *Reading in the Wilderness: Private Devotion and Public Performance in Late Medieval England* (Chicago, 2007), especially 4–25.

[238] For a detailed structural analysis, see Nichols, *Seeable Signs*, 52–55.

The movement of people in the diagram is organized around the two axes, with the passage from this life to the next proceeding from left to right, and the movement between good and evil proceeding up or down. The sacraments lead believers on the spiritual journey from birth to eternal life. Christ crucified, the source of sacramental grace, is at the center-top of the left-hand page. Blood pouring from the wound in his side ramifies into seven streams, one of which goes to each of the sacraments. In the top register on the left, proceeding from left to right, are baptism, confirmation, matrimony, and orders. The sequence continues on the right with eucharist and the anointing of the sick. One procession of the fallen leads from Adam and Eve down to the Great Whore, but another leads up again to baptism, passing around back of the baptismal font to enter the narrative of salvation. The sacrament of confession is the only sacrament placed in the lower register, where it rescues some of those who have succumbed to the charms of the Great Whore, enabling them to rejoin the faithful proceeding toward the celestial Paradise.

In the depiction of matrimony, a priest dispenses the sacrament while bride and groom kneel before him, with their right hands joined together. A witness stands beside the priest. One of the streams of saving blood passes to the spouses' joined hands. No theological argument could better convey the "univocity" of all seven sacraments, including marriage.

1.8.5 The role of the priest

Depictions of the sacrament of marriage and seven-sacrament cycles during the late Middle Ages show a priest administering the sacrament in an ecclesial setting. His ministry was not necessary under canon law for a valid, indissoluble marriage, and theologians maintained that the nuptial blessing and the other liturgical gestures were only sacramentals or solemnities and were not essential. But the image did not contradict the doctrine. To marry without the priestly blessing was an act of impiety, especially in northern Europe, and such a scene would have been incongruous in idealized depictions of the sacraments in the life of the faithful. Moreover, the priest's actions and words manifested the theology of the sacrament and declared what God accomplished through it, reminding the spouses that they were beginning a Christian vocation.

Nevertheless, the way in which artists imagined the sacrament testifies to an idea that was deeper than canon law and the theology of the schools. The depiction of the scene puts a question mark over the role of the priest. Was he only miming God's action to make it evident to everyone, especially the unlettered observers? Or was his role more like that of the priest who "confects" the bread and wine on the altar? In other words, did God himself directly join the spouses together, or did the priest join them as God's instrument?

Some of the early liturgical *ordines* emphasized that it was not the priest but God who joined the spouses inseparably together. Hincmar, as noted earlier, had the minister pointedly say that no human being should separate those whom God is joining together. Similarly, the Raguel prayer emphasizes that it is God himself (*ipse*), and not the bride's father or minister, who joins and blesses the spouses.[239] The popular nuptial petition *Exhaudi nos*, first recorded in the *Verona Sacramentary* (c. 600), expresses the same priestly self-effacement:

> Hear us, almighty and merciful God, so that what has been administered by our office may be fulfilled rather [*potius*] by your blessing. Through [our Lord Jesus Christ, etc.][240]

Exhaudi nos probably originated as a collect said at the beginning of the Roman nuptial mass. It became a feature of the Gregorian tradition and was among the most common and enduring of nuptial prayers throughout the Middle Ages.

During the late Middle Ages, however, a new form of blessing or joining emerged, which seemed to construe the priest as the minister who sacramentally united the spouses. Joining the spouses' hands, the priest now says, "*Ego vos coniungo*" ("I join you together"). The first extant use of this formula is in an *ordo* from Rouen, dating from around the middle of the fifteenth century. Here, after the interrogation, the priest is directed to give the bride to the groom and to say, "I join you together in the name of the Father, of the Son, and of the Holy Spirit."[241] There seems to have been a historical development in which the priest assumed the role of the bride's father in giving her to her husband. Thus, two thirteenth-century nuptial *ordines* direct the priest to say "*ego do*" or "*ego trado*" as he gives the bride to the groom and joins their hands together. The evidence of visual art points in the same direction. The more priestly "I join" replaced the paternal "I give." At the same time, the minister assumed the role of God the Father as the one who joins the spouses.[242]

By declaring that they joined the spouses together, priests during the late Middle Ages took upon themselves a role traditionally attributed to God alone. The notion that God himself joined each couple was the oldest, most traditional way of acknowledging that marriage was holy and inviolable, and it was still commonplace among Protestants as well as Catholics in the sixteenth century. Ambrosius Catherinus, O.P.,

---

[239] "Deus Abraham, Deus Isaac, Deus Iacob, ipse coniungat vos impleatque benedictionem suam in vobis. Per." Ritzer, *Le mariage*, 445. Searle and Stevenson, *Documents of the Marriage Liturgy*, 111. Cf. Tob 7:15.

[240] Ritzer, *Le mariage*, 422: "Exhaudi nos, omnipotens et misericors deus, ut quod nostro ministratur officio, tua benedictione potius impleatur. Per." See also J. Pierce, "A Note on the *Ego vos conjungo* in Medieval French Marriage Liturgy," *Ephemerides Liturgicae* 99 (1985): 290–99, at 293; Stevenson, *The Nuptial Blessing*, 35–37, 39; Searle and Stevenson, *Documents of the Marriage Liturgy*, 40–41.

[241] Pierce, "A Note on the *Ego vos conjungo*," 291. Stevenson, *The Nuptial Blessing*, 75. Molin and Mutembe, *Le rituel du mariage*, Ordo XIV, 304. The original MS is lost.

[242] Pierce, "A Note on the *Ego vos conjungo*," 296–98.

in the treatise on marriage that he addressed to the prelates at the Council of Trent, held that the only minister of the sacrament, insofar as there was any minister, was God himself (Section 18.3.2). Catherinus was staunch adversary of the Protestants, but in this respect he agreed with them. Protestant reformers, too, argued that clandestine marriages were soluble because in that case the devil, and not God, joined the partners together (Section 17.3.6).

Although the *"Ego vos coniungo"* formula was a focus of debate at the Council of Trent, which recommended its use everywhere, the formula was still not in wide use during the first half of the sixteenth century. On the eve of the general council, as far as is known today, it was current only in the dioceses of Normandy and in a region linking Meaux, Metz, and Cambrai. It was still not used elsewhere in France, nor anywhere in Germany. Thomas Goldwell, the bishop of Saint-Asaph, claimed at the council that the formula was customary in England, but there is no other evidence for its use there, and it was not used in York or Canterbury.[243] Its prominence at Trent during 1563 was largely due to the authority of Alberto Castellani's *Sacerdotale ad consuetudinem sanctae Romanae ecclesiae* (also known as the *Liber sacerdotale*), an unauthorized collection of Roman liturgical *ordines* first published in 1523. The *Sacerdotale* served as a standard source of liturgical *ordines* in Italy in the absence of an official *rituale*.[244] The prelates at Trent assumed that the *"Ego vos coniungo"* formula was a fixed and longstanding part of the Roman tradition, to which they attributed special authority. Moreover, Castellani said in his rubric that this formula of solemnization was the form of the sacrament, and that the spouses constituted the matter. Joining the spouses' right hands, the priest should say: "And I by the authority invested in me join you together in marriage."[245] The formula seemed to imply that the priest was the minister of the sacrament in the proper sense, but perhaps the priest was merely enacting and making manifest what God did. Dominic Soto argued that "I join you together" meant only "I approve or bless your joining" (Section 17.7.2). A dozen prelates at Trent considered *"Ego vos coniungo"* to be the requisite form of the sacrament, but a majority even of those who wanted to render clandestine marriages null and void resisted that notion.

The canons of marriage at Trent went through four drafts during 1563, the last of which the council adopted and published in Session XXIV. The formula *"Ego vos coniungo"* made its initial appearance in the second draft, in the first of several canons on abuses. This canon followed immediately after the decree invalidating clandestine marriages. After the reading of the banns, if no impediments have come to light, the couple should celebrate their marriage at a church (*in facie ecclesiae*),

---

[243] A. Duval, "La formule *Ego vos in matrimonium conjungo* ... au concile de Trente," *La Maison-Dieu* 99 (1969): 144–53, at 145–46.

[244] Duval, "La formule *Ego vos in matrimonium conjungo*," 150.

[245] "Et ego auctoritate qua fungor coniungo vos matrimonialiter." Quoted from Duval, "La formule *Ego vos in matrimonium conjungo*," 146n8.

where the parish priest will interrogate them. Having established that they truly consent, the parish priest will say: "I join you together in the name of the Father, the Son, and the Holy Spirit."[246] The same canon required spouses to receive the priestly blessing in church (*in ecclesia*) before consummating their marriage. Although these were meant to be prescribed formalities, they were not intended as conditions of validity. Most of the prelates received these proposals favorably while resisting the universal imposition of "*Ego vos coniungo*," partly because the words themselves suggested that the priest joined the spouses, but chiefly because the insistence on any specific formula of joining might imply that this was the form of the sacrament. Theologically principled prelates objected that the priest's formula was only a sacramental, and not the form of the sacrament. Pragmatists worried that the issue would stir up endless debate and further delay the conclusion of the council. Some of the prelates suggested alternative formulas of joining by which the priest would ask God to join the spouses, such as, "What God has begun in you, may he himself complete,"[247] or "I declare that you have been joined together."[248] According to an amendment that entered in the next draft and survived in the published canons, the priest should either say, "I join you together in the name of the Father, the Son, and the Holy Spirit" or "use other words according to the received rite of each province."[249] The provision for alternatives was a nod to theologians. It sufficed to show that the priest's formula was not part of the essence of the sacrament.

Tametsi, Trent's decree on clandestine marriages, required couples to plight their troth in the presence of the parish priest and at least two witnesses. Absent that condition, there was no marriage. The first draft had only required witnesses, but many prelates had proposed that one of the witnesses should be a priest or, better, the parish priest. Henceforth, there could be no marriage without a priest acting in an official capacity, but the decree did not define what his role was. Careful reading of the decree shows that his role was essentially that of official witness, but by leaving his role unspecified the council satisfied the common intuition that the priest was the minister of the sacrament: an intuition vividly depicted in the two images reproduced here. Solemnities such as the priestly blessing and the rite of *dextrarum iunctio* were not necessary for validity in canon law even after Trent, and they did not belong to the essence of the sacrament according to the theologians, but people could not *imagine* marriage as a sacrament of the church without them.

---

[246] CT 9:683/36–37: "Ego vos coniungo in nomine Patris, et Filii et Spiritus sancti."
[247] Gen. Eremitarum S. Augustini, CT 9:739/37–38: "Quod Dominus in vobis incepit, ipse perficiat."
[248] Larinensis, CT 9:717/10–11: "Verba placent: Ego vos coniungo, vel declaro coniunctos." He also suggested that a marriage should be contracted "ante fores domus sponsae."
[249] CT 9:762/4–6.

PART I

Augustine

2

Marriage in Augustine's writings

Any account of the medieval theology of marriage as a sacrament must begin with Augustine. His writings on this topic, as on many others, were fundamental for medieval scholars. Augustine provided the raw material for the early development of the sacramental theology of marriage during the first quarter of the twelfth century, and that development coincided with the recovery of much of what Augustine had said on the subject, which had been dormant for centuries.

One might argue that what matters for the study of marriage in medieval theology is not Augustine's own thought on the subject, to the extent one can reconstruct and accurately interpret it, but rather the medieval Augustine, who was known chiefly through isolated snippets collected in florilegia ("posies"). Twelfth-century scholars used this material piecemeal, reading the snippets closely but without regard for the original context and sometimes interpreting them in ways that Augustine could not have foreseen or intended. They were living in a world that was far different from Augustine's, and they were addressing current exigencies. They did not share our modern interest in historical verisimilitude and in what it was like to live and work in late-antique Christendom.

Nevertheless, reconstruction of the medieval Augustine would be an impossibly difficult project because of the multiple ways in which medieval scholars had access to his thought. His influence was wide and deep. The original works were available in monastic and cathedral libraries, and monks frequently copied them. Medieval scholars had access to Augustine's ideas not only through the florilegia but also diffusely and indirectly, through countless quotations, allusions, and echoes in the writings of other authors. We should begin, therefore, with a tolerably faithful account of Augustine's own, late-antique thought on the subject, which may be compared and contrasted what medieval scholars made of his words.

2.1 AN OVERVIEW OF AUGUSTINE'S THEOLOGY OF MARRIAGE

The result of Augustine's inquiries into marriage was a coherent theory or doctrine that one might summarize as follows:

First, notwithstanding his ascetical ideology and his conviction that religiously motivated celibacy is superior to marriage, Augustine maintains that marriage is good, and that it is heresy to suggest otherwise. Sexual intercourse and procreation within marriage are likewise essentially good and natural. They were, indeed, part of God's original plan for human kind even before sin entered into the world. The inherited corruption of human nature is especially conspicuous in fallen sexuality, and sexuality even within marriage passes on the contagion of sin from one generation to the next. Nevertheless, the evil of lust does not vitiate marriage. On the contrary, the essential goodness of marriage restrains and mitigates the evil of sexual desire and pleasure.

Second, the religious and moral function of marriage changed as the circumstances of human kind changed. Marriage acquired a remedial function after the fall that would have been unnecessary in the earthly Paradise. The obligation to increase and multiply (Gen 1:28), which was urgent throughout the period of the Old Covenant, passed into abeyance with the advent of Jesus Christ.

Third, the goodness of marriage may be summed up as three distinct benefits (*bona*), which Augustine calls faith, offspring, and sacrament. A brief sketch of each is in order here. The good of faith (*fides*) not only excludes sexual intercourse outside marriage but also requires mutual observance of the conjugal debt within marriage (1 Cor 7:4–5).[1] Augustine uses the term *fides* in this context chiefly because it denotes a virtue pertaining to any transaction, agreement, or partnership.[2] Roughly, the term denotes the dutiful observance of an obligation. Faith as a nuptial good is also related to faith in its religious sense, for the apostate commits spiritual adultery. Although the *bonum fidei* was a feature of marriage from the beginning, according to Augustine, he posits it chiefly to account for the remedial benefit of marriage. The good of offspring (*proles*) consists in the ungrudging begetting of children and in their nurture and education as members of the church. Spouses enjoy this good to the extent that their children are "lovingly received, kindly nurtured, and religiously educated."[3] The good of sacrament entails both the permanence of marriage and the prevention of remarriage.[4]

Christians marry for life, according to Augustine. Neither spouse may remarry as long as the other is alive. Such permanence is fragile. Human nature being what it is, one spouse may illicitly abandon the other *de facto* for no good reason, however committed the latter may remain to the endurance of their marriage. Moreover, in accordance with Augustine's interpretation of the "except for fornication" clause

---

[1] *De b. coniug.* 4(4), CSEL 41:191.   [2] Ibid., 192/4–7.
[3] *De Gen. ad litt.* IX.7, CSEL 28.1:276.   [4] *De b. coniug.* 7–8(7), 197.

in Matthew 5:32 and 19:9, one is permitted to divorce an adulterous spouse. Nevertheless, regardless of the circumstances, something of the marriage bond remains even after a divorce: something that suffices to reduce remarriage to adultery. It is chiefly the good of sacrament, according to Augustine, that distinguishes the Christian practice of marriage from that of Jews and infidels. The *bonum sacramenti* is a sacred aspect of marriage, and it transcends pastoral utility.

Fourth, whereas marriage is good, the celibate vocations have been even better than marriage since the advent of Jesus Christ. The Old Testament patriarchs fulfilled their sacred duty by begetting children for the Lord, but they were holy men, at least equal and perhaps superior in spiritual and moral caliber to the ascetics of the new dispensation.

Fifth, Christian marriage transcends procreation and sexual exigency, for it endures despite sterility and despite the cessation of sexual intercourse. This endurance, which pertains to the good of sacrament, has both legal and moral dimensions. Christians are not permitted to divorce and remarry for the sake of procreation. For example, a man cannot divorce a sterile wife in order to marry a fertile one. Moreover, spouses who mutually agree to abstain permanently, and not only "for a time," as Paul advised in 1 Corinthians 7:5, not only remain married but even enhance their marriages, provided that their motives are pious and their lust has waned sufficiently.

2.2 THE ISSUES THAT OCCASIONED AUGUSTINE'S WORK ON MARRIAGE

Augustine wrote more extensively on marriage than any other western theologian before the Reformation, but he never set out to write a comprehensive treatise on the subject. Instead, each of his discussions of marriage focused on a particular aspect, and what was chiefly at issue was always something other than marriage, and usually something of much broader scope. This is true even of Augustine's *De bono coniugali*. His theology of marriage was the product not of detached reflection but of controversy and debate, and sometimes of campaigns against what he saw as heresy. I shall consider these formative issues in the order in which they arose.

2.2.1 *The Manichees and the goodness of marriage*

The first of the negative influences was the Manichee religion. The Manichees believed that the world was a mixture of Light and Darkness, which they considered to be primordial, irreducibly distinct substances. They sought to liberate Light from Darkness by disengaging themselves from killing and from procreation, as well as from anything that seemed grossly material. The elite members of the movement abstained from marriage and from sexual relations. The members of their outer circle, called Hearers (*auditores*), were subject to a less demanding regime, in part so that they could serve the elite. They were permitted to marry and to have sex within marriage, but they tried to avoid begetting children "lest soul should be entangled with flesh."[5]

Augustine was a Manichee Hearer for just over a decade, having joined the sect around 372 when he was a student in Carthage. In his treatises *De moribus Manichaeorum* (387/89) and *Contra Faustum Manichaeum* (397–98), Augustine rebuked the Hearers for practicing contraception.[6] Augustine's early involvement in Manicheism was a negative influence, encouraging him to affirm the essential goodness of the body, sex, procreation, and marriage. Just as the challenge of Gnosticism during the early-Christian era prompted churchmen and mainstream scholars to curtail their own tendencies to espouse bodily purity, so Augustine found in Manicheism a boundary that defined the limits of moral orthodoxy, keeping the implications of his own abhorrence of sexual desire and pleasure in check.[7] Instead of a dualism whereby the carnal and sexual aspects of human nature were evil, Augustine maintained that human nature, including sexual procreation, was essentially good, although it had become corrupt and distorted because of original sin. Augustine was not ready fully to make that affirmation until the early fifth century. By that time, the threat of Manicheism had receded, and he had become a more confident and less defensive interpreter of the Old Testament.

From the Manichees' point of view, Genesis 1:28 – "And God blessed them, saying: Increase and multiply, and fill the earth, and subdue it" – was an example of the gross materialism of the Old Testament. The Patriarchs, by marrying and begetting children, seemed inferior to the elite of their own movement. In his *De Genesi contra Manichaeos* (388/389), Augustine defended the text from Manichee criticism by applying the methods of spiritual interpretation that he had learned from Ambrose. The words that God spoke do not necessarily imply, he argues, that God commanded our first parents in Paradise to procreate sexually, although they would take on that meaning after the fall, for one may interpret them spiritually as well as carnally. Commenting on Genesis 1:28 and on Genesis 2:18 – "It is not good for man to be alone. Let us make him a help [*adiutorium*] like unto himself" – Augustine suggests that there might have been "a chaste union of male and female" in Paradise "such that the former ruled and the latter obeyed." Or the passage may refer to the proper subjection and obedience of the body and its animal appetites to the rational soul, for Adam and Eve typify reason and appetite

[5] *De mor. Manich.* 65, CSEL 90:146/12–147/4.
[6] *De mor. Manich.* 65, 146/12–147/4. C. *Faustum* XV.7 and XXII.30, CSEL 25:429/22–430/8, 624.
[7] *De continentia* 5(14), 7(18)–8(19), 9(22)–10(24), 12(26)–13(28), CSEL 41:157–58, 161–64, 167–72, 175–78. Although the anti-Manichean passages in this work suggest that Augustine wrote it in the mid- or late 390s, a comparative analysis of its content shows that it more probably came from the same period as his anti-Pelagian treatises, perhaps 418–20. See A.-M. La Bonnardière, "La date du *De continentia* de saint Augustin," *Revue des Études augustiniennes* 5(1959): 121–27; and D. G. Hunter, "The Date and Purpose of Augustine's *De continentia*," *Augustinian Studies* 26.2(1995): 7–24.

respectively. Just as Christ is the head of man, and man is the head of woman (1 Cor 11:3), so also divine wisdom would have ruled human reason, which is the manly (*virilis*) part of the soul; and reason, in turn, would have ruled appetite, the feminine part of the soul. When this order breaks down, "a home is perverse and wretched," both literally and in a spiritual sense. Perhaps the union of Adam and Eve would have filled the earth not with literal offspring but with "a spiritual progeny of intelligible and immortal joys."[8] As for Genesis 2:24 – "Wherefore a man shall leave father and mother and shall cleave to his wife, and they shall be two in one flesh" – this may have had no literal, historical sense in its original setting. The union of Adam and Eve was not originally supposed to be carnal, but the dictum was already a prophecy of Christ and the church, as Paul makes clear in Ephesians 5:31–32.[9]

Augustine's approach to the story of Adam and Eve changed radically during the first decade of the fifth century. Later, in the *Retractationes* (426/27), he would recall his interpretation of "increase and multiply" in the *De Genesi contra Manichaeos* and categorically withdraw it.[10] We see Augustine at a point of change and uncertainty in the preamble to the *De bono coniugali*, probably written around 404 (although a somewhat later date cannot be ruled out). Here, having alluded in the opening passage to Adam and Eve, and having noted the benefits of procreation, Augustine pauses to wonder how children would have been procreated if there had been no sin, and how one should interpret the "increase and multiply" of Genesis 1:28. Sexual intercourse is possible only between mortal bodies, and mortality is a punishment for sin. If there had there been no sin, perhaps people would have begotten children without sexual intercourse, even miraculously. Or one might interpret Genesis 1:28 figuratively, perhaps as referring to a fruitfulness of mind or of virtue, as Augustine himself had done in the *De Genesi contra Manichaeos*. But now Augustine considers a third possibility. Perhaps the human body even in the earthly Paradise was by nature not quasi-angelic but animal and mortal, destined to become spiritual and immortal only when human beings achieved bliss through obedience to God's commands. In that case, there would have been nothing in Paradise to preclude sexual reproduction. If sin had not entered the world, God would have miraculously preserved his people from the aging and death to which they were naturally subject until they had filled the earth with their progeny.[11]

In Book IX of the *De Genesi ad litteram*, composed perhaps around 410, Augustine commits himself to the third theory and elaborates it. He has outgrown the Alexandrian interpretive habit of assuming that the end is a return to the beginning, so that Adam and Eve in Paradise would have been like angels (Matt 22:30). Moreover, without denying that the creation story in Genesis has a

---

[8]   *De Gen. c. Manich.* I.19(30), II.11(15), CSEL 91:97–98, 135–37.   [9]   Ibid., II.13(19), 140.
[10]   *Retr.* I.10.2, CCL 57:30–31.   [11]   *De b. coniug.* 2(2), CSEL 41:188–90.

spiritual, prospective sense, he now emphasizes its historical veracity.[12] As a matter of fact, no children were begotten until after the fall, but Adam and Eve and their descendants were meant to beget children sexually in the earthly Paradise. Commenting on Genesis 2:18 ("It is not good for man to be alone: let us make him a help like unto himself"), Augustine argues that the "help" that Adam needed and which Eve was formed to provide could only have been help in sexual reproduction.[13] Another man would have made a better collaborator, friend, or conversation partner. One might argue, as Augustine had assumed in the *De Genesi contra Manichaeos*, that only between a male and a female can there be a peaceful union in which one commands while the other obeys, so that there is no contrariety of wills. But if God had made another *man* from Adam's side, Augustine now argues, the second man would have been naturally subservient to Adam.[14] Adam's partner was female, therefore, only so that they could sexually reproduce. Yet, just as childbirth then would have been free of pain, so sexual intercourse would have been free of carnal desire and pleasure. And sexuality would have been free of that inner warfare between the law of the members and the law of the mind of which Paul speaks (Rom 7:23).[15] Adam and Eve covered their genitals as soon as they sinned because they recognized the new shamefulness of sexual motions and the sexual act.[16] Had there been no sin, sexual reproduction would have free of shame, and it would have continued, generation after generation, until the city of God was full, and no one would have died. Only then, once the human race had achieved the preordained number of the elect, would human beings have become like angels.[17]

Augustine develops his idea of paradisiacal sexuality most fully in Book XIV of *The City of God*, a treatment that probably already reflects engagement with Pelagianism. Here, Augustine explains at length how the workings of the reproductive organs in Paradise would have been calm and fully under the control of the rational will, and how the loss of control that results from the fall makes the sexual act so shameful that even promiscuous persons are hardly able to do it in public.[18] After the fall, only Jesus Christ was born without carnal concupiscence, for he was

---

[12] *De Gen. ad litt.* VIII.1 and XII.28, CSEL 28.1:229–32, 423. Augustine began writing the commentary around the beginning of the fifth century (perhaps 401) and probably completed it in 415. He seems to have written Book IX during the first decade of the century (perhaps shortly after the *De b. coniug.*), and before his campaign against Pelagianism: see E. A. Clark, "Heresy, Asceticism, Adam and Eve: Interpretations of Genesis 1–3 in the Later Latin Fathers," in E. A. Clark, *Ascetic Piety and Women's Faith* (Lewiston, NY, 1986), 353–85.

[13] Augustine summarizes this argument in *De peccato originali* 40, CSEL 42:198/21–25. Augustine wrote the two-part work of which that is the second part, *De gratia Christi et peccato originali*, c. AD 418.

[14] *De Gen. ad litt.* IX.3–5, 271–73.   [15] Ibid., IX.10–11, 278–81.

[16] *De pecc. orig.* 39 and 41, 198/7–10 and 199/25–26.   [17] *De Gen. ad litt.* IX.6, 273–75.

[18] *De civ. Dei* XIV.10–24, CCL 48:430–48. *De pecc. orig.* 40–41, CSEL 42:198–200. Augustine probably wrote *De civ. Dei* XIV, like the *De gratia Christi et peccato originali*, c. 418.

born of virgin, without sexual intercourse.[19] Carnal concupiscence and the other shameful things that accompany sex have become part of our biology and a subject of medical study, yet they are not strictly part of our nature. When Augustine considers what sexual intercourse would have been like in the earthly Paradise, he observes that a few people even in his own day can control parts and motions of their bodies that most cannot control.[20]

By the early fifth century, Augustine had put Manicheism far behind him. Nothing could be less Manichean than his affirmation that sexual reproduction was essentially good, and that it had been part of God's original plan for human kind. Nevertheless, Augustine steered a difficult middle course between the Manichees' denigration of marriage, on one side, and a wholeheartedly naturalistic and egalitarian affirmation of the goodness of sexuality and marriage, on the other. To defend his own position in the controversies that ensued, Augustine had to show why it was not Manichean or dualistic. In that sense alone, the shadow of his Manichean past remained with him.

2.2.2 *Jovinian*

Augustine tells us in the *Retractationes* that he wrote the *De bono coniugali* (c. 404) to counteract Jovinian's errors, which were still influential in Rome.[21] A Roman monk, Jovinian had been condemned by synods in Rome and Milan in the early 390s and banished by imperial edict in 398. His chief error was an egalitarian theology according to which all Christians in all walks of life – the laity as well as monks and priests, married folk as well as virgins – enjoyed equal merit by virtue of their baptism and would be rewarded equally in the life to come. Augustine's aim in the *De bono coniugali* was to show not only that marriage was good, therefore, but also that celibacy was better.[22] Immediately after writing the *De bono coniugali*, he wrote a companion volume on the superior virtues of celibacy (the *De sancta virginitate*).[23] In 414, Augustine addressed a treatise on widowhood to Juliana, who with her daughter and the widow Proba had fled from Rome to North Africa to escape the sack of Rome by Alaric in 410. They eventually settled in Carthage, where Juliana was consecrated as a widow in 412.[24] The doctrines expressed in the treatise are those of the *De bono coniugali* and the *De sancta virginitate*, but

---

[19] *Epist.* 187 (Ad Dardanum), 31–32, CSEL 57:109/4–110/16.

[20] *De civ. Dei* XIV.23–24, 444–48.

[21] *Retr.* II.22.1, 107. On the Jovinianist background to *De bono coniugali* and *De sancta virginitate*, see D. G. Hunter, "Between Jovinian and Jerome," *Studia Patristica* 43(2006): 131–36; and idem, *Marriage, Celibacy, and Heresy* (Oxford, 2007), 273–77.

[22] *De b. coniug.* 9(9), CSEL 41:199–201. The good/better model for comparing the respective merits of marriage and celibacy is based on 1 Cor 7:38. On the good/better model in Tertullian and Jerome, see MWCh 272–73.

[23] *Retr.* II.23, 109.

[24] D. G. Hunter, "Bono viduitatis, De," in A. D. Fitzgerald(ed.), *Augustine through the Ages* (Grand Rapids, 1999), 111–12.

Augustine puts more emphasis of the organic unity of the church, all of whose members, married folk as well as virgins and widows, are members of Christ.[25]

Marriage is good, Augustine argues, because of its three benefits: faith, offspring, and sacrament.[26] Augustine discovers the threefold structure of the goodness of marriage in the *De bono coniugali* and adheres to it thereafter. Just as contemplation is a foretaste of the next life, he argues, so celibacy is an "angelic exercise" (*angelica meditatio*) that will last forever. Procreation, on the contrary, which is the fundamental reason for marriage, will pass away. Thus, Martha, who was "distracted by many things," represents marriage as well as the active, mundane life, whereas Mary, whose gift would not be taken away from her, typifies virginity as well contemplation (Luke 10:38–42).[27]

Jovinian was not the only target of the *De bono coniugali*. The chief aim of the treatise was to explain why marriage was good, which Jovinian would not have disputed. To some extent, Augustine's agenda still reflected the negative influence of the Manichees, for Jovinian himself had framed his defense of marriage as a rejection of Manicheism.[28] Jovinian assumed that those who valued celibacy above marriage were implicitly Manichean. Augustine mentions toward the end of the treatise that his arguments should suffice to refute the Manichees when they denigrate the polygamy of the Old Testament patriarchs and accuse them of incontinence,[29] and he devotes a large section of the treatise to defending the procreativity and polygamy of the Old Testament patriarchs.[30]

To justify procreation among the Old Testament patriarchs, Augustine developed the already well-established idea of two dispensations: the old dispensation, under which procreation was a religious duty (*officium*), and the new dispensation initiated by Jesus Christ, under which procreation is no longer a duty. Augustine often summarizes the doctrine by quoting or alluding to Ecclesiastes 3:5: there is "a time to embrace, and a time to refrain from embracing." Whereas the holiest people under the old dispensation fulfilled their duty to beget and to raise children, people of the same spiritual stature under the new dispensation should be celibate. Christians should marry, therefore, only if they are otherwise incapable of mastering their sexual appetites. The theory of two dispensations turned on the interpretation of Genesis 1:28: "Increase and multiply, and fill the earth." If the command to procreate went into abeyance with the coming of Christ, then either the earth was already full or there was now a better means of filling it. Augustine generally adopts the second alternative, construing the earth as the city of God, or the church.[31]

---

[25] See especially *De bono viduitatis* 3(4), CSEL 41:307–08.

[26] Augustine summarizes the doctrine at *De b. coniug.* 24(32), 226–28.

[27] *De b. coniug.* 8(8), 198–99.

[28] D. G. Hunter, "Resistance to the Virginal Ideal in Late-Fourth-Century Rome: The Case of Jovinian," *Theological Studies* 48(1987): 45–64.

[29] *De b. coniug.* 25(33), 228.   [30] Ibid., 16(18)–22(27), 210–23.

[31] *De b. coniug.* 9(9)–10(10), 13(15), and 15(17), pp. 200–202, 207–08, and 210. See also *De Gen. ad litt.* IX.7, CSEL 28.1, 275–76; *De nuptiis et concupiscentia* I.14, CSEL 42, 226–27; *De adulterinis*

It is likely, too, that Augustine was mindful of the scandal that Jerome's treatise against Jovinian had recently provoked, although this point cannot be established with certainty. The chief opponent envisaged on the negative side was probably not the Manichees but Jerome, who had seemed to treat marriage as an evil that is permissible only because it is less evil than fornication.[32] In the *De bono coniugali*, Augustine distinguished his own views on marriage, sex, and procreation not only from the egalitarian excesses of Jovinian, but also from certain negative excesses on the other side.[33]

Augustine's defense of marriage under the new dispensation implies that the proper reason for opting to marry and procreate, rather than to devote one's life to Christ through consecrated celibacy, is not procreation *per se* but rather the remedy to sexual desire that marriage offers. Fallen sexual desire is always evil (*malum*), yet Christians can "use" their sexual desire by channeling it toward procreation, according to Augustine, as the patriarchs of Old Testament did. In that case, there is no sin in sexual intercourse at all, although the taint of sexual desire remains. But even if spouses seek sexual intercourse for its own sake, to gratify their concupiscence, the goodness of marriage makes their sin pardonable (*venialis*). It was especially in view of the latter aspect of the remedy, according to Augustine, that Paul advised people to marry and to observe the conjugal debt (1 Cor 7:2–6).[34] Marriage is good even in this "time to refrain from embracing," for it excuses or mitigates the evil of sexual desire.

In short, there are three different valid motives for sexual intercourse within marriage, although these will usually occur in combination. There is no sin when a spouse initiates sex for the sake of procreation. A spouse who agrees to sex in order to render the conjugal debt to the other partner, and not out of lust, is likewise free from sin.[35] And there is pardonable sin in a spouse who requires a partner to fulfill the debt to satisfy his or her own lust, since that is a way to avoid fornication.

The reasons underlying Augustine's negative assessment of sexual desire become clearer in his subsequent controversy with Julian of Eclanum, but one likely reason is already implicit in the *De bono coniugali*, where Augustine divides goods into those that are desirable in themselves (*per se*) and those that are desirable for the sake of something else (*propter aliquid*). Wisdom, health, and friendship belong to the former category. Study, food and drink, sleep, sex, and marriage belong to the second. Study is useful for wisdom, and food and drink are useful for health.

coniugiis II.12(12), CSEL 41, 395–97. On earlier versions of this theory in Tertullian and Jerome, see MWCh 267–68. On "the city of God" as a characterization of the church, see *De nupt. et conc.* I.10(11), 223/2–6.

[32] J. N. D. Kelly, *Jerome*(London, 1975), 182–89. Ph. Delhaye, "Le dossier anti-matrimoniale de l'Adversus Jovinianum et son influence sur quelques écrits latin du XIIe siècle," *Mediaeval Studies* 13(1951): 65–86, at 66–70.

[33] Clark, "Heresy, Asceticism, Adam and Eve" 358–62, 366–68.

[34] *De b. coniug.* 6(6), 194–95.   [35] Ibid., 7(6), 195–96.

Marriage and sex are useful because they are the means of extending the ties of friendship through "the propagation of the human race, the amicable partnership [*societas amicalis*] in which is a great good." Augustine argues that anyone who uses the goods of the second sort (useful goods) for ends other than those for which they were instituted always sins in so doing, whether venially or mortally.[36] Presumably, enjoying them for their own sake is equally sinful. However one might analyze sexual desire (*concupiscentia carnalis*), the deliberate goal is not the begetting and nurturing of children. One might construe it either as a desire for sexual intercourse *per se*, the fulfillment of which results in pleasure, or as a desire for sexual pleasure. Either way, it entails an abuse.

2.2.3 *Pollentius*

Augustine wrote his treatise on divorce and remarriage, the *De adulterinis coniugiis* (419/21), in response to a correspondent called Pollentius, otherwise unknown, who had questioned Augustine's position on divorce and remarriage. Pollentius seems to have known about Augustine's position chiefly from the commentary on the Sermon on the Mount (393/94),[37] where Augustine had argued that spouses are entitled to separate only "because of fornication" (*propter fornicationem*), and not on grounds such as sterility, deformity, blindness, deafness, or disease.[38] Their disagreements turned on the precise interpretation of certain passages from Scripture, especially Matthew 19:9 and 1 Corinthians 7:10–11. It was a friendly, respectful debate, and it severely tested Augustine's position. He confesses toward the end of the first book and again in the *Retractationes* that the questions treated in the *De adulterinis coniugiis* were difficult and complicated, and that he had failed to solve them completely, although he still believed that they were soluble.[39]

A brief sketch of Augustine's doctrine on divorce and remarriage is in order here. Augustine assumed that the texts in which Jesus condemned divorce and remarriage (Matt 5:32, Matt 19:3–9, Mark 10:11–12, Luke 16:18) logically implied that marriage was insoluble.[40] The reason why no one could divorce his or her spouse and marry another, these texts seemed to imply, was that the supposed new marriage would in reality be adultery. Logically, that implied that the divorced partners were in some sense still married.

Augustine maintained, nevertheless, that one had the right, perhaps even the duty, to divorce an adulterous spouse. He based this aspect of his doctrine on Matthew's versions of the admonition, where Jesus makes an exception of some sort in the case of *porneia* ("immorality"), translated as *fornicatio* in the Latin versions

---

[36] Ibid., 9(9), 199–200.   [37] Cf. *De adult. coniug.* I.1(1), 347.

[38] *De sermone Domini in monte* I.18(54), CCL 35:61–63.

[39] *De adult. coniug.*, I.25(32), 379. *Retr.* II.57, 136.

[40] M.-F. Berrouard, "Saint Augustin et l'indissolubilité du mariage," *Recherches Augustiniennes* 5(1968): 139–55.

(Matt 5:32, 19:9).[41] Assuming that the fornication in question is adultery, Augustine deduces that the husband is permitted to divorce an adulterous wife, but that neither partner may remarry as long as the other is alive. By remaining unmarried after divorce, the ex-partners leave the door open for reconciliation, which is a good thing, but the injured party is not obliged to take back a repentant spouse. Such a divorce may be permanent.[42]

If there are any other valid reasons for divorce, these must amount to fornication in some extended sense, for that is the only exception that Christ allows. Augustine accepted the traditional view that idolatry or apostasy was another just cause for divorce because it was a kind of spiritual adultery. His reasoning was partly analogical, for he assumed that the union of Christians with Christ was itself a marriage, but he found biblical proof in the Pauline Privilege: the right of a convert to Christianity to divorce an infidel spouse if the latter is not amicably disposed toward the convert (1 Cor 7:12–15). If the only valid reason for separation, according to Jesus, was adultery, and if Paul permitted a Christian to divorce an unbelieving spouse, then unbelief must be a kind of adultery.[43] In his commentary on the Sermon on the Mount, Augustine considered whether the "fornication" of the Matthean exception might even include unlawful covetousness (*concupiscentia*) of any kind, since covetousness is a kind of idolatry.[44] He rejected that broad interpretation in the *Retractationes*, although he confessed that he did not know exactly what other forms of adultery, besides extra-marital sex and apostasy, might count as valid grounds for divorce.[45]

Augustine was cautious, too, about affirming that a wife could divorce an adulterous husband, but only because he was mindful that he lacked the literal support of Scripture. Augustine seems not to have doubted that all the rules about divorce, adultery, and the conjugal debt applied equally to both partners.[46] But Matthew's version of Jesus' admonition, like Luke's, envisaged only the divorce of a wife by her husband, whereas Mark's version envisaged divorce from both sides.[47] Because Matthew's version alone contained the exception, Scripture alone did not show that the exception permitted wives to divorce adulterous husbands. Indeed, it was not obvious from Matthew that a husband's infidelity even amounted to adultery. Under both Roman and Jewish law, adultery was the injury done to a husband by an unfaithful wife and her lover, and a husband's infidelity to his wife was not, in itself, adultery. Christian writers during the patristic period generally rejected this double standard, and they often extended the term *adulterium* to the husband's infidelity.

[41] On patristic interpretations of the Matthean exception, see MWCh 173–226.
[42] *De adult. coniug.* II.6(5), 387.   [43] *De serm. Dom. in monte* I.16(44), CCL 35:51/1077–1080.
[44] Ibid., I.16(43), I.16(46), pp. 47/1011–1018, 52/1103–1115.
[45] *Retr.* I.19.6, 58/81–59/93. B. Alves Pereira, *La doctrine du mariage selon saint Augustin* (Paris, 1930), 136–39.
[46] Alves Pereira, *Doctrine du mariage*, 79–87.
[47] Mark's version was probably intended for a Gentile audience. Only the husband could divorce a spouse under Jewish law, whereas both spouses had the right of divorce under Roman law.

They did so partly because they were less inclined to allow husbands to find sexual satisfaction outside marriage, and partly in view of the symmetry of the conjugal debt in 1 Corinthians 7:2–4.[48] Nevertheless, the double standard remained as a cultural norm, and most people considered a wife's adultery to be far more heinous than a husband's. Notwithstanding his cautious approach to Scripture, Augustine believed that the rules about divorce and adultery should be applied equally to husbands and to wives, and that any injunctions and biblical texts (such as Rom 7:3) that refer only to a wife's adultery should be interpreted in that light.[49] Pollentius and Augustine seem to have been in agreement on this point.

Pollentius's chief contention was twofold: first, that someone who had divorced a spouse on the grounds of adultery could remarry; and, second, that divorce was permissible on other grounds, besides adultery, but without the capacity to remarry. Pollentius accepted the principle that neither spouse could remarry as long as the other was alive (1 Cor 7:39), but he reasoned that adultery was a kind of spiritual death, which left the wronged partner free to remarry.[50]

Augustine's point of departure in the treatise is their disagreement over the interpretation of 1 Corinthians 7:10–11: "Not I but the Lord commands that the wife depart not from her husband, and if she depart, that she remain unmarried or be reconciled with her husband." How should one interpret the text in the light of the passages from Matthew? Paul does not mention the *porneia* exception. Why not? According to Pollentius, Paul must be referring to divorce on grounds *other* than adultery. It is only in such cases, he reasons, that remarriage is not allowed, whereas a man who divorces his wife for adultery can remarry. According to Augustine, on the contrary, Paul must be referring to divorce on grounds of adultery, since that is the only valid reason for divorce.[51]

There was no way to settle that argument on biblical grounds, but the debate showed Augustine that the Matthean exception was harder to interpret than he had supposed. According to Matthew 5:32, a man who divorces his wife makes her commit adultery, except in the case of fornication. The implied logic, from Augustine's perspective, is obvious. A man who divorces his wife makes her prone to adultery by exposing her to the possibility of fornication or remarriage, for, as Paul says, each man should have his own wife, and each woman her own husband, "because of fornication" (1 Cor 7:2). But if she is *already* an adulteress, a husband cannot be blamed for making his wife prone to adultery by divorcing her.[52] According to Matthew 19:9, however, a man who divorces his wife and marries another except in the case of fornication *commits adultery himself.* Here, the exception seems to apply not to divorce *per se* but rather to remarriage after divorce, and that implies, as Pollentius points out, that a man who has divorced his

---

[48] MWCh 122–23, 125, 145, 174–75, 186.
[49] *De b. coniug.* 7(7), CSEL 41:196. *De adult. coniug.* II.19(20), 407/7–10.
[50] *De adult. coniug.* II.2(2), 383–84.   [51] Ibid., I.1(1), 347–48.   [52] Ibid., I.2–3(2), 348–49.

wife because of her adultery is free to remarry. To save his own interpretation, Augustine is reduced to arguing that a man who divorces and remarries is *less* adulterous when he does so because of his wife's adultery than when he does so on other grounds.[53] Rather than using Matthew 19:9 to prove his doctrine, Augustine is forced to apply his doctrine to determine how the text should be interpreted. The doctrine becomes the premise, and not a conclusion, of his interpretation.

2.2.4 *Pelagianism and Julian of Eclanum*

During the same period as he was corresponding with Pollentius, Augustine found himself under attack for his theory of fallen sexuality. Around 418, Julian, the bishop of Eclanum in Campagnia, wrote a letter to Valerius, a member of the imperial court in Ravenna, arguing that Augustine doctrine's of original sin denigrated marriage. Valerius passed these criticisms on to Augustine, who responded with what would become Book I of the *De nuptiis et concupiscentia* (419/20), which he addressed to Valerius. Augustine later explained that his aim was to defend "the goodness of marriage lest anyone suppose that the fault of carnal concupiscence and the law of the members fighting against the law of the mind [Rom 7:23] belong to marriage, for conjugal chastity uses this evil of sexual desire [*libido*] for procreating children."[54] Julian responded with a treatise in four books addressed to bishop Turbantius, in which he argued that Augustine's theory of original sin was Manichean.[55] Someone sent excerpts from Julian's *Ad Turbantium* to Augustine, who responded with a supplement to the *De nuptiis et concupiscentia* (420/21). This became Book II of the treatise. Shortly after Augustine composed this supplement, he got hold of the *Ad Turbantium* itself and discovered that the excerpts on which he had depended were unreliable. He composed a new, major work of refutation instead, the *Contra Iulianum* (421/22). The debate with Julian preoccupied Augustine for the remainder of his life. When he died, he was working on another treatise against Julian, known as the *Contra Iulianum opus imperfectum* (428–30).

In Augustine's view, the Pelagians failed to appreciate how deeply the fall had wounded and perverted the human will. Augustine wrote about marriage and concupiscence as if he was a physician of the soul, alerting people to the disease of the fallen will and to its symptoms, and advising them about appropriate treatments and regimens.[56] Julian had already become associated with Pelagianism by refusing with eighteen other bishops to subscribe to Pope Zosimus's condemnation of Pelagius. His critique of Augustine's views on marriage took the debate to another level. Julian not only argued that Augustine's position on original sin and sexual

---

[53] Ibid., I.9(9), 354.   [54] *Retr.* II.53, 131/6–10.

[55] The *Ad Turbantium* is lost, but the pieces of it that can be salvaged from Augustine's writings against Julian are gathered in CCL 88, 340–96.

[56] D. F. Kelly, "Sexuality and Concupiscence in Augustine," *Annual of the Society of Christian Ethics* 1983: 81–116, at 82–87.

desire was covertly Manichean; he also presented an alternative, naturalistic position, whereby sexual desire itself was natural and inherently good. For Augustine, on the contrary, carnal desire and saving grace were mutually opposed. Just as everyone except Christ was born with the carnal concupiscence inherited from the first sinful man, Adam, so no one can be reborn without the grace of the second, sinless man, Jesus Christ.[57]

Augustine's dim view of sexual desire troubles the modern reader, but it had a long Christian pedigree. The New Testament is ambiguous in its treatment of marriage and sexuality. As Augustine points out, Jesus confirmed the goodness of marriage by choosing a wedding as the setting for his first miracle (John 2:1–11), as well as by reaffirming the permanence of marriage.[58] Nevertheless, Jesus says to Peter, who had apparently left his wife to follow him: "Amen, I say to you, there is no man that has left house or parents or brethren or wife or children for the kingdom of God's sake who shall not receive much more in this present time, and in the world to come life everlasting" (Luke 18:29–30).[59] Jesus seems to regard marriage as one of the secular entanglements from which true disciples should disentangle themselves. By the end of the second century, at least in the mind of some Christians, the ambiguity had resolved itself into what is known as encratism: a cult of purity presupposing that sexual abstinence was necessary for salvation. Moreover, although the ascetics who proliferated from the fourth century were setting aside not only sex but all the secular entanglements and preoccupations that marriage entailed (cf. 1 Cor 7:32–34), the sexual urge must have been deeply troubling for them, especially during the early years of a religious vocation. Although ascetics had to restrain their appetites for food and drink, they still needed food and drink to survive. Sex, on the contrary, was something to be set aside entirely. Total abstinence, not moderation, was the proper course. Sex, therefore, became the surrogate for everything that had gone wrong in human nature.

Augustine defended his espousal of celibacy on several fronts, but one should keep in mind that the validity of asceticism as an honorable Christian vocation was never a matter of debate. Jovinian himself was a monk. Julian had been married, and both he and his bride were the children of bishops. The *Epithalamium* that Paulinus of Nola wrote to commemorate Julian's wedding is among the earliest records of a nuptial liturgy, but Julian's wife had either died or entered the religious life by the time he became a bishop.[60] Devout couples often agreed to become celibate at some point in their marriage, and the practice was not

---

[57] *Epist.* 187, 31, CSEL 57:109/4–7.   [58] *De b. coniug.* 3(3), CSEL 41:190/10–19.

[59] The parallels are Matt 19:29, and Mark 10:29–30. The term "wife" is absent from Mark's version. It is present in some Greek and Latin traditions of Matthew, but probably only as the result of "contamination" (scribal assimilation) from Luke.

[60] P. Brown, "Sexuality and Society in the Fifth century A.D.: Augustine and Julian of Eclanum," in E. Gabba(ed.), *Tria Corda: Scritti in onore di Arnaldo Momigliano*(Como, 1983), 49–70, at 54.

controversial. Peter Brown suggests that Julian, in contrast to Augustine, represented an older, conventional, more moderate view of sexuality as an "unproblematic" but "detachable" part of human nature. Christians of this mainstream persuasion accepted sexual desire as a natural urge that was necessary for maintaining the continuity of the human species, and they considered it to be a manageable, socializable force, albeit one that could be suppressed for the sake of higher spiritual ambitions. From this point of view, the physiology of the sexual act as described by medical scholars, with arousal, orgasm, and so forth, was not an object of shame and dismay but was rather a normal bodily function. Brown points out that Augustine's ideas about concupiscence had the odd result of separating sexual desire, sexual pleasure, and the experience of orgasm from the natural physiology of the sexual act.[61] Consistent to the last, Augustine argued that the libidinous and ecstatic aspects of coitus were not strictly natural concomitants but rather punishments for original sin.

As Augustine saw it, St Paul's war between the members and the mind was emblematic of the disorder of the fallen condition. The disobedience in human flesh was the penalty for sin. The theory follows a hierarchical logic. When human beings disobeyed God's wisdom, God punished them by making the flesh disobedient to reason.[62] Indeed, at the moment of orgasm, carnal pleasure overpowers reason, the very aspect of human nature whereby humans are made in God's image.[63] Carnal disobedience is vividly apparent in the movements of the genitalia, which sometimes happen despite our wishes but often fail to happen when we need them. Why is it impossible to control the genitalia as one controls the eyes, lips, hands, or feet? Such disorder or weakness is shameful.[64]

Moreover, Augustine assumed that carnal pleasure was the means by which original sin was passed down from parent to child. The proof text for this theory in the Middle Ages was only pseudonymously ascribed to Augustine: in fact, it was by Fulgentius of Ruspe.[65] Nevertheless, Augustine himself implies the idea in several places. For example, he argues in the *De Genesi ad litteram* that Jesus Christ, because of his virgin birth, descended only carnally and not "libidinally" from Abraham, since no act of lust infected Jesus' conception.[66] In the *De nuptiis et concupiscentia*, Augustine explains that his aim is to "distinguish the evil of carnal concupiscence, because of which a man who is born through it contracts original sin, from the goodness of marriage."[67] Later in this work, summarizing his doctrine

[61] In the article cited in previous note. [62] *De nupt. et conc.* I.6(7), CSEL 42:218/13–16.
[63] *De civ. Dei* XVI.16, CCL 48:438–39.
[64] *De nupt. et conc.* I.6(7), 218/22–219/16.
[65] Fulgentius of Ruspe, *De fide ad Petrum* 16, CCL 91A:721. Citing Ps 50:7 ("For behold, I was conceived in iniquities, and in sins did my mother conceive me"), Fulgentius argues that it is not the "fecundity of human nature" that transmits sin from parent to child, but rather the "filthiness of lust."
[66] *De Gen. ad litt.* X.19–20, CSEL 28.1:321–34. [67] *De nupt. et conc.* I.1(1), 212/13–15.

of the three goods, he asks how sin could have been passed on to babies through the conjugal goods of faith and offspring.[68]

Julian assumed that fully to defend the goodness of God's creation, one had to show that carnal concupiscence, as well as marriage, was good. Without denying that sexual desire leads people into sin and needs to be controlled, Julian regards sexual desire *per se* as an essentially natural force. According to Julian's analysis, the libidinous force that moves the genitals is a species of "vital fire." Its "mode" (its proper use and limit) is the conjugal act (i.e., sex within marriage), whereas only its excess (its improper, inordinate use) consists in intemperance and fornication.[69]

It seemed to Augustine, on the contrary, that there was something fundamentally wrong with carnal desire. Lust is not a desire for something evil, but it is *indifferently* attracted to licit and illicit goods, whereas the other senses are capable of distinguishing between fitting and unfitting objects.[70] Touch, for example, discriminates between the rough and the smooth. Only one's understanding, and not one's desire, can distinguish between licit and illicit sexual goods. Consequently, it is only by resisting concupiscence that one can avoid what is forbidden. One must either follow sexual desire into sin or rein it in by keeping it within the bounds of virtue. The only options are sin or an agonizing and distracting internal conflict: St Paul's "war of the members." Neither alternative is happy, and neither is congruent with an earthly Paradise.[71] Augustine marvels that Julian can regard the "appalling shamelessness or rather madness [*amentia*]" of concupiscence as a good.[72] According to Augustine, sexual desire itself, as well as the shame associated with it, is adventitious and does not belong properly to marriage. One should not "impute" sexual desire to marriage.[73]

Augustine does not deny that there would have been concupiscence of some sort in the earthly Paradise, but only that there was any *shameful* concupiscence. But that does not imply that there could have been any *carnal* desire in Paradise. The word *concupiscentia* usually denotes sexual desire, but its basic or etymological sense is "strong desire" or "yearning." As Augustine points out, there can be spiritual as well as carnal concupiscence. For example, there is the concupiscence for wisdom.[74] Augustine seems to be thinking of Wisdom 6:21, which refers to a *concupiscentia sapientiae* that brings one "to the everlasting kingdom." In a letter that he wrote to Atticus, Bishop of Constantinople, probably in the 420s, Augustine argues that the Pelagians conflate two different things: the concupiscence that is proper to marriage (*concupiscentia nuptiarum*), and the concupiscence that belongs to the flesh (*concupiscentia carnis*). The former is characterized by conjugal chastity and includes a desire both to remain faithful to the bond of partnership (*fides*) and to beget children (*proles*). The latter is an indifferent desire for sexual intercourse

---

[68] Ibid., I.21(23) 236/9–10.   [69] *Contra Iulianum* III.13(26), PL 44:715.
[70] *Epist.* 6*.5, CSEL 88:34.   [71] *C. Iulianum* V.16(62), PL 44:818.
[72] *Contra Iulianum opus imperfectum* IV.69, PL 45:1379.
[73] *De pecc. orig.* 39, CSEL 42:198/7–12; 200/7–8.   [74] *De nupt. et conc.* II.52, CSEL 42:308.

per se, regardless of whether it is licit or illicit, and without regard to procreation. That is why Adam and Eve covered their private parts with fig leaves when they began to experience the concupiscence of the flesh, whereas they had not been ashamed of their nakedness before.[75]

The problem with carnal desire, from this point of view, is not that it lusts after evil things, but that its lust is indifferent. One might compare it to the acquisitiveness of a person who does not care whether the goods that he wants to acquire belong to other people. The theory does not explain but rather presupposes the difference between licit and illicit sexual acts. Because lust does not distinguish between licit and illicit objects, one's rational self must either fight it or be seduced by it.

Augustine's preferred view was that there would have no carnal concupiscence in Paradise. Instead, the genitals would have been directly responsive to the rational will. On this view, the point is not that sexual desire has become disordered or corrupt, but rather that sexual desire is itself an adventitious root of disorder and corruption, the curse of original sin.[76] Because the movements of the genitalia would have been directly subject to reason, as the movements of the hands are now, there would have been no need for libido. Nevertheless, Augustine concedes in his late work for the sake of argument that there could have been carnal concupiscence in the earthly Paradise, but only if it was wholly responsive to reason, so that it would have moved only insofar as reason commanded it to move. In that case, there would have been nothing to disturb the tranquility and order of Paradise.[77] This was not a possibility that he found appealing, but he recognized that nothing in his own arguments precluded it.

2.3 THE MEDIEVAL RECEPTION OF AUGUSTINE

One can get some sense of how medieval scholars, especially monks, regarded Augustine's work on marriage by observing the distribution of extant manuscripts. All of his major writings on marriage must have been available in the Middle Ages, for extant manuscripts of the relevant works, especially of the *De bono coniugali*, are plentiful in monastic libraries from the twelfth through the fifteenth centuries.[78]

The works on marriage and celibacy were often compiled in ways that indicate how people used them and considered them to be valuable. The combination of

[75] *Epist.* 6*.5–6, in Bibliothèque Augustinienne, *Oeuvres de saint Augustin* 46B (1987), 130–32 (or CSEL 88:34–35). The asterisk indicates that this letter belongs to the correspondence that Johannes Divjak found in a fifteenth-century MS at the Bibliothèque Municipale of Marseilles in 1975. It was apparently unknown in the Middle Ages.

[76] Kelly, "Sexuality and Concupiscence," 110. But compare the very different view of Brown, "Sexuality and Society," 60.

[77] *C. Iulianum.* V.16(62), PL 44:818. *C. Iulianum imp.* I.68, I.122, CSEL 85.1:75, 253. *Contra duas epistulas Pelagianorum* I.17(34), CSEL 60:450–51.

[78] The exception is *Epist.* 6*, to Atticus. I have gleaned the following information from volumes of *Die Handschriftliche Überlieferung der Werke des heiligen Augustinus* (Vienna, 1969–).

De bono coniugali, De sancta virginitate, and *De bono viduitatis* (usually in that order) is common. It reflects a traditional threefold division of Christians, who were ranked according to merit and eternal reward: first virgins, then widows, then married folk. This and other threefold divisions of the church into orders or estates were popular throughout the central Middle Ages. Medieval collections of *ad status* sermons often include sermons for each of the three estates, even though consecrated widowhood did not have the distinct vocational status that it had enjoyed in the early church.[79]

Larger compilations were made, especially in German-speaking regions. These are of two sorts. Those of one sort, of which there are Carolingian examples, consist of *De bono coniugali, De sancta virginitate, De bono viduitatis, Epistula 130* (to Proba), and *De opere monachorum.*[80] Those of the other sort, which became popular in the twelfth century, consist of *De nuptiis et concupiscentia* (usually prefaced by the relevant passage from *Retractationes* [2.88] and by *Epist.* 200, to Valerius, both of which explain the historical context and composition of the treatise), *De bono coniugali, De sancta virginitate, Epistula* 167 (to Jerome), *Epistula* 172 (Jerome's acknowledgement of *Epist.* 167), and either the entire *Retractationes* or a list of Augustine's works taken from the *Retractationes* (or both).[81] Monastic readers seem to have valued Augustine chiefly as a pastoral authority. Whereas the first type focuses on the celibate vocations, with which even the *De bono coniugali* is largely concerned, the inclusion of the *De nuptiis et concupiscentia* in the second type shows that the collection was designed to comprehend all the estates of the medieval church, both married and celibate.

Epistula 130, to the widow Proba on prayer, was a natural and perennial companion to the treatise on widowhood, but the inclusion of the other letters is harder to explain. *Epistula* 167, to Jerome, is about the correct interpretation of James 2:10: "For whosoever keeps the whole law but fails in one point has become guilty of all it." Here, Augustine critically examines the Stoic doctrine that anyone who truly has any one virtue must have all of them. Perhaps this letter was included because Augustine happened to cite marital fidelity as an example of a virtue that can coexist with vice.[82]

[79] G. Constable, *Three Studies of Medieval Religious Thought* (Cambridge, 1998), 252–53, 329. S. Farmer, *Surviving Poverty in Medieval Paris*(Ithaca, NY, 2002), 111.

[80] MS Cologne, Erzbischöfl. Diözesan- u. Dombibl. Cod. Dom 78 (9th cent.). Vienna, MSS Österr. Nationalbibl. Cod. Lat. 1021 (9th cent.); Zettl, Stifsbibl. Ms. 296 (ca. 1200). The first of these three does not include *De opere monachorum.*

[81] MS Munich, Bayer. Staatsbibl. Clm 14491 (11th cent.); MS Graz, Universitätsbibl. Ms. 270 (12th cent.); MS Vienna, Österr. Nationalbibl. Cod. Lat. 849 (12th cent., before 1145); University of Oregon, Burgess Collection MS 25 (Germany, late 12th cent.); MS Bamberg, Staatsbibl. Ms. Patr. 28 (late 12th cent.: includes *De opere monachorum* and *Epist.* 130 as well as *Epist.* 167 and *Epist. 172*); MS Klosterneuburg, Stiftsbibl. CCl 19 (12th/13th cent.); MS Munich, Bayer. Staatsbibl. Clm 5915 (15th cent.); MS Melk, Stiftsbibl. Ms. 136 (627) (mid-15th cent., or 1451); MS Melk, Stiftsbibl. Ms. 1592 (56) (15th cent. includes *Epist.* 130 instead of *Epist.* 167, 172).

[82] *Epist.* 167.10, CSEL 44:596–97.

Whatever the pastoral influence of Augustine's treatises may have been, the theology of marriage that emerged during the first half of the twelfth century was not dependent on his treatises as such. Instead, the schoolmen took what they needed from florilegia and used excerpts that circulated as *sententiae*. The use of *sententiae* was fundamental in the schools during the first quarter of the twelfth century. The method was not apt to produce accurate interpretations of what Augustine had said, consistent with their textual and historical context, but it met the needs of the day perfectly. It enabled scholars to apply Augustine's words creatively and imaginatively to current exigencies while preserving the appearance of tradition. The most important *sententiae* on marriage during the twelfth century came originally from the *De bono coniugali*, the *De nuptiis et concupiscentia*, and Book IX of the *De Genesi ad litteram*. Among the topics covered by these excerpts, the most conspicuous are the changing function of marriage in relation to the fall of human kind and to the advent of Jesus Christ, and the three goods of marriage: faith, offspring, and sacrament.[83]

---

[83] H. Zeimentz, *Ehe nach der Lehre der Frühscholastik* (Düsseldorf, 1973). B. Matecki, *Der Traktat In primis hominibus* (Frankfurt am Main, 2001). In Matecki, see the chart on pp. 71–75.

3

Bonum prolis, bonum fidei

The utility of marriage

What is the purpose of marriage? Why marry? Fundamentally, according to Augustine, the reason (*causa*) for marriage is the good of procreation: the begetting and rearing of children as members of the church, the body of Christ. In another sense, however, the proper reason for Christians to marry is not procreation but the remedy against lust, which pertains to the good of faith. But that does not imply that marriage has lost its essential relation to procreation. I hope in what follows to clarify the relation between these two teleologies. I begin with procreation.

3.1 *BONUM PROLIS*: PROCREATION

Procreation was the original reason for marriage,[1] according to Augustine. God instituted marriage by creating male and female and by blessing them, telling them to "increase and multiply."[2] The procreative end belongs to the very nature of marriage, and it has to be included in any adequate definition or analysis of marriage. Augustine never departed from that premise. In the *De nuptiis et concupiscentia*, he characterizes the "natural good of marriage" as "the joining of male and female for the sake of begetting children."[3]

Augustine characterizes childrearing as the object of a natural association or partnership: "it pertains to the nature of marriage that male and female are joined in a partnership [*societas*] for begetting children, and that they do no defraud one

---

[1] *De b. coniug.* 17(19), CSEL 41:212/22–23: "qui non quaerunt in conubio nec appetunt, nisi propter quod institutae sunt nuptiae [i.e., prolem]." *De adult. coniug.* II.12(12), 395/20–21: "sint ergo nuptiae causa generandi institutae." *C. duas epist. Pelag.* I.10, CSEL 60:431/5–6: "dicimus a deo nuptias institutas propter ordinatam generationem filiorum."

[2] *De civ. Dei* XIV.22, CCL 48:444/1–9. The verb used here is *constituere*, rather than *instituere*, but the meaning is the same.

[3] *De nupt. et conc.* I.4(5), CSEL 42:215/1–2.

another, just as every partnership naturally shuns a fraudulent partner."[4] He goes on to argue, nevertheless, that higher, supra-natural modes of fidelity are expected from Christian spouses as people of faith. Invoking a philosophical commonplace, Augustine compares marriage to procreative pair bonding in other animals. Male and female birds, for example, form breeding pairs and collaborate in making nests and take turns to look after their young. Whereas some human beings pursue sexual pleasure in a bestial manner, some beasts pursue procreation and raise their young in an almost human manner.[5]

Augustine does not maintain that procreation is the proper reason for choosing to marry rather than to pursue a celibate vocation in the fallen world. He does maintain, however, that couples who intend to prevent procreation when they marry, making that a condition of their agreement, vitiate their marriages and are not truly married. Indeed, as we shall see, Augustine claims that a spouse who begins to practice contraception during a marriage becomes unmarried. His vehement objections to contraception reflect his own experience as a Manichee Hearer. T. D. Barnes suggests that Augustine and his mistress "must have practiced some fairly effective form of contraception," since they begot only one child in a fourteen-year sexually active relationship.[6]

Augustine specifically condemns several methods of preventing procreation, including intercourse during the infertile period (the "rhythm method" espoused in modern Catholicism), *coitus interruptus*, the man's use of a part of his wife not intended for that purpose (i.e., anal or oral sex), the use of contraceptive drugs to prevent the formation of a fetus or to destroy it before it is alive, and the use of abortifacients to kill a fetus after it has become alive.[7] Augustine does not distinguish between licit and illicit means of contraception, for in his view all are equally bad. Indeed, he maintains that the very *intention* to prevent procreation, as well as the actual use of contraceptive methods, is vicious and destroys marriage. In the *De bono coniugali*, Augustine condemns those who are *unwilling* to procreate (the verb is *nolle*) as well as those who *act* to prevent procreation.[8] Similarly, in the *De nuptiis et concupiscentia*, he condemns not only those who prevent procreation through an

---

4 Ibid., 215/11–14. The vocabulary of fraud is from 1 Cor 7:5, although the cheating in question there is abstinence, not adultery.
5 *De nupt. et conc.* 4(5), 215/5–9. Cf. *Dig.* 1.1.1.3 (Ulpian), *Institutes* 1.2, pr.; Cicero, *De officiis* I.4.11.
6 T. D. Barnes, in a review of O'Donnell's commentaries on the Confessions, *Classical Philology* 89 (1994): 293–99, at 297.
7 Use of the sterile period: *De mor. Manich.* 65, CSEL 90:147/2–4. *Coitus interruptus*: *C. Faustum* XXII.30, CSEL 25:624/20–21. Use of the wrong part of a wife's body: *De b. coniug.* 11(12), 203–04. Contraceptive drugs, abortion: *De nupt. et conc.* I.15(17), 230. Augustine assumes that a fetus becomes alive not at the point of conception but later, when it receives a soul. Augustine criticizes contraception also in *C. Faustum* XV.7, 428–30, but without mentioning a specific method.
8 *De b. coniug.* 5(5), 193/15–17.

evil deed (*opus*), but also those who prevent it through an evil *votum*.[9] The word *votum* can mean "prayer," but here it seems to mean "wish" or "intention." Augustine is surely using the term in that sense when he characterizes his relationship with his concubine as "a pact of libidinous love, where offspring are born contrary to *votum*."[10] Augustine may be referring here to partners who agree to marry with the understanding or stipulation that they plan to avoid conception.[11] Be that as it may, it is clear that the intention to prevent procreation is just as bad, in Augustine's view, as the actual use of any preventive method.

Augustine maintains that contraception nullifies even an already-existing marriage, although he is perhaps using an admonitory hyperbole. Criticizing the Manichees for allowing the Hearers to practice contraception, Augustine complains that although they take wives in accordance with the law of marriage and with nuptial tablets proclaiming that they are marrying "for the sake of begetting children" (*liberorum procreandorum causa*), they try to prevent procreation, which is the very reason for marriage. Because they "take away from marriage what belongs to marriage," they are not husbands but depraved lovers, their wives are whores, their marriage bed is a brothel, and their fathers-in-law are pimps.[12] Augustine goes further in the *De nuptiis et concupiscentia*, where he says that spouses who practice contraception are husband and wife (*coniuges*) in name alone. In fact, they do not retain "any of the reality [*veritas*] of marriage, but rather use the honorable name of marriage to draw a veil over their depravity."[13] When the wife alone is guilty, she is her husband's prostitute. When the husband alone is guilty, he is his wife's adulterer.[14] If they married with that intention, they did not come together in marriage but in immorality (*stuprum*). Spouses who marry properly but start to practice contraception later are no longer husband and wife.[15]

Nevertheless, is not the avoidance of procreation in marriage itself that vitiates marriage, in Augustine's view, but rather the effort to prevent sexual intercourse from being productive. As long as they are spiritually and emotionally mature enough to cope with abstinence, there is no harm if married couples practice celibacy. On the contrary, they will elevate their marriage. I can see no way of rescuing Augustine's position from inconsistency on this point, for abstinence as well as contraception must "take away from marriage what belongs to marriage." From Augustine's perspective, though, as we shall see in the following chapter, mutually agreed abstinence sublimates rather than vitiates marriage, raising it to a higher level that transcends its natural utility. Moreover, Augustine assumes that spouses will abstain only after their lust has waned, and not as soon as they marry.

---

[9] *De nupt. et conc.* I.15(17), 229/21: "siue uoto malo siue opera malo."
[10] *Conf.* IV.2(2), CCL 27:41: "pactum libidinosi amoris, ubi proles etiam contra votum nascitur."
[11] According to Gregory IX's decretal *Si conditiones contra*, X 4.5.7 (ed. Friedberg, 684), such an agreement renders the contract of marriage null and void.
[12] *C. Faustum* XV.7, CSEL 25.1:429/26–430/8.
[13] *De nupt. et conc.* I.15(17), 229.   [14] Ibid. I.15(17), 230.   [15] Ibid., 229.

Augustine often points out that a man agrees to take his wife "for the sake of begetting children" (*liberorum procreandorum causa*) when he signs or seals the nuptial tablets (the *tabulae nuptiales* or *tabulae matrimoniales*). He is referring to what was in essence a dowry agreement, or dotal contract, consisting traditionally of a wax-covered wooden diptych on which one would write with a stylus.[16] The parties agreeing to the marriage and their witnesses would sign or seal[17] the agreement at the domestic wedding ceremony, which Augustine must often have attended in Hippo as a witness. Augustine likens the gospels to the nuptial tablets of the marriage between Christ and the church.[18] Use of the phrase *liberorum procreandorum causa* in the tablets, in his view, was proof of the fundamental and necessary relation between marriage and the intention to procreate, and it sufficed to show that spouses who practiced contraception were contravening their wedding vows.[19] In a fundamental sense, therefore, everyone who married did so to beget children, for such was their agreement and such is their partnership. In that sense, according to Augustine, procreation is the *only* legitimate reason for marrying.[20]

Nevertheless, marrying "for the sake of procreating children" was not so much a personal motive as it was an end that belonged essentially to marriage and distinguished it from concubinage. There were implicit cultural assumptions at work here that are difficult for the modern reader to disentangle. In classical Roman law, which did not attempt to prevent divorce, the chief consequence of being married was that it legitimized the offspring. The children that a man "received" (i.e., acknowledged as his own) were his *liberi*: his *own* children, and his natural heirs. Contrariwise, in the absence of nuptial ceremonies and dotal instruments, evidence that a man and a woman were in fact living together as man and wife "for the sake of procreating children" might suffice to show that they were married.[21] Christians regarded marriage as an enduring compact (a *pactum, foedus,* or *confoederatio*),[22] but, as Augustine knew at first hand, concubinage was customary even in Christian societies, and the children that a man had by his mistress were not his *liberi*.

Because no rituals or documents were strictly necessary for a valid marriage either in Roman civil law or in western Christendom, what distinguished concubinage

---

[16] J. Evans Grubbs, "Marrying and its Documentation in Later Roman Law," in THTH 43–94, at 74–94. D. G. Hunter, "Marrying and the *tabulae nuptiales* in Roman North Africa," THTH 95–113, at 103–11.

[17] See B. Nicholas, *An Introduction to Roman Law* (Oxford, 1962), 255–57, on the use of seals and subscriptions in wills. The practice of authenticating a document by writing out a *subscriptio* at the end, instead of applying a seal, was linked to the use of papyrus or parchment instead of wax tablets, although the methods were sometimes combined.

[18] Hunter, "Marrying and the *tabulae nuptiales*," 110–11.

[19] E.g., *C. Faustum* XV.7, 429/26–27.

[20] *De b. coniug.* 24(32), 227/4–5: "causa pariendi: quae ... sola sit qua nuptiae fiunt...." *C. Faustum* XV.7, 430/3–4: "filios autem inuiti [auditores] suscipiunt, propter quod solum coniugia copulanda sunt."

[21] Cf. *Codex Iustinianus* 5.4.9

[22] J. Gaudemet, *L'Église dans l'Empire romain, IV–Ve siècles* (Paris, 1958), 532.

from marriage was a complicated network of laws, conventional norms, and societal expectations. Typically, a man of middle to high social class would take a lower-class or servile concubine (or several in succession) for sexual comfort before he was ready to marry. Augustine had had just such a concubine, whom he abandoned when it was time for him to marry a suitable bride of his own class. Augustine loved their illegitimate child, Adeodatus, and she remained faithful to him after they parted in 385. Through that experience, Augustine explains, he learned the difference between a legitimate marriage, entered into for the sake of begetting children, and a "compact of libidinous love, where children are born against [their father's] intention, although once born they compel us to love them."[23] Augustine recalled fifteen years later how his mistress had been torn from his side, leaving a wound that had not healed.[24] The modern reader is inclined to view Augustine's relationship with his concubine much more generously than Augustine himself did, and to emphasize their mutual affection, the fidelity of the anonymous woman, and the marriage-like features of their relationship.[25] Moreover, Augustine himself may have been thinking of that relationship in the *De bono coniugali* when he remarks on the ways in which concubinage or an informal relationship might approximate to marriage by virtue of the intentions of one or both spouses. Augustine speculates that an informal but monogamous sexual relationship, entered into without the intention of raising children, might perhaps amount to marriage if the partners intended to remain together as long as both were alive, but only if they receive their offspring willingly and do nothing to prevent procreation.[26]

Whereas procreation is naturally inherent in marriage, sexual desire, according to Augustine's preferred view, is not. Libido is a result of the fall, not part of the original condition. Augustine duplicates the conceptual apparatus and vocabulary of desire for rhetorical effect, positing distinct carnal and conjugal desires. Just as the flesh has it appetites, so does marriage. To the flesh belongs the desire for sexual intercourse (*concupiscentia carnis*). To marriage belongs the desire to beget and to raise children (*concupiscentia nuptiarum*).[27] Responding to Julian's objections in the *De nuptiis et concupiscentia*, Augustine complains that Julian confuses the issue

---

[23] Augustine, *Conf.* IV.2(2), 41.   [24] Ibid., VI.15(25), 90.

[25] On the reevaluation of Augustine's relationship with his mistress, see K. Power, "Concubine/ Concubinage," in Fitzgerald, *Augustine through the Ages*, 222–23 (which includes an extensive bibliography); and D. Shanzer, "Avulsa a latere meo: Augustine's Spare Rib — Confessions 6.15.21," *Journal of Roman Studies* 92 (2002): 157–76.

[26] *De b. coniug.* 5(5), 193.

[27] *Epist.* 6*.5, CSEL 88:34. This passage is difficult to translate because of Augustine's multiple use of the genitive case. In *concupiscentia nuptiarum* and *concupiscentia carnis*, the genitive expresses the quasi-possessive relation "belonging to" or "pertaining to"; in *concupiscentia pudicitiae coniugalis* there is a genitive of description (where the genitive term is normally a phrase consisting of a noun with an adjective); and *concupiscentia legitime propagandae prolis* involves an objective genitive (compare, "Augustine's love of Scripture"). The sense of the genitive in *concupiscentiam vinculi socialis* is uncertain: it could be another objective genitive (in which case, "concupiscence *for* the social bond" would be a better translation), or it may be

by saying that what motivates sexual intercourse is a "natural appetite." The term "appetite," Augustine argues (with comical irony), is a fig leaf that Julian uses to hide what he is really talking about: carnal desire. Once one names it and recognizes it for what it really is, one sees that it is shameful and unnatural. There are indeed natural appetites, such as the appetite for health and, in marriage, the appetite for begetting, nurturing, and educating children. But such appetites arise from reason, not from the flesh.[28]

3.2 *BONUM FIDEI*: THE REMEDY FOR CONCUPISCENCE

Augustine's notion of marriage as a remedy is based on 1 Corinthians 7, where Paul, having affirmed that "it is good for a man not to touch a woman," concedes that "each man should have his own wife and each woman her own husband" in order to ward off "the temptation to immorality" (vv. 1–2). Paul treats marriage here as a means of regulating and containing sexual desire, and he says nothing about procreation. To contain their ardor, spouses should render the conjugal debt to each other, for each spouse has power over the other's body (vv. 3–5). Speaking for himself, Paul would prefer everyone to be celibate, but he concedes that God endows different persons with different gifts, or charisms (v. 7). He notes that marriage is the source of tribulations and distractions (vv. 28, 32), a theme that Jerome developed, combining Paul's counsel with anti-conjugal material from Seneca, Plutarch, and a lost treatise by Porphyry.[29] That said, those who are incapable of celibacy may marry with a clear conscience, "for it is better to marry than to burn." Marriage is good, therefore, although celibacy is better (v. 38).

Augustine brought to his interpretation of Paul's counsel some assumptions that are not in Paul or anywhere else in Scripture. With Paul, Augustine regarded marriage as a solution to the problem of sexual desire, and he deduced that people should opt for the lesser good of marriage only if they were incapable of celibacy. Unlike Paul, Augustine assumes that sexual desire and pleasure are not only distracting but also dangerous and contaminating. Nevertheless, marriage renders lustful sex "pardonable" (*venialis*) as long as there is no attempt to prevent sex from resulting in procreation.[30] Augustine read his doctrine of the venial fault (*culpa venialis*) into 1 Corinthians 7:6, where Paul in the Old Latin versions says that he speaks *secundum veniam* ("by way of indulgence"). Later versions have Paul

---

another genitive of description, or it may merely express the relation of "pertaining to." I am grateful for David Hunter's counsel on this problem.

[28]   *De nupt. et conc.* II.7(17), 269–70.

[29]   Ph. Delhaye, "Le dossier anti-matrimonial de l'Adversus Jovinianum et son influence sur quelques écrits latins su XIIe siècle," *Mediaeval Studies* 13 (1951): 65–86, at 68–69. J. N. D. Kelly, *Jerome* (London, 1975), 184.

[30]   *De nupt. et conc.* 1.14(16), 229.

speaking by way of "permission."[31] Augustine seems not to have noticed that Paul was writing in the shadow of the imminent *parousia*, when there was no point in begetting another generation because the time left was too short (1 Cor 7:29).

Augustine used the theory of the two dispensations to explain why the remedy, rather than procreation, had become the primary reason for choosing to marry.[32] The theory was predicated on Genesis 1:28, where God commanded human kind to fill the earth by begetting children. God repeated the command after the Flood (Gen 9:1). Once the earth was full, therefore, there was no longer any need to procreate. Whereas Jerome argued that the literal earth was so full that it could hardly support its population,[33] Augustine argued it was the church, or the city of God, that was now becoming full. Moreover, even if it was not quite full, celibacy was a better way to fill God's city than procreation.

Procreation was a duty (*officium*) under the Old Covenant, Augustine argues, when God commanded his people to "increase and multiply," but there were reasons for that duty then that no longer obtain in the Christian era. Before the advent of Jesus Christ and the mission of St Paul, the city of God was limited to the people of a single race. They practiced endogamy to maintain the purity of their cult, but they needed to procreate until the Messiah came, for he was to be born of that race.[34] God's plan for human kind includes a hidden number of the elect: a number that is at least equal to but may surpass the number of fallen angels. The end will come when the population of God's city, on earth and in heaven, reaches the predetermined number.[35]

Under the New Covenant, the city of God embraces people from all the regions of the earth. The need to beget children for the Lord is no longer urgent, and a celibate vocation is a more effective means of populating God's city and of reaching the hidden number of the elect. Procreation is no longer a duty, therefore, and celibacy has become a higher vocation than marriage.[36] Augustine's argument is partly arithmetical or demographic, but it is also qualitative. The city of God is the church as the bride of Christ, gathering together people from all over the world as her spiritual children. In the end, the city will be the community of all souls unified in the beatific vision. The city of God progresses from carnal to spiritual kinship, therefore, for spiritual regeneration through baptism is a higher goal that mere carnal generation.

Augustine summarizes the numerical aspect of his theory in a seminal passage of the *De Genesi ad litteram*, where he identifies the help (*adiutorium*) that Eve was supposed to give to Adam. Augustine distinguishes here between marriage as a

[31] *Sermo* 354A, 7–9, in F. Dolbeau (ed.), *Vingt-six sermons au people d'Afrique*(Paris, 1996), 80–81. *Epist.* 6*.7, BA 46B:136–36. *De continentia* 12(27), CSEL 41:177.
[32] *De b. coniug.* 13(15), 15(17), 207/12, 210/7–8. *De nupt. et conc.* I.13(14), 226/23–24. *De Gen. ad litt.* IX.7, CSEL 28.1:275/20.
[33] Jerome, *Adv. Helvidium* 21, PL 23:215.
[34] *De b. coniug.* 9(9), 200/24–201/2. *De nupt. et conc.* I.13(14), 226–27.
[35] *Enchiridion* 9(29), CCL 46:65. *De civ. Dei* XXII.1, CCL 48:807.
[36] *De serm. Dom. in monte* I.5, 40–41, CCL 35:43–46.

procreative *officium* (a duty or obligation) and marriage as a remedy. Now that the city of God is open to all races of the earth, there is no need to suffer the indignities of sexuality unless one needs the remedy:

> Therefore I do not see with what help the woman was made to provide the man if one takes away the reason of begetting [*causa generandi*], nor do I see why one should take it away. For whence does faithful and pious virginity have great merit and great honor before God if not that in this "time to refrain from embracing" [Eccl 3:5], when a great abundance taken from all the races suffices to complete the number of the elect, the lust [*libido*] to feel sordid pleasure does not claim for itself what the necessity of providing offspring no longer demands. Accordingly, the weakness of both sexes, with its inclination toward depraved ruin, is rightly corrected [*excipitur*] by the honorableness of marriage, so that what would have been a duty [*officium*] for the healthy is a remedy for the sick.[37]

It is clear from the context that the "number of the elect" is not that of persons alive on earth but that of the citizens of the city of God, including those who have already left this world.[38]

In the *De bono coniugali*, Augustine responds to Jovinian's objection[39] that if everyone became celibate, the human race would come to an end. Although the hypothesis is remote, Augustine replies to the objection, and he seems to accept the consequence that the human race would come to an end, albeit in a sublime sense that Jovinian did not envisage. If everyone became celibate in the right spirit (i.e., not as the Manichees do), "how much more quickly would the city of God be filled and the end of the world be hastened."[40] The reasoning is obscure. Perhaps Augustine assumed that there were already enough people in the world to fill the city of God, so that if all of them became saints, the world would end. Or perhaps he reasoned that the eventuality would occur only when God's preordained plan had been fulfilled.

The subtler, qualitative aspect of Augustine's theory pertains to spiritual kinship. Carnal kinship is obviously among the benefits of marriage. At the beginning of the *De bono coniugali*, Augustine observes marriage is "the first joining of natural human partnership [*prima ... naturalis humanae societatis copula*]," and that all human beings are related by blood inasmuch they share a common ancestor in Adam. Sexual intercourse in marriage extends the web of kinship through children (*conexio societatis in filiis*).[41] Later in the *De bono coniugali*, though, Augustine argues that the duty to procreate has fallen into abeyance, and he posits a spiritual kinship that is better and more sublime than blood relationship. There is no need to fear that celibacy will reduce the population. Because people will continue to

---

[37] *De Gen. ad litt.* IX.7, 275. On completion of the number of the elect, see ibid., IX.3, 272/6–7: "donec certo numero inpleto"; and IX.6, 273/24–25: "ut ita omne humanum genus ... certa numerositate inpleretur."
[38] Ibid., IX.6, 273–75.   [39] See Jerome, *Adversus Iovinianum* I.36, PL 23:259.
[40] *De b. coniug.* 10(10), 201.   [41] Ibid., 1(1), 187–88.

procreate, there will never be any shortage of offspring from which to populate the church and to produce "holy friendship." But the blood relationship resulting from procreation is inferior to the all-embracing spiritual kinship of the church. People from all peoples of the earth are now entering the "holy and pure fellowship" (*sancta et sincera societas*) and are forming a "spiritual kinship" (*spiritalis cognatio*).[42] Similarly, glossing 1 Corinthians 7:29 in the *De nuptiis et concupiscentia*, Augustine says that the people of God "should no longer be propagated carnally by generation, but should rather be gathered spiritually by regeneration."[43]

This spiritual community is hierarchically ordered. Just as celibacy supersedes marriage in the unfolding of human history, so celibacy is a higher calling within the church. Augustine divides Christians into three classes: the married folk, who are the common people (*plebs*) of the church; the clerics, who are the ministers of the church; and the celibates, who have turned away from the world to lead a life of contemplation. Marriage is the humblest of the three callings. Augustine discovered this division in two Scriptural sources, each of which illumined the other.[44] One source was Ezekiel 14:12–23, a record of an apocalyptic vision in which Noah, Daniel, and Job are the only persons who survive the onslaughts of famine, wild beasts, war, and pestilence. Noah, according to Augustine, who guided the ark that carried God's chosen ones to safety, typifies the ministers (*praepositi, rectores*) of the church. Daniel, whom God greatly loved, who understood God's words (Dan 10:11), and who was proven by many trials, typifies the continents: the contemplative Christians who have turned away from mundane distractions to think only about God (1 Cor 7:32–34). Job, both because he was a married man with a family and in view of his tribulations, typifies married folk (*coniugati*).

Augustine discovered a parallel typology by combining Matthew 24:40–41 and Luke 17:34–35, which record variants of a parable about the final judgment. When the Son of Man returns, there will be two men working in a field, two persons asleep in bed, and two women grinding flour at a mill. The persons asleep in bed typify the contemplatives, who are already at rest. The women at the mill typify married folk: their subordinate gender shows that they represent the laity, and the grinding of the mill wheel represents the endless cycle of mundane preoccupations. The men who work in the field typify the clerics. There are two of each because one will be taken and the other left. Augustine says that he cannot think of any other classes of persons besides these three from which the church is composed.[45]

---

[42] Ibid., 9(9), 201.   [43] *De nupt. et conc.* I.14(15), 227/15–16.

[44] See G. Folliet, "Les trois catégories de chrétiens," in *Augustinus Magister*, communications, vol. 2 (1954–55), 631–44. Folliet notes eight places in which Augustine comments on the Ezekiel text or on the parable of Matthew and Luke. See especially *Enarrationes in Psalmos* 132, 4–5, CCL 40:1928–30, and *Quaestiones evangeliorum* II.44, CCL 44B:104–06, where Augustine uses both sources together.

[45] *Quaest. evang.* II.44.2, 106/37–38.

The proper reason for a Christian to marry now, according to Augustine, is not procreation but the remedy.[46] Now that the church is receiving new members from all the races of the world, he argues, "even those desiring to be joined in marriage solely for the sake of children should be urged to use the fuller good of continence instead."[47] Paul did not say, "if they have no children, let them marry," but "if are not continent, let them marry" (1 Cor 7:9).[48] Before Christ came, there was a duty (*officium*) to procreate children through marriage, but that duty no longer exists. Anyone capable of celibacy should remain celibate to avoid the undesirable concomitants of marriage: domestic distractions, tribulation of the flesh, and sexual shame.[49]

John Chrysostom presents the same theory with some differences of emphasis. According to Chrysostom, God instituted marriage in the beginning with two purposes: the preservation of chastity and the procreation of children. Marriage preserves chastity by containing desire, for marriage began when desire began. The first of the two purposes is the more important, for even a childless marriage sanctifies, and it is especially important in these last days. In former times, when people had no hope of the resurrection, they achieved the comfort of perpetuity by begetting children. But the desire for posterity has become superfluous, Chrysostom argues, for the earth is crowded and the resurrection is drawing near. For those Christians who do desire offspring, it is better to beget them spiritually. The only reason to marry now, therefore, is to avoid fornication.[50] Whereas Augustine considered the remedial aspect to be adventitious – a product of the fall that rescued human nature from calamity – Chrysostom considered it to be intrinsic to the institution of marriage.

Augustine assumes, nevertheless, that marriage retains its essential, natural relationship to procreation. Even the remedial aspect of marriage presupposes, at least to some extent, the good of procreation. Augustine envisages a range of possibilities. At one extreme are those, such as the patriarchs of the Old Covenant, who seek sex in marriage only for the sake of procreation.[51] For such persons, the good of offspring *is* the remedy. They commit no sin at all, although what Augustine calls the "wound" (*plaga*)[52] of original sin remains, for sexual intercourse cannot occur without "some bestial motion, at which nature blushes."[53] At the other extreme are those who seek sex for sensual gratification rather than for the sake of procreation, yet only with their spouses and without attempting to prevent procreation. Such persons commit some sin by using sex immoderately, but because they confine sex within marriage their

---

[46] *De b. coniug.* 10(10), 202/5–8.   [47] Ibid., 9(9), 201/5–7.
[48] *De bono viduitatis* 8(11), CSEL 41:316/10–16.   [49] *De b. coniug.*, 13(15), 207–08.
[50] John Chrysostom, *On Virginity* 19, SC 125:156–58; *Homily on Marriage*, 3, PG 51:212–13.
[51] *De b. coniug.* 17(19), 212–13. *De continentia* 12(27), 177.   [52] *De nupt. et conc.* I.13, 226/12.
[53] *De pecc. orig.* 43, CSEL 42:201/19–22. On the "bestial motion" of sex, see also *De Gen. ad litt.* XI.32, 366/11; *De peccatorum meritis et remissione* I.21, CSEL 60:21; and *C. Iulianum* III.47, PL 44:726/8.

sin is pardonable, or permitted "by way of indulgence" (*secundum veniam*, 1 Cor 7:6).[54]

Ideally, therefore, spouses should "use" their lust by channeling it toward procreation. The more their sexual intercourse is directed toward procreation by personal intention, the less tainted it is by sin.[55] But Augustine is realistic. Whereas sexual intercourse would have been directed entirely to procreation in the earthly Paradise, it is almost always at least partly motivated by lust in the fallen condition. Augustine does not expect Christians to copulate rationally and dispassionately. Sexual fervor and the desire to procreate children are mutually competing forces, in his view, but the latter can subjugate the former, and sex is meritorious for those who are completely successful – if any such there be.[56] Although sexual desire itself is never honorable, therefore, its use may be free from any fault.[57] But sexual desire is good only insofar it is *good to use an evil thing well*, just as it is evil to use a good thing badly. Augustine later rejects an idea with which he had flirted in the *De bono coniugali*: that some degree of carnal pleasure in sexual intercourse, as in eating, is harmless and good as long as it is moderated and directed to its proper end.[58]

Young spouses, whose chief motive for sexual intercourse is almost inevitably their lust, can restrain that lust and mitigate its evil by learning to channel it into procreation. Their modesty and shame and their sense of parental responsibility will come to their aid:

> Marriage has this good also: that carnal or youthful incontinence, even though it is depraved, is redirected to the honesty of begetting offspring, so that the union of marriage [*copulatio coniugalis*] may make something good out of the evil of sexual desire. Furthermore, concupiscence of the flesh is repressed and burns as it were with more modesty when it is tempered by parental affection. For a certain seriousness intrudes upon the heat of pleasure when a man and woman, in the very act of cleaving to each other, think of themselves as father and mother.[59]

Here, too, marriage mitigates sexual desire and compensates for its intrinsic evil by directing it in some way toward procreation.

What of spouses who through "immoderate exaction of the conjugal debt . . . have sexual intercourse even besides the purpose of begetting children [*praeter causam procreandi sibi misceantur*]"? In such cases, as long as they do not *prevent* procreation, the goodness of marriage mitigates their fault and makes it pardonable (*venialis*).[60] But contraception puts lust beyond excuse. In effect,

---

54 *De b. coniug.* 6–7(6), 194–95. *De nupt. et conc.* I.15(17), 230/9–11.

55 *De nupt. et conc.* I.12(13), 226. *C. Iulianum* V.16(60), PL 44:817. *De pecc. mer. et rem.* I.57, 56–57. *De pecc. orig.* 38, CSEL 42, 196/26–27. *Epist.* 6*.5, CSEL 88:34. On the idea that reason uses lust, see *De pecc. orig.* 39, 197/26–198/3. On the idea of use in general, see *De doctrina Christiana* I.3(3), CCL 32:8.

56 *De pecc. mer. et rem.* I.57, 56.   57 *C. Iulianum* V.16(60), PL 44:817.

58 *De b. coniug.* 16(18), 210. *Retr.* 2.22.2, CCL 57:108.   59 *De b. coniug.* 3(3), 191.

60 Ibid., 6(6), 194–95.

spouses who practice contraception are having extra-marital sex. For the same reason, to demand sex from one's wife when she is pregnant is "immodest, shameful, and dirty."[61]

What is it about marriage, according to Augustine, that makes even "immoderate" sex pardonable? By definition, there is no personal intention here to channel sexual desire toward procreation. Augustine's answer to this question is unclear. He sometimes implies that marriage mitigates lust merely by containing it within the bounds of fidelity. For example, in his letter to Dardanus, Augustine observes that although Christ "did not destroy the good of marriage" by being born of a virgin, Christ "moderates the evil of disobedient members, so that when carnal concupiscence has been limited in some way, it may at least become conjugal chastity."[62] In the *De bono coniugali*, Augustine explains that the conjugal debt enables each partner to save the other from fornication.[63] But that reasoning as it stands is circular. What is it that makes sex within marriage less sinful than extramarital sex? In the *De continentia*, Augustine argues that marriage mitigates the evil of sexual desire and makes it pardonable by containing it and subjecting it to an orderly discipline, and by preventing a certain disorderly conduct (presumably non-procreative sex) even *within* marriage.[64] In another passage from *De bono coniugali*, Augustine seems to argue that there is something good about marriage itself that mitigates the evil of sexual desire. Here he considers the moral standing of wives who exact the conjugal debt from their husbands for their own sexual gratification even when the latter would prefer to be continent. Even concubines sometimes behave more honorably, Augustine complains (perhaps with his own beloved mistress in mind), but he concedes that such women benefit from the very fact that they are married. Because their concupiscence is confined within the partnership and fidelity of the marriage bond, it does not "flow out, formless and dissolute." Even if "it is obscene for a woman to want to use her husband lustfully, it is nevertheless honorable [for her] to want to have sex with no one except her husband, or to want to have children by no man except her husband."[65]

Although Augustine seems to suggest that the very containment of lust within marriage makes the lust pardonable, quite apart from any procreative intent, the feature of marriage that rescues lust, in his view, may be its inherent relation to procreation. Even if there is no personal intention to procreate, procreation is the proper end of marriage itself.[66] That may one reason why contraception appalls him. As long as one does not try to prevent procreation, the procreative good inherent in marriage succeeds in mitigating the sin even when there is no personal intention to procreate.

---

[61] *De b. coniug.* 6(6), 194.
[62] *Epist.* 187.31, CSEL 57:109/15–18.
[63] *De b. coniug.* 6(6), 195.
[64] *De continentia* 12(27), 177.
[65] *De b. coniug.* 5(5), 194.
[66] *De nupt. et conc.* I.14(16), 229/13–15.

3.3 SUMMARY: THE STORY OF MARRIAGE

According to Augustine's mature position, God instituted marriage in the beginning so that the spouses could procreate and raise children. Sexual intercourse would have been wholly good, and human beings had a duty to "increase and multiply" and to raise children for God. The human race would have multiplied until it reached the preordained number of the elect, when God would have transformed human beings, raising them to the higher, immortal condition of eternal bliss. In the meantime, no one would have died.

With the fall came the evils of lust and death. Sexual intercourse became shameful. Nevertheless, marriage still embodied the duty to procreate. Sexual procreation was the only means of perpetuating and multiplying the human race, which was a sacred duty, for the city of God was limited to a single race, and God forbade exogamy. The people of God had a duty to perpetuate their race until the Messiah came. And they still had a duty to populate the city of God and to reach the preordained number of the elect: the very duty that God commended to Adam and Eve when he blessed them and commanded them to "increase and multiply."

Under the New Covenant, everything changed. The city of God was now open to all the races of the earth. Conversion became a better way to "increase and multiply," spiritual regeneration superseded corporeal generation, and spiritual kinship superseded carnal kinship. Procreation, therefore, was no longer a religious duty. The celestial city of God, in which everyone would be like the angels and there would be neither marrying nor giving in marriage, was already emerging in the midst of mundane care. For those who are strong enough, therefore, celibacy is the proper vocation. For the others, who cannot restrain their lust, marriage is the solution. The innate goodness of marriage remedies the adventitious evil of sexual intercourse. In particular, marriage mitigates the evil of lust by containing it within the bounds of fidelity and of the conjugal debt (the *bonum fidei*), and, ideally, by channeling it toward procreation (the *bonum prolis*).

In one sense, procreation is still the reason for marrying. In another sense, procreation is no longer an adequate or proper reason. Perhaps it would be better to say that procreation is the reason for marriage itself, whereas the remedy is the reason for choosing to marry. Thus, Alves Pereira, using a scholastic distinction to interpret Augustine, argues that procreation is the *finis operis* of marriage, according to Augustine, whereas the other reasons for marrying, including the remedial aspect, are the *fines operantis*: the ends of one who marries.[67]

It may be more helpful to make the same point more concretely. Suppose a Christian is trying to decide whether to marry or to pursue a celibate vocation. Needless to say, this is an idealized scenario, presupposing a freedom to choose that must have been rare in practice. Nevertheless, procreation, according to Augustine,

---

[67] B. Alves Pereira, *La doctrine du mariage* (Paris, 1930), 50.

is not an adequate or a proper reason for choosing marriage. On the contrary, one should marry only if one needs the remedy. Nevertheless, having chosen marriage, one has opted for a way of life that is naturally and innately ordained to procreation. The "good of offspring" is one of the rules. Ideally, one should make that end one's own. Failing that, it suffices that one does not try to cut marriage off from its natural end by preventing procreation: or, more precisely, by preventing sexual intercourse from being productive, for there is another, potentially sublime, aspect of marriage that enables it to flourish in the absence of sex and procreation, and to transcend its original purpose by prefiguring the life to come.

4

Bonum sacramenti

The sanctity and insolubility of marriage

Augustine always regarded Christian marriage from an ecclesiological perspective. He construed it in relation to the other sexually defined vocations that were valid in the church, such as consecrated virginity and widowhood.[1] Sexual activity is good insofar as it is contained by the goods of marriage, especially *fides*. It is less good than vocational continence, but it is the means by which those who are not strong enough for continence can participate in the Christian life and have their own place in the city of God. Moreover, marriage has a figurative relationship to the ultimate realization of the church in the next life, when there will be no marrying or giving in marriage. But spouses should adopt the higher way of continence in this life as soon as their ardor has waned sufficiently. The vertical, hierarchical preference for celibacy in the city of God is mirrored in the horizontal aspiration of spouses toward marital continence.

Augustine emphasizes that marriage – especially a marriage between baptized Christians – transcends its procreative and remedial utility. To be sure, the fundamental reason for marriage as an institution is procreation, and the proper reason for Christians to marry is to take advantage of the conjugal debt, which provides a remedy against fallen sexuality by containing lust. Those two purposes correspond to the goods of procreation and faith respectively. Yet Augustine encourages spouses to practice abstinence as soon as they are able, and he maintains that by so doing they do not vitiate their marriage. On the contrary, they raise it to a sublime level. Augustine argues in some places that marriage can survive and flourish without procreation; in others, that it can do so without sexual intercourse.

Augustine describes two ways in which marriage can survive childlessness or abstinence. On the one hand, the spouses are obliged to remain together as long as they are alive except in the case of adultery, and even in that case neither can

[1] W. Otten, "Augustine on Marriage, Monasticism, and the Community of the Church," *Theological Studies* 59(1998): 385–405.

validly remarry. On the other hand, the partnership becomes stronger, more resilient, and more sublime if the spouses become celibate when their lust has sufficiently abated. These two ideas are closely related in Augustine's mind, but their relationship remains unclear, and each has its own logic. Permanence of the first sort consists in the endurance of an enforceable obligation, although it entails a supra-contractual tie that survives the separation of partners and even a valid divorce. Permanence of the second sort is a matter of fact. It pertains to what we should call a "relationship": an existential and frangible entity that can and often does break down *de facto*. Augustine associates both aspects of marriage with the good of sacrament (*bonum sacramenti*), although it is chiefly the obligatory tie that leads him to posit this good, since it alone transcends human contingency and impermanence.

4.1 MARRIAGE AS AN AMICABLE PARTNERSHIP

Augustine often construes marriage as a *societas*: a partnership or association.[2] The idea had legal connotations, and a partnership would be vacuous without some sense of obligation. Nevertheless, a partnership is an actual, *de facto* state of affairs. It is not a bond that continues to exist *de iure* even when no one is observing it in fact.

In any partnership, two or more individuals come together in pursuit of a shared goal. Marriage is a partnership in that sense, whatever else it may be. The Roman jurist Modestinus defined marriage as "the union [*coniunctio*] of male and female, a *consortium* of the whole of life, a sharing of divine and human law."[3] Like *societas*, the term *consortium* denoted partnership. As Judith Evans Grubbs puts it, Modestinus "expresses the Roman idea of marriage as a joint enterprise, in which each partner has both emotional and financial interests."[4] But Modestinus did not consider this *consortium* to be an enforceable obligation, for marriage in classical Roman law was a "social fact." The law determined the prerequisites and consequences of marriage, but it did not enforce or even define the *consortium*.

Augustine derived his idea of marriage as a partnership partly from philosophical and legal commonplaces and partly from the biblical narrative of the primordial marriage, which he considered to be a record of historical fact. From a biblical point of view, marriage is the union of "two in one flesh." It came into being when God brought the first woman to Adam as his wife, having formed her from Adam's side (Gen 2:22). Augustine is thinking of that narrative when he describes marriage as the "first joining of natural human partnership [*prima ... naturalis humanae societatis copula*]."[5] Eve was made from Adam's side, Augustine explains, to show that she was Adam's partner and not his servant, for marriage is a close relationship between

---

[2]   *De nupt. et conc.* 1.4(5), CSEL 42:215/1–14.   [3]   *Digest* 23.2.1.
[4]   J. Evans Grubbs, "Marrying and its Documentation in Later Roman Law," THTH 43–94, at 43.
[5]   *De b. coniug.* 1(1), CSEL 41:187/8–9. The term *copula* does not usually refer to sexual intercourse in patristic or medieval Latin.

equals wherein each partner should cherish the other.[6] The manner of Eve's formation shows, too, that marriage is in some undefined sense a physical, embodied relationship, although Augustine does not identify the union of two in one flesh specially with sexual union or consummated marriage, as his medieval successors will usually do.

What is the essence or core of this partnership? In what do husband and wife collaborate? What is their shared goal? Fundamentally, according to Augustine, they come together to beget children, to nurture them, and to educate them: all goals that he subsumes under the *bonum prolis*.[7] The partnership of marriage acquired another, secondary goal because of the fall: the containment and mitigation of lust. Spouses owe each other the conjugal debt (1 Cor 7:4), which Augustine likens to "mutual servitude," for each owns the other's body. By marrying, each partner undertakes to satisfy the other's sexual needs, saving him or her from "illicit sexual relations."[8] In a sermon on conjugal abstinence that he probably delivered shortly after writing the *De bono coniugali*, Augustine counsels that even a spouse who is strong enough for abstinence should render the debt to a weaker (i.e., more libidinous) partner. To do so is an act of love and mercy.[9] But it is only by *rendering* the debt, according to Augustine, and not by *requiring* it, that a spouse displays conjugal affection.

Nevertheless, although the partners marry to procreate children and to satisfy each other's sexual needs, their relationship does not come to nothing when they have raised their children and are too old to beget more, or if they are sterile, or if they agree to abstain entirely from sexual intercourse for reasons of piety. Indeed, Augustine encourages Christian couples to abstain as soon as they are able. What endures thereafter is a spiritual partnership that is *gendered* but not *sexual*, for it presupposes the difference between male and female but does not involve coitus. This celibate, spiritual partnership is still natural, for the sexes are mutually complementary.

The idea of an asexual marital partnership appears in two different guises in Augustine's work, respectively anthropological and pastoral. In his early work, as we have seen, Augustine preferred to interpret the command of Genesis 1:28, "Increase and multiply," in a nonliteral manner, especially insofar as it pertained to the situation before the fall. Augustine characterizes this primordial, presexual partnership in the *De Genesi ad Manichaeos* as one in which the male rules while the female obeys.[10] He assumes that two partners cannot be unified and at peace unless

[6]   Ibid., 187/10–188/1. *De civitate Dei* XII.28, CCL 48:384.   [7]   *De b. coniug.* 6(6), 195.

[8]   Ibid., 195/6–10: "debent ergo sibi coniugati … mutuam quodam modo seruitutem.…"

[9]   *Serm.* 354A, 13, in *Vingt-six sermons au peuple d'Afrique*, ed. F. Dolbeau(Paris, 1996), 84. See D. G. Hunter, "Augustine, Sermon 354A: Its Place in His Thought on Marriage and Sexuality," *Augustinian Studies* 32 (2002): 39–60.

[10]   *De gen. c. Manich.* I.19(30) and II.11(15), CSEL 91:97/9–98/14, 136/11–137/27.

they compose a balanced social unit, in which their wills are mutually complementary and their respective needs and inclinations do not compete.

The idea of a pre-sexual union of ruler and ruled appears again in the preamble to
the *De bono coniugali*. Here, Augustine remarks that children are "the fruit not of
the union [*coniunctio*] of male and female, but of sexual intercourse [*concubitus*],"
for even without sexual intercourse there would still have been "a certain friendly
and fraternal union [*amicalis quaedam et germana coniunctio*] of one ruling and the
other obeying."[11] Augustine's speculations about a pre-sexual relationship of ruler
and ruled seem to come to an end in Book IX of the *De Genesi ad litteram*, when he
inquires into the "help" for the sake of which God made Eve (Gen 2:18, 20).
A second man would have been a better companion, collaborator, or conversation
partner for Adam, Augustine argues. Indeed, the two men would have been united
as ruler and ruled, for the man made from Adam's side would have been naturally
subservient to him.[12] It is pointless to ameliorate this passage to satisfy modern
values, but Augustine does not say that men and women cannot collaborate or be
friends. Nor does he claim that the sole purpose of women is procreation. As human
beings (*homines*), women have the same purpose and destiny as men, namely, to
serve God and to achieve ultimate bliss. But Augustine assumes that male–male
partnerships, other things being equal, are likely to be superior to male–female
partnerships, and he reasons that procreation was the reason why Adam's helpmeet
was a female, and not another male. Nevertheless, he seems to have turned his
attention away from the possibility of a primordial asexual relationship at this point.

Elsewhere in the *De bono coniugali* and in later works, Augustine considers the
non-carnal, asexual relationship in marriage in another guise: not as the primordial
norm of an earthly Paradise, but as a practical, post-sexual possibility that arises
eventually within any marriage if the spouses live long enough. Because the chief
reason for sexual intercourse in this "time to refrain from embracing" is remedial,
Augustine reasons, spouses do well to abstain from sex as soon as their ardor has
cooled sufficiently for them to cope without the remedy. They will eventually reach
the point of abstinence naturally, but Augustine encourages them to anticipate this
development by abstaining voluntarily, before their deteriorating physiology renders
them incapable. There is more merit in voluntary than in involuntary abstinence,
and a mutual compact of abstinence is itself an excellent amicable partnership.
Once the partners have set aside coitus and the conjugal debt, their friendship will
flourish, for the affective bond between them will be stronger.

Augustine presents this possibility in the *De bono coniugali* as one of the features
that make marriage good. Immediately after the preamble, Augustine observes that
the compact (*confoederatio*) of marriage was commended in the New Testament

---

[11]   *De b. coniug.* 1(1), 187–88. I take it that *germana* here means "fraternal," although it could mean
       "true," "genuine." Compare *germanus amplexus* ("sisterly embrace") in Apuleius, *Golden Ass*
       5.13. (I am grateful to David Bright for this reference.)
[12]   *De Gen. ad litt.* IX.5, CSEL 28.1:273.

both by Jesus' condemnation of divorce (Matt 19:9 etc.) and by his presence at a wedding in Cana (John 2:2), where he performed the first of his miracles.[13] What is it, then, that makes marriage good? Marriage is valuable not only because of procreation, Augustine argues, but also because of the "natural partnership between the different sexes [*propter ipsam etiam naturalem in diverso sexu societatem*]." Otherwise, there would be no marriage between elderly spouses who can no longer beget children, especially if they had failed to beget children or if their children had died. In fact, the "order of charity" between husband and wife waxes even as their ardor wanes. The more virtuous they are, the sooner they will abstain from sexual intercourse by mutual consent, becoming abstinent through choice instead of through necessity:[14]

> One may justly ask why marriage is good, and it seems to me that this is not only because of the procreation of children but also because of the natural partnership between the different sexes, for otherwise one would not say that there is still a marriage between elderly [spouses], especially if they had lost their children or had not begotten any. But in fact, in a good albeit aged marriage, even if the ardor of youth between male and female has waned, the order of charity between husband and wife nevertheless waxes, for the better they are, the sooner they will begin to abstain from sexual intercourse; and not as happens later, when by necessity they are unable to achieve what they want to do, but because, before that has happened, they deserve praise for being unwilling to do what they would have been able to do.[15]

Augustine characterizes sexual ardor in this passage as a tie between *male and female*, and conjugal love as a tie between *husband and wife*. This is the same distinction as he will make later in the letter to Atticus, where he distinguishes between *concupiscentia carnis* and *concupiscentia nuptiarum*.[16] Sexual desire even within marriage is not a *conjugal* bond, for it attracts men and women indifferently to anyone of the desired gender.

As well as considering voluntary abstinence and the natural abstinence of age, Augustine considers the involuntary abstinence of an amorous spouse whose partner is absent or incapable of rendering the debt because of illness. Here, he takes issue with a double standard. Everyone accepted that a wife should not look for sex outside marriage if her husband was incapable, however passionate her needs might be, but it seemed acceptable and normal for a husband to do so. But men have no such license, Augustine argues, for the obligation (*vinculum*) applies as much to husbands as it does to wives.[17] As long as they have faith in Christ, husbands whose wives are unable to render the debt need not be "frightened by the burden of

---

[13] Augustine develops the same point in *In Iohannis evangelium tractatus* 9.2, CCL 36:91.
[14] *De b. coniug.* 3(3), 190–91.   [15] Ibid.
[16] *Epist.* 6*.5–6, BA 46B:130–32 (or CSEL 88:34–35).
[17] *De adult. coniug.* II.16(19), 18(20), CSEL 41:405–06, 407/7.

abstinence," for Christ will help them to carry the burden. God always gives us sufficient means to do what he demands – and God demands chastity.[18]

4.2 THE MARRIAGE OF MARY AND JOSEPH

To corroborate his counsel of conjugal abstinence, Augustine holds up the marriage of Mary and Joseph as ideal. "Why," Augustine asks rhetorically, "should spouses who *cease* having sexual intercourse by mutual agreement not remain husband and wife if Mary and Joseph, who never *began* to have sexual intercourse, were, nevertheless, husband and wife?"[19] This is an argument *a fortiori*. Augustine does not counsel couples to abstain as soon as they marry, as Mary and Joseph did, but only to do so in due course, when they are ready. The celibate marriage of Mary and Joseph is exemplary not as a model or norm for other couples, but as an ideal to which they should aspire.

The marriage of Mary and Joseph had become a focus of reflection because of its complicated role as a token in debates about the respective merits of marriage and celibacy. Extending the argument, Augustine considered the marriage of Mary and Joseph to be exemplary for spouses who agreed to abstain later in their marriage, having previously been sexually active. The relationship between active sexuality and abstinence in marriage was analogous to the relationship between the vocations of marriage and of celibacy. Although both topics led Augustine to reflect inciden- tally on the formation of marriage and on the point at which a betrothed woman becomes a spouse (*coniux*), he was not preoccupied, as medieval canonists and theologians will be, with questions about the point at which a marriage became irrevocable, or about the impediment of prior marriage.

Mary's marriage came to the fore chiefly in the controversy surrounding the Roman theologian Helvidius, who wrote a treatise in which he argued that virgins and married women had equal merit before God. Most of the little that we know about him we owe to Jerome's *Adversus Helvidium* (c. 383). Helvidius did not question the virgin birth of Jesus, but he argued that Mary must have known Joseph sexually *after* Jesus was born, begetting the brothers and sisters who are mentioned in the gospels (Matt 13:55, Mark 6:3).[20] Once Helvidius had raised the issue, those who defended the perpetual virginity of Mary were bound to say something about her marriage. Some assumed that spouses were not truly married until they had come together sexually but saved Mary's virginity by maintaining that she was never truly Joseph's wife. Others saved Mary's virginity by arguing that spouses were married even without sexual intercourse.

---

[18] Ibid., 407/12–14.   [19] *De nupt. et conc.* I.12(13), CSEL 42:226/18–20. Emphasis mine.
[20] D. G. Hunter, "Helvidius, Jovinian, and the Virginity of Mary in Late Fourth-Century Rome," *Journal of Early Christian Studies* 1 (1993): 47–71.

Jerome took the first course in his treatise against Helvidius, arguing that Mary remained Joseph's betrothed (*desponsata*) and was never truly his wife. The disagreement turned on the meaning of Matthew 1:18: "Mary was betrothed to Jesus, before they came together." Does the phrase "before they came together" imply that they eventually came together (i.e., had sexual intercourse)? Helvidius argued that it did. Jerome rejected that argument on idiomatic grounds. One can prevent something from happening by acting *before* it happens. Moreover, Jerome points out, the term *coniux* is equivocal even in Scripture. Mary is called Joseph's spouse (*coniux*) in Matthew 1:20 and 1:24 in a merely conventional sense, he argues, inasmuch as she *seemed* to his wife.[21]

Ambrose, reacting against Jerome, took the second course. In a homily that he composed for the consecration of a virgin around 390, Ambrose argues that Mary was always a virgin and yet deserved to be called Joseph's wife. Mary is called a spouse (*coniux*) in Matthew 1:24 because a woman "receives the name of wife" when she is betrothed (*desponsata*) to a man. Likewise, a marriage (*coniugium*) is so called as soon as it is begun (*initiatur*), for "it is not the deflowering of virginity that makes marriage, but the conjugal pact."[22] Ambrose does not quite say that Mary was *really* Joseph's wife, but only that she deserved to be *called* Joseph's wife and that they had already realized the very foundation of marriage: the "conjugal pact."

Augustine adopted Ambrose's solution but took it a little further. In his view, the marriage of Mary and Joseph was exemplary in every respect and must have been a true marriage in the fullest sense. Augustine also argues, citing biblical evidence, that Joseph was truly Jesus' father by virtue of his marriage to Jesus' mother, and that their marriage realized all three of the conjugal goods: Jesus was their offspring; there was faith because there was no adultery; and there was sacrament because they did not divorce.[23] Mary was not only *called* Joseph's wife, therefore. She really was his wife. Otherwise, Augustine argues, the angel would have lied when he called her Joseph's wife (*coniux*). Augustine introduces this argument when he extols the virtues of marital abstinence, which strengthen the "conjugal bond":

> When persons agree by mutual consent to abstain permanently from the use of carnal concupiscence, let it not be supposed that the conjugal bond [*vinculum coniugale*] between them is broken. On the contrary, it will be firmer insofar as they have entered into pacts between themselves that must be observed more lovingly and more harmoniously — not with the pleasurable ties of bodies, but with the willing affections of minds. For the angel did not speak falsely to Joseph when he said, "fear not to receive Mary as your wife [*coniux*: Matt 1:20]," for she was called

---

[21] Jerome, *Adversus Helvidium* 3–4, PL 23:194–95. Idem, *Comm. in Mattheum* 1:16, CCL 77:9.

[22] Ambrose, *De institutione virginis* 6(41), PL 16:316B–C: "Cum enim initiatur conjugium, tunc conjugii nomen adsciscitur; non enim defloratio virginitatis facit conjugium, sed pactio coniugalis." Ambrose makes the same point in *Expositio in Lucam* II.5, CCL 14:33/84–86.

[23] *De nupt. et conc.* I.11(12–13), 224–25. Augustine is probably thinking of Matt 1:19: Joseph did not "put her away privily."

"wife" as soon as they were betrothed [*ex prima desponsationis fide*], although he had not known her nor was going to know her sexually. The title of "wife" did not perish or remain as a lie in this case, where there had not been nor was going to be any sexual intercourse.... Because of their faithful marriage, both deserved to be called the parents of Christ: not only his mother, but also his father as the husband of his mother. Both of these things [their marriage and parenthood] were of the mind, not of the flesh.[24]

The clause that includes the memorable if barely translatable phrase *ex prima desponsationis fide* was to become a crucial text in the central Middle Ages, although medieval scholars will cite Isidore of Seville's version of the dictum more often than Augustine's.[25]

When Augustine refers here to a "conjugal bond," he cannot have been thinking (if he was thinking clearly) of the bond that prevents remarriage even after a divorce, for that bond cannot be stronger or weaker; it can only exist or not exist. Nevertheless, the frangible partnership of psychological fact and the indissoluble bond of obligation are closely linked in his mind. This is evident when Augustine returns to the topic in his debate with Julian of Eclanum, using some of the same terminology. Julian argues that the gospels refer to Mary as Joseph's wife, Augustine reports, only because this was how people regarded her, for she *seemed* to be Joseph's wife. Similarly, Joseph took the *name* of husband as soon as they were betrothed (*ex desponsationis fide*), although they were not yet married. Augustine replies that although an evangelist might have spoken at the level of convention and appearances, an angel would hardly have done so.[26] Again, Julian claims that Mary and Joseph cannot have been married because there was no sexual intercourse (*concubitus*) between them. But if that premise were sound, Augustine argues, the cessation of sexual intercourse in marriage would amount to divorce, and elderly couples would have to struggle to keep having sex to save themselves from becoming unmarried. As well as the goods of faith and of offspring, therefore, marriage in the city of God has a third good, that of sacrament. It is by virtue of the *bonum sacramenti* that a man cannot divorce even a barren wife in order to remarry and have children, a choice would seem consistent with the good of offspring. Here, too, Augustine argues that Mary and Joseph exemplified all three goods.[27]

A little later in the same book, Augustine considers Julian's thesis that marriage is by definition "nothing more than bodily intercourse" (*corporum commixtio*). Augustine again argues that if that were so, spouses who are too old for sex, as well as those who, having no more hope of offspring, abstain from sex because it is shameful, would cease to be married. Augustine adds that Julian would have spoken "more

---

[24] *De nupt. et conc.* I.11(12), 224.
[25] *Etymologiarum sive originum* IX.7.9: "Coniuges autem verius appellantur a prima desponsationis fide, quamvis adhuc inter eos ignoretur coniugalis concubitus; sicut Maria Ioseph coniux vocatur, inter quos nec fuerat nec futura erat carnis ulla commixtio."
[26] *C. Iulianum* V.12(47–48), PL 44:810–11.   [27] Ibid., V.12(46), 810.

tolerably" if he had said that marriage must *begin* with sexual intercourse, for it is true that men take wives "for the sake of begetting children."[28]

Whenever he discusses the potential sublimity of marriage, Augustine construes marriage itself or the marriage bond as a frangible partnership, a matter of fact: as something that can be stronger or weaker, that might peter out, and that spouses are encouraged to foster. Augustine claims that this partnership survives and even thrives on a more sublime level in a post-sexual marriage. The partnership that he describes here cannot be the indissoluble bond, yet he assumes that it depends on the good of sacrament. Thus, Augustine says that abstinent spouses should "look after" the good of sacrament "harmoniously and chastely,"[29] and he argues that the sacrament is the *only* reason for the survival of a marriage when there is no hope of begetting children.[30] Contrariwise, he argues that spouses who try or intend to prevent procreation turn their relationship into a filthy sham that retains nothing of the reality (*veritas*) of marriage,[31] for they "take away from marriage what belongs to marriage."[32]

4.3 BONUM SACRAMENTI

Augustine's concept of the good of sacrament is clear as to its extension but elusive as to its intension. In other words, it is easy to grasp what feature of marriage Augustine denotes with the word *sacramentum*, but it is difficult to grasp what he means by calling it a *sacramentum*. Perhaps Augustine himself did not know exactly. The interpreter must remain open to allusions, associations, and rhetoric.

The term "sacrament" had several appropriate and helpfully suggestive connotations. It suggested holiness and significance, for, according to one definition, a sacrament was a sacred sign (*sacrum signum*).[33] It also suggested permanence, for the term had a range of uses in classical Latin pertaining to sureties, solemn oaths, and vows. It was chiefly for that reason that Christian authors before Augustine had used the term "sacrament" to refer to the mutual obligations that bind husband and wife.[34] It reminded Augustine of the enduring "sacrament of faith" (*sacramentum fidei*) that one received through baptism, to which he compared the bond of marriage. As well as suggesting an undefined penumbra of sanctity, the term identified something in marriage that pointed beyond marriage itself to what Augustine called "some greater reality." It is important to note that although the

[28] Ibid., V.16(62), 818.   [29] *De b. coniug.* 13(15), 207–08.
[30] *De nupt. et conc.* I.17(19), 231: "Sacramentum ... quod ... coniuges concorditer casteque custodiant."
[31] *De nupt. et conc.* I.15(17), 229; I.17(19), 231.   [32] *C. Faustum* XV.7, CSEL 25.1:429/26–430/8.
[33] *De civ. Dei* X.5, CCL 47:276–77.
[34] Lactantius, *Epitome* 61, CSEL 19:748. Ambrose, *De Abraham* I.4.25, CSEL 32.1:520. Augustine may sometimes be using the term in precisely this sense when he applies it to the indissoluble aspect of marriage. See E. Scalco, "*Sacramentum conniubii* et institution nuptiale," *Ephemerides Theologicae Lovanienses* 69 (1993): 27–47, at 38–39.

word *sacramentum* in Latin (like *mystērion* in Greek) was used to denote religious and initiatic rites, and although Augustine used the term in that sense to refer to pagan rites as well as to baptism and eucharist, he never called marriage a sacrament in a ritual or liturgical sense.[35]

4.3.1 *The bond itself*

Augustine himself distinguishes between the substance of the sacrament (*res sacramenti*) and the sacrament qua sacrament: the meaning or significance of the feature. Its substance is a twofold rule of permanence. This rule constitutes the peculiar "strength" that Christians attribute to marriage, for it is only in the city of God (i.e., in the church) that people fully observe this rule. Not only is the bond indissoluble as long as both spouses are alive, but it transcends the primary reasons for marriage. For example, a Christian man is not permitted divorce a barren wife to marry another, fertile one.

Augustine states the twofold rule of permanence in a variety of ways, and often incompletely or elliptically, but its content is not in doubt. The following statement of the rule, from the *De bono coniugali*, is a gloss on Matthew 5:32:

> The compact [*foedus*] of marriage, once entered into [*initum*], is the substance [*res*] of a certain sacrament to such an extent that even such separation [on grounds of adultery] does not make it void, for if she marries another while her husband is still alive, she commits adultery, and the one who left her is the cause of that evil.[36]

Once they have married, the spouses remain married to each other in some sense until one of them dies. Being married entails the lifelong mutual obligations of the married life, such as observance of the conjugal debt – *except* in the case of adultery.[37] Even if there is a divorce or separation, and even if the divorce is valid (as it would be on grounds of adultery), any remarriage as long as both spouses are alive is adulterous and invalid.

Considered in relation to this rule of permanence, marriage is not so much a frangible relationship as a binding obligation. That is why Augustine characterizes marriage in this context as a compact (*foedus, confoederatio*) and as something "entered into" (*initum*).[38] It is more than an obligation of mutual service, for the

---

[35] É. Schmitt, *Le mariage chrétien dans l'oeuvre de saint Augustin* (Paris, 1983), 218–19.

[36] *De b. coniug.* 6(7), 196. Augustine uses the term *res* with the same sense in *De nupt. et conc.* I.10 (11), 222/24.

[37] The wronged spouse is permitted but is not obliged to divorce the adulterous spouse, according to Augustine, except perhaps in the case of continued adultery by a non-repentant spouse. See B. Alves Pereira, *La doctrine du mariage selon saint Augustin* (Paris, 1930), 140; and Augustine, *Retr.* I.19.6, CCL 57:59/94–99.

[38] For example, *De b. coniug.* 6(7), 196/7 (note *foedus* on line 6); ibid., 15(17), 209/17. See also ibid., 3(3), 190/12 (*confoederatio*); ibid., 7(7), 197/13 (*confoederatio nuptialis*); ibid., 7(6), 196/6 (*foedus*); *De nupt. et conc.* I.10(11), 223/22–23 (*uinculum foederis*).

partners remain bound to each other in some sense even after a valid separation, when there is no longer any partnership between them, nor any obligation of service such as the conjugal debt. Whatever prevents remarriage after a valid divorce cannot be their exclusive gift of self to each other. He assumes that the twofold rule of permanence follows necessarily from Jesus' condemnation of divorce and remarriage in the synoptic gospels, and he makes no attempt to prove that it exists *a priori*. Nevertheless, he reflects on the rule and tries to explain it. He tries to characterize *how* marriage endures, or *what* endures after a divorce. And he speculates as to *why* marriage has this distinctive "strength" in the church. Conceding that this residual aspect of permanence is difficult to understand or to explain, Augustine approaches it by means of analogy.

Augustine's fullest explanations of the good of sacrament are in two parallel passages, respectively in the *De bono coniugali* and the *De nuptiis et concupiscentia*. The two passages complement each other. In both passages, Augustine compares marriage under three different jurisdictions: divine law, the Mosaic law, and civil law. Augustine assumes that remarriage after divorce is prohibited in the church, which follows the law of the Gospel (i.e., Jesus' prohibition of divorce). The Mosaic law of divorce is the focus of Jesus' treatment of the divorce in the synoptic gospels, to which Augustine alludes.

In the *De bono coniugali*, Augustine asks why the bond (*vinculum*) in marriage is so strong that a man cannot divorce an infertile wife to marry a fertile one. He answers that God must have made "a certain sacrament of some greater reality [*res*]" out of "the weak, mortal condition of human beings." As a result, the bond or nuptial compact (*confoederatio*) remains intact when spouses try to dissolve it, "yet to their punishment, inasmuch as when divorce does occur ... they remain husband and wife [*coniuges*] even after their separation, and they commit adultery with anyone to whom they are joined after divorce, whether it be she with another man or he with another woman." Yet this law is observed only "in the city of our God, in his holy mountain" (Ps 47:2). The laws of the Gentiles (i.e., Roman civil law) are such that when a divorce has taken place, "without any liability to human punishment [*sine reatu aliquo ultionis humanae*], the woman marries whomever she wishes, and the man takes whatever wife he wishes." Likewise, Moses allowed men to divorce their wives and remarry after issuing a bill of divorce (Deut 24:1), albeit only as concession to their "hardness of heart," as Jesus explains (Matt 19:8, Mark 10:4–5).[39]

In the second passage, from the *De nuptiis et concupiscentia*, Augustine describes the sacrament as the greatest of the three goods, transcending procreation and fidelity. The twofold rule of permanence is the substance (*res*) of a certain sacrament, to which Paul referred when he said, "Husbands, love your wives, as Christ also loved the church" (Eph 5:25). Having posited this analogy of love between

39 *De b. coniug.* 7–8(7), 197.

marriage and Christ's union with the church, Augustine applies it to the permanence of marriage. On one side, the living Christ is united perpetually with the living
church, and there will never be any divorce between them. On the other side,
husband and wife are united permanently in the church, for they are members of
Christ's body:

> There is such great observance of this sacrament in the city of our God, in his holy
> mountain [Ps 48:2] (that is, in the church of Christ) and among the faithful married
> persons (who undoubtedly are members of Christ), that although women marry and
> men take wives for the sake of procreating children, a man is not permitted to leave
> an infertile wife to take another who is fertile.[40]

A spouse who divorces and remarries commits adultery, albeit only by the "law of the
Gospel," and not "according to the law of this world [*lex huius saeculi*], where after a
divorce [*repudio*] without offense [*sine crimine*] one is permitted to be joined in
marriage with another." Likewise, Moses permitted men to divorce their wives, but
only because of their hardness of heart (Matt 19:8, Mark 10:4–5). According to the
law of the Gospel, on the contrary, once the "the rights of marriage [*iura nuptiarum*]
have been entered into [*inita*], they remain between husband and wife as long as
they live." Remarriage after divorce, therefore, is adultery. A man who divorces and
remarries is more married to the divorced spouse than to the second woman, and
that can only be because "something conjugal [*quiddam coniugale*] remains
between them as long as they live, which neither separation nor union with another
can to take away."[41]

In the second of these two passages, from the *De nuptiis et concupiscentia*,
Augustine says that under Gentile law spouses may remarry after divorce "without
crime" (*sine crimine*). The phrase is ambiguous. Augustine may be referring to the
absence of any required grounds for divorce (i.e., to what we should call a "no fault"
divorce),[42] but the parallel phrase in the *De bono coniugali* – *sine reatu aliquo
ultionis ultionis humanae* – apparently refers to the consequences and not to the
grounds of divorce and remarriage. There is no human *ultio* ("guilt" or "retribu-
tion") for divorce and remarriage under the *ius civile* of Rome.[43] Augustine seems to
be using the phrase *sine crimine* in this second sense, too, in his commentary on the
Sermon on the Mount, where he says that a husband "may dismiss his wife [on
grounds of adultery], and a wife her husband, *sine crimine*."[44] If we read the passage

---

[40] *De nupt. et conc.* I.10(11), 223/3–9.   [41] Ibid., 222–23.
[42] Ambrose uses the expression in this sense in *Expositio evangelii Lucae* VIII.5 and VIII.7, CCL
14:300.
[43] The term *reatus* originally denoted an accused person, or the offence, or the
charge itself, but as used in late and Christian Latin it denoted a wrongdoer's guilt in the sense
of liability to punishment (as distinct from *culpa*, which denotes guilt in the sense of responsibility for an evil).
[44] *De serm. Dom. in monte* I.46, CCL 35:52/1111–17. Augustine construes the term "fornication"
very broadly here, to include illicit sex of any sort.

from the *De nuptiis et concupiscentia* in the light of these parallels, it seems that *sine crimine* also refers there to the consequences, and not to the grounds, of divorce.

If that reasoning is sound, Augustine assumes in both passages that divorce with the right to remarry is freely available and is not penalized under Roman law. But that assumption presents the interpreter with a puzzle, for Constantine issued a law in AD 331 that determined the permissible grounds for unilateral divorce and set the penalties for invalid divorce. A woman was permitted to repudiate her husband only for homicide, preparing poisons, and tomb robbing, on penalty of forfeiture of her dowry and deportation to an island. A man was permitted to repudiate his wife only for adultery, preparing poisons, and procuring. Otherwise, he should not only return her dowry to her, as under classical law, but also remain celibate. If he did remarry, his ex-wife had the right to secure his second wife's dowry.[45] Augustine's remarks about the free availability of divorce and remarriage *sine crimine* under Roman law seem to be at odds with the regime that Constantine instituted.

The solution to the puzzle may lie in an obscure remark by Ambrosiaster, a contemporary of Augustine's, regarding an edict by the emperor Julian, who had tried to roll back the advances of Christianization and to reinstate traditional pagan norms. According to Ambrosiaster, women were unable to divorce their husbands prior to the edict, but they could do so freely after the edict.[46] The observation suggests that Julian revoked all or part of Constantine's divorce law.[47] If that is correct, divorce and remarriage may have been freely available during the period between Julian's edict and AD 421, when Honorius issued a revised version of Constantine's law.[48] Augustine completed the first book of the *De nuptiis et concupiscentia* two or three years before AD 421, during the more liberal period.

Augustine considers the twofold rule of permanence to be a distinguishing mark of the church. Indeed, he argues in the *De bono coniugali* that whereas all human beings from all races recognize that marriage is good because of the "purpose of begetting" (*causa generandi*) and because of the "faith of chastity" (*fides castitatis*), the people of God alone recognize a third good, the "sanctity of sacrament" (*sanctitas sacramenti*). Although marriages are always for the sake of begetting offspring, the sacrament precludes divorce and remarriage among Christians even if a marriage is infertile, and death alone dissolves the marriage bond.[49] Augustine argues in the same work that an informal alliance may be counted as marriage if the partners intend to raise children and to stay together until parted by death.[50]

---

[45] CTh 3.16.1. See J. Evans Grubbs, *Law and Family in Late Antiquity* (Oxford, 1995), 228–31. The law did not restrict access to divorce by mutual agreement.

[46] *Quaestiones veteris et novi testamenti*, 115, CSEL 50:322.

[47] R. S. Bagnall, "Church, State, and Divorce in Late Roman Egypt," in K.-L. Selig and R. Somerville (eds.), *Florilegium Columbianum* (1987), 41–61, at 42–43. H. J. Wolff, "Doctrinal Trends in Postclassical Roman Marriage Law," *Zeitschrift der Savigny-Stiftung für Rechtsgeschichte*, romanistiche Abteilung 67 (1950): 261–319, at 262.

[48] CTh 3.16.2.   [49] *De b. coniug.* 29(32), 226–27.   [50] Ibid., 5(5), 193.

This argument seems to imply that permanence belongs to marriage by nature, although Augustine probably has Christian partners in mind.

Augustine's approach to the peculiarity of the good of sacrament is less straight-forward in later works. In the *De nuptiis et concupiscentia*, he argues that even the goods of offspring and faith are raised to a higher level in the city of God. Infidel spouses may be faithful to each other and shun infidelity, and they may even have sex only "for the sake of begetting children," as their nuptial tablets suggest, but those are merely natural, carnal goods. Again, infidels may observe the virtue of faith in marriage, but they cannot enjoy "true conjugal chastity" because their minds are turned away from God. Only believers can be truly virtuous. Likewise, infidels are keen to procreate, but what Christians seek in marriage is not only the birth of children but also their rebirth as members of Christ.[51] Later in the treatise, August-ine exhorts Christian spouses to seek not only the birth of children but also their spiritual rebirth. Likewise, no man wants his wife to be unfaithful to him, for such faith is a natural, carnal good, but a Christian man should fear his spouse's adultery more for the *spouse's* sake than for his own, and he should hope to receive a future reward from Christ for his own fidelity. The sacrament, too, Augustine adds, should be observed harmoniously and chastely in the church.[52]

Augustine seems to imply that marriage is insoluble everywhere, perhaps by nature, but that Christians alone observe its insolubility, perhaps because they alone grasp its meaning. In the *De fide et operibus*, discussing the rules regarding people who had unwittingly and in good faith entered into adulterous marriages, Augustine says that the rules should be followed "especially [*maxime*] in the city of our God, in his holy mountain, that is, in the church," where people observe "not only a bond [*vinculum*] of marriage but also a sacrament."[53] In the *Contra Iulianum*, Augustine says that as well as the goods of faith and offspring, there is a third good, the sacrament, which prevents a man from divorcing an infertile wife. This good "ought to exist among married persons, especially [*maxime*] among those belonging to the people of God."[54]

How can partners who have separated still be married? What aspect of their marriage survives? In the *De bono coniugali*, Augustine says simply that divorce cannot break the bond (*vinculum*), or the compact (*foedus, confoederatio*).[55] But it is difficult to understand how the bond can be a mutual obligation if it survives even a valid divorce. His approach is subtler in *De nuptiis et concupiscentia*, where he calls the residual aspect of marriage "something conjugal" (*quiddam coniugale*), which survives even when the spouses, because of divorce and remarriage, are no longer bound by a compact (*vinculum foederis*).[56]

---

[51] *De nupt. et conc.* I.4(5), 215–16.   [52] Ibid., I.17(19), 231.

[53] *De fide et operibus* 7(10), CSEL 41:46/5–6.

[54] *C. Iulianum* V.12(46), PL 44:810. In both passages, Augustine mentions the story about Cato giving his wife to another man.

[55] *De b. coniug.* 6(7), 196; 7(7), 197.   [56] *De nupt. et conc.* I.10(11), 223.

To illumine this enduring but puzzling aspect of marriage, Augustine compares it to the enduring "sacraments" conferred in ordination and baptism. If a cleric is ordained to serve a new congregation, the "sacrament of ordination" will remain in him if the congregation does not materialize, or if the bishop removes him from office because of some fault.[57] Likewise, an apostate retains the "sacrament of faith" that he acquired in baptism.[58] In both cases, according to Augustine, the bond that should have been beneficial becomes a source of guilt and divine punishment, just as the bond that should have united husband and wife becomes the cause of adultery. The analysis of the enduring *sacramentum* in these passages is parallel to Augustine's analysis of baptism in his anti-Donatist works, where he distinguishes between the validity and the efficacy of the sacrament. A baptism conferred outside the true church is valid but ineffective, Augustine argues, since its efficacy depends on membership in the true church. Just so, the indelible brand (*character*) of a fugitive slave and the tattoo (*nota*) of a soldier who deserts will remain but mark him as worthy of punishment. Whereas medieval theologians will construe the mark ontologically, as an *ornatus* imprinted on the soul, Augustine construes it socially and legally, as a token of servitude.[59]

Augustine must assume that his readers concur with his understanding of baptism or ordination, for otherwise the analogies would have no point. The aim of the argument is to extend that understanding to marriage. Perhaps Augustine intends only to clarify what he means, but the rhetorical effect is to introduce the reader to a cultural ethos of faith: to "the way things are done" in the church, where the rules are unlike those of the secular world, for they surpass utility and reason.

4.3.2 *The law of divorce*

Considered in retrospect, Augustine's doctrine of the bond of marriage was decisive in the development of the western doctrine of indissolubility: a doctrine that distinguishes Roman Christianity not only from the other Religions of the Book but also from Eastern Orthodoxy. But it is very difficult indeed to determine what the doctrine meant in practical terms in Augustine's own day.

As Henri Crouzel has shown, Ambrosiaster was the only major patristic authority who explicitly held remarriage after divorce to be permissible.[60] According to Ambrosiaster, a man was permitted to divorce his wife for adultery and to remarry,

---

[57] *De b. coniug.* 29(32), 227.
[58] *De nupt. et conc.* I.10(11), 223. See also *De adult. coniug.* II.4(4), 386.
[59] See N. M. Haring, "St. Augustine's Use of the Word Character," *Mediaeval Studies* 14 (1952): 79–97, and B. M. Peper, "On the Mark: Augustine's Baptismal Analogy of the *nota militaris*," *Augustinian Studies* 38.2 (2007): 353–63. Augustine developed the model in arguing against the Donatists in *In Ioannis evangelium tractatus* 5 and 6 (CCL 36:40–67), preached AD 406–07.
[60] H. Crouzel, *L'Église primitive face au divorce du premier au cinquième siècle* (Paris, 1970). On Ambrosiaster, see 267–74.

whereas a wife could divorce her husband for adultery but could not remarry.[61] Otherwise, those councils and fathers stating a position on the topic during the patristic period accepted that divorce was permissible on grounds of adultery but denied that remarriage was permissible. What one is entitled to deduce from that evidence, though, is disputable. Such statements are few and far between, and there is no evidence of a widely established regime of categorical prohibition. If there was such a regime, would Ambrosiaster have departed from it almost in passing, without apology or defense?[62]

More important, what did the prohibition amount to during the early centuries? It is anachronistic to speak of church law before the fifth century at the earliest, and the validity of marriage was a civil matter. Bishops during the patristic era were not in a position to determine who was validly married, as they would be in the central Middle Ages. The scant evidence that we have regarding ecclesiastical policy during the patristic period suggests that remarried divorcees were reconciled with the church after a period of penance.[63] John Meyendorff explains that the Byzantine church until the ninth century upheld strict monogamy in principle, which excluded remarriage after the death of a spouse, but did not attempt to express that doctrine in legal terms. The contracting and dissolving of marriages was a civil matter, whereas the church approached marital problems "on the level of pastoral, sacramental, and penitential discipline." The remarriage of divorcees as well as of widowers in Byzantium, therefore, was not invalid, but it did require penance.[64]

Augustine's doctrine seems on its face to have been a departure from such norms. Augustine confidently stated that Christians did not remarry after divorce, and he maintained that someone who did remarry did not in fact marry but rather committed adultery. Since death alone dissolved the bond, there should have been no way to solve or to mitigate the sin as long as the sinners were *de facto* living in the new marriage. But was his position in fact different from that of the eastern authorities? Arguments *a silentio* are intrinsically weak, but if the western bishops of Augustine's day had excommunicated remarried divorcees from the church without the possibility (absent celibacy) of reconciliation, there would surely have been marginal communities of such outcasts as well as masses of correspondence on the issue, along the lines of the correspondence between Augustine and Pollentius. Instead, there is silence.

---

[61] *Comm. in 1 Cor* 7:11, CSEL 81.2:74–75.
[62] See the critique of P. Nautin, "Divorce et remariage dans la tradition de l'église latine," *Recherches de science religieuse* 62 (1974): 7–54. Nautin argues (p. 7) that the prohibition was a flexible *"principe moral"* rather than an *"article de code"* to be applied without exception.
[63] G. Cereti, "The Reconciliation of Remarried Divorcees according to Canon 8 of the Council of Nicea," in J. H. Provost and K. Walf (eds.), *Ius Sequitur Vitam* (Louvain, 1991), 193–207. Idem, *Divorzio, nuove nozze et penitenza nella Chiesa primitiva* (Bologna, 1977).
[64] J. Meyendorff, "Christian Marriage in Byzantium," *Dumbarton Oaks Papers* 44 (1990): 99–107, at 101–02. The Byzantine church extended indulgence to those marrying for the second and, with greater resistance, for the third time, but it did not permit a fourth marriage. The eastern resistance to the remarriage of widowers was in marked contrast to Augustine's position.

Caution, therefore, suggests that a nuanced account is needed. I propose the following as a working hypothesis: First, Augustine's claim that remarriage after even a valid divorce was prohibited in the church was widely accepted and uncontroversial in the west, albeit not quite settled to everyone's satisfaction. Nevertheless, those who contravened the prohibition were not usually excommunicated permanently from the church, without hope of reconciliation. Second, Augustine's theory of the insoluble *sacramentum* was an articulation of a rigorist position upheld by a certain faction of reform-minded bishops. Such rigorism would have found more fertile ground in North Africa than elsewhere: a Christian culture that was averse to compromise and had known Montanism's doctrine of strict monogamy, which prohibited the remarriage of widowers.[65] Third, although Augustine treated the existence of an insoluble bond as a premise to be accounted for and interpreted, and not as a conclusion to be defended, his arguments about the figurative, representative meaning of the bond and about its similarity to the enduring *sacramentum* of baptism and ordination were designed, perhaps unconsciously, to articulate and to buttress his rigorist position.

4.3.3 *The bond as sacrament*

The twofold rule or "strength" of marriage, according to Augustine, exists because marriage stands for something beyond itself: something that transcends any merely human matter. In the *De bono coniugali*, Augustine says that the marriage bond would not be so strong "were it not that a certain sacrament of some greater reality [*res*] had been taken from the weak, mortal condition of human beings."[66] Augustine does not say here what the "greater reality" is. Nor does he explain what relation is denoted by saying that one thing is a "sacrament of" the other. But his meaning becomes clear if one compares this passage to its parallel in the *De nuptiis et concupiscentia*, where Augustine, citing Ephesians 5:25, posits an analogy between Christ's marriage to the church (cf. Eph 5:32) and the marriage of individual couples within the church (cf. Eph 5:33).[67] The "greater reality" must be the union between Christ and the church. The idiom "sacrament of" denotes a relationship of signification, whereby marriage is a sacred sign of the greater union.[68] Augustine must have reasoned, then, that God made marriage indissoluble so that it would better signify the union between Christ and the church. The permanence of the former was a sign of permanence of the latter.

---

[65] C. Trevett, *Montanism* (Cambridge, 1996), 111–14.   [66] *De b. coniug.* 7(7), 197/9–11.
[67] *De nupt. et conc.* I.10(11), 222/19–223/3.
[68] Scalco, "*Sacramentum connubii*," 37–38, argues that the greater reality is not the "Christo-ecclesial marriage" but rather the "creation-institution of marriage" in Genesis. But Scalco focuses on the *De bono coniugali* and the *De sancta virginitate*, without taking account of the parallel passages in the *De nuptiis et concupiscentia*.

It was not Augustine but Isidore of Seville who made the figurative explanation of the *sacramentum* explicit. Explaining the three goods of marriage, Isidore says that marriage contains a sacrament inasmuch as it cannot be separated even for the sake of procreation.[69] This insoluble bond is called a sacrament because it analogous to and represents Christ's union with the church:

> There is said to be a sacrament between the spouses because, just as the church cannot be divided from Christ, nor can a wife from her husband. That which is in Christ and the church [Eph 5:32], therefore, is an inseparable sacrament of union in each and every husband and wife [Eph 5:33].[70]

4.4 MARRIAGE AS A SACRED SIGN

Augustine's implied notion that the insoluble bond in a marriage is a sacred sign is congruent with the few texts in which he treats marriage itself, rather than the bond within it, as a sacrament of Christ's union with the church. Thus, Augustine argues in the *De bono coniugali* that the polygyny of the Old Testament patriarchs was a sacrament (i.e., a sign or prefiguration) of the future gathering of many persons from all nations of the earth under one God and under Jesus Christ, whereas the monogamy of the New Covenant is a sacrament of the union of souls with God and Christ that will exist in the next life.[71] The emphasis on monogamy in the New Testament, as reflected in the rule that an elder of the church cannot have had more than one wife (1 Tim 3:2, Tit 1:6), is not so much a matter of morals, Augustine explains, as a reflection of "the sanctity of the sacrament."[72]

In other passages, Augustine construes the union between Christ and the church itself a sacrament. The marriage of any couple within the church, according to Augustine, is the great sacrament writ small. This interpretation depends on a careful reading of Ephesians 5:32–33. Having said that he is speaking of the "great sacrament ... in Christ and in the church" (v. 32), Paul adds: "Nevertheless, let every one of you in particular love his wife as himself" (v. 33). Augustine makes the good of sacrament describe itself as follows in the *De nuptiis et concupiscentia*:

> It was said about me before sin, "a man shall leave father and mother and shall cleave to his wife, and they shall be two in one flesh" [Gen 2:24], which the Apostle

---

[69] From *De nupt. et conc.* I.17(19), 231.
[70] Isidore, *De ecclesiasticis officiis* II.20.11, CCL 113:93/105–09: "Sacramentum autem ideo inter coniugatos dictum est quia, sicut non potest ecclesia diuidi a Christo, ita nec uxor a uiro. Quod ergo in Christo et in ecclesia, hoc in singulis quibusque uiris atque uxoribus coniunctionis inseparabile sacramentum est."
[71] *De b. coniug.* 18(21), 214.
[72] Ibid., 214–15. Augustine also argues that polygyny, unlike polyandry, is natural, and that it was socially opportune during the Old Testament period. Cf. Tertullian, *De exhortatione castitatis* 6.1, ed. Moreschini, SC 319:88, where Tertullian presupposes a figurative rationale for the transition from polygamous to monogamous regimes.

says is a great sacrament in Christ and in the church [Eph 5:32]. Therefore, what is great in Christ and in the church is very small in each and every husband and wife [cf. Eph 5:33] and yet is a sacrament of an inseparable union.[73]

Augustine alludes to the same idea in Book II when he says that Genesis 2:24, as well as prefiguring "the great sacrament of Christ and the church," is a statement about the nature of marriage itself.[74] Here, the genitive idiom "sacrament of" signifies identity or specification, and not the relation of sign to signified. The great sacrament (i.e., the mystery) of Christ and the church *is* Christ's union with the church, whereas the marriage of each Christian couple, or perhaps the marriage bond between them, is a little sacrament (i.e., a sacred sign) of that great sacrament: a sign of the mystery.

In some passages, instead of saying that the union between Christ and the church is *like* a marriage, Augustine construes it as if it were a marriage in its own right. The gospels are the *tabulae nuptiales* of this great marriage.[75] In his commentary on the Sermon on the Mount, inquiring into the manner in which spouses should "hate" marriage (Luke 14:26), Augustine explains that because marriage is one of the things that will pass away, one should not be overly attached to it (Gal 3:28, Col 3:11, Matt 22:30). In the world to come, Christians will all be so united with the one God that the possessive pronoun "my" will have no further use in their vocabulary. Then, Christians will truly be able to address God as *our* Father, the city of God as *our* mother, and each other as *our* brother or sister. Nevertheless, marriage will not have passed away, for, having been brought together in spiritual unity, all Christians will be married to one spouse, Jesus Christ. That is why Paul says, "I have betrothed you to one husband, that I may present you as a chaste virgin to Christ" (2 Cor 11:2).[76] Augustine argues in his treatise on celibacy that consecrated virgins have been truly "betrothed to one husband ... as a chaste virgin to Christ."[77] Commenting on the marriage at Cana in John's gospel, Augustine observes that by changing water into wine, Jesus did three things: he showed that God instituted marriage, he confirmed the goodness of "conjugal chastity," and he showed how marriage is sacramental and belongs to the new wine of the gospel. Indeed, even consecrated virgins participate in marriage, Augustine continues, for although they hold a higher degree of honor and sanctity in the church than married folk do, "they too belong to a marriage along with the whole Church: the marriage in which Christ is the bridegroom."[78]

To sum up: The distinctiveness of marriage in the "city of our God," according to Augustine, is apparent above all in the observance of the twofold rule of permanence, which he identified as the substance of the

---

[73] *De nupt. et conc.* I.21(23), 236. Isidore, in the passage quoted above, prunes this sentence so that it no longer posits a great sacrament between Christ and the church.

[74] Ibid., II.32(54), 311/8–9.

[75] D. G. Hunter, "Marrying and the *tabulae nuptiales* in Roman North Africa," THTH 95–113, at 110–11.

[76] *De serm. Dom. in monte* I.40–41, CCL 35:43–46.

[77] *De sancta virginitate* 2(2), CSEL 41:236.   [78] *In Ioh. evang. tract.* 9.2, CCL 36:91/14–23.

bonum sacramenti. This rule is a sacrament inasmuch it is a sign of a greater, eternal reality, namely, of the immortal union between Christ and the church. That too may be called a sacrament: not as a sign, but as the signified mystery. God has raised marriage to a higher level by making something enduring, significant, and self-transcending out of a merely human, contingent, and intrinsically transient relationship. Augustine cites Ephesians 5:25, and not Ephesians 5:32, to corroborate the analogy, and he does so on only one occasion.

Augustine refers to marriage as a sacrament in several respects, but not with reference to its saving, remedial benefits, which he attributes mainly to the *bonum fidei*. The connection between the sacramentality of marriage and its saving efficacy will not emerge until the thirteenth century. Nor did Augustine count marriage with eucharist and baptism among the ritual mysteries of the church.

PART II

Getting married

Betrothal, consent, and consummation

5

Betrothal and consent

Theologians and canonists of the central Middle Ages held that "consent makes marriage." The maxim, as they understood it, meant that the spouses' mutual consent to marry, and their consent alone, was the efficient cause of their enduring marriage. The maxim had originated in Roman law, but whereas the classical jurists were referring to an intention implicit in the process of marrying, medieval scholars were referring to an external act of consent, which was normally a verbal act: an expression of consent that could be witnessed and later identified as having happened in a certain place at a certain time. Moreover, whereas the Roman jurists were referring to parental as well as to spousal consent, the theologians and canonists of the central Middle Ages were referring only to the spouses' consent, which they considered to be constitutive of marriage. Since marriage itself, in their view, was essentially a union of wills or intentions (*unio animorum*), only the spouses' consent could form it. The "consensualism" of the classical Roman law of marriage was different from that of medieval canon law, therefore, notwithstanding similar terminologies.

The origins of the medieval consent doctrine were theological as well as legal. Theological considerations and controversies helped to shape it, and the doctrine of marriage as a sacrament in turn presupposed it. It is appropriate, therefore, to begin with a definitive statement of the doctrine by a pioneering scholastic theologian, Peter Lombard. Writing in the 1150s, the Lombard defined the consent that made marriage thus:

> The efficient cause of matrimony is consent: and not of just any sort, but expressed in words; and not with reference to the future, but with reference to the present. For if they consent in the future tense, saying: I shall take you as my husband, and I you as my wife, then this is not the consent that makes marriage. Again, if they should consent mentally without expressing themselves in words or with other unambiguous signs [*alia certa signa*], then such consent does not make marriage.[1]

---

[1] Peter Lombard, *Sent.* IV, 27.3.1 (422). The phrase *certa signa* is adapted from the *certa verba* of Roman law, which denotes a prescribed verbal formula.

Typically, according to the Lombard, the partners should say something like, "I take you as my wife," and "I take you as my husband." Nevertheless, although bishops, canonists, and theologians often recommended ideal ways to express consent, regional variation precluded the adoption of any single formula. What mattered, according to Peter Lombard, was not the words as such but their meaning.[2] The partners could even use non-verbal signs if they were deaf or mute or spoke in different languages, relying on custom and context to establish the sense and the tense of their signs, although the spoken word was the norm. Because these words were supposed to express interior consent, the act of agreement was invalid if it was coerced or fraudulent, but episcopal courts were capable of making such judgments only in the external forum. As long as the couple used appropriate words and there was no evidence that either partner had been coerced or tricked into consenting, they were presumed to be married even if they did not will or intend to marry in their hearts.[3]

The temporal reference of the expression was crucial. According to the Lombard, the partners became married only if they entered into a "conjugal pact about the present" (*pactio coniugalis de praesenti*), rather than into a "nuptial agreement about the future" (*nuptiale pactum de futuro*). The terms *desponsatio* and *sponsalia*, Peter Lombard noted, were used to denote pacts of both sorts, although the classical term *sponsalia* properly denoted a solemn nuptial agreement (*pactum nuptiale*), that is, a formal promise to marry in the future.[4] The schoolmen thought in Latin, in which the distinction was a simple matter of tense (e.g., *accipio* vs. *accipiam*). Some vernacular languages had to make do with cumbersome and ambiguous idioms to express futurity, such as the auxiliary verbs of English, but the temporal distinction still applied.

This distinction between *de futuro* and *de praesenti* betrothals was an innovation that emerged in the cathedral schools of the Île de France during the first quarter of the twelfth century. The central-medieval consent to marry, expressed in the present tense, had evolved from the early-medieval betrothal (*desponsatio*). Legal and theological exigencies required medieval churchmen to devise something new and even paradoxical: the present-tense betrothal. Canonists in the Bolognese tradition when the Lombard was writing, however, around the middle of the twelfth century, were still pursuing a different theory, with more emphasis on sexual consummation. The distinction of tense was the result of much discussion and debate, and much work remained to be done before scholars and prelates could reach a position that was universally acceptable. Moreover, the innovation was never fully congruent with how the laity thought about marrying. There are traces of the ambiguities and discrepancies in modern English usage. In classical and medieval

---

[2] Ibid., 28.4.2 (435): "Cum igitur sic conveniunt, ut dicat vir: *Accipio in meam coniugem*, et dicat mulier: *Accipio in meum virum*, his verbis vel aliis idem significantibus, exprimitur consensus...."

[3] Ibid., 27.3.1 (422–23).   [4] Ibid., 27.9.9 (430).

Latin, the term *sponsus/sponsa* denoted a person who was the subject of a promise to marry in the future (compare the modern French *promis/promise*). By extension, the term might denote the groom and bride before the conclusion of their wedding, or even until their marriage was consummated in sexual intercourse. A married man was not a *sponsus* but a *coniux*. Nevertheless, the modern English derivative "spouse" denotes an already married person, and medieval people persisted in referring to what we should call "wedding vows" as *sponsiones, sponsalia,* "spousals," and so forth.

Medieval notions of betrothal and marital consent can seem deceptively familiar today, for similar idioms sometimes disguise fundamental differences. Moreover, their historical development was complicated and resulted from interactions between custom and positive law. In this chapter and the next, therefore, I shall put these notions in a broader, less familiar perspective by tracing their origins to the remote past.

5.1 TRADITIONAL MARRIAGE

The ways in which people married in the pre-Christian cultures that were tributary to Christianity during the first millennium varied widely across different peoples and periods, and, we must presume, across social classes. Our knowledge of such norms and customs is fragmentary at best and restricted chiefly to laws regulating the propertied elites. Nevertheless, there are some prevalent and enduring themes and structures, which remain vaguely discernable even in the customs, imagery, and language of marriage in western cultures today. This pattern is at least sufficiently discernable to establish a provisional conceptual framework or social type for understanding variations and developments.

5.1.1 *The typical pattern*

The core relationship in marriage was a collaborative partnership in which a man and one or more women were joined or "yoked" together as a single social unit: not temporarily or for a fixed period, but in principle for life, although divorce and remarriage were not precluded. The begetting and raising of children seemed to be the most fundamental of marriage's many purposes, even *sine qua non* at some institutional level. It is with this core relationship in mind that the Roman jurist Modestinus, appealing to common sense rather than to civil jurisprudence, charac-terized marriage as "a partnership of an entire life,"[5] and that Ulpian attributed marriage and the begetting and rearing of children to a law that nature taught to all animals, and on which even irrational animals were experts.[6]

---

[5] *Dig.* 23.2.1: "Nuptiae sunt coniunctio maris et feminae et consortium omnis vitae, divini et humani iuris communicatio."

[6] *Inst.* 1.2 pr. (also *Dig.* 1.1.1.3): "Ius naturale est, quod natura omnia animalia docuit. nam ius istud non humani generis proprium est, sed omnium animalium, quae in caelo, quae in terra,

Nevertheless, unlike pair bonding among birds, the marriages of human beings were fraught with considerations of kin, power, and property, and they were regulated by customary and written laws. Traditional marriage was fundamentally asymmetrical. In marrying, a wife left her own family or kinsfolk to join her husband's, and any wealth that was due to her went with her into the marriage as a pre-inheritance. Such transactions among propertied families were typically the result of negotiations and confirmed with pledges. The woman was an object of the negotiations and agreements, not a party to them, and marriage altered her status more deeply than it did her husband's. Adultery, therefore, was an injury done to the husband by his wife and her lover. A husband's extra-marital sex might or might not be an object of opprobrium, according to the mores of a particular culture and class and the circumstances of the coitus, but it was not adultery and did not merit adultery's severe penalties.

A marriage was a contract-like agreement insofar as it entailed pledges or vows that established obligations between husband and wife. Pledges were confirmed in stereotypical verbal formulae (*verba solemnia*), or in the giving and receiving of wealth, or in signs and rituals. The husband paid a "price" (in Latin, a *pretium*) to the father or family of his bride or to the bride herself to solemnize the transaction. But marriage fell short of being a contract in the proper sense because the obligations remained implicit and conventional and were never specified in the agreement or made explicit anywhere else. One might posit the spouses' new status as the determinate object of the agreement, but in that case the object was the married estate, and it would be vacuous to designate being married as the object of the contract of marriage.

In order to manage the negotiations and transitions of marriage in an orderly way, people married gradually or in stages rather than all at once in a single event. What is variously known as "marriage by stages" or "processual marriage" was the norm everywhere, in the east as well as in the west, as it arguably still is today in most pre-industrial societies.[7] In the west, marrying was processual throughout the Middle Ages and well into the early-modern period, notwithstanding ecclesiastical innovations of the central Middle Ages that should have transformed it into a single, all-or-nothing event.[8] But processual marriage has existed in a wide spectrum of forms,

---

quae in mari nascuntur. hinc descendit maris atque feminae coniugatio, quam nos matrimonium appellamus, hinc liberorum procreatio et educatio: uidemus etenim cetera quoque animalia istius iuris peritia censeri."

7　S. Greengus, "Redefining 'Inchoate Marriage' in Old Babylonian Contexts," in T. Abusch (ed.), *Riches Hidden in Secret Places* (Winona Lake, Indiana, 2002), 123–39, at 123–24. J. Gaudemet, *Le mariage en occident* (Paris, 1987), 27–29, 185–86.

8　S. McSheffrey, "Place, Space, and Situation," *Speculum* 79 (2004): 960–90, at 960–69. A. Macfarlane, *Marriage and Love in England: Modes of Reproduction 1300–1840* (Oxford, 1986), 291–317. M. Korpiola, "An Act or a Process?" in L. I. Hansen, *Family, Marriage and Property Devolution in the Middle Ages* (Tromsø, 2000), 31–54.

ranging from strong to weak. In the strongest forms, a betrothal anticipates the agreement on which the marriage will be based and is itself a virtual marriage.

Betrothal was a result of extending a negotiated marriage into a graduated, stepwise process. There were practical reasons for concluding the initial negotiations in a firm agreement that occurred months or even a year or two before the partners came together as man and wife, sometimes even when the partners were still infants. The postponement provided time to make preparations, to test the terms of the agreement, to satisfy any conditions, and to undo the agreement with minimal disruption if the match failed. For the woman, this was an in-between, liminal phase as she embarked on her passage to membership of another family.[9] She was not yet required to fulfill the obligations of marriage – to bear his children, for example, or to satisfy his sexual needs – but she was already bound to her husband, and she was required to be faithful to him. Any other man who violated her, with or without her consent, committed adultery against her husband-to-be. A betrothal was more contract-like than a marriage, therefore, for it committed the partners to a definable obligation: to their forthcoming marriage, or to their living together as man and wife in due course. At the same time, the betrothal anticipated the bond of marriage, separating the initial contracting of a conjugal obligation from the spouses' cohabitation as man and wife, and establishing a conceptual distinction between the *de iure* good faith established by the agreement and the *de facto* reality of cohabitation, sexual intercourse, and procreation. No term in modern English adequately denotes the quasi-contractual bond that existed as a result of a strong betrothal, before the spouses came together as man and wife, but the archaic word "troth," from which "betrothal" is derived, captures the idea precisely.[10]

Once a couple had been joined in a strong betrothal, the parties were bound by their agreement, and there was no need for a second agreement or plighting of troth when the spouses finally came together. Nevertheless, there were good reasons to celebrate or solemnize their marriage in a wedding, and the solemnization might include further vows of confirmation. Their coming together was a public right of passage, especially for the woman, marking a change in status that was fraught with religious meaning. Although betrothals were not necessarily private, they were essentially interfamilial agreements. A fully public celebration was more appropriate at the time of the spouses' coming together, when the woman passed from her parental family to her husband's. Then the community at large could witness the

---

[9] A. van Gennep, *Rites of Passage* (Chicago, 1960), 10–11, distinguishes among three classes of rites: preliminal rites of separation, liminal rites of transition, and postliminal rites of incorporation. The rite of betrothal might be construed as preliminal or liminal, but being betrothed is a "period of transition" between the bride's separation from her own family or kin group and her incorporation into her husband's (ibid., 116–17).

[10] Defined in the *Oxford English Dictionary* (sense I.2) thus: "One's faith as pledged or plighted in a solemn agreement or undertaking; one's plighted word; the act of pledging one's faith, a promise, covenant. Chiefly in phr. *to plight one's troth*, to pledge one's faith; to make a solemn promise or engagement; *spec.* to engage oneself to marry."

transition, recognize its validity, accept the new couple into the fold, and reaffirm the institution of marriage.

In traditional marriage, then, the betrothal established a binding obligation to marry. The marriage was completed in the coming together of the spouses, which might be publicized through religious or secular ceremonies, and it satisfied the betrothal contract. Thus, the betrothal anticipated the agreement on which the marriage would be based. The betrothal was ideally between families, but the chief contractants were normally the suitor and the bride's father. The bride was rather an object of the agreement than a party to it.

5.1.2 *Old Semitic marriage*

The marriage laws of the Babylonians and ancient Israelites exemplify the pattern outlined earlier. Driver and Miles coined the term "inchoate marriage" to describe betrothal in Old Babylonian marriage law, and Judaic scholars have appropriated that term to describe traditional Jewish marriage.[11] Samuel Greengus identifies five distinct phases in the process of Old Babylonian marriage: deliberative, pre-nuptial, nuptial, connubial, and familial. The deliberative phase ended when the negotiations were complete and the husband-to-be sent bridewealth to his wife's family. If her family accepted the bridewealth, the couple was *ipso facto* betrothed and there was already an inchoate marriage. Thus began the pre-nuptial phase, in which the partners were already designated as husband and wife. The bride's father, who was now the husband's father-in-law, could terminate the agreement, but in that case he had to repay twice the bridewealth. The husband's family could prosecute as an adulterer any other man who had sexual relations with the betrothed woman. The nuptial phase began with the marriage ceremony, which involved bride-ale, a written status contract, and perhaps – although this remains controversial – *verba solemnia*, such as "You are my wife/husband." The connubial phase began when the woman left her father's home to live with her husband, but the parental dowry that she took with her was returnable until she bore her husband children. Once she became a mother, the marriage had entered its final, familial phase, for the dowry belonged to her children's inheritance.[12]

The typical Jewish betrothal, too, was an inchoate marriage that bound the spouses together and could be ended only by divorce or by the death of either partner.[13] In the Bible, betrothal began with negotiations between men, typically the

---

[11]   G. R. Driver and J. C. Miles, *The Babylonian Laws*, vol. 1 (Oxford, 1952), 248–50, 322–24.

[12]   Greengus, "Redefining Inchoate Marriage." See also R. Westbrook, *Old Babylonian Marriage Law* (Horn, 1988), 34–38, 48–53. Westbrook (ibid., 48–50), criticizes the argument for *verba solemnia* in S. Greengus, "The Old Babylonian Marriage Contract," *Journal of the American Oriental Society* 89 (1969): 505–32, but Greengus's thesis is widely accepted among Hebrew Bible scholars.

[13]   B. Drachman, "Betrothal," in *Jewish Encyclopedia*, vol. 3 (1903), 125–28.

suitor and his intended's father, although parents, other relatives, and friends might act as go-betweens (Gen 21:21, Gen 24, 38:6, Song 8:8, Judg 14:2–7). To confirm the agreement, the suitor gave his future father-in-law a *mōhar*, or bridewealth (Gen 24:53, Exod 22:16), perhaps to compensate her kinsfolk for the loss of a working family member. Jacob's laboring for his father-in-law served the same purpose (Gen 29:20, 27).[14] Once betrothed, the woman remained in her father's home until the preparations for her new life were complete, but she was legally bound to her husband. Sexual intercourse with another man was adultery, for which the penalty was death (Lev 20:10, Deut 22:22–24), The woman was forgiven if she resisted, however, and she was given the benefit of the doubt if she was violated in a place where there were no witnesses to hear her cries for help (Deut 22:25–27). A man who violated a virgin who was not already betrothed to another man had to pay the *mōhar* to her father for using her, and he had to marry her if her father was willing (Deut 22:28–29, Exod 22:16–17), but he did not deserve to be killed.

Michael Satlow argues that the characteristically strong betrothal of the ancient Israelites largely disappeared during the Second Temple period, when most Jews practiced a weaker betrothal akin to that of the surrounding Hellenistic cultures. Greek peoples, too, had formerly known a stronger institution, in which a formal betrothal (*engyē*) was completed in the handing over (*ekdosis*) of the woman to her husband, but the betrothal of Hellenistic Egypt was a weaker, semi-formal agreement with at most pecuniary force, and the wedding rather than the prospective betrothal was the occasion for making binding pledges. Satlow argues that the translators of the Septuagint failed to understand the archaic betrothal and conflated the *mōhar* with the parental dowry. Josephus and Philo, too, Satlow argues, were unfamiliar with betrothal as inchoate marriage, notwithstanding some appearances to the contrary.[15] A form of strong betrothal or inchoate marriage seems to have been reintroduced by the rabbis, who called it *quiddushin*. This new institution emerged during the second half of the first century AD and was well established by the middle of the second century.[16]

Matthew 1:18–19, Satlow claims, is an isolated contemporaneous witness to the practice of inchoate marriage among Jews during the second half of the first century AD. Matthew says that Mary was betrothed (*mnēsteutheisēs*) to Joseph, and that they had not yet "come together." Joseph, whom Matthew calls Mary's husband, is minded to divorce her as an adulteress when he finds that she is pregnant. Matthew's gospel was probably written for what Satlow calls a "Jewish-Christian audience"

---

[14] On the function of the *mōhar* and on labor or service as *mōhar*, see J. Goody's chapter on Jacob's Marriages in his *The Oriental, the Ancient and the Primitive* (Cambridge, 1990), 342–60.

[15] M. Satlow, *Jewish Marriage in Antiquity* (Princeton, 2001), 69–73. Satlow's thesis has been widely accepted, but D. M. Chapman, "Marriage and Family in Second Temple Judaism," in K. M. Campbell, *Marriage and Family in the Biblical World* (Downers Grove, 2003), 183–239, at 185–86, argues that Josephus envisaged a "change of status" in betrothal such that the woman was already a "familial relation" of her future husband.

[16] On the rabbinic *qiddushin*, see Satlow, 73–82.

during the second half of the first century, perhaps c. AD 85. Luke's gospel, on the contrary, was addressed to a gentile audience, and Luke does not say that Joseph was Mary's husband. Nor does he mention the possibility of Joseph's divorcing her (Luke 1:27–28). Satlow concludes that "at least some Jews in the first century, probably in the rural Galilee, were practicing a form of inchoate marriage."[17] Satlow's thesis has been widely accepted, although some of its details are questionable, and pinning so much on a unique witness is risky. While Matthew was certainly in conversation and conflict with what would soon emerge as the rabbinic tradition (the "Scribes and Pharisees"), we cannot be sure that his community were Jewish Christians. They may have been gentiles who followed the Torah. Moreover, the uniqueness of Matthew's account may make one question whether it was a witness to actual practice. William Loader suggests that it was rather a "result of archaising in story telling," whereby the infancy narratives were "framed and in part generated by biblical models."[18] That said, Matthew 1:18–19, for whatever reason, does presume that Mary and Joseph practiced inchoate marriage, and the text was an important witness for those Christian exegetes who held that Mary and Joseph were fully married even though their marriage was never consummated.

Jews during the early-Christian era usually celebrated the completion of inchoate marriage in a public wedding, although there is no indication in Scripture that Joseph and Mary's union was solemnized. Typical elements included the procession of the bride to her new home, the consummation of the marriage in a bridal chamber, and a period of feasting.[19] The rabbis were chiefly interested in the third of these ritual elements, which they invested with religious significance.[20]

5.2 BETROTHAL AND CONSENT IN ROMAN LAW

The outlines of traditional marriage are still discernable in Roman marriage practices during the period of classical law and jurisprudence, which corresponds roughly to the first two and a half centuries of the Christian era. The vocabulary of marriage presupposed an asymmetrical joining that was founded on an agreement between men. The woman's *paterfamilias* was said to give her in marriage (*in matrimonium dare, collocare*), and she alone, and not her husband, was said to enter into the marriage. Likewise, the verb *nubere*, which is usually translated "to marry," was said of her alone. Etymologically, it meant "to take the veil." Her husband was said to take or receive her and to possess her in marriage (*in matrimonium ducere, accipere,*

---

[17] Satlow, *Jewish Marriage*, 72. Satlow does not explain why the relevant setting was rural Galilee. Current New Testament scholarship favors Syrian Antioch (on the Orontes) as the most likely locale for the gospel: see D. C. Sim, *The Gospel of Matthew and Christian Judaism* (Edinburgh, 1998), 31–62.
[18] W. Loader, *Sexuality in the Jesus Tradition* (Grand Rapids, 2005), 49–50.
[19] Satlow, *Jewish Marriage*, 168–81.   [20] Ibid., 178.

habere).[21] Considerations of age in marriage were similarly asymmetrical. Whereas a son marrying for the first time was already considered an adult and was usually about a decade older than his bride, a daughter was still considered a child, for her marriage marked her transition from *virgo* to *matrona*.[22]

Romans considered the giving and reception of a bride to be a process rather than an event. The typical process, at least among the elite classes, began with the betrothal (*sponsalia*) and was concluded in the public "leading" (*deductio*) of the woman to her husband's home. From a legal point of view, however, the process and its customs were immaterial. All that mattered was consent, which did not need to be expressed in any plighting of troth. Rather, the required consent was implied in the nuptial process or in the attitude of the spouses to each other, and the betrothal was merely an informal promise to marry.

5.2.1 *The Roman betrothal*

The jurist Florentinus defined betrothal as "the announcement and mutual promise of a future marriage."[23] If the partners were still *alieni iuris*, the negotiated agreement was chiefly between their respective *patresfamilias*, although the suitor might also be involved. It was improper for the bride-to-be to take an active role in the negotiations or the agreement, especially if she was still a girl or was marrying for the first time, even when the law regarded her consent as a necessary condition.[24] To celebrate the agreement, the woman's *paterfamilias* gave a party in his home, with the *sponsus* as the guest of honor, and the word *sponsalia* denoted the party as well as the agreement.[25] Gifts between the partners, which were forbidden in marriage, were normal and customary, especially from the man to his betrothed. Men in classical Roman culture sometimes gave rings to their betrotheds, although use of the betrothal ring as a pledge and a symbol of union was more Christian than classical.[26] The process was completed in the *deductio in domum mariti*, also known

---

[21] S. Treggiari, *Roman Marriage* (Oxford, 1991); and "Consent to Roman Marriage: Some Aspects of Law and Reality," *Classical Views/Echos du monde classique*, n.s. 26 (1982): 34–44, at 35–37.

[22] M. Harlow and R. Laurence, "Betrothal, Mid-Late Childhood and the Life Course," in L. L. Lovén and A. Stömberg, *Ancient Marriage in Myth and Reality* (Newcastle-upon-Tyne, 2010), 56–77.

[23] *Dig.* 23.1.1: "Sponsalia sunt mentio et repromissio nuptiarum futurarum." The term *nuptiae* refers etymologically to a wedding, and by extension to the spouses' coming together, but it often denotes the state of marriage. Contrariwise, the word "marriage" in English primarily denotes the state but can also denote a wedding. On the Roman betrothal, see Treggiari, *Roman Marriage*, 125–55; C. Fayer. La familia romana. Aspetti giuridici ed antiquari, *Parte II:* Sponsalia, matrimonio, dote (Rome, 2005), 15–184; and K. H. Hersch, *The Roman Wedding* (Cambridge, 2010), 39–43.

[24] A. Watson, *The Law of Persons in the Later Roman Republic* (Oxford, 1967), 18.

[25] Treggiari, *Roman Marriage*, 147.

[26] L. Anné, *Les rites des fiançailles* (Paris, 1941), 5–62. Treggiari, *Roman Marriage*, 148–50. Pliny the Elder refers to an old custom of giving an iron ring, but Tertullian, *Apologeticum* 6.4 (CCL 1:97), mentions the gold betrothal ring (*anulus pronubus*) as an ancient custom. Because

as the *pompa*: a conspicuous nocturnal procession of the bride to her husband's home.[27] Whereas the betrothal was a transaction among men, women predominated at bridal processions and weddings, which marked the bride's passage from *virgo* to *matrona*.[28]

The Roman betrothal had formerly been a binding contract expressed through the exchange of *verba solemnia* between the bride's father and her suitor or whoever had power over him. Thus, Ulpian tells us that betrothals are called *sponsalia* (from the verb *spondere*, "to pledge") because people in former times used to "stipulate and pledge wives-to-be to each other."[29] There are examples of betrothal by verbal stipulation in the plays of Plautus (d. 184 BC) and Terrence (d. 159 BC).[30] A stipulation in this sense of the term was an elementary verbal contract made by question and answer,[31] and it was the oldest means in Roman tradition to establish a legal obligation. The typical formula was "*Spondes? Spondeo*" ("Do you pledge? I pledge"). Both parties had to be present to each other when they enunciated the formula. Stipulations could not be made between persons who were not present to each other (*inter absentes*), whether through intermediaries or in writing.[32] Nor could mutes or deaf persons stipulate.[33] The literal words were stereotypical and significant, but their semantic structure was more important. The same verb had to be used for both question and answer. The stipulated betrothal, therefore, was a contract between the woman's *paterfamilias* and either the suitor himself, if he was *sui iuris*, or his *paterfamilias*, if he was still *alieni iuris*. The latter asked the former whether he pledged his daughter ("*Spondes?*"), and the former pledged his daughter in marriage ("*Spondeo*"). A stipulation by its very nature established a unilateral obligation (only one side pledged), and there is no clear evidence that Romans made bilateral betrothals by mutual stipulation.[34] Because a formal betrothal made by stipulation satisfied the

---

Romans and Greeks commonly wore rings, the giving of rings in the classical betrothal did not necessarily have any special significance.

[27] Treggiari, *Roman Marriage*, 166–70. Fayer, *La familia romana* II, 500–62.

[28] Hersch, *Roman Wedding*, 10.

[29] Dig. 23.1.2 (Ulpian): "Sponsalia autem dicta sunt a spondendo: nam moris fuit veteribus stipulari et spondere sibi uxores futuras." On the archaic formal betrothal, see Treggiari, *Roman Marriage*, 138–45.

[30] E.g., Plautus, *Poenulus*, act 5, scene 3 (Loeb ed., vol. 4, 1980, p. 114/1156–57): "Spondesne, igitur? Spondeo." Treggiari, *Roman Marriage*, 138–45, quotes several examples.

[31] Gaius, *Instit.* 3.92–94. *Inst.* 3.15 pr. On the law of stipulations, see R. Zimmerman, *The Law of Obligations* (Oxford, 1996), 68–94; and Zimmerman, "*Stipulatio* (stipulation)," in *Oxford Classical Dictionary* (4th edition). Like the central-medieval betrothal, stipulations could be absolute, temporal (to be fulfilled by an agreed time or by the end of certain period), or conditional (to be fulfilled when a certain condition was met, such as a sum of money): see *Inst.* 3.15.2–6.

[32] Paulus, *Sent.* 5.7.2. The prohibition of intermediaries did not prevent representation by slaves: see CJ 8.37.14.1.

[33] Gaius, *Inst.* 3.105.   [34] See P. Corbett, *Roman Law of Marriage* (London, 1930), 8–13.

conditions of a binding contract, one must presume that it was actionable, although there is little direct evidence.

The need for *verba solemnia* in contracts waned and was eventually dispensed with entirely before the classical period.[35] Henceforth, any words could be used as long as both parties understood them in the same way.[36] What made an agreement binding or enforceable in classical law was not its verbal form but the consent of the parties. This premise gave rise to a new law of contracts.[37] Inasmuch as the bare consent of the parties sufficed, without any required form, there was nothing to prevent obligations from being contracted *inter absentes* through intermediaries or in writing.[38] When formal stipulations were still practiced, documentation replaced oral formulas, especially in late Roman law,[39] and the principle that stipulations *inter absentes* were invalid became a legal fiction. Justinian ruled that a written contract, even if arranged *inter absentes*, should be deemed valid unless the parties could be proved not to have been in the same city at all on the day of the agreement.[40]

The Roman jurists applied the principles and logic of consensual contracts to betrothals. Whereas people had formerly become betrothed by stipulation, bare consent (*nudus consensus*) sufficed under classical law. As a result, there was nothing to prevent a betrothal from taking place between absent persons, provided that they knew about the agreement or at least ratified it afterwards.[41] But the informal betrothal was not a legal contract. There was nothing to prevent a woman who was betrothed to one man from marrying another,[42] and the unilateral breach of a betrothal was no longer actionable by the first century BC.[43] The addition of a penalty clause against the separation of either a betrothal or a marriage was considered dishonorable (*inhonestum*) and invalid, on the grounds that marriage ought to be unfettered and a free from coercion.[44] Insofar as marriage was the product of

---

[35] CJ 8.37.10.   [36] *Inst.* 3.15.1.

[37] A. Watson, "The Evolution of Law: The Roman System of Contracts," *Law and History Review* 2 (1984): 1–20.

[38] Gaius, *Inst.* 3.136.

[39] See Zimmerman, *Law of Obligations*, 80–82. Although the chronology of this "degeneration" is disputed, Zimmerman argues that written contracts had superseded oral stipulations by the first century BC.

[40] CJ 8.37.14.2 (AD 531).   [41] *Dig.* 23.1.4 (Ulpian), 23.1.5 (Pomponius).

[42] CJ 5.1.1 (239 AD).

[43] Treggiari, *Roman Marriage*, 143–44. Treggiari speculates that the actionable *sponsio* and the informal betrothal probably coexisted for some time, until the former was abandoned or fell into disuse during the second century BC.

[44] *Dig.* 45.1.134 pr (Paul). CJ 8.38.2 (Alexander Severus, AD 223). Cf. X 4.1.29, a decretal of Gregory IX regarding a girl who was betrothed before her seventh year with a penalty clause stipulated in the betrothal. The other party was trying to "extort" the penalty when the marriage failed to materialize. Such stipulations are invalid, according to Gregory, "because marriages ought to be free." Despite canonical objections, though, such stipulations were apparently common in the Middle Ages: see M. Korpiola, *Between Betrothal and Bedding* (Leiden, 2009), 173 (with the literature cited there).

bare consent, betrothal was among its legally superfluous formalities. But the jurists did not consider even marriage itself to be a contract in any formal sense, for it entailed no binding, actionable bond or obligation.

Although there was nothing in law to make the betrothal binding, it did have some legal consequences, most of which presupposed that betrothal was equivalent to marriage in certain respects.[45] Betrothal sufficed to establish affinity, at least to the extent that a father could not marry his son's betrothed, nor a son his father's betrothed.[46] Being betrothed to two persons at once, like bigamy, carried the penalty of *infamia* (the loss of certain legal privileges).[47] And a man who killed his betrothed's father was guilty of parricide.[48] Septimius Severus and Caracalla ruled in a rescript that a man could prosecute his betrothed and her lover for adultery, since violating the expectation of marriage (*spes matrimonii*) was equivalent to violating a marriage.[49]

The Augustan marriage laws, too, treated betrothal as equivalent to marriage. Augustus, the first Roman emperor, issued laws in 18 BC and AD 9 to encourage legitimate marriage and procreation and to discourage marriage between certain classes of persons and adultery.[50] Persons were expected to be married by a certain age. Under the Papian laws of AD 9, men between the ages of twenty-five and sixty and women between the ages of twenty and fifty were expected to marry.[51] Celibacy (i.e., the state of not being married) entailed certain disadvantages. Contrariwise, marriage entailed certain advantages, especially for men.

The Julian law of 18 BC extended the privileges of marriage to betrothed persons, but men took advantage of that principle by becoming betrothed to very young girls, expecting an indefinitely long period of betrothal. The Papian laws of AD 9, therefore, limited the privilege to two years, and as a result men seeking the advantage would not betroth themselves to girls who were less than ten years old.[52] The Julian law also extended to betrothal the privilege whereby a husband could not be compelled to give evidence against his father-in-law and vice versa.[53]

---

[45] Corbett, *Roman Law of Marriage*, 16–17.   [46] *Dig.* 23.2.12.1–2 (Ulpian).

[47] *Dig.* 3.2.1, 3.2.13.1–2 (Ulpian).   [48] *Lex Pompeia de parricidiis* (55 or 52 BC), *Dig.* 48.9.3–4.

[49] *Dig.* 48.5.14.3. Ulpian applies the principle in *Dig.* 48.5.14.8.

[50] The legislation, which must be reconstructed from the work and the jurists and subsequent revisions and repeals, consists of *Lex Iulia de maritandis ordinibus* (18 BC), *Lex Iulia de adulteriis coercendis* (18 BC), and the *Lex Papia Poppaea* (AD 9). See Treggiari, *Roman Marriage*, 60–80; L. F. Raditsa, "Augustus' Legislation concerning Marriage, Procreation, Love Affairs, and Adultery," *Aufstieg und Niedergang der römischen Welt* 2.13 (1980): 278–339; and D. Nörr, "The Matrimonial Legislation of Augustus," *Irish Jurist* 16 (1981): 350–64. On the adultery laws, see D. Cohen, "The Augustan Law on Adultery," in D. I. Kertzer and R. P. Saller, *The Family in Italy* (New Haven, 1991), 109–26; and E. Cantarella, "Homicides of Honor," ibid., 229–44, at 229–34.

[51] Treggiari, *Roman Marriage*, 66. The ages under the Julian laws are unknown.

[52] Treggiari, *Roman Marriage*, 65. The precise nature of the limitation is disputed.

[53] *Dig.* 22.5.4–5 (Paulus, Gaius).

5.2.2 *The peculiarities of marriage in classical law*

Marriage as regulated in classical Roman law and interpreted in the work of the jurists was remarkably undifferentiated, both as regards the significance of particular actions or stages in the nuptial process and as regards the effect of marriage on the status of the spouses. The principle of bare consent and the weak, dispensable betrothal, discussed earlier, belong to a constellation of such peculiarities. Others pertain to purview, divorce, and power. The purview of law and jurisprudence did not extend to the union of marriage *per se*, which was not regarded as binding in any *de iure* sense. The law was interested in establishing whether or not there was a valid marriage in fact (*matrimonium iustum*), but only in view of its consequences.[54] The most important consequence was the legitimacy of the offspring of the union, which in turn determined which family members were subject to the husband's paternal power and what were their rights of inheritance. Among the more obscure consequences were those pertaining to the prohibition of gifts between spouses,[55] which generated a considerable body of jurisprudence, and to the *tempus lugendi* ("period of mourning"), during which a widow was not permitted to remarry.[56] Similarly, classical law had no interest in restricting divorce but only regulated its consequences. The legal freedom to divorce was presumably an extension of the principle of bare consent, inasmuch as the continuation of a marriage was contingent on the spouses' continued intent to remain married.[57]

Most remarkably, a woman's marriage in classical law did not entail her legal transference from her paternal family to her husband's. Instead, she remained under the power of her *paterfamilias* if she was still *alieni iuris*, or alternatively under the more limited power of a guardian (*tutor*). The principle of paternal power (*patria potestas*) was the foundation of Roman family law,[58] and the *paterfamilias* had extensive rights to control his offspring. Whatever wealth they possessed belonged primarily to him and was subject to his control. One would expect a woman's marriage, therefore, to have entailed her passing from one dominion to another. Formerly, it seems, that had happened as a matter of course. A law in the *Twelve Tables*, the earliest code of Roman law (351–349 BC), recognized that a wife would

---

[54] Corbett, *Roman Law of Marriage*, 112–21. [55] *Dig.* 24.1.1 (Ulpian).
[56] *Dig.* 3.2.11 (Ulpian). CJ 5.9.1–2 (380–381 AD). See Treggiari, *Roman Marriage*, 493–94. The purpose of the rule was to ascertain the paternity of any children.
[57] S. Treggiari, "Divorce Roman Style," in B. Rawson (ed.), *Marriage, Divorce, and Children in Ancient Rome* (Oxford, 1991), 31–46, at 33. It does not follow from the absence of legal constraint that divorce was without social or familial constraint or that it was unusually frequent. On attitudes and frequency, see Treggiari, "Divorce Roman Style" (cited earlier), and *Roman Marriage*, 471–82.
[58] Gaius, *Instit.* 1.55. J. F. Gardner, *Women in Roman Law and Society* (London, 1976), 5–11. Treggiari, *Roman Marriage*, 15–16. On paternal power and property, see J. Crook, "*Patria potestas*," *Classical Quarterly* n.s. 17.1 (1967): 113–22. For a sober reassessment of how much power a *paterfamilias* really had, see S. Thompson, "Was Ancient Rome a Dead Wives Society?" *Journal of Family History* 31.1 (2006): 2–27.

come under her husband's control – his *manus*, literally his "hand" – by *usus* (his *de facto* possession) after one year of marriage. The principle was akin to *usucapio*, whereby ownership was acquired through occupancy (*possessio*).[59] Under *manus*, a wife's legal status in relation to her husband was the same as that of his daughters.[60] If her husband was still *alieni iuris*,[61] she was subject to the power of his *paterfamilias*. But the *Twelve Tables* enabled her to avoid *manus* by staying away from her husband's home for a period of three nights (*trinoctium*) in the year, and she could repeat that ploy indefinitely. The existence of the rule implies that *manus* had formerly been an inevitable consequence of marriage, presumably as the final stage of the process, but that it had become separable from marriage, so that it was now possible for a married woman to remain under her father's power. Although *manus* presupposed marriage, therefore, marriage no longer required *manus*. From the rule about *usus* arose the option of being married without *manus* (*sine manu*).[62]

Modern authors often equate the acquisition of *manus* with marrying, but classical authors treat them as distinct institutions.[63] *Usus* was not a means by which a couple married, but a means by which their marriage acquired *manus*. There were two other means: *confarreatio* and *coemptio*. Four descriptions of the three methods are extant, but they all use the same language and present them in the same order – *usus, confarreatio, coemptio* – indicating that they were dependent on the same lost text: perhaps a law of the *Twelve Tables*.[64] *Confarreatio* was a religious ritual involving the sacrifice of a cake of spelt bread to Jupiter and prescribed verbal forms (*cum certis et sollemnibus verbis*) in the presence of ten witnesses,[65] and it seems to have been a wedding ceremony. *Coemptio*, a fictional sale of a woman (or perhaps of power over her), was based on the contract of *mancipatio*, whereby certain goods were transferred from one person's ownership (*dominium*) to another's.[66] *Coemptio*, too, may have been a means of marrying, but it was also practiced as a means for a husband to acquire *manus* over a woman to whom he was already married.[67]

The classical jurists spoke of *manus* in the past tense, as an archaic practice of former times. It seems that marriage could be either *cum manu* or *sine manu* during the third through second centuries BC, but that *matrimonium cum manu* was obsolete by the beginning of the Christian era. According to Gaius, the acquisition

---

[59] Treggiari, *Roman Marriage*, 18–19.
[60] Gaius, *Instit.* 1.111: "... in familiam viri transibat filiaeque locum optinebat."
[61] I.e., still subject to the paternal power of a *paterfamilias*.
[62] On the laws and history of *manus*, see H. F. Jolowicz and B. Nicholas, *Historical Introduction to Roman Law* (Cambridge, 1972), 114–17; S. Treggiari, Roman Marriage, 16–32; and S. E. Looper-Friedman, "The Decline of Manus-Marriage in Rome," *Tijdschrift voor Rechtsgeschiedenis* 55 (1987): 281–96.
[63] Jolowicz and Nicholas, *Historical Introduction*, 115 (with 115n6). Treggiari, *Roman Marriage*, 18n79, points out that the *trinoctium* prevented *manus*, not marriage.
[64] The fullest account is Gaius, *Instit.* 1.110–113. See A. Watson, "Usu, farre(o), coemptione," *Studia et Documenta Historiae et Iuris* 29 (1963): 337–38.
[65] Gaius, *Instit.* 1.112.   [66] Gaius, *Inst.* 1.113.
[67] Gardner, *Women in Roman Law and Society*, 12–13.

of *manus* through *usus* was abandoned partly through enacted law and partly through desuetude.[68] Since *usus* had applied automatically and by default, Gaius must have meant that the law was no longer observed or enforced.

5.2.3 Whose consent?

Marriage in the classical period required the consent of both spouses, as well as of their respective *patresfamilias* if they were still in power (*alieni iuris*).[69] The consent of the *patresfamilias* alone may formerly have sufficed for the marriage of sons and daughters who were in power, but there is no direct evidence to prove that.[70] Whatever was inconsistent with authentic consent in the nuptial process was in principle inconsistent with the contracting of a valid marriage. Such impediments included insanity, dissimulation (feigned or fraudulent consent), and coercion.[71]

The *Digest* says more about whose consent was required for betrothal than for marriage, presumably because betrothal had formerly been the chief occasion for expressing agreement. Nevertheless, because betrothal was a promise to marry, whatever conditions applied to marriage also applied to betrothal and *vice versa*.[72] Since the consent of a *filiafamilias* was necessary for marriage, therefore, her consent was also necessary for betrothal, even if she was not involved in the process.[73] By the same token, one may assume that most of what the jurists said about consent to a betrothal, other things being equal, was also true of marital consent. But parents often betrothed their children as infants, and what chiefly differentiated the consent to betrothal from the consent to marriage was the required minimum age. Girls could not marry until they were at least twelve years old. If a girl began to live in her husband's home before that age, her marriage was invalid until she was twelve.[74] There was no definition of the minimum marriageable age for boys in classical law, but the norm must have been fourteen, the conventional rule of thumb for puberty.[75] According to an opinion of Modestinus recorded in the *Digest*, however, no minimum age had been fixed for betrothal, and children could be betrothed at any age

---

[68] Gaius, *Inst.* 1.111.

[69] *Dig.* 23.2.2 (Paul): "Nuptiae consistere non possunt nisi consentiant omnes, id est qui coeunt quorumque in potestate sunt." See also *Tituli ex corpore Ulpiani* 5.2, with defines the conditions for a valid marriage as *conubium*, sexual capacity, "and that both should consent, if they are *sui iuris*, and their parents, too, if they are in power" ("et utrique consentiant, si sui iuris sunt, aut etiam parentes eorum, si in potestate sunt").

[70] S. Treggiari, "Consent to Roman Marriage," Classical Views/Echos du monde classique, n.s. 26 (1982): 34–44, at 35–39. On the fact that the consent even of a *filiafamilias* was required, see ibid., 37, 40.

[71] Insanity: *Dig.* 23.2.16.2 (Paul). Dissimulation: *Dig.* 23.2.30 (Gaius). Coercion: CJ 5.4.14 (Diocletian and Maximian, AD 284–305).

[72] *Dig.* 23.1.7.1 (Paul).   [73] *Dig.* 23.1.11 (Iulian).

[74] *Dig.* 23.2.4 (Pomponius). *Dig.* 48.5.14.8 (Ulpian). *Dig.* 23.1.9 (Ulpian). CJ 5.4.24 (Justinian).

[75] Gaius, *Instit.* 1.196. On marriageable age, see Corbett, *Roman Law of Marriage*, 51–52; and Treggiari, Roman Marriage, 39–43.

provided only that they understood what was being done, "that is, if they are not less than seven years old."[76] The last clause, which renders the opinion incoherent, was probably a later addition. It suggests that seven had become the conventional age for minimal discernment, presumably because there was no way to establish later whether an infant had known what was happening. Marriageable age was a function of sexual and procreative capability, and not only of the power of discretion,[77] but a child approaching or entering the second *septennium* would have a stronger capacity to consent or dissent than a seven-year-old. In practice, Romans, especially men, were usually considerably older than the legal minima when they married for the first time. Insofar as generalization is possible, women in classical Rome generally married in their middle to late teens, and men in their middle to late thirties.[78]

The various consents were not of equal force. The power of a *paterfamilias* was greater than that of his children in power, and a son had more liberty than a daughter. In principle, a father could not force his *filiusfamilias* to take a certain woman as his wife, but the son was deemed to have to have agreed if his *pater* made him marry a woman whom he would not have chosen otherwise.[79] Although the principle of paternal power gradually waned during late antiquity, the tension between that principle and the children's right of consent remained.[80] Again, whereas a betrothal was always invalid if a son-in-power dissented,[81] a daughter-in-power had permission (*licentia*) to dissent, according to Ulpian, only if her father chose someone who was unsuitable. The Augustan laws made it more difficult for fathers unreasonably to prevent their daughters from marrying.[82]

A *paterfamilias* had at one time enjoyed the power to dissolve the marriages of his children in power. Likewise, he had the right to dissolve the betrothal of his *filiafamilias*, although he lost that power if he emancipated her.[83] Nevertheless, laws enacted by Antoninus Pius (138–161) and Marcus Aurelius (161–180) prohibited *patresfamilias* from dissolving harmonious marriages of their children-in-power (*bene concordans matrimonium*) while permitting them to dissolve marriages when there was deemed to be good cause.[84] But marriage law was not inflexible.

---

[76] *Dig.* 23.1.17.

[77] A girl was supposed to be *viripotens* (capable of receiving a man): *Dig.* 24.1.65, 36.2.30; *Tituli ex corpore Ulpiani* 5.2. On the enduring conflation of the age of consent with puberty, see Vern L. Bullough, "Age of Consent: A Historical Overview," *Journal of Psychology and Human Sexuality* 16 (2006): 25–42.

[78] R. P. Saller, "Men's Age at Marriage and its Consequences in the Roman Family," *Classical Philology* 82 (1987): 21–34. R. P. Saller, *Patriarchy, Property and Death in the Roman Family* (Cambridge, 1994), 25–34. B. D. Shaw, "The Age of Roman Girls at Marriage: Some Reconsiderations," *Journal of Roman Studies* 77 (1987): 30–46. W. Scheidel, "Roman Funerary Commemoration and the Age at First Marriage," *Classical Philology* 102.4 (2007): 389–402.

[79] *Dig.* 23.2.21 (Terentius Clemens), 23.2.22 (Celsus).

[80] Treggiari, "Consent to Roman Marriage," 43–44.

[81] *Dig.* 23.1.13 (Paul).   [82] *Dig.* 23.2.19 (Marcian).   [83] *Dig.* 23.1.10 (Ulpian).

[84] Paulus, *Sent.* 5.6.15, referring to Antoninus Pius. CJ 5.17.5, referring to a law of Marcus Aurelius.

According to Paulus, although children-in-power could not marry without the consent of their *patresfamilias*, marriages contracted without such consent should not be dissolved because the public good trumped the will of individuals.[85]

5.2.4 *Bare consent*

Bare consent (*nudus consensus*) was sufficient to establish a betrothal, and marriage required the same consent as betrothal.[86] The principle of bare consent had two implications: first, that no formal or predetermined way of expressing or confirming consent was required; second, that the initial intention to marry and the continuing intention to be married had much the same legal force.

In any contracts made by consent alone, it did not matter what words were used or whether the contract was documented, although documents might make proof easier.[87] The same was true of marriage. Moreover, no ceremony or formal enunciation of consent was necessary. Rather, the consent of the parties was implicit in the process. In a routine, uncontested marriage, the consent of the relevant parties would have been assumed. Moreover, the absence of dissent sufficed as consent. Thus, a *filiafamilias* was presumed to have consented to her betrothal if she did not openly oppose the will of her *paterfamilias*.[88] Likewise, a *paterfamilias* was presumed to have consented to the betrothal of his *filiafamilias* unless he made his dissent manifest.[89]

Nevertheless, marriage, unlike betrothal, was more than an agreement. While minimizing the formal requirements for marriage, Roman jurists never lost sight of the elementary fact that marriage was the human equivalent of procreative pair bonding in other animals.[90] There was no marriage until the woman began to live in her husband's home, even if he was absent when she did so. If the receipt of a legacy was dependent on a woman's being married, according to Ulpian, she did not have to go to bed with her new husband to receive it. Rather, she was married as soon as she had been "led" to her husband's home, for "it is not intercourse but consent that makes marriage."[91] Again, although informal contracts could be made *inter absentes* through intermediaries or in writing,[92] and although the man did not need to be present at the conclusion of his marriage, Pomponius held that the woman had to be present so that she could be led into her husband's home.[93] An obscurely worded text in the *Digest* is based on an opinion of Ulpian's regarding a man who took a wife when he was absent but perished in the Tiber while returning

---

[85] Paulus, *Sent.* 2.19.2.   [86] *Dig.* 23.1.4 pr. (Ulpian). *Dig.* 23.1.7 pr. (Paulus).

[87] *Dig.* 20.1.4, 22.4.4 (Gaius).   [88] *Dig.* 23.1.12 (Ulpian).

[89] *Dig.* 23.1.7.1 (Paul citing Julian). Such situations presumably arose when the *paterfamilias* was absent for a long period, when other family members would have arranged the union.

[90] *Inst.* 1.2 pr. *Dig.* 1.1.1.3.

[91] *Dig.* 35.1.15: "nuptias enim non concubitus, sed consensus facit." The same maxim is quoted in *Dig.* 50.17.30.

[92] *Dig.* 23.1.4 (Ulpian).   [93] *Dig.* 23.2.5 (Pomponius). Paulus, *Sent.* 2.19.8.

from dinner. The woman was required to observe the period of mourning as his wife.[94] According to the usual and probably correct interpretation, she had entered his home in his absence and was waiting for him – an action that sufficed to realize the marriage. Some medieval scholars of Roman civil law deduced from these opinions that marriage was akin to a real contract, which had to be completed by the actual handing over (*traditio*) of the property,[95] but the jurists' opinions were based on commonsensical rules of thumb and are not evidence of an underlying contractual theory.

Documentation acquired greater significance in late Roman contractual law, and there was a corresponding tendency to regard documentation as a requirement for the recognition of a valid marriage, at least among certain classes of persons. Such documentation was readily available in the form of dowry contracts (*tabulae nuptiales*), which were customarily sealed or signed at Roman weddings.[96] But legal experts resisted this trend, holding that it was contrary to the principle of bare and unfettered consent.[97] Theodosius II determined in 428 that the absence of documented pre-nuptial gifts (which confirmed the betrothal), or of a dowry contract, or of such ceremonial practices as the procession (*pompa*) to the husband's home, did not call into the question the validity of the marriage or of its offspring. On the contrary, the spouses' consent and the testimony of their friends sufficed to establish that they were married, provided that they were of equally honorable status (*pares honestate*) and that there was no impediment.[98] Another western emperor, Majorian, effectively made marriage without a dowry (*sine dote*) invalid in a law of 548, presumably because dowries entailed documentation, but this law was soon repealed.[99] Subsequent legislation followed a complex course, but under Justinian the requirement of documentation to establish the validity of marriage was limited to *illustres* (men of the highest status).[100]

There was also a tendency in late Roman law to use documentation or ceremonies as proof of legitimacy when an upper-class man married a free but low-class woman. Because people would assume otherwise that the woman was not the man's wife but his concubine, the formalities would demonstrate that the marriage was legitimate. Theodosius's law of 428, summarized earlier, said that there was no need

---

[94] *Dig.* 23.2.6.

[95] C. Donahue, "The Case of the Man Who Fell into the Tiber," *American Journal of Legal History* 22.1 (1978): 1–53.

[96] J. Evans Grubbs, "Marrying and Its Documentation in Later Roman Law," in THTH 43–94, at 74–85.

[97] *Dig.* 39.5.31 (*Papinian*). Quintilian, *Institutio oratoria* 5.11.32.   [98] CTh 3.7.3 = CJ 5.4.22.

[99] Majorian, *Novel* 6.9.

[100] See J. Evans Grubbs, "Marrying and its Documentation in Later Roman law," in THTH 43–94, at 85–94; or Evans Grubbs, "Marriage Contracts in the Roman Empire," in L. Larsson Lovén and A. Strömberg, *Ancient Marriage in Myth and Reality* (Newcastle upon Tyne, 2010), 78–101 (a revised and abbreviated version of the previous paper); and J. Urbanik, "A Broken Marriage Promise and Justinian as a Lover of Chastity," *Journal of Juristic Papyrology* 41 (2011): 123–51.

for formalities when the marriage was between persons of equal status (*pares honest-ate*), implying that formalities might be necessary when the partners were unequal. But Justin I, predecessor and uncle of Justinian, repealed the laws that required, "albeit obscurely," marriages between persons of unequal status (*inter impares honestate*) to be contracted with dotal documents.[101]

The other implication of the principle of bare consent was a lack of any clear distinction between the initial intention to marry and the continuing intention to be married. To live together informally as man and wife, other things being equal, was to be man and wife. A rescript of the Emperor Probus to a certain man called Fortunatus (AD 276–282) clarifies this situation. If a man and a woman who are qualified to marry are living together as if they are married, intending to beget and raise children that the father recognizes as his own (*liberorum procreandorum causa*), and if their friends and neighbors witness the relationship, then their marriage and their children are *ipso facto* valid, even if there has been no nuptial procession (*deductio in domum*) and no written dowry contract (*tabulae nuptiales*).[102]

Whereas the word *consensus* usually denoted the initial agreement by which the marriage was contracted, the jurists called the continuing attitude or intention "marital intention" (*affectio maritalis*), without attempting to define it.[103] Once a marriage had been established through consensual cohabitation, it endured as long as the spouses regarded each other as man and wife, regardless of their circum-stances.[104] When Ulpian said, "it is not intercourse but consent that makes mar-riage,"[105] he was referring to the initial contracting of a marriage. When he said that a marriage endured even if the spouses lived apart, since "it is not coitus but marital affection that makes marriage," he was referring to an already existing relation-ship.[106] Nevertheless, there is no clear difference in nature or function between the two forms of agreement. Similarly, a marriage endures when a man's wife is deported as long as he regards her with a husbandly attitude (*mariti affectio*), and she him with wifely intention (*uxoris animus*).[107]

Other things being equal, marital affection was all that distinguished marriage from concubinage.[108] Such affection could arise during the relationship, but the principle of informality meant that there was no way to mark the moment of its onset. Justinian made two laws about the man who lived with a woman as his

---

[101] CJ 5.4.23.7 (Justin I, 520–523).   [102] CJ 5.4.9.   [103] Treggiari, *Roman Marriage*, 54–57.

[104] Cf. Gaius, *Instit.* 3.151 on the continuance of contractual partnerships: "Manet autem societas eo usque, donec in eodem sensu perseuerant; at cum aliquis renuntiauerit societati, societas soluitur."

[105] *Dig.* 35.1.15: "nuptias enim non concubitus, sed consensus facit." The same maxim occurs in *Dig.* 50.17.30.

[106] *Dig.* 24.1.32.13: "non enim coitus matrimonium facit, sed maritalis affectio." The point at issue was whether gifts between the spouses were still invalid. See *Dig.* 48.20.5.1 for a different application of the same reasoning.

[107] *Dig.* 48.20.5.1 (Ulpian).

[108] *Dig.* 39.5.31 pr. (Papinian). Paulus, *Sent.* 2.20.1: "Concubina igitur ab uxore solo dilectu separatur."

concubine but later, having grown fond of her, decided to make her his wife, drawing up a written contract (*nuptialia instrumenta*) to make the union official. As long as the woman was free and there was no impediment, Justinian ruled, the children born before the partners became formally married were as legitimate as those born afterward, since one must presume that the man had always regarded her with at least some degree of marital affection.[109]

5.2.5 *The law of betrothal in late antiquity*

Betrothals became actionable again under Constantine. Remnants of the new legislation survive in laws of the *Theodosian Code*,[110] which was the chief basis of Roman law in medieval Europe until the rediscovery of Justinian's corpus in the late eleventh century. Most of its laws were included in the influential *Breviary* that the Visigothic king Alaric compiled for his Roman subjects.[111] The *Breviary* included influential explanatory glosses, known as *interpretationes*.[112]

The new laws used betrothal gifts, which came to be known as *arrhae sponsaliciae*, as the basis of penalties for breach of promise.[113] Whereas substantial betrothal gifts formerly had only to be returned if the betrothal broke down, Constantine ruled in 319 that a *sponsus* or *sponsa* who broke off a betrothal, regardless of the reason, would forfeit any prenuptial gifts (*donationes ante nuptiales*) that he or she had given to the other. In other words, the recipient (usually the woman) could keep the gifts. Moreover, if the *sponsus* had given only part of what he had agreed to when he broke off the betrothal, he would have to produce the remainder.[114] The *interpretatio* of this law in the *Breviary* characterizes such gifts as the "betrothal wealth" (*sponsalitia largitas*) that a *sponsus* has agreed to give to his *sponsa* specifically (*specialiter*) for their future marriage. It adds that the law applies only if the *sponsus* has made the gift by means of a written and publicly registered deed, as well as with

---

[109] CJ 5.27.10. CJ 5.27.11 pr.

[110] J. Evans Grubbs, *Law and Family in Late Antiquity* (Oxford, 1995), 156–83. Evans Grubbs, "Marrying and Its Documentation," 65–70.

[111] The *Breviarium Alaricanum*, or *Lex Romana Visigothorum*, is the code or compilation of Roman laws that Alaric II (ruled 485–507) ordered to be drawn up in 506 for the Gallo-Roman subjects of his realm, the seat of which was then in Toulouse. On the relation between the *Theodosian Code* and the *Breviary*, see J. E. Matthews, *Laying Down the Law* (New Haven, 2000), 87–89, 101–18, 123–27.

[112] See J. E. Matthews, "Interpreting the *Interpretationes* of the *Breviarium*," in R. W. Mathisen, *Law, Society, and Authority in Late Antiquity* (Oxford, 2001), 11–32; and J. Gaudemet, *Le bréviaire d'Alaric et les Epitome* (Milan, 1965), 37–41. Because Mommsen used the *Breviary* to fill some of the gaps in CTh, some of the *interpretationes* found their way into his edition.

[113] Corbett, *Roman Law of Marriage*, 19–23. Anné, *Les rites des fiançailles*, 87–135. B. Cohen, "On the Theme of Betrothal in Jewish and Roman Law," *Proceedings of the American Academy for Jewish Research* 18 (1948–1949): 67–135, at 103–05. M. Di Ciano, *Le arrhae sponsaliciae in diritto romano e comparato*, doctoral dissertation, Ferrara, 2009.

[114] CTh 3.5.2 (= *Brev.* 3.5.2).

the consent of his parents if he is not yet legally independent.[115] This interpretation may reflect some other legislation by Constantine requiring that gifts (*donationes*) would not be legally valid unless they were written down and publicly registered.[116] A law that Constantius issued under Constantine's name, which is preserved in the *Theodosian Code* and in the *Breviary*, specifically applied that legislation to betrothal gifts.[117]

Constantine was probably the author of another law, now lost, that required a *sponsa* to pay a penalty of four times the betrothal gifts that she had received from her betrothed if she or her parents broke off the engagement.[118] (A *sponsus* in the same position had only to restore the gifts in full, but such gifts, from *sponsa* to *sponsus*, were less common.) The law has not survived, but we know about it through a surviving law promulgated by Theodosius I in AD 380, which attributed the fourfold penalty to an "old law" (*vetus constitutio*) and waived it when the *sponsa* was less than ten years old.[119] Since girls became legally marriageable at the age of twelve, this restriction must have been a consequence of the principle that betrothals should not last longer than two years. The penalty for breach of promise was later reduced to twice the *arrha sponsalicia*. In a complicated law of 472, the eastern emperor Leo made twenty-five years the critical age for a *sponsa* who broke the promise to marry her betrothed. If she was under that age, she had only to repay the *arrha*, regardless of whether she was a virgin or a widow, and regardless of whether she had received it directly or through someone else, such as a *tutor*. But if she had reached her twenty-fifth year and was *sui iuris*, she had to repay twice the *arrha*.[120]

At first, the terminology used to denote betrothal gifts in Roman law was fluid and inconsistent. A Theodosian law of 380 refers to betrothal gifts indifferently as *arrhae*, *sponsalia*, and *pignera*.[121] By the fifth century, a distinction had emerged between the *arrha* and the prenuptial gift (*donatio ante nuptias*).[122] Whereas the term *arrha* (with its cognates) denoted what the *sponsus* gave to the *sponsa* as a surety or pledge to confirm the betrothal, the term *donatio ante nuptias* denoted the increasingly important counter-dowry given by the husband, which, along with the woman's

---

[115] CTh 3.5.2, interp.

[116] CTh 8.12.1. Evans Grubbs, "Marrying and Its Documentation," 66–67.

[117] CTh 3.5.1 (= *Brev.* 3.5.1). Compare the echoes of CTh 3.5.1 *interp.* in the preamble to *Turon. app. 2*, in K. Zeumer, *Formulae Merowingici et Karolini Aevi*, MGH *Formulae* (Hanover, 1886), p. 163 (a Carolingian formula for a dotal charter).

[118] Evans Grubbs, *Law and the Family*, 162–66. Evans Grubbs, "Marrying and Its Documentation," 69.

[119] CTh 3.5.11 (= *Brev.* 3.5.6). CJ 5.1.3 is part of the same law.   [120] CJ 5.1.5.

[121] CTh 3.5.10–11. The two laws were apparently parts of a single constitution issued on the same day in 380. CTh 3.5.10 is lost and is not in the *Breviarium*, but it survives as CJ 5.1.3. CTh 3.5.11, which was not retained in CJ, = *Brev.* 3.5.6. CTh 3.5.10 rules that the recipient must return any betrothal gifts if the marriage is prevented by the death of either partner, and CTh 3.5.11 (mentioned earlier) cancels the fourfold penalty when the girl is betrothed before her tenth year.

[122] I.e., CTh. 3.5.10 (= CJ 5.1.3) and CTh 3.5.11.

parental dowry, was part of the marriage settlement.[123] The term *arrha* was Semitic in origin, and it came into Latin as a loan word from Greek,[124] although it is not clear that the betrothal gift as regulated in Roman law and practiced in the west was Greek in origin, as some scholars have maintained.[125]

What if one of the parties to a betrothal merely failed to fulfill it rather than renouncing it or marrying someone else? At what point did dilatoriness amount to a breach of faith? The Papian laws of AD 9 limited to two years the extension of the privileges of marriage to a betrothal.[126] That law was designed to prevent men from marrying very young girls in order to benefit from the privileges of marriage during a long betrothal, but as noted earlier Romans regarded two years as a typical or reasonable upper limit for the obligation. The betrothal of girls under ten and of boys under twelve, therefore, would not have been considered binding. Augustine was betrothed to a ten-year-old girl, and he recalls the sexual frustration that he suffered because he would have to wait two years before she was ready for marriage.[127] Gaius notes that there may be a valid reason for prolonging a betrothal beyond one or two years to three or four years or even longer, such as illness, criminal charges, the death of a parent, or a long journey.[128] Nevertheless, Constantine ruled that if a *sponsus* had not yet fulfilled his betrothal pact after two years, no "fraud" should be imputed to the *sponsa* if she married someone else rather than suffer the man to make a mockery of her nuptial vows any longer.[129] As well as saving her honor, the law must have obviated any penalties that she or her father would otherwise have incurred through breach of promise.

5.2.6 *Early-Christian betrothal*

Constantine's new legislation on betrothals was consistent with contemporaneous *mores* shared by pagans and Christians in the Roman Empire and in the early Middle Ages. People were inclined to disapprove of the breaking of betrothals and to reason that betrothal anticipated marriage. Whereas Anné held that the *arrha sponsalicia* and Constantine's defense of the betrothal were the result of Christian influence, Evans Grubbs concludes that "the evidence for either eastern or Christian influence on Constantine's betrothal legislation is circumstantial and … not very

---

[123] Evans Grubbs, "Marrying and Its Documentation," 68–69.
[124] From the Greek, *arrrabōn* ("earnest money"). There are several variant forms of the term in early-medieval Latin sources, including *arra, arrha, arrabo, arrhabo*, and writers often use the plural forms (e.g., *arrhae*) to denote the sum total of the gift (cf. *sponsalia*).
[125] Evans Grubbs, *Law and Family*, 174–82. Note that Constantine was still ruler only of the Western Empire when he passed the law about the return of prenuptial gifts in AD 319 (CTh 3.5.2).
[126] Treggiari, *Roman Marriage*, 65.
[127] Augustine, *Confessions* VI.13(23) and 15(25), CCL 27:89, 90.   [128] *Dig.* 23.1.17.
[129] CTh 3.5.4, = CJ 5.1.2. This law is not included in the Breviary.

convincing."[130] Evans Grubbs notes that "the evidence for Christian disapproval of breaking a betrothal is later and much less abundant" than the disapproval of divorce, and that "it also appears rather localized."[131] It remains true, nonetheless, that Constantine's legislation was congruent with contemporaneous Christian sentiments and practices and with the decisions of early councils regarding the firmness of the betrothal.[132]

Two examples of Christian betrothal practices are important here in view of their reception in the Middle Ages: the kiss (*osculum*) and the veil. Tertullian (c.160–c.225) mentions both of these betrothal rites as well as the joining of right hands (*dextrarum iunctio*) in a treatise on the veiling of women. Like St Paul in 1 Corinthians 11:4–5, Tertullian assumes that all women above the age of puberty wear the veil outdoors, and that wives are veiled in church. Should unmarried women, too, wear the veil in church and at prayer, and perhaps also in certain domestic settings? Tertullian assumes that women wear the veil out of shamefaced modesty, to cover their active sexuality. Taking that principle to its extreme, he argues that pubescent girls, too, should wear the veil because they are becoming sexually capable. As evidence of the same principle of anticipation, Tertullian remarks that even pagan wives are veiled when they are led (*ducuntur*) in marriage to their husbands, and that Christian women are even veiled at their betrothals, because the kiss and the joining of right hands figuratively anticipates sexual union.[133] Elsewhere in the treatise, he cites the maxim, "a betrothed woman is in some way a married woman."[134] In other words, she is already spoken for, or as good as married. Just as the betrothal anticipates marriage, so the betrothal kiss, according to Tertullian, anticipates sexual intercourse. It is striking that Tertullian considers the practice of the kiss and the veil at betrothals to be peculiarly Christian.

There is another reference to the betrothal kiss in a rescript that Constantine sent to the *vicarius* of Spain in 335. The letter concerns what happens to betrothal gifts if one of the partners dies before the marriage. In general, such gifts were returned to

---

[130] Evans Grubbs, *Law and Family*, 181. On the extent of Christian influence on the Christian emperors' laws on marriage and divorce, see Evans Grubbs, *Law and Family*, 253–60, and M. Kuefler, "The Marriage Revolution in Late Antiquity," *Journal of Family History* 32.4 (2007): 343–70. Evans Grubbs concludes (*Law and Family*, 317) that the case for decisive Christian influence on Constantine's legislation is convincing only for the repeal of the Augustan penalization of celibacy and childlessness (320) and for the new penalization of unilateral divorce (331). The argument regarding Constantine depends on the presence or absence of Christians among Constantine's advisors, but it is complicated by the fact that Christians appropriated certain pagan ethical principles, claiming them as their own. On the continuity between pagan, pre-Christian values and the values espoused by ascetics and theologians, see J. Evans Grubbs, "'Pagan' and 'Christian' Marriage: The State of the Question," *Journal of Early Christian Studies* 2.4 (1994): 361–412.

[131] *Law and Family*, 180.

[132] Evans Grubbs, "Marrying and Its Documentation," 72–74; *Law and Family*, 177–83.

[133] Tertullian, *De virginibus velandis* 11.4–5, CCL 2:1221. Tertullian is probably referring to a veil that covers only the head, and not the face.

[134] Ibid. 6.2, p. 1215: "desponsata enim quodammodo nupta [est]."

the donor or to the donor's family if the donor died. According to the new ruling, the
fate of betrothal gifts from the *sponsus* to the *sponsa* depends on the kiss. If it has not
yet taken place, the *sponsa* must return the entire gift. If the kiss has taken place
(*interveniente osculo*), half of what the *sponsus* has given is valid (i.e., the *sponsa* or
her family keeps it), whereas half is invalid and must be returned. If the *sponsa* has
given something to the *sponsus*, "which rarely occurs," she must return it in full
regardless of whether or not the kiss had taken place.[135] Although there is evidence
for the betrothal kiss only in Spain and North Africa, the ruling of 335 and the phrase
interveniente osculo had an odd influence on early-medieval Frankish dowry charters, where the term *osculum* came to denote the dotal charter, presumably because
it confirmed the betrothal.[136]

The betrothal seems to have been especially strong in Christian Spain. According
to an early Iberian council, the parents of a *sponsa* who fail to keep the agreement or
who break it without good cause are to be excommunicated for three years.[137] In
385, in the earliest surviving authentic decretal, Pope Siricius replied to several
questions that Himerius, Bishop of Tarragona, had written to Siricius's late predecessor, Pope Damasus. Siricius says in reply that he has considered Himerius's letter
at a meeting of his colleagues (*in conventu fratrum*), and he asks Himerius to share
his reply with the bishops of other regions. One of the questions concerned "conjugal veiling." Could a man marry a woman who was already betrothed (*desponsata*)
to someone else? Siricius forbids such a marriage, explaining that the faithful
consider the violation of the priestly blessing of a wife-to-be (*nuptura*) to be sacrilege.[138] The text is ambiguous, and there are problems with both plausible interpretations. Siricius either implies that a betrothal becomes irrevocable once a priest has
blessed it (the usual medieval interpretation), or he means that it would be sacrilege
to bless the marriage of a bride who is already betrothed to another man.[139] Either
way, Siricius considered the betrothal to be a sacred bond.

Inasmuch as Christian authorities prohibited remarriage after divorce and considered marriage to be insoluble, one would expect them to have determined exactly
when or at what point a marriage became irrevocable. In fact, there is no evidence of
any consistent policy anywhere during the patristic period. As we have seen (Section
4.2), Ambrose argued that a woman was called a wife (*coniux*) when she was

---

[135] CTh 3.5.6 (= CJ 5.3.16), = *Brev.* 3.5.5.
[136] See the references to *osculum* in the index to Zeumer, *Formulae*, 764.
[137] *Council of Elvira*, Canon 54, in C. J. Hefele and H. Leclerq, *Histoire des conciles* vol. 1.1 (Paris,
1907), 251. The Council of Elvira, in south-west Iberia, took place during the first decade of the
fourth century, but the precise date is disputed: see J. Streeter's appendix to chapter 2 on "The
Date of the Council of Elvira," in G. E. M. de Ste. Croix, *Christian Persecution, Martyrdom,
and Orthodoxy*, (Oxford, 2006), 99–104. M. Meigne, "Concile ou collection d'Elvire?" *Revue
d'histoire ecclésiastique* 70 (1975): 361–87, argues that only the first twenty-one canons came
from this council, and that the remainder were collected from other early Iberian councils.
[138] Siricius, *Epist. ad Himerium*, 4(5), PL 13:1136B (and PL 84:632B).
[139] K. Ritzer, *Le mariage dans les églises chrétiennes du Ier au XIe siècle* (Paris, 1960), 230–32.

betrothed, and that the union was called marriage when it was "begun," because "it is not the deflowering of virginity that makes marriage but the conjugal pact."[140] Augustine argued that Mary was truly called a wife (*coniux*) "as soon as she was betrothed [*a prima desponsationis fide*]," even though she had not experienced nor was going to experience sexual intercourse.[141] Following Augustine, Isidore of Seville said that spouses (*coniuges*) "are more truly so called as soon as they are betrothed [*a prima desponsationis fide*], even though they have not known sexual intercourse."[142] The opinions of Ambrose and Augustine were interpretations of Matthew 1:18–19, where Mary was said to have become pregnant while she was betrothed to Jesus, before they came together. Matthew evidently considers them to be married. But neither Ambrose nor Augustine was claiming, as Ivo of Chartres will do, that a betrothal was already insoluble, or that someone betrothed to one person could not validly marry another. Those were central-medieval and not patristic theses, although the scholars and churchmen proposing them cited the texts from Ambrose, Augustine, and Isidore to make their case. Ambrose and Augustine were responding to the controversy that Helvidius had stirred up about Mary's virginity. They intended to show that Mary and Joseph were truly and even ideally married, and they apparently had in mind and were keen to reject the notion that spouses were not truly married until their marriage was consummated in sexual intercourse. Their reasoning was not legalistic but ideological.

5.3 THE NUPTIAL PROCESS IN THE EARLY MIDDLE AGES

Our evidence of marriage during the early Middle Ages, like that of the patristic period, is disappointingly fragmentary. Moreover, it represents the results of a confluence of influences, and attempts to attribute features to one influence rather than another have been fraught with problems. Regional ethnicities were partly a product of the barbarian invasions and settlements, but the invading cultures were already Christian, and they had inherited, appropriated, and adapted features of Roman law. Thus, although the Germanic races brought with them distinctive legal traditions based on the avoidance of feuds through compensation for injuries, it is difficult to identify with any degree of security the distinctively Germanic traits of early-medieval marriage law. German scholars of the late nineteenth through the first half of the twentieth centuries were overly confident and essentialist in constructing supposedly universal structures of Germanic marriage law that were shared

---

[140] Ambrose, *De institutione virginis* 6(41), PL 16:316C.

[141] *De nupt. et conc.* I.11(12), CSEL 42, 224.

[142] *Etym.* IX.7.9: "Coniuges autem verius appellantur a prima desponsationis fide, quamvis adhuc inter eos ignoretur coniugalis concubitus; sicut Maria Ioseph coniux vocatur, inter quos nec fuerat nec futura erat carnis ulla commixtio." Because there is no obvious correlative of *verius* in the text, it might be interpreted as "very truly," or Isidore may mean that Mary was more truly married than women who experienced sexual intercourse, but if so the comparative is misplaced.

by all the Barbarian peoples.[143] The fashionable trend today is to trace early-medieval peculiarities of marriage to late Roman law and to indigenous contingencies and developments, although old essentialist analysis remains entrenched in historical scholarship.

The laws and customs of marriage during the early Middle Ages, or at least of formal marriages among the propertied elites, shared three general traits. These distinguished early-medieval marriage from marriage in central-medieval canon law and theology. Aside from the dowry, differences from classical Roman marriage law were not categorical but rather a matter of emphasis.

First, as in traditional marriage, the early-medieval betrothal was an interfamilial contract, and the bride was rather an object of it than a party to it, although betrothals were characterized as agreements between the partners as well as their parents and kinsfolk. Children could not marry against their parents' will. The negotiations preceding the betrothal were either between the parents on both sides or between the suitor and the woman's parents. In Lombard law, marriage involved the transference of a male power over womenfolk known in Latin as *mundium* ("hand"). The power passed from a woman's *munt*-holder – that is, her father or, if her father was deceased, her male guardians, such as her brothers – to her husband in return for bridewealth.[144] The Lombardic *mundium* is obviously akin to the old Roman *manus*, but the historical relationship between them is obscure. Whether Germanic peoples other than the Lombards observed a law of *mundium* in marriage is unclear and disputable,[145] but it is safe to say that marriage in Germanic law and custom was more akin to ancient Roman *matrimonium cum manu* than to classical *matrimonium sine manu*.[146]

Second, the early-medieval dowry (*dos*) was not wealth brought into the marriage by a wife from her family, as among the Romans, but wealth given to the wife by her husband. Scholars today often use the term "dower" to denote this gift, reserving the term "dowry" for the Roman-style parental dowry, although that convention has little basis in medieval usage or etymology. The parental dowry became prominent again during the eleventh century. The shifts between the two dotal regimes can be explained demographically and in terms of the competitive economics. Husbands paid a dowry for their wives as long as men outnumbered men on the marriage market,

---

[143] E.g., R. Köstler, "Raub-, Kauf- und Friedelehe bei den Germanen," *Zeitschrift der Savigny-Stiftung für Rechtsgeschichte*, germanistische Abteilung 63 (1943): 92–136; and H. Meyer, "Friedelehe und Mutterrecht," *Zeitschrift der Savigny-Stiftung für Rechtsgeschichte*, germanistiche Abteilung 47 (1927): 198–286. See the critiques of F. Mezger, "Did the Institution of Marriage by Purchase Exist in the Old Germanic Law?" *Speculum* 18.3 (1943): 369–71; Y. Hen, *Culture and Religion in Medieval Gaul* (Leiden, 1995), 123–25; and R. M. Karras, "The History of Marriage and the Myth of Friedelehe," *Early Medieval Europe* 14.2 (2006): 119–51.

[144] MWCh 93–99.   [145] Karras, "Myth of Friedelehe," 122–37.

[146] German scholars constructed the notion of *Friedelehe* after the model of Roman *matrimonium sine manu*. In fact, although Germanic marriages ranged widely from regularity to irregularity and from formality to informality, there is no solid evidence of *Friedelehe* as a recognized category in the Germanic laws.

whereas parents gave a dowry with their daughters whenever women outnumbered men.[147] The written dowry, too, confirmed the betrothal, but the *arrha* was the token betrothal pledge, and it usually took the form of a ring. The term *subarrhatio*, therefore, which originally denoted the gift of an *arrha*, came to denote a betrothal.[148]

Third, marrying was a process by which the parties fulfilled the betrothal. Nuptials or weddings were not occasions for the plighting of troth or for an exchange of vows. Nor did they need to be marked by religious ceremonies.[149] If a priest did officiate, his blessing may have been as likely to occur in the bedchamber as in a church.[150] Nevertheless, a nuptial rite of veiling and benediction was established in the Roman church by the late-fourth or early-fifth century, and the Carolingians adopted it, perhaps continuing a tradition that began during the Merovingian period.[151]

5.3.1 *Marrying in Visigothic culture*

Visigothic laws presupposed a threefold process: the suit (*petitio*), then the betrothal (*desponsatio*), and finally the wedding or marriage (*nuptiae*), when the partners finally came together as man and wife.[152] The betrothal was a witnessed agreement between the partners, their parents, and their kinsfolk. A girl beneath the age of twenty had little say in the matter and could not refuse a betrothal to which her father had agreed.[153] Ideally, the suitor marked the betrothal with a token gift,

---

[147] For a summary of the history and economics of dotation in the Middle Ages, see P. L. Reynolds, "Marrying and Its Documentation in Pre-modern Europe," THTH 1–42, at 30–37. On the *dos ex marito*, see A Lemaire, "La *dotatio* de l'épouse de l'époque mérovingienne au XIIIe siècle," *Revue historique de droit français et étranger*, 4th series, 8 (1929): 569–80. On the demographic explanation, see D. Herlihy, "The Medieval Marriage Market," in D. B. J. Randall, Medieval and Renaissance Studies, *no. 6: Proceedings of the Southeastern Institute of Medieval and Renaissance Studies*, Summer, 1974 (Durham, N.C., 1976), 3–21. Jack Goody's work shows that the hypothesis of a typical evolution from "brideprice" to dowry, which supposedly coincides with an improvement in the bride's status, is flawed and should be treated at best with caution, for dowries and bridewealth often coincide in complex systems. By the same token, the term "brideprice" should be avoided, since such money often passed sooner or later to the bride or her children. The *dos ex marito* of Germanic and early-medieval cultures belonged to the bride, even when it was called a *pretium*, and there is no strong evidence that it evolved from a primitive brideprice.

[148] See F. Brandileone, "Die *Subarrhatio cum anulo*," *Deutsche Zeitschrift für Kirchenrecht* 10 (1901): 311–40.

[149] For a summary history of the western nuptial liturgy, see Reynolds, "Marrying and Its Documentation," 15–29 (with the sources cited there).

[150] The evidence of the blessing of the bed or bedchamber is admittedly tenuous and circumstantial but, to my mind, it remains convincing. It derives much of its force from the expression or rubric *benedictio in thalamo*, but Hen, *Culture and Religion*, 133, argues that the term *thalamus* did not necessarily denote the bed or bedchamber and sometimes denoted marriage itself.

[151] Hen, *Culture and Religion*, 131–37 argues that the Merovingians practiced the nuptial mass, anticipating nuptial customs usually considered to be Carolingian innovations.

[152] P. D. King, *Law and Society in the Visigothic Kingdom* (Cambridge, 1972), 224–25.

[153] *Lex Visigothorum* III.1.2, MGH *Leges Nationum Germanicarum* (Leges I), vol. 1 (1902), 122–23. King, *Law and Society*, 229.

sometimes called an *arrha*, but a written agreement about the dowry, which the bride received from her betrothed, was the chief confirmation that the betrothal had taken place and the only written record of a marriage. King Ervig (r. 680–687) issued a law with the rubric, "Let there be no marriage without a dowry." Unless there is a written dowry, the law explains, there will no way later to establish that the partners entered into an honorable marriage. The wording shows that the object of this legislation was not so much the wealth as its written record.[154]

A law promulgated by King Chindasvind (r. 641–649) notes that people who have entered into a betrothal sometimes err by putting off the completion of the compact indefinitely. In future, once the partners themselves and their parents and kinsfolk have reached a betrothal agreement before witnesses and a ring has been given as an *arrha*, then, even if nothing has been recorded in writing, neither side can revoke the betrothal unilaterally. Instead, once the parties have agreed to a dowry that is in accordance with the law,[155] they should proceed without delay to the public celebration of their marriage (*festa celebritas*).[156] The rubric of the law –"That *arrha*s, having been given, should not be revoked" – suggests not only that the purpose of the *arrha* was to confirm the agreement, even in the absence of documentation, but also that the aim was to prevent husbands-to-be from dissolving the betrothal and recovering the *arrha*, as might happen in other negotiations. In a sale, the vendor was bound to complete the transaction once he had received the *arrha* (in this case, pledge money), but the buyer retained the right to cancel the contract and recover the *arrha*.[157]

As in Roman imperial law, no more than two years should normally elapse between betrothal and marriage. A law promulgated by Chindasvind's successor, Reccesvind (649–672), confirmed the two-year rule but allowed for negotiated delays and adverse circumstances. Normally, no more than two years was to elapse between the day of the betrothal and the day of the marriage. The respective parents and kinsfolk of the partners, or even the partners themselves if they are of age, might agree to postpone the wedding, and a delay might be unavoidable if one of the partners could not be present. Nevertheless, no postponement could exceed two years. The parties might repeatedly negotiate such two-year postponements, but if someone failed to complete the marriage through mere unwillingness, the agreement became void even if it had been recorded in writing, and even if the *sponsus* had already given the *arrha*.[158] The delinquent party had to pay whatever penalty was determined in the betrothal, which could be renegotiated.[159]

---

[154] *Lex Vis.* III.1.9, pp. 131–32.   [155] *Lex Vis.* III.1.5, pp. 126–27, sets upper limits to the dowry.
[156] Ibid., III.1.3, 124.   [157] Ibid., V.4.4, 219.
[158] Here my interpretation differs somewhat from that of King, *Law and Society*, 227, according to whom the obligation to marry remained in force.
[159] *Lex Vis.* III.1.4, 125/14–126/9. The same principles may have applied to the *sponsa*, for the wording of this section of the law is not gender-specific.

Because the *arrha* confirmed the betrothal contract and made it binding, the betrothal ring became an important figure of unbroken conjugal unity. Isidore explains that the *sponsus* gave the *sponsa* a ring "either as a sign of mutual faith, or rather so that their hearts should be joined by the same pledge." That is why the ring is placed on the fourth finger, Isidore adds, for a vein runs thence all the way to the heart.[160]

5.3.2 *Marrying in Frankish culture*

Gregory, Bishop of Tours (d. 594), provides a glimpse of the nuptial process in the Merovingian world when he recounts the story of a saintly nobleman called Iniuriosus, whose bride was dismayed because she had intended to devote her life to Christ.[161] Gregory establishes that they were properly married by narrating a sequence of events rather than a single event. Being a righteous man, Iniuriosus observed all the formalities. Having found a girl of his own class, he asked her parents for her hand in marriage ("*in coniugio ... expetiit*"), he gave her an *arrha* to confirm the betrothal, and the two sides agreed to the date of the wedding.

"When that day came, and the wedding had been celebrated," Gregory continues, "they were placed in one bed according to custom [*in uno strato ex more locantur*]." Gregory is using a variant of a classical idiom. In Roman custom, the matron of honor or family members were said to place (*collocare*) the bride or the couple in the nuptial bed at the conclusion of the domestic wedding ceremony.[162] But this bride was "deeply unhappy. Turning her face to the wall, she wept bitterly."[163] The detail shows that she had had no opportunity to tell Iniuriosus about her feelings until they came together in the nuptial bed, their first intimate moment, and that she had not wanted to marry. The bride's consent to her marriage was relatively unimportant in Merovingian culture.[164] Being a kindly and pious man, however, Iniuriosus asked her what the matter was. She had believed that she was destined to become a bride of Christ, she explained, but now it seemed that Christ had abandoned her. Inuriosus pointed out that as only children they both had a duty to continue their family lines, but the girl persuaded him not to demand his

---

[160] Isidore of Seville, *De ecclesiasticis officiis* II.20.8, CCL 113:92. The explanation about the ring finger is from Aulus Gellius, *Noctium Atticarum* X.10 (Loeb edition, vol. 2, 236) on why the Greeks and some Roman men used to wear rings on the fourth finger of their left hand.

[161] Gregory of Tours, *Historiae* I.47, MGH *Scriptores Rerum Merovingicarum* 1.1 (1937), 30. For a sketch of Merovingian marriage, see Y. Hen, *Culture and Religion in Merovingian Gaul A.D. 481–751* (Leiden, 1995), 122–37.

[162] S. Treggiari, "Putting the Bride to Bed," *Echos du monde classique/Classic Views* 38 (1994): 311–31, at 315. See the article on *collocare* in J. F. Niermeyer, *Mediae Latinitatis Lexicon Minus* (Leiden, 1984).

[163] "Sed puella graviter contristata, aversa ad paritem, amarissime flebat."

[164] Hen, *Culture and Religion*, 127.

rights. They lived together thereafter in amicable celibacy, sharing the same bed: the ideal Augustinian marriage.[165]

Frankish dowry charters from the Merovingian and Carolingian periods, which have survived as formulas, typically record that a betrothal has already taken place before parents and kinsfolk and is a matter of public knowledge. Many of these documents look forward to the future wedding day (*dies nuptiarum*), when the bride will acquire her rights (either full possession or usufruct) over the dowry stated in the charter.[166] For example, a Carolingian dotal charter included in a formulary composed at Tours begins thus:

> Law and custom demand that whatever has been promised or bestowed between a betrothed man and woman for their forthcoming marriage, whether by the consent of their parents or their own if they are legally independent, should be solemnly confirmed in writing. Therefore, I in the name of God So-and-So, since it is well known to many that I have betrothed you So-and-So by your own free will and with the consent of our parents and kinsfolk, it has pleased me that I should give to you something from my estate, confirming it with this certificate of dowry [*libellum dotis*] before the day of our marriage, which I have done accordingly.[167]

A detailed description of the husband's dowry follows. The chief stages in the process presupposed here are petition, betrothal, dotation, and wedding. The act of dotation confirms in writing the results of the negotiations between the two families or kin groups.

5.3.3 *Pope Nicholas I on marriage in the west*

Pope Nicholas I provides a uniquely detailed account of marrying in a response that he wrote to the Khan of Bulgaria in 866. The Khan had not yet decided whether to join the eastern or the Roman branches of Christendom. He was more inclined toward Byzantine Christianity, but there were still Roman missionaries in his land, and he wanted to know how the two branches of the church differed. Nicholas explains, therefore, among other things, how people "contract nuptial compacts" ("*nuptialia foedera contrahunt*") in the west.[168]

Marrying begins with betrothal (*sponsalia*), which Nicholas defines as an agreement to marry in the future.[169] It is "celebrated with the consent both of those who

---

[165] Gregory of Tours, *Historiae* I.47, MGH *Scriptores Rerum Merovingicarum* 1.1, 30.

[166] P. L. Reynolds, "Dotal Charters in the Frankish Tradition," THTH 114–64.

[167] K. Zeumer (ed.), *Formulae Merowingici et Karolini Aevi*, MGH *Legum* V, Formulae (Hanover, 1886), *Tur.* 14 (p. 142). Translation quoted from Reynolds, "Dotal Charters," 151.

[168] Nicholas I, *Epist.* 99 (*Responsa ad consulta Bulgarorum*), c. 3, in MGH *Epist.* 6, *Epistolae Karolini Aevi* 4 (1925), 570. A. E. Laiou assumes in "*Consensus Facit Nuptias — et Non*," *Rechtshistorisches Journal* 4 (1985): 189–201, at 190–91, that when Nicholas speaks of contracting "nuptial compacts" he is referring to the initial betrothal, but I take it that he is to the entire process of marrying, from betrothal to solemnization.

[169] Cf. *Dig.* 23.1.1.

are contracting the marriage and of those in whose power they are."[170] The *sponsus* gives a ring to the *sponsa* both as a pledge (*arrha*) of his intent and to signify their indivisible fidelity. And he gives her a dowry that is acceptable to both sides by means of a written agreement. The contractual phase of the marriage is now complete. It only remains for the spouses to come together.

Next, therefore, either "soon afterwards or at an appropriate time (that is, lest they should presume to do such a thing before the time defined by law)," their union is blessed in a church ceremony. The duration of the betrothal depends on the age of the partners. Other things being equal, it should be brief, but a longer interval is inevitable if the partners are betrothed as infants, for no one can marry before puberty. Nicholas regards bride and groom at the wedding as passive recipients: they are brought (*perducuntur*) to the wedding ceremony and placed (*statuuntur*) at the hand of a priest, and they receive (*suscipiunt*) the priest's blessing and the "celestial veil." There is no mention of wedding vows. The ceremony of veiling and blessing, according to Nicholas, commemorates the blessing of Genesis 1:28, when God, "having placed the first human beings in Paradise, blessed them and said: Increase and multiply." Nicholas also cites the example of Tobias, who prayed to God with his wife before he "knew" her (Tob 8:4, 6–9).[171] Tobias was an example of pious restraint and continence, for Tobias and Sarah prayed for three nights before consummating their marriage. Indeed, Carolingian clergy sometimes encouraged newlyweds to observe the "Tobias nights," abstaining from coitus during the first night or first three nights of marriage. The origins of the custom are obscure, but the earliest unequivocal references to it are Carolingian.[172] The function of a church liturgy was to put some seemly distance between the partners' coming together in holy matrimony and their sexual union. Finally, Nicholas explains, the spouses "leave the church wearing crowns [*coronae*] on their heads," which are otherwise retained in the church, and the priest directs them "henceforth to lead an undivided life[173] with God's help."

Nevertheless, in contrast with eastern practice, Nicholas adds, there is no fault if any of the formalities are omitted. Formal marriages are expensive, and many cannot afford them. Mutual agreement (*consensus*) is sufficient to establish a marriage:[174] "If perchance their consent alone is lacking, everything else, including coitus itself, is

---

[170] Cf. *Dig.* 23.2.2.

[171] The prayers for blessing from the Book of Tobit influenced the early nuptial liturgies. See under "Tobie (bénédiction de)" in the index to J.-B. Molin and P. Mutembe, *Le rituel du mariage en France du XIIe au XVIe siècle* (Paris, 1974), 345. On the three nuptial blessings in Tobit and their influence, see MWCh 371–75. There is a similar allusion to Tobit in a French dotal charter (11th century?), ed. Zeumer, MGH *Formulae*, Extr. I.12, pp. 541/4–5: "Sed et angelum de caelo ad corroborandam nuptiarum copulam ad Tobin venisse legimus."

[172] See J.-B. Molin, "Symboles, rites et textes du mariage du moyen âge latin," *Studia Anselmiana* 93 (1986): 107–27, at 123–24; K. Ritzer, *Le mariage dans les Églises chrétiennes du Ier au XIe siècle* (Paris, 1970), 281–82; Henry G. J. Beck, *Pastoral Care of Souls in South-East France during the Sixth Century* (Rome, 1950), 232–33; MWCh 334, 336–37, 374, 391.

[173] Cf. *Inst.* 1.9.1 (Modestinus).   [174] *Epist.* 99, 3, p. 570/16–21.

celebrated in vain,[175] for, as that great teacher John Chrysostom says, it is not coitus that makes marriage, but volition."[176]

5.4 IVO OF CHARTRES ON CONSENT AND BETROTHAL

The betrothal of the early Middle Ages was typically a negotiated, solemn, and contractually binding agreement to marry in the future, and it was the chief expression of the consent that would constitute the marriage. There must have been numerous local variations and developments during the following centuries. The relationship between the betrothal and such formalities as dotation and the *arrha* was subject to endless variation. The sworn betrothal, in which the parties confirmed their agreement by making a solemn oath (*iuramentum*) with their hands on the Scriptures or on some other sacred object, is conspicuous in some central-medieval sources, as we shall see, and it may have been much older. But there was apparently no fundamental change in the function of the betrothal until the late eleventh century.

At what point in its formation did an early-medieval marriage become insoluble? The answer is unknown, and the question may be anachronistic. Before the Gregorian Reforms and the consequent taking over of marriage by the clergy, bishops were not in a position either to dictate how people at large got married or to prevent marriages from being dissolved. Their sphere of control over marriage, such as was, was limited to the aristocratic elite. They may have assumed that spouses became irrevocably bound to each other in divine law when they came together as man and wife, or when the wife was "led" into her husband's home. If so, a new position comes to light in the letters of Ivo of Chartres, at a time when the bishops and clerics of northern France were affirming in reality the control of marriage that they had long claimed as a right.[177] Ivo's policy was the result of applying theoretical principles that were well established in canon law to the traditional practice of betrothal.

Ivo was the foremost canonical authority of his age: an expert to whom the other bishops and archbishops of northern France turned for legal counsel, and who was not afraid to counsel and admonish royalty. Ivo's canonical collections were more authoritative than any others before Gratian's *Decretum*. I shall focus here on his letters, which spanned the length of his career as bishop of Chartres, from 1091 until

---

[175] Note that coitus is said to be "celebrated." Nicholas may be thinking of the bedding ritual.

[176] *Epist.* 99, 3, p. 570/21–24. Through Nicholas, this became a standard canonical text, as in Ivo, *Decretum* VI.17 (*Panormia* VI.107). Ivo also quotes the dictum from pseudo-Chrysostom in *Epist.* 134, PL 162:144A, and *Epist.* 148, PL 162:154A. The source, traditionally ascribed to Chrysostom, is the *Opus imperfectum in Matthaeum* (PG 56:802), which was probably largely the work of a fifth-century Latin cleric in Constantinople: see F. W. Schlatter, "The Author of the *Opus imperfectum in Matthaeum*," *Vigiliae Christianae* 42 (1988): 364–75. In its original context, the dictum referred to the intent maintaining the continuity of an already established marriage, and not to the consent to marry: cf. *Dig.* 35.1.15 (Ulpian).

[177] My phrasing echoes G. Duby, *Medieval Marriage* (Baltimore, 1978), 20.

his death around 1116.[178] Ivo appears in the letters as forthright and principled but also calm and reasonable, rarely resorting to invective. When he cites authorities, he seems to draw chiefly on his own *Decretum* but occasionally on the *Tripartita* A.[179]

5.4.1 Consent to marry

Ivo emphasizes the importance of consent in marriage, maintaining that the consent of the spouses themselves is necessary, albeit not necessarily sufficient, for a valid marriage. The bride's consent is in principle as important as her husband's. The proper occasion to express that consent is not the wedding but the betrothal. Once the partners are betrothed, their union is insoluble.

Ivo appeals in his letters and canonical collections to the authority of about a dozen consensual proof texts. The most important are the authorities by Ambrose, Augustine, and Isidore, discussed earlier (Section 4.2), which affirm that a betrothal is already marriage, even before the partners come together sexually. Ivo also quotes Pope Nicholas I, including Nicholas's quotation of pseudo-Chrysostom – an authority within an authority – to corroborate the principle that consent makes marriage:

> According to the laws [i.e., to civil, or Roman law], the consent alone of those who are getting married should suffice. If perchance their consent alone is lacking, everything else, included coitus itself, is celebrated in vain, for as that great teacher John Chrysostom says, "It is not coitus that makes marriage, but intent."[180]

In his letters, perhaps because he is writing from memory without checking his sources, Ivo sometimes condenses the twofold authority into the maxim, "Consent makes marriage, not coitus," which he ascribes to Nicholas.[181] This maxim is reminiscent of Ulpian's dictum, "It is not sexual intercourse [*concubitus*] but consent that makes marriage."[182]

---

[178] My source for the letters is PL 162:11–504, which is essentially François Juret's edition of 1647. Jean Leclercq began a revised edition of the letters, chronologically arranged, with facing French translations, but only the first volume of the letters appeared (Paris, 1949), and it includes none of the letters cited later. On marriage in Ivo's letters, see B. Basdevant-Gaudemet, "Le mariage d'après la correspondance d'Yves de Chartres," *Revue historique de droit français et étranger* 61 (1983): 195–215; A. Lefebvre-Teillard, "A propos d'une lettre à Guillaume: La filiation légitime dans l'oeuvre d'Ives de Chartres," *Studia Gratiana* 27 (Rome, 1996): 287–309; and C. Rolker, *Canon Law and the Letters of Ivo of Chartres* (Cambridge, 2009), 211–47. On Ivo's life and work, see Rolker, ibid., 1–49.

[179] On the Ivonian corpus in relation to the letters, see Rolker, *Canon Law* (cited above). Rolker argues convincingly that the *Decretum* was Ivo's own work, but that the *Panormia*, which evinces a different, more systematic method, was the work of another author who drew on the *Decretum*. Ivo was evidently familiar with the *Tripartita* A, but the correspondences between this collection and Ivo's letters are insufficient to show that he was its author (161).

[180] Nicholas I, *Epist.* 99, c. 3, MGH *Epist.* 6, 570/21–24. Ivo, *Epist.* 134, PL 162:144A; *Epist.* 148, 154A; *Decretum* VI.17 (*Panormia* VI.107).

[181] "Matrimonium facit consensus, non coitus." *Epist.* 99, 119A. *Epist.* 243, 251A.

[182] *Dig.* 35.1.15.

To show that consent is the foundation of marriage as well as to show *whose* consent is necessary, Ivo cites a sequence of three opinions about betrothal from the *Digest*.[183] First, according to Julian, betrothal requires the same consents as marriage does, and it follows that a daughter-in-power should comply with her father's will. Second, according to Ulpian, a daughter-in-power is deemed to have consented if she does not dissent from her father's choice, and she is permitted to dissent only if the man that her father has chosen is unworthy. Third, according to Paul, a betrothal is invalid if a son-in-power dissents. Although these texts minimize a girl's freedom of choice, Ivo cites them to show that children cannot be betrothed or married without their consent.[184] In one letter, he extends the third opinion analogically to show that a father cannot arrange for his son to be appointed as a bishop without the son's consent. If a son's consent is necessary for the carnal union between a man and a woman, how much more is it necessary for the spiritual union between a bishop and his diocese?[185] Because parents sometimes betrothed their children as infants, Ivo also cites the next opinion in the *Digest*, from Modestinus. It states that there is no "determined age" for betrothals, which can take place between very young children, as long as they understand what is happening in their name, "that is, that they are not under seven years of age."[186] The final clause – an addition that contradicts what has gone before – sets the age of discernment nominally at seven: the beginning of the second *septennium* in the traditional division of the life span.

Pope Nicholas's definition of betrothal appears in Ivo's *Decretum* and in the *Panormia*, although not as far as I am aware in Ivo's letters: "Betrothal … is the promised compact of a future marriage, and it is celebrated with the consent of those who are contracting marriage and of those in whose power they are."[187] The statement is based on two opinions by Roman jurists: Florentinus's definition of betrothal, and Paul's definition of the consent needed for marriage.[188]

Ivo cites two texts from Julian's *Epitome* that in their original setting showed that consent was sufficient for marriage even in the absence of ancillary formalities.[189] According to one text, a man who "takes a wife by marital affection alone, without dotal instruments," cannot "divorce her except on the legally recognized grounds."[190] The other text refers to the sworn betrothal: "If someone swears to a woman by the holy Scriptures that he will have her as his legitimate wife, or makes

[183] *Dig.* 23.1.11–13. Ivo, *Decretum* VIII.20–21, XVI.182 (*Panormia* VI.11, XVI.13).
[184] *Epist.* 99, 119A. *Epist.* 134, 144A.   [185] *Epist.* 176, 178C. *Epist.* 178, 180A–B.
[186] *Dig.* 23.1.14. Ivo, *Decretum* VIII.22, XVI.183; *Epist.* 99, 119B; *Epist.* 134, 144A (*Panormia* VI.13).
[187] Nicholas I, *Epist.* 99, c. 3, MGH *Epist.* 6, 570/2–4. Ivo, *Decretum* VIII.6 (*Panormia* VI.9).
[188] *Dig.* 23.1.1 (Florentinus), 23.2.2 (Paul).
[189] On the background in Justinianic law, see Evans Grubbs, "Marrying and Its Documentation," 92–94. On the *Epitome*, a Latin summary of Justinian's *Novels* prepared for a lecture course in Constantinople and published in 556, see W. Kaiser, *Die Epitome Iuliani* (Frankfurt, 2004). Since the *Epitome* was in Latin, whereas most of Justinian's *Novels* were issued in Greek, it was the chief source for the *Novels* in the West before the twelfth century.
[190] *Epitome Iuliani*, const. 36.7, c. 137. Ivo, *Decretum* VIII.35.

an oath of this sort in a chapel, then she is his legitimate wife even if there has been no dowry or document."[191] Ivo cites these texts in his letters to show both that consent is the essential basis of betrothal and that betrothal is already marriage "for the most part."[192]

Ivo's adherence to the consensual principle is consistent and uncompromising when he deals with questions about betrothal, such as whether a betrothal to one person is a fatal impediment to marriage with another, and whether infants can be validly betrothed. Ivo insists that consent is the principle cause of marriage, and he knows of only one act of consent in the process of marrying: the "pact" that establishes the betrothal. Betrothal is a union not of bodies but of minds or wills, according to Ivo, whereas marriage is also a union of bodies. Nevertheless, a valid betrothal is a virtual marriage inasmuch as it binds the partners together indissolubly and prevents either partner from marrying another as long both are alive. As Ivo puts it, the betrothed partners are already married "for the most part."

I shall focus here on two letters, while citing others to help explicate them: *Letter 167* (to Hildebert, bishop of Le Mans), and *Letter 99* (to a priest called Gualo).

5.4.2 *Betrothal as an impediment to marriage*

Letter 167, to Hildebert, concerns a man who had entered into a betrothal pact with the father of his intended but later married someone else.[193] The girl's father, a "parishioner" of the Le Mans diocese, had complained to Ivo during a visit to Chartres that "he had given his daughter in a conjugal compact [*coniugali foedere tradidit*]" to certain parishioner of Le Mans, who "swore unconditionally [*absolute iuraverit*] that he was going to take her as his wife [*ducturus*] at an agreed time. But now he has taken [*duxit*] another woman as his wife, breaking the conjugal pact [*pactum coniugale*] that he had previously entered into legitimately with another." Ivo argues that compacts of marriage (*foedera nuptiarum*) are binding under both divine and human law, and that they are legitimate, if there is no impediment of relationship, provided that "a girl-in-power (*filiafamilias*) does not dissent from her father's will." Canonical authority (*canonica sententia*) states that a woman who is betrothed (*desponsata*) to one man cannot marry another, and the text about sworn betrothals from the *Novels* (i.e., from Julian's *Epitome*)[194] shows that the betrothed man is equally bound. If a betrothed person of either sex marries someone else, therefore, the marriage is illegal and should be dissolved, for "that which someone presumes by acting against the laws deserves to be dissolved by means of the laws."[195]

---

[191] *Epitome Iuliani*, const. 67.4, c. 244. Ivo, *Decretum* VIII.44 (*Panormia* VI.7).
[192] *Epist.* 148, 154A. *Epist.* 167, 170C.   [193] *Epist.* 167, 170B–D.
[194] *Epitome Iuliani*, const. 67.4, c. 244. Ivo, *Decretum* VI.7, VIII.44.
[195] A favorite maxim of Ivo's, said to be from a letter from Pope John VIII to Emperor Louis II: see Ivo, *Decretum* IV.230, VI.115; *Epist.* 161, 166A. *Epist.* 185, 186A, *Epist.* 242, 250A, *Epist.* 243, 251D.

The burden of Ivo's argument is straightforward. Because betrothal establishes an inseparable compact, it suffices for the impediment of prior marriage. In this case, a man who was already betrothed to one woman has "led" another woman in marriage and is living with her. Does their marriage trump the prior betrothal? No, Ivo answers. Human and divine laws and the weight of canonical opinion are against breaking a betrothal, and Hildebert must dissolve the subsequent marriage. The jilted girl was a daughter-in-power (*filiafamilias*), but Ivo does not tell us what are the criteria for paternal power. She was probably still considered a minor. Although Ivo regards the betrothal chiefly as an agreement between the girl's father and her suitor, he is mindful that if she had dissented from her father's will, there would have been grounds to question the validity of the first union and thereby to uphold the second.[196] Because she consented, if only by not objecting, the betrothal is binding. The various terms by which Ivo denotes the betrothal here and elsewhere in his letters – *desponsatio, sponsalia, pactum coniugale, foedus nuptiarum, foedus coniugale,* and so forth – show that in his view the betrothal is the proper expression of marital consent.[197] In this case, the pact included a stated time. The marriage was to take place on a certain date, or after so many weeks or months. The conjugal pact into which the man had entered was clearly prospective, for he agreed that he was "going to lead" her in marriage. (Ivo uses the future participle, *ducturus.*) It was, nevertheless, indissoluble.

What marked the coming together of the man with the second woman in *Letter 167*? There is no way of knowing. Ivo says that the man had "led" her, but the verb *ducere* (literally, "to lead") had become a merely conventional idiom for marrying. It did not necessarily refer to a bridal procession or to a wife's entry into her husband's home. Ivo may have assumed that the occasion of their coming together would be a public wedding, but there is no mention of any plighting of troth or exchange of vows in the narrative when the husband "led" his wife. Moreover, there would have been no point in the spouses' exchanging mutual consent at the wedding if they were already inseparably bound by their betrothal. One must assume, therefore, that a marriage was complete when the spouses began to live together, whether or not this eventuality was solemnized in church or marked by any ritual or ceremony.

Letter 167 presupposes that a betrothal was a virtual marriage inasmuch it bound the spouses inseparably. Ivo's use of the term *tradere* ("to hand over") is consistent with his assimilation of betrothal to marriage. A father or family was said to "hand over" a woman in marriage – in other words, to give her away in marriage, or to transfer her to another family – but Ivo used this idiom to refer not only to a wedding but also to a betrothal pact. Thus, in *Letter 167*, a father has "handed over his daughter in a conjugal compact" (*coniugali foedere tradidit*) to a man who swore, in

---

[196] Cf. *Dig.* 23.1.12 (Ulpian).
[197] Basdevant-Gaudemet, "Le mariage d'après la correspondance d'Yves de Chartres," 201–02.

return, that he was "going to take her as his wife" (*ducturus*) at an agreed time.[198] Ivo uses the verb *tradere* in this sense also in a letter to Humbald, bishop of Auxerre, regarding the case of a girl called Mathilda.[199] Here too, a marriage was invalid because of a prior betrothal, but it had another defect: the bride had dissented. She had been "handed over" (*tradita*) in betrothal by her parents to Galerannus, the king's chancellor, but another man, Pontius, had taken her in marriage "struggling and crying." Perhaps her father connived in the abduction, or perhaps he had died, for he took no part in the litigation, and Ivo mentions that her mother opposed the marriage to Pontius. Having sought expert opinions from Ivo and others, the bishop of Paris heard Mathilda's case against Pontius, which was that the marriage was invalid both because she had already been "handed over" to another man, and because she did not consent to it. Pontius repeatedly failed to appear before the court, which eventually decided in favor of Mathilda, who was free to marry whomever she willed. Perhaps her abduction and violation vitiated her union with Galerannus.

Ivo's equation of the handing over (*traditio*) of the bride with the betrothal shows that he considered the betrothal to be a virtual marriage, but his idiom is less clear in a letter to Daimbert, archbishop of Sens, in which Ivo relates how two noblemen agreed to a "conjugal pact" whereby whoever had a daughter first was going to give her (*traditurus*) to whichever son of the other he chose when she reached marriageable age (*ad nubiles annos*).[200] In this case, the *traditio* was still in the future, but the pact did not amount to betrothal, for the girl was not yet born. Even her identity was unknown, and no one knew at the time of the pact whose daughter she would be.

It is noteworthy that the suitor in *Letter 167* solemnizes the betrothal by swearing to it. Ivo remarks elsewhere that someone who "confirms the conjugal pact with an oath has completed the sacrament of marriage for the most part."[201] Peter Lombard will later pose the question, "Whether future consent with an oath makes a marriage."[202] Unlike Ivo, Peter distinguishes between future consent, which makes a betrothal, and present consent, which makes marriage, but custom and tradition causes him to ask whether future consent amounts to marriage when it is solemnized with an oath. In some minds, it seems, an oath made the difference between an informal promise to marry and a binding betrothal. Ivo attributes no specific function to the betrothal oath over and above that of the agreement itself, but he may have assumed that it confirmed the agreement by assuring that it was deliberate and genuine. If so, its function was secondary and evidentiary.

---

[198] *Epist.* 167, 170B.   [199] *Epist.* 166, 169B–170A.   [200] *Epist.* 134, 143C–D.

[201] *Epist.* 161, 165D: "Qui enim juramento pactum conjugale firmavit, ex majori parte sacramentum conjugale implevit." See also *Epist.* 134, 143C–D, where the two noblemen swear that one of them will give his daughter in marriage to the other's son. The *sacramentum* to which Ivo refers is the marriage vow or the bond that results from it.

[202] *Sent.* IV, 28.1 (431).

5.4.3 *The betrothal of infants*

Letter 99, to a priest called Gualo, concerns the status and consequences of betrothals between infants.[203] Are such agreements valid and binding? Do they establish impediments of affinity? Gualo asked Ivo whether infants who have not yet reached the standard age of seven "are able to contract the sacraments of betrothal or marriage between themselves, and whether, if one of them dies after a betrothal [*sponsalia*] has been celebrated, the survivor can enter into a marriage with the sister or brother of the deceased, with whom he or she had previously entered into the bond of betrothal [*desponsationis vinculum*]."

To confirm that a valid betrothal is sufficient to create affinity, Ivo cites a canon from the Council of Tribur: "Therefore, it is decreed that although the woman could not be married [*nupta*] to her legitimate husband, the brother cannot have his brother's betrothed."[204] This case concerned a man who had betrothed a woman and given her a dowry but was unable to have sex with her. His brother had sex with her instead, making her pregnant. Although the text presupposes that a betrothed woman becomes married (*nupta*) when her marriage is consummated, the betrothal is considered sufficient to establish affinity, although the union is soluble. Both Ivo and Gualo assume that a valid betrothal establishes a relationship of affinity, preventing a marriage between either of the partners and a sibling of the other. The question, then, is whether an infant betrothal is valid.

It is clear, Ivo argues, that partners cannot legitimately marry until they are capable of rendering the conjugal debt to each other through sexual intercourse. For proof, Ivo invokes the natural law as expressed in Scripture: "For this reason a man shall leave father and mother and cleave unto his wife, and they shall be two in one flesh" (Gen 2:24, Matt 19:5, etc.). But can someone at least become betrothed before marriageable age? The point was less clear to Ivo than it had been to the Roman jurists.

Although Ivo does not regard betrothals between pre-pubescent children as ideal, he concedes that they are permissible in view of their pragmatic advantages, but only if the partners consent:

> If sacraments of this sort are celebrated before the age of puberty for the sake of enlarging or preserving peace between certain persons, and if there is no legal impediment between the partners, and if both partners consent, we do not forbid this, for as Pope Nicholas says, "It is consent that makes marriage, not coitus."[205]

---

[203] *Epist.* 99, 118C–119D.
[204] 118C–119D. *Decretum* IX.100. The canon is a draft or abbreviation of *Conc. Tribur.* 41, MGH *Leges nationum Germanicarum* 2.2, p. 237 (or Mansi, *Sacrorum conciliorum* 18, 152–53). See G. H. Joyce, *Christian Marriage*, 2nd edition (London, 1948), 61n1.
[205] 118D–119A.

Ivo cites the texts from the *Digest* about the consent needed for betrothals, including the opinion of Modestinus, which makes seven the nominal age of discernment,[206] but he notes that the minimum age for betrothals "is not fully defined in either ecclesiastical or human law." That said, if the partners are old enough to consent to their betrothal, even if they are still infants, then they "receive the name of marriage." Here, Ivo cites the usual proof texts from Ambrose, Isidore, and Augustine. It follows, Ivo argues, that "after a marriage has been contracted for the most part [*ex maiori parte*] in a compact of betrothal [*desponsationis foedus*] entered into between two persons by mutual consent, a brother cannot take his brother's wife in marriage, nor can a sister marry her sister's husband."[207]

Notwithstanding Ivo's reasonable uncertainty about the minimum age for betrothal, his argument is clear. Whereas marriage requires the ability to render the conjugal debt, betrothal requires only consent. The partners need not have reached puberty, therefore, but they must be old enough to know to what they are agreeing. There is no determinate age for that level of discernment. Seven is the conventional norm, but even infants beneath the age of seven can become validly betrothed. Moreover, their consent, especially that of girls, need only be lack of dissent. Be that as it may, once the partners are legitimately betrothed, even as infants, their betrothal amounts to marriage "for the most part" (*ex maiore parte*). They cannot come together as man and wife until puberty, but they have already consented, and "consent makes marriage." Neither partner can marry someone else as long as the other is alive, therefore, and their betrothal establishes the impediments of prior marriage and affinity.

Ivo appeals to the same principles in the letter to Daimbert, archbishop of Sens, about the two noblemen and their conjugal pact.[208] The noblemen agreed that if either had a daughter, he would give her to one of the other nobleman's sons when she reached marriageable age. Is the pact valid and binding? Nature has determined, Ivo replies, and both ecclesiastical and secular law have confirmed, that those who are to be united as one body in marriage must first be of one mind in their mutual agreement. Therefore, the pact is valid and binding only if the girl herself consents to the arrangement when she reaches the age of discernment, whatever that may be. Ivo cites civil and canonical authorities, including a passage from what he says is a letter from Pope Nicholas to Bishop Hincmar – in fact, it is the pope's letter to the Khan of Bulgaria. As to the age of consent, Ivo falls back on civil law, quoting texts from the *Digest* to show, first, that because betrothal requires the consent of those who are to marry, the betrothal of daughter-in-power is not valid unless she consents, and, second, that betrothal can take place at an early age provided only that the partners understand what they are doing.[209]

---

[206] *Dig.* 23.1.11, 23.1.13–14.   [207] 119C.   [208] *Epist.* 134, 143C–144C.
[209] *Dig.* 23.1.11, 23.1.14. Ivo sets the nominal age of discernment here at twelve years, instead of seven (as in Modestinus's dictum and in *Epist.* 99), but this was probably the result of a scribal mistake, for it was easy to confuse XII and VII.

Infantile betrothals were especially prone to non-fulfillment and breach of promise. In such cases, as in *Letter 99*, Ivo has to strike a balance between the indissolubility of betrothals and the need for consent. In another letter to Gualo, Ivo discusses
a spurious marriage between two infants who were still in their cradles. Here too, as
in *Letter 99*, Ivo emphasizes the need for consent in marriage, quoting Nicholas I as
saying: "Consent makes marriage, not coitus. If perchance this consent is absent in
marriage, all the other things, including coitus itself, are done in vain." In a distant
echo, rare for its period, of Augustine on the three goods of marriage, Ivo adds that a
marriage between babies is "without faith, without offspring, without consent,
without every conjugal good."[210]

Gualo asked whether infants "are able to contract the sacraments of betrothal or
marriage between themselves." Ivo uses the word "sacrament" to refer to betrothal or
marriage inasmuch it involves a solemn and permanent vow. He does not include
marriage among the ritual mysteries of the church.[211] In this respect, marriage is
comparable to the other offices or "professions" of the church. For example, just as
the sacrament of ordination remains in someone ordained by a schismatic, Ivo
argues, so the sacrament of marriage remains in a couple whose marriage is consecrated by a disobedient priest.[212] For the same reason, persons who marry illicitly
during an interdict are truly married nonetheless. In a letter to Ralph, Provost of
Reims, and his colleague Odolricus, Ivo discusses another case of a man who
entered into a "conjugal pact" with one woman but later married another.[213] The
second "sacrament," Ivo argues, is spurious and should be dissolved. Until the case
comes to court, the partners should suspend their sexual relations, "for he who
confirms a conjugal pact with an oath has completed the conjugal sacrament for the
most part." For proof, Ivo adapts an argument from Augustine: When the angel
called Mary a wife (*coniux*), she had entered into a conjugal pact with Joseph, but
Joseph had not yet taken her (*traduxerat*) as his wife, and he would never know her
sexually. It follows that a man who is betrothed to one woman cannot marry another.
It is true that a lesser sacrament may cede to a greater one, but this must be done in
an orderly way, following the rules. For example, a married man cannot be consecrated as a priest or ordained as a monk unless he has been separated (*solutus*) from
his wife (presumably by a mutual vow of celibacy).[214] Ivo's use of the term "sacrament" in relation to marriage is dependent on Augustine's talk of the *bonum
sacramenti*, but he uses the term chiefly to denote a vow of betrothal or marriage.
Ivo's use of the term "sacrament" to refer to betrothal or marriage is significant in

---

[210] *Epist.* 243, 250D–251B.
[211] In *Epist.* 242, 250A, Ivo says that a marriage between free and unfree persons "does not contain
the sacrament of Christ and the church." A sacrament in this sense is a sign or mystery, and Ivo
is merely echoing the letter of Pope Leo I to Rusticus (PL 54:1204B–05), which I shall discuss in
Chapter 6. The phrase does not imply, as some have supposed, that Ivo considered a valid
marriage to be one of the sacraments of the church in the proper sense.
[212] *Epist.* 155, 160A–B. This passage is a reworking of Augustine, *De b. coniug.* 24(32), 227.
[213] *Epist.* 161, 165C–166C.   [214] See MWCh 227–38, on separating to serve God.

relation to the development of a sacramental theology of marriage during the first half of the twelfth century, but it would be premature to say that Ivo regarded marriage as one of the sacraments.

5.4.4 *Betrothal as virtual marriage*

We have seen Ivo consider betrothed persons to be already married "for the most part."[215] Another letter to Hildebert is about a man who had kept a woman as his mistress. When she became infirm, he entered into a "conjugal pact" with her. Desiring to regularize their union, he gave her a ring. We know nothing more about the details of the case, and Ivo's argument is hard to follow. He presents a concatenation of texts without explaining why he is citing them. These are: passages from Augustine's *De bono coniugali* about the legitimizing of an improper relationship and about the marital status of a stable but merely sexual relationship; the usual authorities showing that consent, and not coitus, makes marriage (Ambrose, Isidore, Nicholas I, and pseudo-Chrysostom); the constitutions from Julian's *Epitome* on marriages entered into "by affection alone," without dowries and documents; passages from Jerome and Augustine showing that the prohibition of adultery applies to men as well as to women; and a passage from Augustine about reconciliation after adultery. For reasons not stated in the letter, the man later regretted his action. He presumably wanted to marry someone else. Perhaps his former mistress, because of her "infirmity," could not have sex with him. Ivo argues that because the man has "completed the sacrament of marriage with her for the most part," the marriage cannot be broken up except on the grounds of fornication, and that neither can marry again as long as the other is alive.[216]

Ivo assumes that a betrothal is fulfilled or completed when the partners come together by cohabiting or copulating, but he reasons that the betrothal is already binding because it amounts to marriage "for the most part." He knows nothing of the distinction between *de futuro* and *de praesenti* betrothals. In a letter to Odo, Archdeacon of Orléans, Ivo argues that an unmarried woman who is pregnant should ideally not marry[217] until she has begotten and weaned her child, since it is improper for a pregnant woman to have sex with her husband, "without which the rights of marriage [*iura matrimonii*] are not completed."[218] In a letter to Lisiardus, bishop of Soissons, Ivo considers a case involving a man called Peter who, apparently with Lisiardus's approval, had married the sister of a woman to whom he had previously been betrothed. A priest had even blessed the prior betrothal. Ivo refers to

---

[215] *Epist.* 99, 119C. *Epist.* 161, 165D.   [216] *Epist.* 148, 153B–154D.
[217] Presumably someone other than the father of her child.
[218] *Epist.* 155, 159A. Ivo argues, nevertheless, citing the "moderation" of 1 Cor 7:2, that such a woman should be permitted to marry because marriage is not a medicine given to the healthy to conserve health, but rather one given to the sick as a remedy, for marrying is a matter not of command but of indulgence.

the first partner as the man's *uxor*, but the argument of the letter presupposes that their union had not been consummated. In Ivo's view, they were already married and the man cannot marry her sister. Indeed, if the first woman is still alive, the man is not free to marry *any* other woman. "But if you object," Ivo continues, "that where one finds that sexual intercourse had not yet taken place there was no marriage, I respond on the basis of the authority of the fathers that marriage is indissoluble as soon as the conjugal pact has been established." Ivo then cites the same authorities from Augustine, Isidore, Ambrose, and the Council of Tribur as he does in *Letter 99*. Such rules, Ivo adds, apply equally to both sexes. Bishop Lisiardus must have calculated that the man's union with the first woman was not a fatal impediment to marriage with her sister because it had not been consummated: a premise that Ivo rejects. But it is the man's betrothal to the prior woman, and not the blessing of that union by a priest, that precludes the marriage to another woman.[219]

What prompted Ivo to consider the betrothed state in its own right was not, as in Augustine, a desire to defend celibate marriage or the marriage of Mary and Joseph but rather his resistance to the popular assumption that betrothed partners were still free, albeit at the cost of secular or ecclesiastical penalties, to marry others. Most of the cases in which the issue arises in his letters concern what we might call "arranged marriages," in which a father agrees to give his daughter in marriage. For example, in a letter to William, archdeacon of Paris, Ivo considers the case of two knights, one of whom had betrothed his daughter to the other. Apparently the daughter or her father later denied that the betrothal had ever taken place. Here, as elsewhere, Ivo rejects the recourse to duels and ordeals, which people regarded as a means of submitting a case to God's judgment. Not only are such methods manifestly unreliable, Ivo argues, but they are also blasphemous because they tempt God. Their use can be justified, if at all, only as the very last resort.[220] Ivo argues, therefore, that the only way to establish that the betrothal occurred is to bring forward witnesses who can testify under oath that the agreement took place.[221]

---

[219] *Epist.* 246, 252A–254A.

[220] Ivo says that he bases this argument on Augustine "in the book of questions on Genesis," but in fact the quotation is from *Contra Faustum* XXII.36, PL 42:423: "Now it pertains to sound doctrine that when a man has some means in his power, he should not tempt his God [cf. Deut. 6:16]." Notwithstanding the theological rationale and clerical supervision of trial by ordeal, Ivo considered its use to be peculiar to secular law. On the history and rationale of the ordeal, see R. Bartlett, *Trial by Fire and Water* (Oxford, 1986). Bartlett shows that the ordeal in western law was a Carolingian innovation designed to handle cases in which the trustworthiness of witnesses was uncertain: a fatal defect in legal procedures founded on compurgation and oath-helpers. On canonical and ecclesiastical objections in the central Middle Ages, see ibid., 90–102. On ecclesiastical opposition to the judicial ordeal in the late twelfth century and at the Fourth Lateran Council of 1215, see F. McAuley, "Canon Law and the End of the Ordeal," *Oxford Journal of Legal Studies* 26.3 (2006): 473–51

[221] *Epist.* 183, 184A–184C.

Ivo's position was consistent with his principles and with the canonical tradition, but it was arguably impractical and pastorally imprudent. Betrothal agreements customarily included stipulations: either time limits, whereby the partners agreed to come together within a certain period or on a certain date; or conditions, such as an agreement to marry if someone agrees, or if certain financial terms are met. There would be no point in making such stipulations if the agreement was indissoluble in any case. Moreover, marriages among landed families and the nobility were fraught with financial and political implications, which could fail to materialize. The very principle of spousal consent, which Ivo emphasized, implied that the spouses needed opportunities to opt out in due course from a conjugal pact arranged by their parents, especially one that had been arranged when the partners were infants. There had to be *some* way for the partners to agree to a future marriage without thereby becoming irrevocably bound, and there were good practical reasons for allowing the commitment to a lifelong union to be the end result of a process, with opportunities for escape. According to Ivo's position, the process was virtually complete as soon as it had begun. French schoolmen during the first quarter of the twelfth century devised a solution to this problem.

5.5 THE EMERGENCE OF THE BETROTHAL DISTINCTION

New approaches to betrothal emerged during the 1120s, within a decade after Ivo's death. The betrothal distinction, in its various forms, first appears in collections of *sententiae* that reflect the activities of the northern-French cathedral schools during the first quarter of the twelfth century. This literature, which I shall discuss in Chapters 8–9, includes both treatises on marriage such as the *Cum omnia sacramenta*, and florilegia such as the *Sententiae Magistri A.* and the *Liber Pancrisis*. The anonymous authors saved Augustine's principle that spouses were married as soon as they were betrothed, but they distinguished between the full consent that made an inseparable marriage, and a weaker, prospective agreement to marry in due course. The latter was soluble, although its breach was a sin and required penance. The former was irrevocable and precluded another valid marriage. The authors appropriated *sententiae* expressing versions of this distinction to solve particular problems, without working out the theoretical implications of the distinction or trying to integrate it into the rapidly evolving theology of marriage.

The authors propose the distinction chiefly as a solution to the problem of betrothal in relation to the impediment of prior marriage. Marriage itself was among the fatal impediments to marriage, for someone already married to one person could not validly marry someone else.[222] But was a man who was already betrothed

---

[222] *In coniugio figura est*, in F. P. Bliemetzrieder, *Anselms von Laon systematische Sentenzen*, = BGPhMA 18.2–3 (Münster, 1919), 113/4–5: "Tria ... contractum dissoluunt: fides consensus, que est de praesenti, non pactionis, que de futuro; fornicatio; impotentia reddendi carnalis debiti."

(*desponsatus*) to one woman able to take another woman in marriage (*ducere eam in matrimonium*)? Was a woman already betrothed (*desponsata*) to one man able to receive a second man as her husband? The question was not whether they *should* or *were permitted* to do so, for everyone agreed that such a breach would be a sin, but rather whether they *could* do so: Was the later marriage valid? Would it trump the prior betrothal? The consensual proof texts that Ivo cited, especially those from Ambrose, Augustine, and Isidore, seemed to imply that the partners were virtually married as soon as they were betrothed (*ex prima desponsationis fide*), so that the second alliance would have to be annulled. The question was a practical one, and every bishop would have had to adjudicate cases that involved it. There are several real-life examples, as we have seen, in Ivo's letters.[223] According to Ivo, betrothal alone, especially when confirmed with a solemn oath, rendered the partners married "for the most part" (*ex maiori parte*), so that they were already irrevocably bound together until death.[224] I have suggested that this position must have been problematic and impractical. If so, the betrothal distinction offered a new solution.

Modern scholars have been keen to attribute the betrothal distinction to someone.[225] By a historical accident, scholars first noticed primitive versions in *sententiae* ascribed – improbably, as it turned out – to Ivo of Chartres, so the credit went to him,[226] but it soon became apparent that the distinction was inconsistent with Ivo's letters and canonical collections.[227] Because scholars ascribed a related *sententia*, which I shall mention later, to William of Champeaux, some scholars then attributed the betrothal distinction to William. Eventually, scholars agreed that it was Anselm of Laon who formulated the distinction, partly because they had eliminated the other likely suspects (Ivo, William of Champeaux, and Ralph of Laon),[228] but chiefly because a *sententia* expressing the distinction is ascribed to Anselm in a single manuscript.[229] But this evidence is negligible. There is no good reason to ascribe the distinction to anyone in particular.

5.5.1 *Early forms of the betrothal distinction*

At least four versions of betrothal distinction appear in *sententiae* from the early twelfth century. The version that occurs most often in the literature posits two kinds of troth (*fides*): that of a pact or contract (*fides pactionis*), and that of consent (*fides*

---

[223] Ivo, *Epist.* 99, PL 162:118C–119D; *Epist.* 161, 165C–166C; *Epist.* 167, 170B–170D; *Epist.* 246, 253A–254A.

[224] *Epist.* 99, 119C; *Epist.* 148, 153B–C; *Epist.* 161, PL 162:165D.

[225] Reinhardt reviews the arguments in *Die Ehelehre*, 78–86.

[226] Bliemetzrieder, "Autour de l'oeuvre," 475–76. Idem, "Gratian und die Schule Anselms von Laon," 39–40. Georges Duby, *Le chevalier, la femme et le prêtre* (Paris, 1981), 191, still attributed the distinction to Ivo.

[227] Ganshof, "Note sur deux textes," 113.

[228] Ibid., 114. For the preamble to the *Liber Pancrisis*, see Lottin, PsM V, p. 11.

[229] *Paris, Arsenal 93*, fol. 93. Ed. Lottin, PsM V, pp. 135–36, no. 207.

consensus). Modern scholars often assume that this is the primitive version of the distinction. A man who has plighted *fides pactionis* with a woman "ought not to marry another woman, but if he does happen to marry another, he should do penance for the breach of troth and remain with the one whom he has married." A man who has plighted *fides consensus* with a woman, in contrast, not only is forbidden to marry another but also cannot do so validly. If he has married another, he must separate from her and return to the first.

There are several variants of the text making the *fides pactionis, fides consensus* distinction.[230] One variant states the distinction baldly,[231] but most of them add explanations and examples.[232] On the one hand, the sources say, there is *fides pactionis* when the man "gives his troth to a woman, promising that he will marry her if she permits him to have sex with her," or "even for cash." Some of the witnesses generalize by adding the phrase "or without any stipulation" to these examples, negating their effect.[233] There is *fides consensus* when the man, "even if he does not take her by the hand, consents to the bride with heart and mouth, and they both concede, one to the other, and they both receive each other."

What do these explanations tell us? First, although no particular ritual is strictly necessary for *fides consensus*, it should be genuine and expressed in spoken words, and it entails the spouses' mutual, unconditional gift of themselves to each other. Second, whereas the man who plights troth of the first sort *promises* that he *will* marry the woman, the partners who plight their troth in the second way actually accept each other, here and now. The difference of tense is crucial. The examples of conditions attached to *fides pactionis* – sex and cash – are more problematic. They may have been appended as special applications of a general distinction, or they may characterize the original setting from which the distinction became generalized when clerics recognized its broader utility. If the latter is the case, the examples

---

[230] For a detailed analysis of the variants, see François-Louis Ganshof, "Note sur deux textes de droit canonique dans le *Liber Floridus*," in *Études d'histoire du droit canonique dédiées à Gabriel Le Bras*, vol. 1 (Paris, 1965), 99–115, at 106–114. On the early spousal distinction, see H. Zeimentz, *Ehe nach der Lehre der Frühscholastik* (Düsseldorf, 1973), 119–24; and H. J. F. Reinhardt, *Die Ehelehre der Schule des Anselms von Laon*, = BGPhThM NF 14 (1974), 78–86.

[231] A. Wilmart, "Une rédaction française des Sentences dites d'Anselme de Laon," RThAM 11 (1939): 119–44, at 129 (no. 19). The source is a version of the *Cum omnia sacramenta* that occurs in *Vat. Reginensis lat. 241*, among other places. Ganshof, "Note sur deux textes," 108n32, cites a dozen other witnesses to this version of the treatise.

[232] For examples of the fullest version, see the following: F. P. Bliemetzrieder, "Autour de l'oeuvre théologique d'Anselme de Laon," RThAM 1 (1929): 435–83, at 476–77; or idem, "Gratian und die Schule Anselms von Laon," *Archiv für katholisches Kirchenrecht* 112 (1932): 37–63, at 62–63; *Liber Floridus*, in F. L. Ganshof, "Note sur deux textes," 100; *Cum omnia sacramenta*, in Bliemetzrieder, *Anselms von Laon systematische Sentenzen*, 147. A version of the *sententia* in the *Liber Pancrisis* (ascribed to Ivo) ends after the example of sex, without the example of cash and the description of consent: see F. P. Bliemetzrieder, *Zu den Schriften Ivos von Chartres* (Vienna, 1917), 68, no. 15.

[233] Lottin, PsM V, 135–36, no. 207.

suggest that the two agreements were not originally conceived as phases in a normal sequence. Perhaps the purpose was to separate certain personal, domestic, merely secular, or even improper agreements from the sacred agreement that churchmen regulated as marriage.

The *fides pactionis*, *fides consensus* distinction survived in canon law as the text *Duobus modis* (the full version of the *sententia*), which was incongruously ascribed to Augustine. This canon was not in Gratian's original *Decretum*, but the decretists cited it, beginning with Paucapalea, and it was added to Gratian's *Decretum* as a *palea*. It passed thence to the *Compilatio Prima* (completed by 1191) and to the *Liber Extra*.[234] Gratian himself, in the first recension of the *Decretum*, shows no sign that was familiar with any version of the betrothal distinction.

A different but related distinction appears in the *Liber Pancrisis* immediately after a seminal treatise on marriage, the *De coniugiis tractantibus*. In this version, the phrase "troth of marriage" (*fides coniugii*) replaces "troth of consent" (*fides consensus*). The troth of a pact (*fides pactionis*) is that whereby a man "promises to receive a woman as his own," whereas the troth of marriage (*fides coniugii*) is that "by which, with the mutual assent of both, he accepts her as his own, whether during the solemnities or before them." It does not matter, therefore, whether the acceptance occurs before or during a wedding.[235] The crux here is a distinction between promising and accepting or receiving.

Modern scholars generally ascribe this *sententia* and its version of the distinction to William of Champeaux. The *sententia* is improbably ascribed to Ivo of Chartres in the *Liber Pancrisis* and in the closely related florilegium contained in the manuscript *Avranches 19*,[236] but it also occurred in a Paris manuscript that is no longer extant, where the *sententia* itself was unattributed but the section in which it appeared was headed, "Here begin the sentences of William the bishop of Châlons-sur-Marne" (i.e., William of Champeaux).[237] But this evidence is negligible. Even if the section as a whole was indeed composed of William's

---

[234] Gratian, C. 27 q. 2 c. 51 (1078). *Quinque compilationes antiquae* I, 4.4.1, ed. Friedberg (Graz, 1882/1956), p. 46. X 4.4.1 (CIC 2:680). These texts have *vel etiam pro consensu* ("or even for consent") instead of *vel etiam pro censu* ("or even for cash"), although this makes no sense in context.

[235] *Liber Pancrisis*, in MS British Library, Harley 3098, 74v. Printed editions: G. Lefèvre, *Les variations de Guillaume de Champeaux* (Lille, 1898), 74; and F. P. Bliemetzrieder, "Paul Fournier und das literarische Werk Ivos von Chartres," *Archiv für katholisches Kirchenrechte* 115 (1935): 53–91, at 78–79. Because the *De coniugiis tractantibus* begins with a division of topics, which it follows precisely, it is clear that this unrelated *sententia*, which comes next, does not belong to the treatise, although both Lefèvre and Bliemetzrieder present it as if it were the last paragraph of the treatise.

[236] Bliemetzrieder's note at the foot of p. 78 – "W [i.e., MS Paris, BnF Cod. lat. 18113] mit der Überschrift: Juo" – is a mistake. W should be Tr, i.e., MS Troyes 425 (a manuscript of the *Liber Pancrisis* copied from MS Harley 3098). Bliemetzrieder's only access to W was via Lefèvre's edition, since the original codex perished in 1914: see next note.

[237] MS Paris, BnF, Cod. lat. 18113. On the loss of the manuscript, see Ganshof, "Note sur deux textes," 106n25; and Reinhardt, *Ehelehre*, 79n26. One can reconstruct the contents of the

authentic *sententiae*, it included patristic as well as medieval material. There is no reason to suppose, therefore, that William himself composed the text in question.

A third version of the distinction occurs in a *sententia* preserved in the earlier of two recensions of a treatise on marriage known by its incipit, *Cum omnia sacramenta*. The *sententia* occurs immediately before a version of the usual *fides pactionis/fides consensus* text, as if the two formed a single *sententia*, but the respective terminologies are mutually inconsistent. In this third formulation, the word *pactio* denotes the stronger, indissoluble mode of troth. The text begins with a scenario: The partners mutually consent to marry "after one month or some other period, confirming their agreement by oaths with their hands on sacred objects." Are they already man and wife (*coniuges*)? No, for what they have entered into is only a conjugal promise (*promissio coniugalis*), and not a conjugal pact (*pactio coniugalis*).[238]

The fourth version is the enduring distinction between future-tense and present-tense agreements. This, too, first appears in sentential treatises on marriage. Both the *In coniugio figura* and the *Sententiae Atrebatenses* use this temporal distinction to interpret or elaborate the *fides pactionis, fides consensus* distinction. The authors were probably more familiar with the temporal distinction but had come across the *fides pactionis, fides consensus* distinction in the sources that they were adapting. The *In coniugio figura* explains that *fides pactionis* is about the future (*de futuro*), whereas *fides consensus* is about the present (*de praesenti*). The author counts *fides consensus* with a prior partner as one of the three valid reasons for divorce, the others being adultery and the inability to render the conjugal debt.[239] The *Sententiae Abrebatenses* combines the two distinctions when discussing the impediment of nonage. There is *fides pactionis*, according to this author, when a man agrees to marry a woman on condition that she permits him to have sex with her. Oddly enough, the author thinks that *fides pactionis* in that case *would* constitute the impediment of prior marriage, although he concedes that others say the opposite. He next explains that there are two kinds of consensual troth: *fides consensus de futuro*, and *fides consensus de praesenti*.[240] There is *fides consensus de futuro*, for

---

miscellany from its description by V. Cousin, *Ouvrages inédits d'Abélard* (Paris, 1836), appendix 3, 625–26. Cousin knew the manuscript as Paris, Notre Dame 222.

[238] *Cum omnia sacramenta*, ed. Bliemetzrieder, 146–47.

[239] *In coniugio figura est*, ed. Bliemetzrieder, 113/4–7.

[240] O. Lottin, "Les *Sententie Atrebatenses*," RThAM 10 (1938): 205–24, 344–57, at 355/135–139 (or idem, PsM 5, 438/156–160). Cf. Lottin, "Une tradition spéciale du texte des *Sententiae divinae paginae*," in *Studia Mediaevalia in honorem admodum Reverendi Patris Raymundi Josephi Martin* (Bruges, [1948]), 147–69, at 160/16–161/19 (or PsM 5, 365/14–17): "Necessarius autem est ad coniugium par consensus utriusque. Consensus alius in presenti, alius de futuro. Similiter de fide: fides consensus de presenti, non de futuro, facit coniugium." ("The mutual consent of both partners is necessary for marriage. There is consent about the present and consent about the future. It is the same with faith: What makes marriage is faith of consent about the present, not about the future.")

example, when a man agrees to marry a woman if her father pays him twenty marks
by an agreed time. But such conditional troth is not a fatal impediment to another
union, partly because the agreement is not about the present, but chiefly because
stipulated conditions sometimes fail to materialize.[241]

The compiler of a florilegium on marriage known as the *In primis hominibus*
focuses on grammatical tense as the basis of the distinction. When "a man and a
woman swear that they will accept each other as spouses and constitute this either
with some security [perhaps a monetary gift or a signed document] or by the gift of a
ring," such an agreement is "not yet marriage, because 'I *will* take you' is one thing,
and 'I *take* you' is another." To marry, on the contrary, is for a man

> to receive a woman as his own, and [for a woman] to receive a man as her own, by
> consenting and willing that they should not forsake each other as long as they live,
> and that each should hand over his body to the other in rendering the conjugal
> debt; and by expressing this consent with words such as these: 'I accept [*volo*] you as
> my wife' and 'you as my husband,' or by not contradicting those who are
> joining them.

The wording is crucial, but they may use rituals and gestures as well, such as the
traditio (a father's gift of his daughter) and the joining of hands. The consensual
proof texts by Ambrose and Isidore, the author adds, must refer to *de praesenti*
betrothals.[242]

The *Sententiae Berolinenses*, which was dependent on the *In primis hominibus*, is
less clear, and its author seems not to have fully understood the distinction. He
defines marriage as "the indivisible joining of a man and a woman" that occurs
"when the man says to the woman, 'I accept [*volo*] you as my wife,' and the woman
says, 'I accept you as my husband'."[243] This formula is in the present tense, but the
treatise does not posit a distinction between future-tense and present-tense betrothals. In answer to whether a marriage begins when an oath (*iusiurandum*) is sworn,
the author replies, following Augustine, that a marriage begins with "the first troth of
betrothal" (*prima fides sponsionis*), and not when the troth is consummated in sexual
intercourse, since it is troth, and not coitus, that makes marriage.[244]

5.5.2 *The distinction of tense*

Unlike the other versions of the betrothal distinction, the *de futuro, de praesenti*
version is explicitly grammatical. Authors often explained it by suggesting what
words to use, as in the passage from the *In primis hominibus* quoted earlier. They

[241] Ed. Lottin, "Les *Sententiae Atrebatenses*," RThAM 10, 355/140–43 (or PsM 5, 438/161–66).
[242] Ed. B. Matecki, *Der Traktat In primis hominibus* (Frankfurt am Main, 2001), 39*–40*.
[243] F. Stegmüller, "*Sententiae Berolinenses*: Eine neugefundene Sentenzensammlung aus der
Schule des Anselm von Laon," RThAM 11 (1939): 33–61, at 60/35–37.
[244] Ibid., 61/1–3.

always stated the norm in Latin, assuming that clergy would be able to translate it into the vernacular of their parishioners. The verbal emphasis had become standard in northern France by the middle of the twelfth century. According to Hugh of Saint-Victor, writing in the 1130s, a proper expression of *de praesenti* consent might be: "I take you as my own, so that henceforth you are to be my wife, and I your husband. And she says likewise, I take you as my own, so that henceforth I am to be your wife, and you my husband."[245] According to Peter Lombard, writing in the 1150s, they should express their consent by saying, "I take you as my husband," and "I take you as my wife," or "in other words that signify the same thing."[246] But "if they agree about the future, saying, 'I *shall* take you as a husband,' and 'I *shall* take you as a wife,' this consent is not that which makes matrimony."[247]

The verbal turn was congruent with the doctrine of marriage as a sacrament, for every sacrament has its "word," or verbal formula, but it must also have been practically expedient. The betrothal distinction had to be made somehow, and it would be hard to think of a means that was easier to explain and disseminate than the distinction of tense. Examples of verbal formulae superseded conceptual distinctions, although the policy was flexible and did not require any specific verbal formula (*certa verba*). If needs be, a spouse could plight her troth without saying anything. Even in Latin, the phonetic distinction between *accipiam* and *accipio* was small, but the circumstances and the stereotyped idioms associated with present-tense betrothal, such as "to have and to hold," "in sickness and in health," and "until death do us part," which are conspicuous in legal depositions from late-medieval England and Ireland, would have obviated such problems even when the partners plighted their troth in secular settings or with a single witness.

The grammatical norm lent itself readily to promulgation. Richard Poore, as bishop of Salisbury in the early-thirteenth century, and again later, as bishop of Durham, instructed his priests to "teach persons contracting marriage this form of words in French or in English: *Ego .N. accipio te in meum.*" Richard explains that marriage is contracted through such words, and that they have "great power."[248]

---

[245] Hugh of St. Victor, *De sacramentis christianae fidei* II.11.5, PL 176:488B: "ille dicit: Ego te accipio in meam, ut deinceps et tu uxor mea sis, et ego maritus tuus, et illa similiter dicit: Ego te accipio in meum, ut deinceps et ego uxor tua sim, et tu maritus meus."

[246] Peter Lombard, *Sent.* IV, 27.3.1 (423): "Accipio te in virum et ego te in uxorem, matrimonium facit." Ibid., IV, 28.4.2, 435: "Cum igitur sic convenient, ut dicat vir: *Accipio te in meam coniugem*, et dicat mulier: *Accipio te in meum virum*, his verbis vel aliis idem significantibus, exprimitur consensus."

[247] Ibid., IV, 27.3.1 (422): "Si enim consentiunt in futurum, dicentes: Accipiam te in virum, et ego te in uxorem, non est iste consensus efficax matrimonii."

[248] F. M. Powicke and C. R. Cheney (eds.), *Councils & Synods with Other Documents Relating to the English Church II, A.D. 1205–1313, Part I: 1205–1265* (Oxford, 1964), Statutes of Salisbury 1217 X 1219, no. 84, p. 87: "Item, precipimus quod sacerdotes doceant personas contrahentes hanc formam verborum in gallico vel anglico: Ego .N. accipio te in meam. Similiter et mulier

Again, the depositions from marriage litigation of late-medieval England and Ireland provide us with many examples of laypersons faultlessly expressing their *de praesenti* consent in domestic or even in private settings, sometimes with and sometimes without clergy at hand to guide them. For example, a laborer, Niall O'Moregan, was the only witness when John McCann married Anisia FitzJohn in a garden, but John properly said, "I take you as my wife," and she properly replied, "I take you as my husband until death do us part."[249]

5.5.3 *The purpose of the betrothal distinction*

The sudden emergence of the betrothal distinction in northern France during the 1120s is remarkable. When one considers it in relation to the nuptial process of the early Middle Ages, what stands out as novel is not the *de futuro* betrothal, for betrothal had always been prospective, but rather the second, present-tense betrothal. Moreover, whereas traditionally a man had been said to receive his wife at the conclusion of the nuptial process, now each partner received the other, and this act of mutual reception was an explicit exchange of consent. From an ecclesiastical point of view, the partners were already man and wife at that point, even if they did not yet begin to live together.

What provided the model for the present-tense betrothal, I suggest, was the preliminary nuptial rite conducted in the presence of a priest at the door or in the porch of a church: a cardinal feature of the clerical "take over" of marriage in northern France and England.[250] The ritual recapitulated in an ecclesiastical setting the traditional secular betrothal, including the ring or other betrothal gifts and the dowry (or dower) contract. A nuptial *ordo* preserved in a late-twelfth-century liturgical manual for bishops from Canterbury, known as the *Magdalen Pontifical* after the library that holds the manuscript, records this prenuptial betrothal rite in a long rubric. The priest first asks those present whether there is any impediment, such as consanguinity or spiritual affinity. Next, he asks each of the partners in turn whether each freely accepts the other, and whether each will care for the other "in health and in sickness," as befits Christians. Then the bridegroom bestows a dowry upon his bride (presumably as a document), and he offers her a ring and some "spousal" coins. After the priest has blessed the ring, the bridegroom takes it and repeats after the priest: "N., with this ring I honor you, and this silver I give to you, and with my body I espouse you, in the name of the Father (on the thumb), and of the Son (on

---

dicat: Ego .N. accipio in meum. In hiis enim verbis consistit vis magna et matrimonium contrahitur."

[249] From a case in the Armagh registers, quoted here from A. Cosgrove, "Marrying and Marriage Litigation in Medieval Ireland," THTH 332–59, at 351–52.

[250] Molin and Mutembe, *Le rituel du mariage*, 30–47. Ritzer, *Le mariage*, 390–95. K. Stevenson, *Nuptial Blessing* (Oxford, 1983), 68–71. C. N. L. Brooke, *The Medieval Idea of Marriage* (Oxford, 1989), 248–57.

the index finger), and of the Holy Spirit (on the middle finger)." Finally, they proceeded into the church for the nuptial mass.[251] This was the ancient nuptial process, such as Pope Nicholas I described, but performed on single occasion in a church setting.

My suggestion, then, is that the church rite, by enacting or recapitulating a betrothal as the first phase of a church wedding, provided the model for positing a betrothal at which the partners became husband and wife: not at the altar, but at the entrance to the church. This hypothesis presupposes that the preliminary rite emerged a little earlier than the earliest extant example, which is in a manuscript that was written at Bury St. Edmunds between 1125 and 1135, and probably used at Laon.[252] After the distinction became established, the *de futuro* betrothal retained the associations of a negotiated settlement or a business transaction, fraught with financial terms and other conditions and sometimes settled in the bride's absence, whereas the *de praesenti* agreement was a sacred rite, whether it was performed in or in front of a church, with a minister present in his official capacity, or even in an entirely secular setting.

Nevertheless, it is unlikely that twelfth-century clerics supposed that their formulas for expressing *de praesenti* betrothals would always or even usually take place in church. Molin and Mutembe's work suggests that in Paris during the time of Hugh of Saint-Victor and Peter Lombard, the partners would have expressed their consent at the prenuptial rite only passively, replying "I do" to a priest's inquiries, as in the rubric from the *Magdalen Pontifical* summarized earlier. The dialogical form, wherein each partner, following the priest, spelled out that he or she accepted the other, does not appear in extant nuptial liturgies until the fourteenth century.[253] By the sixteenth century, the active, dialogical form was prevalent in northeastern and southern France, and sometimes both forms were used in the same rite, as in the Sarum rite. The passive, "I do" form, however, still prevailed in a large central area of France that included Paris.[254]

It is likely, therefore, that when clerics provided formulas for *de praesenti* consent, they were hoping above all to regulate private or domestic agreements. A marriage contracted in a domestic or private setting, without an officiating cleric, was not clandestine if the spouses completed the requisite formalities, such as the banns, in due course.[255] Even when spouses did solemnize their marriages *in facie ecclesiae*, they were often already married. If a cleric was present at the preceding private or domestic ceremony, he could lead the couple

---

[251] H. A. Wilson (ed.), *The Pontifical of Magdalen College*, Henry Bradshaw Society 39 (London, 1910), 202. Although the text is entirely in Latin, the priest would usually have conducted the dialogue in the local vernacular.

[252] Molin and Mutembe, *Le rituel du mariage*, 289–91 (Ordo V). M. Searle and K. W. Stevenson, *Documents of the Marriage Liturgy* (Collegeville, Minnesota, 1992), 148–55.

[253] Molin and Mutembe, *Le rituel du mariage*, 106–09.   [254] Ibid., 110.

[255] McSheffrey, "Place, Space, and Situation," 968, 970–71.

through a dialogue, but it was incumbent upon the clergy to teach the laity how to contract marriage unambiguously even when no cleric was present, as was often the case, and probably more often than not. The dialogical form seems to have originated not in the liturgy, therefore, but through pastoral instruction and promulgation.

6

Consummation

The principle that consent made marriage did not necessarily imply that nothing else was needed for a fixed, fully established marriage (*matrimonium ratum*). Indeed, since the chief means of expressing mutual consent was the betrothal, which was a prospective agreement to marry in the future, it was reasonable to assume that something else was necessary to complete the marriage by marking the coming together of the spouses. Sexual consummation was an obvious candidate, especially in a Christian context, where marriage was construed as the union of two in one flesh: a union that recapitulated Eve's formation from Adam's body. Nevertheless, there was no explicit ecclesiastical doctrine or theory of consummation until the early twelfth century.

The twelfth-century theory of consummation originated in a new set of proof texts, which first appeared in the work of French and Anglo-Norman scholars during the 1120s. Ascribed to Augustine and to Pope Leo I, these partly spurious, partly misquoted texts purported to show that a marriage was incomplete and did not contain the sacrament of Christ and the church until the spouses had come together sexually. The texts seemed to contradict the principle that spouses were virtually married as soon as they were betrothed, which was well established in the canon law tradition and was embodied, as we have seen, in several proof texts. No one questioned the authenticity of the new coital proof texts. Instead, scholars reconciled the two sets of authorities in various ways, and the reconciliation prompted further theorizing. French scholars saved the sufficiency of bare consent, whereas Gratian and his Bolognese followers argued that sexual consummation completed the work that the exchange of consent had begun. This debate coincided with the early development of the sacramental theology of marriage and turned on the premise that marriage was a sacred sign of Christ and the church.

6.1 THE IDEA OF CONSUMMATION

One should not attribute much influence to texts *per se*. Just as one needs to explain why scholars assembled and misquoted the new proof texts, so one needs a reception theory to explain why other scholars accepted and appropriated them. The coital proof texts articulated and provided a theological rationale for the idea that spouses completed their marriage by going to bed together and becoming "two in one flesh." By reconciling these texts with the consensual dossier – especially the proof texts from Augustine, Ambrose, and Isidore – which was much more firmly entrenched in the canonical tradition, scholars could resolve ancient tensions and uncertainties and articulate positions that satisfied the needs both of canonical practice and of theological speculation.

Although the theory that sexual intercourse "consummated" (i.e., completed, or perfected) the formation of marriage was an innovation of the twelfth century, the idea had been implicit in a mass of tradition, law, custom, and vaguely articulated presuppositions. The idea of consummation itself makes little sense in abstraction from the context of customs and expectations in which it was historically embedded. Moreover, sexual consummation sometimes served as a conceptual surrogate for the sexual relationship in marriage: the active and mutual observance of the conjugal debt.

Marrying in the early Middle Ages was a process that began with betrothal and was completed when the spouses came together as man and wife, when the woman began to live in her husband's home. The husband was said to "lead" his wife in marriage (*ducere eam in matrimonium*), or to receive her (*accipere*) as his wife. People naturally assumed that sexual consummation normally occurred at that point, when betrothal became marriage (*nuptiae*). A *desponsata* or *sponsa* (a betrothed woman) became a *nupta* (a married woman) when the spouses finally came together, and typically when they came together in bed.[1] The nonoccurrence of coitus after marriage, as in Gregory's story of Iniuriosus (Section 5.3.2), was abnormal and remarkable, and the status of an unconsummated marriage was problematic and disputable in canon law. Nevertheless, the role of coitus remained largely undefined in the European laws of marriage throughout the early Middle Ages. There is nothing in Roman law or in the written Germanic law codes to indicate that the partners were not properly married until they came together sexually, although there was plenty of legal precedent for dissolving the marriage if the partners were *unable* to do so.

To conclude their wedding, the spouses went to bed together. Pope Nicholas I included coitus among the things that were "celebrated" in marriage,[2] and the verb

---

[1] J. Gaudemet, *Le mariage en occident* (Paris, 1987), 185–88. C. H. Joyce, *Christian Marriage*, 2nd edition (London, 1948), 610–11.

[2] Nicholas I, *Epist.* 99 (*Responsa ad consulta Bulgarorum*), c. 3, in MGH *Epist.* 6, *Epistolae Karolini Aevi* 4 (1925), 570/20–24.

celebrare implied publicity. The bedding was a feature of secular nuptial rituals. There is scattered evidence for secular bedding customs throughout Southern and Northern Europe, but the clearest evidence is from late-medieval Scandinavia. In Sweden, for example, the bridal company led the couple to their bed in a well-lit chamber and gave them special foods to eat before leaving them to consummate their marriage. A nuptial bed was sometimes made especially for the occasion.[3]

Because the bedding of the spouses was the usual conclusion of the secular celebration of marriage, early-medieval nuptial liturgies included the blessing of the bed or of the couple on or in the bed (*benedictio in thalamo* or *ordo in thalamo*).[4] This rite preceded the wedding in Spain, but it concluded the nuptials in northern Europe, where it seems to have been the earliest situation in which clergy became involved in marrying, although it is possible that the term *thalamus* was sometimes used metonymically to denote marriage.[5] Once the Roman nuptial liturgy became established in France, the bedchamber rite was the sequel to a church wedding and nuptial mass.[6] Nevertheless, there are indications that the bedchamber rite could still function even as late as the tenth century as the only priestly participation in marrying. For example, the nuptial rite of the so-called *Egbert Pontifical*, from tenth-century England, includes prayers for the blessing of the bedchamber, the bed, the couple, and the ring, but it does not include a nuptial mass or any reference to solemnization in or at a church.[7]

Nuptial gifts from husband to wife sometimes appear in the guise of the price of a woman's virginity or modesty. There are references in classical Roman tradition to a *pretium pudicitiae* ("price of chastity"), which a husband gave to his bride on the morning after their wedding night. In post-classical sources, the term *pretium pudicitiae* was sometimes used to denote the husband's counter dowry (the *donatio ante nuptias* or *donatio propter nuptias*).[8] This term is used in the Latin translations of Exodus 21:10, according to which a husband should pay for the wedding and for his wife's clothing and should not "refuse the price of her chastity [*pretium*

---

[3] M. Korpiola, *Between Betrothal and Bedding* (Leiden, 2009), 60–66.

[4] K. Ritzer, *Le mariage* (Paris, 1970), 273–76. For the *Ordo thalami* in the *Sacramentary of Vich* (11th century), in Ritzer, *Le mariage*, 436–37. On the medieval Spanish nuptial liturgy in general, see B. F. Bethune, *The Text of the Christian Rite of Marriage in Medieval Spain* (diss., University of Toronto, 1987). Bethune collates the rubrics and prayers from several sources (210 ff.), ranging from the eleventh-century *Liber ordinum* (extant in codices probably written in the monasteries of Santo Domingo de Silos and San Prudencio de Monte Laturce in the Rioja) to late-medieval sources. On the distinguishing features of the Spanish nuptial liturgy, see ibid., 140–209.

[5] As Y. Hen argues in *Culture and Religion in Merovingian Gaul* (Leiden, 1995), 133.

[6] Ritzer, *Le mariage*, 314–17.

[7] Ibid., 312–13. For the texts, see H. M. J. Banting (ed.), *Two Anglo-Saxon Pontificals (the Egbert and Sidney Sussex Pontificals)*, Henry Bradshaw Society 104 (London, 1989), 133–34 and 140.

[8] B. M. Osuna and C. O. Garcia, "*Pretium pudicitiae* y donación nupcial," *Revista de estudios histórico-jurídicos* 26 (2004): 61–84.

pudicitiae]."[9] A Greek dotal instrument (written dowry contract) written on papyrus in the sixth century AD presupposes a similar custom. The husband states that, having found his wife's virginity intact, he owes a certain amount of money to her as her "*hedna* or gifts on behalf of marriage."[10] The *hedna* was usually a pre-nuptial gift, but here it functions as a *pretium pudicitiae*. The notion that a husband had to compensate his wife for taking away her chastity put marriage in a somewhat negative light. Christian scholars considered any woman's loss of virginity to be precisely that – a loss – even when this was the conclusion of a happy wedding. Leander of Seville says in a treatise on holy virginity that it is customary for men when they marry to "bestow dowries, to confer riches, and to hand over their patrimony" to their brides "in exchange for the modesty that must be lost [*ad vicem perdendi pudoris*]." As a result, "their wives seem to have been rather purchased than married." In contrast, Leander argues, holy virgins are betrothed to Christ, who redeems them with the dowry of his blood without taking anything from them.[11] Leander implies rhetorically that wives are akin to slaves and prostitutes.

Sexual intercourse was sometimes a precondition for the wife's reception of her nuptial gifts. The practice of the betrothal kiss presupposed that sexual union, of which the kiss was a token, confirmed the husband's gift.[12] Hincmar of Reims, as we shall see later, assumed that the husband's dowry became effective only when the partners consummated their marriage. The term *Morgengabe* ("morning gift") indicates that this gift was originally a reward given to a bride after sexual consummation, perhaps in recognition that she had proved to be a virgin, although the customs and rules of the gift remain elusive today. References to a nuptial gift variously called *morgingeba*, *morgengifu*, *morgincap*, and so forth appear in the written laws of most of the Germanic peoples during the early Middle Ages.[13] Husbands gave the morning gift to their brides at the time of their marriage or during the "nuptials," but the term itself suggests that it was originally given on the morning after the first night together, either in recognition that their brides had proved to be virgins or "in exchange for their modesty," as Leander put it.

The scattered evidence from early-medieval legal sources and formulas suggests that when elite people distinguished the morning gift from the dowry given by the husband (*dos ex marito*), the former was typically an optional, smaller, and more portable gift. It might consist of chattels or movables for the wife's personal use as

[9] Quoted from the Douay translation.
[10] J. Evans Grubbs, "Marrying and Its Documentation in Later Roman Law," in THTH 43–94, at 83.
[11] Leander, *De institutione virginum et contemptu mundi*, PL 72:876B–C.
[12] Tertullian, *De virginibus velandis* 11.4–5, CCL 2:1221. CTh 3.5.6 (= *Brev.* 3.5.5, CJ 5.3.16).
[13] L. Feller, "Morgengabe, dot, tertia," in F. Bougard, L. Feller, and R. Le Jan (eds.), *Dots et douaires dans le haut moyen âge* (Rome, 2002), 1–25, at 17. See also the references under *Morgengabe* in the index to *Dots et douaires*, and R. Le Jan, "Aux origines de douaire médiévale (VIe–Xe siècle)," in Le Jan, *Femmes, pouvoir et société dans le haut Moyen Âge* (Paris, 2001), 53–67.

distinct from real estate and other immovable property, which her husband would continue to manage as long as they were married. An elaborate Visigothic dotal formula composed in verse states that the groom agrees to give his bride as her morning gift (*morgingeba*) ten boys, ten girls, ten horses, ten mules, and arms, "among other things." No small gift – but the dowry, which the formula describes next, is immovable and much larger, consisting of real estate and such agricultural property as vines, meadows, pastures, and woodland.[14] A law in the code of the Ribvarian Franks states that if a husband dies and there is no written betrothal contract to determine what his widow should inherit, she is entitled to one third of everything that they earned together as her inheritance, to fifty *solidi* as her dowry, and to any morning gift that he had given to her.[15] An Alammanian law states that if a widow wants to relinquish her late husband's estate in order to remarry and there are no surviving children of the union, she is entitled to take goods worth forty *solidi* in gold, silver, slaves, and so forth as her "legitimate dowry," and in addition to goods worth twelve *solidi* if he had given her a morning gift.[16]

The morning gift does not appear in the surviving Merovingian and Carolingian dotal charters, but that was probably because it had become merged with the dowry (*dos*) provided by the husband. Gregory of Tours records that Chilperic, a brutal Merovingian king, gave Galswinth five cities "both as her dowry and as her *morganebyba*, that is, her morning gift."[17] Gregory's phrase (*tam in dote quam in morganebyba*), which sounds like a standard legal idiom, suggests that dowry and morning gift were still distinct in principle, but that the huge gift of real estate served both purposes in this case. Frankish dotal charters sometimes subdivide the dowry in a manner comparable to that of the Visigothic charter mentioned earlier. For example, a seventh-century Merovingian charter from Angers divides the dowry given by the husband into three parts: (1) real estate and agricultural property, including a house with the surrounding woods, meadows, pastures, waters, and so forth; (2) moveable chattels, including jewelry and a bedspread; and (3) domestic animals, including a horse with all its trappings, oxen, cows, sheep, and pigs.[18] The chattels and other personal, more portable components are probably a vestige of the morning gift.[19] The early-medieval morning gift remains obscure, but the *morgongjäf* of late-medieval Sweden appears, at last, in the clear light of day, for it was well

---

[14] *Formulae Merowingici et Karolini Aevi*, MGH *Legum* V, *Formulae*, ed. K. Zeumer, Vis. 20, 584/13. I am assuming that only the initial items constituted the morning gift, although one might argue that the placement of the term "morning gift" is merely poetic, or even that the initial passage in which the term occurs was taken from another source.

[15] *Lex Ribvaria* 37.2 (39.2), in MGH *Leges* (in folio) 5 (1875–1889), 231–32; or *Lex Ribvaria* 41.2, in MGH *Leges nationum Germanicarum* 3.2 (1954), 95.

[16] *Leges Alamannorum* 54.1–3, in MGH *Leges nationum Germanicarum* 5.1 (1966), 112–14.

[17] *Historiae* IX.20, MGH *Scriptores rerum Merovingicarum* 1.1 (1937), 437. Chilperic also agreed to relinquish his concubines, but he later had Galswinth strangled so that he could marry one of them.

[18] Formula *And.* 1c, ed. Zeumer, p. 5.

[19] As R. Le Jan suggests in "Aux origines de douaire médiévale (VIᵉ–Xᵉ siècle)," 59.

documented. Here, the amount of the morning gift was determined at the betrothal, and the gift was traditionally given before witnesses on the morning after the wedding night, although it was not conditional on successful consummation. The traditional association of the Swedish morning gift with bedding survived better in rural areas, whereas it waned in the towns under the influence of continental laws and customs.[20]

Although there is hardly any evidence from medieval legal sources that couples were not considered to be properly married until they had gone to bed together, there is an exception to this rule of silence in late-medieval Iceland, where a legal marriage required the betrothal (*festar*), the subsequent wedding feast (which usually followed one year later), and the bedding, which implied consummation. The partners were not considered to be legally married until witnesses had observed them go to bed together.[21] Thus, according to the laws of the *Grágás*, "A wedding is celebrated in accordance with law if a legal administrator betroths the woman and there are six men at least at the wedding and the bridegroom goes openly into the same bed as the woman."[22]

During the central and late Middle Ages, bedding probably had more signifi-cance in local secular law than it did in learned canon law and the *ius commune*. Here, too, the evidence is better for late-medieval Sweden, where the husband became his wife's guardian and legal representative and took control over her property only after the bedding.[23] In Italy, the fifteenth-century canonist Panormi-tanus (Nicholaus de Tudeschis) noted that a woman was not usually said to be *nupta* until her husband had "led" her into his house, and that the partners were custom-arily called *sponsi* until they had consummated their marriage. Only at that point did they assume the titles of husband and wife (*vir* and *uxor*). Panormitanus did not question that consent alone was sufficient to create a valid and sacramental marriage under the church's law, but he reasoned that the woman's transition from *sponsa* to *nupta* through consummation was material to the interpretation of local statutes about dowries.[24]

The idea of consummated marriage owed as much if not more to religious ideas as it did to secular laws and customs. In Scripture, marriage is a union of "two in one flesh" (Gen 2:24): a polyvalent idea, to be sure, but one from which sexual union can hardly be excluded. Indeed, Paul warns that a man who has sex with a prostitute

---

[20] Korpiola, *Between Betrothal and Bedding*, 78–85.
[21] R. Frank, "Marriage in Twelfth- and Thirteenth-Century Iceland," *Viator* 4 (1973): 473–84, at 475; and J. Jochens, "The Church and Sexuality in Medieval Iceland," *Journal of Medieval History* 6 (1980): 377–92, at 380.
[22] *Grágás II* in A. Dennis, P. Foote, and R. Jenkins (ed. and trans.), *Laws of Early Iceland*, vol. 2 (Mannitoba, 2000), add. 147, p. 243. *Grágás* is the collective term for written Icelandic laws originating before the Iceland's submission to Norway in the 1260s.
[23] Korpiola, *Between Betrothal and Bedding*, 74–78.
[24] C. Donahue, Jr., "Was There a Change in Marriage Law in the Late Middle Ages?" *Rivista internazionale di diritto commune* 6 (1995): 49–80, at 54.

becomes one flesh with her (1 Cor 6:16). In the fifth chapter of Ephesians, Paul weaves the idea of the union of two in one flesh into a characteristically somatic account of Christ's union with the church, which he proposes as the exemplar for every Christian marriage. A man should regard his wife as his own flesh, Paul argues, for the church is Christ's body. The possible role of consummation in marriage is already implicit in theological arguments during the patristic period. Jerome assumed that to save Mary's perpetual virginity he had to concede that Mary and Joseph had never truly been man and wife.[25] Ambrose and Augustine argued, on the contrary, that Mary was truly Joseph's wife, but their vigorous defense of this position presupposed that some held the opposite.[26]

The role of consummation is implicit in the terminology of Christian marriage. Tertullian's account of the veiling of brides presupposed that a bride became *nupta* ("wedded") when she experienced sexual intercourse.[27] The verb *nubere* (from *nubes*: "cloud," "veil") meant "to veil" as well as "to marry," and the noun *nuptiae* denoted in the first place the nuptials. Nevertheless, both *nupta* and *nuptiae* had sexual connotations even in classical Latin.[28] Archbishop Hincmar of Reims, in a letter to be considered later, characterizes the bride and groom after their wedding but before consummation as *nuptiati sed innupti*: wedded but unmarried.[29] He calls them *nuptiati* – the past participle of the late-Latin verb *nuptiare*, "to marry" – because they had publicly celebrated their nuptials, whereas he calls them *innupti* partly because the term *nupti* (the past participle of *nubere*) had sexual connotations, and partly because he was thinking of 1 Corinthians 7:10–11: "And unto the married I command, yet not I, but the Lord: Let not the wife depart from her husband, but if she depart, let her remain unmarried [*innupta*] or else be reconciled to her husband." Hincmar says that spouses who divorce on grounds of fornication cannot remarry but must either remain *innupti* (i.e., single, celibate) or, if they are not strong enough for continence, do penance and be reconciled.[30] He extends Paul's term *innupti* by analogy from divorcees to newlyweds.

Ivo of Chartres, following Augustine, maintains that spouses become virtually married when they are betrothed, but the shadow of an opposing, coital theory of marriage appears in Ivo's letter to Lisiardus, bishop of Soissons, regarding a man who had married the sister of a girl to whom he had previously been betrothed. In Ivo's view, the marriage is incestuous and invalid even though the first union was not consummated. "If you object," Ivo argues, "that there has been no marriage where it is found that sexual intercourse did not follow, I respond from the authority of the

---

[25] Jerome, *Adversus Helvidium* 3–4, PL 23:194–95. Idem, *Comm. in Mattheum* 1:16, CCL 77:9.
[26] Ambrose, *De institutione virginis* 6(41), PL 16:316B–C; *Expositio in Lucam* II.5, CCL 14:33/ 84–86. Augustine, *De nupt. et conc.* I.11(12–13), CSEL 42:224–25.
[27] Tertullian, *De virginibus velandis* 11.4–5, CCL 2:1221.
[28] MWCh 328–31.
[29] Hincmar, *Epistola* 136, in MGH *Epistolae* 8, = *Epistolae Karolini Aevi* 6, 103/29–32.
[30] Ibid., 104/11–12, 23.

fathers [i.e., the consensual proof texts] that a marriage is indissoluble as soon as the conjugal pact has been settled."[31]

A text from Ambrose that passed into the canonical tradition seemed in the central Middle Ages to imply that coitus had some role in the formation of marriage. "If a man uses a woman who has been betrothed and given to him," Ambrose wrote, "it is called marriage. He who assails the chastity of another man's wife commits adultery."[32] Ambrose was making a point about sex within marriage, and not about the formation of marriage. The original sense of the passage is clear in Ivo's *Decretum*, where he quoted the whole passage in a sequence of canons on adultery.[33] The *Panormia*, though, quotes the first clause alone, without the contrast with adultery, in a sequence of consensual proof texts, including the usual texts from Ambrose, Augustine, and Isidore.[34] In that setting, the text must have unsettled the consensual doctrine and raised a problem for discussion.

Medieval people assumed that coitus established a relationship of fact between a man and a woman, quite apart from anything that it did *de iure*. The partners became biologically related. Indeed, sexual intercourse *per se*, even outside marriage, could establish a relationship of affinity. For example, a man could not validly marry the sister of a woman with whom he had copulated. Bruno the Carthusian (d. 1101), commenting on Ephesians 5:32, explores the natural dimensions of the becoming one flesh. Although a man acquires his flesh from his parents, Bruno explains, he becomes carnally more closely related to his wife. This union of two in one flesh is founded on the created order of things, for the first woman was formed from the flesh of the first man. Moreover, sexual union is so powerful that it unites male and female in a physical manner. Some *physici* report that if blood from a man and from a woman who have had sexual intercourse is put in a vessel, the samples become indivisibly mixed, whereas if they have not had sexual intercourse with each other, their samples will remain separate.[35] A twelfth-century scholar distinguishes between the factual and moral aspects of sexual union in a gloss on 1 Corinthians 6:16, where Paul says that a man who has sex with a prostitute becomes one flesh with her. Paul was making a moral point, the scholar explains, intending to bring disgrace upon such men, but what he said was also literally true in a physical sense. When a man has sexual intercourse, "some of his semen is incorporated into the woman," so that what was a part of his body is now a part of hers. The man "too, contracts certain humors through certain pores, and these humors are incorporated, and so, again, he is made one with her." The scholar cites empirical evidence for this exchange: "If a leper copulates with a woman, the first man who follows him,

---

[31] Ivo, *Epist.* 246, PL 162:253B.   [32] Ambrose, *Epist.* 60 (*ad Paternum*), PL 16:1183B–C.

[33] Ivo, *Decretum* VIII.101.   [34] *Panormia* VI.17. Likewise, SMA 2 (p. 167).

[35] Bruno the Carthusian (of Reims), *Expositio in epistolas sancti Pauli*, on Eph 5:32, PL 153:346B–C. The term *physici* in this period denoted scholars who studied *naturalia* or natural philosophy. Physicians were called *medici*.

whether after a brief or a long time, will undoubtedly contract leprosy."[36] He was probably referring to venereal disease.

6.2 ORIGINS OF THE COITAL PROOF TEXTS

The two earliest extant appearances of the coital proof texts date from the 1120s. One is in a popular florilegium known as the *Sententiae Magistri A.*, the first extant version of which was probably complete by the mid-1120s.[37] The other is in the *Collectio decem partium*, a canonical collection composed in 1123 or shortly thereafter. The latter was probably the work of Hildebert of Lavardin, bishop of Le Mans and archbishop of Tours.[38] Both of these works reflect northern-French scholarship, and both were probably dependent, directly or indirectly, on a common but now unknown source for the coital proof texts.

In the *Sententiae Magistri A.*, the dossier consists of three *sententiae* ascribed to Augustine and Pope Leo I, as follows:

[1] Augustine, on perfect marriage: Marriage is not perfect when sexual intercourse [*commixtio sexuum*] does not follow. [2] Again [Augustine]: Marriage does not have in itself a sacrament of Christ and the church if sexual intercourse [*commixtio sexuum*] does not follow it. Nor is the woman in whom it is shown that there has been no sexual intercourse able to belong to marriage. [3] Pope Leo: Since the partnership of marriage was instituted from the beginning in such a way that without sexual intercourse [*praeter commixtionem sexuum*] it should *not* have in itself a sacrament of Christ and the church [Eph 5:32], there is no doubt that a woman in whom it is shown that there has been no nuptial mystery does not belong to marriage.[39]

The first *sententia* may have originated as a rubric, for it merely states the gist of the next *sententia*, although the phrase "on perfect marriage" could be construed as the title of a treatise. In any case, Augustine said no such thing. The third *sententia* is indeed from a letter by Pope Leo I, but it is misquoted. The word "not" (*non*), italicized in the quotation above, has been inserted, and its insertion alters the meaning of *praeter* ("besides"). The phrase *commixtio sexuum* ("mingling of the sexes") replaces Leo's less specific phrase *coniunctio sexuum* ("joining of the sexes").

---

[36] Lottin, PsM V, pp. 101–02, no. 127. Also MS Oxford, Bodleian, Laud Misc. 216, 145rb.

[37] P. H. J. Th. Maas, *The Liber Sententiarum Magistri A.* (Nijmegen, 1995). See also Robert Somerville's review of Maas's study in *Speculum* 74 (1999): 207–09, at 209.

[38] L. Kéry, *Canonical Collections of the Early Middle Ages* (Washington, DC, 1999), 263.

[39] SMA 60–62 (pp. 185–86): "AVG. DE PERFECTO CONIVGIO. Non est perfectum coniugium, ubi non sequitur commixtio sexuum. ITEM. Non habent nuptie Christi et ecclesie in se sacramentum, si eas non subsequatur commixtio sexuum, nec pertinere poterit illa mulier ad matrimonium, cum qua docetur non fuisse commixtio sexuum. LEO PAPA. Cum societas nuptiarum ita ab initio constituta sit, ut preter sexuum commixtionem *non* haberet in se Christi et ecclesie sacramentum, dubium non est eam mulierem non pertinere ad matrimonium, in qua docetur nuptiale non fuisse misterium." (Emphasis mine.)

Moreover, Leo was concerned about the absence of freedom or equality in a marriage, and not about the absence of sexual intercourse. As we shall see, all of these misunderstandings stemmed from a letter by Hincmar of Reims, which was the proximate source of the proof texts.

In the *Collectio decem partium*, the first two texts, ascribed to Augustine, are the same as the corresponding texts in the *Sententiae Magistri A.*, but the third text, ascribed to Leo, is different:

> Since the partnership of marriage was instituted from the beginning in such a way that it cannot exist without the joining of sexes [*praeter sexuum coniunctionem*], which has in itself a sacrament of Christ and the church, there is no doubt that a woman in whom it is shown that there was no nuptial mystery does not attain to marriage.[40]

The gist is the same, but the added negation is supplied by the phrase *esse non posset* ("it cannot exist"), whereas a relative pronoun (*quae*) appears in place of the *non* of the other version. Contrariwise, the authentic phrase *coniunctio sexuum* appears here instead of the later *commixtio sexuum*. It is this other version of Leo's dictum that appears in the *In primis hominibus*, an important florilegium on marriage dating from the 1120s. Its author was probably dependent on the *Collectio decem partium*. Here, the first pseudo-Augustinian text is missing, but the compiler cites the second of the three texts as an objection to the authentically Augustinian doctrine that spouses who practice abstinence by mutual agreement are no less married, and he adds a gloss to reconcile the objection with the doctrine. Then he quotes the standard *sententia* ascribed to Leo, as translated earlier.[41]

6.2.1 *The remote source: Pope Leo's reply to Rusticus*

Pope Leo I wrote to Rusticus, the bishop of Narbonne, in 458 or 459, responding to several questions about Christian practice that Rusticus had put to him.[42] One question concerned a certain priest or deacon who had given his daughter in marriage to a man who had been keeping a woman as a concubine and had even begotten several children with her. Was the man free to marry another? Or was his

---

[40] MS Vienna, Österreichische Nationalbibliothek, Cod. lat. 2178, 129rb–129va: "Augustinus: Non est perfectum coniugium ubi non sequitur commixtio sexuum. Item [Augustinus]: Non habent nuptiae Christi et ecclesiae sacramentum si eas non sequatur commixtio sexuum, nec pertinere poterit illa mulier ad matrimonium cum qua non docetur fuisse commixtio sexuum. [129va] Ex decreto Leonis papae caput XVIII: Cum societas nuptiarum ita ab initio constituta sit ut, praeter sexuum coniunctionem quae haberet haberet in se Christi et ecclesiae sacramentum, *esse non posset*, dubium non est eam mulierem non pertinere ad matrimonium in qua docetur nuptiale non fuisse misterium." (Emphasis mine.)

[41] *In primis hominibus*, 96, ed. Matecki, p. 43*/4–8.

[42] Leo, *Epist.* 167, PL 54:1199–1209.

concubine in effect his wife? Leo's argument presupposes that the concubine was an *ancilla*: a handmaid or bondswoman.[43]

The cleric had followed a conventional social norm, most familiar to us today from Augustine's case, whereby a free man would keep as his mistress a woman who was either servile or of markedly inferior status, in a quasi-monogamous relationship, until he was ready to marry a suitable bride of his own class.[44] Under Roman law, servile persons did not have the right to form legally recognized marriages, even with others in their own class. Concubinage was an acceptable and monogamous relationship in Roman tradition, but it had no legal consequences. Any children of the union were not their father's heirs, although he could leave something to them by testament if he wished. From a legal point of view, they were not *his* children.

Did the same rules apply within the Christian community, where social distinctions were not supposed to matter (Gal 3:28)? In the early period, patrician families could not always find suitable spouses from their own class for their sons and daughters, but the bishops were in no position to substitute their own law for civil law.[45] Even in the fifth century, the answer was still not obvious. The validity of marriage was not at that time subject to ecclesiastical jurisdiction, as it would be in the central Middle Ages, and the requirements for a valid marriage (*matrimonium iustum*) were still those of Roman civil law. Nevertheless, if the man and his concubine were Christians and they were living as man and wife and raising a family, perhaps they really *were* man and wife in the eyes of God and should be regarded thus by the Christian community. Augustine seems to have entertained this idea.[46] The answer to Rusticus's question, therefore, was not obvious.[47]

Leo proposes a theological rationale to show that from a Christian point of view, just as under Roman law, there can be no valid marriage between a free man and a servile woman.[48] Although Leo does not say whether the *ancilla* belonged to the man who was getting married, his response presupposes that she was subservient to him and not a free agent. There was a clear conflict of interest, therefore, inasmuch as marriage was supposed to be a partnership (*societas*), and partnerships were founded on equality, freedom, and mutual consent. Because the prior concubinage of the cleric was not a legitimate marriage, Leo argues, it is not an impediment to his marrying another woman.

---

[43] Ibid., 1204B–1206B.

[44] See S. Treggiari, *Roman Marriage* (Oxford, 1991), 51–52, on concubinage. Technically, the relationship between a freeman and slave was *contubernium*, but it was also *concubinatus* inasmuch as the man did not intend marriage (i.e., there was no *affectio maritalis*).

[45] MWCh 159–62. [46] Augustine, *De bono coniugali* 5(5), CSEL 41:193.

[47] See J. Evans Grubbs, *Law and Family in Late Antiquity* (Oxford, 1995), 309–16, on the diverse and shifting early Christian attitudes to concubinage and to marriages between persons who differ markedly in social standing.

[48] On the Roman law of *conubium* (the capacity to marry), see Treggiari, *Roman Marriage*, 43–49.

Leo concedes that a man can marry an *ancilla* if she is set free, given a dowry in accordance with the law, and made honorable by the celebration of a public wedding. These formalities would have publicly demonstrated her change of status, removing any ambiguity and making *mulier honesta* of her. Leo did not claim, as some medieval and some modern scholars have assumed, that *every* marriage should be solemnized thus. He was referring only to the special case of the freeborn man marrying a servile concubine, when written dotation was a conventional albeit not legally required way to mark the woman's new status and to advertize the legitimacy of the marriage.[49]

Leo's response was to become one of the most influential and oft-quoted texts in the canonical literature of the Middle Ages. In the following translation, the central passage in bold font is the remote source of the twelfth-century *sententia* about the role of coitus in marriage:

> Not every woman who is joined to a man is the man's wife, just as not every son is his father's heir. A compact of marriage is legitimate when it is between freeborn persons [*ingenui*] and between equals. The Lord instituted this [rule] long before Roman law began. Accordingly, a wife is one thing, and a concubine another, just as a bondswoman is one thing, and a free woman another. It was for this reason also that the Apostle, to make the distinction between such persons clear, cites the passage from Genesis in which [Sarah] said to Abraham, "Cast out this bondwoman and her son, for the son of this bondwoman shall not be heir with my son, Isaac" [Gen 21:10, Gal. 4:30]. **Hence, since the partnership of marriage was instituted from the beginning in such a way that besides [*praeter*] the joining of sexes, it should have in itself a sacrament of Christ and the church [Eph 5:32], there is no doubt that a woman in whom it is shown that there has been no nuptial mystery does not belong to marriage.** Therefore, if a cleric of any rank has given his daughter in marriage to a man who has a concubine, he should not be considered to have given her to a married man, unless perchance it is apparent that the woman has been made freeborn,[50] legitimately endowed, and dignified with public nuptials.[51]

---

[49] Cf. CJ 5.27.10 and Justinian, Nov. 117.3.

[50] The phrase *"ingenua facta"* seems paradoxical, but the privileges of the freeborn could be granted by the emperor to a freed person (*libertinus*) by *natalium restitutio* (Dig. 40.11). The status of freed persons was distinct both from that of the freeborn and from that of slaves. The *Lex Papia* enabled all freeborn men except senators and their sons to marry freedwomen (Dig. 23.2.23), but presumably there was a disqualifying conflict of interest when a patron married his freedwoman, who was still subordinate to him. Jerome, *Epist.* 69.5, to Oceanus (PL 22:658–659), castigates clerics who fail to purchase the imperial rescript to dignify their concubines, assuming that because the women are not their legitimate wives, they can later marry without incurring digamy, which was an impediment to orders (1 Tim 3:2, Tit 1:6).

[51] *Epist.* 167, PL 54:1204B–1205A. Here is the Latin for the translated passage in bold font: "Unde cum societas nuptiarum ita ab initio constituta sit, ut praeter sexuum conjunctionem haberet in se Christi et Ecclesiae sacramentum, dubium non est eam mulierem non pertinere ad matrimonium, in qua docetur nuptiale non fuisse mysterium."

Leo's theological rationale is in two parts. First, he alludes to St Paul's allegorical interpretation of the story of Abraham's two partners: his wife, Sarah, and their handmaid, Hagar. Hagar represents the Old Covenant, for her child was born in slavery, whereas Sarah represents the freedom of the New Covenant. Second, alluding to the great *mystērion* of Ephesians 5:32, which in turn is a gloss on Genesis 2:24, Leo argues that a marriage is more than the "joining of the sexes" (*coniunctio sexuum*). Over and above (*praeter*) that relationship, marriage has sacred meaning. It signifies Christ's union with the church.

Leo's phrase *coniunctio sexuum* does not refer explicitly to sexual intercourse. It is a variant of phrases that characterized marriage in Roman law, such as *coniunctio viri et mulieris* ("union of a man and a woman") and *coniunctio maris et feminae* ("union of male and female").[52] Whereas the "union of the sexes" describes the human institution, the preposition *praeter* ("besides") points to the transcendent, supra-human, figurative aspect of marriage. This figurative dimension existed from the beginning, long before the conventions of Roman law, Leo argues, for we know from Ephesians 5:32 that Genesis 2:24 was a prophecy about Christ and the Church. Because the union of Christ and the church is founded not on slavery but on freedom, therefore, a union between a freeborn man and a bondswoman cannot adequately signify it. The man may liberate his concubine and marry her publicly and with documentation, but no woman can be his bondswoman and his wife at the same time. Leo considered public nuptials to be expedient in "mixed" marriages, when the legitimacy of the marriage would otherwise be suspect.

Leo's argument presupposes a new way of construing the "great sacrament" in Ephesians 5:32. The several variants of Ephesians 5:32 in Latin always use the preposition *in*, but the nouns qualified by this preposition may be either in the ablative or in the accusative case: the great sacrament is either *in* (i.e., between) Christ and the church (ablative reading), or it is a prophetic dictum (Gen 2:24) that refers figuratively *to* Christ and the church (accusative reading). But Leo speaks of marriage itself as a sacrament *of* Christ and the church, where the genitive idiom expresses a relationship of signification. This substituted construction will not become prevalent until the twelfth century.

Leo's response enjoyed a multiple life in the canonical tradition. Two variants of the canon *Non omnis mulier* circulated, one consisting of the response as a whole, and the other of the response without the middle section (quoted in bold font earlier).[53] The canon was an important authority on the role of dotation in the

---

[52] *Inst.* 1.9.1: "Nuptiae sive matrimonium est viri et mulieris coniunctio individuam vitae consuetudinem continens." Modestinus adds that marriage is also a "sharing of divine and human law" (*Dig.* 23.2.1): "Nuptiae sunt coniunctio maris et feminae et consortium omnis vitae divini et humani iuris communciatio."

[53] In Ivo's *Decretum*, the middle section (*Cum societas nuptiarum*) appears alone at VIII.74, but the entire text (including the middle section) appears at VIII.139. In the *Panormia*, the section *Cum societas nuptiarum* appears alone at VI.23, whereas the canon *Non omnis mulier* appears at VI.35 without *Cum societas nuptiarum*.

legitimacy of marriage, as well as on the question of whether marriages between free and unfree persons were valid.[54] The middle section, which is what concerns us here, enjoyed an independent life as the canon *Cum societas nuptiarum*, which showed how marriage could be interpreted as a "sacrament of Christ and the church." In some collections, including the *Dionysiana* and the *Panormia*, the relative pronoun, *quae*, is inserted into the middle section, thus:

> Hence, since the partnership of marriage was instituted from the beginning in such a way that besides the joining of sexes, which [*quae*] has in itself a sacrament of Christ and the church [Eph 5:32], there is no doubt that a woman in whom it is shown that there was no nuptial mystery does not attain to marriage.[55]

It is difficult to make sense of this reading, but the insertion links the nuptial mystery directly to the union of the sexes. Here, the sacrament of Christ and church is not something that exists over and above the union of the sexes, as Leo had argued. Rather, it is a property of that union.

Hincmar of Reims adapted Leo's argument to explain the role of coitus in the formation of a valid marriage.

6.2.2 *The proximate source: Hincmar of Reims*

In November of 860, a regional synod of fourteen Frankish bishops that was meeting at Tusey (Tusiacum), near Toul, received a letter from Raymund, Count of Toulouse. Raymund complained that he had given his daughter in marriage to another Aquitainian nobleman, called Stephen, but that Stephen was not "using her as a wife." All that we know about the case comes from a letter that Hincmar, the bishop of Reims, wrote about it. Stephen's excuse was that intercourse with his wife would be incestuous because he had had sexual intercourse before the marriage with a girl who was closely related to her.[56] Stephen would not disclose who the girl was or how she was related to his bride, but if he was telling the truth the problem was serious.

---

[54] See P. Corbet, "Le douaire dans le droit canonique jusqu'à Gratien," in Bougard, Feller, and Le Jan, *Dots et douaires*, 43–55. The canon *Non omnis mulier* sometimes includes an additional clause: "Women joined to their husbands by their fathers' will are free from blame if the women whom their husbands [already] had were not in matrimony, because a wife [*nupta*] is one thing, and a concubine another." See, for example, *Dionysiana*, decretals, no. 18, PL 67:289A–B; Hincmar, *Epist.* 136, ed. E. Perels, MGH *Epistolae* 8, = *Epistolae Karolini Aevi* 6, 93/12–15; Ivo, *Panormia* VI.35. The addition is an abbreviation of Leo's next two responses to Rusticus: see Leo, *Epist.* 167, inq. 5–6, PL 54:1205A–B.

[55] Thus, *Panormia* VI.23: "Unde cum societas nuptiarum ita ab initio constituta sit, ut praeter sexuum conjunctionem, *quae* haberet in se Christi et Ecclesiae sacramentum, dubium non est eam mulierem non pertinere ad matrimonium, in qua docetur nuptiale non fuisse mysterium." The *quae* is inserted as well in *Decretum* VIII.139 (*Non omnis mulier*), but not in *Decretum* VIII.74 (*Cum societas nuptiarum*).

[56] Hincmar, *Epist.* 136, MGH *Epistolae* 8, 88/15–24. On the circumstances of the synod, see P. R. McKeon, "The Carolingian Councils of Savonnières (859) and Tusey (860) and Their Background," *Revue Bénédictine* 84 (1974): 75–100. See J. Devisse, *Hincmar Archevêque de*

By the ecclesiastical rules of the period, Stephen's marriage was incestuous and would have to be dissolved. The partners would be required to do penance, and they might have to remain perpetually unmarried.

The bishops were not sure what to do. According to the current rules of canonical procedure, they could not conduct a judicial inquiry unless the accuser appeared before the tribunal in person, and the accusation would have to come not from Raymund but from his daughter, for the former had relinquished his power over her by handing her over in marriage. Moreover, the bishops thought that an episcopal tribunal should not consider the case until the aggrieved parties had exhausted other means of resolution: She should seek her father's counsel, and Raymund should try to reconcile the spouses. Nevertheless, they felt obliged to intervene. The affair involved two powerful noblemen, and it had been going on for three years. Because everyone was talking about the affair, the bishops feared that it would become the occasion of "very great scandal in the church and damage in the kingdom."[57] They summoned Stephen.

Stephen willingly appeared, but he asked for a private audience with the bishops as distinct from a public judicial hearing. Having heard what he had to say and reconsidered Raymund's letter, the bishops found themselves unable to advise Stephen or to pass any judgment. There would have to be a public hearing. Stephen expressed his willingness to accept whatever counsel or judgment the synod might offer, provided only that the bishops attended carefully to his side of story.[58] This presumably meant that he had opted to submit the case to an ecclesiastical rather than a secular tribunal and had promised to accept the tribunal's decision as final.[59]

The gist of Stephen's story is as follows:[60] While he was still "in the fragile age of youth," he had had sexual intercourse with a certain girl, "as is customary." Later, when it was time for him to marry, he asked Raymund for the hand of his daughter, although he knew that she was related within four degrees of consanguinity to the other girl. The marriage followed the usual course. After the suit (*petitio*) came the betrothal (*desponsatio*), when Stephen betrothed her "with the consent of my parents and kinsfolk [*cum consensu parentum et amicorum meorum*]." Regretting what he had done and doubting whether his marriage was valid, he sought the advice of his confessor. If they first did penance secretly, he asked, could they then complete their marriage without suffering eternal damnation? Stephen recalled that the priest produced a book entitled *The Canons* and read out a text establishing that his marriage was incestuous.[61] The cleric advised that no penance would be fruitful as long as they remained in such a relationship.

Reims 845–882, vol. 1 (Geneva, 1975), pp. 369–91 on the five marriage cases that preoccupied Hincmar in the 860s, and pp. 432–35 on Stephen's case.

[57] *Epist.* 136, 88/25–36.   [58] Ibid., 88/36–89/7.   [59] Joyce, *Christian Marriage*, 221.

[60] Ibid., 89/8–90/5.

[61] The confessor (or perhaps Hincmar) is referring to the canon *Si quis fratris* from the Roman synod of 721 (under Gregory II), c. 9 (Mansi, *Concilia*, 12:263), or at least to a closely related

Stephen was now in a quandary. On the one hand, his conscience would not allow him to fulfill the betrothal by concluding the marriage in sexual intercourse. On the other hand, because of the wrath of Raymund and his allies, and because he was at odds (for reasons that are not explained) with King Charles the Bald, he dared not renounce the union either. Eventually, having used various ruses to avoid accepting his betrothed in marriage, he gave her a dowry and received her in a public wedding. The formula that Stephen uses here in Hincmar's narrative originated in the canon *Non omnis mulier*, from Leo's rescript to Rusticus: "I endowed her and, once she had been dignified by public nuptials, I received her [*dotavi eam et publicis nuptiis honoratam accepi*]." Variants of this formula recur throughout the letter. Having completed the solemnities, Stephen refused to have sexual intercourse with his wife, believing that he would not only compound his own guilt by adding incestuous sex to fornication with another girl and to an already incestuous marriage, but would also drag his innocent wife down into depravity with him.[62]

The bishops proposed a twofold course of action. On the secular side, Charles the Bald, as king of the western Franks, and his nobles would attempt to make peace between Raymund and Stephen. On the ecclesiastical side, archbishops Rodulf of Bourges and Frotar of Bordeaux, together with their suffragan bishops, would conduct an ecclesiastical inquiry. Stephen willingly accepted the decision. The synod asked Hincmar, an ally of King Charles, to counsel Rodulf and Frotar on the ecclesiastical dimensions of the case.[63]

Hincmar responded with the long epistolary treatise addressed to the two archbishops, which is our only evidence of the case.[64] He advises that the bishops should by all means invite Raymund to the tribunal and hear what he had to say, but that they must interrogate Stephen's wife. He goes over the procedures to be followed,[65] and he provides his colleagues with the information that they will need in order to reach a proper, theologically informed decision that is consistent with ecclesiastical law. Hincmar will say "nothing about secular justice, knowledge of which we bishops do not need to have."[66] Esmein cites the case an example of the dual adjudication of marriage cases under the Carolingian regime, where secular judges or noblemen worked in tandem with bishops. The church's authority was still rather disciplinary than judicial, but the system permitted a litigant to promise to abide by the tribunal's decision: an extension of the old Roman practice of voluntary arbitration.

Much about the case remains obscure to us. We do not know whether Stephen's story was true. Perhaps he regretted the betrothal for some other reason and cleverly fabricated the story about pre-marital sex. We cannot even be sure that his marriage was never consummated. The modern reader may doubt the veracity of Stephen's

---

text. Cf. Ivo, *Decretum* IX.19, as well as *Panormia* VII.57. The canon is hard to interpret because of the uncertain and changeable senses of *cognatio* and *cognatus*. See D. A. Bullough, "Early Medieval Social Groupings," *Past and Present* 45 (1969): 3–18, at 11–12.

[62] *Epist.* 136, 89/30–32.   [63] Ibid., 90/14–18.   [64] *Epist.* 136, 87–107.
[65] 90/25–92/20.   [66] 90/21–23. Esmein-Genestal, 1:18–20.

account and the sincerity of his motives, but that reservation has nothing to do with
the premises and logic of the case. Nor is there any reason to doubt Hincmar's
sincerity. Sadly, we do not know the outcome of the tribunal. Nor is it clear what
prospects of "scandal in the church and damage in the kingdom" troubled the
bishops at Tusey. Nevertheless, such alarm is not surprising. Marriage among the
nobility was always a political as well as an economic arrangement, for it forged new
alliances and was a way of making peace.[67] Factional politics and alliances were
especially fraught in Aquitaine during this period, partly because of Pepin II's prior
claim to be king of the region, and partly because of Charles's inability to maintain
control over remote provinces through centralized government.[68] Hincmar himself
conceded that the facts might or might not be as Stephen had stated, and he noted
that the same facts could be sometimes interpreted in different ways.[69] Nevertheless,
his letter presupposes that Stephen was telling the truth.

After the narrative preamble and a review of judicial procedure, Hincmar devotes
most of the letter to showing why the bishops should decide, if the facts are as
Stephen claims, that the marriage should be dissolved. In Hincmar's judgment,
Stephen was right to have shunned sexual intercourse with his wife. If the impediment of incest had not arisen, Stephen would have been obliged to remain with his
wife *even if they agreed never to consummate their marriage* and to remain celibate.
As things stand, however, if Stephen consummates their incestuous marriage, the
marriage must be dissolved and they must both remain unmarried. Both are free to
separate and then to remarry, although Stephen must first do penance.[70]

Notwithstanding his digressions and convoluted arguments, Hincmar's essay
includes a sustained and original attempt to illumine the role of coitus in the
formation and constitution of a valid marriage. Hincmar located a significant aspect
of marriage, whereby marriage was a sacrament of Christ's union with the church, in
sexual union. Hincmar did not argue, as modern scholars usually assume,[71] that
Stephen's marriage was dissoluble merely because it was not yet consummated. Had
Hincmar thought that, Stephen's would have been an open-and-shut case, and
Hincmar's argument would have been simpler and much easier to follow. In fact,
Hincmar argued that spouses normally became irrevocably bound together as soon
as their nuptials were complete, even if they never consummated their marriage. But
if Stephen had consummated his marriage, their intercourse would have been
incestuous and their marriage would not have contained the "sacrament of Christ

---

[67] Cf. Ivo, *Epist.* 99, PL 162:118D.

[68] J. L. Nelson, *Charles the Bald* (London, 1992), 185, 196–98. On the political situation in
Aquitaine, see also J. Martindale, "Charles the Bald and the Government of the Kingdom of
Aquitaine," in M. T. Gibson and J. L. Nelson (eds.), *Charles the Bald: Court and Kingdom*
(Oxford, 1981), 115–38.

[69] Hincmar, *Epist.* 136, 88/27–28.   [70] Ibid., 98/7–15; 105/24–106/8.

[71] E.g., J. Gaudemet, "Les origines historiques de la faculté de rompre le mariage non consommé," in Gaudemet, *Sociétés et mariage* (Strasbourg, 1980), 210–29, at 215–16; Nelson,
Charles the Bald, 197.

and the church." The point was not that their marriage was still unconsummated, therefore, but that *it could never be truly consummated*. There was no way to realize the sacrament – the "nuptial mystery" of which Leo spoke.

Hincmar's point of departure is a three-part definition of the requirements for a legitimate marriage. First, the marriage must be "between free persons and between equals." Second, the woman must be "asked for from the parents responsible for her, legally betrothed, endowed, and dignified with public nuptials." Third, they must be "associated in the union of marriage" in such a way that "from two is made one body and one flesh, in accordance with the words, 'They shall be two in one flesh, they are no longer two, but one flesh,' and 'What God has joined, man should not separate' [Matt 19:5–6]."[72] Hincmar believed in the importance of formalities in marrying, and he draws here on several sources to characterize the nuptial process, including the forged decretal ascribed to Pope Evaristus, the authentic decretal of Pope Siricius, and Leo's *Non omnis mulier*. But none of these sources mentioned the third requirement, regarding marriage as the union of two in one flesh, and Hincar's argument turned on this.

Although Hincmar insists on the necessity of public nuptials, he does not insist on a priestly blessing. The omission is deliberate, for Stephen's marriage had been solemnized but not blessed. Hincmar explains that he would have said more about the function of the blessing if he had heard that in this case "a priestly benediction had been given in accordance with ecclesiastical custom."[73] Had the marriage been blessed, that would only have complicated the situation, for an incestuous union is not fit to be blessed. Because there can be no genuine "faith" (*fides*) in such a marriage, it should not receive a priest's blessing, for "whatever is not of faith is sin" (Rom 14:23). Indeed, no person who has committed a serious sin is ready to receive a priestly blessing until he has made due satisfaction.[74]

Hincmar's chief argument is based on the premise that marriage is a union of two in one flesh, and it is in two parts. The first part consists of excerpts from Leo's response to Rusticus, including the middle passage on the sacrament of Christ and the church in marriage (*Cum societas nuptiarum*). Hincmar quotes this material accurately, and he does not pretend that Leo was talking about sexual intercourse. In the second part of the argument, Hincmar extrapolates Leo's argument by applying it to sexual union. Hincmar's wording makes it clear where Leo's argument ends and where his own extrapolation begins. I have indicated the two parts of the argument – the restatement and the extrapolation – as A and B respectively in the translation that follows:

[A] Pope Leo the Great writes about this union to Rusticus, bishop of Narbonne, thus: "Not every woman who is joined to a man is the man's wife, just as not every son is his father's heir. A compact of marriage is legitimate when it is between free persons and between equals." And a little later, "Hence, since the partnership of

---

[72] Hincmar, *Epist.* 136, 92/28–32.   [73] Ibid., 106/10–12.   [74] Ibid., 106/11–19.

marriage was instituted from the beginning such that besides [*praeter*] the joining of sexes [*coniunctio sexuum*], it should have in itself a sacrament of Christ and the church [Eph 5:32], there is no doubt that a woman in whom it is shown that there has been no nuptial mystery does not belong to marriage." [B] Now, we can also show on this basis that not every marriage makes a conjugal union, that is, [it does not do so] when the marriage is not followed by sexual intercourse [*commixtio sexuum*], just as not every heir is the son of him whose heir he is known to be. **Nor does marriage have in itself a sacrament of Christ and the church if**, as blessed Augustine says, they do no use [marriage][75] nuptially [*nuptialiter*], that is, if **sexual intercourse [*commixtio sexuum*] does not follow it. Nor is that woman able to belong to marriage in whom, we are taught, there has been no sexual intercourse**, just as [according to Leo] "there is no doubt that a woman in whom it is shown that there has been no nuptial mystery does not belong to marriage."[76]

Hincmar reasons that by applying Leo's reasoning to sexual union one can show that a marriage without sexual union does not contain the sacrament of Christ and the church. Immediately after the passage quoted earlier, Hincmar goes over the whole argument again, albeit without citing Augustine. Since Stephen's marriage cannot be brought to this point, it is invalid and should be dissolved.[77]

Hincmar seems at first sight to be ascribing a spurious dictum to Augustine, which would have begun with the words: "Nor does marriage have in itself a sacrament of Christ and the church." The beginning and end of this statement, which are emphasized in bold font earlier, will appear as a coital proof text ascribed to Augustine in the *Sententiae Magistri A*. As Gérard Fransen points out, however, Hincmar was probably ascribing only the unusual phrase, *uti nuptialiter* ("to use in a

---

[75] G. Fransen, "La lettre de Hincmar de Reims au sujet du mariage d'Étienne," in R. Lievens, E. Van Mingroot, and W. Verbeke, eds., *Pascua Mediaevalia* (Leuven, 1983), 133–46, at 134–35 and 140–41, shows that this sentence contains a textual problem: It is not clear whether the object of the verb *uti*, which must be supplied, should be "marriage" or "each other." The reading that appears in the printed editions of Hincmar's letter is doubtful, and my translation is based on Fransen's reconstruction. Husbands were said "to use" (*uti*) their wives when they had sex with them, and this idiom occurs earlier in the letter, when Raymund complains that Stephen was not "using her as a wife" (88/21–22). Cf. Ambrose, *Epist.* 60, PL 16:1183B–C: "Si quis desponsata sibi et tradita utatur, conjugium vocat.…." Nevertheless, in the passage from the *De b. coniug.* that Hincmar has in mind (23(31), CSEL 41:226/16–18), the object of *uti* is not a wife but marriage.

[76] *Epist.* 136, 92/32–93/10. Section-B (93/3 ff.), with the defective section corrected (in italics): "Et nos e regione hinc etiam ostendere possumus, quia non omnes nuptiae coniugalem copulam faciunt, quas non sequitur commixtio sexuum, sicut nec semper illius est filius omnis heres, cuius esse noscitur heres. **Nec habent nuptiae in se Christi et ecclesiae sacramentum** *si, ut beatus Augustinus dicit, nuptialiter non utuntur,* id est, **si eas non subsequitur commixtio sexuum. Nec pertinere poterit illa mulier ad matrimonium** cum qua docetur non fuisse commixtio sexuum, sicut dubium non est eam mulierem non pertinere ad matrimonium, in qua docetur nuptiale non fuisse mysterium." In Perels's edition, the section italicized above is as follows: "sicut beatus Augustinus dicit, si se nuptialiter non utuntur…."

[77] Ibid., 93/10–20.

nuptial manner") to Augustine, for it occurs in an authentic passage from the *De bono coniugali* that Hincmar cites later in the letter.[78]

Nevertheless, Hincmar interprets Augustine in the light of his own theory. Later in the letter, Hincmar appeals to Augustine's analogy of the cleric ordained to serve a congregation: Just as the "sacrament of ordination" remains in the priest even if the congregation never materializes, Augustine argues, so the *sacramentum* in a valid marriage remains even after a divorce.[79] Hincmar explains that Augustine must have been referring not to an "imaginary" union but to the bodily, "incorporated" union established by sexual intercourse.[80]

To corroborate the argument based on Leo, Hincmar cites Ephesians 5:28–32 and passages from Ambrosiaster, Gregory the Great, and Augustine. Although these texts illumine the theme of marriage as a union of "two in one flesh" and as a sign or figure of Christ and the church, none of them posits coitus as a requirement for a complete marriage. Instead, they use the theme to characterize marriage as an especially close or permanent relationship. For example, the passage ascribed to Ambrose – in fact, it was from Ambrosiaster – is a gloss on Ephesians 5:22–23. It explains how husband and wife through mutual affection and dependence enter a union that is comparable to that between Christ and the church. Like the church, the wife is subordinate to her husband. Like Christ, the husband cherishes and controls his wife. Furthermore, just a man leaves his parents to cleave to his wife, so Christians leave error behind them to cleave to Christ. Ambrosiaster also notes also how the two relationships differ. Because God formed Eve from Adam, husband and wife are in some sense numerically one, and the "wife is consubstantial [*consubstantiva*] with her husband," whereas "the church is able to participate Christ only in name and not in nature." Again, notwithstanding the husband's dominion over his wife, they are equals in certain respects, whereas the same cannot be said of Christ and the church. Having been formed from Adam's side, the wife is "inferior because of her creation, but not because of her nature."[81]

Hincmar argues that Stephen's false marriage fails to conform sufficiently to Christ's union with the church. Instead of the "love of offspring," there is the fear of exile and death. Instead of fidelity and conjugal chastity, there is the fear of committing incest. Stephen's marriage, therefore, cannot achieve "the sacrament of incorporation into the unity of Christ and the church." It is not a true marriage but a sham that serves only as a cover for indecency. Even if Stephen consummated the union, it would not be legitimate, established (*ratum*), or permanent. On the contrary, the partners would have to separate and to do penance "because of the crime of incest . . . which a sacrament of Christ and the church cannot have." Their marriage is "neither mystical nor legal," for it lacks the required conformity to Christ

[78] Fransen, "La lettre de Hincmar," 141. Augustine, *De b. coniug.* 23(31), CSEL 41:226/16–18: "Nec ideo arbitrentur meliores esse primis patribus sanctis qui nuptiis, ut ita dicam, nuptialiter usi sunt." Quoted by Hincmar, 98/35–99/1.
[79] *De b. coniug.* 24(32), 227.   [80] *Epist.* 136, 98/19–32.
[81] Ambrosiaster, *Ad Efesios* 5:22–33, CSEL 81.3:117–19, especially 118/4–6 and 119/26–27.

and the church and it contravenes the laws. Far from figuratively realizing the affinity to Christ's union with the church, consummation would only compound Stephen's guilt, making him guilty of incest as well as of fornication.[82]

To show that a marriage before consummation is illegitimate unless it can be honorably consummated, Hincmar appeals to the canonical rules on the impediment of impotence. If a man who has been properly betrothed and married to a woman cannot render the conjugal debt, and if his incapacity can be proved by their own testimony or by other recognized methods of judicial proof, then they should be separated and the woman may remarry. How much more should Stephen's marriage be dissolved, for he is prevented from having sex with his bride not by any "impotence of the flesh" but rather by a "reverence of the mind."[83] Stephen can do nothing now about the affinity that he had contracted by having sex with his wife's relation. He is already one flesh with that woman, just as a man who has sex with a prostitute becomes one flesh with her (1 Cor 6:16).[84] But his sexual union with his bride can never be a sacrament of Christ and the church. In sum, Hincmar concludes, again adapting Leo's *Cum societas nuptiarum*, "There is no doubt that a woman in whom it is apparent that there has not been a sacrament of Christ and the church (that is, a nuptial mystery) through the union of the sexes does not belong to marriage."[85]

Stephen's marriage should be dissolved not because it is still unconsummated, in Hincmar's view, but because it cannot be consummated honorably or legitimately. When there is no impediment to conjugal union, the celebration of nuptials is normally the point at which a marriage becomes irrevocable and indissoluble and the partners become bound by the conjugal debt. When Matthew said that Mary was betrothed to Joseph "before the came together," Hincmar argues, he was not referring to sexual union. Rather, Matthew meant that they had not yet come together "in a nuptial celebration."[86] Because they had not yet celebrated their nuptials, Mary was not truly Joseph's wife, although she "accepted the name of wife [*coniux*] for pressing reasons."[87]

To illustrate the role of nuptials, Hincmar introduces a familiar legend about the marriage at Cana.[88] The groom was John the Evangelist, and Jesus called John away from the wedding to be a celibate disciple. Hincmar argues that Jesus must have summoned John not only before sexual union took place (*ante carnis unionem*) but even before the wedding was over (*ante nuptiarum percelebrationem*), leaving the bride free to remarry. If the call had come after their wedding but before consummation, they might have separated by mutual agreement to serve God, but neither would have been free to remarry. Likewise, if Stephen's union had not been incestuous, he would not have been allowed to separate from his bride or to marry another once he had "betrothed, endowed, and dignified her with public nuptials."

---

[82] *Epist.* 136, 95/15–28; 95/33–34; 96/23–24.   [83] Ibid., 97/4–14.   [84] Ibid., 95/31.
[85] Ibid., 97/9–11.   [86] Ibid., 92/21–24, 102/39–103/4.   [87] Ibid., 103/35–36.
[88] Ibid., 102/19–29.

Instead, he would have had to remain with her, either observing the conjugal debt, or, with her consent, living in married continence.[89]

Having established that Stephen's marriage should be dissolved, Hincmar makes some pragmatic proposals. The tribunal should find Stephen guilty of abandoning his spouse: an offence that requires both penance under ecclesiastical law and a fine (*multa sponsaliorum*) under secular law.[90] But because Stephen has already given her the dowry that "she ought to have acquired for herself if they were carnally joined" (i.e., the morning gift), Hincmar suggests the girl should keep that in lieu of the fine and go back to her father's custody.[91] Hincmar emphasizes that this dowry will function only as compensation, and not as a way of completing the marriage. No one should suppose that her having received the gift makes them truly man and wife.[92]

To appreciate Hincmar's core argument, one needs to distinguish between two questions. One question is about what constitutes marriage, the other about the point in the process of marrying at which the union becomes irrevocable. Twelfth-century scholars will assume that these coincide, but Hincmar does not. His approach is teleological. He believes that a marriage normally becomes irrevocable as soon as the nuptial celebration is complete, but only if the prospective union can be fully realized in due course, with everything that constitutes a Christian marriage. Extrapolating Leo's argument, Hincmar shows that sexual union established through coitus is necessary to complete the required conformity or correspondence between marriage and Christ's union with the church. If the marriage is still in process of formation but sexual union is impossible, as in cases of natural impotence, the potential for the requisite union does not exist and the marriage is defective and soluble. In Stephen's case, coitus would have been physically possible but it was forbidden. Moreover, because their sexual union would be incestuous and sinful, it would not adequately signify or emulate Christ's union with the church. Because potentiality for the union in question did not exist, therefore, the marriage was soluble, even after the nuptial celebration.

6.2.3 *The derivation of the coital proof texts*

The coital proof texts of the twelfth century, outlined earlier, were derived from Hincmar's letter. To see that, one needs to compare two sources quoted earlier: the three proof texts of the *Sententiae Magistri A.*, and the passage from Hincmar. The

---

[89] Ibid., 102/29–34.

[90] Ibid., 98/10, 29. Esmein-Genestal, 1:19, argues that the *multa* must have been the penalty for divorcing a wife without just cause, which is specified in several Germanic law codes, and that it cannot have compensation for failing to fulfill a *desponsatio* (cf. CTh 3.5.2 and 3.5.11; *Lex Romana Burgundionum* 27.1, MGH *Leges Nat. Germ.* 2.1, 147; and *Lex Visigothorum* III.1.4, MGH *Leges Nat. Germ.* 1, 126/9) because their union had already reached the stage of *nuptiae celebratae*. Although their union was unconsummated, Hincmar considers them to be already married, and Stephen had apparently paid the morning gift.

[91] *Epist.* 136, 98/7–15.   [92] Ibid., 98/15–18.

second proof text, which is ascribed to Augustine, is taken from the second section (B) of the passage quoted earlier, where Hincmar extrapolates Leo's argument but cites Augustine: "Nor does marriage have in itself a sacrament of Christ and the church if, as blessed Augustine says, they do no use [marriage] nuptially [*nuptia-liter*], that is, if sexual intercourse does not follow it. Nor is that woman able to belong to marriage in whom, we are taught, there has been no sexual intercourse." The excerpter has omitted the clause in which Hincmar cites Augustine, but he has ascribed the rest of the dictum, rather than the phrase "use nuptially" alone, to Augustine. In fact, this passage is Hincmar's extrapolation of Leo. The third proof text, ascribed to Leo, is in effect a rewording of the canon *Cum societas nuptiarum* but the immediate source was probably the first section (A) of the passage from Hincmar. The excerpter has read the argument that Hincmar extrapolated from the text back into the quotation from Leo in the first section (A). The phrase *commixtio sexuum* ("sexual intercourse") from Hincmar's extrapolation (B) replaces Leo's less specific phrase, *coniunctio sexuum* ("union of the sexes"). Most significant, the word "not" has been inserted, changing the sense of *praeter*. Thus, whereas Leo originally spoke of a sacramentality that existed in marriage *besides* (i.e., over and above) the "union of the sexes," he now seems to speak of a sacramentality that does *not* exist *without* sexual intercourse.

The derivation of the Leonine text in the *Collectio decem partium* is harder to trace, but this canon is similar to the version of *Cum societas nuptiarum* in the *Panormia*. Both have the inserted relative pronoun, "which" (*quae*), which creates a semantic problem.[93] The *Collectio decem partium* solves the problem by keeping the *quae* but inserting the phrase, *esse non posset* ("it cannot exist").

6.3 THE COITAL PROOF TEXTS IN THE *MAGISTRI MODERNI*

The anonymous masters of the sentential literature recognized the authenticity of both sets of proof texts, respectively consensual and coital, and they noted the conflict between them. The *Coniugium namque* notes the conflict without trying to resolve it. On the one hand, Ambrose says that the betrothal (*sponsio*) or the initial pact (*pactio initialis*) suffices to establish a marriage, and *sententiae* by Pope Nicholas and John Chrysostom corroborate Ambrose's position. On the other hand, Augustine says that "there is no marriage in which the service of carnal coupling is not fulfilled," and Pope Leo says that a marriage "is not legitimate in which it is evident that carnal intercourse is absent."[94] Other sentential treatises try to reconcile the two sets of proof texts. They concede that something sacramental is missing from marriage prior to consummation inasmuch as there is a deficiency in

---

[93] It may be relevant that the inserted *non* of the other version of the proof text (as in the *Sententiae Magistri A.*) is in the same place as the *quae* of this version.

[94] *Coniugium namque*, in H. Weisweiler, "Le recueil des sentences *Deus de cuius principio et fine tacetur* et son remaniement," RThAM 5 (1933): 245–74, at 271/34–272/7.

correspondence and signification, but they affirm that the union, nevertheless, is truly marriage and fully established (*ratum*).

According to the *In primis hominibus*, when Augustine says that a wife does not "belong to matrimony" without coitus, he is referring not to marriage simply but rather "to that kind of matrimony in which there is a sacrament of Christ and the church." Before sexual union, the wife "is not one flesh with her husband, as Christ and the church are [one flesh]."[95] The author assumes that a marriage does not have to include this figurative aspect to be valid, established, and permanent.

The *Sententiae Berolinenses* asks whether marriage begins at the moment of the oath (*iusiurandum*). In reply, the author argues that there is a marriage as soon as there is a betrothal (*fides sponsionis*). To corroborate this position, he cites the usual consensual proof texts from Ambrose, Isidore, and pseudo-Chrysostom. But why does Augustine say that marriage "does not have in itself a sacrament of Christ and the church if there is no sexual intercourse in it," and that a woman "with whom it is found that there has been no sexual intercourse does not belong to marriage"?[96] Augustine does not say that sexual intercourse must follow at once, the author points out. He means only that sexual intercourse normally follows in due course, for the partners have agreed to it in exchanging marital consent.[97]

The *Cum omnia sacramenta* concedes that marriage is imperfect without coitus but distinguishes between two modes of perfection. Marriage has numerous concomitants, such as the betrothal, the gift of an *arrha*, the deflowering of virginity, faith, the hope of offspring, the sacrament of Christ and the church, and so forth. These are all good, and the more concomitants a marriage has, the more complete it is. Nevertheless, whereas some concomitants are necessary conditions without which there is no marriage, others are adjuncts (*adiuncta*), without which there is still a marriage. Consent is a condition of the first sort, whereas the sacramental relation between marriage and Christ's union with the church, which is realized by coitus, is only an accidental benefit.[98] That is why John Chrysostom says that it is "not coitus that makes marriage, but intent," for whereas consent is necessary for marriage, coitus is not.[99] The second recension of the *Cum omnia sacramenta* and

[95] IPH 96, ed. Matecki, 43*/7–8.

[96] "Nuptiae Christi et ecclesiae in se non habet sacramentum, nisi sit ibi amixtio sexuum." "Illa mulier pertinere non potest ad matrimonium, cum qua non est amixtio sexuum." Cf. IPH 96 (43*/4–7) and SMA 61–62 (pp. 185–86).

[97] In F. Stegmüller, "*Sententie Berolinenses*: Eine neugefundene Sentenzensammlung aus der Schule des Anselm von Laon," RThAM 11 (1939): 33–61, at 61/1–13.

[98] *Cum omnia sacramenta*, in F. P. Bliemetzrieder, *Anselms von Laon systematische Sentenzen*, BGPhMA 18.2–3 (1919), at 140/2–13. Likewise, *Cum omnia sacramenta*, second recension, in F. P. Bliemetzrieder, "Théologie et théologiens de l'école épiscopale de Paris avant Pierre Lombard," RThAM 3 (1931): 273–91, at 278/73–84; *Decretum Dei fuit*, in H. Weisweiler, *Das Schrifttum der Schule Anselms von Laon und Wilhelms von Champeaux in deutschen Bibliotheken*, BGPhThMA 33.1–2 (1936), 361–79, at 371/19–21.

[99] *Cum omnia sacramenta*, 140/13–15. Likewise, *Cum omnia sacramenta*, second recension, ed. Bliemetzrieder, 278/84–86. The quotation comes from pseudo-Chrysostom via Nicholas I: see

the *Decretum Dei fuit*, which are dependent on the *Cum omnia sacramenta*, rehearse the same arguments.[100]

6.4 GRATIAN'S THEORY

Gratian devoted the second part of the *Decretum* to imaginary, didactic cases (*causae*). The twenty-seventh case is about a man who had already made a solemn vow of chastity but then became betrothed. Later, his *sponsa* renounced the betrothal in favor of another man, whom she married (*nupsit*). Two questions arise. First, is a prior religious vow an impediment to a valid marriage? Second, can a *sponsa* abandon her betrothed to marry (*nubere*) another man?[101] In what follows, I shall consider the treatment only of the second of these questions, and as it existed the first recension of the *Decretum*, which was completed around 1140.[102] Gratian argues that one must determine, first, whether a betrothed couple is already married, and, second, whether betrothed partners are free to separate and to marry others.[103]

6.4.1 *The role of coitus in marrying*

To determine whether betrothed partners are married, Gratian proceeds by dialectical opposition, citing canons on both sides. First, he shows that betrothed partners are married. Next, he shows that they are unmarried. Finally, he reconciles the two positions by showing they are married in one sense but not in another.

It follows from the definition of marriage, Gratian argues, that betrothed persons are already married.[104] Marriage is defined as "the union of a man and a woman, maintaining an indivisible way of life,"[105] and there is already such a union between

Opus imperfectum in Matthaeum 32, PG 56:802; and Nicholas I, *Epist.* 99, c. 3, in *MGH Epist.* 6, 570/23–24 (= Ivo, *Decretum* VIII.17).

[100] *Cum omnia sacramenta*, 139/12–140/15. *Cum omnia sacramenta*, second recension, ed. Bliemetzrieder, 277/57–278/86. *Decretum Dei fuit*, ed. Weisweiler, 371/7–21.

[101] Gratian, C. 27 q. 1 dictum ante c. 1 (1046).

[102] On the two recensions, see A. Winroth, *The Making of Gratian's Decretum* (Cambridge, 2000). The first recension is sublimely coherent in comparison with the more familiar vulgate recension, which is so muddled as to be opaque and self-contradictory, although one should keep in mind that the Gratian cited in subsequent medieval theology and canon law was Gratian II. Studies of particular texts within the *Decretum*, however, have shown that the first recension was itself the result of complex process of compilation, which sometimes undermined its coherence: See M. E. Sommar, "Twelfth-Century Scholarly Exchanges," in W. P. Müller and M. E. Sommar, *Medieval Church Law and the Origins of the Western Legal Tradition* (Washington, D.C., 2006), 123–33.

[103] C. 27 q. 2 dictum ante c. 1 (1062).   [104] C. 27 q. 2 dictum ante c. 1 & cc. 1–3 (1062–64).

[105] C. 27 q. 2 dictum ante c. 1 (1062): "Sunt enim nuptiae siue matrimonium uiri mulierisque coniunctio, indiuiduam uitae consuetudinem retinens." The definition is from *Inst.* 1.9.1 and was common among the canonists, e.g.: Ivo, *Decretum* VIII.1; *Panormia* VI.1, *Collectio tripartita* B 15.1; SMA 1 (p. 167). Cf. *Cum omnia sacramenta*, ed. Bliemetzrieder, 139/9–11: "coniugium ... quod Isidorus ita describit: Coniugium est consensus masculi et femine,

betrothed partners. Moreover, they have already given their consent to each other, and consent is the efficient cause of matrimony. Gratian cites some familiar authorities. According to a maxim that he ascribes to Isidore, "consent makes marriage."[106] According to John Chrysostom, "it is not coitus that makes marriage, but intent."[107] According to Pope Nicholas I, "their consent alone is sufficient according to the laws ... and if this alone is absent, the other things, including coitus itself, are celebrated in vain."[108] Because the consent expressed in the betrothal makes marriage, such consent is both necessary and sufficient for marriage. In sum, it follows from the very definition of marriage that *sponsus* and *sponsa* are already husband and wife (*coniuges*).[109]

Gratian seems to conflate the definition or essence of marriage with the principle that consent makes marriage, but the two are closely related in his mind. In a different case, regarding a free woman who has unwittingly married an unfree man, Gratian combines the two premises – the definition and the causal principle – in a single, two-pronged argument:

> Marriage, or matrimony, is the union of a man and a woman, committing them to an indivisible way of life. Again, the consent of both of them makes the marriage. Therefore, because these [persons] were joined to keep an indivisible way of life, and because each of them consents to the other, they should be called married.[110]

Gratian assumes, perhaps unconsciously, that the causal principle, "consent makes marriage," is somehow essential to marriage, belonging to it by definition.

Having proved that betrothed persons are married by virtue of their consent, Gratian raises a subsidiary question about marital consent and its relationship to sexual intercourse. Consent makes marriage, but *to what* do the partners consent by marrying? To living together? To sexual intercourse? To both of these things? The object of marital consent cannot be cohabitation alone, for in that case a brother and sister could marry. It must include sexual intercourse. But by that standard Mary and Joseph were not married, for Mary had taken a vow to persevere in lifelong virginity.

---

indiuidualem uite consuetudinem retinens." The last word in *Inst.* 1.9.1 was apparently *continens*, but *retinens* is common in the canonical tradition.

[106] "Consensus facit matrimonium." This common maxim is not in fact in Isidore. Cf. *Dig.* 35.1.15, "Nuptias non concubitus, sed consensus facit." Cf. Ambrose *De institutione virginis* 6(41), PL 16:316C: "Non enim defloratio virginitatis facit conjugium, sed pactio conjugalis." Ivo, in *Epist.* 99, PL 162:119A and *Epist.* 243, 251A, ascribes to Nicholas I the maxim: "Matrimonium facit consensus, non coitus." Ivo is probably thinking of Nicholas I's letter to the Bulgarians (cf. Ivo, *Decretum* VI.17, VIII, 233, and also *Tripartita* B 15.17 and *Panormia* VI.107), where the pope emphasizes consent and quotes ps.-Chrysostom (see below): "Matrimonium non facit coitus sed voluntas."

[107] C. 27 q. 2 c. 1 (1063). Ps.-Chrysostom, *Opus imperfectum in Matthaeum* 32, PG 56:802. There is a fuller quotation of this passage in c. 4 (1064), a *palea*.

[108] C. 27 q. 2 c. 2 (1063). Nicholas I, *Epist.* 99 (*Responsa ad consulta Bulgarorum*), c. 3, in MGH *Epist.* 6, *Epistolae Karolini Aevi* 4 (1925), 570/21–24. Ivo, *Decretum* VI.17, VIII.233, and *Panormia* VI.107, *Tripartita* B 15.17.

[109] C. 27 q. 2 d. post c. 2 (1063).   [110] C. 29 q. 1 d. init. (1091).

To prove the minor premise, Gratian points out, following Augustine, that when the angel told Mary that she would have a child, Mary replied: "How can this be, seeing that I know not a man?" (Luke 1:34) She cannot have meant only that she was still a virgin at that time, for then she could have conceived Jesus sexually in due course. Rather, she meant that she would *never* know a man, having vowed to remain to a virgin. But if she had consented to sexual intercourse in becoming betrothed to Joseph, she would have violated her vow mentally, even if she never did so physically. Augustine tells us that we are forbidden to think such a thing, for Mary made a vow of lifelong chastity in her heart, albeit not in spoken words, subjecting herself in all things to God's will.[111]

Gratian finds his solution to this subsidiary question in Mary's complete subjection to the will of God. Mary was determined to persevere in virginity *unless* God revealed another plan to her. Although she intended to remain a virgin, therefore, she left the matter in God's hands. Mary implicitly consented to sexual intercourse inasmuch as she agreed to render the conjugal debt to Joseph *if* he ever demanded it, although she hoped and confidently expected that he would not do so.[112] Nevertheless, by agreeing to share an indivisible way of life, each partner in a marriage implicitly agrees to be sexually available to the other and to keep nothing hidden from the other. Without her husband's consent, a wife cannot abstain even to devote herself to prayer for a little while (1 Cor 7:5), let alone to take a vow of perpetual continence.[113] This subsidiary question had been a subject of controversy. In the 1120s, the *Cum omnia sacramenta* argued that marital consent included consent to coitus. The treatise considered the same objection about Mary and solved it in a way similar to Gratian's.[114] But Hugh of Saint-Victor argued in the 1130s that Mary did not consent to coitus in any sense when she married, since she was firmly committed to perpetual virginity (Section 10.4).

Returning to the main question, Gratian concludes that because betrothed persons have already consented to marry, and because consent makes marriage, they must already be married.[115] Having proved the thesis by arguments from reason and definition, Gratian turns to arguments from authority. Here, too, his sources are familiar. First there is Ambrose, according to whom "a woman who is betrothed to a man receives the name of wife." Ambrose also says: "It is when marriage is begun [*initiatur*] that the name of marriage is assumed, for it is not the deflowering of virginity that makes marriage, but the conjugal pact."[116] Next, there is Isidore: "Spouses [*coniuges*] are truly so called as soon as they are betrothed [*a prima*

---

[111] C. 27 q. 2, dictum post c. 2 (1063).
[112] C. 27 q. 2 c. 3 (1063). The chapter begins with a paraphrase or summary of several passages in Augustine, including *De sancta virginitate* 4(4). Peter Lombard borrows the whole passage from Gratian and ascribes it to Augustine, *De nuptiis et concupiscentia*, in *Sent.* IV, 30.2.2 (439).
[113] C. 27 q. 2 c. 3 (1063). [114] *Cum omnia sacramenta*, ed. Bliemetzrieder, 147/26–148/8.
[115] C. 27 q. 2 c. 3 (1063–64).
[116] C. 27 q. 2 c. 5 (1064). Ambrose, *De institutione virginis* 6(41), PL 16:316C. Ivo, *Decretum* VIII.2; also *Panormia* VI.14, *Tripartita* B 15.2.

desponsationis fide], although they have not known sexual intercourse."[117] Third, there is the text from Augustine's *De nuptiis et concupiscentia* on which Isidore drew.[118] Gratian bolsters these texts with canonical and biblical texts in which a betrothed woman (*sponsa*) is already called a wife (*coniux*).[119] It follows from all these authorities, Gratian concludes, that betrothed persons are already married partners (*coniuges*).[120]

Next, Gratian sets out to prove the antithesis: that betrothed partners are not husband and wife until they come together in sexual intercourse. He begins with two coital proof texts that he ascribes to Augustine and Leo respectively. According to the text ascribed to Augustine, "There is no doubt that a woman in whom it is shown that there has not been sexual intercourse does not belong to marriage."[121] The other proof text is the canon *Cum societas nuptiarum* itself, correctly ascribed to Pope Leo, but with the famous *non* inserted, exactly as in the *Sententiae Magistri A.*[122] Gratian was probably dependent for both texts on the *Sententiae Magistri A.*, on which he apparently drew frequently,[123] but the dictum that he ascribes to Augustine is apparently somewhat different from what he would have found in that source (unless he was using a version unknown to us). In fact, it is a sentence from Leo's canon, *Cum societas nuptiarum*, but with Hincmar's term *commixtio sexus* in place of Leo's *nuptiale mysterium*.[124] These authorities show that the partners are not married until they consummate their betrothal in sexual intercourse.

Gratian corroborates the coital proof texts with an array of subtle arguments based on canons and precedents. To prove that betrothed partners are not yet married, Gratian cites canons taken from letters by Pope Gregory I. These imply that once the partners are married (*coniugati*), neither of them can opt for the religious life unilaterally, leaving the other "in the world." Instead, they may separate only by mutual agreement, and then both must adopt the religious life. Otherwise, they remain bound by the conjugal debt.[125] Gratian then points to hagiographic episodes in which betrothed persons were considered still free to separate from their partners to pursue a more holy calling, even without the other's consent. For example, St Macarius left his bride after the wedding feast, when he was about to enter the

---

[117] C. 27 q. 2 c. 6 (1064). Isidore, *Etym.* IX.7.9. Ivo, *Decretum* VIII.3. Also *Panormia* VI.15, *Tripartita* B 15.3.

[118] Augustine, *De nupt. et conc.* I.11(12), CSEL 42, 224. Ivo, *Decretum* I.14, VIII.14; also *Panormia* VI.16, *Tripartita* B 15.15.

[119] C. 27 q. 2 dictum post c. 10; c. 11; c. 12 (1065).   [120] Ibid., dictum post c. 15 (1066).

[121] Ibid., c. 16.   [122] Ibid., c. 17. Cf. SMA 62 (186).

[123] Peter Landau, "Gratian und die *Sententiae Magistri A.*," in H. Mordek (ed.), *Aus Archiven und Bibliotheken* (Frankfurt am Main, 1992), 311–26. See especially appendix I (323–26): "Gratian, die *Sententiae* Magistri A. und die *copula*-Theorie der Ehe."

[124] C. 27 q. 2 c. 16 (1066): "Non dubium est illam mulierem non pertinere ad matrimonium cum qua docetur non fuisse commixtio sexus." Cf. SMA 61 (185–86): "nec pertinere poterit illa mulier ad matrimonium, cum qua docetur non fuisse commixtio sexuum."

[125] C. 27, q. 2, cc. 19, 21, 22 (1067–69).

nuptial bedchamber, and he went abroad to become a hermit in the desert.[126] Gratian also cites a canon ascribed to Pope Eusebius: "The parents of a betrothed girl may not give her to another man, but she herself may choose a monastery."[127] If married persons cannot separate in this way but betrothed persons can do so, it follows that the bond between *sponsus* and *sponsa* is not marriage.

Next, Gratian shows that numerous canonical rules and decisions about impotence and incest presuppose that the partners are not married until they consummate their marriage in sexual intercourse.[128] For example, if a husband becomes impotent after coitus has taken place, his marriage is not dissolved, yet if a man is unable to consummate his marriage and if the partners can prove this by canonically prescribed means, then the marriage is dissolved and the woman is free to remarry.[129]

Gratian also appeals to the authority of Ambrose commenting on Luke. Ambrose cites several passages of Scripture to show that Mary remained a virgin, especially John 19:26–27, where Jesus commended Mary and John to each other and John "took her into his own home." Assuming that Mary and Joseph parted company, Ambrose argues that she would never have left him if she had had sexual intercourse with him, for Jesus says that divorce is permissible only on grounds of fornication.[130] Ambrose must have assumed that partners were not married until they come together sexually.[131]

To reconcile the two positions, Gratian presents three mutually compatible solutions. The source of all three is the consensual proof text from Ambrose, which states not only that the conjugal pact is what makes marriage, but also that the betrothed partners are *called* husband and wife and that their relationship is *called* marriage as soon as a marriage is "begun" (*initiatur*).[132]

First, Gratian proposes that marriage "is begun in betrothal and perfected in sexual intercourse." On this view, there is already a marriage between *sponsus* and *sponsa*, but it is only an "initiate marriage" (*coniugium initiatum*) and not an "established marriage" (*coniugium ratum*).[133] That is why Ambrose says that marriage is so called when it is begun (*initiatur*) rather than when the wife loses her virginity. Gratian corroborates this position by citing two other, apparently spurious proof texts. According to Ambrose, "In every marriage there is understood to be a spiritual union that the bodily intercourse of the spouses completes." According to Jerome, marriages are "begun in a betrothal agreement and perfected in bodily intercourse."[134] Gratian shows how the distinction between initiate marriage

---

[126] Ibid., dictum post c. 26 (1070). The story, which Gratian ascribes to Jerome, is from *Vita sancti Macarii Romani*, c. 17, PL 17:422B. Macarius's action would be illicit by Hincmar's standards.

[127] C. 27 q. 2 c. 27 (1071). Ivo, *Decretum* VII.40. Also *Tripartita* B 12.2.

[128] C. 27 q. 2 cc. 28–31 (1071–72).

[129] C. 27 q. 2 dictum post c. 28, c. 29, dictum post c. 29 (1071–72).

[130] Ambrose, *Expositio in Lucam* II, 4–5 (on Luke 1:26–27), PL 15:1554C–1555A.

[131] C. 27 q. 2 dictum post. 29 (1071–72).

[132] Quoted at C. 27 q. 2 c. 5 (1064). Ambrose, *De institutione virginis* 6(41), PL 16:316C.

[133] C. 27 q. 2 dictum post c. 34 (1073).

(*matrimonium initiatum*) and perfected marriage (*matrimonium perfectum*) can be applied to interpret these texts. Before sexual consummation, a wife does not "belong to matrimony" as regards perfect marriage, but she is already in an initiate marriage.[135]

Someone might object, Gratian notes, that according to Augustine "there was a perfect marriage between Mary and Joseph." Gratian may be quoting a spurious *sententia*, or he may be summarizing a passage in *De nuptiis et concupiscentia* in which Augustine argues that Mary and Joseph fulfilled the three goods of marriage, and that Joseph was truly Mary's husband and Jesus' father. Gratian cites the latter passage explicitly in the discussion that follows.[136] To obviate the objection, Gratian argues that there are different modes of perfection in marriage. Mary's marriage was perfect inasmuch as it fulfilled the three goods of marriage, namely, faith, offspring, and sacrament, but these are only accidental benefits, which "accompany" marriage. They are not necessary for the perfection marriage *per se*. The marriage of Mary and Joseph was imperfect inasmuch as they did not fulfill the *officium* of marriage, which is sexual intercourse. Gratian slips easily here from consummation (the single act of coitus that completes the nuptials) to what today would be called the "sexual relationship": either recurrent sexual intercourse or the mutual rendering of the conjugal debt.

In sum, according to the first of the three solutions, marriage begins in betrothal but is completed or perfected (*consummatum*) by the "duty [*officium*] of bodily intercourse." All the authorities and arguments on both sides can be interpreted and reconciled by means of this distinction. Whereas initiate marriage, which has not yet been perfected by the "office" of coitus, is still soluble, consummated marriage is insoluble.[137]

According to the second solution, betrothed partners receive the name but not the actuality of marriage, for they are already potentially married, and potential things are named after the corresponding actualities. Gratian has in mind the rhetorical trope of *anticipatio* (in Greek: *prolepsis*). Betrothal is not yet marriage in reality, but it is *called* marriage through anticipation, for it is a marriage-to-be.[138] Similarly, when the angel said, "Do not be afraid to accept Mary, your wife" (Matt 1:20), he was referring to Mary as a wife-to-be. Betrothed women (*sponsae*) are called wives (*coniuges*) in Scripture not in respect of the "actuality [*effectus*] of present things" but in respect of "the hope of future things." According to Ambrose, therefore, what the spouses receive when they exchange consent is not the "reality or actuality" of

---

[134] Ibid., cc. 36–37.

[135] Ibid., dictum post c. 39 (1074).

[136] Cf. Augustine, *De nupt. et conc.* I.11(12–13), CSEL 42:224–25 (on fulfillment of the three goods in Mary and Joseph); Ivo, *Decretum* VIII.15; also *Tripartita* B 15.16, *Panormia* VI.30. This text is cited also in C. 27 q. 2 c. 10 (1065), but this passage is not in the first recension of the *Decretum*.

[137] C. 27 q. 2 dictum post c. 39 §1 ("Sed obicitur...", 1074).

[138] Ibid., dictum post c. 39 §2 ("Potest et aliter distingui...") through cc. 39–40 (1074–75). Anticipation was a familiar rhetorical trope.

marriage but rather the *name* of marriage. The process has begun. This interpretation, according to Gratian, explains how Mary and Joseph, as Augustine says, were spouses and parents not in a bodily manner but by "an inseparable affection of the mind,"[139] for betrothed partners are already bound by the troth (*fides*) that will eventually make them spouses.[140] Citing Bede, Jerome, John Chryrostom, Origen, and Scripture, Gratian shows that although Mary was not really Joseph's wife in actual fact, she was *called* his wife: partly as a concession to custom and appearance, for she was living with him, and partly to hide her virginity from public attention, but chiefly because she was Joseph's wife-to-be.[141]

The third solution pertains to the role of coitus in relation to consent. Although coitus completes marriage, Gratian argues, the efficient cause that *makes* marriage is consent, or troth (*fides*). The partners express that consent and plight their troth in the betrothal. It is only by virtue of the preceding intention or conjugal pact that coitus instrumentally perfects marriage, for coitus has no such efficacy of its own. Hence, there is no inconsistency between texts showing that consent *makes* marriage and texts showing that coitus *completes* marriage.[142]

6.4.2 *The role of the nuptial blessing*

If one concedes that a betrothed woman (*sponsa*) is not yet a wife (*coniux*), is she permitted to renounce her betrothal and to marry another man?[143] Not necessarily. Gratian finds only a few canons that bear directly on this question. The crucial text, which features also in Hincmar's letter on Stephen's marriage, is from the decretal that Pope Siricius sent to Himerius, bishop of Tarragona, in AD 385. Himerius had asked Siricius whether a certain man could marry a woman who was already betrothed to another man. Siricius replies that he prohibits this entirely, "because the blessing that a priest confers on a wife-to-be [*nuptura*] seems to the faithful to become a kind of sacrilege if it is violated by any transgression."[144] According to Gratian's interpretation, Siricius forbids a betrothed woman from marrying another man once the betrothal has been blessed and she has been led into her husband's home, even before the marriage has been consummated.[145]

Gratian uses this response to interpret some other pertinent texts and to obviate possible objections. For example, when Pope Eusebius says that the parents of a betrothed woman cannot give her to another man, Gratian argues, he is referring to a *sponsa* who has already received the bridal veil and the nuptial blessing.[146] Gratian

---

[139] Ibid., dictum post c. 39 §2 (1074).   [140] Ibid., dictum post c. 45 (1076).

[141] Ibid., cc. 40–45 (1074–76).   [142] Ibid., dictum post 45 §1 (1076).

[143] Ibid., dictum post c. 45 §3.

[144] *Epist. ad Himerium*, PL 13:1136B. *Collectio hispana*. PL 84:632B. Ivo, *Decretum* VIII.169 (also *Panormia* VI.18); Hincmar, *Epist*. 136, p. 103. According to Ritzer, p. 231, Siricius meant that the second union could not be blessed.

[145] C. 27 q. 2 dictum post c. 50 (1077–78).

[146] Ibid., §1 (1078). Gratian has cited the text previously, at c. 27 (1071).

interprets a ruling by Pope Gregory II on impotence in the same light. According to Gregory, a marriage may be dissolved if the husband cannot consummate it, and in that case his bride may marry another man; but if he subsequently has sex with another woman, proving that he is not impotent, the original marriage should be reinstated. But the first marriage was never consummated. What prevents it from being dissolved? Gregory must assume, Gratian argues, that this marriage had already been blessed.[147]

Gratian does not explain how the two parts of this theory fit together. Ideally, a marriage would be blessed first and later consummated. In practice, though, many marriages would never have been blessed at all, and some would not have been blessed until after they were consummated. Thus, the Council of Trent will rule in the decree *Tametsi* that spouses must not begin to live together until a priest has solemnized their marriage in church.[148] The rule must have been intended to prevent something that was happening in fact. Studies of post-Reformation England have shown that despite the best efforts of the clergy, many couples began to cohabit as soon as they had become betrothed with an exchange of *de futuro* consent.[149]

The subsequent tradition largely ignored Gratian's thesis that the priestly blessing rendered a marriage irrevocable. Rufinus, whose commentary on the *Decretum* tended to supplant the original work, treats Gratian's theory regarding the priestly blessing as a minor obstacle. He notes that the decretal of Siricius refers only to priestly blessing, and not to the wife's being led into her husband's home: a detail that Gratian added. A man is prohibited from accepting in marriage a woman who is already betrothed to someone else, but the authority does not say that the marriage should be annulled if he does marry her. And even if that were the intention, the fatal impediment would not be the prior betrothal *per se* but rather the papal interdict. Rufinus confesses that he cannot see the relevance of the authority from Pope Eusebius. It is true that parents are not permitted to give in marriage a girl who is already legitimately betrothed to another man, but if they have done so, neverthe-less, and the second marriage has been consummated, the spouses cannot be separated, "for there are many things that ought not to be done but which if they are done, nevertheless, become valid after the fact."[150]

6.4.3 *Gratian and consent*

Modern scholars characterize Gratian's position as the coital or copular theory in contradistinction to the consensual theory of Peter Lombard, but that terminology can be misleading. Gratian maintained no less than Peter Lombard that the spouses'

---

[147] C. 27 q. 2 dictum post c. 50 §2 (1078). For Gregory's ruling, see C. 33 q. 1 c. 2 (1149), = Ivo, *Decretum* VIII.182 (*Panormia* VI.116).

[148] *Tametsi*, in Tanner-Alberigo 2:756/24–25.

[149] See A. Macfarlane, *Marriage and Love in England* (Oxford, 1986), 304–06.

[150] Rufinus on C. 27 q. 2 c. 50, in *Summa Decretorum*, ed. H. Singer, 452.

own consent was a necessary condition for marriage, its efficient cause, and its essential foundation. But, whereas Gratian reasoned that the act of consent needed to be realized or confirmed in coitus, French scholars during the same period reasoned that betrothal sufficed to make a marriage as long as it was expressed in the present tense. It might be better, therefore, to refer to Gratian's as the "consummation theory," and the French alternative as the "betrothal theory."

Gratian's insistence that spousal consent is a necessary condition for marriage is evident in his simple but radical treatment of the necessity of a daughter's consent and her freedom to marry even without her father's consent or against his wishes.[151] Two principles are at work in his discussion of coerced marriage. The first is pastoral: "Marriages entered into unwillingly usually have bad outcomes." The dictum is a gloss by Ambrosiaster on 1 Corinthians 7:39, the text with which Gratian's discussion begins, where Paul writes that a widow is free "to marry whom she wills" provided only that she does so "in the Lord."[152] Gratian finds the second principle, which pertains to the very nature of marital consent, in a decretal that Urban II sent to Sancho Ramirez. Because, as Urban says, "those who are to become one body should also be of one mind," it follows that no woman should be united to a man against her will.[153]

Gratian's position on spousal consent has been obscured by the accretions of the second recension of the *Decretum*. Gratian II (as the compiler of the augmented version is sometimes known) viewed the daughter's right of consent in a more conservative light, adding texts that obscured Gratian I's position.[154] In a section on whether a marriage is valid if the motive for marrying is not procreation, Gratian II digresses to discuss concubinage and the importance of a father's consent to his daughter's marriage. Here, he cites Leo's canon *Non omnis mulier*, which refers to wives as being "joined to their husbands by their fathers' will." He explicates the principle underlying this phrase, explaining that a father's consent to his daughter's marriage is not only desirable but a necessary condition for legitimate marriage. He also cites Pope Evaristus: "Unless she is given in marriage [*tradatur*] by her parents, her marriage is not legitimate."[155] For corroboration, Gratian II quotes a passage in which Ambrose explains what role Rebekah played when she was married to Isaac. Rebekah was not consulted about her betrothal, for it was not her place to choose a

[151] J. T. Noonan, "Power to choose," *Viator* 4 (1973): 419–34.
[152] C. 31 q. 2 dictum ante c. 1 (1112–13). Ambrosiaster on 1 Cor. 7:39, CSEL 81.2, 90/13–14.
[153] C. 31 q. 2 c. 3 (1113). "Quorum enim unum corpus est, unus debet esse et animus...."
[154] A. Winroth, "Marital Consent in Gratian's *Decretum*," in M. Brett and K. G. Cushing (eds.), *Readers, Texts and Compilers in the Earlier Middle Ages* (Farnham, 2009), 111–121.
[155] C. 32 q. 2 dictum post c. 12 (1123). The compiler is thinking of a spurious decretal based on Leo's *Non omnis mulier*. It first appears in the *False Decretals* ascribed to Pope Evaristus (PL 130:81B–C, = *Panormia* VI.31), where it is ascribed to Pope Evaristus. There is a shorter and probably earlier version of the canon in the forged capitularies of Benedictus Levita, III.463, PL 97:859C. See P. Corbet, "Le douaire dans le droit canonique jusqu'à Gratien," in Bougard, Feller, and Le Jan, *Dots et douaires*, 43–55, at 48–50.

husband, although she was consulted about setting the day for the marriage (Gen 24:55–58).[156] These are conservative efforts to reestablish a father's power over his daughter's marriage, and they distract readers from the position that Gratian I pursued.

Gratian I maintained not only that spousal consent was necessary but also that it was what made marriage. He states his position precisely:

> When John Chrysostom says that it is not coitus that makes marriage but intent, therefore, and when Ambrose says that it is the not deflowering of virginity that makes marriage but the conjugal pact, they should be understood as meaning that neither coitus without the will to contract marriage nor the deflowering of virginity without the conjugal pact makes marriage. Rather, it is because of the preceding will to contract marriage, or because of the conjugal pact, that a woman is said to marry [*nubere*] a man or to celebrate marriage [*nuptias celebrare*] in the deflowering of her virginity, or in coitus.[157]

Coitus perfects the marriage instrumentally, by fulfilling marital consent.

To explain why Gratian adopted his consummation theory, therefore, one must explain why he reasoned that coitus was required *in addition to* consent, and not why it was required *instead of* consent. James Brundage asks why Gratian assigned "a primary role in marriage formation" to sexual consummation, and also why Gratian rejected the distinction between future-tense and present-tense betrothals that contemporaneous French scholars were proposing. Professor Brundage suggests that Gratian may have thought that consummation was easier to prove than consent. On the one hand, proof of consent required the presence of witnesses, and, even if witnesses were present, they saw only the external signs, and not the required intention. On the other hand, although consummation was usually private, "circumstantial evidence to corroborate the sworn testimony of the parties was often available and was used."[158] But coitus had a secondary, instrumental role in the formation of marriage, according to Gratian, and not a primary one. More important, the issue is not whether coitus was easier to demonstrate than consent, for the role of coitus in the formation of a marriage presupposed the authenticity of the preceding consent. Other things being equal, consent *and* consummation are obviously harder to prove than consent alone, since it is easier to prove one thing alone than to prove both that and another, separate thing.

Gratian gives no indication that he was aware of the distinction between future consent and present consent, which would have put the problem in a different light and unsettled much of his argument. If he knew about it, he chose to ignore it. His silence seems puzzling, yet the omission does not necessarily call for much

---

[156] C. 32, q. 2, c. 13 (1124). Ambrose, *De Abraham* I.9(91), PL 14:453B.

[157] C. 27 q. 2 dictum post c. 45 §1 (1076).

[158] J. A. Brundage, *Law, Sex, and Christian Society in Medieval Europe* (Chicago, 1987), 237–38 and 269n59.

explanation. The distinction would have had no relevance to him unless it was congruent with local practice in Bologna or Italy in the 1140s, and there is no reason at all to suppose that it was. If Gratian, like Ivo of Chartres, recognized only one mode of betrothal, then it was eminently reasonable and practical to maintain that the relationship became irrevocable not at the beginning of the process, as Ivo had maintained, but at its conclusion, when the spouses came together – whether in church, in the husband's home, or in bed.

7

From competing theories to common doctrine in the twelfth century

The preceding chapters have traced the development of two different solutions to the same question: Whether a betrothal to one person is a fatal impediment to a subsequent marriage with someone else. For example, Gratian asked whether a girl who had betrothed one man could renounce that contract and marry or become betrothed to another.[1] Several alternative theories circulated or were proposed from around the middle of the twelfth century through the 1170s, two of which dominated the field. Each pertained both to a region and to a discipline. According to the betrothal theory, which originated among theologians of the Île de France, the prior betrothal was a fatal impediment only if it was expressed in words referring to the present or in the present tense (*de praesenti*). According to the consummation theory, which originated among the canonists of Bologna, the prior betrothal was a fatal impediment only if it was perfected in sexual intercourse. These theories were superseded in the 1180s by a common doctrine that combined elements of both.

The Anstey case illustrates the kind of problem that such theories were designed to resolve.[2] William de Sackville, an Essex squire, was betrothed to Aubrey de Tesgoz, who remained in her parental home until they were ready to come together. Meanwhile, however, William married another woman, named Alice. This marriage was solemnized, and they raised a family together, but William later dismissed Alice and had the marriage annulled on the grounds of his prior betrothal to Aubrey. During this first phase of the case, in a decretal written around 1140, Pope Innocent II

---

[1] C. 27 q. 2 dictum ante c. 1 (1062): "... an puellae alteri desponsatae possint renunciare priori condicioni, et transferre sua vota ad alium."

[2] P. M. Barnes, "The Anstey Case," in P. M. Barnes and C. F. Slade (eds.), A *Medieval Miscellany* (London, 1960), 1–23. P. A. Brand, "New Light on the Anstey Case," *Essex Archaeology and History* 15 (1983): 68–83. C. N. L. Brooke, *The Medieval Idea of Marriage* (Oxford, 1989), 148–52. R. C. Van Caenegem, *English Lawsuits from William I to Richard I*, vol. 2 (London, 1991), 387–404. See also Brooke's appendix on the Anstey case in *The Letters of John of Salisbury*, ed. W. J. Millor and H. E. Butler, revised by C. N. L. Brooke, vol. 1, (Oxford, 1986), 267–71.

pronounced in favor of the prior union and against the second. Nevertheless, Mabel de Francheville, a daughter of William and Alice, inherited William's estate in Essex as his legitimate heir. In 1158, Richard of Anstey, another Essex squire and a nephew of William's, successfully contested Mabel's right to the estate in order to secure it for himself on the grounds that she was illegitimate. Only a secular court could award William's estate to Richard, but only a church court could determine who was validly married to whom. Because the crux of Richard's case was Mabel's illegitimacy, Mabel tried to show that the prior union with Aubrey did not amount to *matrimonium ratum*, partly on the grounds that it had never been consummated. This suit, too, went as far as the Holy See. Pope Alexander III upheld William's prior betrothal to Aubrey as a fatal impediment to his subsequent marriage with Alice.

Either of the two dominant theories would have settled the Anstey case. According to the betrothal theory, William's prior betrothal to Aubrey would have been a fatal impediment to his marriage with Alice if and only if the betrothal was about the present (*de praesenti*), or expressed in the present tense. According to the consummation theory, the second union would have trumped the first because the first had not been consummated. But in fact there was no universal, supra-regional agreement about these issues during the years of the Anstey case.

7.1 THE TERMS OF THE SCHOLARLY DEBATE (C.1150–C.1180)

Although other possibilities were still under consideration, the betrothal and consummation theories were the chief contenders after the middle of the twelfth century. Whereas Gratian's was the standard formulation of the consummation theory, Peter Lombard's was the standard formulation of the betrothal theory. The Lombard drew on the insights of Hugh of Saint-Victor among others to develop his version of the consummation theory.

To save his conviction that Mary was firmly committed to perpetual virginity when she married, Hugh of Saint-Victor argued that marriage *per se* was an essentially non-carnal partnership (Sections 10.4 and 10.5). One can consent to marriage, according to Hugh, without consenting to coitus. Likewise, there are two conjugal debts: the essential debt of the partnership, and an optional, super-added debt of sexual intercourse. Hugh accepted that coitus was necessary for the union of two in one flesh and that marriage was not a sacrament of Christ and the church without it. To save the sacramentality of marriage *per se*, therefore, Hugh posited another signification. Whereas the union of two in one flesh was the great sacrament of Christ and the church, marriage *per se* was a *greater* sacrament of the soul's union with God.[3] Hugh was more interested in Mary's virginity and in the sanctity of marriage than in the formation of marriage and legal impediments, but he accepted the distinction between *de futuro* and *de praesenti* betrothals, pointing

---

[3] Hugh of Saint-Victor, *De sacramentis christianae fidei* II.11.3, PL 176:482A–C.

out that promising to do something could not be the same as actually doing the same thing. A future-tense betrothal could not amount to a binding marriage, therefore, even if it was confirmed with an oath.[4]

Following Hugh, Peter Lombard argued that a marriage was a sacred sign even before it was consummated, but he modified Hugh's idea in two ways. First, because the Lombard, unlike Hugh, was chiefly interested in the formation of marriage and the point at which a marriage became irrevocable, he focused on the act of consent and the possible role of consummation, rather than on the condition of being married. Second, to save the unity of marriage as a single sacrament, Peter maintained that both present-tense consent and consummation signified aspects of the same thing, namely, Christ's union with the church. Whereas the *coniunctio animorum* (the joining of the spouses' wills or intentions) signified the union of charity between Christ and the church, subsequent carnal intercourse signified the union that existed between Christ and the church by virtue of the sharing of a common human nature, which Christ acquired through his incarnation.[5] The Lombard assumed that a marriage was established (*ratum*) and insoluble if and only if it was truly a sacred sign of Christ's union with the church. Which aspect of the union was signified, in his view, did not matter.

The Lombard accepted that a future-tense betrothal to one person was not a fatal impediment to subsequent marriage with another, chiefly because promising to do something was different from actually doing it. Gratian had appealed to texts in which a holy person had escaped marriage even after the exchange of vows by entering the religious life. Against Gratian, therefore, Peter argues that the vows in such cases must have been *de futuro*, for a *de praesenti* betrothal is irrevocable. Spouses who are bound together by *de praesenti* vows can enter the religious life only jointly and by mutual agreement, and then neither is able to remarry.[6]

Although the two theories had developed independently, a debate about them ensued from around the middle of the twelfth century until its resolution in the late 1170s. Gratian, writing around 1140, gave no indication that he was familiar with the betrothal theory, but Peter Lombard, writing in the 1150s, was familiar with Gratian's position and wrote in opposition to it. Thereafter, theologians who discussed the matter were content for the most part to restate Peter Lombard's position while denying that consummation was necessary for *matrimonium ratum*.[7] Whereas theologians during this period did not usually draw attention to the existence of two competing theories, canonists compared and contrasted them, and the canonists of Bologna defended their own position against the French. For example, the canonist Rufinus rejected the betrothal distinction as a "two-faced" opinion and castigated its proponents – he was probably referring chiefly to Peter Lombard – as seekers after

---

4   Hugh of Saint-Victor, ibid., II.11.5, 486A–C.   5   Peter Lombard, *Sent.* IV, 26.6.1 (419–20).
6   Peter Lombard, *Sent.* IV, 27.5–8 (424–28).
7   E.g., Peter of Poitiers, *Sent.* V, c. 16, PL 211:1259A.

vainglory. Rufinus adhered instead to the teachings of Gratian, a man "of great memory."[8]

Two northern canonists writing during the 1160s, one a Frenchman and the other a German educated in France, reported that the betrothal theory was the policy of the French, or Gallican church, and that the consummation theory was the policy of the Roman, or Transalpine church.[9] It is not clear whether these northern canonists were referring to all of France, to northern France, or even just to the Île-de-France, but it is reasonable to assume that they knew what was the prevailing policy of their own region. French canonists seem to have adhered to Peter Lombard's position during this period, although they tried to avoid explicitly contradicting the Bolognese position, presumably because they were caught between regional and disciplinary loyalties. Most modern scholars have taken these statements at face value and claimed that the French and Roman churches litigated claims of prior betrothal in different ways, according to the respective theories, but there are reasons to be cautious. There is no evidence that all the provinces south of the Alps consistently maintained the consummation policy.

The Bolognese canonists adhered more or less closely to Gratian's position until the 1170s, albeit with a range of variations and some attempts to accommodate aspects of the betrothal theory, but Rome apparently followed the French policy. Thus, Pope Innocent II upheld William de Sackville's unconsummated betrothal to Aubrey as a prior marriage. Indeed, Innocent affirmed that when a woman has been handed over to a man by her father but remains at her parental home until the agreed day arrives, she is nevertheless the man's wife by virtue of their legitimate consent, "for it was not promised as something in the future, but established as something in the present."[10] It makes no difference, according to Innocent, if the man has subsequently had sex with another partner or even begotten children by her. On the contrary, the soundness of the prior union merely makes his subsequent behavior reprehensible. One might be suspicious about the abrupt appearance of the *de futuro/de praesenti* distinction in Innocent's letter. Perhaps it was a later insertion,[11] for the decretal says nothing to establish that the prior agreement was expressed in the present tense, and the occurrence of the distinction here is exceptional. Aside from this single instance, the first decretals positing the distinction were

---

[8] Rufinus, *Summa decretorum* on C. 27 q. 2, ed. Singer, p. 440: "Vaga multum est harum quaestionum sententia, quam non ministri Christi et divine scripture dispensatores, sed inanis glorie aucupes fecere biftrontem.... Cum ergo ille magne memorie Gratianus...."

[9] *Summa Parisiensis* on D. 11 c. 11 and D. 34 c. 19, ed. McLaughlin, pp. 11 and 33–34. *Summa "Elegantius in iure divino" seu Coloniensis* 13.30–31 and 13.34, ed. Fransen, vol. 4 (Vatican City, 1990), pp. 17–18, 19.

[10] *Super eo interrogasti* (c. 1140), JL 8274, WH 1016, 1 *Comp.* 4.1.10: "Non enim futurum promittebatur, sed praesens firmabatur."

[11] As suggested in C. Donahue, Jr., "Johannes Faventinus on Marriage," in W. P. Müller and M. E. Sommar, *Medieval Church Law and the Origins of the Western Legal Tradition* (Washington, DC, 2006), 179–97, at 195–97.

issued by Alexander III during the 1170s. That said, the distinction was well known during the middle of the twelfth century, and Innocent may have used it to interpret what happened when Aubrey was handed over (*tradita*) by her father, regardless of what words were used. In any case, there can be no doubt that Innocent considered the unconsummated betrothal to have been a virtual marriage because the woman's father had given her away to her husband.

Rome was apparently less inclined than the French bishops to dissolve a marriage on grounds of non-consummation through impotence: a position that is difficult to square with the Bolognese theory of consummation. Pope Alexander III was responsible for three decretals on this topic. Two were addressed to Italian bishops and concerned cases in which the wife was the incapable partner. Alexander III advised that spouses in such situations should remain together, living as brother and sister.[12] The third decretal was addressed to the bishop of Amiens and concerned a husband who could not consummate his marriage because of a prior injury, which was unknown to his bride when they married. Moreover, the husband had subsequently contracted leprosy and was living in a leper colony. His wife sought permission to marry someone else. In stating his judgment, Alexander contrasts the policies of the Roman and French churches:

> But although the Roman church is not accustomed to separate persons who have been lawfully joined together on grounds of natural frigidity or other *maleficia*, nevertheless, if it is the general custom of the Gallican church that marriages of this sort should be dissolved, we shall be patiently tolerant if, in accordance with that custom, you grant the woman permission to marry whom she wills in the Lord.[13]

Alexander is echoing observations found in the sentential literature from the early twelfth century. Clearly, he agreed with those French theologians who observed that the Gallican church, in contrast to the Roman church, permitted a marriage to be dissolved when the partners were unable to consummate it, albeit only if the impotence was due not to "natural frigidity" or to a girl's physical immaturity, but rather to "other causes," such as *maleficium*.[14] Understood literally, the term

---

[12] X 4.15.4, 2 *Comp.* 4.9.2, WH 183, JL 14125, *Consultationi tuae, qua nos* (to the bishop of Bisceglie). 1 *Comp.* 4.16.2, WH 188(b), JL 14075, *Consuluit nos.... Super eo vero* (to the bishop of Andria).

[13] X 4.15.2, WH 822, JL 11866, *Quod sedem apostolicam*. The likely date of this decretal is 1171, during Alexander's so-called French period. The only part of Alexander's decretal that Raymond retained in the *Liber extra* was a note explaining that impotent men are incapable of marriage for the same reason as pre-pubescent boys. In Friedberg's edition, these are the last few lines in roman font, whereas the remainder is in italics. (The words set in italics in Friedberg's edition are *partes decisae*, which Raymond of Penyafort omitted from the *Liber extra* but Friedberg tried to restore.) On the rationale and background of these decisions about sexual incapacity, see W. Kelly, *Pope Gregory II on Divorce and Remarriage* (Rome, 1976), 171–79.

[14] Lottin, "Sententiae Atrebatenses," RThAM 10 (1938), 354/84–89 (or PsM V, 437/96–101). *Cum omnia sacramenta*, second recension, ed. Bliemetzrieder, RThAM 3 (1931), 280/121–30. IPH, 30*/7–31/*15.

maleficium denoted magical impotence, and the crucial canon on the subject was *Si per sortiarias*, from Hincmar's letter about Stephen's marriage.[15] Impotence that resulted from a hex raised a special set of canonical issues. Unlike impotence that resulted from immaturity, nonage was not at issue. More important, unlike "natural impotence," which was due either to injury or to innate infirmity, magical impotence typically occurred after a betrothal, and it was likely to affect only the two persons in relation to each other. A man rendered incapable of consummating his marriage by a hex might still be able to copulate with another woman. Most important, the condition was not necessarily permanent, for hexes could be lifted.[16] The canon *Si per sortiarias* permitted spouses to marry again even in such circumstances, albeit not to each other. The original marriage did not have to be re-established if the incapable partner was able to have sex with someone else – the usual rule in cases of impotence resulting from innate infirmity or injury. The French church had traditionally accepted *Si per sortiarias*, albeit not without controversy. Perhaps the term *maleficium* could denote any acquired or adventitious impotence, in contradistinction to impotence that was either innate or the result of a permanent injury, such as castration. The point to note here is that in cases of non-consummation through impotence, the French church was more flexible and permitted separation and remarriage, whereas the Roman church was more inclined to insist on the permanence of the marriage: precisely the opposite of what one would have expected if Rome was firmly committed to the Bolognese consummation theory.

The canonists' reception of the proof text *Duobus modis*, which they ascribed to Augustine, complicated the polarity between the two theories of marriage formation:

Troth [*fides*] is said in two ways: that of a pact and that of consent. If a man makes the troth of a pact with a woman, he ought not to take [*ducere*] another. If he has taken another, he ought [*debet*] to do penance for his broken troth, but he should remain with her whom he took, for so great a sacrament [*tantum sacramentum*][17] ought not to be rescinded. If he made the troth of consent, however, he is not permitted [*licet*] to take another woman. If he has taken another, he must dismiss her and adhere to the first. The troth of a pact occurs when someone promises to another his troth that he will take her if she allows him to have sex with her, or even for consent [*pro consensu*]. But the troth of consent occurs when, even without joining hands, he consents with heart and mouth to take her, and they assent, one to another, and mutually receive each other.[18]

---

[15] See C. Rider, *Magic and Impotence in the Middle Ages* (Oxford, 2006); and J. A. Brundage, *Law, Sex, and Christian Society in Medieval Europe* (Chicago, 1987), 145, 291n150, 457. For the origin of *Si per sortiarias*, see Hincmar, *Epist.* 136, ed. Perels in MGH *Epist.* 8, = *Epistolae Karolini Aevi* 6, 105/8–20 (= Ivo, *Decretum* VIII.194, also *Panormia* VI.117).

[16] See K. A. Boccafola, *The Requirement of Perpetuity for the Impediment of Impotence* (Rome, 1975), 13–38.

[17] That is, an oath of such great significance.

[18] C. 27 q. 2 c. 51, *Palea* (1078). 1 *Comp.* 4.4.1 (46). X 4.4.1 (680).

Duobus modis articulated an early version of the betrothal theory, which had first appeared in the sentential literature (Section 5.5.1), but which had virtually disappeared from French theology by the second half of the century. Although *Duobus modis* was troublesome for the Bolognese canonists, many of them retained it, beginning with Rolandus, and it was inserted in Gratian's *Decretum* as a *palea*.[19] *Duobus modis* envisages two kinds of agreement. One is the promise to marry, which establishes the "troth of a pact" (*fides pactionis*). It is typically an agreement with conditions attached. Although the original sources had spoken of an agreement "for cash" (*pro censu*), this phrase had become "for consent" (*pro consensu*) in the canon as adopted by legal scholars. The other is the exchange of wedding vows, by which the spouses mutually give and receive each other. This establishes the "troth of consent" (*fides consensus*).

In reality, the debate was not one of simple opposition between Paris and Bologna. On the one hand, canonists in the Bolognese tradition incorporated aspects of the French betrothal theory. On the other hand, some French canonists tried to expound both theories without committing themselves to either, although they were more inclined to favor the betrothal theory. Their position was difficult, for they were caught between their allegiance to regional culture and jurisdiction, and their loyalty to Bologna, the hub of their discipline.

7.2 THE CONSUMMATION THEORY IN THE BOLOGNESE TRADITION

Most French decretists upheld the betrothal theory, whereas Bolognese decretists upheld versions of the consummation theory. Absent evidence to the contrary, one should assume that the betrothal theory was consistent with the prevailing ecclesiastical policy in France and England, and that the consummation theory was consistent with the prevailing policy in Bologna, although there was probably uncertainty, inconsistency, and debate everywhere. Before Rufinus, it was possible for Bolognese canonists to mix elements of both positions. But Rufinus decisively rejected the betrothal theory and made the two positions seem for a while to be mutually exclusive options.

7.2.1 *Decretists before Rufinus*

Paucapalea, the first Bolognese scholar to comment on the *Decretum*, did not explicitly commit himself to Gratian's solution to the betrothal problem when he glossed *Causa* 27, although one may reasonably take his silence as tacit agreement. The decretists began to remark on the divergence when they became aware of Peter

---

[19] Some early additions to Gratian's *Decretum* were marked as *palea* ("chaff") during the Middle Ages, perhaps when they were inserted. Even medieval readers were aware that these were later additions. The term may have been a pun referring to Paucapalea, the first Bolognese canonist after Gratian to teach and comment on the *Decretum*.

Lombard's position, which they rejected. Being as yet unaware of the Lombard's position, therefore, Paucapalea saw no need to defend Gratian's. Nevertheless, he assumed that marriage entailed carnal union. In introducing *Causa* 27, he contrasted the "corporeal marriage" or "carnal joining" of man and wife with the "spiritual marriage" between clerics and the church.[20] More important, Paucapalea maintained that a betrothal could legitimately be dissolved on certain specified grounds, which included entry into religion, failure to consummate, lack of consent, special dispensation by the church, and supervenient incest.[21]

Rolandus, who taught canon law in Bologna during the 1150s and 1160s and may have had some connection with the French school, espoused Gratian's distinction between initiate and consummate marriage, but he also incorporated elements of the French theory.[22] He outlined different but arguably compatible theories in two works: in his *De coniugio*, a commentary on *Causae* 27–36 of Gratian's *Decretum*;[23] and in his *Sententiae*, a theological summary.

In his *De coniugio*, Rolandus adopts Gratian's distinction between initiate and consummate marriage, albeit without explicitly endorsing Gratian's thesis that consummated betrothal to a second person trumps a prior, unconsummated betrothal. Rolandus distinguishes between marriage that is only initiated (*matrimonium initiatum tantum*) and marriage that is both initiated and consummated (*matrimonium initiatum et consummatum*). Only the latter contains the sacrament of Christ's union with the church. Rolandus uses this thesis to explain why the coital proof texts ascribed to Augustine and Leo say that a woman who has not yet had sex with her husband does not "pertain to matrimony." Such a woman does not pertain to *consummated* matrimony, Rolandus argues, or to the matrimony that contains the sacrament of Christ and the church, but she is joined to her husband by an initiate marriage.[24]

Rolandus argues in his *De coniugio* that each union entails its own distinctive troth. The marital pact (*pactio coniugalis*), which is created by consent, entails the troth of betrothal (*fides pactionis*). Consummation establishes the troth of carnal union (*fides carnalis coniunctionis*). Whereas the former obliges the partners to remain chaste for each other, only the latter obliges them also to render the conjugal

---

[20] Paucapalea, *Summa super decretum*, ed. Schulte, p. 110 (on Causa 27). Stephen of Tournai (ed. Shulte, 231) and the *Summa Coloniensis* (ed. Fransen, vol. 4, p. 1) introduce C. 27 in the same way.

[21] Paucapalea on C. 27 q. 2 (115).

[22] The identification of Rolandus with the Bolognese canonist with Rolandus Bandinelli, who became Pope Alexander III (1159–1181), is no longer tenable. See J. T. Noonan, "Who was Rolandus?" in K. Pennington and R. Somerville (eds.), *Law, Church and Society* (Philadelphia, 1977), 21–48; and R. Pennington and W. P. Müller, "The Decretists: The Italian School," in W. Hartmann and K. Pennington (eds.), *The History of Medieval Canon Law* (Washington, D.C., 2008), 121–73, at 131–33.

[23] In Thaner's edition, Rolandus's commentary on C. 1–26 and his *De coniugio* (C. 27–36) form a single *Summa* (known as the *Stroma ex Decretorum corpore carptum*), but these were originally separate works: See Pennington and Müller, "The Decretists," 133–34.

[24] *De coniugio*, on C. 27 q. 2, ed. Thaner in *Summa magistri Rolandi* (Innsbruck, 1872), 128–130.

debt to each other. Consequently, a *sponsa* bound by the first troth is still free to renounce the marriage by becoming a religious, even without her partner's consent, but she cannot marry another man as long as the first is alive. Once their marriage has been consummated, on the contrary, she cannot opt for continence without her husband's consent. Thus, Rolandus differentiates between initiate and consummate marriage by assigning distinct conjugal obligations to each, which are the two components of Augustine's *bonum fidei*: a merely negative, outward fidelity by which each partner shuns sex with anyone else; and a positive, inward fidelity by which each partner is sexually available to the other. But Rolandus does not say in this treatise whether or not an initiate marriage to one person is a fatal impediment to marriage with another.[25]

In his *Sentences*, Rolandus defends Gratian's position, but he adopts elements of the French betrothal distinction when he discusses the impediment of prior marriage. Having defined marriage as the union (*coniunctio*) of a man and a woman that maintains an indivisible way of life, Rolandus explains that there are two sorts of union: a spiritual union resulting from the joining of intents, and a corporeal joining resulting from subsequent sexual intercourse. Both unions are required for a marriage to be perfect, or consummate.[26] Later, Rolandus considers the impediments of prior bonds or obligations (*ligationes*), such as religious vows or a prior betrothal. Here, he explains that there are two forms of *ligatio* in marriage. One is what Augustine calls "troth of consent" (*fides consensus*) in the canon *Duobus modis*. To establish consensual troth, each spouse utters a formula such as, "I will [to have] you as my own." The other obligation refers to the future, and each spouse says something like "I shall will [to have] you as my own" or "I shall take you as my own." The *de futuro* bond is an impediment to the contracting of marriage with someone else, but that impediment is not strong enough to dissolve (*dirimere*) a subsequent union with another *after* it has been contracted. Rolandus implies that the second union would be dissolved if the prior betrothal had been *de praesenti*, which would have established the troth of consent.[27]

An anonymous *quaestio* attributes yet another position to Rolandus. Even a conjugal pact stated in the present tense is not sufficient by itself to establish the marital bond. Thus, a man who says to a woman, "I take you as my wife," is not thereby bound to marry her. But a present-tense agreement becomes fully binding if it is corroborated by an oath, by the gift of a ring, or by sexual intercourse. In that case, the partners cannot be separated except for the sake of religion (presumably by mutual consent). If either marries another, the second marriage must be rescinded and the first reestablished.[28]

[25] Ibid., 128: "Fide pactionis se castos vicissim servare tenentur, unde et si religionem et continentiam sponsa invito sponso valeat eligere, ad alterius tamen copulam sponso vivente transire non poterit...." Ibid., 130: "Verum etsi non liceat sponsae vivente sponso alterius copulam expetere, licet tamen monasterium eligere...."

[26] Rolandus, *Sententiae, De sacramento matrimonii*, ed. Gietl, p. 270.   [27] Ibid., 274.

[28] Q. 26, in Thaner, *Summa magistri Rolandi*, 278.

The position of Gandulph, a canonist and theologian of Bologna, is also mixed. In his *Sentences*, a theological work from the 1160s that is heavily dependent on Peter Lombard, he seems to adhere to the French theory without explicitly stating it, but there are traces of the Bolognese theory.[29] Gandulph interprets the union of "two in one flesh" in a manner that recognizes consummation but is consistent with the French betrothal theory. The phrase may denote the spouses' actual coming together in legitimate sexual intercourse, he explains, but it may also denote either their equality in relation to the conjugal debt or the fact that they may now come together to beget the same legitimate offspring.[30] Gandulph touches on the role of coitus in the formation of marriage incidentally when he inquires into to the manner in which sexual intercourse perfects the spiritual union (*coniunctio spiritualis*) in marriage. Spiritual union may be construed as the bond (*vinculum*) that prevents each spouse from marrying as long as the other is alive and obliges them to render the conjugal debt to each other. Construed thus, it is sufficient in itself and is not perfected by sexual intercourse. Nevertheless, sexual intercourse perfects the spiritual union by establishing the relationship of affinity as well as by enhancing the signification of marriage, for sexual union signifies the union by which Christ completed the church and perfected the faithful.[31] Indeed, coitus within marriage, as long as it is legitimate, is a sacrament of Christ and the church (i.e., it signifies Christ and the church).[32] Gandulph seems to attribute no sacramental signification to marriage before consummation. On the one hand, therefore, he assumes, with the French scholars, that sexual consummation is not necessary to complete the marital bond. On the other hand, he also assumes, with the Bolognese scholars, that sexual consummation is necessary both for affinity and for sacramentality.

7.2.2 *Rufinus and Johannes Faventinus*

Rufinus staunchly defended but also elaborated Gratian's position in his *Summa decretorum*, written in the 1160s (most likely 1164–65),[33] and his version of Gratian's theory became the standard thereafter, superseding the original. Commenting on C. 27 q. 2, regarding the betrothed woman who marries another, Rufinus castigates the proponents of the betrothal theory in a torrent of rhetoric, confessing instead his loyalty to Gratian.[34] Rufinus incorporates not only Bolognese canonical

---

[29] According to Donahue, "Johannes Faventinus," 182, Gandulph "adopted the Parisian theory position fully, though it takes a careful reading to see that he did so."
[30] Gandulph, *Sententiarum libri quatuor*, ed. J. de Walter, IV, §220, pp. 508–09.
[31] Ibid., §244 (530–31). Gandulph discusses the union (*coniunctio*) or bond (*vinculum*) in marriage at IV, §225 (513–14).
[32] *Sent.* IV, §239 (526–27).
[33] On the date of Rufinus's *Summa*, see A. Gouron, "Les sources civilistes et la datation des Sommes de Rufin et d'Étienne de Tournai," BMCL 16 (1986): 55–70.
[34] Rufinus, *Summa decretorum* on C. 27 q. 2, ed. Singer, p. 440.

developments but also a theological rationale for the consummation theory appro-priated from Hugh of Saint-Victor.

Like Rolandus, Rufinus posits two kinds of troth (*fides*) in marriage, one created by betrothal, and the other by subsequent sexual intercourse. The former obliges the partners to remain chaste for each other, whereas the latter obliges them in addition to render the conjugal debt to each other. When Isidore says that the partners are called spouses "from the first troth of the betrothal," therefore, one should keep in mind that there are two kinds of troth:

> For by the troth of betrothal they ought to keep themselves chaste for each other. Hence the *sponsa* is allowed to choose to enter a monastery, even if her *sponsus* is unwilling, yet she ought [*debet*] not to marry another as long as he is alive. By the troth of carnal union they are bound to render the conjugal debt to each other, so that neither may dare to remain continent against the other's opposition, whether indefinitely or for a season.[35]

Inasmuch as the union is not fully established or fixed (*ratum*) prior to consumma-tion, it is not a marriage in the strict sense. Following Gratian to the letter, Rufinus claims that betrothed persons (*sponsi*) are called husband and wife (*coniuges*) only proleptically, in view of the hope of things to come (*spes futurorum*).[36] Rufinus clarifies the distinction between non-diriment and diriment impediments. Although a betrothed person is not permitted (*non licet*) to marry and ought not (*non debet*) to marry, it does not follow that such an illicit marriage must be annulled after it has been contracted. Thus, even if a prior betrothal has been blessed by a priest, that not a sufficient impediment to dissolve a subsequent consummated union.[37]

Like Gratian, Rufinus sees no contradiction between his own position and the principle that consent makes marriage. Consent makes marriage both in the sense that it initiates marriage, Rufinus argues, and in the sense that consent is what makes the marriage when sexual intercourse occurs. Again, one may say that consent alone makes marriage in the sense that consent is the *primary* cause, for consent makes marriage principally (*principaliter*) rather than instrumentally.[38]

Rufinus does not suggest that betrothals can be dissolved at will or even by mutual agreement. Instead, he posits several diriment impediments. These include not only fornication, *raptus*,[39] *maleficium*, entry into the religious life, horrendous crime,

[35] On C. 27 q. 2 c. 9 (450).   [36] On C. 27 q. 2 (443).   [37] On C. 27 q. 2 c. 50 (452).
[38] On C. 27 q. 2 (443). Rufinus develops this analysis in his comments on C. 27 q. 2 c. 1 (449–50) and c. 5 (450).
[39] The precise sense of *raptus* in canon law during this period is debatable, and its relationship to rape (in the modern sense of the term) is complex and problematic. In Roman law, *raptus* included a man's adduction of a woman without her parent's consent in order to make her his wife or partner, whether with or without her consent. Isidore and Gratian include illicit sexual intercourse in the scope of the term, and *raptus* can mean "rape" in medieval Latin. See J. A. Brundage, "Rape and Marriage in Medieval Canon Law," RDC 28 (1978): 62–75; C. Saunders, *Rape and Ravishment in the Literature of Medieval England* (Cambridge, 2001), 33–119; and H.

incurable illness, and indefinite detention, but also consummated betrothal to a second person. Before consummation, therefore, a betrothed woman *ought* not to marry someone else, but if she betroths a second man publicly and the betrothal is consummated, then the second union is *matrimonium ratum*, other things being equal, and it cannot be dissolved.[40] Contrariwise, adultery after consummation dissolves the mutual servitude of the conjugal debt but not the sacramental bond (*ligamen sacramentale*). An adulterer no longer has the right to require sex from his wife, but the spouses remain bound together.[41]

Rufinus's analysis of obligations explains why a betrothal is soluble and can be trumped by a subsequent marriage to another, but he proposes a theological rationale for the difference, which he appropriated from Hugh of Saint-Victor. He posits two significations in marriage. The betrothal (*desponsatio*) signifies the sacrament (i.e., the mystery) of the soul's union with God. Betrothal requires voluntary consent expressed in words, but whether those words are *de futuro* or *de praesenti* is immaterial.[42] Subsequent carnal intercourse (*carnis commixtio*) completes the union formed by consent inasmuch as it signifies the great sacrament of Christ with the church (Eph 5:32), which occurred when Christ and the church became one flesh and one person in the Virgin's womb. Now, whereas the union between the soul and God is violable and impermanent, the union between Christ and the church is permanent. The incarnation is never undone, and nothing can separate the church from Christ. It is only fitting (*non immerito*), therefore, that the two signifiers (*figurae*) should be differentiated in the same way, so that the betrothal is soluble, whereas the consummated union is permanent.[43] Rufinus's rationale seems to be neither a proof of the *de iure* difference nor even an explanation of it but rather a secondary, corroborative argument, designed to show why the difference is fitting.

Rufinus obviates arguments used to support the betrothal theory. Nothing can be deduced from the exceptional features of Mary and Joseph's marriage, he argues, because one may not derive a general rule from a special privilege. Again, the proponents of the betrothal theory argue that a *de praesenti* betrothal suffices to establish affinity, for if man marries a woman and cannot consummate the marriage, the canons forbid his blood relation from marrying her. But the reason for the latter prohibition, Rufinus argues, is not that the prior, unconsummated marriage was perfect or *ratum*, but that the second marriage would be an occasion for public scandal.[44]

Kümper, "Did Medieval Canon Law Invent our Modern Notion of Rape?" in Per Andersen et al., *Law and Marriage in Medieval and Early Modern Times* (Copenhagen, 2012), 111–25.

[40] Rufinus on C. 27 q. 2 (443).   [41] On C. 27 q. 2 c. 1 (450).

[42] On C. 27 q. 2 c. 1 (449–50): "Matrimonium non facit coitus, sed perficit voluntas, i.e., consensus voluntarius per verba expressus, verba dico proposita sive de futuro sive de presenti."

[43] On C. 27 q. 2 (441–42).   [44] On C. 27 q. 2 (445–46).

Rufinus also defends his position against the pseudo-Augustinian canon *Duobus modis* (Section 7.1), which articulates a version of the betrothal distinction. According to *Duobus modis*, a man who has agreed to take (*ducere*) one woman by plighting the troth of consent (*fides consensus*) with her is not permitted to take another woman. If he has taken a second woman, therefore, he must leave her and return to the first. Rufinus's defense is twofold.[45] First, he questions whether the text is really Augustine's. For good measure, he also quotes a decretal by Alexander III to show that sexual intercourse perfects marriage. This decretal is obviously spurious, and it was probably Rufinus himself who concocted it. Perhaps he intended it as a joke.[46] Second, assuming for the sake of argument that *Duobus modis* is authentic, Rufinus proposes that when the man is said to take (*ducere*) the second woman, Augustine is referring to the *in domum traductio*, when the wife is received into the man's dwelling. If the man has received the second woman into his house but has not yet had sex with her, then he must leave the second woman and return to the first. In that case, the prior betrothal trumps the second betrothal. Rufinus considers the man's reception of his wife through *in domum deductio* to be a significant legal step, but one that does not consummate the marriage. When the proponents of the betrothal theory distinguish between promising to marry and actually marrying, he argues, they fail to appreciate the difference between "to contract" (*contrahere*) and "to accept" (*accipere*). The spouses *contract* marriage by exchanging consent, when they agree to sexual intercourse and to an indivisible way of life in the future, whereas the husband *accepts* his wife by receiving her into his house. That is why the angel said to Joseph, "do not be afraid to accept Mary, your wife" (Matt 1:20), for they had already contracted marriage but Joseph had not yet accepted her. The final stage is consummation is sexual intercourse.[47]

Sexual consummation is a necessary but not a sufficient condition for a fully established marriage (*matrimonium ratum*), Rufinus points out. For example, the sacrament (i.e., sacred significance) of marriage is never fully present in a marriage between infidels, which can never be *ratum* even if it is consummated.[48] Where Gratian had divided marriage into initiate and consummate but regarded *consummatum* and *ratum* as coextensive terms, therefore, Rufinus arrives at a threefold division: marriage that is only initiate (*initiatum tantum*); marriage that is initiate and consummate but not *ratum* (as in the case of infidels); and marriage that is initiate, consummate, and *ratum*.[49] The three terms do not necessarily demarcate successive stages in the formation of a marriage in Rufinus, as they will do in later authors.

Johannes Faventinus endorses Rufinus's theory in his own *Summa* on the *Decretum*, which he probably published around 1170, but he grafts onto it the distinction

---

[45] On C. 27 q. 2 (447).
[46] On C. 27 q. 2 (448–49). On this spurious decretal, see the preface to Singer's edition, pp. cvii–cix, and p. cxlvi n. 56.
[47] On C. 27 q. 2 (444).   [48] On C. 27 q. 2 (442–43).   [49] On C. 27 q. 2 (440, 442).

between *de futuro* and *de praesenti* consent. His theory seems to anticipate a position associated today with Pope Alexander III.[50] Commenting on C. 27, q. 2, Johannes first outlines three positions: Rufinus's theory, which he attributes to Gratian;[51] the betrothal theory of the French canonists, for which Johannes is dependent chiefly on Stephen of Tournai;[52] and what he characterizes as a "middle way." The third possibility is new. According to the betrothal theory, Johannes explains, the partners must be either unmarried or married, for the sacrament of marriage is never imperfect or half-formed.[53] On this view, there is no such thing as initiate marriage, and a *de futuro* betrothal is merely a promise to marry. Here, Johannes cites both the canon *Duobus modis* and the *Digest's* definition of *sponsalia* as the "announcement and promise of a future marriage."[54] According to the middle position, betrothal creates an initiate marriage, but betrothal may be either *de futuro* or *de praesenti*. If the betrothal is *de futuro*, the initiate marriage is not *ratum* but soluble. If the betrothal is *de praesenti*, the initiate marriage is *ratum* and there are only two grounds for a valid separation: entry into the religious life and *maleficium*.[55] Johannes himself seems to accept the middle position. Following Rufinus, he attacks the use made of the distinction between *de futuro* and *de praesenti* betrothals, but his chief objection is not to the distinction *per se* but rather to the premise that *de praesenti* consent forms a marriage that is *so* consummate and established that it cannot be dissolved on *any* grounds.[56] A woman who has consented to marry in the future *ought* not to marry another, but if she does so the second marriage must stand and cannot be annulled. That is not the case if she has been betrothed *de praesenti*, for a *de praesenti* betrothal can be dissolved only on grounds such as entry into the religious life and non-natural impotence.

Because Gratian envisaged a *sponsa* who became betrothed to a second man, Johannes considers the logical objection that a woman cannot be betrothed to two men at the same time. It follows that she cannot become betrothed to the second man. Johannes replies that although a woman cannot be married to two men at once, she can be betrothed to two men at once, at least *de facto*. Thus, if a woman who is already betrothed to one man becomes betrothed to another and is "known with marital affection" by him, then her presumptive present consent with the second man makes her his legitimate *sponsa*, and they can consummate their

---

[50] See C. Donahue, "Johannes Faventinus on Marriage," 190–91. The following account is dependent on Donahue's article and on the sections of the *Summa* transcribed there.

[51] Donahue, "Johannes Faventinus on Marriage," 186–87n32, 187n33.

[52] Ibid., 187–88n36.

[53] Ibid.: "nec usquam semiplenam aut imperfectum matrimonium sacramentum esse dicunt." The statement echoes a dictum attributed to Cardinalis in a gloss on C. 27 q. 2, edited in R. Weigand, *Die Glossen zum Dekret Gratians* (Rome, 1991), part 1, no. 777, p. 160. See also Weigand, "Die Glossen des Cardinalis (Magister Hubald?) zum Dekret Gratians, besonders zu C.27 q.2," BMCL 3 (1973): 73–95, at 76n9.

[54] Donahue, "Johannes Faventinus on Marriage," 188n36.   [55] Ibid., 188n37.

[56] Ibid., 188n39.

marriage without sin. Johannes notes a parallel under Roman civil law (*secundum leges*): When two persons purchase the same item, it belongs *de iure* to the first person to whom it is given (*traditum*).[57] Johannes must assume that both of the betrothals in question are *de futuro*, but that presumptive *de praesenti* consent is implicit in the second man's "marital affection," for by receiving her he treats her as his wife.

7.3 THE BETROTHAL THEORY IN FRENCH CANON LAW

French canonists generally upheld the betrothal theory, but they were more reticent than their Bolognese colleagues about taking sides – and with good reason, for Gratian's *Decretum* was the fundamental text of canon law everywhere. Their loyalty to the French schools took them in one direction, and their loyalty to their discipline took them in another.

7.3.1 *The* Summa Parisiensis *and Stephen of Tournai*

The *Summa Parisiensis*, which dated from the 1160s, is among the earliest commentaries on Gratian's *Decretum* written in France. Although it does not include Causa 27, the author touches incidentally on marriage formation and on the two competing theories, and some of his remarks indicate that he adhered to the betrothal theory.[58] Two passages are of special interest in this regard.

In one passage, the author contrasts the respective positions of the French and Roman churches regarding the impediment of a prior betrothal:

> One finds a certain custom that is observed today in one way in France and in other way in the Roman church. For if a man has betrothed a woman in words of the present tense and has received the priestly blessing with her, but if, before he knows her, she is betrothed and known carnally by another man, then the church of France forces her to return to the first man, but not the church of Rome. And as yet it is not known which is better.[59]

The author assumes that Rome adheres to the consummation theory and considers France's policy to be a version of the betrothal theory. But the author himself seems torn between the two policies, for he declines to say which is better. He assumes in the passage quoted above that the prior betrothal has been solemnized, but he does not explain what difference solemnization makes to the permanence of a marriage.

The point of departure for the other passage is an obscure argument from Gratian.[60] Following Titus 1:5–7, the medieval church would not promote to holy

[57] Ibid., 189n40.
[58] T. P. McLaughlin, "The Formation of the Marriage Bond According to the *Summa Parisiensis*," *Mediaeval Studies* 15 (1953): 208–12.
[59] *Summa Parisiensis* on D. 11 c. 11, ed. T. P. McLaughlin, p. 11.
[60] Gratian, D. 34, c. 20 (130), and C. 27 q. 2 dictum post c. 29, 1 (1072).

orders a man who had been married more than once. Canon law extended that impediment to the husband of a widow, since *she* was married at least twice. But according to a decretal ascribed to Pope Pelagius, there was no obstacle if the woman had been veiled with the first man but was not yet his *nupta*, so that she was still a virgin when he died. The decision was open to more than one interpretation, but it seemed to presuppose that she was not the first man's wife because their marriage had never been consummated. The *Summa Parisiensis* summarizes this argument but goes on to explain how the "church of the French" would reply to it.

According to the French policy, there is already a fixed or established marriage (*matrimonium ratum*) if a betrothal has been expressed in words of the present tense, as when each says to the other, "I accept you as my own." If a woman who is betrothed in that way becomes betrothed to a second man, she must still return to the first man, even if the first union is unconsummated and the second is consummated. Thus, a man who has married a widow ought not to be promoted to holy orders even if the prior marriage was never consummated. The author proposes two solutions. First, as Peter Lombard suggests, the prior betrothal in Pelagius's decretal may have been *de futuro*, so that she was not the man's wife. Second, even if she was truly the first man's wife, perhaps marriage alone did not suffice to create the impediment. In other words, the impediment may have required not only that she had been married before, but also that her first husband had known her carnally.[61]

Some incidental remarks indicate that the author himself was an adherent of the French theory. Discussing whether a marriage is valid if the motive for marrying is not procreation but incontinence, he concludes that there is a marriage "as soon as consent has been expressed in the present tense, for whatever reason it is contracted," as long there is no impediment preventing the partners from marrying each other.[62] Again, defending the French position that clandestine marriages are illicit but valid and insoluble, the author explains that "as soon as a man has promised to a woman in words of the present tense that he is going to take her [*ducturus*] as his wife, there is a perfect and established marriage."[63] The latter text reveals the ambiguity of the *de praesenti* betrothal. The words have to be *de praesenti*, according to the *Summa Parisiensis*, but the man *promises* that he *will* receive her as his wife. The same author inquires about the man who promises with an oath (*iusiurandum*) that he is going to take (*ducturus*) a woman as his wife. Is he forced to marry her, or may he marry someone else? Augustine says that someone

---

[61] *Summa Parisiensis* on D. 34 c. 19 (33–34). Cf. Peter Lombard, *Sent.* IV, 27.10 (430–31).

[62] *Summa Parisiensis* on C. 32 q. 2 dictum ante c. 1 (241): "Statim etenim ex quo consensus expressus per verba praesentis temporis, est conjugium, quacumque de causa contrahitur, dum tamen sint personae legitimae ad contradendum."

[63] *Summa Parisiensis* on C. 30 q. 5 dictum ante c. 1 (237): "Statim enim ex eo quod aliquis alicui promisit per verba praesentis temporis se ducturum eam in conjugem, matrimonium est perfectum et ratum."

who has given his troth to a woman cannot be forced to keep her,[64] whereas Justinian's *Novels* seem to say that a sworn agreement to marry is binding.[65] Perhaps Augustine contradicts and overrules Justinian, the author responds, but the two authorities can be reconciled if one assumes that the Roman constitution is referring to a man who swears that is going to marry the woman in words of the present tense, but that Augustine is referring to a man who promises to marry in words of the future tense.[66]

Stephen of Tournai, who returned to France after studying in Bologna during the 1160s, summarizes both positions carefully in his *Summa* on the *Decretum*, written around 1165/66.[67] Those who uphold the consummation theory distinguish among initiate marriage (*matrimonium initiatum tantum*), consummated marriage (*matrimonium initiatum et consummatum*), and fully established marriage (*matrimonium initiatum, consummatum, et ratum*). Others "do not approve of the distinction between initiate and consummate marriage," maintaining instead that "as soon as [the partners] begin to be spouses [*coniuges*], they are true and perfect spouses. Nor, they say, is marriage ever a partly formed or imperfect sacrament." Stephen leaves the reader to decide which theory is correct.[68]

7.3.2 Summa Coloniensis

The author of the *Summa 'Elegantius in iure divino,'* also known as the *Summa Coloniensis*, discusses the two canonical theories at length when he considers whether a woman betrothed to one man can marry another.[69] The treatise was composed in the diocese of Cologne, but the author reveals that he had studied in France. Like the *Summa Parisiensis*, he attributes the consummation theory to the Roman or Transalpine church, and the betrothal theory to the Gallican church. He declines to say which policy is preferable. Since the Roman church conceived him in faith, and the French church educated him in law, he will remain silent for fear of contradicting either his mother or his teacher.[70] Nevertheless, the author is evidently an adherent of the betrothal theory, and he cannot restrain himself from scoffing at the alternative.

---

[64] "Dicit enim, licet aliquis fidem det alicui, non tamen ideo cogendus est eam retinere." The author may be thinking of *Duobus modis*.

[65] Cf. Julian's *Epitome*, Const. 67.4, kp. 244 (probably derived from Justinian's *Novel* 74.5): "Si quis diuinis tactis scripturis iurauerit mulieri, legitimam se eam uxorem habiturum, uel si in oratorio tale sacramentum dederit, sit illa legitima uxor, quamuis nulla dos, nulla scriptura alia interposita sit." This text was added to the second recension of the *Decretum*, C. 30 q. 5 c. 9 (1107).

[66] *Summa Parisiensis* on C. 30 q. 5 c. 1 (237–38).

[67] Stephen of Tournai, *Summa*, ed. Schulte, 235–36.

[68] Ibid., 236: "Lectori autem relinquimus, utram magis approbare voluerit sententiam."

[69] *Summa 'Elegantius in iure diuino' seu Coloniensis*, 13.27–39, ed. Fransen, vol. 4, pp. 15–25.

[70] Ibid., 13.39 (24–25).

The author's initial statement of the problem and of the opposing authorities is dependent on both Gratian and Peter Lombard. On one side, there is the example of Mary's marriage to Joseph, and the authorities showing that consent alone makes marriage.[71] But that raises a subsidiary question: To what do the partners consent? The author's solution saves Mary's vow of virginity. Spouses need not consent to sexual intercourse or even to cohabitation when they marry, but only to a conjugal partnership (*societas coniugalis*), which entails an inseparable way of life (*vitae inseparabilis consuetudo*).[72] But there are other authorities, including the usual texts ascribed to Leo and Augustine, indicating that a betrothed woman "is not a wife before sexual intercourse, and that a marriage initiated only by the conjugal agreement is not perfect."[73]

Having outlined the question, the *Summa Coloniensis* presents the Gallican and the Transalpine theories as opposing solutions to it.[74] His exposition of these policies is extensive and includes many arguments and counterarguments, some of which are unusual. His account is hard to follow, partly because he weaves back and forth between the two sides. A few passages are barely intelligible. In what follows, I shall reconstruct his explanation by presenting each side in turn: first the Transalpine consummation theory, and then the Gallican betrothal theory.

The *Transalpini* maintain that a marriage is initiated in a conjugal agreement (*pactio coniugalis*) and consummated in sexual intercourse. Likewise, they distinguish between two kinds of troth (*fides*). Whereas a betrothal obliges the partners to remain chaste for each other, the consummation of their marriage obliges them to render the conjugal debt to each other. Before she is handed over to her husband (*ante traductionem*), therefore, a betrothed woman is free to choose the religious life but not to take a different husband.[75] It is true that the couple are called married partners (*coniuges*) as soon as they are betrothed, as Augustine and Isidore say, but only by the figure of speech known as *preanticipatio* (i.e., prolepsis), just as we address or refer to a bishop-elect as a bishop.[76] They are already called married because of the hope of things to come, and not because of present reality.[77] Bare consent (*solus consensus*) makes marriage, therefore, but only in the sense that such consent initiates marriage, for it does not perfect marriage.[78]

The author construes this theory in terms of the *traditio* model. The Transalpines regard marriage, he explains, as if it were a contract of sale or other conveyance, which begins with an agreement but is perfected in the *traditio*, when ownership (*dominium*) is transferred.[79] They cite a text from Ambrose as proof: "If a man uses [i.e., has sexual intercourse with] a woman who has been betrothed and handed over [*tradita*] to him, that is called marriage."[80] The author seems to conflate on behalf of

---

[71] 13.27, 28a (15, 16–17).
[72] 13.28 (15–16). Cf. Gratian, C. 27 q. 2 c. 1 §1, and Peter Lombard, *Sent.* IV, 28.3.2 (435).
[73] *Summa Coloniensis*, 3.29 (17).   [74] Ibid., 13.30 (17).   [75] 13.32 (18).
[76] 13.31 (17–18).   [77] 13.39/2–4 (24).   [78] 13.39/10–14 (24).
[79] 13.30 (17).   [80] 13.31/15–16 (18).

the Transalpines the surrendering of a spouse (the *traductio* or *traditio*) and the sexual consummation of the marriage. In a later passage, the author notes that "some Bolognese" posit seven impediments that dissolve a *de praesenti* betrothal, including subsequent consummated betrothal to another man. The list is from Rufinus. The author suggests that this list results more from human ingenuity than from tradition and authority.[81]

Whereas Gallican scholars claim that consent alone creates a perfect marriage, the author explains, the Transalpines object that "perfect" can be understood in three ways: in respect of reality (*veritas*), of signification, or of substance. If a betrothal were a perfect marriage in respect of reality, there would be a true marriage even before consummation. But in that case, the partners would already owe each other the conjugal debt, which is clearly not the case.[82] Contrariwise, Roman churchmen point out that unconsummated marriage does not have the same canonical consequences as consummated marriage. If a woman is betrothed to a man in words of the present tense and he dies, canonical jurisdiction does not regard her as a widow. For example, she is not prevented from receiving the veil as a virgin if she marries another man, nor is he prevented from receiving holy orders.[83] Again, if there has been a *de praesenti* betrothal and she has been led into his home, but he is then unable to consummate the marriage because of some *maleficium*, the marriage may be dissolved.[84]

According to the Gallican theory, the author explains, betrothal alone suffices to create an established marriage. On this view, there is no real difference between a betrothed woman (*sponsa*) and a married woman (*nupta*), and a *sponsa* may not elect to become a religious without her husband's consent. If she does so, her husband may call her back to their marriage.[85] But the Gallicans distinguish between two kinds of betrothal. An agreement about the future creates a secular betrothal (*desponsatio legalis*), which is also known as *sponsalia*. This is defined as an "announcement and mutual agreement about a future marriage" (*Dig.* 23.1.1). But an agreement about the present creates a canonical betrothal (*desponsatio canonica*).[86] The author presumably considers a secular betrothal (*desponsatio legalis*) to be soluble, at least when one of the partners elects to become a religious.

The Gallicans say that when Augustine and Leo say that a woman does not "belong to matrimony" before sexual intercourse, they mean that she does not belong to such marriage as contains the full sacrament of Christ and the church. The author draws on Rufinus as well as on Peter Lombard to explicate this point. The betrothal is a sacrament of the soul's union with God in charity, whereas consummated marriage is a sacrament of Christ's union with the church in conformity of nature. Following Rufinus, but still with reference to the Gallican theory, the author explains that just as the soul's union with God is sometimes broken by

---

[81] 13.36/38–46 (21).   [82] 13.36/5–12 (20).   [83] 13.37/1–11 (22).
[84] 13.37/11–16 (22–23).   [85] 13.36/64–67.   [86] 13.33 (19).

apostasy, so the betrothal, which signifies that union, can be dissolved on certain supervenient grounds (*quibusdam accidentibus causis*). Consummated marriage, on the contrary, is as indissoluble as what it signifies.[87] The author's account is confusing at this point, however, for the doctrine that he describes is more congruent with the consummation theory than with the betrothal theory.

Getting back on track, the author argues that even though betrothal by itself, before consummation, is deficient in signification, according to the Gallicans, it is nevertheless true and holy matrimony, for, as Augustine says, "the sanctity of the sacrament in marriage is worth more than the fecundity of the flesh."[88] According to the Gallican theory, therefore, marriage is indeed initiated in consent and consummated in sexual intercourse, but it is consummated only in respect of its signification, and not in respect of its reality (*veritas*), or substance.[89] A marriage is fully formed (*plenum*) and perfect at once, as soon as the conjugal agreement (*pactum*) has taken place, for nothing then is missing from its substance.[90]

The author presents a battery of arguments to corroborate the Gallican position. A betrothed person who is unfaithful commits adultery, not simple fornication. Again, a woman betrothed to one man cannot marry his blood relation, and that impediment must be the result of affinity, even in the absence of coitus. Again, the first act of coitus in a marriage is often "impetuous" and shameful, and it is absurd to claim that holy matrimony is rendered legitimate by an illicit, sinful act. As Augustine says, a marriage is more holy without sexual intercourse.[91] The author outlines the Gallican responses to the Transalpine jurisprudential arguments. Unlike the Transalpines, the Gallicans hold that betrothal obliges the partners to render the conjugal debt, albeit not at once but in due course.[92]

The author uses the *traditio* model to elucidate the Gallican policy. Contractual ownership (*dominium*) is always transferred at the moment of handing over (*traditio*). At what point in the process of marrying does that occur? The Gallicans reason that *traditio* occurs even in the nuptials, before the partners begin to live together, for each partner says: "I hand myself over to you [*trado me tibi*]." In a sense, therefore, the partners are already two in one flesh. A further *traditio* ensues when the woman is led into her husband's home. As soon as the *sponsa* has been given (*tradita*) to a man, veiled with him, and led (*traducta*) into his home, therefore, she is her husband's flesh, even if the "nuptial mystery" of sexual intercourse never ensues. Gratian himself reached this position eventually.[93] Hence, if a woman who

---

[87] 13.34 (19).
[88] 13.34/15–15: "... ut ait Augustinus: 'In nuptiis plus ualet sanctitas sacramenti quam fecunditas carnis." Originally from Augustine, *De bono coniug.* 18(21), CSEL 41:215/, but probably taken from Peter Lombard, *Sent.* I, 26.6.5 (421): "in nuptiis plus valet sanctitas sacramenti, quam fecunditas ventris." Augustine is contrasting Christian with non-Christian marriage: "in nostrarum quippe nuptiis plus ualet sanctitas sacramenti quam fecunditas uteri."
[89] *Summa Coloniensis*, 13.35 (19).   [90] Ibid., 13.36/3–5 (20).
[91] 13.36 (20).   [92] 13.36/23–29 (20–21).
[93] Cf. C. 27 q. 2 dictum post c. 50 (1077–78): the conclusion of q. 2 in the original recension.

is betrothed in that way (*sic deponsata*) to one man enters into a conjugal agreement with another man, she must be compelled to return to the first man even if the second union, unlike the first, is consummated. Her betrothal to the first man trumps her consummated marriage to the second, showing that it is more powerful.[94] Likewise, if a *sponsa* is permitted to marry another man because her *sponsus* is impotent, and if in due course the first man is found to be potent, then the second marriage is dissolved and the first is reinstated, showing again that the prior, unconsummated betrothal is stronger and trumps the subsequent, consummated marriage.[95]

7.3.3 *Marrying: Event or graduated process?*

What distinguished the betrothal theory was not the principle that consent made marriage, which the Bolognese canonists also upheld, but the claim that bare consent *completed* a marriage, so that the marriage existed and was fully established or fixed (*ratum*), other things being equal, *as soon as* the requisite consents had been exchanged. From the perspective of the betrothal theory, therefore, the distinction between initiate and consummate marriage was misconceived. Whereas the Bolognese considered marrying to be a process of formation leading from betrothal to consummation, the French theorists considered it to be a simple, all-or-nothing event. The *Summa Parisiensis* explains: "We say that marriage is at once initiated, consummated, and established [*ratum*] as soon as consent is expressed in words of the present tense."[96] Their position could never be more than a theory, however, because it was too much at odds with prevailing customs and presuppositions.

An anonymous gloss on C. 27 q. 2. contrasts the Bolognese way of construing marriage with that of a certain "C." Some distinguish among initiate, consummate, and established marriage (*matrimonium ratum*) – here the glossator summarizes Rufinus – but "C. does not accept this distinction, saying that a marriage is either perfect between those who are contracting it, or nothing, for an imperfect or partly formed [*semiplenum*] sacrament is nothing."[97] C. is the canonist referred to in the Middle Ages as Cardinalis, who flourished in the 1150s. He was the author of numerous opinions and glosses on the *Decretum* ascribed to "C." or to "Car." He is now known to have been Raymond des Arènes, a native of Nîmes who was trained in Roman as well as in Canon law and was active in Avignon, Arles, Beauvais, and Montpellier. Pope Hadrian IV made him a cardinal in 1158, and he died around

---

[94] 13.36/29–37 (21).   [95] 13.36/47–51 (21).
[96] *Summa Parisiensis* on C. 32 q. 5 c. 16, ed. McLaughlin, p. 246: "Sed nos dicimus statim matrimonium esse initiatum consummatum et ratum ex quo fit consensus expressus per verba praesentis temporis si contrahentes in contrahendo legitimae fuerint personae."
[97] R. Weigand, "Die Glossen des Cardinalis," p. 80, nos. 50–57.

1176/77.[98] Several glosses ascribed to him suggest that he adhered to the betrothal theory, with its distinction between *de futuro* and *de praesenti* betrothals.

The distinction between a prospective betrothal and a marriage was not so clear in actuality. On the one hand, terms such as *desponsatio*, *sponsio*, and even *sponsalia* (or "spousals" in English) continued to be used for the exchange of consent in the present tense, even though their etymology implied a promise. Wedding vows still seemed like promises, and even spouses bound by *de praesenti* consent did not always begin to live together or consummate their union at once. The dissolution of an unconsummated marriage to enter the religious life was a real option, and not a hypothetical possibility dreamed up in the schools.[99] At the same time, as we have seen, authors sometimes construed an exchange of wedding vows in the present tense as the bodily coming together of the *sponsus* and *sponsa* or as the mutual self-*traditio* of the spouses to each other. From this point of view, the wedding (*nuptiae*) was in some sense a surrogate for the woman's being "led" into her husband's home, when cohabitation began.

A statement of the betrothal theory in an abbreviation of the *Decretum* composed in southern France around 1150 illustrates the fluidity of the concepts:

> Spousals [*sponsalia*] of one kind are about the present, and of another kind about the future. There are spousals about the present when a man gives himself [*tradit se*] to a woman as her husband and enrings her with a ring [*anulo subarrat eam*] and accepts her as his wife, and, likewise, she him as her husband. A betrothal of this kind cannot be dissolved because marriage has already been contracted, and if it is dissolved it ought to be restored. Spousals of the other kind are about the future: for example, when a man simply promises, using words alone, that he will accept her as his wife, and she him, but he does not enring her, nor give himself [*tradit se*] to her as her husband, nor she herself to him as his wife, but instead they simply state this in words. Spousals of this kind ought not to be dissolved, but if they are dissolved it is of no consequence because a marriage has not yet been constituted, although [the partners] ought to be required to do penance for three years....[100]

Although the author distinguishes clearly between the two kinds of agreement and their respective consequences, he calls both of them *sponsalia*. Rather than relying on grammatical tense alone, as will later become the norm, he provides a thick description, noting that the *de futuro* betrothal is made in words alone, whereas the man puts a ring upon the woman's finger in *de praesenti* betrothal. (The ritual of *subarrhatio* was originally a betrothal pledge, but it had become linked to marriage through its being enacted in the prenuptial rite at the entrance to a church.) Whereas the partners

[98] See R. Weigand, "The Transmontane Decretists," in Hartmann and Pennington, *History of Medieval Canon Law*, 174–210, at 178–80.

[99] D. D'Avray, *Medieval Marriage* (Oxford, 2005), 181–88.

[100] On C. 27 q. 2 fin., in R. Weigand, "Die Dekretabbreviatio 'Quonium egestas' under ihre Glossen," in W. Aymans, A. Egler, and J. Listl (eds.), *Fides et ius* (Regensburg, 1991), 249–65, at 262, no. 18.

merely promise something in the *de futuro* betrothal, the abbreviation says that they give or hand themselves over to each other in the *de praesenti* betrothal, which amounts to a *traditio*. And whereas traditionally a father gave away his daughter to her husband, here both spouses give themselves to each other.

Such ambiguity generated uncertainties both in terminology and in practice. When did a *sponsa* become a man's *uxor* (wife), his spouse (*coniux*), or a *nupta* ("married woman")? Was it when they exchanged wedding vows, or when they began to live together, or even after consummation? According to an opinion attributed to Cardinalis, a woman bound by a *de futuro* agreement should be called a *sponsa simplex*, whereas a woman bound by a *de praesenti* agreement should be called a *sponsa non simplex*, because she has already "crossed over to marital affection." Yet she is not called a *coniux* until her husband had known her sexually.[101]

Even where the betrothal theory was the norm and the distinction of tense was observed, therefore, the exchange of consent in the present tense remained an ambiguous event, which could be regarded either as betrothal or as marriage. It was partly because of that ambiguity, I suggest, that the two theories merged in a hybrid policy, which had become established as the common, universal doctrine by the end of the twelfth century.

7.4 THE CIVILIANS' *DEDUCTIO* THEORY

Until the hybrid policy emerged around 1180 in canonical jurisprudence and in the decretals of Alexander III, the experts in Roman civil law rejected both of the prevailing theories and upheld a theory of their own. They argued that the formation of marriage required both the exchange of consent and the subsequent *deductio* (also known as *traductio*), that is, the husband's reception of his bride into her new home.[102] A marriage did not become fully binding, in their view, until that point. Classical Roman law was not enforced in any court, although it informed the learned law practiced in both ecclesiastical and secular courts. The independent line adopted by the civilians was an implicit criticism of their colleagues in canon law. Charles Donahue has shown that the civilians were aware of the theories of the canonists from at least the mid-twelfth century, and that they adapted to their own ends both the Bolognese distinction between initiate and consummate marriage and the French distinction between *de futuro* and *de praesenti* betrothals.[103]

---

[101] Weigand, "Die glossen des Cardinalis," 91.
[102] C. Donahue, Jr., "The Case of the Man Who Fell into the Tiber," *American Journal of Legal History* 22 (1978): 1–53. The study covers the period c.1130–c.1260. For texts predating Alexander III's policy, see p. 13n57 (Bulgarus), 15n62 (Johannes Basianus), 19n81 (Placentinus); and pp. 21n94 and 22n96 (*Summa Tubingensis*).
[103] Ibid., pp. 5, 15, 22–23.

The civilians' doctrine was tenuously based on the *Corpus Iuris Civilis*, and especially on a pair of opinions by Pomponius and Ulpian preserved in the *Digest*.[104] According to Pomponius, a woman can be married to a man in his absence, but only if she is led into his house ("*si in domum eius deduceretur*"), "as if into the domicile of the marriage" (*quasi in domicilium matrimonii*). The opinion from Ulpian sketches the bare outlines of a story, leaving much to the reader's imagination. A man marries a woman *in absentia*,[105] but he dies on his way back home from dinner beside the Tiber. She is obliged to observe the *tempus lugendi* (the period of mourning) as his widow. According to the civilians' reading of this story, the woman was already married to him because she had been led into his home. Even though he was absent and fell into the Tiber and was drowned on his way home to join her, the *deductio* had taken place. The canonists were aware of the *deductio* theory. Gratian had remarked that according to imperial Roman law (the "laws of the princes"), a *sponsa* whose *sponsus* died had to mourn him as her husband.[106] Both Cardinalis and Rufinus deduce from the case of the man who drowned in the Tiber that the *deductio* of the woman was required to make her a wife according to the *leges* (i.e., to Roman law).[107] The phrase "laws of the princes" should refer to the *Codex*, but Rufinus, with the texts cited earlier in mind, says that Gratian must be referring to the *Digest*, wherein the imperial laws were confirmed.

Charles Donahue suggests that the civilians upheld the *deductio* doctrine because it would have maximized the opportunity for parents or families to control their children's choice of marriage partner.[108] The civilians naturally emphasized the importance of family and especially paternal consent for children still under *patria potestas*.[109] Canonical policy, on the contrary, emphasized spousal consent and gave children of marriageable age the right to marry regardless of their families' wishes.[110]

Once the common doctrine was established, the civilians had to accept that *de praesenti* consent sufficed to complete a marriage. Nevertheless, they tried to adapt their own position to the policy or to reconcile the two approaches. For example, they argued that the *deductio* might serve as presumptive proof of a marriage, or that it might be necessary for the secular consequences of a marriage as regards gifts and

---

[104] *Dig.* 23.2.5–6.

[105] The text says that *she* was absent, but the civilians assumed that it was the man who was absent, as do most modern scholars of Roman law. See Donahue, "Man Who Fell into the Tiber," 14.

[106] C. 27 q. 2 dictum post c. 10 (1065): "Item in legibus principum sponsa iubetur lugere mortem sponsi tamquam uiri sui."

[107] Cardinalis in Weigand, "Die Glossen des Cardinalis," no. 13, p. 76: "non enim carnalis copula set ductio in domum uxorem facit secundum legem." Rufinus, *Summa decretorum*, ed. Singer, p. 451: "quia secundum leges ex sola ductione uxor facta videtur...."

[108] Donahue, "Man Who Fell into the Tiber," 5, 34–41, 45–48.

[109] Cf. *Dig.* 23.1.10–13, *Inst.* 1.10 pr.

[110] See C. Donahue, Jr., "The Policy of Alexander the Third's Consent Theory of Marriage," in S. Kuttner (ed.), *Proceedings of the Fourth International Congress of Medieval Canon Law*, Monumenta Iuris Canonici C:5 (Città del Vaticano, 1976): 251–81. The existence of the policy is clear, its association with Alexander III in particular much less so.

property, or that a *de futuro* betrothal plus *deductio* had the same effect as a *de praesenti* agreement.[111]

7.5 VACARIUS'S *TRADITIO* THEORY

Vacarius's treatise on marriage, which he composed in England in the 1160s, survives in only a single manuscript.[112] Maitland noted that there are points of similarity between Vacarius's *De matrimonio* and the *Summa Coloniensis*.[113] Less attention has been given to the similarities between Vacarius's theory of marrying and Huguccio's. The treatise appears to have had little if any influence, however, and in places it is very hard to follow. These might be good reasons for disregarding it or setting it aside as a historical curiosity, and readers impatient to see how the hybrid doctrine emerged may safely skip this section without losing track of the argument. Nevertheless, Vacarius's theory is interesting in its own right, and it may shed some light on how people around the middle of the twelfth century regarded marrying and the exchange of marriage vows in the present tense. Scholars of medieval marriage law have generally assumed that Vacarius upheld the civilians' *deductio* theory, or something very like it. In fact his practical position is closer to that of the French theologians, although his rationale is quite different from theirs. Vacarius was arguably more successful than any other medieval scholar in accounting for the "real" aspect of marrying: the act of mutual self-giving that required face-to-face presence and could not be contracted entirely in writing or through intermediaries. But this real dimension, in his view, was not supra-legal or intrinsically sacramental. On the contrary, he bases his theory entirely on Roman contract law.

Vacarius had studied Roman law in his native Lombardy and perhaps also at Bologna before he joined the household of Theobald, archbishop of Canterbury, in the 1140s. He worked in the households of the archbishops of York from 1159 until his death around 1200.[114] His analysis of marriage in the *De matrimonio* is that of an English cleric whose entire intellectual formation had been in civilian law, and who

---

[111] "Man Who Fell into the Tiber," pp. 5, 26–34.

[112] F. W. Maitland, "Magistri Vacarii *Summa de matrimonio*. Introduction," *Law Quarterly Review* 13 (1887): 133–43, and "Vacarius on Marriage (Text)," ibid., 270–87 (text). On Vacarius's character as a scholar, see J. de Ghellinck, "Magister Vacarius: Un juriste théologien peu aimable pour les canonistes," *Revue d'histoire ecclésiastique* 44 (1949): 173–78. On the *De matrimonio*, see Maitland's accurate but limited introduction, and M. Guareschi, "Fra canones e leges: Magister Vacarius e il matrimonio," *Mélanges de l'École française de Rome: Moyen-Age – Temps modernes* 111.1 (1999): 105–39. On Vacarius's unusual attempt to apply the discipline of civil law to theological questions, see J. Taliodoros, "Synthesizing the Legal and Theological Thought of Master Vacarius," *Zeitschrift der Savigny-Stiftung für Rechtsgeschichte. Kanonistische Abteilung* 95 (2009): 48–77.

[113] Maitland, "Magistri Vacarii *Summa de matrimonio*," 137–38.

[114] On Vacarius's career, see J. Taliadoros, *Law and Theology in Twelfth-Century England: The Works of Master Vacarius (c. 1115/20–c. 1200)* (Turnhout, 2006), 2–9. On the likely date of the *De matrimonio*, see ibid., 56–58.

was skeptical about canon law. He uses his expertise in Roman law and jurisprudence to interpret the policy of the French and Anglo-Norman churches, with their distinction between *de futuro* and *de praesenti* consent. Vacarius regards that policy in the light both of the classical distinction between *sponsalia* and *nuptiae* (Dig. 23.1–2) and of the canon *Duobus modis*, which he ascribes for reasons unknown to Pope Hormisdas.[115] Vacarius advocated the same policy as the French theologians did, but his rationale for it was based entirely on the *Corpus Iuris Civilis* and Roman jurisprudence, which he equated with the natural law. When referring to betrothals, Vacarius avoids the ambiguous Christian term *desponsatio*, which by this time could denote either *de futuro* or *de praesenti* spousals, and uses only the less ambiguous classical term, *sponsalia*.

Vacarius construes *de praesenti* consent as analogous to a *traditio* (a "handing over," or delivery) in a real contract. The notion that marrying was a kind of *traditio* was not peculiar to Vacarius. Rufinus construed marriage as *traditio* when he distinguished between the *contracting* of marriage (i.e., the agreement, or exchange of consent) and the husband's *reception* of the woman as his wife. A husband received a woman as his wife, according to Rufinus, by leading her into his house or by having her in his house. Rufinus accused others conflating these two steps by construing the *de futuro* betrothal as a mere promise, rather than as a contract, and by assuming that a man's contracting a marriage with a woman was the same as the man's receiving the woman as his wife.[116] The *Summa Coloniensis* used the *traditio* model to elucidate both the consummation theory and the betrothal theory. The author seems to have equated the *traditio* with coitus in the consummation theory, and with the exchange of present-tense wedding vows in the betrothal theory.[117] Among the civilians, the *Summa Tubingiensis* (1170s) construed the *deductio* of one spouse into the other's home as analogous to *traditio* in a real contract. The term "marriage," the author argues, denotes a matter not only of *ius* but also of fact, for "what leading [*ductio*] is in contracts of persons, a *traditio* is in contracts of things [*res*]. That is, just as a *traditio* is required after a real contract, so too the leading [*ductio*] perfects a betrothal or espousal contract."[118] What is peculiar to Vacarius, then, is not the notion that marrying is a kind of *traditio* but the conceptual framework of his theory and his notion that *traditio* is a purely consensual act. According to Vacarius, a real contract is a linked pair of contracts, the second of which fulfills the first.

Both betrothal and marriage, as Vacarius saw them, were contracts, but of fundamentally different kinds. Betrothal was a negotiated interfamilial agreement,

---

[115] Vacarius, *De matrimonio*, ed. Maitland, §25 (281), §26 (282), §33 (284), etc.

[116] Rufinus on C. 27 q. 2, ed. Singer, p. 444: "Qui hoc dicunt ita procedunt, quasi idem sit cum aliqua matrimonium contrahere et eam accipere, cum accipere sit traducere vel domi habere."

[117] *Summa Coloniensis* 13.30, ed. Fransen, vol. 4, p. 17. Ibid., 13.36/29–37 (21).

[118] Translated from Donahue, "Man Who Fell into the Tiber," 22n96: "sicut se habet traditio in contractibus rerum, sic se ductio in contractibus personarum. hoc est, sicut traditio exigitur post contractum realem, sic ductio perficit et contractum sponsalitium sive sponsalem."

fraught with conditions and financial terms, and the partners did not have to meet face-to-face. Marrying, on the contrary, was an act of mutual self-giving and reception, and the partners had to be present to each other. The *traditio* was a "real" act, therefore, presupposing bodily presence. Vacarius's notion of real action was flexible. The *traditio* did not necessarily require the *deductio in domum* or a coming-together in a shared home, even if it had taken that form in classical law and custom. Vacarius reasoned that the nuptial act of mutual self-giving – the plighting of troth, or exchange of marriage vows – could function as a *traditio*.[119]

Because Vacarius argued that marriage was completed by the act of *traditio*, many scholars have assumed that he rejected Peter Lombard's betrothal theory as well as Gratian's consummation theory, or that he proposed a version of the civilians' theory, whereby a woman became a wife when she was led into her husband's home.[120] In fact, Vacarius says nothing about the arguments of French theologians and seems to have been unfamiliar with them. In his view, the debate is between canon law and civil law. Vacarius developed his own theory using the Bolognese theory as a foil.

Vacarius apparently had the texts of Gratian and Rufinus at hand and little or nothing else when he wrote the treatise, for he appropriated most of his ecclesiastical proof texts from their writings.[121] He is as hostile to Rufinus as Rufinus was to the proponents of the betrothal theory, and he ridicules the consummation theory. Because a text ascribed to Augustine seemed to say that a woman was not a wife until she has had sex with her husband, Vacarius imagines a comical scenario in which Augustine interrupts a husband who is about to have sex with his bride for the first time, advising him that he should not touch her because they are still unmarried. The husband indignantly defends himself, protesting that he has the right to have sex with her as soon as she has been given to him (*tradita*) in marriage.[122]

Vacarius rejected not only the consummation theory but also the entire methodology of canon law. He was dismayed by the inconsistency and variety of church law,

---

[119] Cf. *Summa Coloniensis*, 13.36/29–37 (21). On real contracts and *traditio* in Roman law, see J. A. C. Thomas, *Textbook of Roman Law* (New York, 1976), 179–83; and B. Nicholas, *An Introduction to Roman Law* (Oxford, 1962), 117–120. In a real contract, an obligation presupposes a previously agreed purpose (*causa*) or agreement but results from the actual giving of something, e.g., as a loan, a donation, a pledge, or a bailment. The obligation to which the preliminary agreement refers is established by actual possession, whereas in a sale the obligation terminates in giving and possessing.

[120] E.g., P. Stein, "Vacarius and the Civil Law," in C. N. L. Brooke, D. Luscombe, G. Martin, and D. Owen (eds.), *Church and Government in the Middle Ages*, 119–37, at 133–35. Donahue, "Man Who Fell into the Tiber," 23–25. Brundage, *Law, Sex, and Christian Society*, 266–67. P. Landau, "The Origins of Legal Science in England in the Twelfth Century," in M. Brett and K. G. Cushing (eds.), *Readers, Texts and Compilers in the Middle Ages* (Farnham, 2009), 165–82, at 172.

[121] Maitland, "Magistri Vacarii *Summa de matrimonio*," 138–40.

[122] Vacarius, *De matrimonio*, ed. Maitland, §21 (280).

both at the level of regional jurisdiction and at the level of theory. Although he cites ecclesiastical authorities when they suit his purpose, he considers Gratian's method of reconciling canons to be pointless. In Vacarius's view, the canons *really are* discordant. There is no point in trying to reconcile them.[123]

Vacarius's way of citing Christian authorities and canons is cavalier and arbitrary. For example, having reviewed texts from John Chrysostom, Jerome, Gregory the Great, and Origen that seem to support the consummation theory, Vacarius makes Origen conform to his own position and then claims that this text trumps the others because it is the oldest.[124] Whereas the use of *auctoritates* in the schools presupposed that the respect due to an author gave authority to what he said, Vacarius independently evaluates the truth of a text or statement and approves or disapproves of its author on that basis. For example, he twice accuses Jerome of erring, and he declines to include him among the "more expert authors of the church," but only because Jerome seems to have supported the consummation theory.[125] Contrariwise, he counts Ambrose as one of the "more expert authors" because Ambrose's position on the formation of marriage is consistent with his own.[126]

Vacarius goes to great lengths to defend the spurious, pseudo-Isidorean decretal *Aliter*, ascribed to Pope Evaristus (Chapter 1.6.2). The canon decrees that spouses should be counted as adulterers or fornicators unless every formality is observed: Her suitor must ask for her hand from those with power over her, and she must be promised by her kinsfolk, given a dowry in accordance with the law, blessed by a priest, and so forth. But the canon seems to say in an apparently contradictory remark attached at the end that the rule does not apply if the spouses give their consent and express their vows.[127] According to Vacarius, the canonists have abused this text by making Evaristus contradict himself. He praises Pope Evaristus as a "provident father" (*providus pater*) and an "expert in both laws" (*vir utriusque iuris peritus*), although Vacarius had no information about Evaristus besides the decretal. According to his interpretation, the final remark does not contradict but confirms what precedes it. It presupposes that the girl has been properly petitioned from her parents, given a dowry, and so forth, and its chief purpose is to exclude the opinion of those who think that consummation is necessary in addition. In any case, the ruling was not intended to apply to adult women or to widows, Vacarius argues, but only to young girls, who cannot be expected to make sound choices on their own. To require the consent of family and kinsfolk in such cases belongs as much to "natural reason" as to civil law. It is contrary to "piety and justice, both natural and civil," to assume that the principle of bare consent (*solus consensus*) in marriage excludes the consent of the parents and kinsfolk.[128]

---

[123] Ibid., §16 (277).   [124] §15 (276).   [125] §10 (274). §23 (280–81).   [126] §4 (271).

[127] Gratian, C. 30 q. 5 c. 1 (1104): "… nisi propria voluntas suffrageuerit, et uota succerrerint legitima." Hinschius, *Decretales Pseudo-Isidorianae*, pp. 87–88.

[128] *De matrimonio*, §16 (276–79).

Vacarius begins his *De coniugio* by noting that the joining and dissolution of marriage is a subject fraught with difficulty. Not only do canon law and civil law teach different doctrines, but some of the canonists – he is referring to Rufinus – have muddled matters by distinguishing among initiate, consummate, and established marriage (*matrimonium initiatum, consummatum, ratum*).[129] The notion of initiate marriage, Vacarius argues, is nonsensical. Either there is no marriage yet or there is already a marriage. A marriage is complete as soon as it has begun. There is no intermediate possibility. If marriage were initiated in the *sponsalia*, then either initiate marriage would not be marriage or the betrothal would not be a promise to marry in the future, as it is defined in the *Digest*.[130] One may say that marriage is initiated in the betrothal, but only in the sense that the betrothal is a preparation for marriage.[131] Properly speaking, one may characterize something as initiate only when it has been fully formed but its powers have not yet been fully actualized. For example, when someone has been fictively baptized (i.e., with spurious intentions or in a schismatic church), the baptism is fully formed but initiate insofar as its efficacy remains unrealized, for it has no saving power but can acquire it in the right circumstances. Likewise, when a priest has been ordained but has not yet exercised his office, his priesthood is fully formed but imperfect and initiate.[132] Thus, an unconsummated marriage is imperfect in the same way as a solemn oral agreement (*stipulatio*) to pay a sum of money is imperfect until the money is paid, although the obligation to pay is perfect even before the payment.[133] Any marriage that is sound according to both nature and law (*ius*) is perfect and *ratum*. Contrariwise, if anything essential is missing, such as when the husband suffers from natural impotence, there is no marriage at all, perfect or imperfect.[134]

Vacarius emphasizes that marriage is a legal entity: a set of obligations. One of his objections to the consummation theory is that coitus is a matter of fact, whereas marriage is a matter of *ius*.[135] Nevertheless, just as a fact begins when it is complete, so does a right or an obligation. There is no such thing as a partial of half-formed *ius*. Like ordination to the priesthood, marriage is complete as a *ius* even before the partners begin to exercise the office of marriage by rendering the conjugal debt. Marriage cannot properly be called initiate, therefore, until all the rights and obligations that marriage entails are present, although the question remains as to when that occurs.[136]

Some authors reason, Vacarius explains, that marriage must be perfected in sexual intercourse because it was instituted for the sake of procreation, or because husband

---

[129] §2 (270).   [130] §7 (273).
[131] §10 (273–74): "non potest doceri quomodo in sponsalibus iniciari possit matrimonium, nisi ponatur iniciatur pro quadam preparatione."
[132] §3 (270–71).   [133] §§29–31 (283).   [134] §38 (286).
[135] §17 (278): "Et cum matrimonium ius tantum sit, nichil ei adici uidetur per concubitum, qui tantum facti est et non iuris."
[136] §3 (271): " non recte dicitur matrimonium iniciatum nisi sit iure perfectum."

and wife are supposed to become one flesh in sexual intercourse. Even some of the popes have erred thus. (Vacarius is probably thinking of Leo I.) But the more expert authors of the church show us why this thesis is wrong. For example, Ambrose says that "it is not the deflowering of virginity that makes marriage, but the conjugal pact," and that spouses are so called as soon as a marriage is "initiated." More important, marriage is defined in civil law as "a union of male and female maintaining an indivisible way of life."[137] It is an error, therefore, to suppose that there is only a betrothal and not marriage until coitus, as Jerome seems to have done, or to suppose that a marriage-to-be becomes a marriage in actuality at the point of consummation. On the contrary, it is "congruous with reason and with civil law" to maintain that the mutual consent of the partners by which they actually give and accept each other is what makes marriage.[138]

To reconcile his theory with the coital proof texts ascribed to Augustine and Leo, Vacarius argues that these refer not to marriage *per se* but rather to the capacity for marriage. When these authors say that a woman does not "pertain to matrimony" without sexual intercourse, they are referring not to actual coitus but to sexual capacity, for no one can validly marry without the natural ability (*potestas naturalis*) to perform or receive the sexual act. In like manner, when a person names someone in a will who does not have the legal capacity to inherit, one might say that that the latter does not "pertain" to the will. Moreover, the coital proof texts are a useful corrective, reminding us that coitus is not incidental to marriage, as some suppose.[139]

Vacarius has more difficulty reconciling a text that Gratian ascribes to Ambrose. It states that in every marriage there is a "spiritual joining" (*coniunctio spiritualis*) between the spouses, which sexual intercourse "confirms and protects."[140] Vacarius proposes two solutions. Ambrose may have meant that sexual intercourse demonstrates the partners' capacity to marry, for they cannot marry unless they are able to have sexual intercourse, although if they are in fact able they are married even before consummation. On this view, Ambrose was pointing out that coitus was not irrelevant to marriage. Vacarius's second suggestion is an example of tortured interpretation. Ambrose may have envisaged a situation in which a man leaves his mistress when he discovers that she is married but then marries her when her husband dies. In that case, having previously become one flesh adulterously, they cannot now undo the past and become one flesh legitimately. The second marriage, therefore, is invalid.[141]

The example of Mary and Joseph was as critical for Vacarius as it was for the French theologians. With that example in mind, he denies that sexual intercourse

---

[137] §4 (271). *Inst.* 1.9.1. [138] §§22–23 (280–81).

[139] §21 (279–80). Vacarius is probably referring Peter Lombard, but the opinion in question is more congruent with Hugh of Saint-Victor.

[140] C. 27 q. 2 c. 36 (1073): "*Item Ambrosius in lib. (I) de Patriarchis.* In omni matrimonio coniunctio intelligitur spiritualis, quam confirmat et perficit coniunctorum conmixtio corporalis."

[141] §18 (278).

within marriage is itself a sacrament, as Rufinus held.[142] Nor can he accept Rufinus's argument that Mary and Joseph were perfectly married only by a unique "special privilege," because of her sanctity. It is not the merits of the spouses that establishes a marriage but the legal properties of their union. Citing *Duobus modis*, Vacarius concludes that marriage is already a sacrament before it is consummated.[143] Nevertheless, it is equally wrong to identify marriage with the *sponsalia*, "as some others think," for a betrothal is an expression of expectation regarding a future marriage (*spes futuri matrimonii*). That much is clear from the definition of betrothal as "the announcement and mutual promise of a future marriage."[144]

According to Vacarius's analysis, the fundamental error of the consummation theory is the assumption that marrying entails a single contract, the making or formation of which begins in a betrothal. On the contrary, one must distinguish, as the *Digest* does, between two contracts: that of the betrothal (*sponsalia*) and that of marriage (*nuptiae*). Vacarius shows how each contract has its own distinctive "properties" and consequences.[145] The partners agree to marry in the betrothal, but other persons are often involved as well. A dotal document is prepared, and the man bestows a betrothal gift (*donatio propter nuptias*) on his bride-to-be. In the marriage, the dowry is not promised but actually conferred, and the two partners mutually obligate themselves to render the conjugal debt. Again, there is no defined minimum age for betrothals, as there is for marriage. Crucially, according to Vacarius, bare consent (*solus consensus*) is sufficient for betrothal, since neither the domicile of the partners nor even their presence is involved. In marriage, on the contrary, a common domicile or at least mutual presence is essential.[146]

The proponents of the consummation theory, Vacarius says, contend that betrothal and marriage are distinct contracts in civil law but not in canon law. Under canon law, they argue, marriage is contracted only once, in the betrothal, although it is perfected and confirmed in sexual intercourse. The first union is of the spouses' wills or intentions, the second of their flesh. Again, they argue that betrothal represents the spiritual union between the soul and God, whereas consummated marriage represents the union between Christ incarnate and the church. Just as the former union is soluble whereas the latter is permanent, so also betrothal is soluble but consummated marriage is permanent.[147] Furthermore, they maintain that a man who swears to a woman that he will marry her has already contracted marriage inasmuch as the partners agree to sexual intercourse and to an indivisible way of life in future. The partners' are already united by their intentions, and they are already bound by the obligations of marriage, but their marriage is still in the future as regards sexual intercourse.[148] To elucidate how that process works, the proponents of the consummation theory use the analogy of simple transactions such as partnerships (*societates*) and donations. In the former, the

---

[142] Gandulph, *Sent.* IV, §239 (526–27) defends the thesis that sexual intercourse within marriage under certain circumstances is a sacrament, i.e., a sacred sign.
[143] §19 (279).   [144] §4 (271). The definition is from *Dig.* 23.1.1.
[145] §5 (271).   [146] §5 (271) and §9 (273).   [147] §6 (271–72).   [148] §8 (273).

partners agree to join forces in a certain transaction, and to share profit and loss. The contract is completed when they have actually done so. Likewise, in a donation, the gift is initiated in an agreement (*pactio donationis*) and completed in the handing over of the property (*traditio rei*). Marriages work in the same way, they argue, except that their objects are not things (*res*) but persons.[149]

Vacarius finds a better analogy in certain real contracts. He argues that marrying entails two successive contracts, the second of which both fulfills and supersedes the first. A contract of *societas* or *donatio* ceases to exist when the transaction is realized, since it has no further purpose. But in a real contract, the handing-over creates a new obligation, so that there is in effect a sequence of two contracts:

> One finds something similar in other transactions [*negotia*], for example, when someone promised to you that he would receive your property for safekeeping, and later he received it for that reason [*causa*]. Before he received the property, his promise to look after it did not obligate him to look after it, but in the second contract — that is, in receiving it — he was absolved from his obligation to receive it and instead became obligated to look after it. In the same way, the *sponsus* does not become bound in the betrothal to render the debt, but rather to receive his *sponsa*. But in marriage, now that the obligation to receive her has been removed, he is bound to render the conjugal debt to her.[150]

Partners in a business deal are no longer bound by their contract once they have shared the profit or loss, and a donor is no longer bound once the gift has been given. Obviously, that is not the case in a "partnership of persons," such as marriage, where the *traditio* marks the transition from the first phase of the contract to the second.

In the normal course of events, a Christian *traditio* occurs at the nuptials, when bride and groom exchange their wedding vows. Vacarius considers a remark that Gratian ascribes to Jerome: The fornication of a betrothed woman is adultery only by anticipation, for marriages "are initiated by the betrothal agreement [*sponsalis conventio*] and perfected by bodily intercourse."[151] Either Jerome erred, according to Vacarius, or he used the term "betrothal agreement" to denote the *traditio*, in which partners profess their will to have each other as husband and wife. Both the betrothal and the exchange of marriage vows refer to the same troth (*fides*), therefore, but in different ways: one in regard to the future (*de futuro*), and the other in regard to the present (*de praesenti*). In the betrothal, the partners promise to plight their troth in the future, at the *traditio*. In the *traditio* itself, they express the same troth in the present tense. The two troths posited in the canon *Duobus modis*, therefore, have the same object but differ in tense.[152]

Because the exchange of mutual consent in the present tense functions as a *traditio*, Vacarius argues, the physical presence of the partners is essential. The same

---

[149] §6 (272) and §8 (273).   [150] §9 (273).
[151] C. 27 q. 2 c. 37 (1073): "in coniugiis ... que sponsali conuentione initiantur, et conmixtione corporum perficiuntur." The same text occurs in Bandinus, *Sent.* IV, d. 25 (PL 192:1106D).
[152] §10 (274).

is not true of the betrothal, which can be validly contracted *inter absentes*. Those who say that marriage is initiated in present consent are closer to the truth than the supporters of the consummation theory, but they err when they argue that the bare consent or the union of intents suffices by itself. If that were true, the partners could marry *in absentia*, communicating through a mediator or by letter.[153] To marry thus, with no real *traditio*, would be contrary to both civil and natural law.[154] Ownership (*dominium*) or possession cannot be conferred without some "bodily apprehension" of the object "at least with the eyes or with affection." The partners cannot be joined in marriage unless there is a "corporeal handing-over and quasi-possession." That is why the canon *Duobus modis* characterizes the second troth, *fides consensus*, as what the partners establish by agreeing to accept each other "with heart and mouth." Marriage is formed by consent, but "it is contracted in reality [*in re*], that is, by mutual reception."[155] It is at that point, when they contract *fides consensus*, that the husband is said to take (*ducere*) his wife, and that quasi-possession begins.[156] Vacarius identifies the leading (*ductio*) with their mutual reception of each other when they exchange marriage vows. It is in that *ductio* or *traditio*, and not in sexual intercourse or even in the *in domum deductio*, that the sacrament of marriage is established.[157]

There can be a *traditio* even without the customary sequence of events. Vacarius considers anomalous cases in which the partners' coming together precedes their act of consent. Leah was never betrothed to Jacob (Gen 29:22–28), but she was handed over to him (*tradita*), and Jacob consented after the fact by approval (*ratihabitatio*). The example shows, Vacarius argues, that betrothal is not strictly necessary for marriage.[158] Again, Mary became Joseph's wife when he received her as his wife (Matt 1:20), but how could he receive her when they were already living together? Vacarius replies that Joseph accepted Mary when he began to regard her with the affection due to a wife.[159] Their mutual *quasi-traditio* joined them in marriage.[160]

---

[153] §11 (274). Cf. *Dig.* 24.1.4 pr. (Ulpian): "Sufficit nudus consensus ad constituenda sponsalia. Denique constat et absenti absentem desponderi posse, et hoc cottidie fieri."

[154] §12 (274): "Que sentencia tam naturali iuri quam ciuili uidetur contraria."   [155] Ibid.

[156] Possessive rights other than *dominium* (ownership) were said to be *quasi in possessione* in Roman law because they were incorporeal (Thomas, *Textbook of Roman Law*, 147), although Vacarius was may not have been using this term in any technical sense.

[157] §19 (279).

[158] §10 (273). Vacarius's explanation is dependent on Gratian, C. 29 q. 1 §3 (1091–92), who argues that because Jacob gave consequent, rather than antecedent, consent to the union with Leah, their marriage was not invalidated by error of person (i.e., mistaken identity). But Gratian assumes that the consent fully established the marriage because of the preceding coitus, which Vacarius denies. On *ratihabitatio*, see A. Berger, *Encyclopedic Dictionary of Roman Law* (Philadelphia, 1953), 667.

[159] §13 (275). Vacarius says that she was handed over to him at that point in a certain sense (*quasi tradita*), for he already had the capacity (*facultas*) to be married to her by virtue of their living together. The *facultas* is obscure, but presumably cohabitation establishes a context in which affection alone amounts to *traditio*.

[160] §17 (278). Vacarius is referring again to the marriage of Mary and Joseph, having picked up the topic of §13 after an extended digression about the canon *Aliter* (ps.-Evaristus). He may not be

The partners become insolubly bound, according to Vacarius, as soon as the *traditio* takes place. He rejects Rufinus's rationale for the dissolution of an unconsummated marriage.[161] Citing *Duobus modis*, Vacarius argues that a wife can unilaterally dissolve the union by entering the religious life only before the *traditio*. Once she has been given in marriage (*tradita*), she is bound to her husband.[162] Regarding the decretal of Siricius, which prohibits a woman from taking another partner in marriage after a betrothal, Vacarius offers two possible interpretations. Either Siricius was referring to *fides consensus* (as defined in the canon *Duobus modis*), which is created by the exchange of present-tense marriage vows, or his prohibition would not impede the legal validity of her marriage (*ius matrimonii*) after the fact, although she would have to do penance for the injury that she had committed.[163]

Vacarius's treatment of divorce led him to inquire into the notion of *matrimonium ratum*. Scholars had usually assumed that a marriage was *ratum* if and only if it was insoluble. Contrariwise, inquiry into the Pauline Privilege had led them to reason that a marriage between unbelievers was not *ratum*. Vacarius argues that if a soluble marriage were not *ratum*, then no marriage, even that of Mary of Joseph, would have been *ratum* until the church outlawed divorce and remarriage, for until then every marriage would have been soluble. To say that something is *ratum* is to say not that it is insoluble but only that it is established, provable, and enforceable. Any legitimate marriage, including that of unbelievers, is *ratum*. Contrariwise, a marriage is *non ratum* whenever it is against the law (*contra leges*), for example, if the union is vitiated by fraud or duress.[164]

Vacarius is acutely aware of the difference between divine law and positive human law. He accepts the scope of human law while distinguishing it sharply from divine law, for only the latter is unchangeable. Human laws should be obeyed, but they are adventitious and changeable and at least partly arbitrary. Regarding Hincmar's *Si per sortiarias*, for example, which permits a marriage to be dissolved if the husband is unable to consummate it because of a hex, Vacarius argues that the second marriage is valid only because the first has been dissolved under a human law.[165] If unconsummated marriages can be dissolved in Vacarius's own day, he argues, even when they might be consummated in due course, that is the result of positive ecclesiastical law, and not because there is anything intrinsically deficient about such marriages.[166] Again, if any *matrimonium ratum* is soluble, that is only as a result of human conventions or of concessions to human weakness. Every *matrimonium ratum* is insoluble in principle, even among infidels. When Jesus said, "those whom God has joined together, let not man put asunder," he was addressing not Christians but Jews. The precept applies in principle to every marriage, therefore,

---

using the terms *quasi tradita* and *quasi traditio* in any technical sense, but in the context of Roman law such terms describe the transference of right, which are incorporeal and cannot literally be delivered or handed over. See Thomas, *Roman Law*, 200.

[161] §24 (281).   [162] §25 (281); §27 (282–83).   [163] §25 (281).
[164] Ibid.   [165] §26 (281–82).   [166] §36 (285).

and not only to the marriages of Christian believers.[167] Contrariwise, the maxim that a marriage without God is not *ratum* refers not to marriage between infidels but to any marriage that contravenes the laws and precepts of God, even when it is between believers.[168] Moses permitted Jewish men to divorce their wives in order to avoid worse evils, but that license belonged to the law of human judgment (*lex fori*), and not to law of the divine judgment (*lex poli*).[169]

If every legitimate marriage is *ratum*, even when it is between infidels, then it seems that every marriage is also a sacrament. In that case, what is peculiar to believers? Vacarius considers a dictum from Augustine that Rufinus had cited: "Whereas the sacrament of marriage is common to all peoples, the sanctity of the sacrament is present only in the city of our God and in his holy mountain."[170] Whereas the sacrament *per se* is the sign of a sacred reality, its sanctity is either a power (*virtus*) to bring rewards to good persons and harm to evil persons, or a certain beneficial effect (*effectus*) that results from the sacrament among good persons. In the same way, a medicine is said to have a power (*virtus*) to do good or ill to recipients, according to their disposition, and both the medicine's power to do good and the beneficial effect are called the *sanitas* of the medicine. Augustine was referring to the sanctity of this sacrament chiefly in the second sense, that is, to its beneficial effects, for the spiritual efficacy of marriage among infidels remains unrealized.[171]

7.6 THE COMMON DOCTRINE

A hybrid policy emerged around 1170–1180 and soon became the universal norm. The reasons for its establishment as the common doctrine are not fully understood, but it is significant that the doctrine was first fully expressed in the decretals of Alexander III, whereas the consummation theory was based on Gratian's *Decretum*. Decretal law (the *ius novum*) had surpassed the *Decretum* as the basis of church law by the end of the twelfth century.[172] The common doctrine was based on the French

---

[167] §37 (285–86).

[168] Gratian, C. 28 q. 1 dictum ante c. 1 (1078–79): "Item Augustinus: "Non est ratum coniugium quod sine Deo est." The original source is Ambrosiaster, *Ad Corinthos prima* 7:15 (CSEL 81:77/3–5), on the Pauline privilege: "non enim ratum est matrimonium, quo sine dei devotione est, ac per hoc non est peccatum ei qui dimittitur propter deum, si alii se iunxerit."

[169] §37 (286). The word *polus* literally denoted the celestial axis (cf. "pole star"), but it was a poetic name for heaven.

[170] Rufinus, ed. Singer, pp. 442–43. Cf. Augustine, *De b. coniug.* 7–8(7), CSEL 41:197; *De nupt. et conc.* I.10(11), CSEL 42:223/3–9; *De fide et operibus* 7(10), CSEL 41:46/5–5. Although Augustine spoke of the "sanctity of the sacrament" (*De b. coniug.* 18(21), 214–15, and 24(32), 226–27), the notion that this sanctity was a separable quality or efficacy of the underlying *sacramentum* first appeared in the early-twelfth-century sentential literature (9.5.2–3).

[171] §37 (286).

[172] K. Pennington, "The Decretalists 1190 to 1234," in Hartmann and Pennington *History of Medieval Canon Law*, 211–45. The outpouring of decretals during the central Middle Ages

distinction between *de futuro* and *de praesenti* betrothals, but it incorporated some features of the consummation theory, especially the principle that an unconsummated marriage could be dissolved unilaterally by entry into the religious life.

There is no evidence that Pope Alexander and his advisors deliberately worked out an advanced, synthetic theory of marriage formation. Rather, the common doctrine must have emerged organically in the effort to apply canonical precedents and jurisprudence to the questions that papal judges-delegate and other prelates put to the Holy See: questions that came from all over Europe and were informed by current thinking and troubled by current uncertainties.[173] The French betrothal theory had overwhelmed the Bolognese consummation theory, presumably because the popes adopted it, but consummation still seemed legally significant. As we have seen, Johannes Faventinus, writing around 1170, adopted Rufinus's theory as the basis of his own but also incorporated the distinction between *de futuro* and *de praesenti* betrothals, which Rufinus had rejected. Johannes outlined and seems to have adopted what he characterized as a "middle way" between the French and Bolognese theories, according to which a *de praesenti* betrothal could be dissolved but on either of two grounds: entry into the religious life, and *maleficium*.[174] Although the dating is tenuous, Johannes seems to have described this middle way a few years before a comparable policy had emerged clearly in the late decretals of Pope Alexander III.[175]

7.6.1 *The decretals of Alexander III*

Numerous decretals by Pope Alexander III pertaining to the formation of marriage have survived. Several of them are preserved, wholly or in part, as *capitula* in the *Decretals of Gregory IX*, usually known as the *Liber extra*, which was compiled by Raymond of Penyafort and first published in 1234. Alexander's decretals are difficult to interpret in the absence of a critical edition, and the cases themselves, having come to the papal court on appeal, are often vexed and complicated, raising multiple issues. The summaries provided in the decretals were intended for readers already familiar with some of the circumstances, and the extracts were designed to illuminate particular points of law, and not to record the narrative of the cases.

Taken as a whole and without regard for chronology, Alexander's decretals evince no consistent policy about marriage formation, and one might suppose that he was applying diverse rules to particular cases in a wholly pragmatic, *ad hoc* manner. But

---

resulted largely from the institution of judges-delegate, who adjudicated cases referred to the Holy See locally, in the province or region of the case. See J. E. Sayers, *Papal Judges Delegate in the Province of Canterbury, 1198–1254* (Oxford, 1971); and J. A. Brundage, *The Medieval Origins of the Legal Profession* (Chicago, 2008), 135–37.

[173] A. J. Duggan, "The Nature of Alexander III's Contribution to Marriage Law, with Special Reference to *Licet preter solitum*," in P. Andersen et al. (eds.), *Law and Marriage in Medieval and Early Modern Times* (Copenhagen, 2012), 43–63.

[174] Donahue, "Johannes Faventinus on Marriage," 188n37.   [175] Ibid., 190–91.

Dauvillier showed in 1933 that Alexander's decisions could be plausibly arranged to reveal a chronological development. Charles Donahue refined Dauvillier's arguments, using the best dating available to avoid circular argument.[176]

Donahue posits three phases: the French period, lasting until 1173 or 1174, during which Alexander adopted the betrothal theory of French theologians and canonists; the solemnity period, from 1173 or 1174 to around 1177, during which he regarded the solemnization of a marriage as a significant and even a critical feature; and the "classical period," from around 1177 until his death in 1181, during which Alexander's policy was congruent with what would become the common doctrine. The entire development unfolded within a decade.

Following Dauvillier, Donahue argues that the "decretals around 1170 betray an exposure to Parisian ideas about marriage."[177] Alexander presupposes the French distinction between *de futuro* and *de praesenti* betrothals, albeit without stating it explicitly, and he assumes that only *de praesenti* betrothals are binding. Thus, he holds in two decretals that a prior unconsummated *de praesenti* betrothal trumps a subsequent, consummated marriage,[178] but he holds in a third that a promise to marry, with or without an oath, can be dissolved by mutual consent, like any partnership made under oath. To be sure, the betrothed persons should be urged to fulfill their promise, but it is better for them to separate than to marry but despise each other.[179] Alexander assumes during this period that bare consent, other things being equal, is sufficient to establish an insoluble marriage. Thus, in a decretal dating from 1170 or 1171, Alexander rules that persons who have married clandestinely should be compelled to sustain their marriage, which may not be annulled on grounds of clandestinity.[180] During the same period, Alexander holds that a betrothed person may enter the religious life prior to consummation without the other's consent, although it seems that the partner left in the world could not marry if the betrothal was *de praesenti*.[181] What sets these decisions apart from those of the

---

[176] J. Dauvillier, *Le mariage dans le droit classique de l'Église* (Paris, 1933), 17–32. C. Donahue, "The Dating of Alexander the Third's Marriage Decretals," *Zeitschrift der Savigny-Stiftung für Rechtsgeschichte* 99, Kan. Abt. 68 (1982): 70–124. Christopher Brooke severely criticized Donahue's "heroic attempt" in *The Medieval Idea of Marriage* (Oxford, 1989), 169–72, but Donahue replied to Brooke's critique in an appendix to "Johannes Faventinus on Marriage," 194–97, maintaining that his earlier analysis was basically sound.

[177] "Dating," 105.

[178] WH 991(a), JL 14235, 1 *Comp.* 4.4.4(6), *Sollicitudini sedis apostolicae* (to Gerard, bishop of Padua).

[179] WH 1013(c), JL 13903, X 4.1.2, *Super eo quod. Praeterea hii* (to Bartholemew, bishop of Exeter).

[180] WH 819, JL 13774, X 4.3.2 and 4.17.9, *Quod nobis* (to the bishop of Beauvais). On clandestine marriages, see 1.6.2, 10.6.1, 11.4.11, 14.7, 17.2.5, 17.6, 17.7.3, and 19–20. A marriage is clandestine when it is contracted without whatever means of witnessing and attestation are required under ecclesiastical law to ensure that there will be adequate evidence of the marriage if it becomes the subject of litigation.

[181] WH 336(b), JL 11865, 1 *Comp.* 3.28.9, *De muliere. Sane super eo* (to William, bishop of St. Agatha). WH 944(f), JL 12293–JL 13874, 1 *Comp.* 4.4.5(7), *Sicut romana. Porro si qui* (to William, archbishop of Sens).

later, classical period is mainly negative: They make no explicit appeal to the role of consummation in marriage formation.

References to the solemnization of marriage appear mainly in decretals from 1173 or 1174 to around 1177. Donahue cites three decretals as his chief evidence. The decretal *Licet praeter solitum* to Romualdus, archbishop of Salerno, is unequivocal.[182] Here, Alexander replies to a double question. First, if a man and a woman have exchanged consent in the present tense, with or without an oath, but they have not consummated their marriage, can the woman marry someone else? Second, if she has married again regardless, and if the second union has been consummated, ought it to be dissolved? Although Alexander notes that others are of a different opinion, his judgment is as follows: If they exchanged consent in the present tense in a recognized manner, with or without an oath, and if they did so before witnesses and with whatever solemnity was practiced locally, whether it be a priestly blessing or the record of a notary, then she cannot lawfully marry another, and the second, consummated, marriage ought to be dissolved.[183]

The evidence of the other two relevant decretals from this period is less clear. In one of them, Alexander upholds a solemnized and consummated marriage. The narrative recalls how Andrew plighted his troth (apparently in the present tense) before a priest, a deacon, some other clerics, and some lay witnesses, sealing the contract with an oath. The partners lived together and raised a family, but Andrew later abandoned his wife. Alexander rules that Andrew must return to his wife and treat her with marital affection.[184] But theirs would have been a valid and insoluble marriage on any interpretation, and the record of solemnization may have been relevant only as evidence that they exchanged consent. The decretal provides no rationale for the decision.

According to Donahue, Alexander "expressly refuses" in the third of these decretals "to maintain a prior *de presenti* marriage in the face of a subsequent solemn one, apparently on the ground that the prior marriage lacked solemnity."[185] But although solemnization is a theme running through the decretal, its role in Alexander's decision is unclear, and he makes no reference to solemnity in his judgment. The narrative is as follows: G. betrothed his daughter Mary to R. in her absence. In due course, R. and Mary contracted marriage together in words of the present tense, holding hands, but they could not solemnize their marriage in church immediately because it was Lent. Meanwhile, despite his marriage to Mary, R. took a second woman, Matilda, as his wife, solemnly marrying her before the church (*in facie ecclesiae*). When the case came before the archbishop, R. conceded that he had married Mary (the first woman), but Mary maintained that "no obligation had

[182] WH 620(b), JL 14091, X 3.32.2, *Licet praeter solitum* (to Romualdus, archbishop of Salerno).
[183] WH620(a), JL 14091, 1 Comp. 4.4.3, X 4.4.3, *Licet praeter solitum* (to Romualdus, archbishop of Salerno). Donahue places this decretal between 1169 and 1179, perhaps 1176 or 1177.
[184] WH 457, JL 13872, X 4.1.9, *Ex parte* (to the abbots of St. Edmunds and Ramsey).
[185] "The Dating of Alexander the Third's Marriage Decretals," 105.

been formed between herself and R. except for the "troth that a marriage was to be contracted" (*fides de contrahendo matrimonio*): in other words, a *de futuro* betrothal. Mary considered herself free because R. had not kept his promise. Although the narrative suggests that the prior agreement had been expressed in the present tense, Alexander agrees with Mary. He rules that R.'s marriage to Matilda should be upheld "if it is clear that there was no impediment besides the consent about the future that is asserted to have taken place between the aforesaid R. and M[ary]."[186] Both Mary and the pope seem to have assumed that her prior betrothal was a *de futuro* contract at least partly because it was not solemnized in church.

From around 1177, Alexander's decretals are consistent with what would soon become the universal doctrine. Not only does a *de praesenti* betrothal, with or without solemnity, constitute marriage and trump any subsequent marriage,[187] but a *de futuro* betrothal becomes a marriage if it is consummated, and a marriage formed thus trumps any subsequent union, including a *de praesenti* betrothal. Among the decretals applying the second principle, regarding consummation, the most influential was *Veniens ad nos Wi.*, a late but undated response to the bishop of Norwich.[188] This decretal includes one of the earliest references to the "steady man" threshold for the impediment of coercion by force and fear (*vis et metus*). A certain man, G., had received a woman into his home as his mistress, and she bore him a child. G. had also plighted his troth with her *de futuro* before witnesses, promising that he would take her as his wife. Later, he spent a night in his neighbor's house, where he had sex with a daughter of the neighbor. The neighbor forced him to betroth his daughter in words of the present tense. Which woman is G.'s wife? Alexander rules that it depends on whether he had sex with the first woman *after* he plighted future-tense troth with her. If so, then the first woman is his wife. If not, the second woman is his wife unless the fear that was applied to coerce him was sufficient to cause a steady man (*constans vir*) to succumb.

Alexander assumes in his late decretals that marriage is soluble under certain exceptional conditions before consummation. Two late decretals pertain to the dissolution of an unconsummated marriage. One of them implies that a *de praesenti* betrothal may be dissolved on the grounds of supervenient affinity by dispensation prior to but not after consummation, but only if the sin is publicly known.[189] (The case involves a man who had sex with his mother-in-law before consummating his

---

[186] WH 439, JL 14311, X 4.16.2, *Ex litteris* (to the bishops of Winchester, Bath, and Hereford). The date range for this decretal is 1175–1181.

[187] WH 954(e), JL 14234, 1 *Comp.* 4.4.6(8), *Significasti. Super eo vero* (to the bishop of Norwich). *Collectio Brugensis* 49.13(a), *Consulit nos . . . de duabus*, to the Chapter of Mainz.

[188] WH 1071, JL 13902 = JL 14159, X 4.1.15, *Veniens ad nos Wi.* (to John, bishop of Norwich). The other decretals in this group are: WH 847, *Collectio Parisiensis* 1, 176 (to the bishop of Worcester and the abbot of Evesham); WH 4(a), JL 13765, X 4.2.8, *A nobis. De illis* (to the bishop of Bath); and WH 973, JL 13937, X 4.7.2, *Significavit nobis O.* (to the abbot of Fountains and master Vacarius). See Donahue, "Dating," 106n44 on the interpretation of the last decretal.

[189] Alexander is invoking the impediment of public honesty.

marriage.) The dispensation would leave the partners free to remarry.[190] More significant is the right of either partner, even if the other is opposed, to dissolve an unconsummated marriage (i.e., a *de praesenti* betrothal) by entering the religious life, leaving the other free to remarry. This right cannot be justified by the betrothal theory alone. Alexander refers to it as an ancient right that he has recently revived. In the decretal *Ex publico instrumento*, which Donahue assigns to the solemnity period, Alexander rules that a wife (*uxor*) in an unconsummated union has two months to decide whether to enter religion or remain with her husband.[191] The decretal *Licet praeter solitum* (perhaps 1176 or 1177), noted earlier for its unambiguous solemnity requirement, states the general principle without mentioning a time limit.[192] Another late decretal presupposes both the general rule and the time limit. It concerns a nobleman who swore to a woman with his hand upon the gospels that he would contract marriage with her in words of the present tense within two years. Meanwhile, he decided that he wanted to become a monk. May he do so rather than fulfilling his promise to marry? It seems so, for even if he had contracted marriage, he would still have two months to become a religious even if she were unwilling, in accordance with the ancient canons that have been renewed in the pope's recent rulings. Perhaps expecting that the man might have second thoughts, Alexander counsels that he should go ahead with the marriage and then reconsider, for he will still have two months to change his mind and become a religious unless he consummates the union.[193]

7.6.2 *The Bolognese tradition after Alexander III: Simon of Bisignano and Huguccio*

Simon of Bisignano, who taught in Bologna during the 1170s, was one of the first scholars to incorporate modern papal decretals into canonical jurisprudence. Simon's commentary on C. 27 q. 2 is based on Rufinus. Like his model, Simon begins by paying homage to Gratian, but he adds that Gratian "spoke well but less fully," for he failed to appreciate the distinction between *de futuro* and *de praesenti* betrothals. Divorce is possible after a *de praesenti* betrothal on only two grounds: entry into the religious life, and *maleficium* (the latter as determined in the canon *Si per sortiarias*). To show that a *de praesenti* betrothal is fully binding, Simon cites Alexander's decretal *Licet praeter solitum*. Simon retains Rufinus's theory of the two troths in marriage: one formed by consent alone, which obligates the partners to mutual chastity; and another formed by consummation, which obligates them to render the conjugal debt. In Simon's view, this theory helps to explain why someone can unilaterally dissolve an unconsummated marriage by becoming a religious.

[190] WH 1066 (1179), JL 14058, X 4.13.2, *Veniens ad nos P.* (to the bishop of Poitiers).
[191] WH 476, JL 13787, X 3.32.7, *Ex publico instrumento* (to the bishop of Brescia).
[192] WH 620(b), JL 14091, X 3.32.2, *Licet praeter solitum* (to Romualdus, bishop of Salerno).
[193] WH 135, JL 13905, X 4.1.16, *Commisum et infra. Significavit nobis* (to the bishop of Exeter).

Moreover, Simon maintains that *de praesenti* consent alone, without consummation, is not sufficient to establish the impediment of digamy, which prevents a man
who has had two wives from being promoted to holy orders.[194]

Huguccio (fl. 1180–1210) rejected the consummation theory of the Bolognese
tradition categorically and provided a rationale for the common doctrine. In his
highly influential *Summa* on the *Decretum*, composed around 1188–1190, Huguccio
summarizes what he calls Gratian's theory, although it is really Rufinus's version of
the theory. Huguccio rejects that and proposes instead a version of the betrothal
theory. On the one hand, the partners may promise to take each other in the future,
saying, "I promise to you that I shall take you as my wife/husband," and agreeing to
marry at a certain time, such as after Lent, or in a year's time, or when one of them
reaches puberty, or if a certain condition is fulfilled, such as a father's permission.
On the other hand, the partners may agree in words of the present tense, saying,
"I take you as my wife," and "I take you as my husband," or by using other words or
even non-verbal signs to the same effect. As soon as a betrothal of the latter sort has
taken place, then "there is at once a perfect and entire marriage between them."[195]
In Huguccio's view, the recommended words spoken in the appropriate tense are
the norm, but there are other conventional ways of expressing both *de futuro* and *de
praesenti* consent, including non-verbal signs and rituals. Thus, he concedes that the
giving of a wedding ring (*subarratio per immissionem annuli*) after a promise to
marry is presumed to imply *de praesenti* consent unless there are indications to the
contrary.[196]

Huguccio sets out the rules of the common doctrine with the utmost clarity.
Clearly, someone who is betrothed to one person *ought* not to marry another. But
what should be done after the fact if the betrothed person does marry another?
According to Huguccio, Gratian proposed two rules: First, if the *sponsa* has already
been "led" by the first man and has been veiled or blessed with him, she must
remain with him. Second, if she has had intercourse with the second man but not
with first, she must remain with the second.[197] Huguccio rejects Gratian's policy and
endorses Alexander's. One needs to establish whether the prior betrothal was *de
futuro* or *de praesenti*. If the first man betrothed her *de praesenti*, then she is bound
to remain with him unless she chooses to become a religious, regardless of whether
the second union is *de futuro* or *de praesenti*, whether it was blessed, whether there
was a *traductio*, or whether it is consummated. If both betrothals were *de futuro* and
the second has not progressed beyond that point, then she should return to the first
man. But she should remain with the second man if the union has reached the stage
of consent in the present tense, and likewise if the second *de futuro* betrothal has

---

[194] Simon of Bisignano, *Summa in Decretum*, ed. Aimone, 412–14.

[195] Huguccio, *Summa* on C. 27 q. 2, in J. Roman, "Summa d'Huguccio sur le décret de Gratien,"
Revue historique de droit français et étranger, 2nd series 27 (1903): 715–805, at 745–46.

[196] Ibid., 747.

[197] Huguccio does not explain what should happen if these rules are in conflict.

been followed by coitus, for in that case consent in the present tense is presumed to have taken place.[198]

Huguccio appropriates Rufinus's argument from analogy to explain why a spouse can dissolve an unconsummated marriage by entering the religious life, even though the marriage is fully formed and *ratum*. Whereas Rufinus had proposed the explanation as a secondary argument that might be proposed not unfittingly (*non immerito*), Huguccio uses the strong idiom *quia ... ideo* ("because ... therefore") to connect the signified to the sign. Whereas unconsummated marriage signifies the union between the soul and God, Huguccio argues, consummated marriage signifies Christ's union with the church through a common human nature. Because the soul's union with God is separable, therefore, unconsummated marriage can be dissolved by the entry of one partner into religion. Likewise, because the union between the incarnate Christ and the church is inseparable, consummated marriage, too, is insoluble, for it serves "as a sign of that reality" (*in signum eius rei*).[199]

Huguccio notes that the *de praesenti* union is called a betrothal (*deponsatio*) only improperly. Properly speaking, one should call it a marriage. Likewise, one should properly call the partners in a *de praesenti* betrothal *coniuges* rather than *sponsus* and *sponsa*. Huguccio notes that that some, such as Cardinalis, call a person obligated by a *de futuro* agreement a *sponsus simplex*, and someone who has "passed over to marital affection," but still prior to consummation, a *sponsus non simplex*. But he claims that these variants are merely different words expressing the same distinction.[200]

Huguccio recovers the ideological implications that had appeared from time to time in the French theological tradition, especially in Hugh of Saint-Victor. Like most of the canonists, he is inclined to regard marriage as a contract of which the chief object is sexual intercourse, or a contract to render the conjugal debt. Thus, glossing the phrase "indivisible way of life" in the standard definition of marriage, he explains that this way of life pertains chiefly to the "mutual servitude of the body."[201] Nevertheless, Huguccio maintains that marriage *per se* transcends sexual intercourse, for the union (*coniunctio*) in the definition of marriage is a joining of wills or intentions (*animorum*), and not of bodies.[202] With the marriage of Mary and Joseph in mind, he argues that the union of minds in marriage is more holy and more honorable (*sanctiores et honestiores*) than the joining of bodies. The partners are called *coniuges*, according to Huguccio, chiefly in respect the former, spiritual joining. That is why Isidore said that spouses were "more truly" so called as soon as they plighted their truth.[203]

Several of the arguments that Huguccio uses to defend the classical policy and to refute Gratian are variants of ones that we have seen in Vacarius. Like Vacarius, he

[198] Huguccio, 799–801.   [199] Ibid., 763–64.   [200] Ibid., 746–47.   [201] Ibid., 747.
[202] *Sunt enim nuptie*, 747.
[203] *Coniuges verius*, 755. Isidore, *Etym.* IX.7.9: "Coniuges autem verius appellantur a prima desponsationis fide, quamvis adhuc inter eos ignoretur coniugalis concubitus; sicut Maria Ioseph coniux vocatur, inter quos nec fuerat futura erat carnis ulla commixtio."

argues that the notion of *matrimonium initiatum* is conceptually flawed. Marriage is an entirely simple thing (*res simplicissima*), as every sacrament is. It cannot come into existence in stages.[204] As soon as there is a marriage at all, it is perfect, entire, and complete (*consummatum*), even before coitus has taken place. Marriage before coitus may be described as initiate in the sense that it has begun to exist, or in the sense that it is still incomplete as regards its signification, but it is already complete in its essence.[205]

Huguccio rejects Rufinus's doctrine that there are two troths (*fides*) in marriage: one of betrothal, which obligates the partners to chastity; the other of carnal union, which obligates the partners to the "mutual servitude" of the conjugal debt. Instead, he argues that there is only a single *ius* in marriage, but he distinguishes between the *ius* itself and its execution. A *ius* consists of certain rights and obligations, whereas its execution consists in the power or license to exercise those rights and obligations. Thus, a priest under an interdict has the *ius* of hearing confessions but not the *executio*.[206] Rufinus's distinction between *ius* and *executio iuris* is similar to Vacarius's distinction between the office *per se* and the exercise of an office, although Huguccio's *executio* is not the actual exercise of the *ius* but rather a power to use that right, which is itself a subsidiary right.[207] Like Vacarius, he cites the law of oral agreement (*stipulatio*) to illustrate how a contract is made and fulfilled. If someone agrees to pay someone else a certain sum within a year, the *ius* exists at once, but the other person cannot demand the money before the agreed time, for the *executio iuris* has not yet come into effect.[208] When does the *executio* of marriage come into effect? Huguccio offers three suggestions: it might occur when there is a *traductio* or *traditio*, or when the marriage is blessed by a priest, or after two months, as proposed in Alexander's decretal *Ex publico instrumento*.[209]

Huguccio's rationale for the common doctrine would endure for centuries. Moreover, the fact that this most illustrious of Bolognese canonists rejected what had been the prevailing doctrine of his own tradition put an end to that line of theorizing.

7.6.3 *Summary of the common doctrine*

The essentials of the common doctrine are simple enough and can be understood without the help of such theorizing as Huguccio's. First, a *de praesenti* betrothal is sufficient for *matrimonium ratum* and makes any subsequent marriage to someone else invalid, even if the first alliance is unconsummated and the second is

---

[204] Cf. Vacarius, §3 (270–71).   [205] Huguccio, 754.

[206] See T. Lenherr, "Der Begriff 'executio' in der Summa Decretorum des Huguccio," *Archiv für katholisches Kirchenrecht* 150 (1981): 5–44. Because of the *ius*, sacraments performed by a priest under an interdict are effective despite being prohibited.

[207] Cf. Vacarius, §3 (270–71).   [208] Huguccio, 756. Cf. Vacarius, §29–31 (283).

[209] Huguccio, 756: "Alexander tamen videtur ibi constituere certum terminum, scilicet spatium duorum mensium, intra quos transeat ad religionem vel subjiciat se marito, i. *Ex publico*." WH 476, JL 13787, X 3.32.7, *Ex publico instrumento* (to the bishop of Brescia).

consummated, and even if the second is solemnized but the first is not. Second, although someone who is betrothed *de futuro* to one person *ought* not to marry someone else, and although he may be compelled to reinstate the first betrothal if he betroths a second person *de futuro*, a *de futuro* betrothal may be legitimately dissolved on certain grounds. Moreover, it is not a fatal impediment *post factum* to a subsequent marriage even in the absence of such grounds. In other words, *de praesenti* vows trump a prior *de futuro* betrothal, notwithstanding the breach of promise. Third, a *de futuro* betrothal automatically becomes *matrimonium ratum* if it is followed by coitus. The canonists construed coitus in such cases as presumptive evidence of *de praesenti* consent, although they recognized that the presumption was little more than a legal fiction. Fourth, although an unconsummated *de praesenti* betrothal suffices to establish *matrimonium ratum*, it is not absolutely insoluble. In particular, either spouse may opt to become a religious prior to consummation, even if the other partner is unwilling, and the partner left in the world is then free to remarry. Whereas the first two rules embodied the betrothal theory of the French tradition, the other rules were in accordance with the consummation theory of the Bolognese tradition.

The term *matrimonium ratum* acquired new significance in this common doctrine. Gratian had assumed that *matrimonium ratum* and *matrimonium consummatum* were the same thing, whereas Rufinus distinguished them on the grounds that a consummated marriage was not fully established, fully valid, and insoluble unless it was between baptized Christians. A marriage might be either *consummatum* only, therefore, or both *consummatum* and *ratum*. According to the common doctrine, a marriage was normally *ratum* before it was consummated, and the three modalities formed a normal sequence: first, a betrothal created *matrimonium initiatum*; then consent in the present tense established *matrimonium ratum*; and, finally, coitus established *matrimonium ratum et consummatum*. Other things being equal, an unconsummated marriage, unlike a *de futuro* betrothal, was considered to be *ratum* and fully sacramental. It was not soluble at the will of the spouses or by marriage to another, therefore, but only in certain special circumstances: certainly for entry into the religious life, and perhaps also for other reasons and under other circumstances.[210] Innocent III declared in *Ex parte tua* (X 3.32.14) that there were no other valid grounds, and he seemed to accept even these grounds only grudgingly or provisionally. Dissolution for promotion to Holy Orders was debated from time to time but rejected in Pope John XXII's decretal *Antiquae concertationi* (1322).[211] The power of the pope to dissolve an unconsummated marriage was sometimes recognized, but it did not become

---

[210] Innocent III declared in *Ex parte tua* (X 3.32.14, 1206) that there were no other grounds, and the pope seemed to accept these grounds only grudgingly or provisionally. Dissolution for promotion to Holy Orders was debated from time to time but rejected by Pope John XXII's

[211] P. Nold, *Marriage Advice for a Pope: John XXII and the Power to Dissolve* (Leiden, 2009).

a reality until the fifteenth century, when it signaled the beginnings of a new regime, with more scope for human authority.[212] Under the central-medieval regime, although the church had the power to introduce and remove impediments to marriage, the spouses contracted their union with the help of God the Father alone, and no one else was authorized to intervene.

---

[212] D. d'Avray, *Medieval Marriage*, 188–99.

PART III

The twelfth century

Origins and early development of the sacramental theology of marriage

8

Introduction to the sentential literature on marriage

The sacramental theology of marriage originated in florilegia and anonymous treatises composed during the first quarter of the twelfth century. These works belong to a body of literature made up of *sententiae*: discrete statements of positions on particular issues. Some of the *sententiae* are ascribed in the manuscripts to patristic or contemporaneous authors. Those who gathered them and the authors of treatises compiled from such material preferred to remain anonymous, but their theological work was constructive and original. For want of any better term, I shall refer to them as the *magistri moderni*: the epithet with which the *Liber Pancrisis* characterized the masters who taught in the cathedral schools of the Île de France during the late eleventh and early twelfth centuries, such as William of Champeaux and Anselm of Laon.

Most scholars in the field today attribute the sentential treatises on marriage to the School of Laon, referring to Anselm of Laon and his disciples,[1] but I can see no adequate reason to do so. Moreover, notwithstanding some welcome recent reassessments,[2] the very notion of the School of Laon remains problematic. This is not the place for a thorough review of the topic, but in view of the historical importance of the sentential literature for the theology of marriage some account both of this literature in general and of the salient traits of the treatises on marriage is necessary here.

The sentential literature of the twelfth century presents the researcher with peculiar difficulties. On the one hand, it is distinctive and unlike any other body

---

[1] See especially H. J. F. Reinhardt, *Die Ehelehre der Schule des Anselm von Laon*, BGPhThMA, n.F. 14 (Münster, 1974), and H. Zeimentz, *Ehe nach der Lehre der Frühscholastik* (Düsseldorf, 1973).

[2] M. Clanchy and L. Smith, "Abelard's Description of the School of Laon: What Might It Tell Us about Early Scholastic Teaching?" in *Nottingham Medieval Studies* 54 (2010): 1–34. C. Giraud, *Per verba magistri* (Turnhout, 2010). A. Andrée, "Laon Revisited: Master Anselm and the Creation of a Theological School in the Twelfth Century," *Journal of Medieval Latin* 22 (2012): 257–81.

of theological writing produced during the Middle Ages, and it evinces a remarkable creative effort. It arguably represents the earliest phase in the discipline later known as scholastic theology. On the other hand, much of the literature is anonymous, and the practices, pedagogical procedures, institutional and ecclesial context, and intellectual milieu that gave rise to the literature as a whole remain at best dimly understood. Readers naturally desire to reduce texts to authors, and historically informed readers desire to assign to any medieval author a biography, a vocation, and an intellectual or institutional milieu. To read the sentential literature without begging any questions, however, the reader must remain on the surface of these texts.

I shall begin, therefore, with a descriptive account of the literature as such, with its salient traits, before turning to the theology of marriage developed in it (Chapter 9). This descriptive account is necessarily detailed and rather dry, but readers should be able to glean as much or as little information as they need, according to their respective levels of interest. Modern scholars who are familiar with the sentential literature usually write about it without describing the medium itself, and by so doing they often convey a misleading impression of the literature to readers who are unfamiliar with it.

8.1 THE *SENTENTIAE*

The use of sentences as a theological medium flourished during the first quarter of the twelfth century, although scholars continued to collect such material throughout the century. The term *sententia* had several senses during this period, including "opinion," "thesis," "judgment," "determination," and even "underlying meaning" (the import or deeper *sensus* of a text). The sentences associated with the *magistri moderni* are typically short, self-contained statements, ranging from a few lines to a page (or two or three columns) of manuscript. Each *sententia* makes a single point on a specific topic, as if in answer to a question. The sentences are not presented as infallible, but the term presupposed some weight of authority. They were readily collectible and transferable, and the same *sententia* is often extant in several different collections. The medium made it possible both to compare and contrast different opinions on the same topic and to compose comprehensive treatments of entire subject areas. Above all, it emancipated reflection on propositions from the *seriatim*, context-dependent exposition of Scripture, although the Bible remained fundamental to the discipline.

As well as independent, free-standing sentences, such as those assembled haphazardly in miscellanies and more deliberately in florilegia, the literature includes treatises on particular topics, in which sentences by both patristic and contemporaneous authors have been woven together systematically with connecting material to compose a coherent treatment of a single topic: a treatment that is comprehensive within certain limits, albeit without much sustained argument or development.

Some of these treatises were later compiled into still larger units, each covering a range of subjects somewhat systematically. This second-order compiling apparently occurred later, probably during the second half of the twelfth century.

8.1.1 A *florilegium: The* Liber Pancrisis

Although current scholarship suggests that the *Liber Pancrisis* was composed around 1140, it illustrates well some of the salient features of the sentential literature and the genre of the florilegium during this era. The collection has an especially formative place in modern research on the so-called School of Laon.

The *Liber Pancrisis*, or "All-Gold Book," is a florilegium extant in two manuscripts: British Library, Harley 3098 (1r–91v) and Troyes 425 (95ra–148vb).[3] The title of the book is a Grecism, from *pan-chryseos* ("all-golden").[4] Careful comparison shows that the Troyes text was a copy of the Harley text. A third manuscript, Avranches 19 (133rb–164vb), contains an abbreviated recension of the same collection. It seems that both the Avranches recension and the *Liber Pancrisis* (Harley 3098) were derived independently from the same lost archetype.[5]

A descriptive preamble to the *Liber Pancrisis* explains that the collection consists of "the golden sentences and questions[6] of the fathers Augustine, Jerome, Ambrose, Gregory, Isidore, and Bede, and of the modern masters [*magistri moderni*] William the bishop of Châlons-sur-Marne,[7] Ivo the bishop of Chartres, Anselm, and his brother Ralph."[8] The term "master" (*magister*) could refer to any person in authority, but it usually denoted a schoolteacher, especially one appointed and licensed by a cathedral. Thus, the preamble presents the four modern authors as schoolmen. Ascriptions to several other ancient and modern masters appear in collection itself, where each *sententia* is ascribed to an author in a rubric, which sometimes includes a subject heading, for example, "Jerome on the Lord's body and blood," "Ivo on consanguinity," "William on the soul," "William: What is original sin?" The

---

3   The *ex libris* on the front page of Harley 3098 is written in a fifteenth-century hand and identifies the manuscript as belonging to the Carthusian priory at Rutila (also known as Rutina), near Sirck, on the river Moselle in the Triers region: "Iste liber est fratrum Carthusiensium in Rutila prope Sirck."

4   Is it coincidence that the Greek term *krisis* and the Latin term *sententia* could both mean "judgment"?

5   O. Lottin, "Un nouveau témoin du *Liber Pancrisis*," RThAM 23 (1956): 114–18. Lottin, PsM V, 10–13. Giraud, *Per verba magistri*, 503–07, provides an index of authors and a table collating the three recensions, which includes references to the authentic patristic sources.

6   Several of the *sententiae* are presented in question-and-answer form. Most of these *quaestiones* are ascribed to William of Champeaux.

7   Known today as William of Champeaux (after his birthplace).

8   Harley 3098, 1r: "Incipit liber pancrisis, id est totus aureus, quia hic auree continentur sententie uel questiones patrum Augustini, Yeronimi, Ambrosii, Gregorii, Isidori, Bede, et modernorum magistrorum Willelmi Catalaunensis episcopi, Iuonis Carnotensis episcopi, Anselmi et fratris eius Radulfi."

preamble to the Avranches recension lists the same authors but in a different order, putting Ivo last: William, Anselm, Ralph, Ivo. Moreover, it subordinates the *magistri moderni* to the ancient authors by saying that the collection consists of sentences or questions by Augustine, Jerome, Ambrose, Gregory, Isidore, and Bede "extracted and expounded" by the modern masters.[9] Much has been made of this difference, as if one preamble represents a later stage of intellectual development than the other, but it is safer to regard them as variants representing different ways of construing the relationship of the modern masters to the ancient sources on which they depended. According to the *Liber Pancrisis*, the modern authors are masters in their own right, adding to the accumulated opinions of the ancient authors and standing on their shoulders. According to the Avranches version, on the contrary, the role of the modern masters is to sift and collect opinions from the ancient authorities.

Scholars today usually regard Anselm of Laon as the leading figure among the four masters named in the preamble and treat the *Liber Pancrisis* as a product of the School of Laon.[10] Three of the modern masters named in the preamble, to be sure, had a Laon connection. Anselm taught at Laon for several decades until his death in 1117, while rising through the ranks of canon, chancellor, and archdeacon. Ralph, Anselm's brother, joined him at Laon, taught alongside him, and continued teaching there after Anselm's death. William of Champeaux studied under Anselm before becoming a master at the school of Notre Dame in Paris. But the preamble does not subsume the four masters under a single school or disciplinary parentage, and it is William, and not Anselm, whose name comes first. The notion that the group represents the School of Laon belongs to the twentieth century, not to the twelfth. The only distinguishing feature that all four of the *magistri moderni* share is that they pursued their careers in the cathedrals of the Île de France.[11]

Odon Lottin, a pioneer in the field, concluded that all three versions – the lost archetype, the *Liber Pancrisis* (Harley 3098), and the Avranches collection – all dated from the period 1120–1125.[12] Recent work, however, has shown that the florilegium came from a later period and from a milieu remote from that of the

9   Lottin, PsM V, 11: "Sententie vel questiones sanctorum Augustini, Yeronimi, Ambrosii, Gregorii, Isidori, Bede extracte uel exposite a modernis magistris Guillelmo, Anselmo, Radulfo, Iuone Carnotensi episcopo."
10 For example, Andrée, "Laon Revisited," 263: "In the incipit of this, the 'All-Gold book,' the sentences of Anselm and his brother Ralph in addition to William of Champeaux and Ivo of Chartres, the 'modern masters,' are called upon to complete those of the Fathers...." (Note how Andrée reverses the order of the masters.) T. Mackin, *The Marital Sacrament* (New York, 1989), 302, describes the *Liber Pancrisis* as "a collection of *sententiae* attributed to Anselm."
11 M. T. Clanchy, *Abelard: A Medieval Life* (Oxford, 1999), 80.
12 See O. Lottin, "A propos de la date de deux florilèges concernant Anselme de Laon," RThAM 26 (1959): 307–14, where the author withdraws his earlier argument (stated in "Un nouveau témoin" and repeated in PsM V, 12) that the Avranches florilegium should be dated before 1113 and the *Liber Pancrisis* after 1113. This argument, first proposed by Bliemetzrieder, turns tenuously on the observation that William is designated merely as a master in the Avranches preamble but as the bishop of *Châlons-sur-Marne* in the *Liber Pancrisis* preamble.

four *magistri moderni* named in the preamble.[13] Circumstantial evidence suggests that the archetype of the collection was composed around 1140. The Harley manuscript was probably Cistercian, and the likely date of its composition was around 1170. The Troyes manuscript was also Cistercian, for it was written at Clairvaux, probably during the decade 1175–1185. The Avranches manuscript dates from the first quarter of the thirteenth century and was originally owned by the Benedictines of Mont-Saint-Michel. Monks, especially Cistercians, continued to collect sentences and to compile sentential treatises throughout the century, long after the more powerful technique of *quaestiones* had superseded *sententiae* in the urban schools. They probably favored the literature because it seemed safer and more conservative than the new modes of theological discourse that were beginning to emerge in the urban schools by the middle of the twelfth century, with their emphasis on questions, disputation, and problematic contradictions, and with their much greater interest in logic, speculative grammar, and metaphysics.

Little large-scale organization is discernable in the *Liber Pancrisis*, although the collection begins with creation and treats the resurrection toward the end, and sentences ascribed to the same author or on the same theme tend to cluster together, such as in the tractate on marriage described later. Some of the questions and sentences ascribed to William of Champeaux are arranged as sequences on the same topic, such as on the soul, suggesting that they had comprised a sustained inquiry in the original source.[14]

Aside from two *sententiae* about original sin and concupiscence that touch on marriage incidentally,[15] all of the material on marriage in the *Liber Pancrisis* is gathered into a single section.[16] This begins with a seminal treatise on marriage, the incipit of which is *De coniugiis tractantibus prius sunt videnda*.[17] Of the thirty-two sentences on marriage that follow, roughly half are patristic. The others are ascribed, not always plausibly, to Ivo or to Anselm of Laon.

8.1.2 *Miscellanies*

Sentences and sentential treatises have been preserved in miscellanies as well as in florilegia. The distinction cannot be sharply drawn, but a miscellany as the term is understood here is the result of haphazard, opportunistic gathering. The result is akin to a modern scrapbook. A florilegium, in contrast, is the result of a more or less

---

[13] Giraud, *Per verba magistri*, 203–11.

[14] Compare the sentences, all ascribed to William, in MS Harley 3098, 35v–37v, LP 107–117 (= PM 247, 249, 257, 248, 254, 252, 250, 267, 259, 260, 244). The phrase "Rursus consequenter quaeritur," which introduces LP 114 (PM 267), suggests the *sententiae* came from a sustained, linear inquiry.

[15] LP 123 (PM 255), Harley 3098, 39r, ascribed to William; and Augustine, LP 75, Harley 3098, 24r–v, = *De peccatorum meritis et remissione et de baptismo parvulorum* I.29(57), CSEL 60:56/ 1–18.

[16] LP 255–287, Harley 3098, 72r–78v.   [17] LP 255–256, 72r–73v.

deliberate effort to gather together all of the most relevant material from a certain author or group of authors, or on a certain topic or range of topics, as if to save readers from the trouble of poring over a library of books: an expensive, cumbersome, and often inaccessible resource during the Middle Ages. Miscellanies were rarely copied, therefore, whereas florilegia are often extant in several manuscripts, which diverged as their scribes continued to gather material.

Two miscellanies composed during the third quarter of the twelfth century illustrate the salient features of the medium and have proved to be important sources of sentential material in modern research. Both are Laudian manuscripts preserved in the Bodleian Library: MSS Laud misc. 277 and 216. The former was apparently written by the Benedictine monks of Durham cathedral,[18] whereas an inscription on the first page of the latter – *Liber Sanctae Mariae de Kyrkesta* – identifies it as coming from the Cistercian abbey dedicated to St Mary at Kirkstall, on the River Aire in Yorkshire (now just outside Leeds). Odon Lottin analyzed both miscellanies in 1947,[19] and Richard Southern has used them recently as evidence for the methods and preoccupations of Anselm of Laon.[20] The two miscellanies are similar in scope and method, although there is more biblical material in the Kirkstall than in the Durham miscellany.

The first item in the Durham miscellany is a compilation with the incipit *Principium et causa omnium* (2ra–23vb).[21] It includes treatises on God and creation, on Paradise and fall, on natural and written law, on faith, hope, and charity, on blasphemy, on Noah, on circumcision, and on providence and predestination. The next item is an important treatise on marriage, which I shall refer to as *Cum omnia sacramenta II*. It is ascribed here to Hugh of Paris (i.e., Hugh of Saint-Victor), presumably because someone noticed that passages from his treatise occur also in Hugh's *De sacramentis christianae fidei*. (In fact, Hugh was dependent on *Cum omnia sacramenta II*.) Next come three sentences on marriage that are extant in other sources.[22] These deal respectively with the betrothal distinction,[23] with impotence as grounds for divorce, and with whether marrying in the earthly Paradise was a matter of precept (cf. Gen 1:28).[24]

---

[18] See H. O. Coxe, *Laudian Manuscripts*, with corrections by R. W. Hunt (Oxford, 1973), 227–29. An addition by Hunt (p. 227) identifies the codex as being "from Durham."

[19] O. Lottin, "Nouveaux fragments théologiques de l'école de Laon: Deux manuscrits d'Oxford," *RThAM* 14 (1947): 5–31.

[20] Southern, *Scholastic Humanism*, 2:39–43.

[21] This compilation is initially identical with but later diverges from the compilation that Bliemetzrieder edited as the *Sententiae Anselmi* (BGPhMA 18.2–3, pp. 47–153), which has the same incipit.

[22] These are NF 509, 510, and 13 (= PM 402) in the numeration of Lottin's "Nouveaux fragments."

[23] F.-L. Ganshof, "Note sur deux textes de droit canonique dans le *Liber Floridus*," in *Études d'histoire du droit canonique* 1:99–115, at 108n32, notes a dozen other witnesses to this *sententia*.

[24] On NF 509 and 510, see Lottin, "Nouveaux fragments . . . Deux manuscrits d'Oxford," *RThAM* 14, at 6n6; and A. Wilmart, "Une rédaction française de Sentences dites d'Anselme de Laon," *RThAM* 11 (1939): 119–44, at 129–30, nos. 19 and 20. The two *sententiae* occur as a pair in

Shortly after these sentences and some other, less interesting material (27vb–28rb), there is a break of about two thirds of a column, after which the Durham manuscript begins again on a new page. There follows a long, florilegium-like sequence composed of many modern sentences and a few sentential treatises (28va–78vb). The first forty-eight of the sentences are notable because the same series, with a few minor variations, occurs also in the Kirkstall miscellany.[25] This florilegium-like passage includes several sentences on marriage, which deal respectively with the following topics: whether there can be a true marriage between infidels; the impediment of fraud; whether Jews and Gentiles (infidels) can truly marry; whether the respective positions of Augustine and Leo on the marriage of adulterers can be reconciled; the betrothal distinction; the dissolubility of the very rule by which marriage is indissoluble; procreation and the avoidance of fornication as the two chief reasons for marrying; and impotence as grounds for divorce.[26] Next come three sacramental treatises, respectively on marriage (*In coniugio figura*), on eucharist (ascribed to Bernard of Clairvaux), and on baptism, which apparently belong to the same florilegium-like sequence.[27] There follow selections from Walter of Mortagne, Hugh of Saint-Victor, and others, until the codex is full.

Six main sections are discernable in the Kirkstall miscellany (Laud misc. 216), although there seems to have been no preconceived plan. The first section (2r–133v) includes texts from Jerome, Ambrose, Augustine, and Gregory the Great, as well a series of biblical glosses that are ascribed in the codex to Anselm of Laon (107rb–108ra). These Anselmian glosses are extant also in some traditions of the *Glossa ordinaria*. Next, beginning on a fresh page, there is a florilegium-like section that includes the series of sentences common to both manuscripts (134r–141vb), noted earlier. The third and fourth sections, each of which begins on a fresh page, include glosses on Scripture as well as theological and canonical sentences (142ra–149vb, 150ra–154ra). The fifth section consists of excerpts from Isidore's *Etymologies* (154vb ff.), and the sixth of excerpts from patristic authors and from Bede (160r ff.).

---

several other manuscripts, and usually immediately after the *Cum omnia sacramenta II*, as they do here. They occur together and after *Cum omnia sacramenta II* in MS Vat. Reg. 241, too, but not *immediately* after it.

[25] Lottin, "Nouveaux fragments ... Deux manuscrits d'Oxford," 7–8. The first *sententia* in the common series is NF 398 (PM 302), and the last is NF 422 (PM 178).

[26] These are in order of (non-contiguous) appearance: NF 502 (PM 131), on the marriage of unbelievers; NF 133, on the impediment of fraud; NF 187 (PM 406), on the marriage of unbelievers; NF 182 (PM 67), on the marriage of adulterers; NF 183 (PM 207), on the betrothal distinction; NF 50 (PM 408), on the solubility of insolubility; NF 437 (PM 401), on procreation and the avoidance of fornication as the reasons for marrying; NF 221, on impotence as grounds for divorce; and NF 58 (PM 208), on the marriage of unbelievers.

[27] The correspondence to treatises in the compilation that Bliemetzrieder edited as the *Sententiae Anselmi* (BGPhMA 18.2–3) is as follows: *In coniugio figura* (52vb–53rb) = *Sententiae Anselmi* 5 (pp. 112–13); *De sacramento altaris* (54ra–54vb) = *Sententiae Anselmi* 7 (pp. 115–20); the treatise on baptism (54vb–55rb) = parts of *Sententiae Anselmi* 6 (pp. 113–15), but in a different order.

The third of the six sections listed above in the Kirkstall miscellany includes some sentences and biblical glosses that have not been found elsewhere. One of them explains the difference between the natural law and the "law of benevolence":[28] an important distinction that the *magistri moderni* apply elsewhere to reconcile Augustine and Leo on whether adulterers can marry after the death of the injured party, as well as to explain why the rules and impediments of marriage have changed and ramified with each phase of sacred history. Glosses on 1 Corinthians 5:9 and 6:18 explain the two modes of fornication, respectively carnal and spiritual, and their effects.[29] A gloss on 1 Corinthians 6:16 and a closely related *sententia* distinguish between the moral and carnal dimensions of becoming one flesh with a prostitute.[30] And a gloss on 1 Corinthians 7:9 ("it is better to marry than to burn") distinguishes between avoidable and unavoidable sexual desire. If the desire is unavoidable, then it is better to marry than to burn, for marrying is good whereas being burned up by lust is evil. But avoidable desire is not a proper reason for choosing marriage over celibacy, for it can be restrained and mastered by virtuous effort.[31]

Richard Southern argues that the two miscellanies must have been dependent on a common source, and that it is "virtually certain" that this common source was "a collection of notes which had been brought to the north of England by a student on his return from the schools of northern France." Southern argues that this student must have gone to Laon, and not to the schools of Paris, because "his material is heavily weighted with sentences attributed to Anselm of Laon and his brother Ralph. This points to a date," Southern argues, "between about 1115 and 1117." Southern summarizes what he calls the "substantial part of the material in these two closely related manuscripts which is attributed to Master Anselm."[32] But aside from some biblical glosses none of the modern sentences is ascribed in these miscellanies to Anselm or to anyone else, although some are ascribed to Anselm in other sources. The proposition that the common source was a collection of notes brought back from France by a student is plausible and interesting, but it is hardly "virtually certain." There is no way of knowing whence the English monks gathered this material.

8.1.3 *The School of Laon?*

Although the modern master whose name appears most frequently in the sentential literature is Anselm of Laon, most of the sentences are not ascribed to anyone. By my very rough reckoning, of the approximately 550 modern (i.e., contemporaneous) sentences that have been edited or documented, including minor monothematic treatises and biblical glosses that circulated independently, roughly two thirds are

---

[28] NF 474 (PM 339).   [29] NF 470 (PM 124), on 1 Cor 5:9. NF 472 (PM 128), on 1 Cor 6:18.
[30] NF 471 (PM 127), NF 476 (PM 468).   [31] NF 473 (PM 129).
[32] Southern, *Scholastic Humanism* 2:39–40.

unattributed, whereas 18% are ascribed to Anselm in one or more witnesses, 7% to William, and 5% to Ivo. Sometimes the same *sententia* is ascribed to different masters in different manuscripts, even to both ancient and modern masters, but the number of these multiple ascriptions is too small to factor into this rough estimate.

Although other schools were active during the period of Laon's flourishing, such as those at Paris and Reims, the prevalence of Anselm's name among the minority of ascribed sentences is not surprising. He was the most highly regarded master of sacred doctrine during the early twelfth century. Ambitious young men from all over Europe came to study with him at Laon, and some of his pupils composed eulogies about him after his death.[33] Abelard's derisory account of Anselm's teaching testifies ironically to his master's contemporaneous prowess. Too many modern researchers have accepted Abelard's evaluation uncritically.[34]

Modern research into the sentential literature began with in the 1890s with the work of Georges Lefèvre. Drawing chiefly on the *Liber Pancrisis* in Troyes 425 but supplementing this source with other manuscripts, Lefèvre edited sentences ascribed in his sources to Anselm of Laon, to Ralph, and to William of Champeaux.[35] In 1917, Bliemetzrieder published sentences ascribed (often implausibly) to Ivo of Chartres in the *Liber Pancrisis* (Troyes 425) and in the Avranches redaction,[36] but it was chiefly Anselm who attracted twentieth-century scholars to the sentential literature, for he was a famous master lacking his own corpus of writings. In 1929, Franz Bliemetzrieder published a critical summary of work on sentences ascribed to Anselm and to William of Champeaux in an effort to illumine the contribution of the former and the relationship between these two masters.[37] From the beginning, therefore, research on the sentential literature was motivated chiefly by the desire to establish a corpus of texts for masters of the late eleventh and early twelfth centuries: especially those, such as Anselm, who had left no books or treatises under their name. Thus began the modern School of Laon.

In the early days of this promising new area of research, scholars emphasized the level of systematization in the sentential literature, seeking at Laon the beginnings of the quasi-historical plan of emanation and return that would later be the framework for Peter Lombard's *Sentences* and for the great *summas* of the thirteenth and

---

[33] J. Ghellinck, "The Sentences of Anselm of Laon and Their Place in the Codification of Theology during the XIIth century," *Irish Theological Quarterly* 6 (1911): 427–41, at 427. Giraud, *Per verba magistri*, 70–75.

[34] Peter Abelard, *Historia calamitatum*, ed. Monfrin (Paris, 1978), p. 68. Abelard, who was a student at Laon during 1113, likened Anselm to a fire that produced smoke without heat and to a tree that was rich in foliage but bore no fruit.

[35] G. Lefèvre, *Anselmi Laudunensis et Radulfi fratris eius Sententias excerptas* (Évreux, 1895); idem, *De Anselmo Laudunensi Scholastico* (1050–1117), diss., Faculté des lettres de Paris (Évreux, 1895); idem, *Les variations de Guillaume de Champeaux* (Lille, 1898).

[36] F. P. Bliemetzrieder, *Zu den Schriften Ivos von Chartres* (Vienna, 1917).

[37] F. P. Bliemetzrieder, "Autour de l'oeuvre théologique d'Anselme de Laon," RThAM 1 (1929): 435–83.

fourteenth centuries.[38] In 1911, Joseph de Ghellinck critically assessed the level of systematization in the *Liber Pancrisis* and in comparable collections, concluding that it was modest and still relatively primitive.[39] Nevertheless, when Franz Bliemetzrieder published editions of two compilations of treatises in 1917, which he entitled the *Sententiae divinae paginae* and the *Sententiae Anselmi* respectively, he described them as "systematic sentences."[40] In a survey of work on the sentential literature published in 1947, René Silvain went so far as to claim that the "merit of the *Sentences* of Anselm of Laon consists in the systematic exposition of the entirety of Catholic doctrine."[41]

The plan of Bliemetzrieder's edition of the *Sententiae Anselmi* is remarkably similar to that of Peter Lombard's *Sentences*, but researchers soon realized that this design was the result of later compilation, probably done during the second half of the twelfth century. Moreover, in his quest to reconstruct a forgotten systematic theology, Bliemetzrieder rearranged his material to enhance its organization without warning his readers. The eleven treatises of his edition discuss God, creation, redemption, the fear of God, marriage (*In coniugio figura*), baptism, eucharist, penance, simony, marriage again (*Cum omnia sacramenta*), and the Last Things, in that order. But in the manuscript that Bliemetzrieder used as his base text (Heiligenkreuz, Cod. lat. 236), the sequence is less orderly: God, creation, penance, creation again, redemption, marriage (*In coniugio figura*), baptism, eucharist, the fear of God, the Last Things, simony, and marriage again (*Cum omnia sacramenta*).[42] To enhance the organization of the treatise, Bliemetzrieder united the two sections on creation and moved the treatise on the Last Things to the end.

Throughout the first half of the twentieth century, several distinguished scholars – most notably Weisweiler, Wilmart, Stegmüller, and, above all, Lottin – described and edited sentences and sentential treatises that they found in manuscripts. The chief attraction motivating this valuable effort was always Anselm and his presumed school. Lottin published a series of articles between 1939 and 1947 (with a hiatus during the war years) under the general title, "Nouveaux fragments théologiques de l'école d'Anselme de Laon." The articles included a numbered catalogue of no less than 580 items, including treatises as well sentences, with editions of those texts (the majority) which had not already been published elsewhere.[43] Lottin reproduced

---

[38] See M. Colish, "Another Look at the School of Laon," AHDLMA 53 (1986): 7–22, at 8–10.

[39] J. Ghellinck, "The Sentences of Anselm of Laon and Their Place in the Codification of Theology during the XIIth century," *Irish Theological Quarterly* 6 (1911): 427–41.

[40] F. P. Bliemetzrieder, *Anselms von Laon systematische Sentenzen*, = BGPhMA 18.2–3 (1919).

[41] R. Silvain, "La tradition des Sentences d'Anselme de Laon," AHDLMA 16 (1947–48): 1–52, at 17 (my translation).

[42] Wilmart, "Une rédaction française," 120–21. Heiligenkreuz (Sancta Crux) is a Cistercian abbey in what is now Austria, founded in 1133.

[43] RThAM 11 (1939): 242–59 [NF 1–15], 305–323 [NF 16–21]; 12 (1940): 49–77 [NF 52–120]; 13 (1946): 185–201 [NF 121–258], 202–21 [NF 259–329], 261–81 [NF 330–97]; 14 (1947): 5–31 [NF 398–491], 157–85 [NF 492–580]. All but one of these articles have the same main heading, "Nouveaux fragments théologiques de l'école d'Anselme de Laon." Each article has a subtitle

most of this material with new numeration in the fifth volume of his *Psychologie et morale* (1959), subtitled *L'école d'Anselme de Laon et de Guillaume de Champeaux*. Here, Lottin sorted the texts into four categories according to their authorship and authenticity: Anselm of Laon's authentic sentences; sentences whose attribution to Anselm is probable, plausible, or merely possible; sentences of William of Champeaux; and sentences of the school of Anselm and William.

When it became apparent that neither the systematization nor much of the content of compilations such as Bliemetzrieder's *Sententiae Anselmi* could be attributed to Anselm, scholars began to speak of the "School of Laon." Even Bliemetzrieder later conceded that the author of the *Sententiae Anselmi* was probably not Anselm himself but one of his disciples.[44] But it has never been clear what kind of historical entity the School of Laon is supposed to have been. Scholars posit it to account for family traits in the literature by associating them with Anselm's work at Laon. Although some have equated the School of Laon with Anselm's disciples, most have interpreted the connection more generously, even nebulously, as a milieu, leaving the material basis of Anselm's presumed influence undefined.[45]

In an important article published in 1976, Valerie Flint questioned the existence and even the meaning of the School of Laon. Distinguishing the School of Laon in modern scholarship from the historical cathedral school *at* Laon, Flint contended that using the phrase "School of Laon" to embrace "a whole phase of biblical and theological enquiry" was "inadmissible."[46] Flint argued that there was no way to correlate historically what was known about practices and pedagogy at Laon with the traits of the sentential literature. She proposed instead a functional approach, setting the literature in the context of a movement of pastoral reform that involved monks as well as schoolmen. A decade after Flint's article appeared, Marcia Colish complained that Flint had overreacted and that Flint's "historical agnosticism" was unwarranted.[47] Yet Colish proposed no argument that would link the literature as a whole to Anselm or to Laon. Instead, assuming that there had been such a connection, Colish pursued, like Flint, a functional analysis. Cédric Giraud has recently shown how the School of Laon can be defended against Flint's specific

designating the source or a class of manuscripts, except for the last, of which the subtitle is "Conclusions et Tables." RThAM 13 (1946): 185–201, belongs to the same series but is entitled, "Pour une édition critique du *Liber Pancrisis*."

[44] F. P. Bliemetzrieder, "Théologie et théologiens de l'école épiscopale de Paris avant Pierre Lombard," RThAM 3 (1931): 273–91, at 289; idem, "L'oeuvre d'Anselme de Laon et la littérature théologique contemporaine," RThAM 7 (1935): 28–51, at 47. On the possible authorship of the compilation, see C. Giraud, "Le recueil de sentences de l'école de Laon *Principium et causa*: Un cas de pluri-attribution," in M. Goullet, *Parva pro magnis munera* (Turnhout, 2009), 245–69.

[45] Andrée, "Laon Revisited," 266, summarizing Giraud, *Per verba magistri*, 389–436, defines the School of Laon as "the scholarly milieu where, during the 1120s–1140s, various collections of sentences were compiled under the doctrinal influence of the teaching of Master Anselm."

[46] V. I. J. Flint, "The 'School of Laon': A Reconsideration," RThAM 43 (1976): 89–110, at 90.

[47] M. L. Colish, "Another Look at the School of Laon," 11.

objections, and he has plausibly traced the likely routes and content of Anselm's influence, but his argument, too, presupposes that there was such an influence, which would account for the family resemblances.[48] In general, proponents of the School of Laon do not demonstrate but rather tacitly presuppose Anselm's influence.[49]

In my own view, the broad outlines of Flint's critique remain sound. As far as I can see, no one has made a convincing positive case for attributing the family traits of the sentential literature exclusively or even principally to Anselm or to Laon. Even if one accepted that all the sentences ascribed to Anselm were truly his, he would remain a vague and shadowy figure. We would still not know enough about his doctrines, idiom, and methods of inquiry and argument to distinguish him from his contemporaries. Laon's role in the glossed Bible is more firmly established, but even so the nature and extent of Anselm's personal contribution remains unclear.[50]

The origins of the sentential literature, therefore, remain obscure. We do not know how or in what circumstances or by whom the early collections and treatises were made, and we have to assume that much of the extant literature is already at several removes from those origins. Nor do we known how the medieval sentences were first articulated and written down. Were they, too, an essentially written medium, or did they result, like the later *quaestiones disputatae*, from pedagogical performance? There is probably no single correct answer to that question, although a much-discussed anecdote in Peter Abelard's *Historia calamitatum* may be a unique record of the *sententia* as an academic exercise. The story begins with Abelard and his fellow students at Laon chatting and joking after attending some "conferences of sentences" (*sententiarum collationes*). They argue about the merits of Master Anselm's expositions (*lectiones*) of Scripture, and Abelard claims that any scholar should be able to expound even the most difficult books of the Bible for himself, using glosses and commentaries, but without slavishly adhering to received authority (*magisterium*).[51] Abelard had grown weary of Anselm's ponderous biblical lectures and was no longer attending them, but it seems that he was still attending the *sententiarum collationes*. Sadly, Abelard does not explain what these conferences

---

[48] Giraud, *Per verba magistri*, 389–405.

[49] Compare J. C. Wei, "The Sentence Collection *Deus non habet initium vel terminum* and its Reworking, *Deus itaque summe atque ineffabiliter bonus*," *Mediaeval Studies* 73 (2011): 1–118, at 33–37. Wei cites parallels with six *sententiae* to establish the likely presence of "Anselm and his school" in the compilation, but only one of these *sententiae* is ascribed to Anselm in the sources. The other five are ascribed to William of Champeaux, regarded here as a student of Anselm. But there is no reason to suppose that William owed these ideas more to Anselm than to his own initiative.

[50] A. Andrée, "Anselm of Laon Unveiled," *Mediaeval Studies* 73 (2011): 217–60, argues that the *Glosae super Iohannem* may, indeed, be Anselm's work. But Andrée, "Laon Revisited," 270–75, is critical of modern scholarly assumptions regarding Anselm's contributions to the *Glossa ordinaria*.

[51] Peter Abelard, *Historia calamitatum*, ed. J. Monfrin (Paris, 1967), 68–69.

were, leaving modern scholars to make educated guesses.[52] Moreover, even if sentences were the medium of an academic exercise at Laon, there is no reason to trace the literature as a whole to that particular exercise or to any known pedagogical performance of the period.

8.1.4 *The sentential literature as literature*

Preoccupation with the School of Laon in modern research emphasizes authors, performance, theories, doctrines, and doctrinal influences, but the twelfth-century scholars and scribes who wrote down the sentences were above all avid collectors. Many of the sentences are patristic, and most of the modern (i.e., medieval) sentences are anonymous. The literary effort was closely related to the ancient tradition of the florilegium: the "posy" of choice items picked (*deflorata*) from other literature. The effort was also akin to the addition of marginal and interlinear glosses to Scripture, which flourished during the same period, but whereas the accumulated glosses were arranged in linear fashion beside the sacred text, the sentences stood on their own and could be arranged to suit a collector's interests.[53]

Nevertheless, the medium itself reveals something about its purpose. The *sententia* is a discrete, self-contained statement, expressing unequivocally a certain position on an issue or a certain answer to a question, which is presented more for rational reflection than for pious meditation. Many of the sentences, especially the patristic ones, are formative, potentially seminal statements, likely to guide thought and stimulate reflection. Freed from context, narrative, rhetoric, sustained argument, and the context and multiple senses of Scripture, the sentences invited medieval scholars to assess different answers to the same question, and they held the promise of coherent, straightforward explanations. One may observe the rational energy of the sentences at work in the sentential treatises. These were not a later development, although they occupy a higher level of organization. The collecting of material into florilegia and the composition of sentential treatises were different modalities of a single effort.

Scholars have remarked that the sentential literature is more practical and less speculative than other scholastic work of the twelfth century.[54] The observation is sound, but the focus of the literature is not exclusively pastoral. Much of the literature seems to have been designed to provide clergy with the material that they

---

[52] Clanchy, *Abelard*, 85, suggests that Abelard was referring to a "discussion of prescribed texts, the equivalent of a seminar." Southern, *Scholastic Humanism*, 2:45–46, suggests that the *collationes* were informal discussions that took place in the evening, and that they were related to the evening *collationes* of the Benedictine tradition, which usually took place in the brief free period before Compline.

[53] See L. Smith, *The Glossa Ordinaria* (Leiden, 2009), for a survey of work on the origins of the glossed Bible.

[54] "School of Laon," 100–07. D. E. Luscombe, *The School of Peter Abelard* (Cambridge, 1969), 173.

would need for doctrinal as well as pastoral instruction of the laity, enabling them to corroborate orthodox doctrines with explanations sufficient to allay doubt and to satisfy curiosity. Nevertheless, the authors speculate about reasons and causes, displaying an inquisitive spirit and a desire to resolve contradictory evidence, although their methods seem rudimentary and restrained by the standards of later scholasticism. For example, a *sententia* ascribed to Anselm in the *Liber Pancrisis* asks whether evil persons can prophesy by means of the Holy Spirit. In a few lines, the author reviews the relevant authorities, which seem contradictory. He wants to affirm that all prophecy depends on the Holy Spirit, but he also wants to allow that evil persons can prophesy in some sense, and it seems illogical to suppose that they too are inspired by the Holy Spirit. The author solves the problem by making some causal distinctions. The Holy Spirit may bestow the gift of prophecy upon a person either (1) only because of the dignity of his office (*ex officio*) regardless of his merits, or (2) only because he leads a good life, or (3) for both reasons. Caiaphas prophesied in the first way (John 11:51–52), Elias in the second, and Jeremiah in the third. There are also those, such as the Sybil, who prophesy not by the Holy Spirit but by a "phitonic spirit,"[55] but even they do so with the permission or at the prompting of the Holy Spirit.[56]

The chief difficulty facing any scholar working with the sentential literature is the distance between the literary genre or medium, which is plain to see, and the intellectual culture that gave rise to it, which remains largely unknown. One should not assume that there was a single underlying culture. The literature probably testifies to two related but separable activities: a widespread practice of gathering, collecting, and compiling texts, which resulted in many florilegia and miscellanies; and certain pedagogical practices in the cathedral schools of the early twelfth century, perhaps especially the school at Laon. Very little evidence regarding those practices has survived. Moreover, as noted earlier, the habit of collecting sentences continued throughout the twelfth century, among monks as well as among the masters and students of the schools. The customary ascription of the sentential literature as a whole to the so-called School of Laon, including the unattributed sentences and the anonymous treatises, fulfills a natural human need to reduce texts to authors but is not warranted by any evidence.

8.2 THE SENTENTIAL LITERATURE ON MARRIAGE

The sentential literature on marriage includes patristic florilegia, specialized treatises, and a few free-standing sentences.

---

[55] The term *phitonicus* is a medieval variant or corruption of *pythonicus* ("pertaining to Pytho [i.e., Delphi]"). Medieval authors associate the *spiritus phitonicus* with divination and magic.
[56] LP 168 (MS British Library, Harley 1098, 51v). PM 83 (p. 72).

8.2.1 *Independent modern sentences*

Among the several hundred independent modern sentences (as distinct from treatises) that Odon Lottin collected in the fifth volume of his *Psychologie et morale*,
only some two-dozen are about marriage. Several are interesting and supplement the
evidence of the treatises, but one could not construct any theory of marriage from
these sources alone. The following are the most significant:

- A *sententia* on why infants are incapable of consenting to marriage.
  Ascribed both to Anselm and, in the *Liber Pancrisis*, to Ivo. (PM 206.
  LP 263, Harley MS 75r.)
- A *sententia* on procreation and the avoidance of fornication as the proper
  reasons for marrying. Unattributed. (PM 401)
- A *sententia* on the three institutions of marriage, pertaining respectively
  to the blessing of the first couple in Paradise, to the precepts of Moses
  and the Apostles, and to the teachings of the "holy fathers" (i.e., the post-
  apostolic bishops). Unattributed. (PM 404)
- A *sententia* on whether marrying was a matter of precept in the begin-
  ning, before the first sin. Unattributed. (PM 402)
- A *sententia* on the two kinds of troth: *fides pactionis* and *fides consensus*.
  Ascribed to Anselm in MS Paris, Arsenal 93 (138r), to Ivo in the *Liber
  Pancrisis* (LP 268, Harley MS 75v), and unattributed in MS Oxford,
  Bodleian, Laud. misc. 277 (42vb–43ra). (PM 207)
- Three sentences on whether the marriage of Jews or infidels is truly
  marriage. Unattributed. (PM 130, 131, 208)
- A record of a disagreement between Anselm and William of Champeaux
  as to whether Jews and infidels can truly marry, with Anselm holding the
  stricter view: that a marriage between unbelievers is invalid. Variously
  ascribed to Ivo, to William, and Anselm. (PM 406, = LP 265; LP 266; MS
  Harley 3098, 76r–v)
- A *sententia* on the subordination of wives to their husbands. Unattributed. (PM 133)
- Sentences on whether adulterers can marry each other after the death of
  the injured party, and on how one can reconcile the apparently contradictory positions of Augustine and Leo on this question. Usually ascribed
  to Anselm, although some witnesses are unattributed. (PM 66 and 67.
  See also PM 409, on a related Old Testament case.)
- A *sententia* on the impediments of consanguinity. Unattributed.
  (PM 407)
- A *sententia* explaining how the precept that marriages cannot be
  dissolved is itself soluble. Unattributed. (PM 408)

Aside from questions about the marriage of unbelievers, these independent modern sentences on marriage provide us with few grounds for attributing any particular thesis or doctrine to Anselm of Laon or to his influence. Perhaps Anselm took a rigorist view of the marriage and infidels (PM 406), and perhaps he reconciled the positions of Augustine and Leo regarding the marriage of adulterers by distinguishing between the natural law and the law of benevolence (PM 66, 67). I have argued earlier (Section 5.5.1) that the evidence for attributing any version of the betrothal distinction to Anselm of Laon or to William of Champeaux is at best very weak.

8.2.2 *Florilegia*

Most of the sentential treatises on marriage were dependent on one or other of two patristic florilegia: the *Sententiae Magistri A.* and the *In primis hominibus.*[57] Both include material gathered from the canons of church councils and from papal decretals as well as from the church Fathers and the Carolingian moralists.

8.2.2.1 Sententiae Magistri A

This florilegium is recognizable as complete in at least ten extant manuscripts, and several other manuscripts contain parts of it. The earliest extant version of the collection was probably complete by the mid-1120s.[58] The collection exists in several versions or branches, each of which continued to grow as it gathered material over many years. Pauline Maas observes that it is impossible to reconstruct a basic text from the witnesses because almost every manuscript of the collection has its own history.[59] For the same reason, it is difficult to assign a precise date to the collection. Nevertheless, its dependence on Ivo of Chartres, on the one hand, and its influence on named authors of the 1130s and 1140s, on the other hand, adequately situate it for present purposes in the first quarter of the twelfth century.

We do not know who collected these sentences. The title by which the florilegium is known in modern scholarship comes from the explicit in a single Paris manuscript: "Here ends the book of sentences of Master A."[60] Anselm of Laon has been proposed as the likely author, but that is only a guess. A marginal note in a Cambridge manuscript and a corresponding catalogue entry refer to the work as the "Compilations of Ailmerus."[61] He may have been the Elmer who

---

[57] On the marriage tract of the *Liber Pancrisis*, see Section 8.1.1.

[58] P. H. J. Th. Maas, *The Liber Sententiarum Magistri A.: Its Place amidst the Sentences Collections of the First Half of the 12th Century* (Nijmegen, 1995), 217–18.

[59] Ibid., 219

[60] MS Paris, BnF Cod. lat. 3881, 230r: "Explicit liber sententiarum magistri A."

[61] MS Cambridge, New Univ. Library Ii.4.19, 29r: "Quidam liber scientialis et sacramentalis. Compilationes Ailmeri. Liber bonus et catholicus." As Maas points out, this use of a personal name in the genitive case does not necessarily mean that Elmer was the compiler. It might

was prior of the Benedictine community of Christ Church in Canterbury from 1128 to 1137.[62]

The *Sententiae Magistri A.* is divided topically into several tractates (i.e., groups of texts on a particular topics), one of which begins, *Quid sit matrimonium?*[63] The material of this tractate, as of the others, is presented without comment or topical headings, but each *sententia* is headed by a rubric identifying the source and the topic, for example: "Augustine in the Book on Virginity," "Augustine on the Baptism of Children," "The Same against Julian."

Although there is little discernable topical organization within the marriage tract, the more theological material, much of it from Augustine, comes before the bulk of the canonical material on the rules and regulations. Nicholas Haring observes that the *Sententiae Magistri A.* as a whole was "composed to fill certain gaps left by Ivo of Chartres."[64] The tractate on marriage includes many canonical texts taken from Ivo, which already include several texts from Augustine, but to these the collector has added a continuous series of hitherto unfamiliar excerpts from Augustine's works, probably taken from an Augustinian florilegium.[65] This material pertains mainly to the three goods of marriage and to the changing function of marriage in relation to the chief phases of sacred history: the earthly Paradise, the fall of Adam and Eve, and the incarnation of Jesus Christ. Much of this theological material is from Augustine's *De bono coniugali* and *De nuptiis et concupiscentia*. A smaller but still considerable amount is from the *De sancta virginitate* and the *De Genesi ad litteram*. There are just a few excerpts from other works by Augustine, such as *De bono viduitatis*, *Enchiridion*, *De peccatorum meritis*, *Contra Iulianum*, and *Epist.* 187.

8.2.2.2 In primis hominibus

This is a florilegium devoted entirely to marriage.[66] It was probably composed, like the *Sententiae Magistri A.*, in the 1120s. The collector seems to have taken at least

---

mean that he was the copyist, the donor, the previous owner, or the person who brought the collection to England.

[62] Maas, *Liber Sententiarum Magistri A.*, 197–206.

[63] Ed. H. J. F. Reinhardt, *Die Ehelehre der Schule des Anselms von Laon*, BGPhThM n.F. 14 (Münster, 1974), 167 ff. Maas (cited above) edits the "dogmatic parts" of the SMA, including the sections on the Trinity, the angels, the creation of human beings, the fall, and original sin. Several other passages from the SMA have been edited elsewhere: see Maas, 33. G. Fransen, in *Revue théologique de Louvain* 9 (1978): 202–04, points out some defects in Reinhardt's edition.

[64] N. M. Haring, "The *Sententie Magistri A.* (Vat. Ms lat. 4361) and the School of Laon," *Mediaeval Studies* 17 (1955): 1–45, at 2.

[65] Most of this material appears in a continuous series: SMA 16–59 in Reinhardt's numeration (pp. 169–85). Next (SMA 60–62) come the three coital proof texts discussed above (6.2). Thereafter the collection returns to the standard canonical material.

[66] Ed. B. Matecki, *Der Traktat In primis hominibus* (Frankfurt am Main, 2001), pp. 1*–55*.

one *sententia* and probably more from the canon law compilation known as the *Collectio decem partium*,[67] which was composed in 1123 or shortly thereafter.

The *In primis hominibus* inhabits the same intellectual world as the marriage tractate of the *Sententiae Magistri A*. To a stock of material taken from canonical collections, especially Ivo of Chartres, the compiler has added sentences from Augustine on such topics as marriage before and after the fall, the three goods of marriage, the remedial value of the conjugal debt, and the possibility of a spiritual, non-carnal relationship in marriage. The fresh Augustinian material comes mainly from the *De Genesi ad litteram*, the *De nuptiis et concupiscentia*, the *De bono coniugali*, and the *De adulterinis coniugiis*. This collector, too, probably gathered the fresh sentences from an Augustinian florilegium.[68] Because the theological material is collected mainly in the first half of the *In primis hominibus*, whereas the remainder is dependent on canonical sources, the treatise appears to consist of two parts, respectively theological and canonical in emphasis.[69]

The collector of the *In primis hominibus* has inserted a few headings, questions, and glosses to help the reader, and he sometimes tries to reconcile contradictory sources. His aim was apparently not to put forward positions of his own but rather to alert the reader to uncertainties and problems of interpretation. A cleric who owned or had ready access to the collection would have had some incentives for reflection and debate as well as ample resources for ministry, legal counsel, and instruction of the laity.

8.2.3 *Treatises*

No western theologian since Augustine had written treatises devoted to exclusively to marriage. Moreover, whereas each of Augustine's works on marriage addressed a particular aspect or implication of the topic, the sentential treatises were manuals or compendia summarizing everything that the clergy needed to know about the subject. The only obvious precedent is the section on marriage in the *De institutione laicali* by Jonas of Orléans (d. 841/842) — especially the first chapter of the second book, much of which was incorporated into the *Cum omnia sacramenta I*.[70]

Most of the extant sentential treatises on marriage belong to two groups or families.[71] One group consists of the *De coniugiis tractantibus* and of treatises dependent both on that treatise and on the *Sententiae Magistri A*. These include

[67] Ibid., 24–85. The *sententia* in question is IPH 97 (p. 43*), ascribed to Pope Leo I, which belongs to the little dossier of coital texts. The *In primis hominibus* version of the canon differs from that of SMA 62 (p. 186), but it is the same as that of the *Collectio X partium*, in MS Vienna, Österreichische Nationalbibliothek Cod. lat. 2178, 129va.
[68] Matecki, 76. See the table on pp. 71–75, where Matecki identifies the material source (the original setting) and the likely formal source (the collector's source) of each *sententia*.
[69] R. Weigand, "Kanonistiche Ehetraktate aus dem 12. Jahrhundert," in S. Kuttner (ed.), *Proceedings of the Third International Congress of Medieval Canon Law* (Vatican City, 1971), 59–79, at 59–61; repr. in R. Weigand, *Liebe und Ehe im Mittelalter* (Goldbach, 1993), 37*–57*, at 37*–39*.
[70] PL 106:167–170.   [71] Reinhardt, *Ehelehre*, 10–39.

two recensions of the *Cum omnia sacramenta* (which I shall refer to *Cum omnia sacramenta I* and *Cum omnia sacramenta II*) and the *Decretum Dei fuit* (which, like *Cum omnia sacramenta II*, is dependent on *Cum omnia sacramenta I*). The other group consists of treatises dependent on the *In primis hominibus*.

8.2.3.1 De coniugiis tractantibus

This treatise survives in the *Liber Pancrisis* and in MS Avranches 19, as noted earlier, as well as in MS Paris, BnF Cod. lat. 3867[72] and MS Oxford, Bodleian Library, Douce 89 (95v–98r). Another manuscript containing the treatise – Paris, Bibliothèque Nationale 18113 – perished during the ravaging of Louvain in 1914, but most of its contents can be reconstructed from a description by Victor Cousin.[73] This was a miscellany that began with the words, "Here begin the sentences of William, bishop of Châlons-sur-Marne" (i.e., William of Champeaux). The first twenty-two folios of the lost miscellany contained a florilegium-like series of texts. Some were excerpts from patristic authors, mainly Augustine and Gregory. The others were apparently modern sentences and treatises, although most of these lacked individual ascriptions. Most of the modern items in this section of the lost codex, including the *De coniugiis tractantibus*, occur also in the *Liber Pancrisis*.[74]

There are two modern editions of the *De coniugiis tractantibus*. Georges Lefèvre included it in his edition of forty-seven texts ascribed to William of Champeaux, published in 1898. Lefèvre took his first forty-two items from the *Liber Pancrisis* (Troyes 425) and the remaining five from the Paris miscellany. Item 43 in this edition is the *De coniugiis tractantibus*, again taken from the Paris miscellany.[75] Bliemetzrieder published a new edition of the *De coniugiis tractantibus* in 1919, using the *Liber Pancrisis* (Troyes 425) as his base text but noting the

---

[72] G. Fransen, "Varia ex manuscriptis," *Traditio* 21 (1965): 515–20, at 517. The correct incipit is *De coniugiis tractantibus*, and not *De coniugiis tractandis*, as Fransen has it. The treatise begins: "De coniugiis tractantibus prius sunt consideranda illa tria bona...." ("Those discussing marriage should first consider the three goods....").

[73] V. Cousin, *Ouvrages inédits d'Abélard* (Paris, 1836), appendix 3, 625–27. Cousin knew the manuscript as Notre Dame 222. On the loss of the manuscript, see F.-L. Ganshof, "Note sur deux textes de droit canonique dans le *Liber Floridus*," in *Études d'histoire du droit canonique dédiées à Gabriel Le Bras*, vol. 1 (Paris, 1965), 99–115, at 106n25; and Reinhardt, *Ehelehre*, 79n26. According to Bliemetzrieder, the manuscript came from the abbey of St Peter at Châlons-sur-Marne: see *Anselms von Laon systematische Sentenzen*, 25*.

[74] The "modern" items in the Paris miscellany in order of appearance are as follows, with the numeration in Lefèvre's *Les variations de Guillaume de Champeaux* and the parallels (if any) in Lottin, PsM V and the *Liber Pancrisis*: A little treatise on simony (Lefèvre no. 18, PM 281, LP 88 27r–28v); the *De coniugiis tractantibus*, with its attached *sententia* on the spousal distinction (Lefèvre no. 43, LP 255 72r–74v); *sententiae* or minor treatises on original sin (Lefèvre no. 44, PM 331), prophecy (Lefèvre no. 45, PM 82, LP 163 49v–50r), charity (Lefèvre no. 46, PM 71 and 72, LP 201 61r–v), pride (Lefèvre no. 42, PM 279), and unintentional homicide (Lefèvre no. 47).

[75] *Les variations de Guillaume de Champeaux*, 68–74.

variants in Lefèvre's edition and in *Avranches 19*. This remains the standard edition today.[76]

On the strength of the general ascription at the beginning of the Paris miscellany, many scholars have attributed the *De coniugiis tractantibus* to William of Champeaux, as well as the *sententia* on the betrothal distinction that follows immediately after it in all the extant witnesses. But the grounds for ascribing the *De coniugiis tractantibus* to William are weak at best.[77] It is unattributed in the other witnesses, and some paragraphs within it are individually ascribed to Ivo of Chartres in the *Liber Pancrisis*, as if they were independent sentences. Moreover, although the section to which it belongs was described as the "sentences of William, bishop of Châlons-sur-Marne" (i.e., William of Champeaux) in the lost Paris miscellany, this section included patristic sentences. Even the compiler, therefore, did not mean to ascribe every item in the collection to William.

The *De coniugiis tractantibus* is a well-organized treatise. As the author explains in the preamble, the treatise covers five topics: (1) the three goods of marriage, as expounded by Augustine; (2) the various "institutions" of marriage that unfolded over time and their relationship to the three goods and to the impediments of relationship; (3) whether an illicit marriage that must be dissolved (e.g., on grounds of consanguinity) is nevertheless an existing marriage before it is dissolved, or rather is null and void; (4) the grounds for dissolving a marriage, and whether remarriage after divorce is permitted or forbidden; and (5) whether persons in the earthly Paradise were commanded or only permitted to marry and procreate. The five topics are interconnected, with each leading naturally to the next, and the threads of the first two run through the remainder.

8.2.3.2 Cum omnia sacramenta

This treatise is extant in several different versions. One version, which I shall refer to as *Cum omnia sacramenta I*, is included in the compilation that Bliemetzrieder edited under the title *Sententiae Anselmi*, which is also known today as the *Principium et causa omnium*.[78] Bliemetzrieder based his edition of the *Sententiae Anselmi* on the manuscript Heiligenkreuz, Cod. lat. 236. As already noted, he rearranged the order of the treatises so that the order approximates as closely as possible to that of Peter Lombard's *Sentences* and the later *summas* (Section 8.1.3).

---

[76] F. P. Bliemetzrieder, "Paul Fournier und das literarische Werk Ivos von Chartres," *Archiv für katholisches Kirchenrecht* 115 (1935): 53–91, at 73–78.

[77] Reinhardt, *Ehelehre*, 10–12, treats the work as anonymous.

[78] Bliemetzrieder, *Anselms von Laon systematische Sentenzen*, BGPhMA 18.2–3 (Münster, 1919), 129–51 (treatise 10). Bliemetzrieder's edition of the compilation is hard to follow because he severely abbreviated the patristic quotations with ellipses (...), presumably in an effort to save paper, for the publication appeared soon after the First World War.

I shall rely on Bliemetzrieder's edition of the *Cum omnia sacramenta I* here, although there are reasons to be cautious. Bliemetzrieder's base manuscript, Heiligenkreuz, Cod. lat. 236, peters out part of the way through the *Cum omnia sacramenta*, which was the last treatise in this source (albeit not in his edition, as already noted). For most of the remainder of the treatise, Bliemetzrieder used another manuscript as his base text: Vienna, Nationalbibl., Cod. lat. 584. He used a third manuscript (Paris, Mazarine, Cod. lat. 731) for the last dozen lines.[79]

The compilation that Bliemetzrieder called the *Sententiae Anselmi* had a complex history. Bliemetzrieder focused on manuscripts that originated in German-speaking regions, but kindred compilations with the same incipit have survived in manuscripts originating in England and in France, and their contents are not always the same.[80] The Heiligenkreuz version is one of a loose family of compilations that share the same incipit and the first two or three treatises but diverge thereafter. Some of these versions were in circulation by the middle years of the twelfth century, although Wilmart suggests that the Heiligenkreuz manuscript was written toward the end of the twelfth century, and not from the first half of the century as Bliemetzrieder supposed.[81]

Wilmart describes a different but related compilation, which is preserved in a French manuscript from the second half of the twelfth century (Vatican Library, Codices Reginenses latini, 241). Here, the first three treatises, respectively on God, creation, and redemption, are the same as the first three in Bliemetzrieder's *Sententiae Anselmi*, but neither the *Cum omnia sacramenta I* nor the treatises on baptism, eucharist, penance, and simony in Bliemetrieder's *Sententiae Anselmi* occur in the Vatican manuscript. Instead, after the three initial treatises, there is a loosely assembled tractate on marriage and, finally, a treatise on the Last Things. The tractate on marriage was composed from several sources: a different recension of the *Cum omnia sacramenta*, which I shall refer to as the *Cum omnia sacramenta II* (see later); the *In coniugio figura* (see later); and some two dozen independent sentences.[82]

The *Cum omnia sacramenta I* is more loosely organized than the *De coniugiis tractantibus*, but it is a longer and more ambitious work. The author sets out a plan at the beginning, promising to treat the following topics: (1) the origin of marriage; (2) the twofold institution of marriage, before and after sin, together with the manner of the different institutions, the reasons for them, and their relationship to the goods of marriage; (3) variations in marrying in respect of time, place, and ritual; (4) the grounds for dissolving marriage; and (5) whether divorced persons may remarry. This plan is discernable in what follows, but it is obscured by digressions and repetitions. Moreover, the many patristic sentences, most of which are from Augustine, tend to overwhelm any argument. The *Cum omnia sacramenta I* was dependent

---

[79] The transitions from one source to another occur at 144/13 and 151/11.
[80] Wilmart, "Une rédaction française," 119–21.   [81] Ibid., 120n6.   [82] Ibid., 123–32.

on the *De coniugiis tractantibus* but drew additional material from the *Sententiae Magistri A.*

Three other extant treatises are dependent on *Cum omnia sacramenta I.* Two have the same incipit, whereas the incipit of the third is *Decretum Dei fuit.*[83] Of the two treatises with the same incipit, one remains unedited, and I shall not refer to it again.[84] The other is the treatise that I shall call the *Cum omnia sacramenta II.* Through an accident of scholarship, the modern edition of this version of the *Cum omnia sacramenta* is divided between two publications.[85] In 1931, Bliemetzrieder published an edition of a treatise with the incipit *Coniugium est secundum Isidorum,* which begins with a definition of marriage ascribed (falsely) to Isidore.[86] But Weisweiler showed in 1936 that this was really another recension of the *Cum omnia sacramenta,* from which a short passage at the beginning was missing. (Isidore's definition occurs in both recensions, and it marks a natural break in the discourse.) Internal evidence suggests that the two parts originally belonged together. Moreover, the complete text of this recension has survived in several sources.[87] Rather than duplicating Bliemetzrieder's work, Weisweiler edited only the beginning of the treatise, since it was missing from Bliemetzrieder's edition.[88] One needs to use Weisweiler's edition for the beginning, therefore, and then Bliemetzrieder's edition for the rest. Internal evidence shows that this recension of the *Cum omnia sacramenta* is dependent on the recension that Bliemetzieder included in his *Sententiae Anselmi* (the *Cum omnia sacramenta I*) and not the other way around, as Bliemetzrieder supposed. The second recension (*Cum omnia sacramenta II*) is a more succinct and better organized treatise than its source (*Cum omnia sacramenta I*). The author has apparently tried to clean up the treatise, chiefly by rearranging some sections.

Both recensions must have been written around the beginning of the second quarter of the twelfth century. The *Cum omnia sacramenta I* was dependent on Ivo of Chartres and on the *Sententiae Magistri A.* As Nicholas Haring has shown, Hugh of Saint-Victor drew on the *Cum omnia sacramenta II* in his own *De sacramentis*

[83] Ed. H. Weisweiler, *Das Schrifttum der Schule Anselms von Laon und Wilhelms von Cham-peaux in deutschen Bibliotheken,* BGPhMA 33.1–2, 361–79.

[84] See Reinhardt, *Ehelehre,* 17n38. It is included in some versions of the compilation *Prima rerum origo* (MS Vienna, Nat. Bibl., cod. lat. 854, etc.).

[85] Edition: for the first part, see H. Weisweiler, *Das Schrifttum,* BGPhThMA 33.1–3 (1936), 33–34; for the second part, see F. P. Bliemetzrieder, "Théologie et théologiens de l'école épiscopale de Paris avant Pierre Lombard," RThAM 3 (1931): 273–91.

[86] F. P. Bliemetzrieder, "Théologie et théologiens de l'école épiscopale de Paris avant Pierre Lombard," RThAM 3 (1931): 273–91, at 274–87.

[87] *Cum omnia sacramenta II* (the entire treatise) occurs in a version of the compilation *Principium et causa omnium* (or *Sententiae Anselmi*) that is preserved in MS Vat. Reginensis lat. 241. It also occurs in MS Oxford, Bodleian Library, Laud misc. 277, immediately after a different version of the *Principium et causa omnium.*

[88] H. Weisweiler, *Das Schrifttum der Schule Anselms von Laon und Wilhelms von Champeaux in deutschen Bibliteken,* BGPhThMA 33.1–2 (Münster, 1936), 33–34.

christianae fidei (and not on the Cum omnia sacramenta I as formerly supposed).[89] Hugh wrote this work between 1130 or 1131 and 1137. The Cum omnia sacramenta II, therefore, was the chief means through which work by the magistri moderni on the theology and canon law of marriage passed to Hugh of Saint-Victor and thence to Peter Lombard and the subsequent tradition.

8.2.3.3 The In primis hominibus Group

The following treatises are dependent on the In primis hominibus: Fecit Deus hominem (from the compilation known as the Sententiae Berolinenses);[90] the marriage treatise from the compilation known as the Sententiae Atrebatenses;[91] and the Coniugium namque (from the compilation Deus de cuius principio).[92] The Coniugium namque is dependent on the Cum omnia sacramenta I as well as on the In primis hominibus.

8.2.3.4 Other treatises

Some extant marriage treatises do not belong to either of these two families, although they inhabit the same intellectual world and share some of the same material. One of them, with the incipit Sed prius videndum, is dependent on the Sententiae Magistri A.[93] Another, with the incipit Huius sacramenti habemus, has obvious affinities both with the marriage treatise from the Sententiae Atrebatenses and with the De coniugiis tractantibus family. It is preserved in some versions of the compilation known as the Sententiae divinae paginae (although not in the version that Bliemetzrieder edited in Anselms von Laon systematische Sentenzen).[94] Finally, there is the In coniugio figura, which is included with the Cum omnia sacramenta I

---

[89] Haring, "Sententiae Magistri A.," 30–36, 44.

[90] F. Stegmüller, "Sententiae Berolinenses: Eine neugefundene Sentenzensammlung aus der Schule des Anselm von Laon," RThAM 11 (1939): 33–61, at 56–61. The collection is named after the Berlin MS in which it is preserved.

[91] O. Lottin, "Les Sententiae Atrebatenses," RThAM 10 (1938): 205–224, 344–57, at 352–55; repr. in Psychologie et morale, vol. 5, 400–40, at 434–39. The collection is named after its MS, now held in Arras (Atrebatum). The marriage treatise, which probably dates from the second quarter of the twelfth century, is not known by an incipit because the opening passage is missing.

[92] Edition: H. Weisweiler, "Le recueil des sentences Deus de cuius principio et fine tacetur et son remaniement," RThAM 5 (1933): 245–74, at 270–74.

[93] MS Bamberg, Staatl. Bibl., Cod. Can. 10 (P I 4). See Reinhardt, Ehelehre, 35–36. Unedited.

[94] O. Lottin, "Une tradition spéciale du texte des Sententiae divinae paginae," in Studia Mediaevalia in honorem admodum Reverendi Patris Raymundi Josephi Martin (Bruges, [1948]), 147–69, at 160–61; repr. in Lottin, PsM V, 365–68 (PM 527–28). Lottin divides the material into two treatises, respectively on marriage (Huius sacramenti habemus initium) and on divorce (Cum Dominus in evangelio), but they comprise a single treatise. It is found in recensions of the Sententiae divinae paginae preserved in MS Paris, Mazarine 708 and MS London, British Library, Roy. 11 A.V.

in Bliemetrieder's *Sententiae Anselmi*.[95] This ingenious little treatise stands apart from the others because of its unusual composition. Beginning with the premise that the family unit of father, mother, and child is an image of the Trinity, the author cleverly reduces each aspect of marriage to a triad of features, rules, or categories.

8.2.4 *Traits of the literature*

The extant sentential literature on marriage consists of about a dozen items, of which three are florilegia (or tractates that included florilegia), whereas the others are treatises. All are anonymous, and we do not know in what milieu or institutional setting they were composed. But that is not to say that we know nothing at all about their origins. First, some were dependent on others, and most of the items can be placed into one or other of two families in light of the relations of dependence, as described earlier. Second, the items that are most important historically can be placed chronologically between Ivo of Chartres in the late eleventh century and Hugh of Saint-Victor in the 1130s. Hugh drew extensively on the *Cum omnia sacramenta II*; the *Cum omnia sacramenta II* was a reworking of the *Cum omnia sacramenta I*; the *Cum omnia sacramenta I* was dependent both on the *De coniugiis tractantibus* and on the marriage tractate of the *Sententiae Magistri A.*; and those works drew extensively on Ivo. Third, most of the items evince an effort both to summarize the rules and regulations of marriage and to frame this canonical information within a theological account of marriage in relation to the life of the church and to God's saving plan. These were manuals designed to tell ministers of the church what they needed to know about marriage at a time when the episcopate was striving to take control over the institution across a wide spectrum of the population (Section 1.5).

---

[95] F. P. Bliemetzrieder, *Anselms von Laon systematische Sentenzen*, BGPhMA 18.2–3, 112–13 (treatise 5). The *In coniugio figura* is extant also in the French version of *Principium et causa omnium* (also known as the *Sententiae Anselmi*) preserved in MS Vat. Reginensis lat. 241 (see Wilmart, "Une rédaction française," 130–31, nos. 20b–25), as well as in MS Oxford, Bodleian Library, Laud misc. 277.

APPENDIX:

Sources cited

Florilegia:

- Marriage tract of the *Sententiae Magistri A.* (*Quid sit matrimonium?*). Ed. Reinhardt, *Die Ehelehre der Schule des Anselm von Laon*, BGPhThMA, n.F. 14 (Münster, 1974), 167–244. Cited here by Reinhardt's enumeration of *sententiae* (SMA), with the page numbers in parentheses
- *In primis hominibus.* Ed. Matecki, *Der Traktat In primis hominibus* (Frankfurt am Main, 2001). Note that Matecki enumerates the patristic *sententiae* (IPH), whereas most of my citations are to comments by the collector. Cited by page numbers, and sometimes by line numbers, with the corresponding IPH number in parentheses.
- *Liber Pancrisis.* MS London, British Library, Harley 3098.

Treatises:

- *De coniugiis tractantibus.* Ed. Bliemetzrieder, "Paul Fournier und das literarische Werk Ivos von Chartres," *Archiv für katholisches Kirchenrecht* 115 (1935): 53–91, at 73–78.
- *Cum omnia sacramenta I.* (Dependent on the *De coniugiis tractantibus* and on the *Quid sit matrimonium* of the *Sententiae Magistri A.*) Ed. Bliemetzrieder, *Anselms von Laon systematische Sentenzen*, BGPhMA 18.2–3 (Münster, 1919), 129–51.
- *Cum omnia sacramenta II.* (Revised version of *Cum omnia sacramenta I.*) Edition: First part ed. Weisweiler, *Das Schrifttum der Schule Anselms von Laon und Wilhelms von Champeaux in deutschen Bibliotheken*, BGPhMA 33.1–2 (Münster, 1936), 33–34. Remainder ed. Bliemetzrieder, "Théologie et théologiens de l'école épiscopale de Paris avant Pierre Lombard," RThAM 3 (1931), 274–87.

- *Decretum Dei fuit.* (Dependent on *Cum omnia sacramenta I.*) Ed. Weisweiler, *Das Schrifttum der Schule Anselms von Laon*, BGPhMA 33.1–2 (Münster, 1936), 361–79.
- Marriage tract of the *Sententiae Atrebatenses.* (Dependent on *In primis hominibus.*) Ed. Lottin, PsM V, 434–39.
- Marriage tract of the *Sententiae Berolinenses (Fecit Deus hominem).* (Dependent on *In primis hominibus.*) Ed. Stegmüller, "*Sententiae Berolinenses,*" RThAM 11 (1939), 56–61.
- *Coniugium namque*: Dependent on *In primis hominibus* and *Cum omnia sacramenta.* Ed. Ed. Weisweiler, "Le recueil des sentences *Deus de cuius principio et fine tacetur,*" RThAM 5 (1933), 270–74.
- *Huius sacramenti habemus* (marriage tract of the compilation *Sententiae divinae paginae*).[96] Ed. Lottin, PsM V, 365–68 (PM 527–28).
- *In coniugio figura.* Ed. Bliemetzrieder, *Anselms von Laon systematische Sentenzen*, BGPhMA 18.2–3, 112–13.

---

[96] The marriage treatise is not included in the version of the *Sententiae divinae paginae* that Bliemetzrieder edited in *Anselms von Laon systematische Sentenzen*, 3–46.

9

The theology of marriage in the *Sententiae*

Most of the sentential treatises on marriage follow the pattern established by two florilegia: the *In primis hominibus* and the *Sententiae Magistri A*. They begin with a theological discussion that sets marriage in the context of salvation history and the Christian life. Then they turn to the rules and regulations regarding impediments, divorce and remarriage, and so forth, not only summarizing them but also reflecting on the underlying rationale and noting areas of disagreement among the authorities. I shall proceed in the opposite order here, beginning with regulation and proceeding to the theology of marriage, for this order better reflects the historical development of the literature. The *magistri moderni* began with a well-established and stable body of rules and regulations but added fresh theological material on the place of marriage in the Christian life and in the church, as well as their own reflections on the rules and regulations.

9.1 THE REGULATION OF MARRIAGE IN THE SENTENTIAL LITERATURE

I begin with a summary of the rules regarding validity and divorce in the sentential literature. As I have noted in the previous chapter, the two seminal florilegia and the treatises on marriage were manuals that provided clerics with what they needed to know in ministry, including who could validly marry whom, the criteria of validity and invalidity, and the possible grounds for divorce.

9.1.1 *Impediments and other grounds for divorce*

As the *Cum omnia sacramenta* puts it (in both recensions), marital consent is legitimate only if it is "legitimately carried out and between legitimate persons," that is, between "those whom the divine law does not prohibit from contracting marriage and who are able [*possunt*] to contract it." The author explains that the last condition, regarding possibility, pertains to the impediment of impotence.[1] The chief impediments are carnal and spiritual cognation, nonage, impotence, incest, fear, and fraud.[2] The *magistri moderni* accepted that blood relationship – the sharing of a common ancestor (*cognatio*) – was an impediment up to the seventh degree (*usque ad septimum gradum*) counted according to the canonical computation (Section 1.6.3): a doctrine that was already well established.[3] The treatises explain the rules by stating or sometimes tabulating which *cognati* cannot marry.[4] The *Cum omnia sacramenta I* is unusual in distinguishing between generations and degrees of generation, but the rules are the same.[5] According to this treatise, the parent (father or mother) is the root of generation; their sons and daughters are the foundation (*fundamentum*) of the *degrees* of generation and comprise the first *generation*; their children (the first cousins) are related in the first *degree* but comprise the second *generation*, and so forth. The impediment extends, therefore, "up to the sixth degree, which is the seventh generation."[6]

Spiritual cognation was acquired chiefly by receiving or sponsoring a child at the baptismal font.[7] The *magistri moderni*'s treatment of this topic is conventional. The impediment was based on two underlying assumptions. First, the sponsor who received a child from the font (the godparent) became a spiritual parent of the child: a change that engendered a new set of parent-based relationships. Second, spiritual and biological relationships should not be conflated.[8] For example, no one should be parent and godparent of the same child. Co-parents, such as the biological father and the godmother of the same child, cannot marry.[9] But the impediment is diriment only if it precedes the marriage in question. Thus, a man who tries to obtain a divorce by receiving his own child from the font or by sponsoring the child's confirmation will not succeed, although he is now husband and co-parent of the same woman. Instead, he must do perpetual penance.[10]

---

[1] *Cum omnia sacramenta I*, 141/2–7. See appendix to Chapter 8 for editions cited in Chapter 9.
[2] *Cum omnia sacramenta I*, 143–49.
[3] P. Corbet, *Autour de Burchard de Worms. L'Église allemande et les interdits de parenté (IXème–XIIème siècle)* (Frankfurt am Main, 2001).
[4] *De coniugiis tractantibus*, 76–77. *Cum omnia sacramenta I*, 143/3–12, 149/14–25. *Cum omnia sacramenta II*, ed. Bliemetzrieder, 279 ff. *Sententiae Atrebatenses*, 437/102–137.
[5] *Cum omnia sacramenta I*, 143/1–14.
[6] *Cum omnia sacramenta I*, 143/1–2: "Dictum est quod nulli liceat cognatam suam ducere. Quod intelligendum est usque ad sextum gradum, quod est septima generatio."
[7] See Reinhardt, *Die Ehelehre der Schule des Anselm von Laon*, BGPhThMA, n.F., Bd. 14 (1974), 118–22. Being a sponsor at someone's confirmation could also establish *cognatio spiritualis* in twelfth-century canon law, but this impediment is rarely mentioned in the sentential literature.
[8] S. Gudeman, "The *Compadrazgo* as a Reflection of the Natural and Spiritual Person," *Proceedings of the Royal Anthropological Institute of Great Britain and Ireland* 1971: 45–71, and *idem*, "Spiritual Relationships and Selecting a Godparent," *Man*, n.s. 10 (1975): 221–37, expounds the logic of this separation and observes its practice in modern Peru.
[9] SMA 162 (p. 220). *Cum omnia sacramenta I*, 142/2–3, 144/19–21. *In primis hominibus*, pp. 31–32 (IPH 71). *Sententiae Berolinenses*, 60/4–11. *Sententiae Atrebatenses*, 437/132–37.
[10] *Sententiae Atrebatenses*, 438/144–146.

Servile persons are capable of forming valid marriages, albeit with certain limitations. According to the *Cum omnia sacramenta I*, servile persons are not permitted to marry unless their lords are willing, and such marriages are soluble in cases of fraud (*dolus*), when the free partner is unaware of the other's servile status.[11] The *Sententiae Atrebatenses* explains that divorce is permitted in such cases to prevent the free partner and the children of the union from becoming servile. The author holds that the divorced partners may remarry, although he notes that others hold that such remarriage is forbidden.[12]

Because consent to marry entailed consent to sexual intercourse, anything that prevented sexual intercourse was *ipso facto* an impediment to marriage. The *magistri moderni* held that persons who had taken solemn vows of celibacy, such as canons regular, monks, and nuns, could not marry. The same was true of clerics in major orders in the Roman church (i.e., priests, deacons, and subdeacons), except perhaps by special dispensation. The authors claimed that the Greeks permitted married men to take holy orders, and they thought that being in holy orders was not a diriment impediment in the east, since the sacrament did not require a vow of celibacy.[13] The *Sententiae Atrebatenses* points out that the effect of holy orders in the west depends on whether the man is ordained before or after his marriage. On the one hand, the church permits, rather than commands, the partners to separate if the husband was already in holy orders when they married. Their union must be a true marriage in that case, for it has the legal consequences of marriage, but the woman is free to remarry if they divorce. On the other hand, if an already-married man receives holy orders, the ordination is valid but the cleric's wife remains in control of the situation. If she demands the conjugal debt, he must render it to her and abstain from the duties of his office.[14]

For the same reason, impotence that resulted from biological causes was a fatal impediment to marriage. An impotent man could not marry, and a wife who could show that her husband was unable to consummate their marriage might ask the church to separate them,[15] notwithstanding the presumption that a man's word was worth more in litigation than a woman's.[16] An impotent man is usually said to be "frigid" (*frigidus*) in the sentential literature. The term strictly denoted a humoral condition – a deficiency of vital heat – but it is not clear that the authors were using it in any technical or medical sense. The *In coniugio figura*, which divides every category regarding marriage into three items, distinguishes among three causes of impotence (*impotentia*): illness (*infirmitas*), defective genitalia, and frigidity.

---

[11] *Cum omnia sacramenta I*, 145/18–146/2. *Decretum Dei fuit*, 378/21–26.

[12] *Sententiae Atrebatenses*, 437/124–31.

[13] *Cum omnia sacramenta I*, 148/28–34. Medieval scholars referred to all Byzantine Christians as "Greeks," intending the term in an ecclesiological and not in an ethnic, geographical, or even linguistic sense.

[14] *Sententiae Atrebatenses*, 437/102–107.

[15] SMA 146–50 (pp. 215–17). *In primis hominibus*, 30/17–31/3 (IPH 69).

[16] SMA 152 (p. 217).

Impotence is one of the three things that "dissolve the contract," the others being adultery and prior *de praesenti* consent to another person.[17]

The *magistri moderni* usually adopted the policy on the impediment of impotence that they found in a decretal ascribed to Pope Gregory II. The gist was as follows (I shall pass over some variations and modifications): If a husband because of frigidity has been unable to consummate a marriage after a reasonable period, such as two years,[18] and if his impotence can be proved by compurgation with six oath-helpers (*septima manu*), then the church may separate the couple. Thereafter, the man should remain single because he is impotent, but his former wife is free to remarry. If he subsequently has sex with another woman, however, even if he has married her, the church must reinstate the original marriage, forcing him to return to his former wife, and the oath-helpers are liable to a charge of perjury.[19] The policy presupposed that a husband became bound by marriage and by the conjugal debt even before his marriage was consummated. Impotence vitiated the marriage because it destroyed the capacity to marry, and not because coitus was necessary to complete the marriage.

Proof of *impossibilitas coeundi* was always difficult, and several methods of verification emerged during the Middle Ages.[20] The usual method prescribed in the sentential literature, as in the canon ascribed to Gregory II, was compurgation with six oath-helpers (*septima manu*). The complainant (who was usually but not always the wife), or both spouses together, and the six oath-helpers swore with their hands on a sacred object. The oath-helpers had to be *propinqui*, that is, persons who were in a position to observe the couple, such as family members. Meeting that high standard of proof without fraud or collusion must have been difficult, notwithstanding the absence of privacy in medieval households. Compurgation had replaced the ordeal of the cross, although the standard canon on the method survived in the canonical and sentential literature.[21] According to that canon, which came from a capitulary of Pippin the Short (Charlemagne's father), both parties or their representatives would go to a cross and hold out their arms as long as they

---

[17] *In coniugio figura*, 113/4–7.

[18] The two-year waiting period was from CJ 5.17.10, = *In primis hominibus*, 30/2–31/3 (IPH 69).

[19] Ivo, *Decretum* VIII.182 (*Panormia* VI.116). SMA 149 (p. 216). *In primis hominibus*, p. 30 (IPH 68). *Cum omnia sacramenta I*, 141/5–10. *Cum omnia sacramenta II*, ed. Bliemetzrieder, 279/ 115–280/12. *Decretum Dei fuit*, 372/21–373/3. *Coniugium namque*, 273/36–39. *Sententiae Atrebatenses*, 436/90–95. *Sententiae Berolinenses*, 59/23–34. *Huius sacramenti habemus* (*Sententiae divinae paginae*), 367/26–28.

[20] Esmein/Genestal, 1:259–96. R. H. Helmholz, *Marriage Litigation in Medieval England* (Cambridge, 1974), 87–90. J. A. Brundage, *Law, Sex, and Christian Society in Medieval Europe* (Chicago, 1987), 224–25, 322, 413, 457.

[21] *Decretum Vermeriense*, c. 17, MGH *Capitularia regum Francorum*, vol. 1 (1883), 41. Ivo, *Decretum* VIII.179 (*Panormia* VI.118). SMA 151 (p. 217). *Cum omnia sacramenta I*, 141/13–16. See R. Bartlett, *Trial by Fire and Water* (Oxford, 1986), 46 (with the references in n. 28); and F. L. Ganshof, "L'épreuve de la croix dans le droit de la monarchie franque," in *Studi in onore di Alberto Pincherle* (Rome, 1967), 217–31.

could, and the one whose arms fell first lost the case. The colorful English impotency test of the later Middle Ages, involving palpation of the man's member by a posse of "honest women," must have been both more accurate than the ordeal and less subject to fraud or factual error than compurgation.[22]

The treatises distinguish between natural and magical impotence, and most of them cite or allude to the famous canon on the subject: *Si per sortiarias*, from Hincmar of Rheims.[23] Some of the treatises note that the French church (*ecclesia gallicana*) and the Roman church have different policies when impotence is the result not of natural frigidity or a girl's immaturity but rather of some unnatural cause, such as a hex. The French church, "condescending to human frailness," permits the partners to separate and the marriage to be dissolved in such cases, as Hincmar prescribed, but the Roman church does not.[24] The *Sententiae Berolinenses* rejects Hincmar's policy. Instead, the partners should "devote themselves to prayers, fasts, and vigils, giving alms generously for God's sake, until God frees them from the spell. If the spell cannot be lifted, he should treat her as his sister, and she him as her brother."[25] According to the *Decretum Dei fuit*, the man stricken by a hex should persevere with his wife for at least five years, beseeching God all the while with tears, prayers, fasting, and almsgiving. If he is still impotent after that, they may separate and remarry, and they should not be forced to return to each other if the hex is broken.[26]

Fornication was in certain circumstances valid grounds for a divorce. The *magistri moderni* distinguish between fornication with and without incest, and they inquire as to whether divorce on the grounds of fornication or incest is forbidden or optional or obligatory, and whether the separated partners can marry others. According to the *De coniugiis tractantibus*, fornication without incest before a marriage, as when a man finds that his bride is not a virgin or that she is already pregnant by another man, is not a valid reason for divorce.[27] Fornication committed by a married person without incest is a valid reason for divorce, but the separation is optional, and there can be no remarriage as long as both partners are alive.[28] Incestuous fornication creates an impediment of affinity. If a man commits fornication with a blood relation of his wife after they have married, the spouses can neither engage in sexual intercourse nor remarry. According to some sources, they may separate and remain single; according to others, they may live as brother and sister.

[22] Helmholz, *Marriage Litigation*, 89.

[23] Hincmar, *Epist. 136*, ed. E. Perels, in *MGH Epistolae* 8, = *Epist. Karolini Aevi* 6 (Berlin, 1939), 105/8–20. Ivo, *Decretum* VIII.194 (*Panormia* VI.117). SMA 150 (p. 217). *In primis hominibus*, p. 31 (IPH 70). *Cum omnia sacramenta I*, 141/12–13. See C. Rider, *Magic and Impotence in the Middle Ages* (Oxford, 2006).

[24] *In primis hominibus*, 30/7–10 (IPH 67). *Cum omnia sacramenta II*, ed. Bliemetzrieder, 280/ 121–27. *Sententiae Atrebatenses*," 437/96–101.

[25] *Sententiae Berolinenses*, 59/35–60/3.   [26] *Decretum Dei fuit*, 373/4–9.

[27] As Ivo explains in *Epist. 155*, PL 162:158C–160B.

[28] *De coniugiis tractantibus*, 77/10–22. *Cum omnia sacramenta I*, 144/3–10, 22–24.

But what if the incestuous fornication occurred before they married? According to the *De coniugiis tractantibus* and some of the treatises dependent on it, the marriage is then invalid, and they are both free to remarry.²⁹ According to the *Coniugium namque*, on the contrary, divorce and remarriage on grounds of pre-marital affinity is an ancient custom that has fallen into disuse. Formerly, if a man had had sex with a blood relation of his wife before their marriage, and if this was proven by the ordeal of hot iron, by compurgation, or by some other customary legal procedure, the marriage would be annulled and both could remarry. But because that policy was too easily abused and sometimes led to perjury and trumped-up cases, divorce is no longer permitted in such cases, and the spouses must remain together. Then the husband may not require his wife (the innocent party in the envisaged scenario) to render the conjugal debt, but she can require it from him. If she does so, he must fulfill her demand and then satisfy for his own incestuous turpitude through remorse and penance.³⁰

If the partners have established a valid marriage by the approved means, and if there are no impediments, there are only two valid reasons for separation: adultery and entry into the religious life. The *magistri moderni* forbid remarriage in both circumstances. The *In primis hominibus* derives these rules from the premise that man should not separate what God has joined together (Matt 19:6, Mark 10:9). Christ's injunction does not apply in cases of adultery because the adulterer has already broken the faith that binds them together. Nor does it apply when the spouses separate by mutual consent so that both can enter the religious life, for then it is not man but God who separates them.³¹

9.1.2 *Variations across time and place*

The *magistri moderni* emphasized that most of the impediments and other rules of marriage were historically contingent and dependent on ecclesiastical authority. Because the rules vary "according to the diverse institutions of the church," certain unions "are licit at one time, and illicit at another time."³² According to the *In coniugio figura*, the power to change the laws of marriage has passed from Abraham, Moses, and Christ to the "holy modern fathers" (i.e., the bishops), who have extended the impediments of consanguinity. The diverse institutions pertain "not to the nature of marriage but to diversity of time and the diverse states of man."³³

---

²⁹ *De coniugiis tractantibus,* 77/23–78/3. *Cum omnia sacramenta* I, 144/11–19. *Decretum Dei fuit,* 377/10–13.

³⁰ *Coniugium namque,* 273/40–274/9.

³¹ *In primis hominibus,* 45/12–16 (IPH 102). *Cum omnia sacramenta* I, 145/3–12.

³² *De coniugiis tractantibus,* 76/21–23: "Confiteri igitur debemus hec omnia esse coniugia, sed secundum diuersas ecclesie institutiones nunc licere, nunc non licere."

³³ *In coniugio figura,* 112/12–24.

By the same token, bishops have the power to dispense couples from many impediments.

The authors note that laws vary regionally as well as over time. According to the *Cum omnia sacramenta I*, the customs (*mores*) and the rituals (*sollemnia*) associated with marrying are matters of local practice and are subject to the authority of local churches. Consent makes marriage, and the partners must above all demonstrate their consent before God, but they should do so "in accordance with the custom of their native land" (*secundum morem patriae*).[34] To take account of local variation, the author defines marriage as "the consent of a man and woman to sexual intercourse, made according to what the church decrees." The author explains that the added phrase – *secundum decretum ecclesiae* – "should be interpreted in a broad sense," that is, as referring to the "custom of a particular region or a particular church." The customs and solemnities of marrying vary from province to province. For example, people marry with a particular form of priestly blessing in certain regions, but with a different blessing or with no blessing at all in other regions.[35]

The oft-cited decretal ascribed to Pope Evaristus (AD 97–105) required every conceivable formality to distinguish a legitimate marriage from concubinage: the suit, the betrothal, the bride's attendants, the nuptial mass, the Tobias Nights, and so forth.[36] To reconcile this decretal with regional variation, the *magistri moderni* characterize Evaristus's policy as *ad terrorem*: a discipline intended to curtail abuses by discouraging clandestine marriage, for those "who take wives in secret freely dismiss them afterwards."[37] According to the *Coniugium namque*, Evaristus was either speaking *ad terrorem* or reflecting how people married in that particular region (*in illa terra*).[38]

To explain temporal variations in the law of marriage, the *magistri moderni* distinguished among several modes of law. Few of the impediments belong to the natural law, in their view. Even marriage between siblings was permissible in the beginning. Whereas the natural law existed from the beginning and has never altered, the other modes of law are contingent and designed to enhance the welfare of the people and of the church according to time and circumstance. The most frequent of these distinctions is between the law of nature and the "law of benevolence," also known as the "law of institution." For example, the church has acted

---

[34] *Cum omnia sacramenta I*, 149/21–24, 31–32.

[35] Ibid., 140/19–31. *Coniugium namque*, 272/22–30.

[36] The decretal was a Carolingian forgery, although Hincmar of Rheims considered it to be authentic (*De divortio Lotharii*, PL 125:649A–B). For the text of the decretal, see Hinschius, *Decretales Pseudo-Isidorianae et capitula Angilramni* (Leipzig, 1863), 87–88 (or PL 130:81B–C). Ivo, *Decretum* VIII.4 (*Panormia* VI.32). SMA 72 (p. 189). *In primis hominibus* 54/1–5, 8–9 (IPH 125–126). For commentary, see G. H. Joyce, *Christian Marriage*, 2nd ed. (London, 1948), 104–05.

[37] *In primis hominibus*, 54/5–8. *Cum omnia sacramenta I*, 140/15–18. *Cum omnia sacramenta II*, ed. Bliemetzrieder, 284/210–13. *Decretum Dei fuit*, 371/21–372/8. *Sententiae Atrebatenses*, 439/183–86.

[38] *Coniugium namque*, 272/10–15.

out of benevolence by extending the impediment of consanguinity to the seventh degree. The extended prohibition was meant both to enlarge the scope of charity (*propter amplificationem caritatis*) and to enhance the decorum of the church. It was beneficial to keep the love that comes through marriage separate from the natural love (*dilectio naturalis*) between members of the same family or kin-group.[39] The term *caritas*, in such contexts, does not denote the supernatural gift of loving God but rather a disinterested, universal love, as distinct from the self-interested, preferential love (*amor*) among members of the same family or kin group.

Laws also vary from region to region. The *Cum omnia sacramenta I* notes that priests, deacons, and subdeacons cannot marry in the West without a dispensation. The reason is that they have to make public vows of celibacy, just as canons regular, monks, and nuns do. Nevertheless, priests can marry in the Greek church, where holy orders do not entail a solemn vow of celibacy. Why is celibacy required in one region and not in another? The *magistri moderni* do not argue that the Greeks were heretics. Such variation is possible and valid, they argue, because the prohibition is "not against the law of nature but against the precepts of ecclesiastical institution."[40] The marriage of priests only "violates the law of benevolence, which advances toward the perfection of the church."[41]

The *magistri moderni* used the distinction between laws of nature and laws of benevolence to reconcile the apparently contradictory traditions on the marriage of adulterers. Augustine said that an adulteress could marry her paramour after her husband had died,[42] but a well-known canon usually ascribed to Pope Leo I says that no one "may take in marriage a woman whom he has previously polluted by adultery." (In fact, it was a decree from the Synod of Tribur in 895.)[43] The *magistri moderni* usually reconcile the two positions by arguing that Augustine was speaking about the law of nature, whereas Leo was speaking about the law of benevolence.[44] There is no natural or absolute prohibition against such marriages, but Leo, speaking *ad rigorem*, prohibited them to avoid scandal and the risk of murder. Rules

---

[39] *De coniugiis tractantibus*, 76/3–6. *Cum omnia sacramenta I*, 141/28–142/3. *Cum omnia sacramenta II*, ed. Bliemetzrieder, 280/132–135. PM 67 (58/7–11).

[40] *Cum omnia sacramenta I*, 148/28–34.

[41] Ibid., 151/17–22. The text of 151/9–22 is extant as an independent *sententia*: PM 408 (p. 288), and MS Oxford, Bodl., Laud Misc. 277, 58rb.

[42] *De nupt. et conc.* I.10(11), CSEL 42:223/18–20: "denique mortuo uiro cum quo uerum coniubium fuit fieri uerum coniubium potest cum quo prius adulterium fuit." *In primis hominibus*, 37/17–18 (IPH 82). Quoted in Ivo, *Decretum* VIII.10A, although some recensions, by inserting a "not" ("*uerum coniugium non potest*"), make Augustine say that adulterers cannot marry.

[43] *Concilium Triburense*, c. 51, in MGH *Leges*, sect. 2: *Capitularia Regum Francorum*, vol. 2.2 (1890–1897), 241. Ivo, *Decretum* VIII.211 (*Panormia* VII.10), attributes the canon to a council held *apud Altheum* or *apud Alpheum* in the presence of King Conrad, and the *In primis hominibus*, 38/12–13 (IPH 85), attributes it to a council held *apud Athenas* (variants: *ateum, antheum*) in the presence of King Conrad. The *Sententiae Berolinenses*, 60/29–34, which reviews the two positions without trying to reconcile them, ascribes the canon to Ambrose.

[44] F. L. Ganshof, "Note sur deux textes de droit canonique dans le *Liber Floridus*," in *Études d'histoire du droit canonique dédiées à Gabriel Le Bras*," vol. 1 (Paris, 1965), 99–115, at 103–06.

based on benevolence can be changed if so doing would extend disinterested love (*caritas*).[45] The *In primis hominibus* proposes a different but related explanation: The church prohibits adulterers from marrying only when their adultery is a matter of public knowledge, for the aim is to avoid scandal and to set a good example.[46]

The reconciliation of Augustine and Leo on the marriage of adulterers was part of a broad effort to classify the norms prescribed for Christians and to relativize them as far as possible, attributing them to the authority of the church. Thus, the *Cum omnia sacramenta I* classifies the Christian norms according to whether they are binding or advisory and whether they are soluble or capable of dispensation. Some are admonitory, non-binding councils of perfection, such as: "Go, sell what you have and give to the poor." Some are indulgent permissions, such as: "Let each man have his own wife because of fornication." Some are insoluble precepts, such as: "Honor your father and mother." Some are soluble precepts, such as Paul's permission to eat meat purchased in the shambles (1 Cor 10:25), for this license might be set aside to avoid scandalizing weaker Christians. Again, there are insoluble prohibitions, such as that against murder, but there are also soluble prohibitions, which may be waived according to person, time, or place, such as the rule prohibiting a priest who has lapsed sexually from serving at the altar.[47]

9.1.3 *The power to dissolve*

If a marriage is dissolved because of some fatal impediment, was it already null and void in reality prior to the divorce? It is a commonplace of modern Catholic thought that the church (more precisely, an episcopal tribunal) has no power to dissolve any marriage. Instead, the church can only determine that the marriage in question has never really existed. The *magistri moderni* consider that position among several others, but they reject it. In many cases, they argue, a marriage that has been dissolved, leaving the partners free to remarry, was real before it was dissolved.

According to the *De coniugiis tractantibus*, such is the case when *cognati* (lateral blood relations) marry within the forbidden degrees. Their marriage really exists until the church dissolves it. The impediment itself does not nullify the marriage because it is historically contingent and was not in force from the beginning, when even siblings could marry.[48] Someone might object that Jesus himself, as recorded in Matthew's gospel, considers adultery to be the only valid reason for the divorce of validly married spouses, although even then the partners cannot remarry. If the

---

[45] *Cum omnia sacramenta I*, 148/35–149/10. *Decretum Dei fuit*, 377/9–13. PM 66–67 (pp. 57–58). PM 66 and 67 are ascribed to Anselm in the *Liber Pancrisis*, 75v–76r, 75v (LP 270, 267). PM 67 (LP 267) is a variant of a *sententia* extant in several other settings, e.g., *Cum omnia sacramenta I*, 146/13–22, and *Sententiae Atrebatenses*, 436/59–67.

[46] *In primis hominibus*, 38/17–18.

[47] *Cum omnia sacramenta I*, 150/14–151/11. *Cum omnia sacramenta II*, ed. Bliemetzrieder, 285/236–286/255.

[48] *De coniugiis tractantibus*, 76/16–23.

partners are validly separated for any other reason, therefore, they cannot really have been married before their separation. The author rejects this line of argument. One should remember, he argues, that Jesus was talking about the Mosaic law of divorce, which permitted husbands to break up even lawful marriages. If a marriage is licit and the spouses are able to come together sexually, adultery is the only valid reason for divorce. Illicit marriage, such as that within the forbidden degrees of consanguinity, is another matter. Here, the impediment is valid grounds for the church to dissolve the marriage, but the marriage exists until the church does so.[49]

The *In primis hominibus* considers the case of blood relations who marry in good faith, without realizing that they are related within the forbidden degrees. If their relationship later comes to light, the church must dissolve the marriage. Nevertheless, they must have been married before their divorce, for then any extra-marital sex would have been adultery. Likewise, sexual intercourse between the spouses would not have been sinful until their relationship became known. Even after the partners have become aware of the impediment, they remain truly married until the church dissolves their union, although in good conscience they should abstain from sexual intercourse.[50] Similarly, if the church dissolves a marriage because the husband cannot consummate it, there must be a true marriage until the church dissolves it because the wife will commit adultery if she has sex with another man before the divorce.[51]

The *Cum omnia sacramenta I* explains that although most true marriages are insoluble, some are soluble. Where there are no impediments under natural or human law, the marriage is insoluble and the church has no power to dissolve it. Augustine was referring to insoluble marriages when he said that "something conjugal" endured after adultery and even after remarriage.[52] But there are also soluble marriages. Some soluble marriages must be dissolved. Others may be dissolved by dispensation. If there is an impediment of relationship, for example, the marriage must be dissolved. In the Pauline Privilege, on the contrary, the believer is permitted to divorce and to remarry but may also remain with the unbelieving spouse. Such a marriage is legitimate but soluble by dispensation. Again, if a merchant goes abroad and has not returned after a long period and his wife does not wish to remain continent, the church may dissolve the marriage by dispensation, so that she is free to remarry. The merchant is presumed dead, but no one knows whether he is alive or dead in fact, and the second marriage is really valid even if the first husband is really still alive. Nevertheless, he has the right to reclaim his wife if he is alive and returns. If he does not wish to do so, the second marriage must be dissolved and both must remain continent.[53] Even the rule prohibiting the

---

[49] Ibid., 76/24–77/8.   [50] *In primis hominibus*, 14/13–15/1.   [51] Ibid., 30/3–5.

[52] Augustine, *De nupt. et. conc.* I.10(11), CSEL 42:223/20–22. Ivo, *Decretum* VIII.12–13 (*Panormia* VI.74). SMA 26 (p. 173/21–22).

[53] *Cum omnia sacramenta I*, 142/12–23. Likewise, *In primis hominibus*, 48/13–17, and *Sententiae Atrebatenses*, 436/68–79.

dissolution of marriage is itself soluble, for Moses waived it because of the Israelites' "hardness of heart" (Matt 19:8, Mark 10:5).[54]

Under what conditions is a soluble marriage null and void? Although the *magistri moderni* do not offer a definitive answer to this question, their usual view seems to be that only the non-contingent impediments, which belong to the law of nature rather than to the law of benevolence, nullify a marriage. For example, father-daughter marriage would be void, whereas brother-sister marriage would only be illicit and soluble. The author of the *De coniugiis tractantibus* seems to imply that the marriage of a man in holy orders is null and void rather than merely soluble, but if so his position is unusual.[55]

9.1.4 *Summary: The power of the church*

The *magistri moderni* emphasize and celebrate both the clergy's power to introduce new laws regulating marriage and the obligation of the laity to obey them. The church, especially the episcopate, has such power over marriage in four respects. First, the church legislates the law of benevolence, causing what was licit to become illicit or vice versa, and some of the impediments that the church imposes vary according to both time and place. Second, the church has the power to waive at least some of the contingent, adventitious impediments. Third, local churches determine the solemnities and other customs required for a valid marriage. Fourth, the church has the power to dissolve illicit marriages that really exist until they are dissolved. Only marriages that contravene unchanging divine or natural laws are null and void before they are annulled.

9.2 CONSENT

The *magistri moderni* maintained that the authentic consent of the spouses themselves and of them alone was essential for a valid marriage. Contrariwise, whatever undermined the spouses' consent invalidated their marriage. According to the *Cum omnia sacramenta I*, a daughter who accepts a husband only because she is afraid of her parents is not really married to him. She should seek the church's protection as soon as possible. If there are witnesses to prove that she agreed out of fear, the church will set her free by declaring the marriage null and void. But such cases are difficult to litigate in practice, for the ecclesiastical authorities depend on external evidence. The church cannot defend the girl if there are no witnesses to verify that she was coerced, and then she may be forced to return to her husband. The clergy cannot judge the hidden things of the heart.[56]

---

[54] *Cum omnia sacramenta I*, 151/9–11. PM 408 (p. 288).

[55] *De coniugiis tractantibus*, 76/7–9: "Ab illis qui sunt in sacris ordinibus, iudicatur non fieri coniugium. In quo notandum, quod non dicitur non debere fieri, sed non fieri, et ideo iuste a se recedunt."

[56] *Cum omnia sacramenta I*, 148/9–18.

Parents do not have the power to contract marriage for their children. According to the *Coniugium namque*, there is no marriage if fathers "contract and promise" marriages for their children without the children's knowledge or consent, for the consent of the partners themselves is the very foundation of marriage.[57] The *Sententiae Berolinenses* considers what should happen if a father swears that he will give his daughter in marriage but she proves to be unwilling. If she marries against her will, the marriage is invalid. Moreover, paternal agreements of that sort are prohibited because "those who are to made one body ought to be of one will." It is better for a father to be guilty of breaking his own oath than to give away his daughter in marriage against her will. If she marries unwillingly and later commits adultery because her marriage is unhappy, the sin "will undoubtedly be imputed to her father as well as to her."[58] Some of this argument is taken from a decretal that Urban II (r. 1088–1099) sent to Sancho Ramirez, the king of Aragon-Navarre, in which the pope enunciates the principle that persons who become one body in marriage ought to be of one mind.[59]

Partners cannot become betrothed until they are old enough to consent, and they cannot marry until they are both mentally and sexually capable of the union. If children are given in marriage while they are still in the cradle, the contract is invalid unless they consent when they reach the age of discretion.[60] Again, no one "is permitted, except by dispensation, to contract the nuptial bond beneath nubile age, that is, at less than twelve years of age."[61] According to the *Sententiae Atrebatenses*, partners who plight their troth when they are too young to marry do not automatically become married when they reach marriageable age. If they still wish to marry, they must plight their troth again. The author considers what should happen if a man who is of age plights his troth with an underage girl, and she still wants the man when she comes of age. Can he refuse? Some say that he cannot be forced to accept her because the marriage was invalid. Others say that the marriage was hitherto invalid on the girl's part but valid on his part. On that premise, he must marry her if she still wants to marry even if he is no longer willing.[62]

The *magistri moderni* consider the mutual consent of the spouses to be constitutive of marriage. It is more than a necessary precondition. The *Cum omnia sacramenta I* even defines marriage (*coniugium*) as a certain consent. For proof, the author quotes a definition that he ascribes to Isidore of Seville: "Marriage is the

[57] *Coniugium namque*, 272/7–9.
[58] *Sententiae Berolinenses*, 61/14–19: "Nam qui debent unum effici corpus, unius debent esse voluntatis."
[59] "Quorum enim unum corpus est, unus debet esse et animus." Mansi 20:713C, or PL 151:373B–C; = Ivo, *Decretum* VIII.24 (*Panormia* VI.109), SMA 145 (p. 215). On the circumstances, see J. T. Noonan, "Power to Choose," in *Viator* 4 (1973): 419–34, at 421 (with n. 4). Cf. Ivo, *Epist.* 134, PL 162:143D: "quorum per conjugalem copulam unum debet fieri corpus, eorumdem pariter animorum debet esse consensus."
[60] *Cum omnia sacramenta I*, 139/15–17. Ivo writes about a cradle marriage in *Epist.* 243, PL 162:249D–251B.
[61] *Cum omnia sacramenta I*, 149/11–13.   [62] *Sententiae Atrebatenses*, 438/170–75.

consent [*consensus*] of male and female that maintains [i.e., commits the spouses to] an indivisible way of life."[63] In fact, the definition is a variant of a description of marriage in Justinian's *Institutes*,[64] but with the word *consensus* replacing the word *coniunctio* ("union," "joining") in the original. The author is defining the married state, and not the act of getting married, but the treatise also identifies consent as the efficient cause of marriage. Mindful that the efficient cause of a thing cannot be identical with the thing itself, the author explains that marriage is defined as consent when it is "described through its efficient cause."[65] The author of the *Decretum Dei fuit*, a treatise that is dependent on the *Cum omnia sacramenta*, elaborates this solution:

> Nevertheless, marriage and consent are not the same; rather, consent is the cause of marriage. It is as if someone says, "day is the sun rising over the earth," meaning not that day and the sun are the same thing, but that the rising sun is the cause of day.[66]

The *Cum omnia sacramenta I* takes the pseudo-Isidorian definition as the pretext for an extended inquiry into the nature of marriage, in the course of which the definition is revised several times and used to explain not only what kind of consent is necessary, but also to what the spouses consent. Marital consent is valid only if it is between legitimate persons and made in a legitimate manner. Later in the treatise, the author repeats the pseudo-Isidorian definition, adding the term "legitimate" (*legitimus*): "Marriage is the legitimate consent of male and female that maintains an indivisible way of life." Their consent is legitimate, the author explains, inasmuch as the marriage is legitimately carried out between legitimate persons, that is, persons between whom there is no legal impediment.[67]

The *Cum omnia sacramenta I* notes that coitus is an object of marital consent but argues that actual coitus is not a necessary condition for being married. In consenting to marry, the spouses agree to sexual union (*in carnale copula*). Thus, marriage may be defined as "the consent of a man and a woman to sexual union made according to what the church decrees,"[68] or alternatively as "the [legitimate] consent of a man and

---

[63] *Cum omnia sacramenta I*, 139/9–11: "... coiugium commune, quod Isidorus ita describit: Coniugium est consensus masculi et femine, indiuidualem uite consuetudinem retinens." *Cum omnia sacramenta II*, 274.

[64] *Inst.* 1.9.1: "Nuptiae autem sive matrimonium est viri et mulieris coniunctio, individuam consuetudinem vitae continens." Ivo, *Decretum* VIII.1 (*Panormia* VI.1). SMA 1 (p. 167). The collector probably confused that definition with Isidore's, *Etym.* IX.7.20: "Coniugium est legitimarum personarum inter se coeundi et copulandi nuptiae." Cf. the free translation of Isidore's definition by S. A. Barney et al. (Cambridge, 2006), 211: "A 'conjugal union' (*coniugium*) is a marital relationship [*nuptiae*] of persons who have met the legal requirements, marked by joining together and sexual intercourse with one another." How one construes the definition turns on the meaning of *nuptiae* and the distinction between *nuptiae* and *coniugium*, which are usually synonyms. The word *nuptiae* has both ceremonial and sexual connotations, and Isidore has just explained (*Etym.* IX.7.10–11) that it referred originally to the wedding veil, which covers the bride's face like a cloud (*nubes*).

[65] *Cum omnia sacramenta I*, 139/11–13.   [66] *Decretum Dei fuit*, 371/4–6.

[67] *Cum omnia sacramenta I*, 141/3–4.   [68] *Cum omnia sacramenta I*, 140/21–23

a woman that maintains an indivisible way of life, that is, it is their consent to remain together indivisibly and to have sexual intercourse without avoiding offspring."[69] But if marital consent includes consent to sexual intercourse, did the Virgin Mary break her vow of perpetual virginity when she consented to marry Joseph? Was her marriage invalid because of the prior vow? According to the *Cum omnia sacramenta I*, Mary did not need to break her vow because her marriage vows were conditional. She agreed that *if* Joseph ever required the debt, she would render it, but she trusted in God that Joseph would never require the debt – and, in fact, he did not.[70] The author explains that he adds the phrase "made according what the church decrees" to the definition to allow for local variations. Specific customs (*mores*) and the rituals (*sollemnia*) associated with marrying, he explains, are not mentioned in the definitions because they are matters of local practice and are subject to the authority of local churches. For example, a priestly blessing is required in some regions but not in others.[71]

Summing up, the *Cum omnia sacramenta I* proposes the following as the gist of the foregoing definitions: "Marriage is the legitimate union [*coniunctio*] of a man and a woman, that is, a bond [*obligatio*] between a man and a woman that has been legitimately contracted."[72] The author explains that a man and a woman are joined legitimately when the "bond [*obligatio*] is contracted for God's sake, with mutual consent, and according to the custom of the native land, between a man and a woman whom neither nature nor the divine law prevents from being united."[73]

The *Cum omnia sacramenta II* abbreviates this inquiry into the nature or definition of marriage, focusing on the consent needed to establish a valid marriage and including sexual intercourse among the objects of consent. What makes marriage is "the consent of a man and a woman to have sexual intercourse and to remain together undividedly."[74] The partners must consent "to live together indivisibly and to have sexual intercourse without avoiding offspring," and their consent must be "legitimate, that is, legitimately carried out between legitimate persons."[75]

---

[69] Ibid., 140/32–141/2. The word *legitimus* is absent from the definition but then immediately glossed, as if it were present: "Coniugium est consensus masculi et femine, indiuidualem uite consuetudinem retinens, id est, indiuidualiter commanendi et carnaliter commiscendi, absque prolis uitatione, *legitimus*, id est, inter legitimas personas legitime factus."

[70] *Cum omnia sacramenta I*, 147/26–148/8. Cf. Gratian, C. 27, q. 2, d. p. c. 2, and ibid., c. 3 (1063–64). The *Cum omnia sacramenta I* seems to contradict a position stated elsewhere in the treatise (147/4–5, 148/28–32): that only public religious vows, and not private ones, invalidate marriage.

[71] *Cum omnia sacramenta I*, 140/24–31. See also 149/21–22, 31–32. Likewise, *Coniugium namque*, 272/22–30.

[72] *Cum omnia sacramenta I*, 149/19–21.   [73] Ibid., 149/21–24.

[74] *Cum omnia sacramenta II*, ed. Bliemetzrieder, 274/3–275/5.

[75] Ibid., 279/110–113: "Coniugium est masculi consensus et femine, indiuidualem uite consuetudinem retinens, indiuidualiter commanendi et carnaliter commiscendi, absque prolis uitatione *legitimus*, id est, inter legitimas personas legitime factus." *Decretum Dei fuit*, 372/16–17: "Coniugium est *legitimus* consensus maris et femine individualem vite consuetudinem retinens."

9.3 REASONS AND BENEFITS

The *magistri moderni* posit two principal reasons (*causae*) for marriage: the "hope of offspring" (*spes prolis*) and the "avoidance of fornication" (*fornicationis evitatio*).[76] The primary and original reason for marriage is the procreation and rearing of children. Nevertheless, the chief reason for choosing to marry in the present day, rather than to pursue celibacy, is the remedy, that is, to avoid fornication. The *magistri moderni* regarded marriage as the solution to the problem of sexual desire. Moreover, they saw a historical development in the distinction between the two chief motives, although they were vague or inconsistent as to the moment when one motive superseded the other. Whereas marriage had formerly been a duty (*officium*) because of the obligation to beget children for the Lord, marriage was now a remedy. The chief purpose of marriage, therefore, had changed from positive to negative: from the blessing of Genesis 1:28 to the remedy of 1 Corinthians 7. Their characterization of the remedy as "avoidance of fornication" echoed the words of St Paul. "It is good for a man not to touch a woman," Paul says, "but because of fornication [*propter fornicationem*], let every man have his own wife, and let every woman have her own husband" (1 Cor 7:1–2).

The theory of the two reasons for marrying, which the *magistri moderni* owed to Augustine, was the keystone of their theology of marriage. They regarded the right to marry in relation to their own celibate ideal. Priestly celibacy was always uppermost in their minds when they considered the rights and wrongs of sexual conduct. Ideally, the Christian should be celibate, focusing on spiritual rather than carnal things, and on the next world rather than on mundane things. But marriage was the legitimate solution for those whose "infirmity" prevented them from espousing a celibate vocation. The critical factor was not so much the intensity of libido as a person's weakness or lack of moral fiber: his or her inability to master sexual desire. The authors recognized that people married for many other justifiable reasons, but they regarded such reasons as incidental.

A passage in the *Sententiae Magistri A.* illustrates both the central thesis and its dependence on Augustine:

> *On the first institution of marriage*: Marriage before sin would have been a duty [*officium*], but after sin it is a remedy. The first institution was for the sake of the propagation of children. *Augustine to Valerium*: "There would be no shameful concupiscence in man if he had not sinned, but there would have been marriage even if he had not sinned, for children would have been begotten in the body of that life without this sickness, without which [procreation] cannot occur now." After sin, marriage is contracted so that fornication can be avoided, as the Apostle says: "Let each one have his own wife because of fornication" (1 Cor 7:2). And this [saying] is like a second institution of marriage.[77]

---

[76] PM 401 (p. 286). MS Oxford, Bodl., Laud Misc. 277, 57rb–58va.
[77] SMA 15–17 (pp. 169–70). The reference to *De nupt. et conc.* I.1(1), 212/15–19.

The first statement, regarding marriage as a duty and as a remedy, is a paraphrase of a passage in the *De Genesi ad litteram*, where Augustine compares marriage before and after the fall and introduces the three goods of marriage.[78] The statement passed from the *Sententia Magistri A.* to the *Cum omnia sacramenta I*, whence it became a maxim of scholastic theology. The *Sententiae Magistri A.* associates each purpose of marriage with a historical institution.

The compiler of the *In primis hominibus* uses quotations from Augustine and his own glosses to explain why the evils of lust and pleasure associated with marriage do not make marriage evil, as the heretics suppose. Not only did God institute marriage in the beginning, but Jesus confirmed its goodness by being present at the wedding at Cana and by prohibiting divorce in the gospels. Whereas marriage was free from lustful pleasure in the beginning, it is now a remedy against lustful pleasure.[79] Marriage excuses or mitigates such evils by its three goods: faith, offspring, and sacrament. Marriage has other goods, as well, such as the avoidance of extra-marital sex, the natural partnership (*societas*) between the sexes, and the "spiritual charity" that proceeds from that partnership. The last benefit enables spouses to sustain a chaste partnership after their sexual ardor has waned.[80] To explain how the remedy works, the compiler assembles *sententiae* from Augustine showing that there is no serious sin when a spouse engages in sexual intercourse for the sake of offspring or to render the conjugal debt. There is inevitably some sin in such situations, but it is minor requires little or no satisfaction. Even when a spouse demands the conjugal debt to satisfy his or her lust, the sin is only venial, and prayer and a mild penance are enough to satisfy for it.[81]

9.3.1 *The goods of marriage*

As well as maintaining that that the chief reasons (*causae*) for marrying were procreation and the avoidance of fornication (*evitatio fornicationis*), the *magistri moderni* adopted Augustine's theory of the three goods of marriage. They equated Augustine's *bonum fidei* with negative fidelity (the avoidance of adultery), failing to grasp that according to Augustine it included the conjugal debt. As a result, they did not understand that the good of faith included the conjugal debt, according to Augustine, and was itself the chief defense against lust.

How were the two causes, procreation and the avoidance of fornication, related to the three goods? Both notions seem to be ways of describing the purpose of marriage. The *Cum omnia sacramenta I* solves the problem by distinguishing the final causes of marriage (*causae*) from its goods (*bona*). Whereas the efficient cause of marriage is consent,[82] the chief final causes of marriage are procreation and the

---

[78] *De Gen. ad litt.* IX.7, CSEL 28.1, 275/20–21: "quod sanis esse posset officium, sit aegrotis remedium."

[79] *In primis hominibus*, 2/7–10.   [80] Ibid., pp. 2–6.   [81] Ibid., pp. 6–8.

[82] Ibid., 139/12–13.

avoidance of fornication, just as victory is the final cause of war.[83] There are other, secondary final causes. When Ambrose said that procreation was the only reason (*sola causa*) for marrying,[84] he did not mean that there were no other valid final causes, but only that procreation was first among those causes (*prima causa*), for it was the reason for the first institution of marriage in Paradise.[85] Augustine's three goods of marriage are neither its final nor its efficient causes but rather the benefits that make marriage good (*quare bonum sit coniugium*). The *Coniugium namque*, on the contrary, equates goods with causes and treats the avoidance of fornication (*evitatio fornicationis*) as another conjugal good, bringing the total to four. The goodness of marriage, the author explains, comprises the avoidance of fornication, the hope of offspring, faith, and sacrament. All marriages have these four goods in some sense. One might object that pagans and the Jews of the Old Covenant enjoy only the first two of these goods: the avoidance of fornication and the hope of offspring. The objection leads the author to divide the goods into two classes, respectively inalienable and alienable. He shows that the good of faith is consistent with polygamy, but he concedes that the Jews of the Old Covenant may have lacked something of the goods both of faith and of sacrament, which "are not among the principle causes of marriage." The principle causes are procreation and the avoidance of fornication, which are fully common to all peoples.[86]

Two treatises add the avoidance of homosexuality to the list of conjugal goods. According to the *Sententiae Berolinenses*, Augustine's faith, offspring, and sacrament are the primary goods, but marriage has many secondary goods. These include not only the "excusing of illicit love" (which Augustine would have included under faith) but also "the natural propriety of both sexes," whereby "a man is coupled with a woman, and a woman with a man," so that "a man does not act with a man against nature, nor a woman with a woman."[87] The "propriety" of the two sexes is their complementary, interlocking relationship. The phrase "the natural propriety of both sexes" (*utriusque sexus naturalis proprietas*) is a distant echo of Augustine's "natural partnership of the different sexes" (*naturalis in diverso sexu societas*), which he posits in the *De bono coniugali* to characterize the aspect of marriage that transcends procreation and sustains a marriage after ardor and the hope of procreation have faded.[88]

The same cluster of ideas occurs in the *Cum omnia sacramenta II*, albeit differently arranged. Citing Augustine's *De bono coniugali*, the author explains that

---

[83] *Cum omnia sacramenta I*, 130/23–25.

[84] Ambrose, *Expositio in Lucam* I.45 (Luke 1:24–25), CCL 14:29/696–98: "pudor est enim feminis nuptiarum praemia [i.e., *proles*] non habere, quibus haec sola est causa nubendi." Ivo, *Decretum* VIII.75 (*Panormia* VI.24). SMA 13 (p. 169).

[85] *Cum omnia sacramenta I*, 130/10–13, 135/26–136/6.

[86] *Coniugium namque*, 273/3–18.   [87] *Sententiae Berolinenses*, 56/27–33.

[88] Augustine, *De b. coniug.* 3(3), CSEL 41:190/19–21: "quod mihi non uidetur propter solam filiorum procreationem, sed propter ipsam etiam naturalem in diuerso sexu societatem...." SMA 40 (pp. 177–78). *In primis hominibus*, 5/12–14 (IPH 10).

there is a "natural partnership between the different sexes" in marriage, which unites the spouses even if they are childless. As they grow older and their lust wanes, "the order of charity flourishes." The author adds there is "never as great a partnership [between members] of the same sex as there is between the different sexes," for "the affection [*caritas*] between a man and a man, or between a woman and a woman, is not as great as that between a man and a woman."[89]

9.3.2 *Procreation as a reason for marriage*

The *magistri moderni* use the phrase "hope of offspring" (*spes prolis*) to characterize the procreative good of marriage, whereas Augustine said simply "offspring" (*proles*).[90] The phrase emphasizes the spouses' intention to procreate rather than procreation *per se*, although Augustine, too, assumed that the benefit included the intention to nurture children lovingly and to raise them to worship God. The *Sententiae Berolinenses* explains that spouses achieve the procreative good when they "come together in the hope of offspring," and when they "nurture and discipline [their children] in the law of God and with reverence."[91]

The *In coniugio figura* counts the "love of offspring" (*amor prolis*) among the efficient causes of marriage. Whereas the three final causes for marrying are procreation, the avoidance of fornication, and the extension of charity through exogamy,[92] the three efficient causes are the "manifest consent of legitimate, present persons" (for the partners cannot marry *in absentia*), the "love of offspring" (*amor prolis*), and the intention to be faithful to each other as long as both are alive. To prove that the love of offspring and the intention to remain together are necessary for marriage, the author cites a passage from the *De bono coniugali* in which Augustine suggests that an informal alliance may amount to marriage if the intentions are right.[93] Whereas the love of offspring is among the efficient causes of marriage, the firm intention to avoid offspring "by an evil wish [*votum*] or an evil deed," as Augustine put it, is incompatible with the intention to marry and, therefore, invalidates a marriage.[94] The partners are not required actively to seek or desire offspring in marrying, but they must at least not intend to prevent procreation.[95]

By including the love of offspring among the efficient causes of marriage, the *In coniugio figura* was invoking a traditional moral theme regarding the criteria for

[89] *Cum omnia sacramenta* I, 132/23–25.
[90] For example, *Cum omnia sacramenta* I, 140/4: "fides, spes prolis, sacramentum."
[91] *Sententiae Berolinenses*, 57/1–2.   [92] *In coniugio figura*, 112/17–18.
[93] Augustine, *De b. coniug.* 5(5), CSEL 41:193/17–19. The citations in Bliemetzrieder's edition of *In coniugio figura* are wrong here.
[94] Augustine, *De nupt. et conc.* I.15(17), CSEL 42:229/21: "siue uoto malo siue opere malo."
[95] *In coniugio figura*, 112/27–113/3.

choosing a partner and the proper motives for marrying. Clerics exhorted men and women to marry for the sake of procreation, not to satisfy sexual desire. Isidore of Seville, following Augustine, counsels that people who are choosing spouses should remember that they are marrying to have children and not out of lust (*libido*), and he notes that the nuptial tablets proclaim that a man takes a wife "for the sake of procreating children."[96] Similarly, some eleventh-century dotal charters from northern France proclaim that the spouses are marrying for the "love of offspring" or "the love of posterity," and not to satisfy their lust.[97] The idiom was derived from Tobit 8:9: "Lord, you know that not for fleshly lust do I take my sister to wife, but only for the love of posterity [*sola posteritatis dilectione*], in which your name may be blessed forever and ever."

If the spouses must have some procreative intent in order to consent to a valid marriage, what about persons who marry knowing that they are incapable of begetting children?[98] The author of the *Sententiae Berolineses* inquires whether a man can validly marry a woman who is too old to beget children, or even a young woman who is known to be infertile. Some say that there is no marriage in such cases because there is no hope of offspring. The author falls back on an *a posteriori* solution, failing to solve the objection. There must be "some conjugal pact" between such spouses "according to the dispensation of the church," for if either partner has a relationship with a third person while the other partner is alive, he or she commits adultery. It follows that their marriage is valid.[99] The church's tolerance for marrying among the elderly and among others who had no "hope of offspring" was difficult – perhaps impossible – to square with the procreative rationale for marriage. The clergy's chief aim was not to enhance procreation, for marital abstinence was always the superior option, but rather to include as many respectable unions as possible within the domain of ecclesiastically regulated marriage.

---

[96] Isidore of Seville, *De ecclesiasticis officiis* II.20.9–10, CCL 113:92–93.

[97] K. Zeumer (ed.), *Formulae Merowingici et Karolini Aevi*, MGH *Leges* V, (Hanover, 1886), *Extr.* I 11, p. 540/19: "and I am determined through love of posterity alone [*solo posteritatis amore*], with God's help, to be united with her in human marriage." Ibid., *Extr.* I 13, p. 542/19–21: "Therefore I, by name ___, a knight of God, desiring to imitate the institutions of the holy Fathers [i.e., the Patriarchs], wish to take you, by name ___, as my wife because of the desire to beget offspring [*propter amorem generandae prolis*], and to abide faithfully by the conjugal rule in matrimony." Quoted from THTH 160, 162. In *Extr.* I. 15, 543/12, the *sponsus* promises to take his *sponsa* as his wife "in fidelity, with legitimate consent, and in the hope of offspring [*in ... spe sobolis*], not motivated by lust" Quoted (ibid., 163).

[98] A heretical group of German laypersons in the mid-thirteenth century maintained that any spouses who copulated "without hope of offspring" (*absque spe prolis*) committed a mortal sin. See M. A. E. Nickson, "The 'Pseudo-Reinerius' Treatise: The Final Stage of a Thirteenth-Century Work on Heresy from the Diocese of Passau," AHDLMA 34 (1967): 255–314, at 298; and P. Biller, "Birth-Control in the West in the Thirteenth and Early Fourteenth Centuries," *Past and Present* 94 (1982): 3–26, at 9.

[99] *Sententiae Berolinenses*, 57/16–20

9.3.3 *Malady and remedy*

The *magistri moderni* accepted Augustine's theory that marriage excused the evils inherent in fallen sexuality or at least reduced them to the level of venial sin. According to the *Sententiae Berolineses*, for example, there is no sin when a spouse engages in sexual intercourse either for the sake or procreation or to render the conjugal debt, but marriage remains good after the fall only because it makes the evil of "shameful ardor" pardonable (*venialis*).[100] What prevents people who have recently had sex from going to church is not sin but ritual impurity.[101]

Although they were aware of Augustine's moral psychology of the remedy, the *magistri moderni* usually considered marriage to be a kind of compensation or waiver for sexual sin. Being less preoccupied with introspective moral psychology than Augustine had been, they were less interested in internal disorder and the breakdown of the hierarchy of flesh and spirit, and they rarely explained how marriage ameliorates the sins of concupiscence. They expected laypersons to follow the rules, not to examine their consciences scrupulously and continuously as priests and religious were expected to do. Marriage did not so much rescue coitus from sin, in their view, as excuse it. From a confessor's point of view, excuse was sufficient. A *sententia* in the miscellany collected by the Benedictines of Durham explains that although the "act of incontinence" is evil and damnable, it is "excused through the sacrament of marriage, which is the remedy."[102] The sexual ethic of the *magistri moderni* was pessimistic and puritanical, but it would have been relatively easy for the laity to follow. It would not have put harsh burdens on pious lay folk. The *magistri moderni* did not encourage couples to practice conjugal celibacy, as Augustine had done. Like Augustine, though, they located the fallen aspect of sexuality in disordered desire. Persons who were strong enough to control their carnal desire should not marry. As already noted, a gloss on St Paul's "it is better to marry than to burn" (1 Cor 7:9) in the miscellany collected by the Cistercians of Kirkstall distinguishes between avoidable (*evitabilis*) and unavoidable sexual desire. Other things being equal, one should marry only if one's desire is unavoidable, for avoidable desire can be restrained without marriage.[103]

The *magistri moderni* located the shameful aspect of sexual intercourse chiefly in pleasure (*delectatio*). The compiler of the *In primis hominibus*, glossing Augustine, explains that although marriage is an occasion for sexual pleasure, it does not follow that marriage itself is evil:

> It seems to some people that marriage is evil because it entails lustful pleasure [*delectatio libidinis*]. But there was marriage before the fall of man, and coitus then was free from indecent yearning [*ardor turpitudinis*]. Hence, it is clear that the evil

---

[100] Ibid., 56/20–26.   [101] Ibid., 57/21–27, 58/1–11.
[102] PM 401 (p. 286). MS Oxford, Bodl., Laud Misc. 277, 57rb–58va.
[103] PM 129 (p. 102). MS Oxford, Bodl., Laud Misc. 216, 145va.

of incontinence does not proceed from marriage but rather from the sin that makes human nature corrupt.[104]

The *Sententiae Berolinenses*, glossing Augustine's "what would have been a duty for the healthy is a remedy for the sick," explains that if there were no sin, "the man would have been joined to the woman without shameful ardor and for the sake of children alone, just as one hand is joined to another hand without pleasure [*delectatio*]." Marriage remains good after the fall, the author explains, but chiefly because it makes the evil of "shameful ardor" pardonable (*venialis*).[105] According to a *sententia* or little treatise on marriage preserved in a version of the *Sententiae divinae paginae*, no one knows whether sexual intercourse occurred in the earthly Paradise, but, if it did, it would have been free from pleasure. After the fall, sinful pleasure in sexual intercourse became irresistible. Why, then, does God permit marriage? The author replies that one might ask the same question about eating and drinking, for they, too, cannot occur without irresistible pleasure. In marriage, as in eating and drinking, there are goods that excuse the pleasure. Just as food and drink sustain the body, so marriage provides offspring and enables the partners to avoid fornication.[106]

Notwithstanding their modest expectations for the laity, the *magistri moderni* assumed that *any* carnal pleasure, and not only sexual pleasure, was evil, and they presented refined analyses and measures of pleasure. Their interest may have resulted in part from their personal religious scruples and from the natural anxieties of celibate clerics, but it also reflected the impossible task of squaring the phenomenology of commonplace pleasures with belief in a primordial earthly Paradise. Moreover, it met the needs of the confessional, wherein clerics had to make judgments about the venial sins of pious, faithful spouses, and to prescribe appropriate penances that would not discourage the laity from availing themselves of the sacrament. To measure the degree of moral culpability in carnal pleasure, a cleric ought to determine whether it involved the complicity of the rational will.

A *sententia* ascribed in some sources to Anselm of Laon presents a subtle analysis of pleasure, invoking the Stoic notion of *propassio*: the reflexive, pre-rational response to a tempting stimulus that is prior to the rational subject's deliberate response.[107] The "sin of pleasure" (*peccatum delectationis*) may be avoidable (*evitabilis*) or unavoidable (*inevitabilis*). Unavoidable pleasure is a *propassio*, that is, an involuntary motion of the mind, which is "subject to the law of the flesh." In general, such pleasure is already a species of sin, but it is pardonable (*venialis*) because it is involuntary, and it is not fatal as long as the "remedy of baptism"

[104] *In primis hominibus*, 2/4–7.   [105] *Sententiae Berolinenses*, 56/20–26.
[106] *Huius sacramenti habemus*, 365/25–29.
[107] The proximate source of this analysis of sin was Jerome, *Comm. in Matheum* 1.5.28 and 4.26.37, CCL 77:30–31, 253. See S. Knuuttila, *Emotions in Ancient and Medieval Philosophy* (Oxford, 2004), 178 ff., and M. Colish, "Another Look at the School of Laon," AHDLMA 53 (1986): 7–22, at 18–19.

precedes it. God himself implanted involuntary pleasure in human beings as a salutary trial, for it is "very useful for the conservation of humility" if one uses it well. Thus, the unavoidable pleasure that spouses experience in sexual intercourse is a *propassio*, and it is pardonable because the sacrament of marriage (*sacramentum nuptiarum*) is the remedy to it. But one ought to regret having experienced even pardonable pleasure. Those who consent to it rather than regretting it show contempt for God, who will justly damn them. Indeed, it is such consent that leads to avoidable pleasure. Nevertheless, one's act of consent to an avoidable pleasure is distinct from the act of pleasure itself, just as one may consent to a pleasure without committing the corresponding pleasurable act, as in a sexual fantasy or in adultery of the heart. Even when the pleasurable act under consideration is not carried out externally, one's consent to the pleasure remains distinct from the pleasure itself. The consent welcomes and fosters the pleasure, just as with any other voluntary action. Serious sin exists not in the action *per se* or in the illicit pleasure but in consent to that pleasure.[108]

9.4 THE SACRED HISTORY OF MARRIAGE

In order to situate marriage and its laws in a historical narrative, the *magistri moderni* analyze the changes that have occurred in the course of the history of salvation. Two themes are discernable. One theme regards marriage in relation to the fall and to the advent of Jesus Christ. The other pertains to the regulation of marriage, such as the rules regarding divorce and the impediments of consanguinity. What the law permits at one time, it may later forbid, and vice versa.

Some of the treatises posit different institutions of marriage to explain how the norms and the rules have changed. The precise meaning of the term *institutio* is unclear, but it is clear that an institution both entails a regime or a set of laws and expresses a reason for marrying: a purpose, an end, or a distinct set of benefits.[109] Institutions are historical occurrences, although it is not always clear whether they are discrete events or regimes that endured over long periods. All the *magistri moderni*, following Augustine, hold that marriage was instituted first *ad officium* (i.e., for the sake of procreation) and later *ad remedium*, but whereas some posit additional institutions to account for legal changes such as the movement from Judaic endogamy to Christian exogamy, others resist the multiplication of institutions, reasoning that a legal change does not necessarily presuppose a new institution.

---

[108] PM 85 (p. 74). MS Oxford, Bodl., Douce 89, 94v. Similar analyses of sin as proceeding from involuntary *propassio* to voluntary consent appear in PM 86 (pp. 75–76), PM 278 (222), and PM 452–54 (304–05). PM 75 and 76 are ascribed to Anselm in the manuscripts, and PM 278 and 453 to William of Champeaux.

[109] *Coniugium namque*, 271/28: "Institutio autem coniugii causa et eiusdem coniugii...."

9.4.1 *Office and remedy as successive institutions*

The *magistri moderni* attribute the procreative and remedial virtues of marriage to two distinct historical institutions. God instituted marriage in the beginning for the sake of a duty (*ad officium*). Later, God instituted marriage for the sake of remedy (*ad remedium*).[110] St Paul refers to the second institution in 1 Corinthians 7. But when did it occur? The idea of two distinct institutions, respectively *ad officium* and *ad remedium*, came from Book IX of the *De Genesi ad litteram*, where Augustine argues that in this "time to refrain from embracing" (Eccl 3:5), there is no longer an urgent need to beget children for the city of God. As a result, "what would have been a duty [*officium*] for the healthy is a remedy [*remedium*] for the sick."[111] Augustine is not comparing two periods, however, but rather a counterfactual situation with the actual one. Moreover, Augustine maintains that the duty to procreate endures throughout the Old Covenant, whereas a remedy was needed as soon as Adam and Eve were expelled from Paradise.

The *magistri moderni* tried to reduce Augustine's partly counterfactual theory to a dichotomy between two actual historical institutions, the second of which superseded the first. According to the *Sententiae Magistri A.*, "Marriage before sin was a duty [*officium*], but after sin it was a remedy for sin."[112] Some of the treatises assume that the second, remedial institution of marriage occurred after the advent of Jesus Christ, whereas others assume that it occurred immediately after the fall.[113]

9.4.2 *Laws as successive institutions*

The *magistri moderni* emphasize that the law of marriage is not unchanging. What was formerly permitted became prohibited, and vice versa.[114] For example, because the entire human race descended from Adam and Eve, there must at first have been no prohibition against the marriage of siblings. Brother-sister marriage was prohibited later, when it was no longer necessary. Again, polygamy was introduced under Abraham, and divorce and remarriage under Moses. Polygamy is forbidden under the New Covenant, and Jesus forbade divorce. Later, the church introduced remote impediments to foster exogamy. The *magistri moderni* may have owed this theme, as well, to Augustine, although the debt is rarely explicit. The *In primis*

---

[110] The preposition, *ad*, designates final causality.

[111] *De Gen. ad litt.* IX.7, CSEL 28.1:275: "quod sanis esse posset officium, sit aegrotis remedium." Quoted in *In primis hominibus*, pp. 1–2 (IPH 2).

[112] SMA 15 (p. 169): "Coniugium ante peccatum esset officium, post peccatum uero est peccati remedium. Prima autem institutio fuit ad propagationem filiorum."

[113] Immediately after the fall: *Cum omnia sacramenta I*, 131/18–20; *Cum omnia sacramenta II*, ed. Weisweiler, 34/20–21, 23–24; *Coniugium namque*, 270/6–20. After the advent of Jesus Christ: *De coniugiis tractantibus*, 74/30–75/4; *Decretum Dei fuit*, 362/23–24.

[114] *Huius sacramenti habemus*, 366/30–54.

hominibus assembles passages from Augustine's *De nuptiis et concupiscentia* to show how God permitted polygamy under the Old Law only for the sake of procreation, and to show how and why the impediments of relationship multiplied under Moses and again under the "institution of the time of grace."[115] The peculiarities of the Old Law met the exigencies of that time, when the people of God had a duty to perpetuate and to enlarge their race but could not marry outsiders for fear of adulterating their cult. Lamech was the first man to have more than one wife (Gen 4:19), the author notes, but he did not do so legally. Unlike the later patriarchs, Lamech was guilty of adultery "because he did not marry the second [woman] with God's permission and in order to multiply the people of God, but rather for the sake of sexual pleasure."[116] Medieval exegetes usually regarded Lamech as the first adulterer, reasoning that it was not his polygamy *per se* that was wrong but rather his adulterous intentions.[117]

Following Augustine, the *magistri moderni* maintain that exogamy extends the scope of *caritas*.[118] Augustine argues in *The City of God* that the purpose of the impediments was to keep familial relationships separate from each other. Because siblings cannot marry, Augustine points out, no man should be both father and father-in-law of the same woman. But such scruples were not practical in the beginning. Augustine considers how a vague discomfort regarding the marriage of close relatives, such as cousins, evolved into a legal prohibition when culture and circumstances favored that advance. The separation of relationships extended universal love (*caritas*) to a greater number and enhanced the "social life" of human beings, among whom "concord should be useful and honorable."[119] Excerpts from this discussion appear in the *In primis hominibus*.[120]

Each of the treatises on marriage works out an account of the history and institutions of marriage in its own way. I shall review in more detail how four of the treatises deal with the topic: the *De coniugiis tractantibus*, the *Cum omnia sacramenta I* (with the treatises that depend on it), the *Coniugium namque*, and the *In coniugio figura*.

[115] *In primis hominibus*, pp. 11–14.   [116] Ibid., 12/15–13/2.

[117] *Sententiae Berolinenses*, 58/20–25. Gen 4:19 mentions that Lamech "took unto him two wives," called Adah and Zillah, but it does not say that he erred in so doing. Medieval scholars assumed that he erred because of the context, which is apparently an account of the rising tide of depravity among the descendants of Cain, although the argument may be circular. On Lamech's adultery, see Nicholas I, *Epist.* 99, c. 51, MGH *Epist.* 6 (*Epistolae Karolini Aevi 4*), 586; Ivo, *Decretum* VIII.227; idem, *Epist.* 153, PL 162:157C.

[118] *De coniugiis tractantibus*, 75/17–21. *Cum omnia sacramenta I*, 141/21–142/9. *Cum omnia sacramenta II*, ed. Bliemetzrieder, 280/132–37.

[119] Augustine, *De civ. Dei* XV.16, CCL 48:476–479. See especially 477/7–14 on the expansion of social harmony and on *caritas* as universal, non-discriminating love. Augustine's theory is cited in Jonas of Orléans, *De institutione laicali* II.13, ed. Dubreucq, 1:422–24 (= II.8, PL 106:183C–D). Augustine touches briefly on procreation as a means of extending friendship in the preamble to the *De b. coniug.*

[120] *In primis hominibus*, pp. 13–14 (IPH 33–35).

9.4.3 De coniugiis tractantibus

According to the *De coniugiis tractantibus*, the first institution of marriage occurred in Paradise, "when God brought forth Eve from Adam's rib a helper who was like him, so that they should beget sons and daughters until the number of the elect was completed with all their posterity." If these human beings had not sinned, they would never have experienced death. Rather, they would eventually have been transformed, taking on angelic form. Likewise, they would have experienced no ardor or lust in sexual intercourse, and their genitalia would have been as obedient to their will as the other members of the body. There were no impediments of blood relationship at first. Indeed, Adam and Eve, the first spouses, were made of the same flesh. Nevertheless, the three goods of marriage – faith, offspring, and sacrament – would have been perfectly fulfilled in Paradise, with nothing superfluous and nothing missing.[121]

Although the author maintains that marriage was a duty (*officium*) before the fall, he takes issue with those who say that marriage was a matter of precept (*praeceptum*) rather than of permission. Sexual reproduction was not strictly necessary for reproduction, for God could have propagated the human race by some other means in Paradise, just as he had made Eve from Adam without sexual procreation. Moreover, some men, such as Elias and Jeremiah, chose to be celibate even under the Old Law, when marriage was still a duty.[122]

The author correlates the various institutions of marriage with the three conjugal goods. Marriage was originally instituted with the union of Adam and Eve in the earthly Paradise, but there were three re-institutions of marriage, each of which diminished or qualified one of the goods of marriage: first faith, then sacrament, and finally offspring. The three re-institutions correspond to Abraham, to Moses, and to Christ, respectively. Although Adam and Eve and their descendants after the fall were unable to procreate without lust, there was no new institution of marriage at first, and they continued to fulfill all three of the goods. Nevertheless, something comparable to a change of institution must have occurred after the Flood, for Scripture recounts how God was displeased when the "sons of God" married "the daughters of men" (Gen 6:2). The "sons of God," the author explains, were the sons of Seth, whereas the "daughters of men" were the daughters of Cain. They belonged to different races, and God wanted to prevent miscegenation. That divine displeasure was the historical origin of the impediment of cult: the prohibition against marriage between believers and unbelievers. But what chiefly displeased God in these mixed unions was not the mixing of cult but the fact that the men were seeking carnal pleasure rather than the goods of marriage.[123]

---

[121] *De coniugiis tractantibus*, 73/26–29.

[122] Ibid., 78/16–26. This passage, which is ascribed to Ivo in the *Liber Pancrisis* (MS British Library, Harley 3098, 74v), is extant as an independent *sententia* in MS British Library, Roy. 11 A. V, 24ra–24rb (= PM 402) and MS Oxford, Bodl., Laud Misc. 277, 27vb.

[123] *De coniugiis tractantibus*, 74/1–15.

Whereas the first institution of marriage occurred with Adam, therefore, the second occurred with Abraham, when the good of faith was relaxed. Abraham was unfaithful to Sarah when he had sexual intercourse with Hagar (Gen 16), and Jacob had sexual relations with both Rachel and Leah (Gen 30:4–5, 9–10). But this falling away from the monogamous ideal was not sinful. God permitted it because there were few believers at that time. The strictly monogamous regime instituted in the beginning was no longer practical. On the one hand, the chosen people had a duty to beget children for the worship of the true God.[124] On the other hand, they were not supposed to marry outside their race because that would have adulterated the cult. It is true that they sometimes married outsiders to bring them into the community of God (Gen 41:45), or even as a way of subverting an enemy (Judges 14:4), but these circumstances were exceptional. Marrying outside the cult was usually forbidden.[125]

The third institution occurred when Moses diminished the good of sacrament by permitting Israelite men to divorce their wives, as Jesus explains (Matt 19:8).[126]

The fourth occurred when the duty to procreate passed into abeyance after the coming of Jesus Christ. The faithful no longer needed to beget children to complete the number of the elect, and virginity became the preferable option. Henceforth, the chief purpose of marriage was to save from fornication those who were not strong enough for celibacy. As Augustine says, "what would have been a duty for the healthy is a remedy for the sick."[127] Christians in the author's own day fulfill all three of the nuptial goods, as in the beginning, yet they marry chiefly in order to avoid fornication, not for the sake of offspring.[128] Moreover, because the church now embraces people from all the races of the world, men no longer need to marry their blood relations. Instead, "because of both the expansion of charity [*propter amplificationem caritatis*] and the beauty of the church, it was instituted that marriage should not take place where there is [already] natural love [*dilectio naturalis*], as among blood relations and people sharing a common parent, but only between non-kin [*extranei*]."[129]

9.4.4 Cum omnia sacramenta I

Although the *Cum omnia sacramenta I* depends on the *De coniugiis tractantibus* for its history of marriage, it approaches the topic in a more theological and less legal spirit. The author begins by considering marriage as one of the sacraments. Whereas all the sacraments were instituted after sin and because of sin, marriage alone was also instituted before sin occurred, and not for a remedy (*ad remedium*), like the

[124] Likewise, *Sententiae Berolinenses*, 58/12–19.   [125] *De coniugiis tractantibus*, 75/22–76/2.
[126] Ibid., 74/25–29.
[127] Ibid., 74/30–75/15. Augustine, *De Gen. ad litt.* IX.7, CSEL 28.1:275.
[128] *De coniugiis tractantibus*, 75/30–76/2.
[129] Ibid., 75/17–21. Likewise, *Cum omnia sacramenta I*, 141/28–142/3 (*propter amplificationem caritatis*); *Cum omnia sacramenta II*, ed. Bliemetzrieder, 280/132–35 (*propter dilatandam caritatem*).

others, but to fulfill a duty (*ad officium*).[130] This opening passage will recur often in twelfth- and thirteenth-century theology.

The treatise distinguishes between the institution and the origin, or source, of marriage. God is the origin of marriage, for God made marriage in Paradise by forming Eve from Adam's rib so that she could help Adam to propagate the human race. Again, when Adam said, "This is bone of my bones" and so forth (Gen 2:23), he was inspired by the Holy Spirit, showing that marriage was the object of a divine decree. God himself blessed marriage when he told Adam and Eve to increase and multiply (Gen 1:28). God blessed marriage again when Jesus "consecrated" it with his bodily presence at the marriage of Cana (John 2). In short, "God is the author and origin of marriage."[131] This argument shows that marriage comes directly from God, but the author's chief concern is to guard against anti-matrimonial heresy. The discussion echoes Augustine's defense of marriage against the Manichees, and it is typical of an anti-heretical discourse that flourished during the twelfth and early thirteenth centuries. Clerics who maintained that sexual desire and pleasure were evil and that celibacy was the proper way to salvation had to distance themselves, as Augustine had done, from heretics who denigrated marriage. The wedding at Cana was a common topos in this context. The heretics suppose that marriage is evil because it entails lust. To confound the heretics, Jesus confirmed marriage both by condemning divorce and by attending the wedding of Cana, where he performed the first of his miracles.[132]

The institutions of marriage, according to the *Cum omnia sacramenta I*, pertain to its final causes. This treatise posits only two institutions, "one before sin, as a duty [*ad officium*], the other after sin, for the remedy [*ad remedium*]. The cause of the first institution was the propagation of offspring. The cause of the second was the avoidance of fornication."[133] The author explains that the preposition *ad* in the phrases *ad officium* and *ad remedium* expresses final causality: "These things — the avoidance of fornication and the propagation of offspring — are the causes for which marriage is permitted to happen, just as a war [is fought] for victory, which is the final cause of war."[134] Although the *Cum omnia sacramenta II* quotes Augustine more sparingly, it conveys more of the remedial psychology underlying Augustine's theory:

---

[130] *Cum omnia sacramenta I*, 129/24–27. *Cum omnia sacramenta II*, ed. Weisweiler, 33/1–3. Cf. *Decretum Dei fuit*, 362/5–6: "Tunc autem institutum fuit ad officium generandi; modo ad remedium."

[131] *Cum omnia sacramenta I*, 129/32–130/2. The *Cum omnia sacramenta II*, ed. Weisweiler, 34/ 6–13, makes the point more simply: "Coniugium ergo a Deo est."

[132] *Sententiae Berolinenses*, 56/16–19. Augustine, *De b. coniug.* 3(3), 190/16–19, = *In primis hominibus*, 5/9–12 (IPH 10). The theme was common topos during the high Middle Ages. It appears in preambles to dotal charters (see references to "Wedding at Cana" in the index to THTH), and it is the topic of many marriage sermons, which were often preached when the relevant gospel as read: see David d'Avray, *Medieval Marriage Sermons* (Oxford, 2001), 1–2, and ff. passim.

[133] *Cum omnia sacramenta I*, 130/6–7. *Cum omnia sacramenta II*, ed. Weisweiler, 34/14–15.

[134] *Cum omnia sacramenta I*, 130/23–25. The *Cum omnia sacramenta II* omits this passage.

It should be noted that marriage provides a remedy against concupiscence in two ways: it moderates the ardor of immoderate lust by limiting sexual intercourse under the definitive rule of a single compact; and it excuses ardor, which is evil in itself, by means of the goods that are attached to marriage. For as Augustine says, "The good of marriage in some way limits and moderates the evil of disobedient members, so that carnal desire at least becomes conjugal chastity."[135] The good moderates the evil in [these] two ways because it restrains it from promiscuity [*vagus concubitus*], not permitting it to flow out into perdition. It does not cause it to be no longer evil, but rather to be not damnable. The good is not culpable because of the evil. On the contrary, the evil is pardonable [*venialis*] because of the good.[136]

Following Augustine, the *Cum omnia sacramenta I* explains that those who marry for the wrong reasons are not really married. Indeed, if the husband marries for the proper reasons but his wife marries for an improper reason, such as lust, then he is truly her husband but she is really not his wife but a whore. Contrariwise, if she marries for the proper reasons but he marries for an improper reason, such as money, then he is really an adulterer, whereas she is truly his wife. Nevertheless, such a marriage is valid in the church's external forum because human beings cannot judge the hidden things of the heart. As long as these unions "have been made with a nuptial celebration [*nuptiarum sollemnitas*], we call them marriages."[137]

Both recensions of the *Cum omnia sacramenta* hold that marriage was instituted as a remedy immediately after the fall but associate that institution with Paul's counsel in 1 Corinthians 7. The first recension is explicit on this point: "From that time, when Adam sinned, it was good for a man not to touch a woman, as the Apostle said [1 Cor 7:1]."[138] According to the *Cum omnia sacramenta II*, just as marriage was instituted only as a duty in Paradise, so also it was instituted only as remedy after the fall, for it was no longer a matter of duty.[139] But the *De coniugiis tractantibus* holds that marriage was not instituted as a remedy until the coming of Christ.[140] Similarly, the *Decretum Dei fuit*, which depends on the *Cum omnia sacramenta I*, holds that marriage was instituted as remedy under the New Law: "The reason for the second institution, after the advent of Christ, was the avoidance of fornication."[141]

Although the *Cum omnia sacramenta I* posits only two institutions of marriage,[142] the treatise repeats what the *De coniugiis tractantibus* said about the development of exogamy and the introduction of impediments of relationship. After the advent of

[135] Augustine, *Epist.* 187.31, CSEL 57:109/15–18. = SMA 19 (p. 170). Quoted in *Cum omnia sacramenta I*, 132/9–10.
[136] *Cum omnia sacramenta II*, ed. Bliemetzrieder, 275/5–16.
[137] *Cum omnia sacramenta I*, 130/25–33. Likewise, *Coniugium namque*, 273/25–35.
[138] *Cum omnia sacramenta I*, 131/18–20.
[139] *Cum omnia sacramenta II*, ed. Weisweiler, 34/20–21, 23–24: "Primam institutionem officium tantum esse et non remedium Augustinus confirmat.... Secundam autem non officium esse sed remedium, alibi ostendit."
[140] *De coniugiis tractantibus*, 74/30–75/4. [141] *Decretum Dei fuit*, 362/23–24. Emphasis mine.
[142] *Cum omnia sacramenta I*, 130/6–7: "Institutio coniugii duplex est: una ante peccatum ad officium, alia post peccatum ad remedium."

Christ, it was no longer necessary for men to marry their near relations. Instead, the prohibition of marriage within seven degrees of consanguinity compels people to find "non-consanguineous" partners.[143] Exogamy enlarges charity by separating different modes of relationship. Marriage is no longer permitted where love already exists by nature, as between blood relations and people sharing a common parent. Nor is it permitted where there is already a spiritual love, such as between co-parents.[144]

9.4.5 Coniugium namque

The *Coniugium namque* follows the *Cum omnia sacramenta I* in positing only two institutions of marriage. The author explains that an institution presupposes a reason (*causa*) for marriage. Now, only two such reasons need to be considered here: procreation and the avoidance of fornication. The author does not insist that there are no other reasons, but he can see no reason to posit any: "If someone says that there are other reasons [*causae*] for marrying as well, we do not object, but we declare that these are probably the two chief reasons."[145] The first institution occurred in Paradise, when God blessed Adam and Eve and told them to increase and multiply (Gen 1:28). Marriage then already entailed the three goods of marriage, but its chief reason was the "multiplication of children" (*filiorum multiplicatio*).

The second institution added the "avoidance of procreation" (*fornicatio evitationis*) as a reason. St Paul was making a concession to people who marry for this end when he said, "Let each one have his own wife because of fornication" (1 Cor 7:2). Nevertheless, the author assumes that the second institution occurred as soon as Adam and Eve were expelled from Paradise, for it was "better not to touch a woman" from that moment:

> Therefore, when Adam was expelled from Paradise and human nature became corrupt, he sensed that the joy of pleasure and vice in the touch of his wife were present in him, but he knew that God had given him a remedy in the benefit of marriage. From that time, when Adam [first] sinned, it was "good not to touch a woman," as the Apostle says [1 Cor 7:1], for we should affirm that it is good to abstain with a patient nature from anything that is accompanied by fleshly pleasure. Accordingly, whereas sin makes human kind prone to the deformity and ruin of turpitude, an honorable union sets it right. Carnal union, which is damnable and illicit in itself, becomes venial and acceptable to God through marriage, the fruitfulness of human nature is displayed, and the perversity of incontinence is covered up. It is clear, therefore, that the institution of marriage among Adam's sons

---

[143] Ibid., 148/19–21.

[144] Ibid., 141/21–142/3. The author is referring to the spiritual relationship (*cognatio spiritualis*) contracted by sponsoring a baptism, such as the relationship between a godparent and a natural parent of the same child.

[145] *Coniugium namque*, 270/30–271/5, 271/28–33.

was not natural but rather a matter of dispensation, so that the immoderate ardor of lust should be removed from promiscuous sexual intercourse and controlled under the definite rule of a single faith. Hence the Apostle says: "Let each one have his own wife because of fornication" [1 Cor 7:1]. See how the humble pastor [*pastor humilis*] concedes through a dispensation that people may marry in order to shun the turpitude of promiscuous sexual intercourse.[146]

The author holds up Paul as a model for the "humble pastors" to whom the treatise is addressed. Although they have chosen the better way of celibacy, that is no reason to be puffed up with pride. They must not disdain married folk, for marriage is the remedy that God himself provided for those who are not capable of resisting their sexual appetites. It saves them from fornication and promiscuity (*vagus concubitus*).

9.4.6 In coniugio figura

The *In coniugio figura* begins with the premise that there is a manifold "figure and trace" (*figura et vestigium*) of the Trinity in marriage. Just as woman came from a man and a child comes from their union, so the Son proceeds from the Father and the Holy Spirit proceeds from both. To sustain that Trinitarian premise, the author divides every aspect of marriage into three. There are three institutions of marriage, and three reasons for marrying. There are three goods of marriage: faith, hope of offspring, and sacrament. There are also three virtues corresponding to the three goods: chastity corresponds to faith, fecundity to hope of offspring, and the signifying of Christ and the church to sacrament. There are three impediments: religious vows, holy orders, and consanguinity. There are three efficient causes: the expressed consent of persons who are present and legally qualified, the desire for offspring, and the intention to remain faithful. There are three valid reasons for divorce: prior consent to another marriage, but only if it was consent about the present and not about the future; adultery; and impotence. There are even three causes of impotence: infirmity, defective genitalia, and frigidity.

The first institution occurred before sin, as recorded in Genesis 1:22 and 1:28. Paul recorded the second institution when he said that each man should have his own wife because of fornication (1 Cor 7:2). The author does not say when this institution occurred. The third institution involves "the precepts of the modern holy fathers" (*precepta sanctorum patrum modernorum*), which prohibit the marriage of blood relations.[147]

The three chief reasons for marrying are the begetting of children, the avoidance of fornication, and the enlargement of love (*maioris dilectionis occasio*).[148] These correspond to the three institutions but not in a straightforward manner. Marriage was instituted for the sake of procreation in the beginning, and procreation was a bounden duty only under the first institution. Nevertheless, because this reason

---

[146] Ibid., 270/6–20 (freely translated).   [147] *In coniugio figura*, 112/7–14.   [148] Ibid., 112/17–18.

pertains to the very nature of marriage, it endures through all periods. As Augustine says, the diversity of institutions does not affect the *nature* of marriage, which remains the same.[149] Each of the other two reasons pertains to both the second and the third institutions, although the third reason, the enlargement of love, pertains more to the third institution (that of ecclesiastical regulation) than to the second.[150]

9.4.7 *Summary*

As well as explaining the rules and norms by setting them in the context of God's plan of salvation, the historical analysis of marriage emphasized the power of the episcopate. Bishops had the power to change the laws of marriage, the power to dissolve some marriages, and the power to dispense from some of the impediments. If marriage were an unchanging institution – a perennial reflection of the Law of Heaven – the clergy would be experts on marriage only in the way that meteorologists are experts on the weather, for they would have had no power over it. But if the institution and the laws of marriage continue to change even after the advent of Christ, so that what was licit becomes illicit and vice versa, then the clergy truly have power over marriage. The patristic authorities and the bishops, whom the *In coniugio figura* calls the "holy modern fathers," inherit their power over marriage from God the Father, the patriarchs, and Jesus Christ, in an unbroken tradition.

9.5 MARRIAGE IN THE CHURCH

The *magistri moderni* considered marriage to be one of the sacraments, in part because marriage was a way of belonging to the church. Married folk, in their view, constituted one of the ranks or orders from which the church is composed.

9.5.1 *The sacramentality of marriage*

The *magistri moderni* used the term "sacrament" to refer both to the insoluble aspect of marriage (Augustine's *bonum sacramenti*) and to marriage as a sign of Christ and the church. In a few places, they used the term to characterize marriage as saving and efficacious. Although they did not articulate a consistent theory of marriage as one of the sacraments, their use of the term reflects current developments in sacramental theology. Augustine's idea of the *bonum sacramenti* was the source of much of what *magistri moderni* had to say about the sacramentality of marriage, but they developed that idea in new ways. The insolubility of marriage, they argued, was itself a sign of a sacred reality. According to the *In coniugio figura*, for example, the

---

[149] Ibid., 112/14–16, 112/18–19, 113/8–14. Augustine, *De nupt. et conc.* II.32(54), CSEL 42:311/15–18, says that marriage now is different in quality but not in nature from what it would have been if there were no sin.

[150] *In coniugio figura*, 112/20–21.

good of faith entails chastity, the good of offspring entails fecundity, and the good of sacrament entails "the inseparable union of Christ and the church," for marriage as a sacrament "is a sign and figure of the union of Christ and the church."[151]

Although the authors usually conflate the sacrament of marriage with the good of sacrament, the *Decretum Dei fuit* differentiates between the two uses of the term. The insolubility of marriage is called the good of sacrament "because of the mystery of a hidden signification, by which Christ and the church is signified," the author explains, but the word "sacrament" is sometimes said of marriage itself, "as when someone says, 'the sacrament of marriage,' that is, sacred marriage."[152] Similarly, a *sententia* on the three goods of marriage presents the two senses as alternatives: the good of sacrament is *either* the indissolubility of marriage, whereby neither spouse can remarry as long as the other lives, *or* it is the signification of marriage, whereby marriage is a "figure of Christ and the church."[153]

The *magistri moderni* adapted ideas from current sacramental theology to illumine the insolubility of marriage. Twelfth-century theologians defined sacrament as "a sign of sacred reality" (*signum sacrae rei*): an elaboration of Augustine's definition, "sacred sign" (*sacrum signum*).[154] Thus, the compiler of the *In primis hominibus* explains that Augustine calls the third good of marriage "sacrament" because "it is a sign of a sacred reality, namely, that the church does not forsake Christ, nor Christ the church."[155] Similarly, the *Sententiae Berolinenses* explains that the sacrament of marriage is "the sign of this sacred reality, namely, that just as a man ought not and cannot be without the woman married to him as long as she lives, nor the woman without the man, so also Christ cannot be without the church, nor the church without Christ."[156] A *sententia* improbably ascribed to Ivo of Chartres in the *Liber Pancrisis* points out that a remarriage after bereavement does not fully signify Christ's union with the church. Marriage has the goods of faith, offspring, and sacrament as remedies against sin, the author argues, for marriage cannot be perfected without carnal pleasure. He explicates each in turn. Marriage has the good of sacrament inasmuch as the spouses signify the union between Christ and the church. Strictly, there is no such sacrament in a second marriage, for Christ has but one bride (*sponsa*), and the church has but one groom (*sponsus*). Nevertheless, there is a certain sacrament in a second marriage inasmuch as the spouses will not be separated as long as they live, just as Christ will never be separated from the church. The "material" union between husband and wife signifies the eternal union between Christ and church, for "what God has joined, man may not separate."[157] The union of "two in one flesh" is also interpreted as a sign of a sacred

[151] Ibid., 112/22–25.

[152] *Decretum Dei fuit*, 366/8–11. Cf. Peter Lombard, *Sent.* IV, d. 31, c. 1.3 (2:443): "the third good of marriage is called 'sacrament' not because it is marriage itself, but because it is a sign of the same sacred thing, that is, of the spiritual and inseparable joining of Christ and the church."

[153] *Huius sacramenti habemus*, 365/6–8.　　[154] Augustine, *De civ. Dei* X.5, CCL 47:276–77.

[155] *In primis hominibus*, 3/12–13 (IPH 5).　　[156] *Sententiae Berolinenses*, 57/3–5.

[157] MS Harley 3098, 76r–v (LP 271). F. P. Bliemetzrieder, *Zu den Schriften Ivos von Chartres* (Vienna, 1917), 69, no. 17.

reality. According to the *Coniugium namque*, for example, a legitimate marriage is a sacrament inasmuch as it signifies the union between Christ and the church, for just as Christ and the church are one body, so husband and wife are one body. Again, just as Christ is superior to the church and rules over her, so the husband is superior to his wife and rules over her. The "sanctity of the sacrament" consists in the union between husband and wife.[158] The *Cum omnia sacramenta I* explains that just as Christ and the church become one body through the sharing of a common nature, so husband and wife become one body, or two in one flesh, through sexual intercourse.[159]

The *magistri moderni* found an alternative definition of sacrament in Isidore's *Etymologies*, whereby a sacrament is a "sacred secret" or "sacred mystery" (*sacrum secretum*). A saving power is hidden under the covering (*tegumentum*) of bodily things.[160] This definition was complementary to *signum sacrae rei*, and not a competing alternative. According to the *Coniugium namque*, marriage is a sacrament inasmuch as it "hides and signifies something in Christ and the church."[161] According to the *Cum omnia sacramenta I*, the "indissoluble bond" in marriage is called a sacrament because it "hides something sacred" (*aliquod sacrum occultat*), for it "signifies the marriage of Christ and the church, because Christ and the church are one body as well, and cannot be separated."[162]

The sacraments sanctify as well as signify. One of the sentences included under William of Champeaux's name in the *Liber Pancrisis* suggests that marriage as a sacrament mitigates the sin of concupiscence. Assuming that original sin is sexually transmitted – that is that the parents' lust in sexual intercourse infects the offspring – the author inquires as to the cause and the justice of that transmission. If the concupiscence that is, the source of the infection is in the parents, why should the child deserve damnation because of the act? The author replies that because marriage excuses the parents' lust without altering its nature, its causal properties remain the same, so that the parents' concupiscence is the "efficient cause" of sin in the child. Nevertheless, their sin is pardonable (*venialis*) both because of their intention to beget a child and because of the "sacrament of marriage."[163]

The most explicit and influential reference to marriage as one of the sacraments appears at the beginning of the *Cum omnia sacramenta*. The original recension puts it this way:

> Whereas all the sacraments originated after sin and because of sin, only the sacrament of marriage is also said to have been instituted before sin: not as a remedy [*ad remedium*], like the others, but as a duty [*ad officium*].[164]

---

[158] *Coniugium namque*, 273/19–24. [159] *Cum omnia sacramenta I*, 139/19–22.
[160] Isidore, *Etym.* VI.19.40. [161] *Coniugium namque*, 273/19–21.
[162] *Cum omnia sacramenta I*, 135/19–23. This passage is absent from *Cum omnia sacramenta II*.
[163] PM 255 (p. 207). MS Harley 3098, 39r (LP 124).
[164] *Cum omnia sacramenta I*, 129/24–27: "Cum omnia sacramenta post peccatum et propter peccatum sumpserunt [*or* sumserint] exordium, solum coniugii sacramentum ante peccatum etiam legitur institutum, non ad remedium, sicut cetera, sed ad officium."

The same passage (with minor variations) occurs in the *Cum omnia sacramenta II*,[165] whence it passed to Hugh of Saint-Victor and Peter Lombard. The *Decretum Dei fuit* divides the proposition into two parts. It begins by affirming, "God has decreed that human beings are saved through the sacraments, of which the first was marriage."[166] A little later, having explained how God was the institutor of marriage, the treatise explains that marriage "was instituted then [in Paradise] for the duty of procreating, and now as a remedy."[167]

The remarkable opening passage of the *Cum omnia sacramenta I* quoted above, which will recur frequently in the theology of marriage throughout the Middle Ages, places marriage in the numerable class of sacraments but then distinguishes it from the other members of the class. Marriage seems to be anomalous. All the sacraments, including marriage, are saving means. Like the other sacraments, therefore, marriage was instituted after sin as a remedy. But marriage was *also* instituted before sin, and then not as a remedy but as a duty. The *Coniugium namque* rewords the passage so that it states a problem. It seems that marriage was not instituted as a remedy, as the other sacraments were, for it already existed in Paradise. Indeed, some say that God first instituted marriage as sacrament when he blessed Adam and Eve (Gen 1:28). The author replies that although marriage was not originally instituted as a remedy, it became a remedy as soon as Adam and Eve were expelled from Paradise, when Adam began to experience pleasure in the touch of his wife. The fact that this sacrament was instituted in Paradise, therefore, is consistent with the premise that all the sacraments were instituted as remedies against sin.[168]

9.5.2 *Marriage outside the church*

If marriage is one of the sacraments, can unbelievers marry? If they are married in some sense, is their marriage insoluble? How does the marriage of unbelievers differ from Christian marriage? Such questions arose frequently in the work of the *magistri moderni* because of their new approach to marriage.[169] They regarded marriage as a sacrament, as a way of participating in the life of the church, and as an institution that was entirely subject to ecclesiastical jurisdiction. Obviously, unbelievers could not truly be baptized or promoted to holy orders. How, then, could they marry? The authors sometimes include the Jews of their own day in the

---

[165] *Cum omnia sacrament II*, ed. Weisweiler, 33/1–3: "Cum omnia sacramenta post peccatum et propter peccatum sumpserint exordium, solum coniugii sacramentum ante peccatum etiam legitur institutum; non tamen ad remedium sed ad officium."

[166] *Decretum Dei fuit*, 361/1–2: "Decretum dei fuit, homines per sacramenta salvari, quorum primum coniugium fuit."

[167] Ibid., 362/5–6: "Tunc autem institutum fuit ad officium generandi; modo ad remedium."

[168] *Coniugium namque*, 270/30–271/15.

[169] *Cum omnia sacramenta I*, 137/15 ff. *Cum omnia sacramenta II*, ed. Bliemetzrieder, 278/87 ff. *Decretum Dei fuit*, 368/27 ff. *In primis hominibus*, pp. 15–29.

category of non-believers and sometimes treat them as a special class, akin to that of believers. The *In primis hominibus*, for example, inquires whether there is "marriage of the sort that cannot be dissolved as long as both are alive" between "infidels, idolaters, the Jews of the present day, and others who do not have faith in Christ," and whether or not one partner in such marriages can remarry if the other leaves the marriage.[170]

Questions about the marriage of non-Christians were more than theoretical. Jews still lived among Christians in Europe, and Christians sometimes married Jews, even when such marriages were forbidden. Moreover, there was always a risk that a Jew who had converted in order to marry a Christian might relapse. That situation was the inverse of the one that Paul had considered, in which one partner converted to Christianity and the other remained an unbeliever. Ivo of Chartres wrote two letters about cases of this sort. In his judgment, the marriage must be upheld: The believer cannot divorce the apostate except on grounds of (literal) adultery, and he or she cannot remarry as long as the other is alive.[171]

Answers to questions about the marriages of non-Christians in the sentential literature depend on the precise interpretation of the Pauline Privilege (1 Cor 7:12–16).[172] Paul counsels that a convert should not divorce an unbelieving partner who does not wish to separate. There were various interpretations of this rule, but churchmen generally accepted that the convert had the right in certain circumstances to divorce his or her spouse and to remarry. Moreover, rather than construing Paul's counsel narrowly as if it pertained only to mixed marriages or to marriages in which an unbelieving partner makes life difficult for the Christian convert, the *magistri moderni* assumed that it revealed a deficiency in any marriage between unbelievers. All such marriages, in their view, were in some sense soluble, or at least were not as insoluble as marriages in which both spouses were Christian.

The Pauline Privilege was crucial because the church permitted such divorces, whereas one could attribute the practice of divorce and remarriage in non-Christian societies to error. The *magistri moderni* were inclined, notwithstanding much variation and uncertainty, to regard all marriages as lifelong in principle, but they reasoned that non-Christian marriages were deficient and "dispensable." To interpret the Pauline Privilege and to articulate the difference between Christian and non-Christian marriage, the *magistri moderni* drew on a canon ascribed to Ambrose. (Its real author was the otherwise unknown commentator known today as Ambrosiaster.) In its original setting, the text was a gloss on 1 Corinthians 7:15: "a brother or sister is not under servitude in such cases." The verse suggests that the marriage of an unbeliever is dissoluble because it lacks a dimension that only faith in the true God can provide. According to Ambrose, therefore, a marriage "that lacks devotion to

---

[170] *In primis hominibus*, 15/2–4. [171] Ivo, *Epist* 122 and *Epist.* 230, PL 162:135A–C, 233B–C.
[172] D. J. Gregory, *The Pauline Privilege* (Washington, DC, 1931). Reinhardt, *Ehelehre*, 69–75.

God is not established [*ratum*], and consequently it is not a sin for the one who is dismissed for God's sake to join himself to another."[173] The *Cum omnia sacramenta* (in both recensions) presents a condensed version of this canon: "A marriage without God [*praeter Deum*] is not established [*ratum*], and therefore it is not a sin to dismiss [an unbelieving partner] for God's sake [*propter Deum*] and to be joined to another."[174]

Granted that a non-Christian marriage is soluble, should one go further and conclude that it is not really a marriage at all? The consequence seemed to follow logically if one assumed that marriage was essentially insoluble. The question was much disputed. A *sententia* preserved in the *Liber Pancrisis* and elsewhere records that master Anselm and master William answered it differently. According to Anselm, there is no marriage among the Gentiles (i.e., among those who are neither Jews nor Christians), for there cannot be true marriage without faith. There was marriage of some sort among Jews *before* the advent of Christ, but there is no marriage among Jews after Christ. William, on the contrary, "with the agreement of the bishop of Chartres," argues that there is truly marriage among Gentiles and Jews. William's *a posteriori* argument depends on a close reading of Augustine on the Pauline Privilege. A Christian woman who is married to an infidel is permitted to divorce him, as Augustine argues, because their relationship is a kind of adultery or fornication. Nevertheless, Paul says that it is better for her to remain with him and to try to convert him *lest he should marry someone else*.[175] Since his remarriage would be illicit, they must be truly married.[176]

A *sententia* preserved in the Kirkstall and Durham miscellanies sets out the strict position in detail. Can there be a marriage between a believer and an infidel? Some say that because marriage is a natural good it exists among all cultures, even among peoples who worship false gods. Against this, the author argues that because marriage is a sacrament, it can exist only among people who worship the one true God. That is why the convert is entitled to remarry (1 Cor 7:13, 14). Augustine says that is "not a sin for someone dismissed for God's sake if he joins himself to

---

[173] Ambrosiaster, *Ad Corinthos prima* 7:15, CSEL 81.2:77: "non debetur reverentia coniugii ei qui horret auctorem coniugii. non enim ratum est matrimonium, quod sine dei devotione est, ac per hoc non est peccatum ei qui dimittitur propter deum, si alii se iunxerit." (". . . the reverence of marriage is not owed to someone who shrinks from the author of marriage, for a marriage that lacks devotion to God is not established, and consequently it is not a sin for the one who is dismissed for God's sake to join himself [in marriage] to another.")

[174] *Cum omnia sacramenta I*, 137/17–19: "Ambrosius: Non est ratum coniugium preter deum, et ideo non est peccatum dimisisse propter deum, si alii coniungatur." Likewise, *Cum omnia sacramenta II*, ed. Bliemetzrieder, 279/102–106. *In primis hominibus*, p. 24 (IPH 62).

[175] The argument presupposes that the infidel is married, for otherwise his remarriage would not be a sin.

[176] PM 406 (p. 287), = LP 265 and 266, ascribed to Ivo and Anselm respectively (Harley 3098, 76r–v). The second disputant is called Gregorius in the *Liber Pancrisis*, perhaps because a scribe thus expanded the abbreviation G for Guillelmus or one its variants (e.g., Guuillelmus, Gwillelmus).

another." (This dictum is not authentic.) The *sententia* includes a syllogism: Marriage is insoluble; but the marriage of unbelievers is soluble; therefore, the latter is not truly marriage. To prove the major premise, the author cites Augustine, according to whom married people may separate only because of fornication, although even then the marriage is not really dissolved, for they cannot remarry. The minor follows from the Pauline Privilege. It follows from the conclusion, the author points out, that unbelieving spouses fornicate whenever they have sexual intercourse. If both spouses convert to Christianity, turning to the worship of the one true God, their relationship automatically becomes marriage. But their relationship is not really a marriage if only one partner converts, for marriage is based on consent, and the partners are not consenting to the same thing. Nevertheless, if the unbeliever is willing to live amicably with the believer, that intention implies that he or she has at least the *beginning* of faith, and then they should remain together. Finally, what about marriage among Jews? Surely, they too worship the one true God. The author resists that logic. It is true that there was marriage among Jews *before* the coming of Christ, but the faith of the Jews who have rejected Christ is tantamount to idolatry. There is no marriage, therefore, among the Jews of the author's own day.[177]

According to another *sententia*, contemporaneous Jews can form valid but imperfect marriages by virtue of their imperfect faith in God. One might argue that there is no legitimate marriage (*rectum connubium*) among Jews because they lack faith, for whatever does not come from faith is a sin (Rom 14:23). Against this, the author argues that Jews have partial faith inasmuch as they worship the one true God and wish to raise children for God. Such faith suffices as the basis of legitimate marriage.[178]

For the most part, the *magistri moderni* rejected the strict position attributed to Anselm and adopted the inclusive position attributed to Ivo and William. Unbelievers can legitimately marry, on this view, and their marriage may even be called a sacrament, although it remains soluble insofar as it is deficient in certain respects. According to the *Cum omnia sacramenta I*, the marriage of infidels is legitimate inasmuch as it conforms at least to the basic definitions of marriage. For example, the definition of marriage ascribed to Isidore – "Marriage is the mutual agreement of male and female, committing them to an indivisible way of life" – is true of all peoples, infidels as well as believers.[179] Ambrose (Ambrosiaster) does not say that there is no marriage at all without God, the author points out, but only that such a marriage is not established (*ratum*).[180] One must distinguish, therefore, between marriage in its basic, minimal form and *matrimonium ratum*. The latter

---

[177] PM 131 (pp. 102–03). MS Oxford, Bodl. Laud Misc. 277, 32vb–33ra. MS Oxford, Bodl. Laud Misc. 216, 139va–139vb.

[178] PM 208 (p. 136).

[179] *Cum omnia sacramenta I*, 139/9–10. *Cum omnia sacramenta II*, ed. Bliemetzieder, 276/48–49.

[180] *Cum omnia sacramenta I*, 138/2–3. *Cum omnia sacramenta II*, ed. Bliemetzrieder, 279/105–106.

includes an extra dimension. A marriage between two infidels is deficient and dissoluble, but it is a valid marriage nevertheless. Contrariwise, Christian believers cannot validly marry unbelievers.[181]

The *Coniugium namque* approaches the question in an *a priori* manner, focusing on the definition and the causes of marriage. Inasmuch as marriage is defined as "the consent of a man and a woman to sexual intercourse made according to the church's decree" (a definition taken from the *Cum omnia sacramenta I*), it seems that two infidels cannot strictly marry, for they do not marry according to the church's decree.[182] Nevertheless, the author concedes that infidel spouses are in fact married. Some scholars maintain that when a believer is married to an unbeliever, the marriage is invalid in the believer but valid in the unbeliever. Against this position, the author points out that it is the unbeliever and not the believer who has the power to end the marriage according to Paul's policy (1 Cor 7:15). If the unbeliever does not resist, the believer should sustain the marriage in the hope of bringing the other into the faith. Again, some say that unbelievers cannot marry because "what is not from faith is a sin" (Rom 14:23), but Augustine maintains that the goodness of marriage (*bonum nuptiarum*) is common to Christians, Jews, and even pagans. Although some interpret Augustine's idea "tenuously and tepidly," the author argues, the goodness of marriage to which Augustine refers consists of the avoidance of fornication, the hope of offspring, faith, and sacrament (i.e., permanence). These goods are common to all peoples at least in some form or to some degree. One might argue that unbelievers do not enjoy the good of fidelity inasmuch they practice polygamy, nor the good of sacrament inasmuch as they practice divorce. In reply, the author argues that divorce and polygamy did not prevent Jewish men from being faithful to their wives, and that they practiced polygamy only by divine decree. Christians should not denigrate that ancient practice of God's people even though they must not imitate it. In any case, the chief reasons for marriage (*principales coniugii causae*) are not faith and sacrament but the hope of offspring and the avoidance of fornication, which are common to all peoples.[183] Later in the treatise, the author suggests that "although a certain sacrament is present in [the marriage of] unbelievers, the figure of Christ and the church is not there."[184] Only a Christian marriage, on this view, can fully signify the sacrament's reality.

The extensive treatment of the validity and sacramentality of infidel marriages in the *In primis homibus* is inconclusive, but the author concedes that a marriage between unbelievers is truly a marriage even though it is soluble. Indeed, infidel marriage is the same in many respects as a valid Christian marriage.[185] Later, though, the author suggests that Augustine may have called unbelievers "spouses" (*coniuges*) only because of the similarities between their unions and the true

---

[181] *Cum omnia sacramenta I*, 138–39, citing Augustine, *De adulterinis coniugiis* 21(26), CSEL 41:373–74.
[182] *Coniugium namque*, 272/22–23.   [183] Ibid., 272/36–273/9.
[184] Ibid., 273/24–25.   [185] *In primis hominibus*, 15/4–6.

marriages of believers.[186] Augustine does not say in the *De bono coniugali* that marriage (*nuptiae*) exists among all peoples, the author points out, but only that the goodness of marriage (*bonum nuptiae*) does. Augustine is probably referring to the begetting of children and the fidelity between the spouses.[187] More precisely, as Augustine himself explains, marriage everywhere has the goods of faith and off-spring, but not in the fully realized forms that are proper to Christians. Unbelievers value offspring, but they do not beget and raise them to worship the true God. Therefore, the good of offspring among infidels is not remedy for sin. Moreover, only Christians enjoy the third good, which Augustine calls the "sanctity of sacra-ment."[188] Despite some vagueness or inconsistency as to whether the marriage of non-Christians is truly marriage, the author maintains that such a marriage is soluble. Paul's policy, he argues, whereby a Christian convert with an unbelieving spouse should remain married, was based on pastoral considerations regarding the well-being of the partners. It did not presuppose that such marriages were *de iure* insoluble.[189]

The *Sententiae Berolinenses* distinguishes between imperfect and perfect mar-riage. Whereas perfect marriage is insoluble, imperfect marriage is "dispensable," for the church has the right to dissolve it. Following Augustine in the *De bono coniugali*, the author argues that the goods of faith and offspring are common to all peoples, whereas the "sanctity of sacrament" belongs to God's people alone.[190] The author refines this position later in the treatise when he considers the implica-tions of the Pauline Privilege. The author's interpretation depends partly on Ambrose (Ambrosiaster) and partly on two sayings that he ascribes to Augustine: "The unbelieving person does not have true friendship with his spouse," and "There can be a true marriage only between persons of one faith."[191] Reflecting on the texts in a pastoral rather than a legalistic spirit, and interpreting them as if they described not mixed marriages but also marriages only between unbelievers, the author argues that although there cannot in the strictest sense be a "true marriage" between two unbelievers, one should distinguish between perfect marriage (*coniugium perfec-tum*) and dispensable marriage (*coniugium dispensatorium*). Only a marriage

---

[186] Ibid., 28/7–10.   [187] Ibid., 29/9–13.
[188] Augustine, *De b. coniug.* 24(32), CSEL 41:226–27. In *primis hominibus*, 4/10–12 (IPH 8).
[189] In *primis hominibus*, 29/15–20.   [190] *Sententiae Berolinenses*, 57/10–15.
[191] "Non est vera amicitia cum coniuge infidelis hominis." "Verum coniugium non potest esse nisi homines unius fidei." These are distant echoes of a *sententia* in the In *primis hominibus* (p. 25, IPH 63) taken from Augustine: "Nec uera pudicitia infidelis hominis cum coniuge dici potest, quia 'omne quod non est ex fide peccatum est' [Rom. 14:23], quamvis ueram fidelis habeat pudicitiam etiam cum infideli coniuge qui non habet ueram." ("The chastity of the unbeliev-ing person toward his spouse cannot be called true chastity, because "everything that does not come from faith is sin," although the believer has true chastity even toward the unbelieving spouse, who does not have true chastity.") The source is Augustine, *De coniugiis adulterinis* I.18 (20), CSEL 41:367/24–368/4. Cf. Gratian, C. 28 q. 1 dictum ante c. 1 (1078): "Item Augustinus: 'Non est uera pudicitia hominis infidelis cum coniuge sua.' Ubi autem uera pudicitia esse non potest, ibi nec uerum coniugium est."

between believers is perfect and indispensible, whereas a marriage between unbelievers is imperfect and dispensable. It is permanent in principle, but divorce and remarriage are permissible, even from the church's point of view.[192]

9.5.3 *Christian marriage in the* Cum omnia sacramenta *family of treatises*

The *Cum omnia sacramenta I* includes an original and innovative attempt to explain the relationship between the sacrament of marriage and membership of the church. Like most of the *magistri moderni*, the author reasons that unbelievers and believers can truly marry, but that marriage among believers has an extra dimension associated with its perfected permanence. Furthermore, the author interprets the difference between Christian and non-Christian marriage by working out the implications of construing marriage as a sacrament.

The argument brings together three ideas. First, following some *sententiae* of Augustine, which are interpreted here in a way that Augustine did not anticipate, the treatise distinguishes between the sacrament of marriage *per se* and the sanctity of that sacrament. Although the author conflates Augustine's *bonum sacramenti* with the sacrament of marriage, he argues that the sacrament exists among all peoples, whereas only Christians – indeed, only good Christians – enjoy the *sanctity* of the sacrament. Second, the treatise interprets that distinction between the sacrament and its sanctity in the light of a distinction between the outward appearance of a sacrament and its *res*, or inner reality. The *res*, or sanctity, of any sacrament is what is realized in those who are properly disposed to receive the sacrament. In this case, the *res* is membership of the church. Third, to show how marriage makes the spouses members of the church, the treatise invokes the traditional theme or topos of the three ranks of Christians. The argument is interesting but not entirely coherent and not easy to follow. I shall review it here, therefore, in some detail.

The author's point of departure is a text from Augustine's *De nuptiis et concupiscentia*, which he quotes in abbreviated form when he expounds the three goods of marriage:

> What is commended to faithful spouses is not only fertility, the fruit of which is offspring, nor only chastity, the bond of which is faith, but also a certain sacrament of marriage. The fact that a man and a woman who are joined in marriage persevere inseparably as long as they live, and that neither is permitted to divorce the other except on the grounds of fornication, is the reality [*res*] of a certain sacrament. This is what is preserved between Christ and the church.[193]

---

[192] *Sententiae Berolinenses*, 58/26–59/8.

[193] *Cum omnia sacramenta I*, ed. Bliemetzrieder, 134/15–19, quoting *De nupt. et conc.* I.10(11), CSEL 42:222–23. The proximate source is probably SMA 56 (p. 183), where the text is abbreviated in a similar manner.

There is no suggestion in this passage that the reality (*res*) of the sacrament is something over and above the sacrament itself, and Augustine seems to identify this reality with insolubility. Nevertheless, the appearance of the term *res* is the germ of a new line of thought, since in sacramental theology it denoted what a sacrament signified or conferred. The author assumes that the *res* of marriage pertains to the union between Christ and the church.

Immediately after the passage quoted earlier, therefore, the author launches into a discussion of the distinction between the external goods (*bona*) of marriage in themselves and the corresponding inward realities in the hearts of the spouses. Only good persons enjoy the reality (*res*) of each good. The reality of the sacrament of marriage is "to become members of Christ":

> It should be noted in these three [goods] that the goods are one thing and their realities [*res*] are another. For just as the sacrament of baptism is one thing and its reality is another, namely, the remission of sins, so also the sacrament of marriage is one thing and the reality of that sacrament is another, for not everyone who has the sacrament [of marriage] has the reality of the sacrament. The reality [*res*] of this sacrament is to become a member of Christ, for those who live legitimately in a legitimate marriage serve God through their marriage as well, and they are his members. Just as virgins through their virginity, and continents through their continence, so good married persons are made members of Christ through their legitimate union.[194]

The author's immediate source for the last idea is probably a text from Augustine's *De bono viduitatis* that appears in the *Sententiae Magistri A.*: "So great is the good of a faithful marriage that even they [married persons] are members of the body of Christ."[195]

Summarizing and explicating the argument, the *Decretum Dei fuit* points out that whereas baptism *per se* is a bodily immersion in water with a spoken blessing, its spiritual reality is the cleansing of the soul from sin. Likewise, whereas marriage is the union of a man and a woman, and the sacrament in itself is the insolubility of that union, the reality of the sacrament is to become members of Christ.[196]

The argument depends not only on a close albeit strained reading of Augustine on the three goods but also on an emerging sacramental theology. The sacrament *per se* is an exterior sign, whereas its reality is a saving effect, which the sacrament veils, signifies, and realizes. Augustine made the same point by distinguishing between a sacrament and its saving power (*virtus*).[197] Twelfth-century theologians used the idea to explain the difference between the sacraments of the Old Law (*sacramenta*

---

[194] *Cum omnia sacramenta I*, 134/20–135/6. *Cum omnia sacramenta II*, ed. Bliemetzrieder, 275/21–276/34.

[195] Augustine, *De bono viduitatis* 3(4), CSEL 44:308. SMA 35 and 20 (pp. 176, 170). Augustine goes on to explain that the consecrated widow has a higher rank.

[196] *Decretum Dei fuit*, 366/8–367/5.

[197] Augustine, *In Ioah. tract.* 26.11, CCL 36:265: "Aliud est sacramentum, aliud virtus sacramenti."

legalia), which were merely signs or figures, and the Christian sacraments. No *res sacramenti* was conferred with the sacraments of the Old Testament.[198] By the same token, a person who is not morally prepared to receive a sacrament receives the outward sacrament without its saving reality. Now, marriage is a sacrament inasmuch as it signifies Christ's union with the church. The marriage of two spouses cannot bring about that union writ large, but it can realize the union between Christ and the church in those individuals who are properly disposed for it. It does so by making them members of Christ.

Just as spouses must be morally good to enjoy the reality of the sacrament (*res sacramenti*), according to the *Cum omnia sacramenta I*, so they must be Christians. The author finds the distinguishing feature of Christian marriage not in the sacrament *per se*, but in the sanctity of the sacrament. The sacrament exists everywhere, for marriage is by definition "the consent of male and female, maintaining an indivisible way of life," which is common to all peoples. But only those who have faith in Christ have the sanctity of the sacrament.[199]

This phase of the argument depends on three texts from Augustine. First, Augustine argues the *De nuptiis et concupiscentia* that infidels do not enjoy the goods of faith and offspring in their fullness, as Christians do. Infidel spouses may shun adultery, but they cannot enjoy "true conjugal chastity" because their minds are turned away from God. Likewise, infidels value procreation, but what Christians seek in marriage is not only the birth of children but also their rebirth as members of Christ.[200] The author extends this line of argument to the good of sacrament, arguing that all married persons have the sacrament but only good Christian spouses enjoy the sanctity of the sacrament. Second, Augustine argues in the *De nuptiis et concupiscentia* that that there is such an "observance of the sacrament" (*sacramenti observatio*) in "the city of our God, in his holy mountain," that men do not even divorce sterile wives for the sake of procreation. Just as there is no divorce between Christ and the church, so also is there no divorce between spouses in the church, which is the body of Christ, for they are members of this body.[201] The passage seems to imply that what is unique in the church is not the sacrament *per se* but rather its "observance." Third, Augustine argues in the *De bono coniugali* that whereas all human beings from all races recognize that marriage is good because of the "purpose of begetting" (*causa generandi*) and because of the "faith of chastity" (*fides castitatis*), the people of God alone recognize a third good, the "sanctity of sacrament."[202] Putting these three ideas together, the author argues that everyone has the sacrament, but that only good Christians have the sanctity of the sacrament.

[198] PM 360 (p. 271).
[199] *Cum omnia sacramenta I*, 139/9–11. *Cum omnia sacramenta II*, ed. Bliemetzieder, 276/48–49.
[200] *De nupt. et conc.* I.4(5), CSEL 42:215–16.
[201] *De nupt. et conc.* I.10(11), 222/24–2233/6. The language of *observatio* comes from this passage.
[202] *De b. coniug.* 24(32), CSEL 41:226–27.

Whereas the author has until now distinguished between a good (*bonum*) and its reality, he now distinguishes between the feature itself (faith, offspring, or sacrament) and its good, as well as between the feature and its sanctity. Each idiom depends on a particular use of the genitive case. If one construes the genitive in a specifying, appositive sense, the phrase *bonum sacramenti* ("good of sacrament") refers to the sacrament itself, which is a certain good (compare, "the nation of France"). But if one construes the genitive in a qualitative, quasi-possessive sense, the phrase refers to an accidental quality possessed by the sacrament, namely, its goodness (compare, "the fragrance of a rose"). The author interprets the phrase "sanctity of sacrament" from the *De bono coniugali* in the second manner, as if sanctity were a separable accident of the sacrament. Moreover, he now interprets the phrase "good of sacrament" in the same way, as if the goodness were a separable accident of sacrament. All marriages everywhere, among infidels as well as believers, have the sacrament, therefore, but not all have the sanctity of sacrament, or the good of the sacrament. There is no indication that Augustine envisaged any such thing. In the original text, indeed, the term "sanctity" is little more than a rhetorical make-weight to match "purpose of begetting" and "faith of chastity."

The argument, then, proceeds as follows: Only those who are morally disposed to receive the sacrament receive the good (or reality, or sanctity) of sacrament. Specifically, they must be good Christians. The argument turns from the moral condition of the recipients and their marital fidelity to their religious faith:

> Therefore, both good and evil persons have the sacrament, but good persons alone have the reality of the sacrament, just as faith is one thing, and the good of faith another. Faith is the observance [*observatio*] of chastity; the reality, or good, of faith is the intention of the one who keeps faith, for anyone who is continent keeps faith, but the good of faith cannot exist where God is not the reason behind that faith. This is the good of faith: that it is kept for God's sake. The good of offspring is this: that offspring are desired for God's sake and are raised religiously in his honor. Faith, therefore, may be common to all people, but the good of faith belongs only to the faithful; so also with offspring; so also with sacrament. And this is what Augustine says: that certain goods of marriage are common to all peoples, but that the sanctity of the sacrament, which is also known as the reality of the sacrament, belongs to the people of God alone, that is, to the faithful.[203]

The author maintains that whether what is in question is the moral condition of the spouses or their religious faith, the principle is the same. He makes the same move when he explains why a marriage between infidels is not established (*ratum*): "It is not surprising that infidels can marry, for evil as well as good persons share the other sacraments too, yet not as regards salvation. Good persons alone share the reality of the sacraments."[204]

---

[203] *Cum omnia sacramenta I*, 135/5–15. *Cum omnia sacramenta II*, ed. Bliemetzrieder, 276/40–44.
[204] *Cum omnia sacramenta I*, 138/4–7. *Cum omnia sacramenta II*, ed Bliemetzrieder, 277/53–56.

The *Cum omnia sacramenta II* pursues the argument further, inverting Augustine's argument. Changing a moral argument into a cultural one, the author points out that whereas fidelity or the hope of offspring may be absent from a marriage, the sacrament is never absent. Therefore, it must exist among all peoples, for "wherever there is marriage, there is the sacrament of marriage."²⁰⁵ Nevertheless, he concludes, invoking Augustine, "the sanctity or reality of the sacrament exists only in the city of our God and in his holy mountain."²⁰⁶ Similarly, the *Decretum Dei fuit* argues that whereas the good of faith can be vitiated in marriage, the good of sacrament can never be vitiated. Following Augustine, the author argues that that the sacrament of marriage, like the sacrament of ordination in a priest, is permanent and indestructible.²⁰⁷

To show how marriage makes people members of the church, the *Cum omnia sacramenta I* introduces the theme of the three ranks of Christians:

> The reality [*res*] of this sacrament is to become a member of Christ, for those who live legitimately in a legitimate marriage serve God through their marriage as well, and they are his members. Just as virgins through their virginity, and continents [*continentes*] through their continence, so good married persons [*coniugati*], through their legitimate union, are made members of Christ. Virgins occupy a certain supreme degree, continents a middle one, and married persons the lowest. These are the three men who alone, Scripture says, will be saved, namely, Daniel, Noah, and Job, that is, virgins, continents, and married persons.²⁰⁸

The author had probably appropriated the theme of the three chosen ones from Jonas of Orléans. The *Cum omnia sacramenta II* and the *Decretum Dei fuit* rehearse the same argument with minor variations.²⁰⁹ The authors did not need to explain the ranking or the typology of Daniel, Noah, and Job, for they were drawing on a familiar tradition. This was a complex tradition that had become somewhat confused, but the confusion did not really matter. All the variants identify marriage and two celibate vocations as the three ranks of membership in the church. I have outlined the history of this theme earlier (Section 1.2).

Beginning with a few *sententiae* from Augustine, interpreted in light of current sacramental theology and of contemporaneous debates about the marriage of

---

²⁰⁵ Cf. *Huius sacramenti habemus*, 365/14: "Ultimum [bonum] sacramentum in omnibus est ad hoc tempus." The author argues (365/9–12) that pagan marriages have the goods of faith and of the hope of offspring not in reality but only in appearance, e.g., to avoid scandal or for the adornment of a household.

²⁰⁶ *Cum omnia sacramenta II*, ed. Bliemetzrieder, 276/49–277/54.

²⁰⁷ *Decretum Dei fuit*, 366/1–7. Cf. Augustine, *De b. coniug.* 24(32), CSEL 41:227. Augustine's argument is not that the *sacramentum* survives, but rather that the conjugal bond (*vinculum coniugale*) survives by virtue of the "sanctity of sacrament."

²⁰⁸ *Cum omnia sacramenta I*, 134/24–135/5. Cf. Jonas of Orléans, *De institutione laicali* II.1, ed. Dubreucq, SC 549, 326–30 (PL 106:169C–170C).

²⁰⁹ In *Cum omnia sacramenta II* (ed. Bliemetzrieder, 276/28–33), Daniel, Job, and Noah typify virgins, *celibates*, and married persons, respectively. In *Decretum Dei fuit* (367/1–5), Daniel, Noah, and Job typify virgins, *widows*, and married folk.

infidels, the *Cum omnia sacramenta I* worked out a theology of marriage as one of the sacraments: a theology, moreover, that explained the role of marriage in the church. There are many loose ends, and the analysis raises as many questions as it solves, but it was a remarkable achievement.

9.6 SUMMARY

Although there is no single theology of marriage in the sentential literature, there are some characteristic theological themes and preoccupations. First, the authors emphasized the spouses' own consent to marry, construing this not only as a necessary and sufficient condition for marriage but also as constitutive of marriage. Some of the *magistri moderni* tried to include consent in the definition of marriage. Second, the authors inquired into the reasons for and the benefits of marriage, and into the proper motives for marrying, emphasizing the "avoidance of fornication." They also elaborated the three conjugal goods – faith, offspring, and sacrament – developing the theme in ways that Augustine could not have envisaged. The authors justified marriage chiefly as a remedy against concupiscence and as a moral safety net for those who were not strong enough to commit themselves to a celibate vocation. At the same time, the notion of the good of sacrament prompted theologians to apply to marriage themes and ideas that were emerging in current sacramental theology. Third, the authors set marriage in the context of the history of salvation, emphasizing that both the law of marriage and the proper reasons for marrying were not fixed but mutable. Fourth, because the authors construed marriage as a Christian vocation and as a sacrament, they inquired into the difference between marriage inside the church and marriage outside it. If marriage was a sacrament, were unbelieving spouses be truly married? Most answered affirmatively, but only with certain qualifications. Without faith in Christ and true moral virtue, grounded in that faith, marriage was still a sacrament in some sense, but it lacked the sanctity, reality, or goodness of the sacrament, which made the spouses members of Christ's body.

10

Hugh of Saint-Victor

Three Parisian clerics – Hugh of Saint Victor (d. 1141), Walter of Mortagne (d. 1174), and Peter Lombard (d. 1160) – assimilated the innovations of the *magistri moderni* on marriage and transmitted them selectively to thirteenth-century theologians. Each composed a treatise on marriage using the model established in the sentential literature, beginning with the topics of special interest to theologians before proceeding to the canonical rules and regulations. The theological topics included the original institution of marriage, the effects of the fall, the definition of marriage, the conjugal goods, the necessity and sufficiency of consent, and the betrothal distinction. Canonical topics included the impediments (especially consanguinity, affinity, spiritual kinship, religious vows, cult, and holy orders), divorce, the Pauline Privilege, and marriages of unbelievers.[1] Hugh and Walter directly appropriated the ideas and some of the words of the *magistri moderni*. In particular, Hugh adopted material liberally from the *Sententiae Magistri A.* and the *Cum omnia sacramenta II.*[2] Peter Lombard was in turn dependent on Hugh and Walter.

---

[1] That is, Hugh of Saint Victor, *De sacramentis christianae fidei* II.11, PL 176:479–520; Walter of Mortagne, *De coniugio*, PL 176:153–174; and Peter Lombard, *Sentences* IV.26–42, in *Sententiae in IV libris distinctae*, vol. 2 (Grottaferrata, 1981), 416–509. I cite Migne's edition of the Hugh's *De sacramentis* because it is the most cited and widely available, but I have also consulted Rainer Berndt's edition, *Hugonis de Sancto Victore De sacramentis Christiane fidei* (Monasterium Westfalorum, 2008), a reconstruction of the lost twelfth-century edition prepared under Abbot Gilduin. Berndt's edition is more authentic in relation to a particular manuscript history, but in some cases Migne's variants make better sense. Walter's treatise, which is less theological than those of Hugh and the Lombard, was appended during the Middle Ages to the *Summa sententiarum* as the seventh and final tractate (tract. 7), *De sacramento coniugii*, and it appears in this guise in the PL edition. The *Summa sententiarum*, which was the work of a certain Odo (probably Odo of Lucca), covered only six of the sacraments, without marriage.

[2] N. M. Haring demonstrates in "'The Sententiae Magistri A (Vat. *Ms lat.* 4361) and the School of Laon," *Mediaeval Studies* 17 (1965): 1–45, that Hugh drew on the second recension of the *Cum omnia sacramenta*, incorporating material from it into his *De sacramentis*. Because most of the texts that Hugh took from the *Sententiae Magistri A.* were ones used in the original *Cum omnia*

These three clerics not only transmitted the work of the *magistri moderni* on marriage to later generations: they also refined it. They were more confident in their use of patristic material, and their treatments were more mature, systematic, and efficiently subdivided. Hugh and Walter cited patristic authors sparingly, using them mainly to confirm key points in arguments that they developed in their own words. They did not usually piece the discourse together from borrowed material, as the *magistri moderni* had done.[3] Patristic quotations make up most of Peter Lombard's discourse on marriage in his *Sentences*, but he distances himself from the sources by raising questions of interpretation and reconciling apparent contradictions.

10.1 HUGH'S CHARACTER AS A THEOLOGIAN

Hugh was probably a native of Saxony, but he spent his entire teaching career in the school of the Canons Regular at the abbey of Saint-Victor, just outside the city walls of Paris. His treatise on marriage is part of his greatest work, the *De sacramentis christianae fidei*, which dates from the period 1130/31–1137. The *De sacramentis* was the culmination and summary of his teaching, and it incorporated some of his previous writings.

Hugh's perspective on marriage was that of a cleric engaged in ministry, but it was also informed by monastic theology. Hugh appropriated the nuptial symbolism that Bernard of Clairvaux had developed in his sermons on the Song of Songs, and he claimed that marriage was the best and closest mundane simile for the intimate mutual love between God and the soul.[4] Whereas Bernard regarded marriage as a literary figure that belonged in the domain of exegesis and imagination, Hugh regarded it as a sacrament practiced by the laity both in the spirit and in the flesh, as well as a sacrament over which the clergy had juridical control. Hugh remarked from personal experience about the difficulties of giving proper counsel and judgment in marriage cases.[5]

Hugh's treatment of marriage was unique in several respects, but it was congruent with the peculiar ethos in which he worked. As clerics who had adopted the regular life of monks, the calling of Canons Regular came from two directions: as cloistered religious, they were committed to contemplation; as clerics, they were committed to pastoral ministry. Whereas sacramental ministry was alien or at most incidental

---

sacramenta but not in the *Cum omnia sacramenta II*, scholars had formerly assumed that the first recension was Hugh's source.

[3] Hugh, *De sacramentis* II.11.9–10 is an exception to this generalization. The passage is composed entirely of Augustinian texts taken from the *Sententiae Magistri A*. Thus, *De sacramentis* II.11.9, on those who marry to satisfy lust, consists of a concatenation of texts from Augustine's *De bono coniugali* taken en bloc from SMA 44. Ch. 10, on polygamy under the Old Law, is pieced together from SMA 44–45, 47–48, and 52 (all from *De bono coniugali*) and SMA 55 (from *De nuptiis et concupiscentia*).

[4] *De beatae Mariae virginitate*, ed. Sicard, p. 250/941–252/950.

[5] *De sacramentis*, II.11.6, 490C–D.

to monks, it was essential to the life of most Canons Regular, including the Victorines. Nevertheless, the Rule of St Augustine was adaptable, and the Regular Canons' vocation was ambiguous. An Augustinian community might pursue a way of life (*conversatio*) that fell at any point on a spectrum between cloistered prayer and parish ministry.

During the twelfth century, the Parisian community of Saint-Victor was in the world but not of it. The canons espoused the contemplative ideals of the Cistercians, but they contributed to the flourishing scholastic life of the city. The founder of the community, William of Champeaux – listed as one of the "modern masters" of the *Liber Pancrisis* – had studied under Anselm at Laon, and he had directed the school of Notre Dame before retiring to Saint Victor. Gilduin, who became the first abbot of Saint-Victor in 1114 and served in that role until his death in 1155, developed the abbey as a contemplative academy, equally devoted to study and to prayer. The abbey school apparently accepted externs during this early period, although it had become closed by the 1170s.[6] Having entered the abbey by 1120, Hugh was a master of the school by 1127, and its head by 1133. He worked in the ethos that Gilduin cultivated.

Hugh's extensive corpus is so varied that he is hard to pigeonhole, but three dominant features are evident: he was a professional teacher, with a deep interest in pedagogy; he used salvation history as the chief organizing principle for a systematic theology; and he regarded theology from the perspective of a cleric engaged in ministry. Salvation history is the story of the church; and the church, as Hugh saw it, was a two-sided entity composed of both clerics and laity, with the former ministering to and ruling over the latter. Monks, therefore, make only fleeting, marginal appearances in Hugh's great *summa*, the *De sacramentis christianae fidei*.

Hugh's soliloquy *De arrha animae*, which he probably wrote around 1139, toward the end of his life and after the *De sacramentis*, contains his last words on marriage and his most sustained exploration of nuptial imagery in the tradition of St Bernard.[7] Hugh dedicated the treatise to the brethren of the Augustinian community of Hamersleben in Saxony, near Halberstadt, to which he had probably belonged before he settled in Paris, although the circumstances of his early life remain uncertain and disputed. The figurative *arrha* (betrothal pledge) of the work consists in the created blessings that the bridegroom, God, bestows upon the bride, his people. God confers the *arrha* in this life, whereas the promised marriage belongs to the next, when the blessed will see God face to face. Nevertheless, Hugh records his own momentary experiences of contemplative rapture, in which he enjoys a foretaste of heavenly bliss.[8]

---

[6] S. C. Ferruolo, *The Origins of the University* (Stanford, 1985), 29–30. P. Rorem, *Hugh of Saint Victor* (Oxford, 2009), 5–9.

[7] D. Poirel, "Love of God, Human Love: Hugh of St. Victor and the Sacrament of Marriage," *Communio* 24 (1997): 99–109.

[8] *De arrha animae*, ed. Feiss and Sicard, pp. 280–82.

The bride's identity in the *De arrha animae* is complex. She is the individual faithful soul, but her relationship with God transcends her individuality. Hugh explores two dimensions of generality and particularity in the treatise. On the one hand, God bestows his gifts with varying extension: some on all creatures, others only on select groups, such all human beings or all faithful Christians, and yet others only on certain blessed individuals.[9] On the other hand – and this is the chief topic of the soliloquy – God's gifts are mysteriously singular, for although every chosen person is individually betrothed to God, the relationship is monogamous.[10]

The *De arrha animae* is the most personal and confessional of Hugh's works, but Hugh wrote less about the contemplative's interior relationship with God than about the church and the sacraments. Assuming that that the "eye of contemplation" had been blinded by the fall, Hugh held that God redeemed human beings by tangible, terrestrial means: the humanity of Christ, the ministry of the clergy, and the sacraments.

Hugh discovered that he could use salvation history as a comprehensive organizing principle for theology. He explains in the prologue to the *De sacramentis* that this work is "like a brief summation of all things," which he has "gathered into a single sequence."[11] But the *De sacramentis* is not comprehensive from the perspective of the natural, created order: it is not a compendium of physics, medicine, or ethics, for example. It is comprehensive only from the perspective of redemption. The organizing "sequence" to which Hugh refers is salvation history, notwithstanding many complications and diversions that tend to distract the reader. The *De sacramentis* consists of two books. The first covers creation and fall, human need of the incarnation and of the sacraments as remedies, and the eras of the natural and written laws with their respective sacraments. The second book covers the incarnation, the church as the body of Christ, the sacraments of the age of grace (i.e., the New Covenant), and the world's end. Salvation history replicates the metaphysical cycle of the emanation of all things from God and their return to God, but it receives it on a historical plane.

Hugh's plan proved to be highly successful. Most of the scholastic *summas* of theology were based on variants of it. Later masters based their divisions not directly on Hugh's *De sacramentis* but on Peter Lombard's *Sentences*, but Peter had arrived as his fourfold schema by imposing onto the chapter topics of John Damascene's *De fide orthodoxa* a fourfold division that that owed much to Hugh: God, creation and fall, the incarnation, and the sacraments and the last things. By the thirteenth century, the plan had lost much of its narrative strength and was used largely as an abstract or quasi-philosophical division of topics. Thirteenth-century masters continued to debate the peculiar circumstances of the Garden of Eden, for example,

---

[9] Ibid., 240, 244–46, 248–50.   [10] Ibid., 248.
[11] *De sacramentis* I, prol., PL176:183: "quasi brevem quamdam summam omnium in unam seriem conpegi."

but they treated the creation and fall of human beings chiefly as an opportunity to discuss theological anthropology, and most of them were much less interested than Hugh had been in the history of God's people before the advent of Jesus Christ.

Although Hugh discusses many things besides the sacraments in the *De sacramentis*, its title is appropriate. A thirteenth-century treatise on the sacraments will necessarily be a narrow, specialist work, but the topic is all-encompassing in Hugh, partly because he recognizes several kinds of sacraments as well as the central Christian rites of the New Law, and partly because he regards the sacraments as the saving means by which God has rescued chosen human beings from damnation throughout the ages, reorienting them toward everlasting bliss. All the sacraments, in his view, refer to Christ: some by heralding his advent, the others by prolonging Christ's presence after his death, resurrection, and ascension. By dividing the sacraments both historically, according to the three periods of the saving economy, and functionally, according to the kind of work that they do in any period, and by including all kinds of sacraments in his narrative, Hugh can attain new levels of exactitude without sacrificing breadth or complexity.

Sacraments presuppose ministers, and Hugh regards the clergy as a people set apart: the ruling class of the spiritual life. They mediate between God and the people, whose salvation depends on them. Clerics in major orders are Christ's knights, defeating Satan's army with the sacraments as their weapons. They are also Christ's medical emissaries, using the sacraments as medicines. Priests do not administer marriage to the laity as they do the other major sacraments, but marriage is dependent on ecclesiastical legislation and jurisdiction. Contrariwise, the celibacy of clerics is a necessary condition for the survival of their class. Without it, not only the clergy but even Christendom itself, Hugh argues, would disintegrate.

10.2 HUGH'S SACRAMENTAL THEOLOGY

Hugh is without equal in the western tradition as a sacramental theologian, towering above his contemporaries, yet his contributions to the subject were complex and can seem muddled to an impatient or unsympathetic reader. The subsequent scholastic tradition only partially assimilated his complex sacramental theology. Hugh's intellect and imagination were so broad and so fertile, and his ambition so great, that he set himself a task that no single author could complete. Moreover, Hugh's theology of marriage was rather loosely related to his analysis of the sacraments in general, although it was wholly congruent with his account of salvation history.

The most fundamental distinction in Hugh's theology is between the work of creation (*opus conditionis*) and the work of restoration (*opus restaurationis*). Whereas the former establishes the order of nature, the latter establishes the order of grace. Each of the two works is the focus of a class of writings. Merely human literature, including natural philosophy, ethics, and so forth, focuses on the work of nature. The Bible and the writings that expound it focus on the work of restoration, devoting only a minimum of space to nature and creation. Hugh is chiefly interested in writings of the latter sort.[12]

This schema owed something to the *magistri moderni*, but Hugh was much more ambitious in his use of salvation history. He projected the metaphysical cycle of emanation and return onto the historical drama of the fall and the atonement. Hugh was indebted for these insights to the pseudo-Dionysius as mediated by John Scottus, also known as Eriugena, who had turned the essentially timeless, ahistorical Dionysian theologies into a cosmic narrative of emanation and return. The endowments (*data*) of nature belonged to emanation, according to Eriugena, whereas the gifts (*dona*) of grace belonged to the return.[13] Hugh wrote a commentary on the *Celestial Hierarchy* in Eriugena's Latin translation, and he was clearly familiar with Eriugena's own commentary on the work, although there are few explicit references to the pseudo-Dionysius in Hugh's other works.[14]

10.2.1 *The sacraments and the work of restoration*

Hugh regards human beings as the most complete of God's creatures, "placed in the middle" of creation.[15] They enjoy both the inward, intellectual cognition of the angels and the outward, sensory cognition of the irrational animals.[16] Human beings are by nature apt to read both the inner Word, which is eternally spoken in God, and the outer word written in creation. Moreover, their ability to read the book of created nature depends on their ability to hear the inner book. Familiarity with the inner book enables them to interpret the language and symbols of the Book of Nature.[17]

Creation was from the beginning a realm of signs, but their function has changed. Before the fall, the human mind understood them in the light of what it already knew, as one might rejoice in reading letters from a loved one. After the fall, their chief purpose is corrective, for they lead the mind back to spiritual things and to God, as one leads a blind person by the hand.[18] God introduced many more signs or symbols of this new sort after the fall, using persuasive rhetoric as well as informative prose.

The human soul, which finds itself at the center of all created things, has three ways of seeing: the eye of contemplation, which sees God and the things that are in God; the eye of reason, which enables the soul to understand itself; and the carnal

---

[12] Ibid., prol., c. 2, 183A–184A, and I.1.28, 203D–204B.
[13] I. P. Sheldon-Williams, "Eriugena's Greek Sources," in J. J. O'Meara and L. Bieler (eds.), *The Mind of Eriugena* (Dublin, 1973), 1–14, at 10–11.
[14] P. Rorem, "The Early Latin Dionysius: Eriugena and Hugh of St. Victor," *Modern Theology* 24.4 (2008): 601–14, minimizes Dionysian influence in Hugh's works. This article appears as an appendix in idem, *Hugh of Saint Victor* (Oxford, 2009), 167–76.
[15] *De sacramentis* I.6.5, 266B–C. [16] I.6.5, 266B–267B. [17] I.3.20, 225A–B.
[18] On the *manuductio* by which the mind is "led by the hand" from visible things to invisible things, see Hugh, *In Hierarchiam caelestem* II.1, PL 175:948A.

eye, with which the soul senses material things.[19] The fall ruined the order and harmony among these three senses. Because the root of sin was pride, God humiliated and punished human beings for that pride not only with mortality but also with ignorance and concupiscence.[20] The eye of contemplation became blind, and the eye of reason, which Hugh associates especially with self-knowledge, became dim. Only the carnal eye retained its natural vigor.[21] Fallen human beings look at creation as illiterate persons look at a book. They see the physical shapes, and they may marvel at them, but they can only dimly grasp their meaning. A "spiritual" person, having recovered some of the primordial sensibility, will not only marvel at created nature but also perceive therein the wisdom of its creator.[22]

Faith and the sacraments restore something of the original harmony without reestablishing it in its pristine form. Whereas mortality is only a punishment, the other two punishments – ignorance and concupiscence – are also moral faults (*culpae*), and they lead human beings into error. Fallen human beings cannot save themselves, but God mercifully and gratuitously provides them not only with the created world as the place and time for correction, but also with the incarnation of Jesus Christ and the sacraments as saving means, and with the saving "spiritual graces" that those means provide.[23]

The work of restoration, which is the chief topic of Scripture, consists primarily in three things: the incarnation of the Word, the things that the Word did in the flesh, and the sacraments of the incarnate Word. Some of the sacraments preceded and prefigured the incarnation and others follow and proclaim it, but they all serve the same end.[24] The incarnation of Jesus Christ, therefore, is at the center of the work of restoration both historically and functionally. All other aids to salvation, such as the precepts of the Old Law (which in Hugh's mind are closely related to sacraments), refer to the central event of Christ's incarnation in one way or another, and they derive their efficacy from it. Hugh works out the different aspects of this ambitious plan in more or less detail, without arriving at a single coherent account. In expounding the redemptive work both of the incarnation and of the sacraments, Hugh has recourse to three levels of explanation, pertaining respectively to justice, to faith, and to cognition.

When Hugh explains the incarnation and the atonement, he follows Anselm of Canterbury and devotes most of his attention to judicial themes. He begins with an account of divine justice, emphasizing the differences between God's justice and human justice. What God does is always just, but it is also gratuitous. God justly but gratuitously saves some persons. There would have been no injustice if God had saved no one, for human beings deserve damnation and cannot merit

---

[19] *De sacramentis* I.10.2, 329C–330A. *In Hierarchiam caelestem* III.2, PL 175:976A–B.
[20] *De sacramentis* I.8.1, 305C–D.
[21] I.10.2, 329C–330A. *In Hierarchiam caelestem* III.2, PL 175:976A–B.
[22] Hugh of Saint-Victor, *De tribus diebus* 4, CCM 177:9/24–10/109.
[23] *De sacramentis* I.8.1, 305C–D, and 1.8.3, 307B–D.   [24] I.1.28, 204A–B.

redemption by themselves. Whereas God is the author of justice, human beings are bound by a restrictive justice that not only makes the commission of certain human acts just but also makes their omission unjust.[25]

To explain the atonement, Hugh envisages a complex lawsuit (*causa*). God, man, and the devil are the principal parties. The devil's persecution of human beings is an act of injustice against God, but the victims justly deserve it. Hugh deduces that man can pursue a just cause against the devil only if God himself intervenes as his patron and advocate. But God must first be placated, for he is justly angry. That in turn requires the sacrifice of a God-man.[26]

The incarnation is also an object of saving faith, for it provides human beings with a deeper understanding of their relationship with God. To explain why the incarnation was the most fitting means of redemption, albeit not the only possible means, Hugh argues that by setting an example of the achievement of glory through self-sacrifice, Christ is the antidote to despair.[27] Christ also restores the primordial unity of the inward and outward senses of human beings, for whereas the created world is an outward book and the eternal Word is an inner book, the incarnate Word is "a book written on the inside and the outside" (Ezek 2:9).[28] Human beings become the body of Christ through the gift of faith, and the gift of love vivifies that mystical body.[29]

Three things are necessary for salvation: faith, the sacraments, and good works. These were necessary before as well as after Christ's advent. Faith is the key, but "faith without works is dead" (Jas 2:20).[30] Moreover, faith is itself a sacrament, not only in the etymological sense that it is a mystery, but also inasmuch a sacrament is a visible simulacrum of an invisible reality, for "faith itself is an image and a sacrament" of the beatific vision. Through faith, as St Paul says, we see "through a reflection and in an enigma" (1 Cor 13:12). To see something through a reflection is to see an image of it, and the mirror in which one sees this image is the human heart, but only after it has been cleaned and polished. The reality that one dimly perceives through its reflection is the beatific vision. The enigma is Scripture.[31] Faith in unseen things takes the place of the eye of contemplation, which became blind in the fall.[32]

The work of the sacraments and its ministers extends the work of Christ's humanity. Christ is like a king riding into a campaign against the devil. The saints who came before Christ are the knights who precede the king, and the saints of the New Covenant are the knights who accompany and follow the king. The sacraments

---

[25] I.8.8–9, 310D–311C.
[26] I.8.4, 307D–309C; I.8.6–7, 310B–D. Hugh of Saint-Victor, *Dialogus de sacramentis legis naturalis et scriptae*, PL 176:29A–30A.
[27] *De sacramentis* I.8.10, 311D–312A.
[28] I.6.5, 267A–B.   [29] II.2.1, 415B–416B.   [30] I.9.8, 328A–B   [31] I.10.9, 342C–D.
[32] I.10.2, 329C–330A. *In Hierarchiam caelestem* III.2, PL 175:976A–B.

are their weapons and armor. The two companies use different weapons, but they are fighting the same fight.[33]

Hugh sometimes considers the sacraments from a moral, judicial point of view, and sometimes from the perspective of faith. God has issued an "edict," ruling that those who are waiting for the Savior's return must demonstrate their good intentions by receiving the sacraments.[34] Those who do not receive the sacraments when they are available show contempt and do not deserve to be saved.[35] In that sense, human beings cannot be saved without the sacraments. But God does not need the sacraments to save his people, and God can and does save some human beings to whom the sacraments are not available. Indeed, it is faith that saves, and not the sacraments per se. Those who deny this possibility, considering the sacraments themselves to be absolutely necessary for salvation, are idolaters who venerate external means. Faith in redemption is a far greater thing than the water of baptism.[36]

Hugh focuses on the cognitive function of the sacraments when he explains in detail how they work. The work of the sacraments is based on the innate human aptitude to perceive the inner sense of material things. Like the deeds of the human Christ, the sacraments mend the damage done by the fall by making invisible things visibly manifest. Human beings lost their inner sense in the fall and can no longer perceive the spiritual meaning of outward, material things. Rather than repairing the eye of contemplation so that human beings can read the natural signs again, God provides them with new signs of a different sort: signs that not only signify but also heal, and which move the heart as well as informing the intellect. Commenting on the Celestial Hierarchy of the pseudo-Dionysius, Hugh argues that God presents signs (simulacra) of two sorts to human beings: those of nature, and those of grace. The signs of grace are the human Christ and the sacraments, which belong to Christ but "existed from the beginning." Sacraments are the medicine with which Christ cures our blindness. When Jesus cured a man's blindness by daubing his eyes with an earthy paste of clay and spittle, the man at once believed that Jesus was the Son of God (John 9:6). Thus, whereas the signs of nature only demonstrate, the signs of grace also illumine, by restoring sight.[37]

Hugh considers the sacraments to be medicines that cure like with like. They operate in three ways: by humiliation, by instruction (eruditio), and by practice (exercitatio). Each way corresponds to a weakness of fallen humanity.

First, humiliation: To punish human beings for their pride and overweening ambition, God made them subject to material things, which are naturally beneath them. Fallen human beings desire material things as ends in themselves. Now, one regards as superior to one's self whatever one desires as an ultimate good, for the good is by definition what completes any agent. In the beginning, the human mind

---

[33] De sacramentis I.8.11, 312C–D; prol., c. 2, 183B–C.   [34] I.8.12, 314A.
[35] I.9.8, 328A. I.9.5, 323D.   [36] De sacramentis I.9.5, 323C–326B.
[37] In Hierarchiam caelestem I.1, PL 175:926C–927A.

was immediately joined to God as to its true good, and it saw God in material things. In the fallen state, material things are a "dividing medium" that separates the human mind from God. The intellect has become cloudy, for it is prevented from knowing God. Love, prevented even from seeking God, has grown cold. Yet God uses human beings' subjection to inferior, material things as a saving means, providing them with corporeal sacraments as an opportunity for humility and devotion.[38]

Second, instruction: Human beings need to be instructed by the sacraments because they can no longer know spiritual things directly. The sacraments are the means whereby they can know them indirectly, through sensible things.[39]

Third, practice (*exercitatio*): Because the fallen mind is scattered over multiplicity and addicted to variety and change, wherein it fruitlessly tries to find rest, the sacraments provide variety of a different, therapeutic sort. The performance of the sacraments – the various sacred spaces and congregations, praise and silence, devotion and stillness, hymns and lessons, and bodily gestures such as standing, prostrating, bowing, turning, and so forth – engages our scattered minds and draws them back to unity, and it draws human beings into community. Whereas secular multiplicity dissipates the mind, sacred multiplicity corrects and concentrates it and unifies the faithful.[40] Christians do not seek God *from* the sacraments, as the infidels suppose, but they do seek God *in* them.[41] What was a dividing medium becomes a uniting medium, which leads faithful souls back to God.

10.2.2 *What is a sacrament?*

Hugh's highly influential attempt to define precisely what the sacraments are presupposes an account of what the sacraments are meant to do. His point of departure is a commonplace definition or gloss: A sacrament is "a sign of a sacred thing" (*signum sacrae rei*). The phrase was a twelfth-century expansion of Augustine's gloss on the word *sacramentum* as "sacred sign" (*sacrum signum*).[42] The advantage of this description, Hugh explains, is that it exposes the essential duality of a sacrament. Something visible, material, and exterior stands for something invisible, spiritual, and interior, namely, a certain "spiritual grace." The latter is the reality (*res*) or the power (*virtus*) of the sacrament. Hugh compares these two aspects of the sacraments both to the body and the soul of a human being and to the letter and the sense of a text.[43]

---

[38] *De sacramentis* I.9.3, 319A–320A.   [39] Ibid., 320A–C.   [40] Ibid., 320C–322A.

[41] Ibid., 320A: "Non enim sciunt quod fideles salutem ex istis elementis non quaerunt, etiam si in istis quaerunt; sed ex illo et ab illo quaerunt in istis a quo jubentur quaerere et credunt se percipere in istis."

[42] Augustine, *De civ. Dei* X.5, CCL 47:277/15–16: "sacrificium ergo uisibile inuisibilis sacrificii sacramentum, id est sacrum signum est." Augustine, *Contra adversarium legis et prophetarum* II.9(34), CCL 49:119/983: "tantae rei sacramenta, id est, sacra signa."

[43] *De sacramentis* I.9.2, 317B–C.

Nevertheless, Hugh argues, the phrase "sign of a sacred reality" is no more than a useful "interpretation or expression" of the term "sacrament." It is not a true definition of what a sacrament is, for the phrase would accurately describe sacred scriptures, sacred pictures, and so forth, which are not sacraments.[44] To capture the essence, one needs a narrower description.

More precisely, then, a sacrament is "a corporeal or material element presented externally to the senses that represents by a likeness, signifies by an institution, and contains from its sanctification some invisible and spiritual grace."[45] It is the third aspect that makes the sign efficacious. This definition is both necessary and sufficient, according to Hugh, for every sacrament meets its requirements, and whatever does not meet them is not a sacrament.[46]

Hugh takes the "water of baptism" as an example. The analysis shows that the threefold definition proceeds from generality to particularity. At the first level is a likeness that is innate in the created stuff of the sacrament. At the second level, the sacrament acquires a ritual context through an institution at some point in salvation history. Finally, the sacrament acquires its efficacy through the particular action of a minister (normally a priest), here and now. Thus, there is a natural likeness between the cleansing of the body with water and the cleansing of the soul with the grace of the Holy Spirit. Any water possesses that likeness, but water did not *signify* the grace of redemption until Christ instituted the rite of baptism. Finally, "a word of sanctification is added to the element, and a sacrament comes into existence."[47] Baptism may be analyzed, therefore, as visible water that represents by corporeal likeness, signifies by institution, and contains by sanctification the spiritual grace of redemption. The likeness in water is a work of God as creator and belongs to the order of nature. The institution of baptism is a work of the Savior, Jesus Christ. Sanctification is the work of Christ's ministers.[48] Hugh says that one should analyze every other sacrament into these three aspects, but he does not try to do so.[49]

To convey how each sacrament is efficacious, Hugh maintains that sanctifying power is "contained" in each sacrament. If Christ is the great physician, the recipient is the patient, grace is the medicine, and the sacrament is like a medicine bottle. God or Christ, and not the minister, is the physician: the agent of the sacrament's saving work. The minister is only the dispenser or emissary. It is the medicine that cures, and not the container or the minister, although what the patient sees is not

---

[44] Ibid., 317C.

[45] Ibid., 317D: "sacramentum est corporale vel materiale elementum foris sensibiliter propositum ex similitudine repraesentans, et ex institutione significans, et ex sanctificatione continens aliquam invisibilem et spiritalem gratiam."

[46] Ibid., 317D–318B.

[47] Hugh is echoing Augustine, *In Iohannis evangelium* 80.3, CCL 36:529/5–6: "accedit uerbum ad elementum, et fit sacramentum."

[48] *De sacramentis* I.9.2, 318B–319A.   [49] Ibid., 319A.

the medicine but only the container. For example, in eucharist one sees only bread and wine.[50]

Hugh does not use his causal definition of sacrament, as his successors will do, to distinguish between broad and narrow senses of the term "sacrament" or between the sacraments of the New Law and those of Old, but rather to distinguish sacraments from other sacred signs such as images and texts, which are not sacraments and are not usually called sacraments. Hugh assumes that the threefold definition is coextensive in scope with the combination of humiliation, instruction, and practice.[51] To make sense of Hugh's argument, therefore, one has to assume that the definition can be applied to a broad range of "saving signs," including the sacraments of the Old Law, but with varying degrees of appropriateness, so that the sacraments of the New Law exemplify the definition more fully than those of the Old. The definition is a paradigm that can be applied to a broad range of things, some immediately and obviously, others as if by extension. Hugh outlines a causal nexus, whereby the old sacraments presupposed the new sacraments and had saving power by anticipating them.

10.2.3 *Divisions of the sacraments*

Hugh divides the sacraments both historically and functionally, and the two divisions cut across each other as if at right angles. Historically, the sacraments are divided among three periods: the age of the natural law, which runs from Adam to Moses; the age of the written law, which runs from Moses to the incarnation of Christ; and the age of grace, which runs from the incarnation to the end of the world.[52] The sacraments of the natural law were certain "tithes, sacrifices, and offerings."[53] These were optional and the object of "counsel," whereas the sacraments of the written law, which included circumcision as well as numerous oblations and observances, were obligatory, as are the sacraments of grace, such as baptism and eucharist.[54]

Hugh tries to reconcile the superiority of the sacraments of grace with the essential unity among the sacraments of all three periods, for all sacraments confer the same salvation. God instituted sacraments as soon as human beings were expelled from Eden, for medicine is needed as soon as a disease is contracted. God never left fallen human beings without the means of salvation. It is a mistake, therefore, to say that the earlier sacraments did not have any "effect of sanctification."[55]

Nevertheless, there is a historical progression, for a wise physician knows what remedies are appropriate in each circumstance.[56] Later sacraments are always

---

[50] I.9.4, 322A–323C. I.9.3, 320A–C.   [51] I.9.4, 322A.   [52] I.8.11, 312D.
[53] I.11.3, 344B.   [54] I.11.3, 344A–B. I.11.5, 345B–C.
[55] I.8.12, 313C–D. Compare Hugh's simile of the king riding into battle with his knights before and after in *De sacramentis* I.8.11, 312C–D, and prol., c. 2, 183B–C.
[56] I.8.12, 314A.

"worthier of the effect of spiritual grace" than earlier sacraments.[57] The reason is that all the sacraments derive their efficacy from the Passion of Jesus Christ. The sacraments of grace do so directly, whereas the pre-Christian sacraments did so indirectly, through anticipation and by predicting the work of Jesus Christ. The closer the sacraments are to the Passion of Jesus Christ, the more direct is the relationship. The sacraments of the natural law were a *shadow* of the truth, the sacraments of the written law were an *image* of the truth, and the sacraments of grace are the very *body* of truth, which anticipates the ultimate "truth of the spirit."[58] Because the old sacraments prefigured the new sacraments, they were visible signs of *visible* things, whereas the new sacraments are visible signs of *invisible* things. The new sacraments contain their own sanctifying power as a result of their benediction, and they confer it on faithful recipients, whereas the old sacraments were sanctified through the new sacraments, by prefiguring them. Those who venerated the old sacraments as signs of future things received "the effects of salvation" from them, but they could not attain the fullness of grace, in part because the risen Christ had not yet opened the gates of heaven. They received instead a sustaining grace (*gratia ad sustentationem*) to keep them going.[59] Hugh traces a progression of the means by which people obtained "expiation and justification," first under the natural law through offerings, then under the written law through ritual observances, and finally under grace through baptism. Each succeeding sacrament is a more explicit, more complete, and more effective sign of spiritual restoration than the one that it supersedes.[60]

Hugh divides the sacraments functionally and synchronically into three sorts: the major, remedial sacraments, which are necessary for salvation; the minor sacraments (which will later be called sacramentals), which help to sanctify but are not strictly necessary for salvation, such as the non-essential rituals that surround the major sacraments; and certain preparatory sacraments, which pertain to sacramental ministry (*officium*). For example, baptism and eucharist belong to the first class, sprinkling with water and the distribution of ashes to the second, and priestly vestments to the third.[61] Sacraments of the second sort provide opportunities for *exercitatio* (practice): one of the three elements in Hugh's division of the work of the sacraments. Furthermore, both the major and the minor sacraments include things (*res*), words, and deeds (*facta*), although Hugh does not insist that each sacrament must include all three constituents. For example, the minor sacraments include *things* such as sprinkling with water, the reception of ashes, and the blessing of palms and candles; *deeds* such as the sign of the cross, exsufflation in exorcism, the spreading of the hands, and the bending of the knee; and *words* such as the invocation of the Trinity.[62]

---

[57] I.11.1, 343B–C.   [58] I.11.6, 345C–347A.
[59] I.11.2, 343C–D; I.11.5, 345B.   [60] I.11.6, 345C–347A.
[61] I.9.7, 327A–B, and II.5.1, 439A. Hugh presents the three classes in a different order (1, 3, 2) in the second of these texts.
[62] II.9.1, 471D–472D. Hugh discusses the minor sacraments in II.9 and vestments in II.4.

Hugh uses these historical and functional divisions to keep sacraments of every sort in view, and to emphasize the historical and ritual context of sacraments such as baptism and eucharist. Their inclusive range compensates for the exclusive force of the threefold causal definition. Hugh uses such divisions not to exclude things, as his successors will do, but to spread his net as widely as possible. Thus, Hugh divides the sacraments of the written law into the same three sorts, major, minor, and preparatory. Circumcision (although it began with Abraham) was the chief major sacrament of the Old Law, peace offerings were minor sacraments, and all matters pertaining to the Tabernacle, including the building itself and the utensils used therein, were preparatory sacraments.[63]

Hugh regarded the sacraments from a much broader and more generous perspective than his successors. The narrowing of focus is apparent if one compares his account of the essential constituents of the sacraments, which he calls their "matter," with the accounts of the *Summa sententiarum* (1138–1141) and of Peter Lombard (1150s). Hugh posits constituents of three sorts: things (*res*), deeds, and words. Things used in the sacraments include the water of baptism, the oil of unction, and the bread and wine of eucharist. Deeds include all the associated "signs of sacred realities": not only the sign of the cross, but also the stretching out or raising of one's arms in prayer, and bodily gestures such as bowing, standing, or turning. Words include not only the invocation of the Trinity but also any words used to "express and signify something sacred."[64] Although Hugh is thinking chiefly of the major sacraments in this account, he includes liturgical actions that are minor sacraments in their own right, and it would be easy to add examples from the sacraments of the written law. Hugh does not insist that every sacrament must have all three constituents. According to the *Summa sententiarum*, on the contrary, every sacrament "consists in three [constituents]: things, deeds, and sayings: things, such as water, oil, and suchlike, deeds, such as submersion and insufflation [in baptism], and sayings, such as the invocation of the Trinity."[65] According to Peter Lombard, "There are two things in which a sacrament consists, namely, words and things: words, such as the invocation of the Trinity; things, such as water, oil, and so forth."[66] Thus, the *Summa sententiarum* narrows the range of ritual gestures (deeds), and the Lombard eliminates this category entirely. And whereas Hugh posits a

---

[63] I.12.10, 362B–C. Whereas Hugh characterizes the three classes as pertaining respectively to *remedium, exercitatio,* and *officium* when he expounds the sacraments of grace, he characterizes the classes here, expounding the sacraments of the written law, as pertaining to *remedium, obsequium,* and *cultum divinum,* since *obsequium* is a species of *exercitatio,* and *cultum divinum* is a species of *officium.*

[64] *De sacramentis* I.9.6, 326B–327A.

[65] *Summa sententiarum* IV.1, PL 176:118C: "In tribus consistit sacramentum: rebus, factis, dictis. Rebus, ut sunt aqua, oleum et similia. Factis, ut sunt submersio, insufflatio. Dictis, ut est invocatio Trinitatis."

[66] Peter Lombard, *Sent.* IV, 1.5.6 (235): "Duo autem sunt in quibus sacramentum consistit, scilicet verba et res; verba, ut invocatio Trinitatis; res, ut aqua, oleum et huiusmodi."

disjunctive list, suggesting a wide and indeterminate range of possibilities and combinations, the *Summa sententiarum* and Peter Lombard replace Hugh's disjunction with a limiting conjunction. Moreover, the Lombard reduces the list to a conjunction of *two* constituents, words and things, omitting liturgical movements and gestures from the analysis, notwithstanding their conspicuous presence in the work of any priest administering the sacraments. These later accounts limit the account to features that are necessary for the validity or the essence of each sacrament.

Hugh does not enumerate the major sacraments of the law of grace or propose a definitive list. In Part II of the work, Hugh discusses the incarnation of Jesus Christ, the life of the church, and finally the last things. His treatment of the church begins with the clergy, orders, and the preparatory sacraments associated with orders. Next, he turns to "a consideration of the sacraments," beginning with "the sacrament of the dedication of a church, in which all the other sacraments are celebrated."[67] Just as the church of stone is a figure of the mystical body of Christ, he explains, so the dedication of a church is a figure of baptism.[68] Hugh then devotes sections of the *De sacramentis* to baptism, confirmation, eucharist, marriage, confession, and the anointing of the sick (in that order), all of which he refers to as sacraments. There is also a section on vows, but Hugh says nothing to imply that vows are sacraments. Hugh emphasizes that marriage was exceptional among the sacraments, for it was the only sacrament instituted before the fall.

10.3 THE ROLE OF THE CLERGY

In the second book of the *De sacramentis*, having discussed the incarnation and the church as the body of Christ, Hugh discusses holy orders and the "spiritual power" (*potestas spiritualis*) that belongs to orders, especially to priesthood.[69] The clerics are responsible for the salvation of the laity. Hugh expounds an elaborated version of the Gelasian doctrine, dividing the church into priestly and royal orders.

10.3.1 *Political theology: The two powers*

The laity and the clergy, Hugh explains, constitute the two sides of the body of Christ. The laity constitute the left side of his body, the clergy the right. Each side has its own hierarchy and its own duties. The clergy are concerned with spiritual and heavenly things, the laity with corporeal and earthly things. The laity are not those on Christ's left to whom he will say on the Day of Judgment, "Depart from me, ye cursed, into everlasting fire" (Matt 25:41)! Rather, they are those to whom Solomon referred to when he said, "Length of days is in her right hand, and

---

[67] *De sacramentis* II.5.1, 439A.   [68] Ibid., 439C.   [69] *De sacramentis* II.3, 421–34.

in her left hand riches and honor" (Prov 3:16). The left is good, therefore, although the right is better.[70]

The tonsure is the emblem of the clergy. It may signify humility, Hugh concedes, but it chiefly signifies regal dignity, for clerics are "a chosen generation, a royal priesthood, a holy nation, a peculiar people" (1 Pet 2:9). The tonsure is the cleric's crown. It is also a sign of the cleric's closeness to God, for the top of the head signifies the mind, and the baring of the head signifies divine illumination. Nothing should veil the cleric's pate from God's influence. As a class, the clerics are privy to the secrets of God, and they are God's messengers to the laity.[71] Monks do not need holy orders or the tonsure by profession, for they are not required to minister to the people. They are admitted into the ranks of the clergy only "by indulgence," so that they can be self-sufficient. Otherwise, they would need priests from outside their communities to administer the sacraments, and the presence of outsiders in a cloistered community is distracting.[72]

Hugh's version of the Gelasian doctrine is hierocratic as well as dualistic. He envisages a separation of powers, citing Matthew 22:21: "Render therefore unto Caesar the things which are Caesar's, and unto God the things that are God's."[73] But the priestly power is also a royal power, and secular rulers owe their authority to priestly rulers. The inferior, earthly order owes its power and its very existence to the spiritual, priestly power, which is prior both in time and in dignity. God first established the spiritual power in the Old Testament, and the spiritual power in turn established the royal power. The spiritual, priestly power "institutes" the earthly power in order for it to exist (*ut sit*), and the spiritual power judges the earthly power when the latter errs, whereas God alone can judge the spiritual power. That is why churchmen bless and anoint kings, for "he who blesses is greater, and he who is blessed, less" (cf. Heb. 7:7).[74]

10.3.2 *Celibacy*

Celibacy sets the clergy apart as a "peculiar people." It distinguishes them from the laity and is obligatory for those in major orders. Hugh reveals how much importance he attaches to clerical celibacy when he discusses the impediments of orders and religious vows. Churchmen during his era generally accepted that these vocations were fatal impediments to marriage. If bishops, monks, and nuns could not validly marry, neither could priests, for they too were vocationally celibate.

The chief obstacle to the doctrine was a perennially controversial passage from Augustine's treatise on consecrated widowhood. Augustine concedes that consecrated virgins and widows who lapse and marry sin grievously. Indeed, it is damnable

---

[70] II.2.3–4, 417A–418D.
[71] II.3.1, 421B–C. The term *corona* ("crown") is a common synonym for *tonsura* in medieval Latin.
[72] II.3.4, 422D.   [73] II.2.7, 420C.   [74] II.2.4, 418C–D.

for them even to *wish* to marry, even if no marriage takes place,[75] and their lapse is worse than adultery.[76] But what is sinful is their deceitful breaking of a vow, Augustine argues, and not their marriage *per se.* Augustine rejects an overly literal interpretation of the idea that the consecrated woman is a bride of Christ, so that marriage to another man is adultery. If that were true, he points out, a married woman who espouses celibacy with her husband's consent would commit adultery with Christ. It is the whole church who is Christ's bride, rather than the individual, and the church includes married folk as well as celibates, all of whom share in the great marriage.[77] The passage suggests that when a consecrated virgin lapses and marries, her marriage is valid and binding.

A distinction between private vows, made covertly to God, and public vows, made before the church, emerged during the twelfth century, and it provided one way of reconciling current policy with Augustine's reflections. Only the public vow was a fatal impediment to marriage. This distinction makes a brief appearance in the *Cum omnia sacramenta I*, where the private vow is compared with the soluble "promise of marriage" (i.e., the *de futuro* agreement) as distinct from the insoluble "conjugal pact."[78] Perhaps that analogy was behind the emergence of a different but closely related distinction: that between the "simple" vow of a novice and the subsequent "solemn" vow by which religious gave themselves to Christ and the church, relinquishing their autonomy (cf. 1 Cor 7:4). The latter distinction eventually absorbed or superseded the former. A letter that Pope Innocent I sent to Victricius, bishop of Rouen, in the early fifth century contained the seeds of both distinctions. If a virgin has "married Christ spiritually" and has been veiled by a priest, and if she later marries a man or cohabits with him, Innocent rules, she commits adultery against Christ. She cannot do adequate penance until her mortal husband has "left this age" (*saeculum*); or, according to some versions, until he has "departed from this life" (*vita*). But if the virgin has not yet received the veil, she should do penance because she has broken a good-faith agreement, namely, her betrothal (*sponsio*) to Christ.[79] This passage, which was well established in the canonical tradition, seems to imply that a virgin who has not yet been veiled can validly marry, albeit sinfully, whereas a virgin who has been veiled cannot validly marry.[80]

Hugh expounds the problem in detail.[81] He concedes that the text from Augustine seems to contradict the policy that he upholds, whereby priests and religious cannot validly marry. But suppose that the church deemed the marriage of a consecrated virgin to be valid. The same principle would apply to

---

[75] Augustine, *De bono viduitatis* 9(12), CSEL 41:317/23–318/3.   [76] Ibid., 11(14), 320/6–10.

[77] Ibid., 10(13), 318–20.   [78] *Cum omnia sacramenta I*, ed. Bliemetzrieder, 147/4–5.

[79] Innocent I, *Epist.* 2.13(15)–14(16), PL 20:478B–480A.

[80] Ivo, *Decretum* VII.17–18. The two sections (c. 17 on veiled virgins, c. 18 on unveiled virgins) constitute a single passage in the letter, but they also circulated as separate canons.

[81] *De sacramentis* II.11.12, 499B–504D.

celibate men, and then the consequence would be dreadful. It would be all too easy for any celibate who experiences the urges of sexual desire to lapse and to marry, claiming plausibly that it is "better to marry than to burn," (1 Cor 7:9). There would soon be no celibates left, and then it would be "impossible for anything to remain stable or established."[82]

The policy of clerical celibacy must remain unshakeable, therefore, but what is one to make of Augustine's opinion? It is better, if possible, not to contradict it but rather to reconcile it with current policy. Hugh discusses two possible solutions. First, the church's policy may have changed: not because ancient traditions are taken lightly, but because of differing circumstances. Perhaps people were made of sterner stuff then, and religious now are more prone to backsliding. Second, Augustine may have been referring to women who had made a private vow of virginity, as distinct from a public vow made before the church, for what cannot be proved to the church cannot be judged by the church.[83] To show that public vows are a fatal impediment, Hugh quotes the first section of the passage from Innocent's letter, which he apparently took from the *Cum omnia sacramenta II*.[84] Why does Innocent say that the woman cannot be admitted to penance until her husband has "left this life" (*ab hac vita decesserit*)? According to Hugh's gloss, the woman cannot satisfy for her sin as long as she and her husband are living together. The life in question is their shared life, and her husband leaves it by separating from her.[85]

10.4 HUGH'S TREATISE ON MARY'S VIRGINITY

Hugh construes both the spiritual union of marriage *per se* and the carnal union that usually follows it as distinct sacraments. Whereas the sacrament of spiritual union is essential to marriage, the sacrament of carnal union is optional. Moreover, the former comes into its own and thrives only when the latter is absent.

Hugh first developed this theory in a polemical treatise on the virginity of Mary, which he addressed to a certain bishop G.: probably Geoffrey, the bishop of Châlons-sur-Marne. The treatise came from the same era as the *De sacramentis*, but it is evident that Hugh first worked out the double sacrament theory in the polemical treatise, where it is better integrated with its context, and then selectively incorporated and elaborated his treatment in the *De sacramentis*, where it became part of a comprehensive account of marriage.

---

[82] Ibid., 500D: "nihil deinceps stabile aut ratum esse poterit."   [83] Ibid., 502A–D, 504B–D.

[84] *Cum omnia sacramenta II*, ed. Bliemetzrieder, 283/198–204. The author cites the text as an authority implying that an adulteress cannot do penance as long as the adulterer is alive.

[85] *De sacramentis* II.11.12, 503C–D. Hugh's second solution is implausible, for Augustine denies that the virgins in question are married to Christ, whereas Innocent affirms it. Augustine's moral condemnation would be excessive if he were referring to those who break private vows.

10.4.1 *The problem*

Hugh explains that bishop G. has told him about an unnamed person who has been raising awkward questions about Mary's virginity.[86] According to Hugh, this trouble-some fellow inquired whether persons who consent to marry must thereby consent to sexual intercourse, or more precisely to render the conjugal debt. Then, assuming that the answer to this question was affirmative, he arrived at a dilemma: either Mary was not truly married to Joseph, or she consented to have sexual intercourse with him. The first arm of the dilemma was contrary to Scripture, which clearly stated that they were husband and wife. The second was contrary to the accepted doctrine that Mary had already made a vow of perpetual virginity before she became betrothed to Joseph, as Augustine taught. Even if she had remained a virgin in the flesh, she would no longer have been a virgin in mind. This, too, was unthinkable.[87] Hugh surmises that the man did not mean to impugn Mary's virginity but only to show off his prowess in dialectics. On the contrary, he has shown himself to be a fool, for he is unable to solve his own dilemma.[88]

The chief problem addressed in the treatise pertains to the nature of the consent that is required to "sanctify" a marriage: to join the partners and to make their marriage *ratum*. The treatise is not about the canonical impediment of prior marriage. Nor is it about the role of consummation in the formation of marriage. The object of Hugh's attack is the thesis that marital consent implies or entails consent to sexual intercourse, or, more precisely, to the conjugal debt. This thesis was widely accepted throughout the twelfth century,[89] although Hugh presents himself as a defender of tradition and heaps opprobrium on the adversary. The first recension of the *Cum omnia sacramenta* defines marriage as "the consent to remain together indivisibly and to have sexual intercourse without avoiding offspring."[90] Similarly, the second recension, on which Hugh himself depended, states that what makes marriage is "the consent of a man and a woman to have sexual intercourse and to remain together undividedly."[91] The *Cum omnia sacramenta* considers the objection that the Virgin Mary would have broken her vow of perpetual virginity when she consented to marry Joseph. The author replies that although Mary agreed that she would render the debt if Joseph ever required it, she also trusted that Joseph would never require it.[92] Hugh pursues a more radical solution, separating marriage *per se* from sexuality.

---

[86] Hugh of Saint-Victor, *De beatae Mariae virginitate*, ed. Sicard, 183/3–8.

[87] Ibid., 186/46–57.   [88] Ibid., 184/23–45.

[89] See J. A. Brundage, "Implied Consent to Intercourse," in A. Laiou, *Consent and Coercion to Sex and Marriage in Ancient and Medieval Societies* (Washington, DC, 1993), 245–56.

[90] *Cum omnia sacramenta* I, 140/21–23, 141/1–2.

[91] *Cum omnia sacramenta* II, ed. Bliemetzrieder, 274/3–275/5.

[92] *Cum omnia sacramenta* I, 147/26–148/8. Cf. Gratian, C. 27 q. 2 dictum post c. 2, and ibid., c. 3 (1063–64).

Hugh sets out three points that must be upheld about Mary's virginity,[93] defending each part in turn. First, Mary did not need to compromise her vow (*propositum*)[94] of virginity when she married, for one can enter into a true and holy marriage without consenting to sexual intercourse.[95] Hugh also shows that Mary had in fact made such a vow,[96] and he explains why, in that case, Mary still chose to marry.[97] Second, Hugh confirms and interprets the doctrine that Mary conceived Jesus not by a man but by the Holy Spirit, so that she did not violate her chastity by conceiving.[98] Third, he explains how Mary gave birth without pain and without violating her physical integrity.[99] Hugh explains that he will devote most of the treatise to the first of these topics because the other two are uncontroversial, requiring only explanation (*expositio*) and not proof (*probatio*).[100]

To prove that Mary had taken a vow to remain a virgin, Hugh develops an argument outlined by Augustine.[101] When Mary heard that she would give birth to a son, she said: "How shall this be, since I know not a man" (Luke 1:34). She cannot have meant only that she had not *yet* known a man, for in that case she could still do so and thereby conceive. She must have meant that she would *never* know a man, which implied that she had taken a vow.[102]

10.4.2 *The solution: A theology of marriage*

How, then, could Mary be both truly a wife and truly a virgin: a virgin not only in the flesh but also in the mind? Hugh pursues two main lines of argument to show that there need be no contradiction between marital consent (*consensus coniugalis*) and a vow of virginity (*propositum virginitatis*). His first argument is based on an analysis of the essence of marriage. The second is an exegetical argument, which Hugh proposes in reply to an objection.

Hugh defines marriage as "a legitimate partnership [*legitima societas*] between a man and a woman, in which each person, through mutual consent, owes him- or herself to the other [*semetipsum debet alteri*]."[103] He explains that this definition posits a twofold debt (*debitum*): the partners save themselves exclusively for each other, and they do not deny themselves to each other. By virtue of the exclusive aspect, neither of them will form a partnership with a third person. By virtue of the

---

[93] *De beatae Mariae virginitate*, 183/10–17.
[94] Later theologians will solve the problem by distinguishing between a *propositum* and a *votum*, the former being a private intention, which is only morally binding, and the latter a solemn, public, and absolutely binding vow. Because Hugh does not make this distinction, "vow" is an adequate translation of *propositum*.
[95] *De beatae Mariae virginitate*, 190/114–212/417.   [96] Ibid., 212/426–228/634.
[97] Ibid., 228/635–653.   [98] Ibid., 230/678–238/784.
[99] Ibid., 238/785–240/804.   [100] Ibid., 230/678–232/686.
[101] Augustine, *Serm.* 291.5, PL 38:1318–1319; *Serm.* 225.2, PL 38:1096–97; *De sancta virginitate* 4(4), CSEL 41:238.
[102] *De beatae Mariae virginitate*, 212/426–218/504.   [103] Ibid., 190/119–121.

inclusive aspect, neither of them will dissociate him- or herself from the partnership. What makes marriage, therefore, is the partners' mutual consent, freely and legitimately given, to serve each other in the manner outlined.[104] Hugh argues that there is nothing specifically carnal in these obligations he has outlined. Indeed, he argues that this partnership flourishes in a celibate marriage.[105]

Consent to sexual intercourse, Hugh argues, whereby the partners obligate themselves to the conjugal debt that St Paul described, is distinct from consent to marriage *per se*. It is a supplementary agreement (*comes*), and not what makes marriage. Consent to marriage establishes the conjugal bond (*vinculum*), whereas consent to sexual intercourse establishes the conjugal duty (*officium*). Like the consent to marry, this secondary consent establishes a debt that is both exclusive and inclusive: the partners will save themselves sexually for each other, and they will not deny themselves sexually to each other. In other words, each gives power over his or her body to the other, as St Paul teaches (1 Cor 7:4).[106] But the spouses are not bound to consent thus when they marry, for it is possible to marry while agreeing to abstain.[107]

Hugh corroborates his analysis with a moral argument inspired directly or indirectly by Augustine. If the partners in a marriage mutually agree to suspend the duty (*officium*) of sexual intercourse, the marriage bond will not wane but rather will become more true and more holy, for it is founded now not on "the concupiscence of the flesh or the ardor of lust," but rather on "a bond of charity." Marriage itself is founded not on sexual desire but on charity.[108]

Hugh emphasizes the affective dimension of the spiritual relationship, as well as its quasi-contractual, legal aspect. Moreover, he tends to conflate the two aspects in the polemical treatise, although he will tease them apart in the *De sacramentis*. As a result of their betrothal, the partners are united in mutual affection and in their loving care for each other. Each looks after each other's body and spirit as if they were his or her own. Those who cherish only "the sweet pleasure of the flesh" do not realize how the spouses in a chaste marriage, by caring selflessly for each other, live more happily (*felicius atque beatius*). By abstaining from sexual intercourse, they exclude servitude, anguish, and many other bad things from their marriage.[109]

Hugh considers an objection. Surely the chief reason for marriage is procreation, for that was why God formed Eve as Adam's helpmeet (Gen 1:28, 2:18, 2:21–24). Hugh's reply to this objection involves a careful interpretation of Genesis 2:24. It is *because* the woman has been made from the man's side that "a man shall leave father and mother, and shall cleave to his wife, and they shall be two in one flesh." The verse suggests that the man must leave his father and mother *in order to* be united with his wife. The latter association cancels the former, as if a husband gives to her something that he formerly gave to his parents. Obviously, that is not sexual intercourse. Nor is it cohabitation, for there is nothing to prevent the couple from

---

[104] Ibid., 190/121–129.   [105] Ibid., 192/150–54.   [106] Ibid., 192/130–139, 144–147.
[107] Ibid., 192/147–149.   [108] Ibid., 192/150–54, 196/187–190.   [109] Ibid., 196/191–196.

living with the husband's parents. Nevertheless, there is something exclusive about the new partnership. The man should not withdraw his love from his parents, but he must subordinate his parental love to his conjugal love, for marriage is "singular partnership" (*societas singularis*).[110]

The man's cleaving to his wife is one thing, therefore, and their becoming two in one flesh is another. The former is the primary reason for marriage, whereas the sexual and procreative aspect of marriage, whereby they are two in one flesh, is a distinct and secondary reason. Before sin, coitus and procreation were added to marriage as a duty (*officium*), so that the primary union had greater merit and would be fruitful and not otiose. After sin, coitus was conceded as a remedy, although it hampers the underlying spiritual partnership.[111]

Hugh acknowledges that the secondary union of two in one flesh is the great sacrament of Christ and the church (Eph 5:32), but he argues that the primary union of two in one heart or one mind is a *greater* sacrament. If carnal union is a great sacrament of the union in the flesh between Christ and the church, then the man's cleaving to his wife is a greater sacrament of the love between God and the soul.[112] The man's leaving his parents to cleave unto his wife is itself a "divine sacrament and a profound mystery," for it signifies a person's adherence to the redemptive, supernatural return of things to God, rather than to the natural emanation of all things from God. By leaving those who gave birth to him and finding rest in his freely chosen spouse, the man is figuratively preferring the end to the origin, election to creation, the return to emanation, and the well-being of beatitude to mere being.[113]

Why does Hugh consider the primary union to be a *greater* sacrament than carnal union? The difference, apparently, lies not in what it signifies but in the intrinsic quality or merit of the union. It is surely better, he argues, to be two in one mind or one heart than to be two in one flesh.[114]

10.4.3 *Virginal conception*

Hugh discusses the sense in which Mary is said to have conceived Jesus "from the Holy Spirit" (*de spiritu sancto*) rather than "from a man" (*de viro*).[115] He proposes an analogy with the normal process of conception. Although the woman's role in conception is relatively material and passive, she contributes a semen-like substance from her own flesh as a result of intense love. Hugh assumes that the woman, like the man, cannot produce her semen unless she is sexually aroused by her partner.[116]

---

[110] Ibid., 196/197–210/398.   [111] Ibid., 206/348–208/354, 210/398–400.
[112] Ibid., 194/172–74, 208/363–369.   [113] Ibid., 204/312–206/338.
[114] Ibid., 194/168–170.   [115] Ibid., 230/678–238/784.
[116] A commonplace assumption, prominent in the medical literature, whereby men should enhance their wives' pleasure to ensure conception, and a woman would not conceive from a rape if she was entirely unwilling. See J. Cadden, *Meanings of Sex Difference in the Middle Ages* (Cambridge, 1993), 93–100; and C. J. Saunders, *Rape and Ravishment in the Literature of Medieval England* (Cambridge, 2001), 29–30.

He likens the woman's seminal contribution to a tax on human nature, which is not coerced but rather is paid freely, out of love (*amor, dilectio*), or, "if I may put it this way, by a voluntary charity." A woman is said to conceive "from a man," therefore, because she conceives out of love for the man. Not only does she receive semen from the man, but she also contributes material from herself by virtue of her carnal love for the man. Analogously, therefore, what caused Mary to conceive Jesus was her intense, burning spiritual love of the Holy Spirit, and not any "libido of the flesh." Unlike the male in carnal generation, the Holy Spirit contributed nothing from his own substance. Nevertheless, through the Holy Spirit's influence and Mary's love, nature caused the material substance of the child to come from Mary's flesh. As Scripture says: "The Holy Spirit will come upon you, and the power of the most high will overshadow you" (Luke 1:35).[117]

10.4.4 *The appendix: Marriage and gender*

In an appendix, Hugh explains that many questions have arisen since he wrote the treatise, and that he has had to add further arguments as if he were patching up an old wall. He devotes most of the appendix to replying to an objection *per reductionem ad absurdum*: If marriage is an essentially non-carnal, asexual relationship, then people of the same sex can marry; but people of the same sex cannot marry; therefore, the premise must be false, and sexual intercourse must be a necessary object of marital consent.[118] To solve the objection, Hugh goes over his argument carefully and develops it in new ways, elaborating his analysis of the sacramentality of marriage.

Scholars have questioned whether Hugh himself wrote the appendix, but I can see no more reason to doubt the authenticity of the appendix than that of the preceding work. It is consistent with Hugh's treatment of marriage in the *De sacramentis*, but it goes beyond that treatment and presumably postdates it. In particular, Hugh argues in the appendix that conjugal love is a sacrament not only of the love between God and the soul but also of the love between Christ and the church.

Restating the position developed in the treatise, Hugh explains that there are two sacraments in marriage: first, the sacrament of marriage itself (*sacramentum coniugii*), which is a compact of love (*foedus dilectionis*); second, the sacrament of the conjugal duty (*sacramentum coniugialis officii*), which consists of sexual intercourse within marriage for the procreation of children. The first is a sacrament of divine, spiritual love: not only that between God and the faithful soul, but also that between Christ and the church and between the Word and Christ's human nature.[119]

---

[117] *De beatae Mariae virginitate*, 236/752–238/784. Hugh repeats this explanation in *De sacramentis* II.1.8, 391D–393A.

[118] *De beatae Mariae virginitate*, 242/812–837.

[119] Ibid., 246/879–248/893, 250/937–941. These loves correspond to levels of interpretation ("senses") of the Song of Songs.

To solve the objection, Hugh points out that the love between God and the soul is not a love between equal partners, although they come together in mutual charity. God loves the soul gratuitously and generously, from a superior position of benevolence (*pietas*) and compassion, and as one bestowing a benefit (*beneficium*). The human soul, in contrast, turns to God out of need (*necessitas*), for she can do nothing without God's help.[120] The love between man and wife is asymmetrical in an analogous way. God endowed the man with greater vigor of reason and greater physical strength than the woman. Contrariwise, because woman was formed from man, she is naturally weaker and naturally subordinate and obedient to her husband. To sustain the signification of gender and marriage, God wanted the woman to be mindful of her own fragility and to rely on the man's strength and foresight. The husband loves his wife from benevolence (*pietas*), therefore, whereas a woman loves her husband from need (*necessitas*).[121]

Hugh's idea is congruent with Paul's counsel in Ephesians 5:22–25,[122] but the verse that he quotes for proof is 1 Corinthians 11:3: "the head of every man is Christ, and the head of the woman is the man, and the head of Christ is God." According to Hugh's gloss, the verse posits a triple analogy among the relations between man and woman, between Christ and the Church, and between the divine and human natures of Christ, or God and Christ-as-man. The "holy love of a man for a woman in the sacrament of a chaste marriage" is analogous to "the love of Christ for the church in the sacrament of faith," and the latter is in turn analogous to "the love of God for human nature in the incarnation of the Word."[123]

It follows, Hugh argues, that conjugal love can exist only between a man and a woman. The essential difference required is not in itself sexual. Rather, it is a difference of natures, which is a consequence of sexual difference.[124] The resemblance between human and divine love is so great, Hugh argues, that when Scripture described divine love in the Song of Songs, nothing more like it can be found among visible things than the love between groom and bride:

> For this reason, when in the Song of Love this eternal charity and ineffable love, whether of God for the soul or of Christ for the church, had to be expressed in words — not as to what it was, but as to how it could be — nothing could be found among visible things or among human affections that resembled it more than the love of groom and bride, nor could the invisible and spiritual love be shown in any other way than through its own sacrament, so that, while the auditory sense was receiving in words what human affection knew, the heart might taste interiorly through love what it did not know.[125]

---

[120] *De beatae Mariae virginitate*, 248/895–250/936.   [121] Ibid., 248/894–913.
[122] Especially Eph 5:23: "For the husband is the head of the wife, even as Christ is the head of the church."
[123] *De beatae Mariae virginitate*, 250/936–41.
[124] Ibid., 252/960–969.   [125] Ibid., 250/941–252/950.

Hugh illustrates the point with quotations from the Song of Songs, tacitly assuming that the human love depicted in these verses is the asexual, spiritual charity between man and wife that he promotes in the treatise. The bride says: "My beloved is mine, and I am his, who feeds among the lilies until the day breaks, and the shadows flee away" (2:16–17, 4:6, 6:3); and "I am my beloved's, and his desire is toward me" (7:10). The bridegroom says: "There are threescore queens, and fourscore concubines, and virgins without number. My dove, my undefiled, is but one. She is the only one of her mother, the chosen one of her that bore her" (6:8–9).[126]

10.4.5 *Influences and precedents*

Hugh does not cite any non-biblical sources in his treatise on Mary's virginity, but what he proposes is a radical version of a theory that Augustine expounded in the *De bono coniugali* and other works. According to Augustine, Mary's example showed that marriage could transcend and outlive sexual intercourse. Augustine drew attention to a "natural partnership [*societas*] between the different sexes," which was independent of procreation.[127] Nevertheless, there is nothing in Augustine's mature work on marriage like Hugh's distinction between marriage *per se* and the sexual dimension of marriage. Augustine argued that procreation was the only sufficient reason for sexual difference; he assumed that procreation with the rearing of children was the primary purpose of marriage; and he argued that persons who married did so necessarily "for the sake of begetting children." Augustine was a keen advocate of celibate marriage, but he assumed that couples would not abstain at first but only in due course, when their lust had waned sufficiently. Mary's was a special case, although Augustine argued that Mary and Joseph fulfilled all the conjugal goods, including the *bonum prolis*.[128]

Hugh may have drawn on the treatment of sexual union by some of the *magistri moderni*. According to the *Cum omnia sacramenta*, sexual union in marriage is necessary for the "sacrament of Christ and the church" but it is nevertheless an "adjunct" or "concomitant" of marriage. Sexual intercourse is not necessary for a marriage to be fully established.[129] But Hugh went much further the *magistri moderni*, who did not try to distinguish between different consents or different conjugal debts.

Hugh must have been aware of the contemporaneous idealization of celibate marriage. In his Life of Marie d'Oignies, composed in the early thirteenth century. Jacques de Vitry recounts how Marie, a pious, austere, but unlettered fourteen-year-old, was forced to marry John. It is not clear whether they consummated their marriage, but Marie persuaded John to renounce the conjugal debt. According to

[126] Ibid., 250/928–252/959.   [127] Augustine, *De b. coniug.* 3(3), CSEL 41, 190–91.
[128] Augustine, *De nupt. et conc.* I.11(12–13), CSEL 42, 224–25.
[129] *Cum omnia sacramenta* I, 140/2–15. *Cum omnia sacramenta* II, ed. Bliemetzrieder, 278/73–86.

Jacques, a former Parisian schoolman in Peter the Chanter's circle who venerated Marie and regarded her as his spiritual guide, John was inspired to treat Marie not as his sexual partner but as someone in his care. God had "entrusted a chaste handmaid to a chaste man."[130] After working together in a leper colony, John and Marie eventually parted company. Nevertheless, Jacques claims that their chastity did not diminish but rather enhanced their marriage: "The more he was separated from her in carnal affection [*affectus carnalis*], so much the more was he joined to her through love [*dilectio*], by a bond of spiritual matrimony."[131]

10.4.6 *Hugh's reasoning*

Hugh arrived at his theory by a certain sublimation. Each feature of his theory was the result of projecting a traditional, well-established model of carnal marriage onto a higher, spiritual plane. The carnal union of "two in one flesh" becomes a spiritual union. The great sacrament of Christ's enfleshed union with the church becomes a greater sacrament of the love between God and the soul. The conjugal debt of 1 Corinthians 7:3–4 becomes a mutual debt of spiritual fidelity, and each debt is analyzed into its exclusive and inclusive aspects. Hugh himself draws attention to the analogy between these two debts.[132] Consent to sexual intercourse becomes consent to marital affection. Replying to the objection that Scripture never describes marriage as a union of two in one spirit, but only as a union of two in one flesh, Hugh replies that our understanding naturally progresses from carnal to spiritual things.[133]

10.5 THE THEOLOGY OF MARRIAGE IN THE *DE SACRAMENTIS*

Hugh's discussion of marriage in the second book of the *De sacramentis christianae fidei* is the first extant example of what was to become the norm among medieval theologians: a comprehensive treatise on marriage included in a series of treatises on the Christian sacraments. But Hugh discussed marriage in two places in this work, as if he had trouble finding the right place for the topic in his theological architecture. Hugh inherited from the *magistri moderni* the anomalous notion that although the sacraments were remedies for sin, this sacrament alone had also been instituted before sin.

---

[130] Jacques de Vitry, *Vita Mariae Oigniacensis*, I, c. 1, § 13, ed. D. van Papebroeck, in *Acta Sanctorum*, June (23), vol. 4 (Venice, 1743), p. 13.

[131] Ibid., § 14: "Quanto autem affectu carnali ab ea divisus est, tanto magis matrimonii spiritualis nexu ei per dilectionem conjunctus est." On celibate marriage during the Middle Ages, see D. Elliott, *Spiritual Marriage* (Princeton, 1993).

[132] *De beatae Mariae virginitate*, 192/135–36: "Quod debitum [carnale] in hoc quoque consensu dupliciter, sicut in priori commemoraui, exhibendum est...." Cf. Augustine, *De b. coniug.* 4(4), CSEL 41:191/17–192/1.

[133] *De beatae Mariae virginitate*, 208/366–210/396. Hugh cites 1 Cor 15:46 and Mal 2:13–16.

Hugh introduces the sacraments when he discusses how human beings are redeemed, toward the end of Part 8 of Book I. He emphasizes that there have been sacraments ever since the fall: "As long as there is sickness, that is the time for medicine."[134] Citing Genesis 2:18, however, Hugh notes that the sacrament of marriage was introduced even before sin, and then not as a remedy but as a duty (*officium*). There was no sickness to be cured yet, but there were virtues to be performed. Marriage was a means of instruction (*eruditio*) and of practice (*exercitatio*): two of the three features that Hugh posits in this general account of the sacraments. The duty (*officium*) of procreation was not essential, but it was attached to marriage as its practice.[135] This sacrament was not yet a means of humiliation, for which there was no need.[136]

Because marriage was instituted twice – before sin as a duty, and after sin as a remedy – Hugh promises to discuss marriage twice. He explains that he will first discuss marriage now, before the fall and the other sacraments.[137] Later, he will discuss marriage from the perspective of its second institution, "when it is associated in time with the other sacraments."[138] Hugh postpones the latter discussion until Book II, where marriage appears in the midst of the sacraments of the age of grace.

Hugh underscores the exceptional aspect of marriage again in Book II, which begins with the opening passage of the *Cum omnia sacramenta II*: "Whereas all the sacraments originated after sin and because of sin, we read that the sacrament of marriage alone was also instituted before sin, yet not as a remedy but as an office."[139] After some introductory remarks on the agenda of the treatise and on the origin of marriage, all taken verbatim from the *Cum omnia sacramenta II*, Hugh summarizes the differences between the two institutions of marriage, supplementing his summary with his theory of the two sacraments in marriage.[140]

When did the two institutions occur? Clearly, the original institution of marriage occurred in Eden. Using material taken from the *Cum omnia sacramenta II*, Hugh affirms that God "decreed" that there would be marriage by making Eve from Adam's side as his helpmeet and by revealing his intentions to Adam, who was in a prophetic trance. Adam knew "in the spirit" for what purpose Eve had been formed when he spoke after his deep sleep (Gen 2:23–24).[141] Hugh does not say

---

[134] I.8.12, 313D: "Si quis igitur quaerat tempus institutionis sacramentorum, sciat quia quandiu morbus est, tempus medicinae est."

[135] I.8.13, 314C–D.   [136] I.8.12, 314B.

[137] I.8.13, 314C–318A. Hugh appends his first discussion of marriage in the *De sacramentis* to Book I, Part 8.

[138] I.8.12, 314A–C.

[139] II.11.1, 479D–480D. Cf. *Cum omnia sacramenta II*, ed. Weisweiler, 33/1–3. The passage that Hugh appropriates from the *Cum omnia sacramenta II* runs through II.11.2 into the beginning of II.11.3.

[140] II.11.3, 481B–482D.   [141] II.11.2, 481A.

when the second institution of marriage occurred, although he does say that Christ "consecrated" marriage at Cana, both by his presence and by using the occasion for the first of his miracles: a common topos of twelfth-century theology.[142]

Hugh proposes a different division of institutions when he considers the impediments of relationship (in particular, what should be done if the spouses become aware of an impediment after they have married). Under the first institution, only two persons were excluded from the sacrament of marriage, namely, parent and child (Gen 2:24). Later, there was a second institution "made by the law," and this excluded certain other persons: either because of what was naturally seemly, or to enhance chastity.[143]

10.5.2 *Marital consent and the essence of marriage*

Hugh begins his account of what marriage is by noting that some (*quidam*) have defined marriage as "the consent of male of female that maintains an indivisible way of life."[144] The remote source is Justinian's *Institutes*, but Hugh' proximate source is the *Cum omnia sacramenta II*, in which the term *consensus* has replaced the original *coniunctio* ("joining," "union") and the definition is ascribed to Isidore (Section 9.2).[145] Hugh adds, again following *Cum omnia sacramenta II*,[146] that one should insert the word "legitimate" into the definition. Marriage is "the legitimate consent — that is, between legitimate persons and legitimately given — of male of female that maintains an indivisible way of life."[147] Like his source, Hugh wants to define marriage as consent. Persons are legitimate when there are no impediments of relationship, and consent is legitimately given when the partners agree about the right things.[148] With that pretext, Hugh inquires into the proper object of consent. Later, he discusses the betrothal distinction.

To what do the partners agree? Hugh argues that the object cannot be sexual intercourse, for then there would be no distinction between fornication and marriage. Instead, they consent to a certain partnership, namely, that which God established in the beginning when he formed woman from man as his helpmeet (Gen 2:21–24). But what is the nature of the partnership? Following Augustine, Hugh argues that God formed Eve from Adam's side rather than from an upper or lower part of his body to demonstrate that there was a certain equality between them. She was not supposed either to dominate over him or to be dominated by him, but

---

[142] Ibid.   [143] II.11.4, 483B–C.
[144] II.11.4, 483A: "ut dicerent conjugium esse consensum masculi et feminae individualem vitae consuetudinem retinentem."
[145] *Cum omnia sacramenta II*, ed. Bliemetzrieder, 274/1–2. Cf. *Inst.* 1.9.1.
[146] *Cum omnia sacramenta II*, ed. Bliemetzrieder, 279/113–15.
[147] *De sacramentis* II.11.4, 485C.   [148] Ibid.

rather be his partner.[149] Nevertheless, the fact that she was formed from Adam demonstrated that she was "in some manner" (*quodammodo*) inferior to him.[150]

As in the treatise on Mary, Hugh analyzes the relationship into its exclusive and inclusive aspects. The partners voluntarily give themselves exclusively to each other, obligating themselves to each other and dissociating themselves from others. But none of that entails sexual intercourse, Hugh points out. Agreement to coitus may be "conjoined" to the agreement to marry, as it usually is by default, but the partners are free to exclude it from their compact by mutual agreement if they wish, as Mary and Joseph must have done.[151]

If marriage is essentially asexual, it follows that the partners are married as soon as they exchange consent, even before sexual intercourse. Once the spouses have made the marriage by consenting to it, a subsequent marriage cannot trump the prior agreement even if it is supposedly more complete: for example, if the first union was unconsummated and the second consummated, and the spouses have even begotten children.[152] Suppose the partners promise, perhaps with an oath, that they will give themselves to each other as husband and wife at an agreed time, but that one of them marries someone else meanwhile, or that both of them do so. Which marriage should be upheld? Hugh's argument is based on the logic of their agreement. Someone who *promises* to do something in the future does not yet *do* it: "*Qui promittit nondum facit.*" In the envisaged scenario, whoever has breached the promise must do penance for the deceit, but the second marriage is valid and indissoluble.[153] Hugh suggests a typical formula for present consent. The man might say: "I accept you as my own, so that henceforth you shall be my wife, and I your husband," and she might reply: "I accept you as my own, so that henceforth I shall be your wife, and you my husband." But they may use other words to the same effect, or even non-verbal signs.[154]

Hugh reviews the chief texts of the consensual dossier in the light of the betrothal distinction, citing Ambrose, Augustine, Isidore, and Pope Nicholas I. He concedes that these texts are ambiguous when interpreted in light of his own theory. Augustine and Isidore affirm that the partners are married as soon as there is a betrothal (*desponsatio*), and Ambrose says that the partners assume the name of spouses (*coniugii*) as soon as their marriage begins (*initiatur*). But the betrothal in question might be either a *de praesenti* or a *de futuro* agreement, and the texts may be interpreted in either sense. A marriage "begins" with both agreements, in different ways. But none of this, Hugh argues, affects the basic point: that the partners are not married until they have actually given themselves to each other through a *de*

---

[149] I.6.35, 284C, and II.11.4, 485A. Hugh gave the same explanation in his earlier *Dialogus*, PL 176:23A. It came form Augustine, *De b. coniug.* 1(1), CSEL 41:187.
[150] II.11.4, 485A–B.   [151] II.11.4, 484D–485D.   [152] II.11.5, 485D.
[153] II.11.5, 486A–C.   [154] Ibid., 488B.

praesenti agreement, and that their marriage is no longer incomplete or imperfect as soon as such an agreement has occurred.[155]

10.5.3 *The sacramentality of marriage*

Much of what Hugh says about the sacramentality of marriage in the *De sacramentis* elaborates the theory that he had briefly proposed in the treatise on Mary's virginity, setting it in a broader context and adding some new vocabulary and some refinements. One finds here, too, the key points of Hugh's fuller treatment of the theme in the appendix to the treatise on Mary's virginity, which probably postdates the *De sacramentis*. These discussions involve a two-part sign-and-signified analysis, such that marriage is construed as a sacrament *of* something: of the love uniting God and the soul, and of the union "in the flesh" between Christ and the church. The analysis is congruent with the notion that a sacrament is a "sign of a sacred reality." More to the point, it belongs to a tradition of interpretation leading from Ephesians 5:32 through Leo I and Hincmar to the coital proof texts and the *magistri moderni*. As noted earlier, Hugh sublimated the model to show that marriage was essentially asexual.

Despite his theory of the two sacraments, spiritual and carnal, Hugh is inclined to attribute the sacramentality of marriage to its spiritual aspect alone. For example, when he differentiates between the diversity of natures necessary for marriage and the sexual diversity necessary for procreation, Hugh says that God consecrated marriage as a "sacrament of eternal love," whereas God created sexual difference "because of the utility of human propagation."[156]

We might ask what makes one sacrament greater than the other. The difference of value cannot reflect a difference between the signified unions *per se*. The incarnation is not less sacred, less magnificent, or less mysterious than the love between God and the soul. Hugh must consider one of the signifying unions to be intrinsically more sacred – i.e., nobler and holier – and more meritorious than the other. Moreover, the two sacraments involve different modes of likeness. Conjugal charity is qualitatively similar to the love between God and the soul and shares it. In some sense, the signified love gives value to the signifier: it is *because* the love between husband and wife is like that between God and the soul that the former love is good and beautiful. But the likeness between sexual union and Christ's union with the church has no such entailments. Hugh does not analyze the resemblance, but we must presume that it consists entirely of analogical comparison. There is no suggestion here either that the signifier depends for its existence on the signified, or that the signifier shares the beauty and holiness of the signified. Hugh esteemed the

---

[155] Ibid., 487A–488A.
[156] Cf. *De beatae Mariae virginitate*, 252/959–961: "Propter sacramentum ergo dilectionis eterne, Deus coniugium sancire uoluit. Propter utilitatem propagationis humane, sexum creauit."

incarnation of Jesus Christ above everything except God himself, whereas he held
the sexual union in low esteem. The former is indispensible, the latter dispensable.

10.5.4 Office, remedy, and underlying essence

Following the *Cum omnia sacramenta II*, Hugh distinguishes between the original
institution of marriage "as a duty" (*ad officium*) and the institution of marriage
"as a remedy" (*ad remedium*) after the fall. As Augustine says in the *De Genesi ad
litteram*, "The weakness of both sexes, with its inclination toward depraved ruin, is
rightly rescued [*excipitur*] by the honorableness of marriage, so that what would
have been a duty for the healthy is a remedy for the sick." The second institution
consecrated marriage as a compact of love so that "through its goods, what
pertained to weakness and to offence in sexual intercourse might be excused."[157]
Whether as a duty or as a remedy, marriage was intended to be a "compact of love"
(*foedus dilectionis*). But whereas it was originally instituted for the "multiplication
of nature," it was re-instituted "so that nature should be rescued [*exciperetur*], and
vice restrained." Whereas God directed Adam and Eve to increase and multiply in
the beginning (Gen 1:28), sexual intercourse now is a matter of indulgence and
compassion.[158]

Hugh elaborates Augustine's twofold explanation of the remedy. As well as
containing sexual ardor by keeping it within the bounds of the marriage compact,
marriage excuses the ardor, which is evil *per se*, by compensating for this evil with
the goods of marriage.[159] There can be no coitus without concupiscence after the
fall, for God destroyed the original order between body and soul as a punishment for
pride, making the soul subject to the body. But life would be impossible if the soul
were entirely subject to the body. Tempering justice with mercy, God caused the
fault of concupiscence and disorder to be concentrated in a single organ of the body,
which would no longer be obedient to the rational will. Hugh likens this punishment to an inscription over a doorway, which reminds everyone who comes into the
world that they have inherited original sin.[160]

As well as distinguishing between duty and remedy, as the *magistri moderni* had
done, Hugh perceives a deeper distinction between marriage itself and the sexual
dimension of marriage, which was formerly a duty but is now a remedy. Marriage is
one thing, and the duty or remedy is another.[161] God originally instituted marriage
both "as a sacrament because of instruction [*eruditio*]" and "as a duty because of

---

[157] Augustine, *De Gen. ad litt.* IX.7, CSEL 28.1:275. *Cum omnia sacramenta II*, ed. Bliemetzrieder,
    34/24–26.
[158] *De sacramentis* I.11.3, 481B–482C.
[159] II.11.7, 494B–C. The passage is a quotation from Augustine, *Epist.* 187, 9(31), CSEL 57:109/
    15–18, but Hugh's source is *Cum omnia sacramenta II*, ed. Bliemetzrieder, 275/10–11.
[160] *De sacramentis* I.8.13, 316B–318A.
[161] Ibid., 314D. The term *officium* was often used to refer euphemistically to coitus in marriage,
    construed as the object of the conjugal debt.

practice [*exercitatio*]."[162] The duty of sexual intercourse and procreation was distinct from the underlying "compact of love." The primary, non-carnal relationship required the polar division of human nature into two types, respectively strong and weak, independent and dependent. That the two types are respectively male and female arises from the secondary, carnal relationship, which was necessary for reproduction.[163] Marriage can be true and holy, therefore, without sexual intercourse. Moreover, whereas the removal of sexual intercourse would have made marriage less fruitful before sin entered into the world, now it makes marriage more pure.[164] For proof, Hugh cites two texts that came originally from Augustine's *De bono coniugali*, although Hugh seems to have taken them from the *Sententiae Magistri A*. First, the goodness of marriage must consist not only in propagation but also in the natural partnership between the sexes. Otherwise, there would be no marriage among the elderly or among those who have lost or cannot beget children, whereas, in fact, the "order of charity" thrives as the "ardor of the flesh" wanes. Second, the "sanctity of the sacrament" is worth more than the "fruitfulness of the womb."[165]

Hugh concedes that the "great sacrament" of Christ and the church of which Paul spoke (Eph 5:32) requires sexual intercourse, but he argues that if carnal union is great, spiritual union must be greater. Whereas "it is the spirit that vivifies," "the flesh profits nothing" (John 6:64).[166]

Even in the beginning, therefore, there were two sacraments in marriage, although Hugh is more inclined to regard one as a sacrament than the other. One was the sacrament *par excellence* of the spiritual partnership of love that already existed "in the spirit between God and the soul," and in which God is the bridegroom and the soul is his bride.[167] The other was instituted as a sacrament of the partnership "in the flesh" that would exist in the future between Christ and the church, in which Christ is the bridegroom and the church is his bride.[168] On both sides of the comparison, the bridegroom is superior and the bride subordinate. Whereas he condescends to the bride by kindness (*pietas*), bestowing a benefit (*beneficium*) upon her, she is drawn to him out of need (*necessitas*), receiving the support and protection that he offers.[169] In the essential conjugal relationship, the husband is the image of God and his wife represents the rational soul.[170]

God added the duty (*officium*) of intercourse and procreation to marriage to make the primary relationship fruitful and to provide an opportunity for obedience and virtue, but the addition was also significant. It showed that the partnership between God and the soul would be fruitless unless God infused into the soul the seeds of virtue. Unlike the primary relationship, the sexual debt is symmetrical. Nevertheless,

---

[162] Ibid., 314C–D.   [163] Ibid., 316A–B.   [164] II.11.3, 482D.

[165] II.11.3, 481D. Augustine, *De b. coniug.* 3(3) and 18(21), CSEL 41:190–91, 215. SMA 40 and 53.

[166] *De sacramentis* II.11.3, 482B–C.

[167] Hugh may be thinking of the Song of Songs, but cf. Isa 62:5.

[168] I.8.13, 314D, and II.11.3, 481B–D, 482C.   [169] I.8.13, 314D–315A.   [170] Ibid., 315A–B.

Hugh finds a comparable asymmetrical relation in the physiology of sexual intercourse. Whereas the man actively propagates from his seed, the woman receives his
seed, conceives from it, and gives birth to what she conceives.[171]

10.5.5 *The inward sanctity of marriage*

Because the primary, pre-sexual relationship in marriage is a sacrament of the love
between God and the soul, Hugh argues, marriage itself must foster and protect an
interior spiritual reality (*res*). The spouses' insoluble juridical partnership, which
they establish by their conjugal pact, is only the outward form of the sacrament. The
interior reality (*res*) of that sacrament is the "the mutual love of souls," which is
"protected" (*custoditur*) by the outward compact. This love is in turn a sacrament of
the union between God and the soul, whereby God joins the soul to himself
through "the infusion of his grace and participation in his Spirit."[172]

As well as distinguishing between the sexual and non-carnal dimensions of
marriage, therefore, Hugh distinguishes between inward and outward aspects of
the non-carnal dimension. Hugh uses this double analysis to interpret the three
goods of marriage: faith, the hope of offspring (*spes prolis*), and sacrament (i.e.,
insolubility). Following the *Cum omnia sacramenta II*, Hugh argues that faith and
the hope of offspring are separable from marriage, whereas sacrament is inseparable.
Marriage exists without faith when someone commits adultery, and it exists without
hope of offspring when the partners take a mutual vow of celibacy or when advanced
age prevents them from begetting children. But because the compact of marriage is
itself insoluble, the good of sacrament cannot be separated from marriage. Hugh
points out that this proposition is congruent with his distinction between the primary
and secondary relationships in marriage. Whereas the first two goods pertain to the
sexual relationship, which is separable, the third good pertains to the underlying
"legitimate partnership," which is inseparable from marriage.[173] Nevertheless,
although every marriage everywhere possesses this sacrament, the marriage of
faithful Christians alone has the *sanctity* of sacrament. All those of every race and
religion who come together in the union that God established in the beginning
possess the sacrament, but only those who dwell "in the city of God, in his holy
mountain" enjoy its sanctity.[174] The exterior sacrament is the spouses' "indivisible

---

[171] Ibid., 315B–C.   [172] II.11.3, 482C–D.   [173] II.11.8, 494D–495A.
[174] II.11.8, 496B: "recte sacramentum conjugii omnibus gentibus commune esse dicitur; sanctitas
autem sive virtus sacramenti, non nisi in civitate Dei nostri, et in monte sancto ejus. Hoc est in
fide et charitate, in Ecclesia videlicet sancta, et inter fideles esse perhibetur. Sacramentum
autem conjugii habent, qui pari consensu ad eam quae a Deo inter masculum et feminam
instituta est societatem indivise adinvicem conservandam convenerunt. Sacramenti vero hujus
sanctitatem non habent nisi ii soli qui per fidem membra Christi facti sunt; et per charitatem
mente et devotione intus Deo uniti sunt." Dependent on *Cum omnia sacramenta II*, ed.
Bliemetzrieder, 275/17–276/43. See Haring, "*Sententiae Magistri A*," p. 32, no. 94, on the
transmission of this text.

partnership," and the corresponding interior reality of the sacrament (*res sacramenti*) is the "steadfastly burning charity of their minds toward each other." The exterior partnership, like sexual union, is a sacrament of Christ and church, whereas the interior love is a sacrament of God and the soul. Only those who have become members of Christ through faith and are united to God through charity and devotion enjoy the "sanctity or power [*virtus*] of the sacrament."[175] Hugh's theory of the outward and inward aspects of marriage enables him to tease apart conjugal love from the enforceable bond. The latter exists insolubly and willy-nilly. The former *ought* always to exist in every marriage, but it can be lost or recovered.

Hugh's idealistic treatment of marriage in the *De sacramentis* is the inverse of his treatment in the *De vanitate mundi*, whose genre requires stark pessimism. Reason guides Soul through four scenarios: a courtly gathering on the deck of a ship, a merchants' caravan, a wedding, and a school. Each scenario seems at first to exemplify the good things of life, but each turns bad, and Reason exposes its vanity. Hugh's depiction of marriage here owes something to the traditional "anti-matrimonial dossier,"[176] emphasizing nagging and violence, the distractions of child rearing, and the pains of childbirth, which compensate for the pleasures of the bed, but his aim is to expose the vanity not only of marriage but of everything that looks promising in this world – even the schools. Reason concedes that there are some good things in marriage, but many evil things are mixed in with them. Everyone knows that the "harmony of wills" (*concordia animorum*) that ought to vivify marriage is rare. Instead, the very partnership that ought to engender concord becomes tiresome to the spouses: a source of hatred and discord. Daily arguments, rows, and beatings follow, but the partners are bound to remain together in misery. Corporeal separation is no obstacle to those who are mentally united by their charity, as when a husband and wife espouse celibacy or the religious life. Conversely, corporeal togetherness is torment for those who are mentally divided.[177] From the perspective of the *De vanitate mundi*, the marriage compact does not protect and foster love but imprisons it. Love usually dies in conjugal captivity. Thereafter, the shell of a marital compact only exacerbates the spouses' mutual animosity. The love that dies here is not the elevated, spiritual love that Hugh envisages in the *De sacramentis*, but a more mundane, carnal love, which offers pleasure at first but then brings pain.

Hugh bases his treatment of the role of the Christian faith in marriage, the Pauline Privilege, and the marriage of infidels in the *De sacramentis* on explanations that he found in the *Cum omnia sacramenta II*.[178] Some argue that a marriage without faith is invalid because "whatever is not from faith is a sin."[179] But if an

---

[175] II.11.8, 495D–496B.
[176] Ph. Delhaye, "Le dossier antimatrimoniale de l'*Adversus Jovinianum* et son influence sur quelques écrits latins du XIIᵉ siècle," *Mediaeval Studies* 13 (1951): 65–86.
[177] Hugh of Saint-Victor, *De vanitate mundi*, PL 176:708C–D.
[178] *Cum omnia sacramenta II*, ed. Bliemetzrieder, 278/87–279/106.
[179] From Rom 14:23, but see also Heb 11:6. Cf. PM 208, Lottin, PsM V, p. 136.

unbelieving man takes a wife to beget and to raise of children, is faithful to her, loves and cares for her, and does not marry another while she is alive, Hugh argues, then the marriage is real. Although the husband does not have faith in Christ, he does nothing by his marriage that is contrary to that faith or to the norms of marriage that God instituted in the beginning.[180]

Hugh compares the marriage of infidels both to baptism among heretics and to eucharist practiced among schismatics. According to some authorities, a schismatic priest cannot confect the true body of Christ. But a sacrament may be true in two ways, pertaining respectively to the consecration and validity of the sacrament *per se* and to the "spiritual effect" of the sacrament: its "power and spiritual grace" (*virtus et gratia spiritualis*). Eucharist among schismatics, as among any Christians who receive the sacrament unworthily, is true in only the first respect. The sacrament truly becomes the body of Christ for them, but it does not help them to be full members of the mystical body of Christ, for that body presupposes unity. Likewise, marriage among infidels, as well as among Christians who lead wicked lives, is true in one sense but untrue in another. They do possess the *sacramentum* of insoluble marriage, but they do not receive the inner "power and spiritual effect" (*virtus et effectus spiritualis*) of the sacrament.[181] Although the sacramental virtue or spiritual effect of marriage is analogous to the virtue of eucharist and baptism, Hugh does not call it a grace. Whereas he says that eucharist confers "a power and a spiritual *grace*," he says that marriage confers "a power and a spiritual *effect*."

Hugh cites patristic authorities, including three passages from Augustine, to support his thesis that infidels possess at least the outward sacrament of marriage.[182] But what is one to make of the statement by Ambrose (i.e., Ambrosiaster) regarding the Pauline Privilege: that because marriage without God is not established (*ratum*), there is no sin if the convert separates and marries another?[183] Hugh points out, following the *Cum omnia sacramenta II*, that Ambrose does not say that there is no marriage at all without God, but only that such a marriage is not *ratum*. Even a *non-ratum* marriage is truly a marriage.[184] Someone has said that the convert may dismiss the unbelieving spouse because "injury to the creator dissolves the *ius* of marriage" (i.e., its legal, *de iure* foundation).[185] But even that proposition presupposes that there is some *ius* of marriage even among infidels. The point is not that the marriage

---

[180] *De sacramentis* II.11.13, 504D, 505B–C.   [181] Ibid., 505A–506B.
[182] Ibid., 506B–C. Augustine, *De b. coniug.* 24(32), 226/25–227/2 (SMA 26); *De adult. coniug.* 18 (20), 367/18–20; and *De div. quaest.*, q. 83, 2–4, PL 40:100 (SMA 140).
[183] *De sacramentis* II.11.13, 506C: "Non est ratum conjugium praeter Deum; et ideo non est peccatum dimissio propter Deum si aliis copuletur." Proximate source: *Cum omnia sacramenta II*, ed. Bliemetzrieder, 279/102–106. Original source: Ambrosiaster, *in I Cor* 7:15, 2, CSEL 81:77/ 2–7. Hugh cites a second authority, which he ascribes to Gregory: "Dimisso [Migne: dimissio] propter Deum non est peccatum si alii coniungatur." In fact, this authority is evidently derived from the same text of Ambrosiaster, although it was often ascribed to Augustine, as was the Corinthians commentary as a whole. See Haring, "*Sententiae Magistri A*," p. 21, no. 47.
[184] A tenuous argument. Is an illegitimate marriage a marriage of a certain sort?
[185] Ambrosiaster, *in I Cor* 7:15, 2, CSEL 81:77/6.

of infidels is non-existent, therefore, or even that it is soluble, but rather that it is trumped by faith in God. Other things being equal, even the marriage of infidels is insoluble, but the duty to serve God trumps every obligation.[186] Hugh illustrates his position with a scenario in which an unbelieving wife resists her husband's new religion or divorces him.[187] The convert may continue in the marriage "as a work of perfection" and to avoid scandal (although Hugh seems to assume that the convert has the right to remarry even if the infidel is peaceable). If they divorce, only the convert has the right to remarry, for nothing stronger has trumped the insoluble bond in the infidel.[188] If the unconverted partner is peaceable, he or she is no obstacle to the sanctity of the marriage, and the believer will sanctify the unbeliever (1 Cor 7:4).[189]

Hugh proposes some policies for more complicated cases. If the convert has divorced the infidel but the infidel later converts, the latter is free either to remarry in the faith or, if the first convert has not remarried, to take up the old marriage again; or both of the converts may remain unmarried. Again, if an infidel divorced by a convert has remarried and both spouses later convert to Christianity, the second marriage remains valid. The old ties no longer present an obstacle, even though both partners are still alive, because baptism washes away sin. Reverence and faith absolve them from any injury to the creator, and the freedom of their new faith wipes away old debts. But if persons who are married within the forbidden degrees of consanguinity convert to Christianity, their marriage is invalid. Conversion does not erase the impediment, for the grace of baptism wipes away only sin, not nature.[190]

Hugh distinguishes, then, between the outer legal structure of marriage and its inner spiritual effect: the sanctity or "virtue" of the sacrament. The latter is comparable to the spiritual grace conferred in eucharist and baptism. The outer partnership is insoluble and present in every marriage *de iure*, whereas only those who dwell "in the city of God, in his holy mountain" can enjoy the inward sanctity, which is akin to the love between God and the soul and, indeed, is a sacrament of that love by signifying it. In another context, however, to show that a defective and soluble marriage may nevertheless exist as a true marriage and a true sacrament before it is dissolved, Hugh equates the inner virtue or spiritual effect of the sacrament with the full realization of its insolubility. I shall outline this argument later (Section 10.6.2).

---

[186] *De sacramentis* 507A: "Sed est causa Dei major adversus quam nulla stare debet causa." Cf. Ambrosiaster, *in I Cor* 7:15, 1, 76/23–24: "major enim causa dei est quam matrimonii."

[187] *De sacramentis* II.11.13, 507A–B.   [188] *De sacramentis* II.11.13, 508B–C.

[189] II.11.9, 496D. The chapter is from Augustine, *De bono coniugali* 11(13), 204–05, which Hugh took from SMA 44.

[190] Ibid., 509C–510C: "baptismi gratia culpam delet, non naturam." Cf. *Conc. Tribur* c. 39, Mansi 17:151E: "crimina enim in baptismo solvuntur, non coniugia."

10.6 THE AUTHORITY OF THE CLERGY

In Hugh's mind, the sacramental system presupposes the power of clerics in major orders. Marriage is an exception insofar as it does not require the blessing of a priest or even the witness of the church to be valid. That said, marriages *ought* to be contracted *in facie ecclesiae*. Moreover, the institutional church has juridical power over marriage. The church has the power to introduce and remove diriment impediments, to dissolve some marriages that truly exist before they are dissolved, and even to make a marriage sacramentally valid in the eyes of God despite an unknown impediment that would make the marriage invalid if it were known.

Hugh approaches problems of invalidity and divorce from the practical perspective of a cleric who was sometimes required to counsel and adjudicate. Suppose a man has had sex with a near relation of his wife, whether before or after the wedding. According to canon law, the marriage is incestuous. If the incest becomes public, and the case comes to a tribunal, the church must order both partners to separate and to remain celibate. But Hugh invokes the idea of "public honesty." As a cleric, he would prefer not to hear about such cases officially, with their scandalous "testimonies and proofs." It is often better to save the "peace of the marriage bed" despite the error.[191]

10.6.1 *Clandestine marriage and the principle of* Solus consensus

Hugh accepted that the expressed *de praesenti* consent of the spouses was the sufficient cause of a valid marriage, provided that they were not disqualified by some impediment and that their consent was genuine. He endorsed that principle only reluctantly, however, for he was deeply troubled by the problem of clandestine marriage.[192] "What is to be done," Hugh asks, "about persons of this sort, who have married secretly, if afterwards one or both of them denies what was done and enters into a partnership with another?"[193] One could avoid problems of that sort if, as some maintain, secret marriages were invalid. Then, if the partners plighted their troth in secret, their supposed marriage would in reality amount to fornication. If they were still willing to be man and wife, they could exchange consent again, but this time publicly. In that case, their secret agreement would have established only an initiate marriage (*matrimonium initiatum*), which their public agreement would complete. Such a policy would obviate many evils, and yet the judgment of the majority, Hugh concedes, maintains a different opinion, namely, that "such consent

---

[191] *De sacramentis* II.11.6, 493C–494A. 493C–D: "Ego quidem quandiu fieri rationabiliter posset propter servandam pacem tori conjugalis eiusmodi, testimonia et probationes declinarem."

[192] II.11.6, 488C–494A.

[193] II.11.6, 488C: "Quid ergo faciendum est de hujusmodi qui clanculo convenerunt, si postea aut alter aut uterque factum negando ad alienam societatem transierit?"

[i.e., in the present tense] between legitimate persons, whether given openly or secretly, is judged to be the perfected sacrament of marriage."[194]

Hugh interprets the oft-cited decretal ascribed to Pope Evaristus in light of that policy. According to the decretal, a marriage is illegitimate and amounts only to fornication or promiscuity (*stuprum*) unless the bride has been petitioned from those with power over her, betrothed by her kinsfolk, given a dowry, blessed by a priest, and married with every customary ritual – unless the union is based on their own free will and supported by legitimate vows.[195] Those who maintain that clandestine marriages are invalid or incomplete interpret the final clause as a reference to subsequent public consent, when the spouses repeat their trothplight in public. But if one follows the opinion of the majority, as Hugh feels compelled to do, one will understand Evaristus to have said that a covert, informal marriage is illegitimate only in the sense that it contravenes legally prescribed norms, and not that it is invalid. Hugh compares such a marriage to a baptism performed without its attendant "minor sacraments," such as the consecration of the font, exorcism, and chrismation. The priestly blessing, therefore, is a minor sacrament.[196]

To illustrate the problems of clandestine marriage, Hugh outlines an especially hard case, which I shall refer to covert prior contract. It will become the standard example of the hazards of clandestine marriage. Suppose that a man has married one woman by consent alone, with no witnesses present, so that there is no proof of their marriage. Then he marries another woman, and this union is public and formal and solemnized before the church. Her parents give the bride away, and a priest blesses the marriage. In due course, they beget children.[197] What should the church do if the first woman contests the second marriage and asks that her husband be returned to her?

Hugh's solution is based on the principle that "secret things cannot prejudice manifest things." An ecclesiastical judge is bound to decide according to the evidence and to uphold the second marriage. Even if the court believes the complainant, it cannot act on that belief because so doing would set a terrible precedent. Couples would make up stories to get out of unwelcome marriages. Although the church cannot uphold the first woman's claim, she must remain

---

[194] Ibid., 489B–C: "Si quis igitur ad hunc modum dicat conjugium occulto quidem consensu initiari posse, sed non nisi manifesta amborum confessione firmari compendiosius mala multa declinat, sed plurium approbatio hoc recipit ut sive in manifesto sive in occulto talis consensus inter legitimas personas factus fuerit, perfectum conjugii sacramentum judicetur."

[195] "nisi voluntas propria suffragata fuerit et vota succurrerint legitima." For the text of ps.-Evaristus, which was well established in the canonical tradition, see PL 130:81B–C. The first author to cite it as an authority was Hincmar of Reims, *De divortio*, PL 125:649A–B. G. H. Joyce, *Christian Marriage*, 2nd edition (London, 1948), 104–05, interprets the text in the same way as Hugh did, but K. Ritzer, *Le marriage* (Paris, 1970), 350–53, argues that the tag contradicts the preceding statement. Ritzer suggests that the forger may have borrowed the tag from another, supposedly authentic source to make the whole thing look authentic.

[196] II.11.5, 486D–487A. What Hugh calls "minor sacraments" were later called "sacramentals."

[197] *De sacramentis* II.11.6, 488C–D.

unmarried, for the church cannot now declare that she is unmarried.[198] The church cannot dissolve the second union even if the man repents and wants to return to the first woman.[199] Hugh maintains in effect that only the first marriage is valid before God and in the forum of conscience, whereas only the second marriage is valid in the judgment of the church and in the public forum. This will become the standard way of describing the situation by the end of the twelfth century. It may mislead the modern reader, who is likely to assume that the church's judgment is false. On the contrary, the church's judgment is just, according to Hugh, and it establishes obligations between the parties, although it cannot miraculously turn the second, defective partnership into a true sacrament.

Hugh recalls his own handwringing when he has had to give counsel in such situations.[200] He rejects subterfuge: The church should not publicly affirm the second marriage while privately counseling the partners to separate.[201] One cannot even counsel the man to practice celibacy, for he owes the conjugal debt to the second woman.[202] There is something wrong with the second union, but does it follow that the church is forcing the man to live in sin, cutting him off from salvation? Surely not! To suppose that anyone is beyond salvation is abhorrent to the Christian faith. The man can still repent and be saved, even while fulfilling the conjugal debt to his second wife.[203] In such cases, the church's judgment in the external forum establishes a certain moral context for the questionable marriage, even when what is known in the internal forum would have invalidated the marriage. Nevertheless, the church is unable either to free the first woman from her marriage vows or to remove the taint of sin from the second union.

10.6.2 *The impediments and the power to dissolve*

Hugh emphasizes that most impediments to marriage are adventitious and did not exist in the beginning. He distinguishes between the perennial, natural impediments that existed from the beginning, and the more exacting impediments added later. The latter were introduced "through the law," either "for the propriety of nature or to enhance chastity."[204] As a result, marriages that had been permitted when nature was the only guide became prohibited and illicit through positive law.[205]

The distinction between perennial and adventitious impediments has consequences regarding both the welfare of the spouses and the church's power to dissolve marriages. If the church dissolves a marriage when a previously unknown

---

[198] Ibid., 488D–489A. Hugh does not say what would happen if she kept mum and married another.

[199] Ibid., 490C ff.   [200] Ibid., 490C–D.   [201] Ibid., 491D–492A.

[202] Ibid., 493B–C.   [203] Ibid., 491A–B.

[204] II.11.4, 483C: "Veni postea secunda institutio, quae per legem facta est; et excepit quasdam alias personas sive ad decorum naturae, sive ad pudicitiae augmentum [*Migne:* argumentum]."

[205] II.11.4, 483B–C.

impediment comes to light, did the marriage exist before the church dissolved it?[206] Some argue that if marriage is truly insoluble in the manner expounded by Augustine,[207] so that persons who separate and remarry commit adultery, a marriage that the church dissolves must never have existed. Hugh's answer is similar to that of the *magistri moderni*.[208] He maintains that the marriage truly exists before it is dissolved in many though not in all cases.[209] Hugh argues that although marriage is insoluble *per se*, it does not follow that every particular marriage is insoluble. The argument based on Augustine, therefore, involves a non sequitur. Hugh compares marriage to baptism and to eucharist. Those who are baptized insincerely, with false motives, are truly baptized,[210] but they do not receive the spiritual effect proper to baptism. That contingent defect does not alter the fact that baptism, of itself, confers remission of sins. Similarly, those who partake of the eucharist unworthily do not receive the "spiritual effects," or virtue, of the sacrament: the "partnership with and participation in Christ." Nevertheless, they do receive the true body of Christ. Eucharist does not have any "efficacy of spiritual grace" for them, but that is not to say that eucharist itself lacks efficacy, for the deficiency is in the recipient and not in the sacrament itself. Extrapolating from those examples, Hugh argues that marriage "requires or rather confers" an indivisible partnership of itself (*quantum in se est*), but that insolubility does not belong to a particular marriage unless that marriage exists where it *ought* to exist.[211]

Hugh concludes that there are "certain marriages" that can "truly be called marriages as long as they are upheld as *ratum* by the judgment of the church," but which, "nevertheless, after legitimate reasons have emerged, are rightly dissolved." (Hugh assumes that the impediment was previously unknown, and that the church dissolves the marriage when the impediment comes to light.) Contrariwise, if the partners remain together after the church has dissolved their marriage, their union is now illegitimate and illicit.

That principle does not apply if there is something naturally abhorrent about the relationship. In that case, once the impediment has come to light, it becomes clear that the union was never valid. It is not clear, though, where Hugh would draw the line. At first, he excludes only parent–child marriages.[212] Later, he excludes sibling marriages as if the matter were obvious, even though they would have occurred in the beginning. Nothing can excuse such unions, Hugh states, which are abhorrent

---

[206] I.11.11, 497D–499A.

[207] Hugh cites Augustine, *De b. coniug.* 15(17)–16(18) and 7(6) (CSEL 41:210/15–211/1, 196/6–9, 197/12–14). Hugh's proximate source may be SMA 52 and 42.

[208] See especially *De coniugiis tractantibus*, ed. Bliemetzrieder, 76/24–77/8, which outlines the problem in the same way and reaches the same conclusion.

[209] Cf. *In primis hominibus*, ed. Matecki, 14/13–15/1: The spouses remain validly married even after the impediment has come to light until the church dissolves their marriage, although they ought to abstain from sexual intercourse meanwhile.

[210] They would not need to be baptized again if they repented and sincerely converted.

[211] *De sacramentis* II.11.11, 498A–D.   [212] II.11.4, 483B–C.

and against reason. Hugh's rule of thumb seems to be that if ignorance of the impediment suffices to absolve the spouses from shame when the impediment comes to light, then the marriage has been valid despite the unknown impediment. Contrariwise, if the impediment is such that "modesty and chastity do not escape confusion" when it comes to light, then the marriage was always invalid.[213] Hugh eventually draws the line before "the seventh, or the sixth, or perhaps even the fifth" degree of consanguinity, for the contravention of the marginal impediments of relationships is merely "venial." They are "not so much against natural or ancient legal institution as against the subsequent legislation [*praeceptio*] of the church."[214] Thus, the principle that unknown impediments do not make a marriage invalid applies only to impediments that the church sometimes waives by special dispensation.

If a marriage truly exists before an impediment comes to light and the church dissolves it, it follows that the marriage was legitimate before it was dissolved. Hugh incorporates the absence of any *demonstrated* impediment into the definition of legitimacy, and thereby into the definition of marriage. Following the *Cum omnia sacramenta II*, he defines marriage as "the legitimate consent of male of female that maintains an indivisible way of life," and he glosses "legitimate consent" as consent that is "between legitimate persons and legitimately given."[215] But which persons are legitimate? His source defines legitimate persons as those "whom the divine law does not prohibit from contracting marriage between themselves, and who are able to contract marriage."[216] But Hugh goes further, defining them as those between whom no reasonable cause *can be demonstrated* as to why the compact of marriage cannot be mutually confirmed.[217] One should remember that Hugh was writing at a time when procedures of inquiry were being introduced in the Anglo-Norman church, which obliged the priest to establish that there were no impediments to a forthcoming marriage – procedures that were eventually codified at the Fourth Lateran Council of 1215.

10.6.3 *The excuse of ignorance*

Apart from certain extreme cases, Hugh argues, "what is entirely hidden as regards the judgment of the church may be said not to exist, because as regards the effecting or the impeding of something it does not differ from what does not exist."[218]

---

[213] Ibid., 484B.   [214] Ibid., 483C.   [215] Ibid., 485D.

[216] *Cum omnia sacramenta II*, ed. Bliemetzrieder, 279/110–15: "consensus ... legitimus, id est, inter legitimas personas legitime factus. Legitime personae sunt, quibus divina lex non prohibet coniugium inter se contrahere et qui possunt contrahere." The final condition probably refers to sexual potency.

[217] II.11.4, 483A: "in quibus illa rationabilis causa demonstrari non potest, quare conjugii pactum mutuo firmare non possint."

[218] II.11.4, 483B: "Quod enim omnino occultum est, quantum ad judicium Ecclesiae, non esse dicendum est, quia ad efficiendum aliquid vel impediendum non differt ab eo quod non est."

The argument presupposes the church's power over the validity of marriage. Hugh is not saying merely that an unknown impediment is effectively non-existent as far as the church is concerned, but rather that an impediment unknown to the ecclesiastical authorities has no effect in reality. The ignorance of the church, and not that of the spouses, is what ensures that the marriage exists. Hugh tacitly assumes that the church, the spouses, and their kinsfolk are equally ignorant, but he emphasizes the church's ignorance in this situation. His argument is hard to follow, but Hugh wants to show that the marriage exists and is legitimate *until* the church dissolves it, even after the spouses have become aware of the impediment.

Hugh defends his position against the objection that ignorance alone should not make a marriage valid. If it turns out later that there was an unknown impediment of relationship, he points out, any children of the union will nevertheless be considered legitimate, at least in certain respects. The same must be true, therefore, of the union itself, for the offspring are legitimate inasmuch as the union is legitimate.[219] Hugh rejects the thesis that the same marriage in such cases is legitimate in the church's judgment but illegitimate in God's judgment. It is true that there is some defective or problematic feature of the marriage that is known to God but unknown to the church, and that this flaw would have caused the church to dissolve the marriage. Nevertheless, as long as God alone knows about the impediment, Hugh contends, the marriage is valid not only under human justice but also in God's justice.[220] As long as the impediment is the result of positive legislation, over and above the law of nature, then "ignorance is excused in transgression," albeit only if "the prohibition is not culpably ignored," for "the power [*virtus*] of the sacrament is not prevented as long as the transgression of the precept is not evident."[221]

10.7 CONCLUSION

Several currents of thought merge in Hugh's ambitious sacramental theology. A sacrament is "a corporeal or material element presented externally to the senses that represents by a likeness, signifies by an institution, and contains from its sanctification some invisible and spiritual grace."[222] This definition emphasizes the power of material stuffs, such as water, bread, wine, and oil, and it is the result of reflection on baptism and eucharist. Hugh considers the sacraments to be the tangible saving means by which God has always provided fallen human beings with a means of escape. Every sacrament restores fallen human nature by providing means of instruction (*eruditio*), practice (*exercitatio*), and humiliation. Hugh's theory of sacramental signs in turn presupposes universal symbolism, whereby every created thing represents its creator. Hugh uses the historical division of sacraments into three ages to show that there have been sacraments ever since human beings

[219] Ibid., 483C–484A.   [220] Ibid., 484C–D.
[221] Ibid., 483C.   [222] *De sacramentis* I.9.2, 317D.

were expelled from Paradise, how God's plan of salvation unfolds over time, and how the incarnation of Jesus Christ is at the center of the plan. Hugh uses the division into major sacraments, minor sacraments (sacramentals), and preparatory sacraments to situate rites such as baptism and eucharist in the context of the multifarious liturgical life of the church.

Hugh's theory of the twofold sacrament of marriage belonged to another current of thought, pertaining especially to Ephesians 5:32. This current ran through Pope Leo I to Hincmar and thence to the coital proof texts of the early twelfth century. Hugh elaborated his theory in order to obviate the coital proof texts and to espouse a neo-Augustinian ideology of chaste marriage.

Viewed from a broad perspective, Hugh's understanding of marriage is congruent with the general features of his sacramental theology. The changing functions and rules of marriage exemplify the historical unfolding of God's saving plan; marriage is the one of the "medicines" of salvation; marriage has an inner spiritual effect, comparable to the grace of eucharist and baptism; marriage, like every sacrament, is a sign of sacred realities; it is a major sacrament, whereas the rites of marrying and the nuptial blessing are sacramentals; even before the fall, marriage was a means of instruction (*eruditio*) and practice (*exercitatio*), and it became in addition a means of humiliation after the fall.

Narrowly regarded, though, the sacrament of marriage is anomalous in Hugh's sacramental theology, albeit broadly comparable to the other sacraments. Marriage was instituted in the beginning, even before the first of the three ages, and even before sin. Again, it requires no stuff, such as water or oil: no "corporeal or material element presented externally to the senses." It signifies two sacred realities, but does it contain or confer them? To a limited extent, it does. Although no priest is needed to administer and sanctify this sacrament, it does confer a spiritual effect or sanctity that is comparable to the "invisible and spiritual grace" of the other sacraments. Hugh never suggests that marriage confers grace, but the spiritual bond of love that in some idealistic sense constitutes the power of sacrament itself is more than merely human love. There are hints in some other medieval theologians, such as Alexander of Hales, that the grace of marriage might itself take the form of conjugal love, but this will not become a standard, widely accepted doctrine until the sixteenth century.

11

The early doctrine of marriage as one of the sacraments

A flurry of theological activity during the 1140s and 1150s resulted in a doctrine of marriage as a sacrament that was widely accepted and rarely challenged during the second half of the century. The doctrine included an orderly and predictable array of topics and questions, and it located marriage within the sacramental system. Nevertheless, marriage remained an outsider among the seven sacraments. Theologians counted marriage as one of the seven, but they assumed that it did not exemplify the distinguishing, salient feature of these sacraments, which was the power to contain or cause the grace that they signified. Theologians from around the 1160s began to treat that exception as an anomaly, but they solved the problem by conceding that marriage was not in the fullest or strictest sense one of the sacraments of the New Law.

Peter Lombard is the central figure in this chapter. Writing in the 1150s, the Lombard assembled his account of marriage chiefly from material that he found in Hugh of Saint-Victor and in Walter of Mortagne's treatise on marriage (which he probably knew as part of the *Summa sententiarum*), and to a lesser extent in Gratian. He shaped this material to suit his own inclinations, which were typical of French theologians around the middle of the century. The treatment of marriage in the 1140s by Peter Abelard's followers and by a certain Master Simon provides us with a sense of the tenor of that conversation. The treatise on marriage in the fourth book of Peter Lombard's *Sentences* would become the framework for the scholastic discussion of marriage as a sacrament after the 1220s, when the *Sentences* began to be used as the textbook of theology in Paris: a practice that soon caught on everywhere.

11.1 PETER ABELARD'S CIRCLE

Although Peter Abelard's extant and reliably authenticated writings do not include an account of marriage as a sacrament, a consistent, fully worked out doctrine of marriage does appear in three works associated with Abelard and his followers: the *Sententiae magistri Petri Abaelardi*,[1] the *Sententiae Parisienses*, and the *Ysagoge in theologiam*.[2] The first of these three sources is probably the most reliable as a witness to Abelard's own thought and teaching, but all three present variants of the same view of marriage, and I shall make no attempt here to determine which variants were closer to the master's own opinions.

The treatment of marriage in these works is little more than a highly abbreviated version of what the *magistri moderni* had said, especially the *Cum omnia sacramenta*. Moreover, unlike the *magistri moderni*, these Abelardians did not engage in complex reflections about the sacramentality of marriage or about the place of the sacrament in salvation history, in God's saving plan, and in church. It is as if they extracted only the most practically relevant and least complicated of the key points. They assumed that marriage was properly included among the sacraments of the New Law as an integral component of a coherent sacramental system, but they held that unlike the other sacraments marriage was merely remedial and did not confer a gift of grace.

Like the *magistri moderni*, the Abelardians observe that most of the rules determining the legitimacy of marriage are changeable and vary both historically and culturally. For example, they observe that ordination to the priesthood is a fatal impediment to marriage in the west, yet not because of any intrinsic incompatibility between marriage and the sacrament of orders but only because priesthood here happens to entail a vow of continence. Where ordination does not entail such a vow, as among the Greeks, priests can marry.[3] Again, the Old Law favored endogamy because that practice befitted a tribal society, but the Romans saw the advantage of a man's taking a wife from another community for the "propagation of charity," and the Christian church adopted that practice from the Romans.[4] While conceding that polygyny was normal under the Old Law, the *Sententiae Abaelardi* points out that even under the Old Law kings were not permitted to have several wives. David and Saul were exceptions, but they contravened the law. Although polygyny is

[1] Ed. D. E. Luscombe in CCM 14 (2006). The treatise on marriage consists of §§ 231–41 (pp. 122–27). On the nature of this work, see C. J. Mews, "The *Sententie* of Peter Abelard," *Recherches de théologie ancienne et médiévale* 53 (1986): 130–84, reprinted in Mews, *Abelard and His Legacy* (Aldershot, 2001). R. H. Rheinwald's edition of these *Sententiae* (Berlin, 1835) is reproduced in PL 178:1695–1758 as Abelard's *Epitome theologiae christianae*. H. Ostlender's ascription of the work to a certain Hermann is no longer plausible.

[2] Editions of the *Sententiae Parisienses* and the *Ysagoge in theologiam* are in A. Landgraf, *Écrits théologiques de l'école d'Abelard* (Louvain, 1934). On the *Sententiae Parisienses* (properly known as the *Sententiae Parisienses I*) and the *Ysagoge*, see D. E. Luscombe, *The School of Peter Abelard* (Cambridge, 1969), 164–68 and 236–44, respectively.

[3] *Sent. Abaelardi* §234 (124) and §237 (125). *Sent. Parisienses*, pp. 44/31–45/7. *Ysagoge*, 197/28–198/4. Orders up to the level of acolyte are not impediments to marriage, although the subject forfeits any benefice if he marries.

[4] *Sent. Abaelardi* §235 (124). *Sent. Parisienses*, 45/8–18. *Ysagoge*, 197/16–22.

sometimes permitted, therefore, monogamy is the royal way. And because Christians are a royal people (1 Pet 2:9), they are monogamous.[5]

Although marriage is a sacrament, the Abelardians point out, even non-Christians can marry. Marriage is a good that exists among all peoples, even infidels, as Augustine taught. Moreover, Paul's doctrine in 1 Corinthians 7:4 shows that there can be a valid marriage between a believer and an unbeliever. The *Sententiae Parisienses* affirms that a Christian can marry a Jew provided only that some "recompense" is made.[6] To solve the problem of Romans 14:24 – "whatsoever is not from faith is sin" – the author argues that the phrase "not from faith" here means "against conscience." Jews and infidels who marry fall short of Christian marriage, but they are not acting against conscience.[7]

The authors adopt the French distinction between *de futuro* and *de praesenti* betrothals, noting not only the form and tense of the agreement but also its object. Whereas the man who promises that he will take a woman as his wife agrees to contract a marriage, the man who actually takes a wife agrees to marriage itself, expressing his consent in a vow such as this: "I deliver myself to you so that as long as you shall live I shall not join myself to another, and I give myself to you for fleshly use."[8]

The authors regard Christian marriage chiefly as a way to avoid sexual sin. Marriage is defined as a "compact [*federatio*] between male and female through which they can have intercourse without sin."[9] The same emphasis appears in the treatment of the three goods of marriage. As usual during the twelfth century, the good of faith is reduced to negative fidelity: the faithful partner is obligated not to have intercourse outside the marriage. But even the good of offspring is construed as remedial, for its purpose is to add seemliness (*decor*) to a marriage that would otherwise be indecent. The spouses compensate for the sin that would otherwise inevitably occur in sexual intercourse by committing themselves to educate any children that they beget "religiously," that is, so that they grow up to serve and worship God.[10]

The authors consider marriage to be a sacrament only in the sense that it is a sacred sign. The *Sententiae Parisienses* explains that the third of Augustine's three

[5] *Sent. Abaelardi* §232 (123).

[6] *Sent. Parisienses*, 47/5–6: "Etiam christianus posset Iudeam ducere, si recompensatio sequer-etur inde." Likewise, *Sent. Abaelardi* §240 (126–27). J. A. Brundage, "Intermarriage between Christians and Jews in Medieval Canon Law," *Jewish History* 3.1 (1988): 25–40, at 32, concludes that canon and secular law strongly discouraged sexual relationships between Christians and Jews, but that "classical canon law prescribed no explicit penalty."

[7] *Sent. Parisienses*, 46/24–47/6.

[8] *Sent. Abaelardi* §231 (123). *Sent. Parisienses*, 44/10–13. *Ysagoge*, 196/27–197/2.

[9] *Sent. Parisienses*, 44/8–9: "Coniugium est maris et femine federatio, per quam licet eis sine peccato commisceri." *Sent. Abaelardi* §231 (123) uses the same definition but with the word "legitimate" supplied ("*maris et feminae federatio legitima*"). See also *Ysagoge*, 196/26–27: "Coniugium est maris et femine legitima confederatio conferens licenciam commiscendi absque culpa."

[10] *Sent. Abaelardi* §239 (126). *Sent. Parisienses*, 46/16–20.

goods, the *bonum sacramenti*, pertains to the signification of marriage, for just as one woman is married to one man, so Christ, a single *sponsus*, is united to the church, his only *sponsa*.[11] The *Ysagoge in theologiam* adds that inseparability is the most salient feature of that signification, for just as neither of the spouses can leave the other to marry another, so the church will never cleave to anyone else except Christ, nor Christ the church.[12] Marriage is among the major sacraments, and it signifies something very great and very holy, but it does not have the spiritual efficacy that distinguishes the other major sacraments. Among the sacraments that Christ left behind to continue his work, the *Sententiae Abaelardi* explains,

> ... some are spiritual, others are not. The spiritual sacraments are the major ones, namely, those that avail to salvation. And yet there is one of those that does not look to salvation and yet is a sacrament of a great reality, namely, marriage. For to take a wife does not have any merit for salvation, yet it is conceded by way of indulgence because of incontinence.[13]

All the sacraments, including marriage, are visible appearances of invisible graces, but marriage alone among the major sacraments is *only* a sign of such grace. It is effective and salutary, but only by excusing coitus.[14] The primary purpose of marriage in the Christian economy is to correct or to obviate faults that would otherwise present an obstacle to salvation. Unlike the other sacraments, therefore, marriage does not confer any supernatural gift (*donum*).[15] Instead, it is a remedy against a particular evil, conferring a certain license or indulgence.[16] Marriage "is given in order to restrain incontinence. Hence, it pertains rather to indulgence."[17] Matthew 19:12 and 1 Corinthians 7:2 show that those who can remain celibate should do so, whereas only those who are not capable of celibacy should marry.[18]

The difference that the Abelardians saw between marriage and the other sacraments exactly matched the difference between marriage and vocational celibacy as ways of life. This was the difference between indulgence and holiness. Assuming that the properly Christian vocation was celibacy, these authors reasoned that marriage was permitted only as the remedy for those who were not strong enough for celibacy.

11.2 MASTER SIMON AND HIS FOLLOWERS

The treatise on the sacraments ascribed to a certain Master Simon, about whom nothing else is known, was written at some point between 1140 and 1165, and most likely during the years 1145–1148. Two anonymous treatises, one on the seven sacraments (*De septem sacramentis*) and the other on marriage (*De matrimonio*),

---

[11] *Sent. Parisienses*, 46/20–23.   [12] *Ysagoge*, 198/22–25.   [13] *Sent. Abaelardi* §201 (107–08).
[14] *Sent. Abaelardi* §233 (123).   [15] *Sent. Parisienses*, 44/5–7. *Sent. Abaelardi* §231 (122).
[16] *Ysagoge*, 197/2–5.   [17] *Sent. Abaelardi* §231 (122–23).
[18] *Sent. Parisienses*, 44/27–30. *Sent. Abaelardi* §233 (123–34).

are closely related to Master Simon's treatise,[19] as is the treatise on the sacraments included in the anonymous *Sententiae divinitatis* (1140/48?), which seems to have been the work of someone in Gilbert of Poitiers's circle.[20]

The treatises of this group are the earliest extant witnesses to the seven sacraments.[21] Master Simon begins by defining sacrament as a sign of sacred reality, although he notes that the term can also denote the signified reality itself (*sacrum signatum*) as well as a sacred sign of that reality (*sacrum signans*). The *De septem sacramentis*, following Isidore, explains that what is signified is called a sacrament because it a "sacred secret" (*sacrum secretum*), such as the hidden reality beneath the appearance of eucharistic bread. Both treatises then divide the sacraments into two groups: the non-common, or special sacraments, in which some but not all believers participate; and the common, or general sacraments, in which all believers participate. Marriage and holy orders belong to the first group. Marriage belongs exclusively to the laity, whereas the sacrament of orders belongs exclusively to those who administer the divine office. The common sacraments are baptism, confirmation, penance, eucharist, and extreme unction. The treatises demonstrate *a priori* the need and sufficiency of the five common sacraments by situating them as successive episodes in a narrative of the individual's spiritual development. In the beginning, baptism cleanses the subject from spiritual pollution. Other sacraments enable the Christian to fight the good fight. Penance, for example, enables someone who has fallen to get up and to soldier on. In the end, extreme unction incorporates the subject into another order, preparing him or her for the vision of God. Another division, into necessary and non-necessary sacraments, is coextensive with the first. The special sacraments are not necessary for salvation, whereas the common sacraments are necessary for salvation. Marriage, then, is a non-common, non-necessary sacrament.[22]

Although there were other vocations besides marriage and holy orders in medieval Christian society, the division of the two non-common sacraments reflects a fundamental and supposedly exclusive choice: between the spiritual, ideally contemplative vocation of celibate holiness, and the secular, active vocation of marriage, which was the only way to remain in the world and yet achieve salvation. The celibate way is to the married way as contemplation is to action. Thus, the *De septem sacramentis*

---

[19] All three are edited in H. Weisweiler, *Maître Simon et son groupe De sacramentis* (Louvain, 1937).

[20] B. Geyer, *Die Sententiae divinitatis: Ein Sentenzenbuch der Gilbertschen Schule*, BGPhMA 7.2–3 (Münster, 1909). The author covers all seven in his account of the sacraments in general (108–09), but there follow treatises on only four: baptism, confirmation, eucharist, and penance.

[21] See É. Dhanis, "Quelques anciennes formules septénaires des sacrements," *Revue d'histoire ecclésiastique* 26 (1930): 574–608, 916–50, and 27 (1931): 5–26, at 26:594 ff. Dhanis assumed that the *septenarium* first appeared in the *Sententiae divinitatis*.

[22] Master Simon, *De sacramentis*, 1–2, 45/5–8. *Tract. de septem sacramentis*, 82/21–83/4. See also *Sententiae divinitatis*, 108/17–109/7.

links holy orders to contemplation, to love of God, and to Christ's divinity, whereas it links marriage to "preparation" for friendship with God, to love of neighbor, and to Christ's humanity. This explanation extends Pope Gregory's account of contemplation and action, taking it from its original monastic setting and using it to divide the people of the church into two main groups: celibate clergy and married laity.[23]

Master Simon and his followers approach marriage both as a quasi-contractual bond and as a sacrament of Christ and the Church. Master Simon's point of departure for his contractual analysis is a definition that he ascribes to Isidore: "Marriage is the consent of a man and a woman, holding together an indivisible way of life."[24] In fact, this is a variant of the definition from Justinian's *Institutes*. It probably came to Simon from the sentential literature, complete with the false ascription to Isidore and the substitution of *consensus* for the original *coniunctio*.[25]

More important than the definition of marriage is Simon's parsing of the consent to which it refers. First, such consent must be between legitimate persons. Second, although the spouses are not strictly required to agree to sexual intercourse, they must agree to the same thing regarding sexual intercourse. Third, the agreement commits each partner to observe the obligations of marriage (*ius coniugii*) insofar as he or she is able.[26] Let us consider each point in turn.

First, a marriage is invalid unless the partners who consent are legitimate, that is, are of sufficient age, are not blood relations, and so forth, in accordance with the laws of a given period, for such laws have changed. The *De septem sacramentis* adds that the spouses must be Christians, for although there can be marriage (*coniugium*) of a sort between infidels, this is not *true* marriage (*verum coniugium*).[27] According to the *De coniugio*, clandestine consent renders the partners illegitimate – a rare anticipation of the Tridentine theory of inhabilitation, although the author does not claim that the resulting marriage is *ipso facto* invalid. A clandestine marriage is *ratum* but not *legitimum*, therefore, whereas a public marriage that has to be dissolved on grounds of consanguinity is *legitimum* but not *ratum*. To corroborate his warnings against marrying clandestinely, the author describes the perils of marrying to satisfy lust or without making the proper commitments.[28]

Second, the spouses must agree about coitus, that is, either to *observe* the conjugal debt or to *abstain* from coitus by mutual agreement. The authors easily obviated the

---

[23] On the several versions and diverse interpretations of this division during the central Middle Ages, see Giles Constable, "The Interpretation of Mary and Martha," in *Three Studies in Medieval Religious and Social Thought* (Cambridge, 1998), 1–141.

[24] Master Simon, *De sacramentis*, 45/21–46/1: "Coniugium vero est, ut ait Ysidorus, consensus viri et mulieris individuam vite consuetudinem retinens etc." Cf. *Inst.* 1.9.1.

[25] Compare *Cum omnia sacramenta I*, ed. Bliemetzrieder, 139/9–11; and *Cum omnia sacramenta II*, ed. Bliemetzrieder, RThAM 3 (1931), 274/1–2: "Coniugium est secundum ysidorum consensus masculi ct femine, indiuidualem uite consuetudinem retinens."

[26] Master Simon, *De sacramentis*, 50–51. The other treatises incorporate this analysis into their definition of marriage: *Tract. de septem sacramentis*, 94–95; *Tract. de coniugio*, 99.

[27] *Tract. de septem sacramentis*, 95/4–7.   [28] Ibid., 99/12–18, 102/12–23.

problems regarding the marriage of Mary and Joseph, who must have agreed to abstain when they married.[29]

Third, mutual consent commits the spouses to cherish and to look after each other to the best of their ability, and not only in the marriage bed. But although both partners are thus obligated, the mutual obligation is differentiated by gender, for husband and wife are related as head and body. Whereas his task is to provide, hers is to serve.[30] Only in respect of the conjugal debt is there equality, so that both spouses are obligated in the same way.[31]

Master Simon posits three institutions of marriage, each with its own reason (*causa*) and its own proof text, although he does not specify when these institutions occurred.[32] The reason for the first institution was the procreation of children. This institution is recorded in Genesis 1:28: "Increase and multiply!" Thus, the man who has sex with his wife for this purpose alone does not sin at all. The reason for the second institution was the avoidance of incontinence. That is why Paul says that those who cannot contain themselves should marry in the Lord (1 Cor 7:9, 39). If the reason for sexual intercourse is to avoid incontinence, there is some sin but it is only venial. Those whose sole motive for sexual intercourse in marriage is lust, on the contrary, sin mortally. Such is the "keen lover" (*vehemens amator*), who is said to commit adultery even with his own wife.[33] The reason for the third institution was so that marriage should be a sacrament, or a sign of sacred reality. Paul articulated this reason when he called marriage "a great sacrament in Christ and in the church (Eph 5:32).[34]

To show how marriage is a sacred sign, Master Simon distinguishes between two elements of marrying: that through which (*per quod*) the partners marry, and that toward which (*ad quod*) they marry. These two elements are respectively essential and non-essential. Thus, a marriage is established through (i.e., by means of) consent, whereas it is celebrated toward, or for the sake of (*propter*), sexual union.[35] At first sight, Simon seems to be referring to the efficient and final causes of marriage, respectively: between what makes marriage and the reason for marrying. Indeed, Master Simon explains that marriage is "effected through the consent [*per consensum*] of both" partners, and that is "celebrated because of [*propter*] carnal

---

[29] Master Simon, *De sacramentis*, 50/19–23. *Tract. de septem sacramentis*, 95/7–14. *Tract. de coniugio*, 99–100.

[30] Master Simon, *De sacramentis*, 51/1–3. *Tract. de septem sacramentis*, 95/15–19. *Tract. de coniugio*, 100/5–10.

[31] Master Simon, *De sacramentis*, 48/8–12.   [32] Master Simon, *De sacramentis*, 46–47.

[33] On the three motives for sexual intercourse, see Master Simon, *De sacramentis*, 53/23–54/14; *Tract. de septem sacramentis*, 96/13–19; and *Tract. de coniugio*, 100/25–101/3. Simon ascribes the maxim about the overly ardent lover to Ambrose, and the *Tract. de coniugio* to Augustine. Peter Lombard, *Sent.* IV, 31.5.3 (2:447), ascribes it correctly to Sextus Pythagoricus. For the original maxim, see W. T. Wilson, *The Sentences of Sextus* (Atlanta, 2012), p. 240, *Sent.* 231, and ibid., pp. 243–44, for commentary. On the versions and interpretations of the maxim circulating during the central Middle Ages, see P. J. Payer, *The Bridling of Desire* (Toronto, 1993), 120–24.

[34] Master Simon, *De sacramentis*, 46/21–47/2.   [35] Ibid., 47/4–7.

union."[36] Similarly, the *De coniugio* says that the spouses' consent is that through which (*per quid*) they marry, whereas that "because of which" (*propter quid*) they marry is twofold: the avoidance of lust and procreation.[37] But Master Simon extends the scope of the distinction so that it includes both the distinction between initiation and consummation and Hugh's distinction between marriage *per se* and sexual union. The *per quod* aspects include volition and love (*voluntas et dilectio*), whereas the *ad quod* aspects pertain to sexual intercourse and procreation.[38] That through which (*per quod*) the partners marry, therefore, is constitutive in the formation of their marriage, whereas that toward which (*ad quod*) they marry pertains to outcomes.

In each respect, Simon argues, marriage is a sign of Christ's union with the church. Three things are required for the *per quod* of marriage: the union of wills, mutual love (*dilectio*), and the reciprocal caring whereby the husband protects his wife and the wife submits to her husband. There is something analogous to each of these three aspects in the relationship between Christ and the church. First, just as the spouses' wills are united in consenting to marry, so the church prays daily that God's will should be "done on earth as it is in heaven," striving to do Christ's will and to be brought eventually into perfect accord with it. Second, just as a marriage is based on mutual love, so Christ loves the church, bestowing upon her grace and the indwelling Holy Spirit, through which the church loves Christ in return. Third, just as husband and wife care for each other, so Christ protects the church (Ps 26:5, 141:6) and the church is submissive in every way to Christ.[39] The *ad quod* of marriage is the union of two in one flesh, which Simon analyzes into two components: the partners' coming together to produce a common offspring, and their equality regarding the conjugal debt. Marriage is analogous to Christ's union with the church at least in the first respect, for Christ and the church have become "two in one flesh," and they beget spiritual children.[40]

Simon uses the same distinction to account for the sacramentality of an unconsummated marriage, such as that of Mary and Joseph. When Leo and Augustine said that there was no sacrament in marriage without sexual intercourse, they were referring to the *ad quod* of the sacrament, and not to its *per quod*. Moreover, as with all the sacraments, one should distinguish between what is necessary, or *sine qua non*, and what adorns an already existing sacrament. Consent is necessary *sine qua non*, whereas sexual union with its signification is an adornment.[41]

Master Simon identifies the *bonum sacramenti* with inseparability, implicitly distinguishing it from the sacrament of marriage.[42] Does marriage ever lack this good, just as it often lacks the goods of faith and offspring? Marriage lacked the good

---

[36] Ibid., 47/6–7.   [37] *Tract. de coniugio*, 100/11–17.

[38] Master Simon, *De sacramentis*, 48/15–20.   [39] Ibid., 47/11–48/3.   [40] Ibid., 48/3–9.

[41] Ibid., 48/12–49/4. See also *Tract. de septem sacramentis*, 95/20–23.

[42] See Master Simon, *De sacramentis*, 51–53, on the three goods of marriage. See also *Tract. de septem sacramentis*, 95–96.

of sacrament under the Old Law inasmuch as divorce was permitted, Simon replies, but it would be rash to say that marriage ever lacks this good under the New Law, even though the church sometimes dissolves a marriage and permits the partners to remarry.[43] The *De septem sacramentis* suggests that the good of sacrament is absent when a woman marries a foreigner without knowing that he already has a wife in his own land. He is married to the second wife, but there is no good of sacrament in that marriage (presumably because it is dissoluble).[44]

11.3 WALTER OF MORTAGNE

Walter was born in Mortagne in Flanders, and he probably received his first education at the cathedral school in Tournai. After studying in Reims and directing the cathedral school at Laon, Walter became a master at the school of Saint Geneviève in Paris in 1136 and taught there until at least 1144. He became dean of the cathedral at Laon in 1150, and bishop of Laon in 1155, remaining in that see until his death in 1174. He must have written his *De coniugio* by about 1140, probably while teaching in Paris.[45] Peter Lombard was heavily dependent on it.

Walter's *De coniugio* was appended at an early stage to the *Summa sententiarum* as its seventh and final tractate, completing that work's treatment of sacraments. (The fifth and sixth tractates cover baptism, confirmation, eucharist, penance, and extreme unction.) The *Summa sententiarum* was one of Peter Lombard's favorite sources, and he probably had access to Walter's *De coniugio* in this guise.[46] Unlike the other tractates of the *Summa sententiarum*, the seventh does not have much in common with Hugh's *De sacramentis*. Instead, Walter drew on the *In primis hominibus* (Section 8.2.2.2). Through Hugh's *De sacramentis* and Walter's *De coniugio*, therefore, Peter Lombard had indirect access to three notable works by *magistri moderni*: through Hugh, to the marriage tractate of the *Sententiae Magistri A.* and the *Cum omnia sacramenta II*; through Walter, to the *In primis hominibus*.

I shall confine my remarks here to the more distinctive features of Walter's treatment of marriage, which pertain to marital consent, to the reasons for marrying, and to the morality of marriage and sexuality. Walter sometimes defends opinions that diverge from the main stream.[47] Walter's account of the rules and regulations of

---

[43] Master Simon, *De sacramentis*, 53/4–10. [44] *Tract. de septem sacramentis*, 96/8–10.

[45] On the date of the treatise, see L. Ott, "Walter von Mortagne und Petrus Lombardus in ihrem Verhältnis zueinander," in *Mélanges Joseph de Ghellinck, S. J.*, vol. 2 (Gembloux, 1951), 647–97, at 653–54. On the treatise itself and its use by Peter Lombard, see also L. Ott, *Untersuchungen zur theologischen Briefliteratur der Frühscholastik*, = BGPhThMA 34 (1937), 140–42.

[46] H. Weisweiler, "La *Summa sententiarum*, source de Pierre Lombard," RThAM 6 (1934): 143–83. The work was written by a certain Odo. Although the matter remains unsettled, he was probably Odo of Lucca: see F. Gastaldelli, "La *Summa Sententiarum* di Ottone da Lucca," *Salesianum* 42 (1980): 537–46. For a brief but judicious update on the problem, see G. Silano's introduction to Peter Lombard, *The Sentences, Book I* (Toronto, 2007), p. 10.

[47] For example, in *De coniugio* 10 (PL 176:163B–C), Walter argues that Mary had not taken a specific vow of virginity when she became betrothed to Joseph, and that both later took such a

marriage is more thorough than Hugh's,[48] but the treatise did not contribute much to the sacramental theology of marriage.

11.3.1 *Marital consent*

Citing the usual proof texts, Walter emphasizes both the necessity and the sufficiency of spousal consent.[49] Consent suffices to make a marriage "in the time of grace," but only if it is truly voluntary, for coerced consent is not really consent.[50] Sexual intercourse is not necessary to establish a marriage, as the example of Mary and Joseph shows. Nor does the absence of a dowry or priestly blessing or nuptial ritual invalidate a marriage.[51] When Pope Evaristus said that such formalities were necessary for a marriage to be legitimate,[52] he did not mean that consent by itself was insufficient. Rather, he was warning against the perils of an irregular, furtive marriage. And when Leo spoke about the need for formalities in his letter to Rusticus, he was referring to the peculiar situation in which a man regularizes his union with a servile concubine.[53]

Walter's account of the betrothal distinction is more empirical than normative. Instead of prescribing what ought to happen, he describes and interprets what customarily happens. His account suggests that the distinction between *de futuro* and *de praesenti* betrothals was not always easy to make in practice. In one mode, the man swears to the woman that he will accept her as his wife in the future, and she makes the corresponding oath to him. In the other, each accepts the other at once and promises to remain faithful to the marriage bed. "It is likely [*verisimile*]," Walter argues, "that an oath about the future does not make a marriage." Walter's argument is the same as Hugh's, albeit spelled out at greater length. If the spouses became married as soon as they plighted their troth, they could not truthfully swear to marry in the future, and their oath would be "foolish and false." But the crux of the distinction, according to Walter, is not the tense of the agreement but rather the object of the promise: in one mode, they promise to marry; in the other, they promise to be faithful. Walter mentions the oath (*iuramentum*) because it is a typical

---

vow together. Hitherto, Mary had entirely submitted herself non-specifically to do anything that God willed, whatever that might be.

[48] Walter treats the following topics in marriage law in the treatise: the variation of marriage law over the course of history (Chapter 5); the indissolubility of marriage (Chapters 9 and 18); the prohibition of marriage between unbelievers and unbelievers, and the inferior standing of marriage between unbelievers (8); the impediment of religious vows, with Pope Innocent I's counsel on the marriage of veiled and unveiled virgins (10); whether persons who have committed adultery with each other can later marry (13); marriage between free and servile persons (14); the minimum age for marriage (15); the impediments of consanguinity up to the seventh degree (11), of spiritual relationship (12), and of madness (16); the grounds for divorce (19); spiritual adultery (20); and the remarriage of widows and widowers (21).

[49] Walter of Mortagne, *De coniugio* 6, 158C–159C.   [50] Ibid., 159A–C.   [51] Ibid., 159C.

[52] Walter's source is *In primis hominibus*, ed. Matecki, p. 54 (IPH 125–26).

[53] *De coniugio* 6, 159C–D.

feature of the customary agreement that he has in mind, and not because the oath itself substantively affects the nature of the agreement. When civil law speaks of a man's swearing in a chapel with his hand on sacred objects that he is going to have (*habiturus*) a woman as his wife,[54] and when Augustine and Isidore say that the spouses are married as soon as the betrothal has taken place, they are referring to the second of the two modes. This occurs "when a man and a woman swear to each other that they are going to observe at once and henceforth the faith of the marriage bed and the other oaths of marriage."[55]

Walter wrote two letters about pacts of betrothal and marriage to Alberic of Reims, his former teacher.[56] According to a report that Walter had received from a third party, Alberic had said publicly that a man who "swears that he will receive a woman in the future" could not marry another woman as long as the former was alive. If he did so, the second union had to be dissolved. Walter outlines a scenario in which a man who has decided to marry a woman "for the sake of peace or for some other honorable reason" swears that he will receive her as his wife after one year. Are they already married? No, for they have not yet promised "the faith of conjugal chastity" to each other, and they have not yet received each other as man and wife. To be sure, the man *ought* not to marry another and he will commit perjury if he does so, but the second marriage would be valid. Walter argues that it would be "foolish and false" to swear to do something in the future if that very oath made it happen at once. Here, too, Walter distinguishes between a pact (*pactum*) or oath that makes a marriage, and pact or oath that establishes only an agreement to marry in the future. The latter, he explains, is what the civil law calls *sponsalia*.[57] Having received no reply, Walter wrote a second letter to Alberic on the same subject, in which he anticipated and refuted an objection: that if a man betroths one woman but later marries another, his perjury must be sufficient reason for the second union to be dissolved. It is absurd to maintain, Walter responds, that the sin of perjury prevents the man from validly receiving the sacrament of marriage, since "good and bad persons share the sacraments equally."[58]

Alberic at last replied, apologizing for the delay and observing that whoever reported his own position must have misunderstood it. A marriage begins (*initiatur*), Alberic argues, when the partners agree to marry, binding each other with mutual obligations. Next, there may be an oath to confirm that agreement. Other formalities follow, such as the dowry or prenuptial gift (*donatio propter nuptias*) and the nuptial ritual. Finally, the union is perfected in sexual intercourse. The question is: At what

[54] Cf. *Iuliani epitome*, const. 67.4, c. 244. Ivo, *Decretum* VIII.44 (*Panormia* VI.7).
[55] *De coniugio* 7, 160A–C.
[56] The letters are undated, but the fact that Walter addresses Alberic as *Dominus* and *Magister* indicates that he probably wrote them after 1131, when Alberic became Archdeacon of Reims, and certainly before 1136, when Alberic became archbishop of Bourges.
[57] In E. Martène and U. Durand, *Veterum scriptorum et monumentorum ecclesiasticorum et dogmaticorum amplissima collectio* (Paris, 1724–1733), 1:834–36.
[58] Ibid., 836–37.

point in the process does this marriage constitute an impediment to another marriage? Alberic reviews the consensual proof texts and he incorporates material from at least one of Ivo's letters (Section 5.4.2). The critical point in the process, Alberic claims, is the solemn oath. Suppose that a man has entered into an initiate marriage with one woman and has confirmed that compact with an oath, but that he then marries another. His perjury and his violation of the first agreement will vitiate the "sacrament of marriage" with the second woman, for, as Ivo says, "one who confirms the conjugal compact with an oath has fulfilled the sacrament of marriage for the most part." The validity of the second marriage is at best questionable, therefore, and it is subject to the judgment of a tribunal. If the man is summoned to a tribunal, the partners should suspend carnal relations until the case is settled.[59] Alberic seems to have been unaware of the new betrothal distinction.

11.3.2 *The reasons for marrying*

Having noted that marriage was originally instituted in Paradise (Gen 2:24, Mark 10:7–8, Matt 19:5),[60] Walter discusses the several reasons (*causae*) for marriage. He broadens the range of motives, and he clears away any doubts about the effects of motive on validity. The primary, original reason for marriage is "the hope of offspring" (*spes prolis*), for God commanded human beings in the beginning to "increase and multiply" (Gen 1:28). After sin, a second reason was added: the avoidance of fornication (*vitatio fornicationis*). But although these are the best known reasons, there are others. Some are honorable, such as the reconciliation of enemies and the reestablishment of peace.[61] Others are dishonorable, such as wealth, good looks, and sexual desire.[62] Some say that marriage is invalid when the spouses marry for dishonorable reasons, but Walter rejects that position, citing biblical precedents: Jacob wanted to marry Rachel because she was more beautiful than her sister (Gen 29:17), and God advised the Israelite men to marry any captive women whom they found beautiful and desirable (Deut 21:11). These were not honorable motives, but the marriages were valid.[63]

Validity is one thing and moral well-being another. Walter considers the negative consequences of bad motives when he discusses the goods of marriage. The best known goods, as Augustine explains, are faith, offspring, and sacrament. The third good is called "sacrament" because it is a "sign of a sacred reality," namely, of the inseparable union between Christ and the church.[64] But there are other goods, too,

---

[59] Ibid., 838–39. From Ivo, *Epist.* 161, PL 165D: "Qui enim juramento pactum conjugale firmavit, ex majori parte sacramentum conjugale implevit." Alberic may be drawing as well on Ivo, *Epist. 148* (153B–154D).

[60] Walter of Mortagne, *De coniugio* 1, 153D. Cf. *In primis hominibus*, 1/3–5.

[61] Ibid., 153D–155A.   [62] Ibid., 155A.   [63] Ibid., 155A–B.

[64] *De coniugio* 4, 157B. Cf. *In primis hominibus*, 3/6–13 (IPH 5), from Augustine, *De Gen. ad litt.* IX.7 (CSEL 28.1:275–76).

such as the friendship between a man and a woman that results from their conjugal partnership, and peace between persons who have been enemies. Some marriages have none of the aforesaid benefits, for some persons do not marry either for the sake of offspring or to avoid fornication. Unions of that sort do not produce peace either for the spouses themselves or for others.[65]

11.3.3 *Sexual ethics*

Walter reiterates Augustine's teaching about the goodness of marriage, and he is less pessimistic about pleasure than the *magistri moderni* had been. Because God commanded men and women in the beginning to increase and multiply, Walter argues, sexual intercourse must be good in itself. Nor was its goodness lost in the fall, for God would not have commanded human beings to increase and multiply after the flood (Gen 9:1) if sexual intercourse was always sinful. Just as almsgiving is a good and meritorious act, so is sexual intercourse – provided that it is free from vice and motivated by the desire to beget children. It is true that fallen men and women cannot have sexual intercourse with experiencing carnal concupiscence, which is reprehensible in itself, but the goodness of marriage excuses that evil. What had been a duty for the healthy is now a remedy for the sick.[66]

Walter inquires whether spouses inevitably sin whenever they have sexual intercourse. There is sin whenever a man has sex with a woman who is not his wife, and he commits an abomination whenever he has sex in a manner that is against nature, whether with his wife or with someone else. Normal sexual intercourse within marriage is intrinsically sinful if the motive is to satisfy lust, but the goodness of marriage makes such sin pardonable, as Augustine taught, and a light penance suffices. Sexual intercourse is not culpable at all if the spouses come together intending to beget children and to raise them in the worship of God.[67]

Some object that sexual intercourse even within marriage cannot occur without carnal pleasure (*delectatio carnis*), and that such pleasure is always sinful.[68] Walter concedes that there is some truth in this argument. Sexual pleasure must in some sense be a bad thing for it is a punishment for original sin. One should note, though, that carnal pleasure is not always sinful. Even Jesus, who was immune from sin, must have experienced pleasure when he was tired and rested or when he was hungry and ate. Such pleasures, which presuppose need, are

---

[65] *De coniugio* 4, 157B–C.

[66] *De coniugio* 2, 155C–D. Cf. *In primis hominibus*, 2/1–5, 1/7–8, and 1/14–2/1 (IPH 2).

[67] *De coniugio* 3, 156A–C. Cf. *In primis hominibus*, 8/14–16 (IPH 20), 6/7–10, and 8/18–9/2 (IPH 21). The first of these three passages (IPH 20) is a fragment from Augustine's *Serm.* 354A (Dolbeau 12.12), and it is extant also as fragment "on the good of marriage" from a gloss on 1 Cor. 7 by Bede or Florus of Lyon (PL 39:1732). The third (IPH 21) is from Augustine, *De bono coniugali* 6(6), CSEL 41:195.

[68] Walter found the argument in the *In primis homibus*, 2/4–11 and 7/4–5.

natural for fallen human beings. Likewise, there is no sin when spouses naturally experience some pleasure in coming together to beget children or to render the conjugal debt, provided that the pleasure is not immoderate. Walter considers an apparently contradictory text from Pope Gregory I regarding an ancient ritual scruple. Gregory counsels that spouses who have had sex should wait a while and then ritually wash themselves before going into a church. Gregory counsels that although marriage itself is not sinful, sexual intercourse entails pleasure (*volup-tas*), which is never free from moral fault (*culpa*).[69] According to Walter's interpretation, Gregory was thinking more of general policy then of individual acts. He was mindful that many couples did not restrain their lust and had sex too often. Moreover, although he did not suppose that every act of intercourse was improperly motivated, he recognized that no spouse could always avoid such error.[70]

Like Augustine, Walter argues that the denigration of marriage is a mark of heresy. The theme was commonplace during the central Middle Ages, when the espousal of purity sometimes resulted in movements that challenged or threatened ecclesiastical authority. It is unusually prominent not only in Walter's *De coniugio* but also in four related preambles to dotal charters, of which he was probably the author.[71] Three of the charters are from the diocese of Laon and are dated 1163, 1176, and 1177, respectively. The fourth is from the neighboring diocese of Soissons and is dated 1170. One should remember that Walter returned to Laon as dean in 1150, having directed the cathedral school during the 1120s, and that he was bishop of Laon from 1155 until his death in 1174. The earliest of these charters formerly carried Walter's seal. Not only do the preambles recall the original institution of marriage and the wedding at Cana, where Christ "commended" marriage by performing the first of his miracles, but they add that these precedents refute the "perfidious and execrable folly" of the heretics who deny that marriage is good.[72] The preambles also echo Walter's belief in the pastoral utility of marriage. Two of them (the first and third) conclude with the observation that although the bond of charity dissipates as it

[69] Walter's source is *In primis hominibus*, 8/4–8 (IPH 19), which is abbreviation of a passage from Pope Gregory I, *Libellus Responsionum*, = *Epist.* 11.56[a], MGH *Epistolae* 2.3 (= *Gregorii I papae Registrum epistolarum*, vol. 2), 340/19–31. On Bede's transmission of the *Libellus Responsionum*, see P. Meyvaert, "Bede's Text of the *Libellus Responsionum* of Gregory the Great to Augustine of Canterbury," in P. Clemoes and K. Hughes, *England before the Conquest* (Cambridge, 1971), 15–33. On the contested authorship of the *Libellus*, see also P. Meyvaert, "Le *Libellus Responsionum* à Augustin de Cantorbéry," in J. Fontaine et al., *Grégoire le Grand* (Paris, 1986), 543–49.

[70] *De coniugio* 3, 156C–157A.

[71] L. Morelle, "Marriage and Diplomatics: Five Dower Charters from the Regions of Laon and Soissons, 1163–1181," in THTH 165–214, at 180–81.

[72] L. Morelle, "Mariage et diplomatique: autour de cinq chartres de douaire dans le Laonnois-Soissonnais, 1163–1131," *Bibliothèque de l'École des chartes* 146 (1988): 225–84 at 266: "... humilis exhibetur obedientia et hereticorum qui nuptiali bono conantur detrahere perfida et execrabilis confutatur insania." (From the Laon charter of 1163.)

passes beyond kinsfolk to strangers, it is "called back, as it were, like a fugitive, by the goodness and the faith of marriage."[73]

11.4 PETER LOMBARD

Peter came from Novara in Lombardy, but he spent his entire teaching career as a master of Notre Dame, where he was a canon from 1145. That career ended only when he became Bishop of Paris toward the end of his life. He completed the earliest version of his *Sentences* in 1154 and published it in 1157. He published a second edition in 1158, having made revisions as a result of teaching.[74]

Peter Lombard begins the fourth book of his *Sentences* with a discussion of the sacraments in general. He explains how the sacraments of the New Law differ from the sacraments of the Old, and he enumerates the seven sacraments of the New Law. He then writes extensively on each of the seven in turn. The last of them is marriage.

This was not the Lombard's first treatise on marriage. He had previously written a shorter, self-contained treatise on the subject, using Walter of Mortagne's *De coniugio* as his model, and he had inserted it into his gloss on 1 Corinthians 7.[75] The primitive treatise covers five topics, which Peter Lombard sets out in the initial paragraph: (1) what marriage is (i.e., its definition), (2) its efficient cause, (3) the reasons for which it ought to be contracted, (4) which persons can legitimately contract marriage, and (5) the goods of marriage "by which sexual intercourse is excused." The Lombard reused all of this material from the primitive treatise in Book IV of the *Sentences*, even including the now redundant initial division of topics, although the material is broken up, and the parts are scattered and disconnected.[76]

Although the Lombard counts marriage as one of the seven sacraments of the New Law, he treats it as an outsider. Marriage does not have the definitive features that distinguish the sacraments of the New Law from those of the Old. Contrariwise, circumcision, a sacrament of the Old Law, meets the description of a New-Law sacrament better than marriage does. Marriage and circumcision, therefore, are to some extent inverse exceptions. To set these apparent anomalies in their proper context, one needs to appreciate how Peter Lombard used Hugh's causal paradigm not as a general account of all sacraments but to distinguish among different sorts of sacrament and to characterize the sacraments of the New Law.

---

[73] Ibid.: "Porro ipsius caritatis vinculum inter extraneos et ignotos etiam per nuptias dilatatur et, ubi karitas ipsa per lineam propinquitatis detineri non potuit, per bonum et fidem conjugii quasi fugiens revocatur."

[74] P. W. Rosemann, *Peter Lombard* (Oxford, 2004), 55.

[75] *Collectanea in epistolas s. Pauli*, PL 191:1585D–1587B. The treatise is edited in the Grottaferrata edition of the *Sentences*, 2:84*–87*.

[76] The first edition of the Pauline commentaries appeared in 1148, although Peter continued to revise them until his appointment as a bishop in 1159. See Rosemann, *Peter Lombard*, 44–45.

11.4.1 *The sacraments of the New Law*

Peter Lombard was dependent on the *Summa sententiarum* as well as on Hugh of Saint-Victor for his analysis of the sacraments in general. Neither Odo, author of the *Summa sententiarum*, nor the Lombard shared Hugh's preoccupation with the signs of created nature or with ritual, and they were less interested in salvation history. Their interests were narrower and more closely tied to clerical and pastoral work.

The *Summa sententiarum* begins with two familiar glosses on the word "sacrament": a sacrament is a "sign of sacred reality" (*signum sacrae rei*), and it is a "visible appearance [*forma*] of an invisible grace." These twelfth-century definitions were derived from Augustine and were often ascribed to him.[77] Assuming that a sacrament is a sign of a special sort, the *Summa sententiarum* inquires as to what distinguishes sacraments from signs in general. First, they are visible signs of invisible graces. Second, they signify by virtue of some likeness. In contrast, a circle inscribed on a door signifies only by an arbitrary convention that wine may be purchased within. A sacrament, therefore, signifies by institution and represents by likeness. But all this would be true of water even before it is sanctified. To capture the third aspect, one must add that a sacrament *confers* what it signifies. In short, a sacrament in the proper sense is a sacred sign that confers what it signifies.[78]

Peter Lombard begins by asking: What is a sign? He adopts Augustine's account from the *De doctrina Christiana*, whereby a sign is a thing that conveys an impression to the mind by presenting an appearance to the senses.[79] But what distinguishes sacraments from signs in general? Augustine distinguishes between natural signs (*signa naturalia*) and given, or expressive, signs (*signa data*). Smoke is a natural sign of fire, whereas utterances are given signs of the thoughts that they express.[80] Sacraments are given signs. Moreover, every sacrament "bears a likeness" of the reality that it signifies. Without a likeness, there cannot be a sacrament. The Lombard has already established that the signified reality is an invisible grace. Thus, he arrives at the following definition: "A sacrament, properly speaking, is that which is a sign of the grace of God, and the appearance of an invisible grace, in such a way that it bears its image and stands as its cause."[81]

---

[77] Cf. Augustine, *De civ. Dei* X.5, CCL 47:277/15–16: "Sacrificium ergo uisibile inuisibilis sacrificii sacramentum, id est sacrum signum." On the origins and variants of these two definitions, see D. Van den Eynde, *Les définitions des sacrements* (Rome and Louvain, 1950), 17–31.

[78] *Summa sententiarum* 4.1, PL 176:117A–C.   [79] *De doctrina christiana* II.1(1), CCL 32:32.

[80] Ibid., 1(2), 32–33. Augustine's term *signa data* does not denote conventional signs, as some translators assume, although the distinction between conventional and natural signs is also ancient. On this point, see G. Manetti, *Theories of the Sign in Classical Antiquity* (Bloomington, 1993), 166.

[81] *Sent.* IV, 1.4.2 (233): "Sacramentum enim proprie dicitur, quod ita signum est gratiae Dei et invisibilis gratiae forma, ut ipsius imaginem gerat et causa exsistat." J. De Ghellinck, "Un chapitre dans l'histoire de la définition des sacrements au XIIe siècle," in *Melanges Mandonnet* (Paris, 1930), 2:79–96, at 83, points out that Peter Lombard combines two customary definitions

The distinguishing feature of the sacraments in the proper sense of the term, according to Peter Lombard, is their efficacy, for they not only signify but also sanctify. According to Hugh, sacraments *contain* and *confer* the grace that they signify. According to the Lombard, they *cause* that grace. The meaning is the same. But whereas Hugh used this insight to distinguish sacraments from mere "signs of sacred realities," such as holy texts and pictures, Peter Lombard uses it to distinguish between different classes of sacraments, especially between those of the New Law and those of the Old: the *sacramenta legalia*. Again, whereas Hugh insisted on the essential unity of pre-Christian and Christian sacraments, Peter Lombard emphasizes the difference. The sacraments of the Old Law, he explains, are improperly called sacraments. Strictly, they were not sacraments but only sacred signs.[82] The Lombard conflates the historical division between pre-Christian and Christian sacraments with a semantic distinction between the improper and proper senses of the term "sacrament." Only the sacraments of the New Law fully realize the definition of a sacrament. The sacraments of the Old Law were circumcision, offerings, and certain "carnal sacrifices and ritual observances."[83] The sacraments of the New Law are baptism, confirmation, eucharist, penance, extreme unction, orders, and marriage.[84] Peter Lombard provides a treatise on each in turn. As we have seen, this set of seven sacraments had first appeared in the 1140s in treatises associated with Master Simon and in the anonymous *Sententiae divinitatis*. The Lombard does not say that these are the only sacraments, nor does he state explicitly that there are seven of them. Nevertheless, the reader is bound to assume that the list is closed.

11.4.2 *Circumcision and marriage as exceptions*

The sacraments of the Old Law were only signs of grace, according to Peter Lombard, whereas the sacraments of the New Law also cause grace. Again, whereas the former signified certain saving realities that would be realized in the future, the latter cause realities that they signify in the present.[85] But although the Lombard counts circumcision among the sacraments of the Old Law, he seems to say that it conferred the same remedy against sin then as baptism does under the New Law, although no one could pass into heaven during the time of the Old Law because the gates were still closed.[86] This argument, which the Lombard appropriated from the

---

of sacrament here: *invisibilis gratiae visibilis forma*, which was favored by the canonists (although the Lombard took it from the *Summa sententiarum*); and *invisibilis gratiae visibile signum*, which was favored by Abelard and his followers.

[82] *Sent.* IV, 1.4.3 (233–34); and IV, 1.6 (235–36).

[83] *Sent.* IV, 1.4.3 (233): "sacrificia carnalia et observantiae caeremoniales veteris Legis." Ibid. IV, 1.6 (236): "sacrificia et oblationes et huismodi."

[84] *Sent.* IV, 2.1.1 (239).   [85] *Sent.* IV, 1.4.2–3 (233–34).

[86] *Sent.* IV, 1.7 (236): "Fuit tamen et inter illa sacramentum quoddam, scilicet circumcisionis, idem conferens remedium contra peccatum quod nunc baptismus." See the apparatus to this edition (Grottaferrata, 1981) for references to Augustine and Bede.

Summa sententiarum, is based on texts from Augustine and Bede.[87] The Lombard discusses how women were saved without the benefit of circumcision, suggesting that their faith and good works would have had the same remedial effect.[88] But although he attributes some efficacy to circumcision under the Old Law, he argues that baptism is superior in efficacy and has superseded circumcision. Both sacraments result in forgiveness and absolution from sin, but baptism alone confers a "helping grace" that fosters an increase of virtue and enables the subject to do good works (*gratia ad bene operandum adiutrix*).[89] The effect of circumcision, therefore, was more remedial than beneficial, for the sacrament corrected a defect without raising the subject to a higher condition.

Marriage is the inverse exception among the sacraments of the New Law. It has the same kind of remedial efficacy under the New Law as circumcision did under the Old. Peter Lombard divides the seven sacraments into three groups according to their manner of efficacy. Some, such as baptism, "provide a remedy against sin and confer a helping grace [*gratia adiutrix*]." Others, such as eucharist and orders, "support us with grace and virtue" (presumably by enhancing graces that have already been conferred). And some, such as marriage, "exist for a remedy alone."[90] Marriage is effective as a remedy, therefore, but it does not confer grace: neither a helping, supporting grace, nor an increase in virtue. Like circumcision, it has a merely remedial efficacy. Whereas circumcision surpassed the standards of the Old Law, therefore, marriage falls below the standards of the New Law.

11.4.3 *The treatise on marriage (Book IV, Distinctions 26–42)*

Peter Lombard's treatise on marriage follows the pattern established by the *magistri moderni*, which he inherited from Hugh and Walter. He begins with the institutions and purpose of marriage, its definition, and marital consent. Topics of special interest to theologians, such as the relation of marriage to God's saving plan and the sacramentality of marriage, arise mainly in the first third of the treatise, after which come the canonical topics, especially the mutual obligations of the conjugal debt,[91] the forbidden seasons when one should abstain from marrying as well as from coitus,[92] and the rules and regulations regarding impediments, divorce, and so forth.[93]

---

[87] *Summa sent.* IV.1, PL 176:119A–C.   [88] *Sent.* IV, 1.8 (237).   [89] *Sent.* IV, 1.9 (238–39).

[90] *Sent.* IV, 2.1 (239–40).   [91] *Sent.* IV, 32.1–2 (451–54).   [92] *Sent.* IV, 32.3–4 (454–56).

[93] The chief topics are as follows: the impediments that nullify consent, namely, coercion (d. 29, pp. 436–37) and error (d. 30.1, pp. 437–38, and d. 36, pp. 473–75); indissolubility and divorce (d. 31.1–2, pp. 442–45); changes in the law of marriage regarding monogamy, indissolubility, and impediments over the long duration of history (d. 33, pp. 456–62); the legitimacy (marriageability) of spouses (d. 34.1, pp. 462–63); frigidity, magical impotence, insanity, incest (d. 34.2–5, 463–67); the impediment of difference of religion, and the marriage of unbelievers (d. 39.1–2, 6–7, pp. 483–87, 490–91); spiritual adultery (d. 39.3–4, pp. 487–88); the Pauline Privilege (d. 39.5, 488–90).

Peter Lombard devotes much more space to marriage than to any of the other seven sacraments. The division of each book into distinctions – a thirteenth-century innovation – provides a rough measure. There is one distinction on baptism, one on confirmation, six on eucharist, nine on penance, one on extreme unction, two on orders, and seventeen on marriage.[94] But the amount of text devoted to each sacrament is an indication not of its perceived dignity or importance but rather of the number of urgent questions that attended it. In the case of marriage, most of these questions are canonical.

The insights of the *magistri moderni* and of Hugh regarding the institutions of marriage, its place in salvation history, and its sacramentality appear mainly in what became the first distinction of the Lombard's treatise on marriage (26), which has the character of a prologue or introduction. The division of five topics with which Peter Lombard began the little treatise now appears immediately *after* the introduction, at the beginning of the next distinction (27). The first distinction (26) covers the advances in the theology of marriage made in the schools of northern France since the early twelfth century. All the topics mentioned in this distinction receive fuller treatments in subsequent passages, although the Lombard did not adequately integrate these theological advances into his treatment of marriage as a whole.

Peter Lombard was an astute, perceptive, and efficient scholar, albeit not a profound or original one. His method is evident in his treatment of two much-debated topics: the Pauline Privilege, and the impediment of vows.

The Lombard's succinct and definitive treatment of the Pauline Privilege is a *quaestio* in the formal sense, based on a contradiction that calls for resolution or conciliation. Two authorities indicate that the convert is not permitted to divorce an unbelieving spouse and remarry. One is a gloss on 1 Corinthians 7:14 by Ambrose (i.e., Ambrosiaster), according to which those converts who dismiss "willing" infidel spouses and remarry are committing adultery and their children are illegitimate. The other is canon that Peter Lombard ascribes to the Council of Meaux, although in fact it is from the Council of Tribur (895): "If a man had a virgin as a wife before his baptism, and she is still alive, he cannot have another wife after his baptism, for what baptism absolves is sins, not marriages." On the contrary, 1 Corinthians 7:15 with its gloss by Ambrose (i.e., Ambrosiaster) indicates that the convert can divorce an unbelieving spouse. If the infidel wishes to separate, Ambrose argues, so be it, for the convert is not bound and can remarry. The reverence of marriage is not owed to one who abhors the author of marriage, and a marriage without devotion to

---

[94] The treatise on marriage comprises distinctions 26–42. In their original form, each book was divided into a continuous series of chapters, and the treatise on marriage consisted of Book IV, chs 157–243. The division into distinctions was probably introduced by Alexander of Hales in the 1220s for the convenience of lecturers and commentators. Its first extant appearance is in Alexander's *Glossa in quatuor libros Sententiarum* (1223–1227). See I. Brady, "The Distinctions of Lombard's *Book of Sentences* and Alexander of Hales," *Franciscan Studies* 25 (1965): 90–116, as well as Brady's *Prolegomena* to the Grottaferrata edition of the fourth book (1971), 143–44.

God is not established (*ratum*). The injury to God on the part of the unbeliever dissolves the legal obligation (*ius*) of marriage on the part of the one who is left. To reconcile these authorities, the Lombard argues, one must make a distinction. If the unbeliever is willing to live with the convert, the convert may divorce the unbeliever, but he cannot remarry as long as she is alive. If, on the contrary, the unbeliever is unwilling to live with him, then he is free not only to divorce her but also to remarry in the faith.[95] Peter Lombard modeled this treatment on Gratian's, which has exactly the same components and reaches the same conclusion,[96] but there are some notable differences. Gratian, perhaps because he was misled by a glossed Bible, ascribed the first quotation from Ambrose (Ambrosiaster) to Scripture and the second to Gregory. Peter Lombard corrects Gratian, ascribing both to Ambrose. Moreover, his version of the second quotation (the canon supposedly from Meaux) is fuller and more accurate.

Regarding the impediment of vows, Peter Lombard presents what had already become the standard position. Someone who marries after making a merely private vow must do penance, but the marriage is valid, whereas someone who has made a solemn vow "in the sight of the church" cannot validly marry.[97] The Lombard seems to have been dependent chiefly on Hugh of Saint-Victor for this argument, although his position is similar also to those of Walter of Mortagne and Gratian.[98] Nevertheless, the obstacle that Hugh posed and tried to resolve has disappeared, namely, Augustine's seminal treatment of the issue. According to Augustine, it is damnable for a woman vowed to celibacy even to contemplate marriage, let alone to marry, but such marriages are valid because a vow of celibacy is not literally a marriage to Christ. Hugh suggests (anachronistically) that Augustine may have been referring to private vows. The Lombard ignores the second part of Augustine's argument and cites only the first, which he uses in support of his own position regarding *solemn* vows and expounds at some length in that light.[99] Such a skewed and partial use of a patristic authority may seem inexcusable to the modern reader, but it was consistent with a natural development. Once the distinction between private and solemn vows had become established, the private vow became only obliquely relevant in canon law, where its function was to help distinguish the solemn vow. Any authorities against remarriage after vows were now enlisted in support of the doctrine on solemn vows.

---

[95] *Sent.* IV, 31.5, 488–90. This is clearly Ambrosiaster's position, although Peter claims that Ambrosiaster seems to contradict himself.

[96] Gratian, C. 28 q. 2 (1089–90). Peter also drew on his own fuller treatment of the topic in his gloss on 1 Cor 7:12–19, PL 191:1591A–1594D, where he had already noted an apparent self-contradiction in Ambrose (Ambrosiaster) and resolved it.

[97] *Sent.* IV, 38.2 (478–82).

[98] Hugh, *De sacramentis* II.11.12, 502D–504C; also II.12.3–4, 521B–D. Gratian, C. 27 q. 1 cc. 9–10 (1050–51); also C. 27 q. 1. c. 2 (1047–48), C. 27 q. 1 c. 7 (1050), and C. 27 q. 1 dictum post c. 43 (1062). Walter of Mortagne, *De coniugio* 10, 162B–C, 163A.

[99] *Sent.* IV, 38.2.2–4 (478–80).

11.4.4 The sacred history and institutions of marriage

Peter Lombard begins with a variant of the introduction that had first appeared in the *Cum omnia sacramenta*: "Whereas the other sacraments originated after sin and because of sin, we read that the sacrament of marriage was also instituted by the Lord before sin, yet not as a remedy but as a duty."[100] Following Hugh, the Lombard finds evidence of the first institution both in the formation of Eve from Adam as his helpmeet and in the prophecy that Adam spoke after he awoke from his deep sleep (Gen 2:21–24).[101] The Lombard does not need to remind his medieval readers that Adam was prophesying about Christ and the church (Eph 5:32).

The introductory section of Peter Lombard's treatise on marriage includes a careful analysis of the moral role of marriage under each of the two chief institutions. He had previously covered the same ground in his gloss on 1 Corinthians 7.[102] In the beginning, when God commanded the first parents to increase and multiply (Gen 1:28), marrying was a matter of precept.[103] Later, as Paul teaches, it became a matter of indulgence (1 Cor 7:6). But there are different kinds of indulgence: lesser goods are conceded, whereas lesser evils are only permitted, or tolerated. Marriage is conceded as a lesser good, for although it is less meritorious than celibacy it is remedially effective. By the same token, marriage confers no positive gift. It does "not merit the palm but serves only as a remedy." Whereas marriage is conceded as a lesser good, coitus is tolerated as a lesser evil.[104] More precisely, coitus is conceded as a lesser good when it is solely for the sake of procreation, whereas immoderate sexual intercourse in marriage is only tolerated, for marriage makes the fault pardonable (*venialis*).[105]

Although Peter Lombard does not attempt to situate the second institution of marriage historically, he does describe the historical development of marriage law in respect of monogamy, divorce, impediments, and so forth,[106] emphasizing the effect of Christ's advent. After the incarnation, when the grace of Christ was spreading everywhere, God not only brought the law of marriage back to its original pristine form but also enhanced and elevated the figurative relationship between marriage and Christ. Strict adherence to monogamy superseded the polygamy of the Old Law, "so that one man should be joined to one woman as a figure of Christ and the church." Virginity became preferable to fecundity, and celibacy became obligatory for priests.[107]

---

[100] *Sent.* IV, 26.1.1 (416).   [101] Ibid., 26.1.2.

[102] See especially, PL 191:1585D, 1587B–C, 1589A.

[103] Here the Lombard contradicts some of the *magistri moderni*, e.g., *De coniugiis tractantibus*, ed. Bliemetzrieder, 78/16–26, or in *Liber Pancrisis*, MS British Library, Harley 3098, 74v. The same *sententia* exists independently, outside the *De coniugiis tractantibus*, in MS British Library, Roy. 11 A. V, 24ra–24rb (= PM 402) and MS Oxford, Bodl., Laud Misc. 277, 27vb.

[104] *Sent.* IV, 26.3–4 (418–19).   [105] *Sent.* IV, 31.6 (447–48).   [106] *Sent.* IV, 33 (456–62).

[107] *Sent.* IV, 33.2.1 (459–60), and IV, 33.4.2 (461).

11.4.5 *The definition of marriage*

Peter Lombard defines marriage as "the marital union [*coniunctio*] of a man and a woman, between legitimate persons, holding together an indivisible way of life."[108] He depends partly on Gratian for this formula, which is a variant of the definition from Justinian's *Institutes*.[109] The addition of "between legitimate persons" follows in the tradition of the *Cum omnia sacramenta* and Hugh. The Lombard reverts to the legal tradition by defining marriage as a *coniunctio* (union or joining), and not as consent, but the term remains ambiguous, for it might denote either the act of marrying, which entails consent, or the resulting marriage.

Peter Lombard abandons Hugh's attempt to separate this definition entirely from the sexual, procreative dimension of marriage, but he shares Hugh's desire to show that marriage is consistent with the practice of continence in general and with the union of Mary and Joseph in particular. He achieves this end in two ways: by weakening without eliminating the integral relationship between marriage and sexuality, and by emphasizing the contractual dimensions of marriage. Following Gratian, Peter Lombard explains that the phrase "indivisible way of life" means not only that the spouses will remain together as long as both are alive and that neither will join with another person, but also that neither will practice continence or devote him- or herself wholly to prayer (1 Cor 7:5) by entering the religious life *without the other's consent*.[110] On this view, the mutual gift of self in marriage implies the conjugal debt, but the partners can waive their sexual rights by mutual agreement without detriment to their marriage. Indeed, the Lombard assumes that the partners can preserve their "indivisible way of life" in some sense even after they have separated permanently to follow the religious life.

11.4.6 *The betrothal distinction*

Peter Lombard carefully and precisely expounds the betrothal theory that had emerged as the position of the northern-French schoolmen. His familiarity with Gratian's account, which he rejected, enabled him to enhance the received French theory and to formulate it definitively.

Citing the customary consensual proof texts,[111] Peter Lombard affirms that consent is the efficient cause of marriage. But consent makes marriage only if certain

---

[108] *Sent.* IV, 27.2 (422): "Sunt igitur nuptiae vel matrimonium viri mulierisque coniunctio maritalis, inter legitimas personas, individuam vitae consuetudinem retinens." Cf. *Institutes* 1.9.1, and Gratian, C. 27 q. 2 c. 1 (1062). The definition was part of the canon law heritage: cf. Ivo, *Decretum* VIII.1, *Panormia* VI.1.

[109] *Inst.* 1.9.1.

[110] *Sent.* IV, 27.2 (422). On the conjugal debt and religious vows, see IV, 27.7–8 (425–28).

[111] *Sent.* IV, 27.3.2–27.4 (423–24). The first of the proof texts is ascribed to Isidore, but it is not authentic: "Consensus facit matrimonium." Peter Lombard apparently got it, with its ascription, from Gratian, C. 27 q. 2 dictum ante c. 1 (1062). The other texts, from Pope Nicholas I,

conditions are met: it must be explicit and expressed in words, or with other signs if needs must; it must be authentic rather than coerced or the result of error or fraud,[112] although authenticity does not require that the partners sincerely wish to marry in their hearts; and it must be about the present and not about the future. If she says, "I *will* accept you as my husband," and he replies, "And I you as my wife," their consent is *not* what makes marriage. But if she says "I accept you as my husband," and he replies, "And I you as my wife," their consent makes marriage.[113] The tense is crucial, although in Peter's Latin it is articulated in a single inflexion: *accipio* ("I accept") instead of *accipiam* ("I will accept"). It is not the words as such that matter, however, but their sense. He allows that other words and even unequivocal non-verbal signs may be used, provided that their sense is clear and they signify the same thing.[114] He probably assumed that regional and class-specific customs, rituals, and conventions would have made the tense clear.

Peter Lombard distinguishes between the nuptial compact (*pactio nuptialis*) and the conjugal compact (*pactio coniugalis*). These correspond respectively to *de futuro* and *de praesenti* betrothals. The Lombard strives to overcome the ambiguity of the term "betrothal" (*desponsatio*), which was used of both compacts. It is true that marriage begins as soon as there is a betrothal (*desponsatio*), as Augustine and Isidore say, regardless of whether that betrothal is preceded or followed by sexual intercourse, but only if the betrothal amounts to a conjugal compact (*pactio coniugalis*).[115]

Some say that the partners are not properly called husband and wife (*coniuges*), except perhaps by anticipation, until they have consummated their marriage in sexual intercourse. As evidence, they point out that by longstanding tradition a betrothed person (a *sponsa* or *sponsus*) can separate from his or her partner to enter the religious life, even if the other is unwilling. Peter Lombard reviews Gratian's arguments and others of the same sort.[116] According to the Lombard's analysis, such arguments depend on a terminological confusion. It is true that the right of unilateral separation exists only between a *sponsus* and a *sponsa* and not between married persons (*coniugati*), but the term *desponsatio* is ambiguous, for it may denote either a *de futuro* nuptial compact or a *de praesenti* conjugal compact. Strictly, the partners should be called *sponsus* and *sponsa* only when the betrothal is the result of a mutual promise to marry in the future, which establishes a nuptial compact (*pactio nuptialis*). Then either partner can still dissolve the union by taking religious vows.

---

ps.-Chrysostom, Ambrose, and Augustine are familiar. Peter seems to have taken these, too, from Gratian, C. 27 c. 2, c. 1, and c. 5 (1063, 1064).

[112] On coercion, see *Sent*. IV, 29 (436–37). On error and fraud, see *Sent*. IV, 30.1 (437–39).

[113] *Sent*. IV, 27.3.1 (422–23).

[114] *Sent*. IV, 27.3.1 (422): "Item, si consentiant mente, et non exprimant verbis vel aliis certis signis, nec talis consensus efficit matrimonium." *Sent*. IV, 28.4.2 (435): "Cum igitur sic conveniunt, ut dicat vir: Accipio te in meam coniugem, et dicat mulier: Accipio te in meum virum, his verbis vel aliis idem significantibus, exprimitur consensus...."

[115] *Sent*. IV, 27.4 (423–24).   [116] *Sent*. IV, 27.5–9 (424–30).

They are *coniugati* as soon their betrothal entails an agreement about the present, which establishes an inseparable conjugal compact (*pactio coniugalis*). The terms *desponsatio* and *sponsalia* are both customarily used to denote agreements of both sorts, the Lombard concedes, but the term *sponsalia* strictly denotes a solemn agreement to enter into a conjugal pact in the future, as the definitions from Roman law make clear.[117]

Peter Lombard asks whether the addition of an oath to a *de futuro* betrothal is sufficient to make it into a marriage. Is a sworn promise to marry at an agreed time sufficient to invalidate the subsequent marriage of either or both partners to someone else? In reply, the Lombard points out that "one who promises something does not yet do it." The partners cannot truthfully agree to do something in the future if that promise makes it happen at once, regardless of whether there is an oath or not.[118] Peter Lombard assembled this passage from material that he took from Walter's *De coniugio*, but Walter mentioned the oath chiefly to clarify what kind of agreement he had in mind.[119] As the betrothal distinction became better established, the oath became associated especially with the *de futuro* betrothal and seemed to some eyes to alter the significance of such betrothals.

Because consent alone suffices, it follows that any other customary formalities, such the handing over of the bride by her parents or the blessing of a priest, are not strictly necessary for a valid marriage. Nevertheless, Peter Lombard notes that these solemnities contribute to the honorableness of the sacrament and obviate the hazards of clandestinity.[120] Bare consent is strictly sufficient for a marriage to exist, but only publicly expressed consent *sanctifies* and *confirms* the union. Indeed, because the church must base judgments on evidence, acting in the external forum, those who marry clandestinely are akin to adulterers and fornicators, *as if* their marriages were illegitimate. The Lombard depends on Hugh for these practical observations, from which he does not try to extrapolate any theoretical conclusions.[121]

11.4.7 *The object of consent*

To what do the spouses agree? If they agree only to live together, then brother and sister or father and daughter could marry, which is absurd. But if they agree to sexual intercourse, then Mary and Joseph were not married, for Mary had taken a vow of virginity, which she would have mentally violated by agreeing to sexual intercourse.[122] Peter Lombard obviates both objections by adopting a modified version of Hugh's theory. The spouses do not specifically agree to sexual intercourse or even to cohabitation. Rather, they agree to a conjugal partnership (*societas coniugalis*). This normally entails the conjugal debt among other things, but it should be left

---

[117] *Sent.* IV, 27.8.8 (428), and IV, 27.9.9 (430).   [118] *Sent.* IV, 28.1 (431–33).
[119] Walter of Mortagne, *De coniugio*, PL176:160A–C.
[120] *Sent.* IV, 28.2.1 (433).   [121] *Sent.* IV, 28.2.2 (434).
[122] *Sent.* IV, 28.3.1 (434–35). The arguments are from Gratian, C. 27 q. 2 dictum post c. 2 (1063).

unanalyzed. That was why Eve was formed from Adam's side and not from his head or his feet, for the wife neither dominates over her husband nor is dominated by him, but rather is his partner. They commit themselves to this equal partnership when each of them vows to accept the other. It follows that they will live together "unless perhaps they have separated by mutual consent for the sake of the religious life, whether for period or until the end."[123] Their partnership normally obliges them to render the conjugal debt, therefore, although they may explicitly waive it by mutual agreement.[124]

Mary and Joseph consented to a conjugal partnership when they married, therefore, but not explicitly to sexual intercourse. According to the Lombard's analysis of Mary's intentions, for which he was dependent on Gratian[125] as well as on Hugh and Walter, Mary and Joseph firmly intended when they married to remain celibate unless God commanded otherwise, although they did not enunciate their intention in words until after they married. Their unconsummated marriage was perfect in sanctity, although it was imperfect in signification.[126]

11.4.8 *Reasons and benefits*

The chief reasons for marriage are the "procreation of offspring" and the "avoidance of fornication," which correspond respectively to two of the three goods of marriage: offspring and faith. Peter Lombard declares that marriage "excuses" sexual intercourse "when these three goods ... occur together," but he makes no reference to the good of sacrament in the explanation that follows, and it is not clear whether it contributes to the excusing power of marriage. Inasmuch as spouses have sex for the sake of offspring, they commit no fault. If they come together to satisfy lust, faith makes their fault pardonable (*venialis*). "When these goods are absent, namely, faith and offspring, there seems to be no way of defending sexual intercourse from guilt."[127] Contrariwise, one who engages in sexual intercourse for the sake of procreation or to render the conjugal debt does not sin at all. If it were impossible for fallen human beings to have sex without sinning, God would not have commanded human beings to increase and multiply after the flood (Gen 9:1).[128] Following Walter of Mortagne, Peter Lombard argues that although concupiscence is always evil (*mala*), it is not always a sin (*peccatum*). Nor is carnal pleasure (*delectatio*) always a sin. Even a "holy man" may experience delight when he rests after labor or eats when he is hungry.[129]

---

[123] *Sent.* IV, 28.3–4 (434–35). The quoted text comes as the end of this section (28.4.2).
[124] *Sent.* IV, 27.2 (422).   [125] C. 27 q. 2 c. 3 (1063–64).   [126] *Sent.* IV, 30.2 (439–41).
[127] *Sent.* IV, 31.5 (446–47). *Sent.* IV, 31.5.2 (447): "Ubi autem haec bona desunt, fides scilicet et proles, non videtur coitus defendi a crimine." On incontinence, the conjugal debt, and the venial fault, see also *Sent.* IV, 31.7 (448–49).
[128] *Sent.* IV, 31.7.5 (449). Cf. Walter of Mortagne, *De coniugio* 3, PL 176:156B.
[129] *Sent.* IV, 31.8 (450). Cf. Walter, *De coniugio* 3, 156C–157A. Whereas Walter said that Christ must have experienced such pleasure, the Lombard says that a "holy man" experiences it.

The Lombard repeats everything that Walter had said about the multiple purposes of marriage,[130] and he adds that there were "other, special reasons" for the marriage of Mary and Joseph. For example, it enabled Mary to give solace to her husband, it concealed the miraculous cause of Jesus' birth from the devil (a crux of some explanations of the atonement), and it protected her from suspicion of fornication.[131] Like Walter, Peter Lombard argues that the immorality of spouses' motive for marrying does not necessarily invalidate their marriage.[132] Following Augustine, he argues that those who marry solely for the sake of sexual intercourse are truly married unless they plan to prevent procreation "by some evil fraud" (i.e., by contraception or abortion).[133]

11.4.9 *The conjugal goods and marriage among unbelievers*

At the beginning of the primitive treatise on marriage, Peter Lombard had argued that the standard definition of marriage as a union or joining (*coniunctio*) that "holds together an indivisible way of life" applied only to legitimate spouses who belonged to the Christian faith. Unbelievers could not be legitimate spouses, "for marriage is one of the sacraments of the church, bearing the image of the union of Christ and the church, as the Apostle says: This, I say, is a great sacrament in Christ and in the church."[134] The Lombard had abandoned that theory when he wrote the *Sentences*, where he argues that unbelievers can validly marry. A marriage between infidels is defective, but it is legitimate, and it is inseparable at least in principle (notwithstanding the Pauline Privilege), for it possesses the good of sacrament, which the Lombard equates here with inseparability. The marriages of unbelievers possess the goods of faith and offspring, too, albeit only in defective form. It is not true, as some suggest, that there is no marriage between unbelievers, but such a marriage is untrue in the sense that "it does not have the triple good that excuses coitus and merits reward." That is why Augustine says that the marriage of unbelievers does not have "true chastity" (*vera pudicitia*).[135] Thus, one may distinguish between offspring (*proles*) and the good of offspring (*bonum prolis*). All spouses who have begotten children or intend or desire to do so may be said to have *proles*, but only those who intend to raise their children in the Christian religion have the *bonum prolis*.[136]

---

[130] *Sent.* IV, 30.3–4 (441–42). Cf. Walter, *De coniugio* 1, PL 176:154D–155B.

[131] *Sent.* IV, 30.4.2 (442).   [132] *Sent.* IV, 30.4.1 (442).

[133] *Sent.* IV, 31.2.5 (445). On contraception and abortion, see *Sent.* IV, 31.3–4 (445–46).

[134] PL 191:1586A: "Conjugium utique, sive matrimonium, est maritalis conjunctio maris et feminae inter legitimas personas, individualem vitae consuetudinem retinens. Hac autem descriptione matrimonium fidelium ac legitimorum tantum includitur, et est bona res conjugium. Est enim unum de sacramentis Ecclesiae, tenens imaginem conjunctionis Christi et Ecclesiae, sicut Apostolus ait: Hoc autem dico magnum sacramentum esse in Christo et in Ecclesia."

[135] Augustine, *De adult. coniug.* I.18(20), CSEL 41:367/20–368/3.

[136] *Sent.* IV, 31.2.4 (444).

Unlike the good of offspring, though, the good of sacrament exists even in infidel marriages. Someone one might object that unbelievers cannot marry because "whatsoever is not of faith is a sin" (Rom 14:23). One may obviate that objection, Peter Lombard argues, in either of two ways. The term *fides* may refer to moral conscience rather than to religious faith. Alternatively, the statement may mean that unbelievers always sin in whatever they do – yet not because their particular actions are sinful *per se*, but rather because they do not perform them with the proper intention, that is, by referring them to their due end.[137]

Peter Lombard distinguishes between corporeal and sacramental separation. The former occurs when there is a divorce on grounds of adultery or when the partners separate by mutual consent to enter the religious life. Corporeal separation does not allow remarriage. Spouses can be sacramentally separated only if their marriage is invalid because of some impediment. The spouses can remarry after a sacramental separation, but only because there is no good of sacrament (*bonum sacramenti*) in a union (*copula*) that that is capable of dissolution. Peter Lombard again equates this good with insolubility.[138] Whereas faith and the hope of offspring may be absent from any marriage, therefore, no legitimate marriage can exist without the good of sacrament.[139]

Whereas Augustine had proposed the good of sacrament to identify what distinguished Christian from non-Christian marriages, Peter Lombard argues that this is the only conjugal good that exists in non-Christian as well as in Christian marriages. There is clearly a difference of approach here, although it may not amount to contradiction. One might argue, for example, that what belonged uniquely to Christian marriages in Augustine was not the good of sacrament *per se* but the *observance* of that good. Be that as it may, the motive for the Lombard's argument is his unexamined conviction that marriage is insoluble by its very essence. A soluble marriage is not truly a marriage. Either infidels are not truly married, therefore, or their marriages, too, are *de iure* insoluble. Having formerly held the first position, the Lombard now holds the second.

11.4.10 *Marriage as one of the sacraments*

Peter Lombard begins his treatise on marriage in the *Sentences* by situating marriage among the sacraments: "Whereas the other sacraments originated after sin and because of sin, we read that the sacrament of marriage was also instituted by the Lord before sin, yet not as a remedy but as a duty."[140] But the Lombard does not explain *how* marriage is a sacrament until he has discussed several other preliminary topics: the dual institution of marriage, its remedial function in the fallen condition,

---

[137] *Sent.* IV, 39.6 (490). Cf. Walter, *De coniugio* 8, PL 176:160D–161B, and Gratian, C. 28 q. 1 dictum ante c. 1 (1078–79). Peter discusses the moral value of actions done by unbelievers in *Sent.* II, 41 (1:561–66).

[138] *Sent.* IV, 31.2.1–2 (442–43). [139] *Sent.* IV, 31.2.4 (444). [140] *Sent.* IV, 26.1.1 (416).

the nature of the indulgence by which sexual intercourse is permitted, and the goodness of marriage, with the opposing error of the heretics. The goodness of marriage is the Lombard's pretext for explaining eventually how marriage is a sacrament. Marriage must be good, he argues, for it is a sacrament, and a sacrament is by definition a "sacred sign."[141]

Marriage is not only sacred in itself. It is also a "sign of sacred reality." Peter Lombard does not explain the relationship between its intrinsic sanctity and its significance. But what reality does marriage signify?[142] Peter Lombard appropriates some of Hugh's insights here, but he abandons Hugh's theory of the two sacraments in marriage, which would not have been consistent with his own enumeration of the sacraments. Instead, reverting to the authority of Ephesians, he posits a single sacrament that signifies different but related aspects of a single reality:

> Therefore, since marriage is a sacrament, it is a sacred sign and a sign of a sacred reality, namely, of the union [*coniunctio*] of Christ and the church, as the Apostle says. For it is written, he says, that "a man shall leave his father and mother and cleave unto his wife, and they shall be two in one flesh. Now this is a great sacrament, I say, in Christ and in the church" (Gen 2:24, Eph 5:31–32). For just as there is a union between the spouses both according to the consent of their wills [*animi*] and according to the intercourse of their bodies, so the church is united to Christ by will and by nature, because she wishes the same as he does, and he took his form from the nature of human beings. The bride [i.e., the church], therefore, is united to the bridegroom [Christ] spiritually and corporeally, that is, in charity and in conformity of nature. There is a figure of both of these unions in marriage, for the consent of the spouses signifies the spiritual union between Christ and the church that comes about through charity, whereas sexual intercourse signifies the union that comes about through conformity of nature.[143]

Just as there is both consent and, in due course, sexual intercourse in marriage, so the union between Christ and the church includes both union through charity and conformity in human nature. Peter Lombard seems to have considered the Christological relationships not as successive as coexistent. On both sides of the comparison, one relationship is spiritual, whereas the other is a union of "two in one flesh."

Unlike Hugh, therefore, Peter Lombard posits a single sacrament of marriage with two aspects, each of which signifies a different aspect of the same union between Christ and the church. Marriage is based on consent, and it typically involves sexual union as well, albeit not necessarily. Whereas Hugh considered the partnership (*societas*) in marriage to be the spiritual sacrament, Peter Lombard identifies the spiritual aspect of the sacrament with the initial act of consent that makes a marriage. Peter Lombard is not interested in Hugh's spirituality of marriage,

---

[141] *Sent.* IV, 26.5 (419): "Constat ergo rem bonam esse matrimonium. Alioquin non esset sacramentum: sacramentum enim sacrum signum est."
[142] *Sent.* IV, 26.6.1 (419).   [143] Ibid., pp. 419–20.

although he invokes it as an afterthought at the very end of the discussion, where he adds that marriage "is also a sign of the spiritual union and love of minds, by which the spouses ought to be united to each other, as the Apostle says: Husbands, love your wives as your bodies" (Eph 5:25, 28).[144]

Peter Lombard distinguishes between the *bonum sacramenti*[145] and the sacrament of marriage itself, but he argues that the two things are said to be sacraments for the same reason. Inseparability is called a sacrament "not because it is marriage itself, but because it is a sign of the same sacred reality, namely, of the spiritual and inseparable union of Christ and the church." Whereas marriage is a sign of that union as such, the inseparability of marriage is a sign of the permanence of the union.[146] The relationship between the good of sacrament and the sacrament of marriage will puzzle theologians during the first quarter of the thirteenth century. Are they different, the same, or different aspects of the same thing?

Peter Lombard deals with the coital proof texts in the light of his theory of the two aspects of sacramentality. When Leo and Augustine say that marriage is imperfect without sexual intercourse, they do not mean that marriage cannot be fully contracted without sexual intercourse. If that were so, there would have been no marriage between Mary and Joseph or at best an imperfect marriage, which is unthinkable.[147] On the contrary, the more a marriage is free from sexual intercourse, the holier it is, as Augustine teaches. That said, a marriage without sexual intercourse signifies the union between Christ and the church incompletely, for although it signifies the charity between them, it does not signify their conformity in a shared nature.[148] Sexual intercourse perfects marriage in respect of its signification, therefore, but not in respect either of its intrinsic validity (*veritas*) or of its sanctity. The marriage of Mary and Joseph was imperfect only in respect of its signification, whereas it epitomized marital perfection in respect of sanctity, and it was perfectly valid.[149] As Augustine says, "the sanctity of sacrament is worth more in marriage than fecundity of the womb."[150]

Peter Lombard does not draw any conclusions from his sacramental theory regarding the function of consummation in relation to the stability of marriage or the impediment of prior marriage. Nor does he claim that the sacred significance of marriage determines what makes a marriage irrevocable and inseparable. He is not troubled by the concession that unconsummated marriage is figuratively incomplete. Nevertheless, because marriage is a sacrament of Christ and the church, any relationship that is not a sacrament of Christ and the church, in his view, cannot be

---

[144] *Sent.* IV, 26.6.5 (421).
[145] *Sent.* IV, 31.2.4 (444/14–15): "illud bonum quod dicitur sacramentum."
[146] *Sent.* IV, 31.2.3 (443).   [147] *Sent.* IV, 26.6.2–3 (420–21).
[148] *Sent.* IV, 26.6.4 (421).   [149] *Sent.* IV, 30.2.5 (440–41).
[150] *Sent.* IV, 26.6.5 (421). Augustine, *De bono coniugali* 18(21), CSEL 41:215: "in nostrarum quippe nuptiis plus ualet sanctitas sacramenti quam fecunditas uteri."

marriage. A marriage would not be established (*ratum*) if it failed to signify the union between Christ and the church in *some* salient way.

11.4.11 *Substance, solemnity, and clandestinity*

The inclusion of marriage among the sacraments of the church presupposed the doctrine of bare consent (*solus consensus*), according to which the mutual consent of the spouses was the sole efficient cause of marriage. Such consent was both necessary and sufficient, therefore, to constitute a valid and indissoluble union. This doctrine relegated to an accidental periphery several aspects of the process that might otherwise have seemed essential, especially among members of the landed elites: on the secular side, negotiated settlements and dowries, the agreement of parents and kinsfolk, the giving in marriage (*traditio*) of daughters by their fathers, and the presence of witnesses, including parents, other members of the immediate families, and *amici* (kinsfolk and friends), all of whom represented the community at the conclusion of the agreement; and, on the sacred side, the ministry of a priest, the nuptial blessing, rites and liturgies, and consecrated settings. The doctrine was in tension, therefore, both with the secular expectations of traditional marriage and with the sacred implications of treating marriage as one of the sacraments.

Medieval theologians and canonists articulated and solved such tensions dialectically, by citing and solving authorities that seemed to require what in their view was *not* required. The decretal ascribed to Pope Evaristus was by far the most important of these authorities. We have already seen that it was a focus of debate among the *magistri moderni* (Section 9.1.2).[151] Peter Lombard quotes the decretal because it seems to contradict the principle that "consent alone makes marriage," which he has already established. His version of the authority is an abbreviated version of Gratian's:

> A marriage is not lawful unless the woman is petitioned as a wife from those who are seen to have authority over her and custody of her, and she is betrothed and given a

---

[151] PL 130:81B–C (= Hinschius, *Decretales Pseudo-Isidorianae et capitula Angilramni* [Leipzig, 1863], 87–88): "Similiter custoditum et traditum habemus, ut uxor legitime viro jungatur. Aliter enim legitimum, ut a Patribus accepimus, et a sanctis apostolis, eorumque successoribus traditum, invenimus, non fit conjugium, nisi ab his qui super ipsam feminam dominationem videntur habere, et a quibus custoditur, uxor petatur, et a parentibus aut propinquioribus sponsetur, et legibus detur, et suo tempore sacerdotaliter, ut mos est, cum precibus et oblationibus a sacerdote benedicatur, et a paranymphis, ut consuetudo docet, custodita et sociata a proximis tempore congruo petita legibus detur, et solemniter accipiatur, et biduo vel triduo orationibus vacent et castitatem custodiant, ut bonae soboles generentur, et Domino in actibus suis placeant. Taliter enim et Domino placebunt, et filios non spurios, sed legitimos, atque haereditabiles generabunt. Quapropter, filii charissimi, et merito illustres fide catholica suffragante, ita peracta legitima scitote esse conjugia. Aliter vero praesumpta non conjugia, sed aut adulteria, aut contubernia, aut stupra, vel fornicationes potius quam legitima conjugia esse non dubitate, nisi voluntas propria suffragata fuerit et vota succurrerint legitima." Ivo, *Decretum* VIII.4 (*Panormia* VI.32). Gratian, C. 30 q. 5 c. 1 (1104).

dowry by her parents, and she is blessed by priest according to custom, and she is accompanied by her paranymphs[152] and solemnly accepted.... Know that marriages are lawful when done in that way. Otherwise, these are presumed to be not marriages but adulteries or fornications, unless their own will, supported by lawful vows, has been expressly stated.[153]

The authority was a Carolingian forgery, but that is hardly relevant. Medieval scholars did not question its authenticity, which was in any case established through reception. Moreover, the text functioned not as proof but as a dialectically useful obstacle. Some discussions focused on the meaning of "lawful" (*legitimum*), and some on the sense of the final qualification, which seemed to contradict what went before. Peter Lombard borrowed his solution from Walter of Mortagne. He explains that the requirements should be understood not as the necessary conditions for a valid marriage (*legitimum coniugium*) but as those without which a marriage lacks seemliness (*decor*) and honor (*honestas*).[154]

   Drawing on Hugh of Saint-Victor as well as on Walter of Mortagne, the Lombard uses the decretal as a pretext for distinguishing between the substance of marriage and its attendant solemnities. In the celebration of every sacrament, he explains, some things are necessary because they belong to its substance, whereas others contribute to its seemliness and solemnity. Consent alone, expressed in the present tense, is necessary for the sacrament of marriage, whereas features such as the handing over of a bride by her parents (*parentum traditio*) and the priestly blessing are accidental solemnities. Without them, the marriage is lawfully entered into *ad virtutem* (i.e., as regards its obligational force and entailments), but not *ad honestam*, since the partners have not followed the prescribed laws and customs. The Lombard emphasizes two categories of solemnity, pertaining respectively to parental authority and to ecclesiastical ritual. Evaristus says that spouses who fail to observe these formalities are presumed to be adulterers or fornicators not because their union is invalid, the Lombard explains, but because they have come together *as if* they were fornicators or adulterers, "as those who marry covertly [*clanculo*]" come together.[155]

   Peter Lombard moves directly from that solution to a comment on clandestine marriages, again drawing on Hugh of Saint-Victor (Section 10.6.1). A marriage is clandestine when there are no reliable witnesses. Evaristus's requirements would

---

[152] These may be bridesmaids or bridesmen. The term *paranymphyus* properly denotes one who ceremonially accompanies the bride.
[153] *Sent.* IV, 28.1.4 (433): "Illi etiam sententiae, qua dictum est solum consensum facere coniugium, videtur contraire quod Evaristus Papa ait: 'Aliter legitimum non fit coniugium, nisi ab his qui super feminam dominationem habere videntur et a quibus custoditur, uxor petatur, et a parentibus sponsetur, et legibus dotetur, et a sacerdote ut mos est benedicatur, et a paranymphis custodiatur, et solemniter accipiatur'. — Item: 'Ita legitima scitote esse coniubia. Aliter vero praesumpta, non conjugia, sed adulteria vel fornicationes sunt, nisi voluntas propria suffragata fuerit et vota succurrerint legitima'."
[154] *Sent.* IV, 28.1.4 (433). Walter of Mortagne, *De coniugio*, c. 6, PL 176:159C–D.
[155] *Sent.* IV, 28.2.1 (433).

ensure, among other things, that a marriage is public and properly witnessed. Even covert consent (*consensus occultus*), provided that is expressed verbally in the present tense, makes marriage. Nevertheless, such a marriage is not an "honorable contract" (*honestus contractus*), for if one of the spouses later abandons the other, the church cannot force him or her to return to the marriage because there are no witnesses to prove that they are married. Covert consent is sufficient to establish a marriage in reality, therefore, but only public consent can confirm that the spouses are married for the purposes of ecclesiastical judgment, so that their marriage is secure and properly regulated. Nevertheless, partners who have married secretly may confirm their marriage later by repeating their expression of mutual consent openly in a public setting. That is why Evaristus added that such unions are considered to be adultery or fornication *unless the partners express their consent with lawful vows*. Evaristus was referring to a subsequent public confirmation for what had been only covertly expressed.[156]

Peter Lombard's treatment of this cluster of issues will be fundamental to all treatments of clandestine marriage by scholastic theologians throughout the Middle Ages and into the sixteenth century. With Evaristus's decretal in mind, theologians approached the problem of clandestinity by distinguishing between the essence of the sacrament and its attendant solemnities. Although clandestinity was by definition the absence of proof through witnesses, they subsumed under the general heading of clandestinity the absence both of ritual and of parental consent: the chief ecclesiastical and secular solemnities respectively. This notion of clandestinity seems today overly rich and even muddled or confusing, but it probably reflected the practical options well enough.

11.5 AFTER PETER LOMBARD

Contributions to the theology of marriage were neither ambitious nor extensive during a period of about three decades after the publication of Peter Lombard's *Sentences*. Theologians generally accepted the findings of the Lombard on marriage without challenging them or pursuing new avenues of inquiry. The section on marriage in the *Summa de sacramentis "totus homo,"* which was probably written between 1170 and 1190,[157] is unusually extensive, but it contains little that could not have been written around the middle of the century. The author was heavily dependent on Walter of Mortagne and Peter Lombard, and he contributed little to the development of the topic. Moreover, such extensive treatments of marriage from this period are rare.

---

[156] *Sent.* IV, 28.2.2 (434).
[157] On the likely date of *Summa de sacramentis "totus homo,"* see Betti's introduction to his edition, pp. lxxvii–lxxix. For the *De coniugio*, see 129–76.

There are at least two plausible reasons for the limited scope and ambition of theological writing on marriage during this period. First, following the achievements of the first half of the century, especially Peter Lombard's synthesis, it was possible to reduce any controvertible issue to a handful of standard, briefly stated arguments. Second, theology and canon law were becoming recognized as distinct disciplines, and as a result the discussion of marriage law in a theological setting, such as in a treatise on the sacraments, could be kept to a minimum. Introducing his *Summa* on Gratian's *Decretum*, composed in the later 1160s, Stephen of Tournai wondered how scholars of law and of theology would respond to his work. Basic information on Gratian will seem tedious and unnecessary to the legal scholar, he fears, whereas basic information on Scripture will seem tedious and unnecessary to the theologian.[158] Writing primarily for scholars in France, Stephen can still assume that theologians as well as canonists will read his work, but he assumes, too, that the two disciplines have diverged and become mutually independent.

Peter of Poitiers (d. 1205), who was a master at Notre Dame by 1167, illustrates the second of those trends, for he left the canonical aspects of marriage to specialists in canon law. His strict segregation of theological from canonical aspects of marriage was extreme, however, and should perhaps be regarded as an innovative but unsuccessful attempt at reform. He explains in his *Sententiae* how and why there are seven sacraments.[159] Following Master Simon rather than Peter Lombard, he divides the sacraments of the New Law into the necessary, or general, and the non-necessary, or special. Orders and marriage belong to the latter category. Peter elaborates a journey of life simile to show why the five general sacraments are needed. Baptism is for persons entering the church, confirmation strengthens those who are struggling in it, eucharist is for those who are making progress, penance for those who are returning from sin, and extreme unction for those who are leaving the church of this life.[160] But Peter explains that he will not discuss orders because that topic is better left to the decretists.[161] He will say something about marriage, but many of aspects of that topic, too, are best left to the canonists.[162]

---

[158] Ed. H. Kalb, *Studien zur Summa Stephans von Tournai* (Innsbruck, 1983), 113–14.

[159] Peter of Poitiers, *Sent.* V.3, PL 211:1229B–C. The date of the work is uncertain. P. S. Moore, *The Works of Peter of Poitiers* (Notre Dame, 1936), 29–41, argues that the work was certainly written before 1176, and perhaps by 1170, but Moore's arguments are questionable and a later date cannot be ruled out. C. I. Beckwith, *Warriors of the Cloisters* (Princeton, 2012), 171–77, critically reviews the evidence.

[160] *Sent.* V.3 (1229C–D).

[161] *Sent.* V.14 (1257B): "de ordinibus, nil hic dicendum eo quod decretistis disputatio de his potius quam theologis deservit."

[162] Ibid.: "Quae circa ... conjugium a theologis solent inquiri, sub compendio sunt perstringenda; nec enim animus nobis est complectendi omnia quae circa conjugium possunt inquiri, cum pleraque decretistarum potius quam theologorum famulentur inquisitioni. Videndum est ergo quid sit sacramentum conjugii, et quid res sacramenti, quae institutio et quae causa efficiens, et causa finalis et causae divortiis animadvertendae: quae clarius patebunt prius cognito per diffinitionem quid sit conjugium."

11.5.1 *Topics*

Writing as a theologian, Peter of Poitiers limits himself to the following questions about marriage: What is the sacrament of marriage, or its definition? What is the reality (*res*) of the sacrament? How was it instituted? What are its efficient and final causes? And what are the grounds for divorce?[163] Theologians also discussed the twofold institution of marriage as a duty and a remedy, the marriage of Mary and Joseph and its implications for Christian marriage in general, and the limited efficacy of the sacrament.

The most popular definition of marriage throughout the central Middle Ages was that of Justinian's *Institutes*: marriage is "the union [*coniunctio*] of a male and a female that holds together an indivisible way of life."[164] Following an innovation of the *magistri moderni*, some theologians added that the union was between "legitimate persons."[165] But the term *coniunctio* was ambiguous, since it could denote either an act of joining or the enduring union that resulted. Gandulph of Bologna argues in his *Sentences* (c. 1170) that *coniunctio* in the definition of marriage is the marriage bond, which entails the conjugal debt and prevents either spouse for being joined to a third party as long as the other is alive.[166] The term here cannot denote coitus, Gandulph notes, although he argues that coitus itself, as the carnal *coniunctio* ("joining") of the spouses, is a sacrament (i.e., a sacred sign) of Christ and the church if it is performed for the sake of procreation.[167]

Theologians accepted the idea of a double institution of marriage, which the *magistri moderni* had proposed, following a passage taken from Augustine's *De*

---

[163] See previous note.

[164] *Institutes* 1.9.1: "Nuptiae autem sive matrimonium est viri et mulieris coniunctio, individuam consuetudinem vitae continens." Gratian, C. 27 q. 2 dictum ante c. 1, and c. 3 (1062. 1064). Peter Lombard, *Sent.* IV, 27.2 (422). Peter of Poitiers, *Sent.* V.14 (1257C). Gandulph of Bologna, *Sent.* IV, ed. de Walter, §225 (513–14).

[165] For example, Peter of Poitiers, *Sent.* V.14 (1257C): "Conjugium est viri et mulieris maritalis conjunctio inter legitimas personas individuam vitae consuetudinem retinens." This definition is from Peter Lombard (cited earlier). Cf. Hugh of Saint-Victor, *De sacramentis* 2.11.4 (PL 176:483A): "Quidam hoc modo conjugium diffiniendum putaverunt, ut dicerent "conjugium esse consensum masculi et feminae individualem vitae consuetudinem retinentem." Cui diffinitioni "legitimum" adjungere oportet; quia si consensus masculi et feminae legitimus, hoc est legitime et inter personas legitimas factus, non fuerit, conjugium in eo consecrari non potest." Cf. *Cum omnia sacramenta II*, ed. Bliemetzrieder, 279/110–113: "Coniugium est masculi consensus et femine, indiuidualem uite consuetudinem retinens, indiuidualiter commanendi et carnaliter commiscendi, absque prolis uitatione legitimus, id est, inter legitimas personas legitime factus."

[166] Gandulph, *Sent.* IV, §225 (513–14). Gandulph must have taught both canon law and theology. He wrote glosses on Gratian's *Decretum*, but his *Sententiae* is a theological compendium based on Peter Lombard's *Sententiae*, of which it is largely an abridgement. See M. Colish, "From the Sentence Collection to the Sentence Commentary and the Summa," in J. Hamesse (ed.), *Manuels, programmes de cours et techniques d'enseignement*, 9–29, at 18–19, on the character and setting of Gandulph's *Sententiae*.

[167] Gandulph, *Sent.* IV, §239 (526–27).

Genesi ad litteram. Marriage was originally instituted to fulfill a duty (*ad officium*), that is, for the begetting and rearing of children, but it was later re-instituted as a remedy against lust, or as a way of avoiding incontinence or fornication. According to Gandulph of Bologna, the duty to procreate was implied when God commanded human beings to "increase and multiply" in the beginning (Gen 1:28) and again after the Flood (Gen 9:1). This obligation remained in effect throughout the period of the Old Law and even into the "time of grace." It was only in 1 Corinthians 7:6 that a new regime was definitively stated. Henceforth, marrying was a matter rather of indulgence than of obligation.[168]

Following Walter of Mortagne, theologians distinguished both between primary and secondary reasons for marrying and between honorable and dishonorable reasons. Some theologians used only one of these divisions, others both. Among secondary reasons, theologians counted reconciliation and peacemaking as honorable, and financial gain and carnal beauty as dishonorable. They cited the example of Jacob, who wanted to marry Rachel because she was beautiful (Gen 29:18), to show that a dishonorable motive for marrying did not necessarily invalidate the marriage.[169] Theologians held diverse opinions about procreation and the avoidance of fornication in relation to such divisions. According to Gandulph of Bologna, the primary reason for marriage is the propagation of the human race; honest secondary motives include the restoration of peace and the remedy against sexual "weakness" (*infirmitas*) through the avoidance of fornication; dishonest secondary motives include good looks and financial gain.[170] The *Summa de sacramentis "totus homo"* presents a similar analysis, but the author argues that in this time of grace "the love of avoiding fornication [1 Cor 7:2] alone is the principal reason for marriage." "It is not necessary," the author explains, "that someone should take a wife for the sake of procreation now, for sons of God can be procreated even from adulterers and barbarians."[171]

Peter of Poitiers divides the reasons for marrying into honorable and dishonorable. Honest reasons include not only procreation but also reconciliation, or the restoration of peace. Dishonest reasons include wealth and good looks. Sexual desire may generate either an honorable motive or a dishonorable motive, according to Peter. If a man marries to satisfy his lust, his reason is dishonorable and even his marrying is a mortal sin, although the marriage is valid and the sin attached to coitus is excused by the conjugal goods: faith, offspring, and sacrament. But if a man marries because he is unable to remain continent (i.e., for the sake of the remedy),

---

[168] Gandulph, *Sent.* IV, §§216–18 (506–08).

[169] For example, *Summa de sacramentis "totus homo," De coniugio* 3, ed. Betti, 132/3–8.

[170] Gandulph, *Sent.* IV, §221 (509).

[171] *Summa de sacramentis "totus homo," De coniugio* 3, 131/4–7. This work is unusual in construing the *bonum fidei* positively, as the conjugal debt (see *De coniugio* 5, 134/13–19), whereas most twelfth-century authors still construed it as fidelity in the restrictive sense, i.e., as the avoidance of adultery.

then his motive is honorable.[172] The refined analysis of motives during this period reflects the development of sacramental confession and penance.

The motive of peacemaking or reconciliation enjoyed a privileged status throughout the central Middle Ages, second only to the fundamental motives of procreation and remedy. Unlike the other motives, this was not usually constitutive of the spouses' "marital affection" (i.e., their regard for each other as man and wife). A decretal from Pope Alexander III to the archbishop of York concerns a certain man, W., who had betrothed a girl who was supposedly under seven years of age. When she came of age, she refused to consent. Later, King Henry "gave the mother of the aforesaid girl to the said W. as his wife, whom the same W., in order that the discord that had arisen between his blood relatives and the woman's blood relatives might be put to rest, accepted and solemnly espoused and took in marriage without opposition from the church, and he begot children from her." Was the marriage valid? The impediment of public honesty prevented someone from validly marrying the parent of a child to whom he or she had been betrothed. The age of the daughter at the time of the betrothal, therefore, was crucial. If she was really under seven, then the betrothal was invalid and there was no fatal impediment to the marriage between W. and the girl's mother. But if the daughter had already completed her seventh year, W.'s marriage to her mother was legally dishonorable (*inhonestum*), even though the man had been validly released from the betrothal by the girl's refusal to consent. That was a potential impediment, but Alexander ruled, regardless of the validity of W.'s betrothal to the daughter, that the marriage should be tolerated and the children regarded as legitimate "lest the discord that had formerly arisen between their blood relatives, which is now put to rest, should be rekindled."[173] Here, peacemaking, as an eminently honorable motive, trumped the impediment of public honesty.

Mary's marriage to Joseph raised questions regarding the purity of her intentions, the validity of her marriage, and the quasi-contractual nature of marrying. To what did one agree by plighting one's troth in the present tense? No major theologian after Hugh of Saint-Victor attempted to separate marriage entirely from coitus, and French canonists and theologians agreed that the inability to consummate a union was a fatal impediment. Did Mary morally break her vow to remain a virgin by marrying? Simon of Tournai solves this problem by distinguishing between a *propositum* and a *votum*, for Augustine had called Mary's vow a *propositum*. A *votum* is to a *propositum*, Simon explains, as the desire for a thing is to *the desire to desire* it. Unlike a vow, a *propositum* is not binding either in the eyes of God or in the court of human justice.[174] Simon's distinction is analogous to that between simple (or private) and solemn (or public) religious vows, as well as to that between

---

[172] Peter of Poitiers, *Sent.* IV.17 (1260C).

[173] X 4.2.5 (673–74, WH 12, JL 13887). The likely date of the decretal is 1173.

[174] Simon of Tournai, disp. 80, q. 6, ed. Warichez, 233–34. Simon studied in Paris under Odo of Soissons from c. 1155, and he taught there from c. 1165 to c. 1201.

de futuro and *de praesenti* betrothals. Peter of Poitiers, too, uses the distinction between a *propositum* and a *votum* to solve this problem. Peter argues that inasmuch as Mary consented to coitus, she did so conditionally, that is, she agreed that she would render the conjugal debt if Joseph demanded it, for then such would be God's will. Nevertheless, following Peter Lombard, Peter of Poitiers argues that what one agrees to in marrying is not coitus or even the conjugal debt but rather an undetermined "conjugal partnership" (*societas coniugalis*).[175]

11.5.2 *Marriage as a sacred sign*

When they discussed marriage as a sacrament, theologians of this period generally used the descriptor "sign of a sacred reality" (*signum sacrae rei*) as their working definition of a sacrament. To determine whether there was a valid marriage, it sufficed to show that its signification was complete or adequate in its salient respects. Marriage might signify many things, but the crucial signification pertained to Christ and the church. Thus, Peter Lombard inquires of what reality (*res*) marriage is a sacrament, and he replies that it is a sign of the union (*coniunctio*) between Christ and the church, as Paul says.[176] Paul was referring to the continuing relationship between husband and wife, but Peter Lombard is referring to the formation of their conjugal bond.

Whereas Hugh posited two sacraments in marriage, each with its own signified reality, Peter Lombard, as we have seen, posited a single sacrament that signified two aspects of the same union between Christ and the church. According to Hugh, marriage itself signified the union between God and the soul, whereas sexual union signified the union between Christ and the church. According to Peter Lombard, the mutual consent, or union of wills, of the partners signified the love uniting Christ and the church, whereas sexual consummation signified Christ's conformity with the church through the sharing of a common nature, for Christ "was made flesh and dwelt among us" (John 1:14).

Theologians during the second half the twelfth century generally followed the Lombard's lead. They sometimes used Hugh's analysis of the signified realities and sometimes Peter Lombard's, but they seem to have regarded these as equivalent: as different ways of saying the same thing. This conflation is apparent in Bandinus's summary of Peter Lombard's analysis:

> marriage is a sacrament and sacred sign of a sacred reality, namely, of the union of Christ and the church: according to the spirit, in respect of its beginning [*initium*]; according to the flesh, in respect of its completion. Hence, it is the sign of a twofold sacred reality, namely, of the joining of the soul with God, which is signified in the betrothal, and of our flesh to God, which is signified in sexual intercourse, that is,

[175] Peter of Poitiers, *Sent.* V.16 (1259A–C). Cf. Peter Lombard, *Sent.* IV, 28.3.2 (435).
[176] Peter Lombard, *Sent.* IV, 26.6.1 (419).

when man and woman are made one flesh, just as Christ and the church became one flesh in the Virgin's womb.[177]

As well as conflating Peter Lombard's analysis of the signifieds with Hugh's in this passage, Bandinus adopts the Bolognese distinction between *matrimonium initiatum* and *matrimonium consummatum*.

Peter of Poitiers follows Peter Lombard more closely. There are two signifiers in marriage, he argues: the mutual consent of the partners' wills (*consensus animorum*), and their carnal union (*copula carnalis*). Nevertheless, these are not two sacraments but two aspects of a single sacrament of the union between Christ and the church, in which there is both a spiritual union formed by charity, and a corporeal union formed by the sharing of a common human nature. An unconsummated marriage, such as that between Mary and Joseph, is imperfect only in the sense that it lacks the second signification, for the two aspects of marriage constitute a single sacrament, just as bread and wine constitute a single sacrament in the eucharist.[178]

Simon of Tournai uses the notion of marriage as a *signum sacrae rei* to determine whether Mary was truly married to Joseph, notwithstanding the absence of sexual intercourse. They were truly married if and only if there was a true sacrament between them, and there was a true sacrament if their marriage signified the requisite sacred reality. But the signification of marriage is twofold. On the one hand, the spouses' mutual consent signifies the union of the faithful soul with God. On the other hand, sexual intercourse signifies the incarnation of Christ. Simon regards the first signification as one of qualitative conformity rather than mere analogy. When two non-believers contract a marriage, the consent of their wills (*consensus animorum*) does not fully signify the union of the faithful soul with God because it does not occur "in the Lord" (1 Cor 7:39). That is why such a marriage can be dissolved when one of the spouses converts to Christianity. Nevertheless, unbelievers unknowingly signify the incarnation when they come together carnally, and in this limited, merely analogical respect their marriage is true. The opposite is true of Mary and Joseph, for their marriage was truly sacramental in the first respect (the divine quality of the union) but not in the second (sexual union).[179] Indeed, they could have divorced – but only by making use of the "canonical tradition" that permits either spouse before consummation to go to a monastery, even if the other is unwilling, and there was no such tradition in their day.[180] Simon's sensitivity to anachronism was unusual for the central Middle Ages.

[177] Bandinus, *Sent.* IV.26, PL 192:1106D–1107A. On Bandinus's *Sententiae*, see P. W. Rosemann, *The Story of a Great Medieval Book* (Peterborough, ON, 2007), 28–33. Bandinus taught in Paris during the second half of the twelfth century. This work was among the earliest and most widespread of many abbreviations of Peter Lombard's *Sentences*, but its date remains uncertain.
[178] Peter of Poitiers, *Sent.* V.14 (1257C–D).   [179] Simon of Tournai, disp. 15, q. 1 (52–53).
[180] Ibid. (53/27–33).

11.5.3 *Sacramental efficacy and the preventive model*

The preventive model of sacramental efficacy assumed several forms, but the gist was that a certain sacrament – such as marriage, or circumcision, or any of the sacraments of the Old Law – removes an obstacle to supernatural well-being without enabling the subject to attain that well-being through a gift of grace. For example, the followers of Peter Abelard, as we have seen, maintained that marriage provided a way to restrain lust and a license to have sex without sin, but that it did not bestow a gift (*donum*).[181] According to Peter Lombard, the power of a sacrament to cause what it signifies is the chief feature that distinguishes the sacraments of the New Law from the sacraments of the Old. Nevertheless, the Lombard makes marriage an exception to the rule by subdividing the seven sacraments of the New Covenant into three groups: those which confer both a remedy against sin and a "helping grace," such as baptism; those which "support us with grace and virtue," such as eucharist and orders; and those which confer only a remedy against sin, such as marriage.[182]

Peter of Poitiers follows Peter Lombard closely when he discusses the difference between the sacraments of the Old Law and of the New and the manner in which circumcision was a partial exception.[183] It is obvious, in his view, that marriage does not cause what it signifies (*efficit quod figurat*), for the marriage of two Christians cannot cause the union between Christ and the Church. But that proposition seems to contradict the principle that the sacraments of the New Law cause what they signify. Peter's solution is that marriage is not strictly a sacrament of the New Law, since it was instituted long before the New Law:

Again, marriage is a sacrament of the New Law. Therefore, it causes what it signifies. Therefore, it causes the unity of Christ and the church. To this it should be said that this sacrament was celebrated under the Old Law as well as under the New, and that it is older than all the sacraments, for it was instituted in Paradise when God said, "Be fruitful and multiply."[184]

Peter's solution is syllogistically sound. If marriage is not a sacrament of the New Law, the premise that the sacraments of the New Law cause what they signify need not apply to it. But Peter does not explain why, in that case, marriage is counted among the seven sacraments of the New Law. Nor does he explain why marriage was not raised to the level of the other sacraments of the New Law when it became one of them. He assumes that his readers will readily accept the minor premise: that marriage is not strictly a sacrament of the New Law.

---

[181] *Sententiae Parisienses*, ed. Landgraf, 44/5–7, 44/27–30. *Ysagoge in theologiam*, ed. Landgraf, 197/2–5. *Sententiae magistri Petri Abelardi*, ed. Lucombe, §201 (CCM 14:107–08), §231 (122), §233 (123).

[182] Peter Lombard, *Sent.* IV, 2.1.1 (239–40).

[183] Peter of Poitiers, *Sent.* IV.2 (1141B) and V.3 (1229B–C).

[184] Peter of Poitiers, *Sent.* V.14 (1257D).

11.5.4 *Conjugal virtue and chastity*

Reflection on the virtue of holy virginity provided theologians with another way of thinking about the moral benefits of marriage, aside from questions about sacramental efficacy. Jerome and Augustine had interpreted the thirtyfold, sixtyfold, and hundredfold fruit in the parable of the sower (Matt 18:23, Mark 4:20) as the rewards of marriage, widowhood, and virginity respectively.[185] That idea suggested to medieval scholars that virginity and marriage, insofar as they were practiced authentically and piously, embodied the same virtue in different ways, with different degrees of merit. Thus, Simon of Tournai argues that a common virtue underlies virginity, conjugal chastity, and vidual continence, namely, a habit of mind whereby one is disposed to serve God with one's whole self, including one's body. A girl who marries does not commit a mortal sin when she loses her virginity. On the contrary, the common virtue remains in a different guise and takes on a different name. That said, the virtue of conjugal chastity entails *proles* as well as *fides*, whereas virginity requires abstinence. The faithful wife serves God through legitimate procreation, as well as by keeping her body pure, but she lacks the "integrity of body and mind" that holy virgins exemplify.[186]

It was natural for twelfth-century churchmen to identify the virtue that characterizes marriage with a kind of attenuated virginity, for lust and sexual pleasure seemed self-evidently bad. They justified marriage chiefly as a remedy to that problem, and as means of excusing sex from culpability. Nevertheless, theologians during the twelfth and thirteenth centuries gradually adopted less negative ways of regarding sexual intercourse and sexual pleasure. We have already seen how Walter of Mortagne resisted the notion of the *magistri moderni* that all carnal pleasure (*delectatio*) was intrinsically evil.

The question whether the act of coitus itself might be meritorious provided twelfth-century theologians with a way to think about the relationship between the sexual act and the holiness of marriage. Needless to say, any such merit presupposed that coitus occurred within marriage and was performed with the best of motives. The ideal motive was procreation, but the rendering of the debt was honorable too. Indeed, it was virtuous, for to give what is due is justice. The use of marital sex to avoid fornication was reasonable and not at odds with the purpose of marriage.

Peter of Poitiers considers the following problem: Marriage is a sacrament. But the performance (*opus*) of a sacrament is meritorious. Therefore, coitus in marriage is meritorious. Against that, Peter marshals two authorities. First, Augustine says that

---

[185] Simon of Tournai, disp. 80, q. 5 (233). Jerome, *Adv. Iovinianum* 1.3, PL 23:223B–224A. See also Jerome's commentary on Matt 13:23 (PL 26:89A), where he refers his readers to the former passage. Augustine, *De sancta virg.* 45(46), CSEL 41:290–91.

[186] Simon of Tournai, disp. 80, q. 1 (231–32). Likewise, Alexander of Hales, *QQ disp. 'antequam esset frater'*, Q. 57, disp. 3.2–3, §§65–79 (1121–27); and Thomas Aquinas, *Summa theol.* I-II.70.3, ad 2[m] (1086).

the entire human being (*totus homo*) becomes flesh in the act of coitus.[187] Second, Gregory the Great implies that sexual pleasure (*delectatio*) cannot occur without sin;[188] but coitus cannot occur without pleasure; ergo, etc. Peter replies that Gregory must have been talking about coitus performed to satisfy lust or because of incontinence, which entails at least a venial sin. If the sole intention is to beget children, which is a work that stems from charity (*ex caritate*), then the sexual act itself is meritorious. To be sure, there will be carnal pleasure in the act, which in other circumstances would be a mortal sin, but this is excused by the goods of marriage.[189] Peter's solution presupposes that in evaluating the sexual act one can separate the motive for the act from the pleasure that ensues, although Peter still assumes that the pleasure itself is evil in some sense.

11.6 THE CONTRIBUTIONS OF CANON LAW

Canon law and jurisprudence made several lasting contributions to the theology of marriage during the twelfth century. I have already discussed their contributions to questions about the nuptial process and the function of consummation. Their contributions to three other areas should be noted here: the marriage of unfree persons, marriage and the natural law, and the sacramentality of marriage.

11.6.1 *The marriage of unfree persons*

If "consent makes marriage," it should follow that unfree persons (*servi*) have exactly the same rights to marry as free persons. In fact, canon law and ecclesiastical policy had come around to that position by the end of the twelfth century, after a long period of inconsistency and uncertainty. In the end, everyone agreed that unfree persons had the same right to marry as everyone else because marriage was a sacrament, for there was no distinction between free and unfree persons in the sight of God or in the mystical body of Christ.

The development was complicated because at least three interrelated issues were at stake. First, was a marriage between two unfree persons valid? Second, was a marriage between an unfree person and a free person valid? Third, did unfree

---

[187] Augustine, *Serm.* 162.2, PL 38:887: "Sic enim totus homo absorbetur ab ipso et in ipso corpore, ut jam dici non possit ipse animus suus esse; sed simul totus homo dici possit quod caro sit, et spiritus vadens et non revertens." Augustine is talking about the man who has sex with a prostitute, but he is describing the orgasm, whatever its context: cf. Augustine, *De civ. Dei* XIV.16, CCL 48:438–39. Peter Lombard uses the text in a gloss on 1 Cor. 6:18 (PL 191:1584B): "Sic enim totus homo absorbetur a carne, ut jam dici non possit, ipse animus suus est, sed simul totus homo dici possit caro." I discuss these texts and their reception more fully later (Section 13.1).

[188] *Libellus Responsionum*, = *Epist.* 11.56ª, MGH *Epistolae* 2.3 (= *Gregorii I papae Registrum epistolarum*, vol. 2), 340/19–31. Cf. Walter of Mortagne, *De coniugio* 3 (156A–157A).

[189] Peter of Poitiers, *Sent.* V.15 (1258B–D).

persons need the consent of their owners or seigneurs to marry? The account that follows is designed to highlight only two points: the uncertainty and inconsistency of canon law before Gratian on the marriage of *servi*, and the eventual triumph of an egalitarian theological argument.

The position of classical Roman law had been clear: Neither a slave (*servus*) nor a bondswoman (*ancilla*) could enter into a legitimate marriage with anyone, free or unfree. That did not mean that such a union was forbidden or even frowned upon, but only that it did not amount to marriage. It was merely cohabitation (*contubernium*), and it had no legal consequences.[190] The Christian emperors tempered without fundamentally altering the bar against marriage between *servi* and between free and unfree persons.[191] Slavery remained a distinct category in law during late antiquity, even as it declined in social and economic importance.[192] In reality, slaves were largely superseded during this period by *coloni* – peasants who belonged to an estate in much the same way as buildings, vineyards, and domestic animals did – but although some *coloni* were legally dependent (*alieni iuris*), others were independent (*sui iuris*). The status of *coloni* was distinct from that of *servi* under Roman law, although the distinction was not a feature of medieval law.[193]

Although patristic authors sometimes questioned whether the institution of slavery was compatible with Christianity, they were not consistently or radically opposed to it.[194] The canon *Non omnis mulier*, which was the response of Pope Leo I to Bishop Rusticus of Narbonne (Section 6.2.1), was the chief obstacle in the canonical tradition to the recognition of marriages between free and unfree persons. Using a theological argument to corroborate the position of Roman law, Leo argued that concubinage between a free man and an *ancilla* did not amount to marriage because it failed adequately to conform to the union between Christ and the church. A free man may take an *ancilla* as his legitimate wife only if he first sets her free, and then he should manifest her honor by giving her a dowry and marrying her with public nuptials.[195]

Notwithstanding Leo's ruling, there seems to have been no consistent ecclesiastical policy regarding the marriages of *servi* until the twelfth century. One reason for this uncertainty was the changing and broadening scope of the term *servus*. There were arguably no slaves in the proper sense of the word in northern continental Europe and England after the Carolingian period. Medieval authors who

---

[190] CTh 12.1.6. P. E. Corbett, *Roman Law of Marriage* (Oxford, 1930), 30–39. J. Evans Grubbs, *Law and Family in Late Antiquity* (Oxford, 1995), 261–316.
[191] J. Evans Grubbs, "Marriage more Shameful than Adultery," *Phoenix* 47.2 (1993): 125–54.
[192] C. Whittaker and O. Grabar, "Slavery," in G. W. Bowersock, P. Brown, and O. Grabar (eds.), *Late Antiquity* (Cambridge, Mass., 1999), 698–700.
[193] M. Mirkovic, *The Later Roman Colonate and Freedom* (Philadelphia, 1997).
[194] On patristic attitudes to slavery, see P. Garnsey, *Ideas of Slavery from Aristotle to Augustine* (Cambridge, 1996), 191–243; and P. Freedman, *Images of the Medieval Peasant* (Stanford, 1999), 73–79.
[195] Leo I, *Epist.* 167, inq. 4, PL 54:1204B–1205A.

discussed the marriage of *servi* during the central Middle Ages were thinking chiefly of serfs.[196] These authors assumed that *servi* could marry, but they debated whether they could marry without the consent or against the wishes of their seigneurs. Again, they usually saw no reason in principle why free and unfree persons should not intermarry, but they did worry about the problem of fraud or error, when a free person did not know that the person he or she was marrying was unfree.

The surviving early-medieval canons on these topics failed to present a consistent policy, but they generally upheld the validity and permanence of marriages in which one or both partners was unfree, albeit within certain limits. *Dictum est nobis*, a much-cited canon from the Second Council of Châlons-sur-Saône (813), dealt with seigneurial power over marriages between unfree persons. The canon affirms that a marriage between two servile persons is valid, and it prohibits lords from dissolving such marriages even if the partners belong to two different lords, for "man may not separate what God has joined together" (Matt 19:6). Yet the last line of the canon limits the ruling to "those between whom a legal union has been made with their lords' will."[197] A canon of unknown origin that the canonists ascribed to the Synod of Tribur (895) concerns a husband who had submitted himself to servitude in order to get a divorce. He must have calculated that his loss of status would make his marriage invalid. The ruling prohibits the divorce. It adds that the wife in question need not become servile with her husband, contrary to what secular law decrees, for she married him as a free man, and he became servile without her consent.[198]

Cases of fraud or error entailed more complicated considerations. A somewhat confused canonical text that originated in Julian's *Epitome* explains what should happen in such cases. The argument begins with the principle that marriages between free and unfree persons are not legitimate: "A marriage cannot be contracted between a free man and an *ancilla*, or between a *servus* and a free woman." The prohibition does not apply if the servile person is set free and the marriage is conducted with the proper formalities (as Leo had argued). The text mentions two scenarios involving fraud and error. In one, the lord of an *ancilla* tricks a free man into marrying her. In the other, the lord is not complicit in the initial misunderstanding, but he knows about it and does nothing to prevent it. In both cases, the marriage is valid and the offspring are legitimate because of the special circumstances, despite the fundamental impediment, and the previously servile woman

---

[196] On slavery and serfdom in the Middle Ages, see Freedman, *Images of the Medieval Peasant*, 79–85. On slavery and marriage in southern Europe during the central Middle Ages, see R. M. Karras, *Unmarriages* (Philadelphia, 2012), 80–100.

[197] Canon 30, in Mansi, 14:99. Benedictus Levita, additio III, 54, PL 97:878A. Ivo, *Decretum* VIII.167, XVI.335 (*Panormia* VI.40); *Collectio tripartita* B 29.255. *Dictum est nobis* was inserted into the second recension of Gratian's *Decretum* as C. 29 q. 2 c. 8 (1095).

[198] Ivo, *Decretum* VIII.212 (*Panormia* VI.99). *Collectio tripartita* B 15.76. Inserted into the second recension of Gratian's *Decretum* as C. 29 q. 2 c. 7 (1094–95). On voluntary servitude, see A. Rio, "Self-Sale and Voluntary Entry into Unfreedom, 300–1100," *Journal of Social History* 45.3 (2012): 661–85.

becomes free in the process. In other words, her lord forfeits his power over her.[199] In general, though, ecclesiastical canons treated servile status as material to a marriage contract. The Carolingian canon *Si quis ingenuus* concerns a free man who unwittingly marries an unfree woman. He can try to buy her freedom. If that fails, he may marry another woman if he wishes. Here, the defect lies not in her status *per se* but in his ignorance of it. There is no impediment or grounds for divorce if a free person of either sex *knowingly* marries an unfree person.[200]

Although Pope Leo had based his argument on Scripture and theology, a different line of theological reasoning, which led to an opposite conclusion, became prominent during the central Middle Ages. As Paul says (Gal 3:28), "There is neither Jew nor Greek, there is neither slave nor free, there is neither male nor female, for you are all one in Christ Jesus."[201] This theological premise entered the canonical tradition with the canon *Si quis ancillam*, which was ascribed to Pope Julius, probably because of a scribal error. The canon was originally a ruling that Justinian directed to Julian, the Praetorian Prefect, in AD 530.[202] Justinian's original ruling concerned the man who liberated an *alumna* (foster daughter) in order to marry her. Modern scholarly interpretations of the law vary widely, but it must have pertained to the impropriety or conflict of interest that resulted when a man liberated and married a slave girl whom he had raised in his household in a fatherly manner, as if she had been his daughter.[203] Be that as it may, the word *alumna* in the original text became *ancilla* in the medieval canonical tradition, so that the canon now concerned any free man who freed an unfree woman in his possession in order to marry her. Is their marriage legitimate? The law resolves an "ancient ambiguity" by determining that such marriages will henceforth be legitimate. Because marriage is based on marital affection, and because there is nothing in unions between free and unfree persons that is impious or that flouts other laws, there is no reason to prevent such marriages.[204]

---

[199] *Iuliani epitome*, Const. 36.3, cap. 133. Ivo, *Decretum* VIII.56 (*Panormia* VI.110).

[200] Ivo, *Decretum* VIII.164 (*Panormia* VI.41). Gratian, C. 29 q. 2 c. 4 (1093).

[201] Medieval authors, quoting from memory, often conflate Gal 3:28 with Col 3:11 or Rom 10:12.

[202] CJ 5.4.26.

[203] On *alumni* and *alumnae*, see B. Rawson, "Children in the Roman *Familia*," in B. Rawson (ed.), *The Family in Ancient Rome* (Ithaca, New York, 1986), 170–200, at 173–86.

[204] Burchard, *Decretum* IX.18, PL 140:818A–B: "Si quis ancillam suam libertate donaverit, et in matrimonio sibi sociaverit, dubitabatur apud quosdam utrum hujusmodi nuptiae legitimae esse videantur, an non. Nos itaque vetustam ambiguitatem decidentes talia connubia legitima esse censuimus. Si enim ex affectu fiunt omnes nuptiae, et nihil impium, et legibus contrarium in tali copulatione fieri potest, quare praedictas nuptias inhibendas existimaverimus. Omnibus vobis unus est pater in coelis, et unusquisque dives et pauper, liber et servus, aequaliter pro se, et pro animabus eorum rationem daturi sunt. Quapropter omnibus cujuscunque conditionis sint, unam legem, quantum ad Deum, habere non dubitamus." Ivo, *Decretum* VIII.156 (*Panormia* VI.37). Gratian, C. 29 q. 2 c. 1 (1092–93). Burchard and Ivo attach *Omnibus vobis unus* immediately to *Si quis ancillam*, so that the original canon and its gloss form a single text. Gratian omitted *Si quis ancillam* in the first recension, quoting only the appended gloss, although *Si quis ancillam* was inserted as C. 29 q. 2 c. 3 (1093) in the second recension.

More important than the canon attributed to Pope Julius itself was a theological appendage to it that is reminiscent of Galatians 3:28. It may have originated as a gloss on Justinian's ruling, but it also enjoyed an independent life as the canon *Omnibus vobis unus*, which was transmitted by Burchard and Ivo, and, in modified form, by Gratian. The appendage rejects the very principle that a person's status should affect the legitimacy of his or her marriage, for all human beings are equal before God. Here is a translation of Gratian's version:

> There is one Father in heaven for us all, and every one of us, whether rich or poor, free or slave, is equally going to render an account of himself and of his soul. Accordingly, we do not doubt that all of us, whatever our status, have one law before the Lord. *But if all have one law, then just as a free person cannot be divorced, so also a slave, once he has been united in marriage, cannot be divorced thereafter.*[205]

The final sentence (set here in italics) does not occur in any extant witness before Gratian, who may have added it as his own comment or *dictum*. When read in connection with *Si quis ancillam*, the appendage seemed to apply Paul's theological egalitarianism even to marriages between free and unfree persons. As a decree ascribed to a pope, it belonged squarely in the canon law tradition, embodying Paul's idea in concrete legislation, and it contradicted Leo's opinion.

Ivo's approach to marriages between free and unfree persons seems, nevertheless, to have been inconsistent, or at best difficult to explain and easy to misinterpret. Ivo was generally egalitarian in applying church law. For example, in a letter to William, Archdeacon of Paris, Ivo applies the egalitarian principle to the procedure in a betrothal case. The letter concerns a knight who denied that he had given his daughter to another knight in a betrothal pact. Instead of "tempting God" in a trial by combat, Ivo counsels, the interested parties should bring forward witnesses, and there should be a proper tribunal. Any honest persons who are in a position to give evidence, regardless of their status, should be summoned as witnesses, for "in Christ there is neither slave nor free, and neither male nor female." The secular status of the witnesses is relevant only in "civil and criminal cases," Ivo claims, whereas a decision about a betrothal is a religious matter.[206]

In a letter to John, the bishop of Orléans, Ivo discusses a case of error: A free man had married a girl without knowing that she was an *ancilla*. Ivo contrasts two positions. On one side are both secular law and "the decrees of the fathers," according to which there can be marriage only between free persons of equal standing, and divorce is permissible only in cases of error. On the other side are

---

[205] Gratian, C. 29 q. 2 c. 1 (1093): "Omnibus nobis unus pater est in celis, et unusquisque, diues et pauper, liber et seruus, equaliter pro se et pro animabus eorum rationem reddituri sunt. Quapropter omnes, cuiuscumque condicionis sint, unam legem quantum ad Dominum habere non dubitamus. *Si autem omnes unam legem habent, ergo sicut ingenuus dimitti non potest, sic nec seruus semel coniugio copulatus ulterius dimitti poterit.*" Burchard and Ivo present the canon as a gloss in *Omnibus vobis unus*.
[206] *Epist.* 183, PL 162:184A–184C.

the natural law and Scripture. Ivo is probably thinking of Leo's response to Rusticus when he refers to "the decrees of the fathers," and of Galations 3:28 when he invokes Scripture. His formulation of the egalitarian argument echoes the constitution *Si quis per errorem* from Julian's *Epitome*. It leaves in doubt the validity or invalidity of knowingly mixed marriages, where there is no error. But because "there is neither slave nor free" (Gal 3:28) according to both Scripture and the natural law, Ivo explains, he is not persuaded that such mixed marriages should be dissolved, even in cases of fraud, and he decides that the marriage should be upheld. Ivo suggests that the man might sacrifice his own freedom in a spirit of "conjugal charity" by remaining with the woman as her husband and losing his free status. Failing that, they may suspend conjugal relations. But neither can remarry because the "conjugal sacrament" between them (i.e., the marriage bond) cannot be dissolved.[207]

That seems clear enough, but in a letter to the bishop of Évreux Ivo responds indignantly to the accusation that he has been dissolving marriages between free and unfree persons. He does not deny that he has separated such unions, but he argues that if he did so it was only because they did not really amount to marriage but only to cohabitation (*contubernium*). Ivo cites Leo's letter to Rusticus to show that there is no sacrament of Christ and the church in these supposed marriages. When one partner is in servitude to the other, they cannot fulfill either the "precept of love" (John 13:34) or the golden rule of reciprocity (Matt 7:12). It is true that man may not separate what God has joined (Matt 19:6, Mark 10:10), but it was not God who joined these persons together but man, and their partnership is not spiritual but merely physical. Having defended himself in these general terms, though, Ivo goes on to argue that marriages between free and unfree persons should not be dissolved unless error is involved. No man should separate what God has joined, but it is man, and not God, who joins the partners when there is fraud. If a free man marries an *ancilla* knowing that she is servile, Ivo argues, citing the law *Si quis per errorem*,[208] he cannot divorce her because "consent makes marriage, not coitus." Since he knew about her status when he consented, his consent was authentic.[209] In this case, the consensual principle trumps any theological argument about sacramental freedom. Since he knew about her status when he consented, his consent was authentic.[210]

Prior to Gratian, then, the canonical tradition provided a complicated set of texts and precedents regarding marriages between free and unfree persons, but there had been two crucial achievements. One was a clear distinction between the impediment of status (*condicio*) and that of error, or fraud. Contrary to Leo's opinion, it seemed that a marriage between free and unfree persons was valid unless the free person was unaware of the other's status. The second was a doctrine of equality. Since everyone is equal in the sight of God, a person's status should not in itself be material to the contracting of a Christian marriage, especially if marriage is construed as a sacrament in some sense of the term.

---

[207] *Epist.* 221, PL 162:226B–C.   [208] That is, *Iuliani epitome* 36.3, c. 133.
[209] *Epist.* 242, PL 162:249C–250D.   [210] *Epist.* 242, PL 162:249C–250D.

Gratian definitively articulated the new doctrine. If a free woman *unwittingly* marries a servile man, the marriage is invalid, but only because of the error of status (*error conditionis*), which vitiates consent, for the partners do not agree to the same thing in a material respect. The same is true when there is an error of person (i.e., mistaken identity). Errors regarding the moral quality or the wealth of a partner, on the contrary, do not vitiate consent, for the partners do not fail to agree in any way that is material to their union.[211] If the free partner *knows* that the other is servile when they marry, then the mutual consent is genuine and the marriage is valid. Gratian insists both on the natural equality of all human beings in the sight of God as creatures made in God's image, and on the gratuitous equality of all Christians as members of the church. Inequality of status *per se* is not an impediment, for there is neither Jew nor Greek, neither slave nor free in Jesus Christ (Gal 3:28). To corroborate this argument, Gratian quotes the canon *Omnibus vobis unus* (discussed earlier), ascribed to Pope Julius.[212] Gratian bolsters the argument with another text from Paul, whereby a woman may "marry whom she wills, only in the Lord" (1 Cor 7:39).[213] Paul was speaking of a widow's right to remarry, but Gratian ignores the context.

Pope Hadrian IV's decretal *Dignum est*, issued in 1155, would become the definitive statement of the theological argument. Hadrian rules that unfree persons are free to marry even against the wishes of their lords. He gives two reasons. First, there is neither bond nor free in Jesus Christ. Second, since no one may deny the sacraments to *servi*, no one may prevent them from marrying, for marriage is one of the sacraments.[214] This position was contested, but it inevitably became established as the doctrine of the church.[215] Bonaventure attributes the freedom of *servi* to participate freely in the sacrament of marriage to "new law" (*ius novum*), that is, to decretal law. Bonaventure explicates and endorses Hadrian's argument.[216]

11.6.2 Marriage and the natural law

Marriage had long been counted as part of the natural law, and canonists during the second half of the twelfth century began to reflect seriously on what that premise implied or entailed. Ulpian had cited marriage as an example in a text that was

---

[211] C. 29 q. 1 (1091–92).   [212] C. 29 q. 2 c. 1 (1092–93).

[213] C. 29 q. 2 dictum ante c. 1 (1092). See also C. 31 q. 2 dictum ante c. 1 (1112–13), where Gratian cites Ambrosiaster on 1 Cor 7:39 (CSEL 81.2, 90/13–14) to establish a daughter's right to consent or dissent to her marriage.

[214] X 4.9.1 (691–92). See P. Landau, "Hadrians IV. Decretale Dignum est (X 4.9.1) und die Eheschließung Unfreier in der Diskussion von Kanonisten und Theologen des 12. und 13. Jahrhunderts," *Studia Gratiana* 12 (1967): 511–53.

[215] A. Sahaydachny Bocarius, "The Marriage of Unfree Persons," in P. Landau (ed.), *De iure canonico Medii Aevi,* = *Studia Gratiana* 27 (1996): 483–506.

[216] Bonaventure, IV *Sent.* 36.1.1, arg. 1c (4:792a): "Ad Galatas tertio [28]: *In Christo Iesu non est servus neque liber*: ergo nec quantum ad Sacramenta Christi et Ecclesiae est distinctio servi et liberi; ergo nec in matrimonio." Ibid., resp.: "Dicendum, quod secundum ius novum conditio servitutis non impedit matrimonium, etiam domino contradicente...."

seminal for the treatment of natural law in general. Both Ulpian's own account and the divergent traditions to which it gave rise included several puzzling features and inconsistencies, which provided medieval scholars with much food for thought. A distinction, sometimes amounting to a tension, between two natural powers runs through this topic: human reason, and the animal or sensory appetite of human beings, presumed to be inherently promiscuous. The ensuing developments were mainly canonical and occurred largely within the literature of canon law during the twelfth century. Theologians took up the inquiry into the natural law of marriage during the thirteenth century and greatly elaborated and deepened it.

In the full text, which is preserved in the *Digest*, Ulpian divides law (*ius*) into three categories: the natural law, the law of the peoples (*ius gentium*), and civil law.[217] The part of this text that describes the natural law occurs also in the *Institutes*.[218] Whereas civil law is peculiar to Rome (or to any particular state or people), the law of races or peoples (*gentes*) is common to all human beings, and the natural law belongs to all animals. Marriage, with the begetting and rearing of children, belongs to the natural law:

> The natural law [*ius naturale*] is what nature has taught to all animals, for this law is not proper to human kind but is common to all animals: those that belong to the land and to the sea, and birds as well. From this is derived [*descendit*] the joining of male and female [*coniunctio maris atque feminae*], which we call marriage, from this the procreation of children, from this their rearing. For we see that the other animals, even the wild ones, are experts in this law.[219]

Irrational animals do not marry, but what we call marriage when it occurs among human beings is a union that occurs *mutatis mutandis* among most animals.

Ulpian's threefold division is unusual. Gaius, in another text preserved in the *Digest*, divides law more conventionally into two categories: the law of the peoples (*ius gentium*) and civil law (*ius civile*). Gaius characterizes the former as "that which natural reason has constituted among all peoples."[220] Whereas Ulpian attributes the natural law to all animals, Gaius implies that the law of the peoples *is* the natural law, that is, the law that is common to all peoples because it is innate in human reason.

Medieval scholars were familiar with Ulpian's opinion and cited it frequently, but they were also familiar with a text from Isidore's *Etymologies*, which Gratian incorporated into the treatise on laws with which he begins the *Decretum*.[221] Isidore in effect combines the opinions of Ulpian and Gaius. He divides the law into three sorts, as Ulpian did: natural law, civil law, and the law of the peoples (*gentes*), but

---

[217] *Dig.* 1.1.1.2–4.   [218] *Inst.* 1.2, pr.   [219] *Dig.* 1.1.1.3.

[220] *Dig.* 1.1.1.9. Compare the binary distinction between natural law and civil law in *Dig.* 1.1.1.11 (Paulus).

[221] Isidore, *Etym.* V.4.1. Gratian, D. 1 cc. 6–7 (2). The *ius gentium* (*Etym.* V.6, D. 1 c. 9) pertains to advanced civic life and to the laws regulating interactions between peoples.

then he defines the natural law as that which is common to all nations (*nationes*), adding that it is maintained everywhere "by an instinct of nature [*instinctus naturae*], not by any constitution." He goes on to cite examples. These include not only the "joining of male and female" and the raising of children, but also the universal freedom of all human beings to enjoy the fruits of the air, the land, and the sea, the right to recover something entrusted to another, and the right of self-defense, for all these things are naturally just and equal:

> The natural law is common to all nations, because it is maintained everywhere by the instinct of nature and not by any constitution, such as the joining of a man and a woman [*coniunctio viri et feminae*], the begetting and rearing of children, the common possession of all things and single liberty of all, the acquisition of whatever is taken from the sky, the earth, and the sea, as well as the return of property that has been entrusted or of money deposited, and the repulsion of violence by force. For this, and whatever is like it, is never unjust but is held to be natural and equitable.[222]

Gratian's version became the *locus classicus* for discussions of the natural law by the canonists, who associated the natural law with innate human reason, although they were familiar with Ulpian's idea of a law common to all animals, and they sometimes considered Gratian's text in the light of Ulpian's.

Ulpian's original text was a *locus classicus* among the civilians. They retained the idea that the natural law was what nature taught to all animals, and they sometimes identified nature with God, who gives all things their particular natures. At the same time, they sometimes differentiated between nature as a universal principle and Isidore's *instinctus naturae*, identifying the latter with pre-rational, sensual impulses, such as St Paul's "law in my members" (Rom 7:23) or the Stoics' *propatheiai*. One reason for this differentiation was their observation, first made by Placentius, that the phrase "*quod natura omnia animalia docuit*" could be construed in two ways: either with *quod* in the accusative case and *natura* in the nominative, so that it meant "what nature has taught to all animals"; or with *quod* in the nominative case and *natura* in the ablative, so that it meant "that which was taught to all animals by nature," that is, through the instinct of nature.[223] According to the latter interpretation, the natural law regulates through a blind but purposeful force that God has providentially implanted in all animals, such as the instinctive urge to copulate that results in procreation.

The canonists, on the contrary, were inclined to identify the natural law not with universal, pre-rational instincts but with an innate and inalienable volition in human reason to do good and shun evil. According to Rufinus, for example, the civilians construe the natural law as what nature has taught to all animals, but the canonists do not care for such generality, reasoning instead that the natural law is peculiar to human beings. Rufinus defines the natural law as "a certain natural

---

[222] *Etym.* V.4.1. Gratian, D. 1 c. 7 (2)
[223] See R. A. Greene, "Instinct of Nature," *Journal of the History of Ideas* 58.2 (1997): 173–98, at 177–79.

power implanted in the human creature to do good and avoid the contrary."[224] Simon of Bisignano, likewise, characterizes the natural law as "a power of the mind" (*vis mentis*). This law cannot be the love (*caritas*) that motivates human beings do good and avoid evil, as some say, because such love is not universal. Nor can it be the underlying power of free choice (*liberum arbitrium*), since that is indifferent, being equally inclined to good and to evil. Instead, Simon concludes, it must be what Jerome called synderesis: the inextinguishable sense of the good that is the uppermost power of the soul.[225] The canonists sometimes retained Ulpian's notion of a natural law that nature teaches to all animals, but they regarded this sense of the term as secondary.

Granting that the natural law included the "union of a man and a woman," the canonists inquired into what kind of union that was. Did the natural law include illicit joining, such as fornication? As regards marriage, was the joining in question that of wills (*coniunctio animorum*, i.e., mutual consent) or that of bodies (i.e., coitus or consummation)? Perhaps the union of wills belonged to the natural law of reason, whereas the joining of bodies belonged to the natural law that regulated all animals. Canonists sometimes identified the instinct of nature with animal appetites. Again, they asked whether marriage belonged to the natural law as a matter of precept or in some weaker manner.[226]

According to Huguccio, the "union of a man and a woman" is not so much a part of the natural law as an effect of it.[227] That is why Ulpian says that marriage is derived (*descendit*) from the natural law. The union in question is primarily that of wills (*coniunctio animorum*), and not carnal union, for the former alone can be identified with marriage. The natural law from which marriage is derived is not the law that nature has taught to all animals. Rather, it belongs to reason. Reason dictates that a man should take a wife only for the sake of procreation or to avoid incontinence. Adam articulated this law when he said, "this is bone of bones," and so forth (Gen 2:23). The law that Paul invoked when he said that every man should have his own wife (1 Cor 7:2) was divine or evangelical, but it was an application of the same natural law. Marrying was a precept of the natural law in the beginning, for God commanded Adam and Eve to "increase and multiply" (Gen 1:28), and he repeated the command after the Flood (Gen 9:1). That said, the "union of a man and a woman" may be understood as sexual intercourse within marriage, which obeys both the sensual "instinct of nature" and human reason. As an animal, a man has a natural pre-rational urge to have sex with a woman. A man's natural reason tells him

---

[224] Rufinus, *Summa* on D. 1, pr., ed. Singer, p. 6. Also in R. Weigand, *Die naturrechtslehre der Legisten und Dekretisten* (Munich, 1967), p. 144, nos 236–37. Rufinus flourished from c. 1150 and completed his *Summa* on Gratian's *Decretum* c. 1164,

[225] Weigand, *Die naturrechtslehre*, pp. 173–73, nos 292–97. Simon of Bisignano taught canon law at Bologna during the 1170s and completed his Summa on Gratian's *Decretum* in the late 1170s.

[226] Weigand, *Die naturrechtslehre*, pp. 285–384.

[227] Huguccio (d. 1210) completed his *Summa* on Gratian's *Decretum* in the late 1180s.

that coitus can be only for the sake of procreation or to render the debt, and that sex for any other end is against the natural law.[228]

11.6.3 *Rufinus and Huguccio on marriage as a sacrament*

Rufinus and Huguccio were more interested in theological questions than most of the Bolognese canonists after Gratian, and both appropriated ideas from theologians such as Hugh of Saint-Victor and Peter Lombard. When one compares them with the main stream of Parisian theology, however, their theological reflections can seem eccentric. Rufinus prefers to use the term "sacrament" to refer not to marriage as a sign but to what it signified: the mystery, or "sacred secret," that is veiled under the outward appearances. Marriage is a *figura* of this sacrament, according to Rufinus, which is hidden (*latet*) under marriage. This idea reflects an Isidorean concept of sacraments that was current during the first half of the twelfth century but had largely fallen out of use among theologians by the end of the century. Isidore derives the word *sacramentum* both from *secretum* and from *sacer* ("holy"), explaining that "a divine virtue very secretly brings about the salutary effect under the covering of corporeal realities."[229] The term *sacramentum* seems to connote a permanent joining or union in Rufinus's mind, and that sense best describes the union between Christ and the church. But by saying that this divine union is hidden under human marriage, Rufinus seems to suggest that it is somehow present in marriage: a notion that Huguccio will reject as regards the insoluble union between Christ and the church while retaining it as regards the union between God and the soul.

Citing Ephesians 5:31–32 and the canon *Cum societas nuptiarum*, ascribed to Pope Leo I, Rufinus argues that two sacraments are signified in marriage: the soul's union with God, and the union between Christ incarnate and the church, which is the "great sacrament" of Ephesians 5:32:

> just as in marriage there are two things, namely, the betrothal and sexual intercourse [*commixtio carnis*], so also two sacraments arise there: one in the betrothal, and the other in sexual intercourse. The sacrament of the soul and God is represented in the betrothal, so that, just as at that point the *sponsa* is joined to the *sponsa* by consent, so also may the soul be understood to be joined to God through the relationship of love.... But the sacrament of Christ and the church lies hidden [*latet*] under sexual intercourse, so that, in the same way as a man is made one flesh with his wife, so also we may believe that Christ became one flesh and one person with the church in the Virgin's womb.[230]

---

[228] Huguccio, *Summa* on D. 1 c. 7, in Weigand, *Die naturrechtslehre*, pp. 290–91, nos 494–97.

[229] Isidore, *Etym.* VI.19.40. See D. van den Eynde, *Les définitions des sacrements* (Rome, 1950), 175–77, on the twelfth-century use of this definition.

[230] Rufinus, *Summa decretorum* on C. 27 q. 2, ed. Singer, pp. 441–42.

The betrothal (*desponsatio*), as a union of wills, represents the sacrament of the soul's union with God. The subsequent "mingling of flesh" (*carnis commixtio*) represents the joining of Christ and the church as one flesh and one person in the Virgin's womb.

Rufinus posits this figurative meaning to explain why *matrimonium intitiatum* is separable on certain grounds whereas *matrimonium consummatum* is inseparable. The sacrament of the soul and God is violable and impermanent, for the soul may fall into apostasy, whereas the great sacrament of Christ and the church is insoluble. The incarnation is never undone, and nothing separates the church from Christ. Just as one of the two sacraments signified in marriage is separable whereas the other inseparable, therefore, so also one of the *figurae* is soluble and the other insoluble:

> But because the first sacrament can be violated (for a soul that was close to God often apostatizes from God), it is not unfitting [*non inmerito*] that its figure, namely, the betrothal, even when it has been initiated between legitimate persons, should also be broken when certain causes arise. But the sacrament of Christ and the church is entirely unbreakable, for as soon as Christ assumed a human being, he never set him aside nor ever will. And marriage, therefore, becomes so rooted in the sign of that [sacrament] — namely, in sexual intercourse performed legitimately between legitimate persons — that it can never be uprooted as long as the other is alive, regardless of whatever might strike at it.[231]

Rufinus does not pretend to demonstrate through signification that consummation makes marriage insoluble. Instead, he offers an argument from signification to explain why consummation makes marriage insoluble. His argument is designed not to prove that the rule exists, but to show why the rule is fitting.

Rufinus extends the argument to show why a marriage between illegitimate partners or between unbelievers is not *ratum*. In both cases, the marriage fails to conform qualitatively to its archetype. If sexual intercourse would be illegitimate between the spouses, the "sacrament of Christ and the church" would not be present in their marriage even if they consummated it.[232] Again, when Augustine says that the sacrament of marriage is common to all peoples whereas the sanctity of the sacrament is present only "in the city of God,"[233] the term "sacrament" does not denote the signified sacred reality (*res sacra*) in marriage but rather marriage itself, inasmuch as marriage has the potential to be a sacramental sign of "holy joining," for it is not that among all people. The signified reality – the sacrament of Christ and the church – "is not [present] in the marriage of unbelievers and is not represented there."[234]

---

[231] Ibid., 442.   [232] Ibid.

[233] In fact, as explained earlier (Section 9.5.3), this dictum was creatively extracted from Augustine by the *magistri moderni*. See *Cum omnia sacramenta I*, ed. Bliemetzrieder, 139/9–11; *Cum omnia sacramenta II*, ed. Bliemetzrieder, 276/48–49; and Hugh of Saint-Victor, *De sacramentis* 2.11.8, PL 176:496B.

[234] Rufinus on C. 27 q. 2, 442–43.

Notwithstanding his attribution of a special, figurative sanctity to Christian marriage, Rufinus seems to adopt the conventional twelfth-century opinion that marriage does not confer sacramental grace – at least where sexual union is concerned. In general, each of the sacraments of the New Law not only signifies a special grace but also contains or causes it. Matrimony alone, although it belongs among those sacraments and is even chief among them in some respects,[235] signifies through sexual intercourse a holy reality that it does not cause, for a "law of turpitude" gets in the way. In that respect, at least, marriage is a not an effective sign of the joining between Christ and the church but only a representative sign, like the sacrifices of the Old Law.[236]

Huguccio adapted Rufinus's rationale to explain why a marriage formed by *de praesenti* consent is still soluble before consummation but insoluble after it. Huguccio's way of formulating this rationale is both more precise and less cautious than Rufinus's. One and the same marriage signifies two things after the consummation, according to Huguccio, whereas it signifies only one thing before consummation. It is not sexual intercourse *per se* that is the signifier but rather marriage itself after sexual intercourse has occurred:

> Note that matrimony is a sacrament of two things and signifies two things. Once the betrothal has taken place, matrimony signifies the joining [*coniunctio*] of a faithful person to God through faith and charity. When carnal intercourse occurs, it signifies the joining of Christ and the church through [the common] nature, a joining that occurred in the Virgin's womb. In this way, therefore, marriage signifies one thing alone before carnal intercourse, and afterwards, when carnal intercourse occurs, it does not cease to signify that, but it signifies something else as well.[237]

According to Huguccio, the sacrament of marriage is not the transient act of forming a marriage but the ensuing marriage, or the marriage bond. It is not the act of mutual consent that is the sacrament of the union between the soul to God, as Peter Lombard held, for that act is transient. Nor is sexual intercourse *per se* a sacrament of the union between Christ and the church, for in that case there would be as many sacraments in marriage as there were acts of coitus.[238]

Huguccio rejected Gratian's consummation theory and adopted instead a version of the Parisian theory, with the distinction between *de futuro* and *de praesenti* betrothals. Nevertheless, he retained Rufinus's theory about the significance of consummation, adapting it to show that whereas a *de praesenti* betrothal is soluble on certain grounds before consummation, especially entry into the religious life, consummated marriage is entirely insoluble:

---

[235] Presumably in the sublimity of what it signifies.   [236] Rufinus, on C. 4 q. 2 c. 3, 481.

[237] Huguccio, *Summa* on C. 27 q. 2, *Non pertinet at matrimonium*, in J. Roman, "Summa d'Huguccio sur … *Causa XXVII, Questio II*," *Revue historique de droit français et étranger*, 2nd series 27 (1903): 715–805, at 764.

[238] Ibid., 765. Similarly, Huguccio argues that the good of *proles* cannot be offspring *per se*, or there would be as many goods as there are children. Instead, it is the hope and intention of begetting children and raising them to worship God (*Ex peccato*, 758).

because [*quia*] the intercourse [*commixtio*] of the faithful soul with God is often violated when the soul recedes from God through sin, therefore [*ideo*] matrimony is often broken before carnal intercourse when one of the spouses passes over to religion. But because [*quia*] the joining of Christ and the church is inseparable, for the human being that has been assumed cannot be separated from Christ, therefore [*ideo*] matrimony is entirely inseparable after sexual intercourse as a sign of that reality....[239]

Whereas Rufinus says that it is not unfitting (*non immerito*) that the sign has the same solubility as the signified, Huguccio, by using the strong idiom *quia ... ideo* ("because ... therefore"), implies that there is a necessary causal connection.

Huguccio is keen to show that marriage is a single, simple thing. One is either unmarried or married. There is no such thing as *matrimonium initiatum*, therefore, for, like every other sacrament, marriage is something entirely non-complex: a *res simplicissima*.[240] One may posit two sacraments in marriage in a loose sense, inasmuch as there are two significations, for marriage signifies only the union of the faithful soul to God in faith and charity before coitus, whereas it also signifies the union of the church to Christ in unity of nature after coitus. But the addition of a new signification does not generate a new sacrament, for the addition of a significa-tion does not multiply the sign. Instead, the sacrament takes on a new aspect. For example, numerically the same baptismal water signifies nothing sacred before it is consecrated but signifies redemption from sin after it has been consecrated.[241]

Correcting Rufinus, Huguccio argues that marriage primarily signifies the two unions absolutely, and not as if these divine relations somehow existed between the human spouses. Obviously, the union between Christ and the church cannot exist between any two spouses, for it had already occurred in the Virgin's womb before any Christians were married.[242] That said, the union of faith and charity by which the soul is joined to God *is* present in a marriage between good Christian spouses, whereas it is *not* present in other marriages. That is what Augustine meant, Huguc-cio argues, when he said that the sacrament of marriage was common to all peoples, whereas the sanctity of the sacrament was present only in the city of God. The sanctity to which Augustine referred is the presence in the spouses of what the sacrament of marriage signifies.[243] In this respect, Huguccio seems to have success-fully articulated what Hugh of Saint-Victor had left implicit.

[239] Ibid., *In omni*, 765.   [240] Ibid., *Cum initiatur*, 754.
[241] Ibid., *Non pertinet ad matrimonium*, 764.   [242] Ibid.   [243] Ibid., *In omni*, 764–65.

PART IV

The thirteenth and fourteenth centuries

Development of the classical doctrine

12

Marriage as union

The prelates at Trent in the sixteenth century presupposed a well-established doctrine of marriage as a sacrament. The doctrine had emerged in the schools during a long century lasting from the last decade of the twelfth century through the 1330s,[1] but its main features were already present in Thomas Aquinas's commentary on the *Sentences*, composed in the 1250s. Peter of Tarentaise and Richard de Mediavilla, writing in the 1260s and the 1280s, respectively, presented the doctrine as something settled and well understood, complete with its standard and predictable equipment of explanations, objections, and solutions.

At the core of this classical doctrine was the premise that marriage was properly and univocally one of the seven sacraments of the New Law, exemplifying in its own specific ways the essential features of the genus. Central to that core was the thesis that Christian marriage like the other sacraments of the New Law conferred sacramental grace *ex opere operato*. But this aspect of the doctrine was not widely known and did not have the status of a teaching of the church until the late thirteenth century at the earliest, and probably for much longer. Nevertheless, it was the logical conclusion of the premise that marriage was one of the seven sacraments, for the power to confer *ex opere operato* the grace that a sacrament signified was the chief feature distinguishing the genus.

12.1.1 *Phases and literature*

The development of the classical doctrine may be roughly divided into three periods, although such divisions are always somewhat artificial: first, a period of exploration, from Peter the Chanter to William of Auxerre; second, a period of

---

[1] Le Bras, "Mariage," 2165, calls this period the *grande époque* in matrimonial theology and canon law.

elaboration, from Alexander of Hales to Richard de Mediavilla; third, a period of consolidation with some fresh debate and controversy as new problems emerged, from Duns Scotus to Peter of La Palu.

12.1.1.1 *The period of exploration*

Theologians who contributed to the exploratory period include Peter the Chanter, Stephen Langton, Praepositinus, Guy of Orchelles, and William of Auxerre.

Peter the Chanter (d. 1197) taught in Paris from the early 1170s. His so-called *Summa* is a compilation of questions that he disputed while he was Cantor of Notre Dame: a position that he held from 1183 until he became a canon and the dean of Reims in 1196. Among the notable scholars who belonged to his circle in Paris were Robert Courson, Thomas of Chobham, and Jacques de Vitry.[2] We know something of Peter's opinions on marriage, but only indirectly: chiefly through Robert Courson, who included a treatise on marriage in his *Summa* and mentioned there what Peter had taught. Peter the Chanter and his followers developed a distinctive field of Christian ethics, focusing on pastoral, confessional, canonical, and ecclesiastical topics. Peter's most important work, the *Verbum abbreviatum*, is a guide to ecclesiastical practices and morals for the Parisian clergy. Work of this sort, which seems to have dominated the theology school in Paris for a brief period around the end of the twelfth century, stands somewhat apart from the main tradition of systematic scholastic theology, which from the second quarter of the thirteenth century would be based on the framework of Peter Lombard's *Sentences*. Other works in the broad genre of practical clerical manuals include the *Compilatio quaestionum theologiae* by Master Martinus (c. 1200), although Martinus was more concerned with questions of canon law than Peter the Chanter had been.[3]

Stephen Langton was a master of theology in Paris from around 1180 until 1206, when Pope Innocent III summoned him to Rome. Innocent appointed him archbishop of Canterbury later in that year, and he was consecrated in 1207, but English resistance prevented him from being installed until 1213. Langton's *Quaestiones theologiae* includes a treatise on the sacrament of marriage.[4] This treatise is not a

---

[2]   See J. W. Baldwin, *Masters, Princes, and Merchants* (Princeton, 1970). See also J. W. Baldwin, *The Language of Sex* (Chicago, 1994), 1–3, for a brief sketch of the Chanter and his circle. The Cantor was responsible for the education of the choirboys, although Peter may have delegated that task to others. See J. W. Baldwin, *Masters, Princes, and Merchant*, 1:3–16, on Peter the Chanter, and 1:13–14 on his *Summa*.

[3]   See J. A. Hall, *The Sacraments in the Compilatio questionum theologie of Magister Martinus* (dissertation, Notre Dame, 2010), 164–69, on the canonical emphasis of the *Compilatio*, which Hall regards as belonging to the "literature of pastoral care."

[4]   On the textual problems surrounding Langton's *Quaestiones*, which are extant in several different configurations, see R. Quinto, "La constitution du texte des *Quaestiones theologiae*," in L.-J. Bataillon et al., *Étienne Langton* (Turnhout, 2010), 525–62. I rely here on two manuscript sources: Cambridge, St. John's College, MS 57 (C.7); and Oxford, Bodleian Library, MS Lyell 42.

record of a single disputation but rather a series of questions, each of which is briefly outlined before Langton states his succinct answer. Langton presumably based his *Quaestiones theologiae* on his teaching in Paris, but he probably continued to work on them after he had become archbishop, especially during his periods of exile from England.[5] Some of Langton's ideas about marriage may be traceable to the Chanter, with whom he must have been personally acquainted in Paris, but his approach to the subject was more in the tradition of Peter Lombard. Langton was not afraid of applying to marriage the highly technical, philosophically informed modes of analysis that were beginning to emerge in the schools of Paris, with close attention to grammar and logic.

The treatments of marriage by Praepositinus of Cremona (d. 1210), Guy of Orchelles, and William of Auxerre (d. 1231) comprise a group or family inasmuch as Guy drew upon Praepositinus, and William drew in turn upon both Guy and Praepositinus. The three treatments share many points in common, although William's is by far the most extensive and detailed. Praepositinus was Chancellor in Paris 1206–1209. His *Summa theologica*, which follows the layout of Peter Lombard's *Sentences*, must have been in part the fruit of lectures that he gave in Paris from around 1190. He was appointed *Scholasticus* of Mainz in 1194. The official duty of the *Scholasticus* was to educate boys in the liberal arts, but Praepositinus seems to have continued to work on his *Summa*, perhaps even into the last year of his life. The third and fourth books are less extensive than the first two, and Praepositinus confesses in Book IV that he is cutting his treatment of marriage short because he is short of time.[6] Praepositinus advanced the new, highly technical approach to marriage with which Langton had experimented, applying the latest analytical techniques emerging in the schools.

Guy's *Summa de sacramentis et officiis ecclesiae* dates from around 1220 (or perhaps a little earlier), when he was a master in Paris as well as a canon of Meaux. Little is known about Guy's life, and the paucity both of records that mention him and of surviving manuscripts of his *Summa* indicate that he was only a minor figure during his day. He was much less adventurous in analytical method than either Praepositinus or William of Auxerre. Nevertheless, William drew extensively on Guy's *Summa* when he composed the fourth book of his highly own influential *Summa aurea*.[7]

William of Auxerre taught in Paris from around 1210 until his death in 1231, and he was a leading figure in the life of the university. He composed his *Summa*,

---

[5] On Langton's life and work and his relationship with Peter the Chanter, see Baldwin, *Masters, Princes, and Merchants*, 1:25–31.

[6] Praepositinus, *Summa theologica* IV (*de sacramentis et de novissimis*), ed. Pilarczyk, p. 113: "Et haec sufficiant de matrimonio quia tempus scribendi non habemus."

[7] See the introduction to Guy of Orchelles, *Tractatus de sacramentis ex eius Summa de sacramentis et officiis ecclesiae*, ed. D. and O. Van den Eynde (St. Bonaventure, NY, 1953), p. XLI.

posthumously dubbed "Golden," in the 1220s, most likely between 1222 and 1225.[8] William was familiar with Peter Lombard's work, but he did not comment on the *Sentences*. In fact, he was the last major theologian to write before the adoption of the *Sentences* as the standard textbook of theology.

Throughout this exploratory period, theologians counted marriage among the seven sacraments of the church while assuming, with their twelfth-century predecessors, that it did not exemplify some of the salient features that distinguished the sacraments of the New Law in general from those of the Old, most importantly the power to confer sacramental grace. They held that marriage was a preventive remedy, which obviated certain sins without sanctifying the soul or conferring any positive gift (*donum*). The preventive model remained unquestioned even in the highly technical mode of theology that flourished in Paris from the last decade of the twelfth century until around 1220.

12.1.1.2 *The period of elaboration*

Theologians who contributed to the doctrine's elaboration include Alexander of Hales, William of Auvergne, Albertus Magnus, Bonaventure, Thomas Aquinas, Peter of Tarentaise, and Richard de Mediavilla.

Our chief witnesses to the teaching of Alexander of Hales on marriage are his commentary on Peter Lombard's *Sentences*, known as the *Glossa*,[9] and his disputed questions on marriage and divorce.[10] These so-called disputed questions are really treatises assembled from several disputations, not always consistently. The *Glossa* and the disputed questions on marriage belong to the period after Alexander had been appointed as a master of theology in Paris around 1220 but before he joined the Franciscan Order in 1236. Alexander probably completed the *Glossa* after 1220 but before 1227.[11]

Although Alexander's *Glossa* and disputed questions testify to the originality and intellectual vigor for which he was justly famous during his lifetime, the texts that have come down to us are problematic and sometimes vexing. The commentary has

---

[8] See Ribaillier's general introduction in William of Auxerre, *Summa aurea* (Paris and Rome, 1985), p. 16.

[9] On the manuscript tradition, style, and modern rediscovery of the *Glossa*, see H. P. Weber, "The *Glossa in IV libros Sententiarum* by Alexander of Hales," in P. W. Rosemann, *Medieval Commentaries on the* Sentences *of Peter Lombard*, vol. 2 (Leiden, 2010), 79–110. On Alexander's life and work, see K. B. Osborne, "Alexander of Hales," in K. B. Osborne (ed.), *The History of Franciscan Theology* (St. Bonaventure, NY, 1994), 1–38. On the date of the *Glossa*, see the editorial prolegomena to Alexander of Hales, *Glossa in quatuor libros Sententiarum* (Quaracchi, 1951), 110*–116*, and K. F. Lynch, "A *Terminus ante quem* for the Commentary of Alexander of Hales," *Franciscan Studies* 10 (1950): 46–68.

[10] *Quaestiones disputatae 'antequam esset frater'* (Quaracchi, 1960), vol. 2, Q. 57, *De matrimonio* (pp. 1096–1127), and Q. 59, *De repudio et divortio* (pp. 1158–81).

[11] The *Glossa* was dependent on William of Auxerre's *Summa aurea* but predated both the *Decretals* of Gregory IX and Hugh of Saint-Cher's commentary on the *Sentences*.

survived in three different versions.[12] The fact that some manuscripts refer to the work not as a *glossa* but as a *lectura* suggests that it was supposed to be a more or less verbatim record (*reportatio*) of Alexander's lectures on the Sentences. It was not a *scriptum*, therefore: a version revised by the author for publication.[13] But the commentary as it has come down to us is often jumbled and inconsistent and seems to have resulted from the haphazard editing or compilation of material collected on different occasions. Different analyses of the same issue appear in close proximity to each other. The disputed questions are generally more internally coherent, but they are often at odds with the *Glossa*.

Alexander is thought to have been responsible for assigning Peter Lombard's *Sentences* as the textbook for students studying theology in Paris, and this practice soon became the norm wherever theology was studied at an academic level, including the mendicant *studia*. Henceforth, bachelors and lectors in theology were required to teach the *Sentences* as part of their formal training, and a newly graduated master would often begin his career by editing his commentary for publication. Although masters were free respectfully to disagree with the Lombard, the array, division, and organization of topics of the *Sentences* became standard.

Alexander was a pivotal figure in a new approach to marriage as one of the seven sacraments. Theologians now regarded marriage as being properly one of the seven sacraments of the New Law, and they strove to apply to marriage a unified theory of the seven sacraments. They analyzed the sacramental composition of marriage, especially its matter and form and the agency by which the form was applied to the matter, and they reasoned that marriage conferred sacramental grace *ex opere operato*. The doctrine of marital grace gained acceptance during the second quarter of the thirteenth century and was a matter of established consensus among scholastic theologians, albeit not among the canonists, by around 1260.

The reasons for this development are not obvious, but two contributing factors are probable. First, thirteenth-century theologians embraced a less pessimistic, more accepting view of sexual intercourse and sexual pleasure within marriage than their predecessors had done, although they continued to maintain both that consecrated celibacy was a higher calling and that carnal pleasure was a bad motive for coitus. Second, they were now more inclined to regard marriage as a vocation in its own right rather than as a moral safety net for those too weak to pursue celibacy. One sign of that change is the assumption that the celibate vocations conferred a *stronger* remedy against concupiscence than marriage did.[14] The old remedial model was no longer adequate to account for the moral efficacy of marriage. These modulations are apparent, too, in the decline of the

---

[12] Weber, "*Glossa*," 86.   [13] Ibid., 90.

[14] Bonaventure, *IV Sent.* 26.2.2, ad 2 (*Opera omnia*, Quaracchi, 4:668b–69a): "in matrimonium datur gratia ad remedium, sed in voto [religionis] disponitur anima, ut gratia detur ad perfectius remedium." Likewise, Thomas, *IV Sent.* 26.2.3, ad 3 (Vivès 11:74b); Richard de Mediavilla, *IV Sent.* 26.2.3, ad 3 (Brescia edition, 4:405b).

Augustinian notion that the "avoidance of fornication" (*evitatio fornicationis*) was the primary motive that justified marriage in a Christian context.

Although William of Auvergne happens to belong within this second period chronologically, he stands apart from progress toward doctrinal definition and consensus. When compared with near-contemporaries in Paris such as William of Auxerre and Alexander of Hales, William of Auvergne seems to have occupied a different intellectual world. He was a master of theology at Notre Dame in Paris by 1223, remaining in that position until he became the bishop of Paris in 1228,[15] and he was keenly attentive to new currents of thought, but he employed an idiosyncratic method of writing and inquiry that owed little to current practice in the schools. He did not articulate his discourse through division and subdivision, and his way of arguing is not typical of what we now regard as "scholastic method." Although he sometimes poses questions and responds to them, he prefers to present a barrage of discrete arguments for his own position, introducing each with the word *amplius* ("furthermore"). His writing is loosely constructed and sometimes difficult to follow, albeit perhaps in part because of our dependence on the faulty Paris edition of 1674.[16] Nevertheless, a sharp and discerning intellect is apparent in the midst of William's bluster and colorful rhetoric, and if one can get past his prejudices and animosities, which were probably normal during his period (albeit offensive to modern sensibilities), one finds a conscientious pastor-scholar.

Although William of Auvergne was familiar with current developments in the schools, he writes above all as a bishop with cure of souls. It was his practical experience as a cleric that led him to conclude that marriage conferred grace only by virtue of the blessing of a priest, which elevated marriage to the level of the other sacraments. Absent that blessing, marriage was a sacrament in some sense, but not in the fullest sense. When William's name appears in treatments of marriage after the thirteenth century, it is almost always as that of the first exponent of the theory that conjugal grace depends on the priestly blessing.

William of Auvergne's treatise on marriage is part of a treatise on the seven sacraments, which in turn is one of the main divisions of his *Magisterium divinale et sapientiale*: the encyclopedic *summa* on which he worked from the early 1220s until around 1240.[17] Although William touches on most of the issues that would

---

[15] N. Valois, *Guillaume d'Auvergne, Évêque de Paris* (Paris, 1880) is still indispensible because of its scope. For a representative sampling of current interest in William, see F. Morenzoni and J.-Y. Tilliette (eds.), *Autour de Guillaime d'Auvergne* (Turnhout, 2005).

[16] *De sacramento matrimonii*, in *Opera omnia*, ed. F. Hotot, vol. 1 (Paris, 1674), 512b–528b. I have compared this edition with MS BnF lat. 14842, 173rb–201va, which includes passages that are missing from the printed text, in some cases apparently through homeoteleuton. Since the MS seems *prima facie* to be superior, I have preferred its readings where there are significant differences. In Latin quotations from the MS later, I have inserted the significant variants of Hotot's edition in square brackets, with the corresponding text from the MS in italics.

[17] On the conception and plan of *Magisterium divinale et sapientiale*, see R. J. Teske, "William of Auvergne on Philosophy as *divinalis* and *sapientialis*," in J. A. Aertsen and A. Speer (eds.), *Was ist Philosophie in Mittelalter?* (Berlin, 1998), 475–81. P. Glorieux, *Répertoire des maîtres en*

prove to be key in the theology of marriage during the thirteenth century, he deals with them in his own peculiar manner, and in the context of a continuous essay rather than through division and subdivision of articles.

William's tone or mood, as well, sets him apart from the schoolmen, for he writes frankly and vociferously, and not in the detached, analytical dialect of the school-room. But his very directness enables us to hear how thirteenth-century Parisian scholars and clerics regarded their world. William does not hide his mood and prejudices behind scholastic conventions. He is fond of colorful images, striking and abrasive turns of phrase, unusual terms, and jarring neologisms.[18] William's comparison of licentious spouses to Christians who lapse into Muslim or Jewish ways of life (Section 12.2.4.2) illustrates his fondness for holding up the mirror of the *other* as a means of admonition. One of his methods in this treatise is indirect proof by contrariety. To demonstrate the goodness of something, William explains, it suffices to depict its absence or its opposite as self-evidently bad. William concedes that it is better to demonstrate the goodness of a thing directly,[19] but his negative approach has greater rhetorical force, for it supplements moral argument with fear of the slippery slope, of alien influences, and of the incipient decline into barbarism.

Albertus Magnus, O.P., treats marriage extensively in two places: in his commentary on Book IV of the *Sentences*, and in the treatise on marriage included in his *De sacramentis*. Albert lectured on the *Sentences* in Paris as a bachelor 1243–1245. He was Regent Master of the Dominican *studium* there from 1245 until the Order sent him to Cologne in 1248. His vast commentary on the *Sentences* is an *ordinatio*,[20] which he prepared for publication after he had graduated as a master. He completed the *ordinatio* on Book IV in 1249 or 1250, when he was already teaching in Cologne. Albert's *De sacramentis* is one of the six parts of what he himself refers to as a *summa*. This *Summa de creaturis* or *Summa Parisiensis*, as it is known today, was based on questions that he disputed as a master in Paris. He had completed it by 1246, before he went to Cologne.[21] Where there are differences between his two treatments of marriage, therefore, it is difficult to know which treatment to regard as later and revised or more considered. My own impression, for what it is worth, is that the sententiary commentary expresses his later, more considered reflections on marriage, into which Albert has quietly incorporated new ideas that he had first tried out in the *De sacramentis*.

---

théologie de Paris au XIIIe siècle, vol. 1 (Paris, 1933), 37, conjectures that William wrote the treatise on the sacraments c.1228.

[18] See L. Smith, "William of Auvergne and Confession," in P. Biller and A. J. Minnis (eds.), *Handling Sin: Confession in the Middle Ages* (York, 1998), 95–107, on William's temperament and style.

[19] *De sacramento matrimonii*, ed. Hotot, C. 5, 515aA.

[20] Whereas a *reportatio* was a more or less verbatim record taken down by a student at the time of delivery, an *ordinatio* was a version that the master subsequently edited and authorized for publication.

[21] See J. A. Weisheipl, "The Life and Works of St. Albert the Great," in Weisheipl (ed.), *Albertus Magnus and the Sciences* (Toronto, 1980), 13–51, at 22.

Bonaventure, O.F.M., lectured on the *Sentences* in Paris as a bachelor 1248–1253. He began to teach informally as a master in 1253, and he was appointed Regent Master of the Franciscan *studium* in that year or in early 1254, succeeding William of Middleton, under whom he had studied. The faculty belatedly received him as a master during the Easter of 1254, following the resolution of a rift between seculars and mendicants. Bonaventure effectively abandoned his scholastic career when he was appointed Minister General of the Franciscan Order in 1257.[22] His published commentary on the *Sentences* is an impeccably polished work, which he must have continued to revise after he had become a master in 1254, probably from 1254 to 1256. His treatment of the sacramentality of marriage in the commentary is typical, evincing irrepressible originality in the service of conservative, old-fashioned sentiments. Bonaventure expounded a peculiar theory of marital grace that owed something both to William and Auvergne and to Alexander of Hales. He conceded that the priestly blessing was only a sacramental and not an integral part of the sacrament of marriage, and he argued that marriage itself, even without the blessing, conferred a certain remedial grace. Nevertheless, he held that marriage conferred grace in the fullest sense only by virtue of the priestly blessing. Bonaventure's *Breviloquium* (1256–1257), a manual or compendium of the essentials of theology that he wrote for the Franciscan students in Paris, includes a treatise on the seven sacraments with a section on marriage, but here Bonaventure says next to nothing specifically about marriage as a sacrament of the New Law or as a means of grace. Familiarity with these topics was still only of academic interest and not yet considered necessary for preaching or the cure of souls.

Thomas Aquinas, O.P., lectured on the *Sentences* as a bachelor in Paris from 1252 to 1256, having returned from Cologne, whither he had gone as Albert's assistant.[23] Thomas was Regent Master of the Dominican *studium* in Paris from 1256 to 1259 (a position to which he would return in 1268). He prepared his definitive, published version of the commentary (his *Scriptum*) after he had become a master in 1256. This youthful treatment of marriage would prove to be Thomas's only extensive one, for he had reached only the sacrament of penance in his *Summa theologiae* when he stopped writing altogether in December 1273. Thomas touched on marriage incidentally elsewhere in his writings: in the unfinished *Summa theologiae*, in his Pauline commentaries, in disputed questions. He included a summary chapter on the sacrament of marriage in Book IV of the *Summa contra gentiles* (Orvieto, 1264–1265). Like Thomas's medieval and Reformation successors, the modern reader is dependent chiefly on Thomas's *Scriptum* for his views on marriage. This early material was later

---

[22] See J.-G. Bougerol, *Introduction to the Works of Bonaventure* (Paterson, New Jersey, 1964); J. F. Quinn, "Chronology of St. Bonaventure (1217–1274)," *Franciscan Studies* 32 (1972): 168–86; J. F. Quinn, "Bonaventure," *Dictionary of the Middle Ages* 2:313–19.

[23] See J.-P. Torrell, *Saint Thomas Aquinas*, vol. 1: *The Person and His Work* (Washington, DC, 2005), 24–27, 36–47.

incorporated into the posthumous *Supplementum* to Thomas's *Summa theologiae*, whence its influence passed to his successors throughout the Middle Ages and beyond.

The inclusion of marriage as a sacrament in the proper sense coincided with a heightened awareness of the dual nature of marriage as an institution or union that was both a human contract, made by the spouses' own volition, and a divinely instituted sacrament. Theologians recognized that marriage had a hybrid composition that distinguished it from the other six sacraments, although some similarities to penance mitigated the difference. Marriage was human as well as divine, for to get married was something that the participants did for themselves: they did not receive marriage passively as a gracious helping hand from God, as they received baptism, eucharist, and extreme unction. Although one may trace the origins of this twofold model to the late twelfth century, Albert and Thomas were its chief exponents. In their view, marriage was both a civil contract and a sacrament of the church. It was subject to natural and civil law in the first respect, and to divine law as elaborated by the church in the second respect. That analysis did not imply that marriage should be subject to dual jurisdiction, however, for they assumed that in this case the church was the relevant civil authority.

Peter of Tarentaise, O.P. (d. 1276), and Richard de Mediavilla, O.F.M. (d. 1302), present similar accounts of marriage in their respective commentaries on the *Sentences*, often using the same words. Peter lectured on the *Sentences* as a bachelor in Paris 1257–1258 and was Regent Master of the Dominican *studium* 1258–1260, but his published commentary on the *Sentences* probably dates from his second regency in Paris, 1267–1269. Peter was appointed archbishop of Lyon in 1272, and he became Pope Innocent V in 1276.[24] Richard's life and origins in contrast remain obscure,[25] although we know that he studied in Paris, that he lectured in the *Sentences* there in the early 1280s, and that he was Regent Master of the Franciscan *studium* in Paris 1284–1287. Richard's mode of writing was clear and straightforward, and his lucid and reliable commentary on the *Sentences* was widely used and regarded as an authoritative guide to doctrine at least until the fifteenth century, especially but not exclusively among Franciscans. Peter and Richard offer a clear, succinct version of the doctrine of marriage as a sacrament that had become established by the mid-thirteenth century, especially in Thomas Aquinas.

---

[24] On Peter of Tarentaise's commentary on the *Sentences*, see H.-D. Simonin, "Les écrits de Pierre de Tarentaise," in *Beatus Innocentius* (Rome, 1943), 163–335, at 163–213. On his life and work, see M.-H. Laurent, *Le bienheureux Innocent* (Vatican City, 1947), as well as the *Beatus Innocentius* volume.

[25] E. Hocedez, *Richard de Middleton* (Louvain, 1925), remains the standard treatment of Richard's life and career. The current consensus is that he almost certainly from Menneville, in Picardy (and not as formerly supposed from one of the many Middletons of England). On Richard's treatment of marriage, see J. Lechner, *Die Sakramentenlehre des Richard von Mediavilla* (Munich, 1925), 364–410.

12.1.1.3 *The period of consolidation and new controversy*

John Duns Scotus, O.F.M. (d. 1308), was somewhat removed from the mainstream
in his treatment of marriage, explicating each of the standard topics from an unusual
and sometimes idiosyncratic point of view. Scotus and his followers insisted more
than any of their predecessors had done on the implications of the unified sacramental model. They suggested, for example, that marriage, like baptism and
eucharist, could not be a sacrament of the New Law without a determinate verbal
formula (*certa verba*). This reasoning suggested that it was possible for Christians to
enter into a purely civil, non-sacramental contract of marriage. Others used similar
reasoning to show or to suggest for the sake of argument that marriage was not in the
full or proper sense a sacrament of the New Law, but Scotus himself affirmed and
did not challenge that doctrine.

The works of Scotus to which I shall refer here are the *ordinatio* of the sententiary
lectures that he gave in Oxford, traditionally known as the *Opus Oxoniense*, and
the *reportatio* of the lectures on the *Sentences* that he gave later in Paris.[26] The
relationship between these two sources is problematic. Scotus lectured on the *Sentences* in Oxford 1298–1299, whereas the Paris lectures probably date from the period
1302–1304. He was teaching in Paris by 1302, and he was appointed Regent Master of
the Franciscan *studium* there in 1304, after a year of exile. (The Order would transfer
him to the *studium* in Cologne in 1307.) But Scotus continued to work on his
ordinatio (the *Opus Oxoniense*) during the early years of the fourteenth century and
perhaps even until he died, incorporating material from the Parisian lectures.[27] The
historical relationship between the respective discussions of marriage in the *Opus
Oxoniense* and in the *Reportatio Parisiensis*, therefore, is unclear. Absent strong
internal evidence to the contrary, it is best to regard them as mutually complementary,
as I shall do here.

The work of two fourteenth-century Dominicans, Durandus of Saint-Pourçain
(d. 1334) and Peter of La Palu (d. 1342), mark the end of the period during which the
classical doctrine emerged. Durandus was a contrarian who resisted, among other
things, the Dominicans' recognition of Thomas as the leading modern authority on
theology. His treatment of marriage is remarkable for its detailed, ingenious proofs
that marriage was not univocally a sacrament of the New Law. Durandus declined
to say definitively whether or not marriage conferred grace, but he insisted that
the question was still open to debate, resisting what had become the established
consensus among theologians, although not, as he pointed out, among the canonists. Durandus's critique owed a good deal to that of a dissident Franciscan, Peter
John Olivi, who had come under censure in the 1280s for questioning several

---

[26] T. Williams, "Introduction: The Life and Works of John Duns the Scot," in T. Williams (ed.),
Cambridge Companion to Duns Scotus (Cambridge, 2003), 1–14, at 9–11.
[27] In his edition of Scotus's *Opera omnia* (1639), Luke Wadding filled gaps in the *ordinatio* with
material from the Parisian lectures.

matters of well-established doctrine, including whether marriage belonged properly and univocally among the seven sacraments of the New Law and, in particular, whether marriage conferred grace.[28]

The printed edition of Durandus's commentary on the *Sentences* is the last of at least three versions, composed after 1316.[29] Durandus sometimes removed offending ideas under censure but later restored them in the course of revision and re-revision. I shall not attempt here to trace the development and vicissitudes of Durandus's treatment of marriage through the several redactions of his *Sentences* commentary.[30] Durandus's objections to the sacramentality of marriage were still a talking point during the proceedings at Trent in the sixteenth century, where the prelates placed them alongside the opinions of the Protestants, noting that even some Catholics, as well as the Heretics, had tried to undermine this doctrine of the church.

Peter of La Palu studied at the University of Paris, becoming Regent Master there in 1314.[31] A sound scholar with a reputation as a reliable defender of orthodoxy, he was a member of the commission appointed by Pope John XXII to examine Peter John Olivi, and he was later a member of the commission appointed by the King of France to examine Pope John's own suspect views on the beatific vision (c. 1332). Peter was consecrated Patriarch of Jerusalem in 1329 and travelled to Egypt in that role, but he was always a scholar at heart, and he returned to his studies as soon as circumstances permitted. Peter's treatment of marriage in his commentary on the *Sentences* includes a point-by-point refutation of Durandus.

12.1.2 *The law of marriage*

The classical doctrine of marriage as a sacrament presupposed a body of church law regarding the role of consent in the formation of marriage.[32] These laws, which only ecclesiastical courts could adjudicate and enforce, were largely settled by the early thirteenth century and underwent little development until the Council of Trent. Medieval theologians questioned them only for the sake of argument. For the most part, they adopted the rules as premises.

---

[28] D. Burr, "Olivi on Marriage," *Journal of Medieval and Renaissance Studies* 2 (1972): 183–204.

[29] T. Jeschke et al., "Durandus von St. Pourçain und sein Sentenzenkommentar: Eine kritische Edition der A- und B-Redaktion," *Bulletin de Philosophie Médiévale* 51 (2009): 113–43.

[30] P. Blažek did so in "*Matrimonium non est sacramentum stricte et proprie dictum*: Durandus of Saint-Pourçain on the Sacrament of Marriage," a paper that he presented in Prague, June 2012, at the conference *Sacramentum Magnum*. It will be published with the proceedings of the conference, to be published by Aschendorff-Verlag. I am grateful to Dr Blažek for letting me read his working version of the paper.

[31] On his life and work, see J. Dunbabin, *A Hound of God* (Oxford, 1991).

[32] See C. Donahue, *Law, Marriage, and Society* (Cambridge, 2007), 14–45, for an excellent summary of this body of laws. See also L. Schmugge, *Marriage on Trial* (Washington, D.C., 2012), 55–98, on marriage law as reflected in supplications to the Papal Penitentiary for dispensations during the fifteenth century.

The core principle was that the free, uncoerced consent of the spouses themselves expressed in the present tense (*de praesenti*) was sufficient as well as necessary to make a valid, fully established marriage (*matrimonium ratum*) between two believers, provided that there was no impediment disqualifying one or both of the partners or the couple from marrying, such as holy orders, prior marriage, or consanguinity. Secular formalities such as parental consent, dowries, and dotal documents were not necessary for a valid marriage. Most theologians generally conceded, albeit with some uncertainty, tension, and vacillation, that ecclesiastical solemnization or witnessing was not strictly necessary for a fully sacramental marriage. In particular, no priestly blessing or invocation of divine things was necessary to make a marriage between two Christians into a sacrament.

The Fourth Lateran Council of 1215 had prohibited clandestine marriages.[33] Parish priests who refused to forbid such unions, as well as any priests whether secular or regular who participated in or were present at them, were to be suspended from office for three years as the minimum penalty, with more severe penalties if appropriate. The offending spouses were to be given an appropriate penance (*condigna poenitentia*) even if there was no impediment.[34] Lateran IV left the conditions required for a properly public, non-clandestine marriage largely undefined, presumably because the pope and his bishops wanted to leave that matter to regional conventions. Nevertheless, the canon extended to the universal church the "special custom of certain places" (*specialis quorundam locorum consuetudo*), whereby parish priests announced forthcoming marriages in church so that anyone who knew of a lawful impediment had time to come forward before a designated date. Meanwhile, the parish priest himself (*parochialis sacerdos*) had to investigate the circumstances of the proposed union. If a potential impediment came to light, the priest had to postpone the marriage until he had he received directions in writing, presumably from the bishop or his official. The "special custom" to which the canon alluded was the reading of the banns, which had originated in the Anglo-Norman church, most likely in England.[35] Typically, the parish priest would announce the forthcoming union in his church on several (usually three) consecutive Sundays or feast days (apart from certain prohibited days), so that anyone in the parish who knew of any lawful impediment had time and opportunity to come forward, but Lateran IV did not specify how the forthcoming contract should be announced, leaving both the interval and the number of announcements to local custom and jurisdiction.

---

[33] Canon 51, Tanner-Alberigo 1:258.

[34] 258/32–34: "Sed et iis qui taliter copulari praesumpserit, etiam in gradu concesso, condigna poenitentia iniungatur."

[35] The Middle English term *bann* in this context means "announcement," "proclamation." On the early history of the institution in England from the Council of Westminster in 1200, see M. M. Sheehan, "Marriage Theory and Practice," in Sheehan, *Marriage, Family, and Law* (Toronto, 1996), 118–76, at 145–54. For a general history, see J. B. Roberts, *The Banns of Marriage* (Washington, DC, 1931).

The canon refers at one point to properly public marriages as those contracted "in the sight of the church" (*in conspectu ecclesiae*):

> But if any persons presume to enter into clandestine or forbidden marriages of this sort in a prohibited degree even in ignorance, the progeny received from such a union shall be judged entirely illegitimate and their parents' ignorance shall be no excuse, since by contracting in that way they are deemed to be not lacking in knowledge or at least persons who affect ignorance. In the same way, the offspring shall be judged illegitimate if both parents, knowing that there is a lawful impediment, presume to contract in the sight of the church [*in conspectu ecclesiae*] a marriage that is contrary to every prohibition.[36]

Nevertheless, there is good evidence that notarization without any ecclesiastical solemnity still sufficed even after Lateran IV to publish a marriage in Italy.[37]

Once lay folk had internalized the idea that marriages should be publicly celebrated in the locally approved manner, most couples who married clandestinely probably knew of some impediment and hoped either to prevent it from becoming known or to get a dispensation in due course, for the ecclesiastical authorities generally preferred to rescue a marriage of questionable validity in order to avoid scandal.[38] The very term "clandestine" may have implied that there was something suspect about the union, but in canon law the term denoted any marriage contracted without the church-approved means of publication, which included the banns.[39]

The Fourth Lateran Council did not suggest that a clandestinely contracted union was invalid or soluble merely because it was clandestine – an absence that seems anomalous to many modern readers and seemed so even to some of the prelates at Trent. Modern historians explain the policy by distinguishing between liceity and validity, but most medieval authors regarded the matter chronologically and modally. In their view, the church prohibited couples *from marrying* clandestinely *before* the event, but the church did not prohibit a clandestinely *contracted* marriage *after* the event.[40] On the contrary, the church recognized and, indeed, enforced the validity of the illicitly contracted marriage. But spouses who married clandestinely had done something forbidden, even if there was no disqualifying personal impediment, and they were now required to solemnize their marriage in the provincially approved manner.

Because medieval people considered marrying to be rather a process than an event, a private contract was not considered to be clandestine or reprehensible if solemnization *in facie ecclesiae* was planned or took place in due course. There

---

[36] Tanner-Alberigo 1:23–29.

[37] See D. d'Avray, "Marriage Ceremonies and the Church after 1215," in T. Dean K. J. P. Lowe (eds.), *Marriage in Italy, 1300–1650* (Cambridge, 1998), 107–15.

[38] Schmugge, *Marriage on Trial*, 93–94, 338–39.   [39] Ibid., 339.

[40] Domingo de Soto, *IV Sent.* 26.1–2 (2:135–43), inquires, first, whether clandestine marriage is valid, and, second, whether it is sometimes licit, i.e., permitted through dispensation.

might be a delay of weeks or months between a domestic *de praesenti* trothplight and the solemnization of the union, which in France and England involved a public plighting of troth at the entrance to a church.[41] But couples who failed to solemnize their marriage formally in whatever manner the local church prescribed, including the reading of the banns, had by definition married clandestinely, however widely known their union may have been, and however public the nuptial celebrations. Lateran IV's canon on clandestinity did not mention the priestly blessing or any nuptial liturgy. The required role of the parish priest was to investigate the circumstances and to witness the spouses plighting their troth on the church's behalf, and not to administer the sacrament.

The efficient cause of marriage was the outward expression, normally in words, of consent regarding the present, or in the present tense (*de praesenti*). In principle, the words were an authentic statement of consent only if they truly expressed the spouses' interior mental act of agreement (*consensus animorum*). Coerced consent was invalid in canon law, therefore, albeit only if it passed the threshold of a level of "force and fear" (*vis et metus*) deemed sufficient to move a steady man (*vir constans*).[42] Feigned or insincere consent was more problematic. Most theologians and canonists accepted that feigned consent, as long as its outward expression could be proved by witnesses, was sufficient to establish a marriage that was valid at least presumptively in the judgment of the church. It would have been impractical to require sincere consent even in the absence of coercion or fraud. The usual rationale for such pragmatism was that the church (in the guise an episcopal tribunal) could make judgments only on the basis of outward evidence, or in the external forum, and not on the basis of inward realities or of matters of the heart, or in the internal forum. God alone was judge in the internal forum. It remained debatable, therefore, whether a feigned or insincere marriage was a marriage in the eyes of God and in reality, or only in the church's judgment, and whether it had the spiritual efficacy of a sacrament.

There were two complications regarding the requirement of *de praesenti* consent (Section 7.6). First, *de futuro* consent followed by coitus established a valid, binding marriage. The same was true of conditional consent, which was construed as a particular mode of *de futuro* consent. (Indeed, conditional consent was arguably the origin of *de futuro* consent.) Pope Alexander III and his advisors may have assumed something like Gratian's theory, according to which coitus consummates an initiate marriage, but thirteenth-century canonists and theologians assumed that the act of

[41] See P. L. Reynolds, "Marrying and its Documentation in Pre-Modern Europe," THTH, 23–29; and Schmugge, *Marriage on Trial*, 95.
[42] See J. Brundage, *Law, Sex, and Christian Society*, references in the index under "Impediments, marital: force and fear" and "Constant man standard"; and S. M. Butler, "I will never consent to be wedded with you!" *Canadian Journal of History* 39.2 (2004): 247–70. Most cases from the records of late-medieval English episcopal courts involve the coercion of a daughter by her parents.

coitus somehow implied *de praesenti* consent "by interpretation." Huguccio was responsible for formulating this theory in canon law, which ostensibly rescued the principle that marriage was made by consent alone.[43] Theologians acknowledged that such coitus did not really express consent in many cases, perhaps even in most, but they pointed out, again, that the church as a juridical authority had to conduct its judgments in the external forum. Canon law regarded a marriage established by *de futuro* consent plus coitus as "presumptive": an ambiguous term that might or might not imply legal fiction. Richard de Mediavilla is unusually explicit on this topic. Richard accepts that there has usually been no real *de praesenti* consent when coitus has followed *de futuro* consent. A presumptive marriage is a marriage only in outward appearance and in the judgment of the church, he argues, and not in reality. It is not a *true* marriage, nor is it marriage in God's judgment. What if the partners in a presumptive marriage separate and marry others? Some say, Richard explains, that although the first marriage was only presumptive, it established a real, true impediment by virtue of the church's law and judgment (*ex constitutione ecclesiae*), so that the second marriage is invalid in reality. This thesis raises questions about the extent of the church's legislative and jurisdictional power over the sacrament. In Richard's view, the theory of implied consent is "probable" but not true, and he claims that most learned authorities (*doctores*) reject it. Richard argues instead that the diriment impediment to a second marriage is as presumptive as the prior marriage. The second marriage is valid in God's eyes and in the internal forum, but it is invalid in the judgment of the church, which will require the partners to return to their first, false marriage. Since the union that the church upholds and enforces is invalid in God's eyes, Richard counsels the spouses to undergo penance and to submit themselves to a kind of self-inflicted excommunication. They should not fear that their apparent disobedience regarding what the church requires, such as their failure to receive eucharist at least once in each year, will be a sin, since they know in their hearts, as God knows, that they are doing the right thing.[44]

The second complication was that each spouse had the unilateral right even without the other's consent to abandon a *matrimonium ratum* before consummation by entering the religious life, leaving the other free to remarry: a right of refusal that I refer to as the Privilege of Religion. Early thirteenth-century authors attributed the rule to Pope Alexander III and specified a time limit of two or three months. By the middle of the century, theologians either took the rule for granted or cited a general source, usually the *Liber extra*, without ascribing it to anyone, and they mentioned a time limit only when its arbitrariness was relevant to the argument.

The policy retained a role for consummation in the formation of marriage, although theologians never agreed on how to account for it. They usually reserved

[43] J. B. Mullenders, *Le marriage presumé* (Rome, 1971), 71–73.
[44] Richard de Mediavilla, *IV Sent.* 28.1.4, resp. (427).

the term *matrimonium initiatum* for *de futuro* contracts, although some still applied that term to marriage after *de praesenti* consent but before consummation. Whereas Gratian had assumed that *matrimonium ratum* and *matrimonium consummatum* were one and the same, thirteenth-century theologians saw a distinction. Consent sufficed by itself to make *matrimonium ratum*, but intercourse was required for *matrimonium consummatum*. In the normal process of marrying, consummation occurred after the formation of *matrimonium ratum*, and the result was a *matrimonium ratum et consummatum*. Nevertheless, the theologians, drawing on the work of Rufinus, preferred to think of a marriage's being *ratum* and its being *consummatum* as independent conditions rather than as successive phases, for any marriage could be consummated, whereas only Christians were able to contract *matrimonium ratum* in the strictest sense of the term. According to Peter of Tarentaise, for example,

> ... three things are required for the completion of marriage, for it is necessary that it be initiated through the consent of their wills [*consensus animorum*], and that it be consummated through sexual intercourse, and that it be established [*ratum*] through the faith of the contractants, that is, through the Christian faith.[45]

Peter of Tarentaise explains that when the Lombard defined marriage as "the marital union of a man and a woman ... holding together an indivisible way of life," he was referring not just to any marriage (*non quodlibet matrimonium*), but to a marriage that was both *ratum* and *consummatum*.

The precise relationship between a marriage's being *ratum* and its being indissoluble was unclear. The term *matrimonium ratum* had originated in discussion of the Pauline Privilege, where it was assumed that to be *ratum* ("fixed," "established") was to be permanent or insoluble. Thus, a marriage between unbelievers was not fully *ratum* inasmuch as it could be dissolved through the Pauline Privilege if one of them converted. But an unconsummated Christian marriage was *ratum* in medieval canon law even though it could be dissolved by entry into the religious life before consummation, at least during the two- or three-month window of opportunity. Theologians accepted that both consummation and the spouses' Christian faith in some sense consolidated the indivisibility of marriage, but they were reluctant to allow that any properly contracted marriage between infidels was *de iure* soluble, still less that an unconsummated Christian marriage was soluble.

Canon law during the twelfth century, as we have seen, established the right of unfree persons to marry, even without the consent or against the objections of their lords (Section 11.6.1). Thirteenth-century theologians emphasized that *servi* had this right, citing Pope Hadrian's decretal *Dignum est*.[46] Marriage belonged to the church of Christ, and "in Christ Jesus there is neither slave nor free" (Gal 3:28). Early in the thirteenth century, Praepositinus proposed three chief reasons why *servi* were free to

---

[45] Peter of Tarentaise, *IV Sent.* 27.1.1, resp. (Toulouse edition, 4:292).   [46] X 4.9.1 (691–92).

marry and to choose spouses for themselves: because marriage is made by consent alone (*solus consensus*); because marriage is a remedy against lust, which unfree Christians need as much as anyone else; and because marriage is sacrament, for all Christians are free in Jesus Christ, as Pope Hadrian had said. Praepositinus conceded there was nothing in law to prevent a lord from separating married *servi* by moving one to a different place or even by selling one of them. In such cases, their only licit recourse as Christians was to remain continent.[47]

Scholastic theologians wrote much more about marriage than about any of the other sacraments, but only because of the complexity of the rules and regulations. Only a small part of what they wrote on the seventh sacrament was devoted specifically to the central topic of this book: the sacramental theology of marriage. Nevertheless, that part when considered historically becomes a vast and complicated field of inquiry. To make this field more tractable, I shall divide it here into three main parts, regarding respectively marriage as a union (*coniunctio*) between a man and a woman (Section 12.2), marriage as a sacrament (Chapter 14), and marriage as a dual institution: both an office of nature or human contract, and a divine sacrament (Chapter 16). Two topics that are in principle covered in that division require such extensive discussion that I shall devote separate chapters to them: sexual ethics (Chapter 13), and whether marriage confers sacramental grace (Chapter 15). The division between *coniunctio* and *sacramentum* is plausible because most theologians during this period regarded the sacramentality of marriage as being in some sense supervenient upon a presupposed union. Moreover, a sacrament by definition refers to something beyond itself, which it signifies. It presupposes something prior, therefore, which is to be considered in itself. A theologian did not need to write about the elemental physics of water in a treatise on baptism, nor about baking and viniculture in a treatise on the eucharist, but he did need to write extensively about the contractual union that the sacrament of marriage presupposed, with its basis in natural law and its entailments in civil law.

12.2 MARRIAGE AS THE UNION OF A MAN AND A WOMAN

Scholastic theologians held that marriage was by definition the union or joining (*coniunctio*) of a man and a woman. Most of them regarded this union as something that could be explained, justified, and understood without regard for the significance of marriage as a "sign of a sacred reality," although a few theologians preferred to situate marriage entirely in the genus of sacraments. Bonaventure, for example, subordinated the notion of union (*coniunctio*) to that of signification, situating marriage in the genus of sacred signs. To explain why marriage is defined as a union of a particular sort, Bonaventure argues that the

---

[47] Praepositinus, *Summa theologica* IV, pp. 104–05. Likewise, Guy of Orchelles, *Tractatus de sacramentis* 9.2, no. 221 (pp. 198–99).

remote genus of marriage is that of sacred signs, whereas marriage is specifically a sign of the union between Christ and the church.[48] But most theologians assumed that marriage could and should be coherently explained first as the union of man and a woman and as a life-long partnership, without regard for its sacred signification, for its efficacy as a means of grace, or for its status as one of the sacraments of the church.

12.2.1 *What is marriage?*

The logical premise for any comprehensive treatment of marriage was a definition answering the question, "What is marriage?" But what is logically first does not have to be presented first. Peter Lombard had raised the question only in the second distinction on marriage (dist. 27), making a fresh start after a preliminary essay summarizing the results of the discourse on marriage as a sacrament that had taken place over the previous half-century: its institution, its signification, and its role in the Christian life. Theologians commenting on the *Sentences* did not usually get to the definition of marriage, therefore, until distinction 27, after a general account of marriage as one of the sacraments under distinction 26, although a few brought discussion of the definition back to distinction 26, where they treated it in tandem with the etymology of the terms *matrimonium* and *coniugium*, a topic customarily treated there.[49]

12.2.1.1 *Definitions of marriage*

The schoolmen cited numerous definitions of marriage, but most of these can be reduced to three options.[50] By far the most popular option was some version of the definition from Justinian's *Institutes*, according to which marriage is "the union [*coniunctio*] of a man and a woman, holding together an indivisible way of life."[51] Following Hugh of Saint-Victor and Peter Lombard, theologians often qualified the union or the partners themselves (or both) as being *legitimate*, and they sometimes substituted "male and female" for "a man and a woman." That substitution was an echo of Modestinus's definition of marriage, but it was also related to Ulpian's attribution of "the joining of male and female, which we call marriage" to a natural law that "nature has taught to all animals."[52] Only human beings can marry, but marriage is the human version of the pair bonding that is common to many species

---

[48] Bonaventure, *IV Sent.* 27.1.1, resp. (4:676a).

[49] E.g., Paludanus, *IV Sent.* 26.1 (Venice edition [1493], 139r–v).

[50] Albertus Magnus reviews all three options in *IV Sent.* 27.2 (Borgnet 30:129a), although he considers only the first and second in *De matrimonio* 1.1 (Cologne 26.154a).

[51] *Inst.* 1.9.1: "Nuptiae autem sive matrimonium est viri et mulieris coniunctio, individuam consuetudinem vitae continens." Most medieval texts have *retinens* instead of *continens*.

[52] *Dig.* 1.1.1.3.

of animal. The second option was Modestinus's definition from the *Digest*: "Marriage is the union of male and female, an association for the whole of life, a sharing in divine and human law."[53] The third was to define marriage as consent of a certain sort. This was what the *Cum omnia sacramenta* had done, ascribing the consensual definition to Isidore (Section 9.2).[54]

Theologians always had such definitions in mind when they discussed marriage. Whenever a theologian referred to marriage as a *coniunctio* or to the spouses as *coniuncti*, for example, he was thinking of one or both of the first two definitions. Again, the theologian who referred to the *individuitas* (indivisibility) of marriage was thinking of the "indivisible way of life." A theologian who said that marriage was subject to "divine and human law" was invoking Modestinus's definition.

Peter Lombard had pursued the first option, defining marriage as "the marital union of a man and a woman, between legitimate persons, holding together an indivisible way of life."[55] Thirteenth-century theologians often answered the question, "What is marriage?" by expounding the Lombard's definition. According to the Lombard, the phrase "indivisible way of life" refers to three things: the conjugal debt, inseparability, and the shared life. First, neither spouse can abstain from sex without the other's consent, even for the sake of prayer. Second, the conjugal bond (*vinculum coniugale*) endures as long as both are alive. Third, each spouse should treat the other as he or she would wish to be treated.[56] The Lombard adds that the definition applies in its strictest sense only to marriages between believers, since infidel marriages are separable at least in the case of the Pauline Privilege.

Theologians characterized definitions of the third sort as causal, reasoning that they stated the essence of marriage only indirectly, via its efficient cause. Defining marriage as consent, according to a familiar explanation, was like describing day as the sun shining over the earth.[57] But one should keep in mind that when theologians referred to the sacrament or to the contract of marriage, they were typically thinking not of the condition of being married but of the act of getting married. From that perspective, the distinction between the efficient cause of marriage and marriage as a contract or sacrament was at best subtle and often blurred or confusing. I shall return to this point below.

---

[53] *Dig.* 23.2.1: "Nuptiae sunt coniunctio maris et feminae et consortium omnis vitae, divini et humani iuris communicatio."

[54] *Cum omnia sacramenta I*, ed. Bliemetzrieder, BGPhMA 18.2–3, 139/10–11: "Isidorus ita describit: Coniugium est consensus masculi et femine, indiuidualem uite consuetudinem retinens." Likewise, *Cum omnia sacramenta II*, ed. Bliemetzrieder, RThAM 3 (1931), 274.

[55] Peter Lombard, *Sent.* IV, 27.2 (422): "Sunt igitur nuptiae vel matrimonium viri mulierisque coniunctio maritalis, inter legitimas personas, individuam vitae consuetudinem retinens."

[56] Ibid.: "et ut invicem alter alteri exhibeat quod quisque sibi." Compare the Golden Rule of Matt 7:12 and Luke 10:25–28.

[57] Robert Courson, *Quaestio de matrimonio*, ed. Malherbe, ch. 1, *solutio*, p. 2. Albertus Magnus, *IV Sent.* 27.2, ad diffin. 3, ad 3 (131a).

A popular definition of the third sort was ascribed to Hugh of Saint-Victor: "Marriage is the legitimate consent of two suitable persons regarding their union."[58] This definition seemed to limit marriage to monogamy, excluding the polygyny of the Old Law, but that was not a serious problem because theologians generally assumed that marriage was intrinsically monogamous. They reasoned that polygyny was either an exceptional adaptation to special historical exigencies or a matter of indulgence. According to Albert, for example, the Hugonian definition strictly applies only to marriage under the New Law, but it holds universally inasmuch as marriage is monogamous by its very nature (*secundum naturam*), for the polygyny of the Old Law was an exceptional, accidental modification designed to meet the special needs of God's people at that time.[59]

Stephen Langton chose the first and third options, defining marriage both as "the legitimate union of male and female that holds together an indivisible way of life," and as "the consent of two persons to the same thing expressed in words about the present."[60] The first of these definitions recurs in Praepositinus, Guy of Orchelles, and William of Auxerre.[61] Despite the substitution of "male and female," which might suggest that marriage belongs to the natural law in Ulpian's sense of that term, Langton argues that this definition strictly applies only to believers, since their marriages alone are inseparable whereas others are legitimately soluble at least by the Pauline Privilege. Indeed, Langton argues, the definition must strictly apply only to consummated marriage, for either of the spouses in a Christian marriage has three months to dissolve an unconsummated union by entering the religious life. Langton claims that definitions of marriage as consent (the third option) do not state the essence of marriage *per se* but rather characterize marriage though its efficient cause.

William of Auvergne chose to work with definitions of his own devising. He begins his treatise on marriage by proposing two definitions, the first of which is the point of departure for the treatise as a whole:

> We shall begin, therefore, with God's help, by saying that marriage is [i] a holy, sanctifying, and perfect partnership of male and female of the human genus, or [ii] the bond or necessity that makes those in such a partnership debtors in mutuality, or one to another.[62]

---

[58] Albertus Magnus, *IV Sent.* 27.2 (129a): "Hugo de sancto Victore sic diffinit: 'Matrimonium est duarum ideonearum personarum legitimus de conjunctione consensus'." Cf. Walter of Mortagne, *De coniugio* 6 (PL 176:158C): "Credimus igitur sufficere [ad contrahendum conjugium] duarum idonearum personarum legitimum de conjunctione consensum...."

[59] Albertus Magnus, *IV Sent.* 27.2, ad diffin. 3, ad 1 (131a).

[60] Stephen Langton, *Quaestiones theologiae*, Oxford, Bodleian Library, MS Lyell 42, 1vb; Cambridge, St. John's Library, MS 57 (C.7), 318vb. "Matrimonium est legitima coniunctio maris et femine, individuam vite consuetudinem retinens." "Matrimonium est consensus duorum in idem per verba de praesenti expressus."

[61] Praepositinus, *Summa* IV, p. 99/4–5. Guy of Orchelles, *Tractatus de sacramentis* 9.1, no. 212 (194) states the definition without inserting *legitima* but then explains why the joining must be legitimate, as if it were included. William of Auxerre, *Summa aurea* IV.1.1 (380).

[62] William of Auvergne, *De sacramento matrimonii*, MS Paris BnF lat. 14842, 173rb [ed. Hotot, C. 1, 512bH–513aA]: "Incipiemus igitur auxiliante Deo et dicemus quod matrimonium est

William seems to have constructed the first definition in order to prevent any tendency to explain marriage independently of its being a sacred union, perhaps even of its being a sacrament. Notwithstanding their novelty, William's two definitions echo principles of Roman law. The second, subordinate definition, which identifies marriage as the bond or conjugal debt, captures something of the notion that an "indivisible way of life" is a trait peculiar to human pair bonding. The first definition reflects Ulpian's description of the natural law as "what nature has taught to all animals," such as "the union of male and female, which we call marriage."[63] Because Ulpian's description seems at first sight to include marriage among the things common to all animals, William characterizes marriage as the "partnership of male and female *of the human genus.*" William's conception of joining or union (*coniunctio*) was predicated on his theory of sexuality. Marriage, in his view, was the specifically human version of the male–female bonding that was universal among animals. He regarded gender as a fundamental law of biology. Contrariwise, sexual sins were usually the result, according to William, of deliberately circumventing the natural teleology of gender (Section 12.2.4.2).

Since marriage is a "bond of perfect partnership," William inquires as to the nature of that partnership and as to the means of its perfection. He argues that the partners share five things in particular: their bodies through the conjugal debt, their temporal goods, their bodily welfare in sickness and in health, the raising of their children, and their religion, or worship of God. It is fitting that they share religion, for human marriage from the beginning signifies the mystical marriage between God and the human soul.[64] William shows how the union of marriage builds sanctity on the foundation of a gendered partnership rooted in the natural law.

Thomas Aquinas explains that the three ways of defining marriage focus respectively on the three chief aspects of marriage that the scholar has to consider: its cause, its essence, and its effects.[65] Peter Lombard's definition describes the essence of marriage, which is a certain *coniunctio*. It specifies "legitimate persons" as the subjects of the union, and insolubility as the special virtue of marriage. Modestinus's definition characterizes the effect or result toward which marriage is ordered, namely, "the common life in family matters" (*vita communis in rebus domesticis*). Every social sharing (*communicatio*) is regulated by laws, but whereas merely secular associations, such as armies and businesses, are regulated by human laws alone, marriage is regulated by both divine and human laws, as Modestinus says.[66] Hugh's definition captures the efficient cause, for marriage itself is not consent but the resultant union of the spouses, or their being united in a common cause. Moreover,

---

sancta et sanctificativa ac perfecta societas maris et feminae in genere humano sive vinculum, sive necessitudo, qui eos huiusmodi societatis facit invicem *sive* [sui] in alterutrum debitores."

[63] *Dig.* 1.1.1.3.

[64] William of Auvergne, *De sacramento matrimonii*, ed. Hotot, C. 6, 520bG–521aB.

[65] Thomas Aquinas, *IV Sent.* 27.1.1, qu^a 3, resp. (Vivès 11:81).

[66] *IV Sent.* 27.1.2, qu^a 1, ad 1 (83b).

marital consent *per se* signifies not the union (*coniunctio*) of Christ and the church, as marriage does, but rather the spouses' will to be joined.

Most theologians based their definitions of marriage on the forms suggested by Roman law and by Peter Lombard, but they adapted these to their own particular needs. Some definitions explicitly included the sacramental dimension of marriage. For example, Duns Scotus defined marriage as:

> the contract made rightly and honorably by the mutual consent of the spouses, whereby they give themselves to each other and bind themselves with a permanent bond to the mutual right and power to be had over each other's bodies for the sake of the begetting of children who are to be religiously brought up, expressed externally through some sensible sign, and directly instituted by God as a sensible sign that efficaciously signifies that a grace is to be conferred on the contractants.[67]

Like Hugh's definition, this is a statement of the transitory contracting of marriage and not of the resulting *obligatio*, or bond. The definition is designed to show how the sacramentality of marriage has been superadded to the contract by a special institution. Scotus maintained that the sacramental aspect of marriage, unlike the contractual aspect, required *certa verba*: a prescribed, definitive form of words (Section 16.7). Peter of Aquila, known as Little Scotus (Scotellus), incorporates this requirement by defining the sacrament of marriage as:

> the voicing [*expressio*] by a male and a female to each other of certain definite words [*certa verba*] that signify the bestowal [*traditio*] of mutual power over their bodies for the sake of properly begetting children, efficaciously signifying through divine institution a grace to be conferred on those who are mutually contracting for the mutual and grace-giving union of their wills.[68]

Both authors construe both the contract and the sacrament of marriage as a transient, initiating event: as the spouses' outward expressions of their inner consent.

Peter of La Palu, who taught at the university of Paris between 1330 and 1340, begins his inquiry into what marriage is by proposing that marriage is the union (*coniunctio*) of male and female. Clearly, that formula is not sufficient as a definition, for other animals as well as human beings form male–female pairs. The definition would be more extensive than the *definiendum*. To add that the partnership must be monogamous and permanent would not suffice, for males and females of some other species, such as storks, pigeons, and turtledoves, are joined together

---

[67] John Duns Scotus, *Rep. Par. in IV Sent.* 28.un., conc. 11 (Vivès 24:382b–83a): "Ex omnibus his concludo, quod matrimonium est contractus rectus et honestus mutui consensus conjugum, mutuo se donantium, et vinculo perpetuo se obligantium ad mutuum jus et potestatem habendum in suis corporibus, quoad procreationem prolis religiose educandae, expressus per aliquod signum sensibile extra, institutus immediate a Deo, sub aliquo signo sensibili significante efficaciter gratiam conferri contrahentibus."

[68] Peter of Aquila, *IV Sent.* 27.1 (ed. Paolini, 4:263).

monogamously until parted by death.[69] Peter proposes a series of five definitions, with each correcting a defect of the one that precedes it. The first is Modestinus's definition from the *Digest* (the second option listed earlier), which Peter ascribes to the old civil laws (*leges antiquae*). The second is the definition from the *Institutes* (the first option), which the canonists prefer. Peter notes that the phrase "union of male and female" in the first definition, which is reminiscent of Ulpian's description of the natural law, is defective inasmuch as it could be applied equally to irrational animals. Among human beings, union is intolerable and "brutal" outside marriage, and "rational" only within marriage. That is why the canonists prefer the next definition, from the *Institutes*, for it emphasizes that marriage is specifically a *coniunctio* between a man and a woman, rather than between male and female. Moreover, by referring to an "indivisible way of life," this definition shows that marriage is in principle a lifelong union.[70] The three remaining definitions, Paludanus explains, clarify what kind of consent is required. The third is Peter Lombard's definition of marriage as "the marital union of a man and a woman, between legitimate persons, holding together an indivisible way of life." This shows that sexual intercourse is not essential. The fourth and fifth definitions, like Hugh's, define marriage as consent. According to the fourth, marriage is the "legitimate consent to a joining between two qualified persons." According to the fifth, marriage is "the consent of a man and a woman expressed about the present."[71] Peter of La Palu notes that this act of "pre-consent" is not the essence of marriage but rather its efficient cause. Nevertheless, such definitions remind us, Peter argues, that consent alone makes marriage. Sexual consummation does not alter a marriage essentially, although it does have legal consequences regarding such as matters as affinity, digamy (an impediment to holy orders), and dissolution through the Privilege of Religion.[72]

12.2.1.2 *The ambiguity of* coniunctio

Expositions of marriage as *coniunctio* during the early thirteenth century stumble over an ambiguity, which Bonaventure was the first clearly to expose. Although the term *coniunctio* in classical definitions of marriage denoted a continuing partnership rather than the transitory act of marrying, the term itself might suggest the transitory act of coming together. Robert Courson and Stephen Langton identify the *coniunctio* of the standard definitions with the continuing condition of being married or with the marriage bond. They contrast such definitions with causal descriptions, which characterize marriage through consent.[73] But Praepositinus seems to

---

[69] Paludanus, *IV Sent.* 26.1, preamble (138v).   [70] *IV Sent.* 26.1.2 (139ra–b).
[71] Ibid. (139rb).   [72] Ibid. (139rb–va).
[73] Robert Courson, *Quaestio de matrimonio*, ed. Malherbe, ch. 1, p. 2. Stephen Langton, *Quaestiones theologiae*, St. John's College, MS 57 (C.7), 318vb; Oxford, Bodleian Library, MS Lyell 42, 1vb.

interpret *coniunctio* as the act of joining or of being joined. In the definition from the *Institutes*, he explains, the *coniunctio* is said to hold together an indivisible life because by exchanging consent the spouses express their intent (*propositum*) never to be separated except by mutual consent.[74] Even unbelievers implicitly commit themselves to this "indivisible way of life" when they consent to marry, Praepositinus argues, for they cannot separate without committing a sin. Separation is legitimate only in the exceptional circumstance of the Pauline Privilege, when the unbelieving spouse of a convert has already separated him- or herself spiritually by hating Christianity.[75] Guy of Orchelles and William of Auxerre rehearse much of Praepositinus's account of how marriage is defined, but they are more inclined to identify the *coniunctio* with marriage itself or with the enduring bond. Thus, they argue that the *coniunctio* holds together an indivisible way of life as least as long as it exists, even if the marriage is subsequently dissolved either through the Pauline Privilege or because the *sponsa* in a still-unconsummated marriage becomes a religious. From their perspective, the indivisibility posited in the definition is closely related to the conjugal debt.[76]

Alexander of Hales, on the contrary, equates the *coniunctio* of the definitions with the initial exchange of mutual consent. Having defined marriage as "the union [*coniunctio*] of a man and a woman holding together an indivisible way of life between legitimate persons,"[77] Alexander argues that this is a *causal* definition, and not an articulation of the essence of marriage. Thus, one may also define marriage, as Hugh did, by substituting the phrase "legitimate consent" for "*coniunctio*."[78] Alexander explains that this second version emphasizes *matrimonium ratum*, for consent is the efficient cause that establishes *matrimonium ratum* "as regards the soul" (i.e., as regards spiritual rather than carnal joining). The first version of the definition, with "union" instead of "legitimate consent," emphasizes *matrimonium consummatum*, for sexual copulation is the perfecting cause (*causa perficiens*) of marriage "as regards the flesh." Nevertheless, this difference is a matter of emphasis, Alexander explains, for each definition implies the other. The notion of maintaining an "indivisible way of life" implies inseparability, which is completed through

---

[74] Praepositinus, *Summa* IV, p. 101.   [75] Ibid., p. 108.

[76] Guy of Orchelles, *Tractatus de sacramentis* 9.1, no. 213 (194–95). At 195/4–5, Guy glosses "individuam vitae consuetudinem retinens" thus: "id est retinere proponens, vel in perpetuum vel quamdiu matrimonium toleratur." He goes on to equate the undivided way of life with mutual observance of the conjugal debt. But at 9.2, no. 224 (201/9–11), reporting Peter Lombard's view that the good of sacrament is the same as *inseparabilitas*, Guy glosses *inseparabilitas* thus: "id est propositum non separandi, quod etiam est in matrimonio infidelium." William of Auxerre, *Summa aurea* IV.17.1 (381/14–15): "sed quandiu durat matrimonium, individuam vite consuetudinem retinet. Unde quantum in se est, semper retinendum exigit." (William is talking about the dissolution of an unconsummated marriage when one spouse becomes a religious.)

[77] Alexander of Hales, *Glossa in IV Sent.* 27.1a (4:463): "Matrimonium est coniunctio maritalis viri et mulieris inter legitimas personae individuam vitae etc."

[78] Alexander, *IV Sent.* 27.1e (465–66).

consummation. Both versions, therefore, describe a validly contracted and consummated marriage (*matrimonium ratum et consummatum*).[79]

According to Albert, Peter Lombard's definition of marriage as "the marital union of a man and woman, between legitimate persons" refers to the essential form and matter of marrying, that is, the verbal exchange and the spouses respectively. Modestinus's definition of marriage as an "association for the whole of life," on the contrary, posits the effect of marrying. Albert is clearly thinking of the act of becoming married whenever he refers to marriage (*coniugium*) in this article.[80]

Bonaventure noticed that the term *coniunctio* was equivocal, and he attempted to resolve the ambiguity. Marriage has both transient and enduring aspects, Bonaventure explains, and both the act of forming a marriage by mutual consent and the resulting bond can properly be called *coniunctio*. These two aspects of marriage are analogous respectively to ablution and to the enduring character in the sacrament of baptism. Bonaventure regards marriage, even when defined as the "union of a man and woman," primarily as a sacrament: as the visible appearance of an invisible mystery. Just as baptism is an outward act of ablution that signifies an interior cleansing, Bonaventure explains, so marrying is an outward act of joining that signifies the mystery of Christ's union with the church. Both sacraments have enduring as well as transient aspects:

> just as in the ablution of baptism there is something permanent (i.e., the impression of an interior character) and something transient (i.e., the exterior washing), so also in matrimony there is something permanent, which is the bond [*vinculum*] by which the man and the woman are tied together, however much they may be separated exteriorly; and there is something transient, i.e., the joining that is first made through an exterior word or through some [other] exterior act. Each is called matrimony, and each is a union [*coniunctio*].[81]

Bonaventure explains that the contract, or exchange of consent, is the proximate cause of the enduring bond, whereas the divine institution of the sacrament is the remote first cause of the bond. It is in that sense that no man may separate what God has joined.[82]

Notwithstanding Bonaventure's recognition that the term *coniunctio* could denote both the act of getting married and the state of being married or the bond, most theologians after around 1250 assumed that the *coniunctio* of the standard definitions was the enduring condition of being married or the marriage bond (*vinculum*).

12.2.2 *The etiology of marriage*

Whereas the efficient cause of marriage was the mutual consent of the spouses, theologians recognized that there were several possible reasons or final causes for marriage and marrying.

---

[79] *IV Sent.* 27.1b (463).   [80] Albertus Magnus, *De matrimonio* 1.1, resp. (Cologne 26:155a).
[81] Bonaventure, *IV Sent.* 27.1.1, resp. (4:676).   [82] *IV Sent.* 27.2.1, resp. (679b).

12.2.2.1 *The reasons for marriage and marrying*

Like their twelfth-century predecessors (Sections 9.3 and 11.3.2), thirteenth-century theologians distinguished between honorable and dishonorable (*inhonestae*) reasons for marrying, as well as between primary and secondary reasons. Stephen Langton, for example, counted procreation, the avoidance of fornication, and the reconciliation of enemies as honorable ends, and avarice and lust as dishonorable ends.[83] A dishonorable reason for marrying did not necessarily invalidate the marriage once it was established. Procreation was obviously primary, for it pertained to the very essence of marriage. Peacekeeping and all the dishonorable ends were secondary since they were accidental. Theologians regarded the remedy that marriage offered against lust or fornication sometimes as a primary and sometimes as secondary reason, depending on the context or the point of view.

Albert divides the final causes of marriage into two basic sorts, respectively essential (*per se*) and accidental (*per accidens*). He sometimes construes the essential causes as reasons for marriage itself as an institution (*causae matrimonii*), and the accidental causes as the motives of the persons who are marrying (*causae contrahendi, causae inclinantes ad contrahendum*). Whereas the essential causes are necessarily honorable, the accidental causes may be either honorable or dishonorable. Canon law generally regulates only the essential causes, according to Albert, and not the accidental ones.[84] Albert cites the reconciliation of enemies and the restoration of peace as examples of honorable accidental causes, and good looks, lust, and wealth as dishonorable accidental causes.[85] Albert leaves the reader to surmise with the relevant texts from the *Sentences* at hand that both procreation and the avoidance of fornication are essential causes. But when he discusses the original institution and development of marriage, Albert argues that procreation is the only essential reason for marriage, since the remedy is a secondary, accidental application of that procreative purpose to a further end.[86] The key notion here is that of an "adjoined" benefit or evil. Just as coitus is good *per se* but may be indecent (*turpis*) because of something "adjoined" to it, so marriage is designed for procreation but has the "adjoined," accidental benefit of excusing the turpitude of coitus, which would otherwise (*aliter*) be sinful.[87] The same structure carries over to the conjugal goods. Albert argues that the three goods are essential benefits inasmuch as marriage is *ad officium*, but that they are only "adjoined" benefits inasmuch as marriage is *ad remedium*, for in that respect the function of the benefits is to excuse concupiscence,

---

[83] Stephen Langton, *Quaestiones theologiae*, St. John's College, MS 57 (C.7), 319ra; Oxford, Bodleian Library, MS Lyell 42, 2ra.

[84] Albertus Magnus, IV *Sent*. 30.13, ad 3–5 (227b).   [85] IV *Sent*. 30.13, resp. (227).

[86] IV *Sent*. 26.1, resp. (98b): "matrimonium non habet substantialem ordinem contra peccatum: sed principaliter est ad officium, in quo tamen inventum est remedium contra vulnus quod accidit ex peccato."

[87] IV *Sent*. 31.19, resp. (252–53).

which is itself accidentally related to marriage and to coitus.[88] The good of offspring
is the greatest of the three goods chiefly because it was what God primarily intended
when he instituted marriage in the beginning, but also because it is "commonly
intended by the users of marriage."[89] Albert's reasoning seems to be that any
remedial virtue in marriage must be an "adjoined good" because it is supervenes
on the original, essential purpose of marriage, which was to beget and to raise
children.[90]

12.2.2.2 *The Aristotelian division of causes*

By the 1120s, theologians were routinely applying Aristotle's divisions of causes to
many topics including marriage.[91] The assignment of causes enhanced the students'
skills of analysis and raised questions for debate. This etiological analysis of marriage
was largely independent of the hylomorphic analysis of marriage as a sacrament into
form and matter, which served a different purpose. The efficient cause was the
spouses' mutual consent. The final cause was procreation and the other reasons for
marrying. Most theologians identified the matter or material cause of marriage with
the "legitimate persons" denoted in Peter Lombard's definition.[92] Theologians
during the early part of the thirteenth century counted as formal causes any features
that adorned or embellished marrying or the married estate but were not strictly
necessary for validity, whereas theologians after around 1225 found the formal causes
of marriage in certain of its intrinsic features, such as its definition through genus
and species. Analysis of marriage in terms of three or four of the Aristotelian causes
enabled theologians to summarize and to emphasize some traditional observations,
but it also opened up new areas for inquiry.

According to Robert Courson, for example, the spouses' consent is the primary
efficient cause, which suffices by itself to establish a marriage. Subsequent coitus is a
secondary efficient cause inasmuch as it perfects or completes a marriage. The
spouses themselves are the material cause. The formal causes are features that do not
make or effect marriage *per se* but rather "inform" it by adorning it. These include
the celebration of a marriage *in facie ecclesiae* and the blessing of the couple, both of
which are desirable as measures against clandestinity.[93] Robert regards procreation
and the avoidance of fornication (*evitatio fornicationis*) as the primary final causes,
since they correspond to the office and the remedy respectively. Robert rejects the
common opinion that procreation is no longer, in the era of grace, a proper reason

---

[88] *IV Sent.* 31.4, resp. (233b).   [89] *IV Sent.* 31.3, resp. (232a). See also *IV Sent.* 31.1, resp. (230a).
[90] Ibid., arg. 2c (233b) and ad 2 (234a). For example, the power of a medicinal herb to heal
wounds is accidental, and not, as it were, what the herb intends.
[91] Aristotle expounds the division in *Metaphysics* I.3 ff. (983a24 ff.), *Metaphysics* V.2
(1013a24–1014b25), and *Physics* II.3 (194b16–195a27). See M. Hocutt, "Aristotle's Four
Becauses," *Philosophy* 49 (1974): 385–99.
[92] Albert, *De matrimonio* 1.1, ad 3 (155a).
[93] Robert Courson, *Quaestio de matrimonio*, ch. 4. p. 12.

for marrying. Secondary final causes include not only the spreading of charity, the reconciliation of enemies, and the confirmation of peace treaties, but also the ways in which marriage enables parents to know who their children and their heirs are, and children to know who their parents are. Such certainty enhances charity in the community, and it enables children properly to honor their parents. Without that certainty, human beings would live like the brutes.[94] This theme will become a common feature of accounts of marriage in natural law.

Praepositinus, too, distinguishes among the efficient, formal, and final causes of marriage. Consent is the sole efficient cause of marriage. Coitus is not an efficient cause, Praepositinus argues, for it does not make marriage but rather completes it, whereas there can be no marriage without an initiating act of consent.[95] One might object that according to Modestinus a man's cohabitation with a free woman was presumed to be marriage without any initial act of consent, but Praepositinus argues that this opinion was only about the validity of inheritance rights, and not about the validity of a marriage *per se*.[96] Solemnities are not efficient but "institutional" causes (*causae institutoriae*), which "do not make marriage itself but rather adorn it." These are a species of formal cause. Their purpose is to obviate the hazards of clandestine marriage.[97] Praepositinus divides the final causes of marriage into honorable and dishonorable, and he subdivides honorable causes into necessary and useful. The necessary honorable causes are the begetting of children and the avoidance of fornication, which pertain respectively to the institution of marriage as an office (*ad officium*) and as a remedy (*ad remedium*). Some scholars, Praepositinus notes, maintain that the begetting of children is no longer a proper final cause today because the remedy has superseded the office, but he rejects that position. Christians still properly marry *ad officium* (i.e., to procreate) as well for the remedy. Moreover, the original command to "increase and multiply" expresses a law of nature, although it amounted to a precept only when God's people were few whereas it had become a matter of permission or counsel by the time Mary married Joseph.[98] Useful final causes include the spreading of peace and the reconciliation of enemies. Dishonorable final causes include the acquisition of wealth and the attraction of a woman's beauty.[99] Guy of Orchelles and William of Auxerre appropriated Praepostinus's analysis of efficient, formal, and final causes with only minor changes, but they completed the analysis by adding as the material cause "legitimate persons." A man and a woman are legitimate when there is no impediment preventing them from marrying each other.[100]

Alexander's etiology is typical of his more elaborate approach to marriage (see Table 12.1). As well as dividing the causes into efficient, formal, and final,[101] he subdivides each class. Efficient causes may be essential (*per se*) or accidental

---

[94] Ibid. (p. 13).   [95] Praepositinus, *Summa* IV, p. 102.   [96] Ibid., p. 106.
[97] Ibid., pp. 105–06. Praepositinus cites the decretal of ps.-Evaristus.   [98] Ibid., p. 103/31–33.
[99] Ibid., pp. 106–07.   [100] Guy of Orchelles, *Tractatus de sacramentis* 9.2, 217 (196).
[101] Alexander of Hales, *IV Sent.* 30.10 (486–87).

(*per accidens*). The essential efficient cause is consent. Motives such as wealth and beauty are accidental efficient causes. Alexander argues that these are not, as other scholars maintain, final causes, but rather motivating efficient causes. Essential efficient causes may be either initiating (*incipiens*) or perfecting (*perficiens*). The initiating efficient causes of marriage include not only *de futuro* consent but also *de praesenti* consent that has not yet been outwardly "expressed" in some recognized manner. Because *de futuro* agreement creates only an obligation to marry, and not a marriage, Gratian's argument that "there is an initiate marriage; therefore, there is a marriage," is a non sequitur.[102] There are two perfecting efficient causes: consent expressed in words of the present tense, which completes initiate marriage in respect of the soul by establishing *matrimonium ratum*; and subsequent coitus, which perfects *matrimonium ratum* in respect of the body. Coitus after future-tense consent is equivalent to present-tense consent, but only by "interpretation."[103] Alexander rejects the opinion that someone who consents to marriage insincerely, without really willing to marry in his heart, is married only in the human forum and not in God's eyes. Absent coercion, the words of consent must be understood "according to their common understanding," and even God regards a feigned trothplight "as if there has been a consent of wills."[104] A formal cause may inform marriage either essentially, "as regards being," or accidentally, "as regards well-being." The essential formal cause is the "union of wills" (*unio animorum*), which holds together an indivisible way of life. Accidental formal causes include procreation and *traductio in thorum*.[105] That phrase traditionally denoted the bedding ritual, but Alexander may be referring to coitus as the rendering of the conjugal debt. Alexander divides the final causes of marriage into necessary and expedient. There are two necessary final causes: the procreation and raising of children to worship God (the *officium*), and the avoidance of fornication (the *remedium*). The expedient final causes include the reconciliation of enemies and the restoration of peace.[106]

Peter of Tarentaise uses the fourfold division to elucidate Peter Lombard's definition of marriage as "the marital union of a man and a woman, between legitimate persons, holding together an indivisible way of life." The joining or uniting (*adunatio*) of the spouses is the formal cause, and the man and the woman themselves are the material cause. The description of the union as "marital" refers obliquely to the efficient cause, since the union must be contracted with "marital affection," that is, with the proper consent. The phrase "indivisible way of life" refers to inseparability, or the *bonum sacramenti*, which is a final cause of marriage.[107]

Scholastic theologians sometimes used Aristotle's schema of causes to show how a particular topic is treated in the *Sentences*. Thus, Bonaventure and Peter of Tarentaise divide the distinctions on marriage in the *Sentences* into four groups, dealing respectively with the definition of marriage, construed as the formal cause

---

[102] *IV Sent.* 26.7d (461).   [103] *IV Sent.* 26.7d (461/12–17).   [104] *IV Sent.* 27.3 (467–68).
[105] *IV Sent.* 30.10 (487).   [106] Ibid.   [107] Peter of Tarentaise, *IV Sent.* 27.1.1, resp. (292a).

TABLE 12.1 *Alexander of Hales: The Causes of Marriage*

Efficient –	essential –	initiating:	*de futuro* consent, unstated *de praesenti* consent
		perfecting:	expressed *de praesenti* consent, consummation
	accidental:		wealth, beauty (as motives)
Formal –	regarding being:		the union of wills (*unio animorum*)
	regarding well-being:		procreation, *traductio in thorum*
Final –	necessary:		the begetting and raising of children to worship God, the avoidance of fornication
	expedient:		reconciliation of enemies, peace-making

(distinction 26); with consent as the efficient cause (distinctions 27–30); with the final causes, especially the three conjugal goods (distinctions 31–33); and with the material cause, namely, legitimate persons (distinctions 34–42, on the impediments).[108] Division of a book or a treatise according to the four causes may seem pointless today, but in the absence of printed books with standard pagination it must have not only honed students' analytical skills but also helped them to find their way around the text.

12.2.2.3 *The efficient cause: Consent*

Theologians recognized that consent was the proximate efficient cause of marriage. In a certain sense, it was even the essence of marriage. Three groups of issues arose from that premise. First, if the consent is defective in some way, what is the consequence? Second, what role does consummation play as an ancillary cause in the formation of marriage? Third, in consenting to marriage, do the spouses *ipso facto* consent to sexual intercourse? Is sexual intercourse included as an object of the consent, and, if so, in what way?

Questions of the first group included the canonical issues of coerced and feigned consent, but theologians also wondered whether tainted consent tainted the resulting marriage. For example, William of Auxerre inquires into the consequences of marital consent that is mortally sinful. Is the marriage that results sinful too, as the fruit of a poisonous tree? Or does something bad cause something good? Because both alternatives seem *prima facie* unacceptable, there is a dilemma. In reply, William points out that every action qua action is good *per se* because it comes from God. Only its accidental defects, which do not come from God, can be bad.

---

[108] Bonaventure, *IV Sent.* 26, divisio textus (661a). Peter of Tarentaise, *IV Sent.* 26, divisio textus (282).

A badly motivated, sinful act of consent causes the marriage to exist not inasmuch as the act is sinful, but simply inasmuch as it is an act of consenting to marry. Since there is no deficiency in that act *per se*, it comes entirely from God. William points out that many beneficial and necessary business transactions on which our economy depends are valid and good in themselves even though they are often motivated in fact by greed.[109]

Theologians regarded consent as the sole primary efficient cause of marriage, and subsequent coitus as an efficient cause only in some secondary sense. But consummation and sexual union were not easy to construe. On the one hand, no theologian after Hugh of Saint-Victor held that sexual union was so incidental or supplementary in relation to marriage that marital consent *per se* had no reference at all to sexual intercourse. Furthermore, everyone accepted that a marriage was invalid if the spouses were incapable of consummating it at the time of their contract. On the other hand, theologians treated the idea that consummation completed or perfected marriage cautiously, in part because it seemed to follow that the marriage of Mary and Joseph was incomplete. A remarkable amount of ink was applied to these problems. Although they all proved to be soluble in one way or another, no one ever arrived at a definitive solution and there was little consensus.

Albert argues that consent perfects marriage because "indivisibility, which is the essence of marriage, is essentially caused by it."[110] Marriage "in and of itself is always the cause of indivisibility," whereas the Privilege of Religion, whereby one spouse dissolves an unconsummated marriage by becoming a religious, is an accidental occurrence. It arises when a stronger spiritual bond trumps the weaker but intrinsically indivisible bond of merely human marriage.[111] Albert concedes that the conjugal goods are present "less fully" before consummation. In particular, the good of sacrament is deficient because the signification of marriage is still imperfect.[112] But Albert distinguishes between extensive and intensive perfection. It is true that consummated marriage signifies *more things*, but it does not follow that is a better signifier of what it signifies. An unconsummated marriage is already perfect in signification inasmuch as it signifies perfectly what it signifies, such as the charity between Christ and the church. Again, unconsummated marriage perfectly signifies the interior mental union of the spouses, as well as the spiritual union of the church to God.[113]

Theologians analyzed the place of consummation or sexual intercourse in relation to marriage ontologically, as if marriage were a substance. For example, Albert argues that consent alone perfects marriage "in first being" (*in esse primo*), whereas coitus perfects marriage "in second being" (*in esse secundo*).[114] Whereas consent

---

[109] William of Auxerre, *Summa aurea* IV.17.2, q. 1 (384–85).

[110] Albertus Magnus, *IV Sent.* 26.15, resp. (125a).

[111] Albertus Magnus, *De matrimonio* 1.1, ad 4 (155a).

[112] *IV Sent.* 31.6, resp. (235b); 33.6, ad 1 (289a).

[113] *IV Sent.* 26.15, ad 4–5 (125b); 28.6, ad 5 (195b).   [114] *IV Sent.* 28.6, ad 1 (195b).

perfects the essential union, subsequent coitus is not so much a perfection as an effect or consequence of marriage (an outcome, we might say).[115] Similarly, Thomas distinguishes between the primary and the secondary "integrity" of marriage. Integrity here is what constitutes the wholeness or perfection of a thing: its necessary and sufficient conditions. The primary integrity of a thing comprises its essence, whereas the secondary integrity consists in its characteristic operations. Sexual intercourse is a characteristic operation of marriage inasmuch as marriage establishes a certain "faculty" for intercourse (i.e., the rights and privileges of the conjugal debt). Consequently, whereas consent alone is sufficient for the primary integrity of marriage, according to Thomas, sexual intercourse belongs to the secondary integrity.[116]

Thirteenth-century theologians continued to inquire into the object of marital consent as well as into the canonical validity of the marriage between Mary and Joseph. The two topics were closely related and overlapped to some extent, but they were not entirely coextensive. The parameters of the former question had been established during the twelfth century.[117] On the one hand, if the spouses consented only to cohabitation in marrying, then it seemed that brother and sister, parent and child, and so forth, could marry. On the other hand, if the spouses consented to sexual intercourse, then the marriage of Mary and Joseph was in doubt. How could Mary have consented to coitus without mentally violating her vow of virginity?

The results of this debate were twofold. On the one hand, regardless of how thirteenth-century theologians analyzed marital consent, they generally accepted that consenting to a marriage implied consent to sexual intercourse in *some* sense. They doubted, therefore, whether one could consistently both agree to marry and be bound by a solemn vow to remain continent. If that entailed problems regarding the marriage of Mary and Joseph, one might solve those in an *ad hoc* manner by applying the strategy of exception used in canon law, for the marriage of Mary and Joseph was a special case to which some of the normal rules and conditions did not apply. Discussion of this topic by Peter Lombard and his successors prompted thirteenth-century theologians to weaken the connection between marital consent and sexual intercourse. Peter Lombard had argued that what the spouses agreed to in getting married was neither sexual intercourse nor cohabitation but an undetermined marital partnership (*coniugalis societas*),[118] although he added that Mary must have consented to coitus conditionally, that is, if God should ever require it.

---

[115] *IV Sent.* 30.9, resp.; ad 5 (222a, 222b).

[116] Thomas Aquinas, *IV Sent.* 26.2.4, resp. (75a). Thomas applies this distinction to the marriage of Mary and Joseph in *IV Sent.* 30.2.2, resp. (115a), and *Summa theologiae* III.29.2, resp. (2605a).

[117] On Gratian, see earlier, Section 6.4.1. The crucial text for thirteenth-century theologians was Peter Lombard, *IV Sent.* 28.3 (434–35). Cf. Robert Courson, *Quaestio de matrimonio*, ed. Malherbe, ch. 4, pp. 12–13. On the treatment of this question in canon law, see J. A. Brundage, "Implied Consent to Intercourse," in A. E. Laiou, *Consent and Coercion to Sex and Marriage* (Washington, DC, 1993), 245–56.

[118] *Sent.* IV, 28.3.2; 28.4.2 (435). Cf. *Sent.* IV, 30.2.1 (439): "Consentit ergo Maria in maritalem societatem, sed non in carnalem copulam, nisi ea specialiter Deus praeciperet...."

Some thirteenth-century theologians found Peter Lombard's non-specific notion of marriage as an undetermined *coniugalis societas* wanting, whereas others refined or elaborated it.

When Robert Courson inquires into the object of marital consent, he poses the usual dilemma: If cohabitation is the object of such consent, then father and daughter, brother and sister, abbot and *conversa*, and so on can marry. Contrariwise, if sexual intercourse is the object, then either Mary and Joseph were not married or else she violated her vow. Following Peter Lombard, Robert solves the dilemma by characterizing the object of marital consent as a marital partnership (*societas maritalis*), although he adds that Mary consented to coitus conditionally, if it so pleased God. Robert maintains, too, that Mary's vow to remain a virgin was not the full public *votum*, which would have been irrevocable, but rather a *propositum*: a firm but essentially private and personal intention.[119]

The canonical problems entailed by Mary's celibate marriage were capable of several conjectural *ad hoc* solutions that had no theoretical consequences regarding marriage in general. For example, Stephen Langton suggests that Mary might not have made her vow firmly until after she married, and also that she could have consented conditionally to sexual intercourse while hoping to remain a virgin. She was ready to render the debt to Joseph if God so wished, that is, if Joseph required it.[120] Praepositinus and Guy of Orchelles rehearse the same solution.[121] Guy concedes that a vow of continence is inconsistent with marrying because it prevents two of the three goods, *fides* and *proles*, but like Rufinus he argues that one may obviate that problem by applying the principle that "the privileges of the few do not make common law."[122] Albertus Magnus concedes that Mary's vow of virginity was conditional inasmuch as it was dependent on whatever would prove to be God's will for her, but he suggests that God revealed to Mary before they married that Joseph was of the same mind and would never demand the debt.[123]

Bonaventure reviews three solutions to the canonical problem of Mary's vow. Some say that it was not a fully-fledged *votum* but only a *propositum*, which could be abandoned without blame if needs must. Others, such as William of Auxerre, say that Mary consented to coitus but only in a general or implicit way, and not in a specific or explicit way. Yet others say that Mary consented to sexual intercourse conditionally, by agreeing to it if God so willed. But the first two positions are not sufficient to save Mary's *moral* integrity, Bonaventure argues, and the third fails because marital consent is by its very nature unconditional. There can be no

[119] Robert Courson, *Quaestio de matrimonio*, ed. Malherbe, ch. 4, pp. 12–14.

[120] Stephen Langton, *Quaestiones theologiae*, Oxford, Bodleian Library, MS Lyell 42, 1vb; Cambridge, St. John's Library, MS 57 (C.7), 318vb.

[121] Praepositinus, *Summa* IV, pp. 103/24–30. Guy of Orchelles, *Tractatus de sacramentis* 9.2, no. 218 (197); 9.3.1, no. 231 (207).

[122] *Tractatus de sacramentis* 9.3.1, no. 229 (205–06).

[123] Albertus Magnus, *IV Sent.* 28.6, ad 7 (196a). Albert discusses the marriage of Mary and Joseph at length in *IV Sent.* 30.4–12 (218–227).

conditions or codicils in a marriage contract. Bonaventure owes his own solution to the canon law of his own day: In the unlikely event that Joseph demanded his rights, Mary could have escaped from the marriage by taking a solemn vow and becoming a nun! But Mary probably knew – either through supernatural insight or because Joseph had assured her – that her husband would never in fact demand his conjugal rights.[124]

Theologians responded in a variety of ways to the broader issue, which required the link between consent and coitus to be retained yet only in some weakened modality. Stephen Langton prefers to obviate the dilemma by arguing, following Peter Lombard and Peter of Poitiers, that what the partners consent to is not coitus but rather a "conjugal partnership," which entails sexual intercourse only in some undetermined manner. Just as a monk might validly make a vow of obedience to an abbot while making a specific exception, such as that he will not attend matins, so the spouses may validly marry while agreeing to abstain from sexual intercourse.[125]

William of Auxerre develops this indeterminacy solution with some care. He concedes that Mary, who was utterly submissive to God's will, must have consented to sexual intercourse conditionally, for she would surely have rendered the debt at any time if God required her to do so. But this concession "seems to be nothing" in the context of the question, for Mary was confident that God would *not* expect it of her. The proposed condition, therefore, would be vacuous. William argues instead that what spouses consent to when they marry is "conjugal union" (*copula con-iugalis*). That union comprehends several specific things, including cohabitation as well as sexual intercourse and the conjugal debt, but in only an undetermined manner, much as a genus comprehends its species. Again, consent to conjugal union is related to the various specific realizations of that union in the same way as knowledge of a genus is related to knowledge of any of its species.[126]

Albert prefers to posit a more direct and explicit relationship between consent and coitus. He argues in the *De matrimonio* that the spouses consent to "a marital joining that includes the rendering of the debt in an opportune time and place" as well as to mutual fidelity.[127] In his *Sentences* commentary, Albert argues that Peter Lombard's definition of marriage as a "marital partnership" (*societas maritalis*) is acceptable only if one assumes that the partnership has some reference to sexual intercourse, albeit in such a way that the spouses may abstain by mutual agreement. The spouses agree to sexual intercourse in a general way (*in communi*), therefore, as well as to a form of cohabitation that is specifically marital.[128]

---

[124] Bonaventure, *IV Sent.* 28.un.6, resp. (695–96).

[125] Stephen Langton, *Quaestiones theologiae*, Oxford, Bodleian Library, MS Lyell 42, 2ra; Cambridge, St. John's Library, MS 57 (C.7), 318vb.

[126] William of Auxerre, *Summa aurea* IV.17.2, q. 2 (385–87).

[127] Albertus Magnus, *De matrimonio* 1.5, ad 3 (158b). Canonists debated whether one spouse had right of just refusal when the other demanded the debt inappropriately, such as on a prohibited day, but they usually concluded that the debt overrode the prohibition. On sins of location, see D. Elliott, "Sex in Holy Places," *Journal of Women's History* 6.3 (1994): 6–34.

[128] Albertus Magnus, *IV Sent.* 28.6, resp. (195).

Thomas Aquinas's point of departure is a premise of startling simplicity: "The consent that makes marriage is consent to marriage." It follows that the intentional relationship between the consent to marry and sexual intercourse (*copula carnalis*) mirrors the relationship between marriage itself (*copula coniugalis*) and sexual intercourse. If it were true that spouses are not fully married until they consummate their relationship, then consent to marry would entail consent to sexual intercourse. But sexual intercourse is not a necessary condition but an effect or a consequence of marrying, toward which marriage is "ordered." Those who say that the partners consent to sexual intercourse but only implicitly, therefore, are correct.[129]

Thomas's conclusion is close to William of Auxerre's, but he derives the framework of his argument from the ontology of substances. As well as analyzing marriage into efficient cause, essence, and consequential effects, as he does to elucidate the three definitions of marriage,[130] Thomas considers marriage to have both first being (*primum esse*) and second being (*secundum esse*), just as a substance does.[131] Again, he argues that initiate marriage is to consummate marriage as a habit or power is to its corresponding act or operation.[132] Marriage is "ordered" to sexual intercourse insofar as the conjugal debt belongs to the essence of marriage, for the debt entails a power (*potestas*) to require sex from one's partner, and a power is related to its use as a cause to its effect.[133] Thus, sexual intercourse is a "certain operation or use of marriage," and each spouse acquires a "faculty" (a moral and legal right) to exercise that use. It follows that "sexual intercourse belongs to the second integrity of marriage, and not to the first."[134] Whereas the term "faculty" embraces both factual and juridical powers, the term *operatio* belongs to the vocabulary of ontology, and the term *usus* to the vocabulary of law and jurisprudence. The conjugal debt is not something to which the partners have committed themselves by contract. Rather, it is a kind of implication or result of being married: an obligation that cannot be adequately accounted for in contractual terms. Moreover, if what the partners agree to in marrying is simply marriage, then marriage itself cannot be analyzed or parsed in contractual terms. Whether Thomas's account of consummation suffices to make sense of Mary's marriage vows is debatable, but it does enable him easily to solve the traditional dilemmas. A brother and a sister cannot marry because they are not entitled to acquire the "faculty" in question. Again, one cannot attach abstinence to marital consent as an explicit condition, for that would be inconsistent with the same faculty.[135]

12.2.3 *The ontology of marriage*

Theologians inquired into what Stephen Langton called the *essentia* of matrimony, referring not to its nature but to its being: its ontology. The topic originated during

---

[129] Thomas Aquinas, *IV Sent.* 28.4, resp. (100b).   [130] *IV Sent.* 27.1.1, quᵃ 3, resp. (81).
[131] *IV Sent.* 27.1.3, quᵃ 2, ad 3 (86a).   [132] *IV Sent.* 28.4, ad 4 (100b).
[133] *IV Sent.* 28.4, resp. (100b).   [134] *IV Sent.* 26.2.4, resp. (75a).
[135] *IV Sent.* 28.4, ad 2–3 (100b).

the late-twelfth or early-thirteenth century as a puzzle about number. Suppose that John is Jane's husband: How many marriages or unions (*coniunctiones*) or bonds (*vincula*) exist between them? Common sense and ordinary usage tell us that they share a single marriage, but logic and philosophical scrutiny suggest that John's being married to Jane is one thing, whereas Jane's being married to John is another. Three solutions to this conundrum emerged during the first quarter of the thirteenth century, respectively positing an assimilation, a convergence, and a polyadic accident (i.e., an non-Aristotelian accident that inheres in several subjects at once). According to the first solution, there are really two marriages but we regard them as one because they are alike. According to the second, there are really two marriages but we regard them as one because they converge in a single goal or outcome, such as a certain signification or the begetting and raising of children. According to the third solution, being married is a single accident that inheres in the two subjects at once and in neither of them independently, much as number exists in numbered things.

The question of number invited scholars to inquire into other aspects of the ontology of marriage, especially the category to which marriage belonged. Was marriage a substance or an accident? If it was an accident, was it a relation or a quality? Since marriage could hardly have independent existence as a substance, it had to be an accident of some sort, and accidents had a dependent mode of being: "The *esse* of an accident is its *inesse*," according to a maxim derived from Avicenna. The most likely candidate was the category of relation, although a case could be made for quality. Now, a relation, as Aristotle understood it, was an accident that existed in one subject in respect of or toward another (*ad aliquid*): for example, a father's fatherhood exists in the father toward his son.[136] A man's being the husband of his wife was one thing, therefore, and his spouse's being his wife was another.

Huguccio of Pisa (d. 1210), a canonist, was among the first to inquire into the ontology of marriage, although it is not clear that the question had any practical implications in canon law. Huguccio asks whether matrimony is a substance or an accident, and, if it is an accident, how there can be a single marriage joining the two partners. If marriage is a relation, there should be two unions (*coniunctiones*) or bonds (*vincula*): one in the husband and another in his wife. Huguccio accepts that a marriage is in reality "not a something [*aliquod*] but some things [*aliquae*], not one but two." Nevertheless, we regard the two relations as one, Huguccio argues, because of the similarity between them, "just as some things are said to be colored with one and the same color."[137] This is an example of what I call the assimilation theory, whereby the two relations are counted as one because they are alike.

---

[136] Aristotle, *Categories* 6a36–8b24. On medieval inquiry into the nature of relations, see M. G. Henninger, *Relations* (Oxford, 1989); and J. Brower, "Medieval Theories of Relations," *Stanford Encyclopedia of Philosophy* (Winter 2010 Edition), URL = <http://plato.stanford.edu/archives/win2010/entries/relations-medieval/>.

[137] Huguccio, *Summa* on C. 27 q. 2, ed. Roman, *Revue historique de droit français et étranger* 27 (1903), 748–49.

Robert Courson and Stephen Langton pursue more adventurous explanations, perhaps drawing on the ideas of Peter the Chanter. Both suggest that marriage is a polyadic accident. According to Robert Courson, marriage itself is "a certain spiritual bond [*vinculum*] of male and female, that is, a certain obligation arising between them from their mutual consent."[138] This bond is not a relation, according to Robert, but a polyadic quality. It is present in both spouses in such a way that it is not present in either as an individual, just as a certain number, such as the threeness of three pebbles, is present in many things at once without being in any one of those things as in an individual. Stephen Langton asks to which of Aristotle's categories matrimony belongs; whether, if the category is relation, there is one relation or two; and whether, if matrimony is somehow one thing, it is in the spouses in such a way that it inheres in each of them individually, or rather in the couple in such a way that it is in neither of the spouses as in an individual. Langton argues that a marriage is not a relation but a single quality inhering in two subjects at once.[139] He concedes that there are two bonds (*vincula*), one in each spouse, and that a bond is a relation, but he maintains that there is only one marriage. Langton does not explain the difference between the marriage and the bond.[140]

Praepositinus proposes as plausible alternatives both the polyadic accident theory and the assimilation theory. He begins his discussion with the proviso that a sacrament of the church does not have to comply with Aristotle's categories! Then, following Langton, he suggests in the first place that a marriage is a single entity that exists in both spouses at once but in neither of them individually. Instead, the partners get their identity as husband and wife from (*ex*) the common property. When someone paints a wall white, the wall is white from (*ex*) the work of the painter, but the painter's work is not in the wall. According to the second hypothesis, marriage inheres in each of the spouses independently as in an individual subject. In that case, there are really two marriages but we regard as one thing because of their similarity, just as two persons who look exactly alike are considered to have the same face.[141]

William of Auxerre proposes a version of the convergence theory. He concedes that there are two numerically distinct relations in matrimony, but he argues that they are regarded as one because they converge in a single effect and in a single signification, as bread and wine do in the eucharist. The common effect of the two matrimonies is the union of two in one flesh, and the common signification is the union between Christ and the church.[142]

---

[138] Robert Courson, *Quaestio de matrimonii*, ed. Malherbe, ch. 1, p. 2.

[139] I assume that Langton intended *qualitas*, but the St. John's MS clearly has *causalitas* (without abbreviation), and the Lyell MS has an abbreviation that can only be expanded as *causalitas*. If *causalitas* is correct, Langton's idea may be that the two relations converge in a single effect.

[140] *Quaestiones theologiae*, St. John's College, MS 57 (C.7), 318vb, and Oxford, Bodleian Library, MS Lyell 42, 1vb.

[141] Praepositinus, *Summa* IV, pp. 100–01.   [142] William of Auxerre, *Summa area* IV.17.1 (381).

Alexander of Hales enlarges the inquiry. His solution to the numerical problem is much the same as William's. He argues there are two distinct unions (*coniunctiones*) but that there is a single marriage both inasmuch as the spouses consent to the same "marital partnership," and inasmuch as their two consents are unified by likeness, as if by a single unifying quality.[143] But questions of a different sort arise when Alexander inquires into the survival of a marriage after the partners have separated. That relationship continues to exist, regardless of whether one construes marriage as relation of wills (*animi*) or of bodies or of both. Yet another set of questions arises, Alexander shows, if one considers marriage not in respect of its essence but in respect of its efficient cause, as when one construes *coniunctio* as the act of coming together. The spouses' mutual consent is the efficient cause of the enduring essence of their marriage. Now, an efficient cause may be temporally related to its effect in any of three ways: it may precede the effect, so that it ceases as soon as the effect comes into being; or it may continue to exist with the effect for a while and then cease, leaving the effect by itself; or it may coexist continuously with the effect.[144] Consent must be related to marriage in the second way. If consent is sometimes considered to coexist continuously with the marriage, that is only because the spouses' prior consent is implied in the dependence of the enduring marriage on the initial act, in which the two wills were joined.[145]

Most theologians during the second half of the thirteenth century defended the thesis that marriage was a relation and worked out the implications of that premise. The problem of number remained, but it lost its urgency, for theologians found unity in convergence. Commenting on the *Sentences*, Albert complains that some of the ontological problems are pseudo-problems. He refutes arguments presupposing that there is something absolute in marriage by which the spouses are bound, like a rope by which two people are tied together. Such arguments, Albert argues, stumble over merely semantic distinctions, such as the difference between abstract and concrete terms.[146] Similarly, it is no more necessary to posit two marriages between the spouses than it is to posit two likenesses between two white things, although there are two accidents of being white.[147] Marriage is a relation of equiparance, inasmuch as husband and wife are equal in what pertains to marriage *per se* albeit obviously not in every way.[148] Albert explains elsewhere that the spouses are equal chiefly in respect of the conjugal debt and the "act of generation," whereas in other marital respects, such as the governance of the household, the husband is the

---

[143] Alexander of Hales, *IV Sent.* 27.1g (466).
[144] Compare these examples: a gunshot causes a death; a lighted match sets fire to some sticks; a virus causes a disease.
[145] *IV Sent.* 27.1f (466).   [146] Albertus Magnus, *IV Sent.* 27.1, ad 1–3; ad 6 (128b).
[147] Albertus Magnus, *De matrimonio* 1.1, ad 1 (155a).
[148] *IV Sent.* 27.1, resp. (128). There is a relation of equiparance in A toward B if and only if the following is true: if A is related thus to B, then B necessarily has the same relation toward A. Standard examples are equality, likeness (with important exceptions), friendship, spouse.

dominant partner.[149] Bonaventure deals with the ontological and categorical issues summarily, conceding that the two partners consent to different things when they marry but noting that their acts of consent are inextricably mutual and convergent. The woman implicitly agrees to be her husband's wife by accepting him as her husband, and vice versa. Each relation implies or presupposes the other.[150]

Thomas Aquinas, too, proposes a version of the convergence theory. There are two relations of equiparance in marriage inasmuch as there are two subjects and two relational foundations, one in each subject.[151] But the essence of marriage is union (*coniunctio*), and the notion of union implies that of becoming united (*adunatio*), or of a coming together in a common purpose. Just as many persons come together into a single army or business to pursue a common end, so a man and a woman come together in marriage precisely as husband and wife, that is, in pursuit of their common begetting and raising of children and of their shared domestic life, which are the natural and civil dimensions of marriage respectively. It is in view of that shared *adunatio* that one construes the relation of a marriage as a single thing.[152]

Peter of Tarentaise accepts that marriage is a relation. To the objection that a sacrament by definition is something perceptible to the senses whereas one cannot see a relation, Peter replies that although the conjugal relation itself is not sensible, its efficient cause is sensible, namely, the expression of consent in the present tense. So also is sexual intercourse, which is an outcome of the relation.[153] To the objection that a relation would be duplicated in the two subjects, just as equality is duplicated in two equal subjects, Peter proposes a version of the convergence theory. Although the relation *per se* is duplicated, he argues, there is a single final cause. Although marriage is intrinsically multiple, therefore, it is single in outcome.[154]

Richard de Mediavilla's analysis is more complicated. There are several different aspects of the union that may be called "marriage," he argues, and they belong to different categories. As a sacrament, marriage can be considered either in respect of the *sacramentum tantum* (the outward appearance), or in respect of its *sacramentum et res* (the interior, mediating aspect); and each of these aspects, again, is twofold. The *sacramentum tantum* is the verbal expression of mutual consent, but any sensible sign can be considered either in itself as a *res* or precisely inasmuch as it signifies. Considered in the first way, as a reality in itself, the outward sacrament consists of verbal sounds. Sound itself comes under the category of quality, but the signification of a sound is a relation. Again, two different things can be construed as

---

[149] *IV Sent.* 27.2, ad 3 (130b); 28.7, ad 4 (196b); 32.1, resp. (269).
[150] Bonaventure, *IV Sent.* 27.2.1, ad 4 (679b).
[151] A foundation is the absolute entity (typically a quality or a quantity) in a subject that underlies the relation. For example, if John weighs 160 lbs and Jack weighs 150 lbs, John's weight is the foundation of the relation heavier-than-Jack in John.
[152] Thomas Aquinas, *IV Sent.* 27.1.1, quᵃ 1, arg. 3; resp.; ad 3 (79b, 80). Ibid., 27.1.2, quᵃ 1, ad 3 (83b).
[153] Peter of Tarentaise, *IV Sent.* 27.1.1, ad 1 (292).   [154] Ibid., ad 2.

the *sacramentum et res*: the interior act of mutual consent, which is expressed outwardly in words; and the mutual obligation to observe the conjugal debt without avoiding procreation. The interior act of consent comes under the category of action, whereas the obligation that ensues is a relation. Among the four aspects posited in this analysis, the last – the *obligatio* – is what is most properly called marriage.[155] Although there are two such relations in marriage, one in each subject, the spouses are considered to share a single marriage because we reasonably regard the two bonds as a single thing. Likewise, if John and Martin are related to each other in the same way (e.g., as cousins), we consider them to share a single common relationship (e.g., of cousinhood), although technically each has a relation of being cousin to the other.[156]

John Duns Scotus's treatment of the topic is characteristically both idiosyncratic and highly technical. Since marriage is defined as a certain union, Scotus asks whether that union is a relation or a passion (i.e., the reception of an action). Properly understood, he replies, the union (*coniunctio*) to which the definitions of marriage refer is a "habitual union" (*coniunctio habitualis*), that is, the enduring obligation that results from conjugal consent.[157] Marriage in that sense cannot be an action or a passion, therefore, for these are transient events, whereas marriage endures even while the spouses are asleep. Nor can marriage be a relation, it seems, for marriage is the end result (*terminus*) of a change, and according to Aristotle a relation can be neither the point of departure nor the terminus of a change.[158] Moreover, if marriage were a relation there would be two marriages, whereas in fact we count only one marriage. Scotus concludes that marriage is best understood as two complementary real relations that are really distinct yet constitute a single whole. In the Oxford commentary, Scotus concludes that marriage is "one by the unity of integrity but not by the unity of indivisibility." The same is true, he argues, of any contract, "because a contract includes two parts, namely, the assent of this person and of that person." Moreover, there are two acts in each person: the interior act of consent and its exterior expression.[159] In the Parisian *reportatio*, Scotus compares marriage to a road (*via*) between two cities, such as between Athens and Thebes. Inasmuch as the way from Athens to Thebes is numerically the same as the way from Thebes to Athens, one may say that there is a single way between them. Nevertheless, the way from Athens to Thebes and the way from Thebes to Athens

---

[155] Richard de Mediavilla, *IV Sent*. 26.4.1, resp. (408a).

[156] Ibid., ad 2. The example of cousin is my own, for Richard's example, *vicinus*, cannot be translated adequately into English. John and Martin are *vicini* ("near-by persons," "neighbors") inasmuch as they share a relation of *vicinitas* ("near-by-ness," "proximity").

[157] Duns Scotus, *Opus Oxon.*, *IV Sent*. 27.1 (Vivès 19:199a).

[158] Cf. Aristotle, *Physics* V, 225b11–13. According to Thomas Aquinas's commentary, *Sententia super Physicam* V, lect. 3, §7 (Leonine 2:237a), Aristotle's reasoning is that the relation of A toward B may change entirely because of a change in B, without any change in the foundation of the relation in A.

[159] Duns Scotus, *Opus Oxon.*, *IV Sent*. 27.1 (199a).

are strictly relations, and as such they are really distinct, since each has a different foundation in its subject and a different terminus *to which* it is related. In short, the two ways are materially identical but formally distinct. Likewise, the union of a husband to his wife and the union of a wife to her husband are materially identical but formally distinct, so that "one marriage is formally two marriages."[160]

The schoolmen's sustained inquiry into the ontology of marriage may seem like an elaborate game with as much import as a modern crossword puzzle, but it might also make one suspect that some theologians were inclined to regard the marriage bond quasi-ontologically as a thing or a fact rather than as a juridico-moral *ius* or *obligatio*. The tendency toward ontological realism is especially evident in Peter of La Palu. Informed by recent work on relations, including nominalist theories, Peter denies that marriage is a relation, arguing instead that it must be an absolute (i.e., non-relative) quality of a special sort. Peter's explicit reason for denying that the marriage bond is a relation is that it disposes the subject for grace, for according to Aristotle a disposition is not a relation but a subdivision of quality.[161] This appeal to authority is weak at best, for a disposition in Aristotle's sense is a propensity to act in a certain way, whereas a sacramental disposition is a receptivity to a certain causal influence. Peter's real reason for denying that being married is a relation, I suggest, is his intuitive sense that relations, as the nominalists held, are not really real.

What disposes the recipient of a sacrament to receive grace, Peter assumes, is typically a qualitative *ornatus* (literally, "adornment") of the soul, such as the character in baptism. The dispositive *ornatus* in marriage is the bond:

> . . . . marriage inasmuch as it is a sacrament of the New Law imprints an *ornatus* that is called a bond [*vinculum*] or a tie [*nexus*], and this is not a mere relation of reason but an absolute reality [*res absoluta*] disposing [the subject] for grace. . . .[162]

The notion of the sacramental "adornment" (*ornatus*) was a feature of the dispositional theory of sacramental causality,[163] but the thing to note here is Peter's insistence that the marriage bond is real. As such, he reasons, it cannot be a relation. Some background information may be helpful here. The scholastics distinguished between real relations, which really existed in their subjects, and "relations of reason," which existed only in the mind as it considered the subjects. For example, the identity between one thing and another, such as between the Evening Star and the Morning Star, must be a relation of reason, for there are not two correspondingly related things in the real world. Most scholastics held that a stone's being seen by a person was a relation of reason in the stone, but that a person's seeing a stone was real relation to the stone in the person. Again, when a mouse moves from one side of a pillar to another, the relational change is real in the mouse but not in the pillar. It seems intuitively evident that having the relation in question "makes no difference"

---

[160] Duns Scotus, *Rep. Par.*, IV *Sent.* 27.2 (Vivès 24:374–75).
[161] Paludanus, IV *Sent.* 31.1.2, conc. 2 (159rb–va).
[162] IV *Sent.* 26.4.3, ad 5 (142ra).   [163] I. Rosier-Catach, *La parole efficace* (Paris, 2004), 100–02.

to the seeing person or to the pillar in these examples, although it would be hard to prove that point without circularity. But the nominalists, most notably Peter Auriol, questioned whether *any* relations were real, and whether any relations were accidents inhering *in* their subjects.[164] If John is taller than James, on this view, then John's height and James's height are both real, and those heights are really different, but John's being taller than James is not something that really exists in John. Instead, the observer mentally imposes the relation on John, so that the mind regards John as if the difference were an accident in him.[165] Because of such inquiries, the reality of relations seemed at best questionable and unsafe.

Peter of La Palu reviews three opinions regarding the manner in which the marriage bond may be said to be (i.e., to exist). Some say, he tells us, that the marriage bond is "purely and only a relation, and perhaps one of reason." On this view, a man is the husband of his wife in much the same way as he is the father of his son. According to the second opinion, the bond is not a relation but an absolute (i.e., non-relative) accident that inheres *in the body*. This view is plausible because the bond disposes the subjects for grace, for conjugal grace is a remedy against carnal concupiscence. According to the third opinion, the bond is an absolute accident that inheres *in the soul*. Peter cannot accept the first opinion because of doubts about the reality of accidents, and he seems to prefer the third theory to second: that is, he prefers to regard the marriage bond as an absolute accident of the soul.

If the bond is not relational but absolute, why does it endure in each spouse only as long as the other is alive? Peter considers how one might approach that question from the perspective of each of the three opinions. Those who accept the first opinion have no problem, for a relation in one subject requires the existence of the term "toward which" it exists. It is easy, too, for those who accept the second opinion to explain why a marriage does not endure in the one who dies, for in death the soul is separated from the body, which becomes lifeless. It is not obvious, though, why the bond ceases to exist in the one who survives. Peter cannot accept that each spouse is the agent causing the bond to exist in the other. He suggests instead that the bond in one spouse may be related to the other spouse in the same way as one's seeing a color is related to the color itself. The vision, construed as a real qualitative modification of the subject, ceases at once if the color is removed, but the color is not the efficient cause of the vision, Peter argues, but rather its terminus, for it is what the sense of vision grasps.

Those who hold the third opinion, Peter argues, are the ones who find it most difficult to explain why the marriage bond ceases to exist when one of the spouses dies. If marriage is an absolute accident of a soul, why does it not continue to exist in

---

[164] Henninger, *Relations*, 119–73.

[165] Perhaps because John's having or not having that relation makes no difference to John. If John remains at the same height while James grows up and surpasses him, John is at first taller and later shorter than James, but it is difficult to see why that entails any real change in John.

the separated soul? Citing examples from physics and cosmology as well as from psychology, Peter suggests that the bond might lapse through desuetude. Any habit or motion, especially one that is under the control of a rational being, naturally ceases when its reason for existence, or final cause, has ceased. Marriage pertains to this life not to the next even as regards the spiritual aspect of the bond. That is why the bond in an unconsummated marriage can be severed by civil death (i.e., by entry into the religious life). One should expect, therefore, that God would allow the bond to fall into non-existence when it is no longer needed. One might counter that the character in baptism, confirmation, and orders is thought to remain in the soul after death even though it is no longer needed as a disposition for grace. Peter replies that sacramental characters remain in the afterlife for the same reason and in much the same way as the cardinal virtues do, for these do not remain *as virtues* in the hereafter but rather as glorious adornments of the soul. (Peter assumes that marriage is not worthy to be a postmortem endowment.) Or the bond might cease to exist after death in the same way as knowledge in the possible intellect ceases when the phantasms on which it depends for actual thought, which are supplied by the brain, are no longer available. This even happens with certain brain disorders, such as lethargy. Some experts hold that acquired but unused knowledge remains indefinitely as an unactualized habit in the possible intellect of the separated soul, but Peter thinks that such habits, absent special divine assistance, probably fade sooner or later through disuse, so that one eventually forgets, much as a body naturally cools when a heat source is removed from it.[166]

12.2.4 *Marriage and nature*

Theologians related marriage to the natural law in two ways, respectively diachronic and synchronic. On the one hand, following twelfth-century scholars such as Hugh of Saint-Victor, they construed the natural law as the first of the three great periods of salvation history, which endured from Adam to Moses. Thus, the natural law came first and was succeeded historically by the written law and the law of grace, otherwise known as the Old Law and the New Law, although marriage endured as a natural institution under the Old Law and the New Law. Whether there was a distinct re-institution of marriage under the New Law or only a renewed approval (*approbatio*) was a matter of disagreement. On the other hand, theologians regarded the natural law more philosophically as something perennially inherent in the nature of things, especially rational things. Synchronic division of laws had largely superseded diachronic division in scholastic theology by the Middle of the thirteenth century, but it never did so entirely. No theologian could think of the natural law of marriage without imagining Adam and Eve in the Garden of Eden, with God the Father joining them as man and wife.

---

[166] *IV Sent.*, q. 1, a. 2, conc. 2 (159rb–vb).

We have seen in the previous chapter how canonists during the second half of the twelfth century discussed the situation of marriage in relation to the natural law (Section 11.6.2). The topic arose because Ulpian had included "the union of male and female, which we call marriage" and the procreation and rearing of children as examples of a natural law that "nature has taught to all animals."[167] Thirteenth-century theologians, too, found the topic of natural law to be a useful tool when they discussed marriage, but it was also a source of difficulties. If marriage belongs to the natural law, why is there so much variation in the law of marriage? Contrariwise, what does the natural law of marriage include? Is there something in nature that distinguishes human sexual bonding from that of irrational animals? Does the natural law distinguish fornication from marriage, or do these distinctions depend on human institutions, or on positive laws that were superimposed on the natural law? How much of what Christians maintain about marriage can be demonstrated by natural reason or through the observation of nature alone? I shall consider in a later chapter the natural-law theory of marriage in Albertus Magnus (Section 16.4) and Thomas Aquinas (Sections 16.5.3 and 16.5.4). Central to those accounts was the purported naturalness of monogamy: a topic of much debate during the first quarter of the thirteenth century.

12.2.4.1 *William of Auxerre on monogamy in the natural law*

William of Auxerre's inquiries into the subject sprang from Guy of Orchelles' remarks on biblical polygyny.[168] Guy had inquired whether the Old Testament patriarchs had sinned in having several wives. It seems so, for marriage was instituted as a union between one man and one woman, and custom cannot excuse what is illicit or sinful. Moreover, Lamech, who was the first man to have two wives at the same time (Gen 4:19), was traditionally despised as an adulterer. Yet Augustine, discussing Jacob's four wives, said that polygamy then "was a custom [*mos*], not a sin." The maxim seems to imply a kind of moral relativism. In response, Guy rehearses arguments that the *magistri moderni* had adapted from Augustine. The underlying assumption of such arguments is that polygyny unlike polyandry enables men to procreate more efficiently than monogamy does. Polygyny was necessary after the Flood, therefore, when God's people were few but were not permitted to marry outside their race. Whereas Jacob and the other patriarchs had several wives so that they could beget children of their race more expeditiously, raising them to worship the one true God, Lamech was motivated by lust. Polygyny is not intrinsically sinful as regards its own nature (*in genere*), Guy argues, but only in relation to a certain historical context.[169]

---

[167] *Dig.* 1.1.1.3. *Inst.* 1.2, pr.
[168] Guy of Orchelles, *Tractatus de sacramentis* 9.2, no. 226 (203–04). Guy's argument follows Peter Lombard, *Sent.* IV, 33.1–4 (456–62).
[169] *Tractatus de sacramentis*, 9.2, no. 226 (204/14–31).

William elaborates these reflections and makes them the basis of an inquiry into the natural law.[170] The example of Jacob's wives poses a dilemma. On the one hand, Jacob's polygyny must have been in accordance with the natural law, for there was no other divinely given law at that time, and custom cannot override the natural law. On the other hand, if polygyny is intrinsically wrong (*malum secundum se*), it must have been as wrong then as it is now, and Jacob and the other patriarchs must have sinned. Contrariwise, if it was not intrinsically wrong then, then it cannot be intrinsically wrong now – which seems false.[171]

In his solution, William suggests "without ruling out a better opinion" that monogamy is a secondary precept of the natural law, and that God may justly dispense people from it because of the exigencies of the times. During the Old Testament period, God's people needed to beget as many children as possible to worship him. The patriarchs practiced polygyny chiefly for that reason, while still practicing moral moderation and the virtue that underlies continence. There were also moral benefits. Because wives were bound to be resentful about sharing husbands, polygyny prompted men to listen rather to God than to their wives. (Uxoriousness was a vice in medieval ethics.) Finally, polygyny was a sacred sign. For example, the example of Abraham's two wives, one of whom was free and the other unfree, has proved to be a powerful simile when one needs to compare sincere, free Christians with insincere, "mercenary" Christians. (William cites Gal 4:22–30, Luke 17:34, and Phil 1:18.)[172] To have several wives is not inherently bad (*malum secundum se*), therefore, but it is bad in itself (*malum in se*), that is, it is forbidden absent justifying circumstances. In the same way, homicide is bad in itself (*in se*), but it can be meritorious when there is an adequate reason, such as in a just war.[173] Moreover, God did not dispense the patriarchs from conjugal chastity, which is the virtue that underlies monogamy, but only from the outward work of monogamy, "for virtue is immutable, whereas works are variable."[174]

Monogamy belongs to the natural law, therefore, although polygyny is contrary to the natural law in the weak sense that it is bad in itself (*malum in se*), absent justifying circumstances. William subdivides the natural law into three ranges: universal (*universalissimum*), general (*universalior*), and special. The universal natural law governs everything, embracing even the rules followed by the permutations of the four elements. The general natural law governs animals alone, but it embraces all animals, irrational and rational. The special natural law is dictated by natural reason and is peculiar to human beings. Marriage belongs to the general natural law inasmuch as it is a "union of male and female" that "nature has taught to all animals," but certain features of marriage, such as monogamy, marital fidelity, and the conjugal debt, belong to the special natural law, which is peculiar to rational beings. William notes, though, that not all irrational animals are

---

[170] William of Auxerre, *Summa aurea* IV.17.3 (390–99).   [171] IV.17.3.1 (391/15–18).
[172] Ibid. (390–93).   [173] Ibid. (393/89–92).   [174] IV.17.3.2 (396/53–59).

promiscuous. Some, such as the turtledove, are human-like in their chastity and monogamy.[175] Medieval scholars were fascinated by the overlapping of *genera*.

Simple fornication does not contravene the general natural law shared by all animals, William of Auxerre argues, but it does contravene the special natural law. For that reason, it is a mortal sin. Natural reason dictates not only that there should be no coitus except for the sake of procreation, but also that there should be no coitus outside the marriage compact (*pactio coniugalis*), and that the compact is insoluble. Because the special natural law dictates that marriage is permanent and exclusive, each husband must "leave his father and mother" (Gen 2:24) to bestow his affection appropriately on his wife. If even some irrational animals mate for life, such as the turtledove, how much more should human beings do so, who participate more fully in the virtue of chastity! Indivisibility (*individualitas*), which William defines as the mutual compact never to separate (*pactio coniugalis de non separando*), belongs to the very essence of marriage.[176]

12.2.4.2 *William of Auvergne: Marriage as the natural convergence of the sexes*

William of Auvergne likens human nature to an oddly formed tree planted and cultivated by God. This tree grows from the convergence of male and female as if from two branches.[177] The two branches come together to produce a single fruit. It is never the case that more than two branches come together to produce such fruit. Nor do two females or two males ever produce fruit together.[178]

In William's view, therefore, carnal human nature is essentially gendered. Indeed, the same is true of the natures of most living things. The nature of each species is complete only when the two branches come together as one trunk, whereas each branch contains only a part of the specific nature. As a sign (*indicium*) of this remarkable fact, the generative power, like the underlying nature, is incomplete in the male and in the female, and the two sexes must come together to produce an offspring, somewhat in the manner that rennet sets milk (Job 10:10). The sexuality of the generative power, William argues, is a feature of living things that is more basic than the mechanics of the genitalia. The fact that in most species the male emits seed while the female receives it is only a sign of the underlying difference, for in a few species the female emits and the male receives.[179]

---

[175] Ibid. (394/21–395/26, 395/41–52). Medieval scholars were fascinated by the overlapping of *genera*.

[176] IV.17.3.3 (398/35–399/50). "Propter hoc de substantia matrimonii est individualitas, scilicet pactio coniugalis de non separando."

[177] William of Auvergne, *De sacramento matrimonii*, ed. Hotot, C. 1, 513aA.   [178] Ibid., 513aC.

[179] Ibid., 513aB.With the MS (173vb), I read *indicium* where the printed text has *judicium* in this chapter. (It occurs several times.) The image of two branches growing together to produce a single tree is unusual but may have come from heraldry or from depictions of the Tree of Jesse. An unusual fourteenth-century tomb at the church of St Martin in Lowthorpe, East Riding of

The partnership of marriage is "social and holy," William argues, because it brings one man and one woman together to generate and to raise the "fruit" of the generative power.[180] Contrariwise, any use of the generative power outside the confines of monogamy is abusive and reprehensible.[181] All such abuses are qualitatively the same and differ only in degree. William uses a slippery-slope argument – a favorite device – to emphasize his point:

> Either this beast is restrained — namely, the beast of carnal concupiscence, of such great wildness and unrestrained impetuosity — or it is not. If it is not restrained or held back at all, what can prevent human nature from deviating into shameful acts of every sort, and not only acts of sodomy but all manner of nefarious abominations and detestable obscenities, so that it will not abstain even from intercourse with brute animals?[182]

Since the proper motive for coitus is procreation, even sexual intercourse between one male and one female is abusive when the motive is lust (*concupiscentia*), for to abuse something is to twist it away from its proper end in order to use it for a different end. Like sodomy, therefore, albeit perhaps not to the same degree, coitus motivated by lust is against nature.[183] A person who abuses the generative power is like a farmer who scatters seed in a field without caring whether it germinates and grows.[184] Such abuse involves a certain contrariety. The point is not merely that one uses a thing for some purpose other than its proper, inherent end, William argues, but rather that one uses it in a way that *prevents* it from achieving its proper end. For example, feet are made for walking, but someone who treads grapes to make wine is not abusing her feet, although that is not their proper end. But it would be wrong to use one's feet for any purpose that *prevents* their proper use.[185] Now, when carnal pleasure is the end sought in the sexual act, the motive is apt to prevent the proper use of the generative power and the goodness of marriage, for intense ardor and promiscuity reduce the likelihood of conception. Carnal pleasure is like a strong wine, which intoxicates the mind, enervating it and sapping its virtue. Contrariwise, those who develop an appetite for spiritual things lose their taste for carnal things.[186]

Yorkshire, depicts a noble couple in bed beneath a coverlet with two branches springing from their necks. These converge in a spine-like trunk running down the center of the coverlet, and side-branches run to thirteen heads arranged along either side of the coverlet. Jessica Barker of the Courtauld Institute, who is making a study of the tomb, has shown that in all probability the spouses are Sir John de Heslerton and Margery de Lowthorpe; that seven of the dependent heads (two laywomen and five laymen) are the couple's progeny; and that the other six, which are tonsured, are the chantry priests of a college that the couple founded in Lowthorpe. I am grateful to Ms Barker for this information.

[180] C. 2, 513bD.   [181] C. 3, 514bF–516aG.   [182] Ibid., 515bA.

[183] Ibid., 514bE–F. William characterizes coitus motivated by lust as *contra naturam* ("against nature"), and sodomy as *inimica naturae* ("inimical to nature"). The difference he posits, I presume, is one of degree, not of kind.

[184] Ibid., 514bF–G.   [185] Traditional Chinese foot binding would be an example.

[186] Ibid., 514bG–H.

William applies these teleological insights to illuminate his conventional account of the proper and improper motives for coitus in marriage. There are only three proper motives for coitus: to procreate, to render the conjugal debt, and to prevent either one's spouse or one's self from committing fornication. It is sinful to pursue sexual pleasure (*voluptas*) as one's goal in coitus, but the sin that a man commits by using his wife for sexual pleasure is venial as long as he does not *exclude* the ends or goods that belong to marriage by nature or institution, for the intrinsic sanctity of marriage will excuse his error. But he will sin mortally if his pleasure seeking is not a momentary lapse but something that he does purposefully, frequently, and keenly. Again, if a man marries chiefly for lust, pride, or avarice, and if he is an adult with sufficient instruction to know what is right, then he commits a mortal sin. With God's help, a husband should "know how to possess his vessel in sanctification and honor (1 Thess 4:4), and not in the passion of desire, like the Gentiles which know not God." One may interpret this "vessel," William explains, either as the man's own body or as his wife's.[187]

Using the method of contrariety, William holds up three sorts of persons as obviously despicable abusers of the generative act and prime examples of bestiality: sodomites, prostitutes, and Saracens (i.e., Muslims). (One should keep in mind here that prostitution was among the most populous trades of medieval Paris.)[188] Sodomites and prostitutes are like wild beasts. William explains that the word *bestia*, as Isidore says, is from *vastare*: "to lay waste," "to ravage,"[189] for "the brutality and the menace of those most hateful and most execrable beasts, namely, of the sodomites and the prostitutes and peddlers in fornication," is too obvious to require proof or evidence.[190] William does not discuss the Sodomites extensively, presumably because he considers their misuse of the generative power to be self-evident and universally recognized. He mentions them only to taint other deviants through moral equivalence, such as prostitutes and overly lustful spouses. But William analyzes the vices of prostitutes in some detail. Prostitutes have no interest in begetting offspring, William complains, and they try to obviate offspring by contraception or abortion. Even when they accidentally beget children, they fail to provide for and to nurture them.[191] But prostitutes "rarely or never conceive, either because they have been burned up by too much ardor, or because the excessive

---

[187] C. 6, 519bD–520aF.
[188] P. Biller, *The Measure of Multitude* (Oxford, 2000), 60–88, discusses the demographic aspects of William's discussion of prostitutes and Muslims. On the circumstances and origins of Parisian prostitutes, see S. Farmer, *Surviving Poverty in Medieval Paris* (Ithaca, 2002), references under "Prostitutes" in the index.
[189] Isidore, *Differentiae verborum et rerum* I, *De littera F*, no. 248 (PL 83:36A). The lemma distinguishes between *fera* and *bestia*: "Omnis bestia fera, non omnis fera bestia. Bestiae namque sunt, quae morsu, vel unguibus saeviunt, ut pardi, leones, tigrides, a vastando dictae."
[190] C. 2, 513bA.   [191] C. 2, 513bA–C; C. 9, 525b. See Biller, *Measure of Multitude*, 76–77.

frequency of their turpitude prevents the seed [implanted] in them from curdling and having life."[192]

William's complaint against the Saracens is focused on polygyny and concubinage: practices that he considers to be conspicuous features of Saracen communities. Mohamet's law permits each man, William says, to have four wives and as many concubines as he wishes.[193] The error of the Saracens, therefore, is a special case of the errors of polygyny and multiple concubinage. Polygyny is contrary to equity and justice. Indeed, because women are by nature more concupiscent than men, polyandry would arguably be more natural. When men and women exist in roughly equal numbers, polygyny is against nature even from a demographic point of view.[194] The Saracens justify polygyny as a means to maximize procreation, but in fact Saracen communities are no more fertile than others.[195] Moreover, no man can adequately care for several women at the same time, especially if they are pregnant, giving birth, and nursing.[196] Even a wealthy and powerful king cannot adequately be a father to twelve or more children at once.[197] Saracen men, William claims, treat their wives like pigs and value them only as breeders. They treat their children as commodities and take them to market to sell them.[198]

Just as promiscuous lust is a ravaging beast, in William's view, so sexual depravity is alien to human nature. The example of polygyny among Saracens and Jews, which is no better than institutionalized fornication, shows how sexual and familial disorder is alien to the Christian community. But that is not to say that Christian communities are immune to such abuses. Extending his simile of human nature as a tree growing from the convergence of two branches, William likens the ideal Christian household to a fruitful tree in a peaceful orchard:

> But you will find that the homes of married folk are like trees that are verdant and laden with fruit, where sodomy has not burned up matrimony, where fornication has not torn it down, and where neither sterility nor anything else that is unfitting has befallen it. But one sees that the households that sodomy has captured from the seemliness of human kind have been burned up, and the households that fornication and harlotry capture have been smashed down, and those which sterility captures are arid or dried up at least as regards the fruit of carnal generation, as it is said in Isaiah 56[:3], "Let not the eunuch say: Behold, I am an arid tree."[199]

---

[192] C. 8, 524G. Compare Albert, *IV Sent.* 31.2.2, resp. (258b), citing Avicenna, on why it is better to abstain from sex during pregnancy: Because the womb is like a living animal, pleasure and agitated motion in sexual intercourse may cause the womb to dilate and semen or an embryo to be spilled out.

[193] C. 3, 515bA–B. [194] Ibid., 515bB–516aG. [195] C. 8, 524aF–H. [196] Ibid., 524bG.

[197] Ibid., 524aH-bF. [198] Ibid., 524bF.

[199] William of Auvergne, *De sacramento matrimonii*, MS BnF lat. 14842, 183va–b [ed. Hotot, C. 5, 518bG]: "Domus vero coniugatorum invenies sicut arbores frondosas ac fructibus onustas, *ubi matrimonium sodomia non exusserit* [quas meretricium aut sodomia non excusserit] aut fornicatio non disrumperit, aut sterilitas seu aliud incommodum non occasionaverit. *Quas vero de decore generis humani* [Quae vero contra decorem generis humani] occupat sodomia, sicut exusta sunt. *Quas* [Quae] vero occupat fornicatio et meretricium sicut conculcata. *Quas*

William likens promiscuous, family-wrecking husbands to Christians who are becoming assimilated to their Muslim or Jewish neighbors:

> In the same way as many Christians live in many respects Saracenically or Judaically, or Saracenize or Judaize, so also many spouses or married folk live in many respects fornicariously or adulterously and fornicate and adulterate.[200]

The neologisms in this passage seem to be used more for rhetorical effect than for clarity or for any terminological convenience. By disrupting whatever smoothness William's prose might otherwise have had, they suggest that the aberrant practices are foreign and outlandish.

If prostitution and sodomy are alien and inimical to human nature because they prevent the tree of human nature from bearing fruit, does it not follow that virginity and continence are also inimical? William's complicated response is predicated partly on the concept of intention, partly on the notion that prostitutes and sodomites abuse the generative act, and partly on the idea of a "happy exchange" (*felix commercium*) whereby one trades the consolation of temporal, corporeal pleasures for the consolation of pleasures that are spiritual and eternal.[201] The celibate's intention is not to prevent fructification but to avoid the perils of sexual pleasure, which lie in wait for anyone who engages in coitus. Motivated by that fear, celibates retain their seed. They do not abuse it by spilling it uselessly or inappropriately. The husband is to his wife as a farmer is to his field. Suppose a farmer does not go into his field to sow seed because someone has warned him that a wolf or a lion waits there. Neither his action nor the action of the one who warns him is inimical to the fertility of the field. Moreover, celibates pursue a "more sublime" vocation, for they set aside mundane things in order to be united with the heavenly bridegroom. They sacrifice even good things, such as offspring, as well as avoiding corrupt things, such as sexual pleasure. When David was parched with thirst, and water was brought to him from the well in Bethlehem, he poured it out as a libation to the Lord (2 Kings 23:15–16). Prostitutes and sodomites, on the contrary, run headlong into the jaws of the beast, submerging themselves in the mire of pleasure. They not only avoid the production of fruit: they also pervert and defeat the productive act.[202]

William posits a hierarchy of conjugal benefits that extends from the natural basis of marriage to the goods that make marriage worthy both to be called a sacrament in

---

[Quae] vero sterilitas sicut arida sue arefacta quantum ad fructum generationis carnalis, sicut legitur Isa. 56, Non dicat eunuchus, ecce ego lignum aridum."

[200] Ibid., 185rb [C. 6, 519bD]: "Et quamadmodum multi christiani saracenice vivunt aut iudaice, sive saracenizant aut iudaizant in multis, *ita multi coniuges seu coniugati vivunt fornicarie sive adultere, et fornicantur et adulterantur in multis.*" The italicized section is missing from Hotot's edition. Albertus Magnus, *IV Sent.* 26.10 (Borgnet 30:111b), refers to "certain Judaizing heretics" who maintain that "increase and multiply" is still a precept for Christians. On Christian anxiety about Jewish influence during this period, see S. E. Murphy, "Concern about Judaizing in Academic Treatises on the Law, c.1130–c.1230," *Speculum* 82.3 (2007): 560–94.

[201] C. 3, 515aB. MS Paris BnF lat. 14842, 177ra–b.   [202] C. 9, 525aD–bB.

the broad sense, and even to be counted as one of the sacraments in the proper sense.[203] Marriage has honorableness (*honestas*), seemliness (*decor*), and sanctity (*sanctity*). It has honorableness inasmuch as it is a natural union. Indeed, even some irrational animals – certain birds, such as pigeons, turtle-doves and storks, and most animals that walk on two legs, especially bears – form enduring monogamous partnerships to raise their young.[204] Moreover, monogamy is honorable through contrariety, that is, by excluding correspondingly dishonorable things, such as polygyny and promiscuity. Marriage has seemliness because of the ways in which male and female complement one another in their respective roles.[205] But marriage owes its sanctity to benefits that transcend the merely natural order and constitute its sacramentality.[206]

12.2.4.3 *Marriage as a divinely instituted union*

Albert and Thomas developed the seminal notion of marriage as an office of nature, designed to foster not only the perpetuity of the human species but also the stability and well-being of civil society (Sections 16.4, 16.5.2 through 16.5.4). A permanent, monogamous union is necessary chiefly, they argued, because of the long period required to raise children, unlike the young of other species, and because parents need to know who their biological children are, and vice versa. Marriage is also necessary to enable men and women to collaborate and to support each other in other matters, since males and females differ as to what work best suits them. This twofold office of nature is prior to the sacrament of marriage both ontologically and rationally, for one may account for it fully without positing the sacred significance or saving power of marriage. Reflection on the definition of marriage and on marriage in the natural order, therefore, led scholastic theologians to posit a merely human partnership that was prior to the sacrament of marriage in at least two senses: first, inasmuch as the sacrament presupposed and was based on the human partnership, which it enhanced or sublimated; second, inasmuch the partnership was fully capable of explanation and rationalization in itself, prior to any consideration of its sacramentality. Those basic assumptions raised several questions, such as whether the human partnership could exist independently of sacramentality, whether it existed before the sacrament in a historical sense, and whether the marriage of unbelievers was the same as the merely human partnership on which the Christian sacrament was based. Such questions surfaced in diverse contexts only gradually and sporadically, and medieval scholars never arrived at consistent solutions to them. Thomas sometimes argues that the utility of marriage as an office of nature requires the union to be insoluble, but this implication is vague and poorly developed.

Reflection on the office of nature led theologians to distinguish between marriage in the natural order and marriage as it was originally instituted in Eden. Marriage as

---

[203] C. 5, 518aG.   [204] Ibid., 518bE.   [205] Ibid., 518bF.   [206] C. 6, 518bG–519aA.

God originally instituted it belonged entirely to the law of nature inasmuch as that law is construed as a phase in salvation history, but it surpassed the natural law construed as principles inscribed in human nature. Thomas Aquinas argues that marriage as an office of nature has a fixed core, but that the office of nature is not unchanging, unlike the divine law regulating marriage as a sacrament. Although the natural law *per se* is unchanging, it is indeterminate and must be adapted to the various conditions of human kind, and extrapolated accordingly in different systems of laws.[207] Thomas cites the example of theft to illustrate how such determination works. The natural law dictates that thieves must be punished, but it does not determine what penalties should be imposed on which kinds of theft, and one cannot punish a thief without applying a determinate punishment.[208] Marriage is capable of multiple institutions even as an office of nature, therefore, aside from its sacred history as a sacrament. Contrariwise, the natural law as such, prior to its determination by positive laws, is an abstraction that has never been realized in fact. The natural law of marriage was already positively determined in the very beginning, in Eden. That is why one says that God *instituted* marriage as an office of nature in Eden, for "what belongs to the law of nature does not need an institution." Infidel societies add their own determinations of civil law. For example, some infidel communities treat disparity of cult as a diriment impediment, whereas others do not. Thomas tacitly concedes that these rules have a certain relative validity, although he notes that mixed marriages among infidels are not necessarily prohibited under the church's law, for the church does not judge anything outside itself (*foris*). Nor are they prohibited by divine law, before which all infidel cults are equally false.[209]

Thomas's treatment of marriage as an office of nature in his *Scriptum* (Section 16.5) became the model for many subsequent treatments. Peter of Tarentaise and Richard de Mediavilla follow it closely when they discuss whether marriage belongs to the natural law. Both authors claim that the original institution of marriage was richer and more specific than the natural law of marriage, and both attribute some of the fundamental properties of marriage not to the natural law as such but to that original divine institution, which all human beings share, infidels as well as believers. Even as an office of nature, therefore, marriage is holy and refers beyond itself to something divine.[210]

To show how marriage is an institution of the natural order, even though whatever "belongs to the natural law does not need institution," Peter of Tarentaise distinguishes between general and special conditions. Marriage is a "dictate of the natural law" only in respect of its general conditions, whereby it is no more than the "union of a man and a woman." Further specifications, such as that such-and-such a

[207] Thomas Aquinas, *IV Sent.* 26.1.1, ad 3 (Vivès 11:68a–b), citing Aristotle, NE V.12, 1134b27–30 (and not Book VII, as the text has it). *IV Sent.* 39.1in.2, ad 3 (226a): "Ea autem quae pertinent ad legem naturae, sunt determinabilia per jus positivum."
[208] *IV Sent.* 26.2.2, arg.1; ad 1; ad 3 (72, 73a).   [209] *IV Sent.* 39.un.2, ad 3 (226a).
[210] Peter of Tarentaise, *IV Sent.* 26.1.1 (283). Richard de Mediavilla, *IV Sent.* 26.1.1 (400–02).

man should only marry such-and-such a woman, as determined by the rules of exogamy, the impediments of blood relationship, and so forth, adapt marriage to special conditions but do not amount to distinct institutions of marriage.[211] Whereas the natural law *per se* never changes, the laws of marriage can and do change in respect of its special conditions.[212] But although the rational inclination to marry is a dictate of the natural law, the fact that each spouse becomes indissolubly the bodily property of the other lies outside the natural law and even transcends any merely human law, although it fulfills a natural inclination. "Nature or the human will," Peter argues, "is not capable of making a perpetual conveyance [*traditio*] of this sort unless a divine institution accompanies it."[213] The act of human consent, therefore, does not suffice as the entire efficient cause of marriage. Instead, it is concurrent with the divine institution of marriage, which is the primary efficient cause. Peter of Tarentaise associates monogamy with the original institution of marriage, when God personally intervened, as it were, joining the first man to the first woman.[214]

Richard de Mediavilla, like Thomas, regards the precepts of the natural law as if they were the first, unchanging principles of a speculative science. The first principles of the natural law are extremely general. More specific laws are either deduced from them as proximate or remote conclusions or follow as "determinations" (applications to specific circumstances). But the natural-law precepts are unlike the principles of a deductive science insofar as they require conventional, perhaps even arbitrary determinations. For example, the natural law dictates that thieves should be punished, but no deduction from the principles of the natural law can show what precise punishment to exact for a certain crime. In both respects, as regards both necessary principles and positive determinations, the "instinct of nature" underlying marriage operates in a manner that befits rational beings who have free choice, and not in the manner that drives merely natural processes, such as the upward movement of fire. Marriage did not need to be instituted in the beginning inasmuch as it belonged to the first principles of the natural law, therefore, but God instituted it because even in the beginning it included certain determinations, as well as expressing the remote conclusions of the first principles "more manifestly."[215] Again, it is chiefly in respect of its determinations that marriage law is changeable, and that the church can modify the laws.[216] Whereas the natural law of marriage is known to all rational beings as regards its first principles and proximate conclusions, their remote conclusions and determinations, even when they follow necessarily, have always been obscure to many persons. Marriage is a union that *holds together an indivisible way of life* only at the level of the remote conclusions, which are necessary but not obvious. It is not surprising, therefore,

---

[211] Peter of Tarentaise, *IV Sent.* 26.1.2, ad 1 (284a).   [212] *IV Sent.* 26.1.3, ad 2 (284b).
[213] *IV Sent.* 26.1.2, ad 1 (284a); 26.1.3, arg. 3c (284b).
[214] *IV Sent.* 26.1.3, ad 3 (284b); 27.2.1, resp. (293a).
[215] Richard de Mediavilla, *IV Sent.* 26.1.2, ad 1 (402b).
[216] *IV Sent.* 26.1.3, ad 2 (403b).

that many persons, such as the primitive savages whom Cicero described, know next to nothing about permanent, monogamous marriages.[217]

Richard argues that the natural order requires human parents, in contrast to those of most other animal species, to stay together for a long time (*magnum tempus*) in order to raise their children and secure their enduring welfare:

> The children of human beings need to be looked after by both parents for a long time, and therefore among human beings nature is inclined to a determinate union of a male and female for a long time.[218]

It follows that marriage must be long lasting at least in some general, merely institutional sense. Nevertheless, Richard does not claim that the doctrine of indissolubility can be deduced from the natural law even as one of its remote conclusions. Indeed, he concedes that inasmuch as any bond has been established by mutual consent, it can *ipso facto* be dissolved by mutual dissent. Contracts are dissoluble by their very nature. But the marriage bond (*vinculum*) cannot be legitimately dissolved, although one spouse is entitled to divorce the other on grounds of fornication, and although they may separate by mutual agreement to enter the religious life or to practice celibacy. The reason, Richard argues, is that consent is not the entire cause (*tota causa*) of marriage and its obligations, for divine institution is a concurrent cause; indeed, it is the *principal* cause of marriage. "God ordained that after their mutual consent, the bond is no longer subject to their will."[219]

We are familiar today with the traditional theory, often associated with Catholicism, whereby indissolubility and monogamy are inscribed in the natural law and for that reason are necessarily required *de iure* always and everywhere. Thomas Aquinas came close to that position, but the issues at stake were the subject of much debate and inquiry and resulted in a broad range of positions during the central Middle Ages.

---

[217] *IV Sent.* 26.1.1, ad 2 (402a). Cf. Cicero, *De inventione* I.2.

[218] *IV Sent.* 26.1.1, resp. (401a–b): "Filii autem hominum indigent cura vtriusque parentis, vsque ad magnum tempus, et ideo in hominibus natura inclinat ad determinatam coniunctionem maris, et faeminae, vsque ad magnum tempus." Cf. Thomas, *IV Sent.* 26.1.1, resp. (68a): "Sed in homine, quia indiget filius cura parentum usque ad magnum tempus, est maxima determinatio masculi et feminam, ad quam etiam natura generis inclinat."

[219] Richard de Mediavilla, *IV Sent.* 27.2.1, resp. (415b). Similarly, Durandus, *IV Sent.* 27.1, §6 [ad 1] (368vb).

13

Scholastic sexual ethics

The discourse on sexual ethics in scholastic theology followed a familiar historical trajectory, becoming fully developed, refined, and elaborated around the middle of the thirteenth century. The contributions of twelfth-century scholars in relation to this trajectory now seem exploratory and seminal, as if they were at the beginning of a development or evolution. Theologians of the late thirteenth through fourteenth centuries left the main outlines of the mid-thirteenth-century discourse intact without making any fundamental changes or additions to it, although they added some details and tried some different approaches to particular issues.

The development resulted from practical and pastoral exigencies as well as from speculative inquiry. The schoolmen assumed that any reasonable and intellectually consequential question was worth answering, notwithstanding their doctrine that curiosity was a vice, and they never limited their discourse on sexual ethics to practical matters. Nevertheless, the theologians' overarching purpose was to situate marriage and sexuality within the church and the Christian life, notwithstanding their conviction that celibacy was the best and most obvious way to serve Christ. Moreover, the ministry of confession and penance required a high degree of refinement regarding sexual matters. Although theologians were speaking mainly about practices from which they were professionally excluded, priests were required to diagnose through probing questions whether and to what degree a layperson's sexual acts or thoughts were sinful and to prescribe appropriate penances, as the Fourth Lateran Council of 1215 explained:

> Let the priest be discerning and cautious, so that in the manner of an expert physician he may pour wine and oil over the wounds of the injured one,[1] diligently inquiring into the circumstances of the sinner as well as of the sin, so that through

---

[1] An allusion to the parable of the Good Samaritan (Luke 10:33–34). Cf. Peter Lombard, *Sent.* IV, 1.1.1 (231).

these he may understand prudently what counsel he ought to give him and what remedies to apply, using diverse treatments [*experimenta*] to heal the sick person.[2]

Theologians discussing the "conjugal act" distinguished between what was culpable and what was merely shameful both in external action and in the imagination; they distinguished among mortal sin, venial sin, and positive merit; they analyzed the moral implications of intentions and circumstances; and they parsed the sexual act and sexual experience in several different ways, assigning moral values to its various components. Some of their academic questions had obvious relevance to the confessional, such as those regarding a person's initial, reflexive responses to tempting stimuli, and those regarding the evaluation of moments within the sexual act in relation to the initial or overarching intention of the act as a whole.

Three main streams of inquiry are discernable in scholastic sexual ethics. One stream pertained to the *causae* of sexual intercourse, especially in marriage: to the motives of the spouse who demanded or initiated coitus or who willingly complied with his or her spouse's demand. Conjugal intercourse was assigned values ranging from mortal sin to merit, depending on the subject's intentions. Another stream pertained to sexual pleasure (*delectatio*), which the schoolmen generally considered to be degrading and shameful but not necessarily sinful. Desire and pleasure were modalities of appetite, and each presupposed the other. To be motivated by lust in sexual intercourse was the same as seeking carnal pleasure in it. Nevertheless, some changes in focus resulted in shifts of emphasis. From around the middle of the twelfth century, treatments of the pleasure problem focused on intense, climactic pleasure, which resulted in a transitory lapse of reason. Mindful that human beings were made in God's image inasmuch as they were rational, theologians were bound to regard any loss of reason as detrimental and dehumanizing. The climactic lapse of reason was also a proxy for lust's promiscuous indifference to persons: the feature that most troubled Augustine (Section 2.2.4).[3] But the schoolmen did not regard such indifference as inevitable. Even the husband who was motivated solely by lust or the pursuit of pleasure in the conjugal act might desire his wife either precisely as his wife or merely as the woman who happened to be most readily available. These two streams merged in a third, which pertained to the ways in which marriage *excused* sexual intercourse. Scholastic theologians reasoned that marriage and the intentions that were integral to it excused coitus by containing turpitude and intense pleasure within a rational and virtuous context.

13.1 THE BASIS IN AUGUSTINE

Augustine provided the scholastics with the framework for their sexual ethics, although they modified and schematized his ideas, eliminating much of their

---

[2] *Concilium Lateranense IV*, canon 21 (Tanner-Alberigo 245/13–17).
[3] Augustine, *Epist. 6*.5*, CSEL 88:34. Idem, *C. Iulianum* V.16(62), PL 44:818.

introspective psychological complexity and disregarding the anxiety with which they were freighted in Augustine's mind. Augustine maintained that sexual desire was a bad thing, but that righteous spouses could "use" it well by channeling it so that it fulfilled righteous motives.[4] Just as it is bad to use a good thing badly, he argued, so is it good to use a bad thing well.[5] To illustrate, Augustine envisaged a person with an injured foot who limped to reach "some good" (*aliquod bonum*). The limping pursuit is good by virtue of the goal, but the limp itself remains a defect. "We ought neither to condemn marriage because of the evil of lust," Augustine explained, "nor to praise lust because of the goodness of marriage."[6]

Augustine developed an account of pre-lapsarian sexuality in which the defects of fallen sexuality were retrospectively put right. In his mature view, men and women would have procreated sexually in the earthly Paradise, but without the distortion of lust that infects coitus in the fallen condition. Augustine was inclined to think that coitus in that state would not have entailed any lust (*libido*), or carnal desire (*concupiscentia carnis*). Men and women would have set about the procreative task calmly, dispassionately, and rationally, as carpenters and farmers perform their allotted tasks even now.[7] Nevertheless, Augustine conceded in debate with Julian of Eclanum at least for the sake of argument that carnal desire could have existed in the earthly Paradise, provided only that it was entirely obedient to the rational will, unlike the desire that we experience now (Sections 2.2.4, 3.1, and 4.2).[8] Scholastic theologians, who fully endorsed the animality of the rational animal, espoused versions of the latter position.

Although sexual desire is depraved, Augustine held, only heretics deduce from that premise that marriage is evil. On the contrary, the intrinsic goodness of marriage mitigates or compensates for the evils that have infected sexuality. Marriage was created chiefly for procreation, but after the fall it became a remedy:

> the weakness of both sexes, with its inclination toward depraved ruin, is rightly saved [*excipitur*] by the honorableness of marriage, so that what would have been a duty [*officium*] for the healthy is a remedy for the sick.[9]

The verb *excipere* in this passage may mean either that lust is corrected or rescued by marriage or that it is excepted, as if marriage somehow provides a license or a waiver. Among the followers of Christ, according to Augustine, this remedy and not

---

4 *Retr.* II.53, CCL 57:131/6–10. *De nupt. et conc.* I.12(13), CSEL 42:226. *C. Iulianum* V.16(60), PL 44:817.

5 *De b. coniug.* 3(3), CSEL 41:191.   6   *De nupt. et conc.* I.7(8), CSEL 42:220.

7 *De civ. Dei* XIV.10–24, CCL 48:431–48. *De pecc. orig.* 40–41, CSEL 42:198–200.

8 *C. Iulianum.* V.16(62), PL 44:818. *C. Iulianum imp.* I.68, I.122, CSEL 85.1:75, 253. *Contra duas epistulas Pelagianorum* I.17(34), CSEL 60:450–51.

9 *De Gen. ad litt.* IX.7, CSEL 28.1:275: "utriusque sexus infirmitas propendens in ruinam turpitudinis recte excipitur honestate nuptiarum, ut, quod sanis esse posset officium, sit aegrotis remedium."

procreation is the proper reason for marrying,[10] for there are better ways to populate the city of God and to bring this world to its predestined end.[11]

Augustine discovered in the *De bono coniugali* that three goods in particular comprised the goodness of marriage: offspring (*proles*), faith (*fides*), and sacrament (*sacramentum*).[12] The *bonum prolis* is the intention not only to beget children but also to raise them to worship God. The *bonum fidei* as Augustine understood it is primarily observance of the conjugal debt (1 Cor 7:3) and only secondarily fidelity in the modern sense.[13] The *bonum sacramenti* is the permanence or insolubility of marriage, construed as something that raises marriage above mundane concerns and makes it sacred. Scholastic theologians emphasized the figurative dimension of the *bonum sacramenti*.

As well as the three conjugal goods, the schoolmen found in Augustine three principal motives for sexual intercourse between spouses. Writing in the *De bono coniugali*, Augustine concedes that continence is always preferable to sexual intercourse, other things being equal, but he warns that by choosing continence and failing to observe the conjugal debt one spouse may expose the other to the risk of adultery. It is salutary to keep in mind, therefore, that sexual intercourse in marriage is not necessarily bad, and that it may even be good:

> Conjugal intercourse for the sake of begetting children has no blame [*culpa*]; when it is for the sake of satisfying lust, provided that this is with one's spouse, it has blame that is pardonable [*venialis*] because of the faith of the marriage bed; but adultery or fornication has mortal blame. And for this reason abstinence [*continentia*] from all sexual intercourse is better even than marital sexual intercourse performed for the sake of begetting offspring, because such abstinence has fuller merit. But there is no crime in rendering the conjugal debt, and to require it beyond what is needed to beget offspring has venial blame, whereas to fornicate or commit adultery is a crime worthy of punishment. Conjugal charity should take care, therefore, lest while seeking to achieve greater honor it leads the [other] spouse into ruin.[14]

---

[10] 1 Cor 7:8–9.
[11] *De serm. Dom. in monte* I.40–41, CCL 35:43–46. *De Gen. ad litt.* IX. 3, 272/6–7, and IX.6, 273/24–25.
[12] See Augustine's summary in *De b. coniug.* 24(32), 226–28.
[13] Although early-twelfth-century theologians construed the good of faith as fidelity in our negative sense (Section 9.3.1), thirteenth-century theologians at least partly recovered Augustine's original, positive sense. See, for example, Albertus Magnus, *IV Sent.* 31.9, arg. 3; resp. (Borgnet 30:237b; 238a).
[14] *De bono coniugali* 6(6–7), 195/19–196/4: "coniugalis enim concubitus generandi gratia non habet culpam; concupiscentiae uero satiandae, sed tamen cum coniuge, propter tori fidem uenialem habet culpam; adulterium uero siue fornicatio letalem habet culpam. ac per hoc melior est quidem ab omni concubitu continentia quam uel ipse matrimonialis concubitus, qui fit causa gignendi. sed quia illa continentia meriti amplioris est, reddere uero debitum coniugale nullius est criminis, exigere autem ultra generandi necessitatem culpae uenialis, fornicari porro uel moechari puniendi criminis, cauere debet caritas coniugalis, ne, dum sibi quaerit, unde amplius honoretur, coniugi faciat, unde damnetur."

Peter Lombard disseminated most of this passage, albeit as two separate excerpts.[15] Although Augustine's characteristically convoluted argument in this passage was not clear enough for medieval confessional practice, he touched on three chief motives for conjugal intercourse, which medieval scholars adopted: to procreate, to render the conjugal debt, and to satisfy lust. The first two carry no guilt. The third is inherently worthy of guilt but the goodness of marriage contains, directs, and compensates for that guilt, making it pardonable (*venialis*).

Augustine considered climactic sexual passion to be evidently horrendous. According to a familiar dictum of scholastic discourse, the "entire human being" (*totus homo*) becomes flesh in the orgasm. The dictum came from a sermon fragment in which Augustine discusses how to interpret 1 Corinthians 6:18.[16] Paul says that the fornicator sins within his own body whereas other sins are committed outside the body. Expounding this text, Augustine keeps in mind Paul's observation that the man who fornicates with a prostitute becomes one body with her, as if they were two in one flesh (1 Cor 6:16). Paul considered fornication to be peculiarly internal to the fornicator's body, Augustine argues, because in that sin more than in any other, carnal desire captures the mind, which is no longer free to think about anything else:

> For it seems that the blessed Apostle in whom Christ was speaking wanted to magnify the evil of fornication above all other sins, which, even if they are committed through the body, do not make human attention [*animus*] so bound and beholden to carnal desire. Only in the action of bodily fornication does the enormous force of lust cause the attention to be mixed with the body itself: to be somehow glued to it and tied to it and made one with it — so much so that in the very moment and experience of this entirely disgraceful act, [lust] does not permit the human being to think about or attend to anything except that to which it has enslaved the mind, which this submersion, as it were — this absorption by lust and by carnal desire — subdues as a captive.[17]

A little later in the discussion, Augustine remarks that in this sin alone "the entire human being [*totus homo*] is so absorbed by the flesh that his attention cannot be said to be his own. Instead, the entire human being becomes flesh, and its 'spirit that goes forth and does not return' (Ps 78:39)."[18]

---

[15] Peter Lombard, *Sent.* IV, 31.5.1 (446); *Sent.* IV, 32.1.2 (452).

[16] *Serm.* 162, PL 885–89. The fragment is preserved in Eugippius, *Excerpta ex operibus s. Augustini* (CSEL 9.1:1024–32). P.-P. Verbraken, "Les fragments conservés de sermons perdus de saint Augustin," *Revue Bénédictine* 84.3–4 (1974): 245–70, at 254 (no. 10).

[17] Augustine, *Serm.* 162.2, PL 38:886–87 (or CSEL 9.1:1026–29). Peter Lombard incorporates an abridged and rearranged version of the passage in his gloss on 1 Cor 7:18–20, PL 191:1584A–B.

[18] Augustine, *Serm.* 162.2, 887: "Sic enim totus homo absorbetur ab ipso et in ipso corpore, ut jam dici non possit ipse animus suus esse; sed simul totus homo dici possit quod caro sit, et spiritus vadens et non revertens [Ps 78:39]." Peter Lombard, on 1 Cor 7:18–20, PL 191:1584B: "Sic enim totus homo absorbetur a carne, ut jam dici non possit, ipse animus suus est, sed simul totus homo dici possit caro."

Although such pleasure distinguishes fornication from other sins, according to Augustine, it does not categorically distinguish fornication from licit sexual intercourse within marriage. To be sure, the goods of marriage and the decency and shame of the spouses ameliorate conjugal intercourse. [19] But Augustine describes in *The City of God* how sexual intercourse in the fallen state is driven by irrational lust even in marriage. Lust arouses the shameful parts of the body, taking over the entire body (*totum corpus*) and stirring up the entire human being (*totus homo*) internally as well as externally. The subject's attention and affections are joined to or mixed with the appetite of the flesh. The result is a sensual pleasure (*voluptas*) greater than any other. When it reaches its climax, it all but extinguishes the mind's alertness and capacity to think. What married person, Augustine asks rhetorically, who is a "friend of wisdom and of holy joys," and who knows "how to possess his vessel in sanctification and honor, not in the sickness of desire like the Gentiles who know not God" (1 Thess 4:4–5) – what person of that sort "would not prefer, if he were able, to beget children without such lust?" Then spouses would control their genitalia calmly, directing them to their appointed tasks, just as now they control all the other members of the body. Then even the genital members would respond not to raging lust but to the bidding of the will. [20] The possibility that Augustine envisages here is merely counterfactual in the fallen condition, but it had existed before the fall.

13.2 THE ENDS OF SEXUAL INTERCOURSE

The schoolmen enhanced Augustine's division of motives in two ways. First, they noted that lust even toward one's spouse might be so untamed and irrational that the goodness of marriage no longer contained it, so that the act of conjugal intercourse was virtually extra-marital. Peter Lombard disseminated the maxim, "Every too-ardent lover of his own wife is an adulterer." [21] It came from *The Sentences of Sextus*, a gnomic moral handbook composed in Greek by an otherwise unknown Christian author during the second century. [22] The maxim circulated in at least three Latin versions, one of which used the positive form, *vehemens amator* ("keen lover,"

---

[19] *De b. coniug.* 3(3), CSEL 31:191.

[20] *De civ. Dei* XVI.16, CCL 48:438/1–439/18.

[21] Peter Lombard, *Sent.* IV, 31.5.2 (447): "Omnis ardentior amator propriae uxoris adulter est." Gratian, C. 32 q. 4 c. 5 (1128–29): "Adulter est in suam uxorem amator ardentior." Jerome *Adv. Iovinianum* I.49, PL 23:281A: "Adulter est in suam uxorem amator ardentior." See also Jerome, *Commentaria in Ezechielem* 6:18 (PL 25:173C): "Adulter est uxoris propriae, amator ardentior."

[22] *Sent.* 231, in W. T. Wilson, *The Sentences of Sextus* (Atlanta, 2012), p. 240. See ibid, pp. 243–44, for commentary, and see H. Chadwick, *The Sentences of Sextus* (Cambridge, 1959), p. 39, for Rufinus's translation. Sextus drew on Pythagorean and Jewish sources among others. Medieval authors, following Jerome (*Epist.* 133.3), usually ascribed the collection to a pagan Pythagorean named Sextus or Xystus, but most Latin MSS of the collection ascribe it to Xystus, Bishop of Rome (i.e., Pope Sixtus II). Despite the work's popularity in the early church, it had a mixed reception among Christian leaders and intellectuals, some of whom considered it to be pagan. Sextus's source for this maxim was apparently Clitarchus, a Pythagorean (*Sent.* 71).

"vigorous lover"),[23] whereas the others used the comparative form, *ardentior amator* ("more ardent lover," or perhaps "very ardent lover").[24] The second form invited scholars to ask: "More ardent than whom, or what?" Albertus Magnus replied that the dictum referred to one whose ardor exceeded the "concession and decency of marriage."[25] Although the schoolmen believed that women were generally less in control of their passions than men were, they usually assumed that the overly ardent lover of the maxim was the husband, who used his wife violently and without affection, forcing himself on her without regard for her wishes.[26]

Second, the schoolmen added another motive to the list in addition to procreation, rendering the debt, and lust. A spouse might also pursue sexual intercourse "because of fornication" (*propter fornicationem*), or "because of incontinence." This motive was usually placed third, with "to satisfy lust" coming last. Raymond of Penyafort presents the list in its standard form in his *Summa de matrimonio* (1241) when he explains how Augustine's conjugal goods excuse sexual intercourse:

> These goods are able to excuse [coitus] from sin if, with the faith of the marriage bed preserved, the spouses come together because of offspring. Hence, one should note that spouses sometimes have intercourse to beget offspring, sometimes to render the debt, sometimes because of incontinence or to avoid fornication, and sometimes to satisfy lust. There is no sin in the first and second reasons, there is venial sin in the third, and there is mortal sin in the fourth.[27]

The schoolmen agreed that the conjugal act was free from sin and even meritorious insofar as the intention was to procreate or to render the debt, and that it was at least venially sinful when the motive was lust, or the pursuit of pleasure.[28] To render the debt was just and meritorious, although it generally presupposed at least venial sin in the one demanding the debt. The addition of *evitatio fornicationis* to the list generated extensive discussion[29] although it had a long historical pedigree. Paul

---

[23] For example, Master Simon, in H. Weisweiler, *Maître Simon et son groupe De sacramentis* (Louvain, 1937), 54/12–14: "*Omnis vehemens amator etiam proprie coniugis, adulter est.* Vehemens vero amator est, qui coniuge sua non ut coniuge utitur sed ut scorto abutitur." (Weisweiler's italics.)

[24] P. J. Payer, *The Bridling of Desire* (Toronto, 1993), 120–24. The Greek calls him simply an *akolastos*, i.e., an intemperate, unbridled fellow.

[25] Albertus Magnus, *IV Sent.* 31.20, arg. 2; resp. (253b).

[26] On the possible tension between theoretical equality and practical male-dominance in relation to the conjugal debt, see J. W. Baldwin, "Consent and the Marital Debt," in A. E. Laiou (ed.), *Consent and Coercion* (Washington, D.C., 1993), 257–70.

[27] Raymond of Penyafort, *Summa de matrimonio*, 2.13 (Rome, 1603, p. 519a): "Valent haec bona ad excusationem peccati, si seruata fide tori, causa prolis conueniant coniuges. unde nota, quod aliquando commiscentur coniuges causa suscipiendae prolis, aliquando causa reddendi debitum, aliquando causa incontinentiae, sive vitandae fornicationis, aliquando causa exsaturandae libidinis. in primo et secundo casu nullum est peccatum: in tertio est veniale; in quarto mortale." Raymond cites Augustine and Scripture for the first three motives, and Jerome and the maxim from Sextus (ascribed here to "the Philosopher") for the fourth.

[28] Payer, *Bridling of Desire*, 118–31.   [29] Ibid., 111–18.

had said that each Christian should be married "because of fornication" (*propter fornicationem*, 1 Cor 7:2), and Augustine had held that the proper reason for choosing to marry after the advent of Christ, rather than to pursue a celibate vocation, was not procreation but the avoidance of fornication (Section 3.2).[30] Early-twelfth-century theologians adopted the same position, proposing the "avoid-ance of fornication" (*evitatio fornicationis*) as the proper reason for Christians to marry, and sometimes as a fourth conjugal good in addition to Augustine's faith, offspring, and sacrament (Section 9.3.1). It was reasonable, therefore, to include the avoidance of fornication among the motives for sexual intercourse within marriage. But the use of coitus to avoid adultery presupposed lust, making the motive flawed and morally mixed, and one that required excuse or mitigation. Moreover, the phrase "because of fornication" was ambiguous. Absent any indication to the contrary, it referred to the avoidance of fornication in the one initiating or demanding coitus, but a spouse might also use sexual intercourse to save the *other* from fornication: to prevent him or her from being tempted to seek sexual satisfac-tion outside their marriage. Some theologians included this additional alternative in the discussion, raising the number of possible motives to five.

Discussion of the proper motives led theologians to ask whether coitus in mar-riage could be meritorious. The only acceptable answer was "yes," but theologians found different ways to reach that answer, and it is not always clear whether they were referring to natural, merely human merit or to supernatural merit, the reward for which was salvation and eternal life. Be that as it may, the question had become a standard item on their agenda by the second quarter of the thirteenth century.

This array of motives for sexual intercourse may seem remarkably limited to the modern reader. As befits a schema designed with private confession in mind and focused on intention, it treats each partner as a separate moral agent and provides no way to construe sexual intercourse as a shared activity, much less as "making love." Coitus was a transaction. Medieval scholars were innocent of everything that would be said today about the healthy function of sexuality in a marriage or other long-term sexual partnership, such as the consolidation of a relationship, the maintenance of partnership over a long period, the expression of affection, resolution of conflict, and recreation. Would the schema have seemed equally out of touch to medieval laypersons?

At least one distinguished medieval scholar, Robert Courson, considered the division of ends or purposes for sexual intercourse to be unrealistic and impractical. Inquiring whether coitus in marriage is ever meritorious, Robert uses the standard fourfold division of reasons as a framework for his discussion. He ascribes this

---

[30] Augustine, *De b. coniug.* 9(9), CSEL 41:201/3–7; 10(10), 202/5–8; 13(15), 207; 17(19), 212. *De bono viduitatis* 8(11), CSEL 41:315/17–316/16.

division to Augustine,[31] but he is also indebted to his mentor, Peter the Chanter, whom he mentions at several points. Robert begins with affirmative arguments showing that coitus can be meritorious when the motive is to procreate, to render the debt, or to avoid fornication. According to Augustine, he notes, there is no sin when coitus is motivated either to procreate or to fulfill the conjugal debt. Robert also proposes several arguments from reason. Conjugal intercourse is natural and was instituted by God. Moreover, procreation has sometimes been a matter of precept even after the fall, as when God commanded Noah and his sons to "increase and multiply" after they came out of the ark (Gen 9:1). To fulfill any divine precept is meritorious. Again, since to marry with these motives is meritorious, provided that the choice springs from charity, the same must be true of sexual intercourse within marriage, which completes marriage by realizing what the spouses intended in marrying. What if coitus is motivated by the desire to avoid fornication in oneself? Most authorities consider this to be a venial sin, Robert notes, but in his view it must be meritorious, too, for one's first duty of moral care is toward oneself. If it is prudent to prevent fornication in one's partner, as everyone agrees, it must be even more prudent to prevent fornication in oneself, and prudence is a virtue. To copulate with one's spouse in order to avoid fornicating instead is like taking food on a journey to obviate any need to steal.[32]

To the contrary, it seems that coitus is not meritorious even when the motive is to procreate or to render the debt. However noble the intention, there is bound to be a "particle" of the deed in which the human being is absorbed by and becomes entirely flesh. But "flesh and blood cannot inherit the kingdom of God" (1 Cor 15:50). Again, an action is meritorious before God insofar as it is directed to God, and it cannot be meritorious if even a small part of it is not directed to God.[33] According to these contrary arguments, the negative value of certain aspects or moments of the action undermines or nullifies the positive value of the action as a whole.

Developing his own position, Robert concedes that coitus in marriage is not meritorious insofar as it is considered as a whole, although he questions whether there is any such morally evaluable entity.[34] I shall review his inquiry into the evaluation of complex actions below, in the context of the pleasure problem. Suffice

---

[31] Robert Courson, *Summa* 42, 31–32, ed. J. W. Baldwin, *The Language of Sex* (Chicago, 1994), 239–45. Baldwin's edition of the passage is from Paris, BnF 14524, 154ra–155vb. The references cited here are to the folios on this MS, which Baldwin indicates parenthetically. In L. Malherbe's edition of the treatise on marriage from the *Summa* (Institut Catholique de Paris, 1924), the equivalent text is ch. 18, pp. 101–06. Malherbe used three other MSS, in addition to the Paris and Bruges MSS that both Müller and Baldwin used. M. Müller, *Die Lehre des hl. Augustinus von der Paradiesehe* (Regensburg, 1954), pp. 153–61, provides substantial excerpts from the passage in the footnotes, with an exposition in the main text. Müller's source was MS Bruges, Stadsbibliotheek, Cod. lat. 247.
[32] 154ra–b.   [33] 154rb–154va.   [34] 154va–b, 155ra–155va.

to say here that although Robert is inclined to think that each particle of the action has its own independent value, his aim is not to encourage scrupulosity but rather, by subverting the conventional moral calculus, to allay any anxiety that momentarily fervid sexual pleasure might prevent coitus between spouses from being meritorious in God's eyes.

Having reflected at length on the motives and the phenomenology of marital coitus, Robert proposes that the division of motives has little relevance in reality. The common man (*vulgus*) does not pursue any particular end when he approaches his wife for sex. Instead, he thinks only that she is his wife and that he wants her. One might argue that such action is a mortal sin because his aim is to satisfy lust, which was a sinful motive according to Augustine. But what did Augustine mean? In reply, Robert initially proposes that the fourfold enumeration is not exhaustive, but his point is that the common man has no clearly defined reason for copulating with his wife. The husband typically has a vaguely formed motive that might be loosely characterized as lust, but this is not the fully intentional, deliberate lust that Augustine condemned as a mortal sin:

> Augustine does not deny, we say, that there are other ways to know one's wife than the aforesaid four. The first three are without mortal sin, and beside those three the fourth [to satisfy lust] can be without mortal sin too, namely, when some simple man who is not expected to know the fine points [*apices*] of law approaches his wife; that is, in simplicity, without tending more to this end than to that, but rather approaching his wife as his own, wishing to make use of her. Laymen should not be condemned for loving their wives too tenderly or for approaching them frequently.[35]

It is true that husbands can sin mortally in approaching their wives to satisfy lust, Robert concedes, but only when their demands are against nature or immoderate in some other way, like the overly keen lover in the maxim. Just as someone incurs the vice of gluttony by eating too much, so too the excessively ardent, immoderate lover incurs a mortal sin by coupling with his wife too much.[36] But the simple man who uses his wife as his wife without any moral reflection commits no sin. Robert likens the clerics who condemn amorous husbands to the meddlesome, overly scrupulous "semi-heretics" who keep finding new theological reasons for abstaining from sex on particular days, until no day remains on which sex is wholly licit. Robert learned the method of parsing complex actions into moral particles from his teacher, Peter the Chanter, but at some point, it seems, he found the method absurd.

Most scholastic theologians of the period accepted the fourfold division of motives, but the avoidance of fornication, which came third in the standard enumeration, proved to be complex and equivocal, and it prompted extensive discussion. Construed as the avoidance of fornication in the agent, it was morally

---

[35] 155vb.   [36] Ibid.

ambiguous, for it entailed two concurrent motives that were respectively vicious and virtuous: lust and prudence. Thus, Robert Courson asks how "prurience" and the prudent desire to avoid fornication work together in motivating the same act. What are their respective roles? Almost everyone, Robert says, accepts that coupling to avoid fornication is a venial sin and cannot be meritorious because of the prurience attached to it. Robert seems to accept that conclusion, but he questions by what reasoning one should reach it. He recalls that his teacher, Peter the Chanter, sometimes distinguished between the deed of coitus considered in itself (*opus ipsum*), which is naturally good albeit not meritorious, and the prurience attached to it, which is a venial sin. Even when the deed is performed out of charity, the Chanter argued, the attendant prurience is a sin and prevents coitus from being meritorious. But the Chanter found it difficult to explain what that prurience is. If it is a sin, it must be an action in its own right rather than an intentional aspect of the action of coitus, but the Chanter was unable to sustain that position.

Robert proposes a different approach, which depends on the role of lust in motivating coitus. If one's motive for coitus is to prevent fornication in one's spouse by rendering the debt, then one's action is to that extent prudent, charitable, and meritorious. When one demands the debt to avoid fornication in oneself, however, the action is not meritorious. The difference is that one has no direct control over one's spouse's lust, whereas one does have immediate access to one's own lust. It is true that one acts "because of God" (*propter Deum*) by trying to prevent fornication even in oneself, but that phrase is equivocal. Whereas the action is ordained immediately and directly to God in the first case, where one acts to save one's spouse, it is ordained to God only indirectly in the second, since the act is motivated primarily by lust and only secondarily by the intention to control that lust for God's sake.[37]

Stephen Langton, who also may be reflecting the teaching of Peter the Chanter, reasons that coitus is good *per se* but that it entails a venial sin when one's motive is to avoid fornication in oneself. Why does the same logic does not apply when one *marries* to avoid fornication in oneself? Perhaps, Langton suggests, because marrying as such is immune to prohibition, whereas coitus is open to prohibition. Langton tries to shed light on why people marry by analyzing the composition of complex intentions. If someone intends a certain action as a means to attain an intended end, how does the intrinsic value of the means contribute to the value of the complex intention? Langton recalls that some scholars (perhaps the Chanter) distinguish formally between (i) marrying to avoid fornication in oneself by means of the conjugal debt and (ii) marrying to have sex to avoid fornication. The latter intention, unlike the former, entails at least a venial sin. Again, some argue that because both the intention to copulate with one's partner and the intention to avoid fornication in oneself are good, the complex intention to know one's partner to avoid fornication

[37] 155ra.

in oneself must also be good. Since to give alms is good, and to feed a hungry person is good, then to give alms to feed a hungry person is good. But Langton replies that this comparison fails because intending to avoid fornication in oneself presupposes a deformed desire.[38]

William of Auxerre, too, tries to analyze complex intentions. He posits the usual four motives for coitus: procreation, the conjugal debt, avoidance of fornication in oneself, and lust. William argues that the first three considered in themselves do not entail any sin at all, whether mortal or venial. Indeed, inasmuch as the sexual act is performed from charity (*ex caritate*) for any of those three reasons, coitus is good and meritorious. Absent charity, it is not bad but merely indifferent. Nevertheless, there might be venial or mortal sin because of circumstances or ancillary motives, even if the basic intentions are good. For example, there would be a mortal sin if the husband intended to raise children for the sake of worldly glory, and the risk of at least momentary venial sin is always present because of the pleasure (*delectatio*) that accompanies coitus. Similarly, the Apostles would have committed a venial sin if they preached out of charity but experienced some vainglorious pleasure in the act of preaching. Even the holy man sins venially when he has sex with his wife from charity but the involuntary carnal pleasure that he experiences in the act "pleases him a little bit" (*aliquantulum placet ei*).[39] William concedes that coitus motivated by lust or pleasure-seeking is necessarily sinful, but he argues that the sin is only venial if the pleasure is sought "matrimonially," that is, when a man desires to experience it exclusively with his wife. If a husband is "moved impetuously," so that he has sex with his wife only because she happens to be available but any woman would do, then his action is not rational but merely animal (*brutalis*), and he commits a mortal sin.[40] Most theologians after William of Auxerre adopted the last insight, holding that the husband who sought pleasure in intercourse with his wife committed some sin, but that the sin was only venial if the man desired his wife *as* his wife, for then intercourse was still implicitly contained within the goods of marriage. No major theologian after William, however, held that a spouse sinned unless he or she was displeased by the pleasure experienced in the conjugal act. If an act *per se* was good, in their view, there could be no sin in finding pleasure in it, even if that pleasure was shameful or stifled reason.

Alexander of Hales posits the usual four reasons for coitus, augmenting the third to include the prevention of fornication in one's spouse. Coitus motivated by procreation, by the conjugal debt, or by the avoidance of fornication in one's spouse is free from sin because of the compensating goods. It may even be virtuous and meritorious, for to render the debt is an act of justice, and to prevent fornication in one's spouse fosters continence. But what if the motive is to avoid fornication in

[38] Stephen Langton, *Quaestiones theologiae*, Cambridge, St. John's College, MS 57 (C.7), 319ra–b, and Oxford, Bodleian Library, MS Lyell 42, 2ra.
[39] William of Auxerre, *Summa Aurea* IV.17.4.2, resp. (403/54–61).   [40] Ibid., 402/41–403/53.

oneself rather than in one's spouse? In that case, the action is good as a way of avoiding sin, but it is not meritorious because lust is the primary motive. As for the husband whose sole motive is lust, he commits a mortal sin if he is determined to satisfy his desire regardless of what his wife wants, but he commits only a venial sin if he would not use his wife if she were unwilling.[41]

Albertus Magnus outlines two different analyses of coital intention in his commentary on Peter Lombard's *Sentences*. Commenting on the second book, Albert argues that the conjugal act is meritorious when it is rationally moved and initiated, whether "in the hope of offspring" or in order justly to render the debt. But what if one's motive is to moderate one's own lust? Albert seems uncertain, but he notes that according to some scholars coitus in such circumstances is only a venial sin, and a small one at that.[42]

Albert outlines a much more complicated account in his commentary on the fourth book, where he proposes three basic motive sources for coitus: virtue, nature, and carnal desire.[43] What Albert refers to as nature here is the innate tendency of all animals to perpetuate their species by reproduction, just as they perpetuate the individual through nutrition. This motive is not the same as lust, in Albert's view, for the object of lust is not procreation but carnal pleasure. There are three possible virtues involved, and they correspond to Augustine's three conjugal goods. The virtue corresponding to the *bonum prolis* is "the good of piety" or "love of the worship of God," whereby the subject intends to beget and raise children to worship God. Corresponding to the *bonum fidei* is the virtue of justice in rendering the conjugal debt. Corresponding to the *bonum sacramenti* is the virtue of "faith in the future union with God in one spirit." Albert seems to envisage here the possibility that sexual intercourse may acquire value from its sacred significance: a very unusual suggestion. Be that as it may, he argues that sexual intercourse may be motivated by virtue alone, by virtue and nature together, by lust and nature together, or by lust alone.[44] Each of the four combinations has its proper moral value. Moreover, when lust and nature work together, either may precede the other. When the motive is virtuous, Albert argues, whether virtue acts alone or with nature, then coitus is not sinful but meritorious. There is some sin when lust and nature work together, but the sin will be less when nature precedes lust, and greater, perhaps even mortal, when lust precedes nature. Thus, forgiveness (*indulgentia*) of the sin is automatic when nature precedes lust, but it requires penance when lust precedes

---

[41] Alexander of Hales, *Glossa in IV Sent.* 30.11 (487), 31.9 (493–94), and 31.10e (496).

[42] Albertus Magnus, *II Sent.* 20.6, resp. (Borgnet 27:345b): "et tunc quidam dicunt, quod est veniale peccatum, sed parvum."

[43] *IV Sent.* 26.11, resp.; and 31.21, resp. (Borgnet 30:114; 256). These two passages outline similar accounts, although they differ in some matters of detail and terminology. The term "motive sources" is my own. Albert construes these both as moving (i.e., efficient) causes and as goals, or final causes. I use the phrase "carnal desire" to denote what Albert refers to as *infirmitas* in the first passage and *libido* in the second.

[44] But not, it seems, by virtue and lust together, nor by nature alone.

nature.[45] When lust is the sole motive for coitus (*"cum sola libido movet...."*),[46] the moral value of the act depends on whether the lust is contained within the honorableness of marriage. If the lust is contained, there is only venial sin. But if it overflows the bounds of marriage, there is mortal sin, for then the agent (presumed to be the husband) is effectively an adulterer.

Albert's experience as a confessor leads him regretfully to discuss positions for coitus, although he confesses that he would much prefer not to do so: "It should be said that obscene questions of this sort would not have to be discussed were it not that the monstrous things we hear about in the confessional these days force us to do so."[47] Albert argues that the physiology of the human body and the layout of male and female genitalia show that nature intends men and women to couple in (what is today known as) the missionary position. He arranges the alternative positions in ascending order of abhorrence: the partners may couple together on their sides, or sitting, or standing, or, worst of all, the husband may approach his wife from behind in the manner of domestic animals. Copulating in these abnormal positions is not mortally sinful *per se* as long as the penetration is vaginal, but it is symptomatic of "mortal concupiscence."[48]

Thomas Aquinas reduces the legitimate motives for coitus to two of Augustine's conjugal goods: those of offspring (*bonum prolis*) and faith (*bonum fidei*).[49] The good of faith encompasses two ends: rendering the conjugal debt and the avoidance of fornication in one's spouse. Insofar as the marital act is motivated by any of these intentions, it is fully excused by the conjugal goods and free from sin. The motive of avoidance of fornication in oneself cannot be entirely reduced to the conjugal goods, for it presupposes a certain excess (*superfluitas*). Such coitus is not excused entirely, therefore, but the sin is only venial because it is still contained within marriage. It is true that marriage itself was instituted partly for the avoidance of fornication in oneself (1 Cor 7:2, 9), but to that extent both marriage and coitus are not honorable but rather are permitted through indulgence (1 Cor 7:6).[50]

Whenever an actual act of coitus is free from sin, in Thomas's view, it must also be meritorious, for no actual, here-and-now deliberate act, as distinct from the species of act considered in the abstract, is indifferent.[51] There is merit in sexual intercourse whenever a spouse's motive is either to render the debt or to raise children to worship God. The former exemplifies the virtue of justice, the latter

---

[45] Albert is more specific in the first account, where he says that sin is venial in one situation and mortal in the other. In the second passage, he says only that the sin is more severe (*gravius*) when lust precedes nature than when nature precedes lust.

[46] Albert considers this possibility only in the second passage.   [47] *IV Sent.* 31.24, resp. (263a).

[48] See ibid., arg. 3c (262b), as well as the response.

[49] Thomas Aquinas, *IV Sent.* 31.2.2, resp. (Vivès 11:126a).   [50] Ibid., ad. 2 (126b).

[51] *II Sent.* 40.un.5 (Mandonnet 2:1022–28). *Summa theologiae* I-II.18.8–9 (817–19).

the virtue of religion.[52] The fact that abstinence is especially meritorious, Thomas argues, does not imply that coitus is sinful or devoid of merit, for the "root" of merit, to which the reward is due, is the virtue of charity in the form of chastity, and the same chastity underlies both celibacy and a faithful marriage. The ascetic person achieves additional merit by overcoming certain difficulties, but such excellence is accidental and does not alter the essential nature of the virtue, whether it is acquired or infused.[53]

Thomas Aquinas considers the theory that a husband sins mortally if lust is what principally motivates him to perform the marital act, but sins venially if lust motivates him laterally (*ex latere*). Thomas may be referring to William Auxerre (see Section 13.3.3). According to Thomas's interpretation of this theory, lust is the principal motive when the man initiates the act to find pleasure in it, whereas lust motivates him laterally (*ex latere*) when the man does not seek pleasure in the act yet accepts rather than resists such pleasure it when it is offered (*oblata*) during the act. On this view, Thomas points out, a husband would not be able to avoid sin entirely when he couples with his wife unless he disdained his own sexual pleasure and was displeased by it (as William of Auxerre held).[54] But if an act is good, Thomas argues, to seek pleasure in it cannot always be a mortal sin.[55] Thomas concedes that there is bound to be some sin when the principal goal is pleasure, but he holds that it will be only venial if the motivation is contained by the conjugal goods. If the principal goal – the reason for engaging in the act – is to procreate or to render the debt, there can be no sin in accepting rather than resisting the pleasure when it arises.[56]

Durandus of Saint-Pourçain refutes the theory about lateral concupiscence in much the same way as Thomas did. Durandus notes that a spouse may pursue the sexual act for procreation, for the "justice" of the conjugal debt, for the avoidance of fornication, or for pleasure alone (*causa solius delectationis*). The conjugal goods excuse the sexual act in any of the first three situations, but what happens when carnal pleasure is the motive? Some say, Durandus explains, that to "seek pleasure principally" in the act (*quaerere in actu matrimoniali delectationem principaliter*) is a mortal sin, whereas to accept concomitant pleasure in the act (*delectationem concomitantem acceptare*) is a venial sin. But if that were true, perfection (the avoidance of all sin) would require the husband to hate his own pleasure, which is absurd. Durandus compares sex to eating, which preserves the individual just as coitus preserves the species. Someone whose only motive for eating is gastronomic pleasure commits some sin, but that sin is only venial as long as the act does not exceed the bounds of what is nutritionally sound. Durandus concludes that the husband

[52] *IV Sent.* 26.1.4, resp. (Vivès 11:71a); 31.2.3, resp. (127).   [53] *IV Sent.* 26.1.4, ad 1–2; ad 4 (71).
[54] *IV Sent.* 31.2.3, resp. (127).
[55] Ibid., 127a: "Unde cum actus matrimonialis non sit per se malus; nec quaerere delectationem erit peccatum mortale semper."
[56] *IV Sent.* 26.1.4, resp. (71a); 31.2.3, resp. (127).

who demands sex from his wife solely for the sake of pleasure does sin, but that the sin is only venial if he desires her precisely as his wife. He commits a mortal sin, on the contrary, if he desires her merely as a woman (who happens to be his wife), for then his actions exceed the bounds of marital fidelity.[57]

Peter of La Palu elaborates Thomas's analysis of the motives for coitus, but he introduces some practical wisdom that he had probably acquired through administering the sacrament of penance. Peter posits four valid reasons for coitus in marriage: procreation, satisfaction of the conjugal debt, the avoidance of fornication in one's spouse, and the avoidance of fornication in oneself.[58] The first pertains to the good of offspring, which is the primary end of marriage. The second pertains to the good of faith as well as to the secondary purpose of marriage: the remedy against concupiscence. There is no sin at all if the motive is to procreate, provided that there is nothing improper about the circumstances of time, place, and so forth. Likewise, all sin is excused when the motive is to render the conjugal debt, even when sterility or pregnancy rules out the possibility of procreation. Coupling to prevent fornication in one's spouse, too, is properly motivated and free from sin, for it is an extension of the conjugal debt and it comes under Augustine's good of faith (*bonum fidei*). It is true that there is bound to be intense, shameful pleasure that overwhelms reason in coitus performed with any motive, but the deleterious effect of pleasure is a penal evil (*malum poenae*), like the experience of hunger, and not a moral evil (*malum culpae*).[59] If the sinless act is also motivated by charity, which presupposes grace, then it is fully meritorious. Otherwise, it is indifferent from the theologian's point of view.[60]

When a person's motive for the conjugal act is to avoid fornication in him- or herself, Peter argues, the value of the act depends on the available means of dealing with the problem. Suppose that a man couples with his wife to avoid committing adultery with another woman whom he finds compellingly attractive, but that he could have obviated the temptation by avoiding the attractive woman or by making sure that he was never alone with her. Instead, he solves the problem by coupling with his wife to assuage his desire. His action is prudent, but he commits a venial sin because he chooses this particular means only because it is the most pleasurable and least arduous of those available. Peter compares him to a man who is thirsty and chooses the more potent of two available beverages because he likes to get drunk. He is guilty of allowing drink to overwhelm his reason, even though he really did need to quench his thirst. But suppose, on the contrary, that the man cannot avoid meeting the other woman or being alone with her, and that he resorts to the remedy of sex with his wife when adultery seems otherwise to be inevitable. Then his prudence does him credit and he commits no sin.[61]

[57] Durandus, *IV Sent.* 31.4, resp., §§4–5 (374rb–va).　　[58] Paludanus, *IV Sent.* 31.3.1 (160vb).
[59] *IV Sent.* 31.2.1 (160ra).　　[60] *IV Sent.* 31.3.1 (160vb).　　[61] *IV Sent.* 31.2.2 (160rb–va).

There is still plenty of opportunity for mortal sin in marriage. Peter considers six possibilities. Four are straightforward: A husband commits a mortal sin when he couples with his wife merely because she is a woman, and any other woman would do; when he couples intending in any way to avoid procreation; when the act occurs in a sacred place, such as a church; or when he penetrates an inappropriate orifice. The fifth possibility is disputable: Some say that coitus during the menses is always a mortal sin, but Peter is not convinced. If a wife demands sex while she is menstruating, for example, there is surely no sin on husband's part if his motive for coupling is to render the debt. Sixth, what if the man uses artificial means to arouse his libido, such as sexual fantasies, manipulation, or aphrodisiacs? Peter outlines three different scenarios. First, the husband may use the techniques to overcome impotence or frigidity in himself in order to procreate or to fulfill the conjugal debt. There is no sin in such cases, for the sexual activity remains subject to the right ordering of moral reason. Indeed, spouses are permitted to use embraces, kisses, and foreplay to facilitate normal coitus, as we observe even among some irrational animals, such as doves. Second, if his sole motive for arousing himself is pleasure but in such a way that his desire remains conjugal (i.e., it is directed exclusively toward his wife as his wife), then he commits a venial sin. Third, he may use these aids in such a way that his desire escapes the bounds of marriage in one way or another. In that case, he commits a mortal sin, just as he would do by masturbating.[62] Paludanus's views on foreplay and on sexual ethics in general were bold and unusually detailed, but they were not revolutionary or groundbreaking. Rather, they were an elaboration or working out of principles that had been firmly entrenched in scholastic theology since at least the middle of the thirteenth century, if not earlier.[63]

13.3 THE PLEASURE PROBLEM

Augustine had focused on sexual desire (*concupiscentia* or *libido*) as the problematic feature of fallen sexuality, although he touched in a few places on sensual passion (*voluptas*) and on the horrendous absorption of the mind in the orgasm. The schoolmen focused on pleasure (*delectatio*), construed as the satisfaction and sometimes as the goal of sexual desire.

13.3.1 *Historical background to the problem*

The focus on pleasure is already apparent in the work of the *magistri moderni* (Section 9.3.3). For example, the compiler of the *In primis hominibus* remarks in the midst of excerpts from Augustine on marriage that although marriage is an

---

[62] *IV Sent.* 31.3.2 (161ra–rb).

[63] J. Dunbabin's judgment in *A Hound of God* (Oxford, 1991), 49–50, that Paludanus's views on sexual ethics amounted to "little more than small concessions on particular issues" is perhaps a little exaggerated, but it is substantively accurate.

occasion for sexual pleasure, it does not follow that marriage itself is evil, for it already existed before such pleasure. There was marriage before the fall of man, but there would have been no indecent yearning (*ardor turpitudinis*) in coitus then. It is clear, therefore, that the evil of incontinence does not proceed from marriage but rather from the sin that makes human nature corrupt.[64] The *Sententiae Berolinenses*, glossing Augustine's "what would have been a duty for the healthy is a remedy for the sick," explains that if there were no sin, "the man would have been joined to the woman without shameful ardor and for the sake of children alone, just as one hand is joined to another hand without pleasure [*delectatio*]." Marriage remains good after the fall, the author explains, but chiefly because it makes the evil of "shameful ardor" pardonable (*venialis*).[65] According to a *sententia* or little treatise on marriage preserved in a version of the compilation *Sententiae divinae paginae*, no one knows whether sexual intercourse occurred in the earthly Paradise, but, if it did, it would have been free from pleasure (*delectatio*). After the fall, sinful pleasure in sexual intercourse became irresistible. Why, then, does God permit marriage? The author replies that one might ask the same question about eating and drinking, for they, too, cannot occur without irresistible pleasure. In marriage as in eating and drinking there are goods that excuse the pleasure: just as food and drink sustain the body, so marriage provides offspring and enables the partners to avoid fornication.[66] These early twelfth-century theologians seem to have assumed that all carnal pleasure was detrimental, even that found in food and drink, perhaps in part because such pleasures presupposed the experience of want (hunger and thirst), but also because carnal pleasure drew the subject's attention toward the body and external things and away from interior and spiritual things and from God.

Some sentences ascribed to William of Champeaux and Anselm of Laon invoke the Stoic notion of *propassio*: the reflexive, pre-rational response to a tempting stimulus that is prior to the rational subject's deliberate response.[67] A *sententia* ascribed to Anselm divides the "sin of pleasure" (*peccatum delectationis*) into two sorts: avoidable (*evitabilis*) and unavoidable (*inevitabilis*). Unavoidable pleasure is a *propassio*: an involuntary motion of the mind, which in our fallen state is "subject to the law of the flesh." Such pleasure is already a species of sin, but it is pardonable (*venialis*) because it is involuntary, and it is not fatal as long as it is mended by the "remedy of baptism." Similarly, the unavoidable pleasure that spouses experience in sexual intercourse is a *propassio*, which is pardonable (*venialis*) because the sacrament of marriage (*sacramentum nuptiarum*) is the

---

[64] *In primis hominibus*, ed. Matecki, 2/4–7.

[65] *Sententiae Berolinenses*, ed. Stegmüller, RThAM 11, 56/20–26.

[66] *Huius sacramenti habemus*, ed. Lottin, PsM V (PM 527), 365/25–29.

[67] The proximate source of this analysis of sin was Jerome, *Comm. in Matheum* 1.5.28; 4.26.37 (CCL 77:30–31; 253). See S. Knuuttila, *Emotions in Ancient and Medieval Philosophy* (Oxford, 2004), 178 ff., and M. Colish, "Another Look at the School of Laon," AHDLMA 53 (1986): 7–22, at 18–19.

remedy to it.[68] Involuntary carnal pleasures are symptoms of the fallen condition, but they are morally indifferent because value enters with the response of the rational will. Spouses ought to regret experiencing even involuntary sexual pleasure, and those who consent to it rather than regretting it show contempt for God, who will justly condemn them. God implanted such pleasures in human beings as a salutary trial. They are "very useful for the conservation of humility" if one uses them well. The subject's consent to his *propassio* results in the full-blown passion of avoidable pleasure, even if the desired action remains in the imagination and is never actualized. Such consent, the author argues, is itself an action, distinct not only from any external action but also from the avoidable pleasure that the consent elicits.[69]

Walter of Mortagne resisted that assessment of carnal pleasure. Even Jesus would have experienced pleasure when he was tired and rested, Walter argues, or when he was hungry and ate. Sexual intercourse within marriage is not necessarily sinful, therefore, although the disorderly aspect of sexual pleasure is a punishment for sin.[70] Peter Lombard repeated Walter's observation, although he cautiously substituted "a holy man" for Jesus.[71] Nevertheless, it was the Lombard who transmitted to the scholastic tradition the key text on the depravity of sexual pleasure, which came originally from Augustine (Section 13.1). In the fervid pleasure of sexual intercourse, the entire human being (*totus homo*) is absorbed by and becomes flesh.[72]

Thirteenth-century theologians agreed that sexual pleasure *per se* was not a bad thing (*malum*) in any sense, but that it had become disorderly in the fall. God had punished human beings for disobeying him by unsettling the order that rightfully exists between human beings and other creatures in the macrocosm, and between reason and the animal and corporeal aspects of human nature in the microcosm. Sexual pleasure had become disorderly, or "immoderate." Bonaventure observed

---

[68] Thomas Aquinas, *IV Sent.* 26.1.4, ad 5 (71b): The "first motion" (*primus motion*) of sexual desire is a venial sin (rather than not a sin at all) only if the correlative pleasure is itself inordinate.

[69] PM 85 (Lottin, PsM V, p. 74); = MS Oxford, Bodl., Douce 89, 94v. Similar analyses of sin as proceeding from involuntary *propassio* to voluntary acceptance and consent occur in PM 86 (pp. 75–76), PM 278 (p. 222), and PM 452–54 (pp. 304–05). PM 85 and 86 are ascribed to Anselm in the manuscripts, and PM 278 and 453 to William of Champeaux.

[70] Walter of Mortagne, *De coniugio* 3, PL 176:156C: "Si autem opponit aliquis dicens omnem carnis delectationem esse malam et peccatum sine qua non potest fieri coitus conjugalis, respondemus equidem quod talis delectatio mala est, quia peccati poena est; sed tamen non omnis carnis delectatio peccatum est. Etenim verisimile est carnem Domini nostri Jesu Christi quae semper fuit immunis a peccato delectatam esse requiescendo post fatigationem, et comedendo post esuriem."

[71] Peter Lombard, *Sent.* IV, 31.8.1 (450).

[72] Peter Lombard, gloss on 1 Cor 6:18 (PL 191:1584B): "Sic enim totus homo absorbetur a carne, ut jam dici non possit, ipse animus suus est, sed simul totus homo dici possit caro." From Augustine, *Serm.* 162.2 (PL 38:887): "Sic enim totus homo absorbetur ab ipso et in ipso corpore, ut jam dici non possit ipse animus suus esse; sed simul totus homo dici possit quod caro sit, et spiritus vadens et non revertens."

that the sexual appetite had become like an unruly horse (*equus lascivus*),[73] which needed to be restrained. If the horse was allowed have its way, the blame lay rather with the weakness of the horseman than with the unruliness and vigor of the horse.[74] From a merely causal perspective, it seems, the problem originated both in the unruliness of the sensitive appetites and in the weakness of the rational will. The schoolmen seem have been uncertain about which factor was more defective. From a moral perspective, however, culpability had to be attributed to the rational will – the horseman of the simile – for it was here that intention became critical. Hedonistic capitulation to unruly desire rose to the level of sin, but the disorder *per se* was involuntary, and the rational agent remained free to use it rightly by heroically restraining it or being chastened by it. That said, a problem remained. If no one could copulate without experiencing rebellious lust and shameful, even orgasmic pleasure, how could the intention to engage in coitus ever be free of sin, let alone meritorious?

13.3.2 *Robert Courson's moral particles*

Does the shameful pleasure experienced in the sexual act prevent the act as a whole from being meritorious? Robert Courson rejects a "well-worn solution" to which he and his master Peter the Chanter once subscribed, namely, that the good intention with which one embarks on a deed, such as when one performs coitus to render the debt, makes the action as a whole meritorious. On this view, the evil of carnal pleasure that is present in righteous marital intercourse, like Augustine's limp, is subordinate to the goodness of the action as a whole. But Robert now prefers the theory that "our master the aforesaid Chanter asserted during the last year of his life, when there was lively disputation about these matters," namely, that each particle of a morally complex, extended action has its own value.[75] If a day begins with sunshine but then turns dull, Robert points out, we do not say that the day as a whole was sunny, as if the outset of the day pervaded the rest. The same is true of the end of a day: We do not extend the manner of its ending to what went before, so that a day that turns dull toward evening is for that reason considered to be dull as a whole. Instead, each moment of the day is independently considered sunny or dull.

---

[73] On the words *lascivus* and *lascivia* and their medieval English equivalents, "wanton" and "wantonness," see M. Dzon, *The Image of the Wanton Christ Child in the Apocryphal Infancy Legends of Late Medieval England*, doctoral dissertation (Toronto, 2004), 23–32; and M. Dzon, "Wanton Boys in Middle English Texts and the Christ Child," in I. Cochelin and K. E. Smyth, *Medieval Lifecycles* (Turnhout, 2013), 81–145. The Latin term *lascivus*, like the term "wanton" in medieval English, implies that the subject is uncontrolled, irrational, wild, or playful. It does not mean "lascivious" in the modern sense.

[74] Bonaventure, *II Sent.* 20.un.3, resp. (2:481b); repeated verbatim in *Summa fratris Alexandri* I-II, no. 496, resp. (2:703a).

[75] Robert Courson, *Summa* 42, 31–32, ed. Baldwin, *The Language of Sex* (Chicago, 1994), 239–45.

Robert argues that the sexual act should be evaluated from moment to moment in the same way.[76]

In his lengthy and meandering exposition of this theory,[77] Robert assumes that a complex action (*opus*) that is played out over an appreciable duration consists in a sequence of moral "particles," each of which is susceptible to evaluation as good or bad, sinful or virtuous, meritorious or demeritorious, or even indifferent. Robert argues that particles of different moral value cannot strictly constitute a single moral action:

> because nothing can be constituted from a sin and a meritorious deed, we say that a single action does not come about from particles that are meritorious and particles that are sinful, nor are they coupled to a common terminus, as, for example, in the case of the action of going to church and the subsequent action of looking at a woman [in the church?] to desire her, for from the latter action and the former a single action does not come about. On the contrary, it is necessarily the case that something intervenes to prevent them from becoming one, for a single thing cannot be constituted from a virtue and a vice, or from merit and demerit.[78]

Robert claims that this has implicitly been his view all along, despite appearances. He has consistently maintained that a deed composed of particles with varying moral value cannot be evaluated as a whole.[79]

As we have seen, Robert is a pragmatic and generous realist as far as laypersons are concerned. He deconstructs the moral action of coitus not to warn that serious sin is unavoidable but rather to show that confessors and spouses do not need to worry. One should not even attempt to perform a single meritorious action that is complex and takes place over an extended period of time. As parallel examples, Robert considers the activities of prayer, psalmody, almsgiving, and martyrdom. If one is distracted from God during prayer or psalmody "by a fly,"[80] or if pain distracts the martyr from God, it does not follow that the deed as a whole loses its merit, for there is really no such moral entity as the *deed as a whole* to be evaluated. It is true that someone who is concentrating on reading the Psalms as a penance might start again if he is distracted, but such penance is an impossible task, and one that is perhaps too dangerous to assign. No reader could possibly direct every syllable, every letter of the Psalms to God. If an entire deed is not meritorious solely because it begins or ends well, Robert argues, then neither does a sinful particle within the action vitiate the entire action. Suppose that a pious spouse engages in coitus to render the conjugal debt, and that the activity begins from good intentions and terminates in a good

---

[76] 154rb.   [77] 154va–b, 155ra–155va.
[78] 155rb. See also 154va: "Nichil enim constat ex peccato veniale et actione meritoria."
[79] 155va.
[80] *musca*. It is not clear whether Robert intends the word to be interpreted literally or metaphorically, perhaps referring to a bothersome person. He also refers to vain "dust" (*pulvis*) in preaching.

result, such as conception. There are bound to be particles in between that entail at least very slight (*levissimum*) venial sin. When Augustine said that coitus performed for good reasons was without crime (*nullius criminis*), he was using a figure of speech, as when one says that Codrus had nothing.[81]

A familiar objection opens up a different line of inquiry. It seems contradictory to claim that something instituted and even commanded by God cannot be accomplished without committing a sin.[82] In response, Robert distinguishes among three kinds of actions: those done simply for God's sake (*propter Deum*), those done against God (*contra Deum*), and those done "under God" (*sub Deo*). Actions done for God's sake, such as prayer, are directed immediately to God and they are wholly meritorious. Contrariwise, actions done against God are wholly sinful. But actions done under God (*sub Deo*), such as plowing and seed-sowing, eating and drinking, are mixed or indifferent. Even perfect persons cannot perform works of this sort in such a way that their action is always meritorious, for they often direct them to God in only an indirect, implicit manner. Imperfect persons usually perform them without regard to God at all, so that their action has neither merit nor demerit, but that does not prevent them from acting *sub Deo*. It suffices that laypersons do not act *against* God when they perform such actions. Marriage belongs to the same broad, intermediate category of things done *sub Deo*. The spouses ideally serve both God and the world in an orderly way without putting the world before God, but lapses into minor sin are unavoidable and need not be a matter for deep concern.[83]

13.3.3 *William of Auxerre's divided-self theory*

William of Auxerre refutes several traditional objections purporting to show that coitus is necessarily sinful even within marriage. According to Pope Gregory, a man who has recently had sex with his wife should ritually wash before entering a church. Does that not imply that coitus is a sin? William replies that Gregory's rule has more to do with decency than with sin. Nevertheless, because coitus rarely occurs in practice without at least a little sin, the man who has recently copulated should acknowledge that he has sinned before going into church to be on the safe side, even if he feels confident that he has not sinned. Again, the "indulgence" to which Paul refers in 1 Corinthians 7:6 does not presuppose that coitus is sinful, for the indulgence to marry is not permissive but concessive. Permissive indulgence applies to evil things, such as divorce under the Mosaic law, whereas concessive indulgence applies to the choice of lesser over greater goods. Conjugal chastity is good, but it is less good than virginal chastity. It is true that the "entire human being becomes flesh in coitus," for then reason is drawn toward the sensory faculty by excessive pleasure

---

[81] 155ra. Codrus was the last legendary king of Athens.   [82] 154ra.   [83] 154ra–154vb.

and cannot contemplate divine things. That is why a prophet cannot receive prophecies during sexual intercourse.[84] But because such clouding is transient, it is not necessarily sinful. Human reason is incapable of contemplating divine things at every moment of every day. Finally, from the fact that coitus is a cause for shame (*erubescantia*), it does not follow that it is sinful, for sin is not the only thing that makes one blush. Sin is a disease, and even the sequelae of that disease are shameful.[85] The "inordinate," unruly motions of the genital organs in coitus are shameful because they are not under the control of the rational will. Such disorder is a result of original sin, and it tempts us to commit actual sins, but in itself it is not sinful but rather God's punishment for the sin of original disobedience. It is not a moral evil (*malum culpae*), therefore, but a penal evil (*malum poenae*).[86]

Carnal sexual pleasure is good in itself, William argues, but it became unruly and disobedient in the fall. God punished human beings by unsettling the proper order between spiritual and corporeal things, introducing a form of disobedience within human nature that mirrored the disobedience that human beings had shown toward God. Sexual pleasure is morally fraught in our fallen world, therefore, yet not because it is more intense but rather because it is has become disordered (*inordinatum*). Inordinate carnal pleasure by definition tends to undo the proper separation that should exist in the human being between animal and rational appetites. Nevertheless, hedonic intensity *per se*, William argues, is morally indifferent. Even inordinate sexual pleasure is not sinful *per se*, for it is pre-rational and spontaneous. Merit or demerit enters only with the response of the rational will to the pre-rational sensory pleasure. If the sensory pleasure in coitus pleases (*placet*) the rational subject even slightly, there is some demerit and sin. William contrasts such lapses with the experience of a "holy man" (presumably an Old Testament patriarch), who copulates with his wife only for the sake of procreation. He, too, is bound to experience some sensory pleasure that is at least potentially inordinate, but such pleasure is displeasing to his rational self, and his displeasure restores righteous propriety.[87] Before sin, it would have been possible to take pleasure in sexual pleasure without sinning. In the fallen condition, one can avoid sin in sexual pleasure only by finding it unpleasant.

William considers objections purporting to show that coitus in the fallen world is necessarily sinful because it entails lust and carnal pleasure. Everyone seems to grant that lust is sinful, and there are many plausible arguments showing that carnal pleasure is sinful. Lust leads a husband to seek and to find pleasure in his wife as an

---

[84] Cf. Peter Lombard, *Sent.* IV, 32.3.3 (455–56): "Unde idem [Hieronymus] ait: 'Connubia legitima carent quidem peccato, nec tamen tempore illo quo coniugales actus geruntur praesentia Spiritus Sancti dabitur, etiam si propheta esse videatur qui officio generationis obsequitur." The source is, in fact, Origen, *Hom. in Numeros* 6 (PG 12:610B–C).

[85] A medical term. A sequela is a deleterious consequence of a disease or injury.

[86] William of Auxerre, *Summa aurea* IV.17.4.2 (401, 403–04).   [87] Ibid., 403/54–61.

end in itself, whereas God alone should be the object of enjoyment (*fruitio*), and everything else should be loved only as a means to God.[88] Again, pleasure-seeking attracts people to illicit acts. It is Paul's law of the members, which is at war with the law of the mind (Rom 7:23). If carnal pleasure were not a sin, it would not displease the holy man who has sex with his wife to beget children for God's sake. Contrariwise, since the holy man does everything for God's sake, even his pleasure in coitus should be meritorious – which is absurd, for such pleasure is "inordinate and even immoderate," lacking the due "mode, species, and order" of things.[89] Perhaps sexual pleasure would not have displeased Adam in Paradise, for he would have known his wife only for God's sake, but it *does* displease the holy man now, and that can only be because it is a sin.[90]

William rejects these arguments. Lust (*libido*) is not simply a motion of the sensitive soul but rather is the result of rational consent to such motion. Carnal sexual pleasure *per se*, therefore, is morally indifferent even when it is disorderly. Suppose that such pleasure were a sin. It must either be sinful in itself (*secundum se*) or because of its relation to something else (*propter aliud*). If it is sinful in itself, it must be sinful either simply inasmuch as it is pleasure or inasmuch as the pleasure is carnal. But pleasure as a genus is not sinful, for one may take pleasure in God. Nor is all carnal pleasure sinful, for, as Peter Lombard says, there is no sin when someone takes pleasure in rest after working, or in food after fasting.[91] If carnal pleasure is always sinful, therefore, that must be because of something extrinsic (*propter aliud*), namely, its relation to reason. But reason does not have to capitulate. For example, the holy man's reason finds his own carnal pleasure in coitus displeasing. Since carnal pleasure is not necessarily sinful either in itself or in relation to something else, therefore, it cannot be a sin at all in itself. Rather, it must be morally indifferent.[92]

William deals with the objections in the light of that conclusion, beginning with the argument that coitus always involves lust (*libido*), which is a sin.[93] He denies the premise. Lust is not just any carnal appetite that results in pleasure. Rather, lust involves *voluntary* appetites, which transcend biological necessity. For example, the glutton is one who continues to eat out of lust (*ex libidine*) when his belly is full and human nature does not demand any more food. Again, carnal pleasure is not illicit

---

[88] Augustine, *De doctrina christiana* I.4(4)–5(5), CCL 32:8–9. Peter Lombard, *Sent. I*, 1.2.3 (56).

[89] *Modus, species, ordo* are correlative to measure, number, and weight, respectively, on which see W. J. Roche, "Measure, Number, and Weight in Saint Augustine," *The New Scholasticism* 15.4 (1941): 350–76; C. Harrison, "Measure, Number, and Weight in Saint Augustine's Aesthetics," *Augustinianum* 28 (1998): 591–602; and L. Ayres, "Measure, Number, and Weight," in A. D. Fitzgerald, *Augustine through the Ages* (Grand Rapids, 1999), 550–52.

[90] William of Auxerre, *Summa aurea* IV.17.4.2 (404–05). I have rearranged and condensed the arguments and replies.

[91] Peter Lombard, *Sent.* IV, 31.8.1 (450).   [92] *Summa aurea* IV.17.4.2 (405–06).

[93] Ibid., 406–07.

on its own level, which is that of the sensory soul. It is true that it attracts one to do things that are rationally illicit, but the rational agent can choose to resist. Similarly, when someone wants to eat during a fast, what is sinful is not the hunger itself but the reasoned intention to satisfy it despite the fast. Moreover, the holy man would prefer not to experience pleasure in coitus. He resists it and does not consent to it. Therefore, his pleasure is not sinful in respect of his reason. Again, it is not true that there must be enjoyment (*fruitio*) in carnal pleasure, for enjoyment is an act not of the flesh but of the rational will. Contrariwise, pleasure is meritorious only inasmuch as the pleasurable act is meritorious, such as begetting children for God. Thus, the acts in which one experiences sexual pleasure are not meritorious *per se* but at best indifferent.

It is true that carnal pleasure now is immoderate, William concedes. Indeed, it is even the means of transmitting original sin, for the flesh corrupts a person's soul, and the soul in turn corrupts the flesh of that person's offspring, and so on. Nevertheless, it does not follow that carnal pleasure is sinful, for there are two kinds of evil: that of guilt (*malum culpae*), and that of punishment (*malum poenae*). Pleasure in coitus displeases the holy man because it is an evil of punishment. Contrariwise, carnal pleasure would not have displeased Adam in Paradise because it would have been orderly and not evil in any sense. Even though the holy man is displeased by his own carnal pleasure, he is pleased that such defects and tribulations are humbling and provide him with an opportunity for merit. In the same way, the Jews were not permitted to expel the Jebusites from their territory but instead had to retain them as tributaries, for such annoyance was salutary.[94]

Carnal pleasure becomes sinful, William argues, only inasmuch as the rational will consents and succumbs to the concupiscible part of the animal soul in a kind of convergence or merging of appetites, so that the will finds pleasure in the same things as animal desire finds pleasure.[95] Then the human being becomes subhuman and brutal. But as long as carnal pleasure remains within the boundaries of the animal part of the soul (*vis brutalis*), then, "howsoever intense it may be," there is no sin. William argues that human nature is hierarchically organized, like an "ordered city." He compares the segregation of faculties and appetites to the separation of the waters in Genesis 1:6. When a lower faculty desires something, it may draw a superior faculty down to its own level. Then the superior faculty will find sinful pleasure in what pleases the inferior faculty. But the superior power may instead use the inferior power for its own superior ends. Although baptism sanctifies the soul

---

[94] 3 Kings 9:20–21 (Douay-Rheims): "All the people that were left of the Amorrhites, and Hethites, and Pherezites, and Hevites, and Jebusites, that are not of the children of Israel: their children, that were left in the land, to wit, such as the children of Israel had not been able to destroy, Solomon made tributary unto this day."

[95] William's use of the term "immoderate" is inconsistent. Here, the term implies sin, but elsewhere in the discussion it is synonymous with "inordinate" and does not necessarily imply sin.

completely, it leaves the troublesome, pre-rational motions intact because these sequelae are humbling and provide opportunities for moral struggle and victory.[96] To restore the original order and to avoid sin in coitus, according to William, one needs to be rationally displeased by one's own disordered carnal pleasure, waging St Paul's war between the mind and the "law in my members" (Rom 7:23).

What if the carnal pleasure were orderly, as it would have been in the earthly Paradise? William concedes that Adam in Paradise would have experienced carnal pleasure in the sexual act, just as he experienced carnal pleasure when he ate to satisfy his hunger. But there are different kinds of desire (*concupiscentia*): irrational animals desire sensible things, and their desire is morally indifferent; angels desire intelligible things with rational desire, which is always good. Human beings experience both kinds of desire, and their desires are mixed and morally fraught. As composite, spiritual–corporeal animals, humans desire both sensible and intelligible things, and both good and bad things. Adam would have experienced carnal pleasure in Paradise, therefore, but purely through the satisfaction of his animal desire. He would not have experienced lust (*libido*), which is a rational desire for carnal things. Reason knows that such desire is forbidden.[97] Again, although Adam would have experienced carnal pleasure when he coupled with Eve in Paradise, he would not have found enjoyment (*fruitio*) in that pleasure, for enjoyment is not carnal delight *per se*, but "only that [delight] which is from voluntary love and is itself voluntary." Innocent carnal delight "is neither meritorious nor demeritorious, nor is it joined to any voluntary act inasmuch as the act is voluntary."[98] Carnal pleasure in the fallen state does not remain with its proper bounds, but there is still no sin if reason is displeased by its encroachment and resists it.

13.3.4 *William of Auvergne's moral exchange theory*

William of Auvergne's view of sexual desire (*concupiscentia*) was more pessimistic than was usual in thirteenth-century theology, although the general outlines of his sexual ethics were conventional. William emphasizes the war of the members, the lack of obedience to reason, and the need to control the rebellion of the flesh.[99] Like William of Auxerre, he argues that carnal pleasure in marriage is bad but not always sinful. Although holy persons would prefer to avoid such pleasure, it is not a sin for them but rather a trial that God justly and providentially imposes.[100] But William of Auvergne likens sexual desire to "a beast that never ceases from beginning to end to devour and absorb the greater part of human kind."[101] Those whom he considers to

---

[96] William of Auxerre, *Summa aurea* IV.17.4.2 (408–409).   [97] Ibid., IV.17.1 (382/48–383/65).
[98] Ibid., II.9.2.4 (252/25–28).
[99] William of Auvergne, *De sacramento matrimonii*, ed. Hotot, c. 7, 521aC–522bE.
[100] C. 8, 523aA–B, 523aC.   [101] C. 7, 521aC.

be conspicuous sexual transgressors – prostitutes, sodomites, and Saracens – appear at every turn of his discourse on marriage, illustrating virtues through their converse vices. I have already described William's theory of gender above, including this sexual ethics, because it is integral to the way he situates marriage in the natural order (Section 12.2.4.2).

William of Auvergne denies that lust can be kept within the sensitive soul so that it does not contaminate reason: a possibility that William of Auxerre envisaged, albeit perhaps only as a feature of the Edenic condition. Carnal and spiritual pleasures, according to William of Auvergne, are mutually opposed. The more one seeks one, the less one seeks the other.[102] Carnal pleasure (*voluptas carnalis*) inebriates and seduces the mind and corrupts its sensibilities, causing one to lose one's taste for spiritual things. Eventually, carnal pleasure causes the mind to turn away from religion entirely: from the God whom human kind was created to worship. Such pleasure is inimical even to human nature.[103] Holy people know from experience, William explains, that whatever one takes from the carnal side is added to the spiritual side, and vice versa:

> it is clear how salutary and how useful is the good of virginity and continence, since whatever is withdrawn from carnal lusts [*concupiscentiae carnales*] is added to spiritual desires [*spiritualia desideria*], and a diminution of corporeal desires and pleasures is an increase of spiritual ones. Wherefore, the consumption and extermination of the former will be the fullness and the completion of the latter.[104]

Contrariwise, when the Psalmist says, "My soul refuses to be comforted," William says, he is referring to the "happy exchange" (*felix commercium*) by which one trades the consolation of temporal, corporeal pleasures for the consolation of pleasures that are spiritual and eternal.[105]

Some argue, William of Auvergne notes, that it is not carnal pleasure itself that is wrong but rather immoderate carnal pleasure. But what is moderate sexual

---

[102] Ibid., 522aH–bE. William's argument presupposes a fixed resource of psychic energy. The same supposition is at work in the medieval notion of rapture, where attention is withdrawn from the body and the senses and focused on divine things.
[103] Ibid., 522aF–H. [104] C. 3, 515aB.
[105] MS Paris BnF lat. 14842, 177ra–b [C. 3, 515aB]: "Ex quo etiam manifestum est quam salubre quamque utile sit bonum virginitatis et continentiae, dum quicquid distrahitur a concupiscentiis carnalibus spiritualibus desideriis additur, et diminutio corporalium desidiorum ac delectationum *augmentum* [augmentatio] sit spiritualium. Quapropter consumptio et exterminatio istorum plenitudo erit et *consummatio* [consumptio] illorum. Ipsa enim experientia certissimum est quod quibus ista minuuntur augentur illa, et e converso. *Et qui ab hiis vacui sunt illis pleni sunt, et e converso* [absent from printed text]. Quod vere intelligebat qui dixit, "Renuit consolari anima mea," volens *utique* [uti] felici commercio *amissione* [amissione, scilicet,] consolationis delectationum temporalium seu corporalium *consolationem* [consolationum] deliciarum spiritualium et aeternarum saluberrimo consilio commutare."

pleasure?[106] If the phrase denotes pleasure that has been restrained by marriage, then William agrees, for marriage limits and excuses concupiscence. But perhaps the phrase presupposes something like the medical model, where moderation is a matter of due proportion in relation to a person's complexion. In that case, too little pleasure as well as too much pleasure would be immoderate, and moderate pleasure would be the mean between two extremes. William considers this to be an absurd suggestion. There is no such thing as too little carnal pleasure, since the less one is subject to carnal desires, the more one is free to pursue spiritual desires.[107] Some argue that carnal pleasure might occur in the animal faculty of the soul without disturbing the spiritual power, just as something can be sensed in the auditory power without affecting the visual power. Each power has its own independent sense of delight. But the comparison is misleading. The very experience of carnal pleasure is not a neutral sensation but an act of rebellion: a way in which the corruptible body weighs down the soul (Wis 9:15).[108]

William argues that carnal pleasure is a false, deceptive pleasure, and that it is only equivocally called "pleasure." One might reason that something that men seek so keenly and acquire at such cost, and from which even the holiest men cannot restrain themselves without divine help, must be truly pleasing.[109] But carnal pleasure is like the pleasure in a dream: the "pleasure of sleep" (Wis 7:2). William cites several familiar examples of false pleasures: charcoal or ashes sometimes taste good to pregnant women, who even prefer them to wholesome food; people with scabies find it delightful to scratch their rashes and scabs, even though they lacerate their skin; and sweet almonds taste bitter to persons suffering from choleric fever because of the bitterness of their own saliva and of noxious vapors.[110] "To the hungry soul, the bitter is sweet" (Prov 27:7). In each case, what seems good is not really good, and what seems pleasing is in fact unpleasant. Seduced by illusory carnal appetites, sensual people lose their taste for spiritual things, whereas in reality the latter are much more pleasant.[111] Sexual pleasure cannot even be justified biologically or demographically. Intensity of lust or of carnal pleasure does not enhance fertility for the heat of sexual ardor burns up the seed, just as prostitutes are rarely impregnated because frequency of intercourse kills the seed by preventing it from curdling and germinating.[112]

---

[106] Literally, *moderated* sexual pleasure, for *moderata* is a past participle. The term *modus* in Latin implies order and limitation. A pleasure that is *moderata*, therefore, is kept within its proper bounds or its proper measure.

[107] C. 7, 522aG–H.   [108] C. 8, 523aB-bB.   [109] C. 8, 522bF.

[110] Cf. Aristotle, NE X.3, 1173b20–31.   [111] C. 8, 522bH–523aA.   [112] Ibid., 524aF–G.

One might object that pleasure is by definition found in the "joining of the fitting with the fitting" (*coniunctio convenientis cum convenienti*),[113] and that the coupling of male and female fits that description perfectly. Indeed, sexual intercourse is customarily described as a "joining" (*coniunctio*) of the partners. Moreover, since carnal pleasure is something that humans experience not as humans but as animals, such pleasure must be natural.[114] William refutes these arguments. One cannot rely on subjective evaluations even to establish what is pleasant. The itch of concupiscence sometimes feigns a fitting joining (*conveniens coniunctio*) when in reality there is no such fit. A truly fitting sexual union exists only within the bounds of marriage, whereas pleasure-seeking is promiscuous. This is obvious in sodomy, "the joining of the unfitting with the unfitting" (*disconvenientis cum disconvenienti coniunctio*).[115]

13.3.5 *Sexual pleasure in Eden*

A few mid-thirteenth-century theologians debated whether sexual pleasure in the earthly Paradise would have been more or less intense than it is in the fallen condition.[116] William of Auxerre, as we have seen, argued that sexual pleasure in Paradise would have been intense but would have remained within the animal, sensory soul, without trespassing into the rational soul. Albert and Thomas rejected William's divided-self theory, but they, too, saw no reason why sexual pleasure should distract or overwhelm the rational soul in an ideal world that was free from sin. Taking that analysis further, they argued that sexual pleasure would probably have been more intense in Eden than it is the fallen condition, but without detriment to reason. Bonaventure and the *Summa Fratris Alexandri* held the opposite position, assuming that the orderly, moderated sexual pleasure of Eden would have been less intense than sexual pleasure in the fallen state.

No major theologian of this period denied that Adam and Eve would have experienced sexual desire and sexual pleasure in Eden. The debate was about the intensity of that pleasure. Moreover, the debate was not so much about quantity as about quantification: about the measure of intensity. Are the ecstatic, irrational features of extreme passions accidental to those passions or integral to their intensity? For example, could there be great anger that is not irrational rage? If pleasure is by definition an experience of "the joining of the fitting with the fitting," and if sexual pleasure is natural – a product of the coupling of male and female genitalia, of the

---

[113] The schoolmen sometimes ascribed this definition to Avicenna and sometimes to Aristotle. Cf. Avicenna, *Metaphysics* VIII.7, in *Avicenna Latinus, Liber de philosophia prima sive de scientia divina*, V–X, ed. S. van Riet (Louvain and Leiden, 1980), 432/67–68: "delectatio non est nisi apprehensio convenientis secundum quod est conveniens."
[114] C. 8, 522bF–H.   [115] Ibid., 523aA.   [116] Payer, *Bridling of Desire*, 31–34.

emission of semen through parts of the body replete with nerve endings, and so forth – then it should follow that human beings in Paradise would have experienced carnal pleasures more intensely than now. As Thomas says, "to the extent that nature was more pure, and the body more sensitive, sensual pleasure would have been greater."[117] But that logic presupposes that an intense pleasure can remain subordinate to reason. If, on the contrary, intense sexual pleasure is intrinsically ecstatic and irrational, so that its very intensity is measured by the way it overwhelms reason and draws reason down into the flesh, then it makes no sense to posit an intense carnal pleasure that remains subordinate to reason. Such is Bonaventure's position.

Albertus Magnus asks in his commentary on the *Sentences* whether human beings would have experienced ardor in Paradise. Peter Lombard, echoing Augustine, said that our first parents in Paradise would have "conceived without ardor and given birth without pain."[118] The term "ardor" literally means "heat." If the ardor in question is the biological heat (*virtus caloris*) necessary for producing an erection, Albert argues, then Adam in that pristine state would have had at least as much ardor as men have now, perhaps more. It makes no sense to say that the rational will would have moved the genitals directly, without help from biological heat, for the role of the rational will is not physically to move the body's members but to command them in a quasi-political manner. What if the ardor in question is not biological heat but "keen pleasure" (*vehemens delectatio*)? Then Adam would still have experienced as much if not greater ardor in that state, Albert replies, for sexual pleasure results in the first place from the passage of semen over prolific nerve endings, and Adam's nervous system then was pristine and more finely tuned than ours.[119] Tacitly accepting the force of these arguments, Albert reconciles his own position with that of Augustine and Peter Lombard. When they said that coitus in Paradise would have been free from ardor, Albert explains, they were referring to the sexual pleasure that suffocates reason, and not to sexual pleasure *per se*.[120]

Albert argues that there would have been "greater and more pure pleasure then in the sexual act" in the earthly Paradise than in the fallen state, but that this pleasure would have remained "under the command of reason." It would not have distracted the spouses from contemplation of the "immutable first good."[121] Carnal pleasure would have aroused the genitals only "to the degree, as long as, and when reason willed it." Sexual pleasure in Paradise, therefore, would have been quantitatively intense but qualitatively moderate. Albert rejects the argument that strong activity in any faculty necessarily diminishes activity in other faculties, as William of Auvergne

---

[117] Thomas Aquinas, *Summa theologiae* I.98.2, ad 3 (604a): "fuisset enim tanto maior delectatio sensibilis, quanto esset purior natura, et corpus magis sensibile."

[118] Peter Lombard, *Sent. IV*, 26.2.1 (417). Cf. Augustine, *De Gen. ad litt.* IX.3.6; 10.18 (CSEL 28.1:271–72; 280).

[119] Albertus Magnus, *IV Sent.* 26.7, arg. 1–2 (Borgnet 30:105b–106a).

[120] Ibid., resp. (106a).   [121] Ibid.

argued. The philosophers thought so, but that was because "they knew only the state of corrupted nature, and not that of innocent nature." The "violence" that reason suffers from carnal pleasure in this life is a consequence of original sin.[122]

Bonaventure defends the alternative position. He reviews two opinions. According to the first, carnal pleasure would have been as great or greater in Paradise than it is now, but it would have been moderate in the sense it would not have absorbed or stifled reason. On the contrary, reason would have subordinated even this intense pleasure to rational ends, such as procreation. There would have been no interior struggle between reason and lust: no "war in the members." According to the second opinion, human beings in Paradise would have experienced some pleasure in the emission of semen and in copulation, but it would have been less intense than it is now, for it would have been tempered by reason and "moderated and measured" so that it did not subvert the uprightness (rectitudo) of human beings. Bonaventure considers the second position to be more probable because it is it is more consonant both with Augustine and with reason.[123]

Thomas clarified what was at stake. Commenting on the Sentences, he distinguishes between two ways of quantifying or measuring carnal pleasure: "absolutely," without regard to its relation to reason; or relatively ("proportionately"), in relation to reason. Thomas points out that the same absolute amount of food may be moderate and reasonable for one person and excessive and unreasonable for another. Measured absolutely, sexual pleasure in Paradise would have been greater than it is now. Measured relatively, it would have been much less, for reason would have retained its vigor and uprightness and pleasure would have been entirely subject to reason.[124] Similarly, Thomas points out in the Summa theologiae that the term "immoderate" as applied to passions and bodily or sensual motions is equivocal. Some use the term in a merely quantitative sense, but Thomas uses it to refer not to quantity per se but to the "measure of reason." The sober eater does not experience less pleasure in moderate eating than the glutton does in overeating, but his concupiscence "dwells less on pleasure of that sort."[125]

13.4 EXCUSATIO COITUS

Scholastic theologians held that the Augustinian goods of marriage (bona nuptiarum) excused the sexual act, causing what would otherwise have been sinful or at best shameful to be pardonable and even meritorious. Although the basis of the doctrine was Augustinian, it emerged in its explicit form, with the verb excusare, during the first half of the twelfth century. Notwithstanding occasional references to

---

[122] II Sent., 20.2 (Borgnet 27:342–43).
[123] Bonaventure, II Sent. 20.un.3, resp. (2:481b). This response recurs verbatim, with the same illustration, in Summa fratris Alexandri I-II, no. 496, resp. (2:703a).
[124] Thomas Aquinas, II Sent. 20.1.2, ad 2^m (Mandonnet 2:507).
[125] Summa theologiae I.98.2, ad 3 (603b–604a).

supernatural merit, the discourse about the excusing of coitus was focused on marriage construed as what Thomas called an "office of nature" rather than on marriage as a sacrament.

The scholastic notion of *excusatio coitus* was a way of interpreting Augustine's doctrine that marriage in the fallen state was a remedy to the problem of lust and depraved sexual pleasure. It was associated in particular with a seminal text from the *De Genesi ad litteram*, where Augustine says that the weakness (*infirmitas*) of fallen human beings is saved (*excipitur*) by marriage. Thus, what would have been a duty for the healthy in a world without sin is now a remedy against lust and incontinence.[126] The notion was also associated with the doctrine that marriage in the final age of human history was not a duty but rather was permitted to those Christians who were not strong enough to be continent, as if they were entitled to marry only through an "indulgence" or as a "concession" to fleshly weakness (1 Cor 7:6). Whereas virginity and continence were good absolutely, a sexually active marriage was good only in relation to something that it corrected.

This cluster of ideas is evident in Hugh of Saint-Victor, although the key term in his writing is not *excusare* but Augustine's verb, *excipere*, used here in the sense not of "to except" but of "to save." Human nature and human weakness have been saved through marriage, Hugh maintains, lust has been contained, and the vice of promiscuity has been checked.[127] But the verb *excusare* appears alongside *excipere* in one of the several passages in which Hugh expounds this point. One might conclude that human beings in the fallen world should abstain entirely from sexual intercourse because it cannot be practiced without "obscene concupiscence and fleshly lust." But that would leave weaker human beings prone to promiscuous lust:

> But because the weakness of human flesh would have flowed out more obscenely to every desire if it had not been saved [*exciperetur*] licitly in something, what was first instituted only as a duty [i.e., sexually active marriage] was afterwards conceded as a remedy, so that while the very evil of weakness that is present in [marriage] is

---

[126] Augustine, *De Gen. ad litt.* IX.7, CSEL 28.1:275/18–20: "utriusque sexus infirmitas propendens in ruinam turpitudinis recte *excipitur* honestate nuptiarum, ut, quod sanis esse posset officium, sit aegrotis remedium."

[127] Hugh of Saint-Victor, *De sacramentis christianae fidei* II.11.3, PL 176:481B: "Institutio conjugii duplex est: una ante peccatum ad officium; altera post peccatum ad remedium. Prima ut natura multiplicaretur; secunda ut natura *exciperetur*, et vitium cohiberetur." Ibid., 481B–C: "Officium autem conjugii in commissione carnis, concessit ut in eo praeter generis multiplicationem generantium infirmitas *exciperetur*." Ibid., 481C–D: "post peccatum aut idem ipsum ad remedium infirmitatis concessum beatus Augustinus testatur his verbis, dicens: Utriusque sexus infirmitas propendens in ruinam turpitudinis recte honestate nuptiarum *excipitur*, ut quod sanis esset officium, sit aegrotis remedium." *De beatae Mariae virginitatis*, ed. Sicard, 210/401–404: "... coniugii sacramentum, in quo tunc non sanctificaretur sed exerceretur coniugalis castitas, et nunc non sanctificatur coniugium sed *excipitur* infirmitas coniugatorum."

practiced through an indulgence in order to avoid a greater evil, it may also be excused [*excusetur*] through conjugal chastity.[128]

Hugh distinguishes here between indulgence and excuse. Whereas an indulgence absolves the sinner while leaving the sin intact, an excuse rectifies the sin itself.

The scholastic notion that the conjugal goods *excuse* coitus is traceable to Peter Lombard and thence to Hugh and to Walter of Mortagne. Through their original transgression, Walter explains, human beings "incurred the carnal concupiscence without which a man and a woman cannot have intercourse." As a result, the sexual act is "evil and reprehensible unless it is excused by the goods of marriage," for, as Augustine said, what could have been a duty for the healthy is now a remedy for the sick.[129] Thus, even if one spouse has intercourse with the other solely in order to satisfy lust, his or her guilt is venial because of the goodness of marriage, and a light penance is sufficient to excuse it.[130] Peter Lombard paraphrases these passages when he introduces the sacrament and institution of marriage,[131] and again when he discusses the goods of marriage, where he emphasizes that the conjugal goods excuse lust-driven coitus from mortal sin.[132] Peter Lombard had said in his primitive treatise on marriage, which was incorporated into his gloss on 1 Corinthians 7, that the conjugal goods *excused* coitus.[133] He used the verb *excusare* and its cognates some twenty-six times in his commentaries on Paul. Thirteenth-century schoolmen discussed *excusatio coitus* in treatises on the conjugal goods, therefore, inquiring whether and how these goods excused the marital act, and sometimes whether the marital act could be excused without the goods.

---

[128] Hugh of Saint-Victor, *De sacramentis* I.8.13 (PL 176:318A).

[129] Walter of Mortagne, *De coniugio* 2 (PL 176:155D). "Quia vero homines trangressione sua carnalem concupiscentiam incurrerunt, sine qua nequeunt vir et mulier commisceri; idcirco factus est actus ille malus et reprehensibilis nisi *excusetur* per bona conjugii. Quod autem per coniugium *excusetur* testatur Augustinus super Genesim ad litteram de conjugio loquens his verbis: Quod sanis posset esse officium aegrotantis est ad remedium."

[130] Ibid., 3 (PL 176:156A): "Coitus etiam cum propria conjuge, si fiat solummodo pro explenda voluptate, culpabilis est; sed per conjugium venialis et per levem satisfactionem excusabilis."

[131] Peter Lombard, *Sent.* IV, 26.2.3 (417): "Quia vero propter peccatum letalis concupiscentiae lex membris nostris inhaesit, sine qua carnalis non fit commixtio, reprehensibilis est et malus coitus, nisi *excusetur* per bona matrimonii." Cf. Walter of Mortagne, *De coniugio* 2 (PL 176:155D).

[132] *Sent.* IV, 31.5.1 (446): "Cum igitur haec tria bona in aliquo coniugio simul concurrunt, ad *excusationem* coitus carnalis valent. Quando enim, servata fide thori, causa prolis coniuges conveniunt, sic *excusatur* coitus ut culpam non habeat; quando vero, deficiente bono prolis, fide tamen servata, conveniunt causa incontinentiae, non sic *excusatur* ut non habeat culpam, sed venialem." Cf. Walter of Mortagne, *De coniugio* 3 (PL 176:156A).

[133] Peter Lombard on 1 Cor 7, PL 191:1587A: "His tribus bonis *excusatur* coitus carnalis, qui est inter conjuges, ita ut vel non sit peccatum vel sit veniale. Quando enim causa prolis conveniunt tantum, sic excusatur ut non sit peccatum, quando vero causa concupiscentiae satiandae et refrenandae, veniale est. Unde Augustinus: Conjugalis concubitus generandi gratia [etc.: *De bono coniugali* 6(6), CSEL 41:195]."

Bonaventure's approach to the theme was relatively conservative among mid-thirteenth-century masters. He reviews and refutes two opposing theories. Some say that coitus, like eating, is harmless in itself but evil when it is immoderate or excessive. Others say that coitus is intrinsically evil and always vitiates marriage. Both extremes, Bonaventure argues, are flawed and potentially heretical errors based on fundamental misunderstandings of the way in which any sacrament is a remedy to a disease. The first error underrates the severity of the disease, whereas the second underrates the efficacy of the remedy. The solution, then, must be a middle way between the two extremes. Bonaventure appeals to the supremacy of God, analyzing both the nature of what is excused and the manner in which God excuses it. Excuse is needed because coitus in the fallen condition is a conspicuously carnal act, causing the subject to become at least momentarily entirely flesh. That entails a lack of due order and a subversion of justice, to which shame is the proper response. Now, a moral order may exist either between human beings and God or entirely within humanity, and there is intra-human order both within a single human being and between two or more human beings. Whereas disorder between human beings and God is necessarily and irremediably evil, God may choose to excuse an intra-human disorder so that what would otherwise have been a sin is not a sin, for God is the author and origin of the rules regulating human morality. God may do so by a mandate imposed upon all the members of a certain community, or by a statute affecting only a certain subgroup of that community, or even by a personal exception that applies solely to an individual. For example, God excused the Israelites' despoiling the Egyptians by a divine mandate, whereas God made an exception for Abraham as an individual when he commanded him to kill his son. Marriage functions in the manner of a statute, for it applies only to a certain subgroup of the Christian community, among whom it excuses the sins of lust and sexual passion.[134]

Other theologians looked for the excusing of coitus within the structure and context of the action, associating it with the restoration of moral order. For example, to the objection that coitus must be sinful and inexcusable because it excludes spiritual influence and absorbs reason, Albert replies that one must distinguish between two modalities of reason: *ratio preambulans* and *ratio concomitans*. Whereas the former leads to or directs an act, the latter occurs within a complex act. The carnal pleasure attached to coitus suppresses *ratio concomitans*, Albert concedes, but it need not suppress *ratio preambulans*, on which the moral value of the act depends. The loss of *ratio concomitans* is not sinful but penal: a *malum*

---

[134] Bonaventure, *IV Sent.* 31.2.1, resp.; ad 7 (722–23; 723). Bonaventure assumes that the reader will know the difference between mandates and statutes, but in fact there is no consistency in medieval theology or canon law regarding the distinctions among statutes, mandates, ordinances and so forth. My reconstruction of the argument, therefore, is somewhat conjectural.

culpae, not a *malum poenae*.[135] Again, to the objection that the "vile pleasure" (*foeda delectatio*) of coitus diverts reason away from the immutable good and toward the mutable good, Albert replies that such diversion is mortally sinful only when *ratio preambulans* is diverted. Because pious spouses keep their sexual activity within the bounds of marriage, unlike the overly keen, pleasure-seeking lover of the maxim, there nothing to prevent *ratio preambulans* from retaining its orientation to the immutable good, regardless of how reason fares in the midst of the act.[136]

Thomas elaborates Albert's theory. He concedes that the fall has damaged sexual activity, but he denies that the damage need be either pervasive or guilt-worthy. Just as marriage itself burdens the spouses with mundane distractions, so coitus within marriage burdens them with intensity of pleasure. Ecstatic sexual pleasure even separates the soul from God, preventing it from receiving prophetic inspiration from the Holy Spirit. Such turpitude is obviously regrettable and it makes coitus shameful, but it does not necessarily make it sinful. Countless mundane activities that distract the soul from its contemplation of God, Thomas points out, are nonetheless meritorious as long as they are properly ordered.[137]

Thomas handles the problem by distinguishing between actual and habitual dysfunction. Sexual pleasure in a good marriage, he argues, suppresses reason only as regards its acts and not as regards its habits.[138] Again, the soul may be joined to God not only by *acts* of contemplation and love but also by *habits* of grace. Sexual pleasure in coitus momentarily prevents contemplative acts by overwhelming reason, but it need not interfere with the habits of grace.[139] The husband who seeks pleasure in coitus with his wife *as his wife* does not enjoy (rather than use) pleasure by pursuing it as an ultimate end, although he fails *actually* to refer the pleasure to God.[140] He actually uses a created thing for his own sake, but he habitually uses himself for God's sake. There is no sin, therefore, if the spouses undertake coitus in the right circumstances – with the right intentions, at the right time and place, and so forth – despite the momentary defects that ensue.[141] One must distinguish, therefore, between the value associated with the "order of reason" and the value of momentary acts considered in isolation. Excessive passions and intense pleasures do not corrupt virtue unless they impede the order of reason, and nothing prevents

[135] Albertus Magnus, *IV Sent.* 31.19, arg. 1c–2c; ad 1–2 (Borgnet 30:252b; 253a). On the distinction between penal desire (*concupiscentia poenalis*) and sinful desire (*concupiscentia vitiosa*), see *IV Sent.* 31.21, qu. 3, ad 2 (257b).

[136] *IV Sent.* 31.20, ad 3 (254a).

[137] Thomas uses the example of sleep to elucidate this argument in *Summa theologiae* I-II.34.1, ad 1 (899), for although it distracts the subject from God and is not desirable *per se*, it is beneficial in the context of daily life.

[138] Thomas Aquinas, *IV Sent.* 31.2.1, ad 1 (Vivès 11:125a).

[139] *IV Sent.* 26.1.3, ad 2 (70a).   [140] *IV Sent.* 31.2.3, ad 3 (127).

[141] *IV Sent.* 31.2.1, ad 3 (125b).

the spouses from ordering the act of coitus toward its proper ends.[142] Even the momentary "superabundance of passion" in the sexual act is not sinful *per se*, for it is not the quantity or intensity of pleasure that is defective but rather the way in which it overwhelms reason. Notwithstanding its momentary submersion, reason can maintain order by subordinating the act to the "prefixed" intentions and limits.[143] Whatever turpitude remains within the act itself is not a sin (*malum culpae*) but a punishment for sin (*malum poenae*).[144]

Carnal pleasure may overcome reason in two ways, Thomas points out: either by enticing the appetites to something that is repugnant to reason, or by a certain fettering of reason (*ligatio rationis*). When reason is fettered, the actual use of reason is momentarily suspended, but nothing prevents the pleasurable action from being reasonable in the sense that it is congruent with habitual reason and a consequence of rational decisions. Only habitual irrationality, which results in disorderly behavior, is morally bad. Reason itself dictates that reason should be suspended from time to time, such as in sleep, which like coitus entails a *ligatio rationis*.[145]

Scholastic theologians rarely attributed any power of excuse, virtue, or mitigation to the third of the conjugal goods, the *bonum sacramenti*, just as Augustine never attributed any remedial power to the third good. But there are occasional exceptions. Albert lists four basic motives for coitus: the hope of offspring (*spes prolis*), faith in rendering the debt (*fides reddendi debiti*), mindfulness of the sacrament (*rememoratio boni sacramenti*), and the remedy to lust (*causa infirmitatis sanandae*). Corresponding to the first three motives, which replicate Augustine's conjugal goods, are three virtues: love of the worship of God, love of justice, and "faith in the future union with God in one spirit" (*fides unionis futurae in uno spiritu ad Deum*). Albert implies that all three virtues excuse or compensate for the defects of the sexual act, and that their capacity to signify holy things can be a proper motive for coitus.[146]

Thomas Aquinas seems inconsistent regarding the role of the good of sacrament in the excusing of coitus. When he discusses whether the conjugal goods are sufficient to excuse coitus, he includes the good of sacrament among the compensatory features of marriage:

> Any human act is said to be good in two senses. In one way, by the goodness of virtue, and thus the act derives its being good from the things that place it in the middle [i.e., the virtuous mean], and this is what faith and offspring do in the marriage act, as is clear from what has been said. In another way, by the goodness of sacrament, inasmuch as the act is said to be not only good but also holy. And the marriage act owes this goodness to the indivisibility of the joining, according to

---

[142] IV Sent. 26.1.3, ad 6 (70b). Thomas develops this argument in *Summa contra gentiles* III.126 (Leonine 14:389–90) and *Summa theologiae* II-II.153.2 (2166–67).

[143] *Summa theologiae* I-II.16, ad 3 (716b).

[144] IV Sent. 26.1.3, ad 3 (70a). IV Sent. 31.2.1, ad 2, ad 4 (125b).

[145] *Summa theologiae* I-II.34.1, ad 1 (899a).

[146] Albertus Magnus, IV Sent. 26.11, resp. (Borgnet 30:114a).

which it [the marriage act?] signifies the joining of Christ to the church. And so it is clear that the aforesaid [goods] sufficiently excuse the marriage act.[147]

Later, though, when he asks whether the marriage act can be excused without the conjugal goods, Thomas argues that the good of sacrament does not excuse sexual intercourse, although all three goods make marriage "honest and holy." The reason for this difference, he explains, is that the good of sacrament belongs to the essence of marriage, whereas faith and offspring pertain to its use.[148] It follows, Thomas argues, that faith and offspring make both marriage and coitus honest, whereas the good of sacrament makes only marriage honest, and not coitus. Thomas insists that coitus has no figurative, sacramental value as a "sacred sign." Coitus is not excused by the sacrament of marriage in the sense that the act is "rendered free of sin because they [the spouses] come together because of some signification."[149] Thomas is wary of the notion that coitus, even within marriage, might be construed as a sacramental act by virtue of its spiritual signification. The significant value of coitus was exclusively literary and figurative.

In what sense did the goods of marriage, especially those of offspring and faith, *excuse* coitus? What kind of excusing is involved? This twelfth-century notion was problematic from the perspective of thirteenth-century ethical theory. Thomas considers the problem in detail. One may excuse either the agent who performs an act or the act itself, Thomas points out. Ignorance excuses in the first way, for it wholly or partly excuses the agent from moral culpability without ameliorating the act itself. But marriage, according to Thomas, excuses the act of coitus itself. Now, something that is evil *per se* is inexcusable, although circumstances and intentions may mitigate the evil. Contrariwise, an action that is indifferent *per se* does not need to be excused, although it is good or evil according to its circumstances. Excusable actions, therefore, occupy some middle territory, being neither evil *per se* nor indifferent. What is it in the act of coitus that needs to be excused yet is not inherently evil?[150]

The crucial defect in coitus, Thomas argues, is that the fervor of carnal pleasure (*vehementia delectationis*) overwhelms reason, just as marriage itself entails "trouble in the flesh" and the burden of mundane cares (1 Cor 7:28, 32). As Aristotle observed, one cannot apply one's intellect to anything during the experience of sexual pleasure.[151] Commenting on Aristotle, Thomas explains that

---

[147] Thomas Aquinas, *IV Sent.* 31.2.1, resp. (125a).
[148] As Thomas demonstrates with qualifications in *IV Sent.* 31.1.3, resp. (123–24).
[149] *IV Sent.* 31.2.2, resp. (126a).   [150] *IV Sent.* 31.2.1, resp. (125a).
[151] Aristotle, NE VII.11, 1152b16–18. Aristotle is arguing that pleasure impedes prudence.

erotic pleasure, which is the greatest of all, impedes reason to such an extent that no one in the actual experience of such pleasure is able actually to think about anything. Rather, the entire attention is drawn to the pleasure.[152]

Thomas compares and contrasts the pleasures of sexual intercourse, which conserves the species, with those of eating, which conserves the individual. Gluttony is a sin, and order and moderation are required in eating, but we do not say that eating needs to be excused. The crucial difference between the pleasure of eating and sexual pleasure is that the former is not so intense that it overwhelms reason. The temporary loss of reason in coitus is in itself a salutary *malum poenae*, and not a *malum culpae*, but no "wise person" (*sapiens*), Thomas argues, would undertake something that entails such a loss[153] unless there were some compensating benefit that is at least as good as what has been lost if not better.[154]

Thomas proposes two explanations for the disruptive power of sexual pleasure. One is pessimistic, moralistic, and Augustinian: Although our desire for food, like everything in the fallen state, has been corrupted, it has not been infected as if by a disease, whereas our desire for sex is infected as well as corrupted, for the generative power is the means by which original sin is transmitted from generation to generation. Hunger, unlike concupiscence, is not a transmissible disease. The other reason is optimistic, medical, and naturalistic: Divine providence has attached greater pleasure in all animals to generative than to nutritive acts because individuals need more incentive to conserve the species than they do to conserve themselves.[155] The schoolmen owed the latter idea to Constantine the African's *De coitu*.[156]

Thomas concedes that one would not construe the correcting influence of marriage as an excuse if the act in question were wholly indifferent, or value-neutral. Nor is an act that is evil *per se* wholly excusable. What requires excuse, Thomas argues, is the *appearance* or *likeness* of evil in an action. Since an action that is evil *per se* cannot be wholly excused, excusable actions are those which only seem to be evil, or which seem worse than they really are:

> ... what is properly said to be excused is that which has some likeness of evil [*similitudo mali*] and yet is not evil, or at least is less evil than it appears to be. And some of these things are excused wholly and some only partly. Because the

---

[152] Thomas Aquinas, *Sententia Libri Ethicorum* VII.11, 1152b16 (Leonine 47.2:425/95–102): "Impeditur autem [prudentia] per delectationes, et tanto magis, quanto sunt maiores, ex quo videtur quod per se et non per accidens impediant; sicut patet quod delectatio venereorum, quae est maxima, in tantum impedit rationem quod nullus in ipsa delectatione actuali potest aliquid actu intelligere, sed tota intentio animae trahitur ad delectationem." See also *Summa theologiae* I-II.34.1, arg. 1 (898a), where Thomas summarizes Aristotle's argument in similar terms.

[153] The term *iactura* literally denoted a "throwing away," but it could also denote a cost or expense, or a sacrifice in the modern sense of that word. Compare the throwing overboard of cargo (*proiectio mercium*) from a ship in a storm in *Summa theologiae* I-II.6, resp. (757b).

[154] *IV Sent.* 31.1.1, resp. (121).   [155] *IV Sent.* 31.1.1, ad 1 (121b).

[156] J. Cadden, *Meanings of Sex Differences in the Middle Ages* (Cambridge, 1993), 63–65, 135–38.

matrimonial act has the likeness of an inordinate act because of the corruption of concupiscence, it is wholly excused by the good of marriage, so that there is no sin at all.[157]

Thomas does not want to say that the act of coitus is intrinsically evil, or evil *per se*, for that would imply that only the actor could be excused, rather the act itself. But he concedes that there is a certain defect in the sexual act: something that is not merely indifferent but rather looks bad or looks worse than it really is. What prevents a person who has recently had intercourse from entering a church is not sin, therefore, but rather the indecency of the mind's being reduced to flesh, which *seems* bad.[158] Thomas's notion of the appearance of evil (*similitudo mali* or *species mali*) originated in 1 Thessalonians 5:22: "restrain yourselves from every appearance of evil [*species mala*]." The notion was prominent in scholastic discussions of scandal. Thomas explains that one may scandalize one's fellow Christians not only by sinning but also by performing actions that have the appearance of sin (*species mali*). That is why Paul counseled Christians not to eat meat offered to idols (1 Cor 8:10).[159]

To bring together his intentional analysis of *excusatio coitus* with the traditional thesis that the goods of marriage excuse both marriage and coitus, Thomas construes the goods of offspring and faith as ends: as motives both for marriage and for coitus.[160] To intend to procreate, in the broad sense of procreation that embraces nurture and education, is to pursue the good of offspring (*bonum prolis*). To intend to render the debt is to pursue the good of faith (*bonum fidei*). Both acts of intention are virtuous, and both excuse coitus by making it honorable. The conjugal goods make marriage decent as habitual ends, whereas they make the conjugal act decent as acts of intention.[161] One might object that philosophers distinguish between the useful good (*bonum utile*) and the honorable good (*bonum honestum*), which is good for its own sake. If the goods of marriage are useful goods, how can they make the marital act honorable? Thomas replies that the right use of a useful good is itself an honorable good, for to use something rightly is good *per se*, and not only as a means to some *other* good.[162] No other benefits of marriage or of coitus itself can excuse coitus, according to Thomas. He concedes that moderate coitus, as the medical scholars teach, might be good for physical health, but such use would be abusive, just as it would be sinful to use baptism to enhance physical health.[163]

[157] *IV Sent.* 26.1.3, ad 4 (70a).   [158] *IV Sent.* 31.2.3, ad 4 (127b).
[159] Thomas Aquinas, *Summa theologiae* II-II.43.1, ad 2 (1641b): "vel quia est secundum se malum, sicut peccatum; vel quia habet speciem mali, sicut cum aliquis recumbit in idolo." On *species mali* and scandal, see also II-II.43.3, ad 2 (1643b); and on 1 Thess 5:22, see II-II.144.4, ad 2 (2128b).
[160] *IV Sent.* 31.1.2, resp. (122).   [161] *IV Sent.* 31.2.2, resp. (126a).
[162] *IV Sent.* 31.1.2, ad 6 (122a); 31.2.1, resp. (125a).   [163] *IV Sent.* 31.2.2, ad 4 (126b).

Durandus and Peter of La Palu used the theory of moral circumstances, of which Thomas Aquinas had been a leading exponent, to explain how marriage excuses coitus.[164] Since coitus is good in some circumstances but bad in others, it is a plausible candidate for indifference. If it were evil in species, it would always be evil, which is not the case. And it can hardly be good in species. The distinction between the species and the circumstances of an act was modeled on the distinction between substance and accident. The circumstances include not only quantity, place, and so forth of the action itself, but also the agent's intention, or motive (the *finis operantis*), as distinct from the "object" in which the act itself terminates (*finis operis*), which defines the natural species. Thomas's treatment of the theory of moral circumstance is complicated and capable of widely differing interpretations, in part because the circumstances of an action can sometimes be specifying. For example, when a sexually immoral act is performed *in a church*, the act is specifically one of sacrilege rather than of fornication, just as an act of stealing from a church is sacrilege.[165]

An individual act, unlike a species of act, according to Thomas, cannot be indifferent. Acts that are good in species can be either good or evil by virtue of their circumstances, and acts that are indifferent in their species are good or bad by virtue of their circumstances. Thomas's usual example of an act that is specifically indifferent is picking up a stick. Construed as a species, the action is indifferent, but one who actually and deliberately picks up a stick in a certain place at a certain time performs an action that must be either good or bad by virtue of its circumstances.[166] But acts that are evil in species can never be good by virtue of their circumstances. Thus, lying, for example, which Thomas considers to be a specifically evil act, is rendered at best venial by mitigating circumstances.[167] Alternatively, if one chooses to construe the circumstances as specifying *differentiae* rather than as accidents, then the genus is indifferent whereas the species is good or bad. The distinction between terminus of the action itself (*finis operis*) and the agent's purpose (*finis operantis*) is akin to (and in some contexts the same as) the distinction between the natural species (*species naturae*) and the moral species of an action.[168]

Durandus and Peter of La Palu use this analytical framework to explain how the conjugal goods excuse coitus and marriage. They assume, with Thomas, that what is excused is the conjugal act itself, and not the agent, and that no act that is intrinsically evil (*malum in se*) can be wholly excused. Contrariwise, no act that is intrinsically good (*bonum in se*) needs to be excused. Since coitus in fornication is sinful, whereas it is meritorious in marriage, it seems to be an indifferent act, the value of which depends on its accidental circumstances. The goods of offspring and

[164] *Summa theologiae* I-II.7.4 (763–64).
[165] See J. Pilsner, *The Specification of Human Actions in St. Thomas Aquinas* (Oxford, 2006).
[166] *Summa theologiae* I-II.18.8–11 (817–21).
[167] See J. Bowlin, *Contingency and Fortune* (Cambridge, 1999), 63n5.
[168] *Summa theologiae* I-II.1.3, ad 3 (713b). Justified self-defense, lawful execution, and murder all belong to the same natural species but to diverse moral species.

faith are the circumstances that make it meritorious. But this explanation is insufficient. Eating is indifferent *per se* and good or bad according to its circumstances, but one does not say that eating needs to be excused. The most salient difference between eating and coitus as moral actions is that eating does not involve fervid pleasure (*vehemens delectatio*). But how is one to accommodate that difference in the calculus of moral circumstance?

Following a suggestion by Thomas Aquinas,[169] Durandus argues that because both conjugal intercourse and fornication belong to the same natural species – since, aside from the agent's intention, they have the same phenomenology – it follows that conjugal intercourse necessarily has at least the appearance of evil (*species mali*), which is a reason for shame (*verecundia*) in righteous spouses. It is because coitus has this appearance of evil, according to Durandus, that the conjugal goods are said to excuse it.[170]

Peter of La Palu rehearses Durandus's theory at length and tacitly accepts much of it, but he finds Durandus's reduction of the *species mali* to the common natural species to be insufficient. There must be something in the act itself that is not good, he argues, even considered in abstraction from its circumstances. Peter goes back to the familiar comparison with eating. Eating is indifferent inasmuch as it can be performed as a bad or a good action according to its circumstances – the time and place, the motive, the amount, and so forth – but we do not say that eating needs to be excused. The reason is that eating unlike coitus does not overwhelm reason. Now, that loss of reason, considered in itself, is a bad thing. We must distinguish, therefore, between two sorts of indifferent acts: those which are entirely indifferent *per se* and in their natural species, such as picking up a stick and eating; and those which considered *per se* and in their natural species are inclined more toward evil than toward good ("*magis tamen de se tendit ad malum quam ad bonum*"), but which are indifferent inasmuch as they can be done well or badly according to circumstances. Due circumstances make such an action good by compensating for its inherent defects, which are in themselves rather detrimental than sinful. Sleep is indifferent in this sense, for the loss of vigilance is a bad thing considered in itself and it would be perverse to seek sleep to that end, yet sleep is a good thing in due circumstances. Both coitus and marriage, Peter concludes, are indifferent in this second sense. Both have defects or disadvantages when considered in themselves, but both are beneficial and meritorious in appropriate circumstances.[171]

All three theologians were struggling to find a middle way between indifference and intrinsic evil. Thomas and Durandus found it in the appearance of evil. Peter of La Palu found it in an intrinsic tendency to evil. All three scholars, it seems to me, had come up against the limits of the moral calculus of circumstances.

[169] Thomas Aquinas, *IV Sent.* 31.1.1, s.c. 2 (121a).
[170] Durandus, *IV Sent.* 31.3, §5 [ad 1] (374rb). Similarly, Paludanus, *IV Sent.* 31.2.3, ad 1 (160vb).
[171] Paludanus, *IV Sent.* 31.1.1 (159ra–rb). Surgery is another example.

14

Marriage as a sacrament

By the middle of the thirteenth century, most professional theologians considered marriage to be a sacrament of the New Law in the proper sense. They conceded, however, that this sacrament was exceptional in several important respects. It did not fit easily into the class of seven, and its oddness generated new fields of inquiry.

Theologians regarded the seven sacraments from three interrelated points of view: historically, as the sacraments of the New Law; ecclesiologically, as the sacraments of the church; and logically and ontologically, as sacraments properly so called. The three designations were usually coextensive, but each entailed its own set of special considerations. The first and second designations were more traditional and construed the sacraments as members of a functional and historical set: as the tangible means of salvation that the ministers of the New Law "dispensed" to the laity, and without which there was no way to salvation. The third designation implied in addition that the seven constituted an exclusive, closed genus, the essential features of which each sacrament instantiated in its own specific way.

14.1 THE THEOLOGICAL TASK

The classical doctrine that marriage was a sacrament in the proper sense was not widely accepted beyond the culture of professional, scholastic theologians at least until the late thirteenth century, and perhaps for much longer. The doctrine was not yet a matter of general concern among prelates and canonists. It was not formally defined and promulgated as dogma until the Council of Trent in the sixteenth century. Thirteenth- and fourteenth-century theologians could not appeal to conciliar definitions or decretals to defend the doctrine, as post-Tridentine theologians would do, but they could cite official statements that at least supported their doctrine. The most frequently cited was a passage from the bull or decretal *Ad abolendam*, which Pope Lucius III issued in 1184 in the wake of the Council of Verona. The document anathematized heretics such as the Cathars and

Waldensians who held or taught opinions "other than what the sacrosanct Roman church preaches and observes" regarding eucharist, baptism, penance, marriage, and "the other ecclesiastical sacraments."[1] Theologians also cited the profession of faith that Pope Innocent III sent to the bishops of the Vaudois in 1208 as a test of orthodoxy for the Waldensians. As well as emphasizing the insolubility of marriage and the right of widows to remarry, this profession required acceptance of all seven sacraments, with marriage among them.[2] Such statements seemed to adherents of the classical doctrine to affirm or to presuppose it, and they seem in retrospect to have been milestones along the way from a theologians' doctrine to an ecclesiastical dogma.

As already noted, theologians discussing the sacrament of marriage were usually referring primarily not to the enduring state of being married but rather to the transient act of getting married, just as when theologians spoke of the sacrament of baptism they were referring primarily to a ritual act of invocation and ablution at the font and only secondarily to the baptismal character. A sacrament was by definition an outward, sensible appearance of an invisible mystery, and the spouses' exchange of consent in the present tense, which properly occurred in a church setting, was the most obvious sensible appearance of a mystery. When theologians referred simply to *matrimonium* or to *coniugium*, on the contrary, without characterizing it as a sacrament, they were usually referring to marriage as an enduring relationship or partnership, for that was how marriage had been defined in Roman jurisprudence (Section 12.2.1.1).

The tripartite analysis of the sacrament, which I shall discuss later (Section 14.6.10), helped to clarify to what the phrase "sacrament of marriage" referred. Theologians assumed that every sacrament involved three things: the *sacramentum tantum* or *signum tantum* (the external sign); the *res tantum* (the ultimate signified reality); and the *sacramentum et res*, or *signum et res*, which mediated between sacrament and it *res*. In baptism, which established the paradigm, the *sacramentum tantum* was external ablution with water with the priest's invocation of the Trinity. In eucharist, it was the visible species of bread of wine with their ritual blessing. Theologians identified various aspects of marriage as the *sacramentum et res* and as the *res tantum*, but they always considered the *sacramentum tantum* to be the outward expression of mutual consent. Many theologians held that the *sacramentum et res* of marriage was the enduring bond (*vinculum*).

John Duns Scotus seems to have been the first explicitly to distinguish between the *fieri* and the *esse* of marriage: between its coming into being and its enduring being. He notes that the term "marriage" (*matrimonium*) is equivocal, for it may denote any of three things: the contract of mutual self-giving, the obligation or bond that results from the contract, or the sacrament. The term properly denotes the

---

[1] X 5.7.9, *Ad abolendam* (CIC 2:780–82).   [2] DS 793–94.

second of those elements, according to Scotus: the enduring bond or obligation, which has enduring existence (*esse permanens*). The terms "contract" and "sacrament," on the contrary, denote different aspects of marriage in its coming-into-being (*in fieri*). Scotus points out that the phrases "sacrament of marriage" and "contract of marriage" are both transitive. When a phrase in the form "X of Y" is used transitively, Y is different from X. For example, Y may be a consequence of X. When "X of Y" is used intransitively, on the contrary, it means the same as "the X that is Y." Now, what the term "marriage" properly denotes in the phrases "sacrament of marriage" and "contract of marriage" is not the same as the sacrament or contract but rather is a consequence of it.[3] The transient sacrament of marriage is the sensible sign chiefly of two things: the permanent bond that results, and the grace that will enable the spouses to fulfill their obligations and remain together until parted by death.[4]

Signification was a necessary and fundamental feature of the sacrament of marriage in the classical doctrine, albeit not a sufficient one. Theologians assumed that sacramental signification was based on resemblance but required in addition some act of divine institution. The seven sacraments were species under a remote genus comprising all things instituted as signs of sacred realities: a genus that included the rites, offerings, and sacrifices of the Old Law (the *sacramenta legalia*) and the sacramentals of contemporaneous liturgical practice as well as the sacraments properly so called. Marriage, too, had been instituted as a sign of a sacred reality, but as one of the seven sacraments it was more than a sacred sign. The feature that most obviously distinguished the sacraments of the New Law from those of the Old was their supernatural efficacy, or the power to contain and confer grace. Their efficacy presupposed their signification. The sacraments of the New Law were supposed to cause the grace that they signified and to do so *ex opere operato*, that is, by virtue of the sacrament itself through its sanctification and reception, rather than by virtue of any pre-existing grace or merit in the subject.

Theologians elaborated and refined the classical doctrine by defending it against objections purporting to show that marriage was not truly a sacrament in the proper sense, or not properly a sacrament of the New Law. Some of these objections involved conjugal grace. It seemed that marriage did not confer such grace, and if that were so it could not be one of the seven sacraments. One might argue, for example, that marriage would entail simony if it conferred grace, since a marriage

---

[3] Scotus's example of an intransitive genitive phrase is *creatura salis*, which means the same as *creatura quae est salis*. Some English examples of intransitive genitive phrases are "a state of war," "the fallacy of undistributed middle," and the "sacrament of baptism." English examples of transitive genitive phrases are "the beginning of the council," "the symptoms of malnutrition," and "the sign of a vintner." Cajetan argues in *De sacramento matrimonii*, q. 1, ad 2 (Leonine 12:370b), that when a marriage between unbelievers is said to be a sacrament, then either (a) the word "sacrament" is being used in its broad sense, or (b) one should understand that the phrase *sacramentum coniugii* is being used intransitively to mean the same as *coniugium* ("*ut dicitur sacramentum coniugii pro coniugio*").

[4] John Duns Scotus, *Rep. Par.*, IV *Sent.* 28.un., conc. 20–21 (Vivès 24:383).

contract was typically the conclusion of financial negotiations. Other arguments pertained to the composition of the sacrament, especially its matter and form and the minister who applied the form to the matter. These objections did not depend solely on definitions of sacrament. Instead, theologians pursued an inductive, paradigmatic method, predicated on the working assumption that the salient features of certain typical sacraments, especially baptism and eucharist, must belong *mutatis mutandis* to every other member of the genus.

By defending the doctrine against objections of dissimilarity, theologians also exposed what was distinctive and peculiar about marriage among the seven. Even if marriage was truly one of the sacraments of the New Law, it was not *only* that, unlike baptism and eucharist. Marriage could also be construed as the joining of a man and a woman, which was instituted in Paradise, or as a joining inscribed in the natural law and universally practiced, or as a union that had been recognized and regulated by Roman civil law.

14.2 MARRIAGE AS A SACRED SIGN

Every theologian accepted that marriage was a sacrament *of* something, for a sacrament was by definition a "sign of a sacred reality." But what sacred reality was the sacrament of marriage instituted to signify? St Paul had provided the basic answer: Marriage was a sacrament of Christ and the church (Eph 5:32). Theologians extrapolated other significations from St Paul's. But what kinds of work did they expect the signification of marriage to do? What did it explain or prove? What was its role supposed to be in practice?

Although theologians from around the middle of the thirteenth century onwards often cited Ephesians 5:32 to prove that marriage was a sacrament,[5] the importance of this source for the doctrine is often been exaggerated or misinterpreted. Scholastic theologians rarely tried to deduce the doctrine from the verse through exposition. Instead, they usually cited the text dialectically, as in the preliminary arguments or the *sed contra* of an article rather than in its corpus, or response. Moreover, they usually cited the verse to prove only that marriage was a sacrament in the broad sense (i.e., that it was a sign of a sacred reality), and not to prove that marriage was one of the seven sacraments. But dialectical quotations, such as in a *sed contra*, often served as complex memoranda by association, bringing many things to mind. Through its use as a standard proof text, Ephesians 5:32 came to connote the associated doctrine. During the sixteenth century, the critiques of Erasmus and Luther and the rising tide of Protestantism prompted Catholics to broaden the biblical supports of the classical doctrine, as well as to clarify what one could safely

---

[5] For example, Thomas Aquinas, *IV Sent.* 26.2.1, s.c. (Vivès 11:71b). Richard de Mediavilla, *IV Sent.* 26.4.2, arg. 1c (Brescia edition, 4:408b).

find in or deduce from Ephesians 5:32. As a result, use of the text as a token for the classical doctrine waned in serious theological work.

Arguments from signification regarding marriage were rather narrowly focused during the central Middle Ages. In its original context, Ephesians 5:32 was a digression regarding the meaning of Adam's prophecy in Genesis 2:24. St Paul used the comparison between marriage and Christ's union with the church in Ephesians 5 chiefly to draw a pastoral lesson. The husband should love and cherish his wife as Christ loves the church, and his wife should submit to her husband as the church submits to Christ. But professional theologians during the central Middle Ages barely touched on the pastoral import of the discourse when they discussed the sacramentality of marriage. Again, theologians rarely regarded the sacrament of marriage as a way in which God revealed how Christ and the church were united. Hugh of Saint-Victor held that the sacraments were designed to educate and instruct (Section 10.2.1). They were sensible lessons by which God enabled human beings, who had lost touch with their inner, spiritual life, to understand divine things, as if leading blind persons by the hand (*manuductio*). But although the *idea* of marriage served as a privileged literary figure or allegory for understanding the church's relationship with Christ, theologians rarely treated marriage in reality — the actual marriages of contemporaneous Christians — as a means of revealing and teaching the mysteries of faith.

William of Auvergne is an instructive exception, illustrating what other theologians might have done. Explaining how marriage is a sacrament in the broad sense of the term (i.e., a sacred sign), and probably drawing on his experience as a homilist, William interprets carnal marriage as an allegory of spiritual marriage, which husbands should strive to emulate in their own lives. Beginning with the premise that a wife is to her husband as the husband is to God (cf. 1 Cor 11:3), William outlines the moral lessons that the husband should "read" in his own marriage, as if in a book. Just as his wife begets his children, so should he be fruitful in good works. Just as his wife cannot beget children without his seed, so he cannot beget good works without God's word and an infusion of divine grace. Just as his wife is subject to his authority, so should he be subject to God's authority. Just as she adorns herself and makes herself beautiful to please him, so should he be adorned with virtues to please God. Just as he regards his wife's chastity jealously, so should he expect God to be jealous about his own chastity. And just as he expects his wife to keep his home clean and tidy and to care for his children, so should he keep his soul clean and tidy and nurture good works.[6]

Aside from the issue of grace, scholastic theologians usually posited the signification of marriage to explain consummation and the role of coitus in the formation of a marriage and to interpret the good of sacrament (*bonum sacramenti*). Indeed, after the acceptance of the so-called Alexandrine rules (Section 7.6), theologians

---

[6] William of Auvergne, *De sacramento matrimonii*, ed. Hotot, C. 6, 519aB–D.

explicitly invoked signification chiefly to explain the right of each spouse before consummation to dissolve their marriage by entering the religious life (the Privilege of Religion).

14.3 THE PRIVILEGE OF RELIGION

Although the so-called Alexandrine rules construed *de praesenti* consent as the efficient cause of marriage, they retained a role for sexual consummation. What difference did consummation make, and why? Theologians accepted that sexual intercourse altered or completed the signification of marriage, for Paul's discourse in Ephesians presented marriage as a union of "two in one flesh." The very notion that marriage signified the joining of Christ and the church had become prominent during the early twelfth century as a way to explain the role of consummation, when theologians drew on Hincmar of Reims and the dossier of coital proof texts (Section 6.2). They also accepted that either spouse had the power to dissolve an unconsummated marriage by entering the religious life even without the agreement of the other, who was then free to remarry. The section on "the conversion of spouses" in Pope Gregory IX's *Liber extra* (1234) included the three most important decretals on this Privilege of Religion: Innocent III's *Ex parte tua* of 1206, Alexander III's *Verum*, and Alexander's *Ex publico instrumento*.[7] Following *Ex publico instrumento*, some theologians assumed that the Privilege was available only for a brief period, usually specified as two or three months. The duration was obviously arbitrary, and not, like consummation, a fact of nature.[8] For evidence of the rule, theologians during the early thirteenth century usually cited Pope Alexander by name and noted the time limit.[9] After the 1230s, theologians usually either cited the *Liber extra* non-specifically, without naming Alexander, or assumed that there was such a rule without citing any authority. Moreover, they usually expounded the right of dissolution without mentioning a time limit.

Opportunities to escape from a marriage by taking religious vows before consummation were not as unusual as a modern reader might suppose. Marrying in the Middle Ages was customarily a process rather than an event. Moreover, customs varied from region to region and were difficult to interpret in canonical terms. People continued to regard a plighting of troth as a betrothal even when it was expressed in words of the present tense. A delay between the exchange of consent and cohabitation was to be expected if the spouses were still young and not ready for

---

[7] Innocent III, X 3.32.14, *Ex parte tua* (CIC 2:583–84). Alexander III, X 3.32.2, *Verum* (579); X 3.32.7, *Ex publico instrumento* (580–81).

[8] Robert Courson, *Quaestio de matrimonio*, ed. Malherbe, ch. 5, p. 22: "Ad quartum, dicimus quod istud spatium duorum vel plurium mensium arbitrarium est."

[9] For example, Stephen Langton, *Quaestiones theologiae*, Cambridge, St. John's College, MS 57 (C.7), 318vb, and Oxford, Bodleian Library, MS Lyell 42, 2ra; Praepositinus, *Summa* IV, ed. Pilarczyk, p. 101/12–13; Guy of Orchelles, *Tractatus de sacramentis* 9.1, no. 213 (194/26–1/295); William of Auxerre, *Summa aurea* IV.17.2.2 (387/56–58, 64–66).

sex, if they had married through intermediaries, if the financial settlements to which the parties had agreed were not yet complete, or if they had married privately in a domestic setting and needed to wait for the reading of banns and eventual solemnization *in facie ecclesiae*, especially if there was to be a grand wedding with many guests.[10] Nevertheless, the Privilege of Religion raised some difficult legal questions in practice. If a wife opted to use the Privilege, was she dead to the world and no longer bound by the conjugal debt as soon as she made her choice or not until she had entered the religious community or taken her solemn vows? What would happen if her husband forced himself upon her after she had opted to use the Privilege, so that she became one flesh with him against her will? Could she still become a religious then? If not, should the marriage be upheld? What light could theology shed on the Privilege? Some canonists and theologians reasoned by extrapolation that a newly married spouse was not bound to render the debt until the statutory period of two or three months had elapsed: a principle that extended the opportunity for escape.[11] The argument made sense if one granted that consummation was in effect a legal conveyance, which completed or confirmed the conjugal obligation of one spouse toward the other, although that reasoning could not explain why the window of opportunity closed after two or three months. Fourteenth-century scholars and prelates debated whether, as Hostiensis suggested, a husband could invoke the same Privilege to be ordained as a priest or a deacon, since ordination, too, entailed a vow of celibacy. Pope John XXII commissioned thirteen experts — cardinals, canonists, and theologians — to consider that question. He incorporated some of their consultative documents in his bull *Antiquae concertationi* (1322), which determined that entry into the religious life was the only valid cause for dissolving an unconsummated marriage.[12]

Many theologians reasoned that the significance of consummation — its figurative meaning — helped to explain its role in the Privilege of Religion, or at least showed why the rule was fitting.

14.3.1 *The double analogy rationale*

According to what I shall refer to as the rationale of double analogy, the Privilege of Religion was possible or fitting because consummation brought about a change in signification. On this view, marriage signifies a separable divine–human union

---

[10] See D. L. d'Avray, *Medieval Marriage* (Oxford, 2005), 181–88, who discusses the first three of these situations. A fourteenth-century case recorded in the York Cause Papers (CP E 79) illustrates how there could be a delay between a domestic plighting of troth and public solemnization even when there was no suspicion of clandestinity: See F. Pedersen, "Marriage Contracts and the Church Courts of Fourteenth-Century England," in THTH 287–331, at 309–12, 320–31.

[11] Peter of Tarentaise, *IV Sent.* 27.3.1, qu. 2, resp. (4:295a): "non tenetur [coniux exactus reddere debitum] infra tempus duorum mensium a iure indultum."

[12] P. Nold, *Marriage Advice for a Pope* (Leiden, 2009).

before consummation, and an inseparable union after consummation.[13] Since the signification of a sacrament depends on resemblance,[14] marriage, too, should be separable before consummation and inseparable after it. The rationale presupposes Augustine's suggestion that marriage is insoluble because God has made it into a sign of Christ's permanent union with the church,[15] but it extends that idea by differentiating between the signification before consummation and after it. This rationale is traceable to Rufinus, who used it to show why it was fitting that consummation rendered an initiated marriage fixed (*ratum*) and inseparable, as Gratian had taught (Section 11.6.3).[16] Theologians during the late-twelfth and early-thirteenth centuries adapted Rufinus's argument to explain the Privilege of Religion in the context of the new doctrine of consent with the betrothal distinction, according to which *de praesenti* consent sufficed by itself, even before consummation, to establish *matrimonium ratum*.

Pope Innocent III articulated the rationale clearly in a letter that he sent to King Philip II of France on December 9, 1208, regarding the latter's contested marriage with Ingeborg.[17] Ingeborg claimed that they had consummated their marriage, whereas Philip denied that they had done so. He had already sent her to a convent, and he considered himself free to marry again. Innocent was inclined to believe Ingeborg's account of the facts, but in this letter he expounded all the issues involved, including the Privilege of Religion and its rationale.

Innocent begins with a learned review of the canon law on separation prior to consummation, citing Alexander III and noting, as Gratian had done, the precedents in lives of the saints. Then he outlines the double analogy rationale:

> ... just as sexual intercourse signifies the union between the Word and human nature, because "the Word became flesh and dwelt among us" [John 1:14], so also the consent of wills may signify the charity between God and the just soul, since the person who cleaves to God is one spirit with him. Therefore, just as the bond of union between the Word and human nature cannot be separated, so also the conjugal bond between man and wife after they have been made one flesh through sexual intercourse cannot be separated as long as they are alive. Contrariwise, just as the tie of charity between God and the soul is often dissolved, so also can the

---

[13] More precisely, marriage signifies only a separable divine–human union before consummation, whereas it signifies both that and an inseparable divine–human union after consummation.

[14] Albertus Magnus, *De matrimonio* 2.5, ad 7 (Cologne 26:163b): "Omnis autem virtus signi est ex virtute significati secundum quod huiusmodi."

[15] Augustine, *De b. coniug.* 7–8(7), CSEL 41:197.

[16] Rufinus, *Summa decretorum* on C. 27 q. 2, ed. Singer, pp. 441–42.

[17] *Regestum XI, Epist.* 177 (182), in *Die Register Innocenz' III*, vol. 11, ed. R. Bösel and H. Fillitz (Vienna, 2010), 286–93 (also PL 215:1494–98). On the history of this case, see G. Conklin, "Ingeborg of Denmark," in A. J. Duggan (ed.), *Queens and Queenship in Medieval Europe* (Woodbridge, 1997), 39–52; and J. W. Baldwin, "La vie sexuelle de Philippe Auguste," in M. Rouche, *Mariage et sexualité au moyen âge* (Paris, 2000), 220–29.

conjugal connection be separated when the consent of their wills is all that exists between the spouses.. . .[18]

Innocent goes on to remind his readers of the biblical foundation of this signification in Genesis, Ephesians, and the gospels. Nevertheless, he concedes that there is no scriptural proof for the Privilege, which seems to contradict Christ's command: "What God has joined, let man not separate" (Mark 10:9, Matt 19:6). It would be presumptuous to allow the Privilege, Innocent concedes, were it not that "the examples of the saints and the statutes of the fathers" provide sufficient precedent.[19] Thus, Innocent does not use the rationale to demonstrate or derive the rule or to prove that it is legally sound and licit. Rather, he uses it to shed light on a rule that can be established canonically only through precedent: to show why the rule, thus established, is fitting.

During the early thirteenth century, theologians who used the double analogy rationale to explain the privilege of religion, such as Robert Courson, Praepositinus, Guy of Orchelles, and William of Auxerre, maintained that unconsummated marriage signified a separable union, such as that between the individual faithful soul and Christ, and that consummated marriage signified an inseparable union, such as the union of natures in Christ, or the union between Christ-incarnate and the church.[20] Contrariwise, those who explained the privilege of religion in other ways, such as Stephen Langton and Alexander of Hales, assigned other significations to the two aspects of marriage, which would not support the rationale. The divergence suggests that the reasoning of the former theologians was circular: that their reason for assigning the significations in question to marriage before and after consummation was that marriage was soluble before consummation and insoluble after it.

This difference of approach is apparent if one compares the treatments of the Privilege by Stephen Langton and by Praepositinus. Langton, who does not invoke signification to justify the Privilege, holds that marriage signifies the union between Christ and the church militant before sexual intercourse, and between Christ and the church triumphant after consummation. Langton explains that there are three signifiers in marriage: the union of wills (*consensus animorum*), sexual intercourse, and marriage itself. The first signifies the union of wills between Christ and the church that existed from Abel to the incarnation; the second, the union in one flesh between Christ and the church established by the incarnation; the third, the marriage that will exist between Christ and the church after the final judgment.[21]

---

[18] *Epist.* 177, 287/24–32.   [19] Ibid., 288/2–8.
[20] Robert Courson, *Quaestio de matrimonio*, ed. Malherbe, ch. 5, p. 20, identifies the separable union as that between the members of the church and Christ as their head, "for the members can be divided from the head." The inseparable union, according to Courson, is between the two natures of Christ, which were united in Mary's womb.
[21] Stephen Langton, *Quaestiones theologiae*, Cambridge, St. John's College, MS 57 (C.7), 318vb; Oxford, Bodleian Library, MS Lyell 42, 1vb.

This assignment of signification does not obviously provide a rationale for the Privilege of Religion, although one might adapt it to that end. But Praepositinus modifies Langton's analysis to explain why consummation completes the inseparability of marriage. Like Langton, he posits three significations, but he alters them to accommodate the double analogy rationale. The spouses' joining of wills (*coniunctio animorum*) signifies the joining of the soul to God through charity, according to Praepositinus; the joining of their bodies through coitus (*coniunctio corporum*) signifies the joining of Christ's human nature to the Word; and their monogamy signifies the unity and exclusivity of the relationship between Christ and the church. Because the first of these signified unions is often separated whereas the second is never separated, Praepositinus argues, a marriage between believers can sometimes be dissolved before consummation but never after consummation. It is because of the third signification that a man who has been married twice or the husband of a widow incurs the impediment of digamy, which prevents him from ordination to the priesthood.[22]

Guy of Orchelles and William of Auxerre adopt a double analysis of marriage as a sacred sign that is akin to Peter Lombard's, but unlike the Lombard they use it to shed light on the effect of consummation on insolubility. According to Guy, the two signifiers are the joining of wills and the joining of bodies. The first signifies the union of the individual faithful soul with Christ, which is separable. The second signifies the union of natures in Christ, which is inseparable.[23] William of Auxerre considers the Privilege of Religion at length, inquiring into the legal and obligational qualities of an unconsummated marriage before it is dissolved (e.g., in regard to the conjugal debt and to the three goods of marriage), as well as into objections to the rule and its rationale. William also considers several related contingencies in canon law, such what should happen if the wife opts to become a religious and declines to consummate the marriage but her husband takes her by force.[24] The chief objection to the rule in William's account is an extended analogical syllogism: Marriage signifies Christ's union with the church; but that union is inseparable; therefore, marriage is inseparable; therefore, marriage "is not dissolved if one of them should enter religion."[25] In reply, William concedes that marriage signifies Christ's union with the church, which is insoluble. Nevertheless, one and the same union may include soluble and insoluble aspects. For example, although the union between Christ and the church is insoluble inasmuch as it is considered as a whole (*simpliciter*), embracing all believers, each of the many particular unions (*coniunctiones*) of individual Christians to Christ is soluble, for any member of the church may commit a grievous sin or become apostate. Consummation alters the manner in which marriage signifies the union, redirecting the sign to a different aspect of the

---

[22] Praepositinus, *Summa* IV, p. 107 (*De tribus bonis coniugii*).
[23] Guy of Orchelles, *Tractatus de sacramentis* 9.2, no. 222 (200).
[24] William of Auxerre, *Summa aurea* IV.17.2.2 (387/55–389/109).   [25] Ibid. (387/69–73).

signified union. Whereas the "spiritual" (pre-carnal) joining of a man and a woman before consummation signifies the union between Christ and the individual faithful soul, which is soluble, consummated marriage signifies the union between the Son and human nature through the incarnation, which is insoluble.[26] The circularity of this argument is obvious.

Although Alexander of Hales is beholden to William of Auxerre for his analysis of what marriage signifies, he does not invoke signification to explain the Privilege of Religion. In the disputed questions on marriage, Alexander maintains that marriage signifies two aspects of the same joining of Christ and the church. The mutual consent of wills (*consensus animorum*) signifies the joining or conformity in charity, whereas sexual union signifies conformity in nature, that is, the union of divine and human natures in Christ. Alexander finds proof of the first signification in Ephesians 5:30: "we are members of his body, of his flesh and of his bones," for it is through charity that Christ is head of both the weak and the strong members of the church, signified respectively in the text by flesh and bones. Alexander finds proof of the second signification in Ephesians 5:31: "they shall be two one flesh."[27] Later, Alexander argues that the joining of wills through consent signifies "the conformity of Christ and the church in charity," whereas sexual union signifies the conformity in nature between Christ and the church, which in turn signifies "God's intimate love for man." Thus, "everything is ordained to one thing, namely, to the conformity of Christ and the church in intimate love."[28]

Alexander makes no attempt to correlate this diversity of signification with the relative permanence of marriage before and after consummation. Instead, he inquires which of the two significations is primary and which is secondary. Marriage primarily signifies the "spiritual conformity" between Christ and the church: the joining in love (*dilectio*) and charity. Alexander's argument is rather convoluted. He assumes that to determine what a sacrament principally signifies, one must first establish what is the principal feature of the sacrament as regards its function. Then, whatever that principal feature best signifies will be what the sacrament principally signifies. Is a sacrament primarily a sacred sign or primarily a cause of grace? The sacraments of the New Law are primarily causes of sanctity, Alexander argues, and only secondarily signs of sacred realities, for whereas the latter aspect pertains to their genus, the former pertains to their species as sacraments in the proper sense.[29] If one regards marriage only as a sacred sign, therefore, the second signification (conformity in nature) is primary and the greater of the two. But continent marriage, such as

---

[26] Ibid., resp. (388).

[27] Alexander of Hales, *Quaestio disputata* 57, disp. 1, m. 1, §3 (1097–98).

[28] Ibid., §10 (1100).

[29] The schoolmen considered the genus of a thing to be secondary and its species or specific difference to primary. For example, human beings are primarily rational and only secondarily animal, since to be rational is the point of being human.

that between Mary and Joseph, is intrinsically more holy than a marriage that includes sexual intercourse:

> ... a sacrament is a medicine, a remedy against sickness. Hence, matrimony is a remedy against carnal concupiscence. But the consent of wills heals carnal concupiscence more when there is no carnal coupling than when there is, for someone who consents [to marriage] but does not have sexual intercourse has more power to resist [concupiscence] than someone who has sexual intercourse.[30]

Since the first signifier, the consent of wills, is more sanctifying than the second signifier, sexual union, and since marriage as a sacrament of the New Law is primarily a cause of sanctity and only secondarily a sign of it, the first signifier (the consent of wills) is primary. And what that feature of the sacrament signifies is the union of charity between Christ and the church. The sacrament of marriage, therefore, primarily signifies the union of charity between Christ and the church.[31]

In the *Glossa*, Alexander begins his analysis of signification by pointing out that marriage as a sacrament signifies not just one but several things. He initially identifies three: the joining (*coniunctio*) or coupling (*copula*) of the faithful soul with Christ through charity; the joining of Christ and the church through conformity of nature; and the union (*unio*) between Christ's divinity and his humanity. The spouses' joining of wills through mutual consent signifies the first union, coitus or sexual union signifies the second, and the inseparability of consummated marriage signifies the third.[32] Shortly after saying that, however, Alexander claims that the spouses' mutual consent signifies the "spiritual joining of Christ and the church." Whereas *de praesenti* consent signifies such joining or union as it exists now, *de futuro* consent signifies it as it will be in the life to come.[33] Elsewhere in the *Glossa*, Alexander says that marriage primarily signifies "the joining either of the faithful soul with Christ, or of the church with the head."[34] Alexander argues in the *Glossa*, too, that there are primary and secondary significations, and that any signification attached specifically to coitus or consummated marriage is secondary. Every sacrament of the New Law principally signifies a specific grace, Alexander argues, and any other significations are subordinate to the primary signification. Alexander proposes several arguments to show that the principal signifier in marriage exists even without coitus. Thus, only mutual consent is essential to the formation of the sacrament, whereas coitus is accidental. Moreover, marriage derives its spiritual efficacy (*vis*) from consent alone. Although an unconsummated marriage is incomplete as regards its signification, inasmuch as its range of signification is smaller, it is *more* complete as regards sanctity, for an unconsummated marriage is an essentially

---

[30] Ibid., §9 (1099).   [31] Ibid., §§ 9–10 (1099–1100).
[32] Alexander of Hales, *Glossa in IV Sent.* 26.7a (458–59).
[33] *IV Sent.* 26.7d (461).   [34] *IV Sent.* 26.5m (455).

spiritual relationship, whereas the human being becomes entirely flesh in the act of coitus. And it is chiefly with reference to their sanctity, rather than to their signifi-cance, that the sacraments of the New Law are called sacraments.[35] Alexander's analysis of signification is arguably inconsistent, but that is of little consequence because he does not use this analysis to explain the Privilege of Religion. Instead, like Hugh of Saint-Victor, he uses it to show that the sacrament of marriage is principally a spiritual partnership based on mutual consent, and only secondarily a carnal union resulting from coitus.

Unlike Alexander, Albertus Magnus uses arguments from signification in his *De matrimonio* to explain the Privilege of Religion. In one place, Albert uses the basic rationale, as proposed by Pope Innocent III. Whereas *matrimonium ratum* signifies the "union of God and the soul in charity," he argues, *matrimonium consummatum* signifies "the union of Christ and the church in nature." Since first of these *significata* is separable, whereas the second is inseparable, *matrimonium ratum* is separable, whereas *matrimonium consummatum* is inseparable.[36] Albert proposes a more complicated explanation elsewhere in the treatise. The union in charity between Christ and the church, which *matrimonium ratum* signifies, is itself the very basis of merit among the faithful, for one merits inasmuch as one's deeds flow from a union with God in charity. Since the Privilege of Religion involves the preference for a more meritorious over a less meritorious way of life, therefore, it dissolves *matrimonium ratum*. The two vows or bonds are commensurate, and one trumps the other because it is more meritorious. But *matrimonium consummatum* adds an additional dimension of signification to marriage, and for that reason a religious vow cannot dissolve the union.[37]

What is one to make of the rationale from double analogy? Modern readers who are unfamiliar with medieval religious thought will find it contrived and unconvin-cing. Contrariwise, readers who are familiar with the medieval use of figures, signs, and allegory may find Pope Innocent III's account of the rationale to be convincing and unexceptionable, at least in its historical context. But the rationale has obvious flaws. Perhaps that was why theologians used it less after 1250 than hitherto, although it never went away entirely during Middle Ages. The problems are of three sorts. First, it is not clear how cogent the explanation is supposed to be either causally or

---

[35] *IV Sent.* 26.7e (461). *IV Sent.* 26.7c (460): "Respondemus quod non minus est de sacramento ratione sanctitatis, sed pauciora sunt ratione significationis. Sacramentum autem a sanctitate dicitur sacramentum. Spiritualior enim est illa coniunctio, ubi non remittitur per carnalem copulam: in commixtione enim fit homo caro." On the absorption of the entire human being into flesh, see also Alexander, *IV Sent.* 31.10f (496), and see earlier, Section 13.1, on the origins of the theme.

[36] Albertus Magnus, *De matrimonio* 2.5, ad 7 (163b–64a). Albert, *De matrimonio* 1.3, resp. (157a/ 18–19), describes the *significatum* of marriage as "the joining of the church with God in charity and in nature," and in *De matrimonio* 1.6, resp. (159a/9–11) as "the twofold joining of the church with Christ."

[37] *De matrimonio* 1.1, ad 4 (155b).

logically. Does the rationale purport to show that marriage *must* be soluble before consummation and insoluble after it? And, if so, is that necessity logical or causal? Or is the rationale supposed to show only that the difference is fitting, on the assumption that it can be established in some other way, such as through precedent? Second, the rationale should show that unconsummated marriage is soluble in many ways, whereas thirteenth-century theologians envisaged only one way: the Privilege of Religion. Canonists considered other possible ways to dissolve an unconsummated marriage, but none became established in practice. The pope's right to dissolve an unconsummated marriage did not become established until the late Middle Ages, although canonists had entertained the idea during the second half of the twelfth century.[38] Third, the rationale is circular. Why assume that unconsummated marriage signifies a separable union, and that consummated marriage signifies an inseparable union? Chiefly, it seems, because unconsummated marriage is separable, whereas consummated marriage was inseparable. Thus, as we have seen, theologians who did not use the double analogy rationale to explain the Privilege of Religion, such as Stephen Langton, William of Auxerre, and Alexander of Hales, did not consistently posit significations that would support the rationale. The rationale, therefore, was rigged — but that was not a fatal objection when its purpose was not to prove or even fully to explain why the rule existed, but only to show that a rule discovered through precedent and confirmed by positive legislation was fitting.

14.3.2 *The spiritual death rationale*

The spiritual death rationale was originally designed to solve an objection: that the Privilege was incompatible with the insolubility of marriage. To solve the objection, theologians pointed out that marriage was inseparable only in the sense that it endured as long as both partners were alive. Just as carnal death dissolves the carnal union established by consummation, therefore, so spiritual death dissolves the spiritual union established by consent alone.[39] Stephen Langton uses this argument to reconcile the Privilege of Religion with Christ's injunction, "what God has joined together, let man not separate." If *de praesenti* consent is sufficient to establish a valid marriage, it seems that God joins them inseparably at that point:

> When it is said, "What God has joined, let man not separate," one may ask how the pope [Alexander] can say on the contrary that a spouse can go over to religion within three months if there has been no sexual intercourse. We say that what the pope says does not contradict what our Lord says. Rather, it [Alexander's rule] may

---

[38] D'Avray, *Medieval Marriage*, 188–97.
[39] Paludanus characterized religious vows as "civil death," reserving the term "spiritual death" for a death of the spirit, i.e., a turning away from spiritual to worldly things.

be fittingly interpreted thus: That there is a spiritual death when one of them dies to the world.[40]

Entry into the religious life was kind of a death, for someone who took religious vows died to the world. Spiritual death could not dissolve carnal union, but it would dissolve a union that was still spiritual, that is, dependent on consent alone. Unlike the double analogy rationale, this explanation was specific to the Privilege of Religion and would not have explained the dissolution of an unconsummated marriage in any other circumstance.

Some theologians used the spiritual death rationale to explain how *matrimonium ratum* was already insoluble before consummation. For example, Albertus Magnus uses it to show that marriage has "indivisibility" (*individuitas*) before consummation, notwithstanding the Privilege of Religion.[41] Similarly, Alexander of Hales uses it to show how the *bonum sacramenti*, identified here with inseparability, is an inalienable property present in every marriage, consummated or unconsummated. Whereas the other two goods can be absent from marriage, Alexander argues, the *bonum sacramenti* is always present. There is really no such thing as a separable marriage, least of all between believers, for whereas the good of offspring results from coitus, and the good of faith from the "indivisible way of life," the good of sacrament results not from a consequence or feature of marriage but from marriage itself.[42] To the objection that a marriage is separable by entry into religion before consummation, Alexander's first response is that such a marriage is at least inseparable as long as it lasts (for the spouses cannot separate and remarry at will), but he goes on to argue that any marriage is inseparable only in the sense that it must endure as long as both spouses are alive, whereas a person who enters the religious life dies to the world. Even in that case, however, a vestige of the original bond (*vinculum*) remains in the one who becomes a religious and cannot be erased, for he or she cannot validly marry again.[43]

There is no explicit appeal to signification in the spiritual death rationale, but it presupposes ways of construing consummation and extending the notion of death that would seem convincing only to minds imbued with signification and allegory. Both William of Auxerre and Thomas Aquinas formulate the argument in analogical terms, using the logic of "just as … so also." Here is William's version:

---

[40] Stephen Langton, *Quaestiones theologiae*, Cambridge, St. John's College, MS 57 (C.7), 318vb–319ra (= Oxford, Bodleian Library, MS Lyell 42, 2ra): "Item, cum dictum sit, 'Quod Deus coniunxit, homo non separet,' queritur quomodo papa in contrarium dicat, quod infra tres menses potest ire ad religionem si non fuerit ibi carnalis copula. Dicimus quod papa non est contrarius verbi domini, sed ea sic interpretatur et congrue: quia ibi est mors spiritualis quando alter moritur mundo."

[41] Albertus Magnus, *IV Sent.* 30.12, ad 1 (Borgnet 30:225b). See also *IV Sent.* 27.3, ad 1 (132b) and 28.6, ad 6 (195b–196a), where Albert uses the spiritual death rationale to explain the Privilege of Religion.

[42] Alexander of Hales, *IV Sent.* 31.2d (490).   [43] *IV Sent.* 31.11e (498).

Again, just as a corporeal marriage, that is, one that has been consummated by carnal coupling, is dissolved by corporeal death, so the spiritual marriage that exists before carnal coupling is dissolved by a spiritual death, namely, when one of the spouses enters religion. For then he or she dies to the world, which is a spiritual death.[44]

Without the well-rehearsed analogies between marriage and Christ's union with the church, which had exposed spiritual and carnal dimensions on both sides of the comparison, the very notion of *matrimonium ratum* as a spiritual relationship would have had little cogency.

The spiritual death rationale had largely superseded the double analogy rationale from around the middle of the thirteenth century, although theologians continued to use both, which they assumed demonstrated different but interrelated things. For example, Thomas Aquinas uses the spiritual death rationale to explain why dissolution through the Privilege of Religion is possible only before consummation,[45] whereas he uses the argument from double analogy to solve the objection that marriage even before consummation is an indivisible union that signifies the perpetual joining of the Christ and the church. Thomas replies that unconsummated marriage signifies the joining of Christ to the individual soul through grace, which is soluble, whereas consummated marriage signifies the joining of Christ to the church through the incarnation, which is insoluble.[46] Contrariwise, Peter of Tarentaise uses the spiritual death rationale to explain the Privilege of Religion,[47] but he resorts to the double analogy rationale to explain why the Privilege is no longer available after consummation:

> ... marital union may be divided in two ways: either as regards the bond, or as regards the bed. Likewise, indivisibility is twofold. The first indivisibility of marriage, which is in respect of the bond, pertains to marriage qua sacrament or a sign, for as long as marriage signifies the divisible union of Christ to the faithful soul, then it too is divisible through entry into religion even as regards the bond, as if through a spiritual death. But after it has signified the indivisible union of Christ to human nature, it is not divisible as regards the bond. Nevertheless, marriage is divisible as regards the bed [*thorus*] in two ways: either because of [what] the other spouse [does], that is, through fornication; or by mutual consent through the reception of [the sacrament of] orders or through entry into religion, but not without the spouse's consent.[48]

Consummation alters the significance of the bond (*vinculum*), according to Peter, with the result that the bond is no longer soluble. Marriage is still soluble after

---

[44] William of Auxerre, *Summa aurea* IV.17.2.2, resp. (388/90–94). Cf. Thomas Aquinas, *IV Sent.* 27.1.3, qu^a 2, resp. (85b–86a).

[45] Thomas Aquinas, *IV Sent.* 27.1.3, qu^a 2, resp. (85a); 39.un.4, ad 2 (228b).

[46] *IV Sent.* 27.1.3, qu^a 2, arg. 1; ad 2m (85a, 86a).

[47] Peter of Tarentaise, *IV Sent.* 27.3.1, qu. 1, arg. 2c; ibid., resp. (4:294b; 295a).

[48] *IV Sent.* 27.3.2, resp. (296a).

consummation, therefore, but only as regards cohabitation and the conjugal debt (the marriage bed), and not as regards the bond itself.

14.3.3 *Formal explanations*

Jurisprudential accounts of consummation depended on the assumption that a stronger or nobler vow, other things being equal, trumped a weaker or less noble vow. Everyone agreed that the religious life was superior to married life. Moreover, it seemed obvious that an obligation to God, other things being equal, should trump an obligation to another human being. For example, Abraham's obedience to God trumped his paternal obligation of care toward his son (Gen 22:1–19). These considerations suggested that consummation introduced something into marriage that rendered the competing unions no longer commensurable, preventing the greater from the trumping the lesser. Such explanations were largely formal inasmuch as they did not purport to prove that the Privilege of Religion was possible, or even to explain why the rule existed or was fitting. Rather, they provided a legal analysis of a spouse's rights before and after consummation. Most arguments of this sort construe marrying as a form of self-giving or conveyance in which the spouses give themselves bodily to each other. Consummation completes the gift.

Alexander of Hales and Albertus Magnus invoke the premise, first proposed by canonists during the twelfth century, that consummation establishes the conjugal debt (1 Cor 7:4–5).[49] This line of argument was originally designed to show why unconsummated marriage was soluble under certain circumstances, although it could not show why it should remain soluble for only a brief period. Alexander posits three modes of "faith" (*fides*) between the spouses. As soon as they are married through present consent, the spouses are bound both by the "faith of mutual chastity," which prevents them from extra-marital sex, and by the *fides mutuae exhibitionis*: the obligation to help and support each other. But they are not yet bound by the third mode of faith: the "mutual servitude" by which they owe their bodies sexually to each other. Whereas the faith of chastity pertains to the soul, Alexander explains, and the faith of servitude (the conjugal debt) to the body, their duty to care for each other pertains to the embodied soul. More precisely, it belongs directly to the soul and indirectly to the body. When one of the spouses enters the religious life before consummation, therefore, a superior spiritual obligation toward God trumps an inferior spiritual obligation toward another human being. But by consummating their marriage and establishing the carnal bond, the partners enter into an *unspiritual* way of life: one in which the spouses are distracted by mundane

---

[49] On the canon law theory that consummation established the conjugal debt, see J. A. Brundage, "Implied Consent to Intercourse," in A. Laiou, *Consent and Coercion to Sex and Marriage in Ancient and Medieval Societies* (Washington, DC, 1993), 245–56.

cares (1 Cor 7:33), and in which the soul is pulled down to the flesh by the pleasures of coitus. Since the union is now carnal, it cannot be trumped by a superior spiritual vow. The two obligations are different in kind and incommensurable.[50] Similarly, Albert argues that a husband's body becomes his wife's property only when they consummate their marriage. Thus, a husband who withdraws from a marriage after consummation to pursue continence, refusing to render the debt, invades his wife's rights, whereas there is no such invasion if he withdraws before consummation.[51]

Thomas Aquinas proposes a contractual analysis, emphasizing the power of positive law. Consent alone, Thomas concedes, other things being equal, suffices for the conveyance (*translatio*) by which the spouses become each other's property. Nevertheless, positive legislation has interpolated a delay, preventing the conveyance from coming fully into effect until two months have elapsed after the exchange of consent in the present tense. Until then, the marriage is in a certain sense conditional. Thomas reasons that some delay between consent in the present tense and the spouses' coming together as man and wife is a useful and salutary convention. As well as providing a window of opportunity for the Privilege of Religion, the delay encourages husbands not to regard the sexual availability of their wives too lightly, and it affords the spouses' families time to prepare for the solemnization of the marriage in public nuptials.[52]

Like Thomas, Peter of Tarentaise posits a conveyance (*translatio*) in which the spouses give bodily power over their very selves to each other, as explained in 1 Corinthians 7:4. Peter reasons that consummation completes the conveyance: "The conveyance of power over one's body [*potestatis corporis translatio*] is made complete and effective through consummation."[53] When St Paul said that each spouse had power over the other's body, therefore, he must have been referring to consummated marriage.[54] Nevertheless, consummation would be insufficient, Peter argues, without divine institution. No voluntary human action would suffice by itself to establish such an act of unconditional self-giving. The gift is possible only because divine institution is a concurrent efficient cause of marriage, working with the spouses' own exchange of consent.[55] Church law has introduced the window of two months as a special "indult," which postpones the inevitable conveyance. As befits such an exception, the duration is arbitrary.[56] Peter seems to assume that

---

[50] Alexander of Hales, *IV Sent.* 27.1c–d (463–64). Alexander reviews the particular features, rules, and problems of pre-consummated marriage, e.g., regarding the wife who wants choose the religious life but is raped by her husband, in *IV Sent.* 27.4 (468–69).

[51] Albertus Magnus, *IV Sent.* 27.3, ad 2–3 (132b).

[52] Thomas Aquinas, *IV Sent.* 27.1.3, quᵃ 2, ad 2 (86a).

[53] Peter of Tarentaise, *IV Sent.* 27.3.2, resp. (296a).   [54] *IV Sent.* 27.3.1, qu. 2, ad 1 (295a).

[55] *IV Sent.* 26.1.2, ad 1 (284a); 26.1.3, ad 3 (284b); 27.2.1, resp. (293a); 27.3.1, qu. 2, arg. 3 (294b).

[56] *IV Sent.* 27.3.1, qu. 2, resp. (295a): "non tenetur [coniux exactus reddere debitum] infra tempus duorum mensium a iure indultum"; ibid., ad 2: "tempus duorum mensium, causa deliberandi, a iure indultum est specialiter."

consummation necessarily closes the window of opportunity that the indult opened. Absent the indult, the conveyance would be complete at the moment of consent in the present tense, and consummation would add nothing to it.

14.4 THE SACRAMENT OF MARRIAGE AND THE GOOD OF SACRAMENT

Augustine's theory of the three conjugal goods had been a central component of the new theology of marriage that flourished during the first half of the twelfth century. Discussion of the theme was largely perfunctory during the second half that century, but thirteenth-century theologians took it up again and developed it extensively, albeit now with hardly any reference to Augustine.

Theologians during the early thirteenth century endeavored to clarify the muddled and ambiguous notion of the good of sacrament (*bonum sacramenti*) that their predecessors had bequeathed to them. Many twelfth-century theologians, including Peter Lombard, had identified the good of sacrament with the inseparability of marriage, but an older tradition, which began in the work of the *magistri moderni* but extended well into the thirteenth century, tended to identify the *bonum sacramenti* broadly with the sacramentality or sacred significance of marriage: with the fact that marriage was a sign of a sacred reality. Theologians during the first quarter of the thirteenth century debated which of those two options was correct or most appropriate, and they inquired into the relationship between the good of sacrament and the sacrament of marriage.

A common point of departure for the inquiry was a problem of identity, which Robert Courson stated as follows:

> If it is asked what this sacrament is — for the third good of marriage is called "sacrament" — very many people say that it is the same sacrament as [the sacrament of] marriage. But this does not seem right to us. How can it both be marriage and at the same time be a good of marriage? Therefore, we say that what is called a good of marriage is stability, that is, the inseparability and firmness of marriage, as a result of which divorce has no place in marriage.[57]

If possession of the third conjugal good is the same as the sacramentality of marriage, then the good of sacrament and the sacrament of marriage are the same thing. But the good of sacrament is a feature of marriage, and no thing can be identical with one of its own features. This problem arguably does not arise if one assumes that the third good is not the sacrament of marriage but the inseparability

---

[57] Robert Courson, *Quaestio de matrimonio*, ed. Malherbe, ch. 5, p. 20: "Si queratur quid sit tale sacramentum, quod dicitur tercium bonum coniugii, respondent plerique quod est idem sacramentum, quod est matrimonium. Sed hoc nobis non videtur. Quomodo enim esset matrimonium, simul et bonum matrimonii? Et ideo, dicimus quod hoc bonum matrimonii dicitur stabilitatem, id est, inseparabilitas et firmitas matrimonii, ex quo in matrimonio non habet divortium, et talis inseparabilitas et firmitas."

of that sacrament. Stated thus, the argument would have invited a semantic solution that explained how the name of a feature of something can become a name for the thing itself.[58] When it first arose, though, the problem seemed substantive, partly because there was a tendency to assume that attributing the *bonum sacramenti* to marriage was the same as counting marriage as one of the sacraments.

One approach to the problem was to identify the good of sacrament with inseparability but to note that the inseparability of marriage was itself a sacred sign, or sacrament, of the inseparability between Christ and the church. Such was Huguccio's solution. Huguccio argues that the sacrament of marriage and the *bonum sacramenti* are distinct things, even distinct sacraments. Some say that they are the same inasmuch as they are sacraments of the same thing, but in that case the relationship of the *bonum sacramenti* to marriage would be different from that of the other two goods, faith and offspring, which seems wrong. Moreover, nothing is a good of itself. Huguccio concludes that the *bonum sacramenti* is not the sacrament of marriage but the inseparability of that sacrament. It embraces both the inseparability of marriage itself and the qualified inseparability of the conjugal debt, which can be revoked only on grounds of adultery or by mutual vows of continence. But this twofold inseparability is itself a sacrament (i.e. a sacred sign) of the inseparability of Christ's union with the church, for it signifies that twofold union: both the union of natures that occurred in the Virgin's womb, and the union between Christ and the church formed by faith and charity.[59]

Theologians during the early part of the thirteenth century resisted the contraction of the good of sacrament to inseparability. Although Praepositinus notes that Peter Lombard identified the good of sacrament with inseparability, he prefers to identify it with the full sacred significance of marriage, whereby marriage signifies the twofold union between Christ and the church: the union of charity, and the union in one flesh or in a shared nature. Praepositinus adds that marriage itself has to be inseparable in order to signify the inseparable aspect resulting from the union of natures in Christ.[60] Guy of Orchelles and William of Auxerre develop Praepositinus's suggestion. The good of sacrament is not the same as inseparability, they argue, but it does entail or include inseparability as a salient significant feature of marriage. William puts it this way:

---

[58] The semantic shift in question was known in the Middle Ages as synecdoche (the transfer of a name from part to whole). In modern as well as in classical semantics, synecdoche is sometimes construed as a species of metonymy.

[59] Huguccio on C. 27 q. 2, *Sacramentum quia nullum divorcium*, in Roman, "Summa d'Huguccio," *Revue historique de droit français et étranger* 27 (1903), 758.

[60] Praepositinus, *Summa* IV, p. 107 (*De tribus bonis coniugii*).

The third good of marriage is the sacrament....[61] Therefore, since marriage signifies the joining of Christ and the church, there is inseparability in marriage for that
reason, and not because the third good is inseparability itself, as many say.[62]

One may be forgiven for wondering whether anything substantive is at stake here.
Either the good of sacrament is the inseparability of marriage, which is called a
sacrament because of its sacred significance, or it is the sacred significance of
marriage, which entails inseparability among other things as one of its salient
features, perhaps even as its *most* salient feature.

In reply to the objection that the sacrament of marriage and the good of sacrament cannot be identical because nothing can be identical with one of its own
properties, both Guy and William resort to semantics. They point out that it is
customary to use the same term to denote both (1) a certain feature of a thing and
(2) the thing itself inasmuch as it possesses that feature. Thus, no real equivocation is
involved.[63] For example, to say that the human being is an image of God in respect
of his reason, and to say that human reason is an image of God, are two ways of
saying the same thing.[64] Inseparability is a significant feature of marriage: a property
or feature by virtue of which marriage is apt to signify the union between Christ
incarnate and the church. With that premise in mind, William argues that the right
to divorce under the Old Law "was contrary to the third good of marriage, namely,
sacrament, which requires inseparability."[65] Despite their refusal to identify the
good of sacrament with inseparability, these authors generally use the phrase "good
of sacrament" with reference to inseparability and rarely with reference to other
significant aspects of marriage. They assume that inseparability is the crucially
significant feature of marriage, even if is not the only significant feature.

Most theologians after 1230, like Huguccio, preferred to identify the good of
sacrament narrowly with inseparability while noting that the inseparability of marriage was itself a sacred sign, or sacrament, of Christ's union with the church.
Alexander of Hales rejects William's solution, therefore, arguing instead that the
good of sacrament is the same as inseparability and that it must be distinguished
from the sacrament of marriage. "The [good of] sacrament," Alexander argues, "is
inseparability, by which the inseparability of the joining of Christ and the church is
signified."[66] Inseparability is itself a sacrament in a certain sense, Alexander explains,
for the term "sacrament" may denote a sacred sign, or the "property or disposition"
in respect of which the sign signifies, or even the sacred reality that is signified. The

---

[61] William of Auxerre, *Summa aurea* IV.17.2.2 (387–88), discusses the signification of marriage
and explains how signification entails indissolubility.

[62] *Summa aurea* IV.17.4.1 (400/12–15).

[63] For example, we sometimes call the sky "the blue," and the sea "the briney."

[64] Guy of Orchelles, *Tractatus de sacramentis* 9.2, no. 224 (201). William of Auxerre, *Summa
aurea* IV.17.4.1 (400/16–26).

[65] *Summa aurea* IV.17.4.4 (413/2–5).   [66] Alexander of Hales, *IV Sent.* 31.11a (497).

bonum sacramenti is a sacrament in the second sense: a significant feature of marriage. Marriage signifies the "joining of Christ and the church," and marriage must be inseparable to signify that joining inasmuch as the latter is inseparable. The term "good of sacrament" singles out a particular significant aspect of marriage, therefore, namely, its inseparability. Alexander concedes, though, that it makes no difference whether one says that marriage is sacrament of Christ and the church in respect of inseparability, or that the inseparability of marriage is itself a sacrament of the inseparability of that union, just as it makes no difference whether one says that the human being is rational in respect of the soul or that the human soul is rational.[67]

Theologians after around 1230 were inclined to treat the good of sacrament as an inalienable feature of marriage and sometimes even as an essential feature, but they also considered it to be in some sense a result of the sacrament of marriage, presumably because they identified the latter with the transient act of getting married. For example, Albert argues that marriage is related to the good of sacrament as cause to effect. The fact that marriage is inseparable follows from the fact that it is a *coniunctio*, and the inseparability of marriage signifies the inseparability of the church's union with God.[68]

Thomas Aquinas agrees with Peter Lombard that the good of sacrament is identical with the inseparability of marriage. More precisely, Thomas argues, one should say that the good of sacrament is the inseparability of marriage inasmuch as the latter signifies the inseparability of the church's union with Christ.[69] Thomas points out that according to this interpretation the identity problem does not arise, for it is clear that the good of sacrament is not the same as the sacrament of marriage. Thomas allows that the *bonum sacramenti* may be construed more broadly, however, so that it includes every aspect by virtue of which marriage apt to signify the union between Christ and the church. In that case, one would solve the identify problem by arguing that it is one thing for marriage to be marriage and another thing for it to be a sign of a sacred reality, since signification is but one aspect of marriage. Indeed, Thomas notes, one might call this particular feature of marriage its "sacramentality." Since the sacramentality of marriage (i.e., its sacred significance) is among the goods that make marriage honorable, it would be reasonable to count this among of the goods of marriage.[70]

The logical problem had largely faded from view by the middle of the thirteenth century. It had proved otiose inasmuch as the competing positions amounted to

---

[67] *IV Sent.* 31.2a (489). See also *Quaestio disputata* 57, disp. 2, m. 1, §§31–32 (1108).

[68] Albertus Magnus, *De matrimonio* 2.6, ad 6 (163b).

[69] For example, Thomas Aquinas, *IV Sent.* 31.1.3, resp. (123b): "indivisibilitas, quam sacramentum importat." *IV Sent.* 31.2.1, resp. (125a): "Et hanc bonitatem [sacramenti] habet actus matrimonii [i.e., coitus] ex indivisibilitate conjunctionis, secundum quam signat conjunctionem Christi ad Ecclesiam."

[70] Thomas Aquinas, *IV Sent.* 31.1.2, ad 4; ad 7 (122b, 122b–123a).

different ways of saying the same, but it had helped to clarify the difference between attributing the good of sacrament to marriage and counting marriage as one of the seven sacraments. Thereafter, theologians usually identified the *bonum sacramenti* with insolubility but reserved the right occasionally to interpret it more broadly as the entire figurative dimension of marriage: the aptness of marriage to signify sacred, mysterious unions such as that between Christ and the church. Similarly, they usually identified the *bonum fidei* with sexual fidelity, especially the conjugal debt, but they sometimes took it to include all the obligations of mutual care and support.

14.5 INSTITUTIONS AND SACRED HISTORY

If marriage was truly a sacrament of the New Law, Jesus Christ himself must have instituted it as a sacrament. We have seen in previous chapters how several themes contributed to the notion that marriage had undergone two or more institutions. Drawing on Augustine, the *magistri moderni* had distinguished between the institution of marriage as an office (*ad officium*) in Paradise and its institution as a remedy (*ad remedium*) after the fall (Section 9.4.1). That theme was prominent in Peter Lombard (Section 11.4.4), and it became a commonplace of the scholastic theology of marriage. The *magistri moderni* also tracked the legal history of marriage and its laws, and some of them assumed that each law or regime of marriage entailed a distinct institution. Twelfth-century theologians correlated marriage with the three historically sequential regimes of sacred history: the law of nature, established in the beginning; the Old Law, established by Moses; and the New Law, established by Jesus Christ. This tripartite division was especially important in Hugh of Saint-Victor's work on the sacraments in general and on marriage in particular (Section 10.5.1).

This idea of institution remained variable and undefined throughout the Middle Ages. Theologians usually assumed that a sacramental institution was a historical event: a moment of intervention, in which God had established something new. But they also regarded institutions as legal entities, each of which presupposed as its context a certain code or realm of law. The two notions were compatible, but they sometimes pulled in different directions. A scholar who focused on the legal aspect could regard different institutions of marriage as synchronic, identifying them with coexisting legislative zones rather than with sequential historical events.

Considered from the historical point of view, institutions entailed innovation. To say that marriage was instituted, therefore, was to say that it was introduced *de novo*. Even so, one might posit successive institutions of marriage if they entailed diverse laws or regimens. Theologians sometimes distinguished between a new institution of marriage and the approval (*approbatio*) of an already existing institution, although they never explained what the distinction was. For example, replying to the objection that marriage cannot be a sacrament of the New Law if the priestly blessing is not essential, since every sacrament of the New Law involves a constitutive blessing,

Peter of Tarentaise distinguishes between sacraments that were "simply instituted in the New Law" and sacraments that were "only approved in the New Law." Since marriage was only approved, the blessing was not essential.[71]

Theologians held various opinions regarding the moment at which God first instituted marriage. Everyone agreed that this institution occurred in Paradise, but in what event or dictum of the biblical record should one locate it? Perhaps God instituted marriage when he blessed the first human beings and commanded them to increase and multiply (Gen 1:28). But the record says that God gave the same command to the sea creatures (Gen 1:23), and theologians assumed that God had given it to all animals. Peter of La Palu reviews the opinions of the canonists. According to Tancred, Peter explains, the original institution occurred Genesis 2:23–24, when Adam said, "This is bone of my bones" and so forth. According to this theory, the "increase and multiply" of Genesis 1:28 was not strictly the institution of marriage but rather a "certain blessing of those who marry" (*quaedam benedictio nubentium*).[72]

Adam was speaking through divine inspiration as a prophet in Genesis 2:23–24, as Paul made clear when invoked the dictum in Ephesians 5:32. But was he speaking as a prophet precisely inasmuch as he was referring to human marriage? Albert thought not. Adam was prophesying only about Christ and the church, according to Albert, for his senses sufficed to inform him that Eve was to be his wife.[73] Whereas twelfth-century theologians instinctively regarded marriage in Paradise as a sacrament that looked forward to the advent of Jesus Christ, Albert instinctively regards it as an "office of nature" that was not yet a sacrament.

The idea of historical institutions had deep roots in sacramental theology. Alexander of Hales elaborated the sacramental history of marriage in the tradition of Hugh of Saint-Victor.[74] Although his account seems in retrospect to have been a late flourishing of an already old-fashioned idea, much of what he said on the subject influenced his successors. The sacrament of marriage "was instituted under the Law of Nature," Alexander explains, whereas the other sacraments "were principally instituted under the Mosaic Law or under the Law of the Gospel."[75] To resolve an ambiguity in earlier accounts of the three laws, Alexander subdivides the Law of Nature into two periods, respectively before and after the fall. Alexander variously characterizes the second of the three great periods as the Old Law, the Mosaic Law, and the Law of Fear, and the third period as the Law of Grace, the Law of the Gospel, and the New Law. Alexander explains that matrimony was introduced first,

---

[71] Peter of Tarentaise, *IV Sent.* 26.3.1, ad 1 (4:286b–287a). Peter suggests as an alternative solution that the original blessing of Gen 1:28 may suffice to meet the requirement that every sacrament includes a blessing.

[72] Paludanus, *IV Sent.* 26.1.3, resp. (139va).

[73] Albertus Magnus, *IV Sent.* 26.4, resp. (102b).

[74] The recension of Alexander's *Glossa* that has come down to us has amalgamated at least two such schemata, without attempting to unify or reconcile them.

[75] Alexander of Hales, *IV Sent.* 26.2b (446).

under the Law of Nature; the sacrament of orders ext, under the Old Law; and the other five sacraments last, under the New Law. But if marriage was the first of the seven to be instituted, why do theologians discuss it last? Alexander replies that whereas God keeps the best until last (John 2:10), theologians discuss the best first. God instituted marriage first, then priesthood, and finally the other five sacraments. But marriage comes last in order of nobility, the sacrament of orders comes in the middle, and the other five sacraments come first. Thus, theologians customarily treat the five first, then orders, and finally marriage, since it is the least of sacraments in dignity and sanctity.[76]

A more complex picture emerges when Alexander considers the relationships among the sacramental systems associated with the three phrases of law. All seven sacraments were instituted in one way or another under the New Law, but with varying degrees of innovation, for none was entirely without precedent. The sacrament of orders existed in some sense under the Mosaic law, but it could not be fully realized without the sacrament of penance, for the keys of absolution were given for the first time to Peter and his successors (Matt 16:19), and penance is properly a sacrament of the New Law. Marriage was instituted in the beginning, but it was re-instituted under the New Law. Alexander rejects the opinion that marriage received only "approbation" under the New Law.[77]

Alexander outlines a different and apparently incompatible schema elsewhere in the same commentary. Only confirmation and extreme unction were new when the seven sacraments were instituted under the New Law, he argues, for these sacraments are uniquely suited to the last age. Confirmation presupposes the fullness of grace and the manifest mission of the Holy Spirit, and extreme unction looks toward the opening of the Gates of Heaven and to the beatific vision. But a form of priesthood already existed under the Mosaic Law, eucharist supersedes the Mosaic sacrifice of the paschal lamb, and baptism supersedes circumcision. Circumcision was already practiced during the second, post-lapsarian phase of the Law of Nature, but it was properly instituted under the Old Law of Moses. The most archaic sacraments are marriage and penance, for they alone existed even before the fall. Penance is a sacrament of the New Law insofar as it involves the Power of the Keys, but its essence is contrition, which can be traced to the warning against sin in Genesis 2:17. Marriage was instituted in Paradise only as an office (*ad officium*), but it was instituted again after the fall as a remedy, just as circumcision already existed under the second phase of the natural law but was instituted again under the Old Law. Alexander correlates the several institutions of marriage both with the

---

[76] *IV Sent.* 26.2b–c (446). The relative order or dignity among the sacraments was a common discussion point. Cf. Bonaventure, *IV Sent.* 7, dub. 3 (4:176b): Marriage is the greatest sacrament in signification, eucharist in content, baptism in efficacy, confirmation as regards the dignity of the minister who dispenses it, and orders as regards the dignity of the consequent state.

[77] Alexander of Hales, *IV Sent.* 26.2b–c (446).

distinction between marriage as a procreative duty (*officium*) and as a remedy, and with the division of the three goods: offspring, faith, and sacrament. The first institution of marriage is recorded in Genesis 1:28, where God told human beings to "increase and multiply." That institution established the *bonum prolis*: the obligation to raise children to worship God. The next institution is recorded in Genesis 2:24, when God said through Adam that a man "shall leave his father and mother" to be joined to his wife. This institution established fidelity, or the *bonum fidei*. The next institution occurred after the Flood, when human beings were again commanded to increase and multiply (Gen 9:1). Alexander conjectures that this was probably when marriage was first instituted as a remedy, although he notes that marrying continued to be an *officium* (i.e., an obligation) until the advent of Jesus Christ.[78]

Bonaventure holds that each institution of marriage entailed a particular way of using marriage. When theologians say that marriage was instituted before the fall *ad officium* and that it was instituted again after the fall *ad remedium*, Bonaventure explains, the prepositional phrase specifies the primary use of marriage under each economy. Moreover, each use signifies a particular aspect of the monogamous union between Christ and the church. The sacrament of marriage is the outward, visible expression of an interior, invisible relationship. Fallen human beings need outward signs to understand interior realities, including even the conjugal partnership itself, which is not apparent to the senses. Even signification, therefore, is a species of use. Marriage was instituted after the fall as a remedy not only against concupiscence but also against ignorance. Extending the parallel, Bonaventure argues that marriage was originally instituted in Paradise not only as an office of the generative potency, to conserve the species, but also as an office of the cognitive potency, so that human beings would have external evidence of their mental and spiritual coming together. To be sure, human beings did not need such external instruction before the fall, but outward manifestations of inward realities would have been a source of delight.[79]

Institutional histories of marriage were also sacramental histories, in which marriage was a sacrament at every stage but in different ways. Theologians tried to ascertain precisely when the sacrament of marriage was instituted in Paradise, as well what sacred reality it originally signified. Robert Courson rejects the standard answers. Some say that marriage was instituted when God blessed Adam and Eve and told them to increase and multiply; others, when Adam awoke from his deep sleep, and God brought Eve to him, and Adam said, "This is now bone of my bones," and so forth (Gen 2:22–24). But neither opinion is correct, Robert argues. It is more likely that God instituted marriage implicitly in the very act of creating human beings, since marriage was at first subject only to the natural law, which is

---

[78] *IV Sent.* 26.3 (447–50).   [79] Bonaventure, *IV Sent.* 26.1.1, resp.; ad 4 (4:662).

inscribed in created nature. Eve's consent to the first marriage is implied in Genesis 2:22, where God brought Eve to Adam, for that act should surely be interpreted as a coming together of wills. Eve probably expressed her consent in words, although these are not recorded.[80]

Bonaventure argues that the original institution of marriage is recorded in Genesis 2:24, when Adam prophesied. The blessing of Genesis 1:28 cannot have been the historical institution of marriage, he argues, for God blessed irrational animals in the same way. Since the sacrament of marriage is based on the spouses' consent, rather than on something external that is received from a minister, it was fitting that the sacrament was revealed to Adam through an interior illumination.[81]

Thomas notes that it was Adam who spoke the words of Genesis 2:24 (as well as of v. 23), for although Jesus says that it was the Creator who spoke (Matt 19:5), Adam was speaking as a prophet, having emerged from a prophetic trance (*sopor*). This interpretation of Adam's dictum was familiar from patristic exegesis.[82] Thomas argues, nevertheless, that marriage was first instituted when God told Adam and Eve to "increase and multiply" (Gen 1:28). To the objection that God gave the same command to the other animals, Thomas replies that human beings were not intended to fulfill the command *in the same way* as other animals.[83]

Theologians usually assumed that marriage was instituted even in Eden to signify the union between Christ and church. But how could it have signified that to Adam and Eve if they did not expect the incarnation? The problem touches on a celebrated question of scholastic theology: Would Christ have become incarnate if there were no sin?[84] Some, including Thomas Aquinas, argued that Christ's incarnation would not have been necessary without sin, for there is no need of medicine when there is no disease. But then it seems to follow that the future incarnation was not foreseeable in Paradise. We cannot be sure that Christ would *not* have become incarnate in that case, for God does what he pleases, but we have no reason to suppose that it would have happened. Perhaps marriage then did not signify the joining of Christ and the church through the sharing of a common nature, but only the union of God and the soul, or the union of charity between Christ and the church. Turning that argument on its head, one might argue that because Adam prophesied about Christ and the church when he spoke of his

---

[80]　Robert Courson, *Quaestio de matrimonio*, ed. Malherbe, ch. 3, pp. 10–11.

[81]　Bonaventure, *IV Sent.* 26.1.2, resp.; ad 3 (664). Cf. Albertus Magnus, *IV Sent.* 26.6, arg. 3 (194b), who also locates the original institution of marriage is Gen 2:24.

[82]　See MWCh, 283–95.　　[83]　Thomas Aquinas, *IV Sent.* 26.2.2, ad 4 (73a).

[84]　On the history of this question ("*Utrum filius Dei esset incarnatus si homo non peccasset?*"), see J.-F. Bonnefoy, "La question hypothétique *Utrum si homo non peccasset?* au XIIIe siècle," *Revista española de teología* 14 (1954): 326–68; W. H. Principe, "Guerric of Saint-Quentin, O.P., on the Question: *Utrum Filius Dei esset incarnatus si homo non peccasset?*" in C.-J. Pinto de Oliveira, *Ordo Sapientiae et Amoris* (Fribourg, 1993), 509–37; and J.-P. Torrell, "Christology in the *Quodlibets* of Guerric of Saint-Quentin," in J. R. Ginther and C. N. Still, *Essays in Medieval Philosophy and Theology* (Aldershot, 2005), 53–66, at 55–56.

marriage to Eve (Gen 2:24, Eph 5:32), it follows that Christ would have become incarnate even if there had been no sin, for everyone concedes that Adam could not have foreseen his own fall.[85]

How theologians construed the significance of marriage in Paradise, therefore, depended on their approach to the Christological problem. Alexander argues that although human beings in Paradise could not have predicted that sin would enter the world, they would still have rejoiced in the very possibility of the incarnation. They would have recognized that the incarnation was the greatest thing that could happen to human nature, the summit of human aspiration, and the greatest possible expression of God's love for human kind. It already made sense, therefore, for marriage to signify the incarnation. Alexander does not explicitly propose that Christ would have become incarnate even in the absence of sin, but he seems to lean in that direction.[86] Thomas reasoned that Christ probably would not have become incarnate in the absence of sin, but that marriage was instituted in Paradise to signify Christ and the church. Adam could have foreseen the incarnation, Thomas points out, without foreseeing that sin would be the reason for it, for there are many other likely or fitting reasons for the incarnation, and nothing prevents God from revealing a future effect without revealing its cause.[87]

Bonaventure offers two subtly different solutions. When he discusses the underlying Christological question in his commentary on the third book of the *Sentences*, Bonaventure recognizes the force of both sides in the debate, but he determines that it is more salutary to assume that Christ would *not* have become incarnate if there were no sin. To affirm the opposite would invite complacency.[88] Replying to the objection that the sacrament of marriage in the beginning would then have been "false," for it would have signified something that would never occur, Bonaventure argues that marriage signifies the "joining of God to the church" in two respects: as regards the union of charity, and as regards the union of natures in one Person. In the fallen condition, marriage signifies the joining in both respects, but marriage would still have signified the charitable aspect of the union if there had been no sin. Bonaventure reasons that marriage as an *officium* chiefly signifies the union of charity whereas marriage as a remedy chiefly signifies the union of natures: "For just as marriage now serves both as an office and a remedy, whereas then it served only as an office, so also marriage now signifies two things, but then only one."[89] When Bonaventure returns to the question in the treatise on marriage in the fourth book, he concedes for the sake of argument that Christ would not have become

---

[85] Bonaventure, *III Sent.* 1.2.2, arg. 8c (3:23a). Thomas, *Summa theologiae* 3.2.1, arg. 5 (2417b).

[86] Alexander of Hales, *Quaestio disputata* 57, disp. 1, m. 3, §§14–17 (1101–1103); m. 5, §28 (1106/17–20).

[87] Thomas Aquinas, *Summa theologiae* III.1.3, ad 5 (2418b). Albertus Magnus, *IV Sent.* 26.4, ad 2 (102b), uses the same argument.

[88] Bonaventure, *III Sent.* 1.2.2 (3:21–28).   [89] Ibid., ad 8 (27).

incarnate if there were no sin, since this is the "more common and more probable opinion."[90] Nevertheless, he argues, it does not necessarily follow that marriage in Paradise was not a "great sacrament" of Christ and the church. God, who instituted marriage, foresaw the fall even if Adam did not. Adam must have foreseen the union between Christ and the church and prophesied about it since he was speaking as the mouthpiece of God. Marriage even in Paradise signified the union of the church with Christ, therefore, as well as the union of the individual soul with God, but it did not do so as evidently then (*non ita expresse*) as it would do after sin had entered the world.[91]

Just as theologians inquired precisely when marriage was instituted in Paradise, so they inquired when it was instituted under the New Law — if indeed it was instituted then, rather than approved. Alexander argues that marriage was "solemnized" by the presence of the "true bridegroom" (*sponsus verus*) at Cana (John 2:1–10), but he does not regard that event as an institution, perhaps because it did not entail any legal innovation. Instead, Alexander argues that the institution occurred when Jesus declared that man should not separate what God has joined (Matt 19:5–6, etc.). By abolishing divorce and remarriage, by insisting on inseparability, and by implicitly restoring monogamy, Jesus perfected the *bonum sacramenti* and instituted matrimony as a sacrament of the New Law.[92]

Albert posits four institutions of marriage as a sacrament in the *De matrimonio*. To that end, he considers the sacrament both as a sacred sign and as a cause of sanctity. Marriage in Paradise was already a sign of the twofold union between God and the church, but it had no reparative power. Any medicinal power that it had then was not reparative but preservative. Next, after the fall but still under the Law of Nature, marriage acquired in addition a certain remedial power, but without conferring any interior grace. The intrinsic honorableness of marriage rescued human nature from concupiscence, saving it from falling into ruin. Marriage under the Old Law was still an external remedial cause, but it was also a sign of the interior grace that it would confer in the future, under the New Law. Signification and causality, therefore, did not coincide then, but they converged under the New Law, where marriage causes the interior grace that it signifies.[93]

Albert argues in his commentary on the *Sentences* that nothing prevents marriage from being instituted "twice or thrice or several times" because it serves several different purposes. These include the "office of nature" (i.e., procreation), sacred signification, and the remedy that marriage confers both through the "faith of

---

[90] *IV Sent.* 26.2.1, arg. 3c (4:666a).   [91] Ibid., ad 3 (667).

[92] Alexander of Hales, *IV Sent.* 26.6b–c (456–57). In *IV Sent.* 31.2c (489–90), Alexander presents a different theory of institutions in relation to the goods, where marriage was instituted in respect of the good of offspring in Gen 1:28 ("increase and multiply"), in respect of the good of faith in Gen 2:24 ("a man will leave father and mother and cleave unto his wife"), and in respect of the good of sacrament in Gen 2:23 ("bone of my bones and flesh of my flesh")

[93] Albertus Magnus, *De matrimonio* 1.2, resp. (159a).

marriage bed" and through "the grace that comes from the betrothal of human nature with the divine nature in the person of Christ." Albert argues here that there were at least three historical institutions: one in the original state of innocence, another under the Old Law, and a third under the New Law. The first institution pertained to human nature as such, the second to corrupted human nature, and the third to human nature inasmuch as God has repaired it through Christ.[94] Albert concedes that the "increase and multiply" of Genesis 1:28 was a precept, but he argues that it was a self-limiting one. Human beings were duty-bound to procreate only as long as there was a "deficiency of inhabitants of the world and of those who serve God." Once the population had reached the sufficient, preordained level, procreation was no longer a matter of precept.[95] Albert concedes that the sacrament of marriage was instituted in Paradise before sin, but he argues that it was not instituted then precisely *as a sacrament*, since sacraments by definition heal as well as signify. Likening the sacraments to the bandages with which the Good Samaritan bound up the wounds of the injured man, Albert argues that although "that which is the sacrament" of marriage (*illud quod est sacramentum*) existed before sin, marriage became a sacrament only after sin.[96] By the same token, marriage is not essentially a remedy to sin, Albert argues, for its essential purpose is the office of procreation. After the fall, the office was found to contain "a remedy for the wound that happened because of sin."[97]

Following Albert, Thomas Aquinas argues that marriage was not properly instituted as a sacrament in Paradise, although it was already a sacred sign. Nor is it a sacrament under civil law. Instead, marriage was instituted as an office of nature in Paradise, and as an office of the civil community (*officium civilitatis*) under the civil law. Although marriage confers grace only as a sacrament of the New Law, it is a sacrament in a broader sense whenever it is both a sacred sign and a remedy. Marriage was instituted as a sacrament in that sense soon after the fall, therefore, when it became a remedy, and again under the Mosaic law, when it received additional determination of persons (i.e., the impediments of relationship). Finally, it was instituted under the New Law as a sacrament in the fullest sense: both as an explicit sign of Christ's union with the church, and as a cause of grace.[98]

Peter of Tarentaise locates the original institution of the sacrament in Adam's utterance of Genesis 2:24. It is true that God did not speak as expressly then as when he commanded human beings to increase and multiply, but the latter command was not specifically human, for God gave it to all animals. Moreover, God "tacitly" referred to the mysteries of faith in Genesis 2:24, for Adam was speaking from prophetic inspiration. Appropriating an insight from Bonaventure, Peter argues that

---

[94] Albertus Magnus, *IV Sent.* 26.5, resp. (103b).   [95] *IV Sent.* 26.10, resp., ad 1, ad 6 (112).
[96] *IV Sent.* 26.1, ad 1–3 (99a).   [97] Ibid., resp. (98b).
[98] Thomas Aquinas, *IV Sent.* 26.2.2, resp. (72b–73a).

the manner in which God first instituted marriage, by inspiring Adam to speak for him, was congruent with the hybrid structure of marriage, which is both human and divine. Whereas the obligation to sexual intercourse is carnal and human, the spiritual power of marriage both to signify holiness and to cause it is divine. Looking at Adam's declaration from the perspective of an exegete, Peter of Tarentaise finds that all three conjugal goods are implied in it: the husband's leaving his father and mother to live with his wife implies inseparability, or the good of sacrament; his cleaving exclusively unto his wife implies the good of faith; and their being two in one flesh implies the good of offspring.[99]

Richard de Mediavilla correlates the institutional history of marriage more closely with Scripture. Richard begins by reviewing a theory that is similar to Thomas's. Some say that marriage has gone through four institutions. It was first instituted before sin *ad officium*, for the sake of procreation and of the spouses' mutual support (*solatium*). Next, marriage was instituted after sin but still during the period of the Law of Nature as a remedy against concupiscence, which is the "wound of sin." Marriage was instituted again under the Law of Moses, which added the "determination of persons" (i.e., impediments of relationship). Finally, marriage was instituted under the New Law as the visible sign of a mystery, namely, the union of Christ and the church.[100] The last of those institutions, according to the proponents of this theory, occurred when Jesus prohibited divorce, saying: "What God has joined, let man not separate" (Mark 10:9, Matt 19:6).[101] But Richard rejects that theory on the grounds that it cannot sufficiently account for the various purposes of marriage. Marriage was a sign of Christ and the church during all four phases, and it was remedy against concupiscence in all but the first phase. Richard proposes instead that there were only two institutions of marriage: that of marriage as an office (*in officium*) before sin, and that of marriage both as an office and as a remedy (*in remedium*) after sin.[102] Richard expounds both institutions in detail, construing each not as a single event but rather as an unfolding series of events.

The process of instituting marriage as an office, Richard explains, began when God declared that it was not good for the man to be alone and that he would make a helpmeet for him (Gen 2:18). God was, in effect, predicting the institution that would follow. Next, God implicitly instituted marriage by forming Eve from Adam's side and by bringing her to Adam as his partner (Gen 2:21–22). Finally, God made the first institution explicit by blessing the first couple and telling them to increase and multiply (Gen 1:28). Although Adam's prophetic utterance (Gen 2:24) was not strictly a moment of institution, according to Richard, Adam contributed to the unfolding of the institution by expressing the purpose and meaning of marriage and

---

[99] Peter of Tarentaise, *IV Sent.* 26.1.3, resp. (4:284b).
[100] Richard de Mediavilla, *IV Sent.* 26.1.2, resp. (402a).
[101] *IV Sent.* 26.1.3, resp. (403a).   [102] *IV Sent.* 26.1.2, resp. (402b)

by predicting through divine inspiration the union of Christ and the church that marriage would signify. Like Peter of Tarentaise, Richard argues that the three conjugal goods were already implicit in Adam's words. It was fitting that God instituted marriage not only directly, by blessing Adam and Eve, but also indirectly, by speaking through Adam, for marriage itself has a twofold structure: there is something carnal in it, namely, the obligation to sexual intercourse, but there is also a "spiritual power" in marriage, for it is both a sacred sign and a cause of sanctity.[103] Even if Adam's prophecy had been the sole institution of marriage *ad officium*, it would still be true that marriage was instituted primarily by God and secondarily by a man. In fact, however, God first instituted marriage directly, without human assistance, and only later completed the institution through Adam.[104]

The institution of marriage as a remedy occurred in stages too, according to Richard. God implied that marriage was a remedy when he warned Eve that she would suffer pain in childbirth and be subject to her husband, and when he admonished Adam for obeying his wife's suggestion (Gen 3:16–17). God made this second institution explicit when he told Noah and his family to increase and multiply (Gen 9:1). Jesus' commandment, "What God has joined, let man not separate," was not, as some say, the moment at which Christ instituted marriage as a sign of Christ and the church. Rather, "Christ said those words to show that marriage had been instituted a long time ago," as well as "to instruct those who did not properly understand the inseparability of marriage."[105] Unlike baptism and confirmation, Richard argues, marriage was not instituted in the proper sense under the New Law but rather approved and confirmed. Nevertheless, a major change took place, for marriage was now for the first time a cause of sanctifying grace (*gratia gratum faciens*).[106]

There was no consensus among scholastic theologians either as to when marriage was originally instituted in Paradise or as to when it was re-instituted as a sacrament of the New Law. Nor did they agree as to where these institutions were recorded in Scripture. There was not even consensus as to whether marriage was instituted or only approved under the New Law, although the difference between *institutio* and *approbatio* remained undefined. Nevertheless, theologians did find plausible candidates for these moments of divine institution (or approval), and they showed that the theory of institutions did not present any insuperable obstacles to the recognition that marriage was a sacrament in the proper sense, or a sacrament of the New Law. These details were not troubling matters of heated controversy but rather opportunities for the free exercise of speculation.

---

[103] *IV Sent.* 26.1.3, resp. (403a).
[104] *IV Sent.* 26.1.3, arg. 1; ad 1; ad s.c. (402b; 403a; 403b).
[105] *IV Sent.* 26.1.3, resp. (403a).   [106] *IV Sent.* 26.4.2, resp. (408b).

14.6 MARRIAGE AS ONE OF THE SEVEN SACRAMENTS

There were two ways to show that marriage was truly one of the seven sacraments. A theologian could either test marriage against a definition of the genus, or inquire whether marriage exemplified what were arguably the salient and distinguishing features of other members of the class, especially baptism and eucharist. The second method was more common. As well as exposing ways in which marriage was akin to the other six sacraments, these inquiries exposed the differences and led to the recognition that marriage was a hybrid institution, part contract and part sacrament.

14.6.1 *The parsing of marriage*

Theologians pursued a unified theory of the seven sacraments, applying to marriage schemata that they discovered in other sacraments. They assumed that all the sacraments shared a certain structure, or composition. Was marriage composed in this way?

Analyses of the composition of the sacraments had evolved rapidly during the twelfth and early-thirteenth centuries.[107] Scholastic theologians parsed the sacraments in two ways: by analyzing the sacrament itself, construed as a transient event, into its formal and material components; and by analyzing the work of the sacrament into three aspects: the sacrament itself as an external, tangible, and manifest sign; the unseen, mysterious reality that the sacrament ultimately signified or effected; and a hidden effect that mediated between those extremes and was sometimes construed as a disposition to receive the sacrament's ultimate efficacy.

14.6.1.1 *Form and matter*

The oldest division of this sort was Augustine's, who said in a discussion of baptism that a sacrament occurred when a *verbum* was applied to an *elementum*.[108] The *verbum* was in essence a spoken formula, although the term had wider connotations in Augustine's thought. The *elementum* was a tangible material stuff, such as water or bread and wine. This division had two peculiarities. First, it did not explicitly include the liturgical action of the minister, although that was implicit in the "access" of the word to the element. Second, the material aspect preexisted the sacrament. The sacrament was made from the element somewhat in the way that a pot was made from a lump of clay.

In the twelfth century, Hugh of Saint-Victor said that a sacrament was composed of three items, not two: *res* (things), such as water, oil, or bread and wine; words

---

[107] D. Van den Eynde, "The Theory of the Composition of the Sacraments in Early Scholasticism (1125–1240)," *Franciscan Studies* 11.1 (1951): 1–20, 117–44, and 12.1 (1952): 1–26.

[108] Augustine, *In Iohannis evangelium* 80.3 (CCL 36:529/5–7): "Accedit uerbum ad elementum, et fit sacramentum, etiam ipsum tamquam uisibile uerbum."

(*verba*), such as the invocation of the Trinity; and *facta* (deeds, or actions). Because of his keen interest in liturgical performance and sacramentals, Hugh interpreted *facta* broadly so as to include the sign of the cross, the stretching out or elevation of the hands, and any motion of the body, such as bending, standing, or turning.[109] The *Summa sententiarum* posited the same division, citing two examples of *facta*: insufflation and immersion.[110] Peter Lombard characteristically reduced the analysis to "words and things: words, such as the invocation of the Trinity; things, such as water, oil, and things of that sort."[111] This was Augustine's twofold division with a different terminology.

Thirteenth-century schoolmen appropriated Aristotle's hylomorphic model and regarded each sacrament as if it were a substance. Just as a substance was composed in essence of form and matter, so also, by analogy, was a sacrament. (One should keep in mind here that a sacrament was a transient, initiating event, not the enduring state that resulted.) The analysis invited theologians to determine what was essential and inalterable in each sacrament, in contrast to what was accidental, customary, or changeable. Theologians assumed that Jesus Christ himself had instituted the essential form and matter of each sacrament, and that the omission or alteration of anything essential would prevent the sacrament from occurring. The notions of sacramental form and matter largely superseded those of *verbum* and *elementum*. The *verbum* was construed as a form because it "determined" the matter to a particular use or efficacy. But whereas the *elementum*, such as the water used for baptism, preexisted the sacrament, the matter in the most technical sense was an essential component of the sacrament, correlative to the form. One might identify the matter of baptism as ritual ablution, for example, although theologians continued to identify the matter as water. Thomas Aquinas distinguished between the proximate and the remote matter of a sacrament. The proximate matter of baptism, for example, was not water but the "act of ablution," whereas the water used in the sacrament was its remote matter. The form, as always, was a verbal formula.[112]

14.6.1.2 *Tripartite analysis*

Reflection on the character in baptism and on the *corpus mysticum* in eucharist led theologians to posit three sequential components in each sacrament, as noted earlier: the *sacramentum tantum*, or *signum tantum*, which was the outward sign; the *res tantum*, which was the ultimate signified reality; and the *sacramentum et res*, or *signum et res*, which was a hidden, mediating component. The relation between the *sacramentum tantum* and the *sacramentum et res* was analogous or comparable

---

[109] Hugh of Saint-Victor, *De sacramentis* I.9.6 (PL 176:326B–C).
[110] *Summa sententiarum* 4.1 (PL 176:117A).   [111] Peter Lombard, *Sent.* IV, 1.6.6 (235).
[112] Thomas Aquinas, *IV Sent.* 3.2, qu^a 1, resp. (ed. Moos, 4:118): "... materiam baptismi proximam quae est actus ablutionis." Thomas refers to water as the (remote) matter in ibid., arg. 7 (118).

to that between the *sacramentum et res* and the *res tantum*, although theologians never adequately explained how a non-sensible reality could be a sign of something. In baptism, which established the paradigm, the *sacramentum tantum* consisted of external ablution with water and the priest's invocation of the Trinity; the *res tantum* was the resulting gracious absolution from sin; and the *sacramentum et res* was the character impressed indelibly on the soul, which disposed the subject to receive grace. In eucharist, the *sacramentum tantum* was the visible species of bread of wine or their ritual blessing; the *res tantum* was a sustaining grace; and the true body of Christ that was present under the species of bread and wine might be construed as a *sacramentum et res*. Once theologians had accepted that marriage belonged properly among the seven sacraments, they began to analyze marriage in the same tripartite manner, identifying the *sacramentum tantum* with the outward expression of mutual consent. Some identified the *sacramentum et res* of marriage with the interior act of consent in the act of marrying, others with the enduring bond (*vinculum*) or obligation (*obligatio*), or the enduring interior union (*coniunctio*). Again, theologians sometimes identified the *res tantum* with conjugal grace and sometimes with a divine–human union, especially the union between the church and Christ.

Alexander of Hales proposed differing tripartite analyses of marriage in his *Glossa* on the *Sentences* and in his disputed questions. In the *Glossa*, Alexander holds that the *sacramentum tantum* is the outward expression of consent, and that the *sacramentum et res* is the interior joining of the spouses' wills. Three different things may be construed as the *res tantum*, according to Alexander: the union of the faithful soul with Christ, the union of the church with Christ as with her head, and the charity that unites the church to Christ. Alexander explains that the *sacramentum et res* (the interior joining of wills) disposes the spouses to receive the grace of conjugal charity, although he does not explicitly identify this charity here with the *res tantum*.[113]

In his disputed questions, Alexander parses both baptism and marriage into *signum tantum* ("sign alone"), *signum et signatum* ("sign and signified"), and *signatum tantum* ("signified only"). In baptism, the three elements are respectively the external ablution, the character, and remission of sins. In marriage, the *signum tantum* is the exterior expression of consent: either the expression of *de praesenti* consent, or the expression of *de futuro* consent followed by coitus. The corresponding *signum et signatum* is the interior act of consent, which in turns signifies the intimate love between Christ and the church, the *signum tantum*. One may also say that the *signum et signatum* is the conformity in nature between Christ and the church, for this is signified by marriage, especially consummated marriage, and it is in turn a sign of the union of intimate love between Christ and the church, the *signum tantum*.[114]

---

[113] Alexander of Hales, *IV Sent.* 26.5m (455).
[114] *Quaestio disputata* 57, disp. 1, m. 2, §13 (1101). Presumably the *signum tantum* signifying the union of natures is coitus or sexual union.

Some theologians identified the *res tantum* of marriage with conjugal grace, others with the union between Christ and the church. According to Albertus Magnus, the *res tantum* is the saving effect of the sacrament, which is a "medicinal grace." The *signum tantum* is the exterior forming of the sacrament by the partners' mutual consent, which is expressed in sensible signs. The *signum et res* is their interior act of consent.[115] According to Bonaventure, the *res tantum*, or *signatum tantum*, is primarily the union of the church to Christ and secondarily the union of the individual faithful soul to God. The chief *signum tantum* is the exterior expression of consent in words or non-verbal gestures, although coitus contributes to the *signum tantum* in a secondary manner. The *signum et res* is the interior union or joining of the spouses, which their outward expression of consent both signifies and enhances. Bonaventure uses this analysis to show how marriage and penance differ from the other sacraments. In these sacraments alone, the *signum tantum* is an outward expression of a prior interior act, which is the *signum et res*, although the outward expression also enhances the interior act. The relationship is reversed in the other sacraments, where an outward act, or *signum tantum*, causes the interior *signum et res*.[116]

Once the doctrine of conjugal grace had become established, theologians construed both grace and the union between Christ and the church as the *res tantum*. According to Thomas Aquinas, the *sacramentum tantum* consists of exterior sensible acts (i.e., the exchange of consent), and the ultimate reality (*res ultima*) includes both grace as the contained reality and the union between Christ and the church as the uncontained reality.[117] The *sacramentum et res*, according to Thomas, is the obligation or tie (*nexus*) established by the exchange of consent. The marriage, properly so called, is this enduring obligation, according to Thomas, whereas the sacrament is the transient outward act that establishes the obligation. The interior obligation (the *sacramentum et res*) disposes the spouses to receive conjugal grace, just as the character impressed on the soul in baptism disposes the subject to receive forgiveness of sins.[118]

Peter of Tarentaise and Richard de Mediavilla proposed modified versions of Thomas's theory. According to Peter, the *sacramentum tantum* is the exterior joining (i.e., the expression of consent), whereas the *sacramentum et res* is the interior joining of wills (*coniunctio animorum*). The primary *res tantum* is grace, but the joining of Christ and the church is the *res tantum* in a secondary sense.[119] Richard de Mediavilla agrees that the *sacramentum tantum* is the exterior expression of consent in words, but he finds two things that may be construed as the *res et sacramentum*: the interior "union of consents," and the mutual obligation that is

---

[115] Albertus Magnus, *De matrimonio* 1.2, resp. (156b/50–53).
[116] Bonaventure, *IV Sent.* 26.2.1, resp.; ad 2 (666).
[117] Thomas Aquinas, *IV Sent.* 26.2.1, ad 5 (72a).   [118] *IV Sent.* 26.2.3, ad 2 (74).
[119] Peter of Tarentaise, *IV Sent.* 26.3.1, ad 5 (4:287a).

established by consent. These dispose the spouses to receive the sacramental grace of conjugal charity, which is the *res tantum*. Marriage causes this supernatural conjugal charity "dispositively." But the union between Christ and the church is also a *res tantum*, for it is the ultimate reality that marriage signifies.[120]

14.6.2 *Objections and solutions*

Whereas application of the tripartite schema to the sacrament of marriage was instructive and not problematic, the division of the sacrament into formal and material components was more fraught, for it highlighted the peculiarity of marriage among the sacraments. It was easy to object that marriage could not be a sacrament because it lacked either form or matter. Scholastic theologians showed that such objections were soluble by demonstrating that various aspects could be construed as matter or as form, although there was never consensus as to what the essential matter and form of marriage were.

The usual setting of such objections was an article on whether marriage was a sacrament properly so called, or a sacrament of the New Law. The objections sometimes originated as arguments intended to show how marriage was not in the fullest sense a sacrament of the New Law, but most thirteenth-century theologians used them dialectically, as a way to develop a more detailed account of marriage as a sacrament. Theologians did not deny that the objections exposed genuine differences between marriage and other sacraments. They defended the doctrine by stretching the criteria to fit marriage, and they mitigated the objections both by explaining ways in which marriage had to be different from the other sacraments and by showing that the features in question were not peculiar to marriage. Albert was a pioneer of this technique. He considered objections pertaining respectively to the absence of form, of matter, and of efficacy. There was no prescribed verbal formula (*verbum*) in marriage, no material stuff (*elementum*), such as wine or oil, and arguably no efficacy, if marriage did not confer grace.[121] Peter of Tarentaise considered five objections: no benediction was essential; there was no material element; marriage did not effect what it signified; it did not conform the subjects to the Passion of Christ, which was the common source of all sacramental efficacy; and it was not capable of tripartite analysis into *sacramentum tantum*, *sacramentum et res*, and *res tantum*.[122] But the most fundamental and formative objections pertained to form, matter, and minister, as Albert had shown.

As noted earlier, sacraments were supposed to involve a verbal formula (*verbum*), with which the minister (normally a priest) consecrated some specific physical stuff (*elementum*), such as water, oil, or bread and wine. The essential *verbum* and

---

[120] Richard de Mediavilla, *IV Sent.* 26.4.2, resp. (408b).
[121] Albertus Magnus, *IV Sent.* 26.14 (120–23).   [122] Peter of Tarentaise, *IV Sent.* 26.3.1 (4:286–87).

elementum were presumed to be unchangeable requirements and to have originated in Christ's institution of the sacrament. But marriage required no prescribed form. Theologians and clerics often recommended formulae for the expression of mutual consent, but no particular words were required. Indeed, theologians and canonists conceded that spouses could validly plight their troth with non-verbal signs — literally, "nods" (*nuta*). This might be necessary if they were mute, if they spoke different languages, if the girl was too shy to speak, or even if such was the convention of the region. Again, some conceded that spouses could express their consent in writing or through intermediaries, and that girls could consent by tacitly complying with (i.e., not resisting or dissenting from) the words or actions of a parent. Marriage obviously did not require any material stuff. Theologians considered several aspects of marriage that might have had the role of matter, including the spouses themselves and actions such as consent or consummation, but such suggestions were less important than theologians' concession that marriage was not constituted from sacramental matter in the usual sense of the term.

Discussion of form and matter underscored the most salient differences between marriage and the other sacraments. Whereas sacraments were normally administered by a priest and received passively (*ex opere operato*) by the one whom the sacrament sanctified, marrying seemed to be an action of the participants themselves. Consequently, insofar as marriage sanctified the spouses, they received its blessings at least partly as a result of their own effort (*ex opere operantis*). Stephen Langton raises this issue when he inquires whether marriage has a sacramental form. True, marriage requires an expression of mutual consent, which is normally stated in words, but such words do not have the same function as a sacramental form. The function of the form in baptism, for example, is not to express the consent of the recipient but rather to *make* the sacrament by virtue of a power invested in the words themselves. Thus, non-verbal signs cannot be used instead of words in baptism, as they sometimes are in marriage.[123] Langton attends to the same difference when he discusses the form of baptism. The utterance of an instituted verbal formula is "more necessary" in baptism than it is in marriage, he argues, which can even be celebrated through letters or with non-verbal signs, as when two mutes marry. The reason is that marrying "is a work of man and consists in consent alone," whereas "baptism is a work of God."[124]

Alexander of Hales develops Langton's argument. Is there anything in marriage that can be construed as its matter? Alexander concedes that there is no matter in the usual sense, but he points out that the same is true of penance.[125] He considers but rejects the popular theory that the sacramental matter of matrimony consists of

---

[123] Stephen Langton, *Quaestiones theologiae*, Cambridge, St. John's College, MS 57 (C.7), 318vb; Oxford, Bodleian Library, MS Lyell 42, 2ra.

[124] *Quaestiones theologiae*, Cambridge, St. John's College, MS 57 (C.7), 308vb; Oxford, Bodleian Library, MS Lyell 42, 46vb.

[125] Alexander of Hales, *IV Sent.* 26.5a (450).

legitimate persons.[126] Rather than extend the notion of sacramental matter to marriage and penance by a somewhat strained analogy, Alexander prefers to explain why these two sacraments differ from the other five and do not require any material stuff. The others involve some exterior, "separate" matter because they were instituted after the fall. Because human beings were seduced by exterior sensible things, it was fitting (as Hugh had explained) that they should also be restored by exterior sensible things, for fallen human beings depend on sensible things for their understanding of interior and spiritual things. But marriage and penance originated before the fall, when human beings were still directly in touch with interior and spiritual things. Consequently, the structure of these sacraments is different insofar as they do not require any sensible matter, such as water, oil, bread, or wine. Instead, they are based on interior mental acts, although these must be outwardly expressed. Spoken words in marriage express inward consent, and words and actions in penance express inward contrition. Instead of receiving these sacraments passively and *ex opere operato*, as they receive the other sacraments, the recipients cooperate with God:

> Furthermore, in these two sacraments a human being cooperates with God, as it were. I am referring to the person who receives the effect of the sacrament, for God does not justify the person [in penance] unless the person does his part. Likewise, the sacrament of matrimony does not exist in someone unless he consents. It is not so with the other sacraments, where, on the contrary, the sacramental actions are done by persons other than those who partake in the sacraments.[127]

Alexander touches here on the role of the minister. Insofar as the spouses are the agents as well as the recipients of the sacrament of matrimony, they do not need to receive the sacrament from a priest who administers it. By pointing out the similarities between marriage and penance, Alexander mitigates the perception that marriage does not belong among the sacraments of the New Law.

Albertus Magnus poses objections pertaining to form, matter, minister, and efficacy when he inquires whether marriage is a sacrament of the New Law. One may object that every sacrament of the New Law has a form that has been "promulgated by divine institution" and is the source of its "sanctification" (i.e., its efficacy). But marriage has no such form. It is true that marriage is normally established by a verbal exchange of consent, but that is not a form in the typical sense, for the words of consent vary "according to the laws of those who contract" marriage, and they have not been fixed by divine institution.[128] Again, every sacrament of the New Law has as its matter "some visible stuff, such as water, oil, and things of that sort." Clearly, there is no such matter in marriage.[129] Finally, marriage does not confer sacramental grace.

---

[126] *IV Sent.* 26.5d (451). [127] *IV Sent.* 26.5f (452).
[128] Albertus Magnus, *IV Sent.* 26.14, qu. 1, arg. 1 (120b). [129] Ibid., qu. 1, arg. 2 (120b–121a).

Albert replies that the paradigmatic requirements apply strictly only to a sacrament that is "purely a sacrament," namely, to one that is received entirely as an *opus operatum*. Both marriage and penance are hybrid sacraments, for they are constituted partly from the *opus operans*: from what the participants do. Thus, they "draw their perfection in some way from us." Although the verbal exchange of consent may be construed as the form of marriage, therefore, it does not need to be a sacramental form in the proper sense because marriage does not draw its sanctification exclusively from the *verbum*. The "perfective form" of marriage is not the expression of consent but the "indivisibility of life" (*individuitas vitae*), which is the effect of the spouses' consent. Similarly, because the other sacraments derive their efficacy exclusively from aspects of Christ's incarnate life — especially from the Passion, but also from other aspects of Christ's human life, such as his baptism and resurrection — these sacraments must have matter in the sense presupposed in the objection: a material entity that is received passively by the subject. The matter of penance and marriage, on the contrary, is not received but rather provided by the subject. The matter of penance is something that the penitent does, namely, the act of sorrow (*dolor*). The matter of marriage is the spouses themselves under a particular disposition, namely, insofar as they are at least potentially united as one flesh through sexual intercourse.[130] Although Albert retains Alexander's observations about the special role of the recipient in marriage and penance, he emphasizes that marriage has acquired a new efficacy from the incarnation of Jesus Christ, through which it became a sacrament of the New Law and a remedy for sin *ex opere operato*, whereas the sacraments of the Old Law were effective solely *ex opere operantis*.[131]

Albert considers the objection that marriage cannot truly be one of the seven sacraments because it does not confer what it signifies, for it cannot cause the union between Christ and the church. Some say, Albert notes, that the principle applies only to sacraments that are purely sacraments, and not to sacraments that are both office and sacrament, such as marriage.[132] But Albert's own view is that marriage is supernaturally efficacious and does cause what it signifies, albeit precisely inasmuch as it is a sacrament of the New Law and not inasmuch as it only an office of nature. Marriage as a sacrament of the New Law fully meets the necessary conditions. Citing a dictum that he ascribes to Hugh of Saint-Victor, Albert says that any sacrament properly so called must "justify *ex opere operato*, signify from its institution, and confer an invisible grace from the sanctification of a word."[133] Elsewhere, Albert routinely assumes that marriage confers grace.[134] He raises doubts and objections regarding conjugal grace only when the thesis itself is the topic of

---

[130] Ibid., qu. 1, ad 1–2 (122a).   [131] Ibid., qu. 2, resp. (122b).

[132] *IV Sent.* 26.14, ad 2 (121b).

[133] *IV Sent.* 1.2, ad 11 (Borgnet 29:10a). Cf. Hugh, *De sacramentis* I.9.2 (PL 176:317D).

[134] For example, Albertus Magnus, *IV Sent.* 26.1, arg. 3 (Borgnet 30:98a); *De matrimonio* 1.2, resp. (156b/51–52).

discussion. To the objection that marriage does not cause the union between Christ
and the church, Albert replies that a sacrament of the New Law need not cause
everything that it was instituted to signify. Albert distinguishes, therefore, between
uncontained and contained signifieds. Marriage signifies but does not contain (i.e.,
does not have the power to confer) the union between Christ and the church,
whereas it both signifies and contains a special sacramental grace.[135] Thomas adopts
the same solution in his commentary on the *Sentences*.[136]

Why is marriage not made by the "work of the ministers of the church," as the
other sacraments are? The chief reason, Albert explains, is that marriage is an office
of nature as well as a sacrament. As an office, it must be the work of those who
contract it. Marriage requires an outward expression of consent because it is a
human compact, not because it is a sacrament, although that expression acquires
the additional role of a sacramental form inasmuch as marriage is a sacrament of the
New Law. The clergy do not strictly act as ministers of this sacrament, therefore,
since only the spouses can contract a marriage. Nevertheless, the laws that govern
this contract "depend on the ministers of the church."[137]

Thomas pursues similar objections regarding the matter and form of marriage,
adapting Albert's solutions to his own ends. To the objection that there is no
material element in marriage, Thomas replies that marriage, like penance, is
completed by the acts of the participants. Those acts, insofar as they are perceptible
to the senses, take the place of the matter. In marriage, therefore, the expression of
consent takes the place of sacramental matter.[138] Consideration of the *verbum*, or
form, calls for a more complicated analysis. Thomas seems unwilling to grant that
anyone can marry without words, or at least something that can be construed as
words or that has the same function: something to which one can attribute meaning.
He concedes that the spouses may marry without voicing their consent when needs
must: for example, when one of the spouses is mute, or when the spouses speak
different languages. In such cases, non-verbal gestures, or "nods" (*nutus*), must
suffice. A shy young bride may comply with her parents' wishes tacitly, merely by
complying. But the nods stand for words, and the shy bride expresses her consent by
complying with the words spoken by her parents.[139] Marriage can be considered
simply as an office of nature, just as penance can be considered simply as an act of
contrition, and then neither marriage nor penance requires any verbal formula
(*forma verborum*). But each can also be considered as a sacrament subject to "the
dispensation of the church's ministers," and then each does involve some words

[135] *IV Sent.* 26.14, resp. (121b); ibid., q. 2, ad 3 (122a–b); *De matrimonio* 1.6, resp. (159a).
[136] Thomas Aquinas, *IV Sent.* 26.2.1, ad 4 (Vivès 11:72a).
[137] Albertus Magnus, *De matrimonio* 1.2, ad 3 (156b): "Actus enim [huius sacramenti] officii est, et
   illud officium non est ministrorum ecclesiae, sed contrahentium in matrimonio; et ideo
   necesse est, quod quantum ad efficientia dependeat a contrahentibus. Nihilominus instituta,
   secundum quae fit contractus, dependent a ministris ecclesiae."
[138] Thomas Aquinas, *IV Sent.* 26.2.1, arg. 2; ad 2 (71b, 72a).
[139] *IV Sent.* 27.1.2, qu^a 2, ad 2–3 (83b–84a).

(*aliqua verba*), or at least signs that are equivalent to words. In penance, these are the priest's words of absolution. In marriage, they are the words by which the spouses express their consent, as well as the "blessings instituted by the church."[140]

Thomas concedes that marriage does not have a sacramental form in the usual sense. Typically, the form is a prescribed verbal formula spoken by a minister. (Baptism *in extremis* is a special case.) The nuptial blessing by a priest seems to be what best fits that description, but it is not essential to the sacrament, whereas a sacramental form is by definition an essential constituent. The indefinite verbal exchange of consent functions as the essential form of this sacrament, whereas the blessing is only an associated sacramental, just as the priest's blessing of baptismal water before the rite of baptism is a sacramental.[141] Such blessings are *de solemnitate* rather than *de necessitate*: they pertain to the solemnity surrounding the sacrament, and not to its essence.[142] There is no reason to fear that attributing grace to marriage risks Pelagianism, for God uses the spouses' consent as an instrumental cause of conjugal grace, just as God uses the act of ablution as an instrumental cause of grace in baptism. In both cases, the instrument acquires its transient power from divine institution.[143] The spouses' expressed consent causes their marriage, but it does not cause the grace of marriage. Conjugal grace flows primarily not through the sanctification of a marriage by a priest, Thomas argues, but through the spouses' mutual consent, and by virtue of the conformity of that consent with Christ's Passion which was itself a mystical betrothal. Just as the water of baptism is said to cleanse the soul when it touches the body because of its historical contact with the flesh of Christ (Plates 1 and 2), so marrying puts the couple in touch with the betrothal between Christ and the church, which took place on the Cross (cf. Plate 3).[144]

Because Thomas seemed to identify both the form and the matter of marriage with the spouses' expression of consent, Reformation and early-modern Catholic theologians sometimes differentiated between two aspects of the expression of consent, construing one as the form and the other as the matter, and ascribing this theory to Thomas. According to the usual view, each spouse's vow is matter insofar as he or she gives himself or herself to the other, and it is form insofar as he or she accepts the other's gift of self.[145] But this insight owes as much to Richard de Mediavilla (see later) as to Thomas, and to perceive it in Thomas one must combine points that Thomas made separately and only to obviate objections. To the objection that there is no form, Thomas replies that the expression of consent serves as the

---

[140] *IV Sent.* 1.1.3, ad 5 (Moos 4:26). [141] *IV Sent.* 26.2.1, arg. 1; ad 1 (Vivès 11:71b, 72a).
[142] *IV Sent.* 2.1.1, quª 2, ad 2 (Moos 4:78). [143] *IV Sent.* 2.1.1, quª 2, ad 1 (Moos 4:78).
[144] *IV Sent.* 26.2.3, ad 1 (Vivès 11:74a).
[145] G. H. Joyce, *Christian Marriage* (2nd edition, London, 1948), 185. Joyce points out that Soto, Bellarmine, Suarez, and Sanchez subscribed to this theory, which Joyce himself ascribes to Thomas.

form. To the objection that there is no matter, Thomas replies that marriage, like penance, has no matter besides the participants' sensible actions (*"non habet aliam materiam nisi ipsos actus sensui subjectos"*) – which presumably include the expressions of consent.[146] There is no indication that Thomas intended the reader to combine these two observations into a single theory, and one should interpret both in light of Albert's demonstration that marriage does not have and does not require form and matter in the usual sense.

Peter of Tarentaise suggests that a priestly invocation is strictly necessary only for sacraments that were "instituted simply" under the New Law, whereas marriage already existed before the New Law. It was only approved under the New Law. Peter also points out that God blessed marriage verbally in Genesis 1:28, implying that one may construe the original blessing as the sacramental form of marriage.[147] Every sacrament, by definition, Peter argues, involves some sensible thing that is presented externally to human perception, which confers *ex opere operato* a "remedy of spiritual sanctification from sin." Marriage fulfills these conditions. Therefore, it is a sacrament in the proper sense.[148]

Richard de Mediavilla proposed a new theory whereby the partners' respective expressions of consent were the matter and form composing the essence of marriage. Richard's theory was to prove seminal, although it was often misinterpreted or modified. One might object, Richard notes, that marriage is not a sacrament because no one can be both minister and recipient of the same sacrament. The priestly blessing cannot be the essential form, for it is only a sacramental. To solve this objection, Richard proposes that the first expression of consent is the matter of the sacrament, whereas the second, said in reply to the first, is the form. Typically, the man initiates the union by saying, "I take you as my wife," and his bride completes the union by replying, "And I take you as my husband," or words to that effect. Here, the man's dictum is the matter, and the woman's is the form, since the second statement determines the sense of the first. What decides whether an expression of consent functions as form or as matter is not the gender of the speaker, however, but the order in which the spouses speak. If perchance the woman speaks first, then her vow is the matter, and her husband's is the form.[149] Each spouse administers the sacrament to the other in a collaborative effort, without confusion. The first one who speaks administers the matter, whereas the second, by accepting what the first one says, administers the form, which gives the matter its determinate sense.[150]

Most medieval theologians conceded that no minister was necessary for the sacrament of marriage. Although some theories, such as Richard's, attributed to

---

[146] Thomas Aquinas, *IV Sent.* 26.2.1, ad 1, on form; ad 2, on matter (72a).
[147] Peter of Tarentaise, *IV Sent.* 26.3.1, ad 1 (4:286b–87a).
[148] *IV Sent.* 26.3.1, resp. (286b).
[149] Richard de Mediavilla, *IV Sent.* 26.4.2, ad 1 (408b–409a).   [150] Ibid., ad 4 (409a).

the spouses work that would be attributed to the ministers of the other sacraments, medieval theologians rarely designated the spouses as ministers, presumably because the spouses were not ministers of the church in the usual sense. They were not ordained and licensed by a bishop. The juridical control of the church over marriage was in some sense a substitute for sacramental ministry, as Albert suggested.[151] Thomas Aquinas even said that the clergy "dispensed" marriage, a verb conventionally used to denote sacramental ministry, although he conceded that the priestly blessing was not essential.[152] Thomas seems to have assumed that the church's exclusive juridical control over marriage was sufficient proof that marriage was a sacrament, but Durandus of Saint-Pourçain rejected that argument as a non sequitur, for the church was a civil and temporal as well as a spiritual power during the central Middle Ages. At best, Durandus counters, the argument would prove only that marriage is a sacrament in a broad sense, and not that it is properly one of the sacraments of the New Law. But even if marriage were a purely civil contract and not a sacrament in any sense, Durandus argues, it could still be wholly and justly subject to ecclesiastical jurisdiction, provided that contravention of the rules was spiritually harmful but not harmful to the republic (i.e., to the public good), being a matter of individual conscience.[153]

14.7 CLANDESTINE MARRIAGE

Clandestinity was in effect a lack of formal proof. Thus, it was about supervision, evidence, witnessing, and testimony. By the term "formal proof," I refer to a mode of proof prescribed and recognized by the relevant legislative and jurisdictional authority, which in the medieval context was ecclesiastical. In the absence of that procedure, the contract might still be proved afterwards through *ad hoc*, contingent evidence, but it was still clandestine. In short, a marriage was clandestine if and only if it was contracted without the legally prescribed means of establishing thereafter that the partners had freely expressed their mutual consent in the present tense.

Hugh of Saint-Victor provided the first extensive discussion of the problem (Section 10.6.1), illustrating it with the extreme case of a covert prior contract (Section 10.6.2). In this scenario, a man marries one woman clandestinely but then marries another publicly in a church ceremony, where a priest blesses the spouses. Only the first marriage is valid in the eyes of God, but unless sufficient evidence comes to light the church must uphold the second: not because it is holier or more sacramental, but because the church's judgments must be made in the public forum on the basis of evidence. Hugh reasons that the second marriage has some

---

[151] Albertus Magnus, *De matrimonio* 1.2, ad 3 (156b), quoted earlier.
[152] Thomas Aquinas, *IV Sent.* 1.1.3, ad 5 (Moos 4:26); *IV Sent.* 39.1.2, ad. 1 (Vivès 11:225b); *Summa contra Gentiles* IV.78 (Leonine 15:246a).
[153] Durandus, *IV Sent.* 26.3, §17 [ad 2c] (368rb).

obligational validity by virtue of the church's judgment, especially in regard to the wife's conjugal rights if the man deceived her. Nevertheless, although the first union cannot be dissolved, the second remains irregular. The scenario was not improbable and must have occurred in fact, but it became the standard example because it illustrated the problem of proof with an extreme case for which there could be no remedy.

Hugh assumed that the alternative to a clandestine marriage was a marriage solemnized in church and blessed by a priest. The function of such solemnizing in his analysis was to provide formal proof, but the adulterous husband may well have assumed that an ecclesiastically solemnized marriage would trump a merely domestic, secular marriage because it was holier and more sacramental. The notion that marriage was one of the sacraments of the church could only have encouraged that misunderstanding.

For thirteenth-century theologians and canonists, the cardinal text on the principles underlying clandestinity was the decretal *Quod nobis* by Alexander III, which was included in the *Liber extra*'s brief section on clandestine espousals:

> Regarding what you have suggested to us, that we should dispense from clandestine marriages: We do not see what dispensation should be applied to them. For if these marriages were contracted so secretly that no legitimate proof is available thereafter, those who contract them should not in any way be compelled by the church. But if the persons who contracted them desire to make them public, the church should accept and approve these marriages as if they had been contracted from the beginning in the sight of the church [*in conspectu ecclesiae*] unless some reasonable and lawful cause prevents this.[154]

Observing the principle that the church cannot judge hidden things (*ecclesia de occultis non iudicat*),[155] Alexander says in effect that the church can do nothing in the absence of any proof. The spouses can neither be compelled to remain married nor prevented from marrying again. Should they choose to make their marriage public, however, the church will regard the marriage as valid not only from that moment but from the moment of the original clandestine union, presuming that the spouses are being truthful. Any offspring begotten before the publication of the marriage, therefore, would automatically be legitimate. Alexander does not say how the spouses should publish their marriage, but both medieval and modern interpreters have generally assumed that he was referring to formal proof. For example, the already-married spouses might solemnize their union *in facie ecclesiae*. Other things

---

[154] X 4.3.2, *Quod nobis* (2:679). I take it that the exception ("unless some reasonable and lawful cause prevents this") refers to the presumption that the marriage exists, and not, as is sometimes supposed, to extenuating circumstances for marrying clandestinely.

[155] On the principle, see S. Kuttner, "Ecclesia de occultis non iudicat," in *Acta Congressus Iuridici Internationalis, Romae 1934* (Rome 1935), 3:225–46; L. Kéry, "Non enim homines de occultis, sed de manifestis iudicant," *Revue de droit canonique* 53.2 (2003): 311–36; and J. Chiffoleau, "Ecclesia de occultis non judicat?" *Micrologus* 14 (2006): 359–81.

being equal, clandestinely married spouses would be given the benefit of the doubt. Moreover, if the clandestine contract was contested in litigation, there might still be ways of proving it, even by the witness of eves-droppers.[156] But there was no presumption in favor of the marriage if it came into conflict with a later, incompatible obligation that was more capable of proof, such as another marriage or a religious vow.[157]

The possibility of marrying clandestinely arose from the principle that the spouses' consent alone (*solus consensus*) was the sufficient cause of a valid marriage. Everything else, no matter how desirable, was incidental. This was much more than a pragmatic selection or delimitation from a list of possible conditions. The sacramental doctrine presupposed that marriage was a union of wills or intentions (*unio animorum*): a union that was in turn perfected in sexual union (*unio corporum*). Each union was sacramental insofar as it signified a comparable aspect of Christ's union with the church. Only the spouses' own acts of intention could constitute their *unio animorum*, just as only sugar and water can constitute sugar water. But the practical reasons for upholding the *solus consensus* principle and its historical relationship to the doctrine of marriage as a sacrament remain obscure, for the principle was in tension with two preconceptions: the traditional assumption that parents arranged their children's marriages and gave them away in marriage, especially their daughters; and the new religious expectation that marriage, like every sacrament, normally required the ministry of priest and was properly conducted in an ecclesiastical setting. The *solus consensus* principle wrested marrying to some extent from the control of families, but it also hindered the church's efforts to take control.[158] Since solemnization of marriage in the west had traditionally been the preserve of the wealthy, landed classes (although there was no reason in principle why solemnization should not have been done cheaply), it is possible that the *solus consensus* doctrine enabled the church to catch as many persons as possible within the net of ecclesiastically recognized, fully sacramental, and indissoluble marriage. Without the principle of *solus consensus* in canon law, many more persons would have remained free to take and to abandon partners at will.

From the thirteenth century until the Council of Trent, the canon law on clandestinity was that of the Fourth Lateran Council (1215), whose canon on clandestine marriages was enshrined in the *Liber extra* alongside Alexander III's decretal *Quod nobis*.[159] The *Liber extra* ascribes it to "Innocent III in the general council." Couples should not marry clandestinely but only "in the sight of the

---

[156] The Armagh register records such a case. See A. Cosgrove, "Marrying and Marriage Litigation in Medieval Ireland," THTH 332–89, at 345 and 354–55.

[157] J. A. Brundage, *Law, Sex, and Christian Society* (Chicago, 1987), 363.

[158] C. Donahue, Jr., "The Policy of Alexander the Third's Consent Theory of Marriage," in *Monumenta Iuris Canonici*, series C: Subsidia, vol. 5 (Vatican City, 1976), *Proceedings of the Fourth International Congress of Canon Law*, 251–81.

[159] Lateran IV, canon 51 (Tanner-Alberigo, 258). X 4.3.3 (CIC 2:679–80).

church" (*in conspectu ecclesiae*). To that end, the partners' parish priest (*parochialis sacerdos*) – or both their priests, if they belonged to different parishes – must follow the practice of certain regions (i.e., the banns of Anglo-Norman custom) by announcing the forthcoming union and setting an appropriate date (*competens terminus*) before which parishioners should bring to his attention any lawful impediment (*legitimum impedimentum*). Meanwhile, the priest himself should investigate. If an impediment came to light, the priest had to report it to his bishop, and the bishop or his vicar or official would determine what remedy to apply and declare it in writing. These norms were introduced as a remedy to the problem of clandestinity, but they were also in effect criteria for clandestinity. In future, a marriage was clandestine in canon law if and only if it was not contracted according to the regional version of that procedure, in which the parish priest had the central role.

Because of the twofold resistance described earlier, clandestinity was closely associated and sometimes conflated both with the absence of parental consent and with the absence of ecclesiastical solemnity. We have seen how Peter Lombard linked the three topics together and distinguished what constituted the substance of the marriage from its attendant solemnities (Section 11.4.11). Thirteenth-century theologians followed Peter Lombard closely in their treatment of clandestinity. It suffices here to mention the similar treatments of the topic by Bonaventure and Thomas Aquinas, both of whom follow the Lombard closely. Thomas's treatment remained definitive until the Council of Trent, which overturned it in the decree *Tametsi* of 1563.

Bonaventure asks whether *de praesenti* consent expressed in secret (*in occulto*) makes marriage. Only two things are essential and necessary for a valid marriage, he argues: the legitimacy of the persons marrying (*legitimitas in personis*), and their being united through consent (*unitas in consensu*).[160] In the constitution of the sacrament, legitimate persons have the role of matter, and their expressed consent has the role of form. The parents' disposing of their sons and daughters in marriage (*traditio parentum*) and the priest's blessing, on the contrary, are solemnities. As such, they contribute to the seemliness (*decor*) of the marriage but are not integral to its essence. A clandestine union is sinful and akin to fornication, as Pope Evaristus said, but it is valid *de facto*.[161] By prohibiting the marriage within certain degrees of affinity or consanguinity, the church introduces *necessary* conditions for marriage. By prohibiting clandestine marriages, on the contrary, the church introduces a merely *exigent* condition.[162]

Bonaventure seems to assume that the absence of the two chief solemnities – the blessing by a priest and the parents' gift of their children – is what makes a marriage clandestine. Although these are not necessary conditions for a valid marriage, they

[160] Bonaventure, *IV Sent.* 28.5, resp. (4:694b).   [161] Ibid., arg. 1c; arg. 1 (694a).
[162] Ibid., ad 2m (694b)

are necessary in the sense that they are prescribed by the church. To marry clandestinely not only contravenes a precept of the church but also incurs grave dangers. To illustrate these dangers, Bonaventure cites the standard example: covert prior contract, where someone who has married clandestinely marries again publicly. In such cases, the church "judges justly" (*iuste iudicat*), but its justice is superficial because the truth is hidden. The second marriage is invalid and adulterous *de facto* but it remains valid *de iure* insofar as the church upholds it. The church has no power to make it valid *de facto* or in the eyes of God.[163]

Thomas's treatment of the same question is similar to Bonaventure's, but he sheds a little more light on the issues involved. Thomas considers parental consent and the priestly blessing in the initial arguments and replies. In the body of the article, he notes that in the performance of every sacrament some things are essential (*de essentia sacramenti*) whereas others pertain to the solemnity of the sacrament (*ad solemnitatem sacramenti*). If the participants omit the former, there is no sacrament. If they omit the latter, the sacrament exists but the participants commit a sin. Now, only two things are essential to this sacrament: consent expressed in words of the present tense, and persons who are qualified to marry legitimately. The verbal consent and the legitimate persons are related as form and matter respectively.[164] If these conditions are not met, therefore, there is no sacrament. If the other formalities are omitted, on the contrary, there is still a sacrament. Clandestine marriages are valid, although they are sinful unless the spouses have a legitimate reason for marrying secretly.[165] They are sinful partly because they are open to fraud and to the error of covert prior contract, and partly because they result from a "species of turpitude."[166] This argument involves *petitio principii* of a sort that is common in scholastic writing. Thomas clarifies the situation, but he assumes, rather than proves, that only the legitimate persons and their verbal consent are essential conditions.

Thomas considers whether a daughter has the power to dispose of herself in marriage. By marrying, the spouses give themselves to each other, handing themselves over into each other's bodily power. But one might object that according to classical law and Old Testament precedents a daughter is not *sui iuris* but rather is in the power of her father. She cannot validly marry, therefore, unless her father consents, whereas there is no paternal consent in the typical clandestine marriage. But Thomas points out that she is her father's daughter, not his slave (*ancilla*).

---

[163] Ibid., resp.; ad 3m.

[164] Thomas says only that they are *de essentia sacramenti* in the response, but he calls them "*debita forma et debita materia*" in the *sed contra* (99a). An argument *sed contra* does not necessarily express the author's own position. Whether or not he regarded them as the correlative components of a hylomorphically conceived essence, he would certainly have considered them to have been related as form and matter in *some* sense.

[165] Thomas Aquinas, *IV Sent.* 28.1.3 (Vivès 11:99).   [166] Ibid., ad 4 (99–100).

A father does not own his daughter, as if he had bodily power over her. Rather, she is free, and her father is entrusted with her upbringing. Just as a daughter is entitled to enter the religious life without her father's consent, so she is entitled to marry without it.[167] In fact, the right of the unfree to marry without their lords' consent or cognizance was well established and had been stated definitively in Pope Hadrian IV's decretal *Dignum est* of 1155 (Section 11.6.1).

Thomas compares and contrasts marriage with the sacrament of penance. In penance, the action of the penitent is essential but the sacrament needs to be "perfected" by a minister of the church, acting in his role as sacramental *dispensator*. If marriage were composed in an analogous manner, the priestly blessing would be essential. But there is a key difference, Thomas argues. The penitent's act of contrition is not sufficient to produce the "proximate effect" of the sacrament, which is absolution from sin. (Since absolution is a species of grace, it must be received passively, *ex opere operato*.) The priest's sacramental ministry, therefore, is necessary for achievement of the proximate effect. But the proximate effect of marrying is the mutual obligation that binds the spouses together, and the spouses are naturally entitled *sui iuris* to obligate themselves to each other.[168] Thomas touches tacitly here on the distinction between contract and sacrament. He reasons, characteristically but unlike many other theologians, that sacramental marriage is constituted first by the natural bond that the partners themselves establish contractually, and only then, secondarily, by what God does with that bond, elevating it and using it as a disposition for grace.

It follows that the church's prohibition of clandestine marriage does not render such marriages invalid, Thomas argues.[169] In the absence of prescribed conditions that are *de solemnitate sacramenti*, there is still a true marriage. In the absence of prescribed conditions that are *de essentia sacramenti*, on the contrary, there is no marriage. Thomas elaborates this point when he introduces the impediments. Impediments entailing the absence of something *de solemnitate*, Thomas explains, "are said to impede the contracting of marriage, but they do not bring to nothing what is contracted." Impediments entailing the absence of something *de essentia*, on the contrary, "are said not only to impede the contracting of marriage but also to bring to nothing what is contracted." Impediments of the former sort include the forbidden seasons for marrying, such as advent. Impediments of the latter sort include those of consanguinity within the prohibited degrees and error of person.[170]

[167] Ibid., arg. 1; ad 1m (99)   [168] Ibid., arg. 2; ad 2m.   [169] Ibid., ad 3m–4m (99–100).
[170] *IV Sent.* 34.1.1, resp. (163b): "impedimenta quae contrariantur his quae sunt de solemnitate sacramenti ... dicuntur impedire contrahendum, sed non dirimunt contractum.... Impedimenta autem quae contrariantur his quae sunt de essentia matrimonii ... dicuntur non solum impedire matrimonium contrahendum, sed dirimere contractum." I assume that *contractum* here is the past participle, and not the fourth-declension noun. The verb *dirimere* is often translated as "to dissolve" in this context, but in Thomas's view there is no marriage to be dissolved. Rather, it is prevented from existing.

Thomas introduces another distinction regarding the impediments. Marriage may be impeded in respect either of the contract or of the contractants: the persons who are marrying.[171] Anything that undermines consent, such as coercion or error as to person, impedes the contract, whereas anything that undermines the persons, such as consanguinity or holy orders, impedes the contractants. Thomas cites both prohibitive and diriment examples of impediments pertaining to the contract. Clandestinity is a prohibitive (rather than diriment) impediment that impedes the contract (rather than the contractants). Trent will reject these theses.

14.8 VOICES OF DISSENT: OLIVI AND DURANDUS

Two notable theologians resisted the inclusion of marriage among the sacraments of the New Law: Peter John Olivi, O.F.M. (d. 1298), and Durandus of Saint-Pourçain, O.P. (d. 1334). Both conceded that marriage was a sacrament in a broad sense but denied that it had "full univocity" with the other sacraments of the New Law. They marshaled versions of the standard objections to that end, but they also developed new, more searching arguments. What is most remarkable about these two cases of contrarianism is the strength of the counterattack. The proposal that marriage was not a sacrament of the New Law in the full or proper sense had been commonplace and uncontroversial until the second quarter of the thirteenth century, but now, a century later, it could seem potentially heretical.

14.8.1 *Univocity, equivocity, and semantic zones*

To appreciate why these dissenters questioned the univocity of marriage among the sacrament of the New Law, one needs to appreciate some semantic and logical background. Two ways of identifying the church's sacraments had been in play in sacramental theology since the mid-twelfth-century: as sacraments of the New Law, and as sacraments properly so called. Thus, Hugh of Saint-Victor developed two conceptual frameworks for understanding the sacraments: a historical account, emphasizing the interrelationships between the sacraments of the Old Law and those of the New Law; and an analytical definition, emphasizing causality as well as signification. Hugh presumably considered that the causal definition was true, *mutatis mutandis*, of every sacrament worthy of the name, at any stage of salvation history. Whatever did not in some way meet the definition was not a sacrament at all.[172] In contrast, Peter Lombard used a condensed version of Hugh's causal account to distinguish the sacraments of the New Law from those of the Old. This theory implied that the word "sacrament" could be validly used either broadly or

---

[171] Ibid., "Potest autem matrimonium impediri aut ex parte contractus matrimonii, aut ex parte contrahentium."

[172] Hugh of Saint-Victor, *De sacramentis* I.9.2, PL 176:317D.

narrowly. The sacraments of the Old Law were sacraments only in the broad sense of the term, according to Peter Lombard. But these two distinctions were not fully convergent in his work, for Peter included marriage among the sacraments of the New Law while maintaining that it lacked the chief distinguishing feature of those sacraments: the power to confer grace. Most theologians after Alexander of Hales assumed that the two classes were identical and coextensive: that every sacrament of the New Law was a sacrament in the proper sense by virtue of its own essence, and vice versa.

Theologians recognized, therefore, that the term "sacrament" was equivocal inasmuch as it was customarily used in a range of senses capturing concentric semantic fields. Every sacrament in the proper sense was a sacrament in the broad sense, whereas the converse was not true. Alexander of Hales posits three such fields, explaining that the term "sacrament" may be said broadly (*large*), strictly (*stricte*), or most strictly (*stictissime*). Broadly understood (*large*), the term embraces all sacred mysteries (*sacra secreta*), including the death and resurrection of Jesus Christ. Strictly understood (*stricte*), the term denotes only sacred mysteries that are also signs, including the rites and offerings of the Old Law (the *sacramenta legalia*). These were imperfect inasmuch as they were "signs of things to come." They pointed to the sacraments of the New Law, which would supersede them. Although each of the old sacraments was an "appearance of an invisible grace," it signified that grace only indirectly, by predicting something that would become a cause of grace after Christ. Most strictly understood (*strictissime*), the term "sacrament" denotes only the seven sacraments of the New Law, which alone "effect what they signify" (*"efficiunt quod figurant"*) and are causes as well as signs of grace. Alexander argues on logical and semantic grounds that causality or sanctification, and not signification, is the chief aspect of a sacrament in the strictest sense, just as rationality, and not animality, is the chief attribute of the human being. Thus, a sacrament of the New Law is principally something that *causes* the grace that it signifies and only secondarily a *sign* of that grace, for its being a sacred sign is its genus, whereas its being a cause of sanctity is its specific difference.[173] Alexander tacitly assumes that the sense that is semantically most properly denoted by the term corresponds to the fullest and richest reality, so that a sacrament in the broad sense must be imperfect both semantically and ontologically.

William of Auvergne asks whether a marriage can be a sacrament in the proper sense of the term when there is no nuptial blessing. Because a sacrament in the proper sense is a cause of grace, William reasons, the question amounts to asking whether an unblessed marriage has "sacramental virtue." In other words, can a marriage entered into without the priestly blessing sanctify the spouses? William

---

[173] Alexander of Hales, *IV Sent.* 1.1 (9) and 1.5 (11). Cf. Albertus Magnus, *IV Sent.* 30.9, ad 4 (222b): An unconsummated marriage is imperfect in signification but perfect as a sacrament of the New Law, since its being a sacred sign pertains to its genus, and not to its species.

posits three sources of conjugal sanctity: contrariety (the exclusion of dishonest or sinful things), merit, and sacramental power. Marriage has contrariety by its very nature, for if properly carried out it excludes such sexual vices as prostitution and sodomy. And marriage can be meritorious even without a nuptial blessing if the spouses are not contemptuous of the church's ministry but rather have a good reason for not receiving the blessing, for example, if they live in a region where there are no priests. Such benefits are sufficient for marriage to be not only a sacred sign (*sacrum signum*) but also a saving sign (*signum sacrans, signum sanctificans*). But without the nuptial blessing, even when one was not available, William argues, marriage is not a sacrament in the most proper, narrowest sense, for it has no intrinsic supernatural power to sanctify. Thus, since it "does not have sacramental power at all . . . it is not a sacrament in the proper sense of the word."[174]

To clarify this semantic claim, William compares the differentiation within the structure of a Christian marriage to the difference between a marriage of unbelievers and a Christian marriage. The term "sacrament" may be said either univocally (in the same sense) or equivocally (in different senses) of the two sorts of marriage:

> Hence, marriage among unbelievers and among believers is said both univocally and equivocally. For among unbelievers [marriage] is not other than we have said, namely, it is a sign that sanctifies but only in the aforesaid manner. But among believers [marriage is a sacrament] both in that way and, over and above that, as something that sanctifies by the grace and power of the benediction, which [power to sanctify] is proper to those things that are true sacraments with full power.[175]

A non-Christian marriage can have the benefits of contrariety and even those of merit, and it can perhaps be said to be a sacred sign and to sanctify the spouses. To that extent, the term "sacrament" can be said univocally of both Christian and non-Christian marriages. But only a Christian marriage is a sacrament in the strictest sense of the term, and in that sense a non-Christian marriage is *not* a sacrament. Marriage is raised to the level of a sacrament in the proper sense of the term, according to William, only insofar as it confers grace, which it can do only when it receives a nuptial blessing from a priest.

Albert, too, assumes that the term "sacrament" is said of marriage both in a broad and in a narrow sense. The narrow and broad senses are respectively primary and secondary. In other words, the broad use of the term is derivative in relation to the proper use. If Peter Lombard, Praepositinus, and William of Auxerre are right when

---

[174] William of Auvergne, *De sacramento coniugii*, ed. Hotot, C. 9, 525aC.

[175] MS Paris BnF lat. 14842, 195rb: "Unde matrimonium apud infideles et apud fideles *et univoce* dicitur *et* equivoce. Apud infideles enim non est nisi sicut diximus, *scilicet, sacrans signum, sed eo modo tantum quo diximus*. Apud fideles autem et illo modo, et insuper sacrans benedictionis *gratia et* virtute, quod est proprium verorum et plenae virtutis sacramentorum." Ignoring minor variations and differences of word order, I have italicized earlier the parts of the text in the MS that do no appear in the printed version (C. 9, 525aC–D), which is less precise as well as half the length.

they claim that marriage does not confer grace, Albert argues, then marriage is a sacrament only in a secondary, derivative sense of the term (*per prius et posterius*), for the sacraments in the primary sense not only signify grace but also cause it.[176] Albert borrows the term *per prius et posterius* from the logic of analogy, positing an order among terms that is logical and not only etymological, and which maps the structure and order of reality.[177]

14.8.2 *Peter John Olivi*

Peter Olivi's unusual perspective on marriage led him to make some controversial and purportedly heterodox statements on the subject, which became a feature of the prolonged debate over his orthodoxy: only one of many such features, to be sure, and perhaps a minor feature in relation to "the persecution of Peter Olivi," but a major matter, nonetheless, from the perspective of the history of marriage as a sacrament.[178]

Olivi preferred to regard marriage not as a transient sacramental event but as an estate (*status*) in the church. Considered thus, marriage was more akin to the celibate vocations of virginity and the religious life than it was to baptism and eucharist. These estates shared an underlying nature pertaining to the constraint of sexuality, although they varied in their degree of dignity and merit. None of that was controversial in itself, but Olivi recognized that the inclusion of marriage among the estates did not square easily with its inclusion among the seven sacraments. If marriage was a sacrament, Olivi reasoned, then so were the other estates of the church, especially consecrated virginity and the regular life. Contrariwise, if those other estates were not sacraments, then neither was marriage. Olivi seems to have been concerned lest the inclusion of marriage among the sacraments would be detrimental to the vocations of religious, which he valued much more highly.[179]

Olivi questioned, therefore, whether marriage was in the fullest sense one of the "sacraments of grace." He marshaled numerous arguments to that end, including some that theologians had been posing as dialectical objections to the sacramentality of marriage, such as those regarding the matter, form, and minister of the sacrament. Olivi did not mean to deny that marriage was a sacrament in *some* sense, nor even that it belonged among the sacraments of the New Law in a functional manner. Instead, assuming that the term "sacrament" was equivocal, he argued that marriage did not have "full univocity" (*plena univocatio*) with the other six sacraments.

---

[176] Albertus Magnus, *IV Sent.* 26.14, q. 2, resp. (122b).
[177] On analogical predication and predication *per/secundum prius et posterius*, see P. L. Reynolds, "Analogy of Names in Bonaventure," *Mediaeval Studies* 65 (2003): 117–62, at 125–27 and passim.
[178] The epithet is from D. Burr's title, *The Persecution of Peter Olivi* (Philadelphia, 1976). See also D. Burr, "Olivi on Marriage," *Journal of Medieval and Renaissance Studies* 2 (1972): 183–204.
[179] See Burr, "Olivi on Marriage," 193.

In a treatise on the sacraments, which probably belonged to his *Summa* on the *Sentences*, Olivi inquires whether marriage confers a special grace "by the power of the sacrament" (*ex vi sacramenti*), as well as a general grace by virtue of the spouses' charity.[180] The phrase *ex vi sacramenti*, which had been prominent in discussions of the sacraments early in the thirteenth century, is synonymous here with *ex opere operato*. Olivi reviews two opinions. Since neither was current at the time as far as we know, these were probably opinions that Olivi himself shared with his students.[181]

According to one opinion, marriage does not confer grace *ex vi sacramenti* because it does not truly belong to the genus of sacraments of grace. Olivi cites four standard objections that tend to support this theory. First, one who consents to marry in exchange for temporal goods does not commit simony. Second, marriage already existed under the Old Law and even in Paradise, and it was only approved, and not instituted, under the New Law. Third, there is no minister. The spouses cannot be ministers, for people cannot administer sacraments of grace to themselves. Fourth, marriage, as compared to celibacy, entails a decline from spiritual perfection, whereas the sacraments of grace entail an advancement in perfection. Olivi considers this first position to be "not improbable."

According to the other opinion, marriage may be considered both as a carnal and as a spiritual institution. As a spiritual institution, it confers special grace *ex vi sacramenti* in two ways: in itself, and by virtue of the added benediction of a minister. Marriage in itself (*per se*) confers the grace of Christ by virtue of three things: Christ's approval, the authority of the church, and the faith in Christ with which the spouses receive the sacrament. But the same could be said, Olivi argues, of the celibate estates. Just as God confers special graces with baptism and confirmation to enable the recipients to carry out the precepts that those sacraments entail, so God confers special graces with the estates of the church to enable those who have taken conjugal or regular vows to carry out the precepts that these estates entail. Olivi finds this second opinion to be attractive because as well as distinguishing between the mundane and spiritual dimensions of marriage, it situates the spiritual dimension of marriage in two settings: that of the seven sacraments, and that of the estates of the church. Whereas marriage belongs among the seven sacraments chiefly by virtue of the priestly blessing, marriage belongs in its own right among the estates. The sacraments and the estates are both means of grace, and in much the same way and for the same reasons. Nevertheless, Olivi cannot commit himself to the second theory because he can see no way to prove that the grace given through marriage itself, rather than through a minister's blessing, is a special grace given *ex vi sacramenti* rather than a general grace given *ex opere operantis*, as with

---

[180] Peter Olivi, *Tractatus de sacramentis*, MS Vat. lat. 4986, 135v. See Burr's exposition, "Olivi on Marriage," 191–93.

[181] I have reversed the order of these arguments in my exposition, treating the second first.

any action performed with a good will. He has no alternative, therefore, but to accept the first theory.

Similar objections to the sacramentality of marriage arise when Olivi asks in the sixth of his *Quaestiones de perfectione evangelica* whether virginity is superior to marriage.[182] Throughout this disputed question, Olivi identifies the sacrament of marriage not with a transient, initiating event but with the enduring union or estate that results. Marriage, according to one objection, is the "inseparable tie caused by mutual consent." In the reply, Olivi argues that marriage is not a sacrament in the proper sense because a sacrament is a certain application of matter through which something else is caused, whereas marriage is rather that which is caused (the *causatum*). Whereas a sacrament is a transient event, marriage is an enduring condition or bond resulting from a transient event.[183] Nevertheless, the position that Olivi defends in the body of this question is traditional and unexceptionable. He posits chastity as the common virtue that underlies both virginity and marriage, which are estates that realize chastity in different modalities and degrees. In essence, chastity is the virtue that regulates the acts of the generative potency and tempers the concupiscible passions associated with it, so that these acts and passions are obedient to the law of God. As a supernatural virtue, chastity directs rational persons in this way toward their ultimate beatitude, whether through marriage or through virginity.[184] This non-controversial thesis stemmed originally from patristic interpretations of the thirtyfold, sixtyfold, and hundredfold yields in the parable of the sower (Matt 18:23, Mark 4:20). According to Jerome and Augustine, the yields respectively signify the rewards of Christian marriage, of consecrated widowhood, and of virginity, which Olivi calls the marital, vidual, and virginal estates.[185] Simon of Tournai and Alexander of Hales had developed the idea, the latter at considerable length, positing continence as the common virtue.[186] In the same vein, Thomas Aquinas argued that conjugal, vidual, and virginal continence, whose acts merited the thirtyfold, sixtyfold, and hundredfold yields respectively, were three degrees of the same virtue.[187]

Olivi argues that virginity in the present day, as long as it is practiced with the right motives, is "simply and of itself" better than marriage because it involves a higher degree of chastity. Nothing drags the soul down from contemplative heights to material baseness as effectively as sexual pleasure, for it is rooted in touch, the most

---

[182] Edited in A. Emmen, "Verginità e matrimonio nella valutazione dell'Olivi," *Studi Francescani* 64 (1967): 11–57, at 21–57 (from MS Vat. lat. 4986).

[183] Ibid., ad 24, e (52–53).   [184] Resp., §§1–4 (ed. Emmen, 28–31).

[185] Jerome, *Adv. Iovinianum* I.3, PL 23:212B–214B. See also Jerome, *Commentariorum in Evangelium Matthaei ad Eusebium libri quatuor*, Book II, Matt 13:23 (PL 26:89A), where he briefly refers to the former passage. Augustine, *De sancta virginitate* 45(46), CSEL 41:290–91.

[186] Simon of Tournai, *Disp.* 80, q. 1; q. 5 (ed. Warichez, 231–32; 233). Alexander of Hales, *Quaestio disputata* 57, disp. 3, mm. 2–3, §§65–79 (1121–27). See also Alexander, *Quaestio disputata* 58, *De triplici fructu* (1128–58).

[187] Thomas Aquinas, *Summa theologiae* I-II.70.3, ad 2^m (1086).

material of senses. Sexual pleasure draws to itself all the energies of the sensitive and vegetative powers and even of the body itself, totally monopolizing a person's attention.[188] Yet it was not always so. Here, Olivi incorporates Augustine's account of fallen concupiscence (Section 3.2). Before the fall, marriage was absolutely (*simpliciter*) superior to virginity, for human beings were required to complete the number of the elect. Marriage then would not have entailed the distracting cares about which Paul warned (1 Cor 7:33), and sexual intercourse would have been rational and innocuous. Every act of intercourse would have been fruitful, and no one would have pursued coitus for the sake of pleasure.[189] Sexual pleasure in Paradise would have been extremely intense (*intensissima*), but it would have remained subordinate to the rational will.[190] Even in the fallen condition, sexual pleasure is not deleterious precisely inasmuch as it is pleasure, nor even by virtue of its quantity or intensity, but rather because it draws all the sensitive powers to itself and causes motions that are not obedient to reason.[191] After the fall, virginity became "absolutely and of itself" superior to marriage because of the baseness of carnal pleasure and the distracting cares (*sollicitudo*) that marriage entails. Because God's chosen ones were still required to raise children to worship him, however, God gave them a "singular perfection of the mind" that enabled them to bear the burdens of marriage "without detriment to their own perfection."[192]

Thus far, Olivi's approach to the relative merits of virginity and marriage was unexceptionable, albeit perhaps a little severe and old-fashioned. What got him into trouble was his extended reply to the twenty-fourth objection to the superiority of virginity. The objection is as follows:

> Again, a sacramental estate is worthier and holier than a non-sacramental estate. But marriage is a sacrament of the church, whereas the virginal or vidual estate is not. Therefore, the former estate is more divine and consequently better.[193]

Olivi's reply is twofold. First, he briefly refutes the objection, distinguishing between symbolic and intrinsic value. Typically, what a sacrament signifies is more divine than the sacrament itself. Thus, although the inseparability of marriage perfectly signifies the inseparable union of the soul with God, the latter union is better than marriage in reality. Now, the virginal estate comes qualitatively much closer to the union of the soul with God in reality than the married estate does. The vow of virginity initiates a mode of perfection in this life, and virginity is a beginning of the beatific union between God and the soul.[194] Thus, the virginal estate realizes qualitatively, to the extent possible in this life, what the conjugal estate only signifies

---

[188] Peter Olivi, *De perfectione evangelica*, Q. 6, §5 (ed. Emmen, 32).
[189] Ibid., §6 (33), §3 (29).   [190] Ibid, ad 18 (45).
[191] Ibid. (43).   [192] Ibid., §6 (32, 33).   [193] Ibid., arg. 24 (26).
[194] Ibid., ad 24, a (51).

analogically. It follows, Olivi argues, that the virginal estate is better and "more divine" than the conjugal estate.[195]

Second, Olivi proposes a battery of arguments showing that although marriage may be called a sacrament, it is not so called "univocally with the other sacraments of grace, through which some grace or sanctification or something holy or divine is conferred."[196] His intention is apparently not to reject entirely but rather to limit or to qualify the claim that marriage is one of the "sacraments of grace," and in that way to blunt the force of the objection, which purports to show that marriage is superior to virginity. Marriage may be one of the sacraments of grace in some sense, therefore, but not univocally. Every sacrament confers or causes what it chiefly signifies, Olivi argues, but marriage seems to signify only a range of unions that it cannot cause, such as that between the soul and God, or between the church and Christ, or between Christ's human and divine natures. Even if marriage does confer grace in some sense, there seems to be nothing in marriage that *signifies* that grace or its conferral. Again, the grace-conferring sacraments are repeatable unless prevented by a character impressed on the soul, and with good reason. If marriage were truly one of the sacraments of grace, it too should be repeatable, for the spouses would be likely to lose the grace that was initially conferred in the sacrament. The same couple would repeatedly marry, receiving the sacrament as regularly as they would eucharist or penance to replenish their supply of conjugal grace and to rectify their lapses. Again, a sacrament is composed partly of the application of a certain matter, which represents the grace or spiritual gift conferred through the sacrament. But the only matter in marriage is the spouses, who cannot represent grace or anything else conferred through the sacrament. Again, a verbal formula is an essential component of a sacrament, but the only words necessary for marriage are spoken by the spouses when they plight their troth, and those words are not the form but the efficient cause of marriage.[197] Again, the essential aspects of all the sacraments are "administered through the ministers of the church," but nothing essential to marriage is bestowed by the church's ministers. They may bestow the nuptial benediction, but that is only an accidental benefit, pertaining not to the substance but to the well-being (*bene esse*) of marriage.[198] Several of Olivi's arguments against the sacramentality of marriage in this reply presuppose that a sacrament is a hieratic, ritual event: one that is a means of grace *ex opere operato* because it involves a minister's verbal invocation and his "application" of some consecrated matter, such as water, oil, bread, or wine, to the recipient.

---

[195] Ibid.

[196] Ibid., ad 24, b (51–52): "Praeterea, quod matrimonium dicatur esse sacramentum, non videtur dici univoce cum aliis sacramentis gratiae, per quae gratia seu sanctificatio aliqua vel aliquid sanctum et divinum confertur."

[197] Ibid., ad 24, c–d (52).   [198] Ibid., ad 24, g (54).

Wandering into more dangerous territory, Olivi critically examines the biblical basis of the sacramental doctrine. There is nothing in Scripture, Olivi argues, that can rightly be construed as a record of the institution of marriage as a sacrament. St Paul's "great sacrament" (Eph 5:32) is not marriage but the union between Christ and the church. That is why Augustine says that what is great in Christ and the church is little between men and women,[199] for literal marriage is great not it itself but in what it signifies. Or perhaps the great sacrament of the verse is the marriage of Adam and Eve, which already existed not only before the law of Christ but even before the Old Law. Either way, one cannot justly use this text as proof that marriage is one of the sacraments of grace.[200] Perhaps marriage is a sacrament but only in the same sense as the bronze serpent, the Tabernacle, the ark of Moses, and other things of that sort were sacraments, "which, however, I do not assert at present."[201] These arguments seem to show that marriage is a sacrament only in the broadest sense. Marriage is a sign of a sacred reality, but the same might be said of countless things in Scripture, especially in the Old Testament. But Olivi is careful to note that he does not assert this thesis: at least, not on this occasion. Instead, he poses it only for the sake of argument: a point on which he will insist in the ensuing inquiry.

One might argue that marriage must be a sacrament because it is wholly subject to ecclesiastical jurisdiction and ordering. Olivi does not try to refute the premise of the argument, as Durandus will do, but he observes that the argument would also prove that the religious estates and the consecration of virgins are sacraments, since those too are wholly subject to ecclesiastical jurisdiction and ordering. Olivi adds that he intends only to obviate the argument that the matrimonial estate is holier or more divine than the virginal estate, which is the point of dispute. He does not mean to denigrate marriage.[202]

Olivi's reply to the twenty-fourth objection concludes with the following uncompromising observation:

> Also, suppose that marriage is a sacrament of grace in the same way as the other [sacraments] are: Then one must certainly hold that a fuller grace is given to those who receive the virginal estate, if they are properly prepared, and much more so to those who receive the religious estate. Furthermore, if the former [the married estate] is a sacrament, then the latter [the virginal and religious estates] seem all the more to be sacraments and to be more divine. That is why the solemn veiling of a virgin or a nun is reserved for bishops alone, who are more divine, whereas the

[199] Augustine, *De nupt. et conc.* 21(23) (CSEL 42:236/22–24): "quod ergo est in Christo et in ecclesia magnum, hoc in singulis quibusque uiris atque uxoribus minimum, sed tamen coniunctionis inseparabilis sacramentum."
[200] Peter Olivi, ad 24, f (53).
[201] Ibid., ad 24, g (54): "Non ergo videtur habere aliam rationem sacramenti quam serpens aeneus vel tabernaculum seu archa Moysi, et consimilia; quod tamen ad praesens non assero."
[202] Ibid., ad 24, h (54).

blessing of persons who are marrying is conceded to priests, who are less divine and less perfect.[203]

Here, too, Olivi's claim is hypothetical, but he evidently wants to maintain that the conjugal and celibate estates must be regarded as inferior and superior species *of the same genus*. Both marriage and the celibate vocations must be sacraments *in the same sense*, according to Olivi, whatever that sense may turn out on further inquiry to be.

Olivi's arguments about marriage came under scrutiny and censure in 1283, when the Minister General of the order commissioned a team of Franciscan theologians to examine his work. They found several errors and doubtful points.[204] The *rotulus* (list of purported errors for examination) is lost, but the commission published its findings in a document known as the *Littera septem sigillorum* ("Letter of the Seven Seals"), which states twenty-two sound positions opposing Olivi's errors. Among them is the avowal "that marriage is a sacrament of the New Law and confers grace. To affirm the contrary is erroneous, to sustain the contrary is heretical, to doubt it is entirely forbidden."[205] Denial that marriage was a sacrament in the proper sense was the only error that the commission treated as potentially heretical.

Responding to the commission's criticisms in Avignon, Olivi confesses that marriage is a sacrament of the New Law. If he has ever denied that doctrine, he now revokes his denial. In fact, however, he has never denied it, Olivi claims. Rather, he only demonstrated for the sake of argument and without assertion (*recitatorie et absque assertione*) that grace is not conferred through marriage and that this sacrament is not entirely univocal with the others. Moreover, the matter has already been settled, Olivi says, for he satisfied Dom Jerome on the subject, and he has not spoken about the matter since that time as far he can recall.[206] Olivi was presumably referring to Jerome of Ascoli (the future Pope Nicholas IV), who was Minister General of the Order from 1274 to 1279.

Olivi explained and defended his position again in an apology that he composed in 1285. He has never denied or doubted, he now claims, that marriage is a sacrament. On the contrary, he has consistently maintained that it is a sacrament. But he has inquired whether marriage has "full univocity" with the other sacraments, and he has proved that it does not – but only "without assertion." Olivi then pursues two lines of argument in defense of his position.[207] In the first place, he outlines several ways in which marriage differs from the other sacraments of the New

---

[203] Ibid., ad 24, i (54–55).

[204] On this process and its consequences, see D. Burr, *The Persecution of Peter Olivi* (Philadelphia, 1976), 35–44.

[205] G. Fussenegger, "*Littera septem sigillorum* contra doctrinam Petri Ionnis Olivi edita," *Archivum Franciscanum Historicum* 47 (1954): 45–53, at 51, no. 6.

[206] *Responsio quam fecit Petrus Ioannis ad litteram magistrorum*, ed. Laberge, *Archivum Franciscanum Historicum* 28 (1935), 127.

[207] *Responsio fratris P. Ioannis ad aliqua dicta*, ed. Laberge, *Archivum Franciscanum Historicum* 28 (1935), 374.

Law. There is no minister of marriage, since no one can dispense a sacrament to himself. Again, marriage already existed under the Old law. Again, marriage in one person is abolished by the death of the other person. Again, marriage before consummation is abolished by entry into the religious life. Again, the same marriage exists in two persons at once, or at least in one person dependently on another. Again, marriage can be contracted through intermediaries between persons who are not present to each other (*inter absentes*). For example, the King of Castile's son married the King of France's daughter through intermediaries when the former was in Castile and the latter in France. But a bishop cannot confer orders, confirmation, baptism, extreme unction, or absolution on persons who are in a far-off place, but only on persons who are present to him. Nor can a priest in Spain consecrate bread and wine on an altar in India.[208]

Next, Olivi respectfully takes issue with the anathema of *The Letter of Seven Seals*, according to which it would be heretical to deny that grace is conferred through marriage and forbidden to question it. Olivi explains that he does mean to deny that grace is conferred through marriage, but only that this is a proposition that must be believed. It cannot be an article of faith, for Peter Lombard and several distinguished canonists, among them Goffredus de Trano, Monaldus of Capo d'Istria, Hostiensis, and Bernardus Parmensis, deny that grace is conferred through marriage.[209] Still less, therefore, is the proposition that grace is conferred through marriage *in the same way as through the other sacraments* an article of faith. God does indeed give a grace to those who marry properly to enable them to fulfill that estate well, just as God gives grace to those who enter the virginal and religious states properly, but the question at issue is whether such grace is given *ex opere operato* or only *ex opere operantis*, as in any good deed. On this point, Olivi confesses, he has been unable reach a definitive conclusion.[210]

Olivi now concedes that he spoke carelessly when he claimed that marriage was a sacrament in the same sense as the bronze serpent, the Tabernacle, and the ark of Moses were sacraments, even though he qualified that suggestion by saying that he did not assert this but was only proposing it dialectically. Clearly, marriage is a sacrament in a very different way from signs of that sort.[211] Olivi elaborates this point in a later redaction of the original question, where he adds after the words "which, however, I do not assert at present" that the offending observation was "too loosely said, because marriage is a holy estate of rational persons that is divinely instituted for their good life and for the propagation of offspring to worship God, which [things] do not belong to the aforesaid examples."[212]

---

[208] Ibid., 374–75.   [209] Ibid., 375–77.   [210] Ibid., 377.   [211] Ibid., 377–78.
[212] Emmen, "Verginità e matrimonio," pp. 12 and 54. A. Maier, "Per la storia del processo contro l'Olivi," *Rivista di storia della chiesa in Italia* 5 (1951): 326–39, at 331–33.

Peter John Olivi died in 1298, but his purported errors became a feature of the struggle between the diverging Conventual and the Spiritual movements in the Order during the early fourteenth century, where his opinions on marriage came under scrutiny again.[213] By that time, his name had become associated with the Spirituals, whom the Conventuals accused of perpetuating Olivi's errors. Pope Clement V appointed a commission of cardinals in 1309 to examine Olivi's errors in relation to the Spiritual movement, and this commission continued its work at Vienne, where the general council began in 1311.[214] The leaders of the Conventual attack produced an *appellatio* in 1311, which contained a list of Olivi's errors,[215] including those pertaining to marriage. The Conventuals accused Olivi of having taught five errors regarding marriage: that marriage is a sacrament in the same sense as the bronze serpent, the Tabernacle, and the ark of Moses were sacraments; that when St Paul spoke of a "great sacrament in Christ and the church," he meant only that marriage signified some great thing, which might be said also of the adultery of Bathsheba (2 Kings 11); that marriage was not a sacrament univocally with the other sacraments of the New Law; that pursuit of the religious life and the consecration of a virgin are more divine and are more appropriately counted as sacraments than marriage; and that no "sacramental grace" is conferred in marriage.[216]

Defending Olivi in a response to the *appellatio*, Ubertino da Casale pointed out that the church had never explicitly defined as an article of faith the doctrine that grace is conferred in marriage *in the same way in all respects* as it is in the other sacraments of the New Law. Nor had the church declared dogmatically that marriage was in every way the same as the other sacraments of the New Law and did not differ from them at all. In fact, Ubertino continues, there are many respects in which marriage is obviously different. For example, it already existed in the state of innocence and under the Old Law; it does not need to be conferred by a minister; it can be contracted between persons who are in different places; and the attachment of pecuniary conditions to the agreement does not constitute simony. Moreover, numerous authorities, including Peter Lombard and the canonists Goffredus de Trano, Monaldus, Bernardus Parmensis, and Huguccio, have taught that sacramental grace is not conferred through marriage. It is hardly likely that these distinguished authors would have taught doctrines that are contrary to the sacred canons. Again, the sacred canons do not state that marriage causes everything that it signifies. Marriage signifies the unions of Christ and the church, of the two natures

---

[213] The Spirituals wanted to recover and adhere to the uncompromising ideals of Francis and his companions, whereas the Conventuals favored the more pragmatic, institutionalized way of life that had evolved in the Order subsequently.

[214] See D. Burr, *Persecution of Peter Olivi*, 35–44, for a narrative this process. See also Burr, *The Spiritual Franciscans* (Pennsylvania, 2001), 111–58.

[215] Ed. F. Ehrle as "Anklageschrift der Communität gegen die Spiritualen und im besondern gegen fr. Petrus Johannis Olivi," in "Zur Vorgeschichte des Concils von Vienne," *Archiv für Literatur- und Kirchengeschichte des Mittelalters*, vol. 2 (Berlin, 1886), at 365–74.

[216] Ibid., 369.

in Christ, and of the human mind to God as his bride, but it does not cause these unions. If it causes the last of them, it is only indirectly and in a remedial manner, by preventing carnal concupiscence from violating the union. That is why St Paul did not command marriage, Ubertino argues, but rather conceded it in the time of grace as an indulgence.[217]

Olivi's position on the sacramentality of marriage may be reduced to three themes. First, he was prepared to assert that marriage was a sacrament at least in the sense that it was "a holy estate of rational persons divinely instituted for their good life and for the propagation of offspring to worship God." Second, Olivi pointed out that the manner in which marriage was a sacrament had not been dogmatically determined, and he denied that the doctrine of conjugal grace was an article of faith. Questions such as whether it was a sacrament in the same sense as the other "sacraments of grace" and even whether it conferred grace *ex opere operato* were open to faithful disagreement. Olivi did not deny that grace was conferred through marriage in *some* sense, for it might at least be conferred *ex opere operantis*, but the same could be said of any deed performed charitably by a Christian. Third, inverting the paradigmatic method, Olivi emphasized the differences between marriage and the other sacraments of the New Law, proposing, albeit without assertion, that marriage did not belong univocally to that class. But Olivi's arguments for the third thesis were weak because he did not articulate any standard by which one might judge which features of the sacraments were essential and which were not. Nor did he show how one might distinguish between the specific and the generic features of the sacraments of grace. Even if one granted that marriage differed markedly from the other members of the class, it did not follow that marriage was not univocally a member of that class. A whiskerless breed of cats may still belong the species *felidae*.

14.8.3 *Durandus of Saint-Pourçain*

Durandus used the paradigmatic method to show that marriage was not univocally a sacrament of the New Law. He adopted some of Olivi's arguments, but he took the method to new heights of subtlety and complexity. Durandus asks whether marriage is a sacrament, or, more precisely, whether it is a sacrament properly so called, or a sacrament of the New Law. He begins with some standard objections. First, marriage does not need to be dispensed by a minister of the church, which is a salient feature of the other sacraments. It is true that baptism, too, can be dispensed by a layperson, but only in dire necessity, whereas spouses can validly marry without a minister of the church even when there is no necessity. Second, marriage is not constituted from sacramental form and matter. Durandus immediately refutes one standard solution to this objection: that the spouses' own expressions of consent are

---

[217] Ehrle, Ed., *Responsio ad predictum libellum diffamatorium*, ibid., 377–416, at 389–90.

the form and the matter. Durandus counters that the man's expression of consent is no more the form or the matter than the woman's, and vice versa.[218] Durandus either misunderstood Richard's theory or was citing a different theory akin to or based on Richard's.

Such arguments are preliminary and not entirely apropos, however, for the term "sacrament" is equivocal. One must affirm as a matter of faith, Durandus concedes, that marriage is a sacrament. Pope Lucius III settled the matter in the bull or decree *Ad abolendam*, which condemned those, such as the Waldensians and Cathars, who held or taught false doctrines about such "ecclesiastical sacraments" as eucharist, baptism, penance, and marriage. It is heresy to deny that marriage is one of the sacraments of the church, just as it is heresy to deny that marriage is licit.[219] But it does not follow that marriage is a sacrament in the proper sense of the term. Durandus's own view is that marriage is a sacrament in a broad sense, but that it is not a sacrament "strictly and properly so called, as are the other sacraments of the New Law."[220] Two questions remain open: whether a grace is conferred through marriage *ex opere operato*; and whether marriage has "full univocation" with the other sacraments of the New Law. The former question is theological, Durandus explains, whereas the latter is logical. One is free to answer either of these questions affirmatively or negatively, and without fear of heresy. Durandus assumes that the questions are separable inasmuch as someone who answers "Yes" to the theological question may still answer "No" to the logical question.[221]

Durandus declines to commit himself "at present" to a position on the theological question, but he insists that denial of the doctrine of conjugal grace would not be "contrary to what the Roman church preaches and observes." Durandus rehearses the simony objection, and he refutes the usual solution: that the money is intended only to help the spouses sustain their mundane burdens. The same might be said of someone who buys his way into a monastery, which would unquestionably be simony. Contrariwise, a priest who receives money for blessing a marriage clearly commits simony, precisely because the blessing is a means of grace.[222] But Durandus's chief point, which he presents with emphasis and rhetorical flourish, is that opinion is divided. There is consensus among the "modern theologians" that marriage confers grace, but Peter Lombard, the College of Cardinals, and most experts in canon law maintain that it does not.[223]

Having declined to answer the theological question (although his preference is clear), Durandus applies himself in earnest to the logical question: Is marriage a sacrament univocally with the other sacraments of the New Law? He begins with a

---

[218] Durandus, *IV Sent.* 26.3, §§1–2 [arg. 1–2] (367va).
[219] X 5.7.9, *Ad abolendam* (CIC 2:780). Durandus, *IV Sent.* 26.3, resp., §5 (367va).
[220] *IV Sent.* 26.3, §15 [ad 1–2] (368vb).
[221] Ibid., resp., §5 (367va).   [222] Ibid. (376vb).   [223] Ibid., §§6–8 (367va–b).

standard account of univocity taken from Aristotle's *Categories*: Things are univocals if and only if they share the same name and the same *ratio* insofar as they are so named.[224] Durandus explains that a *ratio*, as understood here, is a definition (*definitio*).[225] If one defines a sacrament broadly, as a sign of a sacred reality, then marriage is clearly a sacrament univocally with all the other sacraments, and not only with the sacraments of the New Law, for it is a sign of the joining between Christ and the church. But one should keep in mind that what marriage signifies is only a non-contained reality (*res non contenta*) – one that is not conferred by the sacrament – whereas each of the other sacraments of the New Law signifies a contained reality (*res contenta*). Moreover, a sacrament of the New Law may be defined as "some corporeal or sensible sign that is externally applied to a human being to bring about spiritual sanctification," as Augustine and Hugh of Saint-Victor showed. If one considers marriage in light of that definition, it becomes clear that it does not have "perfect univocation" with other the sacraments of the New Law.[226]

Durandus's claim here is a subtle one. He does not claim that marriage cannot instantiate the definition *in any way*, but rather that it does not do so perfectly, that is, *in the same way* as the other sacraments of the New Law do. Rather than extend the definition to make it fit the thing in question, Durandus prefers to consider the ordinary sense that the definition has in the context for which it was intended. Definitions need to be properly interpreted, and to that end they must be considered in their proper context.

Durandus presents five arguments to show that marriage lacks "perfect univocation" with the other sacraments of the New Law. The first three use the paradigmatic method to interpret the chief features that belong to the sacraments by definition, namely, that a sacrament is a sign, that it is externally applied to the recipient, and that it causes spiritual sanctification. First, a sacrament of the New Law is a sign in a special manner, for even what is externally enacted "exceeds the dictate [*dictamen*] of natural reason." The performance or reception of a sacrament entails an implicit profession of faith.[227] But natural reason can explain what takes place in marriage, such as how and why the contractants consent to marriage and express their consent.[228] Second, when a sacrament is said to be something "externally applied" (*extrinsecus appositum*), the point is not only that something apparent to the senses occurs, but also that the subject receives the sacrament from without as an *opus operatum*, as the water and the formative words of consecration are received in baptism. A sacrament is received *from* a minister, who externally applies it. That is

---

[224] Aristotle, *Categories* 1, 1a1–12.

[225] Durandus, *IV Sent.* 26.3, §9 (367vb).

[226] *IV Sent.* 26.3, §9 (367vb–368ra): "sacramentum novae legis est aliquod signum corporale uel sensibile extrinsicus homini appostitum ad effectum sanctificationis spiritualis."

[227] Cf. Thomas Aquinas *IV Sent.* 1.1.2, quᵃ 3, resp. (Moos 4:22), and *IV Sent.* 17.3.1, quᵃ 2, resp. (890): The sacraments even under the Old Law were declarations (*protestationes*) and signs of things of faith and, as such, matters not of natural but of divine law.

[228] Durandus, *IV Sent.* 26.3, §10 (368ra).

true even of penance, despite some parallels with marriage. But the spouses themselves establish their own marriage. Even if one grants that each partner applies the sacrament to the other when they plight their troth, that does not show that the *applicatio* of marriage is univocal with the *applicatio* of the other sacraments. The very notion of sacramental application presupposes that whoever administers the sacrament is really present (*realiter praesens*) to the one who receives it. A bishop cannot confer the sacrament of orders, confirmation, baptism, extreme unction, or penance on persons who are in a far-off land, and a priest in Spain cannot consecrate eucharistic bread in India. Yet a woman in France can validly marry a man who is in Spain, for spouses do not have to be really present to each other to contract marriage. Instead, they can exchange consent through letters or intermediaries.[229] Either there is no "application" at all in marriage, therefore, or the application is not univocal with that of the other sacraments of the New Law.[230] Third, as regards spiritual sanctification, even if marriage does confer grace or sanctify in some way, it does not do so univocally with the other sacraments of the New Law. It does not confer grace *de novo* on those who do not yet have grace, as baptism does; nor does it confer remission of mortal guilt, as baptism and penance do; nor does it augment a grace that the recipient already enjoys. Indeed, inasmuch as celibacy is the more spiritual option, marriage diminishes grace.[231]

Finally, Durandus presents two arguments that depend on what he calls "general reasons" (*rationes generales*). Here, he uses the paradigmatic method more freely, without referring to a definition. First, marriage is subject to ecclesiastical ordinance (the positive law of the church) in a manner in which no other sacrament of the New Law is subject. The clergy cannot change or determine the conditions for a valid baptism, but they can change the rules about who may legitimately marry.[232] Second, marriage does not belong integrally to the sacramental system. Baptism is the gateway to the sacraments of the New Law, which depend on it, but unbaptized persons can marry. Durandus concedes that a marriage between infidels is not *ratum* and that it will become *ratum* automatically if the spouses are baptized, but he points out that the spouses can marry before they are baptized, whereas none of the other sacraments can be validly received by an unbaptized person. An infidel, for example, cannot be confirmed. Moreover, what changes when the spouses convert is not their marriage *per se* but their baptismal state.[233]

---

[229] Cf. Peter Olivi, *Responsio fratris P. Ioannis ad aliqua dicta*, ed. Laberge, *Archivum Franciscanum Historicum* 28 (1935), 374–75.

[230] Durandus, *IV Sent.* 26.3, §11 (368ra).   [231] Ibid., §12 (368ra–b).   [232] Ibid., §13 (368rb).

[233] Ibid., §14.

14.8.4 *Paludanus's refutation of Durandus*

Peter of La Palu rehearses Durandus's arguments at length, conceding that they are "probable and subtle" but refuting them.[234] There is some truth in Durandus's position, he concedes, for marriage "is not as perfect a sacrament as the others are." It is the greatest among them in signification, but it is the least in efficacy and as a cause of grace, and it is their efficacy that distinguishes the sacraments of the New Law from those of the Old. Nevertheless, Peter argues, marriage deserves to be called a sacrament of the New Law as properly as any of the others, for the inclusion of a species in a genus does not depend on the level of perfection with which the species realizes the genus. The human being is a more perfect animal than the ass and realizes the possibilities of animality more fully, yet asses and human beings belong equally to the genus of animal because both fully satisfy whatever the definition may be, such as "animate sensible substance."[235]

What Peter regards as Durandus's folly leads him to question the paradigmatic method itself, whereby one compares and contrasts marriage with other sacraments to see whether it can be assimilated to the group. The method is pointless and absurd, Peter argues, because every sacrament is unique. One might use the method to show that every sacrament is not a sacrament, for "there is no sacrament that does not have something proper to itself in which it differs from every other." For example, one might argue that because baptism alone has one of the four elements as its matter, it does not have matter in the same way as the other sacraments. Again, whereas baptism can be administered by a layperson in dire necessity, the other five sacraments, aside from marriage, can be administered only by a priest. Again, eucharist alone involves the consecration of its sacramental matter. And so forth. What matters, according to Peter, is not whether a sacrament differs in important respects from the other sacraments, but whether it is both a sign of grace and a cause of that grace *ex opere operato*. If it meets that definition, it must be a sacrament of the New Law, regardless of *how* it meets the definition.[236] Peter assumes, albeit without presenting much in the way of proof or evidence, that marriage meets that simple definition.

Peter of La Palu is generally an astute and perceptive critic of Durandus, but he did not share Durandus's analytical and philosophical skills,[237] and in this case he misses the point. Peter correctly says that according to Durandus marriage is not "strictly and properly" one of the seven sacraments, but he fails to notice how

---

[234] Paludanus, *IV Sent.* 26.4, divisio (141ra). On Paludanus's critique of Durandus, see J. Dunbabin, *A Hound of God* (Oxford, 1991), 36–42.

[235] *IV Sent.* 26.4.2 (141rb–va).

[236] Ibid., conc. 3 (141va–b). *The ex opere operato* requirement is stated in the preceding passage, conc. 2 (141va).

[237] According to Dunbabin, *Hound of God*, 41, Paludanus's "attempt to expose Durandus's weaknesses was a like a man trying to trap a rat by throwing a duvet at it."

Durandus presupposes and explicates a *definition* of sacrament, interpreting it in its proper context. To show that marriage is a sacrament in the proper sense, according to Durandus, it is not enough to show that it meets the terms of a definition, for one must also show that it meets those terms *univocally*. Peter treats all of Durandus's objections as if they were on the same level, without noticing that the first three turn on features of a definition, whereas the rest are "general" observations about the differences between marriage and the other sacraments.

Olivi and Durandus were outliers in their treatment of marriage as a sacrament. Both questioned and criticized a doctrine that was becoming established as a norm of faith and practice, although it had not yet been dogmatically defined. Moreover, the mainstream response to Durandus, whose critique would still be a talking point at the Council of Trent, raised awareness that the full sacramentality of marriage was something worth defending as orthodoxy.

15

The question of grace

Few theologians before 1225 seriously questioned Peter Lombard's assertion that marriage unlike the other sacraments was *only* a remedy and not a source of grace or even virtue.[1] They assumed that marriage prevented sin by obviating the occasions for sinning and by excusing the conjugal act, but not by reforming the soul as the other sacraments did. Theologians did not consider this position to be in need of defense or demonstration until the 1220s, and canonists continued to maintain it long afterwards.[2] Gandulph of Bologna, writing during the 1160s, suggested that all the sacraments, including marriage, might confer grace and virtue, but he noted that the "doctors of the church" upheld the Lombard's position.[3]

The preventive model prevailed in scholastic theology only until the second quarter of the thirteenth century. Thereafter, most theologians assumed, on the contrary, that marriage had some supernatural efficacy to reform the soul, enabling the spouses to manage their sexual relationship in a way that was decent and fitting from a Christian point of view, to curb wandering desire, and to sustain marriage until they were separated by death. Some extended the scope to this gratuitous assistance to all the distracting, terrestrial burdens of marriage, but most considered concupiscence to be the most conspicuous of such burdens.

15.1 THE PREVENTIVE MODEL

It seemed obvious to twelfth-century theologians that marriage was only "conceded" as a remedy against concupiscence and that its sanctifying efficacy was merely preventive. When these theologians characterized marriage as a remedy, they were thinking of 1 Corinthians 7:9: "it is better to marry than to burn." The chief purpose

---

[1] Peter Lombard, *Sent.* IV, 2.1.1 (239–40).   [2] Le Bras, "Mariage," 2208, 2213.
[3] Gandulph, *Sent.* IV, §17 (ed. de Walter, 396–97). Gandulph was a master of both theology and canon law.

of marriage in a Christian setting was the "avoidance of fornication" (*evitatio fornicationis*). The notion evoked Paul's counsel that each man and should have a wife, and each woman a husband, "because of fornication" (*propter fornicationem*, 1 Cor 7:2). Marriage was a matter of indulgence (1 Cor 7:6) and a means of excusing the conjugal act. The efficacy of marriage, therefore, was merely remedial. Peter Abelard's followers held that marriage did not confer a supernatural gift (*donum*), as the other sacraments did, but only excused things that would otherwise stand in the way of salvation (Section 11.1).[4] Similarly, a summary account of the seven sacraments that Richard Poore promulgated as Bishop of Salisbury between 1217 and 1219 distinguishes between the five necessary sacraments, which everyone needs, and the two optional sacraments: orders and marriage. Whereas the necessary sacraments have the power to confer remission of sins, and the sacrament of orders confers or enhances sacred powers (*virtutes*) that are saving for others, marriage is only a means by which "the sin of fornication is avoided."[5] Canonists regarded marriage more pessimistically. Rufinus argued that consummated marriage, like the sacrifices of the Old Law, was a merely a sign of something sacred, for a "law of turpitude" prevented it from being a means of grace.[6] The common denominator of all such theories was the premise that marriage obviated sin without reforming the sinner: that it removed an obstacle to salvation without being a means to salvation. It did not repair the wounded soul, still less elevate the soul above its natural condition by making it pleasing to God.

Peter Lombard's statement of the preventive model was fundamental in theology during the late twelfth and early thirteenth centuries. Some sacraments, such as eucharist and orders, the Lombard explains, enhance grace and virtue. Some, such as baptism, confer not only a remedy but also a "helping grace" (*gratia adiutrix*), which enables the subject to do good works (*gratia ad bene operandum*). But the sacrament of marriage confers only a remedy.[7] The Lombard's division was consistent with the framework of values in which he situated marriage under the New Law, for he regarded marriage primarily as a way to avoid fornication (1 Cor 7:1–2). He explains that the New Testament distinguishes between two sorts of permission, pertaining respectively to lesser evils and to lesser goods. Coitus motivated by incontinence is permitted as a lesser evil, for it is tolerated and pardonable (*venialis*) as the alternative to fornication. Marriage is permitted as a lesser good, and not through toleration but through indulgence and concession. Marriage is a remedy, therefore, but it does not "merit the palm."[8] As the Lombard explains in a different

---

4 *Sentaentiae Abaelardi* §201; §231; §233 (CCM 14:107–08; 122; 123). *Sententiae Parisienses*, ed. Landraf, *Écrits théologiques*, 44/5–7. *Ysagoge in theologiam*, ed. Landraf, *Écrits théologiques*, 197/2–5.

5 In Powicke and Cheney, *Councils and Synods* 2.1 (Oxford, 1964), p. 65, §15.

6 Rufinus, *Summa decretorum* on C. 32 q. 2 c. 3 (ed. Singer, 481).

7 Peter Lombard, *Sent.* IV, 2.1.1 (2:239–40). See also ibid., 1.9.5 (238–39), on the efficacy of baptism and circumcision.

8 *Sent.* IV, 26.4 (418–19).

context, "to turn aside from evil always evades punishment, but it does not always merit the palm."[9] To merit the palm of victory is to be destined for the future Paradise: to receive a seminal grace that will eventually blossom as glory. Peter Lombard does not mean that married folk will not get into Paradise but only that marriage will not be what takes them there. It will only enable them to avoid pitfalls on the way.

Early-thirteenth-century theologians elaborated Peter Lombard's preventive theory in diverse ways. Stephen Langton divides the sacraments into those which were instituted for salvation (*ad salutem*), and those which were instituted for a remedy (*ad remedium*). To achieve *salus* (literally, "health") in the sense presupposed here is not only to merit eternal bliss or to be worthy of it but also to anticipate that bliss through grace and the indwelling of the Holy Spirit. Whereas the other sacraments of the New Law were instituted for salvation, Langton argues, marriage was instituted from the beginning as a remedy. At first, before sin, it was a remedy against the paucity of human beings. After sin, marriage was re-instituted as a remedy against incontinence.[10] Similarly, William of Auxerre argues that marriage only conserves already-existing grace by protecting the subject from sin, whereas the other sacraments confer grace. Inasmuch as all the sacraments are medications, William explains, marriage is a prophylactic medicine (*medicina perservativa*).[11]

Peter the Chanter argues that marriage cannot confer a *cumulus gratiae* ("increase of grace") because it was instituted only as a remedy, and not for the sake of any positive benefit (*ad augmentum*). The Chanter characterizes sacramental grace as an *augmentum gratiae* or *cumulus gratiae* because he considers it to be a particular enhancement of an underlying sanctity.[12] God confers *cumulus gratiae* through the other sacraments and through certain ecclesiastical rites, especially those involving the oil of unction or chrism, which is a figure or sign of *cumulus gratiae*. There is probably no *cumulus gratiae* in the consecration of a virgin, therefore, since no anointing is involved. Contrariwise, there probably is a *cumulus* in the consecration of a bishop and in the anointing of a king, since both rituals involve anointing.[13] Marriage is the only "ecclesiastical sacrament" that the Chanter does not include among the *spiritualia*, the buying or selling of which incurs the sin

[9] *Sent.* II, 24.1.8 (1:452). The context is a discussion of the grace and moral condition of Adam and Eve before the fall.
[10] Stephen Langton, *Quaestiones theologiae*, St John's MS 318va–b (= Lyell MS 1vb, 2ra): "Matrimonium vero institutum est ad remedium incontinentiae post peccatum, et in remedium universitatis, id est ad multiplicandum genus humanum, ante peccatum." On the *remedium universitatis*, cf. Albertus Magnus, IV *Sent.* 26.10, resp. (112a): Human beings were commanded to "increase and multiply" because of a "deficiency of population" (*defectus multitudinis*).
[11] William of Auxerre, *Summa aurea* IV, peamble to tract. 17 (380).
[12] Petrus Cantor, *Summa de sacramentis et animae consiliis* 1, §3 (ed. Dugauquier, 1:19–22).
[13] Ibid. (19).

of simony. The Chanter defines *spiritualia* as things "through which the grace of the Holy Spirit is conferred or, having already been conferred, is augmented."[14]

Advances in sacramental theology during the second half of the twelfth century and the first quarter of the thirteenth exposed differences that explained why the sacrament of marriage did not confer grace. Theologians noted that marriage, unlike the other sacraments of the New Law, was not received but enacted by the participant. Again, marriage resulted from an exchange of consent and not from a divinely instituted verbal formula. As Langton puts it, marriage is a human work (*opus hominis*), whereas baptism is a divine work (*opus Dei*).[15] According to the *Ordinaturus magister*, an early gloss on Gratian's *Decretum*, marriage "is not among those sacraments which bestow the consolation of heavenly grace," for whereas the other sacraments require a prescribed verbal formula, marriage requires only mutual consent. The sacraments of the New Law originated in canon law (*ius canonicum*), but marriage received its origin from the natural law, its form from civil law, and only its approbation from the church's law.[16]

Marriage seemed to be too secular to confer grace. Canonists from around the middle of the thirteenth century asked whether the sacrament of marriage risked the sin of simony because of the pecuniary conditions, negotiations, and transactions that led up to the agreement. It was not enough to counter that the spouses needed such support to bear the burden of their obligations, for the same might said of ecclesiastical offices and even of entry into the religious life, the purchase of which certainly did amount to simony. To explain why the negotiations, dowries and so forth that attended marriage did not incur this mortal sin, canonists pointed out that no grace was conferred in marriage.[17] The *Summa fratris Alexandri* solved the simony problem in a similar way, arguing that "no grace is conferred in marriage" because it was instituted as "a sacrament of the natural law, prior to the Old Law and the New Law."[18]

To defend the preventive doctrine against the objection that the sacraments of the New Law conferred the grace that they signified, theologians countered that marriage was not strictly a sacrament of the New Law. This argument had first appeared during the second half of the twelfth century, as theologians reflected on Peter Lombard's division of the sacraments according to their efficacy. Peter of Poitiers noted that marriage did not cause the reality that it signified ("*non efficit*

[14] Petrus Cantor, *Verbum abbreviatum* I.34, CCM 196, 244. For the corresponding passage in the short version, where the sense is less clear, see c. 37, PL 205:126A.
[15] *Quaestiones theologiae*, Cambridge, St John's College Library, MS 57 (C7), 308v.
[16] *Ordinaturus magister* on C. 1 q.1 c. 101, in R. Weigand, *Die Naturrechtslehre des Legisten und Dekretisten* (München, 1967), p. 286, no. 485a.
[17] *Glossa ordinaria* on C. 32, q. 2, c. 13 (c. *Honorantur*), in *Corpus Iuris Canonici* (Rome, 1582), cols. 2113–14. Goffredus de Trano, *Summa super titulis Decretalium* on the title De sacramentis non iterandis (Lyons, 1519, 33va–b). Hostiensis, *Summa aurea* on the title De sacramentis non iterandis (Venice, 1574, col. 217).
[18] *Summa fratris Alexandri* II-II, no. 833, "Ad alius vero …" (Quaracchi 3:799b).

quod figurat"), for it primarily signified Christ's union with the church. Clearly, no couple's marriage could bring about that union. To the objection that all the sacraments of New Law conferred what they signified, Peter of Poitiers pointed out that marriage could not have been instituted under the New Law for it had already been practiced under Old Law. Indeed, it was instituted in the very beginning, in Paradise.[19]

Guy of Orchelles develops the solution that Peter of Poitiers had outlined. Guy notes that both marriage and circumcision seem to be exceptions to the Lombard's claim that efficacy is what distinguishes the sacraments of the New Law from those of the Old. On the one hand, circumcision was a sacrament of the Old Law, but according to Peter Lombard and others it did cause the grace that it signified. On the other hand, marriage is a sacrament of the New Law, but it signifies the "great sacrament of Christ and the church, namely, the incarnation of the Son," which it cannot cause. In reply, Guy distinguishes between institution and approbation: between the institution of a new sacrament and the approval of an already-existing sacrament. Circumcision belonged to the Old Law only by approval, for it had been instituted in the time of Abraham. Likewise, marriage is a sacrament of the New Law only by approval, for it was instituted in Paradise.[20]

Hugh of Saint-Cher, O.P. (d. 1263), was the last major theologian to adhere to the preventive model. Hugh's treatment of marriage in his commentary on the *Sentences* (1220s or early 1230s), like most of the commentary, is heavily dependent on William of Auxerre's *Summa aurea.*[21] His approach to marriage in this and in other works remains true to the tradition of theologians writing during the first quarter of the thirteenth century. Hugh assumes that marriage does not fully belong among the sacraments of the New Law. Commenting on the marriage at Cana in John's gospel, Hugh interprets the six water jars as the six sacraments of the New Law. The seventh, marriage, is not included, he explains, because it does not confer sacramental grace in the proper sense.[22] Again, commenting on 1 Corinthians 7, Hugh considers the objection that marriage cannot be a sacrament because every sacrament causes what it signifies. Marriage signifies the joining of Christ and the church, which it cannot cause. Hugh replies that the major premise is true only of sacraments that were instituted under the New Law, whereas marriage was instituted in the beginning,

---

[19] Peter of Poitiers, *Sent.* IV, c. 2 (PL 211:1141B); V, c. 3 (1229B–C); V, c. 14 (1257D). Similarly, Stephen Langton, *IV Sent.*, dist. 1 (ed. Landgraf, p. 150).

[20] Guy of Orchelles, *Tractatus de sacramentis* I.3, no. 10 (13–14). William of Auxerre, *Summa aurea* IV.2.5.1 (37–38), argues that circumcision continued but was not instituted under the Old Covenant.

[21] See P. Abellán, "La doctrina matrimonial de Hugo de San Caro," *Archivo Teológico Granadino* 1 (1938): 27–56, at 32–33.

[22] Hugh of Saint-Cher on John 2, in *Biblia ... cum postilla domini Hugonis Cardinalis* (Basel, 1504), 5:264va: "Sex hydriae sunt sex sacramenta gratiae collativa. Nam esti sint septem sacramenta, scilicet, baptismus, paenitentia, confirmatio, eucharistia, ordo, extrema unctio, et matrimonium, septimum – id est, matrimonium – non est proprie gratiae collativum." (My punctuation.)

before any explicit law was promulgated. Some say that marriage signifies and confers the remission of certain sins, but if so this is remission only in a weak, preventive sense, according to Hugh. Marriage cannot remit the guilt of sins that have already been committed, as baptism and penance do. It only prevents certain new sins, namely, those that would be committed if coitus took place outside marriage.[23]

15.2 THE DISCOURSE ON SACRAMENTAL EFFICACY

The development and eventual rejection of the preventive theory took place in the context of intense and productive inquiry into sacramental efficacy. Topics of inquiry that shaped the arguments about marriage during the first half of the thirteenth century include the distinction between preternatural grace (*gratia gratis data*) and sanctifying grace (*gratia gratum faciens*), the efficacy of circumcision during the time of the Old Law, the efficacy of the *sacramenta legalia* (the rites and offerings of the Old Law), and the distinction between the *opus operatum* of a sacrament (the objective work done) and the *opus operantis* (the work of the participant or recipient). These discourses established a new field of possibilities within which theologians could locate the efficacy of marriage.

When theologians debated whether or not a sacrament conferred grace, the standard was sanctifying grace (*gratia gratum faciens*), which made the soul pleasing (*grata*) to God. Sacramental graces were in some sense special ramifications of that grace, channeling it to meet particular needs. With the possible exception of baptism, theologians distinguished between the special graces of the sacraments and sanctifying grace, for whereas the former were specifically related to particular powers of the soul, the latter was general and more deeply rooted. As Alexander of Hales puts it, "The diverse sacraments were instituted because of diverse needs."[24] Nevertheless, the sacramental graces are akin to sanctifying grace. In a disputation on the need for seven sacraments, Alexander distinguishes between the universal grace of Christ's passion and the particular graces of the sacraments, which ramify from the universal grace. Each of the sacramental graces is designed to heal a particular wound. Alexander adds that one must also distinguish the sacramental graces from the particular sanctifying graces manifest in the virtues, from the gifts of

[23] Hugh of Saint-Cher on 1 Cor 7, ibid., 6:80rb: "Alii autem dicunt quod et illud efficit quod figurat, scilicet remissionem peccati: non [remissionem] peccati quod est, sed quod esset si alias fieret coitus."

[24] Alexander of Hales, *Quaestio disputata* 57, disp. 1, m. 4, §22 (1104): "sacramenta diversa sunt instituta propter diversas necessitates."

the Holy Spirit, from the beatitudes, and from the preternatural grace (*gratia gratis data*) required for the "perfect order of the church," of which there are nine sub-species (1 Cor 12:8–10). All graces except *gratia gratis data* make the soul pleasing to God.[25]

15.2.1 *Preternatural grace*

Scholastic theologians posited certain graces that enabled persons to act in ways that surpassed their natural capabilities without making them more pleasing to God. Some theologians, such as Bonaventure, used the term *gratia gratis data* ("grace freely given") to denote these supra-natural but value-neutral endowments. Others, such as Thomas Aquinas, limited the term *gratia gratis data* to graces bestowed on a subject for the spiritual benefit of others, such as the charisms of the early church and the sacramental powers of priesthood. In the absence of any consistent medieval usage, the post-medieval term "preternatural" serves well enough.[26]

Theologians posited preternatural grace to account for original justice in the earthly Paradise, and inquiries into this original grace in turn sharpened their ideas about sanctifying grace. Theologians debated whether original justice should be characterized as a natural or as a supernatural condition. Many during the first half of the thirteenth century were inclined to think that human beings were initially established in a condition of natural orderliness and perfection without sanctifying grace, although everyone accepted that there was no argument from reason and no authority from Scripture to settle the matter either way. Most theologians accepted, too, that if the angels had been created with sanctifying grace in the beginning, they would have achieved the beatific vision at once and none would have fallen. Only after some of the angels fell were the others confirmed with sanctifying grace, although the delay was not one of time. There were plausible reasons of fittingness for positing a comparable temporal delay among human beings. Sources of the debate included Augustine, Anselm of Canterbury, the *magistri moderni* and the sentential literature, Hugh of Saint-Victor, and Peter Lombard. Some theologians reasoned that human beings even in that natural state would have had some more-than-natural assistance from God sufficient to prevent fall and corruption.[27] Such

---

[25] *Quaestio disputata* 48, m. 2, §31 (861–62).

[26] See W. H. Principe, "Preternatural," *New Catholic Encyclopedia* (New York, 1967), 11:763–64.

[27] See G. Božitković, S. *Bonaventura doctrina de gratia et libero arbitrio* (Marienbad, 1919); J. Bittremieux, "La distinction entre la justice originelle et la grace sanctifiante d'après saint Thomas d'Aquin," *Revue Thomiste* 6 (1921): 121–50; J. Bittremieux "De instanti collationis Adamo justitiae originalis et gratiae: Doctrina S. Bonaventurae, *Ephemerides theologicae Lovanienses* 1 (1924): 168–73; J.-B. Kors, *La justice primitive et le péché originel d'après s. Thomas* (Paris, 1922); E. Catazzo, *De iustitia et peccato originali juxta S. Bonaventuram* (Vicenza, 1942); W. A. Van Roo, *Grace and Original Justice according to St. Thomas* (Rome, 1955); and B. Marthaler, *Original Justice and Sanctifying Grace in the Writings of Saint Bonaventure* (Rome, 1965).

preternatural assistance deserved to be called "grace" only in a broad sense.[28] It would have prevented someone from falling into sin and it would have preserved the natural order of things, which was otherwise powerless to prevent its own collapse, but it would not have elevated the soul by making it pleasing to God. A text from Peter Lombard's *Sentences* was the basis of this discourse. The Lombard posits a "grace of creation" that would have enabled human beings to "stand":

> Now it is necessary diligently to investigate what grace or power human beings had before the fall, and whether by its means they were able to stand firm [*stare*] or not. One should know, therefore, that help was given through grace to human beings at their creation, as we have said above regarding the angels,[29] and that a power was conferred by means of which they were able to stand — that is, able not to decline from what they had received — but by which they were not able to advance to such an extent that through this grace of creation alone they would have merited salvation.[30]

Such assistance "in natural things" (*in naturalibus*) was gratuitous only in the sense that it was an external, divinely given help supplementing the intrinsic capabilities of nature.

15.2.2 *Objective and subjective efficacy*

Theologians accepted that the sacraments of the Old Law justified and were supernaturally meritorious only by virtue of the spirit of charity and piety through which the subject performed or received them, which was already a form of grace. The sacraments of the New Law, on the contrary, were endowed through institution with their own power to justify, and they justified infallibly as long as the recipient did nothing to obstruct their efficacy. This theory presupposed a distinction between the intentional, voluntary work of the subject who performed or received the sacrament and the work of the sacrament itself: for example, between a subject's intentional act of sacrificing a goat, on the one hand, and the sacrifice *per se* or the sacrificed goat, on the other hand. Theologians used a variety of terms to make this distinction. The objective work was characterized as what a sacrament did in and of itself (*quantum in se est*), or by its own power (*ex virtute sacramenti, ex vi sacramenti*), or "from the work done" (*ex opere operato*). The subjective work was characterized as what was attained "from the work of the doer" (*ex opere operantis*), or from the "working work" (*opus operans*), or "because of intention" (*propter intentionem*). The Council of Trent will consistently use the terms *ex opere operato* and *ex opere operantis* to make the distinction, finding in the former notion the

---

[28] Bonaventure, *II Sent.* 29.2.2, ad 1 (2:704a).   [29] Peter Lombard, *Sent.* II, 5.5 (353).
[30] *Sent.* II, 24.1.1–2 (1:450–51). The Lombard elaborates this theory at *Sent.* II, 29.1 (492).

feature of Catholic sacramental theology that most distinguished it from Protestant theories.[31]

It may seem pleonastic to say that a sacrament causes grace through its own efficacy, or *ex opere operato*. If and only if a sacrament justifies extraneously, it seems, rather than by virtue of the charity or devotion of the one who receives the sacrament, can the work of the sacrament be properly characterized as gratuitous. Indeed, the question for theologians during the early years of the thirteenth century was not whether a sacrament *conferred grace* by its own power, but rather whether it *justified the participant* by its own power. That said, a sacrament might be properly said to cause grace *ex opere operantis* inasmuch as the work of the doer (the *opus operantis*) disposed him or her to receive supernatural grace, whether that work itself was natural or gratuitous. Again, if the disposing *opus operantis* was itself a result of grace, then the doer received "grace for grace" (John 1:6).

The distinction between *ex opere operato* and *ex opere operantis* efficacy meant different things to different theologians and in different contexts, but it had acquired a tolerably clear and consistent meaning during the late-twelfth and early-thirteenth centuries in discourses on the rites and offerings of the Old Law (the *sacramenta legalia*). Theologians inquired whether those old sacraments were efficacious as means of salvation. For example, Peter the Chanter asks whether the sacraments of the Old Law were supernaturally meritorious.[32] It seems not, for the oblations, sacrifices, and rituals of the Old Law were performed only as signs of perfect things in the future, as a yoke for the proud, and as a way of teaching the weak, much as one might teach a child. Moreover, God's people performed them not out of charity (*ex caritate*) but out of "servile fear." Contrariwise, some ritual elements of the old sacramental system, such as incense, are still practiced under the New Law. And who would dare to claim that the Blessed Virgin achieved no supernatural merit when she offered two birds in the temple (Luke 2:24)?

The Chanter reviews several possibilities. Perhaps the rites themselves did not confer any *cumulus gratiae*, but the obedience that people practiced in performing them conferred grace or was at least meritorious in some other way. Some say that the old rites were not meritorious at all because they were only remedies. When a physician prescribes a warm bath, they argue, the bath is remedial but has no positive benefit. If that is correct, the Chanter argues, the sacraments of the Old Law were not performed *from* charity (*ex caritate*) but only *in* charity, as are indifferent (i.e., intrinsically value-neutral) actions in the Christian life, such as the hewing of wood and even venial sins. Others say that the sacraments of the Old Law were performed *from* charity (*ex caritate*) but that they were not meritorious because merit depends on context. The blessed in the next life act from charity, but

---

[31] P. Pourrat, *Theology of the Sacraments* (St Louis, 1910), 162–84. E. J. Kilmartin, "Ex opere operato," *New Catholic Encyclopedia*. P. L. Hanley, "Ex opere operantis," *New Catholic Encyclopedia*.

[32] Petrus Cantor, *Summa de sacramentis* 1, §1 (1:13–17).

they no longer acquire merit through any of their acts. Yet other scholars accept that the old rites were meritorious when performed from charity but maintain that such grace was conferred only rarely and exceptionally under the Old Law, since almost everyone at that time performed the sacraments not from charity but from servile fear. Consequently, even when people of the Old Law practiced the good deeds required under the law, such as almsgiving, most of them would not have experienced the sweetness (*dulcedo*) in such actions that Christians do, for that sweetness is a sign of grace.

To prepare for his own solution, the Chanter parses the performance of a sacrament into three elements: (i) the will to perform the work; (ii) the work (*opus*) that is performed in the sacrament; and (iii) the sacrament *per se*, such as the consecrated bread and wine. The work done in the sacrament links the subject's intention to the sacrament itself. Under the New Law, that work acquires *cumulus meriti* (new grace) from the sacrament itself, although it derives some merit, too, from the subject's volition. Under the Old Law, on the contrary, the work derived its value entirely from the subject's volition. A sacrificial lamb, unlike consecrated bread and wine, was no better in itself than any other lamb.[33] The Chanter's threefold distinction is not easy to grasp, for the work performed in the sacrament seems to collapse into one or other of the two extremes between which it is supposed to mediate: either into the intention of the participant, on the one hand, or into the sacrament itself. But the Chanter was inclined to regard a sacrament not as an action but as sanctified material, for example, as a sacrificed goat, or as consecrated bread and wine.

Praepositinus proposes a simpler, dualistic analysis of the possibilities. He explains that some, such as Peter Lombard, maintain that the sacrifices of the Old Law were only signs and did not justify in any way, even inasmuch they were performed out of charity (*ex caritate*). Others distinguish between the *opus operantis* and *opus operatum* and maintain that only the *opus operantis* justified under the Old Law, whereas both the *opus operantis* and the *opus operatum* justify in "our sacrifices," such as the eucharist.[34] Praepositinus does not choose between these positions, although he seems to prefer the second.

Guy of Orchelles concedes that only the sacraments of the New Law justify by means of a grace that is "contained" in them, yet he cannot agree with Peter Lombard that the sacraments of the Old Law were *only* signs or that they signified without justifying ("*figurabant et non iustificabant*"). Guy agrees with Hugh of Saint-Victor that the descriptor "sign of sacred reality" is only an etymology, explaining why the sacraments are so called and how the term "sacrament" is used. The descriptor is not sufficient to explain what a sacrament is, even a sacrament of the Old Law.[35] Nor can Guy accept that the term "sacrament" is said equivocally

[33] Ibid.   [34] Praepositinus, *Summa* IV, pp. 2–3.
[35] Guy of Orchelles, *Tractatus de sacramentis* 1.1, no. 2 (3/8–11).

of the Hebrew and the Christian sacraments, as when a real human being and a depicted human being are both called "human being."[36] Guy prefers the opinion of certain "great men" (perhaps Praepositinus) who say that the sacraments of the Old Law did not justify in respect of the *opus operatum*, or of the thing itself (*res ipsa*), but that they did justify in respect of the *opus operans* (the voluntary work of the one performing the sacrament) insofar as that work came from charity.[37]

William of Auxerre's position is an elaboration of Guy's. Even the offerings of the Old Law justified those who made them, he argues, but only as regards the act of offering (*quantum ad oblationem*) and not as regards what was offered (*quantum ad ipsum oblatum*). For example, the act of sacrificing a lamb justified but the flesh of the lamb did not. The sacraments of the New Law, on the contrary, justify in both ways.[38] Thus, the body of Christ in the eucharist justifies its recipients not only spiritually, through faith, but also sacramentally or materially (*per modum sacramenti vel materiae*), as if the sacrament were a vial that contained a healing potion or electuary.[39]

Similarly, Alexander of Hales accepts that the sacraments of the Old Law justified the Hebrews insofar as they practiced them "from charity and devotion," but he argues that only the *operatio* of the participant justified, and not the *opus operatum* or *res operata* (the rite itself). Moreover, Alexander argues, the old sacraments were not means of sanctifying grace but only of a preternatural grace (*gratia gratis data*), which enabled the participants to avoid evil and enhanced their temporal, mundane life. The sacraments of the Old Law did not confer the grace that would have enabled the participants to advance in the good and to achieve the eternal bliss of the life to come. The fundamental reason for this difference, according to Alexander, is that the Old Law was a way of "servile fear," whereas the New Law is a way of love.[40]

By the 1240s, theologians generally held that the sacraments of the Old Law justified those who practiced or received them insofar as they acted out of charity (*ex caritate*), but that what justified was not the *opus operatum* (the thing itself, such as the sacrificed animal) but only the *opus operans* (the intentional action of the participant).[41] As regards the sacraments of the New Law, the *opus operantis* is what the recipient actively contributes through volition, intention, and effort, whereas the *opus operatum* is what the recipient passively receives, usually from a minister. Sacraments such as baptism and eucharist were said to confer grace *ex opere operato*

---

[36] 1.3, no. 6 (8/13–16). The equivocity of *homo* in *homo verus* and *homo pictus* was a standard example, originating in Neoplatonic commentary on Aristotle's *Categories* 1, 1a1–12. See P. L. Reynolds, "Analogy of Names in Bonaventure," *Mediaeval Studies* 65 (2003): 117–62, at 124, 125 and passim.

[37] 1.3, no. 7 (9–12).   [38] William of Auxerre, *Summa aurea* IV.1.1 (12/16–19).

[39] Ibid., IV.2.1 (16/42–50, and 17/79–18/92).

[40] Alexander of Hales, *Glossa in IV Sent.* 1.8g (16); 8i (17).

[41] Albertus Magnus, *IV Sent.* 1.8.3, ad 1 (Borgnet 29:21b).

on recipients who received them worthily, without presenting any obstacle. In the early thirteenth century, theologians used the notion of *ex opere operato* efficacy to capture Hugh of Saint-Victor's idea that the very stuff of a sacrament, thanks to the words of consecration, "contains" grace in the way a vessel contains a medicine. By the middle of the thirteenth century, theologians regarded that containment as a figure of speech, to be properly interpreted as a causal relationship. Grace cannot be a property of some material stuff.[42]

Theologians now considered conjugal grace with the distinction between object-ive (*ex opere operato*) and subjective (*ex opere operantis*) efficacy in mind. At first, they held that marriage did not sanctify by its own power (*ex opere operato*), for marriage was not received from a minister but enacted by the recipients. They usually left open the possibility that it might confer grace in another way, as did the sacraments of the Old Law. For example, Jacques de Vitry, who studied under Peter the Chanter in the 1180s, argues that no *cumulus* or *augmentum* of grace is received in marriage through the power of the sacrament itself (*ex virtute sacramenti*), because marriage is only a remedy against fleshly defects. Christians are permitted to marry as a concession to their infirmity, according to Jacques, in the same way as sick persons are permitted to bathe, and infirm monks to eat meat in the infirmary. The other sacraments of the New Law were instituted to sanctify as well as to signify. As long they are not received unworthily, they cause what they signify and bestow an increase of grace in and of themselves (*quantum in se est*).[43] Similarly, Guerric of Saint-Quentin, O.P. (d. 1245), concedes that "grace is not conferred in marriage by virtue of marriage [*virtute matrimonii*], because the conferring of grace is a work of God, whereas the consent that makes marriage is a work of man."[44]

Thomas of Chobham, another of the Chanter's students, developed a similar theory in the manual for confessors that he wrote around 1215. Thomas points out that a sacrament is more than a sign of a sacred reality. If it were only a sign, the church itself would be a sacrament, for it is an image of Christ. Indeed, every creature would be sacrament, for all creation signifies God. A sacrament in the proper sense must satisfy three further conditions: it must be like what it signifies; it must have been instituted in the church; and it must cause the sacred reality that it was instituted to signify. Marriage is not a sacrament strictly so called, therefore, for it does not confer what it was instituted to signify, namely, the joining of Christ and the church. Moreover, although marriage is counted among the seven sacraments

[42] Bonaventure, *IV Sent.* 1.1.un.3, resp. (4:17a).
[43] Jacques de Vitry, *Historia occidentalis*, c. 36 (ed. Hinnebusch, p. 192). Jacques divides the sacraments into those which are voluntary (i.e., orders and marriage) and those which are necessary, in the tradition of Master Simon. On Jacques' life and intellectual formation, see Baldwin, *Masters, Princes, and Servants*, 1:38–39.
[44] Guerric of Saint-Quentin, *Quaestio de matrimonio*, MS BnF 16417, 63va; MS Assisi 138, 155rb. See D. Van den Eynde, *Les définitions des sacraments*, 108n2. Guerric became a Dominican friar at Saint Jacques in Paris in 1225. Following a period as Lector of the priory at Bologne, he taught in Paris as a master of theology 1233–42.

that are practiced "in the church of God," it is not strictly a sacrament of the New Law because it already existed under the Old Law. Indeed, even pagans can marry. But although no grace is conferred by virtue of marriage itself (*ex virtute matrimonii*), Christian spouses can attain supernatural merit through the good intentions with which they marry, for example, if they marry in order to raise children to worship God. Such merit does not come from marriage itself (*ex virtute matrimonii*) but from the devotion to God that the spouses exhibit in marrying (*in opere illo*).[45]

Alternatively, a theologian could argue that marriage did sanctify *ex opere operato*, yet only inasmuch as it was solemnized by the nuptial blessing, for the participants passively received the blessing from a priest in the manner of the other sacraments. William of Auvergne (Section 15.4) and Hugh of Saint-Cher proposed versions of this theory. Commenting on the *Sentences*,[46] Hugh of Saint-Cher suggests that although marriage does not confer grace by virtue of the sacrament itself, it may confer grace "by virtue of the priestly blessing" as well as "because of the intention" of those who contract it (*propter intentionem contrahentium*).[47] Whereas the latter grace is conferred *ex opere operantis*, the former is conferred *ex opere operato*.

15.2.3 *The efficacy of circumcision*

Discussion of circumcision as a sacrament raised the possibility of a grace that sanctified the soul even to the extent of conferring remission of sin, yet without enabling the soul to advance toward salvation or to anticipate ultimate bliss. Peter Lombard had held that circumcision, unlike the other *sacramenta legalia*, was an effective, saving sign under the Old Law, but that it conferred only redemption from sin, without putting anything positive in its place.[48] The Lombard seemed to regard circumcision and marriage as inverse exceptions, with the former behaving like a New Law sacrament under the Old Law, and the latter behaving like an Old-Law sacrament under the New Law. Similarly, Stephen Langton argued that

---

[45] Thomas of Chobham, *Summa confessorum*, a. 4, dist. 2, q. 2 (ed. Broomfield, 90–91). On Thomas's life and work, see J. W. Baldwin, *Masters, Merchants, and Princes* (Princeton, 1970), 1:34–36; and F. Morenzoni, *Des écoles aux paroisses* (Paris, 1995).

[46] On Hugh of Saint-Cher's commentary, see M. Bieniak, "The Sentences Commentary of Hugh of St.-Cher," in Rosemann, *Mediaeval Commentaries on the Sentences of Peter Lombard*, vol. 2 (Leiden, 2010) 111–148. Hugh probably composed this commentary, which is dependent both on William of Auxerre's *Summa aurea* and on Alexander's *Glossa*, during the late 1220s or early 1230s, although the date remains uncertain (see Bienak, 112–13). Two studies of Hugh on marriage include partial transcriptions of *IV Sent.* dist. 26 ff.: P. Abellan, "La doctrina matrimonial de Hugo de San Caro," *Archivo theólogico Granadino* 1 (1938): 27–56; and A. Boureau, "Hugues de Saint-Cher commentateur des *Sentences*," in L.-J. Bataillon et al., *Hugues de Saint-Cher* (Turnhout, 2004), 427–64.

[47] Hugh of Saint-Cher, *IV Sent.*, dist. 26, MS Vat. lat. 1098, fol. 173ra. Cf. Le Bras, "Mariage," 2210, citing the same source in MS Basel, Universitätsbibliothek B II 20, fol. 139. The Vatican MS has "*propter benedictionem contrahentium*," but the reading of the Basel MS ("*propter intentionem contrahentium*") is clearly better.

[48] Peter Lombard, *Sent.* IV, 1.9; 2.1 (238–39; 239–40).

circumcision conferred remission of sins without making the subject worthy of eternal life.[49] Theologians assumed that circumcision was supernaturally efficacious in some sense, but they maintained that it was designed primarily to remove a flaw or a defect, especially that of wounded concupiscence, and not to confer any positive gift. They had two reasons. First, the rite could not have been sufficient for salvation because it was practiced before the Passion and resurrection of Christ and the opening of the Gates of Heaven. Second, sacraments by definition confer the grace that they signify. Now, the external act of circumcision was one not of addition but of removal. Any signified grace of circumcision, therefore, caused only a removal of sin and not an increase in goodness or merit.[50]

A wide range of theories arose to explain how circumcision had some efficacy, even *ex opere operato*, but a grace that was inferior to that of baptism. The discourse revolved around two questions: first, whether circumcision removed a defect without conferring a corresponding benefit; second, whether circumcision was efficacious in some way but not through its own power (*ex vi circumcisionis*). Having raised these questions regarding circumcision under the Old Law, theologians raised them again regarding marriage under the New Law, reaching similar conclusions *mutatis mutandis*.

Guy of Orchelles concedes that circumcision was superior in efficacy to the other sacraments of the Old Law and even that it was in some respects equivalent to baptism.[51] According to one opinion, which Guy attributes to Peter Lombard, circumcision took away guilt without conferring any positive grace, just as Adam in the beginning was free from sin but was not yet adorned with the virtues. Guy rejects this theory, arguing that one cannot be cleansed from sin or absolved from guilt without receiving an infusion of grace and virtue, and vice versa.[52] But from the premise that one thing cannot happen without another thing, Guy points out, it does not follow that the two things have the same cause. For example, someone who commits a mortal sin falls from grace, and the two events (the sin and the loss) are necessarily concurrent, yet it is the sinner who causes the sin, whereas God alone withdraws the grace. Guy suggests that circumcision under the Old Law absolved the subject from sin through its own power (*ex vi sua*), but that it conferred grace through the work of the recipient.[53]

Alexander of Hales attributes much the same efficacy to circumcision as he does to the other sacraments of the Old Law. Grace can work in two ways, he explains: by the way of fear, when the goal is to remove evil; and by the way of love, when the aim is to enhance good. In the first way, grace takes away guilt, and grace and fear

---

[49] Stephen Langton, *IV Sent.*, dist. 1 (ed. Landgraf, p. 151).
[50] Bonaventure, *IV Sent.* 1.2.2.3, resp., opinio 3 (4:43b). Albertus Magnus, *IV Sent.* 1.19, arg. 3c (Borgnet 29:34b).
[51] Guy of Orchelles, *Tractatus de sacramentis* 1.2, no. 11 (14–15).
[52] Ibid. (17/25–26 and 17/30–18/2).   [53] Ibid. (15–16).

together help the forgiven person to abstain from doing further evil. In the second way, grace infuses spiritual life into the soul, conferring a power to do good works, and it elicits good works from that power. Circumcision was effective only in the first way.[54]

Theologians questioned whether it was possible to confer remission of sins without conferring a positive benefit. A common solution involves a distinction between direct and indirect causation. Circumcision caused remission of sins directly, some argue, whereas it caused sanctification only indirectly, as a consequence of remissions of sins. Guy of Orchelles, as we have seen, hinted at this solution. According to William of Auxerre, "almost everyone" says that although both grace and remission of sins were conferred with circumcision, only remission of sins was conferred by virtue of the rite of circumcision itself (*ex vi circumcisionis*), whereas grace was conferred by virtue of the charity of those who performed and received it (i.e., *ex opere operantis*). But William cannot accept this theory. Because vice and virtue are contraries, he argues, as are the meriting of eternal life and the meriting of damnation, it follows that whatever remits sins and guilt must also confer grace and virtue. If circumcision removes sin through its own power (*ex vi sua*), therefore, it must also confer virtue and grace through its own power. It is true that no one could enter heaven until Christ's had risen from the dead and ascended into heaven, so that baptism is in that sense more efficacious now than circumcision was then. But that deficiency pertained not to the efficacy of circumcision *per se* but to the circumstances of the era. William concedes, nevertheless, that because the rite of circumcision, unlike the act of ablution in baptism, was in itself an act of removal, this feature must have been reflected in what the rite signified and in its mode of efficacy. Circumcision conferred a certain grace *ex vi sua*, but grace has many effects, and the immediate effect of the grace of circumcision was rather privative than positive. Nevertheless, the removal of sin makes the subject worthy of eternal life as a consequence. The boy who was circumcised would have merited eternal life as a consequence (*ratione consecutionis*) of the remission of sins. Likewise, when a priest says "this is my body" over the eucharistic bread, the direct effect is the conversion of the bread into Christ's body, but the bread is also converted into Christ's blood as a consequence (*ratione consecutionis*), since whatever becomes the body must become the blood as well.[55]

Bonaventure reviews three theories regarding the grace of circumcision and finds them all wanting. He then proposes his own solution. The first theory seems

---

[54] Alexander of Hales, *IV Sent.* 1.18f, resp. (24). Cf. *Quaestio disputata* 50, m. 2, §19 (885–86), where Alexander seems to make two inconsistent claims: first, that the grace of remission of sin was not conferred *ex vi circumcisionis* but rather came "from the mercy of God and from ordination" because of the covenant (*foedus*) of Gen 17:11; second, that because circumcision, unlike baptism, was not a "vessel of grace," it did not directly cause a grace enabling the subject to do good. Rather, it caused remission of sins, which in turn disposed the soul to receive a positive gift of grace from God.

[55] William of Auxerre, *Summa aurea* IV.2.5.2 (39–41).

reminiscent today of Martin Luther's theology: Circumcision did not mitigate sinful concupiscence itself, but it waived a debt or obligation (*debitum*) so that the guilt (*culpa*) inherent in the act or intention was not "imputed" to the subject. Bonaventure rejects this opinion on the grounds that any change in merit before God presupposes some real change in the soul, whether by removal or by addition. According to the second theory, circumcision removed guilt by its own power (*ex vi circumcisionis*), but positive grace was conferred then not by virtue of circumcision itself but through the bountifulness (*liberalitas*) of God, who in his generosity never removes guilt without also replacing it with grace. According to the third theory, circumcision simply conferred a grace by its own power (*ex vi circumcisionis*). Although this grace was entirely privative, as the significance of the act required, there was a positive effect by way consequence, just as the words of consecration said over the bread have the direct effect only of changing the bread into Christ's body, but the elements must also become Christ's blood as a consequence. But Bonaventure cannot accept even this last use of the distinction between the negative and affirmative powers in circumcision. Any grace that rectifies defects in the soul, he argues, must also make the soul more inclined to do good things, just as light cannot remove the darkness from the air without illuminating it. Bonaventure suggests, therefore, that circumcision conferred grace simply, as baptism does, but only in very small amounts, for even a very little grace suffices to remove guilt, whereas more is required to produce noticeable benefits.[56]

Thomas Aquinas reviews three opinions on the efficacy of circumcision in his commentary on the *Sentences*. They are similar to those which Bonaventure reviews. Having rejected all three, Thomas proposes a fourth.[57] The four positions comprise an ascending sequence, with each presenting a higher estimate of the sanctity and efficacy of the sacrament. According to the first, circumcision in itself (*quantum est de se*), aside from the merits of the agent, removed guilt (*culpa*), but only by forgiving the corresponding debt of punishment (*reatus*), without conferring any grace. The recipient was not justified, but his injustice was not imputed to him. Thomas objects that God would not absolve an imputation while the disorder remained. A grace of some sort must have been conferred. According to the second opinion, guilt was removed and grace was conferred, but in different ways. Circumcision removed guilt by its own power (*ex sua virtute*), and in so doing removing an obstacle to grace. Grace followed, therefore, but by virtue not of the circumcision itself (*ex vi circumcisionis*) but rather of divine generosity (*ex divina liberalitate*). Thomas objects that the distinction posited in this theory exists only in the patient and not in the agent. Whereas the expulsion of a form is prior to the reception of a contrary form on the part of the recipient, the agent expels the former by introducing the latter. If God removed guilt through circumcision, therefore, God did so by

---

[56]	Bonaventure, *IV Sent.* 1.2.2.3, resp. (4:43–44).
[57]	Thomas Aquinas, *IV Sent.* 1.4, qu^a 3, resp. (Moos 4:59–61).

conferring grace. According to the third opinion, grace was conferred through circumcision, but it was a grace that had only privative effects and no positive effects. Thomas rejects this opinion on teleological grounds, for circumcision and baptism have the same ultimate purpose: to prepare the subject for salvation. Thomas proposes, therefore, that circumcision conferred grace not only as regards its privative effects – namely, the removal of guilt (*culpa*) and of its debt (*reatus*) – but also as regards some of its positive effects: some, but not all, for the grace of circumcision was more limited in scope than that of baptism.[58] Thomas concedes, nevertheless, that circumcision was designed principally to remove guilt and that it conferred grace only as a consequence (*ex consequenti*).[59]

Thomas rejects his early theory when he returns to the question in his *Summa theologiae*. Here, too, Thomas reviews three positions before proposing a fourth. According to the first, circumcision removed sin without conferring grace. But that is impossible because remission of sins can only occur through and as a result of grace. According to the second opinion, circumcision conferred a grace that remitted sin without having any positive effects. Thomas rejects this position on two grounds: first, because circumcision and baptism have the same ultimate end; second, because in respect of formal causality positive effects naturally precede privative ones, for a form can remove a defect only by imparting some new form. According to third opinion, circumcision conferred some but not all positive effects (unlike baptism, which confers all of them). In particular, circumcision enabled the subject to attain eternal life, but it did not wholly suppress inherited concupiscence or even enable the subject to obey all the precepts of the law. Thomas confesses that he himself used to hold this opinion, but he rejects it now because it fails to do justice to the boundlessness of God's love. Even a minimal grace has unlimited scope, and a little charity is more pleasing to God than great cupidity is displeasing. Thomas concludes that circumcision and baptism confer the same grace but in different ways, for only baptism confers grace through its own power (*ex virtute ipsius*) as an instrument of Christ's Passion, and only baptism confers a character, which is a sign of the subject's incorporation into the body of Christ (Rom 4:11). Circumcision under the Old Law could not work in that way because it preceded the Passion. It conferred grace, therefore, not by its own power (*ex virtute circumcisionis*) but through faith in the future passion (*ex virtute fidei passionis Christi*).

From the perspective attained through these complicated inquiries into sacramental grace and the efficacy of circumcision, the options regarding conjugal grace became clearer and the old preventive model seemed at best difficult to sustain. One could hardly argue that the sacrament of marriage corrected a defect without conferring any positive benefit, for the only way to remove a defect in a subject was to inform the subject with the contrary benefit. Nor was it reasonable to

---

[58] See also ibid., ad 1–2 (61).   [59] Ibid., ad 1 (61).

maintain that marriage today was not supernaturally sanctifying in any way, since even the sacraments of the Old Law were sanctifying. One could still argue that marriage sanctified but did so only *ex opere operantis*, as did any good deed, or that its chief effect was the prevention and not the remission of sin, but then one might have to concede that marriage under the New Law was less efficacious than circumcision had been under the Old Law. Moreover, this theory would imply that marriage was not univocally one of the seven sacraments: a position that was becoming untenable among theologians during the second quarter of the thirteenth century.

15.2.4 *Theories of sacramental causality*

The theories reviewed earlier did not presuppose any particular theory of sacramental causality, for there was no consensus as to how the sacraments caused or "contained" grace during the medieval period. The distinction between *ex opere operantis* and *ex opere operato* efficacy had more to do with *what* caused grace than with *how* it was caused. The notion of *ex opere operato* efficacy brought together a merely negative concept with a typical practice and an image. First, this efficacy was not a result of the subject's work, intention, or prior merit. Second, the efficacy was congruent with practices of dispensation and reception, in which the subject received the sacrament from a minister. Third, one might validly imagine the power as being somehow contained in the sacrament, as a medicine is contained in a medicine bottle. It was easiest to imagine the sacrament as a container if one could identify it with some material stuff, such as bread, wine, oil, or water, or with a formal invocation.

Thirteenth-century theologians distinguished among three standard theories of sacramental causality, each of which was designed to show how a created, material cause could bring about a supernatural, spiritual effect.[60] According the first theory, the immediate effect of a sacrament is a quality of the soul: the character in baptism, confirmation, and orders, and some equivalent *ornatus* ("adornment") in the other sacraments. The *ornatus* disposes the soul to receive sanctifying grace directly from God. A Franciscan, William of Melitona, proposed the most elaborate version of this theory.[61] According to the second theory, which William of Auvergne and Bonaventure preferred, a sacrament has no power of its own to confer grace, for a material thing cannot cause a spiritual effect. Instead, God consistently uses the occasion of the sacrament to infuse grace directly by virtue of the sacrament's institution and through a certain covenant, so that from the perspective of the recipient the sacrament can be regarded as the means *sine qua non* of the grace.[62] According to

---

[60] I. Rosier-Catach, *La parole efficace* (Paris, 2004), 99 ff.
[61] K. F. Lynch, "Texts Illustrating the Causality of the Sacraments from William of Melitona," *Franciscan Studies* 17 (1957): 238–72.
[62] W. J. Courtney, "The King and the Leaden Coin," *Traditio* 28 (1972): 185–209. I. Rosier-Catach, "Signes sacramentels et signes magiques: Guillaume d'Auvergne et la théorie de

the third theory, developed by Thomas Aquinas, the sacrament is an instrumental cause of grace. God uses material means to bring about a spiritual effect somewhat in the way that a craftsman uses an adze to carve a bench, or that a writer uses a pen to write a manuscript. The sacramental power is "transient," that is, it only passes through the instrument, whereas it is inherent in the primary agent.[63]

By time of the Counter-Reformation, William of Melitona's theory had fallen into desuetude, and versions of the other two held the field. The Dominicans adhered to an exaggerated version of Thomas's instrumental theory, insisting on "physical causality." The Franciscans adhered to a theory of "moral causality," which was in effect covenantal causality construed as instrumental causality.[64] The possibilities had been more fluid during the thirteenth century, when theologians could still resort to the various theories opportunistically. Thus, regardless of which theory they defended when dealing with the question *ex professo*, medieval theologians posited institutions, dispositions, covenants, or instruments in an *ad hoc* manner, whenever and however these seemed to shed light on the workings of a sacrament or to solve a particular problem or objection. In the case of marriage, many theologians, including Thomas Aquinas and his Dominican followers, argued that the marriage bond, established by the spouses themselves, disposed the spouses to receive divine grace in the manner of an *ornatus*. Many held, too, that the primary efficient cause of the sacrament of marriage itself was not the spouses' act of mutual consent but the original institution of the sacrament by God, in relation to which the spouses' consent was a secondary or instrumental cause.

15.3 THEORIES OF CONJUGAL GRACE

15.3.1 *Alexander of Hales*

Alexander inverted the order in which theologians considered the efficacy of marriage as a sacrament. Hitherto, theologians had assumed that marriage lacked the efficacy of the other sacraments of the New Law, solving the apparent contradiction by holding that marriage was not a sacrament of the New Law in the proper sense. Alexander reasoned, on the contrary, that because marriage was a sacrament of the New Law, it necessarily conferred grace in some way. To his mind, the question was not whether marriage conferred some grace that it signified, but what

pacte," in F. Morenzoni and J.-Y. Tilliette, *Autour de Guillaime d'Auvergne* (Turnhout, 2005), 93–144.

[63] P. L. Reynolds, "Efficient Causality and Instrumentality in Thomas Aquinas's Theology of the Sacraments," in Ginther and Steel, *Essays in Medieval Philosophy and Theology* (Aldershot, 2005), 67–84. D. Van den Eynde, "Stephen Langton and Hugh of St. Cher on the Causality of the Sacraments," *Franciscan Studies* 11.3–4 (1951): 141–55, shows that the theory originated in the work of those two authors.

[64] J. Pohle, *The Sacraments*, vol. 1 (St Louis, 1915), 152–54. B. Leeming, *Principles of Sacramental Theology*, 2nd edition (London, 1960), 334–36.

that grace was and how it was conferred. Alexander's extant works contain two different theories about the efficacy of marriage, one in his commentary on the *Sentences*, known as the *Glossa*, and the other in his disputed questions on marriage. In the *Glossa*, Alexander argues that the interior act of mutual consent, which the spouses express in their wedding vows, establishes a disposition for conjugal grace. In the disputed questions, Alexander argues that conjugal grace enhances the remedial and unitive benefits that belong naturally to marriage, since grace perfects nature.

15.3.1.1 Glossa in librum quartum Sententiarum

The theory of the *Glossa* is complicated and subtle, and it is hard to follow and to piece together. It is in the tradition of Hugh of Saint-Victor, with an emphasis on conjugal love as a divine gift, but it incorporates the notion of a sacramental disposition. Alexander assumes that marriage, like any sacrament of the New Law, must cause some grace that it signifies, and that this gift must be a particular grace that is proper to the sacrament, such as the charity that unites the members of the church to Christ as their head.[65] But there are problems. Marriage is not peculiar to the church. How can one maintain that marriage causes the charity that unites the church to Christ when unbelievers can marry?[66] Moreover, Alexander concedes that marriage unlike the other sacraments of the New Law does not confer sanctifying grace in and of itself (*quantum in se est*). That is one reason why marriage is usually discussed last in treatises on the sacraments, Alexander explains, despite the nobility of what it signifies:

> ... the other sacraments confer spiritual grace or an increase of grace [*augmentum gratiae*] in and of themselves [*quantum est de se*] if they are received worthily — and I am referring here to sanctifying grace [*gratia gratum faciens*]. But this sacrament does not confer sanctifying grace even on those who receive it worthily. It is for this reason that it is placed after the other sacraments, as the one that has least efficacy in disposing for grace, although it is greater [than the others] in signifying.[67]

Alexander goes on to explain that if the sacraments were ranked as signs, marriage would come high up on the list, for it signifies the union of Christ and the church and the union of natures in Christ, and there is nothing greater in all of creation. But the most salient feature of the seven sacraments qua sacraments is their efficacy, or their power to sanctify, and in this respect marriage is the least among them and is fittingly placed last.[68]

---

[65] Alexander of Hales, *Glossa in IV Sent.* 26.7f (462).   [66] *IV Sent.* 26.7b (459).

[67] *IV Sent.* 26.2a (445–46).

[68] Ibid. (446/5–7): "Cum ergo sacramentum habeat in se quod sit signum et causa, plus habet ex eo quod est causa quam ex eo quod signum quod est [ultimum] sacramentum." The Quaracchi editors insert the word *ultimum* (placed in square brackets earlier), but it should be

Alexander denies only that marrying does not confer grace in and of itself (*quantum est de se*), and not that it fails to confer grace in any way.[69] Other passages in the *Glossa* show that Alexander did consider marriage to be a means of sanctifying grace in *some* manner. Tacitly assuming that the spouses cause their own marriage, Alexander argues that their joining is the *sacramentum et res*, which disposes the subjects to receive grace (the *res tantum*) from God. Alexander is cautious about attributing any objective sacramental efficacy to marriage because the sacrament depends on the agency of the participants.

As we have seen, Alexander assumes that any sacrament can be parsed into three components: the outward appearance, which is what the term "sacrament" usually denotes (the *sacramentum tantum*); the remote, ultimate signified reality (the *res tantum*); and a mediating component (the *sacramentum et res*). The *sacramentum et res* is a signified reality in relation to the outward appearance, but it is a sacrament in relation to the ultimate reality, being in some sense its sign, although the notion of a non-apparent sign was obscure. In the *Glossa*, therefore, Alexander parses the sacrament of matrimony as follows: The *sacramentum tantum*, or "visible appearance of an invisible grace," is the spouses' exterior verbal expression of consent, which is the form of the sacrament. The *sacramentum et res* is the interior consent or joining of wills, which their words express. The third component, the *res tantum*, is the joining of the faithful soul with Christ, or of the church's members with Christ as their head. Alexander compares the structure of marriage to that of eucharist. In one sense, what is most properly called the sacrament in eucharist, insofar as that term connotes mystery and secrecy as well as sanctity, is not the species of bread and wine but the true body of Christ under the appearance of those species, for the true body is what disposes the subject to receive grace.[70]

What chiefly distinguishes marriage from other sacraments of the New Law, according to Alexander, is the fact that its *sacramentum et res*, which disposes the subject to receive sanctifying grace, is a work of human beings (*opus hominis*). But marriage is not entirely alone in that respect, for the same is true of penance, at least when considered from a certain point of view. That is one reason why neither marriage nor penance has something that can readily be identified as matter, such as water, oil, bread, or wine.[71] Following Hugh of Saint-Victor, Alexander argues that the other sacraments involve external matter because they were instituted after the fall, when human beings had to be restored through exterior sensible things. Marriage and penance were instituted before the fall, when human beings were

---

disregarded, for the observation is about the sacraments in general, not about marriage in particular. Cf. ibid., 26.7c (460/17): "Sacramentum autem a sanctitate dicitur sacramentum."

[69] See K. F. Lynch, "The Theory of Alexander of Hales on the Efficacy of the Sacrament of Matrimony," *Franciscan Studies* 11 (1951): 69–139, at 99–103. Lynch argues that in Alexander's view marriage, like the sacraments of the Old Law, sanctified or conferred grace only *ex opere operantis*, but Lynch misses the role of the *sacramentum et res* as a dispositive cause.

[70] *IV Sent.* 26.5m (455).   [71] *IV Sent.* 26.5a (450).

still in touch with their inner natures. These sacraments are rooted not in any external stuff, therefore, but in an interior mental act that is outwardly expressed. In marriage, the spoken words of consent express the spouses' inward consent. In penance, the penitent's contrite words and actions express inward contrition. Whereas the subject is wholly a recipient of God's work in the other sacraments, receiving it if he or she puts no obstacle in its way, the subject actively cooperates with God in marriage and penance, albeit not in conferring grace but only in establishing the disposition for grace. Whereas the participants receive the other sacraments from a minister, therefore, the participants bring about marriage and penance themselves by cooperating with God.[72]

When Alexander asks whether marriage, like the other sacraments of the New Law, is a cause of what it signifies, he reviews two solutions to the standard objections but finds both inadequate. Some say that only the sacraments that were instituted under the New Law cause the grace that they signify, whereas marriage already existed even before the Old Law. Alexander counters that the same logic should apply to penance, which already existed as contrition under the Old Law. Again, some say that marriage causes a grace that it signifies, but only by virtue of the priestly blessing, which is peculiar to the church. Alexander counters that the blessing is not a sacrament but only a sacramental.[73] He does not say why this is a fatal objection, but his point is presumably that sacramentals are inessential. The blessing is not necessary for a valid Christian marriage, which is what is counted as one of the seven sacraments.

Alexander's own solution is predicated on a quotation that he ascribes to Augustine, although in fact it comes from Peter Lombard: "Marriage is a sign of a spiritual joining and of the love of wills [*dilectio animorum*] by which the spouses ought to be joined to each other."[74] The outward act of marrying is a cause as well as a sign of the love or spiritual joining that ought to unite the spouses. Moreover, that conjugal love may, with God's help, become Christian charity, which is a species of grace. But the manner in which they contract marriage is critical, for that act is the *sacramentum tantum*. If the spouses have an appropriately spiritual motive for plighting their troth, and if they have no dishonorable motives – in other words, if they intend to remain chaste and faithful to each other and do not plan to avoid

---

[72] *IV Sent.* 26.5f (452).

[73] *IV Sent.* 26.7b (459). The "sacramentals" of medieval theology were chiefly ancillary rites and symbols involved in performance of the seven sacraments, whereas today the term usually denotes free-standing but secondary rites and symbols available to the laity, such as candles, holy water, and holy medals.

[74] Ibid. (459–60). The quotation is from Peter Lombard, *Sent.* IV, 26.6.5 (421), where Peter's remark follows immediately after an authentic quotation from Augustine — hence Alexander's mistake.

begetting and raising children for God – then their interior consent "disposes [them] to the spiritual union of charity, which the Lord gives to those who consent worthily."[75]

Without denying that marriage might have had something of that efficacy even before the advent of Jesus Christ or that it may do so even among the infidels of his own day, Alexander reasons that the efficacy is fully realized only under the New Law. That is why an infidel marriage may be dissolved through the Pauline Privilege, for the recalcitrant spouse commits spiritual adultery. Moreover, Christ added a "certain sanctification" to marriage by being present at Cana (John 2:1–10) and by instituting the good of sacrament when he confirmed the insolubility of marriage in the gospels (Matt 19:5–6, etc.). By virtue of that sanctification, a certain "increase of grace" (*augmentum gratiae*) is conferred on spouses who "consent worthily and remain in charity."[76] Alexander assumes that there is some intimate relationship between the sacramental grace of marriage and its inseparability, although he does not explain in the *Glossa* what this relationship is.

In sum, Alexander argues in the *Glossa* that when the spouses marry, their interior consent of wills, which is expressed in and enhanced by their verbal consent, both signifies grace and disposes the subjects to receive that grace in the manner of an *ornatus* or *sacramentum et res*. Conjugal grace takes the form of mutual charity, which supernaturally elevates human love as grace perfects nature. Although both the consent of their wills and the spouses' conjugal love are human acts, spouses who receive the sacrament worthily by consenting with godly intentions also receive divine charity as a gratuitous gift, and this charity enhances their mutual love. But marriage cannot properly be said to confer sanctifying grace in and of itself (*quantum in se est*) because the spouses themselves establish the disposition for grace, whereas the recipients of the other sacraments, with the possible exception of penance, receive the disposition passively from the action of a minister and from extraneous form and matter.

15.3.1.2 Quaestiones disputatae antequam esset frater

As in the *Glossa*, Alexander assumes in the disputed questions that marriage must be a cause of grace because it is a sacrament of the New Law. But a sacrament causes what it signifies. Marriage is a sacrament of the union between Christ and the church, who are joined both by love and by the "conformity of nature" (i.e., through the incarnation). It is obvious that marriage does not cause the incarnation, and the

---

[75] *IV Sent.* 26.7b (459/26–460/4). Note Alexander's emphasis on the initial act of consent, rather than on the relationship of marriage itself.

[76] *IV Sent.* 26.7c (460): "... ratione cuius potest in dignum consentientibus et existentibus in caritate conferri augmentum gratiae."

love that joins the church to Christ is the Holy Spirit, and nothing created can cause something divine.[77] One might counter that marriage betroths the individual soul to God, but that will not suffice, Alexander argues, for all the sacraments do that, whereas each sacrament has been instituted to meet a peculiar need by bestowing its own proper gift. If one had to pick out a particular sacrament as the one most apt to betroth the subject to God, it would be baptism.[78]

In response, Alexander argues that marriage has a dual identity, since it belongs even now, in different respects, both among the sacraments of the Old Law and among those of the New Law. As a sacrament of the Old Law, marriage does not cause what it signifies. It is a sacrament of the twofold union between Christ and the church, which it does not cause. But marriage as a sacrament of the New Law does cause something that it signifies, namely, the grace of "conquering or lessening the corruption of concupiscence, which is a penalty for original sin."[79]

How does marriage signify that grace? Alexander explains that marriage by its very nature raises human beings above carnal corruption. The begetting of children to worship God elevates the spirit, and both the rendering of the conjugal debt and the avoidance of fornication elevate the will (*animus*). Because those are causal benefits that belong naturally to marriage, marriage is apt to signify a grace that achieves the same ends more effectively, supernaturally conquering or lessening the corruption of concupiscence. As a sacrament of the New Law, therefore, marriage causes this grace in those who receive the sacrament worthily. The advent of Jesus Christ either established or greatly enhanced this supernatural efficacy. The grace of marriage became greater and more powerful because the union of divine and human natures in Christ raised human nature as a whole above carnal corruption.[80]

Alexander summarizes this theory in a three-part narrative: Marriage signified the dual conformity between Christ and the church from the very beginning, but it has never caused that union. After the fall, marriage became a remedy and even a "vessel of medicine," but largely through natural means. It retained that natural efficacy under the Old Law and even under the New Law. Finally, however, marriage became in addition "a cause effecting a grace that it signifies" with the advent of Jesus Christ, when the grace flowing from Christ's incarnation and Passion enhanced the remedial benefits of marriage.[81]

15.3.2 *William of Auvergne*

William of Auvergne presents a layered account of marriage, with sacramental grace surmounting at least three levels of conjugal goods. Whereas the prior levels pertain

---

[77] *Quaestio disputata* 57, disp. 1, m. 4, §§18–19 (1103); §23 (1104).   [78] Ibid., §22 (1104).
[79] Ibid., §24 (1104–05).   [80] Ibid.   [81] Q. 57, disp. 1, m. 5, §28 (1106).

to marriage itself as a divinely instituted human partnership, the final level requires in addition the nuptial blessing. At the first level, marriage is based on the difference between male and female and on the coming together of the sexes to procreate. Marriage is the human version of something that belongs properly to all living things. At the second level, marriage has the sanctity of distinctively human benefits, which transcend the natural order: the chaste intention of the spouses when they marry, which drives out turpitude; the begetting, raising, and education of children; and the sharing of responsibilities and burdens, for whereas the wife is the natural homemaker, the husband must not only provide for his wife but also give her moral guidance and, when necessary, correct and chastise her.[82] At the third level, marriage is a sacrament in the broad sense of the term, that is, "a sacred sign of the spiritual marriage that ought to exist between God and the human soul." This is sanctity in properly so called.[83] Finally, marriage may receive in addition a "grace of sanctity," but only from a priest's prayer of benediction at the wedding: a grace that protects the spouses from the contamination of lust and from the "allurements of the flesh." Only the last level prompts William to regard marriage not only as a sacrament but also as one of the sacraments of the church.[84]

William's account of the nuptial blessing owes little either to contemporaneous developments in sacramental theology or to the hylomorphic theory of sacramental composition. Instead, he construes the blessing as a prayer. Just as it would be a sin to eat without asking a priest to bless the meal if a priest is present, he argues, so it is a sin to marry without a priest's blessing if it is available. Echoing the decretal ascribed to Pope Evaristus, William argues that persons who marry without the blessing when they have no valid excuse should be regarded rather as adulterers than as husband and wife, and their children as illegitimate, for prayer is needed to protect the spouses from the temptations of the flesh and to ensure that there is peace and harmony in their relationship.[85] William cites as precedents the holy women in Scripture who prayed for fecundity, such as Sarah, Rebecca, and Elizabeth (Gen 18, 25; Luke 1). He points out that it is customary to pray whenever one faces physical or spiritual dangers. Couples face both when they marry: the physical danger that attends childbirth, and the spiritual danger of lust. A devout person prays even before planting or grafting a tree. How much more should we pray over the coming together of the two branches of human nature to produce a single tree? If it is customary to pray when laying the foundations of a building, how much more should we beseech God for help when laying the foundations of the spiritual building that is constructed from a man and a woman?[86]

---

[82] William of Auvergne, *De sacramento matrimonii*, C. 6, 518bG–519aA.
[83] Ibid., 519aA–B.   [84] Ibid., 520aG–H.   [85] Ibid., 520aH.   [86] Ibid., 520bA–F.

William inquires into what he calls the "sacramental power" (*virtus sacramentalis*) of marriage. Is there really such a power: one that marriage possesses "sacramentally," or inasmuch as it is a sacrament? In other words, does marriage confer grace? And, if so, what does conjugal grace do? To clarify the question, William posits three sources of sanctity in marriage: contrariety, merit, and sacramental power. The first consists in the capacity of marriage by its very nature to exclude sodomy, prostitution, and promiscuity. This is the "essential power" of marriage (*virtus essentialis*). Second, spouses who are faithfully committed to their marriages, who are not led astray by carnal allurements, who faithfully bear the burdens of marriage, and who seek to serve God in this as in all things, deserve merit for their deeds. But neither the contrariety nor the merit of marriage is properly sacramental. Is there an additional, fully sacramental virtue?

William offers empirical evidence to show that marriage can confer a supernatural power that affords "much relief against the ardor of carnal concupiscence." He has acquired this information not from hearsay or gossip, he says, but from firsthand reports, and with the divinely bestowed authority of the sacrament of confession. He is acquainted with young husbands who are well fed, live in luxury, and married to pretty women, yet who are sexually cool toward their wives and frigid toward other women. He has heard the same from women in the confessional. Now, such a power, William argues, cannot be explained by contrariety and merit alone. "We do not know to what else we can attribute so great and so marvelous a gift," William says, "other than to the sacramental power of marriage." Because this power is supernatural and surpasses the natural and moral benefits of marriage, William reasons that no marriage possesses it without the nuptial blessing.[87]

15.3.3 *Albertus Magnus*

Albert was the first major theologian to compose a scholastic *quaestio* as to whether marriage conferred grace. He outlines three plausible positions.[88] According to the first, which Albert ascribes to Peter Lombard, Praepositinus, and William of Auxerre, marriage does not confer any grace. Consequently, it is a sacrament only in a broad and secondary sense of the term (*per prius et posterius*), since the sacraments properly so called cause the grace that they signify. According to the second position, marriage confers a certain grace: some supernatural assistance that is "externally attached" to the sacrament and overcomes concupiscence by preventing it from going beyond the bounds of the honesty and the goods of marriage. This is a grace that enables the spouses only to retreat from sin, and not to advance toward the

---

[87] C. 9, 524bH–525aC
[88] Albertus Magnus, *IV Sent.* 26.14, q. 2, resp. (Borgnet 40:122b–23a).

good.[89] The proponents of this position argue plausibly (*probabiliter*) that when the "fathers" said that marriage did not confer grace, they meant that it conferred a grace that was not "ordered *to* the good but only *from* evil." Marriage is incapable of advancing the good, according to this position, not because of any intrinsic defect, but rather because of the burdens and distractions that are attached to it, which St Paul describes (1 Cor 7:32–35). According to the third position, marriage confers a grace that not only defends the spouses against evil but also promotes the goods that all spouses ought to achieve in marriage. As well as mitigating concupiscence, this grace helps the spouses to support each other, to collaborate, and to raise their children religiously.

Albert declines to say which of the three positions is correct, but he confesses that the second "pleases me more than the first," and he describes the proponents of the third position as "sufficiently expert" (*satis periti*), concluding that this position, too, "is very probable." Elsewhere, though, Albert consistently assumes that marriage confers sacramental grace in the ordinary sense (the third position). The division between the second and third positions does not correspond exactly to any actual division of opinion found in extant writings from the period, although Bonaventure arguably held something like the second position. Albert may have been describing opinions that have not survived in the literature, or even positions that came up in discussion with his students, but it is more likely that he devised the schema himself to cover the range of possibilities. The schoolmen preferred to remain aloof from *ad hominem* engagement with their contemporaries, and their reviews of opinions are not so much descriptions of what their colleagues were actually saying as analyses of the theoretical possibilities that both textual tradition and current debate had brought to light.

Albert can see nothing in marriage that prevents it from conferring grace. Perhaps marriage is "a concession to the infirm," but this infirmity is not one that leaves someone prostrate but rather one that prevents the person from going to greater heights. Marriage is a lesser good, not a lesser evil. There is no reason, therefore, why marriage should not be a means of grace and even of supernatural merit (*praemium*).[90] Albert concedes that the salutary efficacy of marriage is peculiar among the sacraments, but he does not interpret this difference as deficiency. The point is not that marriage confers grace only in some lesser or deficient manner, in his view, but that marriage functions not only as a sacrament of the New Law but also in other ways. Albert draws on two of Alexander's insights to elucidate this position. He argues that conjugal grace enhances or elevates the salutary benefits that belong naturally to marriage, whereas most of the other sacraments are efficacious only as means of grace, being otherwise merely figurative. (Eucharist, for example, does not

---

[89] Ibid. (122b): "... et secundum illos oportet dicere, quod secundum matrimonium sit gratia illa, vel aliquid ei conjunctum exterius, quod mitigat concupiscentiam, ne ferveat ultra nuptiarum honestatem et bona matrimonii."

[90] *IV Sent.* 26.14, qu. 2, ad 2 (123).

suffice as a meal, nor baptism as washing.) But marriage shares some peculiarities of this sort with penance. These two sacraments differ from the others inasmuch as each is based on an action contributed by the recipient of the sacrament. In that sense, both sacraments sanctify not *ex opero operato* but only *ex opero operantis* (Section 14.6.2). Albert characterizes the supernatural effect of marriage as an interior grace that enables the spouses to master concupiscence. Whatever turpitude remains despite that remedy is shameful, but it is only a *malum poenae*, not a *malum culpae*.[91] Albert never rules out the possibility that the conjugal grace may also enhance the good. Indeed, in the *De matrimonio*, explaining how marriage is a sacrament of the New Law, Albert says that conjugal grace "flows from the actual [rather than prefigured] union of natures in Christ," and that it "promotes the goods of marriage and the mitigation of concupiscence."[92]

Albert points out that all the sacraments are remedial. This is not peculiar to the sacrament of marriage, for every sacrament heals a specific wound or disease. It is their remedial aspect that distinguishes the sacramental graces from sanctifying grace (*gratia gratum faciens*), the infused virtues, the gifts of the Holy Spirit. If there were no sin, sacramental grace would be redundant and there would be no sacraments, but there would still be virtues and gifts. Each infused virtue entails a readiness to perform a certain meritorious action.[93] But a movement from evil is *ipso facto* a movement toward the good, for it is a motion from one term to the other, as if between two extremes. Consequently, grace is a single "moving form" (*forma movens*) that brings about both changes, which are really identical: the motion toward good is the same as the motion away from evil. Whereas the virtues expel the disease of sin by *contrarietas* alone (i.e., through being incompatible with them), the sacraments concentrate on the disease by relieving the recipient from spiritual pain, by healing, and by fostering recovery.[94]

Albert likens marriage to a "twofold medicine" against the disease of concupiscence, which infects sexual intercourse. The Lombard only explained how marriage works externally, by containing concupiscence within the honorableness of "exterior divine and human laws"[95] and by preventing it from leading the subject into ruin. But marriage also works from within, conferring on those who marry in the faith of Christ an interior sacramental grace that mitigates concupiscence by abating the *fomes*. Albert finds proof of this interior power in Tobit 6:16–17, where the angel Raphael warns Tobias to fend off the devil by approaching his bride chastely, not like those newlyweds who "shut out God from themselves and from their mind and abandon themselves to their lust, like the horse and the mule that do not have understanding." Working together, the exterior and interior benefits of marriage

---

[91] *IV Sent.* 26.1, q. 2, ad 1; ad 3 (123).
[92] Albertus Magnus, *De matrimonio* 1.6, resp. (Cologne 26:159a).
[93] *IV Sent.* 1.4, resp. (Borgnet 29:12a)
[94] *IV Sent.* 1.4, quaest., "Si dicas . . ." (11b–12a); ibid., ad quaest., ad 2 (12b).
[95] An allusion to Modestinus's definition of marriage, *Dig.* 23.2.1

remove sexual vice, leaving only the spontaneous effects of turpitude, which are a penalty for original sin (i.e., *malum poenae*, not a *malum culpae*). Marriage under the New Law still has exterior salutary benefits such as prevention, excuse, compensation, containment, and legal or customary boundaries, but it also confers an "interior grace."[96]

The sacraments derive their interior strength from specific conformity with Christ's passion.[97] Like all the sacraments of the New Law, marriage owes its efficacy to a certain conformity with Jesus Christ, and especially with Christ crucified (cf. Plate 2). Albert concedes that marriage only signifies and cannot "contain" the union between Christ and the church, but there is no reason to assume that a sacrament contains *everything* that it signifies. To save the principle that all the sacraments confer what they signify, Albert distinguishes between the uncontained signified and the contained signified of marriage. Marriage both signifies and contains the grace that mitigates concupiscence, whereas it only signifies the union between Christ and the church.[98] But there is a close relationship between the two *significata*, for the grace of marriage flows "from the betrothal of human nature with the divine nature in the Person of Christ," a betrothal that was fully realized on the Cross.[99] Each of the sacraments "configures" the members of the church to Christ as head in its own special way, and each sacrament "draws strength" from Christ. It was on the Cross, Albert explains, that Christ stretched out his arms to embrace the church and gave up his life for her. It was on the Cross that blood and water, the tokens of eucharist and baptism, flowed from Christ's side, just as Adam's wife was made from his side as he slept. Whereas penance joins the faithful to the suffering Christ (*Christus patiens*), and extreme unction to Christ rising from the dead (*Christus resurgens*), marriage unites them to "Christ betrothing the church to himself, with his blood as the *arrha*." Albert cites Exodus 4:25 as proof: "A bloody bridegroom art thou to me."[100]

15.3.4 *Bonaventure*

Bonaventure's treatment of marriage and sacramental grace is difficult to interpret and seems inconsistent. On the one hand, he affirms that marriage itself confers grace in the same way as every other sacrament of the New Law, even apart from the effect of the nuptial blessing, which is only a sacramental. On the other hand, Bonaventure emphasizes the role of the nuptial blessing, maintaining that marriage belongs properly among the *sacraments of the church* only inasmuch as a priest has

---

[96] *IV Sent.* 26.8, resp.; ad 1 (Borgnet 30:107). *De matrimonio* 1.6, resp. (159a/18–20, 28–29). On the two kinds of turpitude (*turpe poenae, turpe culpae*), see *IV Sent.* 26.11, ad 5 (114b–15a).

[97] *IV Sent.* 1.1, ad 1 (Borgnet 29:4b–5a).

[98] *IV Sent.* 26.14, ad 2 (Borgnet 30:121b); q. 1, ad 3 (122a–b). *De matrimonio* 1.6, resp. (159a).

[99] *IV Sent.* 26.5, resp. (103b); ad q. 3 (123b). Cf. Plate 2.

[100] *IV Sent.* 1.2, resp. (Borgnet 29:9a).

blessed it. Absent the blessing, marriage is a sacrament but not a sacrament of the church, and it only prevents sin without conferring any grace that reforms the soul.

Bonaventure seems both to affirm and to deny that marriage itself, absent the nuptial blessing, confers grace. The only way to reconcile the two ways of speaking is to assume that "grace" is equivocal. Perhaps when Bonaventure says that marriage itself does not confer grace, he is referring to sanctifying grace, whereas when he affirms that it does confer grace, he is referring to a remedial, preternatural grace (*gratia gratis data*). Some passages support this interpretation, but it does involve an element of conjecture.

Bonaventure explicitly argues elsewhere that the term "grace" is equivocal. Understood in its strictest sense, he explains, the term denotes sanctifying grace (*gratia gratum faciens*), which makes the soul pleasing (*grata*) to God and is the beginning of ultimate glory. Grace in this narrow sense is to be distinguished both from preternatural assistance (*gratia gratis data*) and from future glory. But one may also use the term "grace" broadly, including preternatural assistance or future glory or both.[101] It seems, then, that Bonaventure attempted to sustain a version of the preventive theory of conjugal efficacy, but that he attributed some of the preventive power of marriage to *gratia gratis data* while attributing sanctifying grace in marriage exclusively to the priestly blessing. But this position seems inconsistent with Bonaventure's treatment of the grace of circumcision, where he argues that any grace that prevents evil must also do good.[102]

Bonaventure maintains that the sacrament of marriage exhibits the same structure as the other sacraments insofar as an outward act brings about an interior change, which unites the recipient more closely to Christ. The external act of consent not only expresses and signifies the interior act of consent, Bonaventure argues: it also causes the interior act by enhancing it, just as the outward expression of contrition enhances the inward act of contrition. The interior joining in turn causes the union of the soul to Christ and to God "in some way" (*quodam modo*), for the more the members of the church are charitably united with each other, the more they are united with Christ. But that is the reverse of what happens in eucharist, where the sacrament directly unites the recipients to Christ, who become more united with each other as a consequence. Unlike the other sacraments, marriage directly betroths people not to God but to each other. Nevertheless, that betrothal in turn signifies union with God, and a grace is given with literal marriage to make the resulting betrothal or union with God more effective.[103]

Marriage confers such benefits, Bonaventure argues, only if the spouses receive the nuptial blessing. Grace in the proper sense of the term not only prevents sins but also remits them by liberating the subject from the guilt (*culpa*) of sins that have

[101] Bonaventure, *II Sent.* 27, dub. 1 (2:669a–670b). [102] *IV Sent.* 1.2.2.3, resp. (4:43–44). [103] *IV Sent.* 26.2.2, ad 1; ad 3 (668b, 669a).

already been committed, and even from the sequelae of those sins. Moreover, whatever takes away guilt must *ipso facto* replace it with positive good, especially in the form of virtue, as Bonaventure argues when he discusses the sacramental effect of circumcision.[104] But marriage itself, absent the blessing, is not a remedy to sin in that sense. Instead, it only *prevents* sins that would otherwise occur:

> Something can be a remedy against sin in two ways: either by liberating from a sin that *has been* committed, and this is through a grace that is conferred in it; or by liberating from a sin that *would otherwise* be committed. Marriage is a remedy of the latter sort, for many infirm men would burn with lust if they did not have wives, whereas by knowing their wives they escape the burning up of the flesh. There is no need for grace to be given in such a remedy for it to work, although it is still possible for someone to merit in the [sexual] act.[105]

Marriage itself confers a remedy only by preventing sins that would otherwise occur, or by enabling the subject to evade obstacles to salvation, and not by reforming the soul and making it more pleasing to God. Bonaventure holds that grace is not necessary for such a remedy. But one should remember that the term "grace" is equivocal. Broadly interpreted, it includes preternatural grace, or *gratia gratis data*, which is not the grace that remits guilt. In the quoted passage, I suggest, what Bonaventure attributes exclusively to the nuptial blessing is sanctifying grace.

Like Alexander, Bonaventure argues that the sacramentality of marriage elevates its natural properties, but he attributes such perfection not to marriage itself but to the nuptial blessing. Whereas unbelievers marry to beget legitimate children, he argues, believers beget these children to worship God. Similarly, whereas marriage always confers preventive remedy through its intrinsic, natural structure as a human contract, it also confers sanctifying grace on believers – but only by virtue of the nuptial blessing:

> [Marriage] serves as a remedy because it excuses marital coitus from guilt, and also because a grace is given to remit concupiscence *by reason of the benediction joined to it*. Among infidels who know their wives with marital affection, there is excuse from guilt but no gift of grace, whereas among believers there is both.[106]

Marriage confers a grace of remission from sin, therefore, which is grace in the proper sense, *only* when it is blessed by a priest.

Bonaventure distinguishes between marriage as a sacrament of the law of nature and marriage as a sacrament of the church. The former is remedial even among

---

[104] *IV Sent.* 1.2.2.3, resp. (43–44).
[105] *IV Sent.* 26.2.3, ad 4c (4:670b). My translation of the last sentence is rather free. The Latin reads: "et in tali quantum ad usum non est necesse gratiam dari, quamvis in actu illo possit homo mereri." Presumably Bonaventure means that grace is not required for the remedy *per se* but is required for the remedial act to be meritorious, for he makes this point explicitly at *IV Sent.* 31.2.1, ad 7 (723b).
[106] *IV Sent.* 39.1.2, resp. (834). Emphasis mine.

heretics. The latter is conferred only among orthodox believers by virtue of the priestly blessing:

> To the objection that the sacraments of the church do not have efficacy among the heretics, it should be said that matrimony is not like the other sacraments. For in the other sacraments a remedy is bestowed against the disease that is already present in the subject [*qui iam inest*], so that a grace is given through them, or an effect of grace, by means of which the soul is cured from the corruption that results from the disease. But in matrimony inasmuch as it is a sacrament of the law of nature, a remedy is given that preserves from guilt lest someone in knowing his wife should sin — although inasmuch as marriage is a sacrament of the church, it may also give a grace to those receiving it worthily because of the annexed benediction. Therefore, because unbelievers do not receive sanctifying grace [*gratia gratum faciens*] or its effects as long as they are in unbelief, the other sacraments do not provide them with a remedy. But this sacrament alone is able to provide a remedy to them, albeit not [in its] perfect [form] but only for the avoidance of evil.[107]

Whereas marriage as a sacrament of the law of nature excuses everyone, whether non-gratuitously or through a merely remedial, preternatural grace, marriage as a sacrament of the church confers in addition a sanctifying grace "on those who receive it worthily"(i.e., *ex opere operato*), but only on believers, and then only by virtue of the attached blessing.

Bonaventure considers marriage to be partly a human contract and civil office and partly a divine sacrament. What divides the latter from the former, in his view, is the benediction. On the one hand, marriage is a consensual contract that entails the temporal and costly burdens of childrearing and so forth, as well as the moral burdens and turpitude of sexual intercourse. It is appropriate to base the consent to marry, therefore, on negotiated terms. A person whose chief motive for consenting to marry is a large dowry would commit a sin, but not that of simony: partly because marriage has a "carnal office" attached it (i.e., sexual intercourse), but chiefly because the contractant is not the minister (*dispensator*) of the sacrament. That honor falls to any priest who blesses the marriage. On the other hand, marriage "receives the aspect [*ratio*][108] of spirituality and grace when the consent is joined to a blessing, wherein the signification of marriage is explicated and sanctification is obtained through the benediction." Any attempt to buy or to sell the nuptial blessing would incur the sin of simony, for it is through the blessing that marriage receives its spirituality (*ratio spiritualis*) and bestows sanctifying grace.[109]

Bonaventure finds evidence of this division between the sacred and profane aspects of marriage in the ancient custom of the Tobias Nights recorded in the

---

[107] *IV Sent.* 39.1.3, ad 3 (836).
[108] A *ratio* may be either a certain concept or understanding of a thing (i.e., what a term signifies) or, as in this case, a cognizable aspect of a thing, i.e., the thing's nature inasmuch as it is conceptualized or regarded in a certain way.
[109] *IV Sent.* 26.2.2, ad 4 (669).

canons. To "separate the precious from the base" (Jer 15:19), the groom does not consummate the marriage on the first night out of respect for the recent blessing. Although the blessing is only "annexed" to marriage as regards signification, Bonaventure argues, it belongs to the "complete being" (*esse completum*) of marriage both inasmuch as marriage has efficacy and inasmuch as it is a sacrament of the church.[110] The phrase "complete being" is common in scholastic discourse. For example, matter, as a component of substance, is commonly said to lack complete being not only because it cannot exist on its own, but also because it receives being passively from its correlative form.[111] Again, the *Summa fratris Alexandri* describes the child who is still being nourished in the mother's womb as being on the way to complete being as a human person (*in productione ad esse completum*).[112] Bonaventure emphasizes that the blessing is only "annexed" or "adjoined" to the sacrament of marriage, for it is not a condition for validity. Nevertheless, an unblessed marriage is incomplete as a sacrament in the same way as a human being without the use of a certain faculty is incomplete as a human being. Without the blessing, the full potential of marriage as a sacrament of the church remains unrealized.

Nevertheless, Bonaventure refutes the opinion that marriage confers grace only by virtue of the blessing that is joined to it when inquires whether marriage confers sacramental grace. On the contrary, marriage itself, apart from the nuptial blessing, must also confer some grace.[113] Bonaventure reviews two opinions before proposing his own. According to the first opinion, marriage is a remedy against lust (*concupiscentia*) but only "through indulgence," and not "through efficacy." Marriage does not diminish the habit of concupiscence, according to this opinion, but it limits the scope of concupiscent acts, for "it is better to marry than to burn" (1 Cor 7:9). To the objection that all the sacraments of the New Law confer grace, the proponents of this position reply that the premise is true only of sacraments that were instituted under the New Law, whereas marriage already existed before the New Law. Without refuting this opinion, Bonaventure goes immediately to the second. According to the second opinion, marriage, like every other sacrament of the New Law, confers a grace on those who receive it worthily and with devotion, but only by virtue of the nuptial blessing attached to it, for God uses the minister's blessing as the occasion to bless the spouses.[114] That seems to be a succinct statement of Bonaventure's own position, but here he rejects it: "But this position seems to be invalid," Bonaventure counters, "because the blessing is a sacramental. If the sacramental is effective, how much more is the sacrament?" Bonaventure is echoing Alexander of Hales, but the

---

[110] Ibid.

[111] For example, Thomas Aquinas, *II Sent.* 12.1.4 (Mandonnet 2:314).

[112] *Summa Fratris Alexandri* I-II, no. 502 (2:719b).

[113] Bonaventure, *IV Sent.* 26.2.2, resp. (668).

[114] Ibid. (668a): "Deus enim eis benedicit ad benedictionem sacerdotis." Bonaventure has in mind the institutional, or covenantal, theory of sacramental grace, whereby the sacrament is the infallible occasion, other things being equal, for God to bestow grace directly.

logic of the abbreviated argument is unclear. Bonaventure himself maintains even in this article that marriage confers a fuller grace, which is more worthy of the name "grace," by virtue of the benediction than it does in its own right. Presumably, then, the force of the comparison – which has the form, "if P, how much more Q" – is rhetorical. Bonaventure is not suggesting that marriage *per se* confers a greater grace than it does by virtue of the benediction. Rather, he means that if we attribute grace to the nuptial blessing, there is even more reason to attribute grace to marriage itself.

Bonaventure proposes the third position as his own:

> it should be said that to those who receive this sacrament, as befits its nature as a sacrament, there may be given a remedy that excuses coitus and causes what would otherwise be a sin not to be a sin or to be a venial sin. This can happen without a gift [*donum*] of grace, and the sacrament had that power immediately after the fall. But now, in the time of the New Law, the sacrament bestows not only that remedy but also some gift of grace [*aliquod gratiae donum*] on those who receive it worthily, that is, on those who from charity are united in consenting to procreate children to worship God.[115]

Like Alexander, Bonaventure assumes that the spouses' intentions at the time of the trothplight is crucial. If the spouses consent with good intentions to an indivisible way of life, they may receive "some gift of grace" by plighting their troth, as well as from the priest's blessing. The phrase "on those who receive it worthily" is usually a technical term implying that the recipients are sanctified *ex opere operato*, but the phrase *aliquod gratiae donum* suggests that conjugal grace is grace only in some lesser sense, such as *gratia gratis data*.

Bonaventure explains how the soul is "raised above the corruption of inordinate concupiscence" by the grace that the spouses receive *both* because of their consent to an indivisible way of life *and* through the church's blessing. Here, however, Bonaventure does not separate the two graces. Conjugal grace comes through both means, and it sustains the singularity, utility, and inseparability of the union, enhancing the conjugal goods of faith, offspring, and sacrament. Whereas sexual desire is promiscuous and tends toward multiple partners, grace limits it to a single spouse. Whereas desire is inordinate and seeks coitus only for pleasure, grace causes the spouses to pursue it only for the sake of procreation. And whereas desire is prone to jadedness (*fastidium*) and quickly grows weary of one partner, grace makes it satisfied with the same spouse over the long duration of a marriage.[116]

Despite his affirmation that marriage itself confers such a grace and does so even without the blessing, Bonaventure hesitates simply to call this benefit "grace"

---

[115] Ibid. (668a–b). The phrase *ex caritate* sometimes characterizes *ex opere operantis* efficacy, but the phrase *digne suscipientibus* characterizes *ex opere operato* efficacy. In this case, the charity is presumably a qualification or disposition for receiving grace, and not its source.

[116] *IV Sent.* 26.2.2, resp.; 31.1.2, resp. (668b, 719b).

without qualification. In the passage quoted earlier, he calls it "some gift of grace" (*aliquod gratiae donum*). Replying to the simony objection, Bonaventure argues that what is conferred through marriage is not grace "in the same way as in the other sacraments, but only a help of grace [*auxilium gratiae*] ... except perhaps by reason of the benediction joined to it, which would make someone purchasing it a simoniac."[117] The distinction between grace in the proper sense and a help of grace (*auxilium gratiae*) is obscure, but the latter phrase may echo a passage in the *Sentences* where Peter Lombard discusses original justice. According to the Lombard, neither the angels nor human beings received at the moment of their creation a grace that enabled them to advance (*proficere*) or to merit, yet a "help was given through grace" that enabled them to "stand" (*stare*), that is, to avoid falling into sin. The Lombard calls this preternatural assistance the "grace of creation."[118] According to Bonaventure's vocabulary, this would be is *gratia gratis data* as distinct from sanctifying grace (*gratia gratum faciens*).

Does Bonaventure contradict or undermine himself when he argues that marriage itself confers grace, even aside from the nuptial blessing? Perhaps. But the interpreter should remember that the term "grace," according to Bonaventure, is equivocal. Properly understood, it denotes sanctifying grace, which remits the guilt of sins that have already been committed, and which elevates the soul, making it pleasing to God. Broadly understood, the term includes as well any preternatural divine assistance (*gratia gratis data*) that sustains the soul, protecting it from harm.[119] A divine assistance that enhanced the preventive effect of marriage without causing remission of sins or elevating the soul above its natural state, according to Bonaventure, would not be grace in the proper sense of the term, but it might be preternatural grace, or *gratia gratis data*. When Bonaventure cautiously characterizes conjugal grace as "some gift of grace" and as "a help of grace," therefore, he may be referring to a preternatural grace that enhances the preventive properties of marriage. If marriage also confers sanctifying grace, which remits the guilt of already-committed sins and reforms the soul, it can do so, according to Bonaventure, only by virtue of the nuptial blessing, which raises marriage from being a sacrament in some broad sense to being a sacrament of the church, fully integrated into the system of sacramental ministry.

15.3.5 *Thomas Aquinas*

Thomas's review of existing opinions is similar to Albert's, but he is more explicit than his teacher both about the respective rationales for the three positions and about the inadequacy of the first two. First, some say that marriage is only a

---

[117] *IV Sent.* 30.un.3, ad 3 (711b).   [118] Peter Lombard, *Sent.* II, 24.1.2 (450).
[119] Bonaventure, *II Sent.* 27, dub. 1, resp. (2:669a–70a).

sign and that it does not confer grace in any way. But that must be false, for then there would be no adequate reason to include marriage among the sacraments of the New Law. Marriage under the Old Law was already both a sacred sign and a natural remedy, which restrained concupiscence and made coitus honest. Second, some say that a certain grace is conferred in marriage, but one that achieves only a withdrawal from evil, by excusing an act that would otherwise be a sin. But, again, the same might be said of marriage under the Old Law. Some enhance the second position by arguing that conjugal grace mitigates concupiscence by preventing it from going beyond the limits of the conjugal goods, while still maintaining that no grace is given to help the spouses to do good works. Thomas is apparently summarizing Bonaventure's reasoning. Against it, Thomas proposes an argument that Albert discussed when comparing sacramental grace with the sanctifying grace of the virtues, and that Bonaventure used to show why circumcision could not remove sin without replacing it with something positive: Any grace that impedes evil, Thomas argues, must *ipso facto* foster good, just as the heat that takes away cold is the same as the heat that makes things warm.[120] The third opinion follows from that refutation: A marriage contracted through faith in Christ confers a grace that helps the recipients not only to avoid evil but also to fulfill whatever work is incumbent on them as spouses. This last theory is the most probable, Thomas argues, for whenever God gives human beings the power or right (*facultas*) to do something, he also enables them do to it fittingly, just as God provides the body with members that enable the soul to exercise its powers. Since God, through the divine institution of marriage, gave men the right to marry and to use their wives for the procreation of children, so God will also provide the grace without which they could not do so fittingly.[121]

One might object, Thomas notes, that the third position entails something like Pelagianism, for marriage is not received passively from a divinely instituted sacrament but rather is established by the human act of mutual consent. How can human action or human effort cause sanctifying grace? Thomas provides two different but similar solutions to this objection in the *Scriptum*. In one place, he argues that the exchange of consent (the *sacramentum tantum*) establishes only the tie (*nexus*) between the spouses (the *sacramentum et res*), which in turn disposes them to receive grace "from the power of divine institution." In the same way, the external ablution and the verbal formula in baptism do not cause grace but rather establish

---

[120] Cf. Albertus Magnus, *IV Sent.* 1.4, quaest., "Si dicas . . ." (Borgnet 29:11b–12a); Bonaventure, *IV Sent.* 1.2.2.3, resp. (4:43–44).

[121] Thomas Aquinas, *IV Sent.* 26.2.3, resp. (Vivès 11:73b–74a). See also *IV Sent.* 2.1.1, quᵃ 2, resp. (Moos 4:78), where Thomas presents same range of possibilities (differently organized), and cites 1 Thess 4:4 and Tob 6:17 to characterize the effect of this conjugal grace on concupiscence.

the character, which in turn disposes the recipient to receive grace directly from God.[122] In another place, Thomas replies that every sacrament acts as an instrumental cause that "disposes" the subject to receive grace, whereas the divine institution of the sacrament is the principle cause. Thus, no sacrament causes grace by its own power. Instead, God uses the sacrament as an instrument, and we receive the divine grace by the medium of the sacrament "unless there is a defect on our part" (i.e., *ex opere operato*). One may maintain without contradiction or risking Pelagianism, therefore, both that a human act causes the sacrament of marriage, and that God uses this sacrament as an instrument of grace.[123] These explanations seem to invoke two different theories of sacramental causality, respectively dispositive and instrumental (Section 15.2.4), but Thomas does not differentiate clearly between these theories in his early work. Thomas's view seems to be that the spouses' outward expression of consent causes an interior bond that in turn disposes the spouses to receive grace, just as the outward ablution of baptism causes an interior character that disposes the subject to receive grace immediately from God.

Rather than adding something entirely novel to marriage, in Thomas's view, grace elevates a power that belongs to it by nature. Even without grace, marriage is made honorable through the conjugal goods, it takes away the shameful indecency (*turpitudo*) that attends coitus, and it heals concupiscence by providing a proper outlet for it, for "it is better to marry than to burn" (1 Cor 7:9). Although concupiscent acts considered in themselves tend to augment concupiscence, they are conducive to the virtue of temperance inasmuch as they are repeatedly practiced in an orderly manner, which establishes a good acquired habit.[124] But that remedy is effective chiefly against concupiscent *acts*. Grace alone can heal the habitual "root" of concupiscence.[125]

Like Albert, Thomas maintains that the power of all the sacraments originates in the Passion of Jesus Christ. The sacraments extend the efficacy of Christ's Passion, just as blood and water, representing eucharist and baptism, flowed from the wound in Christ's side (cf. Plate 3). The crucified Christ becomes tangible through the matter of the sacraments.[126] But that continuity presupposes that the sacraments signify the Passion through resemblance and conformity. One might object, therefore, that there is no conformity between marriage and the Passion, for marriage is an occasion for rejoicing and has carnal pleasure "adjoined" to it, whereas the Passion was above all painful. Thomas replies that the required conformity in marriage exists not in respect of the Passion itself as an occasion of pain and suffering, but in respect of the charity that the Passion presupposed. Christ suffered

---

[122] *IV Sent.* 26.2.3 ad 2 (Vivès 11:74).   [123] *IV Sent.* 2.1.1, qu^a 2, ad 1 (Moos 4:78).

[124] But cf. *IV Sent.* 2.1.1, qu^a 2, resp. (Moos 4:78), where Thomas seems to argue that this effect could not happen without grace.

[125] *IV Sent.* 26.2.3, ad 4 (Vivès 11:74b).   [126] Cf. Plate N.

not for the sake of pain but through love, in order to unite the church with himself as his betrothed. Indeed, the charity that unites Christ to the church is itself a mystical marriage.[127] Literal marriage is supernaturally efficacious, therefore, because it enables the spouses to touch the mystical marriage that was realized in the Passion, just as baptismal ablution is said to cleanse the soul through touching the body because it previously touched the flesh of Christ.[128]

Thomas never had another opportunity to discuss conjugal grace in detail, but his incidental remarks on the subject in later works indicate that he did not change his mind. In the questions *De veritate*, which he disputed during his first Parisian regency and while he was still editing the *Scriptum*, Thomas distinguishes between carnal marriage, which is contracted through the spouses' free consent, and "a certain spiritual marriage of the soul with God [that] is contracted through an infusion of grace, as it says in Hosea 2:19: 'I will betroth you to me in justice'." Because consent causes marriage only inasmuch as it is a carnal partnership and not inasmuch it joins the soul to God, free choice does not cause the infusion of conjugal grace.[129] In the *Summa theologiae*, explaining why dowries and nuptial settlements do not incur the sin of simony, Thomas rejects the canonists' negative solution: "Some say that it is permitted to give money for a marriage because grace is not conferred in it, but this is not altogether true."[130]

In the chapter of the *Summa contra gentiles* that would prove to be his last word on marriage as a sacrament, Thomas argues that a grace is given in marriage to enable to spouses to participate fully in the union between Christ and the church. He has already shown that marriage must be subject to the church's governance inasmuch as it is primarily a means for raising children to worship God, and that it must be a sacrament to achieve that end. But if marriage is a sacrament, it must by definition cause a grace that it signifies:

> And just as in the other sacraments something spiritual is signified through the things done outwardly, so too in this sacrament the union of Christ and the church is signified through the union of male and female, as the Apostle says: "This is a great sacrament, but I speak in Christ and in the church" (Eph 5:32). And because the sacraments "effect what they figure," one must believe that a grace is conferred through this sacrament on those who are marrying: a grace through which they may belong to the union of Christ and the Church. And this is especially needful for them, so that they may strive not to be disjoined from Christ and the church by carnal and earthly things.[131]

It follows, then, not only that marriage is a sign of a sacred reality, but also that it causes what it signifies by conferring grace. Since marriage signifies Christ's union

---

[127] *IV Sent.* 26.2.1, arg. 3; ad 3 (71b, 72a).   [128] *IV Sent.* 26.2.3, ad 1 (74a).

[129] *De veritate* 28.8, arg. 7; ad 7 (Leonine 22.3:841b–42a, 844a).

[130] *Summa theologiae* II-II.100.2, ad 6 (1946b).

[131] *Summa contra Gentiles* IV.78 (Leonine 15:246b).

with the church, it must also cause it: not, indeed, by uniting Christ and the church, but rather by helping the spouses to participate in that union in their own special way, as spouses. Does this argument contradict Thomas's earlier claim that marriage *only signifies* the joining of Christ and the church, whereas it *both signifies and contains* a sacramental grace?[132] There is certainly a difference in emphasis, but there is no real inconsistency. Obviously, no marriage between two individuals can cause Christ to be united with the church, for that union existed long before they were born and is the source of all sacramental grace. Nevertheless, Thomas, like Albert, maintains that marriage is "conformed" to the Passion, and that it extends the grace of the mystical marriage to faithful spouses by virtue of that conformity.

15.3.6 *Peter of Tarentaise*

Peter follows Thomas closely in presenting three alternative positions. Some say that marriage is only a sign of grace and not a cause, because it was only approved and not instituted under the New Law. Others say that marriage confers a certain grace, but one that only rescues the spouses from evil without conferring any good, for marriage is a remedy that excuses the sexual act from sin. Others say that the grace of marriage is not only remedial but also fosters good things such as mutual love and fidelity in those who receive the sacrament worthily, namely, those who contract marriage "in faith, or with due intention."[133] Peter does not say which of the three opinions is correct, but he implies that he prefers the third by carrying over its terminology into his replies to objections. His only qualification is that both marriage and orders confer grace *in statu*, that is, to assist persons pursuing a certain vocation or way of life, whereas the other sacraments confer grace absolutely (*simpliciter*).[134] Elsewhere, though, Peter echoes William of Auxerre by stating that marriage confers only a "preservative" remedy, whereas the other sacraments confer a "curative" remedy.[135] Despite that inconsistency, Peter of Tarentaise is careful to explain how marriage exemplifies everything that characterizes the sacraments of the New Law, and why it is a sacrament in the proper sense even though it is unique in certain respects.

Peter's chief reason for maintaining that marriage confers grace is a syllogism that he presents as an argument *sed contra*: "Every sacrament of the New Law confers grace; but marriage is a sacrament of the New Law, consecrated by Christ; therefore,

---

[132] *IV Sent.* 26.2.1, ad 4–5 (Vivès 11:72a). Thomas says here that Peter Lombard mentioned only the uncontained reality because he thought that marriage did not have a contained reality. But in *IV Sent.* 2.1.1, quᵃ 2, ad 3 (Moos 4:79), Thomas reconciles his own position with Peter Lombard's by proposing that the remedy posited by the Lombard presupposed grace.

[133] Peter of Tarentaise, *IV Sent.* 26.3.2, resp. (287).

[134] Ibid., ad 2; ad 4 (287b). Peter says in the response that marriage confers some grace "quoad operationem boni ... licet non boni simpliciter."

[135] *IV Sent.* 26.3.1, resp. (286b).

marriage confers grace."[136] Peter concedes that marriage was not instituted under
the New Law, but he maintains that Christ "consecrated" the sacrament both
through his presence and miraculous intervention at Cana and by rejecting divorce
and remarriage.[137] This consecration suffices to establish the minor premise of the
syllogism: that marriage is a sacrament of the New Law. Like every sacrament
properly so called, marriage confers what it signifies. It is true that marriage does
not confer everything that it signifies, for it does not confer the union of Christ and
the church. As a sacrament, therefore, marriage primarily signifies conjugal grace,
whereas the joining of Christ and the church is a secondary signification.[138] Like
every sacrament properly so called, marriage is composed of something external and
sensible that confers as its effect an inward, spiritual remedy against sin.[139] The
exterior, sensible aspect of marriage is the outward expression of consent, normally
in spoken words. It follows that the interior act of consent alone (the *coniunctio
animorum*), without its outward expression, is not sufficient to establish the sacrament of marriage.[140]

15.3.7 *Richard de Mediavilla*

Unlike Albert, Bonaventure, Thomas, and Peter of Tarentaise, Richard did not
review the possibilities and standard positions when he discussed whether marriage
conferred grace. Perhaps such preliminaries were no longer necessary, for the
doctrine was by now well established among theologians. Richard owes his chief
arguments for the doctrine to Thomas Aquinas. Just as nature never gives something
a certain power without providing dispositions that enable the thing to exercise the
power fittingly, so God would not give human beings a power without giving them
the appropriate disposition. Through its divine institution, marriage gives the
contractants the power to use each other sexually to beget children, but they could
not exercise that power fittingly or worthily without sanctifying grace (*gratia gratum
faciens*). Consequently, Richard concludes, a grace must be conferred through
marriage on those who contract it worthily, and this must be sanctifying grace,
and not only *gratia gratis data* as some argue.[141]

Only sanctifying grace suffices, Richard maintains, because Christian marriage
not only restrains concupiscence, keeping it within decent limits, but also strikes at
its root.[142] Like the other sacraments, marriage causes the spouses to be conformed
to Christ's Passion, albeit not in respect of the pain that Christ endured but rather in

---

[136] *IV Sent.* 26.3.2, s.c. (287a).   [137] *IV Sent.* 26.3.1, ad 1 (286b–87a).
[138] *IV Sent.* 26.3.1, ad 3; ad 5 (287a).   [139] *IV Sent.* 26.3.1, resp. (286b).
[140] *IV Sent.* 27.2.2, resp. (294a).   [141] Richard de Mediavilla, *IV Sent.* 26.2.3, resp. (405b).
[142] *IV Sent.* 26.2.3, ad 1 (405b).

respect of the charity that was Christ's motive for enduring it.[143] Marriage confers a sanctifying grace that is a special form of charity. The marital *obligatio*, which the spouses establish by consenting, is a dispositive cause that enables them to receive that grace from God. Since a sacrament in the proper sense is primarily a cause of grace and secondarily a sign, the reality that marriage primarily signifies is not the union of Christ and the church but rather a certain "charity by which they ought to love each other mutually and with holy love [*dilectio sancta*]."[144]

15.3.8 *Durandus of Saint-Pourçain*

As we have seen, Durandus refined and elaborated Peter John Olivi's critique of the sacramental doctrine, but he was more cautious than Olivi regarding the power of marriage to confer grace *ex opere operato*.[145] Thus, although Durandus denied that marriage was univocally a sacrament of the New Law, he declined to say whether or not it conferred grace. Nevertheless, he insisted that the matter was still open to dispute. It could not be a matter of faith, Durandus argued, because both canon law and the Roman church maintained that marriage did not confer such grace:

> As regards the first [question, whether marriage confers grace], the jurists hold one position, and the theologians another. The jurists — who know the text of the decrees and decretals by which the position of the Roman church is expressed, and who have expounded and glossed the canons and decretals, and some of whom have belonged to the College of Cardinals of the Holy Roman Church — hold that grace is not conferred in the sacrament of matrimony.... But modern theologians hold virtually unanimously that grace is conferred through the sacrament of matrimony unless the contractants present an obstacle, just as with the other sacraments, to which marriage is regarded as equal in this regard. For in their view it is otherwise impossible to maintain that marriage is a sacrament of the New Law.[146]

To say that something confers grace unless the recipient presents an obstacle or does not receive it worthily is to say that it confers grace *ex opere operato*. According to Durandus's account, therefore, the theologians of his era were committed to maintaining both that marriage was in the fullest sense one of the sacraments of the New Law, and that conferring grace *ex opere operato* was an essential feature of that genus and a salient feature of marriage. Durandus declines to express his own position, but he insists that there is no heresy in denying that marriage confers such a grace.

---

[143] *IV Sent.* 26.2.3, ad 2 (405b).   [144] *IV Sent.* 26.4.2, resp.; ad 3 (408b, 409a).
[145] On Olivi's arguments, see earlier, Section 14.8.2.
[146] Durandus, *IV Sent.* 26.3, §6; §8 (367v).

Durandus was undoubtedly accurate when he described the consensus among theologians, but he surely exaggerated in describing an opposite consensus among the canon lawyers. It is true that those canonists who touched on the subject said that marriage did not confer grace,[147] but they were content to repeat old positions without inquiry or elaboration. This was still a theological topic, not a canonical one, and it did not arise inevitably in the study of the *Decretum* and the decretals. The position of Hostiensis is typical. Hostiensis says nothing about conjugal grace in the titles on marriage in Book IV of his *Summa aurea*. Nor does he say anything there about the sacramentality of marriage, although he does treat its sacramentality as a premise for developing other aspects of marriage, such as the church's jurisdiction over it. But in Book I, when he reviews the ways in which the sacraments can be divided into sorts, Hostiensis mentions the distinction between the sacraments that cause grace and those that do not, *such as marriage*. If marriage did confer grace, Hostiensis notes, it would entail simony.[148] But the reference to marriage here is incidental and perfunctory and still entirely conventional in the context of canon law.

Notwithstanding Durandus's express refusal to commit himself to either position, he expounded a version of the preventive theory that prevailed until the 1220s, developing it in his own way and with new clarity. Not every remedy against sin, he argues, need be a sacrament in the proper sense. Nor does a remedy need to confer any positive benefit. Suppose that someone gives money to a pauper. The gift of money is "a remedy for him, lest he be driven by poverty to steal," but it is not a sacrament, and it does not confer grace. In the same way, marriage naturally prevents sin only by retaining coitus within its proper setting:

> So also, since a person may satisfy the concupiscence of matrimony through the marital act, it is a remedy for him lest he should be aroused to other corrupt things, such as fornication or adultery. And the same is true of all things that prevent sin from occurring by the nature of their acts....[149]

Durandus contrasts such merely preventive remedies with the sacraments properly so called, which counteract sin less "by the nature of their acts" than "by divine institution." Natural reason alone cannot explain remedies of this sort, for they depend on a supernatural power that has been conferred on the external, sensible

---

[147] Le Bras, "Mariage," 2208–09. *Glossa ordinaria* on C. 32 q. 2 c. 13 (*c. Honorantur*), in *Corpus Iuris Canonici* [*Editio Romana*] (Rome, 1582), 1:2113–14. Goffredus de Trano, *Summa super titulis Decretalium* on the title *De sacramentis non iterandis* (Lyons, 1519, 33va–b). On the *Editio Romana*, see M. E. Sommar, *Correctores Romani* (Berlin, 2009), especially pp. 26 ff.

[148] Hostiensis, *Summa aurea* I.16.6 (Venice, 1574 edition, 217): "Sacramenta quaedam sunt, in quibus confertur gratia.... Quaedam vero sunt in quibus gratia non confertur, sicut matrimonia, quae contrahuntur quando precia interveniunt ... et conditiones pecuniariae consumantur."

[149] Durandus, *IV Sent.* 26.3, §16 [ad 1] (368rb). Paludanus rehearses and refutes the argument in *IV Sent.* 26.4.2 (141va).

means, and the sacrament must be received in faith. There is no reason, he argues, to attribute any such grace to marriage.

15.3.9 *Peter of La Palu*

Paludanus affirms that marriage confers a grace *ex opere operato* that enables the husband to "know how to possess his vessel in sanctification and honor (1 Thess 4:4)."[150] To show how marriage confers grace, Peter argues that every sacrament supernaturally imprints a character or some comparable "adornment" (*ornatus*) on the soul, which in turn disposes the soul to receive grace directly from God. The *ornatus* of marriage is the bond (*vinculum*) or tie (*nexus*), which God himself, and not the contractants, "impresses" or "imprints" on the soul. The marriage bond disposes the soul to receive the grace by which a spouse knows "how to possess his vessel in sanctification in honor." The bond is not a relation, Peter argues, but something real and absolute, and which exists separately in each partner. In reality, therefore, there are two bonds in each marriage.[151]

Peter offers no proof or evidence that marriage confers sacramental grace, and he confesses that natural reason cannot explain why God gave a greater power of conferring grace *ex opere operato* to marriage than he did to the Lord's Prayer or to the blessing and consecration of a virgin, both of which seem to be "more holy" than marriage.[152] Peter's aim is not to demonstrate the theologians' position but to defend it against Olivi and Durandus. Whereas Durandus argued that marriage was not properly a sacrament of the New Law, partly because its power to confer grace was in doubt, Peter assumes that marriage confers grace *ex opere operato* and deduces from that premise that marriage must be a sacrament of the New Law:

> whatever confers a remedy against sin by conferring a helping grace [*gratia adiutrix*] *ex opere operato* is by definition a sacrament. And this [definition] befits marriage, because it confers grace: not from the nature of the act, although it confers a remedy in other ways, but from divine institution.... Therefore, since every sensible sign that God has instituted to be a remedy against sin by conferring grace *ex opere operato* and to signify that grace is a sacrament of the New Law, and since marriage has all of these things according to the theologians, marriage is properly a sacrament.[153]

Peter emphasizes the importance of definitions because, as we have seen, he rejects the paradigmatic method, whereby marriage is compared and contrasted with other sacraments to determine whether it belongs to the same genus (Section 14.8.4). The method had been central in treatments of the topic since Albert, but Peter rejects it

---

[150] Paludanus, *IV Sent.* 26.4.2, conc. 2 (141va).   [151] *IV Sent.* 26.4.3, ad 5 (142ra–b).
[152] Ibid.   [153] *IV Sent.* 26.4.2, conc. 2 (141va).

because Durandus had used it with some success to show that marriage was not a sacrament. One should always return to the definition of what a sacrament is, Peter holds, and use that to determine whether marriage meets the definition.[154]

Here was a fundamental disagreement about the logic of classes, even if Peter of La Palu did not fully understand Durandus's method (Sections 14.8.3 and 14.8.4). Durandus reasoned that one could not assimilate something to a genus without comparing it inductively with several other members, and that one could not grasp what a definition meant without understanding what it was intended to explain and how it was originally used. To establish univocity one had to determine whether the thing in question met the terms of the definition univocally. The definition alone, considered abstractly, was insufficient. But Paludanus held that inquiring whether marriage was like or unlike the other sacraments was futile, since every sacrament was unique. A definition, in his view, was the only reliable standard.

---

[154] Ibid., conc. 3 (141va–b).

16

Human contract and divine sacrament

By posing and solving objections to the doctrine of marriage as a sacrament, theologians also highlighted and clarified the ways in which marriage was peculiar among the sacraments. Whereas baptism was a purely spiritual, figurative washing, and eucharist a purely spiritual, figurative meal, marriage was a literal, temporal partnership, subject by its very nature to the secular law of any community, whether Christian or infidel. Again, whereas unbelievers could not validly be baptized or receive eucharist, their marriages were valid even from a Christian point of view, and their philosophers and religious leaders regarded the institution in a more favorable light than most Christian clerics did. With some qualifications, Christian scholars even accepted the efficacy of diriment impediments imposed by infidel rulers. Theologians during the second quarter of the thirteenth century mitigated the anomalies by showing why marriage was necessarily peculiar among the sacraments in these respects and how other sacraments, especially penance, shared its peculiarities to some extent. They also recognized that marriage, unlike baptism and eucharist, was not only a sacrament but also an office of nature and a human contract, subject to secular as well as to sacred laws. This distinction between the contractuality and the sacramentality of marriage was to prove crucial at the Council of Trent.

16.1 BELIEVERS, UNBELIEVERS, AND THE BOND OF MARRIAGE

Medieval theologians accepted that marriages between infidels were inferior to Christian marriages in certain respects but equal to them in other respects. Augustine had observed that the *sacramentum*, or at least the full observance of it, distinguished marriage in the church from marriage under both Mosaic and Roman law (Section 4.3.1). The Pauline Privilege seemed to imply that the bond of marriage between unbelievers was not as firm as that between believers. The *magistri moderni* had questioned whether unbelievers could marry at all, since they considered marriage to be in some as yet undefined sense one of the sacraments of the church. Most conceded that unbelievers could marry, noting the quasi-generic features of marriage common to all peoples and expressed in some of the standard definitions, but the question was a serious one and exposed an anomaly. The *magistri moderni* construed the Pauline Privilege as evidence that marriage outside the church was in some way not as insoluble as Christian marriage (Section 9.5.2).

Thirteenth-century theologians, likewise, accepted that infidel marriage was in different respects both the same as and less than Christian marriage, but in their hands the distinction proved to be fraught with difficulty and the solution resisted precise formulation. They, too, assumed that the marriages of Christians were intrinsically superior to those of infidels, and by virtue not only of their legal context but also of their intrinsic attributes, benefits, and merits. Only among Christians was marriage truly a sacrament of the church. At the same time, theologians recognized that unbelievers could validly marry, and most conceded that the marriages of unbelievers were sacraments at least in a broad sense of the term, since God had instituted marriage in the beginning as a sacred sign. What distinguished the marriages of Christians? It seemed that the strength of the marriage bond was a good indicator. Only Christians recognized that marriage was indissoluble, and the Pauline Privilege suggested that infidel marriage was soluble *de iure* at least in this circumstance. The difference between Christian and non-Christian marriage seemed to imply that Christian marriage was itself twofold: that it was peculiar in one respect but shared features with infidel marriage in another respect.

The most obvious indicator of the difference between Christian and non-Christian marriage, therefore, was insolubility, which only Christians – indeed, only Latin Christians – observed. To posit a bond (*vinculum*) in marriage was to say that marriage was permanently binding. Medieval theologians used at least four terms to characterize the special permanence attributed to marriage in the western church: "inseparability" (*inseparabilitas*), "indivisibility" (*individuitas*), "insolubility" (*insolubilitas*), and "indissolubility" (*indissolubilitas*), with the cognate adjectives. The terms were interchangeable, but they had different connotations deriving from their different origins. The term *inseparabilitas* was the oldest and most traditional, for it invoked Jesus' injunction: "What God has joined, let man not separate."[1] Since Jesus was addressing Jews as well as Christians, theologians conceded that inseparability was not peculiar to Christian marriage, but they argued that that it was somehow strengthened through baptism and faith in Christ. The term *individuitas*, which became current in theology during the first half of the thirteenth century, invoked the classical definition of marriage as a union that "holds together an indivisible way of life."[2] Albert explains that *individuitas* embraces all the works

---

[1] Mark 10:9: "Quod ergo Deus iunxit homo non separet."
[2] *Inst.* 1.9.1. "Nuptiae autem sive matrimonium est viri et mulieris coniunctio, individuam consuetudinem vitae continens/retinens."

and burdens that the spouses are obliged to undertake precisely as man and wife ("*communicant coniugaliter*"), even in the absence of sexual intercourse, and that it remains after divorce *a mensa et thoro* (i.e., a legal separation) at least to the extent that neither spouse could remarry.[3] The term *insolubilitas*, likewise, ruled out divorce as regards the bond (*divortium a vinculo*), while leaving open the possibility of a legal separation (*divortium a mensa et thoro*) on certain grounds, chiefly adultery. The emphatic term *indissolubilitas*, an intensified variant of *insolubilitas*, entered during the thirteenth century and had largely superseded the other terms by the time of the Reformation. Discourse about the indivisibility of marriage was intertwined with the discourses about the *bonum sacramenti* and about the signification of marriage. Theologians asked whether a marriage between unbelievers was insoluble, whether it possessed the good of sacrament, and whether it adequately signified Christ's union with the church. Although these three questions were neither the same nor even coextensive, they were interrelated and mutually overlapping.

While recognizing that the bond was stronger between believers and that Christians alone observed the law of insolubility, most scholastic theologians resisted the notion that infidel marriage was soluble *de iure*. Thirteenth-century theologians assumed that marriage possessed a certain indivisibility (*individuitas*) from its original institution and by its very nature and natural utility, for marriage by definition "holds together an indivisible way of life." But most assumed, too, that this indivisibility was in some sense heightened or strengthened in the church. Twelfth-century theologians had enthusiastically appropriated Ambrosiaster's explanation of the Pauline Privilege, whereby a marriage between infidels was not fixed or established (*ratum*) because it was joined without God's help (Section 9.5.2). Similarly, Robert Courson held that marriage outside the church was true (*verum matrimonium*) but not fixed (*matrimonium ratum*).[4] But the notion that only Christians could contract *matrimonium ratum* could not be squared easily with the complex law of the Pauline Privilege. Some held that only the convert was free to remarry, and that the unconverted partner was *de iure* still bound by the former marriage. Moreover, some reasoned that what trumped infidel marriage in the Privilege was not Christian marriage *per se* but rather the new bond between the believer and Jesus Christ.

According to one approach to this problem, which was common but never satisfactorily articulated during the Middle Ages,[5] all marriage is intrinsically or habitually indivisible, perhaps even by virtue of the natural law, but this natural indivisibility was somehow confirmed or strengthened when marriage became a sacrament of the church. For example, Robert Courson argues that the definition of marriage as a "union that holds together an indivisible way of life" is true even of marriages among unbelievers, notwithstanding the Pauline Privilege, just as it is true

---

[3]   Albertus Magnus, *IV Sent.* 27.2, ad diffin. 1, ad 2; ad 7 (Borgnet 30:130).

[4]   Robert Courson, *Quaestio de matrimonio*, ed. Malherbe, ch. 2, p. 8.

[5]   See L. Ryan, "The Indissolubility of Marriage in Natural Law," *Irish Theological Quarterly* 30 (1963): 293–310, and 31 (1964): 62–67.

of unconsummated marriage, notwithstanding the right of either spouse to withdraw by entering the religious life. But the definition of marriage as a "union that holds together an indivisible way of life," Robert argues, means only that the joining is always *apt* to hold together an indivisible way of life, and not that it does so in fact, just as one may define valid argument as reasoning that is *apt* to produce belief in a dubitable proposition, for a valid argument does not always result in belief in fact.[6] Similarly, Praepositinus notes that infidel marriages cannot be simply divisible, as the Pauline Privilege seems to imply, for then unbelievers could not truly marry, since marriage is by definition an "indivisible way of life." If infidel spouses are not really married, they must commit the mortal sin of simple fornication whenever they come together sexually, which seems too harsh. Moreover, Jesus was addressing Jews and unbelievers rather than Christian converts when he said, "What God has joined, let man not separate." Praepositinus argues that the marriage of unbelievers possesses all three of the conjugal goods *de iure*, even including the good of sacrament, which Praepositinus equates here with inseparability. The maxim, "the whole life of unbelievers is a sin [*peccatum*]," is true, Praepositinus argues, but it does not follow, as some suppose, that sexual intercourse between infidel spouses is itself mortally sinful. The three conjugal goods excuse coitus even among unbelievers, compensating for the defects of concupiscence and turpitude.[7] Appropriating and expanding Praepositinus's account, Guy of Orchelles argues that non-Christian marriages possess all three conjugal goods yet do so only partially or incompletely, and not in their full form. The word *peccatum* in the maxim, "the whole life of unbelievers is a *peccatum*," Guy argues, is not used not in its narrow sense, meaning "sin," but rather in its broad sense, as in logic, where it denotes anything that is faulty, defective, or incomplete. The whole life of unbelievers is morally defective because they can do nothing to merit eternal life, but it does not follow that their sexual intercourse *per se* is mortally sinful.[8]

Alexander of Hales argues, on the contrary, that although a marriage between infidels is a true marriage and even a sacrament in a broad sense of that term, it lacks the *bonum sacramenti*. It is a true marriage insofar as marriage belongs to the natural law, which is common to believers and unbelievers. And it is a sacrament inasmuch as it is a sacred sign.[9] Moreover, there is no relevant impediment of "disparity of cult" between two infidels, as there would be between a Christian and an infidel. Nevertheless, an infidel marriage is neither truly inseparable nor truly *ratum*.[10]

---

[6] Robert Courson, *Quaestio de matrimonio*, ed. Malherbe, ch. 1, p. 3.

[7] Praepositinus, *Summa* IV, ed. Pilarczyk, p. 101; pp. 108–09. The maxim, "Tota vita infidelium mortale peccatum est," occurs in the *Glossa ordinaria* on Rom 14:23 ("Everything that is not from faith is a sin"). Cf. Prosper of Aquitaine, *Sententiae* 106, PL 45:1868: "Omnis infidelium vita peccatum est; et nihil est bonum sine summo bono. Ubi enim deest agnitio aeternae et incommutabilis veritatis, falsa virtus est, etiam in optimis moribus."

[8] Guy of Orchelles, *Tractatus de sacramentis*, 9.2, no. 223 (200–01).

[9] Alexander of Hales, *Glossa in IV Sent.* 39.7 (588–91).

[10] *IV Sent.* 39.7b; e–f (589; 590).

Alexander treats this theme both in his disputed questions and in his *Glossa*. The two treatments proceed along somewhat different lines yet are mutually consistent and complementary. Because each is multifaceted and hard to follow, I shall piece together the gist of Alexander's argument from both sources in what follows.

Alexander construes the strength of the bond ontologically as well as juridically. He assumes that the advent of Jesus Christ really transformed the permanence of marriage, and not only the positive laws that regulate it. The relationship between the permanence of a non-Christian marriage and that of a Christian marriage is comparable to the relationship between the sacraments of the Old Law and those of the New. Marriage is always and everywhere inseparable *de iure*, but it acquires an additional, factual solidity from a causal relationship with the incarnation, since faith in Christ is the rock upon which the Christian life is built. It is true that faith itself is soluble (*delebilis*), but the central object of faith, which is the union of natures in Christ, is itself insoluble. Moreover, the baptismal character, which is impressed in the "sacrament of faith,"[11] is indelible, and baptism is the foundation of the inseparability of marriage.[12]

Alexander posits a causal as well as signifying relationship, therefore, between Christ and the conjugal bond (*vinculum*). Since marriage signifies the union between Christ and the church, the inseparability of marriage signifies the inseparability of that union, and the grace of Christ strengthens the bond of marriage.[13] As a sacred sign of Christ and the church, marriage has always contained an inseparable bond (*vinculum*), for God instituted marriage from the beginning to be a sign of the inseparable union of Christ and the church, which is based on the shared human nature. Nevertheless, the marriage bond was transformed when it became a true sacrament under the New Law. It changed *de iure* because Christ confirmed the original inseparability of marriage by rejecting the Mosaic law of repudiation (Matt 5:31, etc.). But it was also transformed factually, for "a power [*virtus*] is given to matrimony from the grace of the inseparability of natures in Christ," a grace that marriage "not only signifies … but also receives." This gracious power confirms the juridical inseparability that always belongs to marriage by virtue of its institution.[14] Alexander does not explain how this real, factual transformation comes about. Perhaps he assumes that the grace of Christ enables the spouses to meet the *de iure* demands of permanence.

There is no such causal connection or foundation in marriages between unbelievers, Alexander argues. Infidel spouses are held together only by their own volition and by the natural law. Infidels spouses who convert to Christianity acquire in addition the supernatural *bonum sacramenti*, since their marriage is now founded on faith in Christ ("*habet fidem substratam*"), for "every grace that is given in the

---

[11] Alexander of Hales, Q. 59, disp. 2, m. 3, §37; §40 (1171; 1172).

[12] *IV Sent.* 39.7g (590–91).   [13] Q. 57, disp. 2, m. 1, §§31–32 (1108).

[14] Q. 57, disp. 2, m. 2, §35 (1109).

sacraments is founded on the grace of faith that is given in baptism." Alexander wonders whether the bond (*vinculum*) of marriage and the *bonum sacramenti* are the same or different things,[15] since infidel spouses possess the former but not the latter. He concludes that they are numerically identical "in substance," since the *bonum sacramenti* is a supernatural enhancement of the natural bond. When infidel spouses accept faith in Jesus Christ, the marriage bond remains in them but receives an additional quality or dimension from Christ, becoming the good of sacrament.[16]

The absence of faith in unbelievers, Alexander argues, limits both the significa-tion and the sanctifying power of marriage:

> For although [infidel marriage] signifies the union of the faithful soul to God by virtue of the consent of wills, and although it signifies the union of Christ and the church in a certain respect [*quoad quid*], yet it does not do so absolutely [*simpli-citer*], for it has not been contracted in the faith of the church or in the sacrament of faith. The good of sacrament is properly said to be present when the motive for [receiving] the sacrament [of marriage] is the church's faith, "which works through love" (Gal 5:6), and it is completed in that love as in its end. Only when that happens is the good of marriage called "sacrament" present.[17]

In sum, the marriage bond always signifies Christ's inseparable union with the church, according to Alexander, whether or not the spouses are aware of its so doing, but the bond fully acquires its identity as the good of sacrament only when it is based on faith in Christ and on the baptismal character, for until then it does not fully participate in the inseparable union that it signifies.

Albertus Magnus argues that all three conjugal goods are present in the marriages of infidels as well as of believers, but in a prior and posterior manner (*per prius et posterius*). They are present "perfectly and wholly" only among believers.[18] As regards the good of faith, monogamy signifies the joining of Christ and the church better than polygyny does. The polygyny of the Old Law signified Christ's union with the church militant, whereas Christian monogamy signifies Christ's union with the church triumphant.[19] An infidel marriage has indivisibility, or the *bonum sacramenti*, but not in every respect (*omnimoda*), for such marriages are soluble at least in respect of the Pauline Privilege. Similarly, divorce was still possible under the Old Law, whereas the complete indissolubility of marriage (*omnimoda indis-solubilitas*) flows from the incarnation of Christ under the New Law, when the law of marriage became stricter because of its use as a remedy against concupiscence.[20] Insofar as the indivisibility of such non-Christian marriages is defective, so too is their capacity to signify Christ and the church. Albert suggests that marriages

---

[15] Ibid., arg. contra, §34 (1109).   [16] Ibid., resp., §35 (1109).   [17] *IV Sent.* 39.7e (590).
[18] Albertus Magnus, *IV Sent.* 31.5, resp. (234b).   [19] *IV Sent.* 33.6, resp. (297b–98a).
[20] Albertus Magnus, *De matrimonio* 3.2, ad 3; 2.5, ad 10 (Cologne 26:166b; 164a).

between unbelievers are "habitually" indivisible, just as circumcision was habitually significant for those Israelites under the Old Law who did not understand its significance.[21] What does the term "indivisible" mean when predicated of infidel marriages? Albert suggests that the privative prefix, *in-*, deprives these marriages of actual but not of potential *de iure* separability, since "in some contingent cases they can be divided" (i.e., by the Pauline Privilege).[22]

Thomas Aquinas, following Albert, argues that all three conjugal goods exist among infidels, but only in an imperfect manner. The same may be said of marriage itself, for although unbelievers as well as believers can aspire to the perfection of nature, only believers can aspire to the perfection of grace. The marriage of unbelievers is "imperfect and material" in relation to that of believers,[23] for unbelievers marry only inasmuch as marriage is an office of nature. One might consider such a marriage to be a sacrament of the church "habitually" (i.e., potentially or seminally), as Albert had said, for although unbelievers do not actually contract marriage in the faith of the church, their marriages have some relationship with that faith through the original institution of marriage. But marriage is subject to "the dispensation of the church's ministers" only inasmuch as it is actually a sacrament, since positive law is binding only for the members of the community subject to it.[24] Likewise, the good of offspring is present everywhere as a "good intended by nature," which pertains to the preservation of the species, but it is fully realized as a benefit of sacramental marriage only among believers, where it entails higher ends, especially the raising of children to worship God. Contrariwise, Christian spouses sin if their sole purpose in coitus is to pursue offspring as a good of nature, for although that goal is good in itself, believers are required to refer all created goods to God.[25]

Although marriage often lacks the goods of faith and offspring in actuality, Thomas argues, it never exists without inseparability. The reason for the difference is that marriage is inseparable in its very essence, whereas faith and offspring pertain to the use of marriage.[26] Nevertheless, the marriage bond between unbelievers is "not entirely firm and established." The bond between believers is firmer because it is "established through the faith of Christ." In the Pauline Privilege, the firmer bond of sacramental marriage trumps the weaker bond of non-sacramental marriage.[27]

---

[21] *IV Sent.* 31.5, art. 1c; ad 3 (234b; 235a); 31.16, resp. (248a).
[22] *IV Sent.* 31.16, resp. (248b).
[23] Thomas Aquinas, *IV Sent.* 39.1.2, resp. (Vivès 11:225b).
[24] Ibid., ad 1. Cf. *Summa contra Gentiles* IV.78 (Leonine 15:246a): "Ea autem quae populo per ministros Ecclesiae dispensantur, sacramenta dicuntur."
[25] *IV Sent.* 31.2.2, ad 1 (126). See also ibid., 39.un.2, resp. (225b)
[26] *IV Sent.* 31.1.3, resp. (123a–24b).
[27] *IV Sent.* 39.un.5, ad 1 (229b): "Unde matrimonium infidelium non est omnino firmum et ratum; sed ratificatur postmodum per fidem Christi." Thomas is apparently referring to remarriage contracted after a prior marriage has been dissolved through exercise of the Pauline Privilege.

Thomas holds that some level of indivisibility is required even under natural and civil law so that marriage can foster the raising of children, lifelong paternal care for sons, and other social benefits. Although such laws are not beneficial in every case, they are beneficial or at least neutral in the majority of cases, which is all that is needed for a just law. Nevertheless, the bond becomes stronger and more demanding in Christian marriage, Thomas argues, where it must also serve as a sacred sign of a revealed mystery. Indeed, the absolute indissolubility of Christian marriage is a revealed truth:

> ... among natural acts, that of procreation alone is ordered to the common good, for eating and the emission of other superfluities[28] pertain to the individual [good], whereas procreation [pertains] to the conservation of the species. Hence, since law is instituted for the common good, those matters which pertain to generation must before all others be ordered by divine and human laws. Now, when positive laws are human, they should follow from the instinct of nature, just as every human discovery in the demonstrative sciences has its origin in naturally known principles. But if they [the positive laws] are divine, they not only explicate the instinct of nature but also make up for the deficiency of the natural instinct, just as whatever is divinely revealed surpasses the capacity of natural reason. Since, therefore, there is a natural instinct in the human species from which it follows that the joining of male and female should be both indivisible and one-to-one, it was necessary for this [joining] to be ordered by human law. But divine law adds to that a certain supernatural reason deriving from the signification of the inseparable joining between Christ and the Church, which is also one-to-one (Eph 5:32).[29]

Natural reason cannot discover the union between Christ and the church, which marriage signifies as a sacrament. Nor can it discover, therefore, the absolute, fully corroborated indivisibility that Christ demands of the faithful when they marry. Contrariwise, because Christian marriage embodies the mystery of Christ's union with the church, its absolute indissolubility, which precludes valid remarriage, cannot be fully explained in terms of the natural utility of marriage.

Peter of La Palu regards the marriage bond as a sacramental *ornatus*, which disposes a spouse to receive conjugal grace from God. As such, Peter argues, the bond is not a relation, as commonly supposed, but rather a non-relative accident (presumably a quality of some sort). But no such *ornatus* is "impressed" or "imprinted" in a marriage between unbelievers. Why, then, is such a union

---

[28] Thomas says "other superfluities" because the schoolmen held, following Aristotle, *De generatione animalium* I.18, that semen itself was a superfluity of nutriment in the final stage of digestion (*superfluitas ultimi cibi*). See P. L. Reynolds, *Food and the Body* (Leiden, 1999), 9, 113, 165, 172, 199, 247, 251.

[29] *Summa contra Gentiles* III.123 (Leonine 14:382b–83a). Human law in this setting is secular law, based on naturally-known premises alone. On Thomas's claim that marriage is "inseparable" even as an office of nature, see also *IV Sent.* 33.2.1 (147–48).

considered to be a true marriage? An unbaptized person who received the sacrament of confirmation or orders would receive nothing "real," for no character would be imprinted. If the same person were later baptized, he or she would have to be confirmed or ordained again, for the sacrament would not spontaneously revivify. How can unbelieving spouses who convert to Christianity and are baptized enter into the sacrament of marriage automatically, without marrying again as Christians?

In his reply, Peter invokes the distinction between contract and sacrament. Marriage without baptism is not "formally and properly" a sacrament, he concedes, but it is "something" (*aliquid*). The same might be said of the sacraments of orders and confirmation. Confirmation without baptism it is not a sacrament, yet it is something, namely, an anointing with oil or chrism. One might even call such anointing "confirmation," although one would be using the term equivocally. So, too, is the term "marriage" equivocal, for it may denote either a merely human contract or a sacrament. But there is a major difference between the two examples. Marriage, unlike anointing or chrismation, has an explicable integrity even without baptism, for the same term, "marriage," is both "the name of a contract and the name of a sacrament." A marriage without baptism is a true marriage insofar marriage is a contract, but it is not a true marriage insofar as marriage is a sacrament. Infidel marriage is not a merely fictive entity, therefore, as confirmation without baptism would be. When unbelieving spouses convert to Christianity, the real but merely human marriage that already exists between them becomes in addition a sacrament, and the merely obligational bond becomes a sacramental *ornatus*.[30]

16.2 BLESSED AND UNBLESSED MARRIAGES

Some theologians reasoned that what distinguished marriage as a sacrament from a merely human, civil marriage, forged by the spouses' consent without any special help from God, was the nuptial blessing. An unblessed marriage, according to this line of thought, was either not a sacrament at all or not a sacrament in the full sense. Only a few theologians were committed to this theory in its full-fledged form, but several others seem to have felt its attraction. The prelates at Trent associated it chiefly with William of Auvergne, who had argued that marriage conferred sacramental grace only by virtue of the nuptial blessing. William did not deny that there could be a valid marriage without the blessing even among Christians, but he held that such a marriage was not a sacrament in the most proper sense of the term (Section 15.3.2).[31] Likewise, Bonaventure held that an unblessed marriage between Christians was a sacrament but did not have "complete being" as a sacrament, and that it was not a sacrament *of the church* (Section 15.3.4).[32] Thomas Aquinas argued

---

[30] Paludanus, *IV Sent.* 26.4.3, ad 5 (142ra–rb).
[31] William of Auvergne, *De sacramento matrimonii*, ed. Hotot, C. 9, 525aC.
[32] Bonaventure, *IV Sent.* 39.1.3, ad 3 (4:836); *IV Sent.* 26.2.2, ad 4 (669).

that the nuptial blessing belonged to marriage not as to a civil contract but as to a "sacrament of the church."[33] The theory that marriage owed its full sacramentality to the priestly blessing enjoyed a sporadic, flickering existence during the second quarter of the thirteenth century, cropping up from time to time without becoming established as a viable alternative in its own right.

Among major thirteenth-century theologians, it was Albert who formulated the fullest and clearest version of this theory, although it is difficult to reconcile this formulation with his sacramental theology of marriage as a whole. He makes it in response to an objection: Every sacrament of the New Law involves a verbal formula (*verbum*) invoked by a priest, whereas marriage is established by the spouses' consent alone. Therefore, marriage is not a sacrament of the New Law.[34] In reply, Albert concedes that marriage requires a priestly formula *inasmuch as it is sacrament of the church*, but he argues that marriage must be considered on three levels: as an office of nature, as something good in the church (*bonum ecclesiae*), and as a remedy. The spouses' expressed consent suffices by itself for marriage at the first and second levels but not at the third, where marriage comes under the Power of the Keys (the priestly power of absolution) and is a sacramental medicine. Marriage cannot be a sacrament of the church, therefore, without the spouses' expression of consent *in facie ecclesiae*, the sacramental "dispensation of ministers" (*dispensatio ministrorum*), and the priestly benediction. It is true that these ministerial aspects are not strictly required for marriage to be a sacrament, but they are required for it to be a sacrament *of the church*.[35] Albert does not explain what marriage as a simple sacrament entails – in particular, whether it confers grace *ex opere operato* – but he implies that marriage owes its efficacy as a supernatural remedy to its ecclesiastical setting and, in particular, to the priestly benediction, although this theory seems to be inconsistent with the position that he presents elsewhere (Section 15.3.3).

16.3 THE DIVINE AND HUMAN DIMENSIONS OF MARRIAGE

Recognition that marriage was in some sense a hybrid entity emerged during the second quarter of the thirteenth century in response to objections to the sacramental doctrine. To show why marriage did not fit the paradigm in every respect, theologians pointed out that marriage required the subjects' active participation, whereas baptism and eucharist were received passively, or *ex opere operato*. But penance was arguably exceptional in much the same way, and because there was less reason to doubt whether penance was one of the sacraments, this comparison mitigated the anomaly.

---

[33] Thomas Aquinas, *Summa theologiae* II-II.100.2, ad 6 (1946b).
[34] Albertus Magnus, *IV Sent.* 1.14, arg. 1 (Borgnet 29:28a).   [35] Ibid., resp.; ad 1 (28b).

Alexander of Hales argues that penance as well as marriage existed even before the fall. Penance is a sacrament of the New Law insofar as it involves the Power of the Keys (priestly absolution), but its essence is contrition, which can be traced to the warning against sin in Genesis 2:17. Similarly, marriage was instituted in Paradise only as an office, but it was instituted again as a remedy after the fall, just as circumcision already existed under the second, post-lapsarian phase of the natural law but was instituted again under the Old Law.[36] The idea that penance existed from the beginning may seem odd or contrived, but Alexander has in mind a salient feature shared by the sacraments of marriage and penance alone. Both sacraments are based on an interior action of the participants: in marriage, on the spouses' interior consent, or joining of wills (*coniunctio animorum*); in penance, on the interior act of contrition. That is why neither of these sacraments includes something material: some external stuff such as water, oil, bread, or wine. Whereas the other sacraments were instituted after the fall, when human beings needed to be restored through exterior sensible things, marriage and penance were instituted before the fall, when human beings, as Hugh of Saint-Victor explained (Section 10.2.1), were still in touch with their inner natures.[37]

Albertus Magnus, too, held that marriage and penance shared features that differentiated them from the other sacraments.[38] The sacraments of the New Law, Albert argues, are of two sorts: those which are *only* sacraments, and those consisting of *both* sacrament and an *officium*. Scholastic theologians appropriated the term *officium* from Ciceronian political theory and used it flexibly, and sometimes as little more than a placeholder. Typically, it denoted a task or duty entailed by a status and regulated by the law of a community. Here, Albert seems to use the term to denote any human task, that is, anything that is intentionally *done* rather than received through divine influence, even including an act that is private and interior. Thus, Albert argues that marriage and penance alone are based on an office performed by the participant, whereas the other five sacraments are simply received. Whereas the plighting of troth in marriage entails an office of nature (*officium naturae*), the contrition required in penance is a personal office (*officium personae*).[39] Again, whereas the other sacraments involve an instituted form that the recipient receives *ex opere operato*, marriage is based on a contract (*pactum*) that the recipients make themselves. Both marriage and penance, according to Albert, presuppose "personal, moral, and civil" actions that were in operation even before the New Law. Replying to objections regarding the form, matter, and efficacy of marriage, Albert argues that the paradigmatic requirements apply strictly only to any sacrament that is "purely a sacrament," namely, to one that is received entirely as an *opus operatum*. Now, marriage and penance "draw their perfection in some way from us," for each is

---

[36] Alexander of Hales, *IV Sent.* 26.3 (447–50).   [37] *IV Sent.* 26.5a; f (450; 452).
[38] E.g., Albertus Magnus, *De matrimonio* 2.5, ad 10 (164a).
[39] *IV Sent.* 26.14, ad 2 (Borgnet 30:121b).

constituted partly by the *opus operans* (the work of the participant). But whereas marriage had remedial power only *ex opere operante* before the advent of Christ, it became in addition a remedy *ex opere operato* under the New Law.[40]

Although the verbal exchange of consent functions as the sacramental form of marriage, Albert argues, a form in the proper sense is not required because marriage does not draw its sanctification solely from the *verbum*. Instead, the "perfective form" of marriage is the spouses' "indivisibility of life" (*individuitas vitae*), which in turn is an effect of the spouses' expressed mutual consent. Similarly, only sacraments that derive their efficacy exclusively from the incarnate Christ have sacramental matter in the proper sense, whereas the persons themselves provide something equivalent to matter in penance and marriage. The quasi-matter of penance is the penitent's contrition, or act of sorrow (*dolor*). The quasi-matter of marriage is the couple "under some disposition," that is, insofar as they are potentially united through their own volition as one flesh through sexual intercourse.[41]

According to Bonaventure, as well, the sacraments are of two sorts, for marriage and penance depend partly on faith and partly on a dictate (*dictamen*) or instinct of nature, whereas the other five depend entirely on faith. Whereas sacraments of the latter kind were instituted by a simple divine mandate, those of the former kind were instituted partly by a divine mandate and partly through some interior act of recognition or illumination. Thus, rather than simply commanding Adam to take a wife, God revealed the purpose of marriage inwardly to Adam, who spoke as a prophet when he awoke from his "deep sleep" (Gen 2:23–24). Adam, therefore, had a role in the institution of the sacrament.[42] Again, the human contractants themselves are the chief causes of the mutual obligations of their marriage, but God as institutor is the chief cause of the indissolubility of their marriage and thereby of its signification, for indissolubility is the chief signifier in marriage.[43] Signification is a "dispositive cause" of insolubility, for marriage signifies the insoluble union that exists between Christ and the church as a result of incarnation, or the sharing of a single nature. But the act of institution by which God commanded that marriage could not be dissolved as long as both spouses were alive is the "effective cause" of insolubility. Jesus Christ himself reminded his followers of the original institution and made its implications explicit (Matt 19:3–9, etc.).[44]

The twofold aspect of both marriage and penance, Bonaventure argues, has implications for the relationships among their components.[45] Every sacrament can be parsed into its proximate *signum tantum*, its mediating *signum et res*, and its

---

[40] *IV Sent.* 26.14, q. 1, resp. (121b–122a).   [41] *IV Sent.* 26.14, q. 1, ad 1–2 (122a).

[42] Bonaventure, *IV Sent.* 26.1.2, resp. (4:664); 26.2.1, resp. (666).

[43] *IV Sent.* 26.1.2, ad 4 (664).   [44] *IV Sent.* 27.3.1, ad 1–2 (682).

[45] I have based the following exposition on Bonaventure, *IV Sent.* 26.2.1, resp. (4:666), except where other references are given.

ultimate *res tantum*. In marriage, the expression of consent is the chief *signum tantum*, although coitus is a *signum tantum* in a secondary manner.[46] The interior act of consent is the *signum et res*. The *res tantum* is twofold: both the union of Christ and the church, and the union of the faithful soul with God. In the five sacraments that depend on faith alone, divine institution is the sole cause both of their signification and of their causality, and the *signum tantum* is composed of some exterior action (*elementum*), which causes the *signum et res*. In baptism, for example, the act of ablution is the *signum tantum* that causes the interior character, which is the *signum et res*.[47] Marriage and penance, which depend on dictates of nature as well as on divine institution, differ in all these respects. First, the *signum et res* (the interior mental act) and its necessary relationship with the *signum tantum* (the external act) result not from institution but from a dictate of nature. Second, the *signum tantum* is not constituted from material stuff because, as Alexander of Hales argued, these sacraments originated in the earthly Paradise, when human beings did not need to perceive internal, spiritual things through sensible things. Third, the *signum et res* (the interior, mediating component) causes the *signum tantum* (the exterior sign), rather than vice versa as in the other sacraments. Whereas the act of ablution causes the character in baptism, for example, the interior act of consent produces its external expression in marriage, although the latter enhances the former.[48] Peter of Tarentaise follows Bonaventure's lead when he argues that the manner in which God first instituted marriage, by inspiring Adam to speak on his behalf, was congruent with the hybrid structure of this sacrament, which is partly human and partly divine. Whereas the obligation to sexual intercourse is carnal and human, Peter argues, the spiritual power of marriage to signify and to sanctify is divine.[49]

Like Albertus Magnus, Thomas Aquinas argues that Christian marriage is both an office of nature and a sacrament of the church. Thomas associates the office of nature with marriage as a contract, and the term "contract" appears with novel frequency in Thomas's treatment of marriage in the *Scriptum*. To explain why a nuptial gift or a dowry does not entail simony, Thomas argues that the money is used only to procure marriage as a contract and as an office of nature, and not as a sacrament of the church. Contrariwise, a priest who demanded remuneration for the nuptial blessing would commit simony, for the priest blesses marriage principally as a sacrament of the church rather than as an office of nature, which he blesses only by implication.[50]

---

[46] Bonaventure discusses the dual signification of marriage in ibid., ad 2 (667a).
[47] *IV Sent.* 26.2.1, ad 5 (667b).
[48] Ibid. Bonaventure concedes in *IV Sent.* 26.2.2, ad 1 (668b) that the *signum tantum* in both marriage and penance enhances the *signum et res*, although it does not cause it.
[49] Peter of Tarentaise, *IV Sent.* 26.1.3, resp. (4:284b).
[50] Thomas Aquinas, *Summa theologiae* II-II.100.2, ad 6 (1946b).

Marriage may be considered as a material contract or as a spiritual contract, Thomas argues. Considered as an exterior, mundane thing that has been elevated to the level of sacrament, it is material contract. Considered simply as a sacrament, instituted by Jesus Christ and subject to the regulation by the church, it is spiritual contract.[51] Although marriage is a uniquely twofold sacrament, being both human and divine, Thomas argues that the relationship between the contractual and sacramental aspects of Christian marriage exemplifies a structure that is found in all the sacraments of the New Law. Every sacrament involves some outward, mundane, material thing that the sacrament presupposes, such as ablution in baptism and bread and wine in eucharist. The conjugal contract, with its civil ramifications, is more than figurative and pertains to an office of nature, but it is related to the sacrament of marriage as the act of ablution is related to the sacrament of baptism. Each is the proximate matter from which the sacrament is composed. Thomas presents this analysis most fully when he demonstrates why spouses must outwardly express their mutual consent to marry, normally in spoken words. In every sacrament, Thomas argues, there is an interior, spiritual operation that corresponds to an analogous exterior, material operation. In baptism, for example, the interior cleansing of the soul corresponds to the exterior ablution with water. The sacrament of marriage is both "a certain spiritual joining, inasmuch as marriage is a sacrament, and something material, inasmuch as marriage serves as an office of nature and of the civil life." Considered as an external, mundane thing, analogous to external ablution in baptism, marriage is a material contract, therefore, and it is subject to the same conditions and regulations as any material contract. Thomas refers to marrying as a "material contract" partly because the contract is related to the sacramentality of marriage as matter to form, and partly because the contract considered in itself is a mundane thing and the object of mundane negotiations. Material contracts must be expressed in words, Thomas reasons, whereas religious vows do not, since they establish a purely spiritual obligation.[52] The primary cause of marriage as a sacrament, as of every other sacrament, is a divine power that bestows salvation (*salus*) through the sacrament. The spouses' material contract, therefore, is an instrumental cause of the sacrament, which acquires efficacy through the divine institution, just as the act of ablution in baptism has been divinely instituted as the instrument of spiritual cleansing.[53] Although the cause of marriage is the spouses' expressed consent, therefore, it does not follow that human actions cause conjugal grace: an implication that would entail the Pelagian heresy.[54]

One might argue that the expression of consent is necessary precisely inasmuch as marriage is a sacrament, for every sacrament requires a verbal formula.[55] Thomas

[51] See Thomas Aquinas, *IV Sent.* 40.un.4, ad 2 (Vivès 11:239–40) on marriage as a spiritual contract.
[52] Thomas Aquinas, *IV Sent.* 27.1.2, qu^a 2, arg. 1; ad 1 (82a 83b).
[53] *IV Sent.* 27.1.2, qu^a 1, resp.; ad 1 (83a; 83b).
[54] *IV Sent.* 2.1.1, qu^a 2, ad 1 (ed. Moos, 4:78).   [55] *IV Sent.* 27.1.2, qu^a 2, s.c. (82b).

does not deny that the spouses' words of consent function as a sacramental form, but he reasons that marriage is joined externally through words or equivalent signs chiefly because it is a contract. Thomas uses the analogy of baptism to elucidate the relationship between the exterior expression of consent and the interior *obligatio*, which disposes the subjects for grace:

> conjugal union is made in the same way as obligations in material contracts. And because material contracts cannot be made unless those who are contracting them communicate their will to each other in words, it follows that the consent that makes marriage must also be expressed in words. Thus, the expression of the words [of consent] has the same relation to marriage as exterior ablution has to baptism.[56]

Here, Thomas compares the expression of consent in marriage not, as one might expect, to the *form* of baptism but to its *matter*: not to the minister's invocation of the Trinity, but to ablution with water. Marriage requires an expression of consent chiefly inasmuch as it is a material contract, for every contract requires an agreement to be outwardly expressed in words or equivalent signs.[57]

Thomas's distinction between contract and sacrament in marriage had become commonplace by the fourteenth century, although theologians held different opinions about the nature and extent of human agency and about what to attribute to each aspect. According to Peter of Tarantaise, marriage is both a "divine sacrament" and a "contract of human obligation." A priest who accepts money for joining the spouses in marriage (*pro coniunctione*) commits simony because his ministry pertains to marriage as a divine sacrament, but a spouse who accepts money as a condition for marrying does not commit simony, since the money is intended to establish the human contract.[58] Peter argues that the spouses' consent is not the sole efficient cause of marriage, for it is concurrent with the positive divine institution of the sacrament. Since a sacrament is by definition the "visible appearance of an invisible grace," every sacrament is twofold, consisting both of something sensible and human and of something spiritual and divine. Marriage depends on the spouses' mutual consent insofar as it is a human contract, but it depends on divine institution insofar as it is divine. The spouses' consent cannot be the sole cause even of *de iure* dimensions of marriage, Peter argues, for these transcend any merely human contract. Peter argues that no act of human will would suffice to make each spouse's body the property of the other (1 Cor 7:4), for human beings as such are not entitled to give themselves bodily to others. Such a gift depends on divine intervention, since each human being belongs first to God. Thus, the conveyance (*traditio*) by which each partner becomes the physical property of the other requires "the concurrent will and authority of the Lord

---

[56] *IV Sent.* 27.1.2, quᵃ 2, resp. (83b).   [57] *IV Sent.* 27.1.2, quᵃ 1, resp. (83a–b).
[58] Peter of Tarentaise, *IV Sent.* 26.3.2, ad 3 (287b).

common to both."[59] According to Durandus of Saint-Pourçain, marriage is both a "civil contract," by which the spouses become mutually obligated to each other, and a sacrament. Each aspect of marriage requires an expression of consent in words of the present tense, or through other signs that take the place of words. On the one hand, marriage requires the expression of mutual consent because every sacrament by definition requires some "sensible sign." On the other hand, the contract requires the exchange because only the spouses themselves have the right to give themselves to each other, transferring ownership of their bodies (1 Cor 7:4), and because the contractual consent of each one to that exchange must be openly expressed, so that it is manifest to the other.[60] Peter of La Palu, as we have seen, argues that in infidel marriages there is a true marriage and a true contract but not a true sacrament. Such a marriage is said to be true only because the term "marriage" is equivocal, Peter argues, for it is both "the name of a contract and the name of a sacrament."[61]

16.4 ALBERTUS MAGNUS ON THE *OFFICIUM NATURAE*

Reflection on the definition of marriage and on marriage in the natural law led scholastic theologians to explore the natural human partnership that the sacrament of marriage presupposed. They discovered that it was fully capable of explanation and rationalization in itself, prior to any consideration of marriage as a sacrament. The elevation of the human partnership to the level of a sacrament of the church took nothing away from the former, theologians reasoned. Rather, it enhanced and perfected the contractual partnership, making something spiritual and divine from something material and human. Those basic assumptions raised several questions, such as whether the human partnership could exist without the sacrament even among Christians, whether it was prior to the sacrament in a historical sense, and whether the marriage of unbelievers was the same as the human partnership on which the sacramentality of a Christian marriage was based. Such questions surfaced sporadically in diverse contexts, and medieval scholars never arrived at consistent answers to them.

Albertus Magnus was the first to distinguish the "office of nature" (*officium naturae*) from the sacrament of marriage. As noted earlier, the schoolmen used the term *officium* flexibly and even equivocally. According to a definition that medieval scholars ascribed to Cicero, who wrote a treatise on the subject

---

[59] Peter of Tarentaise, *IV Sent.* 27.2.1, resp. (293a). On the concurrence of the two causes, see also *IV Sent.* 26.1.3, ad 3 (284b), and 27.3.2, resp. (296a). On the necessity of divine institution for the spouses' unconditional gift (*translatio*) of themselves, see also *IV Sent.* 26.1.2, ad 1 (284a). On the establishment of the conjugal debt as the spouses' *translatio* of their bodies, see also *IV Sent.* 27.3.1, quᵃ 2, arg. 3 (294b).

[60] Durandus, *IV Sent.* 27.1, resp., §5 (368v).   [61] Paludanus, *IV Sent.* 26.4.3, ad 5 (142rb).

(*De officiis*), an *officium* is "an act of a person that is fitting according to the customs and institutes of the state."[62] Typically, therefore, the term denoted a task or duty entailed by a status and regulated by the law of a community. But in Albert's view, as we have seen, marriage and penance are *officia* insofar as each results from a work that the subject does (*opus operans*), whereas sacraments are received passively, as *opera operata*. Albert argues that the sacraments of marriage and penance are based on an office performed by the subject – an *opus operans* – whereas the other six sacraments are based on *opera operata*, which the subject receives passively. Whereas the plighting of troth in marriage or the subsequent partnership is an office of nature (*officium naturae*), therefore, the penitent's act of contrition is an office of the person (*officium personae*).[63] The *officium* of marriage according to Albert, includes both the transient plighting of troth and the permanent relationship or bond that results. To explain why the initial joining (*coniunctio*) of this sacrament endures, whereas the other sacraments are transient events that have distinct enduring effects, Albert points out that in any *officium* the initial act is not merely transient but somehow remains.[64]

Albert notes that marriage participates in both divine and human law, as the jurist Modestinus put it.[65] Civil law regards marriage only as an office (*officium tantum*), and divine law only as a sacrament (*sacramentum tantum*), but canon law regards marriage both as office and as sacrament. Marriage was instituted as an office only once, in the beginning, although the office received subsequent determination under both the Old Law and the New Law regarding the persons who could legitimately marry, and it was further regulated under civil law to enhance friendship and cooperation.[66] Albert cites three sources to shed light on the civil aspect: the Ciceronian definition of an office as "an act of a person that is fitting according to the customs and regulations of the state"; Pope Nicolas's statement that "consent alone according to the laws" (*solus secundum leges eorum consensus*) suffices to establish a marriage between legitimate persons (Section 5.3.3); and Ambrose's characterization of marrying as a "conjugal compact" (*pactio coniugalis*).[67] Any *pactio* presupposes civil laws that regulate the matter to which the parties agree. Considered as a sacrament, marriage embraces not only the interior act of consent and its outward expression through sensible signs, but also the grace signified and conferred by the sacrament. Finally, canon law regulates marriage in relation to the "institutes of divine and human laws," that is, both as an office and as a sacrament.[68]

[62] Albertus Magnus, *IV Sent.* 31.4, arg. 1 (233a): "Ut dicit Tullius, 'Officium est communis actus personae secundum institutae patriae'." *De matrimonio* 1.2, resp. (156b): "Dicit Tullius, quod officium est congruus actus personae secundum mores et instituta patriae."

[63] Albertus Magnus, *IV Sent.* 26.14, ad 2 (121b).

[64] Albertus Magnus, *De matrimonio* 1.2, ad 2 (156b).   [65] *Dig.* 23.2.1.

[66] *IV Sent.* 26.14, ad qu. 1 (121b).

[67] Pope Nicholas I, *Epist.* 99 (*Responsa ad consulta Bulgarorum*), c. 3, in MGH *Epist.* 6, *Epistolae Karolini Aevi* 4 (1925), p. 570/16–24. On Ambrose, see earlier, Section 4.2.

[68] *De matrimonio* 1.2, resp. (156).

The same exchange of consent is central both to the office and to the sacrament but in different ways: as the formation of a contract in the office, and as the exterior sanctification or sensible appearance of an unseen mystery in the sacrament. Moreover, although the ministers of the church do not perform this sacrament, as they perform the others, they do control marriage formation through canon law, for "the institutes according to which the contract is made depends on the ministers of the church."[69] Thus, the efficient cause of marriage both as an office and as a sacrament is the same present-tense consent expressed "in words ordained according to the laws and decrees of the fathers," for these words serve a dual purpose.[70] If consent is the essential cause of marriage (*causa per se*), and good looks or wealth an accidental cause (*causa per accidens*), then civil law is the regulating cause (*causa rectificans*).[71] Although Albert is never explicit on this point, it seems that in his view the church is in some sense also the civil community (the *patria* or *civitas*) within which a Christian marriage takes place.

Albert inquires as to the manner in which marriage as an office of nature is a natural thing, subject to the natural law. Marriage is not natural in the merely corporeal sense that coitus is natural, for then it would not exclude fornication. Nor does marriage belong to the natural order that Cicero attributed to the primordial, pre-civilized human beings, among whom there was no private property,[72] for in marriage each spouse owns the other (1 Cor 7:4). Nor is this the generic law that "nature teaches to all animals," for irrational animals cannot marry.[73] Instead, marriage is natural in a manner that is specific to human beings. In particular, marriage enables human parents to recognize their own progeny for an indefinitely long period.[74] Moreover, the natural law of marriage presupposes reason, which alone can distinguish between the honorable and the dishonorable, between what conserves peace and what incites discord, and between what maintains and what undermines the household and the state.[75] Monogamy is a salient feature of what reason perceives as natural and honorable in marriage, for marriage was originally instituted as a one-to-one relationship. Nevertheless, polygyny was not against nature under the Old Law, for it was consistent with the peculiar exigencies of the Israelites during that period of their history.[76]

Albert's chief sources for his analysis of marriage under the natural law are Ulpian's dictum about a natural law that nature teaches to all animals, and Aristotle's observation that human beings are conjugal animals even more than

---

[69] Ibid., ad 3 (156b).   [70] Ibid., resp. (158a/8–13).   [71] Ibid., ad 4 (158b).
[72] Cicero, *De inventione* I.2.
[73] Albertus Magnus, *IV Sent.* 33.1, arg. 1–4 (289a). Thomas Aquinas repeats these arguments in *IV Sent.* 26.1.1 (Vivès 11:67).
[74] Albertus Magnus, *IV Sent.* 33.1, ad 1 (290b).   [75] *IV Sent.* 33.2, resp. (292b).
[76] *IV Sent.* 33.2, ad 1 (292b).

they are political animals, since the household is prior to and more natural than the civil community (*civitas*).[77] Albert explains that if human beings are naturally political (i.e., naturally constituted to live in communities), they must all the more be naturally conjugal, for the order of the civil community presupposes and is based on the order of the household. In the article devoted to this topic in Albert's commentary on the *Sentences*, a lengthy excerpt from Robert Grosseteste's translation of Aspasius's commentary on the *Nicomachean Ethics* takes up most of the response. In fact, the commentator here was not Aspasius but the translator, Grosseteste, who had completed Aspasius's unfinished commentary.[78] Beginning with the arguably Christian premise that coitus is guilt-free only when the purpose is procreation, the commentator goes on to prove that marriage is the rational setting for procreation. Reason intends the best, and the best in this case is not only the generation of children but also their nurture and education, including their education in virtue and knowledge. Male and female not only must come to together in order to generate children, as in other species of animal: they also must remain together throughout the lengthy process of nurture and education, until the offspring are complete as human beings. That is why the spouses mutually consent to an "indivisible way of life." Marriage belongs naturally to human beings in all those respects.[79]

Albert demonstrates in the same article, drawing on Cicero among others, why a stable, monogamous partnership is necessary for the proper raising of children. Nature teaches all animals to beget and to raise children, but that entails different things in different species. In some species, only the mother cares for her young. Males such as the bull, the ass, and the dog do not have determinate female partners because they do not need to recognize their own children. When nature requires both parents to cooperate in raising the young, the male must have a determinate female partner in order to recognize his own offspring, which he is genetically predisposed to prefer. Such are most birds and many beasts that walk on two legs. The bonding of male and female may even be called marriage in such species, albeit only in a loose sense of the term, for humans alone enjoy marriage properly so called.[80]

---

[77] *IV Sent.* 33.1, arg. 2c (289b). *Dig.* 1.1.1.2. Aristotle, NE VIII.12, 1162a16–19.

[78] See J. McEvoy, "Grosseteste's Reflections on Aristotelian Friendship," in McEvoy, *Robert Grosseteste* (Turnhout, 1995), 149–68; and P. Blažek, *Die mittelalterliche Rezeption der aristotelischen Philosophie der Ehe* (Leiden, 2007), 50–55 (on Grosseteste's version), and 123–32 (on Albert's use of Aspasius's commentary).

[79] *IV Sent.* 33.1, resp. (290). For the passage in Grosseteste's Aspasius, see *Aristoteles over de Vriendschap*, ed. W. Stinessen (Brussels, 1963), 78/93–79/13; or Robert Grosseteste, *The Greek Commentaries on the Nicomachean Ethics of Aristotle*, vol. 3, ed. P. F. Mercken (Leuven, 1991), 182–84. It was Mercken who first noticed the extent of the interpolations. Blažek, *Die mittelalterliche Rezeption*, 52–54, quotes this passage with Grosseteste's interpolations in plain characters and the fragments of Aspasius in italics.

[80] Albertus Magnus, *IV Sent.* 33.1, ad 1; ad 4 (290b); 33.3, arg. 6c (295a).

Albert regards marriage as the necessary building block of an orderly, properly organized, stable community. As Aristotle says, nature inclines men and women even more to conjugal than to political partnerships, for the civil community depends on the family and the household.[81] Polyandry is the extreme case of disorderly bonding, according to Albert, for it transgresses the principle that the female is naturally obedient to the male. If a wife tried to serve two husbands at once, the resulting conflict would undermine both the household and the state.[82] Although marriage as an office of nature is rooted in the natural law and springs from the duty to beget and raise children, therefore, it takes on additional determinations under civil law. Whereas nature teaches its own natural law of marriage, pertaining chiefly to the perpetuation of the species, authors such as Aristotle, Aspasius, and Cicero are the experts on the civil and political dimensions of marriage.[83] Infidels regulate marriage exclusively in relation to these political and civil matters (*secundum politegias et civilitates*), whereas marriage in the church is subject in addition to the "laws of Christ."[84]

16.5 THOMAS AQUINAS ON MARRIAGE IN LAW

The modern literature on Thomas's theory of laws is based chiefly on his treatise on law in the *Summa theologiae*, whereas Thomas's only extensive treatment of marriage is in his early commentary on the *Sentences*, for he stopped writing the *Summa* while he was working on penance. The interpreter must proceed cautiously, therefore, situating Thomas's treatment of marriage law in the context of the theory of laws in his *Scriptum*. But there is no treatise on law in the *Scriptum*, as there is in the *Summa*. Instead, Thomas presupposes and only partially articulates a general theory of law. Some of Thomas's most interesting and informative discussions of law in the *Scriptum* occur when he discusses three features of marriage: its basis in nature, the history of impediments to it, and polygyny. The theory of laws that emerges from the *Scriptum* is fairly well developed, although Thomas's terminology was still fluid. Like William of Auxerre and Albert, Thomas construes the precepts of the natural law as first principles of moral reasoning, and his treatment of positive law is, if anything, clearer than it is in the *Summa theologiae*. But the notion of divine law is still rudimentary and undeveloped in the *Scriptum* in comparison with the *Summa theologiae*, and Thomas says less in the early work than he does in the *Summa theologiae* about the teleology of laws in relation to modes of well-being and about the essential relation between law and the common good.

[81] Aristotle, NE. VIII.12, 1162a16–19.
[82] *IV Sent.* 33.3, arg. 5c (294b): "Ex hoc nasceretur dissidium oeconomicae et politiarum." Ibid., resp. (295b): "hoc ordinaretur ad destructionem oeconomicae et politegiae."
[83] *IV Sent.* 26.14, qu. 1, resp. (121b–122a).   [84] *IV Sent.* 31.5, ad 1 (234b).

16.5.1 *The theory of laws in the* Scriptum

Thomas posits several branches of law, referring to each as a certain *lex* or *ius*: terms that Thomas uses interchangeably. He sometimes refers to the rules within each branch of law as laws in the plural (as *leges* or *iura*), but he prefers to call them precepts, statutes, constitutions and so forth, as appropriate, reserving the singular term "law" (*lex* or *ius*) for a branch of law.

Thomas distinguishes in the *Scriptum* between (i) given, perennial laws that cannot be altered (at least by human beings) and (ii) adventitious laws introduced by human legislators. Both divine law and natural law belong to the first category. Divine law in Thomas may be cautiously equated with what later theorists will call divine positive law, in contradistinction to the natural law, but Thomas rarely refers to divine law as having been "posited," and then only for some special reason. Nor does he count natural law as a branch of divine law, although it is certainly divine in the sense that it is God-given. Thomas uses at least five terms to describe categories of man-made law: positive law, human law, civil law, determinations of the natural law, and ecclesiastical law. It is very difficult to determine how these five categories are interrelated and to what extent the categories overlap. The reason for this apparent muddle is that the terms originated in different contexts, and some of them as paired opposites. Thomas does not provide a comprehensive, analytical division of laws in the *Scriptum*.

The most important branches of law invoked in the *Scriptum* are three: natural, positive, and divine. Thomas sometimes mentions civil law (*lex civilis*), which in theory is the positive law of any civil community (*civitas*), but in practice is usually the law and jurisprudence of Justinian's corpus, as elaborated and interpreted by the medieval civilians (scholars of Roman civil law).[85] Thomas treats natural and positive law as opposites, so that each excludes the other. Divine law and human law (*lex humana*), too, are opposites, but whereas the term "human law" invokes the negation of divine law, the converse is less obvious. What is divine is not human, obviously, but the term "divine law" in Thomas had become somewhat separated from the original pairing. Natural, positive, and divine law arguably comprise a comprehensive threefold system of laws, although the relation of divine law to the other two is sometimes unclear or problematic.

Thomas assumes that a law is composed of rules (*regulae*) designed to guide practical, moral reasoning. Law is intrinsically teleological, therefore, although this aspect of law is less developed in the *Scriptum* than it is in the *Summa theologiae*. All except the first principles are designed to regulate *how* certain presupposed ends should be pursued, whereas the first principles of law determine *which* ends should

---

[85] Scholastic theologians use the term "civil law" exclusively to denote secular law, i.e., the body of laws designed to maintain the temporal public good of the political community (*civitas*), and especially Roman law, but not in contrast with criminal law.

be pursued. Law necessarily exists in reason, therefore, and it exists originally and authoritatively in the reason of a *legis lator*, who is typically a single ruler (the *princeps*), yet not in his own right as a person but as an office holder. The coercive and judicial aspects of law, including enforcement, jurisdiction, and the judicial process, which are central to modern notions of law, are peripheral in scholastic theories of law. In his famous treatise on laws in the *Summa theologiae*, Thomas mentions coercion and punishment rarely and then only in passing, and there is no reference to enforcement in his definition of law.[86]

Thomas adopted and applied systematically the philosophical opposition between natural law (*lex naturae*) and positive law (*lex positiva*). Following Isidore, he sometimes attributes natural law to the *instinctus* (prompting) of nature, but it is composed not of animal drives but of rational principles. The natural law consists chiefly of principles that are obvious and transparent, being comparable to the self-evident first principles of speculative reasoning. It is inescapably obvious to every human being, for example, that the human species ought to be perpetuated.

The term "positive law" had emerged in theology during the 1130s and was well established by the middle of the thirteenth century,[87] but Thomas owed his understanding of the notion chiefly to Aristotle. In Book V of the *Nicomachean Ethics*, Aristotle divides political justice into its natural and legal branches. Whereas natural justice is the same always and everywhere and transcends the diversity of human opinions, Aristotle explains, legal justice is variable and adventitious. Previously indifferent actions become differentiated as prohibited or commanded "when the law is posited" ("*quando lex ponitur*"). Some people, Aristotle notes, reason that all justice is legal, for law always varies, whereas nature is always the same. Fire burns in exactly the same way in Greece and in Persia, for example. Aristotle concedes that everything human is changeable and that only divine things are always the same. (Thomas comments that Aristotle is thinking of separate substances and celestial bodies when he refers to divine things here, since the Greeks regarded these gods.) But Aristotle points out that the natural order of things embraces exceptions. For example, the right hand is naturally stronger than the left although a few persons are ambidextrous.[88]

Thomas comments that Aristotle's distinction between natural justice and legal justice here is the same as the jurists' distinction between natural law and positive law.[89] Explicating Aristotle's terse remarks, Thomas compares laws to the

---

[86] *Summa theologiae* I-II.90.4, resp.: "Ex … praedictis potest colligi definitio legis, quae nihil est aliud quam quaedam rationis ordinatio ad bonum commune ab eo qui curam communitatem habet promulgata."

[87] See S. Kuttner, "Sur les origines du term 'droit positif'," *Revue historique de droit français et étranger* 15 (1936): 728–40; and S. Gagnér, *Studien zur Ideengeschichte der Gesetzgebung* (Stockholm, 1960), 210–70. On positive law in Thomas's *Scriptum*, see J. Finnis, "The Truth in Legal Positivism," in R. P. George, *The Autonomy of Law* (Oxford, 1966), 195–214.

[88] Aristotle, NE V.7, 1134b18–35. Thomas Aquinas, *IV Sent.* 33.1.2, ad 1 (143b), uses this example to illustrate the defeasibility of monogamy as a second-level precept.

[89] Thomas Aquinas, *Sententia Libri Ethicorum* V, lect. 12, on 1134b18 (Leonine 47.2:304/10–15).

propositions of a speculative science. Whereas the indemonstrable first principles of a science and the propositions that follow directly from them are naturally known, the other propositions must be discovered through industry and ingenuity. Similarly, a few laws are known naturally and function as the principles of legislation and practical reasoning, such as that evil should be avoided, that no one should be injured unjustly, and that stealing is wrong. These constitute the natural law. The other laws, which Aristotle calls legal justice and the jurists call positive law, are worked out by human industry and ingenuity.[90] Positive laws do not follow ineluctably from the first principles, in the manner of scientific propositions. To that extent, as Aristotle points out, positive law introduces right and wrong where there was no right or wrong hitherto. A positive law is *virtuosa* (i.e., has force) only among the persons subject to the jurisdiction of the ruler or authority responsible for positing this law.[91]

Although everything human is mutable, Thomas argues, it would be foolish to deny that there is some distinction in human beings between natural and non-natural things. For example, having two feet is natural to human beings, although there are exceptions, whereas wearing a tunic is a non-natural, man-made convention.[92] Following Aristotle, therefore, Thomas points out that many physical and biological things that are considered to be natural, such as the greater strength of the right hand, occur in the majority of individuals (*in pluribus*) but fail in a few (*in paucioribus*). Whatever belongs to the very essence (*ratio*) of the human being is natural without exception, whereas the dispositions, actions, and motions that naturally follow from those principles are mutable insofar as they depart from the norm in a few instances. Similarly, certain very general laws belong to the essence (*ratio*) of justice and are immutable, whereas even what follows immediately and naturally from those rules may fail in a few cases. Thus, the rule that something borrowed or entrusted to one's care should be returned to the owner holds in most cases but fails in a few, such as when one knows that the owner is a maniac who plans to use the weapon to do harm.[93]

The first principles of the natural law correspond to what Thomas calls natural inclinations.[94] Although Thomas holds in the *Scriptum* that these inclinations follow upon natural conceptions,[95] they seem to be the basis of natural law. The

---

[90] Ibid., on 1134b19 (305/49–57).

[91] Ibid. (304/42–45): "iustum vero quod est ex positione alicuius civitatis vel principis apud illos tantum est virtuosum qui subduntur iurisdictioni illius civitatis vel principis."

[92] Ibid., on 1134b27–30 (306/163–68).

[93] Ibid., on 1134b24–27 (306/148–53). This is Thomas's stock example, originally from Plato, *Republic* I, 331c.

[94] On 1134b19 (305/57–59): "Est autem considerandum quod iustum naturale est ad quod hominem natura inclinat."

[95] *IV Sent.* 33.1.1, ad 9 (142b): "naturalis inclinatio in appetiva sequitur naturalem conceptionem in cognitione." This principle explains, according to Thomas, why the males of most species, including humans, regard their female partners more jealously than vice versa.

inclinations are fundamental, existential appetites of reason: the inclination to exist as an individual, as a species, as a rational being, and so forth. But there are two ways in which an inclination may belong naturally to a human being. Some inclinations are common to all animals, such as the inclination of male and female to couple in order to beget and raise children. Human beings obey these generic laws not as human beings but as animals, although they pursue them in a rational manner. There are also specifically human inclinations, which human beings possess as human beings, endowed with rational capacity to distinguish between right and wrong. Thomas notes that whereas Aristotle's natural justice includes both aspects of nature, Ulpian and the Roman jurists used the term "natural law" to refer only to the generic aspects, whereas they attributed the specific aspects to the *ius gentium*.[96] Aristotle himself distinguishes between the generic and specific dimensions of human nature when he discusses marriage as a species of friendship in the *Nicomachean Ethics*.[97]

Whenever Thomas explains in what manner the natural law is natural, he begins with an account of the natural behavior of *naturalia*: of non-rational things such as the four elements, which act in certain predictable, invariable ways by virtue of their natures, without reason and choice. The actions of such things are said to be natural because they proceed necessarily from forms innate in the things themselves rather than from external influences, but such principles may be either generic or specific in relation to the subject. For example, a magnet naturally falls downwards by virtue of its generic nature, whereas it naturally attracts iron by virtue of its specific nature. Thomas points out that the actions of *naturalia* are sometimes said to be natural in another sense, namely, when they proceed not from inherent principles but from superior principles in the natural hierarchy of things, for example, when a body is naturally moved by a higher body in cosmology.[98]

Human action is supra-natural in one way and natural in another. It does not occur inevitably without the intervention of rational deliberation, as fire naturally moves upwards. On the contrary, it involves the "mediation" of reasoning and volition, which together constitute free choice.[99] But although free choice is by definition not predetermined, according to Thomas, it would be unintelligible without a predetermined, innate foundation, such as the natural law.[100] The innate principles of human action, unlike the principles from which the actions of *naturalia* proceed, constitute law in the proper sense, for they are rules of human action promulgated by God.[101]

---

[96] On 1134b19 (305/59–75). Cf. Ulpian, *Dig.* 1.1.1.3.   [97] Aristotle, NE VIII.12, 1162a19–24.
[98] *IV Sent.* 17.3.1, quᵃ 2, resp. (Moos 4:890).   [99] *IV Sent.* 26.1.1, resp. (Vivès 11:67–68).
[100] *Summa theologiae* I-II.10, resp. (774); I-II.91.2, ad 2 (1210b).
[101] *Summa theologiae* I-II.90.4, ad 1 (1209a).

Thomas already maintains in the *Scriptum* that other laws are reducible to, or derived from, the natural law one way or another, although the derivations may be oblique and far from obvious. Reduction and derivation are different ways of regarding the same logical relationship. Positive law is derived from the first principles chiefly through what Thomas calls "determination," that is, the application of general principles to specific situations in light of specific circumstances. Even when the natural law determines that certain actions are wrong or worse than others, the assignment of particular punishments to particular instances of those crimes belongs to the positive law.[102] Again, the legislator aims to inculcate particular virtues. These are not required by the natural law, although the natural law does command one to be virtuous.[103] Explaining in the *Scriptum* how all civil and even all divine laws are reducible to the Decalogue, which he construes here as an expression of the natural law,[104] Thomas compares positive laws to natural phenomena that cannot be explained unless one understands all their circumstances. Thus, Thomas posits three levels of law: self-evident natural laws; laws obviously deducible from the former that hold only in the majority of cases; and positive laws, which have no necessity or sufficient reason when considered in themselves, although they make sense once "all the particular circumstances have been considered."[105] Positive laws ideally "depend on the natural precepts that are the same for everyone," but only "through the mediation of certain circumstances."[106] Thomas leaves the second level of law unnamed in this discussion, but when he discusses Old-Testament polygyny in the *Scriptum* he characterizes the first principles and the principles immediately derived from them as first and second precepts of the natural law respectively.[107] Whereas second-level precepts are deduced from first-level precepts as if they were conclusions deduced from first principles in a speculative science,[108] positive laws are derived through

---

[102] This is Thomas's stock example the derivation of laws through *determinatio*. He uses it in IV *Sent.* 26.2.2, ad 1 (73a) and 36.un.1, ad 3 (181a) to illustrate the difference between (a) the derivation of positive from natural law by determination and (b) the quasi-deductive derivation of second-order precepts of the natural law from first-order precepts.

[103] IV *Sent.* 15.3.2, qu^a 1, resp. (Moos 4:712, §424): Positive law "proceeds" from natural law by determination, for "*intentio cujuslibet legislatoris est inducere homines ad virtutes ... quae pertinent ad jus naturale.*"

[104] III *Sent.* 37.un.3, arg. 2 (Moos 3:1243): "Sed haec [decem] praecepta naturalia sunt, cum sint de lege naturali." The Decalogue consists of secondary precepts of the natural law expressed apodictically and indefeasibly. There are exceptions to the prohibition against alienating another's property, whereas there are no exceptions to the commandment against stealing. But just as it is impossible comprehensively to define which cases of alienation are forbidden, so it is impossible comprehensively to define which cases of alienation are stealing.

[105] III *Sent.* 37.un.3, resp.; ad 3, ad 5 (1244; 1245).

[106] Ibid., ad 5 (1245): "praecepta legis quae apud diversos diversa sunt dependent a praeceptis naturalibus quae sunt eadem apud omnes, mediantibus aliquibus circumstantiis."

[107] IV *Sent.* 33.1.1, resp.; ad 2 (Vivès 11:140b–41a; 141).

[108] IV *Sent.* 33.1.1, ad 1 (141a).

determination.[109] Even second-level precepts are intrinsically open to rare exceptions, although they may acquire universal force through positive human legislation or through divine law.[110]

The positivity of positive law is found not only in change, variation, and apparent arbitrariness, but also in the manner by which the law obligates those who are subject to it: the perceived *force* of law. Whereas the natural law is binding always and everywhere by virtue of a nature that all humans share, positive law introduces obligations where none existed before, and in ways that are rightly, and not only through human error, peculiar to a certain community. The binding force (*vis obligandi, vigor*) of positive laws, therefore, is a function of the legislator's will and authority, although the legislator ought to derive laws rationally from the natural law.[111] The binding force of positive precepts cannot be traced back to the natural law for two reasons. First, whereas whatever contravenes the natural law it is evil in itself (*malum secundum se, per se malum*), the legislator's purpose in positing laws is not to prohibit things that are evil *per se* but either to prevent things that can be occasions for evil or to inculcate virtue.[112] Second, the derivation of positive laws from the natural law is not obvious to the law-abiding subject, whose reason for following the laws is not their reasonableness or their reducibility to the natural law but obedience to authority.[113] Thomas traces some other salient features of positive law to its dependence on the will of a human legislator. For example, although the legislator's ultimate purpose in positing law (the *finis operantis*) is to prevent evil, to promote good, and to inculcate virtue, the end of positive law itself (the *finis operis*)

---

[109] *IV Sent.* 39.un.2, ad 3 (226a): "Ea autem quae pertinent ad legem naturae, sunt determinabilia per jus positivum."

[110] *IV Sent.* 33.1.1, ad 2 (141).

[111] *III Sent.* 37.un.3, ad 2 (Moos 3:1245): "Similiter etiam praecepta caeremonialia vel juris positivi non reducuntur ad naturalia quasi ex ipsa natura vim obligandi habeant; sed hoc habent ex voluntate instituentis, quae in institutione naturali ratione utitur, si recte instituit." Thomas somewhat conflates two narratives in this passage, respectively theological and philosophical: the derivation of the (mutable) ceremonial precepts of the Old Law from the Decalogue, and the derivation of positive law from the natural law. See also *IV Sent.* 15.3.2, qu[a] 1, ad 1 (Moos 4:713) on the *vis obligandi* in positive law. In *Summa theologiae* I-II.95.2, resp. (1232), Thomas argues that whereas the second-order precepts derive their *vigor* from the first-order precepts because they follow from them quasi-deductively, the other positive laws are derived by determination, and their *vigor* is a function of human institution ("*ex sola lege humana vigorem habent*"). The adjective *virtuosus* ("powerful," "effective") in *Sententia Libri Ethicorum* V, lect. 12, on 1134b19 (304/42–45) denotes the same binding force of positive law: "iustum vero quod est ex positione alicuius civitatis vel principis apud illos tantum est *virtuosum* qui subduntur iurisdictioni illius civitatis vel principis."

[112] *IV Sent.* 15.3.1, qu[a] 4, resp. (Moos 4:707): "Praecepto juris naturalis prohibentur ea quae sunt secundum se mala. Sed praeceptis juris positivi prohibentur ea quae possunt esse occasiones malorum; vel praecipiuntur aliqua ordinantia ad virtutem, quam legis positor inducere inten-dit." Thomas tends to regard natural laws as prohibitive, and positive laws as prescriptive, and to assign determinate natural ends to proper actions and natural institutions (see below).

[113] *III Sent.* 37.un.2, ad 4 (Moos 3:1245): "quod lege praecipitur ... aliquando non habet rationem quare sic vel aliter fiat."

is to regulate external actions. Positive laws are binding externally and in the public forum, therefore, but not at the level of intention and conscience.[114] Thus, no one should be punished for obeying positive laws grudgingly or with bad motives. To obey is enough.

Thomas maintains that positive laws are instituted to maximize the good and prevent evil only in the majority of cases (*in pluribus*). Exceptions are unusual but not necessarily rare. This feature of positive laws is a necessary consequence of their derivedness and specification, but it is also a corollary of the dependence of positive law on the will of the legislator. Because positive laws are too specific to be beneficial in every case, there are bound to be cases in which obedience to the law would do more harm than good or be counterproductive, and such eventualities are contrary to the intention of the legislator.[115] It follows that all positive laws, insofar as they are positive, are dispensable. Legislators and "those similar to them" (i.e., those with delegated judicial powers), Thomas holds, have the power to dispense their subjects from the positive laws in such cases. Absent dispensation, however, political life generally requires that one must obey the law regardless, for "the good of the many should not be set aside because of the good of the one, since the good of the many is always more divine than the good of the one." Only in extreme situations is one permitted to disobey positive law without a dispensation.[116]

The distinction between divine law and human law had much deeper roots in Christian tradition. It went back to a period in which the pope and his prelates in the west were becoming acutely aware of the differences between the demands of the Gospel and the requirements of Roman law, which they now perceived as emanating from a remote authority in the east. Gregory the Great used the terms "human law" and "divine law" to distinguish between the secular law of Rome (including imperial laws regulating the church) and the more demanding law of the church, which was based on Scripture and existed for the sake of eternal well-being.[117] Thomas remarks in the *Summa theologiae* that the divine law is "instituted chiefly to ordain human beings to God, but human law chiefly to ordain human beings to one another."[118] Human law in that sense is the same as civil law, at least as the latter is broadly understood. In the twelfth century, the term "divine law" sometimes denoted canon law, but Isidore attributed divine law to nature and human laws to

---

[114] *IV Sent.* 15.3.4, quᵃ 1, ad 3 (Moos 4:723, §493). *IV Sent.* 17.3.3, quᵃ 4, ad 5 (906): "praecepta juris positivi non se extendunt ultra intentionem praecipientis quae est finis praecepti."

[115] *IV Sent.* 15.3.2, quᵃ 1, resp. (Moos 712, §423): "... per praecepta juris positivi ... removentur aliqua quae non sunt de se mala et semper. Unde in aliquo casu possunt esse bona et necessaria quae talibus prohibentur preceptis. Et ideo non fuit intentio legislatoris ut semper observaretur praeceptum suum, nisi in illis casibus in quibus bonum virtutis potest conservari."

[116] Cf. Aristotle, NE I.2, 1094b9–10, in Thomas Aquinas, *Sententia Libri Ethicorum* (Leonine 47.1:7): "Amabile quidem enim et uni soli, melius vero et divinius genti et civitatibus."

[117] MWCh 138–41.

[118] *Summa theologiae* I-II.99.3, resp. (1254b): "lex divina principaliter instituitur ad ordinandum homines ad Deum; lex autem humana principaliter ad ordinandum homines ad invicem."

custom.[119] Glossing Isidore, Gratian characterized natural law as what is "contained in the law and the Gospel," explaining that whereas "divine and natural law" is the same always and everywhere, human law is variable and adventitious.[120] The notions of divine law and of natural law, therefore, became linked and were often conflated in the twelfth century. Thomas explains that although the term "natural law" usually denotes laws inherent in the subject, it sometimes denotes a subject's obedience to God, just as in cosmology a body's being moved by a higher body is said to be natural.[121] Because divine law was divisible into the Old Law and the New Law, it was closely related to Scripture. Thomas uses the phrase "divine law" in the *Scriptum* typically to denote any divine decree that is explicitly or implicitly recorded in Scripture, that no human agent has the power to change, and that is presumed to be essentially inalterable – except perhaps through the power of the Holy Spirit in very rare cases.

Whereas early-modern theorists divided divine law into the natural law and the divine positive law, Thomas and medieval scholars rarely referred to the divine law as positive or posited. Instead, they assumed that positive law was a product of human ingenuity and industry. As such, it was necessarily changeable, variable, regional, fallible, and apparently arbitrary. Moreover, positive law was limited in scope and binding only in the external forum, whereas divine law was binding also in the internal forum of private conscience.[122] Thomas refers to divine law as positive or posited only rarely, and always where divine and human laws are presented as parallel but contrasting systems. In the two clearest examples, respectively in the *Scriptum* and in the *Summa contra Gentiles*, Thomas has in mind the possibility of dispensation as a feature of positive law. In the *Scriptum*, Thomas attributes the practice of sacramental penance, in contradistinction to the underlying act of contrition, to "divine positive law" (*ius positivum divinum*), but his point is that divine law here has the same absolute, indispensable force as natural law, even though the law in question was posited historically under the New Law. The relation of the sacrament to the moral obligation to be contrite is a form of determination. Just as one cannot be dispensed from natural law, so even the pope has no power to dispense people from penance, enabling them to achieve forgiveness of sins without it.[123] Because Thomas still treats divine law as akin to natural law in the *Scriptum*, he sometimes holds that there are no exceptions to it. Just as whatever the natural law prohibits is evil in itself, so whatever the divine law commands is *ipso facto* necessary in itself (*secundum se*) for salvation. But positive precepts of the church derive their binding force from their institution by the church. They are always binding and necessary for salvation, absent dispensation,

---

[119] Isidore, *Etym.* V.2 (= Gratian, D. 1 c. 1).
[120] Gratian, D. 1, dictum ante c. 1; dictum post c. 1. (1).
[121] *IV Sent.* 33.1.1, ad 4 (Vivès 30:141b–42a). *IV Sent.* 17.3.1, qu^a 2, resp. (Moos 4:890).
[122] *Summa theologiae* I-II.91.4, resp., "*Tertio, quia ...*" (1212b).
[123] *IV Sent.* 17.3.1, qu^a 5, ad 1 (Moos 4:888).

but often only because the church has commanded them rather than *secundum se.*[124] Thomas construes the monogamy requirement as a second-level precept of the natural law when he discusses Old-Testament polygyny in the *Scriptum*, reasoning that God used his authority to dispense the Israelites from this law. In this context, therefore, divine law has a positive function, for God himself posited a determination of the law, much as a human legislator would do. Similarly, Thomas proposes in the *Summa contra Gentiles* that God has the authority to dispense people from "divinely posited" laws, just as human authorities have the power to dispense from human laws. For example, God dispensed Israelite men of the Old Testament from the divine laws of monogamy and insolubility.[125] Divine positive laws in this sense are laws that are dispensable by God alone.

16.5.2 *The ends of marriage*

In Thomas's work, the traditional reasons (*causae*) for marriage or marrying become ends (*fines*), or final causes of the institution,[126] and marriage is construed as an instrument for achieving those ends. Thomas's notion of the ends of marriage is akin to Augustine's notion of the conjugal goods, and he invariably identifies the primary end of marriage as the *bonum prolis*, interpreted as the begetting and nurturing of children. But Thomas distinguishes secondary from primary ends in two different ways in the *Scriptum*. From one point of view, the remedy against concupiscence is secondary. From another point of view, the spouses' sharing (*communicatio*) is the secondary end of marriage, that is, their mutual support and collaboration in aspects of their shared life other than procreation. There is no reason why marriage should not have two or more secondary ends, but Thomas does not treat these as collateral members of the same category, and the two distinctions work in different ways. The term "secondary end," therefore, is equivocal. The first distinction is theological in origin. It came originally from Scripture as interpreted by Augustine, who distinguished between the *officium* and the *remedium* of marriage. In central-medieval theology, it was associated both with a narrative of salvation history and with a preference for celibacy. The second distinction came from Aristotle, and Thomas always cites Aristotle when he makes it. Each distinction involves its own conceptual framework. Thomas construes both procreation and the remedy as

---

[124] *IV Sent.* 15.3.2, quᵃ 1, ad 1 (713): "praecepta Dei sunt de eo quod est de necessitate salutis secundum se. Et ideo in quolibet casu observari illa oportet. Sed praecepta Ecclesiae quamvis vim obligandi habeant ex actu praecipientium, non tamen semper obligant propter materiam in qua propopuntur."

[125] *Summa contra Gentiles* III.125 (Leonine 14:388b): "Et si quidem lex sit humana, per homines similem potestatem habentes dispensari potest. Si autem lex sit *divinitus posita*, auctoritate divina dispensatio fieri potest: sicut in veteri lege ex dispensatione indultum videtur uxores plures habere et concubinas, et uxoris repudium."

[126] On earlier treatments of the reasons (*causae*), see earlier, Sections 9.3, 11.3.2, 11.4.10, and 12.2.2.1.

essential ends of marriage, in contradistinction to accidental ends such as peace-making, and he attributes procreation to the natural law, and the remedy to divine law.[127] But Thomas counts both procreation and sharing (*communicatio*) as natural ends of marriage, and he attributes both to the natural order. Following Albert, Thomas attributes the regulation of the secondary, collaborative aspect of marriage to civil law and claims that pagan philosophers such as Aristotle, Cicero, and Aspasius are the experts in this field. The only reason for this ascription, it seems, it that theologians discovered the notion of *communicatio* as a secondary natural end of marriage in the writings of the philosophers, although they might have found it in Augustine (Section 4.1) or even in Scripture.

The chief source of this second, more philosophical distinction was a seminal passage from the *Nicomachean Ethics*, where Aristotle considers marriage as a mode of friendship. Like all friendship, marriage is based on a certain sharing (*communicatio*),[128] which Aristotle finds less in procreation than in mutual support and collaboration:

> The friendship between a husband and a wife seems to be in accord with nature. For a human being is by nature more a conjugal[129] than a political one [*in natura coniugale magis quam politicum*], inasmuch as a household is earlier and more necessary than a city, and the begetting of children is more common to animals. Among the other animals, then, community [*communicatio*] exists to that extent; but human beings live together not only for the sake of begetting children but also for the sake of things that contribute to life, for the tasks involved are divided immediately, those of the husband being different from those of the wife.[130]

The friendship between man and wife is natural because it is based on a natural sharing (*communicatio*). Indeed, the human being is primarily a conjugal animal and only secondarily a political animal, for conjugal life is prior to and presupposed by political life, and it is more natural insofar as it is common to many species of animal, whereas civic life is peculiar to rational animals. Sharing in other animals pertains to procreation alone, but husband and wife come together not only to procreate but also to collaborate and to pool their resources in other ways, for each has distinctive talents to contribute to their common life. (Thomas comments that men are more suited to work done outside the home, and women more to work done in the home, such as spinning.)[131] Thus, pair-bonding is natural among human beings not only generically, inasmuch as it is common to all animals and ordered to

---

[127] *IV Sent.* 40.un.3, resp. (Vivès 11:237).

[128] Aristotle, NE VIII.12, 1161b11, in Thomas Aquinas, *Sententia Libri Ethicorum*, Leonine 47.2:484: "In communicatione quidem igitur omnis amicitia est."

[129] The translators say "coupling" here, but I have substituted "conjugal" because it is more consistent with the Latin and with Albert's and Thomas's uses of the passage.

[130] 1162a16–24, trans. Bartlett and Collins, 182, but slightly modified. For the Latin text, see Thomas Aquinas, *Sententia Libri Ethicorum*, Leonine 47.2:485.

[131] Thomas Aquinas, *Sententia Libri Ethicorum* VIII, lect. 12, on 1162a19–24 (488b/256–63).

procreation, but also specifically, inasmuch as it is serves an economic, familial good, being ordered to what is sufficient in domestic life.[132]

Since the human being is naturally political, according to Aristotle, and since the family or household is the basis of the community (the *polis* or *civitas*), marriage is the natural basis of the more complex associations that are regulated by civil law: the positive law of the political community. The same text from Aristotle, therefore, was the source of a distinction the scholastics make between the natural and civil dimensions of the law of marriage. To these, Thomas added a sacred dimension.

Discussing the church's power to introduce and remove diriment impediments to marriage, Thomas considers the objection that marriage must be inalterable both as an office of nature and as a sacrament, since both natural law and divine law are inalterable. The impediments in question cannot contravene the natural law, for they are not universal and perennial. Nor, it seems, can human law introduce impediments, "because marriage arises not from human but from divine institution, as do the other sacraments."[133] In reply, Thomas argues that marriage as a legally constituted institution is based (*statuitur*) on three branches of law: as an office of nature (*officium naturae*) on the natural law, as an office of sharing and of the community (*officium communitatis*) on civil law, and as a sacrament on divine law. Tacitly conceding that the divine law of marriage is inalterable, Thomas points out that the natural law of marriage is subject to "diverse determinations" according to the diverse conditions and states of human kind, and that the positive law of marriage, which regulates the *officium communitatis*, is also intrinsically variable and mutable:

> Marriage is based on the natural law inasmuch as it pertains to an office of nature; it is based on divine law inasmuch as it is a sacrament; and it is based on civil law inasmuch as it pertains to an office of the community. Therefore, a person may be rendered illegitimate in relation to marriage by any of the aforesaid laws. Nor is marriage sufficiently like the other sacraments, for they are sacraments only [*sacramenta tantum*]. And because the natural law receives diverse determinations according to the diverse states [of human kind], and because positive law, too, varies according to the diverse conditions of human beings in diverse times, the Master [Peter Lombard] asserts that different persons have been illegitimate at different times.[134]

This reply will seem muddled unless one assumes that the terms "positive law" and "civil law" are here synonymous. Marriage is regulated, therefore, by three branches of law: natural law, which regulates marriage conceived narrowly as the basis of procreation and child rearing; civil law, which regulates marriage as a cooperative partnership, aside from procreation; and divine law, which regulates marriage as a

---

[132] Ibid. (488b/263–67).   [133] *IV Sent.* 34.un.1, arg. 4 (163a).   [134] Ibid., ad 4 (164b).

sacrament. Thomas presumably considers the *officium communitatis* to be the basis of the civil order of the community at large (the political community), although it is fulfilled primarily in the shared life of the couple. Divine law is unchangeable; natural (i.e., procreative) law is unchangeable *per se* but subject to additional determinations; and civil/positive law, as a human invention, is intrinsically changeable. Although the spousal partnership, too, as distinct from the procreative relation, is rooted in the natural law, Thomas considers the procreative aspect of marriage to be in some sense the most natural. Divine law, too, must be determinable, but although Thomas touches on this idea, he does not develop it extensively. The passage is confusing, too, because Thomas seems to conflate synchronic aspects of marriage (its juridical layers or strata, as it were) with successive regimes. Only the church could determine the validity or invalidity of marriage in Thomas's day, but Thomas never explains what kind of law the church applies to that end.

In another context, Thomas distinguishes between two branches of law regulating marriage: natural law with its determinations, and divine law. Marriages between two unbelievers of different religions may be invalid as a result of impediments imposed by the infidel rulers. Although a marriage between unbelievers fulfills only an office of nature, the natural law is determinable by positive law. If there is a law among the unbelievers preventing marriage between persons of different religions, such a marriage will be invalid. Thomas recognizes the validity of such laws, for human legislators, as such, have the right and the power to "determine" the natural law. Nevertheless, such marriages are not prohibited by divine law, because the prohibited action does not take the subject any further from the grace of Christ than he or she is already. Nor are they prohibited by ecclesiastical law, for the church does not judge external matters.[135]

16.5.3 *Marriage and the multiplicity of law*

Following Albert, Thomas assigned different aspects of marriage to different branches or categories of law. The basis of such divisions of law is obscure, however, for the schoolmen divided law in at least five different ways without distinguishing clearly among them. First, one category of law may be a determination of a prior category, as positive law is a determination of natural law. Second, laws may be construed in a historical sequence, such as that of the Old Law and the New Law. Third, laws may be identified topically, in relation to the diverse aspects of what is regulated. This third mode of division is akin to the modern identification of topical fields such as family law and corporate law, but it is more akin the scholastic division of disciplines, where each discipline is linked to a definitive body of authoritative literature: philosophy to Aristotle and his commentators, medicine to Galen and Avicenna, and so forth. Civil law is apparently a branch or category of law in this

---

[135] *IV Sent.* 39.un.2, ad 3 (226a).

third sense. Fourth, laws may be divided according who made them. For example, theologians distinguished between *canones* and *leges*, that is, between the laws made by councils and popes and the laws made by temporal rulers, especially the Roman emperors. Fifth, laws may be divided according to different jurisdictions (without separation of powers), that is, according to different classes of judges and courts. Ecclesiastical law, also known as canon law, which scholastic theologians rarely mentioned, might be construed as a branch of law in this last sense. But if so the fifth mode of division was not fundamental, for there was nothing to prevent a church court from applying the *leges* of temporal rulers to an issue when these were not contradicted by the *canones* of councils of popes.

In the initial argument summarized earlier, regarding the church's power to introduce impediments that invalidated marriage, Thomas posits three branches of law: divine, natural, and human. In the reply, he names five: on the one hand, natural law and divine law, which are inalterable; on the other hand, civil law, determinations of the natural law, and positive law, which are changeable and innovative. I have argued that civil law and positive law in this instance are probably coextensive. But to which category or categories does the church owe its power to introduce impediments? The modern reader is likely to assume that when Thomas attributed different aspects of marriage to different laws, he meant that the different aspects of marriage were subject to diverse jurisdictions or to diverse courts, but that would be a mistake. The natural law was not a jurisdiction. Moreover, the only jurisdiction capable of determining whether or not a marriage was valid in Thomas's world was that of the church.

Both Albert and Thomas attributed diverse categories of law to the several institutions of marriage, maintaining that marriage was instituted under each of several laws. Twelfth-century theologians had held that marriage had undergone a historical sequence of such institutions (Sections 9.4.1, 9.4.2, and 10.5.1). Albert and Thomas seem to have started with that idea, but in their hands the division was partly historical and partly functional and synchronic, so that it produced in an oddly mixed set of categories.

Albert claims that marriage was instituted under the natural law, under the Mosaic law, under the law of Christ, and under civil law. The natural law of marriage, according to Albert, pertains chiefly to sexual procreation for the perpetuation of the species. Albert points out that although marriage was instituted under the natural law in Paradise, this law is inherent in human nature and is the basis of all marriage laws in every period. The Mosaic law of marriage was chiefly concerned with the determinations regarding who could marry whom (i.e., with impediments of relationship). The law of Christ regards marriage chiefly as a remedy against the wound of concupiscence. Hitherto, marriage was efficacious only *ex opere operantis*,[136] as were all the sacraments of

---

[136] Albert's term is *ex opere operante*.

the Old Law, but it became efficacious *ex opere operato* under Christ. As a remedy, therefore, marriage belongs especially (*specialiter*) to the New Law. The civil law of marriage is concerned with benefits such as the honor that attends the spouses' mutual consent to marry, the friendship that follows from marriage, and the mutual help that the spouses give each other in sharing the burdens of married life. Albert claims that it is chiefly regarding these civil aspects that philosophers such as Aristotle, Aspasius, and Cicero wrote about marriage.[137]

Thomas bases his division on Albert's, but he inserts a historical institution of marriage between the fall and the Mosaic law, arriving at five institutions. Four of the institutions constitute a historical sequence: marriage was first instituted in Paradise under the natural law for the sake of procreation; it was instituted as a remedy after the fall, but still under the natural law; it was instituted under the Mosaic law as regards the determination of persons (i.e., the impediments of relationship); and it was instituted under the New Law as a sign of Christ's union with the church, whence it is counted among the seven sacraments. But marriage is also regulated by the civil law, which is concerned with the secondary, non-essential advantages (*utilitates*) that result from marriage, such as friendship and mutual service. Whereas Thomas says that marriage "had an institution" (past tense) under the first four laws, he says that marriage "has an institution" (present tense) under the civil law, for this institution does not fit the historical sequence. Thomas argues that marriage was not instituted as a sacrament either in Paradise or under the civil law. Instead, it was instituted as an office of nature in Paradise, and it is instituted as an office of the civil community (*officium civilitatis*) under the civil law. To qualify as a sacrament even in a broad sense, marriage must be a remedy as well as a sacred sign. Thus, marriage became a sacrament in a broad sense of the term in the remedial, post-lapsarian institution, and it was instituted as a sacrament under the Mosaic law. But marriage was instituted as a sacrament in the proper sense only under the New Law, when it began to confer grace.[138]

Thomas's notion that marriage was subject to or constituted by several branches of law remained influential throughout the Middle Ages and into the sixteenth century, although sixteenth-century authors were inclined to reduce the multiple laws to a duality of contract and sacrament, where the contract was subordinate to the "public good" of the *res publica*, and the sacrament healed the soul of the individual person. By that time, theologians had abandoned the odd notion that civil law and jurisprudence was devoted exclusively to the non-procreative aspects of marriage, as Thomas himself may have done in later works.

---

[137] Albertus Magnus, *IV Sent.* 26.14, q. 1, resp. (121b–122a).
[138] Thomas Aquinas, *IV Sent.* 26.2.2, resp. (72b–73a).

16.5.4 *The office of nature*

Thomas not only adopted Albert's distinction between marriage as office of nature and as a sacrament: he also imposed this distinction on Peter Lombard's *Sentences*, dividing up his commentary on Book IV, distinction 26 in a manner that had no basis in the text. Under the heading of the marriage as an office of nature, Thomas inquires whether marriage belongs to nature and the natural law, whether to marry is a still a precept, whether coitus in marriage is always a sin, and whether coitus is ever meritorious. Under the heading of marriage as a sacrament, Thomas inquires whether marriage is a sacrament, whether the sacrament was instituted in the earthly Paradise, even before sin was committed, whether marriage confers grace, and whether its completion as a sacrament requires sexual intercourse.

Although procreation is common to all animals, Thomas points out, it does not belong to them all in the same way.[139] To procreate is not only to beget offspring but also to nurture and educate them until they reach the completeness (*perfectio*) of their species. Among humans, completeness entails formation in moral as well as in intellectual virtue, and it requires many years. Albert had cited two classical authorities when he dicussed marriage and the natural order: Ulpian's characterization of the natural law as what nature teaches to all animals, and Aristotle's observation that human beings are by nature more conjugal than they are political animals, since the household is prior to and more natural than the community (*civitas*).[140] Albert explains that if human beings are naturally political – that is, naturally constituted to live in organized communities, where individuals achieve perfection in the whole – they must be all the more naturally conjugal, since the order of the community presupposes and is based on the order of the household. Thomas appropriates Albert's insights but emphasizes more than his teacher the distinction between the two dimensions of marriage as a natural partnership, respectively generic and specific.

Thomas uses Aristotle's theory of the dual function of marriage in two different ways. To show how marriage is natural, Thomas uses the theory constructively, positing natural ends of the human being and showing how marriage meets those ends. But to show that polygyny is deficient in certain respects, Thomas uses the theory prescriptively and instrumentally, positing Aristotle's two ends as the primary and secondary *purposes of marriage* and showing how marriage can either achieve or fall short of those ends. There is a fundamental but often overlooked distinction here: between (a) the natural end of human beings, which results in practices, laws, and institutions and (b) the natural end of those practices, laws, and institutions.

---

[139] *IV Sent.* 26.1.1, ad 1 (68a): "Sed quantum ad primam rationem inclinat ex parte generis; unde dicit quod filiorum procreatio communis est omnibus animalibus. Tamen ad hoc non inclinat eodem modo in omnibus animalibus...."

[140] Albertus Magnus, *IV Sent.* 33.1 arg. 1c; arg. 2c (289). Aristotle, NE VIII.12, 1162a16–19.

To show that marriage is natural and to construct its identity as an office of nature, Thomas follows Aristotle in arguing that marriage meets both a generic end, which is common to all animals, and a specifically human end. The generic end is procreation, or the *bonum prolis*. Nature intends parents to nurture and to instruct their offspring as well as to beget them.[141] Although procreation is a goal that "nature teaches to all animals," it requires different things from parents of different species. Among some species, the young are either self-sufficient at birth or require only a mother's help, and there is no need for pair bonding. Among other species, such as certain birds, the young need both of their parents for a short time, and male and female form temporary breeding partnerships. Among human beings, on the contrary, the young need their parents' help for a long time (*usque ad magnum tempus*), and permanent pair bonding is necessary. Moreover, children need to have determinate parents and to know who their parents are, and fathers need to know who their children are, especially their sons, even after they have left the parental home. These needs in turn require a determinate, long-lasting, and even permanent union between husband and wife, "which is what marriage does." The secondary natural end that marriage achieves is mutual service in matters of the household. Because no one person can do everything that life requires, natural reason determines that humans should live in communities. Human beings are naturally social or political. Moreover, since the male is more competent to perform certain tasks than the female, and vice versa, nature inclines man and woman to form a gendered partnership, "in which marriage consists." These tasks include mutual observance of the conjugal debt, construed as a remedy to sin.[142]

16.5.5 *Polygyny, proper actions, and instrumental teleology*

A theory of natural law based wholly in the teleology of agents, as outlined earlier, would draw few clear boundaries and provide few grounds for censure and condemnation. Thomas's idea of nature has teeth chiefly because he assigns determinate ends not only to agents but also to their proper actions – the actions that they perform naturally – as well as to institutions such as marriage, which Thomas treats in this context as a proper action.[143] Thus, having shown that the action or institution enables agents to fulfill their natural inclinations, Thomas uses that account

---

[141] Thomas cites Aristotle, NE VIII.11, 1161a16–18.

[142] Thomas Aquinas, *IV Sent.* 26.1.1, resp.; ad 1 (67b–68a; 68a). On the "inseparability" or "indivisibility" of marriage as an office of nature, prior to its absolute indissolubility as a sacrament, see *IV Sent.* 33.2.1 (147–48) and *Summa contra Gentiles* III.123 (Leonine 14:382–83). The argument depends on the premise that all laws apart from the first precepts of the natural law are beneficial only in most and not in all cases.

[143] N. Davidson, "Theology, Nature, and the Law," in T. Dean and K. J. P. Lowe, *Crime, Society and the Law in Renaissance Italy* (Cambridge, 1994), 74–98, at 77: "Thomas Aquinas … argued … that all things had been created by God with a specific purpose." See Davidson's references on pp. 77–78.

to assign determinate ends also *to the action or institution*: ends that the agent should pursue in performing that action or institution. Someone who uses the thing not for its assigned end, or who uses it for some purpose that precludes attainment of the assigned end, even contravenes the natural law, regardless of whether the repurposing fulfills a natural inclination of the agent. Thomas posits an instrumental teleology whereby instruments have their proper uses and must not be used for other ends, especially if these are incompatible with their proper ends.

The assignment of natural ends to practices and institutions is all but alien to the modern mind, although we can get some sense of it by considering the crafts. For example, no self-respecting carpenter would use a chisel to stir paint, since a chisel is designed to pare wood. Nevertheless, when Aristotle constructs a teleological account of eudaimonia in Book I of the *Nicomachean Ethics*, he begins by affirming that each science, art, and craft has its proper end: "of medicine, the end is health; of shipbuilding, a ship; of generalship, victory; of household management, wealth."[144] Aristotle shows that such ends are hierarchically ordered in an architectonic fashion, and he arrives finally at the highest end to which all others are subordinated: eudaimonia, which is the end of human life. Aristotle assumes that the attribution of determinate ends to skills and activities is more obvious than the attribution of ends to agents.

Instrumental teleology has a certain intuitive veracity, therefore, but it is not obvious why a natural law predicated on the agent's natural inclinations requires it. One might argue, on the contrary, that human beings are a naturally adaptive species, able to apply something designed for one purpose to a different purpose. In this respect, medieval and modern sensibilities are very different. For example, whereas we should consider the use of trees to make furniture and of honey as a foodstuff to be cases of artificial repurposing, medieval theologians assumed that God made trees and honey for human use. Even so, it is unclear why each instrument should have a determinate purpose that limits how it may be justly used.

Thomas is most explicit about the extension of teleology from agents to proper actions when he inquires in the *Scriptum* whether Old-Testament polygyny was licit.[145] Thomas's proof is ingenious but difficult and convoluted. He treats polygyny as a particular mode of marriage, assessing the aptitude of polygyny to achieve the ends that he has already assigned to marriage. He assigned ends to marriage by constructively showing how marriage fulfilled certain natural human inclinations. To show why marriage should have determinate ends that may be contravened, Thomas construes marriage as a proper action: as something that an agent does naturally. To heat and to gravitate upwards are proper actions of fire, to attract iron is a proper action specific to the magnet, and to gravitate to the lowest place is a proper

---

[144] Aristotle, NE I.1, 1094a6–9, trans. Bartlett and Collins.
[145] Compare the treatments of polygyny in William of Auxerre (Section 12.2.4.1) and William of Auvergne (Section 12.2.4.2).

action of any predominantly earthy object, including magnets. Thomas posits a
relation of aptness (*proportio*) between the subject's proper action and the
subject's end, assuming that a certain action may be performed in a variety of
ways, efficiently or inefficiently, productively or counterproductively, fittingly or
unfittingly. Whether it follows logically that the actions have determinate ends
regardless of the agent's intentions is debatable, but Thomas proceeds stepwise
from one level to the next, reasoning that a given action's aptness entails a proper
role that nature intends for it. Each proper action is *meant* to achieve something
in particular.

Thomas begins, as usual, with an account of natural action in natural things
(*naturalia*), but in this case his account is more puzzling than illustrative:

> It should be said that in all natural things there are present certain natural principles
> [later identified as innate forms] by which they are able not only to perform their
> proper operations, *but also to render those actions fitting in relation to their end*,
> whether these are actions that follow upon something from the nature of its species,
> or from the nature of its genus. For example, it pertains to a magnet to be borne
> downwards from the nature of its genus, and to attract iron from the nature of its
> species.[146]

Thomas distinguishes here between two powers in a subject: (i) the ability to
perform certain actions, which are proper in relation to the subject's genus or
species and (ii) the ability to make those actions apt in relation to the ends of the
subject for which they were designed. But there is no reason to make such a
distinction among *naturalia*. One does not need to posit in magnets, for
example, an ability to use their powers of attraction appropriately, nor in fire
an ability to use its heat effectively. Natural agents do not *apply* their proper
actions to ends. On the contrary, it is only because humans are rational and free
that they need virtues to predispose them to act in certain ways.[147] Thomas
attributes this second-order, instrumental level of capability to *naturalia* only
because the existence of instrumental capability will prove crucial in his account
of lawfulness among rational beings, who alone are fully capable of using
something as a means to an end.

Human beings alone understand the nature (*ratio*) of their ends and the aptness
(*proportio*) of their actions in relation to those ends, Thomas points out, although
irrational animals have a comparable skill known as "estimation." The rational being
must have "a natural conception in the cognitive power and a natural inclination in
the appetitive power by which an operation that pertains either to the genus or to the

---

[146] *IV Sent.* 33.1.1, resp. (140): "dicendum, quod omnibus rebus naturaliter insunt quaedam
principia quibus non solum operationes proprias efficere possunt, sed quibus etiam eas con-
venientes fini suo reddant; sive sint actiones quae consequantur rem aliquam ex natura sui
generis, sive consequanter ex natura speciei: ut magneti competit ferri deorsum ex natura
sui generis, et attrahere ferrum ex natura speciei."
[147] *Summa theologiae* I-II.55.1, resp. (994b).

species *is rendered apt in relation to the end.*"[148] Thomas is referring here to the subject's end, but he assumes that this is fixed in relation to the proper action, since every proper action is designed to achieve a particular end. Because the natural law is a "conception naturally implanted in human beings by which they are directed to act fittingly in their proper actions," it follows that whatever "renders an action unfitting in relation *to the end that nature intends from a certain work* is said to be against the natural law."[149] Thus, "whatever in marriage renders it inapt in respect of the end *to which it is ordained* is said to be against the [natural] law."[150] The notion that nature intends each *operation* to achieve a certain outcome comes out of nowhere in this discussion. It does not follow from the existence of natural inclinations. Thomas will construe polygyny as deficient in relation to the natural law not because it hinders the natural ends of human beings, but because it hinders the ends that nature has assigned to marriage.

As well as distinguishing between the primary and secondary natural ends of marriage, Thomas distinguishes more tenuously between two kinds of teleological inaptitude. A work's inaptitude may either (i) *prevent* the achievement of its natural end, whether primary or secondary, or (ii) *hinder* the achievement of either a primary or a secondary end by rendering it either difficult or less becoming (*decens*). For example, the primary end of eating is nourishment, and negotiation is a secondary end.[151] Eating too much or too little is inapt in the first manner, Thomas argues, for it *prevents* achievement both of the primary and of the secondary end. But eating at an inappropriate time is inapt only in the second manner, since it makes the achievement of both the primary and the secondary ends more difficult and less becoming. The two distinctions generate four possibilities, since both the primary end and the secondary end may be either prevented or hindered. Only what prevents a primary natural end contravenes a first-order precept of the natural law, Thomas claims, whereas what hinders a primary natural end or either prevents or hinders a secondary natural end contravenes a second-order precept of the natural law. If all this is hard to follow, the following summary may help:[152]

---

[148] *IV Sent.* 33.1.1, resp. (140b): "unde oportet quod in vi cognoscitiva sit naturalis conceptio, et in vi appetiva naturalis inclinatio, quibus operatio conveniens generi sive specie reddatur competens fini."

[149] Ibid.: "Omne autem illud quod actionem inconvenientem reddit fini quem natura ex opere aliquo intendit, contra legem naturae esse dicitur." Thomas seems to use the terms *actio*, *operatio*, and *opus* interchangeably in this article.

[150] *IV Sent.* 40.un.3, resp. (237a): "sicut supra dictum est [*IV Sent.* 33.1.1], in matrimonio illud contra legem *naturae* esse dicitur per quod matrimonium redditur incompetens respectu finis ad quem et ordinatum." The word *naturae* (italicized in the earlier quotation) is suspect, for although the question of the article is whether consanguinity impedes marriage because it is against the natural law, Thomas argues in the response that some relations are excluded by natural law, some by divine law, and some by human law.

[151] An early reference, it seems, to the business lunch!

[152] *IV Sent.* 33.1.1, resp. (140b–141a).

- Prevention of a primary end contravenes a first-order precept.
- Hindrance of a primary end contravenes a second-order precept.
- Prevention of a secondary end contravenes a second-order precept.
- Hindrance of a secondary end contravenes a second-order precept.

Thomas does not explain here why this set of relations must be so, but his (arguably circular) reasoning becomes clearer in the following article. Whereas first-order precepts of the natural law must be obeyed always and everywhere, second-level precepts apply only in the majority of cases (*in maiore parte*), leaving room for exceptions and dispensations – such as the polygyny that God allowed under the Old Law.[153]

To ascertain whether polygyny should be licit, Thomas treats Aristotle's two ends, procreation and communication (the shared life), as the primary and secondary ends of marriage respectively. Procreation, or the *bonum prolis*, is the primary end of marriage, and communication (sharing) is the secondary end. These ends are primary and secondary respectively because humans pursue the first end generically, as animals, and the second specifically, as humans. Pursuit of the first end, therefore, as Aristotle says, is more natural than pursuit of the second. Now, construed as a particular form of marriage, polygyny does not prevent or even hinder achievement of the first end of marriage (procreation), since a single man is capable both of inseminating several women and of raising the children whom he begets by them.[154] Therefore, polygyny does not contravene a first-order precept. But polygyny greatly hinders achievement of the secondary end (communication), although it does not prevent it entirely. Polygyny makes the maintenance of peace in the household more difficult because it is hard for a one husband to satisfy the needs of several wives. The man's several wives are likely to compete and quarrel, as persons pursuing the same craft do: "Potters quarrel with each other," as Aristotle put it.[155] It follows that polygyny contravenes only a second-order precept of the natural law, and then only by hindrance, and not by prevention. Now, because second-order precepts apply not in all but only in the majority of cases, they are open to dispensation and to determination through custom. The practice or prohibition of polygyny, therefore, is matter of custom, for custom may strengthen or diminish adherence to second-level precepts, whereas it has no power over first-level precepts.[156] Again, second-level precepts are not binding *without exception* unless they have been "sanctioned by divine and human law." Augustine was not wrong,

---

[153] *IV Sent.* 33.1.2, resp. (143).

[154] Contrast William of Auvergne, *De sacramento matrimonii*, C. 8, ed. Hotot, 524aH-bG, who argues that a husband is *not* capable of caring adequately for several wives and their offspring at the same time.

[155] NE VIII.1, 1155a35–b1 (also *Rhetoric*, 1381b14–18, 1388a12–16). Aristotle observes that although "birds of a feather flock together," persons pursuing the same goal in proximity tend to compete with one another, as potters do, and that such competiveness even undermines friendship. The well-known proverb was from Hesiod, *Works and Days*, 25: "Potter quarrels with potter, and carpenter with carpenter."

[156] *IV Sent.* 33.1.1, ad 1 (141a).

therefore, when he said that the polygyny of the Old Law did not contravene a precept.[157]

Whereas polygyny is detrimental only by *hindering* the achievement of a *secondary* end of marriage, Thomas argues, polyandry would *prevent* the achievement of the *primary* end of marriage. The primary end embraces both the begetting and the rearing (*educatio*) of children. Polyandry does not entirely prevent the begetting of children, Thomas concedes, but it does greatly hinder it, for although a man can sometimes re-impregnate a woman who is already pregnant, he is likely to harm one or both of the offspring in the process.[158] But polygyny prevents achievement of the other aspect of the primary end (*educatio*), for the paternity of a mother's children would be in doubt if she had several husbands, and it is fathers who are primarily responsible for the education of their children.[159]

Thomas uses the Augustinian division of the three conjugal goods, which he interprets here rather broadly, to illuminate the legitimacy of polygyny. He has already identified the good of offspring (*bonum prolis*) with the primary natural end of marriage, and he attributes the secondary natural end, *communicatio*, to the good of faith (*bonum fidei*). To complete this analysis, Thomas construes the good of sacrament as "the signification of Christ and the church," which lies outside the order of nature. "Hence, the first end corresponds to the marriage of human beings inasmuch as they are animals; the second, inasmuch as they are humans; the third, inasmuch as they are believers." Thomas argues that polygyny destroys the third end entirely ("*totaliter tollit*"), for just as Christ is one, so is the church one.[160] Nevertheless, Thomas argues in the following article that the good of sacrament remained "in some way" (*aliquo modo*) in Old-Testament polygyny, for although polygyny cannot signify the unity of the church, it does signify the distinction of degrees in the church, in which there are "many mansions" (John 19:2). Moreover, such distinction exists not only in the church militant of this life, as some argue, but even in the church triumphant of the next life, where there will still be diversity of rank.[161]

The law of monogamy is dispensable because it expresses a second-level precept of the natural law. God dispensed the Israelites from monogamy at a time when procreation and the purity of the race and of the cult were more important than education. Thomas's argument for this thesis is complicated, for he treats monogamy both as a second-level precept of the natural law and as quasi-positive divine law. The second-level precepts, which are like conclusions drawn from first-level precepts, do not hold universally but only in most cases (*in maiore parte*). Such

---

[157] Ibid., ad 2 (141b): "Unde patet quod illa quae lex naturalis dictat, quasi ex primis principiis legis naturae derivata, non habent vim coactivam per modum praecepti absolute, nisi postquam lege divina et humana sanctita sunt. . . ."

[158] From Aristotle, *Historia animalium* VII.4, 585a.

[159] *IV Sent.* 33.1.1, ad 8 (142).   [160] *IV Sent.* 33.1.1, resp. (141a).

[161] *IV Sent.* 33.1.2, ad 5 (144b). On distinction and hierarchy among the blessed in the next life, see *IV Sent.* 49.2.4 (Vivès 4:491–93); *Summa theologiae* I.12.6 (66–67); I-II.5.2, resp. (744b–745a).

defeasibility is typical of ethics as a whole. Second-level precepts are in principle not binding when they are not beneficial, but because such decisions are difficult to make it is generally better to leave them to those with legislative authority, who permit non-observance through dispensation. But monogamy is a special case, for God himself instituted it as a binding law, albeit not by voicing an explicit precept that would be handed down in writing, but rather by impressing it on the human heart (Gen 2:24). Now, dispensation from a law is usually granted in the same manner as the law itself was instituted.[162] It was fitting, therefore, that God dispensed the Israelites from monogamy not by making an explicit commandment but by inwardly inspiring some of their leaders, who passed on the dispensation not by written laws but by example.[163]

16.5.6 *The church's legislative power over marriage*

Thomas recognizes that the church is a legally constituted, state-like authority with power to make positive laws, which he refers to as precepts, constitutions, or statutes. He does not usually refer to these laws as human, perhaps because term "human" connotes secularity. Thomas refers to the law of the church as canon law (*ius canonicum* or *lex canonica*) and as ecclesiastical law.

Nevertheless, Thomas rarely mentions the church's law, perhaps because he does not regard it as constituting a particular branch of law. Thomas refers to civil law and church law as correlative opposites in two places, perhaps thinking of the two branches of juridical authority of his day.[164] In a third place, Thomas argues that a certain ecclesiastical practice must be permissible because it is neither evil in itself (*secundum se mala*) nor prohibited under the Old Law, the New Law (*lex evangelii*), or canon law (*ius canonicum*). It is clear from the context that Thomas is thinking chiefly of decretal law when he refers to canon law here.[165] Thomas does not mention church law in his treatise on law in the *Summa theologiae*, where he divides law in four main branches: the eternal law in God, the natural law (subdivided into first-order and second-order precepts), human law (which seems to be the same as civil law), and divine law (subdivided into Old and New).[166]

---

[162] *IV Sent.* 33.1.2, ad 3 (144a).   [163] *IV Sent.* 33.1.2, resp. (143).

[164] *Quodlibet* 12.15.2, resp. (Leonine 25.2:419): "alius est finis quem intendit ciuilis legislator, scilicet pacem seruare et facere inter ciues.... Finis autem iuris canonici tendit ad quietem Ecclesie et salutem animarum." The other place is *De malo* 4.8, arg. 15 (Leonine 23:126b), where Thomas refers to "*iura canonica et civilia.*"

[165] *Quodlibet* 4.12.1, s.c. 6 (Leonine 25.2:348). The question is whether children who are not yet adept in keeping the commandments are qualified to enter the religious life or to be bound by religious vows. Nothing disqualifies them, according to Thomas, for the religious life includes education in virtue.

[166] *Summa theologiae* I-II.91 ff.

Thomas's silence regarding canon law was not unusual. Theologians of the central Middle Ages did not develop a general theory of church law, although they did develop a political theology that divided the church or Christendom into two branches of governance, or two realms: the priestly realm, responsible for spiritual welfare; and the royal realm, responsible for temporal welfare.[167]

Two subsidiary factors may go some way toward explaining the lacuna. First, medieval scholars did not, as we tend to do, construe branches or species of law primarily as jurisdictions: as courts, judgment, enforcement, penalization, and so forth. Instead, they characterized species or branches of law chiefly by identifying their respective legislators, teleologies, and epistemologies. They asked who was the legislator, in what texts one could find the laws, what mode of welfare the laws were intended to maintain, and by what manner of reasoning the laws were worked out. Second, scholastic theologians as a class regarded the lucrative learned profession of canon law with suspicion and even hostility, and they were critical of its pretensions to scientific rigor and autonomy.[168]

I suggest that the chief reason for their silence, however, was that canon law was mixed law, since it regulated both spiritual and temporal matters. A wide variety of rights and actions came under the jurisdiction of church courts during the period, including matters temporal as well as spiritual, and the boundaries between ecclesiastical and secular jurisdiction were not always clear. Anything pertaining to the persons and property of clerics came under canon law, as did abstinence from servile labor on public holidays, oaths and testaments, tithes and other ecclesiastical taxes, and some areas of commerce, including just pricing, excess profit (*turpe lucrum*), and usury.[169] As noted earlier, Thomas says that whereas the civil legislator strives to maintain peace (*pax*) among the citizens, the aim of canon law (*ius canonicum*) is to work toward peace (*quies*) in the church as well as toward the salvation of souls.[170] The medieval church was coextensive with Christendom, and peace in the church was partly temporal, and in that respect regulated by the church's own quasi-civil law. Albert says that canon law regards marriage both as an office of nature and as sacrament: aspects that he situates in civil law and divine law respectively.[171] The entire scope of the church's power could be described as spiritual rather than secular, but only in a very broad sense, and not in respect of every detail of the law.

---

[167] See J. A. Watt, "Spiritual and Temporal Powers," in J. H. Burns (ed.), *The Cambridge History of Medieval Political Thought c.350–c.1450* (Cambridge, 1988), 367–423.

[168] See J. A. Brundage, "The Medieval Battle of the Faculties," in U.-R. Blumenthal et al., *Canon Law, Religion, and Politics* (Washington, D.C., 2012), 272–83; G. H. M. Posthumous-Meyjes, "Exponents of Sovereignty," in D. Wood, *The Church and Sovereignty, c.590–1918* (Oxford, 1991), 299–312; and T. Shogimen, "The Relationship between Theology and Canon Law," *Journal of the History of Ideas* 60.3 (1999): 417–31.

[169] See J. A. Brundage, *Medieval Canon Law* (1995), chs 4–5.

[170] *Quodlibet* 12.15.2, resp. (Leonine 25.2:419).

[171] Albertus Magnus, *De matrimonio* 1.2, resp. (156).

Although Thomas does not work out any general theory of church law, he explicates some of the church laws on spiritual matters as determinations of the natural law, and others as determinations of divine law. For example, whereas the prohibition against eating too much or too little belongs to the natural law, the rules regarding abstinence from certain foods at certain times are positive laws instituted by the church. The latter are based on the former, for "positive law is derived from natural law."[172] But when he discusses the sacrament of penance in the *Scriptum*, Thomas argues that the church has added positive determinations to *divine* law.

The sacrament of penance, Thomas argues, unlike the underlying act of contrition, must be a function of divine law (*ius divinum*), for the sacraments are declarations (*protestationes*) of faith.[173] Like all the sacraments, penance was instituted by Jesus Christ himself, who is the church's one foundation (1 Cor 3:11).[174] Because the work of the church's ministers presupposes the church, faith in Christ, and the sacraments, no minister can introduce a new sacrament, just as no minister can introduce a new article of faith. But although the divine law of penance obliges anyone who commits a mortal sin after baptism to receive the sacrament of confession, it does not determine when or how the sinner should confess. The fourth Lateran Council under Innocent III added a positive determination by ruling that everyone must confess at least once every year, regardless of whether or not he had committed a mortal sin.[175] There were three reasons for this determination: because it is salutary for all to acknowledge that they "have sinned and need the grace of God" (Rom 3:25); because everyone should approach the eucharist with proper reverence, for the same council required annual participation in that sacrament; and because parish priests need to recognize who are the members of their flock, lest a wolf is lurking among them.[176] Natural law obliges one to be contrite as soon as one has sinned, and divine law requires sacramental confession, but divine law does not require immediate confession except accidentally, as when one cannot otherwise do something else without committing another sin, such as when a sinner receives communion before receiving penance. Otherwise, indefinite delay is risky but not a mortal sin in its own right under divine law. But since a positive precept of the church now requires confession at least once a year, someone who disobeys that law by waiting more than a year commits a mortal sin. Some say that any delay is a mortal sin under divine law, and that the church's precept is intended only to minimize that evil. In their view, the precept excuses the dilatory sinner not in the internal forum of conscience but only externally, as regards ecclesiastical

---

[172] Thomas Aquinas, *IV Sent.* 15.3.1, qu[a] 4, resp. (ed. Moos, 4:708): "ad jus positivum pertinet quod moderatur hominum actus. Et hoc modo jejunium sub praecepto ecclesiae cadit."

[173] *IV Sent.* 17.3.1, qu[a] 2, resp. (890). On sacraments as *protestationes fidei*, see also *IV Sent.* 1.1.2, qu[a] 3, resp. (22); ibid., qu[a] 5, resp. (23–24).

[174] *IV Sent.* 17.3.1, qu[a] 5, ad 2 (894).

[175] Lateran IV, Canon 21 (Tanner-Alberigo, 245). Thomas calls this canon a "decretal" in *IV Sent.* 17.3.1, qu[a] 4, resp. (893).

[176] *IV Sent.* 17.3.1, qu[a] 3 (891).

penalties such as denial of proper burial. But Thomas considers that opinion both too harsh and contrary to the general principle that any "affirmative precept" obligates not immediately but at a determined time. The church established an obligation regarding frequency of penance at Lateran IV where none existed before.[177] In other words, the council made a positive law that was a determination of divine law.

Can the church or the pope dispense individuals from the obligation to receive the sacrament of penance, so that their sins are forgiven without their receiving or at least intending to receive the sacrament? To answer that question, Thomas argues, one must keep in mind the distinction between divine and positive precepts. No minister can dispense someone from the obligation insofar as it stems from the sacrament itself (*ex vi sacramenti*). One might object that the apostle James instituted the sacrament of penance (James 5:15), and that the pope, as successor to the Apostles, has the power to dispense from the precepts of the Apostles. But James only promulgated the sacrament, Thomas replies. Jesus himself instituted it, although that institution is recorded only implicitly in Scripture (e.g., Matt 3:6, Luke 17:14).[178] The pope has no power to dispense from the divine law of penance so that a sinner might be saved without the sacrament, but the pope does have the power to dispense from the church's positive law of penance by deferring the obligation beyond one year.[179]

Thomas maintains that the church can determine the conditions for a valid marriage inasmuch as it is a contract, since all contracts are subject to positive law,[180] but that the church cannot alter the form of any sacrament.[181] Replying to the objection that the church cannot introduce or remove impediments because marriage is a divinely instituted sacrament, Thomas points out that the implied comparison with other sacraments is invalid because unlike them marriage is not *only* a sacrament, for it is also fulfills an office of nature.[182] Thomas makes the same point when he discusses the church's power to extend the impediment of consanguinity to the fourth degree. Both marriage and baptism are sacraments. The church has no power to rule that someone who is capable of receiving the baptismal character according to divine law is incapable of receiving it according to ecclesiastical law. One might argue, therefore, that the church cannot prevent persons from marrying who are capable of marrying according to divine law. In reply, Thomas points out

---

[177] *IV Sent.* 17.3.1, quᵃ 4, resp. (892–93).   [178] *IV Sent.* 17.3.1, quᵃ 5, ad 2 (894).

[179] *IV Sent.* 17.3.1, quᵃ 5, resp. (893–94).

[180] *IV Sent.* 36.un.5, resp. (185a): "matrimonium, cum fiat per modum contractus cujusdam, ordinationi legis positivae subjacet, sicut et alii contractus."

[181] IV Sent.

[182] *IV Sent.* 34.un.1, ad 4 (164b): "Nec est simile de aliis sacramentis, quae sunt sacramenta tantum. Et quia lex naturalis secundum diversos status recipit determinationes diversas, et jus positivum etiam variatur secundum diversas hominum conditiones in diversis temporibus; ideo Magister ponit in diversis temporibus diversas personas illegitimas fuisse."

that marriage, unlike baptism, is not *only* a sacrament, since it is also undertaken to fulfill an *officium*. Marriage, therefore, is "more subject to the ordination of the church's ministers than baptism, which is only a sacrament." But the task (*officium*) that the church regulates is a spiritual one: "Just as human contracts and tasks are determined by human laws (i.e., secular, or civil law), so also spiritual contracts and tasks are regulated by the church's law."[183]

The notion that sacramental marriage is a spiritual contract may seem to contradict Thomas's distinction between the material contract and its sacramentality. In fact, however, both ways of speaking reflect the same notion: that the contract and its sacramentality are related as matter and form respectively. One may regard the same house either as bricks and their form, or as bricks that been informed in a certain way. Thomas follows a long tradition in maintaining that the goods of marriage are common to all peoples but acquire an additional dimension in Christian context. Thus, he distinguishes between (i) the *bonum prolis* as a natural good, which is common to all peoples and (ii) the *bonum prolis* as a good of the *sacrament* of marriage:

> Offspring inasmuch as it is a good of the sacrament adds something beyond offspring as a good intended by nature. For nature intends offspring as the means of preserving the good of the species, whereas offspring as a good of the sacrament of marriage is understood to include beyond that the directing of the offspring that the spouses have received to God. Therefore, the intention by which nature intends the offspring must be referred either actually or habitually to the intention of offspring inasmuch as it is a good of the sacrament, or else it remains solely at the level of created things, and this is not possible without sin.[184]

In the same way, therefore, the contract of marriage can be construed as a material contract common to all peoples or as a spiritual contract regulated exclusively by the church.

Thomas affirms that church has legislative power over impediments of consanguinity, orders, nonage, and uxoricide. In tracing the history of the impediments of consanguinity, Thomas relates its three main phases both to a division of ends and to a division of laws. There are two essential ends of marriage: procreation, also known as the good of offspring (*bonum prolis*); and the restraint of sexual desire (*repressio concupiscentiae*). The former is primary and regulated by natural law, whereas the latter is secondary and regulated by divine law. The chief accidental ends of marriage are the forging of alliances (*confoederatio hominum*) and the extending of friendship (*amicitiae multiplicatio*), and these ends are regulated by human laws and by ecclesiastical statutes (*leges humanae et statuta ecclesiae*).[185] Only

---

[183] *IV Sent.* 40.un.4, ad 2 (239–40).   [184] *IV Sent.* 31.2.2, ad 1 (126).
[185] *IV Sent.* 40.un.3, resp. (237).

parent–child marriage contravenes the natural law of procreation, Thomas argues, and that alone was prohibited in the beginning. Parent–child marriage does not entirely destroy the *bonum prolis*, for nothing prevents a father from begetting children by his daughter or from raising them. Nevertheless, because the relationship is "inordinate," the children cannot be begotten and raised in a fitting way. (Thomas is perhaps concerned about role models.) Father–daughter marriage is inordinate because the same woman is both the man's partner (*socia*) and subordinate to him as his child. Mother–son marriage entails an even greater conflict of roles, for although a wife is equal to her husband as his partner, she is naturally subordinate to him in some ways (*aliqualiter*).[186] In the next phase, God prohibited family members from marrying each other in order to curb desire. There would be little restraint if a man could marry any woman living in the same household. The divine law of Leviticus not only prohibited marriages between parent and child but also preserved decency by prohibiting any family member from "uncovering the nakedness" of another (Lev 18:10).

Finally, both human laws and ecclesiastical statutes advance alliances and extend friendship by prohibiting marriage among kinsfolk.[187] The endogamy of the Old Law was consistent with the needs of God's people at that time, when it was important that lines of descent should not be obscured (Num 36:6), and when worship of the true God was maintained by passing it on from one generation to the next. But exogamy is more consistent with the New Law of the Holy Spirit and of love (*lex spiritus et amoris*), for the worship of the true God is now passed on not through carnal birth (*carnis origo*) but through spiritual grace (*spiritualis gratia*). To expand friendship, the church formerly extended the impediment of consanguinity to the seventh degree, partly because the recognition of common ancestry peters out at that point, but also because the number was congruent with the seven gifts of the Holy Spirit. But that policy proved counterproductive, for it was fraught with opportunities for malice and deception, and the distinction between kin and non-kin was no longer obvious. The church reduced the impediment to four degrees, therefore, partly because that is the maximum extent to which members of successive generations can be alive at the same time, and partly because of the physics of mixture and the four elements, which suggests that a bloodline peters out after the fourth mixing.[188]

Someone might object that Matthew 19:6 – *"Those whom God has joined together let no man put asunder"* – rules out the imposition of any impediments of consanguinity beyond the four imposed by divine law. If divine law does not separate a couple, nor can any human law.[189] Thomas's reply includes his strongest affirmation of the church's power over marriage:

---

[186] Ibid. (237b). [187] Ibid. [188] *IV Sent.* 40.un.4, resp. (239b).
[189] *IV Sent.* 40.un.4, arg. 1 (238b): "Quos Deus conjunxit homo non separet."

Just as God does not join together those who are joined contrary to a divine precept, so God does not join together those who are joined contrary to precept of the church, which has the same binding force as a divine precept does.[190]

Thomas leaves the reader to decide whether secular extensions of the impediment have any force in the eyes of God, but the secular state had no jurisdiction over the validity of marriage in the Christian society that Thomas envisaged.

The impediments of orders and uxoricide illustrate how the church's positive law introduces obligations through determination. There is a certain fittingness (*congruentia*) between holy orders and celibacy, Thomas argues, for those who handle the sacred vessels should maintain ritual purity through continence (Isa 52:11). But that incongruity is not sufficient to establish an impediment, which is due rather to a statute (*constitutio*) of the church.[191] Moreover, positive church law works differently among the Latins and among the Greeks. Among the Greeks, the impediment arises solely from the sacrament of orders (*ex vi ordinis*), whereas among the Latins it arises also from an implicit vow of celibacy. Among the Greeks, therefore, the sacrament of orders is an impediment to the contracting of marriage, but there is nothing to prevent a married person from receiving orders, nor is being in orders an obstacle to conjugal intercourse. Among the Latins, on the contrary, married men may receive orders only if they abstain from conjugal relations with their wives' consent.[192]

Similarly, uxoricide is an impediment to marriage only by the church's decree (*ex statuto ecclesiae*), although that decree is based on considerations of welfare. If a husband has killed his wife because she committed adultery or even because he hated her, the impediment against another marriage is not sufficient to annul the contract *post factum*, and the church may grant a dispensation from the impediment if there is concern that the man is unable to remain continent. But if the man kills his wife in order to marry a woman with whom he has committed adultery (the impediment of crime), ecclesiastical law disqualifies him from marrying that woman and automatically nullifies the contract if he does marry her.[193]

Thomas attributes a more limited power to the church in the case of nonage. The law is based on the principle that one must be sexually capable and have the required level of discernment to contract marriage. Like every contract, marrying is subject to the ordinance of positive law, and positive law is based on what happens in the majority of cases (*ut in pluribus*). The law presumes that the relevant

---

[190] *IV Sent.* 40.un.4, ad 1 (239b): "sicut Deus non conjungit illos qui conjunguntur contra divinum praeceptum, ita non conjungit illos qui conjunguntur contra Ecclesiae praeceptum, quod habet eamdem obligandi efficaciam quam et praeceptum divinum."

[191] "Sed quod impediat matrimonium, ex constitutione Ecclesiae habet." Gratian, D. 31 cc. 12–14 (114–16), following the lead of the *magistri moderni*, compared Latin and Greek policies regarding clerical celibacy without condemning the Greeks, establishing a pattern of regarding both policies as valid. The most detailed study of Gratian's treatment of clerical celibacy and its influence is F. Liotta, *La continenza dei chierici nel pensiero canonistico classico* (Milan, 1979).

[192] *IV Sent.* 37.1.1, resp. (187).   [193] *IV Sent.* 37.2.2, resp. (190).

minimum age is fourteen years in boys and twelve in girls, but that is only a rule of thumb, for some persons become mentally and physically capable before that age. Consequently, if persons beneath the legal age have contracted marriage but are found to be sufficiently mature in mind and body, the church does not annul their marriage: a situation that usually arises when underage partners have married and have already consummated their union.[194] Here, then, the facts trump the law. It does not follow from the *ut in pluribus* principal that the law must always be followed even when the situation on which the law was predicated does not obtain. Despite appearances, the impediment of nonage pertains not to the persons but to the contract itself. The point is not that immature persons are forbidden to contract marriage, but that they are not able in the very nature of things to perform the contract, since they are neither mentally capable of committing themselves nor physically capable of fulfilling the commitment. The church determines whether there is a marriage only passively, by ascertaining the facts, and not by active legal intervention. Before Trent, canon law regarded clandestine marriage in exactly the same way.

16.6 CONSTRUCTIVE RATIONALES FOR MARRIAGE AS A SACRAMENT

Although thirteenth- and fourteenth-century theologians continued to analyze the legal dimensions of marriage historically, attributing each species of marriage law to a stage in a narrative, they also pursued functional, synchronic accounts, analyzing the multiple ends that Christian marriage was supposed to attain. Thomas Aquinas pursued this structural approach in a novel way in the *Summa contra gentiles*, proposing an *a priori*, quasi-demonstrative proof of the doctrine of marriage as a sacrament, and reducing the traditional division of institutions to a non-historical, synchronic division of purposes, each with its corresponding "directing principle." The method suited the apologetic aims of the *Summa contra gentiles*, for it showed how the sacramental doctrine surpassed but was congruent with the political rationale for marriage that theologians appropriated from philosophers such as Aristotle, Cicero, and Aspasius, and it showed how marriage was properly included among the sacraments of the church. Duns Scotus would later develop his own version of the proof. Both rationales begin with the premise that the chief end of marriage is procreation and on that foundation construct the civil and ecclesiastical dimensions of marriage.

16.6.1 *Thomas Aquinas's rationale*

Procreation, which is the primary purpose of marriage, Thomas argues, must be understood on each of three levels, respectively biological, social, and religious. One

---

[194] I presume this would be the case even if their betrothal were *de futuro*.

may procreate to perpetuate the human species, the civil community, or the church. Thus, marriage may be regarded as an office of nature, as a civil institution, or as a sacrament of the church. Marriage serves three corresponding ends, and each has its own directing, regulatory principle, which guides reason. Inasmuch as marriage perpetuates the species, it fulfills an office of nature and is subject to the natural law. Inasmuch as it achieves civic goods, especially the perpetuity and welfare of the state, it is "subject to the ordination of civil law." Inasmuch as it perpetuates the community of the faithful, marriage is subject to the church's governance (*regimen*). Furthermore, marriage insofar as it is governed by the church must be a sacrament, for whatsoever things are "distributed [*dispensantur*] to the people by the ministers of the church are sacraments." Finally, because marriage is a sacrament, the church's ministers confer their blessing on it.[195] The verb *dispensare* was commonly used to denote sacramental ministry, and a priest administering a sacrament was known as a *dispensator*. Thus, inquiring in the *Scriptum* whether sacramental penance was necessary for remission of actual sins, Thomas argues that the penitent must seek the *dispensatio* of the sacrament from a minister of the church:

> Just as someone in seeking to be baptized submits himself to the ministers of the church, to whom belongs the dispensing [*dispensatio*] of that sacrament, so also a person in confessing his sin submits himself to a minister of the church, so that he may obtain forgiveness through the sacrament of penance dispensed by the minister.[196]

Thomas does not explain in what sense clerics are *dispensatores* of marriage. He does not claim the nuptial blessing is necessary for a sacramental marriage, although he considers that rite to be fitting. The *dispensatio* necessary for marriage is presumably limited to legislation, judging, and teaching.

Construed as a sacrament of the church, according to Thomas, marriage is "the joining of a male and a female who intend to beget and to raise children for the worship of God" – a definition designed to reveal how the sacrament extends the natural office. From the Christian point of view, the good of offspring (*bonum prolis*) pertains chiefly to the perpetuity of the church, and not to the perpetuity of the species or of the state. Moreover, as a sacrament, marriage must be a sign of a sacred reality, and it must confer grace. The reality that the sacrament chiefly signifies is the union of Christ and the church (Eph 5:32), and both monogamy and the goods of faith and of sacrament (indivisibility) are features of marriage required by that signification. "Because the sacraments effect what they signify," Thomas argues, "one must believe that a grace is conferred through this sacrament on those who are marrying: a grace through which they may belong to the union of Christ and the Church. And this is especially needful for them, so that they may strive not to be

---

[195] *Summa contra gentiles* IV.78 (Leonine 15:246): "unde et quaedam benedictio nubentibus per ministros Ecclesiae adhibetur."
[196] *IV Sent.* 17.3.1, quᵃ 1, resp. (Moos 4:889).

disjoined from Christ and the church by carnal and earthly things." Rather than distinguish between contained and uncontained *significata*, as he had previously done, Thomas construes conjugal grace here as a further requirement of the same signification, for this grace enables the spouses to participate fully *as spouses* in the mystery of Christ and the church.

Marriage as a sacrament of Christ and the church must be monogamous, exclusive, and indivisible, Thomas argues, for the sign (*figura*) must correspond to what is signified (*significatum*). One Christ is united to one church. As it says in Song 6:8: "One is my dove, my perfect one." Moreover, this is a union of one male (Christ) to one female (the church) that must be kept perpetually (*unius ad unam perpetuo habendam*). Christ will never be separated from his church (Matt 28:20). Nor will his followers ever be separated from Christ (1 Thess 4:17). Marriage as a sacrament of the church, therefore, is a union of one man to one woman whom he must keep indivisibly (*unius ad unam indivisibiliter habendam*). This indivisible, exclusively monogamous obligation pertains chiefly to the good of faith, whereas the quality of indivisibility *per se* pertains rather to the good of sacrament.

Finally, marriage as a sacrament of the church has the three goods enumerated by Augustine: offspring, faith, and sacrament. Children are begotten so that they can be supported and raised to worship God. There is faith insofar as one man is bound to one woman exclusively and indivisibly. And there is sacrament insofar as there is indivisibility in the union, for in this respect, too, marriage is a sacrament, or sign, of Christ and the Church.

16.6.2 *John Duns Scotus's rationale*

John Duns Scotus developed a similar deductive proof, which is recorded both in the *Opus Oxoniense* and in the *Reportatio Parisiensis*. The two accounts are mutually consistent and complementary, and the summary that follows is based on both.

The primary purpose of marriage is to generate and raise offspring, Scotus argues. Indeed, the desire to raise children is inscribed in human nature in such a way that it would still be a natural, innate desire if human beings were immortal and there was no need to perpetuate their species. In order to ensure the proper begetting and raising of children in a manner that befits humanity, both nature and civil order require that each child should have known parents who have permanently obligated themselves to each other. The natural law requires that marriage should be insoluble, but insolubility presupposes that the spouses give themselves unconditionally to each other: a gift that God himself instituted and approved.[197] Since any gift that

---

[197] Duns Scotus, *Opus Oxon., IV Sent.* 26.un. (Vivès 19:147b–50a). *Rep. Par., IV Sent.* 28.un. (Vivès 24:376b–77a).

results in the recipient's right to own something (*ius habendi aliquid*) must be made through some outward expression, typically in words, it follows that the cause of marriage even as a civil contract is normally mutual consent expressed outwardly in spoken words.[198]

Both God and the human will are causes of a marriage, therefore, but in different ways. Considered as the joining that results from the spouses' mutual gift of self to each other, or from the mutual exchange of power over their bodies, marriage arises more from the will of the partners than from any positive legislation. The gift requires a voluntary contract, which, like every contract, must be expressed unequivocally in sensible signs of some sort.[199] Insofar as this basic contract is a legal entity, the only legislator is God, who first instituted marriage.[200] But marriage even in the beginning was instituted not in its bare, natural form but under the terms of an explicit regimen, for the demands of the contract are arduous and need additional support, and some of the rules required for the contract to work effectively are not evident. Institution and positive legislation added determinations to marriage even as it first existed in the beginning.[201] The precepts of marriage do not belong to the self-evident first principles of the natural law, therefore, nor even to the secondary precepts that can be deduced from them as necessary conclusions. Instead, they belong to a third level of law: that of positive rules that are clearly consonant with the aforesaid principles and conclusions.[202]

Scotus frames this whole argument in the context of an ethical problem regarding procreation and sexual intercourse. By Scotus's exacting standards, the begetting of children is a morally indifferent act. Only acts that are directed immediately to God, such as our love of God, are good *per se*. Indifferent acts are good or bad not in themselves but by virtue of their circumstances, especially the agent's end in view. The only motive for procreation that is sufficient to make it a good act is that of sustaining the community of those who worship God.[203]

To the mutual gift of self for the sake of procreation, God has added sacramentality. The addition was fitting because marriage is intrinsically an arduous commitment, entailing both corporeal and moral tribulations. Spouses cannot achieve its ends without supernatural help.[204] Indeed, Scotus observes, it is far more difficult to sustain marriage for the rest of one's life than it is to sustain the life of a religious. A helping grace (*gratia adiuvans*) is needful, therefore, and to that end marriage was instituted as a sacrament in the proper sense, conferring a grace that it signifies.[205] Marriage

[198] *Rep. Par.*, IV *Sent.* 27.1, arg. contra (374a).   [199] *Opus Oxon.*, IV *Sent.* 26.un. (159b–160a).
[200] *Rep. Par.*, IV *Sent.* 28.un., conc. 5; conc. 8 (379b–80a; 381a).
[201] *Rep. Par.*, IV *Sent.* 28.un., conc. 8 (381a). *Opus Oxon.*, IV *Sent.* 26.un., conc. 3 (160b–61a).
[202] *Opus Oxon.*, IV *Sent.* 26.un. (150a).
[203] *Opus Oxon.*, IV *Sent.* 26.un. (148b–49a). *Rep. Par.*, IV *Sent.* 28.un. (377b–78a).
[204] *Opus Oxon.*, IV *Sent.* 26.un., conc. 4 (147b).   [205] *Rep. Par.*, IV *Sent.* 28.un. (382b).

was instituted in the beginning as a sacrament only in the broadest sense of the term, that is, as a sign of something sacred. It was not yet an *effective* sign. The institution of marriage as a sacrament properly so called occurred under the New Law.[206]

16.7 THE SEPARABILITY OF THE CONTRACT FROM THE SACRAMENT

Some of the objections to the sacramental doctrine pertained to the form of the sacrament. Included in the constitution of every sacrament properly so called, by definition, was its form: a prescribed verbal formula, or *verbum*, that the minister pronounced over the elements. As well as the absence of elements and ministers in marriage, the minimal requirements regarding its sacramental form were obviously problematic. To be sure, marriage required the spouses' outward expression of consent, normally in words, but that requirement fell far short of what was typically necessary in a sacramental form. Whereas the schoolmen inquired into what words were essential for eucharist, for example, assuming that Christ himself had passed on the necessary form when he instituted the sacrament, marriage required no particular formula. Moreover, non-verbal gestures were permissible when spouses could not communicate because they were mute or deaf or spoke different languages, and valid marriages could even be contracted *inter absentes* through intermediaries or in writing.

These minimal requirements were not problematic when marriage was considered as a contract. On the contrary, they were typical and predictable. Contracts did not require any particular formula, and there was nothing to prevent a contract from being enacted *inter absentes* or in writing. Regarded from another point of view, therefore, the same features of marriage suggested that marriage as a contract might be separable from marriage as a sacrament even when the contractants were both baptized believers. In that case, Christian spouses could marry contractually without marrying sacramentally.[207] And, if that was so, there was a real distinction, and not only a distinction of reason, between the contractuality and the sacramentality of a Christian marriage. Separability was a sufficient although arguably not a necessary condition for this real distinction. The distinction was of central importance in the debates over clandestinity at the Council of Trent, when the possibility of separation came up frequently. The possibility first emerged in work of Duns Scotus and his followers.

---

[206] *Opus Oxon., IV Sent.* 26.un. (165–66). *Rep. Par., IV Sent.* 28.un. (382b–83a).
[207] The schoolmen sometimes say that the sacrament is separable from the contract, but that usage is misleading, for whereas every sacrament of marriage is a contract, not every contract, according to this theory, is a sacrament.

16.7.1 *Scotus and the Scotists*

Scotus held that marriage as a contract required some authentic expression of consent, but he pointed out that a contract required no particular form of words. A sacrament, on the contrary, required a prescribed formula of spoken words (*certa verba*), without which it was invalid. It seemed that marriage required such a formula inasmuch as it was a sacrament, therefore, but it was not clear what the formula was. What if Christians married without the prescribed form? Perhaps they would be joined contractually but not sacramentally. Scotus did not pursue the inquiry into *certa verba* very far, but he did insist that at least *spoken words* were essential to marriage as sacrament. Thus, one could not marry sacramentally through non-verbal signs, letters, or intermediaries, although these means obviously sufficed for contracts.

Scotus developed the idea somewhat differently in the *Opus Oxoniense* and in the *Reportatio Parisiensis*, although he reached the essentially the same conclusion in both settings. In the former work, Scotus argues that marriage must have been instituted by Christ under the New Law, perhaps when Christ said, "What God has joined, let not man separate" (Mark 10:9), for marriage is one the sacraments of the church and confers grace. If proof of the latter premise were needed, the decree *Ad abolendam* by Pope Lucius III should suffice.[208] This institution added sacramental efficacy to the contract, which was already a sacrament but only in a broad sense. Now, every sacrament properly so called has a form – a verbal formula instituted to signify the grace that it confers – and the form of marriage can only be the words with which the spouses plight their troth. But sacraments require a determinate verbal formula, whereas any authentic expression of consent will suffice for a contract, even including non-verbal signs or gestures. Did Christ specify a determinate verbal formula when he instituted marriage, such "I take you as mine/and I, you, as mine"? Or did Christ institute the sacrament with an indeterminate form, leaving its determination to us, so that every valid contract between believers is also a sacrament? If the first alternative is correct, there must be many marriages between believers that are valid but non-sacramental. Consider the extreme case of mute spouses, who marry without saying anything at all. Again, a father sometimes speaks on behalf of his daughter at a wedding, who remains silent. It seems unlikely that her father is the minister of the sacrament. Perhaps marriage is not truly a sacrament in such cases, although one should not fear that God would leave the contractants without the grace needed for married life.[209]

Whereas Scotus leaves those questions unanswered in the *Opus Oxoniense*, he makes his case conclusively in the *Reportatio Parisiensis*. The exchange of consent

---

[208] X 5.7.9 (CIC 2:780).   [209] *Opus Oxon.*, IV *Sent.* 26.un (167b–69b).

establishes a contract, and it would do so even if marriage were not rooted in the natural law. But whereas any unequivocal expression of intent suffices for a contract, a sacrament requires a prescribed spoken formula (*certa verba*). There is sacramental matter in marriage in an extended sense of the term, and the spouses may be regarded as the ministers of the sacrament, but what is the essential form? The blessing of the priest is not the form but only a sacramental, for it is not strictly required. The form, then, must be a determine formula spoken by the spouses – presumably "I take you as mine/and I, you, as mine." But what happens when mutes marry, or when a marriage takes place between persons who are not present to each other at the same time (*inter absentes*), or when the marriage is contracted through intermediaries or in writing? The last practice is common among the Saracens, who marry by exchanging signed letters. In such cases, there is a contract, but there cannot be a sacrament. God may still provide a helping grace (*gratia adiuvans*) in such cases, but only by virtue of the partners' merit (*per modum meriti*), and not by virtue of the sacrament itself (*ex vi sacramenti*).[210]

Scotus's followers during the fourteenth and fifteenth centuries either upheld the same theory or at least proposed it, citing a marriage between mutes as the standard test case.[211] According to what came to be regarded as the Scotist position, spoken words, which the spouses must speak face to face, and arguably prescribed spoken words (*certa verba*), constitute the essential form of marriage as a sacrament. Peter of Aquila, for example, requires the expression of a prescribed verbal formula (*expressio certorum verborum*) in his definition of marriage.[212] Without that form, there may be still a valid contract of mutual self-giving entered into for the sake of procreation, but there is no sacrament in the proper sense of the term. The theory raised the possibility of separating the contract from the sacrament.

This is a convenient place to mention two sixteenth-century Dominican theologians who argued that the contract of marriage was separable from the sacrament: Thomas de Vio Cajetan (d. 1534) and Melchor Cano (d. 1560). Each theologian revived an old, largely forgotten theory but developed it in his own way: Cajetan returned to the Scotists, and Cano to William of Auvergne (Section 15.3.2). Each argument represented a current in sixteenth-century theology that would become a formative talking point at the Council of Trent.

---

[210] *Rep. Par.*, IV *Sent.* 28.un (384–86). [211] Le Bras, "Mariage," 2204.

[212] Peter of Aquila ("Scotellus"), IV *Sent.* 27.1 (ed. Paolini, 4:263): "Sacramentum vero matrimonii est *expressio certorum verborum* maris et foeminae ad se invicem significantium traditionem mutuae potestatis corporum ad prolem debite procreandam ex institutione divina efficaciter signans gratiam conferendam mutuo contrahentibus ad conjunctionem mutuam animorum gratiosum."

16.7.2 *Thomas de Vio Cajetan, O.P.*

Cajetan reasoned that the personal, face-to-face presence of the spouses was required for marriage to be a sacrament, but not for marriage to be a contract. The idea that sacraments required personal presence had been crucial for Olivi and Durandus (Section 14.8 and 15.3.8), but whereas they had used it to suggest that marriage was not a sacrament in the proper sense of the term, since personal presence was *not* necessary, Cajetan used it, as Scotus had done, to show that marriage even between Christians could be merely contractual. The reception of a sacrament, Cajetan argues, is a personal matter (*passio personalis*). This is clear if one considers the other sacraments, in which the recipient's actions or passions are personal as well as sensibly apparent. Likewise, the recipient's reception of an interior grace is a personal act. Now, personal actions presuppose physical presence. A marriage contracted through intermediaries (*procuratores*) cannot be a valid sacrament of the church, although nothing prevents a contract from being made through intermediaries. Christian spouses who marry through intermediaries or in writing marry validly, therefore, but only contractually and not sacramentally.[213] Their marriage will become sacramental only if they plight their troth personally at a later date. Cajetan points out that if the partners could enter into the sacrament of marriage through intermediaries, they could receive the sacrament while they are asleep. Then, if they had retired to bed in a state of mortal sin, they would commit sacrilege in their sleep: a supposition that is "not only absurd but unintelligible."[214]

Cajetan analyzes how a merely contractual marriage between baptized Christians would differ from a sacramental marriage. Although one cannot receive the sacrament of penance through intermediaries, a penitent might be judged, bound to a penance, and even absolved through intermediaries. Likewise, Christian spouses marrying by proxy enter into a marriage that is both true (*verum*) and fixed (*ratum*), and it is already a diriment impediment preventing a subsequent marriage, even if the latter is consummated.[215] The chief indicator of the difference pertains to insolubility. Even a merely contractual, non-sacramental marriage between Christians is insoluble, but there are degrees or levels of insolubility. Just as a marriage between unbelievers is more soluble than a marriage between believers, so a marriage of believers contracted through intermediaries is more soluble than one contracted face to face. Consequently, it is easier for the pope to dissolve a marriage contracted *inter absentes* than a marriage contracted by the spouses in person. A proxy marriage owes its permanence not to sacramentality but to the fact that it is established (*ratum*) on baptism as if on a root (*in radice*). Thus, a non-sacramental marriage between believers is "radically" but not "formally" established, for it lacks

---

[213] Cajetan, *Quaestiones de sacramentis: De sacramento matrimonii*, Q. 1, §2 (Leonine 12:370a).
[214] Ibid. (370a–b).   [215] Ibid., §3.

the sacramental form, whereas a marriage contracted between believers in person is established both radically and formally.[216]

16.7.3 *Melchor Cano, O.P.*

Melchor Cano's theory became widely known when his *De locis theologicis* was published posthumously 1563. To illustrate the proper use of the opinions of the great schoolmen as of a *locus* of authority, Cano considers the requirements of marriage. It is commonly supposed, Cano explains, that "all scholastic theologians asserted that even when marriage is contracted without a minister of the church, it is truly a sacrament of the New Law." But Cano argues that this doctrine is neither a matter of faith nor even probable, and that the schoolmen did not assert it unequivocally.[217] Cano critically examines the doctrine on several fronts, showing that it is only a "common opinion" and not a settled matter about which the schoolmen have maintained a consistent position, nor even an opinion on which all the schoolmen without exception have agreed. Above all, it cannot rise to the level of a dogma of faith. Thus, the doctrine is not something that must be believed on pain of heresy.[218]

The possibility of a contractual, non-sacramental marriage between Christians arises incidentally in the course of this discussion. Cano points out that the schoolmen have not unanimously held that marriage confers sacramental grace. Indeed, several distinguished theologians have taught the opposite. Cano cites William of Auvergne, who denied "that marriage is a sacrament in the true sense, or has sacramental power" unless it has been consecrated by a priest. Cano uses some of Durandus's arguments, but he declines to appeal to him as an authority because Durandus went too far in denying that marriage conferred grace in any way.[219] Although most of the major schoolmen, Cano concedes, have maintained that a Christian marriage even without a priestly blessing is a sacrament and confers grace, one finds on closer examination that they did not maintain any consistent analysis of the essential matter, form, and minister of the sacrament: a weakness that undermines their authority in this case. Indeed, the question whether a marriage can be received as a sacrament of the New Law when it is not administered by a minister of the church is one that has never been properly examined, let alone settled. Although the Council of Florence declared that no sacrament is complete without its proper matter, form, and minister, it said nothing about the form, matter, or minister of marriage in particular, whereas it defined the role of these things in the other sacraments. Nor has any council or decretal definitively settled the matter. The church has never held that every valid marriage between believers is a sacrament.

---

[216] Ibid., ad 1, §4 (370b).

[217] Melchor Cano, *De locis theologicis* VIII.3, in *Opera* (Bassano, 1746), 236a. I have also consulted the on-line working text of the *editio princeps* (1563) prepared by Juan Belda Plans.

[218] Ibid., VIII.5 (240b–41a).   [219] Ibid. (245b).

Indeed, Cajetan argued that such was not the case, although his opponents failed to understand him. An opinion of the theologians is a matter of faith only if it is corroborated by Scripture, approved and defined in the Apostolic tradition, or deducible from both sources together – none of which is the case.[220] The doctrine is also intrinsically improbable, Cano argues. Marriage without the priestly blessing cannot cause what it signifies in those who marry worthily – a condition that applies to all sacraments properly so called – for a sacrament is a sacred religious rite. A marriage contracted in a civil, profane manner may be a sign of a sacred reality in the same way as the bronze serpent and manna in the wilderness were signs, but it cannot be a sacrament because it is not a religious rite.[221]

Pursuing the inquiry further, Cano notes that according to the Council of Florence no sacrament is complete without matter, form, and minister. But the only minister of a marriage is the priest who blesses it. It makes no sense to argue that the spouses administer the sacrament to each other. Nor is there a sacramental form, properly so called, when there is no priestly blessing, for such a form passes from God as primary agent through the minister to the recipient. Again, whereas the matter of a sacrament is something natural that exists and can be understood prior to consideration of the sacrament, a sacramental form is a supernatural act calling for an act of faith in response. The words of consent that the spouses exchange, on the contrary, are natural things common to all races, which one can understand without faith. Again, the form of a sacrament is what chiefly signifies its spiritual effect, but the words of consent do not signify any spiritual effect. Again, the form of sacrament is a prescribed, determinate, and invariable verbal formula instituted by Christ (the Scotists' *certa verba*), whereas the spouses may verbally express their consent to marry in countless different ways, even in writing or with non-verbal signs. Since the priestly blessing, in Cano's view, is the form of the sacrament, he suggests that the spouses' exchange of consent is better construed not as the form but as the matter of the sacrament. He emphasizes that what is in question here is the form and matter of the sacrament, which many have conflated with the form and matter of the natural contract.[222] Just as a marriage outside the church is only a civil contract, therefore, so an unblessed marriage between Christians is "contracted civilly and profanely by the words of the man and woman alone." It may be valid, but it is not a sacrament.[223]

---

[220] Ibid. (241b–42b).　　[221] Ibid. (243a).　　[222] Ibid. (243a–45a).

[223] Ibid. (243a): "Cum igitur matrimonium solis verbis viri et foeminae civiliter prophaneque contractum, licet rei sacrae signaculum sit, non sit tamen opus religionis sacrum, certe non est proprie sacramentum."

PART V

The Council of Trent

On the eve of the general council

Protestants attacked and Catholics defended the sacramentality of marriage on the eve of the long-awaited general council. No previous conciliar or papal decree had declared as a matter of dogma that marriage was a sacrament in the proper sense, and no one yet had been anathematized for denying or doubting it, but belief in the doctrine had become established as if it were an article of the Catholic faith, and it was firmly entrenched in Catholic practice. The late-medieval iconography of the seven sacraments depicted marriage as full member of the system, sharing the same dependence on the Passion of Jesus Christ (Section 1.8). When such images were depicted in the tapestries, carvings, and frescos of churches, they were designed not to illustrate the abstruse speculations of professional theologians but to instruct the laity and to celebrate the place of the church and her ministers in the lives of the faithful. Vulneral versions of the theme show blood flowing from the pierced side of the crucified Christ to each of the sacraments, with one stream flowing to the bride and groom or to their joined hands as they plight their troth, while a minister of the church officiates and brings them together (Plate 2). Such images manifested in their own way what Olivi and Durandus had denied: the uniformity and univocity of all seven sacraments, including marriage.

The turmoil of practice and belief during the first half of the sixteenth century elicited fundamental changes in the Catholic approach to the sacramentality of marriage. Erasmus and Luther criticized the biblical foundations of the doctrine, especially the use of Ephesians 5:32 as a proof text. In response, Catholic theologians became more circumspect and critical in their use of Scripture, citing a wider range of texts and insisting that Scripture must be interpreted not in a vacuum but in light of the decrees of councils and popes. But Luther's objections were sweeping, comprehending in their scope not only the sacramentality of marriage but also the jurisdiction of the church over marriage and the institutionalized celibacy of clerics and religious. In light of such attacks, the sacramentality of marriage now seemed to Catholics to be an indispensible pillar of their faith. Explicit definition of the doctrine as a dogma followed when the general council at Trent issued its decrees on marriage in 1563.

17.1 FROM IMPLICIT FAITH TO EXPLICIT DOGMA

Catholics during the first half of the sixteenth century appealed to authority to show that the sacramentality of marriage was a doctrine of the church, and not only an opinion of the theologians. A series of official pronouncements had ascended toward recognition of the doctrine without explicitly affirming it. These included four pronouncements: Pope Lucius III's *Ad abolendam* (1184);[1] the profession of faith that Pope Innocent III sent to the bishops of the Vaudois for the Waldensians in 1208 (Section 14.1);[2] the *Profession of Faith of Michael Palaeologus* from the Second Council of Lyons (1274);[3] and, above all, *The Bull of Union with the Armenians* from the Council of Florence (1439).[4]

Durandus of Saint-Pourçain had pointed out that *Ad abolendam* established only that marriage was a sacrament in some sense, and not that it belonged univocally among the sacraments of the New Law.[5] The same could have been said of *The Profession of Faith of Michael Palaeologus* (1274). It was part of a summary of the Roman faith that Pope Clement IV had sent to Michael VIII, the emperor of Byzantium, in an effort to reunite the Roman and Byzantine branches of the church. The *Profession* affirms that "the Holy Roman church holds and teaches that there are seven ecclesiastical sacraments," one of which is marriage. This was first reference to the doctrine of seven sacraments in an official church document. That said, although the *Profession* declares that polygamy is illicit and that the remarriage of either spouse after the death of the other is licit even to the extent of a third marriage, it says nothing about the manner in which marriage in particular is a sacrament.[6]

Pope Eugenius' IV's *Bull of Union with the Armenians*, which he issued at the Council of Florence in 1439, went further. The bull includes a summary of the doctrine of the sacraments adapted from a little treatise on the articles of faith and the sacraments that Thomas Aquinas had composed for the archbishop of Palermo between 1261 and 1270.[7] The summary follows the plan established by Peter Lombard, beginning with an account of the sacraments in general before expounding each of the seven in turn. Although the inclusion of marriage as one of the seven sacraments had been routine and non-controversial since the middle of the twelfth century, it is remarkable that this bull presented the doctrine as something that the

---

[1] X 5.7.9, *Ad abolendam* (CIC 2:780–82).   [2] DS 793–94.
[3] *Profession of Faith of Michael Palaeologus*, DS 851–61.
[4] *Bulla unionis Armenorum*, Tanner-Alberigo 534–59.
[5] Durandus, *IV Sent.* 26.3, §5; §9 (367va, vb).   [6] DS 860.
[7] Thomas Aquinas, *De articulis fidei et ecclesiae sacramentis*, in *Opuscula theologica*, vol. 1 (Turin, 141–51); and *Opera omnia* (Leonine edition), vol. 42, 245–57.

Armenians would have to accept if they wanted to belong to the Roman church. In the section on marriage, the bull affirms that marriage signifies the joining of Christ and the church, citing Ephesians 5:32; it explains that the efficient cause of marriage is consent expressed in words about the present (*de praesenti*); it summarizes Augustine's doctrine of the three goods, expounding the good of sacrament as a sign of the indivisible union (*coniunctio*) between Christ and the church; and it emphasizes that the marriage bond is perpetual, noting that although spouses may divorce on grounds of adultery, they cannot remarry. But the bull says nothing specific about the sacramentality of marriage, such as its power to confer grace.[8]

What would later be cited as proof that marriage was a sacrament in the proper sense was not in the bull's section on marriage but in its preliminary account of the sacraments in general. The bull affirms that whereas the sacraments of the Old Law only prefigured the grace that would be given in the future through the Passion of Jesus Christ, the sacraments of the New Law not only signify but also contain and cause this grace, conferring it on those who receive the sacraments worthily. This universal statement implied that marriage, too, conferred sacramental grace *ex opere operato*. But the bull raised more questions than it settled, for it affirmed that the seven sacraments resulted from the coming together of three components: "things" (*res*), which serve as matter; words, which constitute the form; and "the person of a minister, who confers the sacrament with the intention of doing what the church does."[9] The minister should intend to do not only what the church *teaches* but also what the church *does* in each sacrament – presumably because he is acting not in his own right but as a minister of the church. The bull adds that no sacrament is complete unless all three components are present: word, element, and minister. Whereas the statement contrasting the sacraments of New Law with those of the Old was a paraphrase of what Thomas Aquinas had said in the source, the statement about the necessity *sine qua non* of the three components was new. Thomas had discussed the matter, form, and minister of individual sacraments as the opportunity arose, but he had presented no general doctrine on the topic. The bull clearly implies that these general features – word, matter, minister, and grace conferred *ex opere operato* – are equally present in all seven sacraments without exception. Catholics during the first half of the sixteenth century and at the Council of Trent frequently cited the bull as proof that marriage was a sacrament in the proper sense, often ascribing it simply to the Council of Florence, but the ministry of a priest was not necessary for a valid marriage, and nothing essential to marriage met the description of a *res* or even of a *verbum*. Despite the problems that it posed, however, the bull came closest to meeting the Catholics' need for a dogmatic affirmation of

---

[8] Tanner-Alberigo, 550/8–29.
[9] Tanner-Alberigo, 542/1–8: "Haec omnia sacramenta tribus perficiuntur, videlicet rebus tanquam materia, verbis tanquam forma, et persona ministri conferentis sacramentum cum intentione faciendi, quod facit ecclesia. Quorum si aliquod desit, non perficitur sacramentum."

the doctrine of marriage as one of the sacraments. Post-Tridentine theologians recognized that the *Bull of Union with the Armenians* fell far short of Trent's decrees as regards both its content and its level of authority.

17.2 *DESIDERIUS ERASMUS*

Erasmus (d. 1536) was familiar with and largely endorsed the medieval theology and canon law of marriage as a sacrament, but he had not internalized and had no taste for the habits of analysis and reasoning that those disciplines entailed. On the one hand, he accepted that marriage was a sacrament, although he recast the doctrine in terms of his own devising. On the other hand, he showed that Ephesians 5:32 was not an appropriate proof text for the sacramental doctrine, he denied that marriage was indissoluble, he questioned the value of institutionalized celibacy, and he cast doubt on the superiority of the virginal over the married state. Most of the moral themes in his writing on marriage were conventional among Catholic pastors, leaders, and intellectuals of his day: complaints about abuse of rules, norms, and customs;[10] pleas for reform;[11] insistence on the need for the ritual solemnity that befitted any sacrament; complaints about impious and bawdy nuptial customs;[12] concern about the scandals resulting from clandestine marriages;[13] and an emphasis on conjugal love. But even in pursuing that conventional moral agenda, which he shared with many Catholic theologians and prelates, Erasmus questioned and sometimes undermined the Catholic understanding of marriage. For example, when Erasmus noted that civil authorities had ceded jurisdiction to the church when marriage became recognized as one of the sacraments, he implied that some aspects of ecclesiastical jurisdiction such as the thicket of impediments had undermined both piety and civic order.[14] His attitude to the received doctrine of marriage was that of a faithful Catholic, but it was also subversive, for Erasmus questioned the very principles and habits of reasoning on which the doctrine had been based. This subversive aspect is especially conspicuous in his treatment of marriages contracted clandestinely and without parental consent (Section 17.2.5), although his anxiety about abuses and his sense of the need for reform were common traits among Catholic pastors and scholars. His writings on marriage drew a good deal of Catholic criticism, therefore, especially after the Protestants had appropriated and polemicized them.[15]

---

[10] Erasmus, *Christiani matrimonii institutio*, ASD V-6:86/623–31.   [11] Ibid., 86/639–42.

[12] Ibid., 180/300–182/382.   [13] Ibid., 90/710–94/811.   [14] Ibid., 86/644–61.

[15] See E. Rummel, *Erasmus and His Catholic Critics* (Nieuwkoop, 1989), 1:59, 2:39, 74–78; and E. V. Telle, *Érasme de Rotterdam et le septième sacrament* (Geneva, 1954), 257–71, on Eph 5:32 and marriage as a sacrament, and 271–92, on the ensuing controversy. For summary treatments of Erasmus's theology of marriage, see J. W. Payne, *Erasmus: His Theology of the Sacraments* (Richmond, Va., 1970), 109–25; G. Bedouelle's introduction to *Collected Works of Erasmus*, vol. 83: *Controversies* (Toronto, 1998), at xxxiii–xlii; and H. J. Selderhuis, *Marriage and Divorce in the Thought of Martin Bucer* (Kirksville, 1999), 36–43.

17.2.1 *The estate of marriage*

Erasmus questioned the value of institutionalized celibacy, and he sometimes seemed to attribute equal if not greater dignity to married life.[16] Praising marriage as a holy estate, he counseled the laity not to be discouraged by the prestige of vocational celibacy. Marriage, too, was a spiritual vocation, and spouses could be justly proud of their way of life as long as they "boasted in the Lord" (2 Cor 10:17).[17] In his early *Encomium matrimonii*, a model letter exhorting a young person to marry, Erasmus praised marriage in the tradition of fifteenth-century Italian humanism (Section 17.6.1), even arguing that the married estate was superior to celibacy.[18] The *Encomium* attracted a good deal of Catholic criticism, but Erasmus pointed out that his argument was rhetorical and addressed to an individual, and not a statement of doctrine. Rhetorical analysis of the *Encomium* corroborates his defense.[19]

Erasmus wrote ambiguously about the respective merits of marriage and virginity. He affirmed that virginity was the superior estate, but he noted that God had raised marriage alone to the level of a sacrament. Although virginity has its own special beauty, which elevates it to "angelic dignity," God bestowed even greater dignity on marriage by making it a sacrament. Marriage is an especially holy estate, therefore, and it enables spouses to maintain the "bed undefiled" (Heb 13:4).[20] Even Erasmus's praise of virginity as angelic invites the reader to wonder whether the vocation is appropriate for mere human beings. Erasmus accepted that there was a special place in the church for those "who have made themselves eunuchs for the kingdom of heaven's sake" (Matt 19:12), but he questioned whether more than a very few Christians were capable of taking on this challenge.[21]

17.2.2 *Divorce*

Erasmus openly criticized the traditional doctrine of indissolubility,[22] arguing that divorce should be more freely available and that remarriage should be permissible in some situations. In particular, the innocent party should be permitted to remarry after a divorce on grounds of adultery. Erasmus accepted that marriage was in

[16] Bedouelle (cited earlier), xxxv–vii.
[17] Erasmus, *Christiani matrimonii institutio*, ASD V-6:78/410–18.
[18] ASD I-5:333–416. The *Encomium* was first published in 1518 but written long before, perhaps as early as 1497.
[19] See M. Van der Poel, "Erasmus, Rhetoric, and Theology: The *Encomium matrimonii*," in D. Sacré and G. Tournoy, *Myricae* (Leuven, 2000), 207–27. See also Van der Poel, *Cornelius Agrippa* (Leiden, 1997), 156–59, on the controversy and on misunderstandings arising from the *Encomium*.
[20] Erasmus, *Christiani matrimonii institutio*, ASD V-6:68/234–69/238.
[21] See H. M. Pabel, "Exegesis and Marriage in Erasmus' *Paraphrases on the New Testament*," in H. M. Pabel and M. Vessey, *Holy Scripture Speaks* (Toronto, 2002), 175–209, especially 185–87.
[22] On Catholic reactions to Erasmus on divorce, see Rummel, *Erasmus and His Catholic Critics*, 2:25–26.

principle a life-long union and that no man should separate what God has joined. Marriage was insoluble inasmuch as it was a figure of the insoluble union between Christ's two natures. But Erasmus could see no good reason for perpetuating the union as a legal fiction after a marriage had broken down.[23] A true marriage is insoluble, but some marriages are soluble because they are untrue. In Erasmus's view, a marriage may be deficient not only as a legal contract but also as a personal relationship. Just as a friendship that peters out was never a true friendship, he argues, so a marriage that may be "disjoined" was never a true marriage. A true marriage is not only one that is properly established according to the laws, but also one in which the spouses are held together by true affections.[24]

Erasmus considered the mediating *sacramentum et res* of marriage to be conjugal love, and not the indissoluble *vinculum* as some theologians still held.[25] Some modern scholars argue that Erasmus inverted the traditional Catholic model by making conjugal affection the essence or *sine qua non* of marriage rather than the contract or the marriage bond,[26] but Erasmus was not a professional theologian. His approach to marriage and divorce was more pastoral than sacramental, and his arguments were more rhetorical than logical. Moreover, the term "divorce" is ambiguous in his work and lacks canonical precision. It is not always clear whether he is referring to a legal separation, or to an unratified, *de facto* separation, or even to a breakdown of marital affection. Erasmus warns the reader in his *Christiani matrimonii institutio* that he is concerned here only with "vulgar marriage," and not with the ideal marriage of Mary and Joseph.[27] That said, Erasmus's pragmatism implied a new approach to doctrine and to law. He seems to have arrived at something akin to our modern, pragmatic notion of divorce as "the severing of a valid marriage after disagreements and conflicts."[28]

17.2.3 *Marriage as a sacrament*

Erasmus's only extensive account of the sacramental theology of marriage is in his *Christiani matrimonii institutio*, which he published in 1526 and dedicated to Catherine of Aragon, first wife of Henry VIII.

The *Christiani matrimonii institutio* is largely devoted to pastoral counsels on marrying and on married life, but Erasmus outlines as his point of departure his own version of the sacramental theory. He begins by locating marriage in the natural

---

[23] On Erasmus on divorce, see V. N. Olsen, *The New Testament Logia on Divorce* (Tübingen, 1971), 15–33; Bedouelle, introduction to *Collected Works of Erasmus*, vol. 83 (Toronto, 1998), xl–xlii; and Selderhuis, *Marriage and Divorce*, 39–43.

[24] *Christiani matrimonii institutio*, ASD V-6, 72/278–83. Erasmus is invoking the classical definition of marriage as *coniunctio individuam consuetudinem vitae continens/retinens* (Inst. 1.9.1).

[25] On the origins and circumstances of the *Annotationes*, see W. W. Combs, "Erasmus and the *Textus Receptus*," *Detroit Baptist Seminary Journal* 1 (1996): 35–53, at 38–41.

[26] Payne, *Erasmus*, 118. Bedouelle, introduction, xxxviii.

[27] *Christiani matrimonii institutio*, 63/119–22.　　[28] The phrase is Bedouelle's, p. xl.

order of things. God created nature, and nature determines that nothing better maintains human welfare than "mutual charity and benevolence." Erasmus surveys the various ties of familial affection that unite human beings: those between parents and children, those between descendants and ancestors, those among siblings, and those among kinsfolk. The community is united through such relationships, but they all flow from marriage, which is the closest union among them. If friendship is the voluntary joining of wills whereby two persons become one soul, how much closer is marriage, in which two persons become one body?[29]

Erasmus defines marriage in this treatise as "the legitimate and perpetual joining of a man and a woman, entered into with the aim of begetting offspring, and entailing the indivisible partnership of life and fortunes."[30] He uses two scholastic divisions to elucidate the definition: that of genus and species, and that of the four causes. The phrase "legitimate joining" denotes the genus of marriage, while the "aim of begetting offspring" is the specific difference. The indivisible partnership is a property, or proper accident, of marriage.[31] Again, the spouses are the material cause of marriage, their legitimate joining is the efficient cause, their partnership of life is the formal cause, and procreation is the final cause. The joining is effective because of the law of marriage, and God made that law. But one should not adhere too strictly to a formal definition, Erasmus warns. The church charitably and rightly regards as valid some unions that are not strictly marriages according to the aforesaid definition, such those between elderly persons or of sterile women.[32]

Erasmus turns from the nature of marriage to the three main sources of its solidity and stability: nature, law, and religion. From nature come the ties of kinship and the innate sense of duty and obligation. From law come the contractual, negotiated aspects of marriage, such as oaths, documents, and penalties. And from religion come nuptial rituals and the aura of pious aspiration that should attend the exchange of consent. If even pagans approach marriage religiously, how much more should the followers of the true religion do so, who seek sanctity and the "bed undefiled" (*thorus immaculatus*) in their marriages? Christians find in marriage not only human affection but also the grace of the Holy Spirit, who breathes the "hidden affection of mutual charity" into those spouses who receive the sacrament worthily when they are joined together. What is more holy or more precious in the church than the sacraments: the seven "mysteries" that Christ gave to his bride as pledges of his return? Accordingly, one should celebrate a Christian marriage in a holy place, where it is dispensed by the ministers of the sacraments with fitting

---

[29] *Christiani matrimonii institutio*, 62–64   [30] 64/110–11.

[31] Erasmus is using the term "property" in its Porphyrian and scholastic sense. A property, or proper accident, is a predicament or attribute that is a necessary and coextensive concomitant of a subject but lies outside the subject's essence or definition, such as the capacity to laugh (*risibilitas*) in the human being, the combination of the hot and the dry in fire, and containing the sum of two right angles in a triangle. See P. L. Reynolds, "Properties, Causality and Epistemological Optimism in Thomas Aquinas," RThPhM 68 (2001): 270–305.

[32] *Christiani matrimonii institutio*, 64–66.

prayers, with readings from a gospel, and with the nuptial mass. Erasmus regrets that some Christians desecrate marriage by treating it as a merely secular institution.[33]

Like the other sacraments, or mysteries, of the church, Erasmus explains, marriage is composed of three aspects: the *imago*, which is a certain congruence or likeness between sign and signified; the *exemplum*, whereby Christians find in that very likeness something to venerate and to imitate; and the *arrha*, or pledge, which is a gift of "spiritual grace." Erasmus's analysis of the composition of the sacrament is akin to the exegetical division of the non-literal senses of Scripture into allegorical, moral, and anagogical. Christ is the archetype of all Christian harmony and the fount of all spiritual gifts. As *imago*, therefore, marriage signifies the joining of divine and human natures in Christ and the union between Christ and the church. This signification not only helps us to understand Christ's union with the church but is also the *exemplum* that Christians should try to emulate. The joining of divine and human natures in the person of Christ is an "indissoluble and ineffable bond." The two become one flesh and are perfectly united, and the strong embraces the weak, yet they remain distinct and unconfused. In the same way, the husband retains his natural superiority and authority over the weaker partner, yet he must cherish and embrace her, so that they can lead a harmonious life based not on dominance but on partnership. Just as the hypostatic union springs from an "ineffable charity," so too the union between husband and wife is based on "mutual benevolence."[34] Christ and the church are joined as groom and bride, and as head and members of the same body. There is no divorce there, just as a true marriage is a lifelong union.[35] Marriage has other meanings, too. It signifies the relationship between God and the Virgin Mary, wherein God the Father was the groom, Mary was the bride, and the angel was the bride's attendant (*paranymphus*).[36] Interpreted "according to the moral sense," marriage represents the union of the individual soul with Christ, which is part of the larger union of the church and Christ.[37]

The *arrha* in Erasmus's account is a grace bestowed by Christ. Christ shows through marriage how Christians should live and what duties they should carry out in imitation of him, but he also bestows a "heavenly gift," which enables them to realize the *exemplum*.[38] Erasmus notes that even reliable, orthodox theologians have in the past held diverse opinions about conjugal grace, but he contends that this diversity of opinion should not be exaggerated. Even those who deny that sacramental grace is conferred must still grant that the *exemplum* teaches spouses about Christian charity and harmony and that it shows them how to practice these virtues.[39] But a sacrament in the proper sense, Erasmus insists, is an efficacious sign: one through which grace is conferred by virtue of a divine pact (*ex pacto*

---

[33] Ibid., 66–70.   [34] Ibid., 70–72.   [35] Ibid., 74.   [36] Ibid., 74–76.   [37] Ibid., 76.
[38] Ibid., 70/244–53; 79/448–53. The gift is presumably called an *arrha* because it is the beginning of future blessing, when the betrothal of Christ and the church will be consummated. Compare (and contrast) Luther's characterization of sacramental grace as a "promise" of justice.
[39] Ibid., 78/440–41.

divinae bonitatis). Marriage is such a sacrament. Earlier theologians had considered marriage to be sacrament only in the weak sense that it was a sacred sign, for they assumed that no special, sacramental grace was infused with it. Later theologians adopted the "more probable" view that a special gift of the Holy Spirit was infused into those who contract marriage rightly. This gift renders the spouses better able to live in perfect harmony, to cope with life's burdens, challenges, and adversities, and to raise and instruct their children so that they, too, may live piously: in short, to realize the *exemplum*. Those who participate in the sacrament improperly, on the contrary, receive not grace but divine wrath.[40] Grace is conferred through marriage *ex opere operato* just as it is through all the sacraments, for "a sacramental gift" is "invisibly infused by a divine pact into those who contract marriage rightly."[41] Erasmus accepted the covenantal theory of sacramental grace and applied it to marriage. The theory of instrumental or "physical" causality, which the Dominicans of his day favored, had no part in his theology.[42] What confers grace in marriage, therefore, is neither the minister nor the sacrament itself but God. God confers conjugal grace in fulfillment of a covenant (*ex pacto*), for he has promised to do so whenever the sacrament is rightly received.[43] The sacrament to which Erasmus refers here is the transient event of getting married and not the enduring estate of being married. Whether a couple receives the sacramental grace of marriage depends on how they marry and on their intentions in marrying.

Erasmus concedes that his terminology is novel, but he shows that it is consistent with scholastic doctrine. His division of *imago*, *exemplum*, and *arrha*, he points out, corresponds roughly to the scholastic division of *sacramentum tantum*, *sacramentum et res*, and *res tantum*. What he calls *imago*, they call "sacrament" or "sign." They call what the sign signifies its "reality" (*res*). Thus, they arrive at a similar tripartite analysis, for the same thing may be both a reality and sign. The *sacramentum tantum* is the outward act of being joined together, with its accompanying gestures and rituals, the betrothal gift (*arrha*), and so forth. The *sacramentum et res* is the mutual benevolence and charity between the spouses that motivates their union. Although this is not an outward, sensible sign, it can be construed as a sign of its exemplar, the *res tantum*. The *res tantum* is twofold, including on the one hand the union of two natures in Christ and the corresponding union between Christ and the church, and on the other hand the "sacramental gift" of interior love, which is infused into spouses who receive the sacrament worthily. Clearly, the *sacramentum tantum* does not cause the exemplar in Christ, but it does cause the interior love between the

---

[40] Ibid., 76–78.   [41] Ibid., 78/425–26

[42] As Payne, *Erasmus*, 97–98, observes. See earlier, Section 15.2.4, on scholastic theories about the causality of grace in the sacraments. On the covenant theory, see W. J. Courtney, "The King and the Leaden Coin," *Traditio* 28 (1972): 185–209; and I. Rosier-Catach, "Signes sacramentels et signes magiques: Guillaume d'Auvergne et la théorie de pacte," in F. Morenzoni and J.-Y. Tilliette, *Autour de Guillaime d'Auvergne* (Turnhout, 2005), 93–144.

[43] *Christiani matrimonii institutio*, 78/437–40.

spouses. The sacrament may be said to cause the gift of grace, therefore, although it does so in a much more obscure way than the other sacraments (*multo magis insensibiliter*). But that should not surprise us. Grace is ineffable, and neither the sacrament nor the minister is an efficient cause in the usual sense. Instead, God uses the occasion of the sacrament to infuse grace by virtue of a covenant (*ex pacto*).[44]

17.2.4 *What is the great sacrament (Eph 5:32)?*

The chief witnesses to Erasmus's critique of the Catholic doctrine of marriage are his annotations on 1 Corinthians 7:39 and Ephesians 5:32 in his edition of the Greek New Testament with Latin translation, which was first published in 1516. Revised editions of his New Testament were published in 1519, 1522, 1527, and 1535.

In a long note on 1 Corinthians 7:39 that he inserted in the second edition of his New Testament (1519), Erasmus questions whether the sacramentality of marriage entails its indissolubility. Here, he even seems to question the sacramental doctrine itself.[45] "The wife is bound by the law as long as her husband lives," St Paul writes, "but if her husband be dead, she is at liberty to be married to whom she will, only in the Lord." The theologians hold, Erasmus notes, that marriage must be indissoluble because it is a sacrament, and they claim that its sacramentality would be undermined if divorce and remarriage were permitted. But the implied argument involves a non sequitur, Erasmus argues. From the premise that marriage is a sacrament, it does not follow that it is indissoluble. Moreover, it is not clear that Christians always considered marriage to be a sacrament in the proper sense. Although Greek and Latin patristic authors wrote voluminously about marriage, they never said that it was one of the sacraments. Augustine, who wrote more extensively on the topic than anyone else, called the third of the conjugal goods "sacrament," but he never said that marriage itself was one of the seven sacraments. Nor does Dionysius mention marriage when he discusses in detail the sacraments with their various powers and rites in the *Ecclesiastical Hierarchy*. Jovinian would have had a perfect argument for his position if he could have claimed that marriage was one of the seven sacraments but that virginity was not. Why did he never pose this objection? And Jerome would not have objected so violently to the remarriage of widows if he had considered marriage to be one of the seven sacraments. Erasmus adds in the third, 1522 edition, that there is no need to labor this point because Durandus recorded that in his own day theologians had only recently begun to count marriage among the sacraments of the church properly so called.[46]

Even those ancients who did refer to marriage as sacrament, Erasmus continues, were following Paul in Ephesians 5:32 and meant only that the coupling of man and

---

[44] Ibid., 78/419–40.
[45] On Catholic responses to this critique, see Rummel, *Erasmus and His Catholic Critics*, 1:158–60.
[46] *Annotationes in I. Cor.* 7,39, ASD VI-8, 176/336–178/360.

wife was a "certain type or image" of Christ and the church. They did not mean that it was one of the sacraments of the church. Just as marriage contains the closest possible bond of friendship, so the church is tightly coupled to Christ as if to her spouse. A good marriage between conscientious spouses is indeed a holy and sacred thing, but even an unholy marriage, such that of David and Bathsheba or of Hosea and Gomer, may be a type of some sacred reality (*rei sacrae*).[47] Signification *per se* does not necessarily entail any equivalence or correspondence of value between signifier and signified.

The convoluted sequence of ideas that follows defies exact analysis, but Erasmus makes three interconnected claims.[48] First, marriage cannot possibly conform to what it signifies *in every respect*, and to expect it to do so is harmful. Erasmus is presumably defending his position against the tacit objection that marriage must be indissoluble because its exemplar, the union between Christ and the church, is indissoluble. If complete conformity were necessary, he points out, there would be no sacrament when a man is married to a sterile wife, or when a woman's husband is a drunkard, a gambler, or disreputable, or when an old man marries an old woman, or when two drunkards marry. In such cases, the bodily marriage does not conform to its spiritual archetype, yet the church still considers it to be a sacrament. Again, husband and wife would not be separated even by death if the figure had to correspond to its archetype in every way. Second, the deterioration or breakdown of an individual marriage does not "injure" the "sacrament of Christ," which continues to exist as a common institutional ideal. Catholics divorce even under current canon law, albeit without the right to remarry, whereas Christ and the church are never separated in any way. Again, just as the sacrament of baptism is not injured because some baptized persons lead unclean lives, so also the sacrament of marriage is not harmed when some spouses live badly or even divorce. Marriage is a human thing, and as such it is bound sometimes to fail. Just as what is granted to a few as an exceptional privilege does not vitiate a general law, so the infidelity of a few does not vitiate the sacrament, which is common to all. Third, what links the fallible individual marriage to the indissoluble ideal is the intention of the spouses and not any law that binds them. Everyone who contracts marriage intends the union to be perpetual. No one marries planning to divorce. Erasmus expands this point in the 1522 edition: The institutional permanence and the sacramentality of marriage, he argues, are safe as long as spouses always marry intending never to separate and as long as marriage is a lifelong union *in the majority of cases*. It is not necessary to eliminate divorce and remarriage absolutely and in every case.

Erasmus cast doubt on the biblical evidence for the sacramental doctrine, especially on the use of Ephesians 5:32 as a proof text. He made this point in his annotation on 1 Corinthians 7:39, but he developed it more fully in an annotation on Ephesians 5:32 in his New Testament. Erasmus notes that the Vulgate's term

---

[47] Ibid., 176/360–67. [48] Ibid., 176/367–180/394.

sacramentum in this verse is a translation of the Greek *mystērion*, which may also be rendered as *mysterium* in Latin.[49] This point in itself was obvious and well known and might have been trivial. Erasmus himself refers to the sacraments as the seven mysteries in the *Institutio*, and he glosses "sacrament" as "mystery" when he writes on the sacramentality of marriage.[50] But Erasmus invites the reader to look at the text from a fresh point of view. The terms *sacramentum* and *mysterium* were largely interchangeable in Erasmus's writing, but their respective semantic fields were subtly different even there, for the latter term was more likely than the former to denote a reality of faith, such as the Trinity, rather than a sign of some sacred reality.[51] More important, Erasmus points out that Paul's aside ("but I speak …") shows that his remark about the "great mystery" was parenthetic. The great mystery of this verse is not the union between husband and wife, which is the topic of the discourse as a whole, but rather the union between Christ and the church. The joining of man and wife is no great mystery, for it happens even among the heathens! Those who cite the text as proof that marriage is one of the sacraments[52] are mistaken, therefore – not because there is any doubt about the doctrine itself, which Erasmus accepts, but only because this particular text is not appropriate as proof.

Erasmus considerably expanded this annotation in the second, 1519 edition, and the additions make his critique more cautious. Where he says that the doctrine itself is not in doubt, he now adds that the doctrine is a tradition that probably came to us from the Apostles and certainly from the "holy fathers." Moreover, Erasmus now corrects some observations about the antiquity of the doctrine that he himself made in his annotation on 1 Corinthians 7:39. Some persons (*nonnulli*) object, Erasmus notes, that Dionysius the Areopagite does not mention marriage when he discusses the sacraments of the church with their particular rites and ceremonies in the *Ecclesiastical Hierarchy*; that Jerome never calls marriage a sacrament in his voluminous writings on the subject; and that Augustine, whose authority on the subject is weightier than Jerome's, does not call marriage a sacrament in this sense when he discusses the goods of marriage. They might find it even more remarkable that Jovinian, the champion of marriage, never called marriage a sacrament, for if he had done so Jerome would surely have mentioned it. Since Jovinian maintained that marriage was equal in dignity to celibacy, he could have argued that marriage was better than celibacy or virginity because the former is a sacrament whereas the latter

---

[49] *Annotationes in Eph.* 5,32, ASD VI-9, 255–58. Erasmus opted for *mysterium* in his own Latin translation of the verse.

[50] See *Christiani matrimonii institutio*, 70/239 on the seven mysteries, and 70/244–45 for the gloss: "quam magnifica res significetur hoc nomine sacramenti, siue vt Graeci vocant mysterii, sciendum est in coniugio legitimo…."

[51] G. Chantraine, "*Mysterium* et *sacramentum* dans le *Dulce bellum inexpertis*," in *Colloquium Erasmianum* (Mons, 1968), 33–45.

[52] Erasmus inserts "seven" ("one of the *seven* sacraments") in the 1519 edition, and he adds "according to the peculiar and exact sense of this term" after this remark in the 1522 edition.

was not. These were all objections that Erasmus himself had made. But now he adds that the learned (*eruditi*) can easily solve such objections. Erasmus was responding to criticism, and he may have used the term "learned" ironically, but he insists again that his aim in reviewing such objections is not to put the sacramental doctrine in doubt but only to point out that one may not cite Ephesians 5:32 as proof.

Erasmus in the 1519 edition also expands his remarks on the significance of the term *mystērion*. Use of the term *sacramentum* invites the reader to think of the seven sacraments of the church, but *mystērion* in the Greek New Testament generally signifies anything that is hidden or secret, Erasmus point out. Paul frequently uses the term to characterize things that are obviously not sacraments in our sense, such as when he speaks of the "mystery of iniquity" in 2 Thessalonians 2:7.[53] Erasmus notes that Augustine identified the "great mystery" of Ephesians 5:32 not with marriage but with the union between Christ and the church. Thus, Augustine remarks in the *De nuptiis et concupiscentia* that what is great in Christ and the church is very small (*minimum*) in individual husbands and wives, but that even this small thing is a sacrament of an inseparable union.[54]

Erasmus added some minor refinements and remarks to this discussion in the third, 1522 edition, partly in response to criticism. He emphasizes again that he intends neither to denigrate marriage nor even to deny that it is a sacrament. He also notes that although he himself does not call the doctrine into doubt, some "orthodox scholastics" used to do so. But these qualifications did little to clarify whether or not Erasmus fully accepted the established doctrine of marriage as a sacrament.

Despite the critique that Erasmus made in his annotations, he seems to revert to the conventional interpretation of Ephesians 5:32 in two later passages.[55] Thus, he uses this verse in the *Institutio* (1526) to conclude his discussion of the sacramental *imago* in marriage:

> Therefore, since there are so many symbols of mysteries in legitimate marriage, Paul rightly said: "This is a great sacrament, but I speak in Christ and in the church."[56]

Although this conventional remark may seem surprising, there is arguably no real contradiction, for Erasmus cites the verse here as a token of the preceding discourse in Ephesians, which as a whole is certainly proof that marriage is an image of Christ and the church. But Erasmus does seem to contradict his own critique in a prayer to be said before marrying that he published in 1535. The supplicant addresses God as the one who instituted marriage, who honored it with the miracle at Cana, and who

---

[53] In the 1527 edition, Erasmus adds Augustine's interpretation of the term *mysteria* in 1 Cor 13:2, which is a more pertinent example. On Erasmus's interpretation of *mystērion* in Paul, see G. Chantraine, "Le mustèrion paulinien selon les Annotations d'Érasme," *Recherches de science religieuse* 58 (1970): 351–82.

[54] Augustine, *De nupt. et conc.* I.21(23), CSEL 42:236/22–24.

[55] Pabel, "Exegesis and Marriage," 179.   [56] *Christiani matrimonii institutio*, 76/394–96.

"has taught through Paul, the chosen vessel, that this joining is a great sacrament in Christ and in the church."[57] Even so, the verse's context and its traditional applications suffice to make Erasmus's use of it in this pious, non-technical context permissible. Whether his several and various observations about the sacramentality of marriage are consistent remains debatable.

17.2.5 Clandestinity and parental consent

Erasmus regarded marriages contracted clandestinely or without parental consent as occasions for scandal, fraud, and distress. In his *Christiani matrimonii institutio*, Erasmus's treatment of this issue is part of a broad critique of the received theology and canon law of marriage. The complexities of the existing law of marriage and many of the supposed givens on which it is based, he argues, are absurd and give rise to numerous abuses and deceptions. Erasmus reviews those complexities in detail and at length: the parsing of the words of consent, the distinction between *de futuro* and *de praesenti* betrothals, the fiction of presumed consent (where a *de futuro* vow is followed by sexual intercourse), dissolution of an unconsummated marriage to enter the religious life, and the many impediments.[58] The more complex the system, he argues, the more opportunities there are for abuse. Part of the solution must be to simplify. The impediments of consanguinity and affinity, for example, should be limited to those of the Leviticus code (Lev 18:6–18, 20:11–21).[59] Another and larger part of the solution is to annul marriages contracted clandestinely or without the parents' knowledge and consent.

Erasmus emphasizes that the laws of marriage are largely human inventions. He does not question either the church's right to make such laws or the obligation of Christian citizens to obey them, but he wants those in authority to change the laws.[60] Only positive legislation, he argues, can establish clear boundaries between what it forbidden and what is permitted. Most of the current abuses could be solved if the popes made *more* use of their legislative and judicial power over marriage:

> In these and many other cases, the authority of the popes has the power to render persons capable or incapable [*habiles et inhabiles*], so that either nothing is done by their contracting, or what has been contracted would be absolutely valid: so that either both persons would be deemed bound by what has been contracted, or both would equally be set free.[61]

Erasmus disregards the fine balance that the scholastics discerned between the inalterable core of marriage, which belonged to natural and divine law, and the areas open to positive human legislation. He enlarges the scope of positive law, assuming that its foundation is not an ontology of essences but a policy designed to

---

[57] *Precationes aliquot novae*, in *Opera omnia*, Leiden edition (1703–09), vol. 5, 1205C.
[58] *Christiani matrimonii institutio*, 74–126.   [59] 124/551–554.   [60] 94/810–11.
[61] 133/793–796.

enhance pastoral and civic well-being. Marriages need to work well. If they fail to work, there is no point in sustaining them.

Erasmus traces what he perceives as the disarray of marriage in his own day to two root assumptions: that consent alone is sufficient for marriage (the principle of *solus consensus*), and that any marriage once validly contracted is insoluble. The principle that consent alone is sufficient for marriage, he argues, is a human decree designed to protect the spouses from abusive coercion. As such, it can be abrogated or modified to meet the changing needs of the times.[62]

Marrying would be less prone to deception, Erasmus argues, if a contract of marriage could be annulled after the fact. The principle that a marriage "contracted with the free and legitimate consent of the spouses must stand" is not a necessary truth but a positive law that can and should be changed.[63] The church rightly forbids clandestine marriages even now, but the church ought to prohibit them henceforth in such a way that they would be deemed not to have been contracted.[64] Erasmus proposes that persons marrying clandestinely should be "inhabilitated," that is, rendered incapable of marriage.[65] The prelates at the Council of Trent will adopt this proposal, but their way of interpreting it will be diametrically opposite to Erasmus's. Affirming that "a marriage contracted with the free and legitimate consent of the spouses must stand," the prelates will reason that persons marrying clandestinely can be disqualified from marrying, as if clandestinity were a personal diriment impediment akin to those of consanguinity and affinity: an obstacle preventing access to marriage. But Erasmus rejects that principle, as well as the distinction between prohibitive and diriment impediments:

> Marriage would be free from many of the snares that surround it, therefore, if the distinction between impeding a contract from being made and annulling a contract that has been made [*impedit contrahendum sed non dirimit contractum*] were abolished. For if a contract ought not to be annulled after it has been made, what is the point of forbidding it from being made? And if the prohibition is strong enough to render the persons incapable [*inhabiles*] of marriage, it should also dissolve what has been contracted.

According to the canonical jurisprudence of Erasmus's day, a prohibitive impediment prohibits a marriage from being contracted (*impedit contrahendum*) but has no effect *post factum*, whereas a diriment impediment annuls a marriage that has been contracted (*dirimit contractum*). But Erasmus can see so point in prohibiting a contract from being made without also rendering it invalid after the fact.

Marrying should be a solemn, public, ritual arrangement managed by the parents, according to Erasmus, and corroborated by oaths and stipulations.[66] Partners should be chosen soberly and prudently, with parents taking the leading role. Erasmus is impressed by the awesome paternal power that he finds in classical law and literature

[62] 94/797–803. 133/787–790.   [63] 133/787–790.   [64] 133/797–798.   [65] 133/794.
[66] 133/797–134/834.

as well as in the Old Testament, including the power of fathers to give their daughters away in marriage. Erasmus concedes that parents in his own day should not coerce their children into marriage, yet not because the spouses' free consent is a non-negotiable given or an essential constituent of the sacrament, as the schoolmen imagined, but because parents should act in their children's best interests. A union contracted against a daughter's will is likely to go wrong. An unmarried daughter should be free to marry or to remain single without coercion, therefore, but her parents should control her choice of partner. Thus, St Paul says of the widow that she is "at liberty to be married to whom she wills, only in the Lord" (1 Cor 7:39), whereas he says of the virgin, "if a virgin marry, she has not sinned" (1 Cor 7:36). He does not say that the virgin, like the widow, may marry whom she wills. Paul tacitly implies that the virgin should be permitted to marry even when her parents are unwilling, but that she is not permitted to choose a husband for herself.[67] A balance must be found, therefore, between children's freedom of consent and their obedience to parents. In his own day, Erasmus believes, the emphasis has shifted too far toward freedom. Children should not be permitted to undertake this sacrament of the church covertly, rashly, or as if drunk or under a spell. "Would that the old [filial] piety between parents and their children still prevailed, so that the former would look after their own as they would wish to be looked after, and the latter would not distrust the forethought of their elders."[68]

17.3 MARTIN LUTHER

Luther insisted on a narrow, univocal use of the term "sacrament," and he refused to count marriage among the sacraments.[69] He denied that marriage conferred grace, that it was subject to ecclesiastical jurisdiction, and that it was inferior to the celibate vocations. Luther abhorred divorce and remarriage, but he rejected the notion of the insoluble bond, or *sacramentum*.

[67] 134/831–34.   [68] 134/828–830.

[69] On marriage and sexuality in Luther and Lutheranism, see O. Lähteenmäki, *Sexus und Ehe bei Luther* (Turku, 1955); P. Althaus, *The Ethics of Martin Luther* (Philadelphia, 1965), 83–100; J. Heckel, *Lex Charitatis* (Grand Rapids, 2010), 102–04; J. Witte, Jr., "The Reformation of Marriage Law in Martin Luther's Germany," *Journal of Law and Religion* 4.2 (1986): 293–351; idem, *From Sacrament to Contract* (Louisville, 1997), 42–73; and S. Hendrix, "Luther on Marriage," *Lutheran Quarterly* 14 (2000): 335–50. J. Buitendag, "Marriage in the Theology of Martin Luther," *HTS Teologiese Studies/Theological Studies* 63.2 (2007): 445–61, explores Luther's conception of marriage as "worldly yet sacred" in light of modern philosophical theology. On Luther's handling of marriage matters during the early 1520s and its influence, see M. Brecht, *Martin Luther: Shaping and Refining the Reformation 1521–1532* (Minneapolis, 1990), 90–95. On Luther's personal and pastoral attitude to marriage and sexuality, see H. A. Oberman, *Luther: Man between God and the Devil* (New Haven, 1989), 272–87. On Luther's own marriage to Katherine von Bora (1525), which scandalized loyal Catholics, see Brecht, *Shaping and Refining*, 195–211, and R. Marius, *Martin Luther: The Christian between God and Death* (Cambridge, Mass., 1999), 436–41.

17.3.1 *Prelude on the Babylonian Captivity of the Church*

When Luther reviewed the Catholic sacramental system in his *Prelude on the Babylonian Captivity of the Church* (1520), he directed his harshest criticisms against the doctrine of marriage as a sacrament.[70] Luther affirms that God instituted marriage in the beginning, and he concedes that marriage is a figure or allegory of things that are invisible and sacred, such as Christ's union with the church. Nevertheless, he denies that marriage is a sacrament. The doctrine cannot be found in Scripture, he argues. Moreover, marriage is essentially the same everywhere, whether it exists among Christians, among the Jews of the Old Testament, or even among infidels.[71] Having argued that marriage is not a sacrament, Luther attacks the entire Catholic regime and ideology of marriage. The Catholic church's laws of marriage are not divine but all too human. They have caught marriage in a net. With their prurient casuistry, their excessive regulation, and their absurdly extended web of impediments, clerics have turned a divinely instituted way of life into a farce. Luther is especially skeptical about the spiritual impediments contracted at the baptismal font.[72]

In the same treatise, Luther considers two areas of marriage law about which he is less certain: divorce, and the impediment of impotence. Luther suggests that the wife of an impotent husband might take another man covertly for sexual satisfaction, retaining the marriage for appearance's sake.[73] And although Luther passionately abhors divorce and remarriage, he accepts the obvious implication of Matthew 19:9: that the spouse of an adulterer has the legal right to remarry. Luther denies that the pope has any right to dissolve an unconsummated marriage. The church has some right to expound what God's judgments about earthly things are, in Luther's view, but it has no power to judge or dispense on God's behalf.[74]

17.3.2 Vom ehelichen Leben

Luther outlined his positive views on marriage in *Vom ehelichen Leben* (1522), customarily known in English as *The Estate of Marriage*.[75] The work is divided into three parts. In the first part, Luther establishes the legal foundations. He begins by situating marriage in the natural order, construing it as a virtually inescapable ordinance of creation. Only a very few persons who are sexually capable are able to remain continent without harm. For the others, celibacy is a work of the devil.[76] Luther then turns to the question of who can marry whom, which is the chief topic of the first part. Luther skeptically reviews eighteen traditional categories of impediments. His treatment is largely inconclusive, although he rejects the impediment of

---

[70] Martin Luther, *De captivitate Babylonica ecclesiae* [hereafter *Bab.*], WA 6:550–560 (*De matrimonio*).

[71] *Bab.*, WA 6:550–53.   [72] *Bab.*, 553–58.   [73] *Bab.*, 558–59.   [74] *Bab.*, 559–60.
[75] *Vom ehelichen Leben*, WA 10.2, 275–303.   [76] Ibid., 275–80.

disparity of religion, which seems inconsistent with his belief that marriage is the same everywhere, among unbelievers as well as believers.[77] Luther devotes the second part of the work to divorce,[78] and the third to pastoral counsels on married life. God smiles on spouses who share their mundane domestic duties with a good grace. Luther contrasts the evils of celibacy with the blessings of marriage, the greatest of which is raising children to worship God.[79]

17.3.3 *Marriage and sacramental theology*

I shall consider three features of Luther's treatment of marriage in greater detail: his denial that marriage is a sacrament, his rejection of the celibate estates, and his conception of marriage as civil estate, regulated ideally not by bishops and clerics but by the magistrates.

Luther maintains that a sacrament is composed of two things: a "word of divine promise," and a divinely instituted visible sign. Luther associates the institution of a sacrament more with the ritual sign than with the word, but the two aspects are mutually complementary and each is hardly conceivable without the other. It is these two aspects above all that distinguish the sacraments from mere "figures and allegories" as well as from non-sacramental ecclesiastical rites, such as ordination.[80] The word of promise corresponds roughly to Augustine's *verbum* and to the scholastics' sacramental form, the sign to Augustine's *elementum* and to the scholastics' sacramental matter. The promise itself replaces the sacramental grace of scholastic theology, for Luther rejects the notion of infused grace. Whereas medieval theologians extrapolated the model suggested by eucharist and baptism to five other sacraments, Luther finds that eucharist and baptism alone are sacraments by the standards of his model.[81]

Baptism was arguably the chief exemplar of Luther's sacramental model, notwithstanding his difficulty in accounting for infant baptism – to which, in opposition to the Anabaptists, he was fully committed.[82] "The first thing to observe in baptism," Luther explains in the *Babylonian Captivity*, "is the divine promise, which says that whoever believes and is baptized shall be saved." Salvation rests entirely on that promise, which is far preferable to all the pomp of works, vows, and religious

---

[77] Ibid., 280–87.   [78] Ibid., 287–90.   [79] Ibid., 295–96; 300–01.

[80] *Bab.*, WA 6:532, 550/27, 572. On Luther's sacramental theology, see Althaus, *Theology*, 345–403. On Luther's critique of the Catholic sacramental system in *Babylonian Captivity*, see M. Brecht, *Martin Luther: His Road to Reformation 1483–1521* (Minneapolis, 1985), 380–85.

[81] *Bab.*, WA 6:571–72.

[82] See J. D. Trigg, *Baptism in the Theology of Martin Luther* (Leiden, 1994), 99–109. Luther proposed several theories to reconcile infant baptism with his doctrine of faith, but Trigg argues that the issue was arguably not crucial because in Luther's view the word and the faith continued throughout the believer's life and were not confined to the moment of receiving the sacrament (ibid., 108). See also M. D. Tranvik, "Luther on Baptism," *Lutheran Quarterly* 13 (1999): 75–90. (Tranvik discusses the infant baptism problem at 84–86.)

orders.[83] Some maintain that there is a hidden power to confer grace in the word or in the water of baptism, and others that grace comes directly from God alone by virtue of a covenant. According to both theories, the sacraments of the New Law are signs of grace that cause what they signify *ex opere operato*. But that notion is fundamentally muddled, Luther argues, for the sacraments are effective not as signs but in virtue of the divine promise.

Luther rejected the sacramental history that had been a central theme in Hugh of Saint-Victor and Alexander of Hales, and with it the distinction between the sacraments of the Old Law and those of the New. According to that theory, the sacraments of the New Law superseded the *sacramenta legalia* of the Mosaic law, but Luther considers the phrase *sacramenta legalia* to be an oxymoron. What chiefly distinguishes a sacrament from a mere sign is the promise attached to it, which presupposes faith in Jesus Christ. No such promise accompanied the rituals and offerings instituted under the Old Law. Luther concedes that Abel's sacrifice and the circumcision of Abraham's descendants were like sacraments inasmuch as a divine promise that required faith was attached to them, but he holds that what saves is never the sacrament itself but always faith in the promise, and that the promise is expressed through the spoken words, not in the material sign.[84] Baptism itself, therefore, never justified anyone. Rather, what justifies is the recipient's faith in the divine promise that accompanies baptism.[85] In sum, "it cannot be true that some efficacious power of justification is present in the sacraments, or that they are effective signs of grace, for all such things are said to the detriment of faith and out of ignorance of the divine promise."[86]

Luther inevitably rejected the Catholic doctrine that the sacrament was a means of grace *ex opere operato*. According to this doctrine, the subject received sacramental grace provided only that the sacrament was "received rightly," or if the recipient "put no obstacle" in the way of grace.[87] In Luther's view, this medieval doctrine falsely attributed the word's efficacy to the sign, and faith's efficacy to works. It was chiefly with Luther and Lutheranism in mind that Trent anathematized those who said that the sacraments were "merely external signs of grace or justice, received through faith," that grace was not conferred through the sacraments *ex opere operato*, or that faith in the divine promise was sufficient for the attainment of grace. Trent reaffirmed that the sacraments of the New Law contained the grace that they signified and conferred it *ex opere operato* on recipients who put no obstacle in its way.[88]

Luther and the Catholics were at cross purposes in any debate over grace, for Luther rejected the very notion of infused, sanctifying grace and put in its place the

---

[83] *Bab.*, WA 6:527/33–37.   [84] *Bab.*, 531/31–37; 532/4–35.   [85] *Bab.*, 532/36–533/1.

[86] *Bab.*, 533/12–15.

[87] *Resolutiones disputationum de indulgentiarum virtute*, conc. 7, WA 1:544/33–41.

[88] Council of Trent, session 8, *de sacramentis in genere*, canons 6 and 8; see also can. 5 (Tanner-Alberigo, 684–86).

"not yet" of a divine promise, to which the recipient responded with faith and hope. Justification itself, in his view, was extraneous. Christ's intrinsic righteousness was imputed to believers but remained alien to them. Their sins remained but were not imputed to them. The sinner was justified not intrinsically, therefore, but "forensically," that is, in God's judgment (*in foro divino*).[89] Justification remained extraneous, for God's chosen ones would be justified only in the final judgment. Luther did not deny that justification made a difference to believers in the here and now, for faith resulted in sanctification and good works. Nevertheless, to avoid any muddling of the eternal with the temporal, Luther replaced medieval inspiration and sanctification with prospective aspiration: the hope in things to come.[90] Whereas medieval theologians construed the efficacy of each sacrament as an infusion of special saving grace, Luther spoke of a divine promise. The sacrament was salutary not *ex opere operato* but because and inasmuch as the believer received the promise in faith.[91]

It is not entirely clear what the sacraments added to the other modalities of God's word, in Luther's view, such as preaching and readings from the gospels. Luther noted that the sacrament was physically applied to the body because humans were corporeal as well as spiritual beings.[92] He also suggested that a sacrament was a personal expression of the word, which was addressed to a particular individual, whereas the word in other modalities was essentially public and addressed all Christians generally.[93] Although the sign itself – the material stuff and its ritual application – does no saving work in Luther's account of sacramental efficacy, the biblical evidence for the sign's institution is crucial evidence that the sign is a sacrament. Luther demands a clear biblical record of the institution of a sacrament by Jesus Christ, as there is for baptism (Matt 28:19) and for eucharist (Matt 26:26–28 etc.). The reference must be explicit, and not evident only in light of liturgical practice or conciliar tradition, for one must let Scripture speak for itself. Luther regards penance as a sacrament in his early work, therefore, albeit with much criticism of Catholic practice, for there is some biblical evidence of its institution by Jesus Christ (e.g., Matt 16:19). Moreover, penance has the appropriate structure of word and sign, although there is no element, or material stuff. But the other four sacraments of the medieval *septenarium* could never meet Luther's criteria, marriage least of all.

Luther puts forward two refutations of the sacramental doctrine of marriage in the *Babylonian Captivity*. First, there is no support for the doctrine in Scripture, although marriage is an earthly figure or allegory of something spiritual and ineffable:

[89] See R. S. Clark, "*Iustitia imputata Christi*: Alien or Proper to Luther's Doctrine of Justification?" *Concordia Theological Quarterly* 70 (2006): 269–310.
[90] *Die Disputation de iustificatione*, disp. 3, n. 23, WA 39.1:83/16–17: "Iustificari enim hominem sentimus, hominem nondum esse iustum, sed esse in ipso motu seu cursu ad iustitiam."
[91] *Bab.*, 529, 550. On faith and the sacraments, see Althaus, *Theology*, 348–52.
[92] *Deudsch Catechismus (Der Große Katechismus)*, WA 30.1:215, 217. *Daß diese Wort Christi "Das ist mein Lieb" noch fest stahen*, WA 23:155.
[93] *Sermon von dem Sakrament*, WA 19:504–05.

We have said that in every sacrament there is a word of divine promise, which must be believed by the one who receives the sign, and that a sign by itself cannot be a sacrament. One does not read anywhere [in Scripture] that someone who has taken a wife will receive any grace from God. Nor is there is any divinely instituted sign in marriage, for one does not read anywhere [in Scripture] that marriage was instituted by God to signify something. It is true that all things that happen visibly can be interpreted as figures or allegories of invisible things, but figures and allegories are not sacraments in the sense that we use the term "sacraments."[94]

This argument is muddled but it can be clarified. Luther's model requires the institution of the sacramental sign, and the Catholic model requires that the recipient should receive grace from the sacrament, which in Luther's model becomes faith in the divine promise. There is no evidence in Scripture that marriage has either of these features.

The second refutation goes to the supposed distinctiveness of marriage under the New Law. Luther presents a sequence of three arguments that has some rhetorical force, although it is logically defective and contains several examples of *petitio principii*:

Moreover, since marriage has existed from the beginning of the world and remains to this day among unbelievers, there are no reasons for saying that it is a sacrament of the New Law and of the church alone. The marriages of the fathers [i.e., the Old Testament patriarchs] were no less holy than ours, and the marriages of unbelievers are no less true than ours, yet one does not posit a sacrament among them. Moreover, even among believers there are some impious spouses who are worse than any gentiles. What entitles one to say that marriage is a sacrament here but not among the gentiles?[95]

In Luther's view, marriage itself is essentially the same always and everywhere, whether it is practiced among Christians, among the Jews of the Old Testament, or among heathens. Christian spouses are called to higher standards, which they often fail miserably to meet, but the institution itself is essentially the same among all peoples.

Some may object, Luther notes, that he is contradicting Paul, who says that marriage is a "great sacrament" (Eph 5:32). Luther is dependent on Erasmus for his response. He argues that this is a misunderstanding resulting from an accident of translation. The corresponding Greek word in the original New Testament is *mystēr-ion*, which in the Latin versions was rendered sometimes as *sacramentum* and sometimes as *mysterium*. The choice of terms was arbitrary, but if the word *mysterium* had been used in Ephesians 5:32 instead of *sacramentum*, Luther claims, interpreters would not have assumed that Paul was referring to a sacrament of the New Law.[96]

---

[94] *Bab.*, 550/25–32.   [95] *Bab.*, 550/33–551/2.

[96] *Bab.*, 551/17–18: "Quae res fuit occasio, ut sacramentum novae legis intelligerent, longe aliud facturi, si 'mysterium' legissent, ut in graeco est." Luther does not quite claim that the doctrine of marriage as a sacrament itself is dependent on the accident of translation, but only that the misinterpretation of this particular verse depends on the translation.

Moreover, Luther argues, neither *sacramentum* nor *mysterium* in Scripture ever denotes a sacrament in the accepted Christian sense. Scripture uses these terms to denote a sacred reality itself, whereas we use the term *sacramentum* to denote the sign of such a reality. (Luther cites 1 Tim 3:16, 1 Cor 2:7–8, and 1 Cor 4:1 as examples.) A sacrament or mystery in the biblical sense is "a mystery and a secret thing that is declared in words but grasped by the faith of the heart." St Paul uses the term *mystērion* to denote "the wisdom of the Spirit, hidden in mystery," which pertains to Jesus Christ. The mystery to which Paul refers in Ephesians 5:32 is not marriage but Christ's union with the church, as the wording clearly indicates. Marriage is a figure and a "real allegory" of that mystery, but only in the same way as the sun is a figure of Christ, or as waters in Scripture are a figure of God's people. Such things are not sacraments because there was no divine institution and no divine promise is attached to them.[97]

Although marriage is indeed a figure of Christ and the church, Luther concludes, the sacrament of marriage was not divinely instituted but rather was "invented by human beings in the church." Churchmen have been carried away by their ignorance both of the meaning of the word "sacrament" and of the thing that the word signifies. Perhaps one should charitably tolerate their foolish error, but they expose the Christian faith to ridicule and they distort the sense of Scripture.[98]

17.3.4 *Marriage and celibacy*

Luther denied that the celibate estate was superior to the married estate.[99] Indeed, there was no rightful place in Christendom, in his view, for a celibate estate. He conceded that celibacy was an exalted condition, as St Paul advised, but he held that it was intended only for a very few individuals, whom God had specially called. Everyone else – the vast majority – should marry and raise families. Celibacy that was institutionalized or practiced on a large scale, such as that of priests and religious in the Catholic tradition, was a pernicious folly.

Luther articulates his position on celibacy most fully in his treatise on married life, *Vom ehelichen Leben*. Having created human kind as male and female, Luther explains, God blessed them and told them to "increase and multiply" (Gen 1:27–28). Luther separates these two aspects of creation – gender and the procreative impulse – in order to compare them. Sexual difference, with the features that distinguish each gender from the other, is a Godly work (*gottlich Werck*), for it is one of the things that God created in the beginning and recognized as very good (Gen 1:31). The man should not disdain the woman or her body, just as the woman should not disdain the man or his body. Rather, each must honor the other as a good creation that is

---

[97] *Bab.*, 551/36–552/20.   [98] *Bab.*, 553/9–20.

[99] *Von den Konziliis under Kirchen*, WA 50:651–62. J. Witte, Jr., *God's Joust, God's Justice* (Grand Rapids, 2006), 386–97.

pleasing to God. Individual men and women receive their gender from God and must accept it gratefully as God's gift. The same is true, Luther argues, of the command to "increase and multiply." This is something more fundamental than a precept, for it, too, is a Godly work (*gottlich Werck*). It is as fixed and necessary as the division into male and female. One can no more choose whether to "increase and multiply" than one can choose whether to be male or female. Even among the celibates, the procreative impulse remains as an irresistible fact of nature, driving them into sexual immorality.[100] Luther's argument may seem contrived, for whereas begetting children is something that a person usually does voluntarily and does not have to do, a person's gender is congenital fact of life. But Luther is faithful to the text. Genesis treats both sexual difference and the command to increase and multiply – which God had previously given to irrational animals (Gen 1:22) – as features of the original created order of things. They are similar features in a narrative that explains how and why things are what they are and must be.

Luther concedes that persons of three sorts are exempted and should not be expected to marry: the impotent, who have been eunuchs since birth; the castrated, who have been made eunuchs by other men; and those who have "made themselves eunuchs for the kingdom of heaven's sake" (Matt 19:12). Eunuchs of the third sort are those spiritually exalted persons whom God has called to remain continent even though they are sexually capable. Paul was of that sort, and he wished that others were. But such persons are extremely rare. Absent that special calling and gift, no vows or cloistering can save celibate persons from the procreative instinct and from the devil's work.[101]

17.3.5 *Marriage as a worldly thing*

Whereas the sacramental doctrine focused on the transitory act of marrying (*hochzeit*), Luther, like Peter John Olivi and Erasmus, focused on the estate of marriage (*ehestand*). Moreover, Luther regarded that estate chiefly as a necessary constituent of civil society. Luther abandoned the hybrid notion of marriage that had prevailed since the thirteenth century, whereby marriage was both a civil contract and a sacrament of the church. Marriage, in his view, was entirely a "worldly matter" (*weltlich geschefft*), designed to foster temporal and not eternal well-being.[102] Luther argues in the *Babylonian Captivity* that marriage cannot be a sacrament of the New Law because it is the same everywhere and always: among heathens, among the Jewish patriarchs of the Old Law, and among Christians. It is the same today in Christendom as it was in the beginning when God created it.[103] Pursuing that logic, Luther rejects the impediment of disparity of cult. Nothing prevents a Christian

---

[100] *Vom ehelichen Leben*, WA 10.2:275–76.   [101] Ibid., 277–80.
[102] *Von Ehesachen* WA 30.3: 205/12–14. *Traubüchlein*, WA 30.3/74/2.
[103] *Bab.*, WA 6:550–51.

from validly marrying a non-Christian.[104] The notion of marriage as a sacrament always went hand-in-hand with the notion that the marriage of baptized Christians was in some way categorically different from the marriage of infidels, and even from the marriage of the Jews before Christ. Theologians since the early twelfth century had struggled to account adequately for this difference while conceding that non-Christian marriage was truly marriage. Moreover, the distinctiveness of Christian marriage went hand-in-hand with episcopal jurisdiction over marriage. The sacramental doctrine was a sufficient albeit not strictly necessary condition for the ecclesiastical regulation of marriage, and in practice sacramentality and ecclesiastical jurisdiction went together. Luther rejected all of this.

Luther's claim that marriage was the same always and everywhere should be understood in relation to the political theology of the two kingdoms, or two realms.[105] Luther's treatment of the theme was inconsistent and not well developed, and the theme was soon overshadowed in the Lutheran tradition by the schema of three orders (also known, albeit less accurately, as the three estates): the economic (i.e., familial) order, the political order, and the ecclesial order (*oeconomia, politia, ecclesia*).[106] Nevertheless, his treatment of marriage is unintelligible without reference to the two kingdoms. Luther preferred to regard the church as a spiritual authority entrusted with care of eternal well-being and tasked with preaching and with announcing the promise of grace. He did not deny that the visible church was a human corporation with temporal responsibilities and entanglements, but he was wary of anything that seemed to muddle or to mix the two realms. Luther rejected, therefore, two closely related themes of the Catholic tradition: that of the anticipation of the next life in this life, and that of the quasi-incarnate presence of the divine authority amidst human authority. Luther's version of the Gelasian doctrine, which he extrapolated from St Paul's division of the Law and the Gospel, was extremely dualistic, although he recognized that the two realms interpenetrated in the lives of law-abiding Christian citizens. On the left is the earthly realm, preoccupied with things that are external, material, and temporal. On the right is the heavenly realm,

---

[104] *Bab.*, 556/9–16.

[105] On Luther and the two kingdoms, see Heckel, *Lex Charitatis*, 25–42. On marriage in relation to the two kingdoms, see Witte, *From Sacrament to Contract*, 51–53. On the reception history of the two realms theme in Protestantism, see Witte, *Law and Protestantism* (Cambridge, 2002), 87–117. On the two realms in Luther and Lutheranism, see Althaus, *Ethics*, 43–82; J. R. Stephenson, "The Two Governments and the Two Kingdoms in Luther's Thought," *Scottish Journal of Theology* 34.4 (1981): 321–37; H. J. Berman and J. Witte, Jr., "The Transformation of Western Legal Philosophy in Lutheran Germany," *Southern California Law Review* 62 (1989): 1573–660; and P. T. McCain, "Receiving the Gifts of God in His Two Kingdoms," *Logia* 8.3 (1999): 29–40. For an overview of the long history of the theme with its many variants, see R. Kolb, "Two-Kingdoms Doctrine," in E. Fahlbusch (ed.), *Encyclopedia of Christianity* (Grand Rapids and Leiden, 2008), 8:569–75.

[106] On the three orders, see R. Saarinen, "Ethics in Luther's Theology: The Three Orders," in J. Kraye and R. Saarinen, *Moral Philosophy on the Threshold of Modernity* (Dordrecht, 2005), 195–215.

preoccupied with things that are spiritual and eternal. Both realms come from God and are ways in which God governs his people,[107] but whereas the former uses coercive means, the latter operates in the freedom of the Gospel.[108] The Christian is subject to the earthly kingdom as a public person, and to the heavenly kingdom as a private person.[109] Human beings are naturally capable of temporal, civic righteousness in the earthly kingdom, whereas eternal righteousness comes to them by imputation in the heavenly kingdom, whence they derive their "passive justice" from Christ's "active justice."[110]

In Luther's view, therefore, the jurisdiction that the church claimed over marriage was as muddled as the papal prerogative of granting posthumous indulgences. On the one hand, although the empirical, visible church belonged to the earthly realm, the church's chief task was to foster the heavenly realm through preaching and the sacraments. The church had no business with jurisdiction and coercion in public life.[111] On the other hand, since marriage belonged to the earthly realm, it was properly subject not to the church but to the civil magistrates.[112] Marriage was an outward, earthly, secular estate.[113] Luther saw the problem of clandestine marriage in the same light, emphasizing parental and especially paternal consent as the link between the marriage of minors and the political community, with its common good (usually referred to in this era as the public good). Although parents should not coerce their children into marriage, parental consent was vital for maintaining familial and civic control over marriages.[114] Marrying by its very nature should be a public, external event, for it belonged to the earthly realm, and not to the inner, spiritual order that the church fosters.[115]

17.3.6 *Marriage as a godly thing*

None of that was to say that the married life of Christians could be divorced from their faith.[116] Luther expected nearly all Christians to marry and to live out their faith

---

[107] *Wochenpredigten über Matth. 5–7*, WA 32:390/8–18.

[108] *Von weltlicher Oberkeit*, WA 11:249, 251. *Wentzeslaus Linck Dem Christlichen Leser Gottis gnade*, WA 15:724–34. *Ob Kriegsleute auch in seligem Stande sein können*, WA 19:629. *Auslegung des 101. Psalms.*, WA 51:238. *Der 117. Psalm ausgelegt*, WA 31.1:238–41.

[109] Althaus, *Ethics*, 66–69.

[110] *In epistolam S. Pauli ad Galatas Commentarius*, WA 40.1:42–48.

[111] Berman and Witte, "Transformation of Western Legal Philosophy," 1589–90.

[112] Althaus, *Ethics*, 89–90.

[113] *Ein Traubüchlein für die einfältigen Pfarrherr*, WA 30.3:74–75. *Von Ehesachen*, WA 30.3:205. WA 32:376.

[114] *Von Ehesachen*, WA 30.3:213–14. *Daß Eltern die Kinder zur Ehe nicht zwingen noch hindern, und die Kinder ohne der Eltern Willen sich nicht verloben sollen*, WA 15:167. Luther considered the *de futuro/de praesenti* distinction to be foolish meddling on the church's part, in part because he considered it to be grammatically unclear in German: see Witte, *Reformation of Marriage Law*, 323–30.

[115] *Von Ehesachen*, WA 30.3:207.

[116] Althaus, *Ethics*, 89–90; Hendrix, *Luther on Marriage*, 340–42.

within the context of marriage and family, just as they would do so in the context of a state headed by a Christian prince. The household "replac[ed] the monastic community as the seat of the highest praise of God."[117] The subtle relationship that Luther posits between the spiritual and the civil dimensions of marriage is apparent in his treatment of divorce and remarriage. Although Luther abhorred divorce as contrary to Jesus' teaching and was convinced that marriage was a lifelong union,[118] he accepted on the basis of Matthew 19:7 that the spouse of an adulterer had the legal right to divorce and remarry, albeit only with license from a civil magistrate. Christian spouses should do their best to be privately reconciled before turning to public, civil divorce proceedings before a magistrate as the last resource.[119] Luther would have preferred adulterers to be put to death, but since civil law was lax on that point it made sense for them, too, to remarry if they could not remain continent after divorce.[120]

Marriage was the most religious way of life, according to Luther: far more so, indeed, than that of the so-called religious orders. Luther develops this idea in a playful gloss on 1 Corinthians 7:7: "For I would that all men were even as I myself. But every man has his proper gift of God, one after this manner, and another after that." Luther's exegesis turns on the distinction between the inner, private life of the spirit, and the outer, public life of the body. Paul regards marriage as inferior to celibacy, which is, indeed, a marvelous gift and an elevated way of life. But one should distinguish between the divine gift of celibacy and the institutionalized celibacy of Catholicism, especially that of the religious orders, which Luther as a former Augustinian Friar despised with a passion.[121] Although Paul justly wished that everyone shared his own gift of celibacy and chastity, he recognized that most did not. Moreover, by counting both celibacy and marriage as gifts, Paul praised them equally. Celibacy has more dignity than marriage inasmuch as one compares each with the other, but they are equal under God inasmuch as they are both divine gifts. Similarly, although the man is superior in dignity to the woman, they are equal under God inasmuch as both are creatures who acknowledge God as their creator and Lord.[122] Celibacy is special divine gift, which no one can acquire by choice or by taking vows. Nuns are not brides of Christ, but brides of the devil. They rely more

---

[117] The quotation is from Kolb, "Two-Kingdoms Doctrine," 572b.

[118] *Bab.*, WA 6:555. *Wochenpredigten über Matth.* 5–7, WA 32:378.

[119] *Vom ehelichen Leben*, WA 10.2:287–89. *Von Ehesachen*, WA 30.3:241. *Wochenpredigten über Matth.* 5–7, WA 32:379:27–29. Althaus, *Ethics*, 97–99.

[120] *Vom ehelichen Leben*, WA 10.2:289–90.

[121] Legends, propaganda, and German usage, combined with Luther's own characterization of his former life as monk-like, have conspired to make Luther into a former monk: a vulgar error in English. He was a friar, i.e., a member of a mendicant religious order. See K. Hagen, "Was Luther a 'Monk'?" *Lutheran Quarterly* 24.2: 183–85.

[122] M. L. Mattox, "Luther on Eve, Women, and the Church," in T. J. Wengert, *The Pastoral Luther* (Grand Rapids, 2009), 251–70, shows that Luther's view of women in the church and in the home was "distinctive but nevertheless quite traditional and even restrictive," but that Luther "seemed to suggest that women could or should preach" (p. 252).

on their status and circumstances than on faith in Christ or on the grace of God, and they abuse their celibacy. Rather than using celibacy in order to free themselves from mundane distractions and to devote themselves to God, as Paul intended, they use it arrogantly, pretending to be superior in God's eyes to married folk. It is wrong, therefore, to regard married life as inferior to the religious life. In the primary, most fundamental sense, religion is something inward and spiritual, pertaining to faith, whereas an empirical religious order is something outward, temporal, and corporeal. But a way of life may be called religious in another sense: when it is conducive to faith and thence to the good works that flow from faith. In that sense, marriage is a more truly religious "order" than any of the religious orders. Whereas the members of religious orders enjoy sheltered lives with lifelong security and bodily sustenance, married folk have to face challenges and earn their keep day by day. As a result, they are constantly thrown back on trust in God. And because married folk have to labor, whereas the religious are freed from labor, marriage is superior as an opportunity for good works. In sum, the outward state of married folk enhances and deepens the spouses' inward faith of the heart, whereas the outward state of religious stunts their inner spiritual growth. Marriage is the most religious of orders, whereas the religious orders are the most secular of ways of life.[123]

Just as the estate of marriage (*ehestand*) was a "worldly matter" (*weltlich geschefft*), so also was the wedding (*hochzeit*).[124] As such, it was wholly subject by right to secular jurisdiction and supervision. Although Luther was vehemently opposed to clandestine marriages, he held that the church had no essential role in marrying and weddings. Marriage did not need to be witnessed or solemnized in the sight of the church, but only in the sight of the people or their legal representatives. Luther recognized, nevertheless, that couples would ask their pastors to bless their unions, and he saw no harm in such piety. While emphasizing that there was no required rite for marrying and that people should follow their various regional customs, Luther provided a simple betrothal rite for use by common pastors in his *Traubüchlein*, published in 1529. It lacks the nuptial mass and blessing that would normally follow in the Catholic tradition, presumably because such solemnities would invite the people to regard marrying as a sacrament. Having ascertained that the partners truly consent to marry, the pastor joins their right hands together and observes, "What God has joined together, let not man separate" (Matt 19:6).[125] The liturgical *ordo* makes it clear that the minister has only a limited, ancillary role, and not an instrumental one as he does in baptism and eucharist. He guides the spouses, helps them to plight their troth, witnesses their actions, announces that their union has

[123] *Das siebente Kapitel S. Pauli zu den Corinthern*, WA 12:104–07.
[124] *Traubüchlein*, WA 30.3:74/2.
[125] *Traubüchlein*, WA 30.3:77. Cranmer followed Luther in his Anglican marriage service of 1549 by inserting Matt 19:6 into a service based on the Sarum rite (*The booke of the common prayer* [London, 1549], fol. 14v). Cranmer uses the *quos* variant of the verse: "*Those whome* god hath ioyned together: let no man put a sundre" (my italics).

taken place, and reminds the spouses and others present of the purposes and obligations of holy matrimony. It is not the pastor who joins the spouses, however, nor even the spouses themselves, but God alone. The minister's words and actions only mime what God himself does when the spouses express their mutual consent, as God joined Adam and Eve in the primordial wedding (Gen 2:22).

Luther's rejection of the sacramental doctrine does not imply that marriage is secular in the modern sense of that term. He did not consider marriage to be godless or devoid of theological meaning. All authority comes from God (Rom 13:1–7), and the civil political community that Luther presupposed was typically Christian and ruled by a Christian prince. Luther emphasized that God had instituted marriage, but he maintained that God had done so only once, in the earthly Paradise.[126] Marriage was part of the divinely constituted natural order, and God inscribed the duty to marry and to procreate in human nature. By the same token, marriage was a Godly work and a holy estate, which God himself had instituted in the beginning. The Bible says that *God* joins the spouses, Luther points out (Matt 19:6), and not that their union joins itself. The partners are truly married if and only if they are joined "through God's word." Contrariwise, partners who are so impious as to marry clandestinely or "under cover of darkness," especially if they are minors marrying without parental consent, do not marry through God's word, for they contravene the Decalogue. By failing to honor their parents, they also fail to honor God, and their parents have the right to annul their union. Matthew 19:6 is no defense, for God has not joined them together.[127] Those who were no longer subject to paternal authority should plight their troth before witnesses to avoid marrying clandestinely, but Luther associated clandestinity above all with the absence of parental consent. Parents were the mediators of the community's control over a child.

Martin Bucer and Johann Brenz took up Luther's arguments about clandestinity, developing them in their own ways.[128] Both maintained, as Luther did, that God did not join spouses who contracted clandestinely.[129] Like Luther, Brenz points out that when Christ prohibited divorce, he referred not merely to those who have been joined together but to those whom *God* has joined together (Matt 19:6). Roman civil law as well as Scripture comes from God (Rom 13:1–7), and it, too, requires children to honor their parents by marrying only with their parents' consent. Minors who marry clandestinely, Brenz argues, whether through lust, fraud, or the foolishness of youth, dishonor their parents and transgress the law. Such a union is not "divinely contracted." Indeed, it "proceeds rather from Satan than from our God, since it is consonant neither with divine nor with civil law."[130]

---

[126] *Bab.*, WA 6:550/33–551/2.   [127] *Von Ehesachen*, WA 30.3:213/20–214/24.
[128] On Bucer on marriage as instituted by God, see Selderhuis, *Marriage and Divorce*, 165–93.
[129] On Bucer on clandestinity, see Selderhuis, *Marriage and Divorce*, 197.
[130] Brentius, *Libellus*, c. 2, fols. 8v, 10r–12r. Fol. 12r: "... potius a sathana quam a Deo nostro proficiscatur, cum neque Iuri diuino, neque Civili consonum sit." On Brenz on marriage, see M. Brecht, *Die frühe Theologie des Johannes Brenz* (Tübingen, 1966), 308–13.

17.4 KING HENRY VIII'S REFUTATION OF LUTHER

Henry's *Assertio septem sacramentorum adversus Martinum Lutherum* (1521) was among the earliest Catholic responses to Luther's *Babylonian Captivity*. A widely read, controversial, and influential work, it provoked a violent riposte from Luther, which in turn elicited counter-responses by Thomas More and John Fisher on Henry's behalf.[131]

The extent of Henry's authorship is uncertain, and we do not know who, if anyone, gave him expert advice. There has been debate ever since the treatise first appeared about the role of others in its composition, but it was apparently not the work of Thomas More, and there is no reason why Henry should not have been the principal author.[132] Estimates of its worth, too, have varied widely. In Scarisbrick's estimation, the treatise "is not a piece of theology of the highest order.... its erudition is unremarkable ... its grasp of Lutheranism defective, its exposition of Catholic teaching on the sacraments sometimes unimpressive."[133] But that assessment is unjust. The author's treatment of marriage is well informed, and it is effective in the general direction of its criticism, especially regarding the use of Scripture. I shall assume in what follows that Henry himself composed the treatise.

Henry deals with each of Luther's three main arguments about marriage in turn before examining the question of conjugal grace.[134]

First, Henry criticizes Luther's dependence on Scripture alone as arrogant and misguided. Luther rejects some sacraments because there is no instituted sign, and others because there is no promised grace. Luther rejects the sacrament of marriage on both counts, arguing that one cannot find evidence in Scripture either of the institution or of the promise of grace. But the church is a more fundamental source of authority than Scripture, Henry argues, for we can be confident in Scripture only because the church has established certain writings as Scripture. For example, we are sure that John was really the author of John's gospel only because the church teaches us so. Luther claims that he believes only what he can find in the writings of the Evangelists, although he is selective even in his use of them. But why believe an individual member of the church, such as John, but not the body of which that member is a part? The *church* teaches that God instituted the sacrament of marriage in the beginning, that Christ re-instituted it, and that it was passed on from Christ to the Apostles and from the Apostles to the bishops until the present day. This

---

[131] On the circumstances and consequence of the work, see J. J. Scarisbrick, *Henry VIII* (Berkeley, 1968), 110–117; R. Marius, *Martin Luther*, 339–44; and R. Marius, *Thomas More: A Biography* (Cambridge, Mass., 1984), 276–91.

[132] Scarisbrick, *Henry VIII*, 112. R. Marius, "Henry VIII, Thomas More, and the Bishop of Rome," *Albion* 10 (1978): 89–107.

[133] Scarisbrick, *Henry VIII*, 111.

[134] *Assertio septem sacramentorum adversus Martinum Lutherum*, in *Corpus Catholicorum* 43 (Münster, 1992), *De sacramento matrimonii*, 193–205.

sacrament will be continue to be passed on, as if from hand to hand, until the world's end. None of Luther's protests can alter that.[135]

Second, Henry notes, Luther argues that marriage is as true among non-believers and among the Jews both before and under the law as it is among Christians. Since it is not a sacrament among those peoples, Luther argues, it cannot be a sacrament among us. But the premise is false. And even if it were true, the conclusion is a non sequitur. Marriage *was* a sacrament among the Jews, just as circumcision was. Perhaps marriage is even a sacrament among infidels, although Henry concedes that this is a difficult issue. It is true that marriage among infidels is dependent on the laws and customs of each people, so that what counts as a valid marriage in one society may be invalid or even unthinkable in another. Yet Augustine says that whereas the sanctity of the sacrament exists only "in the city of our God, in his holy mountain," the sacrament itself is common to all peoples. The reader will find a full explanation of that point, Henry adds, in Hugh of Saint-Victor.[136]

Even if one grants that marriage exists but is not a sacrament among unbelievers, it does not follow that marriage is not a sacrament also among believers. Marriage among infidels is a merely human matter (*res humana*), regulated by human laws. That is why they freely permit divorce and remarriage. But marriage among the people of God has always been holier, from the beginning of the world until now. It is true that Moses permitted men to repudiate their wives and remarry, but he did so only as a concession to their hardness of heart and not as if they were really entitled by right to do so. Christ restored marriage to its pristine sanctity (Matt 19:4–9 etc.). Assuming that sacramentality and insolubility are coextensive, and that marriage was insoluble *de iure* even under the Old Law, Henry argues that marriage among God's people has always been a sacrament, whether before the law, under the law, or in the age of grace. The sacramentality of marriage has unfolded and evolved historically among God's people.[137]

Third, Henry refutes Luther's argument that Ephesians 5:32 cannot be interpreted as proof that marriage is a sacrament. Luther argues that the "great sacrament" of this verse is not marriage but Christ's union with the church.[138] But is Luther's interpretation of Ephesians 5:32 correct, even if one disregards the argument of the discourse as a whole?[139] According to Luther, the great sacrament "in Christ and church" is not marriage but the union between Christ and the church. But to say that the sacrament of baptism is great in the cleansing of the soul does not imply that baptism is not present in the body as well. To say that the sacrament of eucharist is great in Christ's body does not imply that the sacrament is not great also in the species of bread and wine. Besides, if Paul meant to say that the great sacrament

---

[135] *Assertio*, 193.
[136] Cf. Hugh of Saint-Victor, *De sacramentis christianae fidei*, PL 176:496A, 496B. The dictum is not in fact Augustine's, although it compiled from Augustine's words. It first appears in the work of the modern masters (Section 9.5.3), whence Hugh acquired it.
[137] *Assertio*, 193–94.   [138] Ibid., 195–96.   [139] Ibid., 196–97.

existed *only* in Christ and the church and did not pertain *in any way* to the union of male and female, that would lessen the force of his comparison, which he proposed in order to commend marriage.[140]

Even if Luther's interpretation of the verse were correct, one must consider the verse in the context of the entire discourse (Eph 5:22–32). This shows that marriage must be construed as a special sign of Christ and the church:

> You see how the blessed Apostle teaches throughout [*undique*] that the marriage of a man and a woman is a sacrament that represents the joining of Christ with the church, for he teaches that marriage was consecrated by God to be a sacrament of Christ inasmuch as he is joined with the church. Paul compares the husband to Christ, therefore, and his wife to the church.[141]

How does the husband imitate Christ? Surely, by loving his wife, just as the wife imitates the church by revering her husband. This religious motive for conjugal love is more cogent even than the natural complementarity of male and female, although that, too, incites love. It is not true, therefore, as Luther would have it, that the comparison between marriage and Christ's union with the church is a mere illustration or figure of speech. On the contrary, it is a reality (*res vera*): a true sacrament (*verum sacramentum*) that was foretold by the prophets. By quoting Adam's dictum in a discourse on marriage and by interpreting it as a prophecy of Christ and the church, Paul implies that marriage is a special sign of Christ and the church:

> Even if Luther obstinately insists that what the Apostle calls a sacrament in these words [Eph 5:32] is not marriage but only Christ's union with the church, yet he can hardly deny that the joining of man and woman is at least a sign of that holy joining by which Christ is joined to the church, and that it was such from the moment of God's institution, when the first parents were joined together, with God uniting them. It was not something invented later by human ingenuity.[142]

However one might interpret Ephesians 5:32, therefore, the passage as a whole reveals both that marriage is a sign of Christ and the church in some special, normative sense, and that it was instituted to signify that union from the beginning, when God joined Adam and Eve.

Finally, Henry develops his own biblical proof that marriage is a means of sacramental grace, citing several texts.[143] Marriage could not be a "bed undefiled" (*thorus immaculatus*), as Hebrews 13:4 requires, without the help of grace. To corroborate this interpretation, Henry rehearses a rationale proposed by Thomas Aquinas. God in his bountiful goodness provides all creatures, even those that lack reason and sense, with whatever is necessary for them according to their various capacities. But the defilement of concupiscence inevitably infects the sexual act unless the spouses have God's gracious help. It is unthinkable that God would

---

[140] Ibid., 196/11–16.   [141] Ibid., 196/6–10.   [142] Ibid., 200/16–21.   [143] Ibid., 200 ff.

expect his people to marry without providing them with conjugal grace, so that those who receive this grace with a good will can be faithful to the marriage bed and avoid the defilements that would otherwise occur, and can even make progress in merit.[144]

Other texts corroborate the argument from need.[145] If God blessed all his creatures according to their various capacities, would he not have blessed with grace the marriage of human beings, who are made in his image (Gen 1:28)? At Cana, Jesus turned the water of a merely human relationship into the wine of something supernatural (John 2:1–11), bestowing a cleansing grace through marriage so that the marriage bed is preserved not only from fornication but also from the defilements of concupiscence. Again, how are women saved by bearing children (1 Tim 2:15), and how does a convert sanctify an unbelieving spouse (1 Cor 7:12–14), if not through grace? We know from Matthew 19:6 – "What God has joined together let not man separate" – that God himself joins the spouses together. If God joins the spouses, will he not also infuse the grace that they need to sustain their union? One must accept, therefore, that God confers grace on marriage, albeit only when spouses are joined in a legitimate marriage (i.e., with due solemnity) and with "God himself assisting" in the rite. They should not dare to be joined merely by the "ceremonies of mortals."[146]

Henry concludes that marriage is a sign of a sacred reality, that it confers grace, and that it is more than a figure of something sacred. Even if what Paul calls a "great sacrament" is not marriage – which Henry does not concede – one must still accept that it is a sacrament in the proper sense.[147]

Henry quotes Hugh of Saint-Victor to corroborate these claims: an author rarely cited in sixteenth-century theology.[148] Perhaps Henry's evident familiarity with Hugh was a result of his own reading, for there is no reason to attribute it to Thomas More's influence.[149] Hugh concedes that the office of marriage (the sexual and procreative aspect) is a "great sacrament" of the union between Christ and the church as "two in one flesh," and he argues that marriage itself is a greater sacrament of Christ and the church, or of God and the soul as two in one spirit, wherein God is the groom (*sponsus*), and the church is his bride (*sponsa*). Henry quotes a passage in which Hugh, having delineated the dual sacramentality of marriage in his usual way, parses the spiritual sign into two aspects, respectively exterior and interior. The outward sacrament (i.e., the *sacramentum tantum*) signifies an inner love between the spouses, Hugh argues, which in turn (as the *sacramentum et res*) signifies the union of grace between God and the soul (the *res tantum*). According to Hugh,

---

[144] Ibid., 200/32–201/9.   [145] Ibid., 201–04.

[146] Ibid., 203/22–24. Henry uses the verb *assistere* in its liturgical sense, as if God the Father were the minister of the sacrament.

[147] Ibid., 204/16–21.   [148] Ibid., 204–05. Cf. PL 176:482A–D.

[149] Marius, "Henry VIII, Thomas More, and the Bishop of Rome," 93.

the partnership itself, which is preserved in marriage externally by their agreeing to a compact, is a sacrament; and the *res* of that sacrament is the mutual love of minds [*dilectio mutua animorum*], which is guarded between them by the bond of their partnership and their conjugal compact. And again, that very love, by which male and female are united in their minds by the sanctity of marriage, is a sacrament and a sign of the love [*dilectio*] by which God is joined inwardly to the rational soul through an infusion of grace and through participation in his Spirit.[150]

Henry is not interested here in Hugh's theory of the twofold sacrament but only in the notion that there is a bond of spiritual love in marriage that emulates the mystery of divine love: an emphasis congruent with the sixteenth-century theology of marriage. The existence of this marvelous love, according to Henry, proves that marriage is a sacrament.

17.5 JOHANN GROPPER

Gropper's *Enchiridion christianae institutionis* is a practical manual of theology written to meet the needs of parochial clergy. Its chief parts are an exposition of the Apostles' Creed; an extensive treatise on the seven sacraments, to which the treatise on marriage belongs; a treatise on prayer, which includes an exposition of the Lord's Prayer; and a treatise on law, which includes an exposition of the Decalogue.[151]

Like many of the cathedral clergy of his day, Gropper was professionally qualified only in law.[152] He had a degree in civil law from Cologne, but he had no formal training in theology, and he was neither erudite nor skilled as a theologian. Nevertheless, he was an astute pastor and a capable administrator, and he applied his native wit and his legal training to theological problems with some success.

Gropper joined the archdiocesan clergy of Cologne in 1525 and was quickly ordained to the priesthood. He became a canon priest of the cathedral chapter in 1534, and soon afterwards vicar general and assistant to the archbishop, Hermann of Wied. In that office, Gropper organized the provincial council of Cologne in 1536. When the decrees of the council were published in 1538, Gropper's *Enchiridion* was appended anonymously as if it summarized the reforms that the council desired or planned to execute. Consequently, Gropper's own ideas were often ascribed to the

---

[150] Hugh of Saint-Victor, *De sacramentis christianae fidei* II.11.3, ed. Berndt, 427/4–9 (= PL 176:482C–D).

[151] The edition cited here is *Enchiridion christianae institutionis in Concilio prouinciali Coloniensi editum* (Paris, 1550). The treatise *De matrimonio* occupies ff. 174r–192v.

[152] On Gropper's life and work, see W. Lipgens, *Kardinal Johannes Gropper* (Münster, 1951); and R. Braunisch, "Johannes Gropper (1503–1559)," in Sebastian Cüppers (ed.), *Kölner Theologen* (Cologne, 2004), 172–99. On Gropper on marriage, see A. Willsch, *Das Verständnis der Ehe im Enchiridion des Johannes Gropper* (St. Ottilien, 1990); and H. Filser, *Ekklesiologie und Sakramentenlehre des Kardinals Johannes Gropper* (Münster, 1995), 365–87.

provincial council.[153] Gropper remained a faithful Catholic when his archbishop, having failed to establish a workable agreement with Rome, went over to the Protestant side.

17.5.1 *The treatise on marriage in the* Enchiridion

Although the *Enchiridion*'s treatise on marriage evinces little familiarity with technical scholastic writing on the subject, it echoes current debates, and it is an original and thoughtful work in its own right. Gropper gives us a glimpse into how the issues that would be debated and settled at Trent looked to diligent, reform-minded pastors during the second quarter of the sixteenth century. Gropper regarded Cologne's decisions about marriage as important and authoritative but provisional. He looked forward keenly to the long-awaited general council, which would surely take place soon. The prelates at Trent cited his treatise on marriage frequently during the deliberations of 1563, usually conflating it with the decrees of the provincial council.[154]

Gropper concentrates on matters that the need for reform and the challenges of Protestantism had made urgent. He has little to say about the rules and regulations regarding the impediments, divorce, and so forth, which took up at least half of the typical theological or pastoral treatise on marriage, presumably because he did not consider them to be in need of serious reform. He does note the difficulty and importance of the impediments in the brief conclusion (c. 24), but he declines to say anything specific about them, advising clergy who are in any doubt to seek advice from their bishops, who alone have judicial authority over such matters.[155] Instead, he focuses on marriage as a sacrament.

The chief topics that Gropper addresses are as follows (with the chapters devoted to them noted in parentheses):[156] the meaning and etymology of the terms *matrimonium, coniugium,* and *nuptiae,* and the logical distinction between marriage and the sacrament of marriage (1); the institutions of marriage and their reasons, or causes (2–3); the distinctiveness of Christian, sacramental marriage in relation to marriage among pagans and among Jews (4–11); proof that Christian marriage is a sacrament of the New Law (12); the *verbum* (verbal formula) of the sacrament (13–14); the *elementum* (15–16), and the role of consummation (17); the role and importance of nuptial rites (18–20); the three conjugal goods, the proper reasons for intercourse, and sexual ethics (21–22); and the minister of the sacrament (23).

---

[153] A. Duval, "Contrat et sacrement de mariage au Concile de Trente," *La Maison-Dieu* 127 (1976): 34–63, at 50–51. For the proceedings and decrees of the Cologne council of 1536, see *Acta Reformationis Catholicae,* vol. 2 (Regensburg, 1960), 118–318.

[154] Duval, "Contrat et sacrement," 50–56. Willsch, *Verständnis der Ehe,* 215–29.

[155] Gropper, *De matrimonio* c. 24 (192v). The Cologne council re-affirmed Lateran IV's impediments and advised parish priests who were in doubt about them to consult persons with more expertise (*peritiores*): *Conc. prov. Colon.* 1536, 7.46, in *Acta Reformationis Catholicae,* 2:270.

[156] The chapters are not numbered in the cited edition, but the start of each new chapter is clearly indicated.

Gropper's chief aim is twofold: to confirm that marriage is properly one of the seven sacraments, and to demonstrate the importance of getting married under ecclesiastical supervision and in a church setting. Gropper is as vexed by the problem of clandestine marriage and by the medieval policy that generated it as he is by the Protestant contention that marriage is not a sacrament.

On what sources did he draw? Gropper quotes Scripture more extensively than had been usual in medieval scholastic treatises on marriage, frequently citing the Book of Tobit as well as the usual dossier of proof texts from Genesis, the gospels, Ephesians 5, and 1 Corinthians 7. He quotes from Augustine several times, albeit usually without attributing the texts. Herbert Filsner identifies Gratian's *Decretum* and Peter Lombard's *Sentences* as Gropper's chief medieval sources, and Gerhard Lorich's *Institutio catholica fidei orthodoxae* and King Henry VIII's reply to Luther (the *Assertio septem sacramentorum*) as his chief sixteenth-century sources.[157] But it would be hard to demonstrate any direct dependence on or even familiarity with the *Sentences* and the *Decretum*, for the themes and phrases that Gropper shared with these works were common property. Gropper does seem to have drawn on Henry VIII and on Lorich (a Catholic reformer and priest of Hadamar who died not long before 1553), although in both cases the differences are as notable as the similarities. The treatise on marriage in Lorich's *Institutio* is a very different work from Gropper's. Although both authors defend the status of marriage as a sacrament, Lorich focuses more on ethical than on pastoral matters, and his treatise includes an account of the impediments. Nevertheless, Gropper's extensive discussion of the reasons for sexual intercourse appears to be a reworking of a passage from Lorich's treatise, unless perhaps both were dependent on a third source.[158] There are no verbatim parallels between Gropper's treatise and Henry's *Assertio*, but the two treatises cover similar ground in their different ways, and some distinctive phrases occur in the same contexts in both works.[159]

17.5.2 *Marriage as one of the sacraments*

Gropper marvels at the madness (*dementia*) of those who deny that marriage is one of the sacraments of the New Law.[160] God instituted marriage from the beginning as

---

[157] See Filser, *Ekklesiologie und Sakramentenlehre*, 365–87, passim, and especially the concluding paragraph on 386–87. Lorich, *De sacramento coniugii*, in *Institutio catholicae fidei orthodoxae* (Frankfurt, 1536), 75r–84v.

[158] Cf. Lorich, *De sacramento coniugii*, 75v–76v, and Gropper, *De matrimonio* c. 21 (190b–91b). The three reasons are procreation, rendering the debt, and lust, of which the first two entail no guilt and the third carries only venial guilt, thanks to the compensating conjugal goods. Both authors cite the familiar maxim about the overly keen lover from the *Sentences* of Sextus, and both cite Tobit 6 to exemplify sexual propriety.

[159] For example, both authors argue that marriage is a sacrament only among the "people of God" (*populus Dei*): cf. Henry VIII, *Assertio*, 195; and Gropper, *De matrimonio* c. 4 (176r).

[160] Gropper, *De matrimonio* c. 12 (179v).

a sign of the union between Christ and church,[161] but whereas marriage under the Old Law only foreshadowed that union, Christian marriage is an "express" sign of it. It is conformed to the mystical marriage between Christ and the church, and such conformity would be impossible unless marriage conferred some "assisting grace," as do the other sacraments of the New Law. Gropper claims that all the reliable orthodox authorities in the east as well as in the west have upheld the doctrine that marriage is a sacrament in the proper sense.[162]

For biblical proof that marriage is truly a sacrament, Gropper appeals to Ephesians 5:32: "This is a great sacrament ... in Christ and the church." Focusing narrowly on this verse rather than reviewing its context and parallels, and tacitly assuming that a sacrament *in* something is a sacrament *of* it, Gropper asks to what the demonstrative pronoun, "this," refers. He argues that it cannot refer to the mystery of Christ and the church, as some maintain, for then something would be sacrament of itself, which is impossible: The union of Christ and the church would be a sacrament of the union between Christ and the church. The pronoun can only refer to marriage, albeit in the context of Adam's recognition of Eve.[163] This exegesis is weak and betrays Gropper's limitations as theologian and biblical scholar. He assumes that the preposition "in" expresses the relationship between sacramental sign and signified reality, and he overlooks other plausible candidates for the reference of "this," such as Adam's dictum. He seems unaware of the possibility, recognized not only by Erasmus and Luther but also by Peter Lombard, that the term "sacrament" sometimes refers not to a sign but to a signified mystery. Gropper's understanding of the text is clearly inconsistent with Augustine's observation that what is great in Christ and the church is little in individual couples, although he quotes this text elsewhere in the treatise.[164] Henry's defense is more convincing because he quotes and expounds the entire discourse on marriage (Eph 5:22–32), whereas Gropper focuses on the sense of verse 32 alone.[165]

Gropper uses several schemata to illuminate the distinctiveness of marriage as a sacrament. At the outset, he distinguishes logically between marriage and the sacrament of marriage. Marriage has a much larger extension than the sacrament, he argues, for not every marriage is a sacrament, just as not every penitential act is sacramental penance.[166] The obvious example of non-sacramental marriage is that of pagans, but Gropper suggests that even Christians who marry improperly, such as those who marry clandestinely or without the priestly benediction, may marry validly

---

[161] *De matrimonio* c. 3 (174v–75r).   [162] *De matrimonio* c. 12 (179v–180r).

[163] Ibid. (180r–v).

[164] Augustine, *De nupt. et conc.* I.21(23), CSEL 42:236. Gropper, *De matrimonio* c. 16 (186v–87r). *De matrimonio* c. 16 is in effect an exposition of Eph 5:22–32, which Gropper has already quoted in full in c. 15 (186r–v).

[165] Henry VIII, *Assertio*, 195–96.

[166] Gropper, *De matrimonio* c. 1 (174a). Henry VIII, *Assertio*, 194–95, criticizes Luther for arguing that because marriage is not a sacrament among unbelievers, it is also not a sacrament among believers, since marriage is essentially the same thing in both cultures.

without receiving the sacrament of marriage.[167] Gropper compares the marriages of Gentiles (i.e., unbelievers), Jews, and Christians, and the comparison reveals both similarities and differences among them.

The Gentiles do not regard marriage as a sacrament or appreciate its true sanctity, which is why they divorce freely. Failing to grasp that marriage is a divine gift, they locate it entirely within the human laws of particular cultures, assuming that a marriage valid in one society may be invalid in another.[168] But even unbelievers are dimly aware that marriage is holy and permanent, for these features are inscribed in the natural law. They abhor adultery and indecency (*stupra*), they value moderation and modesty, and they are aware that marriage is more than a human invention. Unbelievers and Christians also share some of the standard definitions of marriage, such as Modestinus's definition in the *Digest* and Ulpian's in the *Institutes*.[169] They agree that marriage is a "legitimate joining" (*coniunctio*) of male and female, that consent rather than sexual intercourse is the chief cause, that marriage entails a mutual, amicable association (*mutua societas ac familiaritas*), and that this association prevents promiscuity and is the proper basis for raising children. But the marriage of unbelievers is not a sacrament of the New Law, conferring grace on those who receive it in the proper way. Moreover, Christianity is distinctive in its exclusion of polygamy and its prohibition of divorce. Divorce is permitted here only on grounds of adultery, and even then only corporeal divorce is permitted, and not sacramental divorce, which would enable the spouses to remarry. Gropper laments the fact that new heretics such as the "fanatical Anabaptists" are so "wretchedly deluded" that they fail to grasp the distinctive features that make Christian marriage a sacrament: especially the power to confer grace on those who receive the sacrament worthily.[170]

Jewish marriage – here Gropper is thinking chiefly of marriage in the Old Testament – lies somewhere between Christian marriage and Gentile marriage. Marriage had greater sanctity among the Jews than it has among the Gentiles, for the Jews married not out of lust nor simply to procreate but to raise children as God's people. Again, whereas unbelievers pursue outward honor in marriage, the Jews pursue inward piety.[171] The right to divorce under the Mosaic law was a lesser evil conceded to prevent worse evils, for otherwise men would have murdered unwanted wives. Polygyny was justifiable as a proper response to the necessity of procreation, and it had a mystical sense, for it signified the future union of all the faithful with Christ.[172]

---

[167] Gropper, *De matrimonio* c. 13 (181r–v).

[168] *De matrimonio* c. 4 (176b): "... sed sibi omnia tribuerunt, ex re sacra rem fecerunt prophanam, adeo ut matrimonium non ex Dei, sed a moribus ac legibus cuisque populi totum penderet: eoque talia erant apud alios legitima coniugia qualia haberentur alibi per absurda." Cf. Henry VIII, *Assertio*, 194: "De gentibus alia quaestio est, quorum coniugium totum pendebat a moribus ac legibus cujusque populi. Eoque talia erant apud alias legitima conjugia, qualia haberentur alibi perabsurda."

[169] Gropper, *De matrimonio* c. 4 (176r–v).   [170] *De matrimonio* c. 10 (179r).

[171] *De matrimonio* c. 5 (176v), c. 10 (179r).   [172] *De matrimonio* cc. 5–9 (176v–78v).

Jewish marriage under the Old Law prefigured Christian marriage, and it was a sacrament in the same way as the other rites and offering of the Old Law were sacraments. These not only prefigured things to come but also cleansed and sanctified the participants, albeit not by virtue of a power inherent in the sacrament itself (i.e., not *ex opere operato*) but only through faith in Christ-to-come. Even the crossing of the Red Sea and the manna in the wilderness can be counted as sacraments in this broad sense. Just as the polygyny of the Old Law signified the coming together of the synagogue with the church, and of all races into union with Christ, so the monogamy of the New Law signifies the unity of the blessed in a single celestial city.[173] Gropper construes Christian marriage not as something entirely new but rather as the full realization of marriage as it was originally instituted. Infidel marriage falls short of the institution without entirely escaping it, whereas Jewish marriage fulfilled it in a lesser way: a step toward the ultimate realization.

There were four reasons for the institution of marriage, according to Gropper. Marriage was instituted before sin to establish mutual, amicable support between the spouses, with one commanding and the other obeying,[174] and so that there would be a "very close union" to serve as the basis for raising children. After sin had entered into the world, marriage was re-instituted as a means to overcome the weakness that lust entailed and to avoid fornication. But God had instituted marriage from the very beginning also as a sign of the joining between Christ and the church, which God foresaw and preordained before the ages began as the future solution to sin. Gropper argues that this signification was the first and most fundamental reason for instituting marriage.[175] As proof, he presents a concatenation of texts from the Old and New Testaments that illuminate the long courtship, the betrothal (*desponsatio*), and the eventual marriage between Christ and the church.[176] When water and blood flowed from Christ's side on the Cross, signifying the sacraments of baptism and eucharist, the church became his wife, and Christ consummated the marriage that had been promised and preordained since the beginning. The long betrothal was at last fulfilled. Only the people of God understand the sacred significance of marriage: the Jews who lived before Christ as well as the followers of Christ.[177] But the original significance of marriage could be not be

---

[173] *De matrimonio* c. 11 (179r–v).

[174] Gropper, echoing Augustine, defines marriage as "*prima humanae societatis copula, quae germanum atque amicabilem quandam coniunctionem, alterius quidem regentis, alterius autem obsequentis complecteretur.*" Cf. Augustine, *De bono coniugali* 1(1), CSEL 41:187/8–9, 188/1–2.

[175] *De matrimonio* c. 3 (174v–75r).

[176] Ibid. (175r–76r). The chief texts are Hos 2:21[19], Song 1:1, John 1:29–30 (where John the Baptist is the *paranymphus*), John 3:29–30 (where John as an *amicus sponsi* distinguishes himself from the *sponsus*), Ps. 44 (which tells of a royal wedding), Matt 22:1–14, Luke 14:1–24 (Christ on the cross, and the piercing of Christ's side, as compared with the formation of Eve from Adam in Gen. 2:21–24), and John 19:28–37, especially "I thirst" (v. 28) and "it is consummated" (v. 30).

[177] *De matrimonio* c. 4 (176r).

fully realized without the assistance of grace, which would make conformity between marriage and the union of Christ and the church possible. This sacramental grace is peculiar to Christian marriage, for Christ not only recalled marriage to its pristine dignity but also sanctified it with an "increase of grace."[178]

Gropper argues that Christian marriage is truly one of the seven sacraments of the New Law. These are the "mysteries that are rightly and properly called sacraments," for they are sensible signs of invisible graces that they both signify and cause *ex opere operato*. They are "visible signs of the invisible grace of God, a grace God brings about in them efficaciously and assuredly as long as the sacraments are handled and received properly and not unworthily."[179]

17.5.3 *The composition of the sacrament*

Since marriage is a sacrament in the proper sense, it must not only confer grace but also be composed of a *verbum* (a verbal formula) and an *elementum* (the matter from which the sacrament is composed).[180] Gropper prefers these patristic terms to the scholastic terms "form" and "matter." The *verbum* of this sacrament consists of the words by which the spouses plight their troth, Gropper argues, but these words must be said in the right way and with the right intention to qualify as the *verbum*. What is essential is not the exact words but the intention behind them. It does not matter whether the partners plight their troth in Latin, in the vernacular, or in Greek, as long as they marry *in the Lord*.[181] They must say the words when they are present together rather than in writing or through intermediaries, and they must "piously give and receive each other with due respect to God." Indeed, they must be joined "not just in any way, but in God's name . . . or in the name of Father, Son, and Holy Spirit," as befits any sacrament performed "in his holy mountain, in God's city." Even the Jews under the Old Law married "piously and religiously with God as witness, in faith, and in fear of the Lord." How much more, then, is such piety called for under the New Law, where God ties the spouses together inseparably as "two in one flesh" and gives them a grace enabling them to remain chastely together, for "what God has joined, man may not separate."[182] By including the religious intentions of the spouses and the due solemnity of the context, Gropper cleverly develops his notion of the *verbum* so as to exclude clandestine marriage. I shall return to this feature of his argument.

The *elementum* of marriage must be some outward, sensible aspect. Specifically, it is the "exterior joining [*coniunctio*] of the man and the woman," or "that exterior

---

[178] *De matrimonio* c. 12 (179v), c. 14 (183r).

[179] Gropper, *Enchiridion: De sacramentis novi testamenti*, 33v: "signa visibilia inuisibilis gratiae Dei, quam Deus efficaciter et certo in ipsis operatur, modo rite nec indigne tractentur et accipiantur."

[180] *De matrimonio* c. 12 (180v).   [181] *De matrimonio* c. 13 (180v).

[182] *De matrimonio* c. 13 (180v–81r, 181v), c. 14 (183r).

gesture and action by which the spouses are coupled together in the Lord's name," professing that they will be two in flesh and will serve each other in perpetual conjugal fidelity. Gropper is probably referring to the nuptials (i.e., to marriage *in fieri*) when he refers to *coniunctio* here, but one cannot be sure. Nor is it clear whether the *elementum* includes the verbal exchange. Gropper holds that sexual consummation completes the *elementum*. He reasons that the phrase "two in one flesh" denotes sexual union only by implication. It denotes in the first place an exceptionally close partnership in which male and female are joined as a single social unit: a partnership that was instituted in the beginning but is enhanced among Christians. The phrase connotes sexual union secondarily, as the normal outcome of the former joining.[183]

The external aspects of marriage that constitute the *elementum*, Gropper explains, signify both the twofold union between Christ and the church and the compact or indissoluble bond of faith between the spouses. The second of these significations presupposes the first. The bond is indissoluble because God provides grace with the sacrament, infusing love and affection into the minds (*animi*) of the spouses to conserve their partnership and to enable them to preserve their bodies and their minds from fornication. That is why Paul commends faithful spouses in Ephesians 5:22–32 to cultivate and to quicken the grace of mutual love, which is a gift from God.[184]

An unconsummated marriage, Gropper argues, such as that between Mary and Joseph, is imperfect only in respect of the first of those two significations. Christ is united to the church not only spiritually and in charity, but also as the head of a body, through his reception of human flesh.[185] Because an unconsummated marriage does not perfectly signify the second aspect, Pope Leo, as quoted by Peter Lombard and Gratian, says that a wife who has not had intercourse with her husband does not "pertain to matrimony." But nothing prevents an unconsummated marriage from being perfect in respect of sanctity and conjugal love. Moreover, it signifies the spiritual aspect of Christ's union with the church more adequately than sexual union can do. To determine whether a marriage is perfect, therefore, one must consider three distinct aspects: its validity, or truth (*veritas*), which pertains to the firmness of the bond; its sanctity; and its signification in relation to Christ and the church. The unconsummated marriage of Mary and Joseph was imperfect in respect of the third aspect, but it was perfect in respect of the first two aspects. Following Augustine, Gropper reasons that Mary was inspired to make a personal, private vow (*propositum*) of virginity in her mind (*in mente*) before she married, and that she expressed her intention orally only later, after she had conceived Jesus.[186]

---

[183] Erasmus, *Responsio ad annotationes Eduardi Lei* (resp. 1, n. 19), ASD IX-4, 112, prefers *"duo in carnem unam"* to the Vulgate's *"duo in carne una"* in Mark 10:8 and Matt 19:5, partly because the phrase refers to the making of one person out of two, and not explicitly to sexual intercourse. In this sense, Mary and Joseph were two in one flesh.

[184] *De matrimonio* c. 15 (186r).   [185] Ibid.   [186] *De matrimonio* c. 17 (187r–88r).

The minister of marriage, according to Gropper, is the priest who blesses the union. Gropper accepts that the spouses themselves establish the marriage, supplying both *verbum* and *elementum*. He does not consider whether the spouses might be construed as ministers, presumably because that term generally implied an appointed cleric who fulfilled his duties *ex officio*. Gropper does not suggest that the priest's ritual performance is integral to the sacrament, but he tries to show indirectly that the priest's role in the performance of the sacrament is normal and fitting. Some maintain, Gropper notes, that there is no need for any minister of this sacrament, but in his view they go too far. Even under the Old Law, a father – or, in his absence, the nearest male agnate – joined together the spouses on God's behalf, as recorded in Tobit 7. Under the New Law, priests have assumed the paternal role that the bride's father had under the Old Law, and the priest's ministry includes his duty to instruct the contractants. He should tell them about the institution of marriage, citing Genesis; about the sanctity and saving efficacy of marriage, drawing on the gospels; and about the mystery of marriage, citing Paul's letter to the Ephesians. He should remind them, too, of the burdens and the troubles that attend marriage, for these are penalties for original sin and should be borne with patience and equanimity.[187]

17.5.4 Solemnity and clandestinity

Gropper emphasizes the importance of the proper church formalities. He laments the lax standards and customs of his own day, which he regards as a decline from the high standards maintained in former times. Whereas people formerly married with due honor and reverence, now "uncouth gesticulations" have taken the place of "holy congratulation," and couples are joined amid profane dancing and drunkenness. Parish priests should try to prevent such abuses with "pious admonitions."[188] Gropper is echoing decisions of the Council of Cologne, which condemned the lewd horseplay (*ludicra*) that sometimes occurred in church after the priest had joined the couple and declared that such behavior was inconsistent with the religious import of the event.[189] The provincial council also insisted, citing Tobit, that spouses-to-be should approach their marriage piously and religiously and not out of lust. Ideally, couples should prepare for marriage by fasting and receiving eucharist.[190]

Gropper directs his strongest and most extended warnings against clandestine marriage, which he considers to be a result of declining religious and civic standards. Marriage among the Jews of the Old Law was public and inter-familial. The

---

[187] *De matrimonio* c. 23 (192r–v). Cf. *Conc. prov. colon.* 1536, 7.40 (268): Parish priests joining partners in matrimony should explain, citing Gen 2 and Matt 19, how marriage was instituted by God and confirmed by Christ, and how marriage is a sacrament, citing Eph 5.

[188] *De matrimonio* c. 19 (189v–90r).   [189] *Conc. prov. colon.* 1536, 7.47 (270).

[190] Ibid., 7.41 (269/4–20).

practice of the early church is preserved in the "most beautiful canon" of Pope Evaristus, who was the third or, according to some, the fifth successor to Peter.[191] According to this decretal, a marriage was no more than fornication or adultery unless all the formalities had been observed: the suit, the betrothal, the attendants, the nuptial mass, the Tobias Nights, and so forth.[192] But for a long time now the church has upheld clandestine marriages as valid provided only that there are witnesses to prove that the marriage took place. Gropper mentions with approval some current practices designed prevent illicit marriages from taking place, such as the reading of the banns and the refusal to marry wayfarers or persons unknown in the parish unless their identity is documented.[193] Nevertheless, the church fosters lax behavior by recognizing clandestine marriages as valid. As a result, young people marry casually, without taking proper counsel and without parental consent. Instead of thinking of the consequences and the meaning of what they are doing, they marry foolishly and impetuously, moved by the emotion of the moment, by lust, or even by the prompting of the devil. Such unions are prone to deceit and to fraud. Clandestine marriages are entirely lacking in sacramentality (*ratio sacramenti*), Gropper argues, and the church should declare them null and void, or at least decree that they lack "firmness" unless they are confirmed by a fresh act of consent performed with due solemnity.

Gropper recalls that for all those reasons the fathers at Cologne "wanted this holiest of canons [i.e., the decretal of pseudo-Evaristus] to be renewed in the church at a general council."[194] Although the imprecise term "general council" is sometimes used even of a provincial council, which was general in relation to a cathedral chapter, Gropper presumably has in mind a universal council, or at least a council convened by the pope.[195] He was referring to the long-expected general council, which would eventually begin at Trent in 1545. Efforts to organize a general council that would reform the church and fortify it against schisms and the new heresies went back decades. In 1536, Pope Paul III convoked a general council that was to begin at Mantua in 1537, although political and religious troubles prevented it.[196] In Gropper's view, the provincial council at Cologne was a provisional, interim measure, which identified and ameliorated abuses that would need to be solved definitively in due course by a general council, speaking for the

---

[191] *De matrimonio* c. 18 (118r–v).

[192] Hinschius (ed.), *Decretales Pseudo-Isidorianae*, 87–88; and PL 130:81B–C. See G. H. Joyce, *Christian Marriage* (London, 1948), 104–05; Reynolds, MWCh, 406–09.

[193] *Conc. prov. colon.* 1536, 7.45 (270) requires "legitimate testimony" before a parish priest can marry travelers (*peregrini*).

[194] *De matrimonio* c. 19 (188r–90r).

[195] On the several senses of the term *concilium generale*, see H. Fuhrmann, "Das Ökumenische Konzil und seine geschichtlichen Grundlagen," *Geschichte in Wissenschaft und Unterricht* 12 (1961): 672–95, at 682.

[196] H. Jedin provides a detailed account of these developments in *History of the Council of Trent*, vol. 1: *The Struggle for the Council* (London, 1957). See pp. 288–312 on Paul III and the convocation of the council at Mantua.

whole church. One of the canons of the Cologne council expressed the German prelates' desire that the forthcoming general council would renew Evaristus's decree and abolish clandestine marriage entirely, since the harm that it did was all too obvious. Meanwhile, persons marrying clandestinely should be excommunicated. A later revision adds that priests should whenever possible decline to marry couples without parental approval.[197] The council also declared that, except in cases of dire necessity, couples should marry "according to the ancient canons," that is, in church, after the completion of such formalities as the banns, with a priest who blesses the marriage, and with a nuptial mass. Couples who chose to marry without such solemnities "despise the church of God" (1 Cor 11:22).[198]

Gropper cannot be persuaded that clandestine marriages are truly sacramental. Even among Christians, he argues, one must distinguish between marriage and the sacrament of marriage. Christians who marry clandestinely enter into a valid contract of marriage but do not receive the sacrament. Gropper distinguishes between the *verbum* necessary for marriage as a contract and the *verbum* necessary for marriage as a sacrament. Words are used to express *de praesenti* consent even among the infidels. The pious requirements outlined earlier are not necessary for marriage *per se*, therefore, but they are necessary for the sacrament of marriage. The words of contract and of sacrament are the same, but only with right intentions do they constitute the sacramental *verbum*.[199] Again, legitimate consent suffices to establish *matrimonium legitimum*, but the spouses do not enter into *matrimonium ratum* unless they consent and marry in the Christian manner (*more christiano*).[200] Gropper notes at the end of the treatise on marriage that human law and divine law are so mixed together that it is hard to separate them, and he expresses the hope that a general council will discern which aspects of marriage pertain to which law.[201] He suggests in passing that clandestine consent is not even true consent, for so casual an action is inconsistent with the gravity of the commitment, whereby the partners are bound together for life.[202] But his chief argument is that certain religious intentions are necessary if the partners are to marry in the Lord. Absent such piety, their words of consent constitute only a contractual *verbum*, and not a sacramental *verbum*.

As noted earlier, Gropper's aversion to clandestine marriage was widely shared among German reformers, Catholic as well as Protestant. His argument about the invalidity of clandestine marriages is very similar to Gerhard Lorich's. Lorich begins his treatise on marriage with a simple definition: "Marriage is the legitimate joining of a man and a woman through free consent, entailing an indivisible and blessed way of life."[203] Lorich then expounds the meaning (*sensus*) of that definition, focusing on the legitimacy and blessedness of marriage. Fully interpreted, the

[197] *Conc. prov. colon.* 1536, 7.43 (269).   [198] *Conc. prov. colon.* 1536, 7.44 (270).
[199] *De matrimonio*, c. 13 (181r–v).   [200] *De matrimonio* c. 17 (187v).
[201] *De matrimonio* c. 24 (192v).   [202] *De matrimonio* c. 19 (189r).
[203] Lorich, *Institutio*, 75r: "Matrimonium est maris et foemine per liberum consensum legitima coniunctio indiuiduam et beatam uitae consuetudinem importans."

definition implies that the partners, whether brought together by their parents or by their own volition, accept each other faithfully; that they plight their troth with God as their witness, professing to serve each other perpetually; and that they marry before the church (*in facie ecclesiae*), with the blessing of a priest. Only in that way do they marry in the fear of God, entering into a union that by the grace of God is meritorious, *ratum*, indissoluble, and honorable in the sight of both God and men.[204] Lorich goes further later in the treatise. Echoing Evaristus, he argues that to contract a marriage properly and legitimately the Christian *sponsus* must ask his bride's parents for her hand in marriage and accept a dowry for her, and their consent must be genuine and not coerced.[205] It may be true that even a covert expression of consent validates (*sanciat*) a marriage, but that practice is fraught with danger, in part because there will be no witnesses to the union if one of the partners later abandons the other.[206]

Gropper goes further even than Lorich, construing the spouses' pious intentions and the due circumstances of solemnization as conditions that elevate their exchange of consent from contractual *verbum* to sacramental *verbum*. Gropper does not argue that the priestly blessing is the sacramental form. On the contrary, he maintains that the spouses' expression of consent and not the priestly blessing is the sacramental *verbum*. But clandestine contracts are contrary to the church's norms, they result from impure motives, and they are not fully founded on faith, for the partners marry with no respect for God.[207] Absent such conditions, the spouses may validly marry, therefore, but they do not marry "in the Lord." The *verbum* that is required for a sacramental marriage is an expression of the spouses' intention to marry *under God and in fear of the Lord*, for it is God alone who can so unite the spouses that no man can separate them.[208] The honorable intentions for marrying include fear of the Lord, the desire to maintain a chaste, honorable marriage, the desire to procreate children to worship God, and the desire to avoid promiscuity and uncleanness. Gropper allows (on the basis of Gen 21:17–18 and Deut 21:11) that a groom can acquire these honorable intentions even if he was initially drawn to a woman by her beauty, but the partners should be mindful above all that God is the "author and joiner" of marriage, and that it is God who joins them together in marriage.[209] A clandestine marriage is not a *sacrament* of marriage, therefore, although the union will become sacramental if the spouses later exchange their consent piously in a church.[210] It is God who really joins and blesses the spouses in sacramental marriage. The priest ritually enacts God's action to make it known to those present.[211]

No section of the treatise of marriage is devoted to the problem of grace, and Gropper's promise to prove that marriage confers grace remained unfulfilled.[212]

---

[204] Ibid.   [205] Ibid., 81v.   [206] Ibid., 83r.   [207] *De matrimonio* c. 13 (181v).
[208] *De matrimonio* c. 13 (180v–81v); c. 19 (188v).   [209] *De matrimonio* c. 22 (191v–92r).
[210] *De matrimonio* c. 19 (188v).   [211] Ibid. (189r).
[212] *De matrimonio* c. 12 (180v): "Superest itaque, ut et verbum et elementum huius sacramentum indicemus, et gratiam insuper in eo conferri demonstremus."

Nevertheless, Gropper mentions conjugal grace frequently in the course of the treatise, maintaining that marriage confers grace *ex opere operato* on those who receive it worthily. Gropper's understanding of conjugal grace is linked to his conviction that sacramental marriage is a solemn, religious act. Insofar as one can piece together the outlines of his theory of conjugal grace, it has three chief features. First, conjugal grace is conferred through a power that is inherent in the sacrament itself (i.e., *ex opere operato*) and peculiar to Christian marriage. Marriage under the Old Law would have sanctified the spouses, but only by virtue of their faith, as with any sacrament of the Old Law.[213] As well as recalling marriage to its pristine condition, Christ made it more holy by "applying" a new grace to it.[214] Second, conjugal grace is conferred only on those who enter into the sacrament properly and worthily.[215] They must marry piously, religiously, and in the Lord, acknowledging that God joins them together and binds them so firmly that no man can separate them, for marriage is divine as well as human.[216] Third, Gropper identifies conjugal grace with an affection that enriches the marital partnership and makes it sustainable. Citing Ephesians 5:22–32 as evidence, Gropper identifies conjugal grace with a gift of mutual love.[217] Without grace, the union of matrimony could not be an "express sign" of the union between Christ and the church.[218] Furthermore, the gift of conjugal grace enables the spouses to sustain their commitment to each other, living chastely together until parted by death.[219] The provincial council at Cologne expounded the Christological dimension of conjugal grace more fully, directing priests to instruct couples who marry that all those who receive this sacrament in the proper way, with the blessing of a priest, will receive a gift of the Holy Spirit: a gift that enables the husband to love his wife with a chaste love, as Christ loved the church, and that enables the wife to love and revere her husband as her lord for Christ's sake.[220]

The rich theology of marriage that Gropper articulated in his *Enchiridion* was reduced to its bare essentials in the *Regensburg Book*, which he helped to prepare as the basis for the Diet of Regensburg in 1541: one of several attempts to restore religious unity in Germany.[221] The *Book* characterizes the *verbum* only as being "situated" in Jesus' discourse on marriage in Matthew 19, and it specifies as the *elementum* the "exterior joining of a man and a woman, by which they are coupled

---

[213] *De matrimonio* c. 11 (179r–v); c. 10 (179r).   [214] *De matrimonio* c. 14 (183r).

[215] *De matrimonio* c. 10 (179a): "Verum hoc solo ab utriusque, tam Ethnico quam Iudaico, matrimonium distat Christianum, quod est novae legis sacramentum, gratiam conferens iis qui id rite auspicantur."

[216] *De matrimonio* c. 4 (176r–v).   [217] *De matrimonio* c. 15 (186r–v).

[218] *De matrimonio* c. 12 (179v).   [219] *De matrimonio* c. 13 (181r); c. 15 (186r).

[220] *Conc. prov. colon.* 1536, 7.40 (268/20–25).

[221] *Acta Reformationis Catholicae*, vol. 6 (Regensburg, 1974), 21–88. See H. Eells, "The Origin of the Regensburg Book," *Princeton Theological Review* 26 (1928): 355–72; and R. Braunisch, "Die 'Artikell' der 'Warhafftigen Antwort' (1545) des Johannes Gropper," in R. Baümer, *Von Konstanz nach Trient* (Munich, 1972), 519–45.

in God's name and in the church of Christ." The spouses should know that they have been joined by divine authority and not by any human authority. They should know, too, that they have received a special grace, for it is by virtue of this grace that a convert sanctifies even a gentile partner, and that their children are made holy (1 Cor 7:14).[222]

17.6 SOLEMNITY, CLANDESTINITY, AND REFORM

Catholics and main-stream Protestants shared anxieties about how people were marrying, and churchmen of both traditions called for reform. Both were opposed to the excesses of the radical Protestants, such as Gropper's "fanatical Anabaptists," who were inclined to regard marriage not as a civic institution but as a personal and communal matter and to deny the jurisdiction of civil as well ecclesiastical authorities.[223] Some Anabaptists had even experimented with polygyny and group marriage. In response, Catholics and mainstream Protestants insisted on the rule of law and on the civic importance of marriage. For the same reasons, both sides were troubled by perceived conjugal and sexual abuses, especially by clandestine marriages, which they regarded as the most prevalent and harmful abuse and the one most in need of prevention through reform and legislation. The fact that Luther blamed the problem of clandestinity on Catholic canon law and on the sacramental doctrine only heightened the Catholics' sense that something had to be done about it.

17.6.1 *The ideology of marriage and the dream of order*

Anxiety about clandestine marriages during the sixteenth century should be understood against the background of an ideology surrounding marriage and sexuality. Churchmen, intellectuals, and orators, troubled by change and uncertainty, dreamed of an orderly political community rooted in marriage and the family, in domestic virtue and tranquility, and in the firm but benign rule of the *paterfamilias*. Marriage, in their view, was fundamental to familial and civic well-being. Contrariwise, abuses of marriage and of the sexual act were subversive.

Most of the themes of this ideology had emerged during the central Middle Ages, and we have seen how they flourished in the thirteenth century. William of Auvergne likened the ideal Christian household to a tranquil, fruitful orchard, contrasting it with the unholy vices of prostitutes, sodomites, and Saracens. To be drawn into promiscuity was like allowing one's faith to be adulterated by Jewish or Muslim influence: to become "Judaized" or "Saracenized." And William emphasized the subversive influence of lust and promiscuity, depicting lust as a beast that

---

[222] *Regenburger Book* c. 16 (71).
[223] See G. H. Williams, *The Radical Reformation*, 3rd edition (Kirksville, Mo., 1992), 755–98.

was devastating the Christian community. The person who pursued a celibate vocation, according to William, was like a farmer who stayed at home rather than going out to cultivate his fields: not because he did not consider the work worth doing, but because he had been warned that a wolf was lying in wait (Section 12.2.4.2). Albertus Magnus and Thomas Aquinas developed the notion of marriage as a civil contract designed to foster political well-being and regulated by civil law. Lifelong monogamy, they argued, as well as providing the optimal conditions for the begetting, raising, and caring for offspring, also enabled men and women to collaborate by combining their respective talents. Albert and Thomas claimed that marriage as a remedy and as a sacrament was revealed in Scripture and expounded by Christian authorities, but that pagan philosophers such as Aristotle, Cicero, and Aspasius were the chief experts on the familial and civic dimensions of marriage. The sacrament presupposed and supernaturally enhanced the contract (Sections 16.4 and 16.5).

Little if anything was strictly new in the sixteenth-century ideology of marriage, therefore, but it flourished throughout Europe during this period, acquiring new rhetorical means of articulation and new urgency. Everyone assumed that the household was the foundation of civic order and well-being. Legists found a rationale in Roman law, in classical philosophy, and in the theory of the common good, but on a practical level the preoccupation reflected patterns of local governance. In some regions, especially in Italy and France, what was chiefly at stake was the ascendancy and perpetuity of elite, noble families. In others, such as in England and Germany, local governance presupposed the bourgeois householder, who not only controlled his wife and family as their *paterfamilias* but also helped to maintain justice and order in the community as a churchwarden, a juryman, or a councilor.[224]

A discourse extolling the virtues of marriage and preferring marriage to celibacy sprang up and flourished in the warm climate of Italian humanism during the fifteenth century. These humanists affirmed the value of marriage, incorporating and modifying elements of Christian tradition but correcting the cautious, qualified, and sometimes pessimistic evaluation of marriage and sexuality that had prevailed throughout the patristic and medieval periods. St Jerome's pessimism regarding sex and marriage was a particular target. Secular scholars as well as clerics and prelates commended the ideal household headed by a God-fearing *paterfamilias* who ruled over his children and servants justly and piously, preserving a stable household.[225] As Emlyn Eisenach says, this was not a depiction of the *status quo* but "a dream of

---

[224] S. Rees Jones, "The Household and English Urban Government in the Later Middle Ages," in M. Carlier and T. Soens, *The Household in Late Medieval Cities* (Leuven-Apeldoorn, 2001), 71–87. S. McSheffrey, *Marriage, Sex, and Civic Culture in Medieval London* (Philadelphia, 2006), 138–40.

[225] E. Eisenach, *Husbands, Wives, and Concubines … in Sixteenth-Century Verona* (Kirksville, 2004), 1–2, 27–33.

the establishment of clear lines of authority in a complex and often problematic (though certainly patriarchal) reality."[226] The Italian humanists were thinking of extended, elite families, including servants and even animals as well as children; they emphasized the virtues of nobility and the duties of noblemen; and they regarded marriage as the means to perpetuate the excellence of the ruling elite. Humanist treatises extolling marriage first appeared in the Italian republics during the early fifteenth century.[227] In Venice, where "the family was the gateway to the political life,"[228] Giovanni Caldiera wrote a treatise on the household (*De iconomia*), which he construed as a microcosm of the political community (*politia*). Following Aristotle, Caldiera argued that the family and the political community were interdependent. Fransesco Barbaro, a Venetian nobleman, wrote a treatise focusing on marriage itself (*De re uxoria*), and he presented it as a wedding present to the Florentine ruler Lorenzo de' Medici and his bride, Gínerva Cavalcanti. In the first of its two books, after an introductory chapter on the nature of marriage, Barbaro describes the endowments and virtues that a man should seek in his future wife. In the second book, he describes the wife's duties and the management of an orderly household.

The affirmative themes that originated in such treatises were elaborated in wedding orations: a genre that was peculiar to the courts of fifteenth-century Italian dynastic principalities.[229] The orators praised the prince, the bride's father, and the institution of marriage, and they commended the bride's virtues and gracefulness. Anthony D'Elia points out that Guarino Guarini, author of the earliest surviving wedding orations, introduced the triad of *honestas, utilitas, iucunditas*, which became a common feature of the genre. D'Elia argues that this triad had a role comparable to that of Augustine's *fides, proles, sacramentum*. Classical ethicists divided goods into honorable and useful, the former alone being valuable for their own sake. To these, Quintilian, a favorite resource of Renaissance rhetoricians, added pleasure: *voluptas* or *iucunditas*. In the wedding orations, marriage possesses *honestas* inasmuch as it encloses sexual desire and activity, and *utilitas* inasmuch as it fosters interfamilial and political alliances, enhancing the aggregation and transmission of wealth. These were variants of traditional themes from medieval theology, but the orators developed the theme of *utilitas* more fully. The third good, *iucunditas*, embraced the pleasures of beauty, companionship, and sex, which the orators celebrated in a manner opposed to the grudging endorsement of sexual pleasure and feminine charms among medieval theologians and moralists.[230]

---

[226] Ibid., 1.
[227] M. L. King, "Caldiera and the Barbaros on Marriage and the Family," *Journal of Medieval and Renaissance Studies* 6 (1976): 19–50. See also M. L. King, "Personal, Domestic, and Republican Values in the Moral Philosophy of Giovanni Caldiera," *Renaissance Quarterly* 28.4 (1975): 535–74.
[228] King, "Caldiera and the Barbaros," 19.
[229] A. F. D'Elia, *The Renaissance of Marriage in Fifteenth-Century Italy* (Cambridge, Mass., 2004).
[230] Ibid., 40–41.

Themes in praise of marriage passed from fifteenth-century Italian humanism into sixteenth-century northern-European thought, most obviously in Erasmus.[231]

Reformers in the pre-Protestant and Protestant territories of northern Europe, too, praised the estate of marriage and dreamed of an orderly community rooted in the family, adapting southern humanist themes to their own more severe ideologies. Lutherans in particular espoused a paternalistic, hierarchical model of social order, composed of three concentric realms, each headed by its father: the household by the *Hausvater*, the state or principality by the *Landesvater*, and the universe by the *Gottesvater*.[232]

On the dark side of that ideology was the civil prosecution of sex crimes, which intensified during the late-medieval and Reformation periods and verged on communal hysteria. Authorities attempted to purge their communities of sins that seemed inherently impious and destabilizing. Guido Ruggiero shows that in fifteenth-century Venice the rhetoric associated with ordinary sex crimes such as fornication included talk of the "dishonor done to God, [to] civilizing forces in general, and [to] Venice in particular," whereas hitherto it had focused on the dishonor done to families and individuals.[233] Sodomy seemed especially dangerous and threatening.[234] People feared that sexual misbehavior in general but especially heinous sexual crimes and crimes against nature would bring down the wrath of God on their communities. They associated heinous sexual crimes with heresy and sometimes attributed them to heretics.[235] Thus, the French word *bougres* (the origin of the English word "bugger") originally referred to the Cathars (associated with the Bogomils) but was transferred to sodomites.[236] Similarly, the Norwegian term *kjetteri* ("heresy") was transferred to heinous sexual crimes.[237] Sodomy belonged in the

---

[231] Ibid., 131–34.

[232] J. F. Harrington, "*Hausvater* and *Landesvater*: Paternalism and Marriage Reform in Sixteenth-Century Germany," *Central European History* 25.1 (1992): 52–75. Harrington incorporated much of this article in *Reordering Marriage and Society in Reformation Germany* (Cambridge, 1995), in which see especially 41–47. See also S. Ozment, *When Fathers Ruled* (Cambridge, Mass., 1983), passim, on Lutheran paternalism.

[233] G. Ruggiero, *The Boundaries of Eros: Sex Crime and Sexuality in Renaissance Venice* (Oxford, 1985), 17–18.

[234] N. Davidson, "Theology, Nature and the Law," in T. Dean and K. J. P. Lowe, *Crime, Society and the Law in Renaissance Italy* (Cambridge, 1994), 74–78, at 86–87. Ruggiero, *The Boundaries of Eros*, 70–88. M. Korpiola, "Rethinking Incest and Heinous Sexual Crime," in A. Musson, *Boundaries of the Law* (Aldershot, 2005), 102–17, at 108–09 and 112. S. McDougall, "The Prosecution of Sex in Late Medieval Troyes," in A. Classen, *Sexuality in the Middle Ages and Early Modern Times* (Berlin, 2008), 691–713. M. Boone, "State Power and Illicit Sexuality: The Persecution of Sodomy in Late Medieval Bruges," *Journal of Medieval History* 22.2 (1996): 135–53, at 153, suggests that such campaigns "helped to shape the collective mentality and to strengthen the grip of the ruling elites of both state and city."

[235] J. A. Brundage, *Law, Sex, and Christian Society* (Chicago, 1987), 473.

[236] R. Conner, "*Les Molles et les Chausses*," in A. Livia and K. Hall, *Queerly Phrased* (Oxford, 1997), 127–46, at 129–33.

[237] A. I. Riisøy, *Sexuality, Law and Legal Practice and the Reformation in Norway* (Leiden, 2009), 50–53.

special legal category of *nefandum*: the wicked, heinous, abominable, and impious.[238] Non-procreative sex between men and women (such as anal intercourse), homosexual sodomy, and bestiality were comparable inasmuch as they abused nature. These activities were qualitatively comparable, therefore, but they constituted an ascending scale of incongruity, according to whether sexual activity was performed in the wrong manner, with the wrong gender, or with the wrong species.[239] In practice, though, sodomy seemed to be by far the most threatening and subversive of all sexual crimes. Efforts systematically to purge communities of sodomy began during the central Middle Ages and were especially intense during the fifteenth and sixteenth centuries, when they occurred all across Europe but most extensively in the republics of Florence and Venice.[240] Secular authorities were the chief agents of the vigorous efforts to extirpate sexual crime during the late Middle Ages and the Reformations, although ecclesiastical authorities concurred.

Religious and secular anxieties converged in the prosecution of sexual crimes and misdemeanors. Jurisdiction over such crimes had always been unclear or mixed, falling somewhere between the domain of the spiritual and ecclesiastical and the domain of the temporal and civil. Crimes such as simple fornication and adultery might be prosecuted in either ecclesiastical or civil courts, or in both (a valid form of double jeopardy); or each jurisdiction might pursue its own peculiar interests in the same crime. Shannon McSheffrey examines the case of Thomas Rote and Joan Chylde, who were prosecuted for fornication in London in 1472 at a ward mote inquest (the ward's civic court, consisting of twelve jurors appointed by the alderman). When Thomas and Joan pleaded in their own defense that they were planning to marry, the jurors called their bluff, proposing that that they should plight their troth at once, before the court. Their only alternatives were to marry or to confess that their defense was a sham. They chose to marry. Their marriage was canonically valid under the medieval regime of *solus consensus*, but Thomas later denied that he had married Joan, and Joan sued him in the consistory court. Only an ecclesiastical judge could determine whether or not there was a valid marriage.[241] Civic interest in sexual morality was a catalyst of reform in Protestant Germany, where groups of citizens, both clerics and laymen, formed lay synods to prosecute sexual crimes and misdemeanors.[242]

---

[238] See J. Chiffoleau, "Dire l'indicible. Remarques sur le catégorie de *nefandum* du XIIᵉ au XVᵉ siècle," *Annales ESC* 45.2 (1990): 289–324.

[239] Korpiola, "Rethinking Incest and Heinous Sexual Crime," 106–07.

[240] M. J. Rocke, "Il controllo dell'omosessualità a Firenze nel XV secolo," *Quaderni Storici* 66 (1987): 701–23. M. J. Rocke, *Forbidden Friendships: Homosexuality and Male Culture in Renaissance Florence* (New York, 1996). Ruggiero, *The Boundaries of Eros*, 109–45.

[241] McSheffrey, *Marriage, Sex, and Civic Culture*, 113, 160–61. The circumstances of civic inquest are known only through the depositions of the consistory court. For translations of excerpts from the depositions, see McSheffrey (ed.), *Love and Marriage in Late Medieval London* (Kalamazoo, 1995), 84–85.

[242] Harrington, *Reordering Marriage*, 114–18, 122–24, 139–40, 153–73.

All of these trends converged in a heightened emphasis on the role of marriage and the family as building blocks of an orderly political community. One should render unto Caesar what is Caesar's (Matt 22:21), but all government came from God (Rom 13:1–7). The divine order was comprehensive and all embracing. It was not the private concern of a subgroup within the temporal community. Although the understanding of temporal goods and of civil legislation was accessible in principle to such infidels as the pagan sages of antiquity, reformers assumed that the Christian faith had enhanced and corrected that understanding. Protestant reformers assumed that Christian princes rightfully controlled the temporal realm.

17.6.2 *The pastoral problem of clandestine marriages*

Catholic and Protestant Churchmen on the eve of Trent feared that clandestine marriages were undermining civic order. Clandestine marriages and the marriages of minors without parental consent seemed to sever marriage from the community at large. They were offensive to those who considered marriage and the family to be the foundations of the political community.[243] The very term "clandestine" was pejorative. The words *occultum* and *secretum* did not necessarily have negative connotations, but the word *clam* ("secretly") was pejorative, and the word *clandestinum* almost invariably denoted something evil: something that was underhand, impious, or treacherous: something that needed to be covered up because it was shameful.[244]

Until the Council of Trent, the canon law on clandestinity was that of the Fourth Lateran Council of 1215 (Section 14.7)[245] Couples should not marry clandestinely but only "in the sight of the church". (*in conspectu ecclesiae*). To that end, the partners' parish priest (*parochialis sacerdos*) should announce a forthcoming union, setting an appropriate date before which the parishioners should bring any lawful impediment (*legitimum impedimentum*) to his attention. Henceforth, a marriage was clandestine in canon law if and only if it was not contracted according to that procedure.

Bishops and provinces adapted Lateran IV's minimal, non-specific requirements to local traditions and customs. In France and England, the norm included the reading of the banns on three successive Sundays or feast days before the marriage was contracted, and eventually solemnization before witnesses *in facie ecclesiae*, when the parish priest would conduct the pre-nuptial rite at the entrance to the church or in the porch.[246] Then the party proceeded with the newlyweds into the church for the priestly blessing and the nuptial mass. In Italy, where members of

[243] Selderhuis, *Marriage and Divorce*, 194. [244] Chiffoleau, "Dire l'indicible," 359–62.
[245] Lateran IV, canon 51 (Tanner-Alberigo, 258). X 4.3.3 (CIC 2:679–80).
[246] Contrary to what is often written, this council did not require witnesses, triple banns, or marriage *in facie ecclesiae* (i.e., administered by the parish in or at the entrance to a church).

the clergy were generally less involved and less conspicuous in marrying, notarization fulfilled among the elite a role comparable to that of marrying *in facie ecclesiae* in the north.[247]

Although Lateran IV prohibited couples from marrying clandestinely, it did not deem such marriages to be null and void after the event. A simple exchange of consent in the present tense (or in the future tense followed by sexual intercourse) sufficed to establish a marriage that was indissoluble and fully sacramental according to ecclesiastical law. The existence of such a marriage could not be established in the public forum without witnesses who could testify that the exchange had taken place, but that necessity arose only if the marriage became the subject of litigation, such as in cases of prior contract.

The motives behind the desire to eradicate clandestine marriages on the eve of Trent are difficult to determine and are still not fully understood. The field is crisscrossed by some crucial but difficult distinctions, such as those between civil and secular jurisdiction, between persons in authority and their subjects, and between implicit motivation and explicit rationale. Moreover, while everyone in authority agreed that clandestine marriages were a major problem, they differed as to *why* they were a major problem.

Catholic and Protestant reformers during the sixteenth century wrote about clandestine marriage as if it had reached pandemic proportions and was undermining the welfare of the family and the community. But historians have as yet discovered no convincing evidence that clandestine marriages frustrated the economic or civic ambitions of parents or secular administrators on so large a scale. The relations among real or perceived hazards, ideology and polemics, and litigation regarding clandestinity in the various cultural regions, ecclesiastical provinces, and linguistic communities of Europe during late Middle Ages and the sixteenth century are still not fully understood. Much work remains to be done, especially in the fields of social history and history of law: fields that lie largely outside the purview of this book. But it is likely that the campaign against clandestine marriage was motivated as much by the ideology described earlier as by actual hazards or frustrated ambitions. Just as marriage featured in a dream of order, so also clandestine marriages, with their associations of lust, rashness, disobedience, deception, impiety, and individualistic disdain for authority and the common good, featured in a nightmare of disorder.

We have no way of knowing what the relative frequencies of clandestine marriages were in Catholic communities during the first half of the sixteenth century. We may assume that the lower the social stratum to which the couple belonged, the less likely the partners were to solemnize their union. Although many of the marriage cases that came before episcopal courts in the late Middle Ages involved

---

[247] See D. d'Avray, "Marriage Ceremonies and the Church after 1215," in T. Dean and K. J. P. Lowe (eds.), *Marriage in Italy, 1300–1650* (Cambridge, 1998), 107–15; and T. Kuehn, "Contracting Marriage in Renaissance Florence," THTH, 390–420, at 394–95.

clandestine unions, prosecution of clandestinity itself *ex officio*, as far as one can tell from surviving records, was rare. What brought such unions into litigation was usually a claim of prior contract or the failure of one of the parties, usually the husband, to fulfill the obligation, when the court might enforce the contract if it could be established through witnesses. Clandestine marriages were much more likely to run into problems than marriages contracted *in conspectu ecclesiae* after the banns were read.[248] The marriages that came before the Papal Penitentiary during the fifteenth and sixteenth centuries were often clandestine, but these couples were usually seeking dispensation from an impediment.[249] It is likely that many of them married knowing about the impediment but hoping to get a dispensation after the event, for ecclesiastical judges preferred not to dissolve existing marriages so as to avoid scandal.[250]

Clandestine marriage and the principle that the spouses' consent alone (*solus consensus*) was sufficient to establish a valid marriage must have subverted ecclesiastical law, parental care, and simple prudence in many ways, but concrete historical evidence of such mayhem before the sixteenth century is sparse. The reforms of Lateran IV did not in fact prevent persons who were already married from marrying again. Sara McDougall describes how the episcopal courts of Champagne during the late Middle Ages – especially those of Troyes, but also those of Paris, Rouen, Cambrai, and Châlons-en-Champagne – pursued a campaign against illegitimate remarriage during the late Middle Ages: cases in which separated men and women had married again either in the knowledge that their spouses were still alive, or without having ascertained that they were dead. The penalty was exposure on the ladder of the scaffold followed by incarceration. Most of these illicit second marriages were clandestine.[251] The *officialités* of this region seems to have been unusually proactive – at least in contrast to England, where marriage litigation usually began with an instance suit, which was brought to the courts by litigants seeking redress, whereas *ex officio* prosecution was more common in northern France.[252] Connecting this late-medieval French campaign to *Tametsi*, McDougall suggests that the problem of bigamous remarriages was the chief reason everywhere

---

[248] For the English situation, see M. M. Sheehan, "The Formation and Stability of Marriage in Fourteenth-Century England," in idem, *Marriage, Family, and Law in Medieval Europe* (Toronto, 1996), 38–76. On enforcement of contract cases in relation to clandestinity, see R. H. Helmholz, *Marriage Litigation in Medieval England* (Cambridge, 1974), 25–73.

[249] L. Schmugge, *Marriage on Trial* (Washington, D.C., 2012), 388–39. J. Sperling, "Marriage at the Time of the Council of Trent (1560–70)," *Journal of Early Modern History* 8.1–2 (2004): 67–108.

[250] Schmugge, *Marriage on Trial*, 92–94.

[251] S. McDougall, *Bigamy and Christian Identity in Late Medieval Champagne* (Philadelphia, 2012).

[252] C. Donahue, Jr., "English and French Marriage Cases: Might the Differences Be Explained by Differences in the Property Systems?" in L. Bonfield, *Marriage, Property, and Succession* (Berlin, 1992), 339–66. Idem, *Law, Marriage, and Society in the Later Middle Ages* (Cambridge, 2007), 598–622.

for the suppression of clandestinity. But there is as yet no clear evidence that similar campaigns occurred elsewhere. Moreover, the unions in the cases that McDougall examines were clandestine *second* marriages, whereas *Tametsi* singled out as the most conspicuous abuse those cases in which the first union was clandestine and the second was public. The abuse that the church was trying to eradicate in Champagne illustrates one way in which people used clandestine marriage to make the most of their circumstances. Emlyn Eisenach shows how the people in Verona, especially (but not exclusively) ordinary people of the majority as distinct from members of the elite (who were more likely to contract public and notarized marriages), used clandestine marriage strategically. A son might marry clandestinely to establish his independence from his parents, for example, or a daughter to advance her social standing.[253]

What was wrong with clandestine marriages in the eyes of those who tried to prevent them? Around the time of Lateran IV, it seems, the concern was about control. With the church assuming legal, judicial, and supervisory control over marrying, churchmen wanted to make sure that people who could not validly marry would not marry in fact. Such was the explicit purpose of the banns, although that practice must also have helped to bring cases of non-fulfillment and subsequent bigamy to light. But many of those who were keen to suppress clandestine marriages during the first half of the sixteenth century, including most German Protestant and Catholic reformers and most French proponents of reform, focused on the marriage of minors without parental consent as the chief abuse. They objected that clandestinity enabled minors to marry rashly, without proper supervision and guidance, and without their parents' consent and supervision, contravening children's obligation to honor their parents. They argued that minors were too immature to make such an important decision without guidance, or too driven by their passions, or too prone to deception. Children needed the advice of persons who were older and wiser and above all of their parents, who had a valid interest in the matter. It is clear that parents in many parts of Europe around the time of the Reformations, especially among the elites, were anxious to control their children's choice of partner. Some secular governments were keen to help them.[254] Obviously, it was much harder for minors to marry without their parents' knowledge or against their wishes if they met the church's requirements for a public marriage. Moreover, the notion of clandestine marriage in polemical and reformist discourse of the era was coextensive with the principle of *solus consensus*, which made clandestine marriage possible. The somewhat illogical result was that clandestine marriages and the marriage of minors without parental consent were treated as two distinct species of abuse under the general heading of clandestine marriage.

---

[253] Eisenach, "Husbands, Wives, and Concubines," 87–133.

[254] Selderhuis, *Marriage and Divorce*, 194, reports that the marriage court in Zurich between 1525 and 1531 had to "deal with ninety cases in which parents filed a complaint against a marriage secretly contracted by their underage children."

Protestants regarded the parental supervision of marriage both as an implication of the fourth (or fifth) commandment – "Honor your father and your mother" (Exod 20:12, Eph 6:2) – and as the vital bridge between the individual and the political, God-fearing community.[255] Martin Bucer argued that secret marriages were contrary to the very nature of marriage.[256] Protestant reformers complained about disorder in the process of marrying, but they were more concerned to affirm parental and especially paternal authority, and they wanted to use secular law and state coercion to achieve that end.[257] Notwithstanding Luther's objection to the involvement of the church and canon law in marriages, the result was "a typically Protestant merging of the secular and the religious into a new, common standard for all Christians."[258]

The French, too, opposed clandestinity chiefly because it enabled minors to marry without parental consent. Sarah Hanley has shown that French laws suppressing clandestine marriages and especially the marriage of minors without parental consent grew from a tradition of secular case law, civil jurisprudence, and royal statutory law, the origins of which can be traced to the 1530s. The case law was fundamental and expressed the will of the elite citizenry.[259] The chief aim was to manage the assets of dynastic families. In 1556, a statute of the Parlement raised the age of majority for marriage from twenty to thirty years for males, and from seventeen to twenty-five for females. On July 24, 1563, when the prelates assembled at Trent to discuss the first drafts of the doctrinal and disciplinary decrees on marriage, the secretary read out a petition from the King of France. The king beseeched the council to invalidate not only marriages contracted without the proper solemnities in church, or at least in the presence of the parish priest and two or three witnesses, but also the marriages of minors contracted without parental consent.[260] Johann Baptista Fickler, a layman who kept a diary of the proceedings, recalled that the prelates went on to voice opinions about clandestine marriage that were "extremely pleasing to the French."[261] The first three drafts of the decree on clandestine marriages included invalidation both of clandestine marriages and of the marriages of minors contracted without parental consent, just as the French king has asked. The two impediments were never conflated either in the drafts or in

---

[255] Harrington, *Reordering Marriage*, 91–92, 187–90, 197–204.

[256] Selderhuis, *Marriage and Divorce*, 196. On clandestine marriage (*Winkelehen*) in Protestantism, see ibid., 26–27 and 194–201; and Harrington, *Reordering Marriage*, 28–31, 60–61, 91–92, 98–99, 180–81, 187–89.

[257] Harrington, *Reordering Marriage*, 38–47.   [258] Ibid., 39.

[259] S. Hanley, "The Jurisprudence of the Arrêts: Marital Union, Civil Society, and State Formation in France, 1550–1650," *Law and History Review* 21.1 (2003): 1–40. See also B. B. Diefendorf, *Paris City Councillors in the Sixteenth Century* (Princeton, 1983), 155–70; and S. Hanley, "Family and State in Early Modern France: The Marriage Pact," in M. J. Boxer and J. H. Quataert, *Connecting Spheres* (Oxford, 1987), 53–63.

[260] Le Plat, *Monumentorum ad historiam Concilii Tridentini*, vol. 6, 166. On France and the issue of clandestinity at Trent, see A. Tallon, *La France et le Concile de Trent (1518–1563)* (Rome, 1997), 679–86.

[261] Le Plat, *Monumentorum ad historiam Concilii Tridentini*, vol. 7 pars altera, 383.

discussion, but the prelates treated them in tandem as if the defense of either entailed defense of the other. But when the third draft of the decrees was presented, the legates included a new, alternative decree on clandestinity, which the delegates could opt for instead of the revised version. This strengthened the requirements for publicity, but it made no reference to parental consent. The new version with only minor revisions became the council's decree *Tametsi*.

There were also objections of a different sort, which did not apply specifically to minors and did not suppose that the absence of parental consent was an impediment in its own right. Instead, they focused on the possibilities of deception and seduction. It was too easy for clandestinely married spouses to separate and to remarry, and too easy for men to seduce women with private marriage vows in the present tense and then to abandon them, and even to marry again. The scenario of covert prior contract enjoyed a long and central history in reforming literature on clandestinity. Typically, a man marries the first woman clandestinely and the second publicly. Such men may have deceived one or both of the two wronged women, but the abuse was consistent with a vernacular tendency to regard a public or solemnized marriage as more complete, more formal, and even more sacramental than a clandestine one. People naturally assumed that the second, public contract would trump the former, clandestine contract. This was the only abuse that *Tametsi* cited to explain why clandestine marriages should be prevented. Hugh of Saint-Victor had used it to illustrate the hazards of clandestinity in the first extended discussion on the topic (Sections 10.6.1 and 10.6.2). Hugh asks the reader to suppose that a man marries one woman clandestinely but then marries a second woman *in facie ecclesiae*. If there are no witnesses to the first union, Hugh argues, the church may be forced to uphold the second union even if the man repents. Then the man is forced to remain in an adulterous marriage, and the first woman is unable to remarry in good conscience.[262] The reasoning of *Tametsi* involved the same elements: the same sequence of clandestine and public unions, and the same limitation of the judicial process, based on the principle that the church could pass judgments only in the public forum. This abuse must sometimes have occurred, and there a few cases of it in the extant episcopal records, but it is unlikely that this was the prevailing or the most detrimental abuse, or even the one that most vexed the officials of episcopal courts in practice. *Tametsi* was not recalling a prevalent problem when it rehearsed the scenario but rather citing a standard, textbook illustration, hallowed by long tradition.

Giovanni Matteo Giberti, bishop of Verona, begins the section on marriage in his *Constitutiones* (1541) with reforms designed to prevent clandestine marriages, but he makes no mention of the absence of parental consent. Nor, Emlyn Eisenach points out, does a similar, slightly later secular law of the Venetian republic.[263] Instead,

---

[262] Hugh of Saint-Victor, *De sacramentis* II.11.6, 488C–491B.
[263] E. Eisenach, *Husbands, Wives, and Concubines* (Kirksville, 2004), 98–99.

these sources focus on the abuses of men who use clandestine marriage as a subterfuge to despoil virgins and to seduce credulous women, leaving them ruined, destitute, and begging in the streets.

Italian prelates and reformers were less concerned about the marriage of minors without parental consent than their counterparts in France and Germany, although they were not libertarians who did not care whether minors had their parents' consent to marry. Studies of the marriage cases that came before the Papal Penitentiary indicate that clandestine marriages were relatively rare in Italy but common in Germany, Spain, and Portugal.[264] Perhaps parents' control over their children's marriages was more secure in Italy, where written notarial records were the chief evidence of a marriage's validity, whereas the clerical control of marriages through the measures of Lateran IV had proved ineffective in northern Europe.

17.6.3 *Bishop Giberti's reforms*

Giovanni Matteo Giberti was bishop of Verona from 1524 until his death in 1543, during the period when Verona was part of the Venetian republic. Giberti's *Constitutiones*, published in 1541, are his reforming guidelines for the clergy of his diocese. Many of Giberti's reforms anticipated those of the Council of Trent. Agostino Valier, bishop of Verona from 1565 to 1606, a reformer tasked with implementing Trent's decrees, was content to republish Giberti's *Constitutiones* with his own annotations. Some of these were for clarification, but in most of them Valier noted the similarities and differences in the decrees of Trent.[265]

Giberti shared the anxieties of Veronese and Venetian noblemen, but he was an outsider, being the illegitimate son of a Genoese nobleman.[266] He was concerned as much with lawlessness, poverty, injustice, and the abuse of power as with church reform.[267] Emlyn Eisenach explains how the customary process of marrying did not square easily with the canonical doctrine of *de futuro, de praesenti*, and presumptive consent, especially among the ordinary people who made up the majority of the population. A Veronese marriage customarily began with a private or domestic promise or plighting of troth that was construed as a marriage (*maridazzo*) and regarded as a contractually binding agreement. The tense of the agreement was immaterial. The spouses were then husband and wife, but not irrevocably so. Separation was still possible if the partnership failed, even if it had been consummated. The partners would spend time together and sometimes begin to engage in

---

[264] L. Schmugge, *Marriage on Trial* (Washington, D.C., 2012), 388–39. J. Sperling, "Marriage at the Time of the Council of Trent (1560–70)," *Journal of Early Modern History* 8.1–2 (2004): 67–108. Sperling argues that the peculiarities of the Italian dowry system made it more difficult for minors to marry without parental consent.

[265] Eisenach, *Husbands, Wives, and Concubines*, 48. Giovanni Matteo Giberti, *Constitutiones Gibertinae cum animadversionibus Cardinalis Augustini Valerii, aliorumque Episcoporum Vernonsium*, in Giberti's *Opera* (Ostiglia, 1740), 1–152.

[266] Eisenach, *Husbands, Wives, and Concubines*, 14.   [267] Ibid., 4.

sexual intercourse during the gradual transition from a private arrangement to a
publicly recognized union, which would ideally be celebrated at last in a public
wedding (*nozze*).[268] Giberti emphasizes the distinction between the future-tense
betrothal (*sponsalia per verba de praesenti*) and the present-tense betrothal (*sponsalia
per verba de praesenti*), but rather than attempt to simplify the customary process of
marrying, he tries to embrace all of its moments.

Giberti deals separately in the *Constitutiones* with clandestine marriages and with
marrying despite an impediment. In both respects, Giberti insists on the role of the
parish priest and his bishop in supervising and regulating marriages. Giberti regrets
that spouses often marry with some undisclosed impediment of relationship between
them, such as consanguinity, affinity, public honesty, spiritual cognation, or legal
cognation.[269] He devotes the longest chapter of the treatise on marriage to a
catalogue of these impediments.[270] To prevent such abuses, Giberti elaborates the
policies of Lateran IV. Once the partners have become betrothed in the future tense
or even in the present tense, the parish priests of both partners should announce the
forthcoming union to their congregations on one Sunday during mass. The priest
should say that since "N., the son of such-and-such, and N., the daughter of such-
and-such, have contracted a betrothal and intend to marry in due course through
words of the present tense," anyone who knows of a lawful impediment that may
prevent them from validly marrying should come forward within eight days.[271]
Notaries should not presume to record the *sponsalia de praesenti*, *subarratio annuli*,
or the *instrumentum dotale* until the contract has been announced publicly in the
sight of the church and its validity established.[272] In addition to announcing the
octave bann before each contract, as Lateran IV required, the parish priest should
make a general bann once a year, advising his congregation that they should make
known any impediments to marriages that are going to be contracted or even have
already been contracted, on pain of excommunication.[273] If an impediment comes
to light, the parish priest must refer the matter to his bishop. No one else, whether
ordained or lay, should presume to make such judgments, on pain of excommunication, unless he has a special mandate to do so from the bishop or his vicar.[274]

Giberti begins the treatise with constitutions designed to eliminate clandestine
marriages. In insisting on the role of the parish priest in marrying, Giberti opposed
the prevailing notion of his region that notarized written records sufficed to make a

---

[268] Ibid., 93–100   [269] Giberti, *Constitutiones*, tit. 7, cap. 6 (121–22).   [270] Cap. 10 (123–26).
[271] Cap. 6 (122).
[272] Cap. 8 (123). Kuehn, THTH 392, notes that there were three types of written marriage contract
     in fifteenth-century Florence: the future-tense betrothal (*sponsalitium*), the exchange of vows in
     the present tense with the bestowal of a ring (*matrimonium*), and the deed of dowry (*instru-
     mentum dotale*, *confessio dotis*). Giberti presumably had no objection to notarization of the
     future-tense betrothal as long as the church intervened as that point.
[273] Cap. 4 (121).
[274] Cap. 5 (121). Valier notes that Trent prohibited anyone other than an ecclesiastical judge from
     hearing matrimonial cases (sesssion 24, can. 12).

marriage public. Giberti warns that clandestine marriages do great harm. Parish priests should warn all the members of their congregations but especially unmarried girls that clandestine marriages give rise to scandals, quarrels, and murders. A union intended to foster kinship and friendship results instead in enmity and conflict. Girls should not believe men who plight their troth to them clandestinely, for such men are deceivers. Having taken away a credulous girl's virginity, they deny that they ever made the promise and leave the girl disgraced and destitute, begging for food and regarded by all with contempt.[275] To prevent clandestine unions, Giberti counsels that henceforth every phase of the process, including future-tense betrothals and the bestowal of a ring (*sub annuli subarratione*) as well as present-tense betrothals, should occur before the parish priest in an appropriate setting, such as a church, a municipal building, or a parental home. The parents of the spouses should be present if they are still alive. Failing that, the nearest relatives of both spouses should attend if they are willing, as well as several trustworthy witnesses.[276] If a priest learns from talk (*fama*) that a couple in his parish has married clandestinely, whether the talk is reliable or only plausible, he should order the spouses to make their union public as soon as possible. Failing that, unless the couple had good cause to keep their contract secret, the ordinary of the episcopal court should declare their union invalid.[277]

If a couple has married clandestinely and the parish priest discovers that there was an impediment, whether the spouses knew about it or not, and if they had not first obtained a dispensation from the bishop, the priest should warn them without delay. They have nine days to separate once the priest has given them warning. If they fail to separate, they are automatically excommunicated. The priest should also ask *homines et concilliarii locorum* to impose suitable fines.[278]

Couples must approach each phase of the process of marrying with due propriety. A future-tense betrothal is not insoluble and may be dissolved by mutual consent, but it is a solemn, binding contract and must be taken seriously. When a man has made his promise to a woman, especially if he has confirmed the promise with an oath, he must not abandon her if she is unwilling without seeking license to dissolve the betrothal from the bishop or his vicar. The bishop will not deny the petition if there is good cause.[279] Giberti regrets that a long period often elapses after a future-tense betrothal, during which the spouses spend time together, frequent each other's homes, and even have sexual intercourse. In future, they should not presume to come together until their betrothal has been confirmed publicly in the manner defined earlier.[280] Valeri explains in an annotation that Giberti must be referring to

---

[275] Cap. 1 (120).

[276] Ibid. (119). Valier notes that the Council of Trent went further by making clandestine marriage invalid.

[277] Cap. 3 (120–21).   [278] Cap. 11 (126).   [279] Cap. 4 (121).

[280] Cap. 2 (120). Valier notes that Trent prohibited spouses from cohabiting in the same home before receiving the nuptial blessing in a church (*ante benedictionem sacerdotalem in templo*).

present-tense betrothals, but Giberti is conspicuously silent as to the tense, and the rules on clandestinity and publicity outlined in the first chapter embrace future-tense betrothals. Although Giberti does not insist that marriages must be solemnized with a priestly blessing or in a church, he commands clerics of all ranks when they bless spouses to do so not in profane buildings but only in churches, with both of the spouses present. No priest should presume to bless a bride from another parish.[281] Furthermore, the blessing should take place in the morning, after sunrise, and in the full light of day, and it should be followed at once by the nuptial mass, as has always been customary. There should be no lewd goings on or ribaldry or anything else at the wedding that might be "an occasion for regarding so excellent a sacrament with contempt."[282]

17.6.4 *The ritual tendency:* "Ego vos coniungo"

As noted earlier, some of the prelates at Trent regarded marriage as a religious rite that required the ministry of a priest. They assumed that in a properly conducted marriage a minister joined the hands of the spouses, spoke the appropriate form, and blessed the union, and that the rite should take place in a church. Some of those who took this line were inclined to overstate their case by claiming that marriages contracted clandestinely or in a merely secular manner rather than *in facie ecclesiae* had always been invalid, but most recognized that that claim was unsustainable. If sacramental ministry was essential, very many marriages that the church had hitherto considered valid would in fact have been invalid. But perhaps only professional theologians were troubled by scruples of that sort. Most of those who insisted on the ritual formalities were not professional theologians, and they may have regarded the matter and form of a sacrament not as aspects of a sacramental ontology but as terms to be used in the parsing of a practice. Most of the prelates at Trent who wanted to invalidate clandestine marriage agreed with the Protestants that its hazards were more social and political than religious.

Those who considered the ministry of a priest to be in some sense an integral component of marrying emphasized the ritual act of joining. Acting on God's behalf, the priest joined their right hands saying, *"Ego vos coniungo"* ("I join you together," or "I join you in marriage"). Interpretations of the minister's role in joining the spouses varied widely, and even those who insisted that this liturgical performance was essential rarely explicated its theology or explained how it contributed to the composition of the sacrament. Did the minister join the spouses as God's instrument, or did he merely mime what God alone did, manifesting God's action to instruct the spouses and others present? Such questions seemed

---

[281] Ibid.: "nullus [clericus] fit tam audax, et temerarius, quod sub quovis praetextu praesumat benedicere sponsam, quae non fit de sua parochia."
[282] Cap. 13 (127–28).

crucial to professional theologians, but others at Trent were less careful, and some regarded the questions with impatience.

The performative formula, "*Ego vos coniungo*," seemed ancient and even perennial. It invoked the first marriage in Eden, to which Jesus himself was referring when he said, "What God has joined together, let not man separate" (Mark 10:9). Nevertheless, its first recorded use in the marriage liturgy is in an *ordo* from Rouen dating from around the middle of the fifteenth century. Here, after the interrogation, the priest is directed to give the bride to the groom and to say, "I join you together in the name of the Father, of the Son, and of the Holy Spirit."[283] The formula probably emerged because the priest had assumed the role traditionally performed by the bride's father when he gave her in marriage to the bridegroom. Thus, two thirteenth-century nuptial *ordines* direct the priest to *give* the bride to the groom (rather than to *join* them), saying "I give you" "(*ego do*" or "*ego trado*") as he joins their hands together. At some point, it seems, the more priestly "I join" began to replace the paternal "I give" through the influence of Mark 10:9, and the minister assumed or enacted the role of God the Father as the father figure who joined the spouses.[284]

Although some of the prelates at Trent spoke as if the "*Ego vos coniungo*" formula was ancient and universal, it was still not in wide use during the first half of the sixteenth century. On the eve of the Council of Trent, it was current in all the dioceses of Normandy and in a region linking Meaux, Metz, and Cambrai, but it was still not used elsewhere in France or anywhere in Germany.[285] Thomas Goldwell, the bishop of Saint-Asaph, claimed during the proceedings that the formula was normal in Rome, that it was an Apostolic tradition, and that it was customary in England.[286] It would be rash today to contradict him absolutely regarding the current English situation, but there is no other evidence for its use there. It does not occur in the extant rites of York and Canterbury.[287]

The prominence of the formula at the Council of Trent during 1563 was partly in response to the exigencies of the moment, but it was also due to the authority of Alberto Castellani's *Sacerdotale ad consuetudinem sanctae Romanae ecclesiae*, also known as the *Liber sacerdotalis*. This was an unauthorized collection of Roman

---

[283] J. Pierce 1985, "A Note on the *Ego vos conjungo* in Medieval French Marriage Liturgy," *Ephemerides Liturgicae* 99 (1985): 290–99, at 291. K. W. Stevenson, *The Nuptial Blessing* (New York, 1983), 75. J.-B. Molin and P. Mutembe, *Le rituel du mariage* (Paris, 1974), Ordo XIV (p. 304). The original manuscript of the *ordo* is lost. Pierce, p. 291, explains why the *ordo* was not from the mid-fourteenth century, as Molin and Mutembe assumed (following Martène), but rather from the mid-fifteenth.

[284] Pierce, "A Note on the *Ego vos conjungo*," 293–96.

[285] A. Duval, "La formule *Ego vos in matrimonium conjungo* ... au concile de Trente," *La Maison-Dieu* 99 (1969): 144–53, at 144–45.

[286] Asaphensis, Aug. 17, 1563 (CT 9:716/43–717/2): "Quoad decreta de abusibus placet illa forma: *Ego vos coniungo* etc., quia est consuetudo ecclesiae Romanae, quae consuetudo est etiam in Anglia, et credit, quod sit traditio apostolica. In *sacerdotali* dicitur: *Pronunciet sacerdos verba, quae sunt forma huius sacramenti.*"

[287] Duval, "La formule," 150.

liturgical rites that was first published in 1523. It served as a standard source of liturgical *ordines* in Italy in the absence of an official *rituale*.[288] Castellani's *Sacerdotale* became invested with special authority at Trent because the prelates assumed that it represented the norms and traditions of Rome. The *Sacerdotale* prescribed "*Ego vos coniugo*" as the form of the sacrament. Like Melchor Cano, Castellani interpreted the spouses as the matter of the sacrament, and the minister's formula of solemnization as the sacramental form. Joining the spouses' right hands, the priest should say: "And I by the authority invested in me join you together in marriage."[289]

The late-medieval notion that a priest joins the spouses in marriage testifies to the ritual trend in the common understanding of marriage as a sacrament. The minister at the wedding, who is amply illustrated in depictions of the seven sacraments, had not only taken on the role of the human father who gave away his daughter or his children in marriage; he had also ritually taken on the role of God the Father, marrying the spouses as God married Eve and Adam. Most professional theologians resisted the notion that the priest's ritual action was more than an accidental "solemnity," but in the eyes of many bishops, parish priests, and laypersons, the priest must have seemed to join the spouses in reality and in the eyes of God. The obscure and ambiguous notion that a human third party acting *ex officio* joins, betroths, or marries the spouses remains with us to this day. Professional theologians were caught between their sense of the need for reform and their grasp of the well-established sacramental theology of marriage, which included the principle of *solus consensus*.

17.7 DOMINIC DE SOTO

Domingo de Soto (d. 1560), O.P., attended the Council of Trent during the first of its three periods (1545–1547) as a theologian appointed by the Holy Roman Emperor, Charles V (who was also Charles I of Spain). Soto led the Dominican theologians at the council on behalf of their minister general, and he represented the school of Salamanca, where he had occupied the primary chair in theology since 1532.[290]

Soto discusses marriage in his commentary on the fourth book of the *Sentences*, which he composed toward the end of his life.[291] He mentions what the prelates said

---

[288] Duval, "La formule," 145–46.

[289] "Et ego auctoritate qua fungor coniungo vos matrimonialiter." Quoted from Duval, "La formule," 146n8.

[290] On Soto's life and work, see V. Beltrán de Heredia, *Domingo de Soto* (Madrid, 1961); and idem, "Soto (Dominique de)," in *Dictionnaire de théologie catholique*, 14.2:2423–31. On Soto at Trent, see Beltrán de Heredia, *Domingo de Soto*, 117–73. On theology and scholarship in Salamanca, see A. Pagden, "The School of Salamanca," in G. Klosko, *Oxford Handbook of the History of Political Philosophy* (Oxford, 2011), 246–57.

[291] *Commentariorum Fratris Dominici Soto Segobiensis . . . in quartum Sententiarum tomus secundus* (Salamanca, 1566). The commentary on the fourth book is in two parts: t. 1, published in 1557–1558; and t. 2, published in 1560.

about marriage at the Council of Trent, noting that they had made no decisions when the proceedings ceased[292] (i.e., when Pope Paul III prorogued the council in 1547). These were probably not personal reminiscences, for the discussion of marriage took place in Bologna during 1547, whither the pope had transferred the council. Soto remained in Trent with the prelates loyal to the emperor, who refused to accept the legitimacy of the proceedings in the new venue.[293]

Soto's treatment of marriage is typical of theologians and other learned clerics loyal to the Catholic tradition around the middle of the sixteenth century, before the council at Trent discussed marriage in depth at the twenty-fourth session. Soto emphasizes the divergences between the Catholic tradition and Protestantism and the importance of adhering faithfully to the former; he affirms that marriage is properly one of the seven sacraments of the New Law, and that it confirms grace *ex opere operato*; and he rejects the ritualist notion that the sacrament is in essence a religious rite, of which the minister's words of blessing and joining constitute the form. Although he understands why some prelates at Trent wanted to make clandestine marriages null and void, he finds that proposal theologically unacceptable, considering it to be both too much of a departure from traditional practice and too much at variance with the principle that consent makes marriage. Both the matter and the form that constitute the essence of this sacrament are to be found in the spouses' verbal expressions of mutual consent, Soto argues. The spouses themselves are the *materia circa quod* of marriage (its subject matter), and not its essential, constitutive matter. The expression of consent also constitutes the *sacramentum tantum*, and the invisible bond between the spouses is the *sacramentum et res*. Both conjugal grace and Christ's betrothal with the church, in their different ways, have the role of *res tantum*. No minister is essential besides the spouses themselves, therefore, and no new form was added when Christ instituted marriage as a sacrament of the New Law. Indeed, the essential components of the sacrament of marriage are the same as those of the contract.

17.7.1 *Marriage as one of the sacraments*

Is marriage one of the sacraments? Soto observes that although there are many heretics such the Lutherans who deny that marriage is a sacrament, Catholics should find the question easy to answer affirmatively.[294] The question is really twofold, Soto points out. First, one must ask whether marriage is a sacrament at least in the broad sense of the term, which befits the sacraments of the Old Law as

---

[292] Soto, *IV Sent.* 28.1, resp. (2:136b), on whether clandestine marriage should be made invalid: "De qua utique re in Tridentino concilio exiit saepe sermo inter patres." *IV Sent.* 26.2.3, resp. (90b), on the thesis that marriage confers sacramental grace: "Et si oecumenica Synodus fuisset progressa, id ipsum definisset: nam sic erat patribus in animo."

[293] Beltrán de Heredia, "Soto," 2424; idem, *Domingo de Soto*, 166–72.

[294] *IV Sent.* 26.2.1, resp. (2:84b).

well as those of the New. Does marriage at least *signify* some sanctification or sacred thing? Second, one must ask whether marriage confers a grace that it signifies.

In fact, however, Soto addresses the question in three stages, not two. First, he argues that marriage has the salient features that characterize the sacraments of the New Law, also known as the sacraments of the church. (Soto uses the two terms interchangeably.) The distinctive manner in which these sacraments signify sacred realities, Soto argues, distinguishes them from sacraments in other, broader senses of the term. Having established that marriage is a sacrament of the New Law, Soto raises two further, subsidiary questions: whether marriage was instituted under the New Law and, if so, when; and whether marriage confers grace. Soto takes Luther as his chief adversary when he addresses the second question, and Durandus when he addresses the third. But Soto attempts neither to demonstrate his own, Catholic theses categorically nor even to refute the theses of his adversaries. Instead, he provides a rationale for the Catholic position and he solves the objections of Luther and Durandus, exposing the weaknesses of their respective arguments.

Soto uses three lines of argument to show that marriage has the salient characteristics of the sacraments of the New Law. The first and most extensively developed argument assumes that these sacraments are mysteries that signify the holiness (*sanctitas*) of the Gospel in a specially intimate way. (Soto uses the terms *mysterium* and *sacramentum* interchangeably in this article, perhaps to undercut Luther's objections.) Whereas the sacraments of the Old Law remotely signified *future* holiness, "our sacraments," or the sacraments of the church, intimately signify *present* holiness. Now, marriage is a sacrament of the latter sort; ergo, and so on. What Paul says about marriage in Ephesians 5 is sufficient proof of the minor premise of the syllogism, Soto argues. Christians should be subject to one another in the fear of Christ[295] (Eph 5:21); wives should be subject to their husbands "as unto the Lord, for the husband is head of the wife, even as Christ is the head of the church" (Eph 5:21–23); and husbands should love their wives "even as Christ also loved the church, and gave himself for it" (Eph 5:25), for the joining of Christ and the church, Soto explains, springs from "mutual love" (*amor mutuus*). The love (*dilectio*) that joins husband and wife signifies the love that joins Christ and the church. Paul illuminates the comparison by referring to Eve's formation from Adam's side and the dictum of Genesis 2:24: "henceforth, the man will leave his father and mother to become one flesh with his wife." Husband and wife are joined in two ways: first, in charity and love; then, through sexual intercourse, in nature and the flesh. The same is true of Christ and the church. As a result of this assimilation, the twofold joining of husband and wife signifies the twofold joining of Christ and church. Paul's comment about the "great sacrament" in Ephesians 5:32 – which Soto has already cited as the argument *sed contra* – is a fitting conclusion to Paul's discourse on marriage in the chapter, and it expresses a "Catholic truth."[296]

---

[295] Soto does say "Christ," although the word in Eph 5:21 is in fact "God."
[296] *IV Sent.* 26.2.1, resp. (84b–85a).

It is important to understand, Soto argues, that Paul describes an unfolding: a progression from shadowy images to reality. Otherwise, one might reason that the "great sacrament" was primarily the original marriage of Adam and Eve, which took place when there was no sin and no need for sacraments in the proper sense. Whereas that first marriage was a "mystery and a figure of the future union of Christ and the church," marriage received its full sacramentality (*vis sacramenti*) only after Christ died on the cross, when the "new sacraments" flowed with the blood and water from his side, and when the Church was formed from Christ as his wife, just as Eve was formed from Adam's rib.[297]

Soto considers Luther's objections to this use of Ephesians 5:32: first, that Paul did not say "sacrament" but "mystery"; second, that the "great mystery" is not marriage but the joining of Christ and the church. The first objection is trivial, Soto points out, for the terms *mysterium* and *sacramentum* are interchangeable. And the second is pointless, for the whole discourse presents one joining as the sign of the other. We should not consider Ephesians 5:32 out of context, as Luther does. Moreover, there is a long, well-established tradition of using the discourse as whole and this verse in particular to prove that marriage is a sacrament.[298]

The premise of the second of Soto's three lines of argument is that every sacrament of the New Law is a "sign of some hidden remedy against some sin"; but marriage is of that sort; ergo, etc. Soto's proof of the minor is an argument from reason. Marriage is the means by which human kind is propagated, and this propagation is vital because humanity was created for ultimate beatitude and has been recreated for beatitude through Christ. Because propagation cannot occur without concupiscence, it was entirely fitting that Christ instituted marriage as a remedy against concupiscence. To the objection that there are many sins for which no special sacramental remedy has been instituted, Soto replies that concupiscence is uniquely pervasive. It affects "the whole of nature," and it is virtually innate in human beings.[299] Surely, God would not leave his people in the last age without any supernatural remedy.

The third line of argument is an appeal to the authority of tradition. Many canons have affirmed that marriage is one of the sacraments, such as *Ad abolendam* and the Council of Florence (in *The Bull of Union with the Armenians*.)[300] But have Christians always believed that marriage was a sacrament of the New Law? Soto argues that the belief has always been at least implicit. Erasmus confessed that he did not know whether marriage was numbered among the sacraments in Jerome's day, and he pointed out that Dionysius did not mention marriage when he discussed the sacraments in *Ecclesiastical Hierarchy*. But Erasmus, unlike Luther, prudently expressed his own uncertainty without making any categorical denial. In fact, Soto argues, the fathers of the church such as Augustine and Jerome wrote about

---

[297] Ibid. (85a).   [298] Ibid. (85a–85b).   [299] Ibid. (85b).   [300] Ibid. (85b).

marriage in ways implying that they revered marriage as if it were a sacrament of the New Law, even if they did not explicitly affirm that it was.[301]

Turning to the second question, regarding the institution of marriage as a sacrament of the New Law, Soto assures his readers that this question, too, is easy (*facilis*) for any Catholic to answer.[302] It suffices to compare marriage under the New Law with marriage under the Old Law and among the Gentiles. To understand its sacred history, one should note that marriage provides three *bona* or *munera*: procreation, remedy, and signification.[303] Marriage was instituted for the office of procreation in the very beginning, even before sin. In that respect, marriage is inscribed in the universal natural law. Marriage became in addition a remedy against concupiscence after sin. That benefit too belongs to the natural law, although the light of natural reason does not suffice to reveal clearly some of the determinations that it requires, for example, that persons should not marry within certain degrees of consanguinity, or that only one woman should be married to one man. The law of Moses added some of those determinations, although Moses permitted polygyny.[304] (Soto seems to regard these developments not as new institutions but as ramifications of the original institution.) The third benefit is the ability of marriage not only to "point to the mystery of the betrothal of Christ with the church," but also, through that signification, to become "an instrument of the same redeemer, infusing grace in those who use it properly." Marriage acquired this third benefit only when Christ instituted it as a sacrament of the New Law, for Christ instituted all seven sacraments as "instruments of his Passion."[305]

Soto notes in passing that marriage has several other benefits, as well as the three outlined earlier. The temporal commonwealth (*res publica*) fosters marriage in order to perpetuate itself. Roman civil law, secular laws in general, and the *lex gentium* foster the mutual service and support between the spouses: for example, through laws about dowries and inheritance. Unlike the other six sacraments, marriage existed even before it was instituted by Christ as a sacrament of the New Law. Nevertheless, it acquired a new sacramentality (*nova ratio sacramenti*) from that institution.[306] To the objection that no sacrament can be instituted more than once, Soto replies that marriage was instituted only once *as a sacrament of the New Law*.[307]

When did the new institution occur? Where is that institution recorded? Some locate it in Jesus' discourse on divorce (Matt 19:3 ff., etc.), but Scripture shows that Jesus was not introducing anything new but restoring marriage to the original, pristine condition in which it was created: an origin that is common to marriage

---

[301] Ibid. (85b–86a).   [302] *IV Sent.* 26.2.2, resp. (87a).

[303] Soto's schema of office, remedy, and significance or sacramentality was apparently a variation of Augustine's schema of *fides, proles, sacramentum*.

[304] *IV Sent.* 26.2.2, resp. (87a).

[305] Ibid. (87a–b). Soto introduces this argument in the *sed contra* (87a).

[306] Ibid. (87b).   [307] Ibid., ad 1m (88a).

among all peoples everywhere. Jesus was explaining marriage in light of the natural law, which had become obscured.[308] But an institution is not necessarily a historical event. In this case, the institution of marriage is the force or significance that marriage possesses in a particular system of laws and according to other presupposed norms. Soto concedes that he cannot point to any place in the New Testament where Christ instituted marriage as a sacrament of the New Law, but he can say that Christ revealed by his presence at Cana that there had been such an institution. The transformation of water into wine signified that what had hitherto been only an office and a remedy would henceforth be celebrated as a sacrament and as a means of grace. Jesus foresaw that without grace the wine of joy and friendship in marriage would lose its taste, becoming cold and lifeless. To remain true to Jesus' example, spouses should be concerned less with dowries, gifts, and finery when they marry, and more about "virtue, which is guardian of perpetual conjugal joy and friendship."[309]

The third of Soto's three main questions is whether marriage confers sacramental grace. In fact, he has already shown as much in demonstrating that marriage is a sacrament of the New Law. Nevertheless, he raises the question more explicitly now as an opportunity to demonstrate how his position on conjugal grace is a doctrine of the Catholic church. It is true that whether marriage confers grace has been controversial even among Catholics. Durandus argued that although marriage was certainly a sacrament in the sense that it was a sign of Christ's betrothal to the church, as described in Ephesians 5, one might still argue without risk of heresy that marriage did not confer grace. Indeed, Durandus considered this negative position to be more probable, chiefly because it was held by canonists such as Goffredus de Trano, Hostiensis, and Bernard of Pavia. These scholars argued that if marriage conferred grace, the financial transactions attending marriage, such as the dowry, would entail simony. Soto notes, too, that Durandus's position underwent a certain evolution. In the first edition of his commentary, he argued that marriage did not confer grace and was not a sacrament of the New Law, but Durandus modified his position in the second edition to avoid accusations of heresy, arguing instead that marriage was not univocally one of the sacraments of the New Law, and that it was still permissible to maintain that it did not confer grace.[310] Nevertheless, Soto marvels that Durandus attributed so much authority to the scholars of church law, whose expertise does not extend to the divine law (*ius divinum*). The simony objection is easily solved, for the financial settlements pertain to marriage as a civil contract, not to marriage as a sacrament.[311]

Soto reviews what Peter Lombard and Thomas Aquinas said about conjugal grace. According to Thomas, three opinions were current in his day: that marriage conferred no grace at all; that it conferred a grace only for the removal of evil, by

---

[308] Ibid., arg. 2 (87a); resp. (87b).   [309] Ibid., resp. (87b).   [310] Ibid. (89b).
[311] Ibid. (90b).

excusing the marriage act; and that it conferred a grace that helped the spouses to do good. The most probable position, according to Thomas, was the third: that marriage "simply confers grace."[312] Peter Lombard seems to have assumed that marriage did not confer any grace. If so, he was inconsistent, for he included marriage among the sacraments of the New Law, and he made the power to cause grace the distinguishing feature of those sacraments.[313] The Lombard may have held the second of the positions that Thomas reviews, but that, too, is unsustainable, partly because any grace that removes evil must also assist the subject to do good, and partly because this position does not sufficiently distinguish marriage under the New Law from marriage under the Old Law, nor even from marriage under the law of nature, for marriage has always been a remedy that excuses concupiscence.[314]

Soto affirms that marriage confers grace in the same way as the other sacraments of the New Law. Such has been the "common opinion" of theologians such as Thomas Aquinas, Duns Scotus, Bonaventure, and Richard de Mediavilla. More important, the church has formally counted marriage among the seven sacraments of the New Law, most notably at the Council of Florence (i.e., in the *Bull of Union with the Armenians*), which emphasized the distinction between the sacraments of the Old Law and those of the New and counted marriage among the latter. St Paul's teaching in Ephesians 5 shows that Christ added a "new power" (*vis nova*) to marriage.[315] Just as Eve was formed from Adam's rib as his wife, so the church was formed from Christ's side on the cross. The children who are begotten through the sacrament of Christian marriage to worship God become the adopted sons and daughters of God. Just as the sacrament of orders was instituted so that priests could administer the sacraments fittingly, so the sacrament of marriage was instituted so that the conjugal act could be performed fittingly.[316] As Bonaventure said, the grace of marriage helped the spouses to overcome concupiscence in three ways: by enabling each spouse to be satisfied with a single partner; by enabling them to observe the conjugal debt properly, and not to pursue sexual intercourse only for the sake of pleasure; and by preventing them from growing tired of each other, so that they can sustain their relationship until parted by death.[317] Conjugal grace is conferred at the moment when the spouses exchange consent in the present tense.[318]

[312] Ibid. (89a).

[313] *IV Sent.* 26.2.3, resp. (88b–89a). Later in the response (89b), Soto says that there was an evolution of Durandus's position. In the first edition of his commentary, according to Soto, Durandus argued that marriage did not confer grace and was not a sacrament of the New Law. In the second edition, to avoid accusations of heresy, he argued that marriage was not univocally one of the sacraments of the New Law, and that it was still permissible to maintain it did not confer grace.

[314] Ibid. (89a–b).   [315] Ibid. (89a).   [316] Ibid. (89b–90a).

[317] Ibid. (90a). Cf. Bonaventure, *II Sent.* 26.2.2, resp. (668b); 31.1.2, resp. (719b).

[318] Soto, *IV Sent.* 26.2.3, resp. (90a): "Quod si scisciteris quando nam eiusmodi gratiam conferat, respondetur, quod tunc, dum consensus de praesenti amborum coniugum simul concurrunt, ut paulo inferius repetetur."

Formal objections to this Catholic position are easily solved, Soto argues. One might object that if marriage confers grace as a remedy against concupiscence, then everyone should marry, for the problem of concupiscence is universal. Now, it is clear from St Paul's counsel (1 Cor 7:32–33) that marriage is not meant for everyone.[319] But this objection involves a non sequitur, for virgins and celibates control their concupiscence in other ways, mortifying themselves with fasting and vigils and devoting themselves to prayer and contemplation as their vocation requires.[320] Again, one might object that if marriage is a true sacrament that confers grace, only baptized believers can marry, since baptism is the gateway to the sacraments (*ianua sacramentorum*). But according to Paul's counsel (1 Cor 7:12–13) a believer should not divorce an infidel spouse if the latter is peaceable, and this counsel presupposes that infidels, too, can participate in the sacrament.[321] But that objection amounts to nothing, Soto replies. If by calling marriage a sacrament one means that it is a legitimate bond that sustains the office of procreation and signifies Christ's union with the church, then clearly the marriage of infidels is a sacrament, for marriage was instituted with those properties in the beginning. It is on that basis that the believer should remain with an infidel spouse as long as the latter is peaceable. But if one uses the term "sacrament" properly, meaning a sacrament of the New Law that confers grace, then the marriage of infidels is not a sacrament.[322]

There is no doubt in Soto's own mind, therefore, that marriage confers grace, but he wonders whether this proposition attains the level of a "catholic truth," so that its denial would be heresy. Durandus thought not. Soto concedes that this is a difficult question. On the one hand, he does not want to condemn as heretics the aforesaid canonists or even Durandus, "their champion," and he concedes that the doctrine is not stated in so many words in Scripture or even in the canons of the councils. Even the great schoolmen such as Thomas Aquinas, Bonaventure, and Duns Scotus held only that this was the "more probable" position. On the other hand, the church has affirmed in *Ad abolendam* and at the Council of Florence that marriage is truly one of the sacraments of the church, and one must now take into account how Catholic doctors such as John Fisher[323] and Johann Eck and local councils at Paris and Cologne have condemned the Lutherans for denying that marriage confers grace. The Council of Trent would have come to the same conclusion if it had reached marriage in its determinations, for such was the opinion of most of the prelates. Soto concludes that it would now be "at least rash and very dangerous" to deny that the error in question – the thesis that marriage does not confer sacramental grace – is a heresy.[324]

Given that marriage is a sacrament of the New Law in the proper sense, fulfilling all the necessary criteria, Soto inquires into the matter and the form of this

---

[319] *IV Sent.* 26.2.3, arg. 3 (88b).   [320] Ibid., ad 3 (93a–b).   [321] Ibid., arg. 4 (88b).
[322] Ibid., ad 4 (93b).   [323] Identified here as Roffensis (i.e., the bishop of Rochester).
[324] Ibid., resp. (90a–b).

sacrament. According to the Council of Florence in the *Bull of Union with the Armenians*, every sacrament is constituted from its proper matter and form, which a minister brings together. If any of these three features is missing, according to the bull, the sacrament is invalid. Now, marriage does not require a minister in the usual sense of the term, but the spouses' words of consent function as both the matter and the form of the sacrament, and they perform the role that a minister of the church performs in the other sacraments. Soto argues that Durandus went too far when he assumed that the matter of marriage must be some tangible stuff. Marriage has no *res* in that sense, but neither has penance. Soto quickly dispenses with two competing theories. Some theologians, such as Peter of La Palu, maintain that the spouses themselves are the matter, but according to Soto the spouses are not the essential matter that is correlative to the form of the sacrament, but rather its subject (i.e., its *materia circa quam*). Others argue that the matter of the sacrament is the interior act of mental consent, whereas the form is the exterior expression of consent. But Soto points out that both the form and the matter of any sacrament are exterior, sensible things, which together compose the *sacramentum tantum*. Soto agrees with Durandus that one cannot identify one spouse's expression of consent as the matter and the other's as the form, as Richard de Mediavilla had held. In Soto's view, each spouse is both agent and recipient. Thus, each spouse's *verbum* is the matter that is informed by other's *verbum*.[325]

The mutual expression of consent, therefore, constitutes the exterior sacrament (*sacramentum tantum*), whereas the "union and tie" (*unio et nexus*) that binds the spouses together is the invisible *sacramentum et res*. Two things have the role of ultimate *res tantum*: the betrothal between Christ and the church, and conjugal grace. The sacraments of the New Law are said to cause what they signify, but marriage does not cause the betrothal between Christ and the church. Does it follow that marriage is not a sacrament of the New Law? No, because the betrothal of Christ and the church is an exterior signified reality, whereas conjugal grace is an interior signified reality, and the sacraments cause only the interior things that they signify. In other words, grace is the contained reality (*res tantum contenta*) of the sacrament, whereas the betrothal of Christ and the church is an uncontained reality.[326]

17.7.2 *The nuptial blessing and the sacramental form*

Soto notes that the Council of Florence's inclusion of a minister among the necessary conditions of all the sacraments seems to imply that Christian marriage is invalid unless the couple receives the blessing of a priest, who ritually unites them with the words, "I join you together, in the name of the Father, the Son, and the Holy Spirit." The form of the sacrament, on this view, is the priest's words, and not

---

[325] *IV Sent.* 26.2.1, resp. (86a–b).   [326] Ibid., ad 2–3 (86b).

the spouses' words. It would follow that any clandestinely contracted marriage is invalid.[327] Soto concedes that there is a reasonable case to be made for this theory. It seems fitting that marriage would have received a new form and a new minister when it became a sacrament under the New Law. The words by which the spouses contract marriage seem to have a merely contractual force, as in a transaction of buying or selling. Thus, the Scotists hold that no specific words were required for the contract between the partners, whereas marriage as a sacrament should require a prescribed formula, which the minister enunciates. Again, sacramental actions are "acts of religion" by which the recipients are "divinely sanctified." Thomas Aquinas seems to apply that standard to marriage when he says in the *Summa contra gentiles* that marriage as a sacrament of the church is not only subject to ecclesiastical law but also dispensed by the church's ministers.[328] Finally, William of Auvergne seems to have held that although marriage without the priestly blessing was a sacrament in some sense, it lacked sacramental efficacy (*virtus sacramenti*) and was not a sacrament in the proper sense (*veri nominis*).[329]

Having reviewed the evidence for the ritualist theory, Soto rejects it. Thomas Aquinas clearly considered the priestly blessing to be an accidental solemnity and not part of the essence of the sacrament. William of Auvergne's position was eccentric (*singularis*), and theologians today rehearse it only for the sake of argument, without asserting it.[330] Soto suggests later in the discussion that William and Thomas may have been referring not to the priest's act of ritual joining, which follows immediately after his interrogation and the spouses' exchange of consent at the entrance of a church, but rather to the blessings that occur during the nuptial mass in the sanctuary (*templum*), for such blessings bear witness to the religious act of marrying. That consideration may have moved William to commend such blessings as proper testimony to the sanctity of marriage, and to regard with contempt those who chose to go without them.[331]

If the priestly blessing were the sacramental form, then some prescribed formula, such as "*Ego vos coniungo*," would be universal in the church, but that is not the case. In some places, the priest says, "I betroth you and confirm this sacrament"; in others, "Those whom God has joined let no man separate," and so forth. Soto points out that no specific formula for marriage has ever been prescribed in the canons of councils or in the writings of Christian authorities, although some exchange of consent by the spouses in the present tense has often been prescribed as necessary for marriage, sometimes with a typical formulae such as "*Ego te accipiam in meam/*

---

[327] *IV Sent.* 26.2.3, resp. (90b–91a); 26.2.1, ad 1 (86b).

[328] Thomas Aquinas, *Summa contra gentiles* IV.78 (Leonine 15:246).   [329] *IV Sent.* 26.2.3 (91a).

[330] Ibid., resp. (90b–91a). Soto discusses the formula "*Ego igitur vos coniungo in nomine patris*, etc." at 91b–92a. In fact, Melchor Cano, whom Soto succeeded as the principal professor of theology at Salamanca in 1152, would famously defend William's position in his *De locis theologicis*, published posthumously in 1563. Soto was either unaware of Cano's views or was speaking ironically or mischievously.

[331] *IV Sent.* 26.2.3, resp. (92b–93a).

meum" to illustrate how they might express such consent. Even the Council of Florence, which declares that the presence of a minister is necessary for all the sacraments, makes no mention of the priestly formula in the section of marriage, whereas it does require the spouses' exchange of consent in the present tense.[332]

No new form was added, therefore, when marriage became a sacrament of the New Law, and no minister is required besides the spouses themselves. The same exchange of consent, which was formerly a mere compact or contract, became a religious act (*actus religionis*) when marriage became a sacrament of the New Law. One need not fear that a kind of Pelagianism is implied, for the act has the power to cause grace not of itself but only insofar as Christ instituted it as a sacrament.[333]

Soto notes that if the priestly joining or blessing were the form of the sacrament, any marriage that was not blessed by a priest, such as a clandestine marriage, would lack sacramentality (*ratio sacramenti*). It would confer no grace, and the marriage would be invalid until the partners repeated it in the prescribed setting with the priestly blessing. Furthermore, clandestine marriage would be forbidden not only in positive canon law (*ius pontificum*) but also in divine law (*ius divinum*). In fact, there is nothing in the canons or in the writings of the Christian authorities to say that clandestine marriage is invalid and must be repeated. Clandestine marriages are forbidden only in canon law, and not in divine law. If no grace is conferred through a clandestine marriage, as William of Auvergne supposed, that is only because the disobedience of the spouses or their excommunication makes them unworthy to receive grace *ex opere operato*.[334] One should not interpret the formula "*Ego vos coniungo*" literally, therefore, as if the priest really joined the spouses together. Instead, it means something like "I approve or bless your joining." The verbal form of any sacrament primarily signifies its immediate effect. For example, the formula "I baptize you [etc.]" signifies the baptism that results. Thus, the spouses' own expression of consent sufficiently signifies its immediate effect, namely, their being united or joined together (*coniunctio*).[335]

17.7.3 *The problem of clandestine marriages*

Soto raises the question of clandestinity in another setting. Are clandestine marriages valid? And can they be licit in particular cases through dispensation? It seems that they must be valid, for Pope Nicholas I said that the spouses' consent was the sufficient cause of marriage.[336] As the scholastic maxim has it, once a cause is posited, so is its effect ("*posita causa ponitur effectus*").[337] But it seems that every sacrament must be "perfected" by a minster of the church. This is true even of

---

[332] Ibid. (91b).   [333] *IV Sent.* 26.2.3, resp., ad 1 (92b).   [334] *IV Sent.* 26.2.3, resp. (91b).

[335] Ibid. (91b–92a).

[336] Gratian, C. 27 q. 2 c. 2 (1063): "Sufficiat solus secundum leges consensus eorum, de quarum quarumque coniunctionibus agitur."

[337] *IV Sent.* 28.1, s.c. (135b).

penance, in which the subject's own actions, and not something applied to the subject by the minister, constitute the matter of the sacrament. Baptism may be performed by a layperson but only in cases of dire necessity. The decretal of Evaristus seems to confirm that only a properly solemnized marriage is valid.[338]

Soto begins his response by clarifying what the term "clandestine marriage" means. The canonists recognize at least six ways in which a marriage can be clandestine, but some of these are not relevant to the present inquiry, such as when the spouses are under the minimum age and marry against the church's prohibition, or when a couple cohabits without getting married. Only two senses of the term are relevant here. In the strictest sense, a marriage is clandestine when there are no witnesses to prove that it took place. In a broader sense, even a witnessed marriage is clandestine if the procedures that the church requires have not taken place, especially the banns. To say that a marriage is clandestine, therefore, is not to say that all solemnities such as those to which Evaristus referred are missing.[339]

Soto concedes that a good case can be made for making clandestine marriages null and void, as Erasmus and some of the schoolmen have contended. The prelates at Trent, too, discussed this possibility, he recalls. The damage that such marriages do is obvious. Moreover, as long as clandestine marriages are valid, children will be able to marry without their parents' consent, whereas the natural law dictates that children must obey their parents. Civil law, too, requires parental consent for a valid marriage.[340] Only a general council or the pope can settle this matter definitively, Soto concedes, but in his opinion a clandestine marriage, however undesirable, must be valid because the consent of the spouses is sufficient, as Pope Nicholas said.[341] In no other sacrament is the action of the subject more essential and central than it is in marriage, or the action of an appointed minister more accidental and peripheral. Because the actions of the recipients constitute the matter as well as the form of this sacrament, it is complete without the ministry of priest, which is essential in the other sacraments and even in penance. A marriage contracted without the blessing of a priest, therefore, is valid and sacramental and can confer grace[342]

One might object that clandestinity is comparable to marrying within the forbidden degrees of consanguinity. Since the prohibition of the latter makes marriage invalid, so, too, should the prohibition of the former.[343] Soto replies that the two cases are not parallel. The impediments of consanguinity pertain to the persons who marry as to the matter presupposed by the sacrament (the *materia circa quod*), whereas the invalidation of clandestinity would pertain not to the matter but to the *modus* of marriage: to the manner in which it is contracted.[344] Soto touches here on a cluster of arguments that will preoccupy the prelates at Trent during the

---

[338] Ibid., arg. 2 (135b)   [339] Ibid., resp. (135b–36a).   [340] Soto cites *Dig.* 23.1.11 and 23.2.2.
[341] *IV Sent.* 28.1, resp. (136a–37a).   [342] Ibid., ad 2 (137b).   [343] Ibid., arg. 1 (135b).
[344] Ibid., ad 1 (137a–b).

penultimate session in 1563. The proponents of invalidation will find the best precedent in the church's power to introduce diriment impediments, whereas the opponents will reply that it is one thing to disqualify the persons from contracting marriage, and quite another to invalidate the manner (*modus*) in which they contract marriage.

17.8 THE CATHOLIC AGENDA ON THE EVE OF THE GENERAL COUNCIL

When the prelates and theologians at the Council of Trent turned to the sacrament of marriage, the challenges of Protestantism and the exigencies of governance had already established a clear agenda. Three areas of concern stand out in the proceedings: the sacramentality of marriage; the evidence for the sacramental doctrine, especially its biblical proof; and the problem of clandestine marriages.

First, Catholics affirmed against the Protestants that marrying was truly one of the sacraments of the New Law and that it conferred grace *ex opere operato*. The married estate, too, was truly holy, but it was not as holy as the vocational celibacy of clergy in major orders and of religious. The relative excellence of holy virginity had to be reaffirmed.

Second, Catholics responded to the criticisms of Erasmus and Luther regarding the biblical basis of the doctrine. They conceded that Ephesians 5:32 considered in itself was not proof that marriage was one of the sacraments, even if St Paul's phrase *sacramentum magnum* referred to marriage: a matter that was now uncertain and contested. They recognized that they had to adduce as evidence the entire discourse about marriage in Ephesians 5 and several other passages from Scripture. Favorite texts included 1 Thessalonians 4:4, where Paul admonishes the Christian husband to "know how to possess his vessel in sanctification and honor"; the story of Tobias, where the angel Raphael warns the young suitor not to follow the example of those "who in such manner receive matrimony as to shut out God from themselves and from their mind, and to give themselves to their lust, as the horse and the mule, which have not understanding," for "over them the devil hath power" (Tob 6:17);[345] and Hebrews 13:4: "Let marriage be held in honor by all, and the bed undefiled [*thorus immaculatus*], but fornicators and adulterers God will judge." The phrase *thorus immaculatus* alone sufficed to invoke this last verse and the special way in which it was now being interpreted. Only sacramental grace, theologians reasoned, could enable spouses to maintain an undefiled bed as well as to sustain a life-long union without straying outside the marriage or regarding each other with boredom and contempt.

---

[345] Thomas Aquinas, *IV Sent.* 2.1.1, quᵃ 2, resp. (Moos 4:78). Paludanus, *IV Sent.* 26.4.2, conc. 2 (141va).

Rejecting Luther's purported reliance on Scripture alone, Catholics insisted that such texts should be understood in light of authority and tradition: the authority of patristic and scholastic theologians and exegetes, and tradition as articulated through papal and conciliar decrees. Scholastic theologians of the central Middle Ages had exercised a finely tuned sense of authority, but they cited authorities chiefly in the peripheral, dialectical parts of an article: the arguments pro and contra. Sixteenth-century theologians, responding to Protestant critique, considered the use of authorities more deliberately and brought it into the center of theological argument. Scripture was authoritative par excellence, but one had to interpret Scripture with the guidance of conciliar and papal decrees and of past masters, which spoke for the whole church, the community of faith.

Melchor Cano (d. 1560) was a pioneer of the new approach to authority (Section 16.7.3). Cano's *De locis theologicis* was published posthumously in Salamanca in 1563. His *loci* were neither the first principles of a science nor the main topics or subject headings of theological discourse (as were Melanchthon's *loci*) but rather were the major sources of data, evidence, and information on which the theologian should draw. These had to be distinctively understood and appropriately applied, whether separately or in combination. Cano enumerated ten *loci*. Seven were proper to theology and fully authoritative for the theologian: Scripture, unwritten tradition, the Catholic church, the general councils, the Apostolic Roman church, the great patristic authors, and the scholastic theologians and canonists. The other three *loci* were secondary and supportive from a theologian's point of view: human reason, the secular philosophers and the scholars of Roman civil law, and human history. Cano subjects each *locus* to critical analysis, explaining how it should be applied and what weight it carried.

No text from Scripture declared in so many words that marriage was one of the seven sacraments. Having established *a priori* what a sacrament was in the proper sense of the term, one had to show how the key biblical texts could not be interpreted adequately or convincingly without attributing to marriage the very properties that were necessary and sufficient for its being one of the sacraments. That marriage was a sacred sign was obvious, and it was not difficult to show that its causes and its composition were at least consistent with its being a sacrament. The crucial question was whether it conferred sacramental grace. The Thomistic principle that God provides his faithful with the means to do faithfully and fittingly whatever he demands of them was important. More important, though, was the new emphasis on the sacred *quality* of marriage. Sixteenth-century theologians routinely identified the sacramental grace of marriage with conjugal love, referring not to passive, romantic love, but to an active love that enabled spouses to fulfill their obligations toward each other patiently and steadfastly until death. The resemblance between marriage and its sacred archetypes, such as Christ's union with the church, entailed not only analogy, therefore, but also a qualitative assimilation. Without grace, the argument went, no merely human marriage could adequately emulate its divine archetype, and the marriage bed could not be a *thorus immaculatus*. This approach to the interpretation of the Scripture presupposed a general theory of the fulfillment of ancient promises in the Gospel, especially through the grace flowing from Christ's Passion. Thus, even texts regarding the marriage of Adam and Eve could be adduced as evidence that marriage was a sacrament, since they were interpreted in relation to God's unfolding plan. If God joined the spouses in matrimony and proposed their union as an image of Christ's union with the church, would he not realize that union in the Gospel to the fullest extent, fulfilling its promise?

Third, most Catholic churchmen considered clandestine marriages to be perilous and subversive and wanted to suppress them as much as possible, ideally to eradicate them. To that extent, they agreed with the Protestants. But what could be done? The root of the problem was the principle of *solus consensus*, which had been firmly entrenched in canon law and theology since the twelfth century, and which was closely associated with the sacramental doctrine. Marriage was the joining of the spouses' own wills (*unio animorum*), by which they gave themselves bodily to each other. The sufficient, constitutive cause of a marriage, therefore, was the consent of the spouses themselves. This principle relegated all other conditions that might be required – betrothal gifts and dowries, documentation, judicially recognized publication, ritual solemnization, parental consent, and the consent of temporal lords to the marriages of persons in their service – to the accidental periphery of "adornments" and "solemnities." Ecclesiastical courts refused to uphold clandestinely contracted marriages when there was no proof and the marriage came into conflict with another vow or contract, but that was a matter of presumptive judgment, and it did nothing to alter the reality of the prior union in the eyes of God. A maxim of canon law was crucial here: *"Ecclesia de occultis non iudicat"* ("The church does not adjudicate hidden matters"). The maxim divided the church's judgment from God's judgment. *"Iudicabit Deus occulta hominum"* ("God will judge the secrets of men," Rom 2:16). Medieval canonists and theologians tried to distinguish between what was valid in the church's judgment and what was valid in the eyes of God, whereas Trent abolished that distinction in the case of clandestinity.[346]

Protestants attributed the abusive practices to the sacramental doctrine, which in their view enabled ecclesiastical judges, canon lawyers, and other clerics to meddle in an essentially worldly matter about which they knew little, wreaking havoc. Contrariwise, the point of departure for Trent's treatment of the issue was a condemnation of the Protestants' invalidation of marriages contracted clandestinely or without parental consent, which from the Catholic point of view was a heresy.

Most Catholic scholars and prelates did not believe that church law was written in stone and could never be altered. On the contrary, theologians and canonists had been emphasizing since the twelfth century that church law, unlike its foundations in divine and natural law, had always adapted to changing needs and would

---

[346] Chiffoleau, "Dire l'indicible."

continue to adapt. The obvious examples in the case of marriage were the diriment impediments. When the Fourth Lateran Council reduced the range of diriment impediments in 1215, it explained that changing circumstances sometimes required changes in ecclesiastical law:

> It ought not to be judged reprehensible if human laws [*statuta*] are sometimes changed according to changing times, especially when urgent necessity or evident utility demands it, since God himself changed in the New Testament some of the things that he had commanded [*statuerat*] in the Old Testament.[347]

This statement stepped clumsily over the distinction between human law and divine law, but the precedent was sound, and the canon was enshrined in the *Liber extra*.[348] No one doubted that Lateran IV had the right to make marriages valid that had hitherto been invalid, or that the church before Lateran IV had held the converse right.

New possibilities would emerge rapidly at the general council, where the rules of the game required the prelates and *theologi minores* to parse marriage into essence and solemnity, matter and form, contract and sacrament, and so forth. I shall consider these developments in Chapters 19 and 20. Suffice to say here that on the eve of the council two avenues toward invalidation presented themselves.

To those of the ritual tendency, the solution was to define the priest's ritual action of joining and blessing as the form of the sacrament, absent which there was no sacrament, although there might perhaps be a contract. Gropper had proposed a subtle rationale for this move – by extending the notion of the sacramental *verbum* to include the piety and obedience of the spouses – but subtlety of that sort eluded the prelates of the ritual tendency at Trent. Most professional theologians rejected this possibility entirely. If the solution were possible, then either (i) marriages that had been contracted without the ministry of a priest over the centuries had not been sacraments or (ii) the church had the power to alter the form of a sacrament. Few dared to entertain either position.

For those who rejected the ritual tendency, the only way to make a plausible, theologically consistent case for invalidation lay with the uncontested power of the church to introduce and remove diriment impediments beyond those of natural and divine law. Prelates and *theologi minores* at the general council revisited the body of theory regarding this precedent. Thomas Aquinas had argued that the church had such a power over impediments because marriage unlike the other sacraments was not *only* a sacrament. It was also a contract, and contracts were subject by their very nature to positive law (Section 16.5.6). But was the church's power regarding diriment impediments pertinent to clandestine marriage? It was one thing, surely, to disqualify certain persons from marrying, and quite another to invalidate a certain manner of marrying.

---

[347] Lateran IV, can. 50 (Tanner-Alberigo, 257).   [348] X 4.4.8 (CIC 2:703–04).

18

The sacrament of marriage at Bologna and Trent

The general council began to discuss the dogmas and disciplines of marriage during its sojourn at Bologna in 1547.[1] Although no decisions about marriage were reached there, some seminal ideas emerged, especially regarding clandestine marriage. The council returned to the sacrament of marriage in 1563 and published the decrees on the doctrine and reform of marriage in Session XXIV (Nov. 11, 1563).[2] In this chapter, I shall follow the council's treatment of the sacramentality of marriage during those two periods, focusing on the doctrine on marriage as one of the seven sacraments. In the next two chapters, I shall follow the council's treatment of the problem of clandestine marriage, first at Bologna (Chapter 19) and then at Trent (Chapter 20).

18.1 PROCEDURES

A summary account of the procedures at Trent is in order here.[3] Much of the best modern literature on the council presupposes that the reader is already familiar with the procedures, and the information in older and cursory treatments is often inaccurate or inconsistent.

---

[1] For a narrative of the council at Bologna, see O. de La Brosse et al., *Latran V et Trente*, Histoire des conciles oecuméniques 10 (Paris, 1975), 348–95.

[2] For a good summary of marriage at the Council of Trent, see J. Bernhard, "Section V. - Le mariage," in Bernhard et al., *L'Époque de la réforme et du Concile de Trente* (Paris, 1989), 212–302. On the proceedings of 1563 that culminated in the Session XXIV, see Lecler et al., *Le concile de Trente 1551–1563*, Histoire des conciles oecuméniques 11 (Paris, 1981), 415–84.

[3] On the council as a whole, see especially H. Jedin, *Geschichte des Konzils von Trient*, 4 vols in 5 (Freiburg, 1949–1975), partially translated by E. Graf as *History of the Council of Trent*, 2 vols (London, 1957–1961); and J. W. O'Malley, *Trent: What Happened at the Council* (Cambridge, Mass., 2013). For a brief review of the place of Trent in the Counter-Reformation, see B. Thompson, *Humanists and Reformers* (Grand Rapids, 2007), 514–21.

The council took place in three phases: 1545–1547, under Pope Paul III (Sessions I–X); 1551–1552, under Pope Julius III (Sessions XI–XVI); and 1562–1563, under Pope Pius IV (Sessions XVII–XXV). The council was transferred to Bologna on March 12, 1547, partly to escape an outbreak of plague, but the prelates loyal to the emperor remained in Trent, which was nominally on German soil, refusing to recognize the authenticity of the proceedings.[4] The prelates at Bologna agreed to suspend the proceedings at a general congregation on September 14, 1547,[5] although some of them continued to deliberate through January, 1548. Paul III gave the remaining bishops leave to return home on September 17, 1549.[6] The "Council of Bologna" published no substantive decrees.

The papal legates were responsible for preparing the agendas and for the presentation and revision of draft decrees. The legates during the first phase (1545–1547) were Giovanni Maria Ciocchi del Monte, who presided, Marcello Cervini, and Reginald Pole. Pole left the council on June 28, 1546, and did not return.[7] Del Monte became Pope Julius III in 1550 and reconvened the council in 1551. Marcello Crescenzio was the only legate during this second phase (1551–1552), but he was assisted by archbishop Sebastiano Pighino and bishop Luigi Lippomano as papal nuncios. Pope Pius IV had appointed five legates to the council when it reconvened 1561: Ercole Gonzaga (prince-bishop of Mantua), Girolamo Seripando (Superior General of the Augustinian Friars), Ludovico Simonetta, Stanislaus Hosius, and Markus Sittich von Hohenems.[8] Gonzaga was supposed to be the presiding legate, but he died during the night of March 2, 1563, and Pius IV appointed Giovanni Morone to replace him.[9] Pius appointed Bernardo Navagero as a legate around the same time, and Seripando died on March 17, 1563. During the concluding months, when the council worked on the dogmas and reform of marriage, the legates were Giovanni Morone, Ludovico Simonetta, Stanislaus Hosius, and Bernardo Navagero, with Morone as "first president." Cardinal Morone overshadowed the other three and energetically directed the work of the council during an especially busy and fraught period, bringing the proceedings to a close.[10]

The role of the papal legates was crucial to the council's constitution. The spirit of conciliarism, which had reached its zenith at the Council of Constance (1414–1418), was among the factors motivating the early demands for a general council.[11] Conciliarism was a complex movement, but it may be broadly characterized as the

---

[4] On the circumstances of the move, see John W. O'Malley, *Trent*, 121–26. O'Malley writes that the "momentous decision had been taken without consultation of pope, emperor, or even the officials of the city of Bologna" (124).

[5] CT 6.1:460–64.   [6] O'Malley, *Trent*, 137–38.

[7] O'Malley, *Trent*, 108. Cervini would become Pope Marcellus II in 1555, but he died three weeks after his election.

[8] O'Malley, *Trent*, 173–75.

[9] See A. P. Robinson, *The Career of Cardinal Giovanni Morone* (Farnham, 2012), 137–38, on Morone's appointment; and see ibid., 148–61, on his role during the remainder of the council.

[10] O'Malley, *Trent*, 206.   [11] H. Jedin, *History of the Council of Trent*, 1:5–165.

contention that supreme power in the church regarding both doctrine (*de fide*) and discipline (*de moribus*) is invested not in the papacy but in a general council. The popes had successfully reasserted their authority by the mid-sixteenth century, but the matter was not entirely resolved and divisions remained. The popes maintained their authority over the council not only by convening it but also through the authority of their legates. On January 18, 1562, the Spanish bishops, led by arch-bishop Pedro Guerrero of Granada, protested against the papal legates' exclusive right to set the agenda and to prepare draft decrees, as defined in the principle of *proponentibus legatis*.[12] The council abstained from defining the constitution of the church and the authority of the papacy, leaving the authority of the published decrees undefined.

The council itself determined its standard procedures during the early general congregations. These evolved as needs were met, problems solved, and disputes settled.[13]

The voting members of the council were the prelates: the members of the episcopal hierarchy (who made up the majority), the generals of the mendicant orders and the Society of Jesus, and the abbots of Clairvaux and of a few representative Benedictine monasteries. The recorded *acta* refer to these prelates collectively as the fathers (*patres*) of the council. The prelates were advised by experts in theology and in canon law, who had no vote. These experts either attended as personal assistants to the prelates or were appointed to the council by the pope or the emperor. The theologians among them, who were more numerous than the canon-ists, were called *theologi minores*, chiefly to emphasize that they had a merely advisory role, but perhaps also to distinguish them from the prelates qualified in theology.[14] The "theologian-prelates" were a minority. It was more common for bishops to be qualified in canon law.

The final vote on each decree or set of decrees took place at a Session: a solemn, ritual event, which usually included a mass, an oration, a sermon, and a reading of the decrees, as well as the final vote. Sessions took place in the cathedral of St Vigilius. Voting was usually predictable, for the work of reaching sufficient consensus had already been done during the general congregations. Prelates could submit their votes orally or as a signed document. Many of the decrees published at the Sessions were procedural decisions and announcements regarding openings, post-ponements, prorogations, resumptions, scheduling of the next session, and so forth. The substantive decisions of the council comprised decrees both of doctrine (the dogmas) and of reform. Other things being equal, the prelates voted in a standard

---

[12] CT 8:291. D. Coleman, *Creating Christian Granada* (Ithaca, 2003), 170–71. O'Malley, *Trent*, 176. The legates had published the principle of *proponentibus legatis* earlier on the same day in the decree of Session XVII (Jan 18, 1562). See Tanner-Alberigo, 723.

[13] O'Malley, *Trent*, 77–81.

[14] N. M. Minnich, "The Voice of Theologians in General Councils from Pisa to Trent," *Theological Studies* 59.3 (1998): 420–41.

order. The cardinal legates voted first; then the episcopal prelates in order of rank: cardinals, patriarchs, metropolitans, and finally the bishops, who made up the majority; and at last the heads of religious orders and the abbots.

The main business of the council took place in plenary meetings known as general congregations, each of which occupied the morning or afternoon of a particular day. The morning meetings usually lasted for three or four hours and the afternoon meetings for three. During the first and second periods of the council, the general congregations took place in the great hall of the Palazzo Giroldo. Because this hall could not accommodate all the prelates participating in the third period of the council, a special amphitheater was built to accommodate them at the church of Santa Maria Maggiore.[15]

The work of each series of general congregations began when the papal legates presented a draft of the decrees on a particular topic or topics to the prelates. The prelates would then meet in general congregations, often twice in a day when the agenda was heavy, voting in turn until everyone had spoken. Votes ranged from simple expressions of approval (*"placet"*) or disapproval (*"non placet"*) to detailed speeches. The number of general congregations devoted to a particular draft is a rough measure of how much the prelates had to say about it. The process might take many days. For example, voting on the first draft of the decrees on marriage in 1563 required fourteen general congregations, which were spread over an eight-day period (July 24–31).

The process was unlike a debate or a modern committee meeting, for every participant normally spoke just once in a pre-established order. The prelates usually came with prepared remarks if they had substantive contributions to make, and they sometimes apologized for coming unprepared. Some of the written texts of their votes (*vota scripta*) have survived, and a few of these were recorded in the *acta*. Nevertheless, because the prelates responded to what others had said before them, the deliberations evolved and new themes emerged. How the secretarial reporting was related to what was said and written remains largely obscure. The wide differences between *vota scripta* and the corresponding recorded *acta* are disconcerting. Nevertheless, I shall assume for simplicity's sake that the recorded *acta* accurately convey what the prelates said. To say that a prelate said something during a general congregation is an abbreviated way of saying that the secretary reported that the prelate said it.

Questions about the relationship between dogma and reform were controversial at the beginning of the council.[16] A decree of reform, strictly so called, was a declaration not about faith (*de fide*) but about practice (*de moribus*). Those who had been advocating a general council since the 1520s looked to it chiefly for ecclesiastical reform, but the challenge of Protestantism made doctrine and discipline inseparable. The prelates agreed on January 22, 1546, that dogma and reform

---

[15] O'Malley, *Trent*, 176.   [16] O'Malley, *Trent*, 81–82.

should be treated together but that doctrines would come first. Every decree about doctrine (*de dogmatibus*) would be followed by a corresponding decree of reform (*de reformatione*).[17] A decree on doctrine typically consisted of a general statement followed by canons expressing particular dogmas as anathemas condemning anyone who denied each dogma. The general statement might be an introduction to the canons or an extensive essay in several chapters. Since doctrinal edicts were decisions about truth and falsehood and were presumed to be incorrigible, their acceptance was obligatory always and everywhere, on pain of heresy. Reform edicts, on the contrary, could be rescinded by the pope or another general council and were binding only in provinces where the local churches promulgated them.

As well as the general congregations and the sessions, there were more or less private meetings of various sorts, official and unofficial. The papal legates commissioned *theologi minores* to meet in their own *congregationes theologorum*, which the prelates might attend as auditors. Such meetings were usually preparatory and took place before the prelates began to vote on a draft. The aim was to provide some indication of the current consensus of the profession regarding contentious topics or Protestant heresies, and to bring to light what issues were at stake.

The legates also deputed groups of prelates to undertake special tasks, such as preparing the agenda and drafting decrees, and they commissioned prelates qualified in theology or in law to meet in particular congregations, sometimes called private congregations in the record. These meetings were especially useful when difficult or divisive issues had come to light during the general congregations. Freed from the task of resolving differences, of finding common ground, and of reaching a decision, a commission of appropriately qualified prelates could focus on the issues. On October 11, 1547, for example, during the council's sojourn at Bologna, the legates appointed a deputation of prelates who were qualified in either or both laws to review the agenda for sacramental reform. These prelates recommended on October 26 that "private congregations" of prelates with appropriate expertise could often resolve the difficulties of fact that had come to light during the general congregations. Prelates qualified in theology should be commissioned to discuss the "dogmas of faith," whereas those qualified in canon or civil law were better suited to matters of "morals and reform." Once a private congregation had clarified the issues, the jurist-prelates recommended, the matter could be taken back to the general congregations for their decisions.[18] The procedure at particular congregations and at *congregationes theologorum* was similar to that of the general congregations inasmuch as each member of the commission normally spoke only once, in a prearranged order.

The proceedings of the general and particular congregations were recorded by or under the direction of Angelo Massarelli, secretary to the council, who had formerly been Marcello Cervini's secretary. Massarelli was appointed bishop of Telese o Cerreto Sannita in 1557, however, and he voted in that capacity at Session XXIV,

---

[17] CT 4:572/3–5.   [18] CT 6.1:529.

endorsing the decree invalidating clandestine marriages.[19] The Roman Curia, wanting to maintain the impression that the decrees were apodictic and fearing lest the minutes might diminish and complicate the impact of decrees, declined to publish the proceedings and restricted access to them until the 1880s.[20] They are now available with related records and documents in fine editions published under the aegis of the Societas Goerresiana.[21]

18.2 BOLOGNA, 1547

The council at Trent defined the doctrine on the sacraments in general at Session VII (March 3, 1547), as well as the doctrines on baptism and confirmation in particular. The prelates at Trent went on to discuss the agenda for the other five sacraments,[22] and the *theologi minores* met to discuss the sacrament of eucharist, but at this point the council was transferred to Bologna (March 20, 1547).

Although the council at Bologna published no decrees, their deliberations prepared the ground for future debates and decisions. The prelates discussed the eucharist, which the *theologi minores* had already discussed at Trent, and both the prelates and the *theologi minores* began working on the other four sacraments. The prelates' discussion of marriage touched on most of the key points that would preoccupy the council during 1563, when their deliberations culminated in the canons and decrees on marriage in Session XXIV.

18.2.1 *The doctrine of the sacraments in general (Trent, Session VII)*

According to the general doctrine of the sacraments defined at Trent, there are exactly seven sacraments of the New Law: baptism, confirmation, eucharist, penance, extreme unction, orders, and matrimony, and no one may add or subtract any from the list. Furthermore, all were instituted by Jesus Christ, and each one is "truly and properly" a sacrament (canon 1), although they are not all equal in dignity (canon 3). The seven sacraments are more than a means of fostering faith (canon 5). They differ fundamentally from the sacraments of the Old Law, and not only in respect of ceremonies and external rituals (canon 2). The sacraments of the New Law are necessary for salvation, and "faith in the divine promise" is not sufficient. All of these sacraments contain the grace that they signify and confer it *ex opere operato* on those who put no obstacle in its way (canons 4, 6, 8). Their efficacy is

---

[19] CT 9:975/28–29: "Cotronensi [et aliis] ... mihi ep. Thelesino ... placent omnia."

[20] See O. Chadwick, *Catholicism and History* (Cambridge, 1978), 46–71.

[21] *Concilium Tridentinum: Diariorum, actorum, epistularum, tractatuum nova collectio* (Friburgi Brisgoviae, 1901–). CT 9, ed. S. Ehses, published in 1924, contains the proceedings of 1563, but CT 6.1, ed. S. Merkle, which contains the proceedings at Bologna in 1547, was not published until 1950. Consequently, accounts of marriage at Trent written before 1950 usually say little or nothing about the Bologna proceedings.

[22] CT 1:623 (diary of Massarelli).

independent of the moral state of the minister (canon 10), although they are ineffective unless the minister intends to do what the church does through the sacrament (canon 11).[23]

The doctrine on the sacraments in general was partly a confirmation of the *Bull of Union with the Armenians* (*Exultate Deo*), where canon 11 originated, and partly a defense of Catholic doctrines against the Protestants, especially Luther and his followers. It might be construed in part, like the *Bull of Union*, as a generalization that did not necessarily apply to every sacrament in every respect. For example, the council had not said that each and every sacrament was necessary for salvation or required a minister. Nevertheless, the canons explicitly stated that all seven were fully and univocally sacraments of the New Law, and that all conferred grace *ex opere operato*.

No one at Bologna disputed that marriage was truly one of the seven divinely instituted sacraments of the New Law or that it conferred grace. This much had already been established in the decree on the sacraments in general. By the same token, everyone agreed that the Catholic doctrine could be defined by anathematizing anyone who denied that marriage was a sacrament in the full and proper sense. The Lutherans were perpetrating a heresy. What remained to be settled regarding the doctrine of marriage was the evidence for the sacramentality of marriage, especially in Scripture, the composition of the sacrament, its institution, and so forth. These were not matters of heated controversy, although some of them resisted consensus. The issue of clandestine marriage, on the contrary, proved to be fraught with difficulty. Discussion of the topic at Bologna brought to light fundamental and irreconcilable disagreements about reform, which in turn presupposed divergent conceptions of the sacramentality of marriage.

18.2.2 Theologi minores

The proceedings on marriage began in Bologna on April 26, 1547, when the legates put before the *theologi minores* a list of heterodox articles regarding the sacraments of extreme unction, orders, and marriage. The document included quotations from Luther and Melancthon illustrating the errors.[24] Thirty-four theologians discussed these articles in five successive *congregationes theologorum*, which took place during the evenings of April 29 and May 4–7. But the theologians spoke mainly about extreme unction and orders. Only a few spoke about marriage, perhaps because they did not anticipate serious doubt or controversy.

The catalogue of errors was apparently based on a fuller summary that Girolamo Seripando, Superior General of the Augustinian Friars, had prepared earlier, probably at Trent.[25] Seripando's document had included fifteen heterodox articles on marriage. The first four pertained to sacramentality. These included the claim that

---

[23] Session VII (March 3, 1547), *Canones de sacramentis in genere*. Tanner-Alberigo, 684–85.
[24] CT 6.1:95–99.   [25] Ibid., 90–95.

marriage is not a sacrament in the proper sense because it carries no promise of grace. Marriage may be loosely called a sacrament inasmuch as it is the subject of a divine mandate and has certain salutary promises attached to it, but the civic power of the magistracies, too, is the subject of a divine mandate, and the promises attached to marriage are merely temporal, pertaining rather to bodily than to spiritual life. Marriage, therefore, is not a sacrament of the New Law. Again, although it is true that marriage has become *de facto* one of the sacraments of the church, it was not God but human beings who instituted this sacrament. A marriage between infidels is no less truly a marriage than one between Christians. According to the fifth of Seripando's articles on marriage, parents have the power to annul the clandestine marriages of their children.[26] According to the last article, secular rulers have jurisdiction over matrimonial cases.[27] The other heterodox articles on marriage pertained to the impediments of consanguinity and affinity, which should be reduced to those of Leviticus; to remarriage after divorce, which is possible at least in the case of adultery; to polygamy, which is valid and permissible; and to the impediments of holy orders and clerical celibacy, which are abusive.

The six heterodox articles on marriage that the legates eventually put before the *theologi minores* was comparatively skimpy.[28] The articles focused on law and discipline. The first article stated that clandestine marriages were illegitimate and that as a consequence parents had the right to annul them.[29] Most of the theologians who discussed this article rejected this article as false and potentially heretical, and all agreed that parents did not have the power to annul a marriage that their children had contracted with their own free consent (Section 19.2). The other articles touched on polygamy, the possibility of remarriage after divorce,[30] and the impediments of relationship. There was nothing in this list regarding the jurisdiction of civil authorities over marriage cases, an issue that Seripando had included and that would return to the agenda in 1563. Nor was there anything regarding the sacramentality of marriage, although denial that marriage was a sacrament was at the center of the Protestant heresies. The *theologi minores*, nevertheless, affirmed that marriage was truly a sacrament of the New Law.

Mindful of the critiques of Erasmus and Luther, and tacitly conceding that Ephesians 5:32 could not stand alone as a sufficient proof text, the theologians broadened the supports of the sacramental doctrine in Scripture and tradition. Vincent de Placentia, O.P., began his statement by appealing to the authority of the councils and invoking Ephesians 5:32.[31] Vincent concedes that the terms

---

[26] 92/26.: "Parentes posse irritare omnia clandestina matrimonia, quidquid doceat papa."
[27] 95/4: "Causas matrimonii spectare ad principes saeculares."   [28] 98–99.
[29] 98/8: "Matrimonia clandestina non esse legitima ac proinde a parentibus irritari posse."
[30] 98–99, *De sacramento matrimonii*, art. 3–5.
[31] Vincentius de Placentia, 109/18–19: "Matrimonium sacramentum esse probatur ex concilio Constantiensi, Florentino etc. *Ad abolendam* de haereticis." Vincent is presumably referring to the condemnation of Jan Hus in the bull *Inter cunctas* (1418) as well as to the *Decree of Union with the Armenians* (1439) and the bull *Ad abolendam* (1184).

"sacrament" and "mystery" are synonyms, as Erasmus and Luther argued, but he protests that the point is trivial, for *mystērion* is the Greek term for what the Latins call *sacramentum*, and vice versa. St Paul says that marriage is "a great sacrament or mystery" in Christ and the church because the union of wills (*unio animorum*) that makes marriage is akin to what unites Christ and the church. Moreover, marriage is a sacrament of the New Law, and as such it must confer grace.[32] Francis Salazar, an Observant Franciscan, declared that the articles on marriage were all heretical "because marriage was instituted by God." For proof, he invoked the original institution of marriage in Genesis 1:27–28, and he cited both Paul's treatment of marriage in Ephesians and First Corinthians and Hugh of Saint-Victor's *De sacramentis*.[33] Augustine of Montalcino, an Augustinian friar, proposed as biblical supports not only Ephesians 5:32 but also Hebrews 13:4 (the "bed undefiled"), 1 Timothy 2:15 ("she shall be saved in childbearing"), and 1 Corinthians 7:14 (where the convert sanctifies the infidel spouse through their marriage). All these texts, he claimed, showed that marriage was both holy and sanctifying. Friar Augustine also invoked the original blessing of Genesis 1:28, which, he explained, should be considered in light of its invocation by Jesus (Matt 19:6 etc.).[34] Since God himself joins spouses together in matrimony, "it follows that marriage is from God and is a holy thing."[35]

18.2.3 *Particular and general congregations*

The prelates began to consider marriage on August 29, 1547, when the legates put before them two articles articulating erroneous and potentially heterodox policies. These were respectively about clandestine marriages and remarriage after divorce.[36]

On September 9, turning from the reform of abuses to matters of doctrine, the legates proposed drafts of six dogmatic canons on marriage, framed as usual in the form of anathemas.[37] The prelates devoted eight general congregations to these canons (September 10–24). The first canon anathematized anyone who denied that marriage was truly one of the sacraments of the New Law; the second, anyone who denied that freely contracted clandestine marriages were valid and indissoluble *post factum*. The other canons anathematized those who said that remarriage was permissible after a divorce on grounds of adultery, that priests were permitted to bless second marriages, that polygamy was licit even for Christians, and that the impediments ought to be limited to those of the Leviticus code. I shall review the prelates' discussion of clandestinity in the next chapter (Section 19.3). Suffice to say here that although most of them held that clandestine marriages were necessarily valid, a few wanted the council to render clandestine marriages null and void henceforth.

---

[32] 109/21–110/2.   [33] Franciscus Salazar, 113/13–16.   [34] Augustinus de Montealcino, 107–08.
[35] 108/5–6: "Si enim Deus coniungit homines in matrimonio, ergo matrimonium a Deo est et sancta res est."
[36] CT 6.1:407.   [37] CT 6.1:445–447.

The first of the draft canons anathematized anyone who said that marriage was not a true sacrament of the New Law but rather was a merely human institution:

Canon 1 (1547, original version): If anyone says that marriage is not a true, divinely instituted sacrament of the evangelical law but rather is something invented in the church by human beings, let him be anathema.[38]

Such was Luther's doctrine, and most of the prelates readily endorsed this canon. Not only was Luther's denial evidently heretical, but his heresy could only confirm, conversely, that the opposite doctrine was an important truth and a matter of faith for Catholics.[39] But what was the evidence for the Catholic doctrine? When did God or Jesus Christ institute this sacrament? Whereas some located the institution in the Gospel or the New Law, others found it in Eden, especially in God's joining together of the first man and woman.

The prelates cited several sources from both Scripture and tradition as proof that marriage was truly one of the seven sacraments: councils such as Constance, Florence (in the *Bull of Union with the Armenians*), and Trent itself (in the canons on the sacraments in general); Augustine of Hippo; St Paul, especially in Ephesians 5; and the words of Jesus: "What God has joined together, let not man separate."[40] Franciscus Romeo, Master General of the Dominicans, found sufficient proof that marriage conferred grace in Hebrews 13:4 (the "bed undefiled").[41] The archbishop of Aix pointed out that Trent's own doctrine on the sacraments in general, defined at Session VII on March 3, already implied that marriage conferred grace and had been instituted "by God and Christ."[42] The bishop of Sarsina suggested for the same reason that the proposed canon was redundant.[43] The bishop of Feltre said that marriage could not have been "invented by human beings in the church" because God himself had instituted it when he created Adam and Eve. Jesus invoked and confirmed that primordial institution when he said, "What God has joined together, let not man separate" (Matt 19:6, Mark 10:9).[44]

Several prelates argued that the canon on the sacramentality of marriage was not specific enough, and some proposed ways of strengthening it. Ambrosius Catharinus Politus, O.P., who was present as bishop of Minori, proposed that the canon should define the manner in which marriage was a sacrament, "since it does not have all the qualities that the other sacraments have."[45] It is clear from Catharinus's treatise

---

[38] CT 6.1:445/22–23: "Si quis dixerit matrimonium non esse verum sacramentum legis evangeli-cae divinitus institutum, sed ab hominibus in ecclesia inventum, a.s." Cf. 447/36–37, an earlier version: "Si quis dixerit matrimonium non esse verum sacramentum a Christo Domino nostro institutum, sed ab hominibus in ecclesia inventum, a.s."

[39] Veronensis coadiutor, 452/19–25. Alyphanus, 471/7–17.

[40] Sibinicensis, 450/33–35. Veronensis coadiutor, 452/18–19. Albinghanensis, 475/10–11. Portuensis Portugallensis, 477/9–12. Gen. Praedicatorum, 478/3–6. Gen. Heremitarum s. Augustini D. Seripandus, 479/8–10.

[41] Gen. Praedicatorum, 478/15–16.   [42] Archiep. Aquensis Gallus, 473/18–19.

[43] Sarsinensis (i.e., Sarsinatensis), 474/5–6.   [44] Feltrensis, 449/32–35.

[45] Minoriensis, 471/39–41.

on marriage that although he did not question whether marriage was truly a sacrament of the New Law, he emphasized that it was peculiar among these sacraments in certain respects (Section 18.3.1). The bishop of Bertinoro, on the contrary, who seems to have been more in tune with the mood of the gathering, wanted the canon to affirm that "there is no difference between this sacrament and the others."[46] Several proposed that the canon should anathematize anyone who denied that marriage conferred sanctifying grace.[47] Some wanted the council to be more specific about how this sacrament had been instituted. To say that marriage had been *divinely* instituted was too general. Instead, the canon should state that Jesus Christ had instituted it.[48]

Some prelates were troubled by the implication that marriage had not been a sacrament under the Old Law, and they wanted the canon to be reworded so as to leave room for that possibility. Sebastiano Leccavella, O.P., archbishop of Naxos, was the first to express this view, and several others supported him or expounded the same idea.[49] Benedetto de Nobili, O.P., bishop of Accia, remarked that the scholastics considered questions such as whether God had instituted the sacrament under the Old Law and whether it conferred grace then to be matters still open to debate.[50] Similarly, Catharinus noted that according to some theologians – he seems to have been referring to himself – marriage was already a true sacrament among the "holy fathers" of the Old Law, when it conferred grace through faith in Christ-to-come (*Christus venturus*).[51] Catharinus will develop this theology in his treatise on marriage (Section 18.3.3).

Others argued, on the contrary, that the council should emphasize the difference between marriage under the Old Law and marriage under the New Law, for only on that basis could the church affirm that marriage now was truly one of the seven sacraments. Marriage was a sacrament in some sense under the Old Law, but not in the fullest sense. Robert Wauchope, archbishop of Armagh, contradicted the archbishop of Naxos and claimed that marriage under the Old Law was not a sacrament but only a sacramental.[52] Others more cautiously held that it was already a sacrament then but only in a broad sense of the term, for the sacraments properly so called derived their supernatural efficacy from Christ's Passion. Marriage under the Old Law, therefore, did not confer grace. It was only a sign or prefiguration of

---

[46] Britonoriensis, 474/25.

[47] Feltrensis, 449/32–33. Veronensis coadiutor, 452/24–25. Caprulanus, 455/4–5. Bituntinus, 455/23–24. Lavellanus, 458/1–2. Archiep. Aquensis Gallus, 473/15–19.

[48] Britonoriensis. 474/24–25. Gen. Heremitarum s. Augustini D. Seripandus, 479/27–28.

[49] Naxiensis, 449/4–5. Bononiensis, 450/28. Chironensis, 451/6–7. Aquensis Vorstius (Petrus Vorstius, auditor rotae curiae Romanae), 451/27. Alyphanus, 471/9–14.

[50] Aciensis de Nobilibus, 450/15–16.   [51] Minoriensis, 471/41–472/2.

[52] Armacanus, 449/18–21: "Primus placet, ut iacet. Neque obstat, quod dicit Naxiensis, quia in veteri lege matrimonium non erat sacramentum, sed sacramentale; neque conferebat gratiam. Sed in lege evangelica aliter est, ut declaratum est Tridenti de sacramentis in genere primo canone." The word *sacramentum* is supplied by the editor.

something that would come to fruition under the New Law: perhaps marriage itself as one of the seven sacraments.[53] Luigi Lippomano, coadjutor bishop of Verona, said that marriage under the Old Law prefigured something (presumably marriage) under the New Law in the same way as escaping in Noah's Ark from the Flood was a prefiguration of baptism.[54]

Girolamo Seripando used the canon as a pretext to summarize his own theology of marriage. According to the secretary's record, Seripando posited both a *sacramentum minimum* and a *sacramentum magnum*, ascribing the distinction to Augustine. Marriage as the union between two individuals is a *sacramentum minimum*, whereas marriage as a sign of Christ's union with the church is a *sacramentum magnum*.[55] The composition of marriage as a sacrament is the same as that of the other sacraments of the New Law, according to Seripando. Marriage is composed of *verbum* and *elementum*; it is an object of faith; and it is a "visible form of an invisible grace," which it confers. The sacramental *verbum* is what the partners say to express their mutual consent, although this *verbum* presupposes Christ's own words, "Those whom God has joined, let not man separate." The *elementum* consists of everything visible and exterior that is used to join and to manifest the contract: the bestowal of a ring, the kiss, the handclasp, and so forth. Many authorities might be cited as proof that marriage confers grace, Seripando claims. He identifies the sacramental grace of marriage with a special, supernatural love that unites the spouses: a love that with God's help will last until they are parted by death. It is because of this love that they are no longer two but one, for husbands must love their wives as if they were their own bodies (Eph 5:28). The same supernatural love supports the raising the children and enables the spouses to abstain from fornication (1 Cor 7:9, 7:2). Like the other sacraments, marriage is an object of faith, for one knows only through faith that God joins the spouses' wills (*animi*) in mutual love and charity (*dilectio et charitas*). Seripando is refuting Durandus here, who argued that marriage was not an object of faith, but his thesis would have reminded contemporaries of Luther's contention that every true sacrament expresses a "word of divine promise," which must be received in faith. Seripando adds that only a marriage between Christians is a sacrament in this special sense. Neither a marriage between infidels nor even one between Jews is truly a sacrament because marriage derives its efficacy from the reality of Christ's Passion, as do all the sacraments. Absent that real, causal connection, a marriage is only figuratively related to Christ's union with the church.[56]

Whereas the prelates had found it easy to agree that marriage was truly a sacrament, the issue of clandestine marriage proved to be unexpectedly fraught,

---

[53] Maceratensis, 459/24–25. Aprutinus, 459/32–34. Albinghanensis, 475/12–13.

[54] Veronensis coadiutor, 452/20–22.

[55] Perhaps Seripando meant that Christ's union with the church (the signified) was the *sacramentum magnum* (Eph 5:32), whereas the marriage between any two members of the church (Eph 5:33) was a *sacramentum minimum*.

[56] Gen. Heremitarum s. Augustini D. Seripandus, 479/9–27.

and the legates commissioned particular congregations to work on some of the questions that arose (Sections 19.5 and 19.6). On October 12, a particular congregation of prelates qualified in theology or canon law met to discuss whether the canon on clandestine marriage should be handled under dogma as a matter of faith, or be recast as a decree about abuse and reform.[57] They established that the decrees must include a dogmatic canon on clandestine marriages, although this might refer to a corresponding decree of reform. The next question was how to modify the draft canon so as to identify more precisely what was heretical in the Lutheran position on clandestinity. The prelates who were qualified in theology met on October 14 to discuss this matter.[58] The same prelates met again on October 15 to discuss revisions to the third of the dogmatic canons that had been presented to them on September 9, regarding remarriage after a divorce on grounds of adultery.[59]

Revised versions of the first three of the canons on the sacrament of marriage, respectively on sacramentality, clandestinity, and indissolubility, were put before the theologian-prelates on October 18.[60] At some point before November 7, Franciscus Romeo, Master General of the Dominicans, proposed further amendments to these revised canons, so that three versions of each of these canons are extant.

Whereas the original version of the first canon, on sacramentality, had said simply that the sacrament of marriage had been "divinely instituted," the revised version now specified that Jesus Christ had instituted it, and that marriage conferred grace. In the following translation, the substantive additions or modifications are in bold font:

> Canon 1 (1547, revised version): If anyone says that **the sacrament of** marriage is something introduced into the church by human beings, or that it is not truly a sacrament of the evangelical law instituted **by our Lord Jesus Christ, or that it does not confer spiritual grace on those who contract it with due observance [*rite*]**, let him be anathema.[61]

Franciscus Romeo proposed that the canon should say not just "*rite*" but "*rite et digne*" ("with due observance and worthily"). In his view, the term *digne* ("worthily") was needed explicitly to preclude those who presented an obstacle to grace. This requirement was consistent with the claim that marriage conferred grace *ex opere operato*. But Romeo also wanted to excise the word "spiritual" to accommodate "the difficulties of theologians regarding the sacrament of marriage, which seems to have little in the way of spirituality."[62]

---

[57] 529–32.   [58] 532–34.   [59] 534–35.
[60] 537. For the original versions of Sept. 9, see 445–47.
[61] 537/3–5: "Si quis dixerit **sacramentum** matrimonii ab hominibus fuisse in ecclesia invectum, aut non esse vere sacramentum legis evangelicae **a Domino nostro Iesu Christo institutum, aut rite contrahentibus spiritualem gratiam non conferre**, a. s." The additions are in bold font. Cf. 447/36–37, an earlier amendment that has the more specific "*a Christo nostro Domino nostro institutum*" instead of the original "*divinitus institutum*."
[62] 537/21–23.

There was now no question of publishing any decrees at Bologna, but the legates presented the prelates with a dossier of abuses, remedies, and related disciplinary provisions regarding marriage on November 29, 1547, which they discussed in general congregations through December 25 (Section 19.7).

18.3 AMBROSIUS CATHARINUS ON THE SACRAMENT OF MARRIAGE

Catharinus (1484–1553) had gone to the Council of Trent in 1545 as a papal theologian and an adviser to Cardinal Del Monte, but Pope Paul III made him bishop of Minori in 1546. It was in that office that he participated at Bologna during 1547.[63] Catharinus's *De matrimonio quaestiones plures* is one of several treatises that he addressed to the prelates during the second phase of the general council, having reflected on what had ensued during the first phase. The date of publication is 1551, but it was distributed with the author's *Enarrationes*, published in 1552.[64] Catherinus developed and modified in this treatise positions that he had outlined at Bologna. I shall consider the work's treatment of clandestine marriage in the next chapter (Section 19.9.2) and focus here on the sacramentality of marriage.

Lancelotto Politi took the name Ambrosius Catharinus when he entered the Dominican Order in 1517, abandoning a promising career in law. His reputation as a cleric and author of distinction was based largely on his campaign against the Lutherans.[65] Catharinus was a vigorous opponent of some of the luminaries of his own order, including Cardinal Cajetan, and he made himself unpopular among his brethren. Indeed, he made enemies everywhere, but he enjoyed preferment in the church, partly because of his services against the Lutherans, but also because he was a staunch adherent of the papal side in the tension between papalists and conciliarists.

As a theologian, Catharinus was eccentric and largely self-taught. He was qualified in both laws, but he had no formal qualifications in theology, and whatever theological training in Thomistic theology he received when he joined the Dominican Order must have been abbreviated.[66] Nevertheless, he had a sharp and perceptive intellect, and he was able to assimilate the theories of scholastic theologians and to take them in new directions, unfettered by received wisdom.

---

[63] Pope Julius III appointed him archbishop of Conza in 1552, but he died in the following year.

[64] *Enarrationes R. P. F. Ambrosii Catharini Politi Senensis Archiepiscopo Compsani in Quinque priora capita libri Geneseos* [etc.], Rome, 1552. Repr. Ridgewood, New Jersey, 1964.

[65] See P. Preston, "Catherinus versus Luther, 1521," *History* 88.3 (2003): 364–78; and G. Caravale, *Sulle tracce dell'eresia. Ambrogio Catarino Politi (1484–1553)* (Florence, 2007).

[66] Caravale, *Sulle tracce dell'eresia*, ch. 1, sketches Catharinus's early formation and entry into the Dominican Order. See also A. K. Jenkins and P. Preston, *Biblical Scholarship and the Church* (Aldershot, 2007), 150–52, on Catharinus's background; and ibid., 150–72, on Catharinus's polemic against Cajetan.

The treatise addresses twelve questions. The first seven are about the sacramentality of marriage, which Catharinus considers in relation to the various stages of sacred history, to sexual consummation, and to clandestinity. The remaining chapters are devoted to the impediments (consanguinity, affinity, disparity of cult, and vows), to polygyny, and to whether remarriage is permitted after a divorce on grounds of adultery. I shall consider only the questions on marriage as a sacrament in this chapter.

Catharinus's theology of marriage is based on the premise that marriage is holy because God instituted it in Eden, when he joined the first spouses together. The primordial union is reenacted in every sacramental marriage, for God the Father really joins each couple in a union that no human being can sever. This was an ancient and popular notion, but Catharinus adjusts it to accommodate the medieval doctrine that marriage is one of the seven sacraments of the New Law.

18.3.1 *Marriage as a sacrament*

Is marriage a sacrament? The Protestant attack on the Catholic doctrine had turned on the interpretation of Ephesians 5:32 and on the traditional use of the verse as a proof text of the doctrine. Catharinus begins his defense, therefore, by considering this text and its meaning. Since St Paul says that marriage is a "great sacrament," the question seems to be settled at once. The objection that Paul said *mystērion*, and not *sacramentum*, is ridiculous and trivial. Paul wrote in Greek, and *sacramentum* is a Latin word, but *mystērion* is the word that the Greeks use when they talk about what the Latins call *sacramentum*. This glib rebuttal hardly does justice to Erasmus's arguments about the semantic fields of the two terms, although it may be an adequate response to Luther's polemical reduction of Erasmus's arguments. But Catharinus outlines a more serious version of the objection. The terms *sacramentum* and *mysterium* are synonyms, but both are used in the New Testament only to denote things that are not sacraments in the current sense but rather are mysteries of the church: the ultimate objects of faith. For example, Scripture refers to truths regarding Christ as sacraments or mysteries, such as his bodily resurrection (Eph 3:3, 3:9, Col 1:27, 1 Tim 3:16, Apoc 1:20).[67]

Some argue, Catharinus, notes, that the phrase *sacramentum magnum* in Ephesians 5:32 refers not to marriage but to Christ's union with the church, or perhaps even to the primordial marriage between Adam and Eve. Catharinus reviews their objections. It is true that Paul likens husband and wife to Christ and the church in order to commend both the love (*dilectio*) that the husband owes to his wife and the reciprocal service (*observantia*) that the wife owes to her husband. But Paul goes on to invoke the prophetic words that God spoke through Adam: "Because of this, a man shall leave his father and his mother, and shall cleave unto his wife, and they

---

[67] Catharinus, *De matrimonio*, Q. 1, 225/1–37.

shall be two in one flesh" (Gen 2:24).[68] It is here that Paul speaks of a "great sacrament."[69] But perhaps the phrase *magnum sacramentum* refers to Christ's union with the church, or even to the mystery of the incarnation.[70] Moreover, even if the phrase *magnum sacramentum* denotes a human marriage, then surely it refers to Adam's marriage to Eve. Just as Eve was formed from Adam as his helpmeet, so Christ left his father by emptying himself and taking on human flesh, becoming a servant;[71] and just as Eve was formed from Adam's side while he slept, so water and blood, tokens of the sacraments of baptism and eucharist, flowed from Christ's side on the cross. These analogies are peculiar to the primordial marriage, for no other wife was formed from her husband's rib.[72] Even if the phrase *magnum sacramentum* does refer to human marriage as sign of that sacred reality, it does not follow that marriage causes what it signifies or that it confers grace, which are necessary conditions if marriage is to be counted among the sacraments of the New Law.[73]

In reply, Catharinus concedes that this verse, considered in itself, is not sufficient to prove that marriage is one of the sacraments of the New Law. Nevertheless, careful examination of the biblical evidence in light of the church's traditions shows not only that the doctrine is something that the faithful ought to believe but also that it stands to reason. However one might construe the "great sacrament" of Ephesians 5:32, Paul's discourse on marriage in this chapter suffices to show that marriage is a sacrament in the proper sense. Even if the phrase *magnum sacramentum* does denote Christ's union with the church – which Catharinus does not concede – the discourse as a whole still links together the union of Adam and Eve, the union of Christ and the church, and Christian marriages in a way that makes sense only if marriage is one of the sacraments. One may even identify the *sacramentum magnum* with Christian marriage, therefore: an interpretation that Catharinus finds "more pleasing," although he does not insist on it.[74]

Catharinus points out that although Adam was speaking solely about his relationship with Eve when he said, "this is now bone of my bones" etc. (v. 23), he was speaking about future marriages in the following verse (v. 24), as well as about Christ and the church, for Adam himself did *not* leave father and mother when he married. Again, God was referring not only to the marriage of Adam and Eve but also to every future marriage when he said, "Be fruitful and multiply, and fill the earth" (Gen 1:28). Paul presents both the first marriage and Christ's union with the church as norms for every marriage. Christian marriage signifies the church's union with Christ.[75]

---

[68] Q. 1, 225/46–226/1: "Propter hoc relinquet homo patrem suum et matrem, et adhaerebit uxori suae, et erunt duo in carne una, sive in carnem unam." Catherinus consistently quotes the text with the "*Propter hoc*" of Matt 19:5 and Eph 5:31, and not the "*Quam ob rem*" of Gen 1:24.
[69] Q. 1, 225/38–46.   [70] Q. 1, 226/23–37.   [71] Q. 1, 227/56–228/4.
[72] Q. 1, 226/15–22, 226/46–227/20.   [73] Q. 1, 225/28–37.   [74] Q. 1, 228/26–44.
[75] Q. 1, 227/21–228/25.

One might object that marriage cannot be a sacrament in the proper sense, or one of the seven sacraments of the New Law, unless it causes what it signifies. A couple's marriage may signify the union between Christ and the church, but it can hardly cause that union, which already existed before the couple married.[76] Catharinus replies that marriage signifies the union between Christ and the church not absolutely (*simpliciter*), as if the reference stopped there, but inasmuch as the latter is the exemplar for the former. Marriage signifies the union of the Christ and the church, and God supernaturally enables Christian spouses to imitate that exemplar – but only if they marry with the right intentions, that is, in the fear of God and intending to beget children for God, for the participants of this as of all the sacraments do not receive grace if they put an obstacle in its way.[77] There are really two relations between the sacrament and its *res*, therefore, which come together in a single *motus reflexus*: an analogical relation by which the marriage signifies or figures Christ's union with the church; and an exemplary, causal relation by which God enables the subject to emulate that union as its exemplar. Now, this divine assistance is a species of grace. The canonists denied that marriage confers grace. Indeed, even some of the theologians did so, such as Peter Lombard, although the "better theologians" maintain that marriage does confer grace. Be that as it may, we must hold that God supernaturally blesses and assists the spouses when he joins them together, enabling them to sustain the bond of obligation between themselves, to raise their children religiously, and to preserve the "undefiled bed" (*thorus immaculatus*) of Hebrews 13:14.[78] Catharinus's argument here echoes that of Erasmus in the *Christiani matrimonii institutio*. Erasmus argues that marriage as a sacrament is not only an *imago* revealing how Christ is united with the church, for what marriage signifies is in turn the *exemplum* to which the *imago* should conform. Furthermore, Erasmus claims, God provides a grace, or *arrha*, with the sacrament, which enables Christian spouses to emulate Christ's union with the church and to achieve the "undefiled bed" (Section 17.2.3).

18.3.2 *The composition of the sacrament: Matter, form, and minister*

Other objections to the sacramental doctrine had arisen within the Catholic tradition. Catharinus's account of these objections is dependent on Durandus of Saint-Pourçain, but unlike Durandus he uses them not to cast doubt on the doctrine but to show that marriage is one of the sacraments of New Law *in a peculiar manner*. Every sacrament is composed of a form that determines some indefinite matter. Moreover, there should be a minister who brings the form to the matter, acting as an instrument of God. According to Pope Eugene's *Bull of Union with the Armenians*, therefore, all the sacraments require three components: things as the matter, words as the form, and a minister who acts "with the intention of doing what the church

[76] Q. 1, 228/52–229/11.   [77] Q. 1, 229/12–39.   [78] Q. 1, 229/40–230/9/

does." If any of these is missing, according to the bull, there is no sacrament. But marriage seems to require no form, no matter, and no minister.

Catharinus reviews the standard solutions to such objections, but he finds them wanting. Almost everyone says that the sacramental form of marriage consists of the words by which the spouses express their mutual consent, but the form that determines the matter of any sacrament is a definitive formula prescribed by Christ and passed on by the church: a formula that specifically signifies the reality that the sacrament both signifies and causes. Christian spouses do not need to say anything different from what infidels say to contract a sacramental marriage, and such words do not specifically signify the sacramental effect of marriage. It is true that sacramental words constitute the form only when they are spoken in faith (as Gropper pointed out), but that does not solve the objection, for the words used to establish a marriage are the same among Christians and infidels. Moreover, words are not strictly necessary for marriage. It is absurd to suggest, as Scotus and his followers did, that a deaf or mute person cannot contract a sacramental marriage. Nor does a girl's silence when she is too shy to answer the minister's questions prevent her from contracting the sacrament.[79] Consider what happens when an infidel couple converts to Christianity, or when even one of them does. Their marriage becomes a sacrament without the benefit of any fresh *verbum*.[80]

It is equally difficult to say what is the matter of this sacrament. The objections posed above rule out Richard de Mediavilla's theory, whereby the words of the first partner who speaks comprise the matter, and the other's response is the form. What if the bride is too shy to speak and remains silent?[81] Thomas Aquinas rightly said that in marriage, as in penance, there was no matter besides the acts of the spouses. But since a sacrament is an outward sign that is apparent to the senses, the matter cannot be the spouses' interior acts of consent. It can only be their outward expression of mutual consent, normally in words. But that is the form, and the matter cannot be the same as the form.[82]

Nor need there be any ministering priest or liturgist (*mysta*) in the proper sense, for such assistance is not essential. Nor do we ever say that the spouses *receive* this sacrament. Instead, we say that they make it or perform it. It is absurd to suppose that the spouses themselves are the ministers of the sacrament, for no one can both give and receive the same thing at the same time. Moreover, according to the *Bull of Union with the Armenians*, the spouses would have to intend to do what the church does in the sacrament. Most faithful Christians for centuries did not consider marriage to be a sacrament, and even now many of the faithful do not intend or even understand this, yet all these marriages are valid and sacramental.[83]

Catharinus's solution is radical and unusual. Like Melchor Cano, he argues that the matter of the sacrament is the spouses' expression of mutual consent inasmuch

---

[79] Q. 1, 230/10–231/21, 232/40–233/3.   [80] Q. 1, 231/52–232/2.   [81] Q. 1, 233/46–50.
[82] Q. 1, 233/27–45.   [83] Q. 1, 231/26–232/40.

as it establishes and sanctifies both the bond of marriage between them and their conjugal obligations. In other words, it is their contract, normally expressed in words.[84] But the form, or *verbum*, consists not in the priest's words, as Cano argued, but in the very words that God spoke through Adam, and by which God instituted the sacrament in the beginning: "Because of this a man shall leave his father and his mother, and shall cleave unto his wife, and they shall be two in one flesh" (Gen 2:24).[85] To the objection that these words were spoken but once in the remote past, Catharinus replies that Scripture and the law are perennial and always speak to us. That is why Christ reminded us that what God has joined together, no man should separate.[86] Christ is the source of marriage's sanctity and efficacy, as he is for every other sacrament.

Insofar as there is a minister of this sacrament or a liturgist (*mysta*), therefore, he is God the Father. God "assists" at the sacrament: a liturgical idiom implying active presence. But why is there no human minister in this sacrament, as there is in the others? It is because the other sacraments cannot be effected unless a minister disposes the matter to receive the form. But the matter of marriage is the contract. If the contractants are believers, this matter is already disposed by its very constitution to receive the form, and their marriage will be a means of grace as long as they do not present an obstacle to it.[87] When unbelievers contract marriage, on the contrary, their marriage is only potentially a sacrament – or "habitually," as Thomas puts it. It is not a sacrament yet, but it will become one automatically if they become Christians, or even if only one of them does, for the believer, as St Paul says, will sanctify the unbeliever.[88] The blessing of a priest is not strictly necessary for the sacrament, therefore, although Christian spouses ought to receive the blessing because the priest's words and actions articulate the mystery of marriage.[89] Replying to Erasmus's objection that Dionysius did not include marriage when he discussed the sacraments in *Ecclesiastical Hierarchy*, Catharinus replies that Dionysius was concerned with the sacramental ministry of liturgists, and not with the sacraments *per se*.[90]

According to Pope Eugene's bull, all the sacraments require a minister who intends to what the church does in the sacrament. One might expect Catharinus to solve the problem by proposing that God the Father is the minister of marriage, but the minister of a sacrament in the normal sense is God's instrument or mediator. To say that God is the only minister of marriage, therefore, is to say that there is no minister in the usual sense. Catharinus concedes that marriage is an exception to Pope Eugene's statement, therefore, and this presents him, as a papalist, with a dilemma. Some people respect the pope too much, he concedes, but others too little. The pope is infallible only when he formally defines a matter of dogma, for

---

[84] Q. 1, 233/19–27.   [85] Q. 1, 234/5–10.   [86] Q. 1, 234/11–17   [87] Q. 1, 234/17–44.
[88] Q. 1, 234/51–235/9.   [89] Q. 1, 235/41–45.
[90] Q. 1, 234/44–51. See ibid., 225/34–37, for the objection.

then the faithful should believe his statements as firmly as they believe the Gospel. But when the pope expresses his own opinion, as Eugene did in the *Bull of Union of the Armenians*, he is not infallible. Nevertheless, in these troubled times, when the devil attacks the faithful on every side, it would be rash to say that Pope Eugene made a mistake and said something false. Instead, one should perform what Catharinus calls a "reduction to the truth," accepting the pope's words but interpreting them so as to eliminate any implied error. The problem, then, is that there is no minister of the sacrament of marriage, whereas Pope Eugene said that all the sacraments require a minister. To eliminate the contradiction, one should interpret the word "all" collectively rather than distributively. Just as one cannot avoid all sins but one can avoid any individual sin, so all the sacraments as a class require a minister, but not every one of them considered individually does.[91]

18.3.3 *The sacramental history of marriage*

Many theologians, Catharinus notes, teach that marriage was instituted in Paradise only as an "office of nature," and not as a sacrament, and that it would never have become a sacrament if human beings had not sinned. But Catharinus cannot accept this theory. It is contrary to his view that marriage was holy from the beginning, when God himself joined together and blessed the first parents in marriage, just as he joins all believing couples even now. Adapting that premise to the sacramental theology of marriage, Catharinus argues that marriage was already fully sacramental in the earthly Paradise, where it even conferred grace. That is why St Paul refers to the original institution of marriage when he explains how marriage is a sacrament.[92] It is true that there was no need then for a remedy against concupiscence,[93] but couples would still have needed a "divine blessing" to enable them to sustain their partnership and to sanctify their children. God would have bestowed this assistance through an interior influence that each generation would have passed on to the next: the counterpart of original sin.[94]

One might object that human beings in Paradise would have needed no mediation from material, sensible things, since they would have received spiritual influence immediately from God. Sacraments are in the first place sacred signs. But Catharinus can see no reason why human beings in Paradise should not have learned about God through sensible signs. He concedes that exterior mediation would have been incongruous if the sacraments were instruments of grace through some inherent, quasi-physical property (as sixteenth-century Thomists generally maintained, especially Cardinal Cajetan), but Catherinus can make no sense of the Dominican theory that sacraments are "physical" instrumental causes, and he even ridicules it.[95]

---

[91] Q. 1, 235/46–237/3.   [92] Q. 3, 243/1–26.   [93] Q. 3, 243/31–34.   [94] Q. 3, 245/16–25.
[95] Q. 3, 243/34–38, 243/50–245/2.

If marriage was a sacrament in Eden, it must already have signified the union between Christ and the church. And it seems that Adam himself, speaking as a prophet, was referring to Christ's incarnation when he said: "Because of this a man shall leave his father and his mother," and so forth (Gen 2:24): words that constitute the sacramental form, or *verbum*, of marriage. One might object that Adam could not have foreseen the incarnation of Christ, for he did not foresee his own sin, and Christ became incarnate to save sinners.[96] Catharinus might have replied, following Thomas Aquinas, that Adam could have foreseen the effect without foreseeing its cause, but instead he opts for a theory that the Franciscans favored: that Christ would still have become incarnate even if there had been no sin.[97]

When sin came into the world, marriage ceased to be a sacrament for a while, for "every sacrament presupposes open commerce between human beings and God."[98] Only the matter of the sacrament remained: the merely human contract, which served no worthier end than the "office of nature." This contractual matter, or "marriage itself" (*ipsum matrimonium*), was formless and devoid of the original blessing. But God soon restored the blessing, so that marriage became a sacrament again:

> After sin, however, the matter of the sacrament remained, which is marriage itself, whereas the blessing by which marriage was made to be a sacrament was destroyed. Whenever this blessing is restored, marriage begins to be a sacrament again.[99]

The matter was sufficient to establish the continuity of the institution, but absent the blessing this matter alone could not properly be called "marriage," just as a corpse is only equivocally a human being.[100] Marriage immediately after the fall, therefore, was only a vestige of the marriage that God instituted in Paradise. The Gentiles are witnesses to this vestigial institution. Deprived of the light of faith, they practice concubinage, polygyny, divorce and remarriage, incestuous relationships, and even free promiscuity. Indeed, such is the weakness of unaided human nature that even some of the philosophers and others considered to be wise saw nothing wrong in polygyny (*communitas mulierum*), although in reality it is inconsistent even with human nature and with the office of nature.[101]

Marriage remained in its formless state only until God called his chosen ones to redemption through Jesus Christ, but Catherinus argues that this restoration must have happened soon after the fall. As soon as marriage regained God's word and blessing, it recovered its sacramentality and conferred grace again. But now the supernatural efficacy and sanctity of marriage was primarily remedial. Its purpose was to rescue sexuality from sin and to restore the "undefiled bed" (*thorus immaculatus*).[102]

---

[96] Q. 3, 243/27–30.   [97] Q. 3, 243/43–50.   [98] Q. 4, 246/33–35.   [99] Q. 6, 253/30–34.
[100] Q. 4, 246/18–22: "Sed quodcumque fuisset matrimonium, nullum alium honestiorem habuisset finem, quam in officium naturae: et adhuc nescio an fuisset coniunctio digna matrimonii nomine...."
[101] Q. 4, 246/24–32.   [102] Q. 4, 246/33–247/38. Q. 6, 253/19–30.

Catharinus concedes that the sacraments of the Old Law, which Moses instituted, were merely signs, and that they did not confer the grace that they signified. Such sacraments were practiced out of fear, or as a punishment, or for earthly advantage, and not out of love or as a means of grace. But Catharinus argues that marriage was never one of the sacraments of the Old Law that Moses instituted, for God the Father had instituted it as a sacrament in the beginning. Marriage was already a sacrament of the New Law in the time of the Old Law, since it already conferred a grace derived prospectively from the Passion of Jesus Christ. The same is true of circumcision, which was instituted not by Moses but by Abraham, although ritual circumcision ceased with Christ's advent because baptism superseded it. The great patriarchs whose deeds are recorded in the Old Testament belonged in reality to the New Law and to the New Testament. In other words, they were Christians.[103]

Most theologians, Catharinus notes, hold that the sacraments could not have been efficacious before Christ died because their efficacy depends on the reality of Christ's Passion. An effect may follow its cause temporally or be simultaneous with it, but it cannot precede it.[104] The theologians concede that faith in Christ was sometimes a means of grace even before Christ's advent, but they construe Christ in that case not as the efficient cause of grace but as its final cause, inasmuch as those who received grace before the Passion looked forward to the Passion and desired it.[105] But Catharinus rejects that entire theory, along with the theory of "physical" causality that it presupposes. Instead, he espouses the theory of moral causality, which the Franciscans favored. If marriage was not truly a sacrament before Christ's Passion, then Mary and Joseph would not have been sacramentally married when Mary conceived Jesus, which is unthinkable.[106] Worse, Christ's own baptism would not have been a true sacrament, since his Passion had not yet occurred.[107] Nor does Catharinus accept that Christ or his Passion before Christ's advent was only a final cause of grace.[108] Instead, he argues that Christ and his Passion were already efficacious before Christ's advent. How can that be? Partly because God transcends time, but chiefly because the mode of efficient causality involved is that of merit, and not that of physical causality. God foresaw from the beginning that human beings would sin, and that Christ would merit their salvation.[109] There is no reason, therefore, why the faithful should not have benefitted from Christ's merit even before Christ became incarnate, provided only that they had at least implicit faith in Christ-to-come. The names of the elect are "written in the book of life of the Lamb, which was slain from the beginning of the world" (Apoc 13:8).[110]

Rather than positing two or more institutions of marriage, therefore, as the scholastic theologians had done, Catharinus posits a single institution in Eden followed by several successive restorations (*instaurationes*). Each restoration follows

---

[103] Q. 5, 251/15–54. [104] Q. 5, 247/50–248/7. [105] Q. 5, 248/7–19. [106] Q. 6, 252/28–40.
[107] Q. 5, 248/20–32. [108] Q. 6, 249/34–55. [109] Q. 5, 248/53–249/18. [110] Q. 5, 249/19–34.

a lapse and restores the divine benediction. Catharinus searches Scripture for evidence of these restorations, and some his instances are puzzling. The first is recorded immediately after the fall, in Genesis 3:16–18, when God told the woman that he would make her suffer pain in giving birth and that she would be subservient to her husband, and when God said to the man, "cursed is the ground for thy sake." These words, Catharinus observes, "can be applied very appropriately to marriage" (*"quae quidem verba aptissime ad matrimonium accomodantur"*). Catharinus finds further evidence of a restoration in Genesis 4:1, where Eve, after giving birth to Cain, says, "I have begotten a man through the Lord." Again, a restoration is recorded in Genesis 9:1, after the flood, when God repeated the blessing of Genesis 1:28, exhorting human beings to be fruitful and multiply. What of the New Testament? One might suppose that Jesus restored marriage when he said, "What God has joined together, let man not separate," but Catharinus points out that Jesus was reminding his audience of the original institution of marriage, and not establishing anything new. Instead, Catharinus finds the restoration of the sacrament at Cana (John 2), where Christ turned water into wine. The water signified people who had grown spiritually unstable and "insipid" and who lacked grace. Christ chose a wedding as the setting for the first of his miracles because, as the Son of God, he had been with the Father in the beginning and was coauthor of marriage. The feast-master (the *architriclinus* of John 2:8) signifies the pope, whose task it is to make sure that the people have the "good wine" of the true faith to drink.[111]

Catharinus agrees with Luther, Bucer, and Brenz that God does not join together couples who marry clandestinely – or, more precisely, without their parents' consent. His rationale, however, is based on sacramental theology. Such unions are immoral and contrary to divine law, and the partners manifest their lack of filial piety and show contempt for God. These marriages do not receive the sacramental blessing from God, yet not because the error vitiates the sacramentality of marriage *per se* or because some essential component of the sacrament is lacking, but rather because the sin puts a moral obstacle in the way, preventing the reception of grace *ex opere operato* (Section 19.9.2).

18.3.4 *Indissolubility and sacramentality*

Is marriage already a sacrament before the spouses are carnally united through intercourse? This was old question, albeit one no longer the subject of extensive inquiry or debate during the sixteenth century. Catharinus's attempt to answer it leads him to take a fresh look at the relationship between sacramentality and indissolubility. Catharinus proposes two chief theses: first, that marriage is a sacrament even before it is consummated; second, that such a marriage still does not have

---

[111] Q. 6, 253–55.

absolute indissolubility.[112] But his discussion is difficult to follow, and some of his arguments seem half-formed or self-undermining.

He begins by posing two problems. First, the doctrine of marriage as a sacrament, which is predicated on Paul's treatment of marriage in Ephesians 5, presupposes that marriage is a sign of Christ and the church. The sacramentality of marriage is based on this signification. But surely what properly signifies that union is the joining of "two in one flesh" (Eph 5:32), which is established through sexual intercourse.[113] Second, the theologians hold that the sacramentality of marriage is coextensive with and even derived from its absolute indissolubility (*indissolubilitas omnimoda*). If marriage is a sacrament even before intercourse, therefore, it must already be "entirely indissoluble and indispensable." But marriage before intercourse is dissolved automatically (*ipso iure*) by the entry of either spouse into the religious life. Moreover, some of the canonists hold that the pope has the power to dissolve a marriage before (but not after) intercourse, and Cardinal Cajetan was of the same opinion. Whether the pope had such a power of dispensation was still controversial in Catharinus's day, but in his view that debate was no longer relevant because some of the popes, including Martin V, Eugene IV, and Alexander VI, had in fact exercised the power, as recorded in the official *regesta*.[114] As a staunch papalist, he could not accept that these pontiffs had erred.

Does Catharinus himself agree or disagree with the theologians' premise that indissolubility and sacramentality are coextensive? In fact, he contradicts himself, and I can see no way to resolve the contradiction. In the chapter on marriage before intercourse, he teases the two aspects of marriage apart. He points out in an *ad hominem* argument that those who hold, contrary to his own view, that marriage was not a sacrament during the era of the Old Law are logically compelled to hold, as he does, that the indissolubility of marriage does not depend on its sacramentality, for marriage was indissoluble, Catharinus maintains, even then:

> If, therefore, marriage was not a sacrament before the advent of Christ, but it had, nonetheless, absolute indissolubility, as the Lord confirms, it should then be clear that indissolubility — even the absolute indissolubility that is not capable of dispensation — would proceed not from the power of marriage as a sacrament but from its nature, and above all from its divine institution. But I have said this only in passing, not as if I meant to hold that marriage was not a sacrament before the advent of Christ, as some teach. Rather, I meant to show that those who do hold that position are forced not to attribute indissolubility, even absolute indissolubility, to the sacrament: which, nevertheless, they do.[115]

---

[112] Q. 2, 239/53–240/1: ". . . duas ponimus circa praedictam conclusiones. Prima est, matrimonium etiam ante copulam esse sacramentum. Secunda est, etsi matrimonium illud fit sacramentum, non habere tamen omnimodam indissolubilitatem."

[113] Q. 2, 237/6–13, 37–47.   [114] Q. 2, 237/14–25.   [115] Q. 2, 239/23–34.

But when Catharinus demonstrates in a later chapter that marriage was a sacrament under the Old Law, he assumes that the premise is true: that the indissolubility is derived from or coextensive with its sacramentality. Since marriage was indissoluble during the era of the Old Law, he argues, then either (i) marriage was a sacrament then or (ii) it derived its indissolubility both then and now from some other cause. But the second hypothesis is not credible:

> Therefore, if marriage had been a sacrament only after the advent of Christ, it is clear that either marriage would not have been entirely indissoluble [*omnino indissolubilis*] before the advent, since it was not a sacrament; or, if perhaps it was indissoluble, that it would have been so for some other reason than because it was a sacrament, and the same would be true even now; which, however, is not conceded.[116]

Catharinus could consistently maintain that the sacramentality of marriage is a necessary but not a sufficient reason for indissolubility, but he would still contradict himself. What he affirms in the second passage cited earlier (on the sacramentality of marriage during the era of the Old Law) is exactly what he denies in the earlier chapter (on the sacramentality of marriage before intercourse), namely, that indissolubility is not derived from or coextensive with sacramentality.

Nevertheless, Catharinus makes some interesting and cogent points in the chapter on marriage before intercourse, where he subjects some traditional assumptions and arguments to effective criticism. By focusing on what Catharinus explicitly affirms, and by skirting around some of the more difficult features of his discussion, one can see that he formulates a position that is both coherent and subtle. God instituted marriage in the beginning, Catharinus argues, as a union that was entirely indissoluble (*omnino indissolubilis*), or that had absolute indissolubility (*indissolubilitas omnimoda*). This permanence cannot be abrogated under any circumstances as long as both spouses are alive, not even by a papal dispensation. Marriage is absolutely indissoluble because God instituted it thus in the beginning, when he spoke the words of institution through Adam (Gen 2:24) and joined Adam and Eve together in marriage. Jesus reminded his listeners of that institution when he said: "What God has joined together, let not man separate" (Matt 19:6), explaining that husband and wife are no longer two, but one flesh.

The notion of absolute indissolubility presupposes that there might be a non-absolute, or "not quite" indissolubility. Now, to posit an indissolubility that is less than absolute may seem to be an oxymoron, but theologians and canonists had been implying that there was such a thing since the twelfth century. Catharinus does a better job than most of articulating and explaining how indissolubility can be

---

[116] Q. 5, 252/7–13 : "Si ergo matrimonium esset sacramentum solummodo post Christi adventum: certe aut non fuisset ante adventum omnino indissolubile matrimonium, cum sacramentum non esset: aut si forte fuisset indissolubile, ex alia causa fuisset, et simili modo etiam nunc esset, quam quia sacramentum: quod tamen non conceditur."

incomplete or soluble. Although marriage passed through a relatively formless condition immediately after the fall, because of the loss of the original blessing, it still retained a certain natural indissolubility: a shadow of the real thing. The pagan jurists recognized this indissolubility when they defined marriage as an "indivisible way of life."[117] Moreover, the goods of procreation and fidelity are universally recognized, and divorce is inconsistent with them.[118] To be sure, the utilitarian reasons for indissolubility may not apply in particular cases, but laws are made to regulate what happens often, or in the majority of cases, and not what happens always. The wise consider the permanent natures of things, and not what happens occasionally.[119] Civil law permits divorce and remarriage on specific grounds, therefore, but only to avoid worse evils and scandals, and because human reason alone cannot discern the higher standard that prohibits divorce and remarriage entirely. Only through the light of revealed divine law can human beings perceive and reaffirm the absolute indissolubility of marriage.[120] One reason for holding that the indissolubility of marriage does not depend on its sacramentality, therefore, is that marriage is indissoluble by its very nature, for it retains its indissolubility even when it has ceased to be a sacrament, although natural human reason cannot fully perceive that quality.[121] Permission to divorce under the Mosaic law, according to Catharinus, was a concession of a quite different sort. By explaining that Moses permitted divorce because of men's "hardness of heart" (Matt 19:8), Jesus implied that Moses, who knew the divine law, was permitting the Israelites to do something that he knew was prohibited by divine law. In fact, marriage was absolutely indissoluble even under the Old Law.[122] In short, marriage among infidels is not a sacrament, and it is indissoluble but not absolutely so. Marriage among the Jews of the Old Covenant was both a sacrament and absolutely indissoluble, as it is among Christians, although only Christians fully recognize and observe that absolute indissolubility.

Catharinus's chief reasons for denying that the indissolubility of marriage derives from its sacramentality pertain to the signification of marriage, since any sacrament is in the first place a sacred sign. Some theologians argue that marriage before intercourse is soluble because it signifies a soluble union, such as that between Christ and the individual soul, whereas marriage after intercourse is indissoluble because it signifies an indissoluble union, such as that between Christ and the

---

[117] Q. 2, 238/41–54.   [118] Q. 2, 239/18–20.

[119] Q. 2, 239/20–23: "Licet autem in particularibus coniugiis cessare possit haec ratio, leges tamen ad id quod frequenter accidit aptari solent: quoniam rei naturam speculabantur sapientes, non autem quod interdum contingit."

[120] Q. 2, 238/54–239/8, 239/35–41.

[121] Q. 2, 238/41–46: "Primum ergo constituendum esse mihi videtur, indissolubilitatem matrimonii, absolute loquendo, non inde venire quia ipsum matrimonium sit sacramentum significans illam copulam Christi cum ecclesia. Nam matrimonium absolute et suapte natura id habet ut sit indissolubile."

[122] Q. 2, 239/9–13. Q. 5, 251/55–252/2.

church. As we have seen, this was a common way to explain the Privilege of Religion (Section 14.3.1). But Catharinus shows that the similarities between signifier and signified are not adequate to support the rationale. Whereas the union between the individual Christian and Christ is dissolved by the individual's sin, for example, the spouse who enters the religious life before consummation does not sin but rather advances in goodness. Again, whereas the separation comes from one side alone in the signified union, it can come from either side in the human signifier. And whereas the separation between the soul and Christ through sin is reparable, the separation brought about by entry into the religious life is irrevocable. Finally, whereas the pope may dissolve an unconsummated marriage on many grounds, sin alone separates the soul from Christ.[123]

Catharinus rejects the double analogy rationale, therefore, but he accepts the alternative rationale: that entry into the religious is a spiritual death (Section 14.3.2). This death brings about the end of a merely spiritual marriage, whereas only carnal death can terminate a carnal marriage.[124] He also proposes an alternative theory of signification, which he finds more plausible. On this view, marriage before intercourse signifies the union of Christians with Christ in this world through grace, a union that "has the promise of future perfection through glory," whereas marriage after intercourse signifies the union between Christ and his faithful that will exist after the resurrection. While the former union is not "entirely indissoluble," at least in individuals, the latter will be everlasting in everyone.[125]

The purpose or gist of these complicated arguments is not entirely obvious. Catharinus intends to show that marriage signifies Christ and the church even before consummation, and, therefore, that nothing prevents it from being a sacrament then.[126] Thus, he points out that Paul did not propose that the relevant signification of marriage existed only after sexual intercourse, since much of the signification that Paul had in mind was peculiar to the manner of Eve's formation from Adam. But since, as Catharinus next observes, this signification belongs uniquely to the first couple, its relevance to the case he is defending is unclear.[127]

The strongest reason for indissolubility, according to Catharinus, lies in the divine institution of marriage in the beginning, which is a matter of revealed divine law. Natural reason is not able to perceive the absolute indissolubility of marriage, for it considers marriage only as an "office of nature," whereas God ordained from the beginning that marriage is also a sacrament:

> ... divorce would have been permissible, it seems to me, if we were not instructed by the law of God but instead had considered natural reason alone. For absolute indissolubility [*omnimoda indissolubilitas*] is from divine law, and not only from

---

[123] Q. 2, 238/2–40.   [124] Q. 2, 240/20–32.   [125] Q. 2, 240/37–47.
[126] Q. 2, 240/8–10: "... dicimus, matrimonium ante carnalem copulam significare coniunctionem Christi cum Ecclesia tua."
[127] Q. 2, 240/48–241/6.

natural law, since God himself joined male and female: a thing that no human reasoning is able to infer. For he joined them not only for the office of nature, but also so that offspring should be begotten for himself in another life, and accordingly so that marriage should be a sacrament.[128]

Sacramentality and indissolubility are closely linked, therefore, but they are not entirely coextensive, and indissolubility is not a consequence of sacramentality. Instead, it depends directly on God's word:

> Even if that marriage [before sexual intercourse] is a sacrament, nevertheless, it does not have absolute indissolubility. The reason for this is that the absolute indissolubility of marriage comes not from the sacrament but from the word of God, and what the word of God made indissoluble was marriage that has been consummated through sexual intercourse.[129]

The same words that constitute of the form or blessing of marriage are also a statement of law: "Because of this, a man shall leave his father and mother and cleave unto his wife, and the two shall be one flesh." God decreed through these words that marriage would be become absolutely indissoluble only through consummation, when the partners become in the fullest sense "one flesh." In Catherinus's view, therefore, indissolubility and sacramentality are independent concomitants, which run as if along parallel historical tracks.

18.3.5 *Summary*

Notwithstanding some obscure points and some inconsistencies, Catharinus proposed a coherent, legally informed account of the sacramentality of marriage.

The sacrament of marriage presupposes an underlying natural union. This union is inscribed in the natural law and elaborated in Roman civil law. Nevertheless, it is above all a matter of divine law, for God instituted marriage in the beginning by making Eve from Adam and by bringing her to him as his wife.

Indissolubility is rooted in this natural partnership, but it depends, too, on the revealed divine law of marriage. Catharinus attributes absolute indissolubility (*indissolubilitas omnimoda*) to a divine law that is known only through revelation. Indissolubility and sacramentality are related and largely coextensive, but indissolubility does not depend on sacramentality but on revealed divine law alone. There is nothing to prevent a fully sacramental marriage from being dissolved if the divine law permits the dissolution, as it does in some cases of non-consummated marriage.

The sacramentality of marriage consists chiefly in a supernatural blessing, which enables the spouses to sustain the demands of marriage and to overcome the moral defects attached to the sexual act. God instituted the sacrament, too, in the beginning, and not, as most theologians assumed, in the Gospel, or after the advent of

---

[128] Q. 2, 239/43–51.   [129] Q. 2, 239/55–240/4.

Jesus Christ. The matter of the sacrament is the underlying contract, and its formal *verbum* is Adam's prophetic dictum, which St Paul invoked in Ephesians 5:32. The sacramental blessing was lost when Adam and Eve sinned, but it was restored later, and the cycle of loss and restoration has recurred at several points in sacred history. The most complete restoration occurred during the marriage at Cana, when Christ turned the water of human instability and coldness into the wine and warmth of the Gospel. The sacrament of marriage requires no minister in the usual sense, for the minister's job is to dispose the matter to receive the form, and in this case the material contract is already predisposed to receive the form. Insofar as there is a minister, however, he is God the Father, who joins each couple together now as he did in Eden.

18.4 TRENT, 1563

Work on the sacraments began again at Trent during the second phase (1551–1552), but the council did not get to the sacrament of marriage before it was suspended. Session XIII (Oct. 11, 1551) published the principal decree on the sacrament of eucharist. Session XIV (Nov. 25, 1551) published decrees on the sacraments of penance and extreme unction.[130] The publication of decrees was suspended on January 25 at Session XV. The aim was to give Protestant representatives more time to come to the council. The council granted them safe passage but warned that they would be welcome only if they came to learn the will of the universal church, and not to attack the church. Hope of reconciliation was fading by this time. It had become clear that Catholics and Protestants had passed a decisive parting of the ways, even though they shared many desires for reform.[131] Assuming that the prelates would continue to deliberate in general congregations meanwhile, the council at Session XV announced that the next Session, scheduled for March 19, 1552, would include decrees on the sacrament of marriage, as well as on some matters of general ecclesiastical reform.[132] But proceedings came to a halt when the council was prorogued on April 28, 1552.

Marriage returned to the agenda during the third phase on March 11, 1562, when Cardinal Gonzaga as the chief legate put before the prelates twelve articles on questions of reform.[133] Most were about reform of the clergy, but two were on clandestine marriage.[134] The same questions on clandestine marriage were

[130] See Tanner-Alberigo, 693–98 (on eucharist), and 703–13 (on penance and extreme unction).
[131] O'Malley, *Trent*, 157–58.
[132] Tanner-Alberigo, 719/24–27. CT 7.1:474, 494/19–21: "Interea vero de matrimonii sacramento agendum et de eo praeter superiorum decretorum publicationem definiendum esse eadem sessione statuit et decernit, et prosequendam esse materiam reformationis." The first mention of these decisions came at the close of a general congregation on the evening of previous day, Jan. 24, CT 7.1:474/49–50: "Et decernitur subsequentem indicandam ad festum divi Iosephi, quod erit 19. mensis Martii, et in ea praeter alia agendum esse de sacramento matrimonii."
[133] CT 8:378–79.   [134] Cap. 10–11, ibid., 379/3–5.

reformulated for consideration by the *theologi minores* on March 13,[135] but there seems to have been no formal discussion of marriage during 1562. The two articles on clandestine marriage were mentioned on April 17 and 21 of that year, but only as matters that would have to be handled later.[136] The proceedings on marriage began in February, 1563.

18.4.1 Theologi minores

On February 3, 1563, Cardinal Gonzaga announced that the council would be prorogued until April 22, but that meanwhile the *theologi minores* would dispute certain articles pertaining to the sacrament of marriage, while the prelates would discuss the reform of abuses pertaining to the sacrament of orders. The *theologi minores* would meet in the mornings, and the prelates later in each day, in the hope that council would soon be brought to a conclusion.[137] This arrangement left the prelates, who were then discussing reform of the sacrament of orders, free to attend the *congregationes theologorum* as auditors during the mornings. Eight articles summarizing the chief heretical or questionable positions on marriage held by the Protestants were put before the theologians on February 4.[138]

The legates divided the sixty-two available theologians into four "classes," assigning two articles to each class. The classes met sequentially, albeit in a different order : the first class from February 9 through 16, the second from February 17 through 25, the fourth from February 26 though March 2, and the third from March 4 through 22. The two articles assigned to the first class were about marriage as a sacrament and clandestine marriages respectively. To the second class were assigned articles on divorce and polygamy. The third was given an article proposing that marriage was preferable to celibacy and that God gave more grace to married folk than to others, as well as an article on the marriage of priests. The theologians of the fourth class were to consider the impediments. According to the first of their two articles, the impediments of consanguinity and affinity should be limited to those of the Leviticus code. The second article included two propositions: that the only diriment impediments to marriage (besides those of consanguinity and affinity) were those of impotence and "ignorance of the contract"; and that matrimonial cases were subject to the jurisdiction of secular rulers (*"causasque matrimonii spectare ad principes saeculares"*).[139]

I shall focus here on the work of the first class,[140] which comprised fifteen theologians: six Spaniards, two Portuguese, four Frenchmen, and three Italians. Theirs would be the liveliest and most fruitful discussion, chiefly because of the subject matter, but perhaps also because of the superior caliber of the theologians. The most distinguished among them was the Spanish Jesuit Alfonso Salmerón, a

---

[135] Ibid., 379/14–17.   [136] CT 8:458/41–44 and 465/15–18.   [137] CT 9:376/9–21.
[138] Ibid., 380–81.   [139] 380.   [140] 382–89, 395–408.

biblical scholar and a companion of Ignatius Loyola, who was present as a papal theologian. Four of this class were friars: Pedro Fernández, a Dominican appointed to the council by Philip II of Spain; Antonius de Gragnano, a Conventual Franciscan; Aloysius de Burgo Novo, an Observant Franciscan; and Taddeo da Perugia, an Augustinian Hermit who was attending as advisor to the bishop of Saint-Papoul. Four were secular clerics from Spain: Pedro Mercado (advisor to Acisclo de Moya y Contreras, bishop of Vic),[141] Joannes del Gado (who was representing the bishop of Tuy in his absence), and Cosme-Damian Hortolà (Hortolanus) and Ferdinando de Bellosillo (both of whom had been appointed to the council by Philip II).[142] Two were secular clerics from Portugal: Antonius Leytanus, who accompanied the bishop of Coimbra, and Diego Andrada de Payva, whom King Sebastian had appointed to the council. There were also four secular masters of theology from the university of Paris: Nicholas Maillard, Nicholas de Brys, Antonius Coquier, and Simon Vigor (who would later become archbishop of Narbonne). These were all learned theologians, familiar with the works of the great medieval schoolmen, whom they cited frequently but not always accurately, apparently from memory. All but two of them were open to the possibility of invalidating clandestine marriage henceforth: an indication of a shift that had been taking place since around 1550. Antonius de Gragnano and Antonius Coquier, on the contrary, maintained that the church did not have the power to render clandestine marriages null and void.

The first of their two articles was a summary of Luther's contentions in his *Babylonian Captivity*:

> That marriage is not a sacrament instituted by God but rather was introduced into the church by human beings, and that it does not have the promise of grace.[143]

According to Luther, a sacrament was by definition a divinely instituted sign that had a divine promise attached to it. But Scripture provided no reason to believe, Luther argued, either that marriage had been divinely instituted to signify something, or that anyone had ever received grace by marrying (Sections 17.3.1 and 17.3.3). The theologians considered Luther's position to be unacceptable and even heretical.[144] Marriage was a sacrament in the proper sense, and it conferred grace.[145]

---

[141] 381/10: "Petrus Morcattus cler. saec. Hispanus, cum ep. Vicensi." Acisclo de Moya y Contreras is listed among those who attended Session XXIII, but he was apparently not present during the proceedings of Session XXIV. The "ep. Vicensis" who took part in the latter was Domenico Casablanca, O.P., bishop of Vico Equense in Italy.

[142] Whether absent prelates were entitled to commission others to represent them had been a matter of debate, the outcome of which was that representatives could attend and speak at general congregations, but that they had no vote.

[143] CT 9:380/3–4: "Matrimonium non esse sacramentum a Deo institutum, sed ab hominibus in ecclesiam inventum, nec habere promissionem gratiae."

[144] Alphonsus Salmeron, 382/34–35: "Primus igitur articulus haereticus est."

[145] E.g., Nicolaus Maillard, 386/34–35: "Matrimonium igitur est sacramentum a Deo institutum et gratiam confert."

But what was the evidence for the Catholic doctrine? What texts from Scripture could be cited as proof? Mindful of the arguments of Erasmus and Luther, the theologians reviewed the biblical supports cautiously. They regarded Ephesians 5:32 as a crucial text, and some maintained that the word *sacramentum* in the verse denoted marriage as one of the sacraments, notwithstanding the range of senses attached to *mystērion* in the original Greek.[146] Nevertheless, most of the theologians accepted that this verse by itself was not sufficient proof that marriage was a sacrament in the relevant sense. Only Taddeo da Perugia held that Ephesians 5:32 was a sufficient proof text by itself, and his argument rested not on Paul's use of the word *sacramentum* but on an analysis showing that the verse expressed "everything required" for marriage as a sacrament, that is, both the sign and the sacred reality that it signified.[147]

Rather than citing Ephesians 5:32 in isolation, therefore, the theologians built up a dossier of texts, citing especially Genesis 1:28, Hebrews 13:4, 1 Timothy 2:15, 1 Thessalonians 4:4, and Ephesians 5:22–33, which they considering in light of the patristic and medieval authorities, papal decretals, and conciliar decrees. According to Salmerón, it was not Ephesians 5:32 by itself that sufficed as proof, but rather verses 25 and 32 considered together, and then only if one interpreted them in light of Paul's use of Genesis and with the corroboration of papal decretals, conciliar decrees, and patristic writings.[148] Similarly, Nicholas Maillard held that Ephesians 5:32 was the key text, but he too conceded that it was not sufficient proof by itself. The crux of the issue, according to Maillard, was whether marriage was a sacrament under divine law as well as according to the church's human law. Now, there are three possible reasons for affirming that a premise belongs to the divine law: because Scripture explicitly says so; because it is a necessary consequence of what Scripture explicitly says; or because the decrees of sacred councils have established the premise as a dogma. To illustrate proof of the second sort, Maillard pointed out that because Scripture says that Christ had a body and blood, one may affirm on the basis of Scripture alone that Christ must have had blood vessels. Maillard concedes that one cannot prove in the first way that marriage is a sacrament in the proper sense or that it confers grace, for Scripture does not say so explicitly. But one can prove the doctrine in the second way as well as in the third. Marriage would not adequately signify the joining of Christ and the church (Eph 5:25, 32) unless it conferred grace, as the other six sacraments do. Marriage is not a "dead sign," as were the sacraments of the Old Law. Rather, it receives living efficacy from Christ's Passion, as do the other sacraments of the New Law. Again, marriage could not result in a "bed undefiled" (Heb 13:4) "if the contractants were in mortal sin and without grace."[149]

---

[146] Alphonsus Salmeron, 383/22–24. Simon Vigor, 395/33–36.
[147] Thaddaeus Perusinus, 408/24–32.   [148] Alphonsus Salmeron, 382/35–384/5.
[149] Nicolaus Maillard, 386/7–12.

Like Salmerón and Maillard, Ferdinando de Bellosillo emphasized the importance of tradition as a guide to the interpretation of Scripture. He conceded that Scripture did not explicitly say that marriage was a sacrament or that it conferred grace, but he pointed out that Scripture did not explicitly say that baptism was a sacrament either. We know that such propositions are true only thanks to the traditions of the Apostles and of the church, which show us how to interpret Scripture.[150]

The theologians explored how one might use rational arguments to tease out the implications of Scripture. According to Cosme-Damian Hortolà, the Protestants define a sacrament as a divinely mandated rite, composed of certain ceremonies, to which a promise of grace is attached. But that definition fits marriage, Hortolà argues, for marriage was divinely mandated in Genesis 1:28 and in 1 Corinthians 7:9, and God would not mandate a way of life without promising some "eternal grace" to support it.[151] One may arrive at the same result, Hortolà argues, by beginning with a traditional Catholic definition, for example, that a sacrament is a sign of a sacred reality, or the visible appearance of an invisible grace. Marriage could not be an adequate sign of Christ's joining with the church unless the spouses loved each other in mutual spiritual friendship, and they could not do that without grace. Nor could their marriage result in the "undefiled bed" of Hebrews 13:4 without grace. Hortolà invokes the Song of Songs to depict the spiritual friendship in marriage.[152]

Several other theologians argued that God must have given Christians the grace to fulfill their marriages in a fitting and holy way. How else would God do that than by bestowing a sacramental grace? Thus, Antonius Coquier argues that without grace the husband could not love his wife as Christ loves the church, which is what Paul demands (Eph 5:25). It stands to reason that Christ must have given Christian spouses the means to do what he demanded and to follow his example.[153] Similarly, Antonius de Gragnano, echoing Thomas Aquinas, argues that God does not impose heavy burdens without also bestowing the grace to bear them: "Where there is laborious work, it is fitting that God should bestow grace, which comes through a sacrament."[154] Gragnano concedes that Ephesians 5:32 suffices to prove only that marriage is a sign of Christ's joining with the church, and not that it is a sacrament in the proper sense. Nevertheless, the authority of the church entitles us to take that extra step, which is predicated on Matthew 19:6: "What God has joined together, let not man separate." What God himself "joins together" in the sacrament is not so much the contract as the grace that unites the spouses.[155]

Most of the theologians maintained that Jesus Christ had personally instituted marriage as a sacrament of the New Law.[156] Ferdinando de Bellosillo refuted the

---

[150] Ferdinandus de Bellosillo, 403/41–44.
[151] Cosmas et Damianus Ortolanus, 387/28–388/2.   [152] Idem, 388/2–33.
[153] Antonius Cochier, 398/18–21.   [154] Antonius de Gragnano, 407/12–13.
[155] Idem, 407/16–22.
[156] Cosmas et Damianus Ortolanus, 388/1–2. But Nicolaus Maillard, 386/31–35, finds the institution of the sacrament in Gen 1:28.

Protestant contention that Christ had only restored marriage to its pristine condition, without raising it to the level of a sacrament.[157] Antonius de Gragnano affirmed, against Luther, both that Christ instituted marriage and that marriage carried the promise of grace. Gragnano questioned whether marriage conferred a "greater grace" under the New Law than it had under the Old, but he held, nonetheless, that marriage had been instituted under that law and, therefore, was a sacrament of the New Law. The benediction recorded in Genesis 1:28, he argued, was not the institution of marriage precisely *as a sacrament*, for although God's blessing was itself supernatural, what it referred to was something natural that all animals shared, namely, procreation.[158] Simon Vigor took as his point of departure the Protestant thesis that a sacrament was a sign instituted by God that held the promise of grace. Adam's monologue in Genesis 2:24 marked the original institution of marriage, Simon Vigor argued, but marriage had become a sacrament of the New Law through a "new promulgation by Christ," which established the promise of grace.[159]

The theologians discussed the composition of marriage as a sacrament, especially its matter, form, and minister. They agreed that it was possible to identify these aspects of marriage, and that the objections of Durandus and of the Protestants regarding the composition of marriage were soluble. Nevertheless, there was little unanimity among them as to what the matter, form, and minister of marriage were.

Salmerón argued, with Durandus in mind, that marriage had matter, form, and minister in its own peculiar manner. That was only to be expected, for although marriage belonged univocally in the genus of the seven sacraments, it differed specifically from the others. Salmerón proposed that the matter of marriage was the handclasp and the giving of a ring – a thesis that he attributed, oddly enough, to Thomas Aquinas.[160] The form was the words by which the spouses expressed their mutual consent, or whatever other signs they used in place of words. The priest's blessing was not the form of the sacrament but only a sacramental. He also argued that even a marriage contracted through intermediaries was a true sacrament. As to the old objection that the financial negotiations and settlements surrounding a marriage would amount to simony if marriage were a sacrament, Salmerón replied that wealth of that sort was not given in exchange for the sacrament but rather to enable the couple "to sustain the burdens of marriage, as when a consecrated chalice is sold, or a priest contracts to fulfill his office."[161]

Most of theologians accepted that marriage itself conferred grace, regardless of whether or not the spouses received the priestly blessing. As Antonius Coquier puts

---

[157] Ferdinandus de Bellosillo, 403/35–39.   [158] Antonius de Gragnano, 407/3–4, 24–28.
[159] Simon Vigor, 395/19–396/24.
[160] Cf. Thomas Aquinas, *IV Sent.* 26.2.1, ad 2 (72a), where Thomas argues that because the sacrament of marriage, like penance, is caused "by the act of the one who uses the sacrament," there is no other matter than "the very acts that are apparent to the senses," which take the place of a material element. But Thomas is presumably referring to the mutual expression of consent.
[161] Alphonsus Salmeron, 384/6–18.

it, "the blessing of a priest does not constitute the sacrament."[162] On this view, the spouses' expression of their consent was the form of the sacrament. But two theologians, Pedro Fernández and Simon Vigor, considered the priestly blessing essential to the sacrament of marriage. Their analysis was similar to Melchor Cano's. According to Pedro Fernández, the consent of the spouses establishes only a "contract of nature," whereas marriage as a sacrament receives in addition a certain sanctity from "Christian law" through the blessing of a priest, just as baptism includes a cleansing of the soul over and above the physical act of ablution. The priest is the minister of the sacrament, and the formula with which he blesses the union – *"Ego vos coniungo"* etc. – is its form. The spouses' exchange of consent is not the form of the sacrament, therefore, but its matter. Fernández adduces several supporting arguments. If the words of the spouses constituted the form, they would be prescribed and invariable, but in fact consent can be expressed in many ways. Again, the sacraments of the New Law are "ceremonies of a certain religion, by which we worship God." Clearly, marriage has those characteristics solely by virtue of the priestly blessing. Again, only a priest can administer sacred things, by virtue of the "supernatural power" of his office. No "profane" person can do. That is why the priest blesses the couple in the Roman nuptial rite with the words, "And I, by the power of the church invested in me, join you together." Fernández is referring to the *Liber sacerdotalis* by Alberto Castellani (Section 17.6.4).[163] Fernández claims, too, that Council of Cologne decreed that marriage without the priestly blessing was not a sacrament of the New Law. He must have been thinking of Johann Gropper, whose treatise on marriage was often conflated with the Cologne proceedings, to which it was appended. Fernández suggests that Thomas Aquinas seems to have held the same opinion.[164]

Like Fernández, Simon Vigor argues that the form of the sacrament consists of the words spoken by the priest, who is the minister of the sacrament, whereas the spouses' words of consent constitute the matter. Simon Vigor concedes that a marriage may be validly contracted without the priestly blessing, but he argues that such a marriage is a mere contract and does not confer grace. Although marriage is indissoluble even as a contract, it confers grace by virtue of the priest's blessing. Without it, the union is not a true marriage (*matrimonium verum*), although it is a valid marriage. Indeed, even a clandestine marriage between free persons is valid, for it is contrary neither to the law of nature nor even to the divine law but only to human law.[165]

---

[162] Antonius Cochier, 398/5: "benedictio sacerdotis non constituit sacramentum."

[163] "Et ego auctoritate ecclesiae qua fungor coniungo vos." See A. Duval, "La formule Ego vos in matrimonium conjungo … au Concile de Trente," *La Maison-Dieu* 99 (1969): 144–53, at 145–146n8.

[164] Pedro Fernández, 405/9–23, 405/26–406/6. The record includes some citations to Thomas's *Scriptum* and *Summa contra gentiles*, but they do not make sense. Fernández may have had in mind *Summa contra gentiles* IV.78 (Leonine 15:246), where Thomas argues that priests bless marriage because like all sacraments it is "dispensed to the people by the ministers of the church."

[165] Simon Vigor, 396/24–397/13

Regardless of their diverse positions on the matter, form, or minister of marriage, all the theologians agreed that some distinction should be made between the contract and the sacrament. Thus, Salmerón, who identified the form of marriage with the spouses' exchange of consent, pointed out that both the contract by which the spouses gave themselves to each other and the bond (*vinculum*) or joining (*coniunctio*) that resulted from the contract belonged to the law of nature and could not be identified with the sacrament. The contract of marriage existed among all peoples, whereas the sacrament existed only among believers. Marriage became a sacrament, over and above the contract, inasmuch as it consisted of "sensible signs ordained by God to confer grace."[166]

18.4.2 *The general congregations*

On June 21, the legates commissioned thirteen prelates to draft the decrees on the sacrament of marriage: seven Italians, two Spanish, two French, one Portuguese, and one Croatian. Pedro Guerrero, archbishop of Granada, was one of the Spaniards.[167] The legates put the commission's first draft of these decrees before the council on July 20, 1563. The draft underwent three revisions during the course of their deliberations, the last of which became the council's formal declaration on marriage, made at the twenty-fourth session on November 11. As usual, the dogmatic canons came first in each draft, followed by the decrees on reformation. The former, as statements of truth, were in principle universal and inalterable, whereas the disciplinary rulings were alterable, and they would be binding only where they were promulgated. The proceedings were fraught and protracted, largely because of irreconcilable differences over clandestine marriage.[168]

18.4.2.1 *The four drafts*

A conspectus of the phases of these proceedings will provide some context for what follows:

- The first draft, presented to the council on July 20, consisted of eleven dogmatic canons and decree on the reform of clandestine marriages. Voting required fourteen general congregations (July 24–31).[169]
- The second draft, presented on August 7, consisted of twelve dogmatic canons, a revised version of the decree on clandestine marriage (now

---

[166] Alphonsus Salmeron, 382/30–34.   [167] CT 9:590–91.

[168] On the progression of these drafts, known in French as *projets*, see L. Bender, *Forma iuridica celebrationis matrimonii* (Rome, 1960), 14–20; and Le Bras, "Le Mariage," 2236–42. For a narrative of the proceedings at Trent 1561–1563, see K. M. Sutton, *The Papacy and the Levant* (Philadelphia, 1984), 4:769–828.

[169] First draft: CT 9:639–40. General congregations: 641–79.

beginning with the word *Tametsi*), and several canons on other abuses (*super abusibus*). Voting required twenty general congregations (August 11–23).[170]

- The third draft, presented on September 5, consisted of a preface, twelve dogmatic canons, a new, alternative canon on the reform clandestine marriage (*Tametsi*), and twelve canons *super abusibus*, the second of which was a revision of *Tametsi* from the second draft. Voting required seven general congregations (September 7–10).[171] It was the new, alternative version of *Tametsi* that went through to the fourth draft. The council abandoned the old version, and with it the requirement of parental consent.

- The fourth draft, presented on October 13, consisted of a preface, twelve dogmatic canons, and ten canons *de reformatione*, the first of which was the decree *Tametsi*. Voting required two general congregations (October 26–27).[172]

I shall concentrate in this chapter on three features of these drafts: the preface, the dogmatic canon on marriage as a sacrament (canon 1 in all versions), and the canon on jurisdiction. I shall discuss the decrees on clandestinity in the following chapter. Whereas the discussion of clandestine marriage brought to light irreconcilable differences among the prelates, the other matters proved relatively straightforward.

18.4.2.2 *The doctrinal preface*

There was no doctrinal preface in the first and second drafts. The first began immediately with the anathemas.[173] The second began with a brief preamble introducing the anathemas, explaining that having condemned the heresies and false dogmas regarding six of the sacraments – errors that the devil has insinuated into the church in this stormy season – it remains to condemn the diabolical errors and heresies that have arisen regarding the sacrament of marriage.[174] Some of the prelates proposed that the decree should be prefaced with a summary of the doctrine regarding this sacrament. For example, Diego Gilberto Nogueras, bishop of Alife, called for a preface that would explain which aspects of marriage belonged to divine law and which to human law, and that would identify the matter, the form, and the minister of the sacrament. His own view, he explained, was that the priest was the minister of the sacrament, and that the words by which he consecrated a marriage were its form.[175]

---

[170] Second draft: 682–85. General congregations: 685–741.
[171] Third draft: 760–65. General congregations: 779–95.
[172] Fourth draft: 888–90. General congregations: 898–906.   [173] 639.
[174] 682/1–6.   [175] Aliphanus, 674/44–675/3. See also Auriensis, 663/16.

The preface appeared in third draft, which began with the original preamble on heresies and false dogmas but appended a draft of a "new preface" after the anathemas.[176] This did not touch on any controversial issues but instead developed three main points. First, Adam, inspired by the Holy Spirit, declared that marriage was a "perpetual and inviolable tie" when he said, "This is bone of my bones" etc. (Gen 2:23–24). Second, Christ explicated and corroborated what Adam had said and confirmed the strength of the tie by adding, "What God has joined together, let not man separate" (Matt 19:4–6, Mark 10:9). Third, a certain sanctity was added under the evangelical law to perfect the natural love (*caritas*) between the spouses. As evidence, the preface cites Ephesians 5:25 and 32, where Paul commanded husbands to love their wives as Christ loves the church (v. 25) and explained that marriage was a great sacrament in Christ and the church. Paul indicated (*innuit*) not only that marriage represented the joining of Christ and the church, therefore, but also that it was sanctifying, conferring the grace of Christ on those whom Christ joins together. Finally, the preface noted briefly that it was necessary to condemn certain heresies by anathematizing the schismatics who proposed them. The last statement was the link to the anathemas that would follow when the preface was moved to its proper place.

This preface touched on the chief themes regarding the sacramental doctrine of marriage that had emerged during the Middle Ages: the sacred history of marriage, beginning in Eden; the indissolubility of marriage, linked in some undefined way to its sacramentality; the sacred signification of marriage; and Christ's raising of marriage to the level of a sacrament of the New Law, with the power to sanctify. Christ not only restored marriage to its pristine condition, therefore, but also strengthened its insolubility and added the efficacy of grace. The statement also embodied some recent advances, especially the identification of the grace of the sacrament with strengthened conjugal love, and a cautious and circumspect reference to Scriptural proof. Paul did not state but rather indicated or hinted (*innuit*) that marriage was one of the sacraments in Ephesians 5:32, and the interpreter should read Ephesians v. 32 in light of v. 25.

The preface of the fourth draft retained the same outline and composition, but it was improved and augmented.[177] It was now placed in its proper place, at the beginning of the decree. The third part was reworded to highlight conjugal grace, which flowed to the sacrament from the merit that Christ had earned through his Passion (Plate 2), perfecting the natural love that had belonged to marriage from the beginning:

> The same Christ, institutor and perfector of the venerable sacraments, merited for us by his own Passion a grace that would perfect that natural love [*amor*], confirm the indissoluble union, and sanctify the spouses themselves.[178]

[176] 761. [177] 888–89.
[178] 888/30–32" Gratiam vero, quae naturalem illum amorem perficeret, in indissolubilem unitatem confirmaret ipsosque coniuges sanctificaret: idem Christus, venerabilem sacramentorum institutor et perfector, sua nobis passione promeruit."

This is what Paul indicated (*innuit*) in Ephesians 5:25 and 32 by saying that husbands should love their wives as Christ loved the church, and that marriage was a great sacrament in Christ and the church. By virtue of the grace received from Christ, marriage under the Law of the Gospel is raised above what it had been under the Old Law, so that it is one of the sacraments of the New Law. The concluding statement of errors and heresies, which was designed to introduce the canons, was expanded to replace the now-redundant preamble of the second draft. Whereas "our holy fathers, the councils, and the universal tradition of the church have always taught" that marriage is one of the sacraments of the New Law, impious and insane heretics have been attacking the church's doctrine, pursuing the liberty of the flesh under the false pretext of the Gospel. The perpetrators of these errors must be anathematized.

18.4.2.3 *Marriage as a sacrament (canon 1)*

The first version of this canon was narrowly directed against the Protestants, especially Luther:

> Canon. 1 (1563, first draft): If anyone says that marriage is not a true, divinely instituted sacrament of the evangelical law, but has been introduced into the church by human beings, let him be anathema.[179]

This was the same as the first of the dogmatic canons on marriage discussed at Bologna.[180]

It became clear during the deliberations that this statement was too thin and not specific enough to capture what Catholics considered to be the salient, non-negotiable features of their sacramental doctrine. Moreover, it was not strong enough to rule out even some erroneous Catholic opinions, especially those of Durandus. Several prelates called for additions and changes to strengthen the canon. The Cardinal of Lorraine, who voted first, proposed that the canon should anathematize anyone who denied that marriage was "properly one of the seven sacraments of the evangelical law."[181] Several prelates concurred and proposed other additions along the same lines, such as that marriage was instituted by Christ, or that it conferred grace.[182] Some wanted to emphasize that marriage was properly or

---

[179] CT 9:639/21–22: "Si quis dixerit, matrimonium non esse verum sacramentum legis evangelicae divinitus institutum, sed ab hominibus in ecclesiam invectum: anathema sit." The variants "*in ecclesiam invectum*" and "*in ecclesia inventum*" seem to have the same meaning, although their precise sense is debatable. Luther's term had been *inventum*, not *invectum*. On this point, see Ehses's note, 682n2.

[180] CT 6.1:445/22–23: "Si quis dixerit matrimonium non esse verum sacramentum legis evangelicae divinitus institutum, sed ab hominibus in ecclesia inventum, a.s."

[181] Card. Lotharingus, CT 9:642/23–24. Card. Madrutius concurred, 643/21–22.

[182] Hydruntinus, 644/5–6: marriage was instituted by Christ and confers grace. Segobiensis, 656/31–32: marriage is among the seven sacraments of the evangelical law. Parisiensis, 658/17–18,

univocally one of the seven sacraments. This was in order to contradict Durandus, who held that marriage was only equivocally one of the sacraments.[183] The general of the Servites proposed that the phrase "confers grace" should be added to distinguish the council's position from Peter Lombard's, who had said nothing about the grace of marriage and perhaps misled Durandus.[184]

Several proposals regarding the first canon were never incorporated. Some of the prelates wanted to include the phrase "promise of grace" in the anathema: a term that Luther had popularized. For example, Nicolas Pseaume, bishop of Verdun, proposed that the canon should anathematize anyone who says that "marriage is not truly and properly a sacrament with the promise of grace instituted by Christ the Lord."[185] Antonín Brus von Muglitz, archbishop of Prague, proposed that the canon should say when "Christ instituted marriage, namely, when he said, 'What God has joined together let not man separate'" (Matt 19:6).[186] But there was no agreement among theologians as to when Christ instituted the sacrament or where in the New Testament that institution was recorded. The gospel text that the archbishop cited seemed rather to mark the recalling of marriage to its original, pristine condition. Some prelates wanted the canon specifically to refer to marriages between Christians or faithful Christians,[187] but Vincenzo Giustiniani, Master General of the Dominican Order, resisted this proposal, noting that according to some authorities not every marriage between Christians was a sacrament. For example, fra Giustiniani explained, some theologians maintained (he was probably thinking of Cajetan) that a marriage between Christians contracted through intermediaries was a true marriage but not a sacrament, and "Gropper in the Council of Cologne" had denied that clandestine marriage was a sacrament, at least until it was publicly celebrated. To obviate such questions, Giustiniani proposed that the canon need only refer to marriages that had been "properly and legitimately celebrated under the evangelical law."[188]

The prelates generally agreed that four points should be more explicit in the canon: that marriage was one of the seven sacraments; that it had been instituted not only "divinely" but also *by Jesus Christ*; that it was a sacrament of the New Law in the proper sense, and not only equivocally, as Durandus had argued; and that it conferred sacramental grace *ex opere operato*. These four points were embodied in the revised version of the second draft (translated here with the additions in bold font):

Canon. 1 (1563, second draft): If anyone says that marriage is not **truly and properly one of the seven sacraments** of the evangelical law, **instituted by Christ**, but has

and Gebennensis, 663/30–31: marriage was instituted by Christ. Guadiscensis, 672/2–3: marriage is truly and properly a sacrament of the New Law and confers grace. Usellensis, 677/26: marriage confers grace *ex opere operato* on those who do not present an obstacle.
[183] Bracarensis, 650/18–20. Leriensis, 661/5.   [184] Gen. Servorum, 679/39–40.
[185] Virdunensis, 657/21–22. Likewise, Brugnatensis, 656/17; Leriensis, 661/5–6.
[186] Pragensis, 651/28–30.   [187] Parisiensis, 658/17–18. Atrebatensis, 661/34. Montisfalisci, 662/40.
[188] Gen. Praedicatorum, 678/32–679/1.

been introduced in the church by human beings, **and that it does not confer grace**, let him be anathema.[189]

This version remained essentially unchanged in the subsequent drafts, and little more was said about the first canon. It was in the above form that it finally appeared in Session XXIV.

18.4.2.4 *Ecclesiastical jurisdiction*

The last dogmatic canon in the first draft declared that the church had jurisdiction over marriage:

> Canon 11 (first draft): If anyone says that matrimonial cases do not belong to ecclesiastical judges, let him be anathema.[190]

This canon was not the subject of extensive debate or discussion. The bishop of Quimper endorsed the canon and claimed that many councils had established the competence of the ecclesiastical forum in matrimonial cases.[191] Nevertheless, most of those who referred to this canon were more or less opposed to it.[192]

The prelates who questioned or raised doubts about the canon pursued three main contentions. First, some proposed that the topic was not suitable for a dogmatic canon, leaving open the possibility that it might be dealt with as a disciplinary matter.[193] Second, some argued that the scope of the church's judgment would need to be defined, and a division between the spiritual and the secular domains established. The bishop of Larino proposed that the canon should refer specifically to "matrimonial cases *concerning the sacrament*."[194] The bishop of Guadix said that the canon should state which cases the church was competent to judge.[195] Third, some held that the canon might be retained but with a more narrowly focused anathema. The patriarch of Jerusalem proposed that the canon should anathematize anyone who "dares to defer matrimonial cases to a secular

---

[189] 682/7–9: "Si quis dixerit, matrimonium non esse **vere et proprie unum ex septem** legis evangelicae sacramentis, **a Christo institutum**, sed ab hominibus in ecclesia invectum [*sic!*], **neque gratiam conferre**: anathema sit." It is arguable that *invectum* should be *inventum*: See 682n2. Both forms appear in textual witnesses to the subsequent drafts and in Session XXIV.

[190] 640/29–30: "Si quis dixerit, causas matrimoniales non spectare ad iudices ecclesiasticos: anathema sit."

[191] Corosopitanus, 672/31–673/3.

[192] Se Le Bras, "Le mariage," 2244–46. Le Bras perceives here an anticipation of early-modern regalism.

[193] E.g., Ilerdensis, 666/18: "11. non ponatur sub anathemate." The following concurred with Illerdensis: Elnenensis, 667/10; Nemausensis, 667/41; Aliphanus, 675/11; Rossensis, 676/6–17; Usellensis, 677/29. Others with the same opinion include Hyprensis, 669/24–25, and Namurcensis, 669/42. Prelates who asked for this canon to be excised during discussion of the second draft include Aurelianensis, 714/9.

[194] Larinensis, 662/19–20.   [195] Guadiscensis, 672/13–14.

tribunal."[196] Some prelates wanted the canon to anathematize those who held that the church's claim to have such jurisdiction was tyrannical,[197] or who said that matrimonial cases did not belong *in any way* to ecclesiastical judges,[198] or who said that the church erred in saying that matrimonial cases pertained to the ecclesiastical forum.[199] Some had merely strategic concerns and were worried that they would seem to overreach or might gratuitously offend the secular authorities. The bishop of Orléans, no doubt with French law in mind, argued that the canon should be removed "lest we seem too ambitious" and "annoy the secular [authorities]." He also pointed out that matrimonial cases had not been subject to ecclesiastical jurisdiction in the primitive church: a premise implying that the matter was not suitable for a dogmatic anathema expressing a timeless and universal truth.[200]

It is far from clear what was at issue. On the one hand, there is ample reason to suppose that the exclusive jurisdiction of ecclesiastical judges over the bond of marriage was highly contestable at the time of Trent. The Lutherans initially wanted marriage to be entirely subject to secular authorities. Johann Gropper remarked at the end of his treatise on marriage that human and divine law were so mixed up that it was hard to separate them, and he expressed the hope that a general council would soon discern which aspects of marriage pertained to which law.[201] On the other hand, the church claimed exclusive jurisdiction through its courts only over marriage *per se* (i.e., the validity of marriages, the enforcement of the bond, and separations *a mensa et thoro*). It was hardly controversial to claim, as the bishop of Oppido Mamertina did, that *not all* matrimonial cases belonged to the church.[202]

Despite the objections of a small minority, outlined earlier, the canon on ecclesiastical jurisdiction survived unchanged through the other three drafts and was eventually published in Session XXIV.

18.5 DECREE ON THE SACRAMENT OF MARRIAGE (SESSION XXIV)

Session XXIV took place on November 11. As well as twenty-one canons on general ecclesiastical reform, the Session published the decree on marriage, which apart from some insignificant corrections was that of the fourth draft. It consisted of a preface on the doctrine of marriage, twelve dogmatic canons, and ten chapters *super reformatione*, the first of which was the new version of *Tametsi*.[203]

---

[196] Hierosolymitanus, 666/32–33.
[197] Civitatensis, 668/31–34. Civitatis Castelli, 669/4–5, and Barcinonensis, 670/43, concurred with Civitatensis.
[198] Columbriensis, 673/15: "nullo modo pertinere." The secretary noted this proposed modification in his summary, 680/30.
[199] Archiep. Hydruntinus, 688/32–34 (second draft).   [200] Aurelianensis, 660/8–12.
[201] Gropper, *Enchiridion christianae institutionis*, c. 24 (Paris, 1550), 192v.
[202] Oppidensis, 673/37–38: "In 11. non est verum, quod omnes causae matrimoniales pertineant ad ecclesiam."
[203] Tanner-Alberigo, 753–59. CT 9:966–71.

The preface outlines the traditional doctrine. Adam, inspired by the Holy Spirit, declared that marriage was a "perpetual and inviolable tie" when he said: "This is now bone of my bones, and flesh of my flesh. For this reason a man shall leave his father and mother and shall cleave unto his wife, and they shall be two in one flesh" (Gen 2:23–24). Christ explicated and corroborated what Adam had said when he said, "they are no longer two but one flesh," confirming the strength of the tie by adding, "What God has joined, therefore, let not man separate" (Matt 19:4–6, Mark 10:9). "The same Christ, institutor and perfector of the venerable sacraments, merited for us by his own Passion a grace that would perfect that natural love [*amor*], confirm the indissoluble union, and sanctify the spouses." This is what Paul indicated (*innuit*) by saying that husbands should love their wives as Christ loved the church (Eph 5:25), and that marriage was a great sacrament in Christ and the church (Eph 5:32). By virtue of the grace received from Christ, marriage under the Law of the Gospel is raised above what it had been under the Old Law, so that it is properly counted among the sacraments of the New Law, as "our holy fathers, the councils, and the universal tradition of the church have always taught." But recently diabolical errors have beset the church, and heretics have rejected the church's teaching:

> Against this [tradition], impious and insane men of our time not only have held false opinions about this venerable sacrament but also, introducing the freedom of the flesh under the pretext of the Gospel as is their wont, have asserted in writing and in speech many things that are alien to the mind of the Catholic church and to proven custom since apostolic times, and not without doing great damage to Christ's faithful. Desiring to confront their rashness, lest their pernicious contagion draws more persons to itself, this holy and universal synod has decided to exterminate the more conspicuous errors and heresies of the aforesaid schismatics by decreeing the following anathemas against those heretics and their errors.[204]

The first of the ten canons on dogma affirms that marriage is one of the sacraments in the proper sense:

> Canon 1: If anyone says that marriage is not truly and properly one of the seven sacraments of the evangelical law, instituted by Christ, but has been invented in the church by human beings, and that it does not confer grace, let him be anathema.[205]

The other canons anathematize those who say (2) that Christian men may practice polygamy; (3) that the impediments of consanguinity and affinity should be limited to those of the Leviticus code; (4) that the church has no power to introduce diriment impediments; (5) that either spouse may dissolve a marriage on grounds of the other's heresy, irksome cohabitation, or continued absence; (6) that an

---

[204] Tanner-Alberigo, 754/15–23. CT 9:967/8–15.
[205] Tanner-Alberigo, 754/25–27. CT 9:967/16–18. Several sources have *invectum* instead of *inventum*, but *inventum* is the preferred reading today.

unconsummated marriage is not dissolved by the entry of the either spouse into the religious life; (7) that the church errs in teaching that a marriage cannot be dissolved on grounds of adultery; (8) that the church errs in teaching that a divorce cannot be granted on certain grounds "as regards the bed or as regards cohabitation," whether for a determined or indefinite period; (9) that men in holy orders and religious may marry; (10) that the married estate is not preferable to that of celibacy or virginity; (11) that the church's prohibition of the solemnization of marriage during certain seasons stems from pagan superstitions and is tyrannical, and that the church's nuptial blessings and ceremonies should be condemned; and (12) that "matrimonial cases do not belong to ecclesiastical judges."

After the dogmas comes the decree on reform, which begins with *Tametsi*. This renders clandestine marriages null and void, defines the conditions for a validly public marriage, and prescribes further procedures and solemnities as norms. The second, third, and fourth chapters on reform revise and reduce the impediments of spiritual relationship, public honesty, and affinity, respectively. The fifth through ninth chapters deal with abuses: persons who knowingly marry within the forbidden degrees expecting a dispensation *post factum*; *raptus*; men who wander from place to place, abandoning one wife and taking another; concubinage; and temporal lords who coerce into marriage the men or women who serve them. The final chapter reaffirms the prohibition of weddings during Advent and Lent, adding that bishops should make sure that weddings are celebrated modestly and decently, "for marriage is a holy thing, and it should be conducted in a holy manner."

19

Clandestine marriage

Bologna, 1547

The principle of *solus consensus* was at the root of the problem of clandestine marriage, for it was both what prevented the church from eradicating such marriages and what enabled couples to marry without parental consent. Because the two abuses – marrying clandestinely and marrying without parental consent – were connected by this common root, Catholics as well as Protestants were inclined either to conflate the two abuses or to regard marriage without parental consent as a special mode of clandestinity.

19.1 THE RULES OF THE GAME

The prelates and *theologi minores* at the general council treated the issue of clandestine marriage within the parameters that the scholastic theologians of the central Middle Ages had established. Some of the prelates found this constraint irksome, but such were the rules of the game.

It was virtually axiomatic that the church had no power to alter the essence, or substance, of any sacrament. The church had some power to alter the liturgical solemnities and even the received liturgical form, such as the words by which the priest consecrated the bread and wine in eucharist, but only if these changes did not touch the essence, which had been instituted by Jesus Christ. Thus, the Council of Trent decreed in Session XXI on July 21, 1562, that the clergy and the laity were not required by any divine command (*nullo divino praecepto*) to receive communion under both species, whatever the biblical evidence for the practice might be, and that the church always had the power, acting under the guidance of the Holy Spirit, to make changes to how any sacrament was received, provided that the substance was not changed (*salva illorum substantia*).[1] Presupposing a distinction between inalterable divine law and mutable but valid ecclesiastical law, the decree implied

---

[1] Session XXI, cap. 1–2 (Tanner-Alberigo, 626).

that whether the laity received the bread alone or both the bread and the wine was not a matter of divine command and, therefore, did not pertain to the inalterable essence of the sacrament. Consequently, the church had the power to determine which of these alternative practices should be followed.

The assumption that each sacrament had an inalterable essence took on new importance at Trent, where the prelates were defending the sacramental system against Protestant attack. A sacrament of the church, from their point of view, did not emerge through a historical process but rather was instituted by Jesus Christ at the dawn of the church's history, and it had not changed essentially thereafter.[2] For the most part, the prelates who proposed the invalidation of clandestine marriages at the general council conceded that the essence of this sacrament, too, was inalterable and tried to show that their proposal would not entail or imply any alteration to that essence.

The medieval schoolmen had regarded the sacraments as if they were Aristotelian substances. The essence of each sacrament was composed of form and matter, where the form was an invocation, and the matter was something actualized or determined by the form. Typically, the minister disposed the matter to receive the form and applied the form to the matter. The scholastic analysis of the sacraments into form and matter served two functions: it covered the same ground as the Augustinian analysis into *verbum* and *elementum*, which it largely superseded (although the latter survived and appeared occasionally even during the sixteenth century, especially in the work of amateur theologians); and it elicited inquiry into which features of the received liturgical forms were strictly necessary and which were not. There would be no sacrament if any of the necessary features was omitted or altered.

The changes that this doctrine ruled out were not physical, such as occurred when water became air. Rather, they were changes regarding the constituent conditions that were necessary and sufficient for a certain sacrament. The schoolmen applied the hylomorphic model to the sacraments only in an extended, analogous manner. That the essences of physical substances were inalterable, such as that of water or of angels of a particular rank, was tautologous, for an essence was the quiddity, or *quid est*, of a substance. To change the essence of a physical substance would entail changing its real definition, which was absurd. But it was not absurd to change the necessary and sufficient conditions of an institution or a legal property. The law could change the conditions of ownership, for example, provided that the modified definition was just and did not contradict natural or divine law.

---

[2] The notion that Jesus Christ had instituted the sacraments was itself open to a range of interpretations. Ruard Tapper, for example, held that Christ instituted some sacraments personally (*immediate*) and others indirectly, through a power that he imparted the apostles. See W. A. Newman, *Jus Divinum and the Sacrament of Penance* (diss., Washington, DC, 1969), 206–06.

Moreover, it was not unthinkable that *God* might change the essence of a sacrament. Thomas Aquinas envisaged this possibility in his commentary on the *Sentences*, although the passage was rarely cited during the sixteenth century because it was not included in the *Supplementum* to the *Summa theologiae*. Thomas inquires into the sin committed by someone who omits or alters part of the received liturgical form of a sacrament, such as some of the words used to consecrate the bread and wine of eucharist. He argues that the implications depend partly on whether the words in question belong to the liturgical form through divine law or through the church's positive law:

> It should be said that the sacraments owe their efficacy to divine institution, and that form is primary in sacraments, even in relation to matter. Therefore, just as no one is permitted to change or to institute a new sacrament, so no one is permitted to change the form of a sacrament in respect of what belongs to the essence of the form without special counsel from the Holy Spirit, who does not bind his power to those words. If [the essential form] is changed [by any human agent], the sacrament is not enacted, and in addition guilt is incurred. But if something is changed that belongs to the form through a determination by the church, there is a sacrament nevertheless, but guilt is incurred.[3]

Thomas distinguishes here between two possible sources of valid change: a change to the essential form introduced by the Holy Spirit acting through the church, and a change introduced by the church on its own authority (albeit, no doubt, under the guidance of the Holy Spirit). An intervention of the first sort – a very rare thing – pertains to divine law and might even alter the essential form. An intervention of the latter sort pertains to ecclesiastical law, or the positive law of the church, and the church has no power to alter the essential form of the sacrament. But no one at Trent claimed that the Holy Spirit was about to invalidate clandestine marriage by changing divine law.

To determine what constituted the essence even of baptism or eucharist was no easy matter. There were no hylomorphic definitions of the sacraments in Scripture. Scholastic theologians had tried to determine what aspects of the received liturgical *ordines* and related practices were essential by examining them theologically in light of the biblical evidence. They generally assumed, moreover, that the *ordines* of the Greek (i.e., Byzantine) tradition were equally valid, so that their analyses had to accommodate those differences. They were aware, too, that the grammatical peculiarities of Latin were incidental, although they unconsciously assumed that Latin was the norm. The form might be expressed in any language.

The principles outlined earlier were embodied in some well-known texts about marriage in the writings of notable scholastic theologians. Duns Scotus said that the church introduced impediments to marriage "only as regards the persons, because the church has determined nothing regarding the form or the matter of the contract

---

[3] Thomas Aquinas, *IV Sent.* 3.2, qu[a] 2, resp. (ed. Moos, 4:121).

itself but has only rendered certain persons illegitimate by making them incapable of this contract."[4] Scotus's logic implied that if the church validly decreed that there was no sacrament of marriage when some feature was missing from the sacrament itself, then that feature would *ipso facto* be essential, for the church would not have changed anything essential to the sacrament but rather would have defined what had always been true. That in turn seemed to preclude the possibility of changing the necessary and sufficient conditions of a valid sacrament of marriage. There were two ways to overcome the objection: either (1) the church *could* alter the essence of this sacrament, at least within limits or in special circumstances or (2) marriage without the feature in question had *never* been a valid sacrament. Neither alternative was acceptable in the debate over clandestine marriages. There were then two possible solutions, both of which would be explored during the general council. Perhaps clandestinity should be construed as a personal impediment, that is, one that inhabilitated the persons, preventing them from marrying (i.e., disqualified them, or rendered them incapable). Or perhaps the church had the power to invalidate the contract of marriage as such, without altering the conditions of the sacrament. The first possibility emerged at Bologna in 1547, and it appeared again at Trent in 1563. Although it lost ground and faded into the background during the proceedings of 1563, a vestige of the theory remained in the decree *Tametsi.* The proponents of invalidation at Trent in 1563 relied chiefly on the second possibility.

Thomas Aquinas, whom the general council regarded as the "scholastic doctor" par excellence, provided a more complicated set of requirements (Section 14.7). Following Peter Lombard, Thomas distinguished between the essentials of a sacrament, without which the sacrament would not occur, and the solemnities, without which there was still a sacrament, even if their omission was prohibited.[5] What was essential to marriage, according to Aquinas, was "consent expressed in words of the present tense between persons who can legitimately contract marriage."[6] Any other customary or traditional features of the event, even if the church prescribed them, were solemnities. Clandestine marriages were necessarily valid, therefore, although they were sinful unless the spouses had a valid reason for marrying secretly.[7] In the same article, following Peter Lombard, Thomas excluded parental consent and the priestly blessing from the list of things that were necessary for this sacrament. These were only solemnities.[8] But that would not prevent the church from introducing or removing diriment *personal* impediments. Thomas himself argued that the church

---

4   Duns Scotus, *Opus Oxon., IV Sent.* 42.un. (Vivès 19:560a): "Ex statuto Ecclesiae sunt tantum-modo impedimenta ex parte personarum, quia Ecclesia nihil determinavit circa formam vel materiam istius contractus, sed solum personas aliquas illegitimavit, faciendo eas non capaces hujus contractus."

5   Thomas Aquinas, *IV Sent.* 34.1, resp.; ad 4 (Vivès 11:163, 164).

6   "ita consensus expressus per verba de praesenti inter personas legitimas ad contradendum, matrimonium facit."

7   Thomas Aquinas, *IV Sent.* 28.1.3 (Vivès 11:99).   8   Ibid., ad 1m; ad 2m.

had that power because marriage, unlike the other sacraments, was not *only* a sacrament but was *also* a contract, for the conditions of contracts were naturally subject to positive law (Section 16.5.6). In short, the fact that legitimate persons were essential to the sacrament did not prevent the church from determining which persons were legitimate. Some of the prelates at Trent maintained that clandestinity invalidated the persons.

Although most of the prelates at Trent assumed that the essence of marriage, like that of the other sacraments, was inalterable and had been instituted by Jesus Christ, a few of them perceived some areas of latitude. Scholastic theologians had had to stretch the hylomorphic model to apply it to the sacrament of marriage. Most professional theologians agreed that the form of marriage was the expressed consent of the spouses, and only a very few of them followed the ritual tendency by identifying it with the priestly blessing, notwithstanding the precedents in William of Auvergne and Bonaventure. But the Scotists had drawn attention to the lack of any prescribed and necessary verbal formula, or *certa verba* (Section 16.7.1), which the other sacraments required. Nor was there consensus regarding the matter of marriage, about which several theories were in circulation (Section 14.6.1.1). The medieval schoolmen had been content to obviate objections to the sacramentality of marriage by showing that there were plausible candidates for the form and the matter of the sacrament, without insisting on any particular theory. Nor was there consensus as to when Jesus Christ instituted the essence of marriage or where in Scripture that institution was recorded. Perhaps the form or the matter of the sacrament was still open to some further determination.

Such questions were germane to the arguments about clandestinity at the general council, especially during 1563, when the discourse reached its most technically advanced level. Since marriage did not apparently require any *certa verba*, a few prelates suggested that Jesus Christ had left the form or the essence of this sacrament indeterminate and open to determination. In that case, the church had the power further to define how marriages were contracted by adding some procedure of solemnization as a feature of the essential form. Moreover, the schoolmen had been inclined to attribute the identity of a substance more to its form than to its matter, since the form actualized the matter. As we have seen, Thomas had observed that "form is primary in sacraments, even in relation to matter."[9] Prelates during the debate over clandestinity more often affirmed that the *form* of a sacrament was inalterable than the *essence* was inalterable. Some prelates questioned whether the matter necessary for marriage was as fixed and inalterable as that of baptism and eucharist. Perhaps the essential matter was alterable, therefore, at least within certain limits. This possibility appealed especially to those who construed the matter of a sacrament in Augustinian fashion as its *elementum*, to which the minister applied

---

[9] *IV Sent.* 3.2, quª 2, resp. (ed. Moos, 4:121): "principalius est in sacramentis forma quam etiam materia."

the *verbum*. (On this view, the matter of baptism, for example, was water, rather than the act of ablution, as Thomas Aquinas had held.) The quasi-*elementum* of marriage seemed to be the partners who were marrying (both before and during their coming together), and the church clearly had the power to render persons incapable of the sacrament who had hitherto been capable, and vice versa. For example, Lateran IV had reduced the scope of the diriment impediment of consanguinity from the sixth to the fourth degree.

The point of departure for the council's deliberations on clandestine marriages at Bologna was a twofold doctrinal error, presumed to be Protestant heresy: that clandestine marriages were invalid, and that in consequence parents had the power to annul them. This clumsy formulation was a source of difficulty, for it tended to conflate clandestinity with the absence of parental consent. Moreover, it gratuitously introduced a question of judicial authority into the discussion, which would have been better treated separately. The formulation was not satisfactory even as a summary of a Protestant contention, as some of the prelates pointed out.

Discussion of this purported heresy raised a secondary question of reform: What could or should the Catholic church do to prevent such marriages? In particular, did the church have the power to render them invalid? Opinion swung in favor of invalidation during the proceedings, but that possibility generated an apparent anomaly. If the Catholic church was going to make clandestine marriages invalid henceforth, the Protestant claim that such marriages were already invalid might be unauthorized and presumptuous, but where was the heresy?

19.2 PRELIMINARY DISCUSSION BY THE *THEOLOGI MINORES*, APRIL 26 THROUGH MAY 7

The first articulation of the double error was one of the heterodox articles put before the *theologi minores* on April 26, 1547, according to which "clandestine marriage is not legitimate and hence can be annulled by the parents."[10] The *theologi minores* did not discuss marriage extensively at this stage, for most of them focused on extreme unction and orders, but they did review the fundamental issues surrounding the problem of clandestinity. None of them disputed that marrying clandestinely was an abusive practice. The Portuguese friar Georgius a Sancto Iacobo, O.P., spoke for most when he said that "clandestine marriages should be prohibited because of the scandals that arise from those which cannot be proved."[11] Nevertheless, most of the theologians who discussed the article rejected it as false and potentially heretical, and all agreed that parents did not have the power to annul a marriage that their sons and daughters had contracted freely.[12] More important, most maintained that

[10] CT 6.1:98/8: "Matrimonia clandestina non esse legitima ac proinde a parentibus irritari posse."
[11] Georgius a Sancto Iacobo, 106/16–17.
[12] As the secretary records in his summary, 121/26–30.

clandestine marriages, other things being equal, were valid.[13] This was still the consensus among professional theologians, who assumed that invalidation would be inconsistent with the sacramentality of marriage. Several argued that the article was false because marriage was "perfected by consent" ("*consensu perficitur*"), or because the consent of the spouses sufficed for a valid marriage, or because a clandestine marriage included everything essential to the sacrament. Even if a marriage had been clandestinely contracted, therefore, neither the parents nor even the church had the power to dissolve it.[14]

Some of the theologians argued that clandestine marriages were valid and insoluble *because* marriage was a sacrament. Peter-Paul Caporella, a Conventual Franciscan, argued that because marriage was a sacrament instituted by Christ, the marriage bond was indissoluble, and no one could annul it.[15] Similarly, Peter Canisius (a Jesuit) and John-Baptist Moncalvius (another Conventual Franciscan) invoked the God-given character of marriage. Provided that the spouses freely consented when they married, even if they married clandestinely, then God himself has joined the spouses together, and no human agent, not even the church, can separate them.[16] To the objection that marriage without parental consent was invalid among the gentiles and the heathens (*ethnici*), Moncalvius responded that marriage was a sacrament only "in Christ and the church," as St Paul had put it (Eph 5:32). Marriage among gentiles or heathens was only a civil institution (*quaedam politia*), subject to civil law and jurisdiction. What rendered marriage impervious to annulment by any human agent, in his view, was its sacramentality.[17]

Claudius Zaius, a Jesuit, noted that the term "clandestine" was equivocal. It might denote a marriage without witnesses, or one without certain customary formalities, or one not contracted *in facie ecclesiae*. Zaius cited sources showing that each of these modes of clandestinity was prohibited. He also pointed out that because the church already prohibited clandestine marriages, the first part of the article, whereby "clandestine marriage is not legitimate," was technically not heretical but true. Validity and legitimacy, in his view, were not coextensive. Once such marriages had been contracted by mutual consent, they could not be dissolved, even though they were not lawful.[18]

In sum, the *theologi minores* agreed that the spouses' parents had no power to dissolve a marriage, and they agreed that although the church prohibited clandestine marriages, the church had no power to dissolve them. Such unions were insoluble because marriage was a sacrament, because the spouses' consent was

[13] A possible exception is Ioannes Consilii, 107/5–8, who conceded that parents had no power to annul a marriage but said that marriage according to Evaristus required "legitimate vows" and expressed the desire that "clandestine marriages would be prohibited by this holy synod."
[14] Augustinus de Montealcino, 108/6–8. Gaspar de Valentia, 112/30–32. Gentianus Hervetus, 115/25–28. Claudius Zaius, 116/30–117/9.
[15] Petrus-Paulus de Potentia, 108/28–109/2.
[16] Petrus Canisius, 118/27–30. Ioannes Baptista Moncalvius, 118/2–5.
[17] Ioannes Baptista Moncalvius. 118/5–9   [18] Claudius Zaius, 117/1–9.

sufficient as well as necessary to establish a valid marriage, and because no human agent could separate those whom God had joined together. But the theologians had failed to distinguish between preemptive invalidation, which would have prevented the contracting of a valid marriage, and the dissolution of an already contracted marriage.

19.3 GENERAL CONGREGATIONS ON CLANDESTINITY AND DIVORCE, AUGUST 29 THROUGH SEPTEMBER 6

On August 29, the legates put before the prelates two articles stating erroneous and potentially heterodox policies regarding both clandestine marriage and remarriage after divorce. These were Protestant errors, but the presiding legates noted that even some Catholics had proposed them. A dossier provided with the articles included biblical and patristic evidence both for and against each of the statements. Discussion of this material required six general congregations (August 30 through September 6).

The first article elaborated the double error that had already been put before the *theologi minores*: "Clandestine marriages are not true, legitimate marriages, and hence parents have the power to annul them unless those who have covertly contracted them entreat their parents to recognize them as valid."[19] As before, the formulation invited confusion by failing to distinguish between clandestinity and the absence of parental consent. The appended authorities went to show, on one side, that the spouses' consent sufficed and, on the other side, that parents and especially fathers had the right to give their children away in marriage or to withhold their permission.[20] The second article proposed that remarriage was possible after a divorce on grounds of adultery.[21] These were *prima facie* matters of reform, and some prelates proposed that clandestinity should be handled entirely in a decree on reform (*de reformatione*) and not treated as a matter of dogma.[22]

The prelates' opinions about the validity of clandestine marriage varied more widely than those of the *theologi minores*. Most but not quite all of the prelates denied that parents had the power to annul clandestine marriages *post factum*,[23] and most held that clandestine marriages were valid in principle, by virtue of the very constitution of marriage. Nevertheless, a few of the prelates proposed that the church should invalidate clandestine marriages henceforth. Four alternative

---

[19] CT 6.1:407/7–9: "Matrimonia clandestina non esse vera et legitima matrimonia, ac proinde esse in potestate parentum ea irritandi, nisi qui clam contraxerunt impetrarent a parentibus ea rata haberi."

[20] 407–09.

[21] On the discussion of this topic at Bologna, see L. Bressan, *Il canone tridentino sul divorzio per adulterio e l'interpretazione degli autori* (Rome, 1973), 79–120.

[22] Bellicastrensis, 427/29–30. Archiep. Armacanus, 431/4–5. Salutiarum, 431/38–39.

[23] For example, Materanus, 419/16–22; Sibinicensis, 421/9–12; Chironensis, 421/18–22; Maiorciensis, 421/28–30; Armacanus, 431/4–13. See also the secretary's summary, 434/16–18.

positions emerged. Most held (i) that clandestine marriages were valid by their very constitution and could not be rendered invalid.[24] At least one seems to have held (ii) that clandestine marriages were *invalid* in principle, and that parents had the power to annul them (the converse of the first position).[25] A few held either (iii) that clandestine marriages were valid, but that the church could and probably should make them invalid henceforth, or (iv) that clandestine marriages were valid in some generic or merely civil sense but were not sacramental.[26]

Most of the prelates who considered this article held the first position: that clandestine marriages were valid by virtue of the very constitution of the sacrament. They maintained that the mutual consent of the spouses was sufficient to establish a valid and indissoluble marriage, provided that it was expressed in the present tense or in the future tense followed by coitus. The absence of parental consent, however regrettable, was not a diriment impediment, in their view, because no man could separate what God had joined.[27] They conceded that the church prohibited clandestine marriages and that many evils and scandals arose from them, but they reasoned that clandestinity was an impediment only to the making of the contract in the future, and not to an already contracted marriage. Once the spouses had plighted their troth, even if they had done so clandestinely and contrary to the church's prohibition, no human agent could separate them.[28] Angelo Pasquali, O.P., bishop of Mottola, argued that an already-contracted clandestine marriage was necessarily true, sacramental, and legitimate because the essentials of the sacrament, especially the matter and the form, were present, although he conceded that clandestine marriages were prohibited *before* they were contracted:

> Clandestine marriages are true marriages when they have already been contracted [*cum iam contracta sunt*], although they are prohibited and illegitimate before they are contracted [*antequam contrahuntur*], because what is required for a true sacrament is the requisite matter and form — that is, the contractants themselves and their consent — and these are present in clandestine marriages. A clandestine marriage, therefore, is not only a true marriage but also a legitimate marriage and a sacrament.[29]

According to the secretary's summary of the proceedings, some of those who upheld this position claimed that clandestine marriages "could not be dissolved by any human power" because Jesus had said, "What God has joined together, let not man

---

[24] Summary, 434/5–11.   [25] Summary, 434/18–21.   [26] Summary, 434/11–15.

[27] For example, Materanus, 419/26–28; Sibinicensis, 421/12–14; Alyphanus, 428/8–10.

[28] For example, Sebastensis, 424/5–6: "Clandestina matrimonia licet prohibita sint, contracta tamen tenent et vera sunt matrimonia." Likewise, Chironensis, 421/19–20; Motulanus, 424/11–15; Parentinus, 424/25–27; Veronensis coadiutor, 425/13–16; Mylensis Ferrettus, 425/21–24; Caprulanus, 425/28–29; Mylensis Graecus, 426/29–30; Feltrensis, 427/18–19; Card. de Monte, 433/9–10.

[29] Motulanus, 424/11–15.

separate." But others – the secretary was probably referring to Ambrosius Catharinus – countered that it was not God but the devil who joined such marriages.[30]

The decretal ascribed to Pope Evaristus soon became a focus of discussion, partly because it seemed to show that the church had in the past invalidated marriages contracted clandestinely or without parental consent, and partly because it suggested that such was the ancient practice of the church. Some argued that Evaristus must have only prohibited such marriages without invalidating them, since what he had required were solemnities, which were not of the essence of the sacrament.[31] Moreover, they pointed out, the final words of the decretal (*"nisi voluntas propria suffragata fuerit, et vota succurrerint legitima"*) showed that the consent of the spouses was sometimes sufficient even according to Evaristus.[32] Those who held that clandestine marriages were valid *post factum* could still maintain that they were illegitimate or unlawful inasmuch as they contravened a prohibition.[33] Some of those who considered clandestine marriages to be necessarily valid wanted the council to suppress them as far as possible by imposing more severe penalties, such as denial of support or of dowries.[34]

Alvaro della Quadra, bishop of Venosa, seems to have upheld the second position: that clandestine marriages had always been invalid. Not only should they be "entirely prohibited and detested," he argued, but they were already "illegitimate" – by which he seems to have meant that they were invalid. Such marriages failed to meet the requirements of Evaristus's decretal. They also lacked parental consent, "which is required by every law." It was true that the spouses' mutual consent sufficed to make marriage, but only if it was *legitimate* consent, and clandestine consent was illegitimate. Parents had the power, therefore, to annul the clandestine marriages of their children.[35] Ambrosius Catharinus, O.P., who participated at Bologna as the bishop of Minori, would later develop a carefully nuanced version of this position in his treatise on marriage (Section 19.9.2), but as far as one can tell from the secretary's record he did not make this claim during the proceedings at Bologna.

Four or five of the prelates upheld versions of the third position: that clandestine marriages were currently valid and indissoluble, but that the church, acting through this general council, had the power to make them invalid henceforth. Furthermore,

---

[30] Summary, 434/24–27. Cf. Alyphanus, 428/6–10: "Quoad clandestina matrimonia, an sint valida et rata, respondet, quod sic, cum sint in eis omnia, quae ad essentiam matrimonii requiruntur, i.e., consensus proprius nubentium. Quae matrimonia a parentibus irritari non possunt, quia, cum sint vera matrimonia, *quod Deus coniunxit, homo non separet.*"

[31] Aquensis Vorstius, 421/40–41. Caprulanus, 425/29–31.

[32] For example, Motulanus, 424/15–16.

[33] For example, Sibinicensis, 421/9–10: "Quoad clandestina tenet valida esse, licet non legitima ex iam aductis."

[34] Aquensis Vorstius, 421/38–38. Veronensis coadiutor, 425/18. Mylensis Ferrettus, 425/23–24. Aquinatensis, 426/13. Feltrensis, 427/13–14.

[35] Venusinus, 425/40–426/4. The secretary seems to be referring to Venusinus when he summarizes this position at 434/18–21.

they contended, the church probably *ought* to do so, in view of the evils and scandals that resulted from such marriages. Sebastiano Leccavella, O.P., archbishop of Naxos, was the first to articulate this position. He was also the first in the Bologna proceedings to speak of *inhabilitatio*, although he seems to have been referring not to the contractants but to the contract itself. He concurred with the arguments used by the majority to show that clandestine marriages were valid, but he argued that if the church at Lateran IV had been able to "habilitate" the more remote degrees of relationship, so that a formerly invalid match was now valid, why should the church not have the converse power to decree that clandestine marriages were henceforth entirely invalid?[36]

Four other prelates proposed variants of the same position: the bishops of Accia, Bologna, and Minori (Ambrosius Catharinus), and the archbishop of Uppsala. Benedetto de Nobili, bishop of Accia, who spoke next after Sebastiano Leccavella, questioned whether any determination on the two articles would be possible with so few prelates present. Nevertheless, he expressed the desire that all clandestine marriages should be entirely prohibited and eliminated henceforth because of the "countless evils that arise from them daily." It was not unusual, he argued, for the church to introduce new regulations when new reasons and circumstances become apparent and existing remedies had proved ineffective. The church arguably had the power to determine that any clandestine marriage would henceforth be invalid until it had been properly confirmed before the church. Benedetto de Nobili pointed out that marriage might be construed in two ways: either inasmuch as it is common to all peoples, or inasmuch as it is a sacrament. Whereas simple consent (*consensus simplex*) suffices for marriage in the first sense, the sacrament requires other, circumstantial conditions that alter the significance of consent, such as "religion, faith, and church."[37] Ambrosius Catharinus conceded that clandestine marriages were valid in current canon law. Nevertheless, he confessed that he found it very difficult to accept that they were valid in the sight of God, since they lacked the proper solemnities and were contracted without the parents' knowledge or against their wishes. The council should be able, he argued, to raise the level of the prohibition by making clandestine marriages invalid after they have been contracted, just as marriage in the fourth degree of consanguinity was at one time permitted but is now prohibited.[38]

According to the fourth position, which presupposed an analysis of the sacrament akin to Melchor Cano's (Section 16.7.3), a clandestine marriage was valid in some merely secular or generic sense but was not sacrament. As noted earlier, the bishop

---

[36] Naxiensis, 420/17–19.

[37] Aciensis de Nobilibus, 420/29–37. Bononiensis, 421/6–7: "... quod clandestina matrimonia non valerent ob tanta mala, quae inde oriuntur." Upsalensis archiepiscopus, 433/2–4: "Quoad primum [articulum, de clandestinis] tenet cum ecclesia valida esse clandestina matrimonia; sed prohibenda sunt a synodo, ne rata sint, propter multa scandala."

[38] Minoriensis, 432/31–37.

of Accia, Benedetto de Nobili, took this view, as well as holding that clandestine marriage should be rendered null and void henceforth. Likewise, Giacomo de' Giacomelli, bishop of Belcastro, argued that marriage might be construed either inasmuch as it is common to all peoples or inasmuch as it is a Christian sacrament. A clandestine marriage contracted improperly and impiously by consent alone, merely to satisfy lust, is not a Christian sacrament because it lacks features that Christian piety requires, such as faith, the church, and the involvement of parents. Clandestine marriages, therefore, are valid marriages in some sense, but they are not "true, Christian marriages."[39] Robert Wauchope, archbishop of Armagh, refuted this position. Clandestine marriages between Christians are themselves Christian and sacramental, he argued, even if the partners have contracted them from inappropriate motives, such as lust or wealth. In the same way, a Jew who receives baptism to achieve greater honor in the community or for financial gain has erred but has nonetheless been truly baptized.[40]

19.4 GENERAL CONGREGATIONS ON THE DOCTRINE OF MARRIAGE, SEPTEMBER 9–24

On September 9, 1547, the legates presented drafts of six dogmatic canons on marriage, and the prelates devoted eight general congregations to them (September 10–24). I have already described the discussion of the first canon, on the sacramentality of marriage (Section 18.2.3). The second canon anathematized anyone who said that freely contracted clandestine marriages were not true and settled (*rata*) and that parents, therefore, had the power to annul them:

> If anyone says that clandestine marriages that are entered into with the free consent of the contractants are not true and settled marriages, and hence are in the power of the parents to make them valid or invalid, let him be anathema, although [*tametsi*] the church has always judged with good reason that such marriages should be prevented.[41]

The heresy that this canon condemned was another version of the double error that the *theologi minores* and the prelates themselves had already discussed, but the canon now included a reservation introduced by the conjunction *tametsi*. Its purpose was to obviate a possible misinterpretation of the anathema, which should not be taken to imply that the Catholic church approved of such marriages. The

---

[39] Bellicastrensis, 427/30–36. This bishop held the office of *commissarius apostolicus in concilio* (467/1–2).

[40] Archiep. Armacanus, 431/4–13.

[41] CT 6.1:446/1–4: "Si quis dixerit clandestina matrimonia, quae libero contrahentium consensu fiunt, non esse vera et rata matrimonia, ac proinde esse in potestate parentum ea rata vel irrita facere, a. s.; tametsi sancta ecclesia matrimonia huiusmodi bonis et rationabilibus causis inhibenda esse censuerit." The canon survives in several alternative forms: see 446/11–26, 447/1–11, 36–37.

addition was descriptive but indirectly normative, since by recalling that the church had always and with good reason tried to prevent clandestine marriages, it implied that clandestine marriages were evil and should be prohibited, and it brought the issue of reform into the foreground. What could or should the Catholic church do to prevent such marriages?

The other canons anathematized anyone who said that a man whose wife had committed adultery could remarry; anyone who blessed second marriages or presumed to teach that such marriages might be blessed, holding the church in contempt; anyone who said that a man could have several wives; and anyone who said that the impediments of consanguinity and affinity should be reduced to those of the Levitus code.

The prelates outlined and defended rationales for the anathema on clandestine marriages. No one at this stage in the proceedings, it seems, wanted to maintain that clandestine marriages were already invalid or less than sacramental. For some, indeed, the anathema did not affirm the validity or sacramentality of such marriages strongly enough. Angelo Pasquali, bishop of Mottola, proposed that the wording should be modified so as to affirm that a clandestine marriage between legitimate partners was a sacrament.[42] The bishop of Alatri argued that a clandestine marriage was valid and insoluble because God had witnessed it, even if there had been no human witnesses, for what God has joined together no man may separate.[43]

What decisions could or should the council make in order to suppress clandestine marriages more effectively? Some of the prelates articulated the standard canonical interpretation of the Catholic prohibition: that the church forbade couples from marrying clandestinely *before* the fact yet recognized such marriages as valid and indissoluble *after* the fact.[44] With that analysis in mind, the bishop of Albenga proposed that the anathema should refer not to clandestine marriages in the present tense, as those which *"are* entered into with the free consent of the contractants," but rather in the past tense, which *have been* entered into clandestinely.[45] Tommaso Caselli, O.P., bishop of Bertinoro, proposed that the *tametsi* clause should say that the church had prohibited them to prevent them from happening (*prohibuit, ne fieret*), and not that the church "judged that such marriages should be prevented" (*inhibenda esse censuerit*).[46]

The prelates recognized that the church's current prohibition of clandestine marriage was ineffective, and some wanted the church to do more to prevent them. Olaus Magnus, archbishop of Uppsala, declared at the outset of the discussion:

---

[42] Motulanus, 452/13.   [43] Alatrinus, 475/38–40.

[44] For example, Feltrensis, 449/36–37: "licet clandestina matrimonia sint prohibita, ne contrahantur, contracta tamen tenent." Likewise, Maceratensis, 459/25–26.

[45] Albinghanensis, 475/13–21.

[46] Britonoriensis, 474/35–36. The same bishop, 474/33–35, proposed that the *tametsi* clause should explain *why* the church prohibited clandestine marriages, as did Maioricensis, 451/20–21, and Motulanus, 452/13–14.

"There ought to be a more effective remedy to condemn such clandestine marriages because of the many scandals that arise from them." He proposed that the church should reinstate Pope Evaristus's policy and require the same solemnities.[47] Attention turned from the validity of clandestine marriages to the importance of suppressing them, and from the anathema to the appended *tametsi* clause. Some prelates proposed that this clause, which was appended to a canon on doctrine, should refer to or be replaced by a separate decree on the reform of clandestine marriages.[48] But how would the church suppress them? The most popular remedy at this stage of the discussion was to penalize them more severely, for Lateran IV had said the persons marrying clandestinely would suffer an "appropriate penance" (*condigna poenitentia*), leaving local jurisdictions to determine the specific penalty.[49] A few of the prelates were more specific about penalties. The bishop of Pistoia proposed that erring daughters should be deprived of their dowries: a fitting penalty if absence of parental knowledge or consent was the salient defect of clandestinity.[50]

Some of the prelates proposed that the church, in view of the many evils and scandals to which clandestine marriages gave rise, ought to eradicate them entirely (*omnino tollere*), or to eradicate *all* such marriages (*tollere omnia*)[51] The idiom is ambiguous. It might refer either to all *particular* clandestine marriages or to all *modes* or *kinds* of clandestine marriage. If the prelates were referring to all particular clandestine marriages, they must have been advocating invalidation, for there was no other way to make sure that no one would marry clandestinely. The key term may be the verb *tollere*, implying eradication. It was stronger than *prohibere*. Luigi Lippomano, who was present as the coadjutor bishop of Verona, opposed invalidation and argued that clandestine marriages should not be "eradicated absolutely" (*prorsus tollenda*), but rather should be discouraged (*inhibenda*) with severe penalties.[52]

---

[47] Upsalensis, 449/13–14.

[48] Armacanus, 449/21–23. Bononiensis, 450/28–31. Aquensis Vorstius, 451/27–29. Salutiarum, 453/11–12.

[49] Bononiensis, 450/28–31. Chironensis, 451/7–8: ". . . esset tamen prohibendum matrimonium clandestinum sub gravibus poenis, praesertim illud, quod per testes non probatur." Mirapicensis, 453/35–36. Caprulanus, 455/8–9. Aprutinus, 470/5–6. Veronensis coadiutor, 452/26–27: "Quae matrimonia clandestina gravibus poenis sunt inhibenda, non tamen prorsus tollenda." Lavellanus, 458/2–4, proposed more severe penalties but precluded invalidation. Minoriensis (Catharinus), 472/5–12, proposed more severe penalties *and* invalidation. Camerinensis, 452/5–7, proposed that there should be no change to the current policy (presumably that of Lateran IV): "matrimonia clandestina sunt prohibenda in futurum, prout hactenus factum est in ecclesia." Those who said that penalization was the proper remedy without explicitly calling for reform, such as Mylensis Graecus, 459/22–23 ("et quod clandestina prohibeantur sub poenis etc."), probably assumed that there would be additional or more severe penalties. Cf. Lateran IV, canon 51, Tanner-Alberigo 1:258/32–34: "Sed et iis qui taliter copulari praesumpserit, etiam in gradu concesso, condigna poenitentia iniungatur."

[50] Pistoriensis, 459/14–16.

[51] For example, Mylensis Ferrettus, 425/23–23: "Essent tamen matrimonia ipsa clandestina omnia tollenda a synodo propter multa scandala, quae inde oriuntur." Likewise, Grossetanus, 451/4–5: "Sed clandestina matrimonia cuperet omnino tolli."

[52] Veronensis coadiutor, 452/26–27: "Quae matrimonia clandestina gravibus poenis sunt inhibenda, non tamen prorsus tollenda."

Those who wanted to prohibit clandestine marriages entirely were not necessarily advocating invalidation and may have been referring to all modes of clandestine marriage. For example, Thomas Stella, O.P., bishop of Lavello, was apparently not advocating invalidation when he said, "clandestine marriages should be entirely prohibited [*omnino prohibeantur*] because of the scandals and evils that arise from them, and because they are contracted and occur only because of the flesh," for he noted that invalidation would imply concurrence with Lutheran heresies. Thomas Stella advocated more severe penalties rather than invalidation. He added that some provision should be made to protect sons and daughters from unreasonably stubborn or coercive parents.[53] It is less clear what Richard Pate, the bishop of Worcester, meant when he declared that clandestine marriages ought to be "entirely prohibited in the future" because of the scandals and evils associated with them, especially marriage without parental consent. He explained that the "holy fathers" – perhaps he was thinking of Evaristus – had assumed that marriages should not be contracted without parental consent, and that this prohibition had been scrupulously observed in England up to his own day.[54] Both Richard Pate and Thomas Stella demanded at a later stage in the proceedings that clandestine marriages should be "entirely eradicated."[55]

Three prelates explicitly proposed that the church should make clandestine marriages invalid henceforth while conceding that such marriages had been and still were valid. The first to propose this solution was Catharinus, developing an idea that he had put forward tentatively on September 4 during the discussion of erroneous articles on clandestinity and divorce.[56] Concurring with the anathema, Catharinus conceded that clandestinely contracted marriages were currently valid and sacramental, but he emphasized that to contract a marriage clandestinely was a sin. The chief defect of such marriages, in his view, was the absence of parental consent. To marry against one's parents' knowledge or without their consent contravened natural, human, and divine law. Catharinus cited as proof Exodus 20:12 ("Honor thy father and mother") and 1 Corinthians 7:36–38, where Paul affirmed (according to the standard interpretation) that a virgin's father had the right to give or not to give her away in marriage.[57] Furthermore, because clandestine marriages were a source of enmity and scandal, they undermined civic order. For all those

---

[53] Lavellanus, 458/5–6: "Et clandestina matrimonia omnino prohibeantur propter scandala et mala, quae inde oriuntur, et cum tantum propter carnem contrahantur et fiant."

[54] Vigorniensis, 455/16–19: "Cuperet tamen omnino in futurum prohiberi matrimonia clandestina propter scandala, quae fiunt et propter eorum impuritatem et foeditatem, praesertim cum matrimonia sine consensu parentum contrahi non debeant iuxta sanctorum patrum sententiam, quod ad unguem observatur in Anglia (unde ipse Vigorniensis ortum habet)."

[55] Vigorniensis, 530/49–50: "non curat, quo in loco ponatur, dummodo clandestina matrimonia omnino tollantur." Lavellanus, 531/10–11: "Cuperet omnino tolli clandestina matrimonia."

[56] Minoriensis, 432/34–36.

[57] Most modern interpreters assume that St Paul was referring the virgin's betrothed, and not her father, but the old interpretation makes good sense.

reasons, severe penalization was appropriate, but it was not sufficient. Clandestine marriages ought henceforth to be rendered invalid (*irritari*), for the church had the necessary power.[58] Antoine Filhol, archbishop of Aix, conceded that clandestine marriages were currently valid and that parents did not have the power to annul their children's marriages, but he proposed that the *tametsi* clause should be amended so as to inhabilitate persons marrying clandestinely.[59] This was the first explicit reference to the theory of inhabilitation, according to which clandestinity would become a diriment personal impediment comparable to the impediments of consanguinity and affinity. Franciscus Romeo, Master General of the Dominicans, argued that parents could not annul their children's marriages because parental consent, like the bestowal of a dowry and the priestly blessing, was only a solemnity, and not part of the substance of the sacrament. But he added that the pope had the power to render such marriages null and void.[60]

Others resisted the idea that the church should or even could make clandestine marriages invalid.[61] To Sebastiano Antonio Pighini, bishop of Alife, it would be incoherent to anathematize those who said that clandestine marriages were invalid but then to affirm that the Catholic church would invalidate such marriages. The anathema was correct, and it implied that the church had no right or power even to prohibit clandestine marriages. Clandestinity could not be included among the impediments. Such a marriage might be found invalid in due course, when the circumstances were investigated, but only because some other defect had come to light.[62] In the nature of things, clandestinity was likely to disguise serious impediments, such as a prior contract, blood relationship, or acquired affinity. But clandestine marriages as such could not be prohibited, much less invalidated, Pighini argued, because matrimony belonged to the divine law, "which neither the pontiff nor the church is able to alter." Diriment impediments to marriage such as consanguinity, affinity, and religious vows were permanent conditions that inhered in one or both of the persons, whereas transitory obstacles, such as the clandestine circumstances of the contract, were not impediments in the proper sense.[63] This counter-argument regarding inherence would prove to be the chief objection to the theory of inhabilitation during 1563.

[58] Minoriensis, 472/10–12.

[59] Archiep. Aquensis Gallus, 473/22–23: "Quod dicitur in fine *tametsi* etc., cuperet inhabilitari personas, ne matrimonia huiusmodi clandestina valerent." He may have been referring to marriages without parental consent.

[60] Gen. Praedicatorum, 478/22–23: "Posset tamen pontifex prohibere ista matrimonia, ne fierent, et facta irritare."

[61] Veronensis coadjutor, 452/26–27. Lavellanus, 458/2–4. Sarsinensis, 474/9–10: "Neque censet irritanda matrimonia clandestina."

[62] Pighini cites Alexander III's decretal *Quod nobis*, X 4.3.2 (2:679), which was cited in the dossier of Aug. 29 accompanying the two heretical articles (408/6–10). Portuensis Portugallensis, 477/12–13, 16–18, proposes that the canon should anathematize those who say that clandestine marriages are not true and valid *inasmuch as they are clandestine*.

[63] Alyphanus, 471/17–29.

Tommaso Caselli, O.P., bishop of Bertinoro, refuted the arguments for invalidation being put forward, although he did not explicitly deny that the church had the necessary power. Affirming that such marriages were valid and could not be annulled by the parents, Caselli considered how one should interpret 1 Corinthians 7:37: "Nevertheless, he that stands steadfast in his heart, having no necessity, but has power over his own will, and has so decreed in his heart that he will keep his virgin, does well." Some cited this text as proof that fathers had the right of giving away their daughters in marriage, but Tommaso argued that Paul described fathers as "having no necessity" because they did not have the right to control their daughters' marriages. A daughter was not obliged either to marry or to remain unmarried at her father's bidding, and her father could not prevent her from marrying without his knowledge. It was not her father, therefore, and but the virgin herself who was said to "have power over her own will" (*habens potestatem suae voluntatis*). As for the decretal of Evaristus, Tommaso argued, the exception referred to the contractants, for their will was sufficient, whereas the parents' consent was not necessary.[64] The purpose of these counter-arguments was to show that absence of parental knowledge or consent was at most an accidental defect, which could not amount to proper grounds for invalidation.

The bishop of Albenga conceded that the church had the power to invalidate clandestine marriages even after they had been contracted (*postquam sunt contracta*), but he argued that the church ought not to use this power. He put forward two reasons. First, the invalidation of clandestine marriages would result in even more scandals and improprieties than the existing policy generated. Second, none of the problems being cited as reasons for invalidation was new. If invalidation was appropriate now, why had the church, which had always prohibited such marriages, reluctantly conceded until now that they were valid? It would be rash to depart from the longstanding policy, which was consistent with the traditional doctrine that the partners' consent was what made their marriage and that any other desirable customs were only solemnities.[65]

The prelates voiced a range of opinions regarding the role of parental consent in marriage. Everyone seems to have assumed that parental consent was important, but how should its absence be understood in law and in theology? Some cited evidence from Scripture and tradition to show that children were obliged to honor and obey their parents. They deduced that to marry without parental consent was a contravention of natural and divine law. Again, marriage was a civil contract as well as a sacrament, and marriages that were clandestine or contracted without parental consent undermined civic order and well-being.[66] Those who regarded marriage

[64] Britonoriensis, 474/26–33. 474/31–33: "Et verba Evaristi non obstant, cum ipsemet dicat: *nisi voluntas* contrahentium *suffragetur propria*; et tunc non requiritur consensus parentum."
[65] Albinghanensis, 475/14–21: "Ecclesia tamen irritare posset huiusmodi matrimonia clandestina; sed non deberet...."
[66] Thermularum, 453/27–29. Vigorniensis, 455/17–19. Minoriensis, 472/6–10.

more as a sacrament than as a civil contract, on the contrary, considered parental consent to be incidental. They cited not only Jesus' injunction, "What God has joined together, let not man separate," (Matt 19:6, Mark 10:9) but also the text that marked the original institution of marriage in Paradise: "For this reason a man shall leave his father and mother and cleave unto his wife" (Gen 2:24, Matt 19:5, etc.). Marriage was what *separated* children from their parents: the point of transition at which children left the sphere of parental control and began to make their own way in the world. It was incongruous, therefore, to insist that parents had the right of consent and refusal.[67]

The discussion of the draft anathema on clandestinity revealed the absence of any common understanding of how the defect should be defined or what its criteria were. Some prelates assumed that what made a marriage clandestine was the absence of proof; others, the absence of due solemnity. And the prelates were conflating clandestinity with the absence of parental consent. Only Benedetto de Nobili, O.P., bishop of Accia, proposed criteria for clandestinity. In his view, a marriage was clandestine when both proof (presumably through witnesses) and the customary solemnities were missing.[68] Cornelio Musso, O.F.M. Conv., bishop of Bitonto, proposed that the word "clandestine" should be taken out of the anathema, since in his view some clandestine marriages even now were not "true," including those contracted without the ministry of a priest. Nevertheless, the bishop argued, marriages contracted without parental consent, other things being equal, were true marriages.[69] Antoine Filhol, archbishop of Aix, questioned whether clandestine marriages should be deemed *matrimonia rata*, although he conceded that parents had no power to annul them.[70] The bishop of Saluzzo objected to the *tametsi* clause on the grounds that not all clandestine marriages were prohibited. He proposed that the canon should specify *which* clandestine marriages were prohibited, namely, those contracted without trustworthy witnesses.[71]

19.5 DOGMA OR REFORM? THE PARTICULAR CONGREGATIONS OF OCTOBER 12 AND 14

The discussion of the canon on clandestine marriages had raised the question of reform. What should the Catholic church do to prevent such marriages? The prelates accepted that there would need to be a decree of reform regarding clandestine marriages, and a few prelates were now calling for invalidation. But if the church rendered clandestine marriages null and void, the value of the anathema would be debatable. Why condemn the Protestants as heretics for a practice that the Catholic church was going to introduce? To be sure, the Protestants had no right to

---

[67] Sarsinensis, 474/8–9. Portuensis Portugallensis, 477/14–16.
[68] Aciensis de Nobilibus, 450/21–22.   [69] Bituntinus, 455/24–26.
[70] Archiep. Aquensis Gallus, 473/20–22.   [71] Salutiarum, 453/12–14.

deem clandestine marriages invalid, but perhaps the Protestant policy should be condemned as an error not of faith (*de fide*) but of practice (*de moribus*).

To clarify these issues, the legates on October 12 commissioned the prelates qualified in theology or canon law to discuss whether there should be a dogmatic canon on clandestine marriages, given that there would now be a reforming decree.[72] They devoted one evening to this question. Cardinal Del Monte remarked in wrapping up the discussion that it had been appropriate to include experts in law as well as theologians because this was a "mixed" topic, albeit primarily a theological one.[73]

Most of the prelates at this particular congregation held that condemnation of the Protestant error entailed a matter of dogma, and that the anathema should be retained. Some affirmed simply that there should be a dogmatic canon on the issue;[74] some added that the matter should be treated both under dogma and under reform;[75] and some proposed that the dogmatic canon should include some reference to reform, with the penalties spelled out in a corresponding decree of reform.[76] These positions were obviously mutually compatible. Richard Pate, bishop of Worcester, showing signs of impatience with the theological arguments, declared that he did not "care under which heading it was put, as long as clandestine marriages were entirely eradicated."[77]

The chief task of this particular congregation was to decide whether a dogmatic canon on clandestine marriages should be retained in some form, and most agreed that it should. In their view, the Lutheran policy entailed a heresy, whatever the Catholic church's own policy might turn out to be.[78] There was little attempt at this stage to identify what the Lutheran heresy was, although Pighini, bishop of Alife, cited the *Bull of Union with the Armenians* and argued that whether clandestine marriages were valid was a question of dogma because it pertained to the substance of a sacrament.[79]

A few prelates wanted the issue to be treated solely under reform, with no dogmatic canon. Thomas Stella and the bishop of Nevers were in this party, although both said that they wanted clandestine marriages to be "entirely

---

[72] CT 6.1:529–32.   [73] Ibid., 532/1–3.

[74] Upsalensis, Abricensis, 530. Albinganensis, Ebriocensis, Calvensis, 531.

[75] Materanus, Armacanus, Cesenatensis, Amalfitanus, Feltrensis, Chironensis, Sarsinensis, Maioricensis, Aquensis Vorstius, Carinolae, Motulanus, Parentinus, Pisauriensis, Veronensis, Thermulanus, Mylensis Ferrettus, 530. Chissamensis, Aquinatensis, Mylensis Graecus, Abbas Lucianus Pomposiae Ferrariensis, 531.

[76] Bononiensis, Sebastensis, Camerinensis, Caprulanus, 530. Britonoriensis, Aprutinus, Alyphanus, Minoriensis (Ambrosius Catharinus), Sulmonensis, Gen. Praedicatorum (Romeo), Gen. Hermitarum (Seripando), Gen. Servorum, 531.

[77] Vigorniensis, 530/49–50: "non curat, quo in loco ponatur, dummodo clandestina matrimonia omnino tollantur."

[78] Upsalensis, Abrincensis, Chironensis, Aquensis Vorstius, Sebastensis, Veronensis, 530. Britonoriensis, Aquinatensis, Ebriocensis, Aprutinus, Sulmonensis, Calvensis, Gen. Servorum, 531.

[79] Alyphanus, 531/23–26.

eradicated."[80] They accepted that the Lutheran position on clandestinity had to be condemned, but they did not want that condemnation to be expressed as a dogmatic anathema. The bishop of Nevers protested that according to the Lutherans a marriage without parental consent was invalid even if a thousand witnesses were present. In his view, it seems, the Lutherans erred in focusing on the absence of parental consent when the critical defect was absence of proof. But the concern of this minority was mainly strategic. They feared that the anathema would become a source of further scandal by suggesting that the Catholic church approved of clandestine marriages, whereas in fact, as Benedetto de Nobili put it, "all the doctors and councils of the church" had prohibited such marriages.[81]

Cornelio Musso, bishop of Bitonto, argued that the matter could not be one of dogma because dogmas were inalterable, whereas the church's position on clandestine marriage was and should remain changeable (*mutabilis*). He added that the church had always prohibited clandestine marriages because of the scandals to which they gave rise.[82] Seripando refuted Musso's argument. The fact that the mutual consent of the spouses was sufficient to establish a valid marriage, Seripando claimed, was a "perpetual truth" and, therefore, a matter of dogma.[83] Ambrosius Catharinus, too, refuted Musso, but from a different point of view. Catharinus agreed that the church's position on clandestine marriage could change. He conceded that clandestinely contracted marriages were currently valid, but he argued that church had the power to invalidate them henceforth. Nevertheless, a matter of dogma was at stake. The Protestant heresy was ecclesiological, for they declared that clandestine marriages were invalid when the church still held that they were valid.[84]

The particular congregation of October 12 had established there should be a dogmatic canon anathematizing those who already held that clandestine marriages were invalid. The next question was how to modify the dogmatic canon so as to identify more precisely what was the heretical in the Lutheran position. The prelates who were qualified in theology met on the evening of October 14 to discuss this matter.[85] Some of those qualified in law remained to hear the discussion, and the theologian-prelates invited them to share their thoughts on the matter.[86]

The theologian-prelates considered three alternative proposals (*censurae*): (1) to take out the equivocal term "clandestine" from the canon and to focus on parental consent, so that the canon would anathematize only those who said that marriages "made without the will of the parents" were invalid; or (2) to declare that a clandestine marriage would be condemned when its invalidity had come to the church's notice; or (3) to leave the canon as it stood.[87] The first amendment was

---

[80] Aciensis, Placentinus, Sancti Pauli, 530. Lavellanus, Niverniensis, 531.

[81] Aciensis, 530/21–22.   [82] Bituntinus, 530–31.   [83] Gen. Hermitarum, 531/38–41.

[84] Minoriensis, 531/28–31.

[85] 532–34. The same theologian-prelates discussed the third canon, regarding remarriage after adultery, on the following day.

[86] CT 6.1:534/21.   [87] Ibid., 532.

straightforward. At the outset of the discussion, Robert Wauchope, archbishop of Armagh, suggested what the anathema might look like without any reference to clandestinity:

> If anyone says that marriages that are entered into with the free consent of the contractants without the agreement of the parents are not true and valid marriages, so that it is in the power of the parents or magistrates to make them valid or invalid, let him be anathema.[88]

The purpose and even the meaning of the second proposal is unclear. Nor is it clear how the prelates construed it. On the face of things, it might invalidate either (i) any marriage found to be clandestine in the sense that it lacked witnesses or proper solemnization (or both)[89] or (ii) a clandestine marriage once it had been examined and found deficient because of some *other* impediment. Both positions had already been in circulation. In fact, discussion of the second proposal turned on the functions of proof and solemnization. Marrying before the church (*in facie ecclesiae*) was considered to be a means of *probatio* or *approbatio*: terms that are difficult to construe or to translate adequately because they convey at once the notions of proof, endorsement, and approval, with varying emphasis. The need for proof, however, was always uppermost. The theologian-prelates asked themselves whether such proof (or approval) was necessary for validity, at least in the church's public forum.

A few prelates were inclined to favor the first proposal and were prepared to adopt Robert Wauchope's amendment. In their view, this revision would have correctly identified the crux of the Lutheran error.[90] Giacomo de' Giacomelli, bishop of Belcastro, proposed that the term "clandestine" should be included if and only if the Lutherans included it when stating their own, erroneous position.[91] Cornelio Musso, bishop of Bitonto, endorsed Robert Wauchope's amendment. There should be "no mention" of clandestine marriages, he argued, but only of marriages without parental consent, since clandestine marriages were valid as marriages albeit not as sacraments.[92] Several prelates contradicted the bishop of Bitonto on this last point, affirming that clandestine marriages were not only valid but also sacramental.[93] Thus, Franciscus Romeo, Master General of the Dominicans, argued that clandestine marriage "is not only true and valid, but also a sacrament, as blessed Thomas and other theologians hold." Such a marriage was imperfect as a sacrament, he

---

[88] Armacanus, 533/1–3: "Si quis dixerit matrimonia libero contrahentium contracta consensu sine voluntate parentum non esse vera et rata matrimonia, ita ut sit in potestate parentum vel magistratus ea irritandi, a. s."

[89] This is the editorial interpretation: See 532n5, referring to the summary on 484/21–24.

[90] Aciensis, Abrincensis, Chissamensis, Lavellanus, 533. Minoriensis, 534/2–3.

[91] Bellicastrensis, 533/26–27.

[92] Bituntinus, 533/21–25. Musso added that, as Cardinal Del Monte had said in a previous congregation, only marriages endorsed (*probata*) by the church are legitimate.

[93] Britonoriensis, Lavellanus, Aprutinus, 533. Gen. Minimorum, 534.

argued, but only in the same sense as a child was an imperfect human being. Clandestine marriages did not confer grace, Franciscus Romeo conceded, yet not because the marriage itself was not a sacrament but only because the sin of marrying clandestinely was an obstacle to grace.[94]

Most of the prelates wanted to retain the reference to clandestinity in the anathema, partly because the Lutherans themselves used the term in articulating their own policy.[95] Some would have preferred a declaration that a freely contracted clandestine marriage was valid "in general," without specifying what manner of clandestinity came under the anathema. These favored the retention of the canon as it stood (the third option). By making the condemnation too specific, they reasoned, one would risk implying either that some other modes of clandestine marriage were invalid when in fact they were valid, or, on the contrary, that the only prohibited mode of clandestinity was the absence of parental consent, which was false.[96] Seripando argued that the canon should condemn exactly what the Lutherans said, or at least the gist of what they said, without any attempt to parse the notion of clandestinity. He proposed the following minimal version, which included the word "clandestine" but left its sense indefinite: "If anyone says that clandestine marriages are not settled [*rata*] unless they are approved by the parents, and hence that it is in the power of the parents to make them valid or invalid, let him be anathema."[97]

It was becoming clear that clandestinity and the absence of parental consent were not coextensive abuses and might have to be distinguished or even treated separately. But if the absence of parental consent was not a sufficient and perhaps not even a necessary condition of clandestinity, what *was* the essential defect? Contrariwise, what made a marriage public in the approved manner? Such questions became more urgent as minds were turning toward the possibility of invalidation. Olaus Magnus, the archbishop of Uppsala, wanted to include some mention of those whose marriages were "approved *in facie ecclesiae*, since those are truly settled and valid marriages."[98] But what was the salient feature of marriage contracted *in facie ecclesiae*, absent which the marriage was clandestine? Aside from the minimal requirements of Lateran IV, the conditions that made a marriage public rather than clandestine had always been a regional or provincial matter.

Some considered the ministry or blessing of a priest to be the salient feature that ought to distinguish properly contracted marriages from clandestine marriages. But the prelates who discussed this idea seem to have conflated questions about the introduction of new positive law with questions about the inalterable constitution of

---

[94] Gen. Praedicatorum, 534/5–10.

[95] Britonoriensis, 533. Gen. Praedicatorum, 534. Also Feltrensis, 534, who was present only as an auditing *iurisperitus*.

[96] Motulanus; Veronensis; Aprutinus, 533. Generalis s. Augustini (Seripando), 534.

[97] Gen. s. Augustini, 534/16–18: "Si quis dixerit matrimonia clandestina non esse rata, nisi a parentibus probentur, ac proinde esse in potestate parentum ea irrita vel rata facere, a. s."

[98] Upsalensis, 532/18–19: "Placeret fieri mentionem de iis, quae in facie ecclesiae approbata fuerint, cum illa vere sint rata matrimonia et valida."

the sacrament. Catharinus inquired whether clandestine marriage was a sacrament. He noted in response that according to *The Bull of Union with the Armenians* a minister was necessary in all the sacraments. Inasmuch as no minister of the church officiated at clandestine marriages, they were valid but non-sacramental. Catharinus conceded, nevertheless, that his position was unusual. It was the "common opinion of theologians" that clandestine marriages were sacraments.[99] Giovanni Giacomo Barba, O.S.A., bishop of Teramo, insisted that the priest's role was accidental. Clandestine marriages were true and sacramental because consent alone made marriage, regardless of whether or not a priest was present:

> Clandestine marriages are sacraments because consent makes marriage, and a valid marriage is a sacrament. Nor is a minister necessary for this sacrament, because the form does not need to be proffered by a minister as in the other sacraments. Instead, the form of marriage is the words expressing the free consent of the contractants. Where there is free consent, therefore, there is a sacrament, because what makes the sacrament is neither the priest nor the endorsement [*probatio*] of the church but the Holy Spirit.[100]

Tommaso Caselli, bishop of Bertinoro, proposed that there should be some mention of clandestinity in the canon because clandestine marriage was a sacrament, even if the practice was reprehensible. Furthermore, consent, and not the priestly blessing, was the sufficient cause of marriage. He pointed out that if clandestine marriages were not sacraments because they were not blessed by a priest, then neither would second marriages be sacraments, since they too were customarily not blessed by a priest.[101]

Proof by witnesses was a more promising candidate for what was missing in clandestine marriages, but Robert Wauchope and others pointed out that it was illogical to make proof a condition for validity, since proof was posterior to what needed to be proved, namely, whether a valid marriage had taken place. Proof itself could not be what made a marriage valid or invalid: *"probatio non facit validitatem."* If a marriage was proven but the proof was false, it would be valid in reality and in God's eyes even though the church judged it to be invalid.[102] Developing the same argument, Dionysio de Zanettinis, bishop of Chironissa (known as the "Little Greek"), pointed out that when the church declared a marriage to be null and void because of inadequate proof, what could not be proved was mutual consent. If there had in fact been such consent, then, regardless of the church's judgment, the marriage was valid in the sight of God.[103]

The particular congregations had revealed a remarkable lack of consensus among the prelates regarding clandestine marriages, but they had at least established two

---

[99] Minoriensis, 533–34.   [100] Aprutinus, 533/42–47.   [101] Britonoriensis, 533/30–32.
[102] Armacanus, 532/20–23.
[103] Chironensis, 533/11–14. Aprutinus, 533/47–49, argued that the church could judge hidden things, and that clandestine marriages might be true marriages.

points: that the anathema should be retained in some form, although a separate decree of reform clandestine marriage would be needed as well; and that the anathema should refer to clandestine marriages as well as to marriages without parental consent. The prelates had not agreed as to what made a marriage clandestine, but the discussion had brought two defects into focus: the absence of proof, and the absence of the priestly blessing. Discussion of the first defect revealed that it would be absurd to make proof a condition of validity (although the council would eventually make it so at Trent). Discussion of the second defect brought back the question of whether the blessing was what made marriage sacramental. The prelates' considered answer was as always negative, but the notion had an intuitive attraction that could not be ignored. Finally, the problem of whether questions about clandestinity should or should not be construed as matters of dogma was beginning to come into focus.

19.6 REVISION OF THE CANONS: THE PARTICULAR CONGREGATIONS OF OCTOBER THROUGH NOVEMBER

The agenda now turned to revision of the dogmatic canons on marriage. The theologian-prelates met again, beginning on October 15, to discuss revisions to the third of the dogmatic canons presented to them on September 9, regarding remarriage after a divorce on grounds of adultery. Revised versions of the first three canons were put before them on October 18, including the canons on sacramentality (canon 1) and on clandestinity (canon 2). At some point before November 7, Franciscus Romeo, Master General of the Dominicans, and Agostino Bonucci, Superior General of the Servites, proposed their own further amendments to the first two revised canons.

The revised version of the canon on clandestinity (canon 2) extended the list of agents who might be falsely be said to annul marriage, and it dropped the term "clandestine," notwithstanding the opposition of most of the theologian-prelates to this proposal during the particular congregation of October 14. The *tametsi* clause was also omitted, for since it had referred to clandestine marriages it was now redundant:

> If anyone says that marriages between legitimate persons contracted with free consent are not true and valid, but are in the power of the parents or guardians or magistrates to make them valid or invalid, let him be anathema.[104]

Franciscus Romeo objected that the proposed version raised more problems than it solved, and he proposed that the gist could be better captured as follows:

---

[104] CT 6.1:537/6–8: "Si quis dixerit matrimonia **inter legitimas personas** libero consensu contracta fiunt non esse vera et rata, sed esse in potestate **parentum aut tutorum** aut magistratuum ea rata vel irrita facere, a. s." Additions are in bold font.

If anyone says that marriages contracted with free consent but without the knowledge or even against the wishes of parents or guardians or magistrates are not true
and valid, let him be anathema.[105]

Agostino Bonucci, who explained that he was making his proposals after carefully
studying Johann Brenz's pamphlet on marriage,[106] offered two new, alternative versions of the canon, which in his view would better capture the gist of the Protestant
heresy. Both versions anathematized those who held that *judges appointed by magistrates* had the power to inquire into and annul the marriages of minors (*iuniorum*)
contracted without the consent of their parents. According to the second, longer
version, the Protestants conducted this inquiry before the couple had sexual intercourse and before they celebrated their nuptials in a church wedding.[107]

The record of these proceedings is incomplete, but they were apparently inconclusive.

19.7 GENERAL CONGREGATIONS ON ABUSES AND REMEDIES,
NOVEMBER 29 THROUGH DECEMBER 25

On November 29, 1547, the legates put before the prelates a dossier of abuses,
remedies, and related provisions regarding marriage, which had been prepared by
four bishops deputed for this task.[108] The list of abuses captures the specter of nuptial
disorder that troubled many Catholic clerics as well as Protestants.[109] Because
clandestine marriages gave rise to "many grave scandals and dangers," they are at
the head of the list of six major abuses. A narrative explains how the church has
found no way effectively to curb clandestine marriages, notwithstanding many
admonitions and prohibitions, beginning with the decretal of Pope Evaristus. The
very fact that valid marriages must be contracted freely and not coerced has made
the abuse difficult to prevent.

The dossier includes two remedies to clandestinity. First, any minors who marry
clandestinely and without parental consent shall be disinherited, and girls shall be
deprived of their dowries. For the first time, the reform specifies the age of majority:
twenty years for daughters and twenty-two for sons. Second, if a girl is betrothed

---

[105] CT 6.1:537/16–17: "Si quis dixerit matrimonia libero consensu contracta nescientibus aut etiam
discentientibus parentibus seu tutoribus aut magistratibus non esse vera et rata, a. s."

[106] I.e., *Libellus casuum quorundam matrimonialium elegantissimus Ioanne Brentio autore* (Basel,
1536), this being the Latin translation of Brenz's *Wie in Eesachen, und in den fellen, so sich
derhalben zutragen, nach götlichem billichem rechten christenlich zu handeln sey* (Staß-
burg, 1529).

[107] Gen. Servorum super canonibus matrimonii, 538.

[108] CT 6.1:619–21. The deputies were the bishops of Casena, Fiesole, Bitonto, and Nevers (ibid.,
583/15–16, and 586/5–8, 630/1–2).

[109] In addition to the abuses presented for discussion, the bishop of Saint-Malo (Macloviensis, 627/
11–12) mentions another, whereby "spouses come to a church late at night to receive the
blessing from a priest without being seen," an abuse associated with clandestine marriages.
Reformist clerics insisted that church weddings should take place during the hours of daylight.

when she is still under the age of twelve without the consent of her parents or legal guardians, whether in words of the future or of the present tense, the betrothal is invalid, and her suitor will be treated as an abductor and will face the penalties for *raptus* as defined in civil law, as also will his accomplices.[110] Since the suppression of clandestine marriage was in tension with the freedom to marry, one of the attached provisions confirms that marriages ought to be entirely free and warns that a girl approaching marriage can become so encumbered by the obligations and agreements negotiated on her behalf by her parents, including settlements such as the *arrha*, that her consent is no longer truly free. Such arrangements must not curtail her freedom, for her authentic consent is essential.[111]

The other abuses are concubinage, knowingly marrying within the forbidden degrees in the expectation of getting a dispensation later,[112] and three species of nuptial impropriety: pre-nuptial intercourse, unseemly ribaldry at weddings, and the public mockery of men who marry widows. In some places, the document explains, obscene banter and lewd singing even breaks out in the sanctuary of a church after the blessing of the couple. This practice should be suppressed by severe penalties, even to the extent of excommunication, for "my house shall be called the house of prayer, but you have made it a den of thieves" (Matt 21:13). In some places, too, it is customary for couples not to receive the nuptial blessing until several days after they have come together and consummated their marriage. In future, couples who have already consummated their unions will not be permitted to receive the nuptial blessing, and priests who do bless them will face suspension.[113] This remedy would presumably have applied to all cases of pre-nuptial intercourse, but the aim was to prevent couples who had become betrothed (whether *de futuro* or *de praesenti*) from cohabiting or spending time alone together and beginning to have sexual intercourse before the marriage was confirmed in a church ceremony, for solemnization was the point of no return in popular understanding.

The prelates met in general congregations from December 1 through 25 to discuss these abuses and remedies. I shall limit my commentary here to their treatment of clandestine marriage. They soon realized that there would be no consensus on this topic. The question of a remedy could not be treated wholly as a matter of reform, for any policy presupposed a theological position on the causes and the composition of the sacrament, and there was insufficient consensus regarding the presupposed doctrines.

Several of the prelates resisted even the introduction of new penalties and considered severe penalties, such as disinheritance, to be inappropriate.[114] Sebastiano

---

[110] Abuse I (§§ 1–3), 619/1–23.   [111] Provisions (§ 13), 621/17–22.

[112] Abuse VI (§ 9), 620/27–35. See also Provisions, §§ 10–11 (621).

[113] Abuse V (§ 8), 620/21–26. Cf. Jonas of Orléans, *De institutione laicali* II.2 (SC 549:330–40): Couples indulging in pre-marital intercourse are not entitled to receive the blessing by which God blessed Adam and Eve.

[114] Sebastensis, 627/1–5. Macloviensis, 627/10–11. Mylensis Ferrettus, 631/. Myrapicensis, 631/15. Calvensis, 633/8–9 (". . . sed reliquenda sunt in iure antiquo, cui standum est").

Leccavella, O.P., speaking on the first day, agreed that clandestine marriages should be prevented, but he suggested that disinheritance and deprivation of dowry were too severe. In his view, the council should not attempt to prescribe any new canonical penalties but rather should leave them to "the disposition of the *ius commune.*"[115] Others defended the penalty of disinheritance. Lippomanus, citing Ephesians 6:1 and 1 Corinthians 7:38, argued that it was appropriate because children ought to obey their parents,.[116]

A major and irreparable fissure regarding invalidation soon emerged, dividing most of the prelates into two opposing parties. On one side were those who not only favored the suppression of clandestine marriage through penalties but also maintained that the church could and probably should invalidate such marriages.[117] Giovanni Michele Saraceni, archbishop of Acerenza e Matera, and Robert Wauchope, archbishop of Armagh, presented different versions of this position on the first day. Saraceni considered the age and status of the spouses to be crucial. If those who married clandestinely had reached the age of majority (*in perfecta aetate*), their marriage should be considered valid. But if they were still minors (*non ... in aetate matura*) and were still subject to parental power (*sub aliena ... potestate*), their marriage was defective and should be annulled. Moreover, a girl in this situation should be deprived of her dowry, and her seducer should be punished as an abductor (*raptor*).[118] Robert Wauchope, archbishop of Armagh, after apologizing for coming to the congregation unprepared, declared that clandestine marriages ought to be entirely eradicated ("*omnino tollantur*"), adding that the council had the power to achieve this if the prelates saw fit. He maintained that there were adequate precedents for the innovation, especially the invalidation of certain degrees of relationship that had not been prohibited under divine law.[119]

Some on this side were forthright advocates of invalidation, whereas others proposed it only as a possibility to be considered. And whereas some were willing to settle for suppression through more severe penalties if that turned out to be what the majority wanted, others maintained that there was no point in relying on penalization alone since the policy of prohibiting clandestine marriages without rendering them null and void had proved ineffective. Alvaro della Quadra, bishop of

[115] Naxiensis, 622/15–17.
[116] Veronensis coadiutor, 629/26–30. Others who endorsed more severe penalties and disinheritance include Briocensis, 633/6–7, and Maceratensis, 633/33–34.
[117] Archiep. Materanus, 622/2–11. Armacanus, 622/29–35. Archiep. Aquensis, 623/7–8. Feltrensis, 623/21–26. Aciensis, 623/28–30 ("potest [ecclesia] tamen, antequam contrahantur, personas inhabilitare"). Grossetanus, 624/35–36. Portuensis Portugallensis, 628/1–3 ("concilium possit (et expediat) ea irritare"). Salutiarum, 631/4–6. Thermularum, 631/8–10. Caprulanus, 631/ 26–29. Vigorniensis, 632/4–6. Venusinus, 632/16–21. Aquinatensis, 632/27–32. Bituntinus, 634/ 9–14. Minoriensis (Catharinus), 652/13–653/5. Lucianus abbas Pomposiae Ferrariensis, 653/ 24–654/3. Gen. Praedictorum, 654/14–17.
[118] Archiep. Materanus, 622/2–8. I presume that "*imperfecta aetate*" at 622/4–5 should be "*in perfecta aetate.*"
[119] Armacanus, 622/29–35.

Venosa, was among this latter group. He proposed that "clandestine marriages that are without parental consent" ought to be entirely eradicated (*omnino tolli*) and rendered invalid. The proposed penalty of disinheritance would not suffice. "If clandestine marriages are bad," he protested, "they should be entirely eradicated. If they are good, they should not be penalized." "The church has the power to invalidate and entirely to eradicate such marriages."[120]

Others argued that clandestine marriages should not and probably could not be rendered null and void, partly because such marriages had everything required for the sacrament, and partly because the church had no right to prevent persons from marrying freely, since the union was founded on the spouses' consent.[121] Prelates on this side not only denied that the church had the power to invalidate clandestine marriages but were even wary of trying to suppress them through more severe penalties. The desire to stamp out clandestine marriages entirely, in their view, was inconsistent with the freedom to marry (*libertas matrimonii*).[122]

A third position emerged. A few prelates conceded that the church might have the power to invalidate clandestine marriages in theory but argued that invalidation would be rash and overly novel, and, therefore, inexpedient.[123] For example, Claude de La Guiche, bishop of Mirepoix, said that the church had the power to make clandestine marriages invalid but that using the power would be contrary to what the "holy fathers" had said regarding consent to marry. Moreover, he pointed out, the invalidation of such marriages would itself become a source of scandal. He even considered the penalty of disinheritance to be too severe.[124]

Most of the prelates who wanted clandestine marriages to be rendered null and void conceded that such marriages were currently valid. That matter had already been settled in the second of the dogmatic canons on marriage, which the prelates had discussed during September (Section 19.3). This affirmed that clandestine marriages contracted with the free consent of the spouses were true and settled (*rata*), and that parents did not have the power to annul them, although it added (in the *tametsi* clause) that the church had always prohibited and endeavored to suppress such marriages.[125] The discussion of the canon had exposed a lack of consensus regarding its underlying principles, but no one had rejected the canon outright by proposing that clandestine marriages were invalid or less than sacramental.

---

[120] Venusinus, 632/16–21.

[121] Abricensis, 624/4–9. Chironensis, 625/6–18. Fesulanus, 625/29–32. Sarsinatensis, 625/37–43. Malfectensis, 629/4–5. Motulanus, 629/10–13. Albinganensis, 632/34–36. Niverniensis, 633/15–19. Aprutinus, 634/19–37. Alyphanus, 651/28–652/11.

[122] Chironensis, 625/18–19. Fesulanus, 625/29–30. Motulanus, 629/10–11. Aprutinus, 634/27–29.

[123] Maioricensis, 626/27–30. Camerinensis, 628/. [124] Myrapicensis, 631/21–24.

[125] 446/1–4: "Si quis dixerit clandestina matrimonia, quae libero contrahentium consensu fiunt, non esse vera et rata matrimonia, ac proinde esse in potestate parentum ea rata vel irrita facere, a. s.; tametsi sancta ecclesia matrimonia huiusmodi bonis et rationabilibus causis inhibenda esse censuerit."

By what right or power could the church render such marriages null and void now? The notion that such marriages were prohibited but were valid once they had been contracted retained a strong hold. But several prelates obviated that objection by arguing that the church had the power to inhabilitate the persons who were about to marry clandestinely, as if clandestinity were a diriment personal impediment. Antoine Filhol, archbishop of Aix, had said in September that he wanted the canon to inhabilitate persons marrying clandestinely, so that such marriages would be invalid.[126] He returned to this proposal on December 3. He conceded that clandestine marriages were true and valid, and he said that marrying without parental consent was an abuse condemned only in civil law, and not in canon law. He was willing to settle for penalization as the remedy, if that was the best that could be achieved. Nevertheless, he argued, it would better to deem persons marrying clandestinely to be illegitimate: in other words, to disqualify them from marrying by declaring that they were not *personae legitimae*.[127] Some other prelates pursued versions of the same argument, claiming that the church had the power to inhabilitate or to render illegitimate persons who were marrying clandestinely.[128] Benedetto de Nobili, O.P., bishop of Accia, conceded that clandestine marriages were valid *after* they had been contracted, but he proposed that the church had the power to inhabilitate the persons *before* they contracted their marriage.[129] Similarly, Catharinus conceded that the church could not invalidate or dissolve already-contracted clandestine marriages but argued that the church could invalidate to-be-contracted clandestine marriages (*matrimonia clandestina contrahenda*) by inhabilitating the persons.[130] Catharinus considered the absence of parental consent rather than secrecy *per se* to be the crucial defect of such marriages. Giovanni Giacomo Barba, bishop of Teramo, argued that parental consent should not be required because a man leaves his father and mother to cleave unto his wife (Gen 2:24).[131] Catharinus replied that this text referred not to marrying *per se* but to a consequence of marrying. The son is said to cleave to his *wife*, and not to cleave to a woman by making her his wife.[132]

Some proponents of invalidation argued instead that the church should invalidate the contract itself, or the manner (*modus*) in which the spouses contracted marriage.

---

[126] Archiep. Aquensis Gallus, 473/21–22: "Quod dicitur in fine *tametsi* etc., cuperet inhabilitari personas, ne matrimonia huiusmodi clandestina valerent." Sebastiano Leccavella, O.P., the archbishop of Naxos, 420/17–19, had been the first to use the terminology of *inhabilitatio*, but he was apparently referring to the habilitation or inhabilitation of certain degrees of relationship, and not of persons.

[127] Archiep. Aquensis Gallus, 623/4–8.

[128] Aciensis, 623/28–30. Salutiarum, 631/4–6. Bituntinus, 634/13–15. Minoriensis, 653/1–3.

[129] Aciensis, 623/28–30: "Ad articulum, an ecclesia possit in totum irritare matrimonia clandestina, respondet, quod potest, quia, licet iam contracta sint valida, potest tamen, antequam contrahuntur, personas inhabilitare." Benedetto de Nobili also wanted to reinstate the policy of Evaristus but to take out the specification of threshold ages, replacing it with "*quacumque aetate.*" Aquensis Vorstius, 626/34, too, proposed that Evaristus's policy should be reinstated: "Cuperetque innovari canonum Evaristi."

[130] Minoriensis, 653/1–3.   [131] Aprutinus, 634/23–26.   [132] Minoriensis, 652/19–25.

The bishop of Feltre cited impediments of status and relationship as precedents, but he argued that the church had the power to invalidate even free consent to marriage when that consent was clandestine.[133] The bishop of Angoulême proposed that there should be a prescribed ecclesial form for marrying, and that the sacrament should be administered by a priest. Failing that, the marriage would be invalid.[134]

The proponents of invalidation cited other examples of such innovation, where the church had modified or waived a rule inscribed in natural or divine law. The bishop of Caprulae (Caorle) found precedents in canon law's handling of precepts such as "Thou shalt not kill" (Exod 20:13) and "Thou shalt not steal" (Exod 12:15). The church permitted people to kill in the church's defense, and to steal in cases of dire need.[135] Pierre van der Worst, bishop of Acqui, who was among those seeking the reinstatement of the policy of Pope Evaristus, found a precedent in the pope's power to dissolve a non-consummated marriage. He cited the canonist Hostiensis (Henry of Segusio) on this point.[136] But the bishop of Nevers, who was among the opponents of invalidation, refuted Pierre van der Worst's argument. He questioned both the authority of Hostiensis and the power of popes to dissolve unconsummated marriages, and he argued that the parallel was not sufficiently apposite. The invalidation or eradication of clandestine marriages would require the church to abrogate divine law, which it had no power to do.[137]

Franciscus Romeo, Master General of the Dominicans, distinguished between a defect of the contract or sacrament of marriage *per se*, and a detrimental *consequence* of that union. Considered in themselves, he conceded, clandestine marriages were truly and properly marriages, for they had the form and the matter essential to the sacrament, as many of the scholastic doctors had maintained. It was true that the Council of Florence (in the *Bull of Union with the Armenians*) had emphasized that the ministry of a priest was necessary for the validity of the sacraments in general, but the council had not applied that principle to marriage. Romeo argued, nevertheless, that the church could and should invalidate clandestine marriages henceforth, especially those without witnesses: not because such marriages were intrinsically sinful or defective, but because of their social consequences, such as the scandals to which they gave rise. In the same way, he pointed out, the church invalidated the more remote degrees of relationship not because there was anything wrong in such unions *per se*, which were not incestuous, but in view of the beneficial consequences of the restriction. The church was able *a fortiori*, therefore, to invalidate clandestine marriages.[138] Romeo was touching on an important consideration,

---

[133] Feltrensis, 623/21–26.   [134] Angolismensis, 626/20–22.   [135] Caprulanus, 631/26–35.

[136] Aquensis Vorstius, 626/31–35. Vorstius is referring to Hostiensis's gloss on Alexander III's decretal *Ex publico*, X 3.32.7 (580–81), on which see K. Pennington, *The Prince and the Law, 1200–1600* (Berkeley, 1993), 65–67. On the canon law of papal dispensation from an unconsummated marriage, see W. Kelly, *Pope Gregory II on Divorce and Remarriage* (Rome, 1976), 232–41.

[137] Niverniensis, 633/15–26.   [138] Gen. Praedicatorum, 654/7–19.

which would emerge again during 1563. Many assumed that positive law could validly prohibit only things that were intrinsically evil (*mala per se*), rather than accidentally or consequentially evil. Whereas some thought that this principle would prevent the church from invalidating clandestine marriages, others maintained that a statistically predominant evil consequence – that is, one that occurred *in the majority of cases* – amounted to an intrinsic evil.

The subtle arguments of the proponents of invalidation prompted the opponents to reclaim and elaborate the position of the medieval schoolmen (Section 14.7). The result was a formidable barrage of traditional objections and arguments. As well as questioning whether the suppression or eradication of clandestine marriages would be pastorally expedient, opponents denied that the church had the power to make them invalid. They also denied that children required their parents' consent to marry, and, for that reason, they did not consider disinheritance to be an appropriate penalty. According to Giacomo Ponzetti, bishop of Molfetta, "clandestine marriage could not be rendered invalid by the church because it was a true sacrament."[139] Dionysio de Zanettini, bishop of Chironissa, argued that the church could not invalidate clandestine marriages because everything essential to the sacrament was present in them, namely, the free mutual consent of legitimate persons. Nor could the church alter the essential composition of this or of any other sacrament. Nor was the parents' dissent a fatal flaw, for the man who married, according to Scripture, left his father and mother to cleave unto this wife. Dionysio de Zanettini denied that adequate precedents could be found in the impediments of relationship or in the church's power to dissolve an unconsummated marriage. On the contrary, the invalidation of clandestine marriages was inconsistent with tradition and with the decisions of many councils and popes. Even the effort to suppress clandestine marriages through draconian penalties would curtail the freedom to marry (*libertas matrimonii*), which was a fundamental good.[140]

The bishop of Nevers held that the freedom to marry was a matter of divine law (*ius divinum*). Because of this freedom, the spouses' free consent sufficed by itself for a valid marriage between legitimate persons. Since the church had no power to alter divine law, it had no power to invalidate clandestine marriage. The absence of witnesses, he pointed out, was a defect of proof and not of the marriage itself. Moreover, canon law had established that in such cases the church should presume in favor of the marriage's authenticity, so that the partners' confession that they had mutually consented, other things being equal, was sufficient.[141] The penalty of disinheritance was not appropriate because paternal consent was not required under canon law. Indeed, what was being proposed was more restrictive even than the

---

[139] Malfectensis, 629/4–5: "tenet clandestinum matrimonium non posse ab ecclesia irritari, cum sit verum sacramentum."

[140] Chironensis, 625/6–23.

[141] Cf. Alexander III's decretal *Quod nobis*, X 4.3.2 (679), which was cited in the dossier accompanying the two heretical articles on Aug. 29 (408/6–10).

relevant Roman civil law. Again, the remedy was supposed to apply only to children in power (*filii in potestate*), but that was a category of Roman and not of canon law. Indeed, it was not current in the secular laws of many peoples today, even including the French (*Galli*).[142]

Sebastiano Pighini, bishop of Alife, conceded that the elimination of clandestine marriages was desirable, other things being equal, but he argued that the church did not have the power to prevent them entirely. He granted that clandestine marriages should be suppressed through penalties, but he held that the church was not able to invalidate them because marriage was a sacrament, and the sacraments were inalterable. He considered the impediments of relationship to be a false precedent, for such impediments were inherent in enduring qualities of the persons. They were not based on transient circumstances. The church could not make clandestine marriages invalid without altering divine law, which the church had no power to do. Nor did the church have the power to alter the form of this or any other sacrament. God himself made the union of marriage, and what God has joined together, no man can separate.[143]

Giovanni Giacomo Barba, O.S.A., bishop of Teramo, perceived a contradiction between the doctrinal canon, which affirmed that clandestine marriages were valid, and the remedy, which was aimed at preventing them. He also claimed that the remedy was contrary both to divine law and to the freedom to marry (*contra ius divinum et libertatem matrimonii*). Clandestine marriages, he argued, included everything essential to the sacrament, namely, the form and matter "by which the sacrament is perfected." The essential form of the sacrament is the contractants' mutual consent expressed in words, and the essence of any sacrament is inalterable. The presence of witnesses, on the contrary, is not of the essence but rather is a matter of solemnity and of proof. The church can change the impediments of relationship because such changes do not affect the essence of the sacrament. But parental consent is not essential, and for that reason the penalty of disinheritance is "against the substance of marriage itself." If unfree persons (*servi*) are entitled to marry without the consent of their lords, why should children not be entitled to marry without the consent of their parents?[144] Giovanni Giacomo Barba argued that the biblical texts being cited as proof of parental control over marriage were not convincing. A man *leaves* his father and mother to cleave unto his wife (Gen 2:24).[145] Moreover, even if there were precedents for paternal control over marriage in the Old Testament, Christians were no longer in servitude to the Law. Paul said that the widow could marry whomever she willed (1 Cor 7:39). He did not add, "with her father's consent."[146]

---

[142] Niverniensis, 633/15–26.   [143] Alyphanus, 651/25–652/5.

[144] Minoriensis (Catherinus), 652/23–25, refutes this argument, citing Thomas Aquinas and arguing that that the bonds of matrimony and of servitude are not sufficiently alike.

[145] Minoriensis, 652/19–22, refutes this argument also.

[146] Aprutinus, 634/19–635/2.

Those who were keen to eradicate clandestine marriage, whether by invalidation or by severe penalties, were not of one mind regarding the relation of parental consent to clandestinity and its reform. Some considered the absence of parental consent to be the crucial defect associated with clandestine marriages.[147] Others were less concerned about parental consent than about clandestinity as such, which they construed as the absence either of proof through witnesses or of marriage *in facie ecclesiae*. Alvaro della Quadra, bishop of Venosa, said that he wanted "entirely to eradicate clandestine marriages entered into without the parents' consent, since there is no way in which they can be done in a seemly way." Foreseeing an objection, Alvaro della Quadra conceded that there were special circumstances in which it was expedient to marry without parents' knowledge, and he proposed that some provision should be made for such eventualities. It should be possible to give bishops or their ordinaries the power to authorize marriages without parental knowledge when the parents were cruel or unreasonable. In such cases, a cleric would take on the role of father.[148] The bishop of Albenga held that marriage should not strictly require parental *consent*, but he argued that children ought not to marry without their parents' *knowledge*. He interpreted the notion of marrying secretly (*clam*) in the latter sense. Disinheritance was not the appropriate remedy for those who contracted marriage without their parents' consent, but it was appropriate for those who married without their parents' knowledge.[149]

Both Luigi Lippomano and Luciano degli Ottoni, the abbot of Pomposa (near Ferrara), cited texts from the Old and New Testaments to prove that the parents' right of consent was inscribed in the divine law, especially the father's right to give away his daughter in marriage. It followed, in their view, that the church had the right entirely to eradicate by invalidation the marriages of minors who contracted without parental consent.[150] Luciano degli Ottoni held that a girl's expression of consent to her marriage was less important than her father's: "If a father says to someone, 'I give my daughter to you as your wife,' the marriage is complete [*perfectum*], but if, on the contrary, a daughter marries without her father's consent, the marriage is invalid."[151] The record may have distorted what he said, but Thomas Aquinas had observed that the father's or parents' words could be construed as the sacramental *verbum* if the girl was too shy to speak up at her wedding.[152]

---

[147] Materanus, 622/2–8. Archiep. Aquensis, 623/4–5. Venusinus, 632/16–17. Minoriensis, 652/19–22.

[148] Venusinus, 632/16–21. The need to make provisions for such cases was a topic of discussion during the proceedings of 1563.

[149] Albinganensis, 632/34–36.

[150] Veronensis coadiutor, 629/28–29, citing Eph 6:1 and 1 Cor 7:31. Lucianus abbas Pomposiae Ferrariensis, 653/29–30, citing Exod 22:16–17 and 1 Cor 7:38.

[151] Lucianus abbas Pomposiae Ferrariensis, 654/1–3. The abbot may be referring to *Dig.* 13.1.11–12 (which is about *sponsalia*, but *Dig.* 13.1.11 implies that the same rules apply to *nuptiae*);

[152] Thomas Aquinas, *IV Sent.* 27.1.2, quⁿ 2, ad 2, ad 3 (Vivès 11:83b–84a).

Whereas some proponents of invalidation focused on the absence of parental consent, others focused on the circumstances and solemnities of the contract itself, such as witnesses or other means of proof, the presence of a priest administering the sacrament, a prescribed liturgical form, or ecclesial approbation through marriage *in facie ecclesiae*.[153] For example, the bishop of Porto, who argued that the invalidation of clandestine marriage was both possible and expedient, conceded that the absence of parental consent was a serious defect, but he was worried that even the penalty of disinheritance would curtail the freedom to marry (*libertas matrimonii*). He proposed instead that the presence of witnesses should be required for a valid marriage, for without proof there was no way to prevent already-married persons from falsely marrying again.[154] Cornelio Musso, bishop of Bitonto, returned to a theory that he had outlined on September 13, during the discussion of the draft doctrinal canons on marriage. He maintained that parental consent could not be required and that its absence should not be penalized. He was opposed, therefore, to the remedy of disinheritance. But what made a marriage clandestine and worthy of prohibition, in his view, was the absence of witnesses and of a ministering priest. Such marriages ought to be invalidated because they were not true sacraments, although they might be true marriages in some generic sense. He conceded that the church probably did not have the power to invalidate such marriages after they had been contracted, but he held that the church did have the power to invalidate them preemptively by deeming the persons illegitimate, following the precedent of the personal impediments. Furthermore, he argued, the church would not invalidate the sacrament as such but rather the underlying contract that the sacrament presupposed, for "although the church cannot introduce anything new regarding the sacrament of marriage, it can do so regarding the contract."[155] This theory would become the chief rationale of the proponents of invalidation during 1563 and the focus of much debate.

19.8 SUMMARY

The discussion of clandestine marriage at Bologna was limited by the muddled formulation of the anathema, which conflated clandestinity with the absence of parental consent, as well as by a lack of shared assumptions. Further progress would require the two defects to be disentangled and treated separately, as they would be at

[153] Feltrensis, 623/24–26 (without witnesses). Grossetanus, 624/35–36 (without proof, unspecified). Angolismensis, 626/20–22 (without a prescribed liturgical form administered by a priest). Portuensis Portugallensis, 628/1–3 (without witnesses and parental consent). Salutiarum, 631/6 ("*id est sine testibus et absque facie ecclesiae*"). Caprulanus, 631/28–29 (without witnesses and marriage *in facie ecclesiae*). Bituntinus, 634/10–11 (without witnesses in the presence of a priest). Gen. Praedicatorum, 654/14–15 (without witnesses).
[154] Portuensis Portugallensis, 628/17–23.
[155] Bituntinus, 634/14–15: "Et licet ecclesia non possit innovare aliquid circa sacramentum matrimonii, potest tamen circa contractus." Cf. Bituntinus, 455/22–27 (Sept. 13).

Trent in 1563. Nevertheless, some important questions and principles emerged. Most of the prelates agreed that the Protestant policy of invalidation entailed a heresy, although they were unable to identify what that heresy was. They had also begun to consider what the Catholic church's own remedy should be. At first, most assumed that the church had no power to invalidate such marriages and that invalidation was inconsistent with the sacramentality of marriage, but during the deliberations a plurality of the prelates endorsed invalidation. Their explorations in turn prompted the opponents of invalidation to restate the traditional position in exhaustive detail. A new possibility emerged, which would circumvent the standard objections: that the church might prevent partners from marrying clandestinely by rendering them incapable (*inhabiles*) of contracting marriage, as if clandestinity were a personal impediment akin to those of consanguinity and affinity. At least six proponents of invalidation espoused this theory. Pighini, bishop of Alife, who opposed invalidation, objected that the personal impediments were based not on transient circumstances but on qualities that inhered in the persons.[156] This counter-argument, too, would become a focus of debate during 1563. Toward the end of the proceedings, Cornelio Musso touched on what would become the chief defense of the proponents in 1563: that a clandestine marriage might be invalidated not as a sacrament but as a contract.

Finally, the so-called "Council of Bologna" had added to the condemnation of the Protestant heresy a descriptive *tametsi* clause, emphasizing that the church had always tried to prevent clandestine marriages. This grammatical device will reappear in the decree on clandestine marriages in 1563, albeit with a different purpose and in a different configuration. The lineaments of the decree *Tametsi* of 1563 are retrospectively discernable in the drafts of the canon on clandestine marriage discussed at Bologna in 1547.[157]

19.9 AFTER BOLOGNA: RETROSPECTIVE TREATISES ON CLANDESTINE MARRIAGE

Giovanni Antonio Delfini and Gentian Hervet, who had participated at Bologna as *theologi minores*, and Ambrosius Catharinus, who had participated as bishop of Minori, wrote treatises on clandestine marriage shortly after the proceedings. Delfini, who apparently had said nothing about clandestine marriage at the council, published his treatise in the following year (February, 1548). Hervet and Catharinus published theirs after the council had reconvened at Trent in 1551, addressing them to the assembled prelates in the expectation that the council would soon take up the issue of clandestine marriages again.

---

[156] Alyphanus, 651/28–29; 652/7–9.
[157] G. di Mattia, "Il decreto *Tametsi* e le sue radici nel Concilio di Bologna," *Apollinaris* 53 (1980): 476–500.

19.9.1 *Giovanni Antonio Delfini*

The pretext of Delfini's treatise was the "great controversy among the fathers regarding clandestine marriage" that had unfolded at Bologna in the previous year.[158] He later incorporated an extended version of the treatise into his *De matrimonio et caelibatu*.[159] Delfini was a Conventual Franciscan, and he had already established himself in his order as a capable theologian, educator, and administrator.[160] He had been present at the opening session of the general council, and he helped to draft the decrees on Scripture, original sin, and justification.[161] Delfini had spoken during *congregationes theologorum* on the sacraments of extreme unction, orders, and marriage, but apparently he had not spoken on the problem of clandestinity (Section 19.2).[162] In the treatise, he argues that the church rightly prohibits clandestine marriages but has no power to render them null and void.

The treatise begins with four theses (*conclusiones*). First, a clandestine marriage, however the term is interpreted, is by its very constitution both true (*verum*) and settled (*ratum*). Second, the church may justly prohibit clandestine marriages and punish those who marry secretly. Third, when someone marries one person covertly but then marries another publicly – the scenario of covert prior contract – the church, dependent on external evidence, may judge the second marriage to be true and settled when in fact and in the eyes of God the first marriage is true and settled. Fourth, the church can prohibit clandestine marriages, but it cannot annul them. Nor does the church have the power to illegitimize the persons because of the manner (*modus*) in which they contract their marriage.[163]

To prove that a clandestinely contracted marriage is necessarily valid, Delfini exhaustively analyzes the components, conditions, and consequences that make up marriage as a sacrament: its four causes, the minister of the sacrament, the three nuptial goods, and the essential effects. All of these are present, he argues, in clandestine marriages.

Whereas the remote, universal efficient cause of the sacrament is its divine institution, the proximate, particular efficient cause is the spouses' consent expressed in words of the present tense.[164] The partners' mutual consent, therefore, and not

---

[158] *De clandestino matrimonio*, CT 13.1:72–81.
[159] *De matrimonio et caelibatu* (Camerini, 1553), 1:60–70.
[160] He is identified in the proceedings as regent of the Order's house of studies in Padua, a position to which the Order appointed him in 1547. Later in the same year, he became minister of the Order's province of Bologna. He had previously been a lector in Bologna and regent of the houses of study in Brescia (1542–1545) and Venice (1545–1546). See R. Zaccaria, "Delfini, Giovanni Antonio," in *Dizionario Biografico degli Italiani*, 30:546–50, for these details.
[161] These decrees were published in fourth, fifth, and sixth sessions, respectively. Delfini spoke on justification at a *congregatio theologorum* on June 26, 1546 (CT 5:274), and again on the sacraments in general on January 27, 1547 (CT 5:859).
[162] Ioannes Antonius Delphinus, CT 6.1:102/5–13.
[163] *De clandestino matrimonio*, 73.   [164] 73/25–36.

the consent of their parents, is the efficient cause,[165] and their verbal expression of consent, regardless of who speaks first, is the form. The matter "to which the sacramental words are applied" consists in "legitimate persons." The persons may be construed, therefore, as the *elementum* of the sacrament. Whoever may be said to join the spouses is the minister of the sacrament. A priest who officiates at their wedding may properly be called the minister of the sacrament, therefore, but marriage is peculiar among the sacraments insofar as the matter itself – that is, the persons – applies the *verbum* to the *elementum*. Consequently, the spouses themselves perform of the role of sacramental ministers when no ordained minister is present. Now, when God instituted marriage in the beginning, he determined only that the spouses' "free and mutual consent expressed in words of the present tense" would be the "proximate and particular cause of marriage." God did not institute marriage as something that would have to be done openly or covertly, for example, but simply as marriage.[166] Everything else is accidental.

Delfini arrives at the same conclusion by considering the purpose, benefits, and effects of marriage. Its final cause is threefold: procreation (Gen 1:28), remedy (1 Cor 7:2, 7:9), and signification, whereby it is a "figure of the mystical joining of Christ and the church" (Eph 5:32). Its goods are those enumerated and expounded by Augustine: faith, offspring, and sacrament, or inseparability. Marriage has two essential effects. One is the voluntary joining of their wills (*coniunctio animorum*), which entails the spouses' mutual gift of their bodies to each other:

> Paul says regarding this effect: "The wife has not power over her own body, but the husband, and likewise also the husband has not power over his own body, but the wife" (1 Cor 7:4). And so this free and mutual gift or conveyance [*traditio*] of bodies is a certain spiritual or matrimonial contract, as if it were a drawing together of their two wills [*voluntates*] into a free and mutual sharing of bodies. Thus, it is fitting that the spouses, through the perpetual joining of their wills [*animorum coniunctio*], are like a single heart and a single soul. Nay, it is fitting, I say, that they should love each other mutually with perpetual and chaste benevolence, yet in such a way that wives are obedient to their husbands, in the manner that Paul describes: "Wives, submit yourselves unto your own husbands, as unto the Lord. For the husband is the head of the wife, even as Christ is the head of the church, and he is the savior of the body. Therefore as the church is subject unto Christ, so let the wives be to their own husbands in everything. Husbands, love your wives, even as Christ also loved the church and gave himself for it that he might sanctify it" (Eph 5:22–25).[167]

The other essential effect is sanctifying grace.[168] Delfini concedes that spouses who marry clandestinely do not receive sanctifying grace through the sacrament, but this exception is not fatal to his argument. Only baptism and penance, he argues, confer "grace itself" (*gratia ipsa*), or "first grace" (*prima gratia*). Because the other

---

[165] 75/54–55.   [166] 75/25–28.   [167] 74/25–36.   [168] 73–74.

sacraments presuppose baptism and penance, they augment or perfect a grace that is already present. Sacraments of this second kind do not have the "necessity" of those of the first (i.e., they are not absolutely necessary for salvation), and they remain valid even if the participant receives no "grace or intention of grace" from them.[169] Because persons who marry contrary to a prohibitive impediment of the church, such as those who marry clandestinely or during an interdict or a prohibited season, commit a mortal sin, grace is not augmented or perfected in them. They may even be excommunicated. Nevertheless, their marriage is sacramental and "entirely settled and firm before God," for nothing essential is missing.[170] A clandestine marriage may be invalid in the church's judgment (*forum ecclesiae*), which is the relevant judicial forum (*forum iudicale*), but only because in such cases the church presumes that there has been no marriage. If there is no personal impediment and the spouses freely plight their troth clandestinely in the present tense, their marriage is valid before God and in the forum of conscience (*forum conscientiae*), also known as the penitential forum (*forum poenitentiale*), even if the church cannot recognize it.[171]

Although the church cannot alter anything belonging to the "form or nature of the sacraments," the church does have the power to introduce impediments that render persons incapable of marrying.[172] How can the church exercise this power without altering the essential matter of a sacrament? Delfini's solution is ingenious and presupposes a grasp of scholastic ontology. The persons are the matter of the sacrament, and he concedes that the church cannot directly change or make illegitimate the proper matter of any sacrament.[173] Nevertheless, the church does have a special but limited power indirectly to modify the matter of marriage, for the persons are members of the body of Christ, and the church has a certain "power of jurisdiction" (*potestas iurisdictionis*) over that body. By the same token, the church has no power to illegitimize persons who do not belong to the church, for it has no jurisdiction over them. The church's power even over the matter of Christian marriage is limited and indirect. Christians cannot be prevented from marrying "without reasonable grounds" (*sine rationabili causa*), namely, some feature or defect that is "inseparably joined to the persons." Indeed, the church has no direct power over the sacramental matter *per se*, but it has an indirect power over certain features that are "inseparably joined to the persons, such as consanguinity, holy

---

[169] 74/16–21, 75/50–55.
[170] 75/14–19. Delfini inserts a passage on excommunication as the appropriate penalty for clandestine marriage in *De matrimonio et caelibatu*, I, 66–67.
[171] 78/27–40. 77/8–11.
[172] Delfini expands the argument of this section in *De matrimonio et caelibatu* I, p. 68, where he notes that the church has the power to prevent a sacrament by entirely withdrawing its matter. For example, excommunication by the pope or a senior prelate prevents someone from receiving the sacrament of penance from his parish priest, whereas relaxation of excommunication restores that ability. Thus, excommunication withdraws and relaxation restores the matter of penance. The same argument occurs in Adrian Florensz, discussed later.
[173] For example, by determining that the *elementum* of baptism is chrism, or that the matter of marriage is bread and wine.

orders, vows, and other things of that sort." These are not part of the essence but are "reducible to the essence of marriage in some way." The circumstances of marrying, on the contrary, such as clandestinity or a forbidden season, are merely accidental. Consequently, these do not constitute reasonable grounds for invalidation, for they are not things that are inseparably joined to the persons.[174]

Because clandestinity is a defect only in the manner of contracting marriage, therefore, it does not pertain to the essence of the sacrament in any way. But the church is entitled to prohibit the manner of contracting (*modus contrahendi*) in any way that advances the "honesty, decency, and solemnity of marriage" (*matrimonii honestas, decor, et solemnitas*), and there are good reasons for prohibiting clandestine marriages. It is folly for young people to undertake an action of such great moment covertly, without witnesses and without the guidance of their elders. Clandestine marriages give rise to many scandals, they have at least the appearance of fornication, and they result all too easily in adultery – for example, when the spouses regret their ill-considered union and separate to marry others.[175] Following Peter Lombard, Delfini interprets the decretal of Evaristus as entailing a simple prohibition, for the conditions that Evaristus requires are only solemnities. The marriages that he prohibits have the appearance of fornication and may even be deemed to be fornication in the church's external judgment, but they are valid in reality and in the eyes of God. The final clause – *nisi voluntas propria suffragata fuerit et vota succurrerint legitima* – preserves the principle that consent is the sufficient cause of marriage.[176]

19.9.2 *Ambrosius Catherinus*

Catharinus addressed his *De matrimonio quaestiones plures* (1551) to the prelates who had assembled at Trent for the second phase of the council.[177] I have already outlined his treatment of the sacramentality of marriage in this work (Section 18.3).

According to the secretary's record, Catharinus conceded on September 6, 1547, at Bologna (Section 19.2) that clandestine marriages were valid in canon law, but he questioned whether they were valid in the sight of God:

> In regard to clandestine marriages (about which he had said nothing on the previous day), he responds that he maintains as others do that they are valid marriages, although he finds it very difficult to determine whether they are true marriages before God, since [the partners] do not contract them in accordance with the lawful solemnities, especially when their parents are unaware and unwilling.

---

[174] 79/11–30. Delfini provides a long quotation from Scotus in support. See also 75/18–19: "Nimirum talia [i.e., impedimenta dirimentia] non referuntur ad matrimonii essentiam, vel [scd?] ad aliquid inseparabiliter coniunctum cum essentia referuntur."

[175] 77/31–78/11. [176] 76/10–15. 76/22–77/2. Peter Lombard, *Sent.* IV, 28.1.4–2.1 (433).

[177] Printed with *Enarrationes R. P. F. Ambrosii Catharini Politi Senensis Archiepiscopo Compsani in Quinque priora capita libri Geneseos* [etc.], Rome, 1552.

Accordingly, the council should be able, if it wishes, to prohibit them and impose an impediment such that they will be invalid even after they have been contracted, as happened with the fourth degree [of consanguinity], which was prohibited although it had formerly been permitted. Accordingly, the council ought to prohibit clandestine marriages severely, lest they are deemed to be established marriages [*matrimonia ... rata*].[178]

On December 22, 1547, Catharinus concurred with those who claimed that the church had the power to invalidate clandestine marriage by inhabilitating the contractants:

Although the church does not have the power to invalidate already contracted marriages [*iam contracta matrimonia*] even when they are clandestine, it does have the power, nevertheless, to invalidate and to prohibit to-be-contracted marriages [*contrahenda*] and to inhabilitate persons contracting in that way.[179]

It is possible that the secretary missed some of the nuances of what he said at Bologna, but Catharinus seems to have been caught between his personal conviction that such marriages were invalid before God, on the one hand, and his recognition that the church had been recognizing them as valid for centuries, on the other. The position to which he was inclining, therefore, was that a clandestinely contracted marriage was invalid before God but valid in the church's judgment.

Catharinus poses a twofold question in the treatise: whether clandestine marriages are valid; and, if so, whether their validity is such that they merit the term "sacrament."[180] His definition or characterization of clandestine marriages is twofold: They lack "witnesses and the priestly blessing," and they lack the consent of the parents in whose power the contractants are (i.e., to whom they are legally subject).[181] But Catharinus's case for invalidation turns entirely on the absence of parental consent, which in his view entails injury to parents, disregard of the proper interests of family and kin, and impiety. He assumes that solemnization is important chiefly as the proper means of making sure that couples marry with the supervision of their parents, who are the bridge between the couple and the political community.

Catharinus now argues that clandestine marriages are in reality neither valid nor sacramental because they contravene natural law, divine law, civil law, and the *ius gentium*. He does not deny that they are currently valid under canon law, and some of his arguments against clandestine marriages presuppose that couples who marry clandestinely are married in some legally and morally relevant sense. For example,

[178] CT 6.1:432/31–37.   [179] Ibid., 653/1–3.
[180] Q. 7, 255/30–31: "An valida sint, et ita rata ut mereantur dici sacramentum."
[181] Q. 7, 255/22–29. Catharinus does not mention the age of sons and daughters as a relevant consideration, but his reference to children in the power of their parents in the definition implies that he is thinking of sons and daughters "at home," i.e. *filii familias* (a term he uses at 255/44).

he argues that clandestinity makes adultery more likely, since a third party may have a relationship with someone without realizing that he or she is clandestinely married.[182] Insofar as the second union is adulterous, I presume, the first union may properly be construed as a marriage. Nevertheless, Catharinus builds a juris-prudential case for the intrinsic invalidity of clandestine marriages, appealing to natural and civil law, to reason, and to Scripture. These reflections lead him to propose a policy. He confesses that if he himself had responsibility for making the appropriate "decision or reformation," he would immediately declare such mar-riages to be invalid and pass a law to that effect, since they contravene civil law, natural law, "good morals," the Law of Moses, and canonical decrees. Such a law would prevent the intolerable abuse whereby persons marry clandestinely under the false assumption that the intrinsic sacramentality of their marriage will make the union decent and honorable.[183] He urges the general council and the pope, therefore, to pass the appropriate laws.[184]

Notwithstanding his emphasis on solemnization, Catharinus is closer to Luther-ans such as Johannes Brenz (Sections 17.3.5 and 17.3.6) in his general approach to the problem than he is to most Catholic theologians and canonists of the period. He is concerned less with the presence or absence of a sacramental essence than with the familial and political deficiencies of marriages without parental consent, which render them at best suspect from a legal point of view. He maintains that clandestine marriages, especially when they are contracted without the parents' consent, are invalid by their very nature. Although the church has been treating them as valid, they have always been invalid in reality as regards both divine and natural law. No man may separate what God has joined, but God does not join together those who marry clandestinely.

Catharinus takes the civil laws of the Christian emperors (*principes christiani*) as his point of departure. One should assume by default, he argues, that these laws are sound, and they prohibit clandestine marriages as invalid.[185] Catharinus is presum-ably referring here not only to laws made by the Christian Roman emperors and to the *Epitome Juliani* but also to the classical jurisprudence collected in Justinian's *Digest*. Moreover, he would have understood this body of civil law and jurisprudence as it was interpreted and elaborated in the tradition of civilian scholarship. But he must be referring to the absence of parental consent, and not to clandestinity *per se*. The solemnities of marrying counted for little or nothing under Roman law and in Roman jurisprudence, whereas sons and daughters (especially daughters) who were "in the power" of their fathers needed their fathers' consent to marry validly.[186]

---

[182] Q. 7, 258/5–9. [183] Q. 7, 258/50–55. [184] Q. 7, 262/50–55. [185] Q. 7, 255/31–33.
[186] *Dig.* 23.2.2: "Nuptiae consistere non possunt nisi consentiant omnes, id est qui coeunt quorumque in potestate sunt." That general principle was interpreted in light of *Dig.* 23.1.10–13 regarding *sponsalia*, since according to *Dig.* 23.1.7.1 the consents required for *sponsalia* and *nuptiae* are the same. See also CJ 5.1.2 (= CTh 3.5.4), 5.4.18 (= CTh 3.7.1, *Brev.* 3.7.1), and 5.4.20; CTh 3.5.5 (*Brev.* 3.5.4) and 3.5.12 (*Brev.* 3.5.7).

According to the jurists, a daughter-in-power was at least morally obliged to consent to her father's will in this matter, and her lack of opposition could be construed as her consent.[187]

Some might object, Catharinus notes, that as Christians we should obey the church's canons, and not the *leges* of the Roman emperors. But civil law is what natural reason deduces from the natural law as if from first principles. Moreover, the *Corpus Iuris Civilis* is especially reliable because it was codified under the aegis of Christian rulers. Catharinus concedes that canon law sometimes contradicts civil law, but he argues that it may do so only when civil law contradicts natural or divine law.[188] Aside from such rare exceptions, civil law should be respected for its regulation of civic well-being, and canon law should embrace it. Catharinus asks, therefore, whether the civil laws that prohibit clandestine marriages – more precisely, marriages without paternal consent – contradict natural law or divine law. He argues that they do not. It follows that the church ought to respect and embrace the civil law on clandestine marriages.[189]

Some cite Genesis 2:24 or Matthew 19:5 – "For this reason a man will leave and his father and his mother" – as proof that under divine law sons and daughters do not need parental consent to marry. (The bishops of Sarsina, Porto, and Teramo had made this argument during the proceedings at Bologna.)[190] But it is ridiculous, Catharinus argues, to suppose that the Bible would in its very opening pages give license to children to dishonor their parents and to treat them with contempt. What the text from Genesis characterizes is not the contracting of marriage but the change in status that results from the contract. A son leaves his father and mother to cleave to his *wife*, and not to a woman by making her his wife. She is already his wife when he leaves his parents to join her.[191] The Old Testament shows us that fathers had the right to give away their daughters in marriage. Catharinus cites the Mosaic Law and the stories of Isaac and Rebecca and of Jacob and his two wives. In the New Testament, 1 Corinthians 7:38 shows that a father has the right to give or to refuse to give his daughter in marriage.[192]

Again, some argue that the civil laws in question contradict a law of nature, whereby the mutual consent of the spouses is the sufficient cause of a valid marriage. Even if children are naturally obliged to honor their parents, therefore, it would be unjust for civil law to abrogate this natural law.[193] But if consent alone were strictly sufficient for marriage, parents could contract marriage with their own children, and the prohibitions against incestuous unions would be inventions of merely human

[187] *Dig.* 23.1.11–12.
[188] Q. 7, 255/33–42. On civil laws as deduced from the natural law as from first principles, see Q. 7, 256/30–33.
[189] Q. 7, 256/35–48.
[190] Sarsinensis, 474/6–9. Portuensis Portugallensis, 477/12–16. Aprutinus, 634/23–26.
[191] Q. 7, 255/43–256/8. Catharinus had proposed this argument at Bologna, CT 6.1:652/19–25, chiefly in response to the bishop of Teramo (cf. Aprutinus, 634/23–26).
[192] Q. 7, 257/4–33.   [193] Q. 7, 260/37–43.

law. Clearly, such marriages are invalid because they are inconsistent with the honor that blood relatives owe to each other, regardless of whether the partners consent. Why should there not also be laws preventing children from marrying clandestinely "because of the honor that they owe by right to their parents"? And what is to prevent such laws from rendering the marriages null and void?[194] Clandestine marriages violate the father's right (*ius paternum*) to control the marriage of his *filii familias* (the sons and daughters who are subject to him): a right that "natural reason teaches to everyone."[195]

It is true that parents cannot prevent their children from choosing to enter the religious life, provided only that the child is old enough to make the vow. Some deduce by extrapolation that parents have no right to prevent their children from marrying whomever they choose. But the parallel is false, Catharinus argues. Becoming a religious, unlike marrying, is a simple, unmixed good. The person who enters the religious life advances to a higher, more excellent way of life, which is more in accord with the Gospel: the "better part" of Luke 10:42. Moreover, this elevation has no effect on kinship or interfamilial relationships. Those who enter the religious life pass from this world to another. It is the "children of this world" who marry (Luke 20:34), on the contrary, and marriage establishes new relationships of affinity between families. A person entering the religious life cannot properly be said to injure his or her parents, even if they are unwilling. Indeed, persons pursuing a religious vocation should sometimes be *advised* to take vows without their parents' prior knowledge, for carnal love and attachment often make it hard for parents to let go, so that one's family members become one's enemies, as Jesus said (Matt 10:36).[196]

The *ius gentium* on this matter concurs with the divine law of Scripture as well as with natural law, Catharinus argues. Everywhere, except perhaps among the most barbarous and irrational peoples, parents give away their daughters in marriage, and children are expected to seek and to respect their parents' counsel in marrying. Daughters especially are rightly considered subject to their parents' judgment because of the natural weakness of their sex, their inexperience in the ways of the world, and their natural shyness.[197]

Finally, Catharinus argues, reason tells us that marrying publicly has many advantages. Because marriages establish new relationships of affinity between families, families have a legitimate interest in them. Persons who marry secretly are often motivated only by lust, and they may come to regret their marriage and illicitly marry again. Clandestinity increases the possibility of marrying within the forbidden

---

[194] Q. 7, 256/9–28. Catharinus writes *ius naturae* at 256/10, but *ius divinum* at 256/17. I assume that he means to refer to the law of nature throughout, since sixteenth-century scholars sometimes counted the natural law as a species of divine law.

[195] Q. 7, 256/30–35. Catharinus is alluding to *Dig.* 1.1.3: "Ius naturale est, quod natura omnia animalia docuit" ("The law of nature is what nature taught to all animals").

[196] Q. 7, 260/37–261/15.   [197] Q. 7, 256/49–257/4.

degrees. It may result in abortion if the husband dies or absconds leaving his wife pregnant. And it may lead to adultery – for example, when a man has a sexual relationship with a woman without knowing that she is secretly already married. And because the children of clandestine unions are illegitimate, clandestine marriages are injurious to the spouses' children as well as to their parents.[198] Thus, clandestinity undermines the goods of fidelity and progeny. There are no good reasons for contradicting the civil laws that prohibit clandestine marriages, therefore, for these are rational and consistent not only with natural law and with the *ius gentium* but also with divine law. Catharinus concludes that clandestine marriage is not really marriage at all but promiscuity (*stuprum*) or mere cohabitation (*contubernium*), as Evaristus declared.[199]

Catharinus argues that clandestine marriages lack the third good, the *bonum sacramenti*, as well as the goods of fidelity and progeny. He construes the *bonum sacramenti* here as the sacramentality of marriage: the special properties that marriage possesses as one of the sacraments of the New Law. Chief among those properties is the power to confer heavenly grace. Now, a sacrament confers grace *ex opere operato* only when the recipient presents no obstacle to it. Clandestinity is an obstacle of that sort. How can someone who marries secretly, dishonoring his parents and contravening natural law, civil law, and the canons of the church, merit grace? It is not God who joins such unions, therefore, but unbridled lust or an unclean spirit.[200]

Notwithstanding the church's current recognition of clandestine marriages as valid, Catharinus maintains that the church's canons on this subject are historically consistent with civil law and the *ius gentium* in prohibiting clandestine marriages. After reviewing the canonical prohibitions of clandestine marriages from Evaristus to the Fourth Lateran Council, Catharinus concludes that such marriages are already illegitimate (i.e., against the law) "in the sight of the church."[201] He emphasizes, too, that the Roman rulers who made or adopted civil laws against clandestine marriage were Christian. He challenges the experts in theology and canon law to show what was wrong with such laws. Did the rulers not have the power to pass laws that fostered familial and civic concord? If they had that power, what prevented them from exercising it? Catharinus points out that some of the eastern fathers, such as Basil of Caesarea, adopted the same laws as the canons of the church.[202] If someone can prove that the validity of clandestine marriages pertains properly and exclusively

---

[198] Q. 7, 257/39–258/28.   [199] Q. 7, 258/42–49.

[200] Q. 7, 258/28–40; 258/38–40: "De his autem recte dici potest, quod eos non Deus, sed immundus aliquis Daemon et libido flagitiosa coniunxit." Cf. Johannes Brenz, *Libellus casuum quorundam matrimonialium*, ch. 2, p. 12: "... quis ibit inficias, quin huiusmodi Matrimonium, absque parentum consensu et uoluntate contractum ... potius a sathana quam a Deo nostro proficiscatur, cum neque Iuri diuino, neque Civili consonum sit."

[201] Q. 7, 258/55–259/20; 259/10–11: "Ex quibus satis constat, saltem coram Ecclesia non esse matrimonia."

[202] Q. 7, 259/21–260/15.

to their sacramentality, then the issue would have to be submitted to a "pontifical tribunal." But that is not so, Catharinus argues. It is not a matter that is alien to secular rulers and legislators, for it pertains to civic behavior (*mores civiles*) and to the proper ends of the commonwealth (*res publica*).[203] Clandestine marriage contravenes social justice as well as the honor due to parents. Suppose that a son of the nobility, moved by lust, secretly marries a servant girl, or a woman who is notoriously promiscuous, or an adulteress, or a prostitute. Or suppose that a daughter of the nobility secretly marries a servant, or an adulterer, or a pimp. Such "inequalities" are unjust, and they are the proper concern of secular rulers and legislators.[204] The secular Christian legislators who decreed that clandestine marriages were invalid for purely secular, civil reasons did not trespass on sacred ground, as if plying a sickle in a neighbor's cornfield (Deut 23:25). They eradicated the contract, not the sacrament. Natural and civil laws, albeit corroborated by the canons of the church, suffice to determine that in such cases there is no marriage. And if there is no valid contract of marriage, there will be no sacrament. Contrariwise, if there is a valid contract, other things being equal, there will be a sacrament.[205] It remains only for the pope to give his approval to such laws by incorporating them into canon law.[206]

Catharinus concedes that parents often abuse their right of consent by unjustly preventing their children from marrying. A father may prevent his son from marrying because he desires a larger dowry or a daughter-in-law with more advantageous connections. In pursuit of his own advantage, a father may even coerce his son into marrying a woman who is notoriously promiscuous or too old. Such injustices should be prevented, but not in a way that contradicts the parental right of consent. If a man unreasonably prevents his son from marrying a suitable woman of the son's own choosing, the son should first try to persuade his father. If he fails, others should try on his behalf. Failing that, canon law should permit the son to testify to an episcopal tribunal, explaining whom he wants to marry, how his father had no just cause to reject this woman as his daughter-in-law, how he has shown due honor and respect to his father, and so forth. Then the bishop, assuming the father's role, would have the power to permit the son to marry against his father's wishes – but publicly, *in facie ecclesiae*, and with the father's knowledge. Then the unwilling father would not be entitled to disinherit his son. Because he had been acting unjustly, he would not suffer injustice or injury.[207] Catharinus is aware, too, of a worse and all too frequent abuse. Sometimes parents or siblings in search of large dowry try to coerce a girl to marry against her wishes by threatening to send her to a convent. If they fail to get their way, they may even force her to become a nun and falsely to make her profession before God. The church should prevent such abuses both by regulating the size of dowries and by making sure that a marriageable girl's monastic profession

---

[203] Q. 7, 260/16–37.   [204] Q. 7, 261/16–30.   [205] Q. 7, 261/31–41.

[206] Q. 7, 261/42–262/4. Catharinus is suggesting, I take it, that a papal decretal might settle the matter, even without a general council.

[207] Q. 7, 262/5–32.

is sincere and authentic. Whenever a family gives a daughter to a monastery, the bishop should make sure that she is free to express her will without fear and ascertain that she is truly willing. The bishop should also admonish parents in his diocese not to use coercion or threats when they give their daughters in marriage.[208] Such abuses should be suppressed through regulation and good practice, but it remains true that parents have a natural right to give away their sons and daughters in marriage, especially if they are minors.

19.9.3 *Gentian Hervet*

Hervet recalls in the preface to his treatise how clandestine marriages had been the subject of much controversy at Bologna. Because the proceedings had been suspended, however, he did not have the opportunity to present his own position on the subject to the prelates. He addresses this treatise to the prelates now assembled again at Trent. The dedication is dated January 20, 1552, in Rome.[209] Hervet published a revised and expanded version in 1561, dedicating it to Jean de Morvillier, who was bishop of Orléans, whence Hervet had originated, and France's ambassador to the general council.[210]

Although Hervet participated at the council as one of the *theologi minores*[211] – he is listed in the proceedings as a "secular cleric" – he was not a theologian but a classical scholar and philologist, renowned chiefly for his translations of classical and patristic Greek texts. He had gone to the council initially as an advisor to Cardinal Pole, in whose Roman household he happened to be serving.

Hervet describes the "great controversy" about clandestine marriages that had taken place at Bologna. On one side were those who claimed that clandestine marriages were entirely unsound and ought to be declared null and void. On the other were those who claimed that although clandestine marriages were prohibited, they were settled and valid if the contract could be proved. The question, according to Hervet, is not whether the church has the power to render such marriages invalid, but whether such marriages already are invalid. During the *congregationes theologorum* on extreme unction, orders, and marriage (Section 19.2), Hervet had said that

---

[208] Q. 7, 262/32–50.

[209] This original version is printed in CT 13.1:145–52.

[210] *Oratio ad Concilium qua suadetur, ne matrimonia quae contrahuntur a filiis familias sine consensu eorum in quorum sunt potestate, habeantur deinceps pro legitimis* (Paris, 1556). In the later version, Hervet considerably augmented the fifth and final part of the treatise, regarding examples and counterexamples from patristic and early-Christian sources. This augmented passage is appended to the original version in CT 13.1:153–59.

[211] During the proceedings of 1546–1547, Hervet spoke extensively on imputed justice and the certitude of grace (Oct. 20, 1546, CT 5:566–69) and briefly on the sacraments in general (Jan. 29, 1547, CT 5:861–62), on eucharist (Feb. 12, CT 5:923), and on penance (April 25, CT 6.1:74).

clandestine marriages could not be annulled *after* they had been contracted because the spouses' consent was the sufficient cause of marriage.[212]

To settle the matter, Hervet now argues, one needs first to define what clandestine marriages are. Hervet stipulates that marriages are clandestine when they are "contracted not publicly, with the ceremonies required by law, but secretly and covertly."[213] Now, if there is no impediment disqualifying the persons, who constitute the matter of the sacrament, such marriages are obviously prohibited but valid *post factum*. The deficiency is not an impediment but an absence of proof. If the fact that the partners have married can be proved, or if both confess they have married, then their marriage is known to be true, settled, and indissoluble even though it was contracted clandestinely, and any children begotten before the church recognized their union will be legitimate.[214] It is absurd to propose that legitimate children can be born from an illegitimate union.[215]

The real difficulty pertains not to clandestine marriages, as defined here, but to marriages without parental consent. Hervet proposes a scenario. Suppose that a *filia familias* (i.e., a girl who is still "at home," or a minor) contracts marriage with someone without parental consent; both partners confess to the union, so that the problem of proof does not arise; and they seek to have their marriage made public through the appropriate solemnities and ceremonies. Nevertheless, their parents withhold their consent. Is the marriage nevertheless "firm and legitimate"? Hervet argues that it is not. Any marriage of children who are still in power (*in potestate*) without the consent of those who have power over them should not be regarded as valid in any way. Rather, as Evaristus said, they are committing fornication and promiscuity. But such a marriage will become valid if neither of the partners wishes to renounce the union and their parents give their consent to it.[216]

Hervet claims not that the church has the power to render such marriages invalid but rather that they are already invalid. There is sufficient proof, he argues, in the Old and New Testaments, in civil law, and in the *ius pontificium* (i.e., canon law, especially decretal law), all of which show that parental consent is necessary.[217] For biblical proof, Hervet cites Genesis 24:50–58 (on Rebecca's betrothal to Isaac), Genesis 29:21 (on Jacob's marriage to Leah), and 1 Corinthians 7:36–38 (on the man who gives "his virgin" in marriage). As to civil law, "what could be clearer than that a *filius familias* and a *filia familias* cannot legitimately marry unless those who have power over them consent?" This claim about Roman civil law was not controversial, but Hervet cites only one law, by which a daughter who had reached

---

[212] CT 6.1:115/25–28: "Quoad matrimonium: primus articulus falsus est, quia sacramentum matrimonii, postquam est contractum, a nemine dirimi potest. Sed in clandestino adfuit consensus, qui matrimonium perfecit; ergo clandestinum dirimi non potest."

[213] CT 13.1:146/15–17: "Ea autem ego esse statuo, quae non publice et cum iis, quae a iure requiruntur, ceremoniis, sed clam et in occulto contrahuntur."

[214] This follows from Alexander III's decretal *Quod nobis*, X 4.3.2 (679).

[215] CT 13.1:146/11–147/2.   [216] 147/2–10.   [217] 147/38–40.

her twenty-fifth year was free "to join herself in marriage" without suffering the penalty of disinheritance if her father had not found a husband for her. Hervet is thinking of a *Novel* of Justinian regarding the circumstances in which sons and daughters may validly be disinherited.[218] But someone might object that if daughters who marry inappropriately may be disinherited, does that not imply that daughters who marry appropriately, even without their parents' consent, may not be disinherited, and that parental consent is not entirely necessary? Hervet finds his solution in a gloss by Theodore Balsamon, a twelfth-century Byzantine scholar of civil and canon law, according to which fathers may always dissolve unsuitable marriages of their sons and daughters but may disinherit them only if they have suffered "atrocious injury."[219]

Hervet's chief evidence from canon law is the decretal of Evaristus (Section 11.4.11), although he finds corroboration in Theodore Balsamon and Basil of Caesarea.[220] Some claim that the final clause of the decretal, *"nisi voluntas propria suffragata fuerit et vota succurrerint legitima,"* shows that the consent of the spouses was sufficient. But then Evaristus would have contradicted himself: an absurd and impertinent suggestion. Hervet proposes instead that the phrase *voluntas propria* ("their own will") refers to the partners' continued will to remain married, whereas the phrase *vota legitima* ("lawful vows") refers to parental consent. If those who have married without parental consent still want to be married and their parents give their consent, their marriage becomes valid.[221]

Hervet and Catharinus held similar positions on clandestine marriages. Both assumed that what was really at stake was not clandestinity *per se* but marriage without parental consent. Both considered the issue to be essentially one of civil law, and not of sacramental theology. And both argued that such marriages were already invalid by their very nature, whether or not the church rendered them null and void through positive legislation. To their mind, the invalidity of marriages contracted without parental consent was an essentially civil, temporal matter, rooted in ancient and perennial divine law. It only remained for the church to bring its canons into line with that mundane reality.

---

[218] *Nov.* 115.3.11.   [219] 148/1–16.   [220] 148/35–49.   [221] 148/17–35.

Clandestine marriage

Trent, 1563

Clandestine marriage returned to the agenda at Trent on March 11, 1562, when Cardinal Gonzaga put before the prelates twelve questions regarding ecclesiastical reform (Section 18.4). The tenth and eleventh were on clandestine marriage: whether clandestine marriages should be declared null and void in future, and what the church should define as the necessary conditions distinguishing a marriage contracted *in facie ecclesiae* from one contracted clandestinely.[1] The legates proposed a related question for the *theologi minores* (recorded on March 13):

> Whether clandestine marriages, which according to Evaristus and the Lateran Council have no stability in the tribunal and judgment of the church, can be declared null and void by the ecumenical council, so that this secrecy may be counted among the diriment impediments to marriage.[2]

But there were apparently no formal deliberations on marriage during 1562. Clandestine marriage was mentioned again on April 17 and 21, but only as a matter that would have to be handled later.[3]

The posing of these questions in the context of ecclesiastical reforms, even before the council had reached the sacrament of marriage, is a sign of a new sense of priorities. The point of departure for the council's deliberations on clandestine marriage at Bologna had been a twofold Protestant heresy: that clandestine marriages were invalid, and that in consequence parents had the power to annul them. But what could the Catholic church do to prevent such marriages? That question had arisen in the course of deliberations over the anathemas, and it had led the

---

[1] CT 8:379/3–5.
[2] CT 8:379/14–17: "An sicut clandestina matrimonia nullam habere firmitatem quoad forum et aestimationem ecclesiae, declarunt Evaristus et concilium Lateranense, ita simpliciter nulla esse et irrita ab oecumenico concilio posset decerni, ut occultatio haec inter impedimenta coniugium dirimentia connumeraretur?"
[3] CT 8:458/41–44 and 465/15–18.

prelates to ask whether the church had the power to render such marriages null and void henceforth. When the council reconvened in 1562, the priorities were reversed. The question of what should be done to prevent clandestine marriages now came first. Contrariwise, condemnation of the Protestant heresy, which was never definitively identified, would prove to be a secondary topic during 1563. The most urgent question was whether the Catholic church had the power to render clandestine marriages or marriages without parental consent null and void henceforth.

The council eventually declared at Session XXIV that clandestine marriages would henceforth be invalid, but the issue proved to be unusually fraught. All but two of the fifteen *theologi minores* who considered the issue at the outset (Section 18.4.1, February 9–16) conceded that the church had the power to invalidate clandestine marriages henceforth. But a persistent minority of prelates resisted this reform, which would entail a departure not only from the policy and canon law of the preceding centuries but also from the teachings of the most revered scholastic theologians. A few prelates did not take a position, but those who did may be divided for convenience into proponents and opponents, that is, those who called for invalidation, and those who resisted it.

Modern literature on the council includes exact counts of how the prelates voted on this and on other issues, but the recorded *acta* are not amenable to such exactitude, and the numbers are a matter of interpretation. The *acta* do not include an official tally of who voted *pro* or *contra*. Moreover, the prelates were voting not on a single issue but on a complicated document with many parts, including matters of both dogma and discipline. They could and often did say "*placet*" to one part and "*non placet*" to another, but their votes were often complicated or qualified, and there were several possible reasons for endorsing or opposing the decree on clandestine marriages. Invalidation was not the only issue at stake. That said, the proponents of invalidation during 1563 consistently outnumbered the opponents roughly in the ratio of five to two.[4] If allowance is made for random variations resulting from the presence or absence of particular prelates at various stages and from ambiguities and lacunae in reporting, this ratio remained constant throughout the voting on each of the four drafts and at Session XXIV. *Tametsi* became law despite a persistent minority of opponents who continued to vote and argue against the innovation until the end. The division did not run entirely along regional or provincial lines, but most of the opponents were Italians, and roughly half of the Italian prelates were opponents.[5]

---

4 On average, 136 prelates endorsed invalidation and 55 opposed it (+/- 1, according to interpretation) during voting on each of the four drafts and at Session XXIV. A few (never more than a dozen) abstained from taking a position at each stage, whether by voting to go with the majority, or by deferring to the pope, or by not taking a position on this particular issue.

5 I follow convention in identifying the prelates as French, Spanish, Portuguese and so forth on the basis of their sees rather than of their personal origins or native tongues, although these categories were largely coextensive. I count as Italian all the sees lying within the modern nation state of Italy and those across the Adriatic in the Venetian Empire and along the Dalmatian coast: communities sometimes described as the Italian Diaspora.

20.1 AN OVERVIEW OF THE ISSUES

The prelates pursued many lines of argument regarding clandestinity, and new arguments and counterarguments emerged in the course of debate. Nevertheless, it is possible to identify the chief lines of argument without unduly distorting or simplifying what was said. I refer here only to the issue of clandestinity *per se*. At first, the prelates considered including parental consent among the necessary conditions for a valid marriage, but that requirement was abandoned in the third draft.

Opponents restated the doctrine of the medieval schoolmen again and again. Many of them reasoned that if the church now rendered marriages null and void that would hitherto have been valid, she could do so only by altering the essence of marriage, especially the essential form, which the church had no power to do. The force of this argument depended on what was being proposed as the distinguishing feature of a non-clandestine, legitimately public marriage. If the distinguishing feature was the solemnization of marriage *in facie ecclesiae*, the opponents reminded the prelates of the scholastic distinction between the essence of a sacrament and its solemnities. Solemnities could be changed, but that would not affect validity. The essence was inalterable. If the distinguishing feature was the testimony of witnesses, that was clearly a matter of proof, and it was logically absurd to incorporate proof into what was to be proved. The church might judge that a clandestinely contracted marriage was invalid or non-existent through lack of proof or on the basis of a presumption about its circumstances, but that was merely a judgment made in the public forum. It did not make the marriage invalid in the forum of conscience or before God: a region into which the church's judicial arm had no power to intrude. At its core, therefore, the debate was about the scope and limits of positive law and ecclesiastical jurisdiction.

A small minority of proponents adhered explicitly to the ritual tendency, reasoning that marriage, like any other sacrament, required the ministry of a priest, who joined the spouses and blessed their union. One of the *theologi minores*, Pedro Fernández, also defended this position. The idea had broad appeal as a model for good practice, but few of the prelates maintained it literally and unequivocally because it implied that countless marriages recognized by the church over the centuries had been invalid or at best non-sacramental. Those who were inclined to uphold this theory regarded the decretal ascribed to Pope Evaristus as crucial, for they saw it as evidence of the ancient, more authentic practice of early church, which had prevailed before lax deviations had crept in.

The proponents in the main stream pursued three chief lines of argument, predicated respectively on the notion of inhabilitation, on the distinction between contract and sacrament, and on the principle of exigent power. These were mutually compatible but independent and separable rationales. Each was designed to pave the way for innovation by obviating traditional objections. According to the first line of argument, the church could make clandestinity a diriment personal impediment akin to those of consanguinity and affinity. By contracting marriage clandestinely, on this view, the partners would disqualify themselves from marrying. (Among the *theologi minores*, Aloysius de Burgo Novo defended this position.) The argument was important because virtually everyone accepted that the church had the power to introduce diriment personal impediments, although to treat clandestinity as an impediment of that sort seemed forced and artificial even to some of the proponents. Those pursuing the second line of argument conceded that the church probably had no power to alter the essence of this or any other sacrament, but they pointed out that marriage was also a contract, and that contracts, as Thomas Aquinas had showed, were naturally subject to positive law. A commonwealth was free to impose on the making of contracts any conditions that fostered the common good, including the presence of witnesses. As the Christian commonwealth (*res publica christiana*), the church could invalidate the contract without "touching" the necessary conditions for the sacrament *per se*, one of which was a valid contract.[6] This line of argument was historically related to the first, for it extended a rationale that Thomas Aquinas had used to explain the church's power to introduce personal impediments. According to the third line of argument, the church necessarily had the God-given power to pass whatever laws were necessary for the welfare of the Christian community. If clandestine marriages constituted a serious evil, if the existing prohibition and penalties had proved ineffective, and if the invalidation of clandestine marriages would be beneficial in the majority of cases – for every just new law was disadvantageous in a few cases – then the church necessarily had the power to eradicate them by rendering them null and void. How that power could be explained in terms of sacramental theology was a secondary matter.

The proponents were breaking new ground, and their theorizing evolved during the proceedings. As we have seen, the inhabilitation theory had emerged at Bologna. It was prominent at Trent in 1563 chiefly during voting on the first draft. It lost ground thereafter, although a vestige remained in the published decree *Tametsi*. The exigent power theory (the third of those outlined earlier) came to the fore during discussion of the second draft, partly as a result of frustration and impatience. Some proponents wanted to steer a course around the theological debate. The claim that the church could invalidate marriage as a contract without touching marriage as a sacrament incorporated a body of political theory about the legislative power of a commonwealth (*res publica*) or its ruler (*princeps*) over contracts and other voluntary agreements and obligations made by the citizens. This proved to be the most important line of argument, and the prelates developed it in considerable detail, although there is no trace of it in the published decree. I shall describe this theory and its origins more fully later (Section 20.2).

---

[6] A. Duval, "Contrat et sacrement de mariage au concile de Trente," *La Maison-Dieu* 127 (1976): 34–63.

The opponents resisted such innovation. They were not proposing anything new, but the arguments of the proponents forced them to shift ground and to develop new counterarguments. In response to the inhabilitation theory, the opponents argued that personal diriment impediments were necessarily based on features that were permanently inherent in the persons. Giovanni Battista Castagna, archbishop of Rossano, stated this principle clearly at the council, drawing on the work of Giovanni Antonio Delfini (Section 19.9.1). In the course of debate, emphasis shifted from the permanence of the underlying trait to its inherence. The basis of the impediment would have to be a "quality" that was really present in the persons, the opponents argued, and not something contrived through legislation. The proponents countered that the new diriment personal impediment of clandestinity would indeed be founded on some enduring quality really inherent in the persons, such as their disobedience, their impiety, their contempt for the church, or their guilt.

The focus on exigent power made many of the opponents cautious about claiming outright that the church was not able to invalidate clandestine marriages. Any tendency to limit or diminish the church's power at this point seemed discordant in the context of the general council. Instead, they criticized the proponents' position as rash, overly novel, and imprudent at the present time. If this course of action was both possible and expedient, they asked, why had the church not taken it before? Giovanni Battista Castagna, archbishop of Rossano, was the chief exponent of this position, too, which he already proposed during voting on the first draft. During voting on the second draft, it became a full-fledged theory in its own right.

The prelates on both sides repeatedly invoked the distinction between the church's *power* to invalidate clandestine marriages and the *expedience* of the reform. If the action was both possible and expedient, it followed that the church *ought* (*debet*) to execute it.[7] It was one thing to determine whether the church was able to invalidate clandestine marriages, and another to determine whether that reform was needed and whether it would be beneficial. Some of the opponents questioned the claims of expedience, pointing out that the proposed policy would generate new scandals and abuses of its own. But even a just law, according to a widely accepted legal doctrine, was beneficial only in the majority of cases, although (absent dispensation) it was binding in all cases. The argument, therefore, was partly statistical. Would the benefits of invalidation predominate over the drawbacks? On a deeper level, some of the opponents assumed that a new law, especially one invalidating a contract, required grounds stronger than contingent consequences or

[7] For example, the following proponents declared that invalidation is both possible and expedient: Card. Lotharingus, 642/29; Clugiensis, 655/26–27; Leriensis, 661/8–9; Augustensis, 664/4–5; Venetensis, 665/1–2; Namurcensis, 669/42–670/1; Salamantinus, 673/8–10; Monopolitanus, 675/42–676/1; Parisiensis, 658/23–24; Fesulanus, 659/36–37; Aurelianensis, 660/11; Insulanus, 660/17; Montismarani, 660/35; Barcinonensis, 670/44–46. Compare the *Oxford English Dictionary*'s second sense of the term "expedient": "Conducive to advantage in general, or to a definite purpose; fit, proper, or suitable to the circumstances of the case." The usual Latin idiom involves an intransitive verb, *expedire*.

"inconveniences." It was not clandestine marriages *per se* that had evil consequences, one opponent argued, but rather the malice of those who married clandestinely.[8] What was to be invalidated had to be intrinsically evil (*malum per se*).
Contrariwise, some proponents argued that something that had evil consequences
in the majority of cases was *ipso facto* intrinsically evil. But perhaps the very
distinction between power and exigency was unsustainable. The opponents
reasoned that a new policy that transgressed well-established sacramental theology
and overturned centuries of precedent could hardly be expedient, regardless of what
its pastoral or political consequences might be. Contrariwise, the very fact that
reform was sorely needed seemed to imply from the perspective of the exigent
power argument that the church had the power to accomplish it. The distinction
between expedience and power was clear enough in principle, but it proved to be
fraught and perhaps unsustainable.

The distinction between dogma and reform, which had already arisen at Bologna
(Section 19.5), was crucial and highly contested. It came to the fore during discussion
of the second draft, in which there was no longer a dogmatic canon anathematizing
those who said that clandestine marriages were invalid. Whereas a dogma, which
could not be rescinded, required something close to total consensus, a substantive
majority was sufficient for a reform. The proponents, therefore, who were in the
majority, insisted that the invalidation of clandestine marriages would be purely a
matter of reform. The opponents countered that this reform presupposed a matter of
doctrine. To be sure, if the reform was consistent with sacramental theology, then it
was purely a matter of reform. But whether the church had the *ability* to invalidate
clandestine marriages was a theological question about doctrine. Whereas the reform
per se would be expedient or inexpedient, the premise that the reform was *possible*
was either true or false and, as such, a matter not of reform but of doctrine. The
proponents replied that on that basis *every* reform was also a matter of doctrine, since
any rescindable disciplinary edict presupposed that the reform was possible.

The two main opposing positions that emerged at Trent were equidistant from the
Protestant position. Opponents and proponents agreed that the sacrament of marriage was untouchable, but whereas the opponents deduced that the church could
not render clandestine marriages invalid, the proponents argued that the church
could preempt clandestine marriage as a sacrament by invalidating the contract.
Some opponents objected that the proponents were only agreeing with the Protestants, whom the Catholics condemned for claiming that clandestine marriages were
invalid, but that was hardly fair. According to most of the proponents, the church
would render clandestine marriages invalid henceforth *by introducing new positive
law*. The Protestants, on the contrary, denied that the church had power of that sort
and maintained that the sacrament of marriage had been "invented in the church by

---

[8] Cavensis, 701/29–30: "Mala enim, quae proveniunt ex clandestinis, non proveniunt ratione
clandestinorum, sed potius malitia hominum."

human beings." They wanted to return to the bedrock of the primordial natural law, which God had both inscribed in human nature in the beginning and revealed in the Old Testament. They were inclined, therefore, to cancel the personal impediments "invented" by the church and to return to the Leviticus code. The opponents, too, insisted on a bedrock that the church had no power to change or annihilate, but unlike the Protestants they found it chiefly in the New Testament, construed as divine law: in the institution by Jesus Christ of marriage as a sacrament.

20.2 MARRIAGE AND THE CHRISTIAN COMMONWEALTH

The contractual theory had many parts, and no speaker at the council stated it in every detail. Nevertheless, it is possible to reconstruct the argument in a manner that is consistent with the recorded *acta*. Its purpose was to show that the church had the power to invalidate clandestine marriages and was wholly entitled to do so if that action was expedient and legally justified, that is, an urgently needed reform that would be beneficial in most cases. Most of the prelates, including the opponents, shared the conviction that clandestine marriages were harmful and subversive and ought to be prevented as much as possible. Because that premise was not controversial, no one thought it necessary to make much of a case for it. The prelates mostly relied on conventional, stereotypical characterizations of the perils of clandestinity, although the secretary may have accidentally enhanced this feature in abbreviating for the record what was said or proposed.

20.2.1 *The argument in outline*

Since marriage is both a contract and sacrament, the proponents reasoned, and since the two aspects are really distinct, one may put sacramentality to one side and consider marriage solely as a contract between citizens of a commonwealth (*res publica*). This was an abstract, theoretical conception pertaining to the commonwealth as understood in political philosophy, although it approximated to the situation of marriage in non-Christian cultures. Any commonwealth or its ruler (*princeps*) has the power to determine the conditions of validity for the contracts, vows, oaths, and so forth of its citizens through laws that serve the public good (*bonum publicum*), to which the private goods of individuals, of couples, and even of families are subordinate. The contract of marriage is no exception. The distinction between essence and solemnity has no relevance here, for the commonwealth is entitled to require any formalities it chooses as necessary conditions for the validity of a contract, including solemnities and the presence of witnesses, as long as that requirement advances the public good and does not undermine the free consent of the contractants. Clandestine marriage is a case in point, for although it serves the personal desires of the spouses – desires that are likely to be imprudent, irrational, and overly carnal – it is contrary to the public good.

Now suppose that marriage is also a sacrament. That sacrament presupposes the contract in the same way as the sacrament of baptism presupposes ablution with water. In other words, the contract is a material cause of the sacrament. The sacramentality of marriage enhances the contract, directing it to higher ends, just as grace perfects nature. The contract may, indeed, now be regarded as a spiritual contract. But that enhancement does not destroy or take anything away from the contract. Everything that constitutes the contractuality (*ratio contractus*) of marriage remains intact, including the contract's subjection to regulation by the commonwealth in the interests of the public good. Invalidating the contract will subtract matter that is essential to the sacrament without altering the essence of the sacrament. Suppose, for example, that the wine placed on the altar at eucharist became vinegar before the priest consecrated it.[9] There would be no sacrament, since wine and not vinegar is the essential matter of eucharist, but the intervention would not have altered the essential conditions of the sacrament. On the contrary, it is because those conditions are inalterable that the changing of wine into vinegar would prevent the sacrament from taking place.

That line of argument might conceivably had led to the conclusion that secular authorities should determine the conditions of validity for this contract. They would have presumably exercised this power on a regional level, since there was in fact no universal secular power in Catholic Christendom. The King of France, for example, would have the power to invalidate marriages contracted without parental consent in his kingdom. But none of the prelates at Trent considered this possibility. Nor did the French crown claim such a right even after Trent, although the king and the Parlement tried to subvert Trent's decisions in other ways. Why had the church largely, perhaps even exclusively, assumed the power to regulate this particular contract? This link in the chain was the least well developed at Trent, but two considerations took the place of a fully developed argument. First, the church regulated this contract because marriage was also a sacrament, just as the church regulated and had jurisdictional authority over the civil contracts, transactions, privileges, rights of ownership, and so forth of clerics and religious. Second, the commonwealth to which this contract was subject was specifically the Christian commonwealth: the *res publica christiana*.

20.2.2 *Presuppositions*

The argument outlined earlier was solidly based on well-established principles, now put in the service of a novel policy. It presupposed three areas of theory.

One area of theory pertained to the distinction between the contractuality (*ratio contractus*) and the sacramentality (*ratio sacramenti*) of marriage. This area was

---

[9] This was the standard example, presumably because wine did naturally turn into vinegar. If it seems insufficient, consider what would happen if the wine turned into water or even into olive oil. The principle at stake is the same.

based on some teachings of Thomas Aquinas regarding the church's power to introduce diriment personal impediments (Section 16.5.6). If sacraments were subject exclusively to inalterable divine law, Thomas had asked, how was the church able to introduce personal impediments? In reply, Thomas pointed out that marriage, unlike the other sacraments, was not *only* a sacrament. It was also a contract, and contracts were subject by their very nature to human, positive law. Considered in itself, the contract was an essentially mundane, secular thing, rooted in the natural law and fulfilling an "office of nature." Aristotle had fully expounded it. But it was also related to the sacrament of marriage as ablution with water was related to the sacrament of baptism. Considered in itself, therefore, it was a "material contract": both in the sense that it was a mundane, secular arrangement, and in the sense that it was a material cause of the sacrament. The fact that Christian marriage could also be considered holistically as a spiritual contract did not destroy the material aspect.

The second area of theory pertained to the political notion of a *res publica*, or commonwealth. The commonwealth is founded on legislation, and the purpose of law is not the private good of any individual, family, or association but rather the public good (*bonum publicum*): the good of the community as a whole. The ruler of a commonwealth enhances this good through laws that regulate actions and instill civic virtues. This was a theory that Aristotle emphasized, and it was one that Thomas Aquinas had espoused, although he had spoken of the community (*communitas*) and its common good (*bonum commune*) rather than of the commonwealth (*res publica*) and its public good (*bonum publicum*): the preferred terminology during the sixteenth century. Aristotle characterizes politics, which in his view is essentially the art of legislation, as the architectonic science in relation to all other fields of ethics.[10] The art of a master craftsman (*architektōn*) subsumes and is the reason for the subsidiary arts. For example, the equestrian art is architectonic in relation to the arts of making bridles, shoeing horses, and so forth. Law is by definition, according to Thomas, "an ordinance of reason for the common good, promulgated by one who has care of the community."[11] And the reason for law is that each human being is "a part of the perfect community," for "every part is ordained to the whole as imperfect to perfect."[12]

---

[10] R. Bodéüs, *The Political Dimensions of Aristotle's Ethics* (Albany, N.Y., 1993), 63–68.

[11] Thomas Aquinas, *Summa theologiae* I-II.90.4, resp. (1209a): "[lex] nihil est aliud quam quaedam rationis ordinatio ad bonum commune, ab eo qui curam communitatis habet, promulgata."

[12] *Summa theologiae* I-II.90.2 (1207a), resp.: "omnis pars ordinetur ad totum sicut imperfectum ad perfectum, unus autem homo est pars communitatis perfectae." This principle as Thomas expounds it is an extension of eudaimonism, for the individual is by nature part of a political community and, therefore, is perfected in it, but sixteenth-century authors seem inclined to treat the community as more important than the individual. On Thomas's understanding of the political part-whole relation, see A. P. D'Entrèves, *The Medieval Contribution to Political Thought* (New York, 1959), 24–31.

The third area is the notion of a *res publica christiana*. The Christian common-wealth of sixteenth-century Catholic thought was not Christendom, as is sometimes said, but the church. Nevertheless, the terms *ecclesia* and *res publica christiana* were not synonyms. The term *res publica Christiana* denoted the church considered *as* a commonwealth or political community: an institution fully expounded by philoso-phers such as Aristotle and Cicero. What that assimilation meant was often more suggested than explicit, for the Christian commonwealth was an ideal projected partly by rhetorical means. It is significant that Catholics during this period extended terms that normally denoted secular authority, such as *res publica, magistratus*, and *politia*, to ecclesiastical authority, although precisely what the transference signified is hard to define. Because there was by definition only one universal, Catholic church, this church could be construed as a commonwealth only to the extent that it was a single, effectively governed visible community. An invisible community of isolated Christian communities might be construed as the mystical body of Christ, but it would not be a commonwealth.

The idea of the Christian commonwealth presupposed a hierocratic political theology, such as that expounded by in the twelfth century by Hugh of Saint-Victor (Section 10.3.1) or in the sixteenth by Giovanni Antonio Delfini (Section 19.9.1). The point of political theology during the Middle Ages and the Counter-Reformation was to reconcile the principle of separation – that one should render unto God what is God's, and unto Caesar what is Caesar's (Matt 22:21) – with the principle that all power comes from God (Rom 13:1–7). The visible church as the body of Christ includes two distinct but analogously hierarchical powers, one royal (the *regnum*) and the other priestly (the *sacerdotium*). Authority over the body ecclesiastic is twofold, therefore, with the royal power caring for the temporal welfare of the community, and the priestly power caring for its spiritual, eternal welfare. According to the hierocratic model, some separation is necessary for the orderly coexistence of the two powers and the health of each, but the royal power is subordinate to the priestly power, to which it owes its very existence. The royal power may even be regarded as a necessary evil resulting from war, coercion, and the harmful aspects of city building. Secular rulers must recognize both their own limitations and their duty to foster the eternal, spiritual welfare of the citizens, which they do by protecting the ecclesiastical power and when necessary using coercive, even deadly force on its behalf. Such is the gist of the Two Swords theory, first proposed by Bernard of Clairvaux. Ecclesiastical authority retains the supreme, architectonic power, and it mediates between human beings and God. To be effective, ecclesiastical authority must separate itself as far as possible from secular matters by delegating power over them to secular authorities: not because it has no right to regulate them, but so that it can preserve the spiritual priorities of its mission.[13]

---

[13] W. Ullmann, *The Growth of Papal Government in the Middle Ages* (London, 1970). J. A. Watt, "Spiritual and Temporal Powers," in J. H. Burns, *Cambridge History of Medieval Political Thought c.350–c.1450* (Cambridge, 1988), 367–423.

Giovanni Antonio Delfini was typical. He explains that the ecclesiastical power is older and nobler than the civil power, which originated as a response to violence. It is the efficient cause of the civil power, which it brought into existence.[14] It is the formal cause of the civil power, just as charity is the form of the virtues. And it is the final cause of the civil power, which it regulates and directs to its ultimate end.[15] The two powers normally work together in harmony, and both are necessary for the welfare of the Christian commonwealth. The personal separation of ecclesiastical from temporal power is crucial only at the level of the papacy, according to Delfini, and even there it is not complete. There is nothing to prevent ministers of the church from also holding civil authority, or magistracy, for "whatever [offices] are useful in a Christian commonwealth and are pleasing and acceptable to God can be legitimately assumed by any persons who are suited and apt."[16] But the pope should exercise as little temporal power as is consistent with his mission. He must hold *some* temporal power, Delfini concedes, but he should not have as much power over temporal things as he has over spiritual things.[17]

With a hierocratic model in mind, the prelates at Trent did not feel any urgent need to explain why the church had authority over the contract of marriage, which had spiritual and sacramental consequences. Since secular power originated in the priestly power, the church was entitled to take back or "remove" civil powers whenever appropriate.

This complex of political theory and sacramental theology was not new. The proponents applied it to show that church could invalidate clandestine marriage, which was a fairly new idea, but Thomas Aquinas has already proposed the theory to explain the church's power to introduce personal impediments. Two doctors of Louvain, Adrian Florensz (the future Pope Hadrian VI, d. 1523) and Ruard Tapper (d. 1559), developed Thomas's theory in ways that anticipated the arguments that the proponents used at Trent in 1563, especially the contractual theory. Both theologians took the still-conventional view that the church had no power to invalidate clandestine marriages, and opponents during 1563 cited Florensz and Tapper as well as Delfini, Henry of Ghent, and others to support their own position.[18] Nevertheless, all the major pieces of the political theory expounded by the proponents were already present in Florensz's and Tapper's analysis of the church's power over impediments. Both emphasized the power of a commonwealth over the contracts of citizens, and Florensz argued that an impediment could subtract the matter of the sacrament without altering its essential conditions.

---

[14] Giovanni Antonio Delfini, *De potestate ecclesiastica* (Venice, 1549), 4b–6a.
[15] Ibid., 6b–7a.   [16] Ibid., 152b–153a.   [17] Ibid., 153a–154b.
[18] Archiep. Rossanensis, 647/7–9, 649/1–3. Faventinus, 676/23–24, 735/30–37. Britonoriensis, 703/21–23. On Tapper on clandestine marriage, see R. Lettmann, *Die Diskussion über die klandestinen Ehen* (Münster, 1966), 94–97.

20.2.3 *Adrian Florensz*

Commenting on Peter Lombard's treatment of the sacraments, Florensz inquires whether marriage is a sacrament of New Law, instituted by God.[19] In the body of this article, adapting his analysis from Duns Scotus, Florensz distinguishes among three aspects of marriage: the contract, the bond, and the sacrament.[20] The contract and the sacrament are numerically the same inasmuch as one and the same action of marrying can be construed both as a contract and as a sacrament. Nevertheless, the two terms denote different aspects of marrying. The contract is the transient action by which the spouses give themselves bodily to each other. The sacrament, too, is a transient event, just as the sacrament of baptism is a transient act of ablution. The bond is the enduring, insoluble mutual obligation established by the contract and confirmed through consummation, although this insolubility is fully realized only between believers. Considered as a sacrament, marriage is a sign both of the union between Christ and the church and of conjugal grace. Florensz argues that marriage was *instituted* only as a sacrament, and not as a contract. Because contracts arise naturally from the natural law, they do not require any special act of institution. Signs, on the contrary, do require institution. Marriage was instituted in the beginning as a sign of Christ's union with the church, and it was instituted again in the Gospel as a sacrament of the New Law. Florensz concedes that theologians do not agree as to when or where in Scripture Jesus Christ instituted marriage as a sacrament of the New Law, but he does not consider that to be a crucial problem. He notes that there is even some debate as to when and how Christ instituted baptism.

As well as the standard objections to the sacramentality of marriage, such as those regarding the verbal form, the priestly blessing, and dependence on the Passion of Christ, Florensz poses the objection that marriage cannot be a sacrament in the proper sense because the church has introduced many changes to it, such as those regarding the impediments of consanguinity and affinity. The constitution of a sacrament is defined under unchangeable divine law, to which the law of the church is subordinate. Now, an inferior law cannot abrogate a superior law.[21]

Replying to this objection, Florensz concedes that an inferior law cannot abrogate or alter a superior law, but he argues that the inferior law can provide or withdraw the matter that is subject to the superior law. To illustrate this principle, Florensz considers what happens when the pope or a senior prelate excommunicates someone. That person is *ipso facto* prevented from receiving absolution from a parish priest through the sacrament of penance, yet not because the conditions of the sacrament have changed, for they are the subject of divine law and, as such, inalterable. Contrariwise, the pope or a senior prelate may render the subject capable of receiving

---

[19] Adrian Florensz, Quaestiones de sacramentis in Quartum Sententiarum librum, 5: De matrimonio, Q. 1 (Rome, 1522: 188r–189v).

[20] Resp. (188va–b). Cf. Scotus, *Rep. Par.*, IV *Sent.* 28.un., conc. 20–21 (Vivès 24:383).

[21] Florensz, arg. 1b (188va).

absolution again by lifting the excommunication. Even a baker can turn wheat, which is not the matter essential to eucharist, into bread, which is the matter essential to eucharist. The manner in which sacraments are subject to the church's law depends on the nature of the sacramental matter. For example, the matter of confirmation and of extreme unction is consecrated oil, but the church has the power at least to determine how the oil must be consecrated, for Christ left those details undetermined. In every case of such change, though, the church does not alter the essence of the sacrament but rather subtracts or supplies the matter essential to the sacrament.[22]

Nevertheless, Florensz argues, marriage is unique among the sacraments as regards the extent to which its essential matter – legitimate persons – can be defined through legislation. This is because the sacrament presupposes a contract, for contracts are naturally subject to positive law because individual goods are subordinate to the public good. Florensz asks the reader to disregard the sacramentality of marriage for a moment and to consider how marriage would be regulated if it were a mere contract regulated by a commonwealth:

> Marriage inasmuch as it is a contract of persons [*contractus personarum*] is subject by natural law to the regulation [*ordinatio*] of the church, whereas marriage as a sacrament adds signification and causality to the contract as if onto a foundation. If marriage were not a sacrament, it would be subject to human statute just as any contract of things [*contractus rerum*] is subject. The human being by his very essence [*id quod est*] belongs to the community and ought to risk his life for the commonwealth if necessary.[23]

Just as the commonwealth can make laws preventing certain persons from alienating their property to others by a contract of things, Florensz points out, so also the commonwealth can determine which persons are entitled to give themselves bodily to each other in marriage: a contract of persons. The sacramentality of marriage adds a new dimension over and above the contract, but it does not take anything away from the contractuality of marriage. By withdrawing from certain persons the contractual right to give to each other power over their own bodies (1 Cor 7:3–4), or conversely by providing that power, the church "is able to change the matter of the sacrament accidentally."[24]

20.2.4 *Ruard Tapper*

Tapper was a doctor of theology and the rector of the university of Louvain, as well as Inquisitor General of the Low Countries.[25] In 1544, the theology faculty of

---

[22] Ibid. (189rb–189va).   [23] Ibid. (189rb).

[24] Ibid.: "Sic quia materia matrimonii est homo potens dare potestatem corporis sui, ecclesia quia potest ei illam facultatem dandi potestatem sui corporis auferre vel non habenti dare, potest per accidens mutare materiam sacramenti."

[25] For brief accounts of Tapper's life and work, see J. Etienne, "Ruard Tapper (1487–1559)," *Louvain Studies* 5 (1975): 284–86; and W. A. Newman, *Jus Divinum and the Sacrament of Penance in Two Tridentine Theologians: Melchior Cano and Ruard Tapper* (doctoral diss., Washington, D.C., 1969), 188–200.

Louvain published under his direction a list of fifty-nine articles of faith at the request of the emperor, Charles V, and Tapper later wrote an exposition of the first twenty.[26] The text to be considered here is his exposition of the twentieth article: "Marriages contracted contrary to canons that annul them are absolutely null and void."[27] The article affirms the power of the church to introduce diriment impediments, for some Protestants held that the only impediments that were truly diriment were those of the Leviticus code, which expressed the natural law. After a general introduction, Tapper pursues a detailed critique of Erasmus, Luther, Brenz, and Bucer, but only the introduction matters here. Tapper was unusually learned and he had a powerful intellect, but his prose is disorderly, meandering, and repetitive. In what follows, rather than following the course of his presentation, I have taken pieces from it and rearranged them to arrive at a tolerably coherent argument.

Marriage is a contract whereby the spouses give themselves bodily to each other in order to procreate, Tapper argues. It is because of that uniquely contractual basis, and not because of the sacrament *per se*, that there are many more impediments to marriage than there are to any other sacrament.[28] Tapper classifies the impediments according to the cause of the contract that each impedes. Error and coercion impede the efficient cause of the contract, which is mutual consent. Impotence impedes the final cause, which is procreation. Consanguinity, affinity, holy orders, and solemn vows impede the material cause, or the persons.[29] Furthermore, some impediments are diriment whereas others are merely prohibitive. The reason for this difference is that some impediments pertain to things that are essential to marriage, whereas others pertain to the solemnities of the sacrament, which are accidental.[30] Nothing can dissolve the bond of marriage once it has come into existence, but some things can prevent it from coming into existence.[31]

The church prohibits couples from marrying clandestinely or without the announcement of the banns. It does so in order to prevent persons from marrying when there is an impediment between them, especially one that would nullify their union, and to ensure that the sacrament is regarded with due reverence.[32] But is

---

[26] Ruard Tapper, *Explicatio articulorum venerandae Facultatis Sacrae Theologiae Generalis Studii Lovanien[sis] circa dogmata ecclesiastica ab annis triginta quatuor controversa, una cum responsione ad argumenta adversarorm*, 2 vols, Louvain and Paris, 1555–1557. The *Explicatio* was republished in Tapper's *Opera*, Cologne, 1582–1583. The latter is the version of the *Expositio* that is usually cited because it was published in facsimile by Gregg Press (1962), but it is inferior to the earlier edition, which the Hathi Trust makes available via the internet. In what follows, I provide page numbers for the earlier version first, followed by the page numbers in the Cologne *Opera* in square brackets.

[27] "Matrimonia contracta contra canones ipsa dirimentes, simpliciter sunt irrita et nulla."

[28] *Explicationis . . . tomus primus*, art. 20, 495/3–10 [305a].   [29] 494/23–34 [305a].

[30] 494/34–40 [305a].   [31] 493/1–4 [304a].

[32] 494/20–23 [305a]: "Prohibent autem duntaxat ne clandestine contrahatur, vel ante bannorum proclamationem, ne fortassis impedimentum sit inter eos, qui matrimonium inire desiderant, et propterea cum sacramenti irreverentia nulliter contrahunt."

clandestinity itself a diriment impediment? Does the church have the power to render clandestine marriages null and void? Tapper concedes that this is a difficult question:

> But whether the clandestine contract of marriage can be universally annulled because of the many dangers and scandals that arise from it, just as this has been prohibited by the sacred canons, and, likewise, [whether] a conjugal contract entered into without the parents' consent [can be annulled] because of the irreverence and neglect shown to the parents — these are difficult questions.[33]

Tapper notes that although clandestine marriage and marriage without parental consent are often conflated, "there is a great difference between them." Some couples marry clandestinely *with* their parents' consent. Others marry publicly and solemnly after the announcement of the banns *without* their parents' consent. But neither deficiency, Tapper argues, is a diriment impediment.[34] Some hold that the church has the power to invalidate such marriages and that it did so for a long time, but Tapper reasons that the case for invalidating such marriages is no stronger than the case for invalidating civil contracts, vows, and oaths, for these are invalidated only on the presumption that there has been fraud or some other irregularity. When such a presumption is found to be contrary to the truth, the contract is judged to be valid. Even when there are no witnesses to a contract, it is still binding in the forum of conscience. Thus, a clandestine marriage is valid in principle and annuls a subsequent marriage even when the former is unconsummated and the latter consummated.[35] Similarly, those who marry without paternal consent sin against their fathers, who are justly indignant, but the marriage is settled (*ratum*), nonetheless, for "irreverence to the parents is not a reason for annulling a marriage."[36] To prove that clandestinity is not a diriment impediment, Tapper treats marriage not, as one might expect, as a sacrament, but as a contract. His argument is not absolute or *a priori* but rather based on an empirical observation about civil contract law. Contracts, in his view, are so fundamentally based on the free consent of the contractants that the commonwealth can do little to alter the sufficient and necessary conditions of a contract *per se*. What the commonwealth can do, however, is to change the preconditions of a contract, such as who is entitled to make it.

The magistracy of any commonwealth has the authority to introduce diriment impediments to marriage, Tapper argues, only insofar as it has the power to regulate the preconditions of any contracts made by its citizens. It uses this power to foster virtue and the public good by securing the peace and welfare (*salus*) of the community as a whole.[37] Thus, every well-ordered commonwealth (*res publica bene ordinata*) has laws that prohibit certain marriages or render them invalid.[38]

---

[33] 503/23–27 [310b].   [34] 502/41–46 [310a].

[35] 503/27–38 [310b]. 503/3–12 [310a]. Tapper cites the decretal *Si inter virum*, X 4.1.31 (672). He ascribes it to Alexander III, but in fact the author was Gregory IX.

[36] 502/38–41 [310a]. 503/36–37 [310b].   [37] 495/10–15 [305a–b].   [38] 493/35–36 [304b].

Tapper uses the term *magistratus* here not to denote a particular office or office-holder, but rather to embrace the ruling authority of the commonwealth, however that might be constituted.[39] The term primarily denotes secular authorities, but Tapper uses it by extension to denote ecclesiastical authorities, especially when he wants to emphasize the hierarchy's quasi-political role as governor and legislator of the Christian community. Magistracies require good cause to introduce just laws, and they introduce marital impediments to foster the welfare of the commonwealth, rather than that of individuals or couples. Aristotle explains how marriage is regulated both by the *ius naturale* and by the *ius civile*, or *ius legitimum*. Every magistracy has the power to introduce impediments in order to foster the "peace, tranquility, and public welfare" of the commonwealth.[40]

After the Gospel had abrogated the Mosaic laws of marriage, Tapper argues, new modes of authority and new laws had to be introduced, such as the laws of the Christian emperors, for marriage is the contract on which inheritance and succession depend.[41] The natural laws that remained after the abrogation of the Mosaic law were ambiguous and too general. Consider, for example, the general principle of Leviticus 18:6: "No man shall approach to her that is near of kin to him, to uncover her nakedness." It expresses a natural law, but it cannot be applied effectively without determination. What should count as "near of kin"? Christian magistracies, both "political and ecclesiastical," supplied such determinations through their *leges* and *canones*, defining precisely which degrees of kinship would be impediments.[42] These determinations were necessarily changeable, for the needs and circumstances of human communities are themselves changeable.[43]

Every magistracy, too, has the power to introduce both prohibitive and diriment impediments to marriage. Diriment impediments require stronger causes than prohibitive impediments.[44] Tapper considers this choice to be a universal tool of all legal systems, and he notes precedents in the Old Testament. The prohibited relationships of the Leviticus code were diriment impediments, and Ezra interpreted disparity of cult as a diriment impediment (Ezra 9). But although Esau sinned when he took Canaanite women as his wives, and although his parents, Isaac and Rebecca, dissented, there is nothing in Scripture to indicate that Esau's marriages were less than valid (Gen 36:2–5).[45]

Tapper explains that magistracies are of two sorts: political and ecclesiastical. These pursue different ends, but they are equivalent insofar as both the *leges* of the political magistracies and the *canones* of the ecclesiastical magistracies are designed to foster peace and public welfare and to inculcate virtue in a community:

---

[39] Tapper's term *magistratus* is synonymous with Luther's *oberkeit* (*Obrigkeit* in modern German).

[40] 493/42–494/1 [304b].   [41] 493/38–41 [304b].   [42] 495/47–496/23 [305b–306a].

[43] 496/23–31 [306a].   [44] 493/39–494/3 [304b].   [45] 493/1–34 [304a–b].

The magistracy is able to regulate, therefore, whatever pertains to public welfare: and not only the secular but also the ecclesiastical magistracy, each in relation to the end and scope of its regime. For the faculty to govern and to rule the community subject to it is common to both, and this entails the power to make laws.[46]

The respective powers of the two magistracies are interdependent and overlapping. A universal social compact (*generale pactum societatis humanae*) requires that people should obey their rulers (Heb 13:17), and that lesser powers are subject to higher powers.[47] On the one hand, Scripture teaches that the power of kings comes from God (Prov 8:15) and that kings must rule justly (Isa 10:1–2). Even secular rulers are "ministers of God and of his kingdom."[48] On the other hand, bishops are pastors, and they must care for the virtue and welfare of their flocks (Acts 20:28, John 21:17, 1 Pet 5:2). The church pursues nobler, more spiritual ends than the political magistracy, but the regimes are equivalent insofar as they both use laws to achieve the peace and welfare of a community.

The church is in its own way a magistracy ruling over a commonwealth, therefore, and it must use that power to regulate whatever contracts come within its legislative scope. Its duty of care includes the spiritual welfare of the faithful in this life, as well as their blessedness in the next life:

> Just as the secular authority [*potestas saecularis*] has the faculty to prohibit some civil contracts and to render others invalid, such as the contracts of minors, and just as fathers [*patresfamilias*] have the faculty to annul the vows and oaths of their children, so also the ecclesiastical authority [*potestas ecclesiastica*] has the faculty to regulate marriage as an office of Christ's own family and to invalidate some marriages for the sake of the honor and the good of the church, in order to achieve both the celestial fatherland as the ultimate goal and the peace and honor of the members of Christ's family.[49]

Individuals are subject to the rulers of these regimes because their personal welfare is subordinate to the welfare of the community:

> For the sake of public welfare, all are subject to the magistracy as regards their persons, contracts, and faculties. For the part exists naturally because of the whole, and it ought to bear loss and detriment for the welfare of the whole, for by a law of nature the part will put its own very existence at risk [for the sake of the whole]. As the Apostle says, we ought not "to please ourselves." Rather, "each one of us should please his neighbor for his [the latter's] good" (Rom 15:1–2). And elsewhere, "you are not your own, for you have been bought with a great price" (1 Cor 6:19–20). It is no wonder, then, that everything regarding the life, behavior, and marriages of Christ's family members is regulated [by the ecclesiastical magistracy] for his honor and for the welfare, tranquility, and honor of his family, especially where Christ himself left no rules but rather left them to be constituted in accordance with the

---

[46] 495/24–29 [305b].   [47] 495/30–40 [305b].   [48] 495/21–24 [305b].   [49] 495/40–47 [305b].

diversity of the times and places of the faithful, through those whom he appointed as ministers over his family after himself and in his place.[50]

Only the prelates of church have the power to regulate the "contracts and offices of church" inasmuch as these are spiritual and serve the welfare of the faithful. That power includes exclusive jurisdiction over even the civil contracts of "ecclesiastical persons." But "imperial laws" regulate merely earthly offices and contracts.[51]

Tapper argues that marriage in the Christian commonwealth is subject to the church's laws (*canones*) in some respects and to the civil laws (*leges*) in other respects:

> The conjugal contract that is a sacrament and an office for propagating the church is necessarily subject to ordination and invalidation by the ecclesiastical magistrate for the sake of the peace of the church and the welfare of the faithful, although at the same time it is subject to ordinances and laws of the civil power inasmuch as it is referred to the peace, honor, and good of the commonwealth.[52]

Tapper cites Thomas Aquinas to corroborate this claim. Thomas recognizes that the rulers of non-Christian communities have the right to invalidate contracts of marriage among their people. And Thomas also says that marriage is subject to the law of nature inasmuch as it fulfills an office of nature, to divine law inasmuch as it is a sacrament, and to civil law inasmuch as fulfills and "office of community."[53] Tapper agrees. The two regimes pertain to different aspects of marriage, respectively earthly and celestial:

> Insofar as the union of male and female belongs to the genus of mortals, therefore, it is a certain seedbed of the city, but whereas the earthly city needs only generation, the celestial city also needs regeneration in order to escape from the harm done by generation.[54]

Tapper notes that the *Institutes* of Justinian, after a summary of the impediments of consanguinity and affinity, adds that those who marry contrary to these prohibitions will not be considered man and wife, that their marriage and dowry will not be considered valid, and that their children will be illegitimate. Tapper remarks that the "imperial power always uses the right of prohibiting and invalidating marriages" insofar as they fulfill "an office of nature and propagation" and foster "the peace and honor of the commonwealth."[55] Neither the sacred canons nor the doctors of the church contradict those civil laws. On the contrary, they commend them.[56]

---

[50] 496/31–41 [306a–b].   [51] 496/41–45 [306b].   [52] 497/9–13 [306b].

[53] 497/13–22 [306b]. Thomas Aquinas, *IV Sent.* 39.un.2, ad 3 (226a); *IV Sent.* 34.un.1, ad 4 (164b).

[54] 498/18–21 [307a].

[55] 497/41–48 [307a]. *Inst.* 1.10.12: "Si adversus ea quae diximus aliqui coierint, nec vir nec uxor nec nuptiae nec matrimonium nec dos intellegitur. Itaque ii, qui ex eo coitu nascuntur ... solent ... spurii appellari."

[56] 498/1–2 [307a].

Tapper maintains that whenever civil law prohibits marriage for the sake of the public good, that prohibition is generally valid also in church law, although he notes that not all canonists have agreed. Tapper cites Guido de Baysio (d. 1313) and Philipus Franchus de Perusio (d. 1471) in support of his own position, and Hostiensis in support of the opposite position.[57] He holds that the church's law is superior to civil law and has the power to abrogate it. For example, the church has abrogated the *tempus lugendi* of Roman civil law (the obligation of a widow to wait for a year or more before remarrying).[58] Absent incompatibility or explicit abrogation, however, the civil regulation of marriage remains in force. Tapper discusses at some length this division of the ecclesiastical and civil aspects of marriage, whereby marriage is still subject in certain respects to "the secular magistracy" and in others to "the prelates of the church."[59] For the most part, he seems to be referring to the power to legislate, and not to the power the judge cases, although decretal law straddled that division. A gloss on the decretal *Si quis ancillam*, ascribed to Pope Julius (Section 11.6.1), establishes the point that Tapper wishes to make. Julius judged that a marriage between a free man and a formerly servile woman whom he had liberated was valid because there was nothing in the union that was impious or contrary to the civil laws (*leges*). According to the gloss, such marriages would indeed be invalid if they were contrary to civil laws (*leges*), but only if no church laws (*canones*) abrogated the civil laws.[60]

Tapper insists that although marriage is subject to ecclesiastical law inasmuch as it is a sacrament, its sacramentality does not prevent it from being subject to civil or imperial power:

> It is clear from what has been said that the sacramentality [*ratio sacramenti*] in Christian marriage does not in any way prevent the secular power from being able to make laws about it inasmuch as it fulfills an office of the commonwealth. Yet the ecclesiastical power, which is architectonic and considers marriage in relation to a higher end and rationale, has the power to derogate, revoke, and invalidate the constitutions [of the secular power] if they are contrary to or inconsistent with the sacred duty [*religio*] and scope of the ecclesiastical regime.[61]

The civil law to which Tapper refers is chiefly the *Corpus Iuris Civilis* of Justinian, which was the basis of the *ius commune*, or learned law. But here Tapper's position is far from clear. Whether he would extend this power to kings or to his own emperor is unclear. Nor is it clear what power over the existence and validity of marriage, if any, he would concede to secular magistrates of a Christian commonwealth.

[57] 497/28–43 [306b–307a].   [58] 498/32–41 [307b].
[59] 498/25–23 [307a]: "Ubi satis insinuatur qua ratione coniugium subsit magistratui seculari, et qua ratione prelatis Ecclesiae." The passage on the division runs from 497–502 [306b–310a].
[60] 497/22–28 [306b].   [61] 498/26–31 [307b].

20.3 *THEOLOGI MINORES*

On February 3, 1563, Cardinal Gonzaga announced that the council would be prorogued until April 22, but that meanwhile the *theologi minores* would dispute several articles pertaining to the sacrament of marriage (Section 18.4.1).[62] The articles were announced on February 4. The theologians were divided into four classes, with two articles assigned to each class. The article on clandestine marriage was assigned to the first class, which met from February 9 through 16. As noted earlier, there were fifteen theologians in this class. Six were from Spain: Alfonso Salmerón, S.J. (a biblical scholar and a companion of Ignatius Loyola), Pedro Fernández, O.P., Pedro Mercado (advisor to Acisclo de Moya y Contreras, bishop of Vic), Joannes del Gado, Cosme-Damian Hortolà, and Ferdinando de Bellosillo. Two were from Portugal: Antonius Leytanus and Diego Andrada de Payva. Four were secular masters of theology from Paris: Nicholas Maillard, Nicholas de Brys, Antonius Coquier, and Simon Vigor. And three were Italian friars: Antonius de Gragnano, O.F.M. Conv., Aloysius de Burgo Novo, O.F.M. Obs., and Taddeo da Perugia, O.S.A.

The article stated that "parents have the power to annul clandestine marriages, and that marriages contracted thus are not true marriages, and that it is expedient that marriages of this sort should be rendered invalid in the church in future."[63] This article expressed the same twofold error that had been the focus of discussion at Bologna but the order of the two components was reversed, with the power of parents to annul such marriages coming first.

Most of the theologians affirmed, against Luther, that clandestine marriages were valid and sacramental. Alfonso Salmerón noted that clandestinity might be characterized in several ways. A marriage may be clandestine inasmuch as there are no witnesses, as in the decretals of Alexander III, or inasmuch as it is not solemnized ecclesiastically, as required by the decretal of Evaristus, or inasmuch as the banns have not been read, as Lateran IV required. But are clandestine marriages invalid, as Luther holds? If we consider the laws of marriage, Salmerón explains, we find that clandestine marriages are literally illegitimate, since they are contracted in a manner contrary to those laws.[64] But if we consider "the essentials of marriage," we find that

---

[62] CT 9:376/11–12: "Deinde ut theologi disputarent de his articulis, qui pertinent ad sacramentum matrimonii...."

[63] 380/5–6: "Parentes posse irritare matrimoni clandestina, nec esse vera matrimonia, quae sic contrahuntur, expedireque, ut in ecclesia huiusmodi in futurum irritentur." The verb *posse* in this context has the sense of "to have power." It was commonly used to express both active potency (the ability of an agent to do something) and neutral potency (the possibility that something may happen, or the statistical fact that it sometimes happens). It was rarely used to express passive potency (the capacity of a subject to receive a causal influence, or to be affected in a certain way).

[64] Alphonsus Salmeron, 384/25–385/1: "Si respicimus leges, quae matrimonia praescribunt, sunt illegitima, quia contra eas contrahuntur." I take it that the word *leges* here includes ecclesiastical law, although it usually denotes civil law, for Salméron is distinguishing between *leges matrimonii* and *essentialia matrimonii*, not between *leges* and *canones*.

clandestine marriages are established and stable (*rata et firma*). To corroborate this position, Salmerón cites Genesis 2:24 ("where," he comments, "nothing is required except consent"), the example of Tobias (who contracted marriage without his parents' knowledge), decretals by Alexander III and Innocent III, and the standard consensual proof texts from Nicholas I and pseudo-Chrysostom.[65]

The theological experts assumed that marriage, like every other sacrament, had an inalterable essence composed of matter and form, although as noted earlier there was little consensus as to what those constituents were (Section 18.4.1). According to Salmerón, the form was the spouses' expression of consent, that is, the words of consent or whatever non-verbal gestures served instead of words, and the matter was the joining of right hands with the bestowal of a ring. The spouses themselves took the place of the minister, since the priest's action was only a sacramental.[66] Antonius de Gragnano, too, held that the words of consent constituted the form, and Diego de Payva said that the spouses were the ministers of the sacrament.[67] But both Simon Vigor and Pedro Fernández held that the spouses' verbal expression of consent was only the matter of the sacrament.[68] Fernández claimed that the priest was the minister of the sacrament.[69]

The decretal ascribed to Pope Evaristus came up several times during the discussion of clandestinity.[70] A marriage will not be legitimate, according to the decretal, unless the groom petitions for his bride from those with power over her and a priest blesses the marriage with prayers and oblations. Otherwise, the result will not be a legitimate marriage but rather adultery, concubinage, promiscuity, or fornication. But the decree adds, apparently in self-contradiction, that such a marriage will be illegitimate unless what is missing is made good by the spouses' own will (*voluntas propria*) and by legitimate vows.[71] Although the theologians agreed that the decretal was crucial, they disagreed over its interpretation, which was certainly problematic. What was meant by "legitimate"? To whom did the ruling apply? Was the rule merely disciplinary or did it make clandestine marriages invalid? Why did the final clause apparently contradict what went before? Furthermore, the decretal seemed to require parental consent, a notion that most of the theologians resisted.

Both Nicholas de Brys and Pedro Fernández held that clandestine marriages were invalid, although their respective criteria for clandestinity differed. According to Nicholas de Brys, clandestine marriages and marriages contracted without parental consent were already invalid by their very nature. He emphasized the importance of

[65] 384/20–385/24.   [66] 384/6–13.
[67] Antonius de Gragnano, 407/17. Didacus de Payva, 401/15.
[68] Simon Vigor, 396/25–26. Petrus Fernandez, 405/27–31.
[69] Petrus Fernandez, 405/14–16.
[70] For example, Alphonsus Salmeron, 384/23, 385/7; Cosmas et Damianus Ortolanus, 388/35–389/3; Simon Vigor, 397/19–22; Didacus de Paiva, 400/23–29.
[71] PL 130:81B–C. On the decretal, see Joyce, *Christian Marriage* (London, 1948), 104–05, and MWCh 406–07. On its significance in Protestant–Catholic debate on the eve of Trent, see Joyce, ibid., 116–18, 120–22.

marrying publicly, noting that even non-Christians did not consider a marriage to be true if the partners had married secretly. Nicholas proposed that the last clause in Evaristus's decretal, which seemed to contradict what went before, referred to the parents' consent, not the contractants'. A clandestinely contracted marriage was null and void not only by divine law, he argued, but also by the law of nature, by the *ius gentium*, and by civil law. Unless a marriage had been contracted openly and publicly *with the consent of the parents*, Nicholas claimed, it was not firm or settled, it was not from God but from Satan, and the church should annul it.[72]

Whereas Nicholas de Brys emphasized the primordial natural law and the *ius gentium*, Pedro Fernández distinguished between contract and sacrament, expounding a theory akin to Melchor Cano's (Section 16.7.3).[73] Marriage was not a sacrament of the New Law, Fernández argued, unless the spouses were joined and blessed by a priest. In any sacrament, there is a natural basis to which a sanctifying power has been added supernaturally. In baptism, for example, the external ablution is a natural act, to which has been added the sacramental power to cleanse the soul. Every sacrament is a religious ceremony (*caeremonia religionis*), which must normally be administered by a priest. Priests alone possess the required supernatural power, which is the efficient cause of the sacrament. Members of the laity are prohibited from profaning the sacraments by administering them. In marriage, therefore, the contract, which consists in the spouses' expression of consent, is the natural basis and matter of the sacrament. The form is not the spouses' words of consent, for they can express their consent in many different ways.[74] Rather, the form is spoken by the priest. According to the Roman tradition, the priest informs the sacrament by saying, "And I by the authority of the church invested in me join you together" (Section 17.6.4).[75] As the Council of Cologne held – Fernández is referring to Gropper (Section 17.5.4) – a marriage contracted by the spouses alone, without the ministry and blessing of a priest, is not a sacrament of the New Law and does not differ from the marriage under the *ius gentium*. One might have expected Fernández to argue that clandestine marriages were at least contractually valid, but instead he agrees with Evaristus that they amount to nothing more than promiscuity and fornication (*stupra et fornicationes*). Fernández cites Pope Nicholas's letter to the Khan of Bulgaria (oddly enough) and the decretal of Evaristus to corroborate his position.[76]

The other members of this class, however, unlike Nicholas de Brys and Pedro Fernández, accepted that clandestine marriages were currently valid, although some

---

[72] Nicolaus de Bris, 387/20–24.   [73] Petrus Fernandez, 405–06.   [74] 405/22–23.

[75] 406/5–6: "*Et ego auctoritate ecclesiae, qua fungor, coniungo vos,* quibus verbis formam sacramento ipsi dat." Fernández takes this formula from Alberto Castellani's *Sacerdotale ad consuetudinem sanctae Romanae ecclesiae,* but Fernández, as Duval points out, omits Castellani's "*cum assensu utriusque.*" See A. Duval, "La formule Ego vos in matrimonium conjungo... au concile de Trente," *La Maison-Dieu* 99 (1969): 144–53, at 148.

[76] 406/6–7.

did so only grudgingly, as if the policy went against the flow of prudence or even against the nature of marriage. Hortolà noted that both Evaristus and the Council of Cologne (i.e., Gropper, Section 17.5.4) had said that clandestine marriages were not sacraments. Nevertheless, he argued that parental consent was not strictly necessary, and that clandestine marriages were valid as long as the spouses themselves consented, as the final clause of Evaristus's decretal seemed to say. Even if Evaristus had meant to invalidate clandestine marriages, his rule must have been subsequently abrogated by the traditions of the church.[77] Antonius Coquier argued that clandestine marriages were necessarily true marriages, for otherwise the church would have erred by failing to annul them. Nor was parental consent a necessary requirement.[78]

None of the experts doubted that clandestine marriages were hazardous and highly undesirable. Antonius Leytanus lamented that such marriages were a source of discord, hatred, and enmity, whereas marriage was supposed to be a bond of peace. It was often difficult to ascertain whether any contract had been made with proper consent, and marriage was no exception. One should not leave young people to make their own choices without supervision when they married.[79] Ferdinando de Bellosillo said that clandestine marriages were the source of indecency, adultery, scandals, enmity, strife, and feuds.[80] Taddeo da Perugia conceded that clandestine marriages were valid, but he argued that they were detrimental to the goods of offspring, faith, and sacrament, and that they were the source of countless evils (_infinita mala_).[81] Joannes del Gado said much the same, although he was evidently referring not to clandestinity _per se_ but to the absence of parental consent.[82]

Granted that clandestine marriages were prohibited and perilous but currently valid, the theologians asked whether the church had the right or the power to render them null and void henceforth. There was less clarity and unanimity on this point, but most seem to have been open to the possibility. Antonius Leytanus argued that because the church already regarded clandestinity as a mortal sin, it ought to be possible to raise clandestinity to the level of a diriment impediment.[83] Pedro Mercado argued that church's policy of regarding clandestine marriages as valid could not be construed as a truly Catholic, universal tradition (_consuetudo_) because it had not been upheld in Evaristus's day. A tradition was truly Catholic if and only if it was observed by everyone, always, and everywhere. The church probably did have the power, therefore, to make the clandestine marriages of children beneath a certain age invalid henceforth.[84]

---

[77] Cosmas et Damianus Ortolanus, 388/34–389/5.   [78] Antonius Cochier, 398/21–24.

[79] Antonius Leitanus, 398/40–399/3.

[80] Ferdinandus de Bellosillo, 404/27–29: "ad tollenda tot incommoda et mala, quae ex eis oriuntur, stupra, adulteria, scandala, odia, caedes, inimicitae, etc., quae mala retulit."

[81] Thaddaeus Perusinus, 408/32–43.

[82] Ioannes del Gado, 402/21–23: "Et praeterea non nisi adulteria, contentiones, caedes, odia, calamitates plurimaque scandala ex huiusmodi matrimoniis oriuntur."

[83] Antonius Leitanus, 398/46–48.

[84] Petrus Morcatus, 403/23–29. Mercado was invoking the Vincentian criteria for catholicity: "_quod ubique, quod semper, quod ab omnibus creditum est._"

Some theologians considered the proposed impediment of clandestinity to be a defect of the contract, that is, of the manner (*modus*) in which the spouses contracted marriage, whereas others suggested that it would be a personal impediment. Joannes del Gado considered clandestinity to be a defect of the contract, akin to those of coercion and insanity. Citing evidence from the Mosaic law (Exod 22:17, Deut 7:3, Num 30:6, etc.), del Gado argued that clandestinity ought to be counted among the diriment impediments because of the absence of parental consent, which he considered to be a fundamental constituent of the union. He accepted the principle that "consent makes marriage," but he argued that one ought to construe the required consent as legitimate consent. The partners' consent was unlawful if they did not have the agreement of their parents. Those who married solely because of romantic love (*causa amoris*) were out of their minds (*amentes*), and insanity was a well-established defect of consent in both Roman and canon law. Persons marrying solely because they were in love were irresponsible and could not be expected to make rational decisions about their future.[85]

Aloysius de Burgo Novo argued that a new diriment impediment of clandestinity would make the persons illegitimate, preventing them from marrying validly. He conceded that clandestine marriages were currently valid, but he argued that the church had the power to alter sacraments by determining who was capable of receiving them. This was clearly so in the case of marriage. For example, the church no longer recognized marriages between believers and unbelievers as valid, but St Paul had done so. Again, a council of Aix-la-Chapelle had ruled that a marriage between an abductor and the woman whom he abducted was no longer valid, but it had hitherto been valid.[86] What the church rendered invalid in such cases was not the manner in which the persons married but the persons themselves. Aloysius de Burgo Novo questioned also whether the church had no power to modify a sacramental form, as most theologians assumed. He suggested that the church had modified the sacramental form of baptism. That being so, the church was able *a fortiori* to alter the matter of the sacrament of marriage, namely, the persons. In short, the church had the power to prohibit clandestine marriage by making the persons illegitimate (*"potest personas illegitimare"*).[87]

Some theologians predicated the case for invalidation on the presumed power of civil authorities to invalidate clandestine marriage. If civil law had by right the power to invalidate clandestine marriages, they argued, then church law had this power *a fortiori*. Diego de Payva was one of those who proposed this argument. He reasoned that the church had greater power over marriage than secular rulers because she

---

[85] Ioannes del Gago, 401/31–37, 402/18–21. Del Gado cites Hosea, apparently thinking of Hosea 4:11.

[86] Aloysius is dependent on Gratian C. 36 q. 2 c. 11 (1292). The original source is in fact *Benedictus Levita*, III.395 (see Ehses' note, 406n7). It is not clear whether Aloysius meant that this canon itself represented a change in the church's law or that the law had changed later.

[87] Aloysius de Burgo Novo, 406/25–31.

regarded marriage as a spiritual thing. "Just as civil laws have the power of prohibiting clandestine marriage for the sake of the political good," he argued, "how much more is the ecclesiastical power able to prohibit them for the sake of the spiritual good."[88]

Ferdinando de Bellosillo pursued a similar *a fortiori* argument, but in his view the church's power to invalidate clandestine marriages pertained to the contract rather than to the sacrament. The premise of his argument was that ecclesiastical power (*potestas ecclesiastica*) was greater than civil power (*potestas civilis*). In other words, ecclesiastical power was plenary in relation to secular power. Since the civil power was able to invalidate contracts in general, he argued, so also was the ecclesiastical power able to invalidate this contract. What the church would invalidate was not the sacrament *per se* but the underlying contract, for contracts were by their very nature subject to new laws. When Christ instituted marriage as a sacrament by adding grace to the contract, he left the contract itself unaltered, with all its conditions. Clandestine marriage could be annulled as a contract, therefore, and if there was no contract there would be no sacrament.[89] To the objection that the contract was subject to the natural law, which was invariable, Bellosillo replied that although the divine law was entirely invariable, the natural law was invariable only in its first principles and in the rules that followed immediately from them. For example, no one could be dispensed from any of the Ten Commandments. But secondary rules derived from the natural law were changeable, and people could be dispensed from them.[90] Bellosillo reasoned that the church had assumed control over the civil dimension of marriage. Pedro Mercado was explicit on this point. He conceded that parents had no right to annul clandestine marriages, but he argued that the church did have that right because "she has her own *politia*" (i.e., her own regime or political governance).[91]

Only two members of the class, Antonius de Gragnano and Antonius Coquier, maintained that clandestine marriages could not be rendered null and void. Antonius de Gragnano rejected the explanations of the proponents of invalidation, agreeing instead with medieval doctors such as Thomas Aquinas and Duns Scotus. Furthermore, he argued, because the church had no *power* to invalidate clandestine marriages, it followed that invalidation would not be *expedient*.[92] Marriage was a sacrament, and the church did not have the power to change the sacraments. Gragnano based his argument on an analysis of the composition of marriage. The spouses' expression of consent and not the priestly blessing was the form of the sacrament; their bodies constituted the matter; and they themselves, and not the priest, were the ministers. To the standard objection that no subject could both administer and receive numerically the same thing, Gragnano pointed out that the

---

[88] Didachus de Paiva, 401/3–5.   [89] Ferdinandus de Bellosillo, 404/4–11, 35–36.

[90] 404/34–35, 38–41.   [91] Petrus Morcatus, 403/5–7.

[92] Antonius de Gragnano, 407/28–30: "Ad 2. articulum respondit, ecclesiam non posse irritare matrimonia clandestina, ergo et non expedit ut fiat, clandestinum sc. iam contractum."

eyes both produced vision and received it. And to the tacit objection that the form of a sacrament was prescribed and unvarying whereas spouses could plight their troth in countless different ways, Gragnano replied that one must distinguish between essential and accidental conditions. The forms of both baptism and penance had changed historically, but only in accidental ways, leaving the essence unchanged. Some of the impediments to marriage, such as holy orders, solemn vows, and affinity, pertained to essential conditions, which were unchangeable. The solemnities were changeable but only accidental. Their omission was a sin, but not one that invalidated the resulting union. Gragnano rejected the theory that the church could make clandestinity a diriment impediment by invalidating the persons.[93]

Antonius Coquier reasoned that because marriage was a sacrament, clandestine marriage could not be rendered null and void. Having shown that clandestine marriages possessed all the essentials of the sacrament, Coquier considered the objection that civil law invalidated such marriages, and that civil law was extrapolated from the law of nature. Coquier replied that civil law and the church had fundamentally different interests in marriage. Civil laws were designed to enhance peaceful interaction among citizens in the political community. Since the consent of parents to their children's marriage was conducive to such peace, civil laws required it. But the church was concerned only with whatever was "substantial" in marriage (i.e., with its sacramental essence).[94] It followed that the church did not require parental consent as a *sine qua non*, although this was certainly seemly and desirable. Parental consent was expedient, but it would not be expedient for the church to make such marriages invalid or to render the persons illegitimate and incapable of marriage, for "these are true marriages."[95]

The distinction between contract and sacrament seems to have arisen again when the fourth class of theologians discussed their second article, according to which matrimonial cases were in the domain of secular rulers (*principes saeculares*). It is not clear how this happened. Some of the theologians were absent, and the contribution of only a single theologian was recorded, and his identity remains unclear. His name was Jacobus Alatri (or perhaps Alani). He may have been the Conventual Franciscan who accompanied the bishop of Vannes. He was not listed as a member of the class.[96]

Jacobus is said to have "adduced the same distinction that had been adduced by many others, namely, that two things should be considered in marriage: the contract and the sacrament." Jacobus said that he could not agree with a certain argument that some had used to show that clandestine marriage was a sacrament. The gist of this argument, according to Jacobus, was as follows:

---

[93] 407/30–408/3.
[94] The clause, "ecclesiam autem spectare tantum ad substantialia matrimonia," is a marginal addition (see the apparatus, 398, note d), but the argument requires it.
[95] Antonius Cochier, 398/26–31.
[96] On his identity, see Ehses's note, 422n1. On the circumstances, see Le Bras, "Mariage," 2244.

Only things that contain something supernatural pertain to the church. Since clandestine marriage pertains to ecclesiastical rulers, it follows that such marriage contains something supernatural and, therefore, that it is a sacrament.[97]

Rejecting that argument, Jacobus maintained that "cases involving sacraments do not pertain to the church unless they are against divine precepts."[98] He cited biblical evidence to corroborate his thesis: Acts 15; Deuteronomy, where "it is explicitly said that all arduous and difficult cases were referred to the high priest"; 1 Corinthians 6:2–4 ("Know you not that the saints shall judge this world" etc.);[99] and Luke 22:38, "Behold, here are two swords." "One [sword is] *in* the church," Jacobus explained, "and the other is [used] *on behalf* of the church, that is, [the sword] which the [secular] rulers should use to help the church."[100] (Jacobus was invoking the hierocratic Two Swords allegory, which Bernard of Clairvaux elaborated to encourage the pope to support the crusades.)[101] Secular powers, therefore, must use the material sword to protect the church.

Jacobus's argument is interesting but obscure. According to Le Bras' interpretation, he held that the church had competence only over those aspects of marriage which pertained to the sacrament, whereas clandestinity was a matter subject to secular law or jurisdiction.[102] That would have implied that the validity of marriages in a Christian commonwealth was partly subject to secular law and jurisdiction, as Tapper may have held. But all the sources that Jacobus cited seem to support the unrestricted right of ecclesiastical authorities to remove civil matters to themselves. Perhaps his contention was that the church's jurisdiction included not only the strictly sacramental aspects of marriage but also anything that was spiritually or ethically fraught, including whatever contravened such "divine precepts" as the duty of children to obey their parents.

20.4 THE FIRST DRAFT

On June 21, 1563, the legates deputed thirteen prelates to draft the decrees on the sacrament of marriage: two French, seven Italian, one Hungarian, one Portuguese, and two Spanish.[103] One of the Spaniards was the redoubtable Pedro Guerrero,

---

[97] 424/36–39: "Ad ecclesiam non pertinent nisi ea, quae habent in se aliquid supernaturale, et quod, cum matrimonium clandestinum pertineat ad principes ecclesiasticos, dicendum erat, quod tale matrimonium haberet in se aliquid supernaturale et sic quod est sacramentum...."

[98] 424/39–41: "et ideo dixit, quod sibi non placebat illa ratio ex eo, quod concludebat, quod tantum sacramentorum causae pertinebant ad ecclesiam; quae sunt contra praecepta divina."

[99] This is according to Ehses' correction and note. According to the record, Jacobus cited 1 Cor 5. Another possibility would be 1 Cor 2:15, which (with Luke 22:38 and Rom. 13:1–2) was a crucial proof-text in Boniface VIII's *Unam sanctam*.

[100] 424/32–45.

[101] On the Two Swords allegory, see Watt, "Spiritual and Temporal Powers," 367–423, at 370–74; and D. VanDrunen, *Natural Law and the Two Kingdoms* (Grand Rapids, 2010), 32–36.

[102] Le Bras, "Mariage," 2245.   [103] CT 9:590–91.

archbishop of Granada. The same commission was presumably responsible for the three subsequent drafts. How the drafts evolved is not always apparent from the recorded *acta*, for we have no record of the commission's deliberations, and it is not always evident that amendments were made in response to voting during the general congregations. To some extent, at least, the evolution of the commission's thought seems to have been autonomous. It is significant, therefore, that most were proponents. Only two of them, Paolo Emilio Verallo[104] and Ugo Boncompagni, bishop of Vieste (and the future Pope Gregory XIII), were opponents. Verallo voted emphatically against the decree at Session XXIV, although Boncompagni finally deferred to the judgment of the pope.[105]

In the first draft, the decrees comprised twelve dogmatic canons on the sacrament of marriage, expressed as anathemas, and a decree of reform. The third of the canons and the reform decree were about clandestine marriage. Voting required fourteen general congregations (July 24–31). The dogmatic canon, which was a variant of one that the prelates had considered at Bologna in 1547, was as follows:

> Canon. 3 (first draft): If anyone says that clandestine marriages that have been contracted with the free consent of the partners are not true and established marriages [*matrimonia vera et rata*], and hence that it is in the parents' power to make them valid or invalid, let him be anathema.[106]

The corresponding decree of reform begins with a narrative describing the perils of clandestine marriage, singling out in particular the scenario of covert prior contract, where a man marries one woman clandestinely but then marries another publicly and "lives with her in perpetual adultery." This was the standard extreme case, which Hugh of Saint-Victor had expounded in the first extended account of the hazards of clandestinity (Section 10.6.1). It was extreme because there was no remedy, for the church could only make judgments based on the evidence of witnesses in the public forum. Mindful of such hazards, the decree explains, the church has tried to prevent clandestine marriages with "very grave penalties." All such laws remain in force, but because the council recognizes that the remedies

---

[104] Verallo, who is mentioned at CT 9:644 as "*unus ex deputatis*," is listed here as the archbishop of Rossano, and he is identified as the senior archbishop of Rossano in the list of prelates who participated in Session XXIII on July 15 (CT 9:634: "*Paulus Aemilius Verallus archiep. Rossanensis senior*"). He had been appointed archbishop of Rossano in 1551, but he was appointed archbishop of Capaccio in 1553 (a personal title, for Capaccio was a diocese), when Giovanni Battista Castagna (the future Pope Urban VII) succeeded him as archbishop of Rossano. He is usually identified in the *acta* by his name, Verallus (whereas metropolitans and bishops are usually designated by their sees), although he is identified as Caputaquensis (bishop of Capaccio) in the record of Session XXIV.

[105] Caputaquensis, 972/29: "Decretum de clandestinis nullo modo probare possum." Vestanus, 975/36–37.

[106] 640/3–5: "Si quis dixerit, clandestina matrimonia, quae libero contrahentium consensu fiunt, non esse vera et rata matrimonia, ac proinde esse in potestate parentum, ea rata vel irrita facere: anathema sit."

have proved ineffective, it decrees that henceforth marriages that are contracted in secret (*clam*), that is, without three witnesses present, will be null and void.[107] In addition (*insuper*), the council renders null and void marriages contracted by minors (*filii familias*) without their parents' consent (*sine parentum consensu*). This prohibition applies to sons under the age of eighteen and of daughters under the age of sixteen.[108] The effect of this decree would have been to invalidate any marriages henceforth that were not contracted (i) in the presence of at least three witnesses and (ii) with parental consent for sons under the age of eighteen and daughters under the age of sixteen.

The draft decree also proposed new criteria for the publicity that the church would require henceforth. Hitherto, the criteria would be those of the fourth Lateran Council, which required the parish priest to announce the forthcoming marriage and to invite those who knew of any lawful impediment to come forward by a certain date. Meanwhile, the priest should make his own inquiries. Spouses who failed to meet that requirement sinned against the church, and their children would be illegitimate until they had ratified their marriage in the approved manner, but their marriage was valid and insoluble. The new decree required three witnesses to be present as a condition for validity. The norms of Lateran IV remained in force, for the new decree stated that any previous laws against clandestine marriage were to remain in force,[109] although that provision was easy to overlook. Moreover, there was nothing in the new decree to make the ministry of the parish priest or marrying *in facie ecclesiae* or even the reading of the banns necessary for validity. Only the presence of witnesses and, for minors, parental consent were *sine qua non*, and the witnesses would usually be laypersons.

Although the anathema still combined the issues of clandestinity and parental authority, the reform decree separated the two issues and stated criteria for each deficiency, although both laws were included within the same "decree on clandestine marriages." In the ensuing deliberations, the prelates treated clandestinity and lack of parental consent as distinct defects and did not conflate them, but they seem to have assumed that an argument in favor of prohibiting either of them was by implication an argument in favor of prohibiting the other.

On July 24, the day on which deliberations over the first draft began, emissaries from Charles IX, King of France, brought a petition on clandestine marriage to the council, and it was read out to the prelates. The king beseeched the council to reestablish the ancient ceremonies of marriage and to decree that marriages must be solemnized publicly in church. If dire circumstances made it permissible to dispense a couple from these requirements, their marriage should not be deemed legitimate until it had been celebrated in the presence of three or more witnesses by the parish priest (*parochus*) or by some other priest. Likewise, the marriage of minors

---

[107] 640/31–39.

[108] 640/40–42. On the issue of parental consent at Trent, see Le Bras, "Mariage," 2241–42.

[109] 640/42–44: "Aliis tamen legibus, quae contra clandestine contrahentes promulgatae sunt, suo loco et robore permanentibus."

(*filii familias*) without parental consent should be rendered null and void, although the fathers of the council might want to limit this restriction by defining an age of majority.[110] What chiefly distinguished the French proposals from the decree under consideration was the requirement that a priest should be present (preferably the parish priest) to solemnize the union. The layman Johann Baptista Fickler, who kept a diary of the proceedings, recalled that the prelates went on to express opinions about clandestine marriage that were "extremely pleasing to the French."[111]

Voting on the first draft began. Charles, Cardinal of Lorraine, voted first, and he emphasized the expediency of invalidating clandestine marriages. His position was entirely consistent with that of the French crown.[112] He could not endorse the dogmatic canon with its anathema, but he had no doubt about the corresponding decree of reform. The proposed law would be expedient for many reasons, among which the he mentioned six. First, if such marriages are not entirely eradicated, many of the benefits of marriage will be prevented, especially the good of friendship (*bonum amicitae*). Marriage is supposed to extend friendship, but clandestine marriages are a source of discord and litigation, and they engender enduring animosity between families. Second, the resulting uncertainty about dowries is also source of litigation. Third, if there are no witnesses, it is too easy for the spouses to separate and remarry at will. Fourth, those who marry clandestinely are often motivated by lust, and as a result their marital bed (*thorus maritalis*) is not a "bed undefiled" (Heb 13:4). Fifth, such marriages are a cause of adultery, since someone may not know that a potential spouse or sexual partner is already married, just as Abimelech did not know at first that Sara was married to Abraham (Gen 20:3–4). Sixth, they undermine the good of offspring (*bonum prolis*), for the spouses are deprived of their inheritance, and parents sometimes murder children who marry without their consent. Again, marriage without parental consent contravenes the precept, "Honor your father and mother" (Exod 20:12, Matt 15:4). There are many examples in Scripture of fathers giving away their daughters in marriage, the cardinal pointed out, whereas neither canon nor civil law had ever approved of marriages contracted without parental consent. There is nothing to prevent the church from rendering such marriages invalid, just as the church has ruled that certain degrees of consanguinity are diriment impediments.[113] The new policy would be open to new abuses, but appropriate means of redress could be stipulated. For example, if a father tried to make his daughter choose between marrying a man of his own choosing and becoming a nun, she could appeal to her bishop, who would protect her.[114]

---

[110] Josse Le Plat, *Monumentorum ad historiam Concilii Tridentini ... collectio*, vol. 6 (Louvain, 1786), 166. See also the secretary's note on this petition, CT 9:680/40–43.

[111] Le Plat, Monumentorum ... collectio, *vol. 7, pars altera* (Louvain, 1787), 383.

[112] One should keep in mind that the prelates were voting on all the decrees about marriage, both dogmatic and reformatory. Clandestine marriage was one of many topics.

[113] Card. Lotharingus, 642–43.   [114] 642/28–643/19.

What distinguished a properly solemnized marriage from a clandestine one? Some prelates wanted to enhance the designation of the lay witnesses: there should be more of them, they should be citizens, and so forth.[115] Replying to the objection that witnessing was logically posterior to what was being witnessed, Francisco Delgado López, bishop of Lugo, argued that witnesses would be present not only to testify but also "to constitute the essence of the sacrament."[116]

Several of the prelates proposed that the decree should require some ecclesiastical involvement: a notion that appealed especially to those who were inclined to regard the sacrament as a ritual event. Some proposed that one of the three witnesses should be a priest (*sacerdos, presbyter*) or the parish priest (*parochus*).[117] Several proposed that the couple must receive the priestly blessing.[118] Charles d'Angennes de Rambouillet, bishop of Le Mans, proposed that a parish priest should be present to "confirm the consent with his blessing," for "this belongs to the essence of this sacrament."[119] Marcantonio Bobba, bishop of Aosta, accepted the decree as it stood but wanted to add that marriages contracted without the priestly benediction would be deemed illegitimate in respect of inheritance.[120] Some proposed that marriages should be invalid unless contracted *in facie ecclesiae*. Franciscus Bachodius, bishop of Geneva, proposed that marriage should be "publicly celebrated in church."[121] Antoine Havet, bishop of Namur, said that *all* clandestine marriages should be rendered null and void, and not only those without witnesses. Then marriages would be invalid unless they were celebrated *in facie ecclesiae* according the custom of the region (*iuxta conditiones diversarum nationum*).[122] Some proponents considered the ministry of a priest to be integral to the sacrament. Germanico Bandini,

---

[115] For example, Chironensis, 658/34–35: witnesses should be citizens, and one should be a *presbyter*.

[116] Lucensis, 674/26–28: "Respondit ad argumenta dicentium, quod testes sequuntur sacramentum: quod testes adducuntur non tantum ad testificandum, sed ad constituendam essentiam."

[117] One of the witnesses should be a *sacerdos*: Card. Lotharingus, 642/41–643/1; Insulanus, 660/19; Metensis, 662/37; Brixiensis, 668/5–9; Aliphanus, 675/15. One of the witnesses should be the *parochus*: Naxiensis, 652/3–4; Parisiensis, 658/23–24; Mutinensis, 659/9; Atrebatensis, 661/44; Anglonensis, 670/26.

[118] Calamonensis, 659/20–22: *parochus* and benediction. Ebroicensis, 653/10–11): marriages should be invalidated when they lack priestly benediction. Oscensis, 654/10: five witnesses and priestly benediction. Segobiensis, 657/11–12: the partners are not married until they receive the benediction. Aurelianensis, 660/10–11, and Ilerdensis, 666/19–20: there is no marriage without *benedictio ecclesiae*. Ostunensis, 667/5–7: the priestly blessing should *sine qua non*, for it is what distinguishes Christian marriage from a marriage of gentiles. Senecensis, 674/41–42: the minister of the sacrament is the priest, and the necessary form consists of the words with which he blesses the couple, i.e., either *"Ego vos coniungo matrimonialiter"* etc., or *"Quod Deus coniunxit, homo non separet."*

[119] Cenomanensis, 663/38–40: "Quoad testes dicatur, quod adsit parochus, qui consensum sua benedictione confirmet. Tenet enim, hoc pertinere ad essentiam huius sacramenti."

[120] Augustensis, 664/5–7.

[121] Gebennensis, 663/34. Likewise, Oppidensis, 673/38–39, proposes that the marriage must be *in facie ecclesiae*.

[122] Namurcensis, 670/11–13,

bishop of Siena, claimed that the words with which the priest joined the spouses was the form of the sacrament, whereas the spouses' expression of the consent was its efficient cause. The priest should say either "I join you together in marriage" ("*Ego iungo vos matrimonialiter*") or "What God has joined, let man not separate."[123] Diego Gilberto Nogueras, bishop of Alife, who spoke next after Germanico Bandini, claimed that the minister of this sacrament was the priest, and that the form was the priest's words of joining or blessing. Citing the decretal of Evaristus, he suggested that clandestine unions had never been true marriages and that their issue had always been illegitimate in reality, although he accepted that they were currently valid in the church's judgment. Nogueras proposed that the dogmatic canon should either be removed or be reworded so that it anathematized anyone who said that clandestine marriages *approved by the church* were not true marriages.[124] But some who advocated the presence of a priest thought of him less as a liturgical minister than as an official witness. Diego de Covarrubias y Leiva, bishop of Ciudad Rodrigo, objected that priests were "prohibited by the canons" from witnessing contracts, and he proposed instead that the number of lay witnesses should be increased.[125] The bishop of Tortona, reflecting the custom prevalent in parts of Italy, proposed that one of the witnesses should be either a priest or a notary, and that all the witnesses should be trustworthy.[126]

To many of the prelates, the anathema and the decree of reform seemed mutually contradictory. To say that clandestine marriages *are* valid (in the present tense) but *will* henceforth be invalid is not contradictory or paradoxical. But to *anathematize* those who were already practicing the proposed new policy was surely incongruous, even if the Protestants had overreached their authority or misunderstood the rationale. Several of the prelates, therefore, were unhappy with the dogmatic canon as it stood, and some wanted it to be removed entirely. Others proposed that it should be reworded to make it more consistent with the reform decree, or even that it should be incorporated into the decree.[127] Some thought that the canon was inconsistent with earlier Catholic practice, for they assumed that clandestine marriage had formerly been invalid, and they feared that the canon would retroactively anathematize Pope Evaristus! For example, Martín Pérez de Ayala, bishop of Segovia, objected that canon contradicted Evaristus and Clement III. He claimed that the church had maintained for 1,200 years that marriages contracted clandestinely or without parental consent were invalid. A clandestine marriage was not truly a marriage, as Evaristus said, and it was invalid until the parents of the spouses consented to it.

---

[123] Senecensis, 674/40–43 (cited earlier). Others of this persuasion include Segobiensis, 657/10–12, and Cenomanensis, 663/39–40.

[124] Aliphanus, 674/44–675/3, 675/5–8.. [125] Civitatensis, 668/41–42.

[126] Tortonensis, 656/29–30.

[127] Theanensis, 663/42–43. Almeriensis, 665/35–36. Ilerdensis, 666/14. Ostunensis, 667/1–2. Clusinus, 667/18–19. Dolensis, 667/25–26. Nivernensis, 667/28–29. Tutellensis, 668/19–20. Calaguritanus, 668/25. Nimosiensis, 670/35–36. Nucerinus, 673/23. Pisauriensis, 673/40–41. Torcellanus, 677/37. Gen. Eremitarum S. Augustini, 679/4.

Children were subject to their parents by the law of nature, and Scripture showed that fathers had the right to hand over their daughters in marriage (1 Cor 7:38). Sons and daughters had no right to act without the guidance and consent of their parents in a matter of such great moment. This bishop rejected the anathema entirely.[128] Diego de Covarrubias y Leiva, bishop of Ciudad Rodrigo, proposed to overcome the tension between the anathema and the reform decree by making the former more restrictive. He suggested that the canon should anathematize anyone who said that the ecclesiastical legislation on clandestine marriages was "tyrannical" (a term that the Protestants applied freely to whatever they found objectionable in Catholic canon law).[129] Pedro González de Mendoza, bishop of Salamanca, proposed that the contradiction should be resolved by inserting the word *hactenus* into the dogmatic canon. Then the decree would anathematize those who held that marriages contracted clandestinely had *hitherto* or *until now* been invalid.[130] Some wanted the canon to anathematize those (i.e., the Protestants) who held that clandestine marriage was invalid "by divine or natural law," rather than by the positive law of the church.[131] As already noted, some wanted it to be removed but with a suitably modified version of its gist relocated in the decree of reform.[132]

As noted earlier, Evaristus's decretal appeared frequently in the general congregations at this stage, as it had done in the deliberations of the *theologi minores*. But the evidence of the decretal was moot, and some of the arguments regarding it were circular. In fact, the decretal proved nothing. Those who were inclined to endorse the decree of reform assumed that Evaristus had decreed that clandestine marriages were invalid,[133] whereas the opponents interpreted him in other ways. Ottaviano Preconio, O.F.M. Conv., archbishop of Palermo, pointed out that the final clause ("*nisi voluntas propria suffragerit*") implied that partners could marry freely and informally, and he suggested that Evaristus had spoken "hyperbolically" when he declared that informal marriages amounted to no more than fornication and promiscuity.[134]

---

[128] Segobiensis, 656/31–39. See especially 656/32–35: "3. canon non placet. Evaristus enim, Clemens III et concilcium Carthaginense 4. sunt contrariae opinionis. Per 1200 annos ecclesiae tenuit, clandestina non esse matrimonia, neque matrimonia esse rata, antequem succedat consensus parentum."

[129] Civitatensis, 668/28–30.

[130] González de Mendoza, *Lo sucedido en el concilio de Trento*, CT 2:689/28–34 (*votum scriptum*).

[131] Auriensis, CT 9:663/18–19. Likewise, Legionensis, 665/21–25, wanted the canon to anathematize those who said that clandestine marriages were untrue by their very nature: "Dixit, tertium canonem debere manere ad condemnandos haereticos, qui dicunt, clandestina ex natura sua non esse vera matrimonia. Probavit, quod irritatio clandestinorum potest fieri ex ratione potestatis rei publicae, ad quam pertinet determinare, quid expediens sit, etiam contra voluntatem particularium, a fortiori id potest ecclesia, in qua adest potestas supernaturalis."

[132] Ostunensis, 667/1–2. Clusinus, 667/18–19. Comensis, 680/14–15.

[133] For example, Almeriensis, 666/3–5; Lucensis, 674/20–21. Likewise, Clodiensis, 704/17–19, and Segobiensis, 707/5–10, during voting on the second draft.

[134] Archiep. Panormitanus, 664/30–32. Nemausensis, 667/45–668/1, argued that Evaristus was referring not to clandestine marriages in general but to *raptus* (marriage by abuction, or of a girl without her parents' consent).

Most of the proponents accepted that clandestine or unwitnessed marriages had been fully valid at least for several centuries but proposed that the church should make such marriages invalid henceforth. But did the church have the power to make a new law of that sort? The opponents thought not, but archbishop Pedro Guerrero argued that the church did have the required power. Guerrero expounded this argument fully in his treatise on clandestine marriages (Section 20.6), and only its bare outlines appear in written proceedings. Experience has shown, Guerrero said, that merely prohibitive impediments (*impedimenta prohibentia tantum*) to clandestine marriage have been ineffective. It follows that diriment impediments (*impedimenta irritantia*) must be introduced. In Guerrero's view, prohibitive and diriment impediments were on a sliding scale. Wherever a prohibitive impediment is valid, a diriment impediment would also be valid. Again, if secular rulers have the power to invalidate clandestine marriages, then the church *a fortiori* must possess it. Again, if the church has the power to make certain degrees of consanguinity and affinity and even legal relationship (contracted through adoption) diriment impediments, the church must *a fortiori* have the power to invalidate clandestine marriages. Consider the diriment impediment of cult, which prevents a believer from marrying an unbeliever. The church, and not divine law, has made such marriages invalid. Even the diriment impediment of nonage is to some extent a positive human invention, for some twelve-year-olds are more capable of making rational decisions than some twenty-year-olds.[135] Others, too, emphasized the power of the church to introduce laws that went beyond or were more determinate than divine or natural law.[136] To the objection that the decree would entail agreement with the heretics, Thomas Stella, O.P., now bishop of Capo d'Istria, replied that it was absurd to demand that Catholic policies should always contradict Protestant policies. To the objection that the decree would constrain freedom, he replied it would take away "not freedom of the spirit, but only freedom of the flesh."[137]

Several prelates argued that the church already exercised the same power in other situations. Some saw a precedent in the power of the church or the pope to dissolve an established but unconsummated marriage (*matrimonium ratum et non consummatum*), for such a marriage was already a true sacrament.[138] Several pointed out that the church had already introduced new diriment impediments, such as those of consanguinity. Surely the church is equally or even more able to make clandestinity a diriment impediment.[139] Some deduced that the proposed degree would invalidate the persons by rendering them unfit (*inhabiles*) to marry each other. To

---

[135] Granatensis, 644/17–23.

[136] Granatensis, 644/28–29. Iustinopolitanus, 654/22–23. Abbas Lunaevillae, 678/23–27. Gen. Eremitarum S. Augustini, 679/33–35.

[137] Iustinopolitanus, 654/24–26. Thomas Stella had attended the proceedings at Bologna as bishop of Lavello. He became bishop of Capo d'Istria in 1549.

[138] Barcinonensis, 670/44–46. Guadiscensis, 672/14–17.

[139] Card. Lotharingus, 642/38–39; Leriensis, 661/15–20; Auriensis, 663/21–24.

invalidate a manner (*modus*) of contracting marriage that had hitherto been valid would be unprecedented,[140] but everyone accepted that the church had historically altered the rules about who could marry whom. It was Daniello Barbaro, Patriarch of Aquileia, who introduced the inhabilitation theory into the discussion, and many prelates followed his lead.[141] But Antonio Corrionero de Babilafuente, bishop of Almería, argued that annulment of the contract was better than inhabilitation of the persons because it was "more universal."[142]

The argument from exigent power emerged explicitly only once in voting on the first draft, although it may have been present in the background. Francisco Delgado López, bishop of Lugo, claimed that God must have given the church "authority over all things that are expedient." If the invalidation of clandestine marriages is expedient, therefore, it must also be possible.[143]

According to the contractual theory, invalidation would alter the conditions of the contract and not of the sacrament as such. If there is no contract, there is no sacrament, just as if there is no ablution with water, there is no baptism.[144] Pierre Duval, bishop of Sées, articulated this rationale clearly:

> There are two things in marriage, namely, the contract [*pactio*] and the sacrament. The contract is not valid if it is rendered invalid by a superior law. These contracts are changeable according to the diversity of times — even in marriage, as is apparent in the degrees of consanguinity. Hence, just as the church has illegitimized [certain] degrees of consanguinity, so also she has the ability to illegitimize clandestine marriages. Nor does the church render the sacrament invalid, but only the contract.[145]

The reference to a "superior law" seems redundant here, but again the notion will become clear in Guerrero's treatise (Section 20.6.3). A ruler of a commonwealth has legal authority over the necessary conditions for all contracts, including the contract of marriage, unless a superior ruler or law removes that authority to itself. In the Christian commonwealth, ecclesiastical law is superior to secular law. Thus, Jacopo Nacchianti, O.P., bishop of Chioggia, distinguished between the contractuality of marriage and its sacramentality (*ratio sacramentalis*), which presupposes the

[140] Dertusensis, 671/11. Niochensis, 671/37–44. Rossensis, 676/7–8.
[141] Aquilegiensis, 643/32–34. Granatensis, 644/17–25. Tarentinus, 651/7–8. Messanensis, 651/36. Hierapetrensis, 654/5–6. Vulturariensis, 660/26–27. Auriensis, 663/23–24. Theanensis, 664/1–2. Niochensis, 671/42–45. Pisauriensis, 673/41–42. Ventimiliensis, 676/4. Rossensis, 676/7–8. Abbas Euticius Cassinensis, 678/6–9. Abbas Augustinus Cassinensis (S. Benedicti de Ferraria), 678/14–16. Gen. Praedicatorum (Vincenzo Giustiniani), 679/1–6.
[142] Almeriensis, 666/7–8.   [143] Lucensis, 674/15–18, 28–30.
[144] Iadrensis, 645/14–16. Bracarensis, 650/25–26. Lancianensis, 651/39–43. Sagiensis, 654/31–33. Clugiensis, 655/26–36. Brugnatensis, 656/20–22. Mutinensis, 659/8–11. Leriensis, 661/9–14. Metensis, 662/30–32. Auriensis, 663/24–25. Cotronensis, 665/19. Legionensis, 665/23–25. Uxentinus, 667/32–33. Civitatensis, 668/34–40. Civitatis Castelli, 669/1–5. Namurcensis, 670/5–7. Columbriensis, 673/16–18. Lucensis, 674/21–25. Monopolitanus, 675/40–42.
[145] Sagiensis, 654/28–33. Likewise, Gebennensis, 663/33; Cortonensis, 665/19.

contract. The church has the power to change the former, not the latter.[146] Leonardo Marini, O.P., archbishop of Lanciano, conceded that the decree would invalidate the persons rather than the contract, but he argued that the persons would be invalidated as the matter not of the sacrament but of the contract.[147] "We do not touch the sacrament," claimed Bartolomé Fernandes dos Mártires, O.P., archbishop of Braga, "but only the contract."[148] Others repeated this claim about not "touching" the sacrament.[149] Francisco Delgado, bishop of Lugo, argued that the addition of grace and sacramentality (*ratio gratiae seu sacramentalis*) to marriage under the New Law took nothing away from the contract, for grace perfects nature without destroying it. Contracts could be regulated so as to favor whatever was expedient for the commonwealth (*res publica*). The sacramentality of marriage did not take away the commonwealth's power to regulate the contract, which the church has removed to herself.[150]

The written vote of Pedro González de Mendoza, bishop of Salamanca, includes the fullest surviving statement of the contractual theory. His votes as recorded in the *acta* are brief and unremarkable, but he preserved the written texts in his diary. Here, González de Mendoza endorses the decree invalidating marriages contracted clandestinely or without parental consent. The church has the necessary power, and the reform would be extremely expedient (*"vehementer expedit"*). González de Mendoza then proves each of these two claims in turn, appropriating material from Ruard Tapper for his proof of possibility (Section 20.2.4), and from Catharinus for his proof of expedience (Section 19.9.2). The church has the power to invalidate such marriages because "the human being is a political animal and part of the commonwealth." It follows that "all his actions, contracts [*pacta*], and agreements can be directed to the public good by those who have care over public matters," so that these things neither injure other citizens nor harm the commonwealth as a whole. For example, a person has the right to alienate his own property under the natural law, but the commonwealth can abrogate this right if alienation would harm the public good. The contract of marriage is related to the sacrament as matter to form, and the church has the power to cause a matrimonial contract that would harm the commonwealth not to be the matter required for the sacrament. For the same reason, the church can require that conditions such as the presence of three witnesses and the content of parents are *sine qua non*. The contract of marriage is subject both to civil and to ecclesiastical law. "Insofar as marriage is a civil contract, it is subject to civil power, whereas inasmuch as it is a contract between Christians and the matter of the sacrament of marriage, it is subject to ecclesiastical power."

---

[146] Clodiensis, 655/25–36.   [147] Lancianensis, 651/39–43.

[148] Bracarensis, 650/29–32: "Non enim tangimus sacramentum, sed pactum."

[149] Brugnatensis, 656/22–22: "et ita tangemus contractum matrimonii, non autem sacramentum." Auriensis, 663/25: "sic non tangitur sacramentum, sed contractus tantum, ut praeintelligitur sacramentum." Uxentinus, 667/32–33. Monopolitanus, 675/40–42.

[150] Lucensis, 674/23–26.

To prove that invalidation is expedient, González de Mendoza shows that clandestine marriages and especially marriages without parental consent violate natural law, the *ius gentium*, and civil law; that they undermine the three goods of marriage; that they subvert the peace of the commonwealth and concord among its citizens; and that they give rise to scandals, feuds, adultery, and other evils, as he can testify from his own experience in his diocese.[151]

The contractual theory was associated at this stage of the proceedings with arguments *a fortiori*. If a secular ruler (*princeps saecularis*) has the power to invalidate the marriage contract, Pedro Guerrero argued, then all the more must the church possess it.[152] Bartolomé Fernandes dos Mártires, archbishop of Braga, argued that if the church was able to invalidate the persons, as in the impediment of consanguinity, and even to invalidate their consent, as in the impediment of force and fear, the church was all the more able to invalidate the contract that the sacrament presupposes. Again, if even pagan rulers could invalidate matrimonial contracts, the church was all the more able to do so. Again, if a ruler could pass an edict preventing people from subjecting themselves to servitude, they were all the more able to prevent them from subjecting themselves to the servitude of a marriage that was not contracted it a prescribed manner. Invalidation of the contract would not touch the sacrament. Nor would it convert a sacrament into a non-sacrament.[153] Egidio Foscherani, O.P., bishop of Modena, said that it would be rash to deny that the church had the power to invalidate clandestine marriages, for if a commonwealth was able to do so, the church was *a fortiori* able to do so.[154]

Two *modi loquendi* emerged as ways of articulating the church's power over the marriage contract. The contractual theory presupposed that any commonwealth had the power to regulate the contracts of its citizens in order to foster the public good. Some prelates assumed that a commonwealth was by definition a secular body and argued that if a commonwealth had this power, then *a fortiori* the church did so. For example, Andrés de la Cuesta, bishop of León, argued that if the commonwealth (*res publica*) could override individual interests to pursue the public good, how much more could the church do so, for it was invested with "supernatural power."[155] Others collapsed the comparison by construing the church itself as a Christian commonwealth (*res publica christiana*). Gaspar do Casal, O.S.A., bishop of Leiria, argued that Christian marriage did not lose its contractuality (*ratio contractus*) when it acquired sacramentality (*ratio sacramenti*), and that any contract was subject to the law of the commonwealth (*res publica*). The commonwealth had the power "to ordain all its parts to the public good." "The only difference is," he went on,

---

[151] Pedro González de Mendoza, *Lo sucedido en el concilio de Trento desde el año 1561 hasta que se acabó*, CT 2:689/35–690/40 (*votum scriptum*).
[152] Granatensis, 644/18-19: "Princeps saecularis posset irritare matrimonia clandestina, ergo a fortiori ecclesia."
[153] Bracarensis, 650/22–33. Likewise, Metensis, 662/31–32.   [154] Mutinensis, 659/8–11.
[155] Legionensis, 665/23–25.

"that outside the Christian commonwealth [*res publica christiana*] it [marriage] is a secular contract, whereas in the Christian church it is an ecclesiastical contract because of its sacramentality."[156]

The public good of the commonwealth as a whole trumped the private or particular good of any of its parts, even of the family. François Richardot, bishop of Arras, argued that the church's power over the marriage contract was fundamentally different from that of secular rulers over secular contracts, for "the matrimonial contract is ratified by God and is a divine contract." He endorsed the decree because he found the comparison with impediments of consanguinity and the inhabilitation theory convincing, but he argued that the good of a commonwealth trumped the good of any part of that commonwealth. Whereas consanguinity was detrimental only to the individual family, he explained, clandestinity was detrimental to the commonwealth as a whole. If the church was able to invalidate consanguineous marriages, she was *a fortiori* able to invalidate clandestine marriages.[157]

Antoine Havet, bishop of Namur, replied to those opponents who were appealing to the medieval scholastic doctors. According to Thomas Aquinas, the opponents pointed out, the spouses' consent by itself (*solus consensus*) was sufficient to establish a marriage. But Havet countered that they were committing the fallacy of reasoning from actuality to possibility (*a facto ad posse*). Consent sufficed in Thomas's day, but it would no longer suffice after the church had annulled clandestine marriages. Moreover, the opponents were overlooking other passages in Thomas that could be cited to support the proposed policy. Thomas said that God did not join together those whom the church did not join together; that marriage, unlike baptism, was not only a sacrament but also a contract; and that marriage as a contract came within the scope of the church's legislative power.[158]

Even some who were open to the possibility of invalidation had doubts about the rationales being proposed. François Richardot, bishop of Arras, endorsed the decree of reform but could not accept the contractual theory.[159] Carlo Grassi, bishop of Montefiascone, conceded that the church ought to able to invalidate clandestine marriage "because the human part of marriage is mutable," but he found the proponents' arguments unconvincing. If the church had the power to prevent the matter and form of marriage from becoming a sacrament, why had she not used it before? He pointed out that according to Thomas Aquinas, solemnities were only

---

[156] Leriensis, 661/8–14: "[661/13:] tantum est haec differentia, quod extra rem publicam Christianam est saecularis contractus; in ecclesia autem Christiana ratione sacramenti est ecclesiasticus contractus." Note that terms *res publica Christiana* and *ecclesia Christiana* denote the same body ecclesiastic.

[157] Atrebatensis, 661/37–40.

[158] Namurcensis, 669/42–670/13. Thomas Aquinas, *IV Sent.* 40.un.4, ad 1 (Vivès 11:239b); *IV Sent.* 34.un.1, ad 4 (164b); *IV Sent.* 36.un.5, resp. (185a).

[159] Atrebatensis, 661/37–43. Colimbriensis, 655/3–4, 13–15, was unconvinced by the inhabilitation and contractual theories, but his critique is difficult to reconstruct. At this stage, he confessed that he was undecided but voted to defer to the majority.

accidental. Clandestinity, therefore, did not undermine the essence of marriage. The theory that the decree would invalidate the contract without touching the sacrament failed, Grassi argued, because the contract was the exchange of consent, which was the form of this sacrament. Grassi also refuted the bishop of Segovia's claim that clandestine marriages had been invalid from the time of Evaristus to the time of Clement III. The examples of Peter Lombard and Thomas Aquinas, he argued, sufficed to show that his colleague was mistaken. (Grassi himself seems to been confused about the dates, however, for Clement III reigned 1130–1191.)[160]

The opponents maintained that it was impossible to invalidate clandestine marriages without changing the essential form or matter of the sacrament. Everything essential to marriage was present in a clandestine marriage, whereas the missing features were accidental solemnities. The form of the sacrament had been instituted by Jesus Christ and was inalterable.[161] Clandestine marriages also had the essential salutary goods and benefits of marriage, such as the remedy against lust.[162] Moreover, the decree was inconsistent with the anathema.[163] It would entail a new doctrine, and one that the heretics had introduced.[164] There was precedent in Scripture for treating relationships as diriment impediments, but there was no precedent there for treating clandestinity as one.[165] On the contrary, there were instances of clandestine marriage in the Old Testament.[166] Martin Baudouin, bishop of Ypres, pointed out that witnesses could not be part of the essence of the sacrament, since what they were supposed to witness was the sacrament. Cardinal Cristoforo Madruzzo, Prince-Bishop of Trent, pointed out that a change to the circumstances or the solemnities of the contract would not invalidate it. The only remedy available, therefore, was to suppress clandestine marriages by penalizing them.[167] Giovanni Trevisan, Patriarch of Venice, added that the decree would imply that Catholics now agreed with the Protestant heretics.[168] Antonio Elio, Patriarch of Jerusalem, opposed invalidation on the grounds that it was a "new dogma" introduced by the Protestant heretics, that there was much doubt among the theologians as to whether it was possible, and that the inconvenience of a law was not a sufficient reason for abrogating it.[169] Ottaviano Preconio, O.F.M. Conv., archbishop of Palermo, argued that the decree contradicted Bonaventure, Thomas Aquinas, and Richard de Mediavilla, and that it would require changing the matter and form of a sacrament. He also rejected the inhabilitation theory. If the church invalidated clandestine marriages, Preconio argued, it would do so by invalidating the manner

---

[160] Montisfalisci, 662/43–663/11. Segobiensis, 656/31–39.   [161] Clusinus, 667/20–22.
[162] Madrutius, 643/23–29. Venetiarum, 643/38–39. Rheginensis, 651/23–24. Interamnensis, 655/ 45–656/7. Lucerinus, 660/41–46. Larinensis, 662/20–21.
[163] Venetiarum, 643/36.
[164] Venetiarum, 643/37–38. Philadelphiensis, 653? Hierosolymitanus, 666/34–37.
[165] Larinensis, 662/21–24. Hyprensis, 669/33–34.   [166] Interamnensis, 655/45–46.
[167] Madrutius, 643/23–29. Abbas Claravellensis, 677/41–678/1. Generalis Minorum Conv., 679/ 18–19.
[168] Venetiarum, 643/35–44,   [169] Patriarcha Hierosolymitanus, 666/34–37.

(*modus*) in which they contracted the sacrament, and not by disqualifying the persons. He also rejected the use of Evaristus's decree, pointing out that the final clause contradicted the rest and suggesting that the pope was speaking hyperbolically.[170]

Giovanni Battista Castagna, archbishop of Rossano, was among the most astute and careful opponents of invalidation.[171] On July 24, 1563, he refuted the theory of inhabilitation, appropriating the objection of Antonio Delfini (Section 19.9.1). According to the secretary's summary, Castagna "responded to those who said that the church inhabilitated the matter" of marriage (i.e., the persons), arguing that a personal impediment of that sort "acted in relation to a cause that inhered inseparably in the person." The invalidation of clandestine marriages would pertain not to the persons but to the manner (*modus*) in which they contracted marriage.[172]

Archbishop Castagna's analysis is more fully expounded in the written text of his vote (*votum scriptum*).[173] The question is not whether clandestine marriages should be prevented, Castagna argues. They give rise to many evils and scandals, and the church justly prohibits them. The question, rather, is this: If two persons who are capable (*habiles*) of marrying have freely expressed their mutual consent, does the church have the power to render their marriage null and void on the grounds that it was not contracted before three witnesses or with the consent of their parents? If that were so, what has been until now a true and valid marriage and a sacrament of the church will not be so in future. But is that possible? The proposal to invalidate clandestine marriages, Castagna argues, is inappropriate because its premise is unsafe and controversial. He concedes that most of the *theologi minores* who considered the question agreed that the church did have such a power, and he declines to say whether or not the church has this power in his own opinion. The fact remains that many distinguished scholars who have discussed the question, such as Ruard Tapper and Antonio Delfini, have held that the church does not have such a power. Even in the secular realm, uncertainty about fundamental premises suffices to prevent new legislation. How much more, then, should one be cautious about altering the conditions of a sacrament! Every aspect of the issue should be fully explored first. Meanwhile, in the absence of certainty or consensus, the council cannot justly invalidate clandestine marriages.[174] Moreover, Castagna went on, even if one grants that the church has the necessary power, its use is not expedient in the current circumstances, when the Protestant heretics are attacking the church. They would only gain strength from a declaration that what had been a sacrament for

[170] Archiep. Panormitanus, 664/32–33: "Non irritetur igitur sacramentum, sed irritetur modus." Likewise, Quinqueecclesiensis (bishop of Pécs), 665/13–15: "Quoad decretum de clandestinis dixit, quod synodus non tollit clandestina, sed tollit modum clandestinorum, puta ut tollantur clandestina, quae non constant esse clandestina."
[171] Giambattista Castagna became Pope Urban VII on Sept. 15, 1590, but he died on Sept. 27.
[172] Rossanensis, 644/51–53.
[173] Archiep. Rossanensis, 645–49. The discussion of clandestine marriage begins at 646/23.
[174] 647/3–33.

1,563 years would no longer be a sacrament. Even if the proponents' case were philosophically and theologically sound, therefore, the proposed legislation would be inexpedient.[175] Why innovate in this matter where previous councils declined to do so, even when they invalidated marriages on other grounds? This is hardly an opportune time to introduce novelties regarding the sacraments.[176] Clandestinity cannot impede a marriage by inhabilitating the persons, as the impediments of orders, of consanguinity, and of spiritual and legal relationship do. These are necessarily founded on causes that inhere in the persons. If clandestinity is to be a diriment impediment, it will impede the manner (*modus*) in which the persons contract marriage, and not the persons themselves. One should be honest, therefore, about what is at stake. How can the church invalidate marriages that are freely contracted by legitimate persons without altering the essential form and matter instituted by Jesus Christ?[177] Some other opponents agreed that the decree would be rash and inopportune because the power of the church to invalidate clandestine marriage was doubtful and controversial.[178]

Martín de Córdoba Mendoza, O.P., bishop of Tortosa, and Giulio Magnani, O.F.M. Conv., bishop of Calvi, posed the same objection as Castagna to the theory of personal inhabilitation: that it presupposed that the impediment was inherent in the contractants.[179] Fray Martín opposed the decree despite the position of his archbishop, Pedro Guerrero, who led the Spanish delegation. Three things must be considered in this sacrament, Fray Martín argued: its form and its matter, which constitute its essence, and its subject matter (*subiectum circa quod*). The church has no power to alter the essential form or matter of any sacrament. The council needs to define, therefore, what the form of marriage is. Some say that the form consists in the words spoken by the priest, namely, "I join you together in the name of the Father, the Son, and the Holy Spirit." Others say that it is the spouses' expression of consent.[180] If the form is what the priest says, then clandestinity is already a diriment impediment. But if the form is the spouses' consent, as most assume, then the invalidation of clandestine marriages is not possible. Fray Martín rejects the theory that the church can invalidate the contract without touching the sacrament, for the two aspects are inseparably joined. Moreover, the contract consists in the exchange of consent, which is the form of the sacrament. The impediment cannot remove the *subiectum circa quod* by rendering persons who marry clandestinely incapable (*inhabiles*) of marrying. Some argue that their disobedience toward their parents is the inherent defect that disqualifies the spouses, but according to Genesis 2:24 marriage is what separates sons and daughters from their parents. Because they are not bound to obey their parents in this matter, there is no disobedience if they marry without their consent. Still less is the absence of

---

[175] 647/34–648/9.   [176] 648/10–18.   [177] 647/23–28.
[178] Britonoriensis, 654/1–2. Hierosolymitanus, 666/35–36. Civitatis Castelli, 669/12. Hyprensis, 669/25–29. Soranus, 675. Abbas Claravellensis, 678/1–2.
[179] Dertusensis, 671. Calvensis, 671/31–32.   [180] Dertusensis, 671/1–4.

witnesses an inherent obstacle. Fray Martín found that in good conscience he had to say *"non placet"* to the decree, although if the majority of prelates favored it he would not oppose them.[181]

Because the contractual argument presupposed that the contractuality and the sacramentality of marriage were really distinct, some of the opponents challenged that premise on the grounds that contract and sacrament were simultaneous and only conceptually distinct. Giulio Magnani, bishop of Calvi, argued that although there was a real distinction between the contract *in fieri* (the transitory contracting of marriage) and the enduring bond that resulted, there was no real distinction between contract and sacrament, "for the contract does not precede the sacrament in time but only in reason."[182] Francisco Delgado, bishop of Lugo, countered that contract and sacrament were separable not only conceptually but also "in reality and in time." They were separate in reality, for example, when persons married through intermediaries, since, as Cajetan showed, they would then marry only contractually and not sacramentally.[183] There were other reasons, aside from questions about the distinction between contract and sacrament, for parsing the temporal composition of the sacrament. To the objection that witnessing was posterior to the formation of the sacrament, Francisco Delgado argued that witnesses were brought in not only to testify but also "to constitute the essence of the sacrament."[184] The bishop of Almería claimed that the decree would invalidate marriage "before there is a sacrament" and not "after there is a sacrament."[185]

Some of those who rejected or were doubtful about the power of the church to invalidate clandestine marriages suggested that the church might annul them through judicial presumption. Hitherto, an unproven marriage was presumed valid, other things being equal, if the spouses "confessed" to it, but that presumption could be reversed. Paolo Emilio Verallo argued that this was the only way in which the church could annul clandestine marriages. He suggested that the church might presume that a clandestine marriage had been contracted through fraud or under duress.[186] Scipione Bongalli, bishop of Città di Castello, was inclined to agree with Verallo, but he was troubled by the absence of precedent. If our predecessors made the opposite presumption, Bongalli asked, why should we take it upon ourselves to reverse it now?[187]

Some opponents questioned the pastoral expediency of invalidation. Clandestine marriages did not always entail the inconveniences that the proponents attributed to them. Giovanni Giacomo Barba, O.S.A., bishop of Terni, conceded that it was

---

[181] Dertusensis, 671/6–20.   [182] Calvensis, 671/25–32.

[183] 674/21–24. He did not say what the temporal distinction was, but it may have been historical, inasmuch as marriage was already a contract before it became a sacrament of the New Law.

[184] 674/26–28.   [185] Almeriensis, 666/5–8.

[186] Verallus, 644/39. Faventinus, 735/30–36, citing Ruard Tapper, will make the same argument when he votes on the second draft.

[187] Civitatis Castelli, 669/5–17.

sinful to marry clandestinely, but he pointed out that a clandestine marriage was still a remedy to many evils, and he argued that it could be a means of grace.[188] Martin Baudouin, bishop of Ypres, who would eventually endorse the decree, summarized the unresolved objections and theological questions, and he cautioned that the council should not act rashly regarding a matter of such great moment. Even if the reform was expedient, the fathers could not be sure that the church really had the power to enact it. The church could not change the essence of a sacrament. Nor could the church make witnessing part of the essence of the sacrament. It was not even clear that rendering clandestine marriages null and void would be pastorally expedient. The policy might encourage promiscuity, for young men would feel free to fornicate without fear of being caught in the bonds of marriage.[189] Antonio Savion, Minister General of the Conventual Franciscans, was not necessarily opposed to the decree and would eventually endorse it, but he questioned the argument from expedience. To argue, "it is expedient, therefore the church is able to do it," he pointed out, was a non sequitur. Again, even if it was expedient to eliminate the evils that *resulted* from clandestine marriage, it did not follow that it was expedient to render clandestine marriage itself invalid. The presence of witnesses at a marriage could itself be a source of strife. For example, there was sometimes conflict between witnesses and parents. It would be better to eradicate clandestine marriage entirely (*omnino*) by requiring marriage *in facie ecclesiae*.[190]

The opponents challenged the proponents to explain why, if the action was both possible and expedient, the church had not invalidated clandestine marriages before.[191] The proponents had not been able to show that such marriages did more harm now than hitherto. Such marriages might be the source of many scandals, but scandals were inevitable in this world (Matt 18:7).[192] The bishop of Nimes confessed that although he did not "dare to say" that the church lacked the power to invalidate clandestine marriages, he could not bring himself to support the decree. If the church had such a power, why had she not used it before?[193] Pedro Guerrero and Thomas Stella, O.P., bishop of Capo d'Istria, countered that if everything unprecedented or innovative was precluded, as the opponents seemed to be arguing, the church could never introduce new laws.[194]

The opponents agreed that clandestine marriages were generally harmful and should be suppressed as much as possible, but in their view the only available remedy was to impose more severe penalties, such as disinheritance or even

[188] Interamnensis, 655/44–656/56.
[189] Hyprensis, 669/25–39. Likewise, Namurcensis, 669/42–670/1.
[190] Gen. Minorum, 679/18–24.
[191] Rheginensis, 651/23–25. Milopotamensis, 652/21–24. Interamnensis, 656/4–5. Lucerinus, 660/ 45–46. Vestanus, 667/13–17. Hyprensis, 669/34–37. Urbevetanus, 676/43–677/1. Gen. Minorum Conv., 679/19–21.
[192] Milopotamus, 652/21–24. Lucerinus, 660/42–46.   [193] Nemausensis, 667/42–45.
[194] Granatensis, 644/28–29. Iustinopolitanus, 654/22–23.

excommunication.[195] For example, Giovanni Giacomo Barba, O.S.A., bishop of Terni, held that the church did not have the power wholly to eradicate clandestine marriages through invalidation. Instead, there should be a new statute requiring spouses who had married clandestinely to appear before an ecclesiastical judge within one month. Failing that, they would be disinherited.[196]

Most of the prelates assumed that clandestine marriages and marriages without parental consent would stand or fall together. An argument for invalidating one was an argument for invalidating the other, and an argument against invalidating one was an argument against invalidating the other. The Cardinal of Lorraine argued that parental control over the marriages of their children was a matter of natural law, and he noted the precedents in Scripture.[197] Thomas Stella, O.P., bishop of Capo d'Istria, reminded the prelates that God had made the first woman from Adam and brought her to him to show that women were the weaker sex. Since their minds were weaker, they ought not to contract their own marriages. Instead, their parents should give them away in marriage.[198] Some proposed that the decree should include a provision enabling children to appeal to the bishop if parents were unreasonable, so that the bishop could assume the father's role.[199] Twenty-one of the proponents endorsed the threshold ages for marrying without parental consent stated in the draft decree, namely, eighteen for sons and sixteen for daughters, but twelve prelates wanted to raise them.[200] The Cardinal of Lorraine proposed that the ages should be "brought back" to twenty-five years for sons and twenty for women.[201]

To the mind of the opponents, on the contrary, requiring parental consent would be contrary to the natural law and to the freedom of the Gospel. Marriage was what separated children from their parents (Gen 2:24).[202] Children should obey their parents, but their obedience was less servile than that of unfree persons to their lords. If the unfree can marry without their lords' consent, then *a fortiori* children can marry without their parents' consent.[203]

---

[195] Card. Madrutius, 643/26–27. Hydruntinus, 644/11. Materanus, 650/16–17. Rheginensis, 651/25–26. Senonensis, 652/34–653/2. Cathaniensis, 653. Philadelphiensis, 653. Colimbriensis, 655/6. Recanatensis, 655/24–25. Interamnensis, 655/45, 656/7. Cenetensis, 656. Lesiensis, 659/41–43. Lucerinus, 660/44–45. Nemausensis, 668/1. Niochensis, 671/41–42. Urbevetanus, 676/31–32.

[196] Interamnensis, 655/44–45, 656/5–7.   [197] Card. Lotharingus, 643/11–13.

[198] Iustinopolitanus, 654/19–21.

[199] Card. Lotharingus, 643/15–18. Almeriensis, 666/1–2. Ilerdensis, 666/20–21. Venciensis, 670/17–18. Niochensis, 671/43–44. Corosopitanus, 673/5–6. Aemoniensis, 675/31. Rossensis, 676/8–9. Gen. Praedicatorum, 679/10–11.

[200] Segobiensis, 657/14 (24 for sons, 20 for daughters). Parisiensis, 658/25–26 (20, 20). Calamonensis, 659/22, Aurelianensis, 660/12, Guadiscensis, 672/20, Aliphanus, 675/14–15 (20, 22). Cenomanensis, 663 (25, 20). Sibinicensis, 664 (20, 18). Oppidensis, 673/39, Pennensis, 673/47 (raise daughter's threshold to 25). Trivicanus, 677/13–14 (23, 20).

[201] Card. Lotharingus, 643/5–7.

[202] Venetiarum, 643/39–41. Clusinus, 667/21–22. Nemausensis, 668/3–4. Hyprensis, 669/37–39.

[203] Panormitanus, 664/36–37. Urbevetanus, 677/1–4.

The secretary summed up this first round of discussion as follows:

> But as regards the decree on clandestine marriages, there was great dispute and
> controversy among the fathers. For some judged that clandestine marriages ought to
> be entirely eradicated so that they were not marriages, and that the church was able to
> do that and ought to do so. Others took the opposite view: that these should not be
> eradicated because they were true and established marriages. Some added that the
> church did not have the power to make them invalid. There was much controversy,
> too, as to whether it would be expedient. Some said that the persons ought to be
> illegitimized [i.e., rendered legally incapable] from contracting marriage in that way,
> regardless of whether the marriages themselves were nullified or made invalid; others,
> that clandestine marriages should continue in the church as they are now, but that
> very grave penalties should be introduced against those contracting marriage in that
> way. Orators from the sovereigns desired and entreated that the aforesaid clandestine
> marriages should be rendered invalid. Thus, orators from King Charles [of France]
> had presented the document described above on July 24.[204]

20.5 THE SECOND DRAFT

The legates presented the second draft of the decrees on marriage on August 7.
Voting required twenty general congregations (August 11–23). The proceedings
were unusually prolonged chiefly because the issue of clandestine marriage proved
to be intractable. Far from resolving their differences, the two sides not only
maintained their respective positions but also put forward new arguments and
counter-arguments.

There was no dogmatic canon on clandestinity in the second draft. Instead, the
gist of the canon was incorporated into the decree of reform, as some of the prelates
had proposed during voting on the first draft. What had been expressed as an
anathema was now recast in a descriptive preamble beginning with the word
tametsi, which described the current policy of the church in the present tense.
Although (*tametsi*) the church does not doubt that clandestine marriages contracted
with the free consent of the partners are valid and true and justly condemns those
who claim that such marriages are false, as well as those who claim that parents can
annul marriages contracted secretly without their consent, nevertheless (*nihilominus*) the church is acutely aware that clandestine marriages have given rise to many
evils, especially cases of covert prior contract, and the church desires to eradicate
such marriages. Henceforth, therefore, the church will render those who attempt to
contract marriages or spousals[205] secretly (*clam*), rather than in the presence of at

---

[204] 680/33–43.

[205] This version refers to what is being contracted as *matrimonium sive sponsalia* (683/14, 683/14), as
does the revised-original version in the third draft (763/45, 763/50, 763/1). The new, alternative
decree included in the third draft reverts to the simple *matrimonium*, which will be retained in
the fourth draft and in Session XXIV. The reason for the disjunction is unclear. These spousals
must be *sponsalia de praesenti* (a term that was still in current use, although theologians and

least three witnesses, incapable (*inhabiles*) of marrying, and the contract null and void. Likewise, the church will render sons under the age of twenty and daughters under the age of eighteen who try to marry without parental consent incapable (*inhabiles*) of marrying, and the contract null and void, although they may appeal to an episcopal judge if their parents' resistance is unreasonable.[206] The notion of inhabilitation was now incorporated into the decree, and the age of majority was raised from eighteen years for sons and sixteen years for daughters to twenty and eighteen. Only three lay witnesses, as before, were strictly required to make the marriage non-clandestine. The second draft includes a new promulgation clause: Bishops and their pastors must publish the decree immediately in their parishes and explain it to the faithful, and they should continue to do so on a monthly basis, so that no one need be ignorant of its provisions.[207]

Several new canons on abuses (*super abusibus*) followed that decree, the first of which was also about clandestinity. This confirms and elaborates the norms established by the Fourth Lateran Council, including the banns. If no impediments come to light, the couple should celebrate their marriage at a church (*in facie ecclesiae*), where the parish priest will interrogate them. Having established that they truly consent, the parish priest will say: "I join you together in the name of the Father, the Son, and the Holy Spirit."[208] The spouses should receive the priestly blessing in church (*in ecclesia*) before consummating their marriage. (Whether the joining formula and the blessing are the same thing is not clear.) The canon also provides alternative procedures for difficult cases and warns that the parish priest must not receive a fee for his blessing.[209] These were prescriptions directed to the universal church and not recommendations or a record of regional practices, but they were not proposed as necessary conditions for validity. Only the presence of the lay witnesses and parental consent for minors were strictly necessary in that sense, although he inclusion of marriage *in facie ecclesiae* under the canons *super abusibus* would have gone some way toward satisfying those who had demanded the presence of a priest or the nuptial blessing as a necessary condition for validity.

The first three prelates who spoke were the Cardinal of Lorraine, Cardinal Madruzzo, and the Patriarch of Jerusalem. They articulated the two competing positions that had emerged, with the Cardinal of Lorraine endorsing the invalidation of clandestine marriages and the other two opposing it. The Cardinal of Lorraine insisted that *all* clandestine marriages should be rendered invalid, namely, all marriages that were not contracted *in facie ecclesiae*. (In the idiom of the council, to invalidate *all* clandestine marriages was synonymous with ruling that only marriages solemnized *in facie ecclesiae* or in the presence of the parish priest would be

canonists since the 13th century had considered it to be improper). Perhaps the term *sponsalia* referred to a present-tense contract after which the spouses remained apart, rather than coming together immediately in cohabitation or consummation.

[206] 683/1–24.   [207] 683/25–28.

[208] "Ego vos coniungo in nomine Patris, et Filii et Spiritus sancti."   [209] 683/29–684/7.

valid.) Minors should be prevented from marrying without their parents' consent, but they should be able to appeal to their bishop if their parents were negligent.[210] The Cardinal of Lorraine spoke on the canons *de abusibus* at a later congregation, when he objected to the specification of any particular form for solemnization, such as *"Ego vos coniungo."* He proposed instead that the partners should be "joined by a priest according to the rite of holy church and according to the custom of the region."[211]

Cardinal Madruzzo and the Patriarch of Jerusalem opposed invalidation. Madruzzo rejected the decree entirely and affirmed the validity of clandestine marriages. He proposed a battery of arguments as proof. The prelates cannot be certain that the church has the power to inhabilitate the partners on grounds of clandestinity, and the solemnities that constitute the manner (*modus*) in which the partners marry are clearly inessential. The decree, therefore, is at best unsafe. Again, because divine law, which no human law can alter, permits everyone freely to choose between the vocations of celibacy and marriage, no one has the right to prevent someone from marrying. Again, the distinction between contract and sacrament is unsound, for marriage is always subject to divine law by virtue of its original institution in Eden. Even among the pagans, therefore, marriage is more than a contract. And there are alternative remedies to the bad consequences of clandestine marriage. "We must beware," Madruzzo concludes, "lest through our desire to cure human vices we destroy and abandon divine medicines."[212]

Antonio Elio, Patriarch of Jerusalem, wanted the dogmatic anathema (the third canon of the first draft) to be restored. The revised decree was now internally contradictory, he argued, for the preamble (the *tametsi* clause) implied that clandestine marriages were valid, whereas what came next rendered them invalid. Indeed, the new policy of the decree was precisely what had been put before the *theologi minores* as a heresy. He conceded that the decree might be pastorally expedient, but he agreed with Cardinal Madruzzo that the church probably did not have the power to invalidate either the persons or their consent. Antonio Elio conceded that minors should not be permitted to marry without parental consent, but he argued that new penalties could prevent them from doing so.[213]

Giovanni Battista Castagna, archbishop of Rossano, elaborated the agnostic position that he had proposed during discussion of the first draft.[214] There are three chief opinions regarding the decree of invalidation, Castagna points out. Some hold that invalidation is both possible and expedient; others, that the church does not

---

[210] Card. Lotharingus, 687/12–18.
[211] Card. Lotharingus, 695/3–5: "contrahentes coniungendos a sacerdote iuxta ritum sanctae ecclesiae et iuxta consuetudinem patriae." Similarly, Brixiensis, 726/31–32, and the Gen. Eremitarum S. Augustini, 739/37, wanted the words *"Ego vos coniungo"* to be erased, but Ventimiliensis, 734/26–27, wanted them to remain.
[212] Card. Madrutius, 687/27–44.   [213] Patriarcha Hierosolymitanus, 687/47–688/8.
[214] Archiep. Rossanensis, 691–94 (votum scriptum).

have the necessary power; others, that invalidation is not expedient at this time, whether or not the church has the necessary power.[215] The archbishop had already proposed the last of these positions during discussion of the first draft.[216] Now he explains what differentiates the third position from the second, and he confesses that he is still personally inclined toward the third position.[217] Whereas the decree has the unqualified approval of those who hold the first position, Giovanni Battista Castagna explains, those who hold the second position consider the first to be artificial, fabricated, and deceptive. Talk of inhabilitation, in their view, is playing with words. In reality, what was formerly a sacrament would no longer be a sacrament. It is true that the church can invalidate marriage by inhabilitating the persons that constitute its matter, but personal inhabilitation must satisfy three requirements: it must result from the interpretation of existing principles and not from wholly new laws; it must be based on real characteristics that are permanently inherent in the persons; and those characteristics must obstruct the intrinsic purpose (*intentio*) of marriage. For example, impotence undermines the *bonum prolis*, a prior marriage obstructs union with another person, orders and sacred vows are incompatible with conjugal vows, and endogamy limits the capacity of marriage to extend the scope of friendship and charity. To require witnesses or parental consent is something quite different. Such obstacles are not permanent, inherent features of the persons that prevent them from marrying. Rather, they are adventitious and transitory. Marrying clandestinely is a sin, even a crime, but this error does not precede the consent but rather coexists with it. Those who hold the second position, therefore, argue that what the decree would entail is not inhabilitation of the persons but the constitution of a new sacramental form. Things that had hitherto been only solemnities or means of proof would become part of the very essence of the sacrament. But the church has no power to make such changes.[218]

Those who hold the third position, Giovanni Battista Castagna explains, do not insist that invalidation is impossible, but they maintain that it would be too much at odds with the weight of tradition and too risky for both doctrinal and tactical reasons. They note that the church has never made parental consent a necessary requirement, whereas civil law has done so. Why? Surely not because the church has lower standards or is more lax, but rather because the church regards marriage as a sacrament of the New Law. The church already prohibits clandestine marriages, but reverence for the sacrament holds her back from invalidating them. Again, the decree and the removal of the anathema would imply that the church now agrees with Erasmus and the Protestant heretics. Castagna reviews the Protestant arguments extensively, citing Ruard Tapper. Obviously, the fact that these heretics consider marriages contracted clandestinely or without parental consent to be

---

[215] 691/1–3.   [216] 647/34–648/9.

[217] 692/11–12: "Tertia opinio illorum est, qui non insistunt in hoc, an ecclesia possit, an non, sed iudicant, hoc tempore irritari haec matrimonia non expedire. Inter eos ego fui."

[218] 691/4–692/10.

invalid is not in itself a sufficient reason for maintaining that such marriages are valid. Nevertheless, their position is part of sustained critique of Catholicism. The decree would at best be a tactical error, therefore, and one that would only confuse uneducated and simple folk. What is to prevent the same reasoning from being extended to religious vows, which the church has always protected from parental disapproval?[219] Finally, it is difficult to square the decree with the church's teaching about the moral purpose of marriage. Marriage is a remedy against lust, and good physicians do not limit their capacity to cure diseases by withholding their remedies. Contrariwise, parents cannot always be relied upon to do what is best for their children.[220] The archbishop proposes that the dogmatic canon (the anathema) should be restored, and that the council should either remove the decree or moderate it so that its remedies fall short of invalidation.[221]

The absence of the dogmatic anathema from the second draft was itself a subject of much disagreement. Many opponents and even a few proponents wanted it to be restored.[222] The removal seemed especially troublesome to those who held that the decree presupposed a doctrine. Debate on the latter issue became crucial at this point, for it was becoming clear that there would never be sufficient consensus to proclaim any *doctrine* regarding clandestine marriages. Some of the proponents insisted that the invalidation of clandestine marriages was purely a matter of reform, which implied no new dogma.[223] Martín Pérez de Ayala, bishop of Segovia, "reprehended those who said that this determination was a dogma." If even the possibility of this reform was a matter of dogma, he argued, then every reform would presuppose a dogma, which was absurd.[224]

Most of the proponents were happy to see the anathema removed, for they perceived an inconsistency between the anathema and the policy that they supported. But that inconsistency was not entirely resolved, for the gist of the anathema was now included in the *tametsi* clause. Pedro González de Mendoza, bishop of Salamanca, a staunch proponent of invalidation, could not endorse the *tametsi*

---

[219] Iustinopolitanus, 706/18–22, considers the argument that just as people cannot be prevented from entering religion, so they cannot be prevented from marrying. He replies that the comparison fails, for whereas one is an ascent toward a more perfect life, the other a descent toward lust.

[220] 692/11–694/45.   [221] 694/46–51. 690/40–41.

[222] Opponents calling for the restoration of the anathema include Patriarcha Hierosolymitanus, 688/5–6; Venetus, 688/16–17; Hyruntinus, 688/34–35; Florentinus, 690/12; Rossanensis, 690/40–41; Barensis, 701/6; Cavensis, 701/26–27; Britonoriensis, 703/27–28; Castrensis, 703/36; Castellanetensis, 704/35–37; Racanatensis, 707/3–4; Interamnensis, 707/26–27; Cenetensis, 707/31; Umbriaticensis, 708/16; Marsicensis, 711/29–30; Segniensis, 712/21; Lesinensis, 713/7; Lucerinus, 715/16; Larinensis, 717/4; Civitas Castellanae, 728/29–31; Faventinus, 735/28–29. Proponents calling for its restoration include Sulmonensis, 707/36, and Tortonensis, 708/22.

[223] Mutinensis, 711/5–6. Legionensis, 721/9–10. Namurcensis, 730/5–8, 21–22.

[224] Segobiensis, 709/14–16: "Reprehendit eos, qui dicunt, hanc determinationem esse dogma. Si enim hoc esset, omnes determinationes possent reduci ad dogma, quia semper potest dici, an hoc possit vel non possit fieri."

clause because it seemed to contradict the decrees invalidating marriages contracted clandestinely and without parental consent, just as the dogmatic canon had done. Recasting the canon as a descriptive preamble to a reform decree had not solved the problem, in his view. He, too, proposed that the dogmatic canon should be restored. Failing that, he suggested, the *tametsi* clause should be reworded with the word *hactenus* ("hitherto," "until now") inserted. Then it would be clear that although clandestine marriages had been valid hitherto (*hactenus*), they would henceforth (*deinceps*) be invalid.[225]

The anathema had seemed especially troublesome to proponents who maintained that the church had invalidated clandestine marriage in former, more disciplined times, perhaps even since the beginning, and the *tametsi* clause did not necessarily solve the problem. Jacopo Nacchianti, O.P., bishop of Chioggia, argued that clandestine marriages had never been legitimate, for they were sinful and sacrilegious. The church had only treated them as if they were legitimate and tolerated them *propter oeconomiam*, judging it was not expedient to condemn them as null and void.[226] Some prelates continued to argue that the decretal ascribed to Evaristus was a crucial witness of earlier practice.[227] From their point of view, the dogmatic canon had seemed to anathematize Pope Evaristus, so they were happy to see it removed. Thomas Stella, O.P., bishop of Capo d'Istria, objected that even the descriptive *tametsi* clause contradicted Evaristus.[228] Martín Pérez de Ayala, bishop of Segovia, and Sebastiano Antonio Minturno, bishop of Ugento, maintained that the church had deemed clandestine marriages null and void at least from the reign of Evaristus to the reign of Clement III. The latter cited this supposed fact as evidence that clandestine marriage was intrinsically evil (*per se malum*).[229] Antonio Agustín, bishop of Lleida, claimed that the church had deemed clandestine marriages to be invalid until the reign of Alexander III.[230]

Other prelates on both sides refuted historical claims of that sort. In their view, the final clause of Evaristus's decretal – "*nisi voluntas propria suffragata fuerit et vota succurrerint legitima*" – affirmed the principle of *solus consensus*. Christophori Patavini, general of the Augustinian hermits, explained that he was happy to endorse the *tametsi* clause because he did not believe that Evaristus had rendered clandestine marriages null and void. Diego Laínez, general of the Society of Jesus, argued that clandestine marriages had never before been invalid, citing evidence from the

---

[225] Pedro González de Mendoza, *Lo sucedido en el concilio de Trento*, CT 2: 692/42–693/3 (*votum scriptum*). González de Mendoza had also wanted the term hactenus to be inserted into the third canon (the anathema) of the first draft: ibid., CT 2:689/28–34.

[226] Clodiensis, CT 9:704/22–25.

[227] S. Severinae, 690/43–46. Caiacensis, 702/37–40. Clodiensis, 704/18. Iustinopolitanus, 706/17–18. Verdunensis, 709/26–27. Vicensis Hispanus, 719/22–33. Augustensis, 720/11–12. Vaurensis, 720/27. Almeriensis, 722/12–13. Ilerdensis, 722/41–723/5. Tutellensis, 727/5. Civitatensis, 727/31–32. Anglonensis, 730/35–36. Aliphanus, 734/19–21. Gen. Minorum Obs., 738/25–26.

[228] Iustinopolitanus, 706/17–18.   [229] Segobiensis, 709/5–10. Ugentinus, 725/28–30.

[230] Ilerdensis, 722/41–723/1.

Old Testament and from patristic sources. He argued that Tertullian, who lived only shortly before Evaristus, considered clandestine marriages to be valid. Evaristus wanted to protect daughters from the hazards of marrying without parental guidance, Laínez argued, but the final clause showed that he considered the spouses' consent alone to be sufficient for a true marriage.[231]

The anathema had made little sense also to those who considered marrying to be an essentially ritual event, in which the priestly blessing was the sacramental form. From their point of view, clandestine marriages had always been intrinsically invalid, even if the church had for centuries treated them as valid. Most of these prelates, too, believed that Evaristus had rendered clandestine marriages null and void. They were pleased to see the "*Ego vos coniungo*" form included as a recommended practice, for it had acquired special authority through Alberto Castellani's *Sacerdotale ad consuetudinem sanctae Romanae ecclesiae* (Section 17.6.4), and it was congruent with the iconography of the sacrament (Section 1.8.3). Thomas Goldwell, bishop of St Asaph, endorsed this formula, claiming that it was traditional not only in the Roman church but also in England. Indeed, he believed that it was an apostolic tradition. He noted that according to the *Sacerdotale*, this was the form of the sacrament.[232] Antonio Savion, Minister General of the Conventual Franciscans, compared "*Ego vos coniungo*" to the formula of penance, "*Ego te absolvo*." Just as marriage requires the spouses' consent, so penance requires the subject's contrition. Nevertheless, the priestly formula is still necessary. Bartolomé Fernandes dos Mártires, O.P., bishop of Braga, hoped that the formula would be "included among the ceremonies to be observed throughout the world."[233] Other prelates resisted such enthusiasm. Francisco Zamora de Cuenca, Minister General of the Observant Franciscans, endorsed the formula but conceded that it was "only ceremonial."[234] Others could accept "*Ego vos coniungo*" as the recommended formula, but they pointed out that other suitable formulas were available, and they did not want to exclude the diverse received rites of regional churches.[235] According to the secretary's summary of amendments (*censurae*), forty-two prelates concurred with the Cardinal of Lorraine's suggestion that spouses should "be blessed by the parish priest according to the received rite of holy church and before the consummation of marriage."[236] A "received rite," in this sense, was one practiced as a local custom.

The stipulation of "*Ego vos coniungo*" as the standard formula aroused concern because it seemed to imply the priest was the essential minister of the sacrament, and that his words constituted the sacramental form. The meaning of the formula as

---

[231] Gen. Iesuitarum, 740/42–741/10. Vestanus, 724/34–35, and Clusinus, 725/6–7, also denied that Evaristus had invalidated clandestine marriage.

[232] Assaphensis, 716/43–717/2.   [233] Bracarensis, 697/27–28.

[234] Gen. Minorum Obs., 738/19–20: "Quod Dominus in vobis incepit, ipse perficiat."

[235] Card. Lotharingus, 695/3–5. Iustinopolitanus, 706/9–12. Metensis, 717/29–30. Ilerdensis, 722/36–37.

[236] 744/2–8.

well as the imposition of a prescribed formula pointed in that direction. All of the opponents and most of the proponents did not believe that the priest was minister of the sacrament in that sense. Thus, Pedro González de Mendoza, bishop of Salamanca, wanted the formula to be excised "because many will think that the holy synod judged that this was the form of the sacrament of marriage, just as 'I baptize you' was the form of baptism, 'I absolve you' of penance, and so forth." People would infer that there was no sacrament of marriage unless a priest said these words, the bishop argued, and this inference "would stir up great controversies and dissensions in the schools."[237] Some of the prelates proposed alternatives that made the priest's role seem more ceremonial and less instrumental. Christophori Patavini, general of the Augustinians (and a proponent), suggested: "What God has begun in you, may he himself complete."[238] This formula originated in Philippians 1:6, but variants were current in rituals for the commissioning of missionary brethren, the bestowal of habits, and so forth.[239] Moreover, it was reminiscent of two blessing prayers used in two old nuptial *ordines*, *Exaudi nos* and the Raguel prayer, in both of which the priest asks God to join the spouses.[240] Antonio Corrionero de Babila-fuente, bishop of Almería (another proponent), suggested: "They have been joined in marriage as Christ's servants, in the name of Father, Son, and Holy Spirit."[241] Belisario Baldevino, bishop of Larino (an opponent) suggested that the formula "I declare that you have been joined" might be included as an optional alternative to "I join you together."[242]

Many prelates wanted the decree to require not only that witnesses were present but also that the marriage was contracted *in facie ecclesiae* or with the blessing of a priest.[243] Those who proposed that clandestine marriages should be entirely (*omnino*) or thoroughly (*penitus*) invalidated were in effect demanding that

[237] González de Mendoza, *Lo sucedido en el concilio de Trento*, CT 2:693/14–22 (*votum scriptum*).

[238] Gen. Eremitarum S. Augustini, 739/37–38: "Quod Dominus in vobis incepit, ipse perficiat."

[239] Phil 1:6: "Confidens hoc ipsum quia qui coepit in vobis opus bonum perficiet usque in diem Christi Iesu." Cf. Cf. G. G. Meersseman, *Dossier de l'Ordre de la Pénitence au XIIIe siècle*, 2nd edition. Spicilegium Friburgense, Textes pour servir à l'hisotire de la vie chrétienne, 7. (Fribourg Suisse, 1982). p. 145, §8.

[240] Veronese (Leonine) Sacramentary, in K. Ritzer, *Le mariage* (Paris, 1970), 422: "Exaudi nos, omnipotens et misericors Deus, ut quod nostro ministratur officio, tua benedictione potius impleatur; per…." The earliest extant uses of the Raguel prayer (cf. Tob 7:15) are in the Spanish *Sacramentary of Vich* and the French *Benedictional of Archbishop Robert* (probably from Rouen), both dating from the 11th century, Ritzer, 441 (§1425), and 445 (§12e): "Deus Abraham, Deus Isaac, Deus Iacob, ipse coniungat vos impleatque benedictionem suam in vobis. Per…."

[241] Almeriensis, 722/4–5: "Sint iuncti servi Christi matrimonialiter in nomine Patris et Filii et Spiritus Sancti."

[242] Larinensis, 717/10–11: "Verba placent: Ego vos coniungo, vel declaro coniunctos." He also suggested that a marriage should be contracted "ante fores domus sponsae."

[243] Granatensis, 690/8–9 ("in praesentia ecclesiae"). Aurelianensis, 714/15–16 ("in facie ecclesiae"). Vulturariensis, 714/22 ("in facie ecclesiae"). Tiburtinus, 715/29 ("in faciem ecclesiae"). Lavellinus, 732/37 ("in faciem ecclesiae"). Senecencis, 734/6 ("in faciem ecclesiae"). Aliphanus, 734/17–23 ("sacerdotum benedictione firmata").

marriages had to be solemnized *in facie ecclesiae* or before a parish priest, for these were two ways of saying the same thing.[244] Antonio Agustín, bishop of Lleida, argued that to require witnesses alone would engender new problems and would not eliminate clandestine marriages. Witnesses could be fraudulent or untrustworthy, and their testimonies were sometimes inconsistent. The council should require marriages to be contracted either *in facie ecclesiae* or in the presence of two witnesses and a notary, who would record the contract in an *instrumentum*. If the council adopted the latter policy, every diocese should retain an episcopal notary who would record each marriage and report it to the bishop within a few days.[245]

Only a few proponents advocated the inhabilitation theory at this stage,[246] but they still considered diriment personal impediments, such as those of relationship, to be the most pertinent precedents. They suggested several others, however, such as the pope's power to dissolve an unconsummated marriage, a father's power to dissolve a conditional marriage, and the impediment of force and fear.[247] Some proponents argued that the new impediment would invalidate not the persons but their consent or the manner (*modus*) in which they contracted marriage.[248] Nevertheless, because opponents continued to criticize the inhabilitation theory, proponents continued to defend it against their objections. Some opponents objected, as before, that a personal impediment had to be founded on something enduring and inherent in the persons.[249] The prelates debated whether some of the traditional personal impediments, such as *cognatio spiritualis* (acquired through baptism) and *cognatio legalis* (acquired through adoption), were based on any real, inherent, enduring quality, since they seemed result to entirely from positive legislation and from the commonwealth's power over contracts. Contrariwise, moral qualities associated with clandestine marriage, such as disobedience and crime, did inhere in the persons.[250] Scipione

---

[244] Messanensis, 698/36–37. Ebroicensis, 702/20–21. Caiacensis, 702/37–38. Verdunensis, 709/23–26. Chironensis, 710/33–34. Sanctonensis, 710/40–41. Mutinensis, 711/9–10. Calamonensis, 712/1–3. Sanctonensis, 710/40–41. Mutinensis, 711/9–11. Calamonensis, 712/2–4. Insulanis, 712/25–26. Cassertanensis, 716/16–17. Adriensis, 716/22. Auriensis, 718/29–30. Cenomanensis, 719/35–36. Sibinicensis, 720/32–33. Suessionensis, 720/38–39. Cotronensis, 720/43–44. Ostunensis, 724/10–12. Ugentinus, 725/25–28. Tutellensis, 727/5–6. Civitatensis, 728/15–17. Acerrensis, 728/24–25. Namurcensis, 730/22. Venciensis, 730/26–28. Anglonensis, 730/34–36. Parmensis, 730/37–40. Niochensis, 731/28–30. Guadiscensis, 732/8–9. Papiensis, 732/15–16. Barcinonensis, 731/3–4. Columbriensis, 732/24–25. Rapotensis, 734/43. Abbas Lunaevillae, 738/5–8. Generalis Minorum Obs., 738/26–28. Gen. Minorum Conv., 738/45–46.

[245] Ilerdensis, 723/8–11.

[246] Granatensis, 690/4. Theanensis, 719/42. Gen. Minorum Conv., 738/43–44.

[247] Bracarensis, 697/20–26. Lancianensis, 699/7–14. Leriensis, 713/21–22, 714/1–2. Atrebatensis, 715/16. Asturicensis, 716/36–38. Auriensis, 718/38–47.

[248] Mutinensis, 711/9–10. Metensis, 717/22–25. Civitatensis, 727/35–728/2. Gen. Minorum Conv., 738/44–45. Gen Minorum Obs., 738/26–28.

[249] Interamnesis, 707/24–26. Rheginus, 700/24–27.

[250] Lancianensis, 699/10–14. Iustinopolitanus, 706/29–31. Mutinensis, 711/14–15. Auriensis, 718/43–719/10. Ugentinus, 725/30–36. Vestanus, 724/32–34. Clusinus, 725/10–11. Civitatensis, 728/1–13. Hyprensis, 729/29–32.

Bongalli, bishop of Civita Castellana, argued that the impediment of *cognatio legalis* was founded on a real inherent quality. He conceded that the crime of disobedience inhered in persons who married clandestinely, but this was not a "sufficient reason" for invalidation. A diriment personal impediment, he argued, resulted from "a law founded on an inherent quality in such a way that when that quality is absent, the marriage cannot be invalidated." Just as the church could not cause a marriage to exist without the spouses' consent, so the church could not invalidate a marriage without some impeding quality inherent in the persons. Furthermore, the decree would take away the freedom (*libertas*) of sons and daughters to contract marriage.[251]

Proponents continued to defend the contractual theory, arguing that the church could assume the power of a commonwealth and invalidate the contract.[252] Whenever a commonwealth justly prohibits a contract without annulling it, the commonwealth has the power to annul it if mere prohibition has proved ineffective.[253] Invalidation of the contract would not touch the sacrament. Antonio Corrionero de Babilafuente, bishop of Almería, proposed a helpful illustration. Suppose that the wine that was going to be consecrated in the sacrament of eucharist were converted by some "art" into vinegar. Its conversion would prevent the sacrament by subtracting the necessary matter. Likewise, the sacrament of marriage presupposes legitimate consent, and the church has the power make clandestine consent no longer legitimate, "since the illegitimizing of political matters [*rerum politicarum*] belongs to the commonwealth [*res publica*]."[254] This line of argument drew some of the prelates into a debate about ontology. Opponents objected that it was impossible to invalidate the contract without touching the sacrament because the two things were simultaneous and inseparable. The sacrament of marriage was related to the contract as species to genus, or even as heat is related to fire. To destroy the contract, therefore, was *ipso facto* to destroy the sacrament.[255] Proponents countered that the sacrament was related to the contract accidentally or by addition, and not as species to genus.[256]

The exigent power argument, which had made only a brief appearance during voting on the first draft, now became conspicuous and fully developed. God would not have left the church without the means to do whatever was expedient or to prevent a mortal sin, the proponents argued.[257] This argument was partly a symptom

---

[251] Civitatis Castellanae, 729/3–9.
[252] Bracarensis, 697/16–27. Tarentinus, 698/14–16. Lancianensis, 699/7–9. Clodiensis, 704/11–17. Cauriensis, 712/9–13. Leriensis, 713/37–38. Montis Marani, 715/2–4. Ostunensis, 724/10–22. Oppidensis, 732/38–41. Lucensis, 733/32–33.
[253] Catholonensis, 716/31. Ilerdensis, 722/44–723/1. Usellensis, 737/15–17. Gen. Minorum Obs., 738/29–30.
[254] Almeriensis, 722/15–18.
[255] Cavensis, 701/38–39. Interamnensis, 707/21–22. Montisfalisci, 717/41–43. Clusinus, 725/11–12.
[256] Columbriensis, 732/19–24. Ostunensis, 724/15–22.
[257] Aquilegiensis, 688/12–13. Archiep. Cretensis, 688/27–29. Hyrdruntinus, 688/39–40. Tarentinus, 698/15–17. Philadelphiensis, 703/17–18. Iustinopolitanus, 706/22–25. Sulmonensis, 707/39–40. Mutinensis, 711/11–12, 21–24. Calamonensis, 712/1–4. Leriensis, 713/30–44. Theanensis, 719/38–39. Augustensis, 720/13–15. Montis Marani, 715/3–6. Albinganensis, 715/31–33. Legionensis,

of frustration and impatience. It seemed to many of the proponents that pointless, merely academic theological questions where preventing the council from reaching an expedient conclusion. François Richardot, bishop of Arras, urged the prelates to care less about their own opinions and more about the truth.[258] The exigent power argument was mingled, too, with tactical considerations. Whereas the opponents maintained that the decree of invalidation would imply capitulation to the heretics, the proponents maintained that it would demonstrate the power of the church, which the heretics denied. This was not the moment to confess that the church was powerless. But there was also a serious theological, even metaphysical basis to the argument, as Pedro Guerrero will explain in his treatise on clandestine marriages. If God would not leave his church without "necessary things" – that is whatever was needed for the welfare of his people – then one could argue thus: "It is expedient. Therefore, it is possible." (*"Expedit. Ergo ecclesia potest."*) Carlo Grassi, bishop of Montis Falisci, countered that one could just as validly argue: "It is not possible. Therefore, it is not expedient." (*"Non potest. Ergo non expedit."*)[259]

In response to the emphasis on the church's power and authority, many opponents pulled back from making theological claims about the form and matter of the sacrament, confessing that they would not dare to say that the church lacked the power to invalidate clandestine marriages.[260] Instead, they adopted the prudential, agnostic position that the archbishop of Rossano had expounded while continuing to oppose the proponents' own theological arguments. For example, Salvatore Pacini, bishop of Chiusi, outlined the standard objections to invalidation but declared that he "did not wish to speak about the power of the church."[261] Scipione Bongalli, bishop of Civita Castellana, said that the question was not whether the church was able to invalidate clandestine marriages but whether she was able to do so "in this way."[262] Martin Baudouin, bishop of Ypres, and Sebastiano Vanzi, bishop of Orvieto, conceded that the church had the necessary power in some *general* way, but they doubted whether the proponents' explanations of how the church would exercise this power were plausible.[263]

721/9–13. Almeriensis, 722/12–13. Vicensis Italus, 723/23–24. Civitatensis, 727/32–35, 728/14–15. Barcinonensis, 731/4–5. Niochensis, 731/28–29. Gen. Minorum Obs., 738/28–29.

[258] Atrebatensis, 715/42–45.

[259] Montisfalisci, 717/45–46.

[260] Racanatensis, 707/5–6: "quamvis non audeat dicere, ecclesiam id non posse statuere." Clusinus, 725/8: "Dixit, se nolle loqui de potestate ecclesiae." Calvensis, 731/21–23: "Quoad decretum de clandestinis dixit, quod non vult loqui, an ecclesia possit, sed an expediat, et quod sibi videtur, quod non expediat, et ideo non placet decretum." Urbevetanus, 745/40–746/30.

[261] Clusinus, 725/6–13.

[262] Civitatis Castellanae, 728/45–46: "non est disputandum, an ecclesia possit, sed an ecclesia possit hoc modo."

[263] Hyprensis, 729/29 ff.: "Quoad decretum de clandestinis dixit, quod, quamvis non dubitet de potestate generali ecclesiae, tamen...." Urbevetanus, 735/39 ff.: "Quoad decretum de clandestinis non placet ea irritari.... Dixit se non dubitare, ecclesiam posse in genere inhabilitare aliquem ad clandestine...."

Rather than arguing that invalidation was impossible, therefore, several of the opponents now argued that it was overly novel and unprecedented. They objected that Catholics had not demanded it until the Council of Cologne and Johann Gropper, or that it was a practice of the heretics, or that it was contrary to traditional practice and to the teachings of the scholastic masters, or that the very possibility was uncertain and still controversial among theologians.[264] The conclusion was the same: The decree must be rejected, and the anathema must be restored. Conceding that invalidation might be possible, they maintained that it would not be expedient. They were referring not to political welfare but to prudence, rules of procedure, and tactics. Reversing the direction of the first round of discussion, Gian Vincenzo Micheli, bishop of Minervino Murge, said that the question was not whether the church had the power to invalidate clandestine marriages but whether exercising that power would be expedient. In his view, it was not.[265] This cautious, agnostic, and pragmatic mode of opposition, predicated on procedural and contextual propriety, became a position in its own right during discussion of the second draft, as the archbishop of Rossano had suggested on the first day.

20.6 ARCHBISHOP PEDRO GUERRERO ON CLANDESTINE MARRIAGE

Guerrero was archbishop of Granada from 1546 until his death in 1576, and he led the Spanish delegation during the council's second and third phases.[266] A treatise on clandestine marriage that he wrote to explain his own position and the various arguments and counterarguments at the council show not only that his own position was very well developed, but also that what seem like incidental remarks made by him in the recorded *acta* were actually fragments of a carefully worked out theory.

Guerrero was a qualified theologian as well as a capable administrator. He had studied and taught theology at Salamanca, and he held the primary chair of theology at Sigüenza from 1535 to 1546, where he was a canon of the cathedral.[267] Guerrero was also a keen reformer. He collaborated and corresponded with Juan de Avila, a controversial reformer and preacher and an advocate of devotional and evangelical

---

[264] Card. Madrutius, 687/24–25. Rheginus, 700/24–27. Barensis, 701/8–10. Cavensis, 701/26–27. Philadelphiensis, 703/14–16. Interamnensis, 707/13–14. Clusinus, 725/6–13. Nemausensis, 726/19–22. Comensis, 726/41–43. Civitas Castellanae, 728/45–729/3. Faventinus, 735/36–37. Hyprensis, 729/32–34. Gen Jesuitarum, 741/15–23

[265] Minerbiensis, 702/53–703/1.

[266] On Guerrero's life and work, see C. Herreros González and M. C. Santapau Pastor, *Pedro Guerrero: Vida y obra de un ilustre riojano del siglo XVI* (Logroño, 2012). On Guerrero's work as a reformer and his role at Trent, see D. Coleman, *Creating Christian Granada* (Ithaca, 2003), 145–76.

[267] See Herreros González and Santapau Pastor, *Pedro Guerrero*, 135–75, on Guerrero's intellectual and theological formation.

renewal.[268] They had become acquainted as students at Alcalá in the 1520s. In 1551, Juan de Avila wrote to Guerrero describing the appalling consequences of marriages contracted clandestinely or without parental consent, urging the archbishop to pursue the matter at Trent. The only solution, Avila maintained, was to invalidate all marriages contracted without witnesses.[269] Guerrero championed this and other reforms at Trent. After the council, he strove to realize Trent's reforms in his archdiocese, as well as to assimilate the Moorish citizens of Granada more fully to the dominant Christian culture.

Guerrero acquired a reputation for being troublesome and intransigent during the third phase of the council.[270] Pedro González de Mendoza, bishop of Salamanca, noted in his diary on October 31, 1563, that the Italian prelates despised Guerrero so much that his wanting something to be done was sufficient reason for them to propose the opposite.[271] On January 18, 1562, Guerrero had led the Spanish bishops in a protest against the papal legates' exclusive right to set the agenda and to prepare draft decrees, as defined in the principle *proponentibus legatis*.[272] Shortly after this protest, he wrote a brief treatise on the subject, which he addressed to the legates.[273] Guerrero was convinced that the cause of reform would be blocked unless the bishops took control of the agenda, but his fear was exaggerated, for the legates deputed the drafting of decrees to prelates. As noted earlier, Guerrero was himself one of the thirteen prelates whom the legates deputed on June 21, 1563, to draft the decrees on the sacrament of marriage.[274]

20.6.1 *The treatise*

Guerrero's treatise on clandestine marriages survives in a single manuscript.[275] Juan López Martín, an authority on Guerrero, identifies the hand as that of Guerrero's secretary, Juan de Fonseca: the cleric and theologian who assisted Guerrero at Trent.[276]

---

[268] Coleman, *Creating Christian Granada*, 148–50. Herreros González and Santapau Pastor, *Pedro Guerrero*, 125–31. For Guerrero's correspondence with Avila, see J. López Martín, *Don Pedro Guerrero: epistolario y documentación* (Rome, 1974).

[269] H. Kamen, *The Phoenix and the Flame* (New Haven, 1993), 279.

[270] Coleman, *Creating Christian Granada*, 145–48, 166–76.

[271] González de Mendoza, Lo sucedido en el concilio de Trento, CT 2:707/35–36.

[272] CT 8:291. Coleman, *Creating Christian Granada*, 170–71.   [273] CT 13:572–74.

[274] CT 9:590–91.

[275] MS Biblioteca Universitaria de Granada, Caja B-4, 346r–383v. J. López Martín, "El voto de Don Pedro Guerrero sobre el sacramento del matrimonio en el Concilio de Trento," *Archivo Teológico Granadino* 44 (1981): 147–219, provides an edition (pp. 155–219), for which I am very grateful, but because it contains quite a few transcription errors, I have used the manuscript as my preferred source. I shall cite the folio of the manuscript first, followed by the corresponding page reference in López Martín's edition in square brackets.

[276] The *acta* record that Ioannes Fonseca, "clericus saecularis Hispanus cum archiep. Granatensi," spoke on communion under both kinds at a *congregatio theologorum* on June 22, 1562 (CT 8:612), and again on the sacrament of orders on October 1, 1562 (CT 9:31–32). He is also listed in the *acta* as one of the *sacrae theologiae doctores et magistri* who contributed to Session

The manuscript includes marginal and interlinear notations in the hands both of Fonseca and of Guerrero himself.[277]

It is likely that Guerrero or his secretary (or both) worked up the treatise from the notes or *vota scripta* that he used during the proceedings. The treatise reflects the state of argument during voting on the second draft. Guerrero refers to the proceedings in the past tense, and he writes as if he is explaining them to outsiders, but he does not mention the decree *Tametsi* of Session XXIV (Nov. 11, 1563). After *Tametsi*, Guerrero's chief task would have been to implement the reforms in his archdiocese and not to argue for invalidation or to reply to objections. Moreover, the treatise reflects the state of the question before the presentation of the third draft on September 5, for Guerrero assumes throughout that what is at stake is the invalidation both of clandestine marriages and of the marriages of minors without their parents' consent. The first two versions of the decrees on clandestine marriage, presented on July 20 and August 7, took the same approach, but the third set of drafts, presented on September 5, included a new, alternative version of the decree that did not require parental consent (Section 20.7).[278] Proponents who expressed any preference in their votes, including Guerrero,[279] opted for the new version, which passed into the fourth draft and eventually became law in Session XXIV (Section 20.8). Because the treatise presupposes most of the arguments that circulated during the proceedings, it must have been composed well after July 20, 1563, when the legates put the first draft of the decrees on marriage before the prelates. It is likely, therefore, that the treatise originated in voting on the second draft, August 11–23.[280] By that time, the chief arguments and counterarguments were all in circulation. The argument from exigent power, which Guerrero expounds in the treatise, flourished during this second stage of the proceedings. Contrariwise, the proponents no longer relied on the inhabilitation theory by this time, although they continued to defend it against objections. Guerrero's approach in the treatise is exactly the same. Guerrero's attitude to the debate, too, is consistent with what was happening during voting on the second draft, when it was becoming clear that the two sides would never be reconciled. Guerrero addresses his treatise as if to a third party, I suggest, because he was not trying to persuade the opposing prelates at this stage – a lost cause – but only to justify the position of the proponents and to make it seem unassailable.

The treatise comprises three main sections followed by an appended essay on divine law. First, after some preliminary remarks, there is a numbered series of seven

XIX (CT 8:500). J. López Martín, *La imagen del obispo en el pensamiento teológico-pastoral de don Pedro Guerrero en Trento* (Rome, 1971), includes editions of Tridentine treatises by Guerrero on ecclesiastical residence (201–301) and by Juan de Fonseca on the sacrament of orders (302–45).

[277] López Martín, "El voto de Don Pedro Guerrero," 148–49.   [278] CT 9:761–62.

[279] CT 9:781/1.

[280] López Martín, "El voto de Don Pedro Guerrero," 149–50, reaches the same conclusion through different reasoning.

brief statements.[281] Guerrero characterizes these as premises,[282] but they might be better described as cruxes or key points. Guerrero adds some further key points after the numbered premises. Second, Guerrero presents a sequence of five extensively developed theses (*conclusiones*), which together constitute a single five-step argument. The third section consists of objections to invalidation with Guerrero's replies to them. There are twelve of these objections, although the series is not numbered. Finally, there is a brief but original essay on the multiple senses of the terms "canon law" and "divine law." The topic arises incidentally from Guerrero's reply to the last of the objections.

Three salient and interconnected themes run through the treatise: the twofold character of Christian marriage as both contract and sacrament; the relationship of human law to divine law; and the changeability of all human law, ecclesiastical as well as secular, which must adapt to the exigencies of each era.

The exposition that follows is in three parts. In the first part (Section 20.6.2), I shall summarize Guerrero's narrative of the circumstances and describe his intentions and methods. In the second part (Section 20.6.3), I shall attempt coherently to reconstruct the central five-step argument. To that end, I shall rearrange some of the material and incorporate material from elsewhere in the treatise, for Guerrero's writing is repetitive, non-linear, and digressive. Finally, I shall outline the theory of laws that Guerrero outlines in the appendix (Section 20.6.4).

20.6.2 *Guerrero's intentions and methods*

Guerrero explains his intentions concisely at the beginning of the treatise:

> Among many matters that were subjects of inquiry and controversy when the Council of Trent under Pius IV deliberated over the sacrament of marriage, the question of clandestine marriages and of the marriages of minors [*filii familias*] contracted without the consent of their parents was debated for a long time, and it greatly vexed the fathers of the council. Did the church have the power to render them null and void, whether by making the persons illegitimate and rendering them incapable [*inhabiles*] of contracting marriage, or by annulling their consent, or in some other way? Also, was it expedient for the church to do so?[283]

Guerrero was an advocate of the inhabilitation theory at the council,[284] but here he seems to avoid committing himself to it. Nor does he commit himself to it in the body of the treatise, although he defends it against objections.

---

[281] There is an error of enumeration in the manuscript, where two successive premises, the fourth and fifth, are both counted as the fourth, so that the numbering is out of step from the fifth premise onwards. In the notes that follow, I shall add Guerrero's number in parentheses, for example, Premise 5 (4) is the fifth premise, although Guerrero assigned the number 4 to it (348r, 158).

[282] 346v/5 [156]: "Pro clariori autem harum quaestionum enodatione sunt aliqua praemitenda."

[283] Guerrero, *De matrimonio*, f. 346r (ed. López Martín, p. 155).

[284] CT 9:690/3–7, 781/3–4.

Guerrero explains that some of the *theologi minores* discussed these questions first, and that only two of them denied that the church had the power to invalidate clandestine marriages. Moreover, only a few doubted that invalidation would be expedient, and even those were prepared to leave the matter to the prelates.[285] This account is broadly consistent with what we know from the *acta* (Section 20.3), although Guerrero arguably exaggerates the openness of the theologians to invalidation.[286] The two members of the first class who opposed invalidation, as we have seen, were Antonius Coquier and Antonius de Gragnano. When the prelates considered the question, Guerrero continues, 137 held that the church both could and should invalidate clandestine marriages henceforth, whereas 57 contradicted them, maintaining either that the church did not have the power to invalidate or that invalidation would not be expedient. But very few of the latter, Guerrero adds, dared to say that the church lacked the power. Although we do not know whence he came by these numbers or how he calculated them, the ratio is close to what one finds in the recorded *acta* at any stage. But Guerrero arguably oversimplifies the division of opinions. His use verb "to dare" (*audere*) points to what actually happened. Because the proponents increasingly emphasized the church's God-given power to do whatever was needful for pastoral and civic well-being, many opponents were forced to concede that invalidation was theoretically possible while maintaining that it would be rash and repugnant to tradition and that its theological presuppositions were not yet established.

The question that Guerrero addresses in the treatise, he explains, is twofold: first, whether the church is able to raise the level of prohibition from simple prohibition to invalidation; second, whether doing so is expedient now. Guerrero emphasizes that the church already prohibits the marriages in question and penalizes them. What is in question is not a new prohibition but the enhancement of an existing prohibition.[287] Guerrero maintains that in any legal system, whether secular or ecclesiastical, there will be both prohibitive impediments and diriment impediments, and that there is a natural progression from simple prohibition to invalidation. When a contract or other voluntary institution is harmful, the relevant authority first tries to prevent it through simple prohibition, without invalidating it *post factum*. If that proves ineffective, the authority raises the level of prohibition to invalidation. If an authority has the power to prohibit, it also has the power to invalidate.[288]

Throughout the treatise, as in the opening passage quoted earlier, Guerrero couples clandestine marriages in the proper sense – that is, marriages contracted secretly (*clam*) – with the marriages of minors (*filii familias*) contracted without parental consent. The two categories are loosely included under the general heading

[285] 346r [155].   [286] CT 9:397–98, 407–09.   [287] 346v [155].
[288] Guerrero states this principle briefly as premise 6 (5), 348r–349r [159–60], and he develops it extensively in his reply to the twelfth objection, 376v–378r [206–08].

of clandestinity, but Guerrero neither conflates nor separates them. He tacitly assumes that the two errors stand or fall together, so that an argument for invalidating one is implicitly an argument for invalidating the other, perhaps because he considered the second error to be the chief hazard of the first. As we have seen, the first two drafts of the decree on clandestine marriages at Trent took the same approach.

Guerrero explains what the term "clandestine marriage" means. In general terms, a marriage is clandestine when it is contracted without whatever formalities (*solemnitates*) the church normally requires, and without a dispensation from observing them (which might be granted in cases of parental coercion, for example). More precisely, marriages may be contracted clandestinely in any of three circumstances, which constitute a descending scale of clandestinity: (i) when there are no witnesses, and consequently no proof that the spouses are married if they choose to deny it; (ii) when there are witnesses present but no priest; and (iii) when there are witnesses and a priest, but he is not the "proper" priest, that is, the contractants' parish priest or his appointed ordinary. In addition, Guerrero notes, the marriages of minors without parental consent are customarily said to be clandestine even if they are contracted publicly – indeed, even if the partners plight their troth *in facie ecclesiae*.[289] Guerrero does not advocate any particular way of construing clandestine marriage in the treatise. The first two drafts of the decree construed clandestinity in the first of three ways outlined above, although some of prelates wanted to include the ministry of a priest or the parish priest in the requirements. The new version of the decree introduced with the third draft will abandon the parental consent requirement and make the presence of the parish priest as well as of witnesses a condition for validity.

Whereas the couplet of errors is conjunctive, three other couplets that occur throughout the treatise are disjunctive: the commonwealth (*res publica*) or its ruler (*princeps*), "natural or divine law" (*lex naturalis aut divina*), and human or ecclesiastical law. The first disjunction reflects the assumption that although law exists to enhance the common good of the community, there must be a particular legislator, namely, the person with "care of the community," also known as the *princeps*. Guerrero mentions the pope's power to legislate and adjudicate at several points in the treatise, but he does not espouse any particular constitutional theory of the church. In the appendix, he seems to go out of his way to avoid mentioning the papacy. Instead, he says that the author of church law is the ecclesiastical *politia* or *magistratus*, just as the author of the civil law is the civil *politia* or political *magistratus*.[290] The most persistent disjunction is that of natural or divine law. Until the appendix, Guerrero always posits these laws together. The couplet comprehends the unchangeable givens of law, in contrast to the positive laws introduced by human agents, which are rescindable and generally capable of dispensation. Guerrero uses the third disjunction – that of ecclesiastical or human laws – to

---

[289] Premise 2, 346v–347r [156].   [290] 318r [215].

characterize laws that are positive and changeable. In the appendix, Guerrero argues that natural law is a branch or species of divine law, and that ecclesiastical law is a branch or species of human law.

Guerrero handles the issue of dogma and reform judiciously in the treatise, articulating here a concern that does not explicitly emerge in the *acta*. He points out that a dogmatic edict or an anathema requires something close to unanimity, whereas the requirement for an edict of reform is much lower. A vote of 137 to 50 would suffice for a disciplinary edict, therefore, but not for a definition of doctrine or an anathema.[291] A decree invalidating the marriages in question would in itself be a *de facto* and not a *de iure* matter, Guerrero says: a matter of practice, not of doctrine. If a *de facto* edict turns out to be counterproductive, the pope can easily rescind it.[292] Guerrero concedes, nevertheless, that such a decree would presuppose that invalidation is possible: a premise that if true is necessarily true, and if false is necessarily false. But he points out that this truth is asserted only indirectly and by implication. There is a great difference, he argues, between (i) declaring dogmatically that the church has the power to do something and anathematizing those who deny this and (ii) tacitly presupposing that the church has this power by making a decree of reform. What Guerrero and his fellow proponents are advocating is an action of the second kind. The church already grants dispensations from certain impediments without condemning those, such as Thomas Aquinas, who considered them to be indispensible. Moreover, it is not the case that there are as many presupposed doctrines of possibility as there are impediments to marriage, for all the impediments of ecclesiastical law presuppose one and the same legislative power. And even if the decree of invalidation did presuppose a peculiar possibility, Guerrero argues, the problem would not be fatal, for very few of the prelates and only two of the *theologi minores* denied that the church had the *power* to invalidate. Many argued that invalidation would not be expedient, but that is a matter not of dogma but of fact (*res facti*), for which a simple majority (*maior pars*) would suffice.[293]

According to the recorded proceedings, Guerrero said that clandestine marriages and marriages contracted without parental consent were "evil of themselves" (*mala de se*) inasmuch as they were evil in the majority of cases (*in pluribus*). As such, they could be rendered null and void.[294] This observation reflects the assumption of some opponents that clandestine marriages could not justly be rendered null and void unless they were intrinsically evil. The fact that something had merely contingent evil consequences was not sufficient grounds, they contended, for making it illegal. In response, Guerrero schematizes the moral categories. Some actions are intrinsically indifferent but may be bad or good according to circumstances, such as

---

[291] Objection 3, 367r [191].   [292] 364r [187].   [293] 368r [193].

[294] Granatensis, CT 9:689/25–26 (2nd draft): "Item matrimonia clandestina de se sunt mala, et similiter contrahere absque licentia parentum.…" Granatensis, 781/7–8 (3rd draft): "Probavit, quod clandestina sunt de se mala, cum ut in pluribus sint mala; ergo, convenienter irritantur."

picking up a stick,[295] whereas other actions are intrinsically good or evil (*de se*). But one must make two further distinctions. Some intrinsically evil actions are necessarily and always evil, whereas others are usually evil but are good in exceptional circumstances. Likewise, some intrinsically good actions are necessarily and always good, whereas others are usually good but are evil in exceptional circumstances. Now, every just human law is beneficial not in all but only in the majority of cases, and special dispensations can be made in exceptional cases. Clandestine marriages and marriages without parental consent, then, are intrinsically evil in the sense that they are usually evil but are good in exceptional circumstances.[296] When necessary, a bishop can remove responsibility for overseeing a marriage contract from the parents to himself and take the place of the bride's father by giving her away.[297]

20.6.3 *The five-step argument*

Guerrero maintains that one may intelligibly construe any marriage solely as a contract, even when that marriage happens also to be a sacrament in the proper sense.[298] His entire argument depends on that premise. Thus, one may regard even a Christian marriage solely in respect of its contractuality (*ratio contractus*), which is by its very nature subject to natural and civil law. One may disregard its sacramentality (*ratio sacramenti*), which is exclusively subject to inalterable divine law. Such was the method that Adrian Florensz and Ruard Tapper used to show how the church had the power to introduce diriment personal impediments (Sections 20.2.3 and 20.2.4). But this conceptual separation would not be relevant, Guerrero notes, if the distinction were *merely* conceptual. To prove that there is a "real distinction," one has to show that the contract can be separated from the sacrament in fact.[299] To that end, it suffices to show that marrying is sometimes a non-sacramental contract, especially if that separation occurs among God's people, including the Jews of the Old Covenant, and above all if it occurs among Christians. Guerrero reviews several circumstances in which marriage is only a contract and not a sacrament in the proper sense. In some of these it is a sacrament in the broad sense – that is, a sign instituted to signify a sacred reality (*signum sacrae rei*) – but I shall ignore that complication here. Guerrero explains that he will not discuss Cajetan's theory that a marriage contracted through intermediaries is only a contract and not a sacrament. Nor will he discuss the theories of those such as William of Auvergne and certain *moderni* – presumably Melchor Cano and other doctors of Salamanca – who

---

[295] This is the standard scholastic example, which Thomas Aquinas cites in *Summa theologiae* I-II.18.8, resp. (817b).

[296] Premise 7 (6), 359r–v [160–61]. Cf.   [297] Objections 5–7 (4–6), 369r–370r [194–96].

[298] Guerrero introduces the distinction between contract and sacrament as the third premise (347r [156–57]), and he posits their real separability as the fourth premise (347v [157–58]).

[299] Likewise, Clodiensis, CT 9:704/13–17, argued that the distinction was real and not merely conceptual.

attribute the sacramentality of marriage (*ratio sacramenti*) to the priestly blessing. Such theories are too controversial for his purpose. Having set them aside, Guerrero argues that marriage would have been a contract but not a sacrament in the proper sense if human beings had remained in the original, sinless condition. In the actual world, all marriages before Christ, even among God's people, were merely contractual, as are all marriages after Christ between non-Christians or between a Christian and a non-Christian. Again, Protestants who marry intending not to receive the sacrament, which they deny, marry only contractually, as do Catholics who marry intending only to receive some temporal benefit, even if they do not intend *not* to receive the sacrament.[300]

Having established that there is a real distinction, Guerrero asks his readers to put the sacramentality of marriage out of mind for the moment and to consider marriage simply as a contract. He claims that his chief argument at this point is not theological but "physical," or a matter of moral philosophy.[301] He reintroduces the sacramentality of marriage at the third step of his argument, but he does so only negatively, to show that it is not an obstacle to invalidation.

Guerrero posits a twofold metaphysical axiom, which he describes as a dogma that is both "Catholic and certain." God neither (a) lacks necessary things nor (b) abounds in superfluous things.[302] As Guerrero notes, the second part of the axiom is a version of the familiar scholastic maxim that God or nature does nothing in vain.[303] Guerrero's wording of these maxims suggests that he acquired them directly or indirectly from the medieval Aristotelian florilegium known as the *Parvi flores*, composed by Johannes de Fonte, O.F.M., around 1300, which was still popular in the sixteenth century.[304] Guerrero claims that one may validly argue either from expedience to possibility or from possibility to expedience, according to context, as follows:

(a) A certain action of the church can sometimes be expedient. But God is not lacking in necessary things. Therefore, the church has the power to perform the action now.

(b) The church has a certain power. But God does nothing in vain. Therefore, exercise of that power can sometimes be expedient.[305]

---

[300] 347v [157–58].   [301] 349v–350r [161–62].

[302] Conclusion 4, 363v/24–25 [186]: "... ex illo dogmate certo et catholico, quod deus neque deficit in necessariis neque abundat in superfluis." Guerrero also states the first of the two axioms at the beginning of the treatise, immediately after the introductory narrative translated earlier.

[303] 363v/19–20: "Deus autem et natura nihil faciunt frustra."

[304] Cf. Joannes de Fonte, *Parvi flores*, in J. Hamesse (ed.), *Les Auctoritates Aristotelis* (Louvain and Paris, 1974), p. 188, §168: "Natura nihil facit frustra, unde non deficit in necessariis, nec abundat in superfluis." Ibid., p. 161, §18: "Deus et natura nihil faciunt frustra." On the authorship of the collection, see J. Hamesse, "Johannes de Fonte, compilateur des Parvi Flores, le témoignage de plusieurs manuscrits de la bibliothèque vaticane," *Archivum Franciscanum Historicum* 88 (1995): 515–31.

[305] 363v/20–25: "Quare sicut valet argumentum potest expedire quandoque, ergo iam est talis potestas in ecclesia (alias enim non sufficienter esset provisum) ita valet, est potestas iam data,

Guerrero uses both lines of argument: the first to show that the church has the power to invalidate marriage, and the second to show that exercising that power can sometimes be expedient. The proposition that something "can sometimes be expedient" is hard to interpret, but Guerrero seems to construe this neutral potency in a statistical manner. Thus, whereas what is necessary always occurs and what is impossible never occurs, what is possible sometimes occurs.

The argument then proceeds in five steps, or *conclusiones*, as follows:

(i) Every commonwealth (*res publica*) or its ruler (*princeps*) has the power preemptively to render null and void both marriages contracted clandestinely and marriages contracted by minors without their parents' consent, unless a superior law or judicial authority prohibits this invalidation. This thesis follows from the axiom that God is not lacking in necessary things (i.e., God will provide what is needful).

(ii) The church, too, must possess this essentially political power.

(iii) The sacramentality of marriage does not detract from that power.

(iv) The exercising of the power "can sometimes be expedient." This thesis follows from the axiom that God and nature do nothing in vain.

(v) The exercise of the power is expedient *now*.

I shall now attempt to reconstruct Guerrero's argument for each step.

(i) Every commonwealth (*res publica*) or its ruler (*princeps*) has the power to render clandestine marriage contracts and the marriages of minors contracted without parental consent null and void, unless prohibited by a superior law or judicial authority.[306] The crux of Guerrero's argument is that every *res publica* as the term itself implies has the power to do whatever is expedient for the common good, since all particular, private goods are subordinate to that good.[307] The power to regulate contracts belongs naturally to the commonwealth, and it is a right bestowed by God. No one doubts, Guerrero maintains, that a commonwealth has the power to order that contracts are invalid unless certain solemnities or observed, or unless the parties have reached a certain age, or unless a certain number of witnesses is present.[308] This power extends to all civil contracts, ranging from bequests and sales to voluntary servitude.[309] If this is true of other contracts, why should it not be true of marriage?[310] Unlike sexual intercourse, Guerrero argues, marrying is public by its very nature. Among all the peoples of the world, no event is

---

ergo et quandoque potest expedire illa uti, ex illo dogmate certo et catholico, quod Deus neque deficit in necessariis neque abundat in superfluis."

[306] Conclusion 1, 350r–353r [162–168].   [307] 351v [164–65].

[308] 503/3–12, 27–38 [310a, 310b]. This is the converse of Tapper's argument: that because commonwealths have no such power over secular contracts, nor does the church over marriage contracts. See Ruard Tapper, *Explicationis … tomus primus*, 503/27–38 [310b], and 503/3–12 [310a].

[309] 350v [163].   [310] 352r [165–66].

more public, more celebrated, more witnessed, and more surrounded by formalities and solemnities. Marriages are contracted publicly in every well-governed commonwealth, for people need to know who has legitimately begotten whom.[311]

Guerrero discusses at length the manner in which subordinate positive human law determines what is either indifferent or not fully determined in the superordinate natural or divine law. What the superior law concedes or permits, the subordinate law may prohibit or command. Only when the superior law commands or prohibits is the subordinate law constrained from making a determination of this sort. Guerrero illustrates this legal principle with parallels from physics and logic. The influence of one and the same universal cause, such as the sun or the heavens, is indeterminate until it is determined through diverse secondary causes to result in diverse specific effects: generating another human being through a human parent, for example, or a fire through a fire. Similarly, one and the same major premise in logic can yield diverse conclusions through diverse minor premises. The opponents, Guerrero argues, fail to appreciate the flexibility of human laws in relation to natural or divine law.

The flow of determination is not arbitrary. Here, Guerrero invokes the first axiom: God is not deficient in necessary things. It follows that God will always provide the commonwealth with whatever is expedient for its welfare.[312] One must concede that the commonwealth has the power to invalidate the marriages in question, therefore, *unless* one can show that such invalidation is repugnant to natural or divine law. Now, everyone concedes that such marriages have always been and are prohibited, although at least during recent times the prohibition has not been diriment. If simple prohibition is not repugnant to the superior law, then neither is invalidation.[313] The burden of proof, therefore, is with the opponents of invalidation, and not with the proponents. Unless they can show that invalidation is repugnant to natural or divine law by using proofs based on reason or on Scripture, then one must assume that invalidation is possible.[314]

(ii) The church, too, must have the power to render clandestine marriage contracts null and void.[315] Commonwealths have the natural right to regulate contracts *unless* they are prohibited from so doing by a superior commonwealth

---

[311] Objection 11, 373r [200].

[312] Conclusion 1, 351v/2–4 [164]: "... cum non sit potestas haec supernaturalis, nec supervacanea sed potius expediens et necessaria in ipsa republica. et deus numquam deficiat in necessariis et valde expedientibus."

[313] 351v [164].

[314] Premise 1, 346v [156]. Cf. Granatensis, CT 9:781/2–6, where Guerrero argues that it is difficult to prove that the church is unable to invalidate clandestine marriages because it is difficult to prove a negative. On the contrary, those who claim that the church is not able must prove that invalidation is contrary to divine or natural law.

[315] Conclusion 2, 353v [168].

or authority, for example, by the removal of cases or by the annulling of judgments. Now, the church is the plenary authority in relation to the secular commonwealth. If an emperor has the right to suppress the marriages in question by imposing grave penalties, then he also has the right to invalidate them – "unless the church has removed such power from him." As a "son of the church," a Christian emperor will cheerfully cede the right of invalidation to the church because marriage is a sacrament.[316] The reason why the church assumes legislation and jurisdictional authority over this contract is that marriage is also a sacrament, but Guerrero puts no limitations of principle on the church's superior authority. "If the commonwealth has the power to do something," Guerrero claims, "so also does the church."[317] The church has removed to itself the essentially civil power of regulating marriage contracts and of rendering some of them null and void. Contrariwise, take whatever regulations and impediments the church has in fact imposed on marriage contracts: a commonwealth would also have the right to impose these if it were left to exercise its authority independently. The claim that the church has plenary power over the commonwealth or its prince makes sense only if one assumes that Guerrero espoused a hierocratic political theology.

   (iii) **The sacramentality of marriage does not detract from the church's power to annul clandestine marriage contracts.**[318] The opponents hold that invalidation is impossible because the church has no power to alter whatever is essential to any sacrament, such as its matter and form, which Jesus Christ instituted. Guerrero accepts the premise of the argument, but he argues that the church has exactly the same power over the validity of the sacrament of marriage as it has over the validity of the contract, and for the same reasons. Thus, the church has the same power over the sacrament as a commonwealth would have over the contract if marriage were not a sacrament. The church does not have this power inasmuch as marriage is a sacrament, but inasmuch as it is a contract. The reason is that the Gospel of Jesus Christ did not take away anything from the natural order, for grace perfects and does not destroy nature.[319] The contractuality of marriage remains intact and is naturally subject to the same conditions, just as the water of baptism is still water.[320] The church may invalidate marriage as a contract, and if there is no contract there is no sacrament, "for

---

[316] Conclusion 1, 353r [167].

[317] Conclusion 2, 353v/6–7 [168]: "si enim respublica quaecumque potest, ergo et ecclesia." Cf. Granatensis, CT 9:644/18–19: "Princeps saecularis posset irritare matrimonia clandestina, ergo a fortiori ecclesia." Likewise, Leriensis, CT 9:661/11–14; Legionensis, 665/23–25; Lancianensis, 699/16–18; Clodiensis, 704/19; Bracarensis, 697/19–20.

[318] Conclusion 3, 353v–363v [168–86].

[319] Cf. Granatensis, CT 9:644/25–27: "Nec his contrariatur, quod dicitur matrimonium esse sacramentum, quia gratia non destruit, sed perficit naturam."

[320] Premise 4, 347v–348r [158]. Conclusion 3, 353v–354v [168–69].

marriage considered as a contract is prior both in reality and conceptually to the sacrament, which presupposes it. Thus, whatever power the church has over marriage as a contract, it also has *in consequence* over marriage as a sacrament."[321] To illustrate this point, Guerrero asks the reader to reflect on two imaginary scenarios. Suppose that some other secular contract, such as a sale or a donation, were raised to the level of a sacrament. Again, suppose that someone prevented the sacrament of eucharist from taking place by intervening and turning the bread or wine into some other stuff.[322] As we have seen, Antonio Corrionero de Babilafuente, bishop of Almería, proposed the latter illustration during the proceedings.[323]

To corroborate the third thesis, Guerrero reviews the history of the impediments of relationship.[324] The church has historically both extended and reduced the impediments of consanguinity at different times, and the church has even invented new impediments, such as those of spiritual relationship, legal relationship, crime, and public honesty. These did not come from the natural law or from the divine law of the Leviticus code.[325] Whenever the church introduced an impediment of relationship, it rendered persons illegitimate or incapable (*inhabiles*) of marrying who had previously been legitimate and capable, and it prevented marriages that would hitherto have been valid sacraments.[326]

Some object that such impediments must be based on some quality that inheres in the persons, such as their being first cousins, and that the impediments must already exist in the persons before they contract marriage. The defect of clandestinity, they argue, pertains to how marriage is contracted and entails no inherent quality. But they exaggerate the difference, Guerrero argues. What inherent quality comes between the spouses in the more remote degrees of blood relationship, or in spiritual or legal relationship, or in public honesty?[327] Moreover, the impediments of relationship are imposed not because of anything that exists prior to the contract but in view of the consequences of the contract, especially the goods that accrue from exogamy. Clandestine marriages and the marriages of minors without parental consent, too, are prohibited because of the consequences of the contract.[328] Just as

---

[321] Conclusion 3, 354r/14–17 [169]: "Matrimonium enim in ratione contractus est prius re aut ratione ipso sacramento et illi praesupponitur, quare quaecumque potest ecclesia super matrimonium, ut est contractus, ex consequenti potest ut est sacramentum."

[322] 354v [169].   [323] Almeriensis, 722/15–18.   [324] Cf. Granatensis, CT 9:644/21–25.

[325] 354v–355r [170–71].   [326] 354r [169].

[327] Lancianensis, CT 9:699/10–14, countered that a spiritual relationship (acquired through sponsoring a baptism) comes to exist in the persons not from nature but only through the church's institution. Likewise, Iustinopolitanus, 706/29–31, countered that *cognatio legalis* (acquired through adoption) has no enduring inherent cause in the persons. Cf. Granatensis, CT 9:690/ 3–7: If one who contracts marriage with a blood relation is *inhabilis* because the consanguinity remains in him, how much more *inhabilis* is the one who has within himself the disorder of wishing only to follow his lust without obeying either the church or his parents.

[328] 355v–357r [171–74].

the purpose of the impediments of relationship is to prevent enmity and to extend friendship through exogamy, so the purpose of prohibiting the marriages in question is to prevent scandals and enmity.[329]

(iv) **The exercising of that power can sometimes be expedient** (*"potest expedire quandoque"*). Here, Guerrero applies the second axiom. Since the church has the power to invalidate the marriages in question, the exercise of that power can sometimes be expedient. "Such a power would be in vain if its use and execution were not sometimes permitted and expedient," for "God and nature do nothing in vain."[330]

(v) **The exercising of that power is expedient** *now*. The marriages in question are extremely harmful, and simple prohibition has proved ineffective. Invalidation is the only remedy. Moreover, only a general council, with its universality, the broad range of expertise that it represents, and its special authority, has the authority to raise the level of prohibition to invalidation. If invalidation is expedient in the present age, therefore, enacting such a law *now* is urgently expedient.[331]

The errors in question undermine all the goods and goals of marriage, Guerrero claims. Consider Augustine's three goods of marriage: faith, offspring, and sacrament. As a result of clandestinity or lack of parental consent, the offspring are illegitimate, fidelity is missing, and the sacrament is profaned by sacrilege. Marriage is supposed to reconcile families and to extend peace, but these marriages cause disputes, dissent, and enmity, especially among noble families. People are murdered, witnesses perjure themselves, and fathers die from grief. Moreover, such marriages often turn out badly, leading to mutual hatred or adultery. Elsewhere, Guerrero cites covert prior contract as the most serious hazard of clandestine marriage. There is no remedy in such cases, and invalidation is the only way to prevent the abuse.[332] This was the classic example of the dangers of clandestinity, which Hugh of Saint-Victor had expounded at length in the 1130s,[333] and it was the only hazard specifically cited in the decree *Tametsi*.

20.6.4 *Guerrero's theory of laws*

Guerrero's theory of laws is broadly Thomistic, and he cites Thomas to substantiate several of the key points of his argument. No other schoolman is cited more than twice in the treatise, whereas Guerrero cites fifteen texts from Thomas explicitly: two from the *Summa theologiae* and the others from Thomas's *Scriptum* on Book IV of Peter Lombard's *Sentences*. Guerrero could have found the latter in the posthumous *Supplementum* to the *Summa*, but in fact he provides references to the *Scriptum* itself.

---

[329] 399v [178].   [330] 346r [155].   [331] 364r [187].   [332] 359v–360r [178–79].
[333] Hugh of Saint-Victor, *De sacramentis christianae fidei* II.11.6, PL 176:488C–490D.

Most of the passages from Thomas that Guerrero cites pertain to the rightful power of human authorities, whether secular or ecclesiastical, to make positive laws. Two texts, taken together, seem in retrospect to contain the germ of Guerrero's own theory. In one, from a discussion of nonage, Thomas says that marriage is "subject to the ordination of positive law, as are other contracts."[334] In the other, Thomas considers a complex objection to the church's ability to introduce impediments, one strand of which is that no impediments can be introduced because marriage is a divinely instituted sacrament. In his reply, Thomas points out that marriage, unlike the other sacraments, is not *only* a sacrament, and that positive human law must adapt to the changing circumstances of human kind.[335] Guerrero deduces from these texts that human law may prohibit what natural or divine law concedes or permits.[336]

Guerrero follows Thomas in maintaining that human law introduces precepts of right and wrong where the natural law is indifferent.[337] The purpose of human law, nevertheless, is to embody and to realize the natural law. Human laws that are close to the natural law are derived from it in a quasi-deductive manner, but most positive laws arise through a process of "determination," whereby the extremely general principles of the natural law are applied to particular situations and circumstances in a particular community.[338] The more distant the laws are in relation to the first principles of the natural law, the more they are prone to exceptions. Positive laws are beneficial only in the majority of cases, therefore, and they are capable of dispensation.[339]

Guerrero, like Thomas, emphasizes that the church's laws must adapt to current exigencies. Only natural or divine laws are perpetual, whereas human laws, even those of the church, are and must be changeable.[340] Some of the opponents objected that by invalidating the marriages in question the church would be agreeing with the Protestant heretics and implicitly committing the same heresy. Guerrero replied at Trent that whereas the Protestants claimed that the *natural law* invalidated clandestine marriages, the council was proposing that the *church* should invalidate clandestine marriages. This policy would affirm precisely what the Protestants deny: that the church has legal authority over marriage.[341] In the treatise, Guerrero refutes arguments purporting to show that the necessary conditions of

---

[334] Thomas Aquinas, *IV Sent.* 36.un.5, resp. (Vivès 11:185a).

[335] *IV Sent.*, 34.un.1, ad 4 (164b). [336] Objection 11, 374r–v (201).

[337] Aristotle, *Nicomachean Ethics* V.7, 1134b18–35. Thomas Aquinas, *Sententia Libri Ethicorum* V, lect. 12, on 1134b18–19 (*Opera omnia*, Leonine edition, 47.2:304–05); *III Sent.* 37.un.3, ad 2 (ed. Moos, 3:1245).

[338] Thomas Aquinas, *IV Sent.* 26.2.2, ad 1 (Vivès, 11:73a) and 36.un.1, ad 3 (181a).

[339] *IV Sent.* 15.3.2, qua 1, resp. (ed. Moos, 712, §423).

[340] Objection 2, 366v–367r [190–92]. Cf. Granatensis, CT 9:644/28–29: "Respondit ad id, quod dicitur, numquam id fuisse factum in ecclesia: quia nihil fieret de novo, si semper attenderetur ad ea tantum, quae facta sunt."

[341] Granatensis, CT 9:781/11–15.

marriage are unchanging, and he ridicules the opponents for using them. They argue, for example, that if the church were able to invalidate the marriages in question, she would have done so before,[342] and even that marriage is a natural rather than a civil contract.[343] Guerrero marvels that they cannot grasp how weak such arguments are.[344] Everything that the church does or teaches changes and evolves over time according to the circumstances of each place and each era. Even the truth about God is revealed and made explicit only gradually and partially at appropriate times and places under the providential guidance of the Holy Spirit.[345]

Guerrero is especially interested in the determination of human or ecclesiastical laws in relation to their foundations in natural or divine law. Human or ecclesiastical law has the power to prohibit or command what natural or divine law concedes or permits. In developing the first of his five conclusions, as we have seen, Guerrero argues that the proposed decree would determine natural or divine law by changing concession into prohibition. He likens this determination to what happens when a universal cause, such as the sun or the heavens, works through a secondary cause, such as a generating parent or a fire.[346] Guerrero extends this simile later in the treatise to illumine the natural progression from simple prohibition to invalidation. When a universal physical cause prohibits something, it may concur with a secondary cause that causes what is prohibited, or it may prevent that outcome. For example, although God prohibits evil acts, he usually concurs with their secondary causes, but he sometimes intervenes miraculously, as when he prevented the three men from being consumed in the fiery furnace (Dan 3:19–27). In the same way, the church formerly concurred with the clandestine marriage contracts that it prohibited, but there is nothing to prevent the church from invalidating them now. God also bestows something akin to his universal power on the commonwealth and on the church, to which the actions of individuals are subordinated. Whether in the workings of nature or of grace, therefore, and whether in the universe as a whole or in the body politic as a whole, God disposes everything sweetly and everything is coordinated, just as a hand or other member of the human body does not act without the subject's consent and concurrence.[347]

Guerrero pursues a different but not incompatible approach in developing the third of the five theses. The proposed decree, which invalidates marriages contracted clandestinely or without parental consent, determines natural or divine law. Nevertheless, the superior law is not merely indifferent. There are three possibilities to be

---

[342] Objection 1, 365r–366r [188–90]. Guerrero develops this argument in his reply to objection 12, 376r–v [205–207].

[343] Objection 10, 371r [197].

[344] Ibid., 371v/15–16 [198]: "Mirum est, quod hii homines non intelligant suarum rationum fragilitatem."

[345] Objection 1, 366v/17–20 [190]: "Sic spiritus sanctus docet ecclesiam omnem veritatem suis locis et temporibus prout ipsi expedit scire, non omnia simul, sed ordinate et quando necessarium est...."

[346] Conclusion 1, 350r–351r [162–64].   [347] Objection 4, 368v–369r [193–94].

considered. Natural or divine law may (1) concede or permit people to marry thus, or (2) command them to so do, or (3) prohibit them from doing so. Obviously, the superior law in this case does not command, for then even the church's current prohibitive prohibition of clandestine marriages would be iniquitous. Nor can the higher law concede or permit clandestine marriage, for in that case the church would be free to *command* people to marry clandestinely or without parental consent, by determining at the lower level what is indefinite at the higher level. The only possibility that remains, therefore, is that natural or divine law *prohibits* the marriages in question without invalidating them. That being so, what prevents the church from further determining the superior law by raising the level of prohibition to invalidation?[348]

Until the appendix, Guerrero treats natural and divine law as an unanalyzed inclusive disjunction, and he treats human law and ecclesiastical law in the same way. Guerrero resolves this lack of definition at the end of the treatise, when he explains the multiple senses of the term "divine law." It becomes clear now that natural law and what he calls positive divine law are both branches of divine law,[349] and that civil law and ecclesiastical law, likewise, are both branches of human law. Guerrero explains that a species or branch of law gets its name from the legislator. Human laws are made by human beings. Divine laws are made by God.[350] This is a departure from Thomas in the *Summa theologiae*, who defines the branches teleologically: Human law leads to the natural, temporal perfection of human beings as human beings, whereas divine law leads to eternal beatitude.[351]

In the order of created reality, Guerrero explains, everything is the work of God in a broad sense, but some things are more properly said to be God's work than others, for God works on three levels. First, God makes some things without working through secondary, created causes. God makes the angels, the heavens, the four elements, and human souls in this way, and he justifies existing souls in the same unmediated manner. Second, God sometimes works through creatures to achieve things that are beyond their powers. In some cases, as in the miracle of the fiery furnace, the power that God supernaturally bestows is natural *per se*. In others, as with the sacraments, God bestows supernatural powers on created things.[352] Third, God sometimes works through secondary natural causes in a natural way, using the innate powers that he instilled in them by creating them. Such are the mundane

---

[348] Conclusion 3, 359v–361r [178–80].

[349] 381v/18–19 [215]: "Est etiam ius divinum duplex, naturale scilicet sive naturae, et positivum, quod vocatur ut condistinguatur naturali." Medieval theologians usually reserve the term "positive" for human laws in contradistinction to natural law.

[350] Objection 12, 381r–v [215].   [351] Thomas Aquinas, *Summa theologiae* I-II.91.4 (1212a).

[352] Guerrero is presupposing the theory that the sacraments are physical instrumental causes, which the Dominicans espoused. The Franciscans preferred the theory of covenantal or moral causality.

physical motions of generation and corruption. These, too, are works of God, but they are less properly so than works of the first and second kinds.[353]

Similarly, all law is divine law in the broadest sense, but some branches of law are more properly called divine than others. First, God promulgates some laws directly, without using human mediators. Such is the Decalogue and the natural law: both the natural law that human beings share with all animals and the *ius gentium*. Such, too, are the laws that God reveals directly to angels, prophets, and holy persons, inasmuch as he reveals them thus. Second, God sometimes uses human beings as messengers (*nuncii, praecones*), who announce his laws to the people. Then an angel or a prophet begins by saying, "Thus says the Lord," and St Paul says, "The Lord says, not I" (1 Cor 7:10). Such laws are properly called laws of God (*leges Dei*) or divine laws (*iura divina*), although human beings announce them. Third, God sometimes appoints human beings to make their own laws, endowing them with the necessary power. Then they are not messengers but legislators. St Paul says, "I say, not the Lord" (1 Cor 7:12). Moses, too, promulgated precepts in his own name (*suo nomine*). Kings and other secular legislators have this role, as well as prophets and apostles, for all regulatory power comes from God (Rom 13:1–7). These human laws, too, are divine, but in a secondary sense. Moreover, some of them deserve the term "divine" more than others. Canon laws are more properly called divine than civil or political laws because they are more closely related to the supernatural law revealed in Scripture, and because they are more immediately directed to the supernatural end of human beings. Even within the field of ecclesiastical law, laws that regulate matters that are more spiritual or more arduous, such as those regarding fasting and almsgiving, are more properly called divine than the other ecclesiastical laws.[354]

Just as civil laws determine and are subordinate to the law of nature, Guerrero claims, so ecclesiastical laws determine and are subordinate to divine law. "Ecclesiastical or canon laws," he writes, "are related to the supernatural law of God as civil laws are to the law of nature."[355]

20.7 THE THIRD DRAFT

The legates presented the third version of the draft decrees on marriage on September 5, and the prelates voted on them in seven general congregations (September 7–12). They spoke more briefly than before, for most of what they needed to say had already been said. No new substantive arguments emerged. Nevertheless, many did not limit themselves to saying *placet* or *non placet*, as the legates wanted them to do at this stage, and several opponents took the opportunity to claim yet again that the church had no power to do what was being proposed.

---

[353] 382r–v [216–17].   [354] 382v–383r [217–19].
[355] 383v/1–2 [219]: "Habent enim se ecclesiastica seu canonica iura ad legem Dei supernaturalem, ut civilia ad legem naturae.…"

In the third draft, the decree *Tametsi* is relocated as the second of the canons on abuses (*super abusibus*). The first of these canons, as in the second draft, explains the proper procedures for marrying and confirms the policy associated with the Fourth Lateran Council. After the banns, the couple proceeds to the celebration of their marriage *in facie ecclesiae*, when the parish priest interrogates the partners to establish their free consent. Once that has been established, the priest should say, "'I join you together in matrimony in the name of the Father, the Son, and the Holy Spirit,' *or use other words according to the received rite of each church [ecclesia]*."[356] The provision for alternatives (indicated here in italics) is new. It was a response to the concern of several prelates that insisting on the formula "*Ego vos coniungo*" might imply that this was the sacramental form and that the priest was the instrumental minister, although this procedure is prescribed only as a recommended norm and not as condition of validity.

The second canon is the decree *Tametsi*. Two alternative versions are provided: a revised version of the original, and a new version. I shall paraphrase the revised original version first, with the only significant modification in italics: Although (*tametsi*) there is no doubt that clandestine marriages contracted with the free consent of the partners are valid and true (present tense), albeit only "*as long as the church wished them to be valid*" (past tense: "*quamdiu ecclesia ea rata esse voluit*"): a new qualification. The church justly condemns those who claim that such marriages are false, as well as those who claim that parents can annul marriages of marriages contracted secretly without their consent, nevertheless (*nihilominus*) the church is acutely aware that clandestine marriages have given rise to many evils, especially cases of covert prior contract, and the church desires to eradicate such marriages. After this long narrative introduction, constructed as before around the idiom "*tametsi ... nihilominus*," comes the new policy. In future, the church will render those who attempt to contract marriages secretly (*clam*), rather than in the presence of at least three witnesses, incapable (*inhabiles*) of marrying, and the contract null and void. Likewise, the church will render sons under the age of eighteen and daughters under the age of sixteen who try to marry without parental consent incapable (*inhabiles*) of marrying, and the contract null and void, although they may appeal to an episcopal judge if their parents' resistance is unreasonable.[357] The anathema of the first version is restored to some extent through a description of the church's current position.[358]

---

[356] *Canon super abusibus* 1, 762/44–763/29. For the formula, see 763/5–7.

[357] 763/30–764/12. The term *inhabiles* appears at 763/46 (on clandestine marriage) and 764/2 (on marriage without parental consent).

[358] 761/29–32 (also 763/31–34, in the new version of *Tametsi*): "... et proinde iure damnandi sint illi, ut eos sancta synodus *anathemate damnat*, qui ea vera ac rata esse negant, quique falso affirmant, matrimonia, a filiis familias sine consensu parentum contracta, irrita esse, et parentes ea rata vel irrita facere posse...." Compare the third draft, 683/2–5: "... ac proinde iure damnandi sunt illi, prout ab hac sacrosancta synodo damnantur, qui huiusmodi matrimonia vera ac rata esse negant, quique falso affirmant, matrimonia a filiisfamilias clam sive alio quocumque modo sine parentum consensu facta parentum voluntate irritari posse...."

The heresy is now identified as declaring such marriages invalid as long as the church still considered them to be valid.

The age of majority is brought back to eighteen for boys and sixteen for girls, as in the first draft. The rationale behind the raising or lowering of the age of majority is not explicit in the proceedings, but it reflected a difference of rationale. If the purpose of requiring parental consent was to permit parents to manage their assets and to control kinship in the interests of familial well-being and the common good, it would be better to have no age limit. Failing that, the threshold age should be as high as was consistent with adulthood and independence. But if children needed parental consent because of their immaturity – because they were imprudent, inconsiderate, lacking in discernment and foresight, gullible, slaves to their passions, and so forth – then a lower age of majority was appropriate.

The promulgation clause requires, as before, that bishops should make sure that the decree is published in the parish churches of their dioceses as soon as possible in the first year, and again as often as seems expedient. But the clause now specifies, too, that the decree "shall begin to take effect in each parish after thirty days, to be counted from the first day of publication in the same parish."[359]

The new version of *Tametsi* shares some of those revisions but it includes several innovations of its own, and it was substantially reconfigured.[360] It, too, interpolates the phrase, "*as long as the church wished them to be valid*" in the description of existing policy, and it notes that the council condemns *with anathema* those who either deny that freely contracted clandestine marriages are true and valid or hold that parents can annul the marriages of minors made without their consent. The new version of the decree then incorporates the norms of the first canon *super abusibus*. Having noted the perils of clandestinity, the decree explains that this council, following in the footsteps of Lateran IV, requires the parish priest to announce the banns on three successive feast days. There is provision for the parish priest to modify or even to waive the reading of the banns in special circumstances. If no lawful impediment comes to light, the partners should marry *in facie ecclesiae*, where the priest should interrogate them and then either say, "I join you together in matrimony in the name of the Father, the Son, and the Holy Spirit" or use "other words, according to the received rite of each church." The essential requirement comes next. Henceforth, the council renders persons incapable (*inhabiles*) of marriage and their contract null and void unless they marry in the presence of the parish priest (or his properly designated representative) and of two or three witnesses. The decree adds some further norms of good practice. The spouses should not begin to live together until their marriage has been blessed by the parish priest, and the parish priest should record their names and the names of the witnesses, with the date and place, in a book reserved for this purpose. Couples should confess and attend eucharist before they marry or, failing that, at least three days before they

---

[359] 764/10–12.   [360] 761/23–762/43.

consummate their marriage (a vestige of the Tobias Nights), as well as observing whatever other salutary customs are practiced in their region. The clause on promulgation is the same as in the revised-original version except that the decree is to come into effect twenty (rather than thirty) days after its first publication in each parish.

As regards what was required for a valid marriage, the new decree was different in two substantive respects. First, the presence of the parish priest (or his designated representative) was required, as well as the presence of witnesses. Some of the prelates even during discussion of the first draft, as we have seen, had proposed that the presence of a priest should be required, or, better, the presence of the parish priest, as well of lay witnesses. Only his presence as official witness was strictly necessary, however, and not his ritual actions or words of solemnization. Second, parental consent was *not* required, although the *tametsi* clause still noted that the church condemned and anathematized those who held that the marriages of minors made without parental consent were invalid.

In the voting that followed, prelates referred to the new decree both as the second form (*forma secunda*)[361] and as the version that invalidated all (*omnia*) clandestine marriages, or that eliminated them entirely (*omnino*). Some 134 prelates endorsed the invalidation of clandestine marriage, whereas 60 opposed it.[362] Seventy-six of the proponents said that they preferred the new version (although some of them said that they could accept either version), and fifty-two expressed no preference. Only five of them preferred the revised-original version. The opponents expressed no preference regarding the two versions of the decree. Cristoforo Madruzzo said that to require parental consent would comply with civil law but would transgress divine law, which protected the freedom of sons and daughters in contracting marriage.[363]

Why did the legates or those responsible for drafting the decrees propose this alternative? Nothing in the recorded *acta* provides an answer to that question. According to one modern account, Cardinal Morone devised it as a way to reconcile the two sides.[364] If that was his intention, however, he failed, for the ratio between proponents and opponents remained the same. Nor, it seems, would he have had any reason to expect the opponents to find the new version more acceptable than the revised-original version. Perhaps this was the version that Cardinal Morone and the other legates were willing to support or, at least, not to oppose.

Why did the proponents quietly accept that parental consent would not be required? During the discussion of the first two drafts, several proponents of invalidation had tried to show that parental consent was both urgently expedient and

---

[361] In the printed edition of the *acta*, the new version appears first (761, at n. 5) and is labeled as the first version (*prima forma*), but it is clear that the prelates refer to the new version, and not to the revised-original version, as *forma secunda*.

[362] According to Bernhard, Lefebvre, and Rapp, *L'Époque de la réforme* (Paris, 1989), pp. 257–58, 134 prelates out of 203 endorsed the decree, with great majority opting for the new version, whereas 63 were hostile to the decree and rejected both versions.

[363] Madrutius, 779/41–44.

[364] J. Bossy, *Christianity in the West 1400–1700* (Oxford, 1985), 24–25.

inscribed in natural and divine law and in Scripture. Moreover, the argument about the subordination of individual choice to the common good presupposed that parents were the link between the commonwealth and their sons and daughters and would control their choice of spouses. But now a plurality of proponents voted in favor of the new version, and there was little mention of parental consent. Even the Cardinal of Lorraine, who voted first, did not object to the removal of the parental consent requirement, although the King of France had demanded it. He said only that he preferred the second version, but that he could accept the first if a majority of prelates preferred it.[365] Martin Baudouin, bishop of Ypres, said that the second version displeased him less than the first because he could not accept that the marriages of minors contracted without parental consent should be rendered invalid. He still found the arguments against clandestine marriages unconvincing, although he would say nothing about the power of the church to invalidate them, and he conceded that invalidation was not a matter of dogma.[366]

Most of the proponents must have considered the presence of the parish priest more important than parental consent, although some would have preferred both. They had good reason. On the one hand, the new decree satisfied the widely held conviction that marriages ought to be solemnized by ministers in church, and it must have gone some way toward appeasing even those, such as Thomas Goldwell, who considered marriage to be a religious rite. On the other hand, because the decree also required the parish priest to read the banns and to join the couple and bless their union (although these formalities were not necessary for validity), it would now be virtually impossible for minors to marry without their parents' knowledge, and much more difficult for them to marry without their parents' consent. At the same time, the decree preserved the appearance of *solus consensus* by limiting the necessary role of the parish priest to his presence as a witness and by eliminating the need for the consent of anyone other than the spouses. The new decree was the more comprehensive of the two options – which may partly explain why the prelates characterized this as the version that would invalidate *all* clandestine marriages.

Nevertheless, there were signs of an incipient crisis during the general congregations on the third draft as prelates faced the fact that arguments for and against invalidation were not going to achieve anything.[367] Some opponents still insisted that the decree presupposed a matter of dogma, which could not be settled with more than fifty prelates opposed to it. Several prelates, including Daniello Barbaro, patriarch of Aquileia (a proponent), and Giovanni Trevisan, Patriarch of Venice (an opponent), proposed that in such circumstances no conclusion could be reached and the matter would have to be referred to the pope for his decision.[368]

---

[365] Card. Lotharingus, 779/27–28.   [366] Hyprensis, 791/38–41.
[367] Le Bras, "Mariage," 2239–40.
[368] Aquilegiensis, 780/13–15. Venetus, 780/17–20. Archiep. Verallus, 781/26–28. Feltrensis, 791/4–6. Civitatis Castelli, 791/27–28. Praemisliensis, 793/18–19. Urbevetanus, 793/39–40.

Two of the Spanish prelates spoke forcefully against that proposal. Pedro Guerrero, who assumed that the role of the papacy in a general council was limited to convening it, pointed out that the very purpose of a general council was to solve difficult questions, and that the pope had convened this council to that end. If the invalidation of clandestine marriage entailed a matter of dogma, Guerrero argued, then only a general council was capable of making that determination. If it was a matter of reform, the only question was whether that reform was expedient, and there was no better forum for that decision than a general council. It was pointless to cite old laws, for a general council was capable of changing human laws according to the needs of the time. To say that the council should refer the question to the pope was the same as saying that no action should taken.[369] Martín Pérez de Ayala, bishop of Segovia, elaborated Guerrero's argument. The pope is present *virtually* at the council, he argued, both by convening it and through the representation of his legates. To refer a matter from the council to the pope, therefore, would be to refer it from the pope *with* his council to the pope alone, which was pointless. Clandestine marriages should be eradicated because they were "against justice, against honor, and against the church both eastern and western." The disagreement among the prelates was not a sufficient reason for abandoning the effort to reach a determination regarding such an important matter. Even in matters of dogma, the majority always prevailed. The bishop asked the legates to urge those claiming that the church lacked the power to invalidate clandestine marriages to put their arguments in writing so that they would be easier to follow and to refute.[370] Because those arguments were straightforward and traditional and had been stated again and again, one has to assume that Martín Pérez de Ayala was trying to scare his opponents.

The opponents continued to make the same objections as before. Cardinal Madruzzo said that although he would not say whether the church had the power to invalidate such marriages, he marveled that many prelates were willing to accept the invalidation of clandestine marriages, which entailed many difficulties, rather than suppressing them with heavier penalties.[371] Many opponents continued to demand that the third dogmatic canon of the first draft (the anathema) should be restored.[372] Although most of those who explained their position declined to argue that the church did not have the power to invalidate clandestine marriages, they argued that exercising that power would be rash and overly novel, that the theological presuppositions were still uncertain, and that the policy would imply

[369] Granatensis, 780/39–45: "Idem autem est dicere: *Remittatur Papae*, quam: *Nihil fiat*."
[370] Segobiensis, 785/39–786/3.   [371] Madrutius, 779/44–47.
[372] Madrutius, 779/34. Hierosolymitanus, 780/10. Venetus, 780/16. Archiep. Verallus, 781/24. Materanus, 782/9. Nicosiensis, 782/32. Panormitanus, 782/50. Barensis, 783/13. Pientinus, 783/23. Cavensis, 783/16. Cattarensis, 783/21. Milopotamensis, 783/28–29. Catanensis, 783/31. Marsicensis, 784/12. Britonoriensis, 784/23. Castrensis, 784/31. Racanatensis, 784/47. Cenetensis, 785/5. Bovensis, 786/18. Segniensis, 786/44. Lesiensis, 787/7. Lucerinus, 787/41. Ilcinensis, 788/8. Larinensis, 788/28. S. Leonis, 788/33–34. Clusinus, 790/21. Comensis, 790/42. Troianus, 792/10. Paphensis, 793/1. Pennensis, 793/27. Gen. Iesuitarum, 794/30.

agreement with the Protestant heretics. Invalidation would be inexpedient. Instead, they proposed harsher penalties as the remedy. They also questioned whether invalidation would have the beneficial consequences presumed by the proponents.[373] Giovanni Battista Castagna, archbishop of Rossano, pointed out that the decree conflated proof with validity, and he wanted to preserve the traditional distinction between invalidity before God and invalidity before the church. He proposed that the imposition of more severe penalties, even including excommunication, was the only appropriate remedy.[374]

Several prelates on both sides still objected to the formula "*Ego vos coniungo*" and wanted it to be removed, even though allowance was now made for regional alternatives. Most did not state their reasons, but Cristoforo Madruzzo probably spoke for most when he objected that these words might seem to constitute the form of the sacrament.[375] Pietro de Petris, bishop of Lucera, proposed that the decree should require only that marriages "should be contracted *in facie ecclesiae* according to the custom of the regions."[376] Giovanni Giacomo Barba, O.S.A., bishop of Terni, suggested that the original form of the sacrament had been the husband's words, "I take you as my wife, that you shall be bone of my bones and flesh of my flesh" (Gen 2:23), but that the church had changed the form. He proposed that the priest should now say, "May the Lord complete what he has begun in you."[377] The general of the Augustinians, Christophori Patavin, had proposed the same formula during voting on the second draft.[378]

20.8 THE FOURTH DRAFT AND SESSION XXIV

When the legates presented the fourth draft, on October 13, it included only the new, alternative version of *Tametsi*, which was now the first of ten canons on the reform of marriage (*de reformatione*).[379] Voting was predictable and required only two general congregations (October 26–27). By my count, 125 prelates endorsed the decree invalidating clandestine marriage, 51 opposed it, and 10 declined to take a position.

Although the legates wanted the prelates to confine their votes to expressions of approval (*placet*) or disapproval (*non placet*),[380] some of them still had objections

---

[373] Madrutius, 779/41–47. Archiep. Hydruntinus, 780/31–32. Florentinus, 781/17–18. Senonensis, 783/5–8. Rheginus, 783/41–44. Ierapetrensis, 784/27–28. Lesiensis, 787/38–41. Nemausensis, 790/31–32. Praemislienis, 793/20–21. Pennensis, 793/26. Urbevetanus, 793/41–794/1.
[374] Rossanensis, 781/36–40.
[375] Madrutius, 779/37–38. Archiep. Hydruntinus, 780/34. Archiep. Verallus, 781/26. Callaritanus, 782/15. Nicosiensis 782/33. Philadelphiensis, 784/16. Britonoriensis, 784/21–22. Cenetensis, 785/8. Pactensis, 785/23. Lucerinus, 787/42–44. Brixiensis, 790/39. Faventinus, 791/2–3. Gen. Iesuitarum, 794/35–36.
[376] Lucerinus, 787/42–44.
[377] Interamnensis, 784/51–785/2: "Dominus, qui incepit, ipse perficiat."
[378] Gen. Eremitarum, 739/37–38: "Quod Dominus in vobis incepit, ipse perficiat."
[379] 889/27–890/34.   [380] 902/6–7.

and incidental amendments to share. Some wanted the decree to include provision for Catholics living in regions were there were no parish priests or even no priests at all.[381] Diego Gilberto Nogueras, bishop of Alife, still pursuing a lost cause, wanted the decree to make some "mention of fathers, lest it is permitted to contract [marriage] when the parents are unwilling."[382] The bishop of Caorle (Caprulae) wanted the decree to require the presence of a notary instead of a parish priest.[383] Pedro del Frago Garcés, bishop of Ales-Terralba, objected to the qualification, "as long as the church has not rendered them invalid," and proposed instead: "as long as the church tolerated them or dissimulated."[384]

Antonio Elio, patriarch of Jerusalem, spoke forcefully against invalidation. The legates had urged the prelates to limit themselves to expressions of "*placet*" or "*non placet*," but Elio protested that such brevity was not consistent with the gravity of the matter before them. He could not endorse the decree because it entailed a "new dogma" and contradicted a "true and Catholic dogma." The anathema described in the *Tametsi* clause, notwithstanding the phrase "as long as the church did not render them invalid," expressed that Catholic truth, and dogmas were perennial and could not be altered. The contractual theory, whereby the church would invalidate the contract without touching the sacrament, was specious. In good conscience, he felt bound to state his objections again. Neither fear nor self-interest could compel him to steer to the right or to the left. He would rely only on almighty God to teach him what was true, for God "is terrible in his counsels over the sons of men" (Ps 65:5).[385]

Apart from a few minor, non-substantive alterations, the decrees of dogma and reform published on November 11 in Session XXIV were the same as those of the fourth draft.[386] By my count, 134 prelates endorsed invalidation, 55 opposed it, and 10 declined to take a position, most of them by deferring to the majority or to the judgment of the pope.[387] Most of the opponents, as before, were Italians. Giovanni Trevisan, Patriarch of Venice, voted against the decree. The Patriarch of Jerusalem and two of the legates, Ludovico Simonetta and Stanislaus Hosius, confessed that they could not endorse invalidation, but they deferred to the judgment of the pope. Among those voting *non placet* were Cardinal Cristoforo Mudruzzo (Prince-Bishop of Trent), Diego Laínez (general of the Society of Jesus), and the archbishops of Bari, Otranto, Acerenza e Matera, Palermo, Reggio Calabria, Rossano, and Nicosia. The bishops of Nicastro and Paphos endorsed all the decrees on marriage but confessed that they would have preferred not to have made any decision about clandestine marriages.[388]

---

[381] Segobiensis, 901/12–13. Mutinensis, 901/38–39. Albinganensis, 903/4–5. Atrebatensis, 903/12–13. Assaphensis, 903/17–18. Hyprensis, 904/40–41. Pisauriensis, 905/21–22. Monopolitanus, 905/37–38.

[382] Aliphanus, 905/33–34.   [383] Caprulanus, 904/36–37.   [384] Usellensis, 906/4–5.

[385] Hierosolymitanus, 902/6–32 (*votum scriptum*).   [386] 971–77.

[387] According to Le Bras, "Le mariage," 2241, 136 prelates voted in favor on invalidation, 55 were opposed, 4 elected to go with the majority, and 4 deferred to the judgment of the pope.

[388] Neocastrensis, 976/8. Paphensis, 977/32–33.

Several of the opponents took this last opportunity to articulate their objections to a reform that they would soon have to realize in their dioceses. Antonio Elio, Patriarch of Jerusalem, and Giovanni Trevisan, Patriarch of Venice, restated their objections in written votes. Antonio Elio objected that there was insufficient consensus, and that the objections of Cristoforo Madruzzo and others had not been adequately resolved. Contrary to what the proponents argued, invalidation of the contract would "touch" the sacrament by purporting to alter its inalterable form. The decree would contravene an ancient custom of the church, and it would contradict a dogma that the church has perpetually maintained.[389] Giovanni Trevisan made similar claims even more forcefully. He could not endorse the invalidation of clandestine marriages because Christ alone had the power to institute new species of sacrament. Christ had not shared that power with the church. The church had never dared to invalidate clandestine marriages in the past, knowing that the action would be inexpedient. There was no "just and rational cause" for invalidation that was "certain, indubitable, and universal."[390] Others opponents, too, objected that the decree of invalidation would "touch" the sacrament, that the church could only prohibit and could not invalidate clandestine marriages, that the new law would overturn a long-standing practice, that it was a departure from tradition and from the teachings of the great scholastic doctors, including Thomas Aquinas, that it would require the institution of the new sacramental form, and so forth.[391] The opponents who spoke out at this stage were no longer cautious about denying that the church had the necessary power.

Costantino Bonelli, bishop of Città di Castello, reduced the case for opposition to five points. First, the church has always taught that the consent of the spouses is the sufficient cause of marriage. To require in addition the presence of the parish priest and of witnesses implies that the form of the sacrament has been changed, and that what until today has been required only as proof will from tomorrow be part of the sacramental essence. Second, the decree will undermine the principle of free consent. It is contradictory to affirm that the spouses' free consent is the efficient cause of marriage but that in future it will be subject to the will of the parish priest and witnesses. Third, divine law instituted this sacrament as a remedy against concupiscence, and the church has no right to refuse this remedy. There may be no parish priest or no witnesses at a certain time and place, whereas the disease of concupiscence will always exist everywhere. Fourth, a transitory impediment or an impediment based on a transitory cause can never invalidate marriage, as almost all scholars of canon law have maintained. (Bonelli cites Innocent III's decretal, *Cum inhibitio.*)[392] Fifth, in all other cases in which the church was able to render marriage invalid, a simple prohibition was sufficient, without a decree that explicitly

---

[389] Patriarcha Hierosolymitanus, 972/7–14.   [390] Patriarcha Venetiarum, 972/17–24.
[391] Rheginus, 973/22–32. Lesinensis, 974/33–34. Larinensis, 974/54–55. Montisfalisci, 975/4–16. Feltrensis, 975/49–976/6. S. Marci, 977/24–27.
[392] X 4.3.3 (679–80).

invalidated marriage. There is no precedent for raising an impediment from a merely prohibitive prohibition to invalidation.[393]

When voting on the sacrament of marriage was complete, Cardinal Giovanni Morone, as first president, announced that all the prelates had approved the summary of doctrine and the canons on the sacrament of marriage. In fact, most had endorsed the decree on clandestine marriages, although more than fifty prelates had disapproved. One of those was Cardinal Ludovico Simonetta, apostolic legate to the Holy See, but he deferred to the judgment of the pope.[394] Opinion among the legates was divided equally, with two in favor and two against. Morone himself gave his approval, subject to that of the pope. Bernard Navagero also approved.[395] Stanislaus Hosius was unable to attend Session XXIV because of ill health, but he submitted his vote in writing on the following day. He confessed that he had to say "*non placet*" to the decree of invalidation because he could see no new reason to depart from the long-standing tradition of the church. Nevertheless, like Simonetta, he deferred to the judgment of the pope.[396]

20.9 THE MEANING OF *TAMETSI*

The decree on clandestine marriage, known today as *Tametsi*, is in two parts, although the division is easy to miss on a first reading. The first part, after a narrative preamble, defines the conditions that distinguish public from clandestine marriages:

> Although [*tametsi*] there should be no doubt that clandestine marriages made with the free consent of the contractants are valid [*rata*] and true marriages as long as the church has not rendered them invalid, so that those are justly to be condemned who deny that such marriages are true and valid and who falsely affirm that the marriages of minors [*filii familias*] contracted without the consent of their parents are invalid and that parents have the power to render them valid or invalid, nevertheless [*nihilominus*], the holy church of God for most just reasons has always detested and prohibited them. But since the holy synod recognizes that those prohibitions have proved ineffective because of human disobedience and is troubled by the grave sins that arise from those same clandestine marriages, especially those of persons who remain in a state of damnation when, having abandoned a first wife with whom they had contracted secretly, they publicly contract with another and live with her in perpetual adultery: an evil that cannot be remedied by the church (which is not able to make judgments about hidden things) unless some more efficacious remedy is applied; therefore, following in the footsteps of the sacred Lateran Council celebrated under Innocent III, it [the present council] commands that henceforth, before a marriage is contracted, the contractants' own parish priest shall announce those between whom it is to be contracted three times during solemn mass, on three successive feast days; then,

---

[393] Civitatis Castelli, 976/9–37. [394] 977/45–52. For Simonetta's vote, see CT 9:1563/31–33.
[395] Card. Navagerio, 971/34. [396] Card. Varmiensis, 1008/3–11.

after those announcements have been made, if no lawful impediment has come to light, they will proceed to the celebration of marriage before the church [*in facie ecclesiae*], where the parish priest, after the man and the woman have been questioned and their mutual consent established, shall either say, "I join you together in marriage, in the name of the Father, the Son, and the Holy Spirit," or use other words according to the received rite of each province. But if there has at some time been probable suspicion that the marriage might be maliciously prevented if it is preceded by so many announcements, then either let there be only one announcement, or at least let the marriage be celebrated in the presence of the parish priest and two or three witnesses; and then, before its consummation, let there be announcements in church, so that if there are any hidden impediments they will more easily be detected, unless in the judgment of the ordinary it is expedient to dispense with the announcements, which the holy synod leaves to his prudence and judgment. Those who attempt to contract marriage otherwise than in the presence of the parish priest — or of some other priest with the license of the parish priest or his ordinary — and of two or three witnesses: these the holy synod renders entirely incapable [*inhabiles*] of contracting thus, and it declares such contracts invalid and null, and accordingly by the present decree it renders them invalid and annuls them.[397]

This part of the decree establishes three circumstantial conditions that make a marriage public rather than clandestine: the parish priest announces the banns, he solemnizes the union, and there are at least other two witnesses (usually lay folk). The first requirement (the banns) is subject to an elaborate set of provisions for exceptional cases. It is not included among the conditions necessary for validity. Nor is solemnization necessary. The only necessary condition is the presence of the parish priest or his delegate and of at least two (other) witnesses.

The decree retains the anathema, but it states it only indirectly. It does not declare, "*Anathema sit!*" – which would not have been appropriate in a decree of reform. Instead, the decree reports, as if referring to a dogmatic canon stated elsewhere (although it had been removed), that the church anathematizes those who say that marriages contracted clandestinely or without parental consent are invalid *as long as the church still declares that they are valid*. The *tametsi* clause contains remnants of unresolved debates about the anathema, but it is sufficiently clear that the heresy of the Protestants is to claim that such marriages are invalid *when the church holds that they are valid*. The heresy in question, then, had been to jump the gun by declaring that clandestine marriages were invalid before the church herself did so. Nevertheless, an important point of doctrine was at stake here. Clandestine marriages would henceforth be invalid not by their very nature or according to divine or natural law, as the Protestants supposed, but only as a result of positive legislation by the church. Thus, the decree affirmed the ecclesiastical power that the Protestants were inclined to deny. The council did not merely *declare* that

---

[397] Tanner-Alberigo, 755–56.

clandestine marriages were invalid. Instead, it annulled them and rendered them invalid, as the final clause in the earlier quotation explicitly states. How does it do so? The decree retains the highly questionable notion of inhabilitation while adding that the church annuls the contracts. The use of an inclusive *vel* would have eliminated this flaw, although it might have diminished the rhetorical force of the decree.

The second part of the decree prescribes some corollaries and related norms:

- Penalties are imposed on priests or laypersons who participate in a marriage that does not follow the required procedures, such as one contracted in the presence of fewer witnesses or of an unauthorized priest.
- The parish priest should retain and carefully preserve a book in which he records the date and place of each marriage and the names of the spouses and the witnesses.
- Only the parish priest (or another priest licensed by the parish priest or his ordinary) is permitted to bless the couple. No other priest, secular or religious, may *join or bless* them, regardless of any ancient customs.
- Spouses should not begin to cohabit until their marriage has received the priestly blessing in a sanctuary (*in templo*).
- Couples should receive the sacraments of penance and eucharist before they marry, or, failing that, at least three days before they consummate their marriage.
- Any other nuptial practices or solemnities that are customary in the region should be observed.
- Bishops should make sure that these rules are promulgated throughout their dioceses as soon as possible during the first year, and again as often as they consider expedient. The decree will take effect thirty days after its first publication.

Priestly benediction is mentioned only in this ancillary part of decree. Whether the blessing is the same as or different from the priest's joining the partners (typically by linking their right hands), is unclear, but such vagueness may have been necessary to accommodate regional variations.

The cardinal requirement of *Tametsi* is the presence of the parish priest. The provisions of Lateran IV, too, hinged on the role of the parish priest, but now his presence is *sine qua non*. The decree makes no provision for couples belonging to two different parishes: a detail that required subsequent interpretation and elaboration by canon lawyers.[398] I have suggested earlier that the required role of the parish priest must have made it virtually impossible for minors to marry without their parents' knowledge, and much more difficult for them to marry without their parents' consent.

---

[398] A. Esmein, *Le mariage en droit canonique*, revised version, vol. 2 (Paris, 1935), 202–07.

Nevertheless, *Tametsi* did not make parental consent a necessary condition, and as a result it was not acceptable to the French. The French church refused to promulgate *Tametsi* for thirty years. The crown and the Parlement – the supreme court of France – respected the exclusive right of the church to determine the validity of marriage through canon law and through episcopal courts, but they subverted ecclesiastical law and jurisdiction by constraining the civil consequences of a valid marriage. Moreover, the Parlement effectively removed marriage litigation to itself by hearing cases appealed from the ecclesiastical courts, and it introduced new laws suppressing marriages contracted without parental consent, albeit without explicitly claiming the power to invalidate the sacrament.[399] Minors who married without parental consent could be deprived of family support and disinherited. The Ordonnance de Blois of 1579, promulgated by Henry III, adopted but supplemented Trent's requirements for a public, non-clandestine marriage, requiring four witnesses where Trent had required three, and requiring the parish priest to have proof both of the partners' ages and of the their parents' consent. Minors who married without parental consent and their accomplices were guilty of the crime of *raptus*, which was punishable by death. If the girl was unwilling, she was innocent and the man's crime was *rapt de violence*. If she was willing, she, too, was guilty and the crime was *rapt de séduction*. Canon law since the central Middle Ages had regarded the absence of the girl's consent as critical and construed *raptus* as something akin to rape in the modern sense,[400] but French civil law retained the classical notion of *raptus* as elopement, whereby a man took a girl as his wife without her father's consent. French legists, working on the basis of Roman law, justified the need for parental consent by invoking the public good, to which the wishes of individuals and couples was subordinate. The case law and legal theory that suppressed such marriages was explicitly the national law of France, which its advocates contrasted not only with the laws of other nations and also with the transnational law of the church.[401] In contrast, Spanish bishops in Spain and Mexico during the sixteenth and seventeenth centuries not only enforced *Tametsi* but also respected the right of sons and daughters to marry without their parents' consent, when necessary protecting minors from their parents. For them, too, their version of the law was a matter of national pride and identity. They accused "French Catholics of heresy because

[399] See B. B. Diefendorf, *Paris City Councillors in the Sixteenth Century* (Princeton, 1983), 155–70; and S. Hanley, "Family and State in Early Modern France: The Marriage Pact," in M. J. Boxer and J. H. Quataert, *Connecting Spheres* (Oxford, 1987), 53–63.

[400] H. Kümper, "Did Medieval Canon Marriage Law Invent our Modern Notion of Rape?" in P. Andersen et al., *Law and Marriage in Medieval and Early Modern Times* (Copenhagen, 2012), 111–25.

[401] See S. Hanley, "Engendering the State: Family Formation and State Building in Early Modern France," *French Historical Studies* 16.1 (1989): 4–27; and "The Jurisprudence of the Arrêts," *Law and History Review* 21.1 (2003): 1–40. Prof. Hanley tells me that she is currently working on a book that will trace the development of explicitly national French marriage law, emphasizing the importance of judicial decisions and legal opinions from court cases, to be entitled, *The Social Sites of Political Practice in France: Law, Litigation, and Local Knowledge, 1500–1800.*

of their failure to adhere to the orthodox norms of individual consent as set forth by the Council of Trent."[402]

The function of the parish priest as well as of the witnesses in *Tametsi* was strictly evidentiary. He witnessed the marriage on behalf of the church, and his testimony proved that the marriage had taken place. Although the decree created an impression of sacramental ritual, it subverted it. By recommending that the priest should use the formula "*Ego vos coniungo*," the decree depicted the priest as the minister who ceremonially joined the partners. One can easily imagine such a marriage taking place in church in the presence of *proximi et amici*, as in the ideal wedding (Plate 1). Nevertheless, nothing ceremonial was strictly necessary, and any competent adults would do as witnesses. The fact that *Tametsi* permitted other customary formulas to be used instead of "*Ego vos coniungo*" suggests that the parish priest was not the instrumental minister of the sacrament: that he did not "marry" the spouses by joining them sacramentally. It was still possible to hold after Trent that an unblessed marriage was valid only as a contract and not as a sacrament, and a few notable theologians endorsed Melchor Cano's theory (Section 16.7.3), but that position was as improbable as it was unusual.[403] The parish priest's essential function was to oversee and to witness the union on behalf of the church, whereas the spouses themselves established their sacramental union. The first part of the decree, describing a marriage conducted openly rather than secretly, required the priest to *say* something appropriate, but it made no mention of joining or blessing. These liturgical actions appeared only the second, ancillary part of the decree. Only the *presence* of the parish priest was necessary for validity.

The decree *Tametsi* set aside the principle of *solus consensus*, and with it a way of understanding marriage that had seemed immovable and indispensible in theology, canon law, and ecclesiastical practice since the early twelfth century. No one else's *consent* was required, but something else was required. The principle of *solus consensus* had checked the advance of ecclesiastical power over marriage during the Middle Ages and complicated the development of the sacramental theology of marriage, but churchmen had considered it to be immoveable. Medieval clerics, canonists, and theologians did not celebrate the possibility of marrying clandestinely.

---

[402] P. Seed, "The Church and the Patriarchal Family: Marriage Conflicts in Sixteenth- and Seventeenth-Century New Spain," *Journal of Family History* 10.3 (1985): 284–93, at 285. On the church's defense of marriage choice against parental interference, see also P. Seed, *To Love, Honor, and Obey in Colonial Mexico* (Stanford, 1988), 75–91

[403] For example, Guillelmus Estius (Willem Hessels van Est, d.1613), *IV Sent.* 26.10 and 29.5 (Venice, 1777–1778, 6:109–13, 157–59). Estius concedes that according to the "common opinion of the later scholastics," the spouses themselves are the ministers, but he confesses that he considers Cano's position to be "very true," and he contends that it provides a more probable way of dealing with the *inter absentes* question than Cajetan's theory. Estius agrees with Cano that although marriage can be validly contracted without the blessing of a priest, such a marriage is not a sacrament in the proper sense of the term and does not confer grace. The treatment of the question by Sylvius, on Thomas Aquinas, *Suppl.* 42.1, q. 1 (Douai, 1645, pp. 170–73), is largely a rehearsal of Estius's.

They came from the same social strata as the parents who wanted to control their children's marriages, and they considered clandestine marriages to be hazardous and reprehensible. Nevertheless, they reluctantly accepted that there was no way to make them invalid. The opponents at Trent had good reason to ask why, if the invalidation of clandestine marriages was both possible and expedient, the church had not taken this action before. None of the proponents tried to explain why invalidation was more expedient in the sixteenth century than hitherto.

The opponents at Trent adhered to the traditional principle of *solus consensus*. They argued repeatedly that marrying was one thing, and proof that a marriage had occurred another. It followed that a marriage might be valid in the judgment of the church and in the public forum yet invalid before God and in the forum of conscience, or vice versa. When he outlined the scenario of covert prior contract, which *Tametsi* rehearses, Hugh of Saint-Victor had reluctantly conceded that in the judgment of the majority (*plurium approbatio*), "consent between legitimate persons whether given openly or secretly is judged to be the perfected sacrament of marriage."[404]

Tametsi abolished such distinctions, and with them a piece of the realism that had characterized the medieval theology of the sacraments. The council proclaimed that in this case what the church had not witnessed would henceforth not exist. *Because* unwitnessed marriages could not be upheld as valid in the judgment of the church and in the public forum, they would *ipso facto* be invalid even in the forum of conscience and before God.

---

[404] Hugh of Saint-Victor, *De sacramentis* II.11.6, PL 176:489C: "plurium approbatio hoc recipit ut sive in manifesto sive in occulto talis consensus inter legitimas personas factus fuerit, perfectum conjugii sacramentum judicetur." Hugh describes the marriage as *perfectum* because he has just suggested (and reluctantly denied) that a clandestine marriage might be considered as *matrimonium initiatum* until the spouses confirm it by restating their vows publicly.

Bibliography

MANUSCRIPTS CONSULTED

Assisi, MS 138.
Cambridge, St. John's College, MS 57 (C.7).
London, BL, Harley 3098.
Oxford, Bodleian Library, MS Laud Misc. 216.
Oxford, Bodleian Library, MS Laud Misc. 277.
Oxford, Bodleian Library, MS Lyell 42.
Paris, BnF lat. 14842.
Paris, BnF lat. 16417.
Vat. lat. 1098.
Vat. lat. 4986.
Vienna, Österreichische Nationalbibliothek, Cod. lat. 2718. Bibl. Universidad Granada Caja B-4.

PRIMARY LITERATURE

Abbo of Fleury. *Liber apologeticus.* PL 139:461–71.
Acta Reformationis Catholicae ecclesiam Germaniae concernentia saeculi XVI. Die Reform-verhandlungen des deutschen Episkopats von 1520 bis 1570. Ed. Georg Pfeilschifter. 6 vols. Regensburg, 1959–1974.
Aelred of Rievaulx. *Opera omnia 3: Sermones 47–84.* Ed. Gaetano Raciti. CCM 2B. Turnhout, 2001.
Albertus Magnus. *Opera omnia.* Ed. August Borgnet. 38 vols. Paris, 1890–1899. ["Borgnet edition."]
    Opera Omnia edenda curavit Institutum Alberti Magni Coloniense. Münster, 1951–. ["Cologne edition."]
    De sacramentis, tract. 9: De matrimonio. Ed. A. Ohlmeyer. *Opera omnia,* Cologne edition, vol. 26 (1958), 154–70.
Alexander of Hales. *Glossa in quatuor libros Sententiarum Petri Lombardi.* Nunc demum reperta atque primum edita studio et cura PP. Collegii s. Bonaventurae. 4 vols. Quaracchi, Florence, 1951–1957.

Quaestiones disputatae 'antequam esset frater.' Bibliotheca Franciscana Scholastica Medii Aevi, 19–21. Nunc primum editae studio et cura PP. Collegii s. Bonaventurae. 3 vols. Quaracchi, Florence, 1960.

Ambrose. *De institutione virginis.* PL 16.

Ambrosiaster. *Ambrosiastri qui dicitur commentarius in epistulas paulinas.* Ed. H. J. Vogels. CSEL 81.1–3 (1966–1969).

[Pseudo-Augustine.] *Quaestiones veteris et novi testamenti CXXVII.* Ed. A. Souter. CSEL 50 (1908).

Archiv für Literatur- und Kirchengeschichte des Mittelalters. Ed. Franz Ehrle and Heinrich Denifle. 7 vols. Freiburg im Breisgau, etc., 1885–1900.

Aristotle. *Nicomachean Ethics.* Trans. Robert C. Bartlett and Susan D. Collins. Chicago, 2011.

Aristotle; Aspasius; Michael. Trans. by Robert Grosseteste. *Aristoteles over de Vriendschap: Boeken VIII en IX van de Nicomachische Ethiek med de commentaren van Aspasius en Michaël in de Latijnse vertaling van Grosseteste.* Ed. Wilfried Stinnisen. Brussels, 1963.

Aspasius: See also Robert Grosseteste.

Augustine. *Confessiones.* CCL 27.

Contra duas epistulas Pelagianorum. CSEL 60.

Contra Faustum Manicheum. CSEL 25.1.

Contra Iulianum. PL 44.

Contra Iulianum opus imperfectum. PL 45.

De adulterinis coniugiis. CSEL 41.

De bono coniugali. CSEL 41.

De bono viduitatis. CSEL 41.

De civitate Dei. CCL 47 (Books I–X), CCL 48 (Books IX–XII).

De continentia. CSEL 41.

De doctrina christiana. CCL 32.

De fide et operibus. CSEL 41.

De Genesi ad litteram. CSEL 28.1.

De Genesi contra Manichaeos. CSEL 91.

De gratia Christi et de peccato originali. CSEL 42.

De moribus ecclesiae et de moribus Manichaeorum. CSEL 90.

De nuptiis et concupiscentia. CSEL 42.

De peccato originali: See *De gratia Christi*

De peccatorum meritis et remissione peccatorum et de baptismo parvulorum. CSEL 60.

De sancta virginitate. CSEL 41.

De sermone Domini in monte. CCL 35.

Enchiridion. = *Liber de fide, spe, et caritate.* CCL 46.

Ennarationes in Psalmos. CCL 38–40.

In Ioannis evangelium tractatus. CCL 36.

Quaestiones Evangeliorum. CCL 44B.

Retractationes. CCL 57.

Vingt-six sermons au peuple d'Afrique. Ed. F. Dolbeau. Paris, 1996.

Avicenna *(Ibn Sina): Avicenna Latinus. Liber de philosophia prima sive de scientia divina, V–X.* Ed. S. van Riet. Louvain and Leiden, 1980.

Bandinus. *Sententiarum libri quatuor.* PL 192:965–1112.

Banting, H. M. J. (ed.). *Two Anglo-Saxon Pontificals (the Egbert and Sidney Sussex Pontificals).* Henry Bradshaw Society 104. London, 1989.

Barbaro, Franceso. *De re uxoria.* Ed. Attilio Gnesotto. *Atti e memorie. Accademia patavini de scienze, lettere ed arti*, N.S. 32 (1915–1916).

Bellarmine, Robert. *Opera omnia, ex editione Veneta*. 12 vols. Paris, 1870–1874. [Repr. Frankfurt, 1965.]

    Disputationes de controversiis christianae fidei adversus hujus temporis haereticos: Controversiarum de sacramento matrimonii liber unicus. In *Opera omnia*, vol. 5 (1873), pp. 37–151.

Benedictus Levita (pseudo-). *Collectio capitularium*. PL 97:699–912.

Bernard of Pavia. *Summa Decretalium*. Ed. Ernst Th. Laspeyres. Regensburg, 1860. [Repr. Graz, 1956.]

Bonaventure. *Opera omnia*. Ed. Fathers of the Collegium s. Bonaventurae. 9 vols. Quaracchi, Florence, 1882–1902.

The booke of the common prayer and administracion of the Sacramentes, and other rites and ceremonies of the Churche: after the Churche of England. London, 1549.

Brenz (Brentius), Iohannes. *Libellus casuum quorundam matrimonialium elegantissimus*. Basle, 1536.

Breviarium Alaricanum: See *Lex Romana Visigothorum*.

Burchard of Worms. *Decretum*. PL 140:537–1065.

Cajetan: See Thomas de Vio Cajetan.

Cano: See Melchor Cano.

Catharinus, Ambrosius (Lancellotto Politi). *De matrimonio quaestiones plures*. Published in an addendum to *Enarrationes R. P. F. Ambrosii Catharini Politi Senensis archiepiscopi Compsani in quinque priora capita libri Geneseos*, cols. 225–62. Rome, 1551–1552. [Repr. in facsimile under the title *Enarrationes Assertiones Disputationes*, Ridgewood, New Jersey, 1964.]

Chaucer, Geoffrey. *The Works of Geoffrey Chaucer*. Ed. F. N. Robinson. 2nd edition. Boston, 1957.

Codex Theodosianus. Ed. Paul Krueger, Theodor Mommsen, Paul Martin Meyer. 2 vols. Berlin, 1905.

Collectio decem partium. MS Vienna, Österreichische Nationalbibliothek, Cod. lat. 2718.

Collectio Tripartita (ascribed to Ivo of Chartres). Working text, ed. Martin Brett and Przemyslaw Nowak, URL: http://project.knowledgeforge.net/ivo/tripartita.html (last accessed June 2, 2013).

Commentarius Cantabrigiensis in Epistolas Pauli e schola Petri Abaelardi. Vol. 2: In *Epistolam ad Corinthos, I^{am} et II^{am} ad Galatas, et Ephesios*. Ed. Artur Landgraf. Publications in Mediaeval Studies 2. Notre Dame, Indiana, 1939.

Concilium provinciale Coloniense anno 1536 celebratum: Acta Reformationis Catholicae, 2:118–318.

Concilium Tridentinum: Diariorum, actorum, epistularum, tractatuum nova collectio. Edidit Societas Goerresiana Promovendis inter Germanos Catholicos Litterarum Studiis, Friburgi Brisgoviae 1901–.

Corpus Catholicorum. Werke katholischer Schriftsteller im Zeitalter der Glaubensspaltung. Münster in Westfalen, 1919–.

Councils and Synods with Other Documents Relating to the English Church. 2 vols. in 4. Oxford, 1981, 1964. [Vol. 1 (1981), 871–1204, ed. D. Whitelock, M. Brett, and C. N. L. Brooke (Pt. 1, 871–1066; Pt. 2, 1066–1204). Vol. 2 (1964), 1205–1313, ed. F. M. Powicke and C. R. Cheney (Pt. 1, 1205–1265; Pt. 2, 1265–1313).]

Corpus Iuris Canonici. 3 vols. Rome, 1582. [Vol. 1, *Decretum Gratiani*. Vol. 2, *Decretales D. Gregorii Papae IX*. Vol. 3, *Liber Sextus Decretalium*.]

Corpus Iuris Canonici. Ed. Emil Friedberg. 2 vols. Leipzig, 1879, 1881.

Corpus Iuris Civilis. Ed. Theodore Mommsen, Paul Krueger, Rudolf Schoell, and Wilhelm Kroll. *Institutiones, Digesta*: vol. 1, Berlin, 1911. *Codex Iustinianus*: vol. 2, Berlin, 1906. *Novellae*: vol. 3, Berlin, 1904.

Cum omnia sacramenta I. In F. P. Bliemetzrieder, *Anselms von Laon systematische Senten-zen*, BGPhMA 18.2–3 (Münster, 1919), 129–51.

Cum omnia sacramenta II. First part: ed. H. Weisweiler, *Das Schrifttum der Schule Anselms von Laon*, BGPhMA 33.1–2 (Münster, 1936), 33–34. Remainder: ed. F. P. Bliemetzrie-der, "Théologie et théologiens de l'école épiscopale de Paris avant Pierre Lombard," RThAM 3 (1931), 273–91.

De coniugiis tractantibus. Ed. F. P. Bliemetzrieder, "Paul Fournier und das literarische Werk Ivos von Chartres," at 73–78.

De coniugiis tractantibus. MS British Library, Harley 3098, 72r–74v.

Decrees of the Ecumenical Councils. 2 vols. London, 1990. (Latin text from G. Alberigo et al., *Conciliorum Oecumenicorum Decreta*, with parallel English translations by Norman P. Tanner.) [Cited as Tanner-Alberigo.]

Decretales Gregorii IX (Liber extra). In *Corpus Iuris Canonici*, vol. 2. [Cited as X.]

Decretum Dei fuit. Ed. H. Weisweiler, *Das Schrifttum der Schule Anselms von Laon*, BGPhMA 33.1–2 (Münster, 1936), 361–79.

Delfini, Giovanni Antonio. *De clandestino matrimonio.* CT 13.1:72–81.

De matrimonio et caelibatu. Camerini, 1553.

De potestate ecclesiastica. Venice, 1549.

Denifle, Heinrich and Franz Ehrle (eds.). *Archiv für Litteratur- und Kirchengeschichte des Mittelalters.* 7 vols. Berlin, 1885–1900. [Repr. Graz, 1955–1956.]

Dennis, Andrew, Peter Foote, and Richard Perkins (eds. and trans.). *Laws of Early Iceland, Grágás: The Codex Regius of Grágás, with Material from other Manuscripts.* University of Manitoba Icelandic Studies 3 and 5. Winnipeg, 1980.

Denzinger-Schönmetzer: See *Enchiridion Symbolurum, Definitionum et Declarationum.*

Domingo de Soto. *In quartum librum Sententiarum.* 2 vols. Salamanca, 1566–1579.

Durandus of Saint-Pourçain (Durandus de Sancto Porciano). *In Petri Lombardi Sententias theologicas commentariorum libri quatuor.* Venice, 1571.

Editio Romana: See *Corpus Iuris Canonici.* Rome, 1582.

Écrits théologiques de l'École d'Abélard. Textes inédits. Ed. Arthur Landgraf. Spicilegium Sacrum Lovaniense, Études et Documents 14. Louvain, 1934.

Ehrle, Franz. "Zur Vorgeschichte des Concils von Vienne." In *Archiv für Literatur- und Kirchengeschichte des Mittelalters*, vol. 2. Berlin, 1886.

Enchiridion Symbolorum, Definitionum et Declarationum de rebus fidei et morum. Ed. Heinrich Denzinger and Adolf Schönmetzer. 34th edition. Barcelona, 1965. [Cited as DS]

Enchiridion christianae institutionis in Consilio prouinciali Coloniensi editum: See Gropper.

Enarrationes in Matthaeum. PL 162:1227–1500.

Erasmus, Desiderius. *Christiani matrimonii institutio.* Ed. A. G. Weiler (2008). ASD V.6:1–252.

Desiderii Erasmi Roterodami Opera omnia. Ed. Jean Leclerc. Leyden, 1703–1706. [Repr. Hildesheim, 1961–1962.] [Abbr. LB.]

Opera omnia Desiderii Erasmi Roterodami. Amsterdam, 1969–2008, and Leiden, 2009–. ["Amsterdam edition," abbr. ASD.]

Estius, Guillelmus (Willem Hessels van Est). In *Quatuor libros Sententiarum commentaria.* 6 vols. Venice, 1777–1778.

Fecit Deus hominem [marriage treatise included in the *Sententiae Berolineses*]: In Stegmüller, "Sententie Berolineses," RThAM 11 (1939), 56–61.

Florensz, Adrian, of Utrecht (Hadrian VI). *Quaestiones de sacramentis in Quartum Senten-tiarum librum.* Rome, 1522.

Formulae Merowingici et Karolini Aevi. MGH *Leges*, sect. V. Ed. Karl Zeumer. 1882–1886.

Gandulph of Bologna. *Magistri Gandulphi Bononiensis Sententiarum libri quatuor.* Ed. Ioannes de Walter. Vienna and Breslau, 1924.

Giberti, Giovanni Matteo. *Jo. Matthaei Giberti Episcopi Veronensis Ecclesiasticae Disciplinae ante Tridentinam Synodum instauratoris solertissimi Opera . . . Editio altera auctior, & emendatior.* Ostiglia, 1740.

Constitutiones Gibertinae cum animadversionibus Cardinalis Augustini Valerii, aliorumque Episcoporum Vernonsium. In *Opera* (1740), 1–152.

Goffredus de Trano. *Summa super titulis Decretalium.* Lyon, 1519. [Repr. Aalen, 1968.]

Gomes, Gulielmus [William] Z. *De matrimoniis clandestinis in Concilio Tridentino: cum appendice de forma celebrationis matrimonii apud Indos.* Rome, 1950.

González de Mendoza, Pedro. *Lo sucedido en el concilio de Trento desde el año 1561 hasta que se acabó.* CT 2:635–719.

Gratian. Concordia discordantium canonum (Decretum). In *Corpus Iuris Canonici.* Ed. Friedberg, vol. 1.

Gregory I, Pope (?). *Libellus Responsionum* (= *Per dilectissimos filios meos*). MGH Epistolae (in Quart) 2, = *Gregorii I papae Registrum epistolarum*, vol. 2 (1892–1899), *Epist.* 11.56ᵃ, pp. 332–43.

Gregory of Tours. *Libri historiarum X.* Ed. Bruno Krusch and Wilhelm Levison. MGH *Scriptores rerum Merovingicarum*, vol. 1.1 (1937–1951).

Gropper, Johann. *Enchiridion christianae institutionis in Consilio prouinciali Coloniensi editum, opus omnibus verae pietatis cultoribus longe vtilissimum.* Paris, 1550.

Guerrero, Pedro. *Tractatus de matrimoniis clandestinis.* MS Biblioteca Universitaria de Granada, Caja B-4, 346r–383v. [Edited in J. López Martín, "El voto de Don Pedro Guerrero," 155–219.]

Guerric of Saint-Quentin, *Quaestio disputata de matrimonio.* MS Paris, BnF lat. 16417, 63ra–63va. MS Assisi 138, 155ra–156va.

Guido of Monte Rochen. *Manipulus curatorum.* Novissime parisius impressus et emendatus. Paris, 1501.

Guy of Orchelles (Guido de Orchellis). *Tractatus de sacramentis ex eius Summa de sacramentis et officiis ecclesiae.* Ed. Damian and Odulph Van den Eynde. Franciscan Institute Publications, Text Series no. 4. St. Bonaventure, N.Y., 1953.

Hadrian VI, Pope: See Florensz.

Henry VIII (King). *Assertio septem sacramentorum adversus Martinum Lutherum.* Ed. Pierre Fraenkel. *Corpus Catholicorum*, vol. 43. Münster, 1992.

Hervet, Gentian. *De matrimoniis clandestinis.* CT 13.1:145–59.

Oratio ad Concilium qua suadetur, ne matrimonia quae contrahuntur a filiis familias sine consensu eorum in quorum sunt potestate, habeantur deinceps pro legitimis. Paris, 1556.

Hostiensis. *Summa aurea.* Venice, 1574. [Repr. Turin, 1963.]

Hincmar of Reims. *Epistolae: Die Briefe des Erzbischofs Hinkmar von Reims (Hincmari Archiepiscopi Remensis Epistolae)*, vol. 1. Ed. Ernst Perels, 1939. MGH *Epistolae* 8.1, = *Epistolae Karolini Aevi* 6.1.

Hinschius, Paul (ed.). *Decretales Pseudo-Isidorianae et Capitula Angilramni.* Leipzig, 1863. [Repr. Aalen, 1963.]

Hugh of Saint-Cher (Hugo de sancto caro). *Commentarius in libros I-IV Sententiarum.* MS Vat. lat. 1098.

Postillae in totam Bibliam: In Biblia Latina continens textum bibliae cum postilla domini Hugonis Cardinalis. 6 vols. Basel, 1504.

Hugh of Saint-Victor. *De arrha animae.* Ed. H. B. Feiss and P. Sicard in *L'oeuvre de Hugues de Saint-Victor, 1: De institutione novitiorum; De virtute orandi; De laude caritatis; De arrha animae*. Ed. H. B. Feiss et P. Sicard. French translation by D. Poirel, H. Rochais, and P. Sicard. Introductions, notes, and appendices by D. Poirel. Sous la règle de saint Augustin series. Turnhout, 1997.

De beatae Mariae virginitate: Ed. Patrice Sicard (from MS Troyes 301) in *L'oeuvre de Hugues de Saint-Victor, 2: Super Canticum Mariae; Pro Assumptione Virginis; De beatae Mariae virginitate; Egredietur virga, Maria porta*. With introduction, notes, and French translation by Bernadette Jollès. Sous la règle de saint Augustin series. Turnhout, 2000.

De sacramentis christianae fidei. PL 176:173–618.

De sacramentis christianae fidei. Ed. Rainer Berndt. *Corpus Victorinum*, vol. 1. Monasterium Westfalorum, 2008.

Huguccio, *Summa*, C. 27 q. 2: In Roman, "Summa d'Huguccio."

Huius sacramenti habemus. Ed. O. Lottin, "Une tradition spéciale du texte des *Sententiae divinae paginae*," in *Studia Mediaevalia in honorem admodum Reverendi Patris Raymundi Josephi Martin* (Bruges, 1948), 147–69, at 160–61. Repr. in Lottin, PsM V, 365–68 (PM 527–28).

In coniugio figura et vestigium trinitatis. In F. P. Bliemetzrieder, *Anselms von Laon systematische Sentenzen*, BGPhMA 18.2–3 (Münster, 1919), 112–13.

In primis hominibus. In Matecki, *Der Traktat In primis hominibus*. [IPH]

Innocent III, Pope. *Between God and Man: Six Sermons on the Priestly Office*. Translated with an introduction by Corinne J. Vause and Frank C. Gardiner. Washington, D.C., 2004.

De quadripartita specie nuptiarum liber. Ed. and trans. in Munk, *A Study of Pope Innocent III's Treatise*. [Also PL 217:921–68.]

De quatuor speciebus desponsationum. Ed. and trans. in Munk, *A Study of Pope Innocent III's Treatise*. [Also PL 217:659–66.]

Die Register Innocenz' III. Ed. Othmar Hageneder et al., Publikationen des Historischen Instituts beim Österreichischen Kulturinstitut in Rom. Graz, 1964–.

Epistolae. PL 214–216.

Innocent V, Pope: See Peter of Tarentaise.

Ioannes Maior. *Quartus in Sententiarum*. Paris, 1509.

Iohannes de Fonte: See Hamesse, *Les Auctoritates Aristotelis*, under secondary literature.

Isaac of Stella. *Sermons*. Tome 1. Ed. Anselm Hoste. Trans. Gaston Salet. SC 130. Paris, 1967.

Isidore of Seville. *De ecclesiasticis officiis*. Ed. C. M. Lawson. CCL 113. Turnhout, 1989.

The Etymologies of Isidore of Seville. Trans. with introduction and notes by Stephen A. Barney et al. Cambridge, 2006.

Etymologiarum sive originum libri XX. Ed. W. M. Lindsay. 2 vols. Oxford, 1911.

Iulianus (Julian). *Projet Volterra*, "The Epitome of Julian," ed. Simon Corcoran, URL: www.ucl.ac.uk/history2/volterra/julianintro.htm#volt (accessed June 13, 2013). [This web edition is based on *Iuliani Epitome Latina Novellarum Iustiniani*, ed. Gustav F. Hänel (Haenel). Leipzig, 1873.]

Ivo of Chartres. *Decretum*. Working text ed. Martin Brett and Bruce Brasington, URL: http://project.knowledgeforge.net/ivo/decretum.html (accessed June 2, 2013).

Epistolae. PL 162:11D–288.

Jacques de Vitry. *Historia occidentalis*. John F. Hinnebusch (ed.). *The Historia Occidentalis of Jacques de Vitry: A Critical Edition*. Spicilegium Friburgense, Texts Concerning the History of Christian Life 17. Fribourg, Switzerland, 1972.

Jaffé, Philipp (ed.). *Regesta pontificum romanorum ab condita ecclesia ad annum post Christum natum MCXCVIII*. 2nd edition, revised by S. Loewenfeld, F. Kaltenbrunner, and P. W. Ewald. Leipzig, 1885–1888. [Abbr. JL]

Jerome. *Adversus Helvidium de Mariae virginitate perpetua*. PL 23:183–206.

    Adversus Iovinianum. PL 23:211–338.

    Commentariorum in Mattheum. CCL 77.

Johannes de Fonte, *Parvi flores*: See Hamesse, *Les Auctoritates Aristotelis*.

John Duns Scotus. *Opera omnia*. *Editio nova iuxta editionem Waddingi XII tomos continentiam*. 26 vols. Paris, 1891–1895. ["Vivès edition."]

    Opus Oxoniense. In *Opera omnia*, Vivès edition, vols 8–21.

    Reportatio Parisiensis (Reportata Parisiensia). In *Opera omnia*, Vivès edition, vols 22–24.

John of Salisbury. *The Letters of John of Salisbury*. Ed. W. J. Millor and Harold E. Butler, revised by C. N. L. Brooke. 2 vols. Oxford, 1986, 1979.

Jonas of Orléans. *De institutione laicali: Instruction des Laïcs*. Ed. Odile Dubreucq. SC 549, 550. Paris, 2012, 2013.

Julian: See Iulianus.

Lactantius. *Epitome*. CSEL 19.

Lancellotto Politi: See Catharinus.

Landgraf, Arthur (ed.). *Écrits théologiques de l'école d'Abélard. Textes inédits*. Spicilegium Sacrum Lovaniense, Études et Documents 14. Louvain, 1934.

Leander of Seville. *Regula, sive liber de institutione virginum et contemptu mundi, ad Florentinam sororem*. PL 72:871–894.

Leo I, Pope. *Epistolae*. PL 54:551–1218.

Le Plat, Judocus [Josse] (ed.). *Monumentorum ad historiam concilii Tridentini potissimum illustrandam spectantium amplissima collectio*. 7 vols. Louvain, 1781–1787.

Lex Romana Visigothorum. Ed. Gustav F. Hänel (Haenel). Leipzig, 1848. [Repr. Aalen, 1962.] [Abbr. *Brev.*]

Leges Visigothorum. Ed. Karl Zeumer. MGH *Leges Nationum Germanicarum* (= *Leges*, sect. I), vol. 1 (1902).

Liber pancrisis. MS London, BL, Harley 3098, 1r–91v.

Littera septem sigillorum: See Fussenegger.

Lorich, Gerhard. *Institutio catholica fidei orthodoxae et religionis sanae*. Frankfurt, 1536.

Luther, Martin. *D. Martin Luthers Werke: kritische Gesammtausgabe, Schriften*. Weimar, 1883–1948. ["Weimarer Ausgabe," abbr. WA.]

Major, John: See Ioannes Maior.

Mansi, Jean-Dominique. *Sacrorum Conciliorum Nova et Amplissima Collectio*. 31 vols. Venice, 1759–1798.

Martène, Edmond. *De antiquis ecclesiae ritibus libri ex variis insigniorum ecclesiarum: pontificalibus, sacramentoriis, missalibus, breviariis, ritualibus, seu manualibus, ordinariis se consuetudinariis, cum manuscriptis tum editis*. 4 vols. Antwerp. 1736–1738.

Martène, Edmond and Ursin Durand (eds.). *Veterum scriptorum et monumentorum historicorum, dogmaticorum, moralium, amplissima collectio*. Paris, 1724. [Repr. New York, 1968.]

Martinus, Magister. *Compilatio quaestionum theologiae*, treatise on the sacraments: In J. A. Hall, *The Sacraments in the* Compilatio questionum theologie.

McSheffrey, Shannon (introduction and translations by). *Love and Marriage in Late Medieval London*. TEAMS Documents of Practice series. Kalamazoo, 1995.

Melchor Cano. *Opera, in hac primum editione clarius divisa*. Bassano, 1746. [*De locis theologicis*: pp. 1–457.]

    De locis theologicis. Texto de la editio princeps [Salamanca, 1563] preparado pro Juan Belda. Documenta Catholica Omnia, URL: www.documentacatholicaomnia.eu/03d/1509-1560,_Cano_Melchior,_De_Locis_Theologicis,_LT.pdf (accessed April 14, 2014).

Missale Romanum ex decreto sacrosancti Concilii Tridentini restitutum, S. Pii V. Pontificis Maximi jussu editum, Clementis VIII. et Urbani VIII. auctoritate recognitum. Regensburg, 1862.

Ordines Coronationis Franciae: Texts and Ordines for the Coronation of Frankish and French Kings and Queens in the Middle Ages. Ed. Richard A. Jackson. 2 vols. Philadelphia, 1995.

Nicholas I, Pope. *Epist.* 99 (*Responsa ad consulta Bulgarorum*). Ed. Ernst Perels. MGH *Epistolae* (in quart.), t. 6, = *Epistolae Karolini Aevi* 4 (1925), 568–600.

Nicholas of Clairvaux, *Sermo in dedicatione ecclesiae*: Published as Peter Damian, *Sermo 69*, PL 144:897–902.

Paludanus: See Peter of La Palu.

Panormia (ascribed to Ivo of Chartres). Working text ed. Martin Brett and Bruce Brasington, URL: http://project.knowledgeforge.net/ivo/panormia.html (accessed June 2, 2013).

Paucapalea, *Summa: Summa über das Decretum Gratiani*. Ed. Johann F. von Schulte. Giessen, 1890. [Repr. Aalen, 1965.]

Peter Abelard. Sententiae (formerly known as Sententiae Hermanni). In Petrus Abaelardus, *Opera Theologica VI: Sententie – Librum Sententiarum*. Ed. D. E. Luscombe, J. Barrow, C. Burnett, K. S. B. Keats-Rohan, and C. J. Mews. CCM 14 (2006).

Peter John Olivi. *De perfectione evangelica, Q. 6: An virginitas sit simpliciter melior matrimonio*. In Emmen, "Verginità e matrimonio," 21–57.

 Responsio fratris P. Ioannis ad aliqua dicta per quosdam magistros parisienses de suis Quaestionibus excerpta (Responsio secunda, 1285). Ed. D. Laberge, "Fr. Petri Ioannis Olivi, O.F.M., tria scripta," *Archivum Franciscanum Historicum* 28 (1935), at 130–35, 374–407.

 Responsio quam fecit Petrus Ioannis ad litteram magistrorum sibi praesentatum in Avinione [= Responsio prima, 1283]. Ed. Damasus Laberge, "Fr. Petri Ioannis Olivi, O.F.M., tria scripta," *Archivum Franciscanum Historicum* 28 (1935), at 126–30.

 Tractatus de sacramentis. MS Vat. lat. 4986, 128r–156v.

Peter Lombard. *Collectanea in epistolas s. Pauli.* PL 191:1297–1696, PL 192:9–520.

 Sententiae in IV libris distinctae. 2 vols (tom. 1, pars 2; tom. 2). Spicilegium Bonaventurianum 4–5. Grottaferrata (Rome), 1971, 1981.

 Sententiae in IV libris distinctae (tom. 1, pars 1): *Prolegomena.* Spicilegium Bonaventurianum 4. Grottaferrata (Rome), 1971.

 The Sentences. Translated and annotated by Giulio Silano. 4 vols. Toronto, 2007–2010.

 Tractatus de coniugio. In *Sententiae in IV libris distinctae* (Grottaferrata edition), 2:84*–87*. [Also PL 191:1585D–1587B.]

Peter of Aquila (Scotellus). *Commentaria in quatuor Libros Sententiarum Magistri Petri Lombardi.* Ed. Cypriano Paolini. 4 vols. Levanto, 1907–1909.

Peter of La Palu (Petrus Paludanus, Petrus de Palude). *Scriptum in quartum Sententiarum.* Venice, 1493.

Peter of Poitiers. *Sententiarum libri quinque.* PL 211:789–1280.

Peter of Tarentaise (Pope Innocent V). *In IV librum Sententiarum commentaria.* 4 vols. Toulouse, 1649–1652.

Peter the Chanter (Petrus Cantor, Peter of Hordenc). *Summa de sacramentis et animae consiliis.* Ed. Jean-Albert Dugauquier. 3 vols. in 5. Louvain, 1954–1967.

 Verbum Abbreviatum: Textus Conflatus. Ed. Monique Boutry. CCM 196. Turhout, 2004

Philip of Harveng. *De institutione clericorum.* PL 203:665–1206.

Praepositinus. *Praepositini Cancellarii de Sacramentis et de novissimis (Summae Theologicae Pars Quarta).* Ed. Daniel E. Pilarczyk. Collectio Urbana, Series III, Textus ac Documenta 7. Rome, 1964.

Quinque compilationes antiquae nec non Collection canonum Lipsiensis. Ed. E. Emil Fried-berg. Leipzig, 1882. [Repr. Graz, 1956.] [Cited as *Comp.*]

Raymond of Penyafort. *Summa de poenitentia et matrimonio.* Rome, 1603.

    Summa on Marriage. Translated with an Introduction by Pierre Payer. Medieval Sources in Translation 41. Toronto, 2005. Rome, 1964.

Das Regensburger Buch: Acta Reformationis Catholicae, 6:21–88.

Richard de Mediavilla. *Super quatuor libros Sententiarum Petri Lombardi quaestiones.* Brescia, 1591. [Repr. Frankfurt am Main, 1963.]

Regesta pontificum romanorum [abbr. JL]: See Jaffé.

Robert Courson. *Quaestio de matrimonio* (from his *Summa*). In Malherbe, *Le mariage au début du XIIIème siècle d'après la Summa du cardinal Robert de Courson.* [Note: A section from the same treatise is edited in Baldwin, *Language of Sex,* Appendix 1, 239–45.]

Robert Grosseteste (trans.). *The Greek Commentaries on the Nicomachean Ethics of Aristotle in the Latin Translation of Robert Grosseteste, Bishop of Lincoln* († 1253), vol. 3: *The Anonymous Commentator on Book VII, Aspasius on Book VIII, and Michael of Ephesus on Books IX and X.* Critical edition with an introductory study by H. Paul F. Mercken. Corpus Latinum Commentariorum in Aristotelem Graecorum 6.1. Louvain, 1991.

Robert Paululus. *De ceremoniis, sacramentis, officiis et observantibus ecclesiasticis.* PL 177:381–456.

Robert Pullen. *Sententiarum libri octo.* PL 186:639–1010.

Rolandus of Bologna. *De coniugio.* Ed. Friedrich Thaner, *Summa magistri Rolandi mit Anghang Incerti auctoris quaestiones,* pp. 115–234. Innsbruck, 1872–1874. [Repr. Aalen, 1973.]

    Sententiae. Ed. Ambrosius M. Gietl. *Die Sentenzen Rolands nachmals Papstes Alexander III.* Freiburg im Breisgau, 1891. [Repr. Amsterdam, 1969.]

Rufinus. *Summa decretorum.* Ed. Heinrich Singer. Paderborn, 1902.

Sanchez, Thomas. *Disputationum de sancto matrimonio libri decem.* 3 vols. Venice, 1612.

    De essentia et consensu matrimonio in genere, = Disputationum de sancto matrimonio, Book II, in vol. 1, pp. 145–220.

Scotus: See John Duns Scotus.

Sentences of Sextus. Ed. Walter T. Wilson. Atlanta, 2012. [Earlier edition by H. Chadwick, *The Sentences of Sextus.*]

Sententiae Atrebatenses. In Lottin, "Les Sententiae Atrebatenses"; and in PsM V, 400–440.

Sententiae Atrebatenses, marriage treatise from: In Lottin, "Les *Sententiae Atrebatenses*" and in PsM V, 434–39.

Sententiae Berolinenses. In Stegmüller, "*Sententie Berolinenses,*" RThAM 11.

Sententiae divinae paginae, marriage treatise from: In Lottin, "Une tradition spéciale," (1948), 160–64; and in PsM V, nos. 527–28.

Sententiae divinitatis. In Geyer, *Die Sententiae divinitatis: Ein Sentenzenbuch der Gilbertschen Schule,* BGPhM 7.2–3. Münster, 1909.

Sententiae Magistri A., De matrimonio. In Reinhardt, *Die Ehelehre,* 135 ff. [Abbr. SMA]

Sententiae magistri Petri Abelardi. CCM 14.

Sententiae Parisienses. In Landgraf, *Écrits théologiques de l'école d'Abélard,* 3–60.

Sextus: See *Sentences of Sextus.*

Simon, Master. *Tractatus magistri Simonis de sacramentis.* Ed. Weisweiler, *Maître Simon et son groupe De sacramentis,* 1–81.

Simon of Tournai. *Les Disputationes de Simon de Tournai.* Spicilegium Sacrum Lovaniense, Études et Documents, 12. Ed. Joseph Warichez. Louvain, 1932.

Simon of Bisignano. *Summa in Decretum*. Ed. Pier V. Aimone. Fribourg, 2007. URL: www
.unifr.ch/cdc/summa_simonis_de.php (accessed June 3, 2013).

Siricius, Pope. *Epistolae et decreta*. PL 13:1132–96.

Stephen Langton. *Der Sentenzenkommentar des Kardinals Stephan Langton*. Ed. A. M.
Landgraf. BGPhThMA 37.1. Münster, 1952.

   Quaestiones theologiae. Cambridge, St. John's College, MS 57 (C.7) and Oxford, Bodleian
Library, MS Lyell 42.

Stephen of Tournai (Stephan von Doornick, Stephanus Tornaciensis). *Die Summa über das
Decretum Gratiani*. Ed. Johann F. von Schulte. Giessen, 1891. [Repr. Aalen, 1965.]

   Summa: Prologus. Ed. H. Kalb, *Studien zur Summa Stephans von Tournai*, 113–20.

Suarez, Franciscus. *Commentariorum ac disputationum in tertiam partem divi Thomae*. 5 vols.
Mainz, 1616–1619.

Summa Coloniensis: See *Summa "Elegantius in iure diuino" seu Coloniensis*.

Summa de sacramentis "totus homo". Spicilegium Pontificii Athenaei Antoniani 7. Ed.
Umberto Betti. Rome, 1955.

Summa 'Elegantius in iure diuino' seu Coloniensis. Ed. Gérard Fransen and Stephan Kuttner.
Monumenta Iuris Canonici, Series A: Corpus Glossatorum. 4 vols. New York, 1969;
Vatican City, 1978, 1986, and 1990.

Summa sententiarum. [Odo of Lucca?] PL 176:41–174.

Summa Parisiensis: The Summa Parisiensis on the Decretum Gratiani. Ed. Terence P.
McLaughlin. Toronto, 1952.

Sylvius, Franciscus (François de Bois). *Commentarii in tertiam partem s. Thomae
Aquinatis ... et in eiusdem supplementum*. 2 vols. Douai, 1645.

Tancred. *Summa de matrimonio*. Ed. Agathon Wunderlich. Göttingen, 1841.

Tapper, Ruard. *Ruardi Tapperi ab Enchusia ... Opera*. 2 vols. Cologne, 1582–1583. [Repr.
Ridgewood, N.J., 1962.]

   *Explicatio articulorum venerandae Facultatis Sacrae Theologiae Generalis Studii Louaniens
[is] circa dogmata ecclesiastica ab annis triginta quatuor controversa, una cum responsione ad argumenta adversariorum*. 2 vols. Louvain, 1555–1557.

   Explicatio Articulorum viginti, venerandae facultatis Sacrae Theologiae Generalis studii
Lovaniensis, circa dogmata Ecclesiastica, nostro hoc tempore controuersa, vna cum
responsione ad argumenta aduersariorum. In Tapper, *Opera*.

Tertullian. *De virginibus velandis*. CCL 2.

   Le mariage unique (De monogamia). Texte critique et traduction de Paul Mattei. SC 343.
Paris, 1988.

Thomas Aquinas. *Doctoris angelici divi Thomae Aquinatis Opera omnia*. Ed. S. E. Fretté and
P. Maré. 34 vols. Paris, 1871–1880. ["Vivès edition."]

   De articulis fidei et ecclesiae sacramentis ad archiepiscopum Panormitanum. *Opera omnia*,
Leonine edition, 42:245–57.

   Expositio et lectura super epistolas S. Pauli. Ed. Raphael Cai. 2 vols. Turin and Rome, 1953.

   Sancti Thomae Aquinatis doctoris angelici Opera omnia iussu Leonis XIII P. M. edita.
Rome, 1882– ["Leonine edition."]

   Scriptum super libros Sententiarum. In *Opera omnia*, Vivès edition, vols 7–11. [Vol. 11 cited
here for *IV Sent.* 23 ff.]

   Scriptum super Sententiis. Ed. P. Mandonnet and M. F. Moos. 4 vols in 5. Paris, 1929–1947.
[Cited for *Book II Sent.* through *IV Sent.* 22, where the edition ceases.]

   Sententia Libri Ethicorum. In *Opera omnia*, Leonine edition, vol. 47.1–2.

   Summa contra Gentiles. In *Opera omnia*, Leonine edition, vols 13–15.

   Summa theologiae. 5 vols. Ottawa, 1941–1945.

Thomas de Vio Cajetan. Quaestiones de sacramentis. In Thomas Aquinas, *Opera omnia,* Leonine edition, 12:341–75. [*De sacramento matrimonii triplex quaesitum*: ibid., 370–73.]

Thomas of Chobham. *Summa confessorum.* Ed. F. Broomfield. Analecta Mediaevalia Numurcensia 25. Louvain, 1965.

Tobit: A New Translation with Introduction and Commentary by Carey E. Moore. Anchor Bible 40A. New York, 1996.

Tractatus de coniugio (anon.) Ed. Weisweiler, *Maître Simon et son groupe De sacramentis,* 99–102.

Tractatus de septem sacramentis ecclesiae (anon.) Ed. Weisweiler, *Maître Simon et son groupe De sacramentis,* 82–98.

Ubertino da Casale. *Responsio ad predictum libellum diffamatorium.* 377–416

Vacarius, *Summa de matrimonio.* Ed. F. W. Maitland, "Vacarius on Marriage (Text)." *Law Quarterly Review* 13 (1887): 270–87.

Vázquez, Gabriel. *Commentariorum ac disputationum in [partes] sancti Thomae.* 8 vols. Alcalá, 1598–1615. / *Commentariorum ac disputationum in tertiam partem sancti Thomae, tomus secundus*: Vol. 6 (1611). / *Commentariorum ac disputationum in tertiam partem sancti Thomae, tomus quartus*: vol. 8, 1615.

Tractatus de sacramento matrimonii inchoatus. In *Commentariorum ac disputationum in tertiam partem sancti Thomae, tomus quartus* (vol. 8, 1615), pp. 466–566.

Walter of Mortagne. *De coniugio.* PL 176:153–174.

William of Auvergne. *Opera omnia.* Ed. F. Hotot, with supplement ed. Blaise Le Feron. 2 vols. Orléans and Paris, 1674. [Repr. Frankfurt am Main, 1963.]

De sacramento matrimonii. In *Opera omnia,* 1:512–28.

De sacramento matrimonii. MS Paris BnF lat. 14842, 173r–201v.

William of Auxerre. *Summa aurea.* Spicilegium Bonaventurianum 16–20. Ed. Jean Ribaillier. Paris and Grottaferrata, 1980–1987.

Ysagoge in theologiam. In Landgraf, *Écrits théologiques de l'école d'Abélard,* 63–285.

SECONDARY LITERATURE

Abellán, Pedro M. *El fin y la signifación sacramental del matrimonio desde S. Anselmo hasta Guillermo de Auxerre.* Granada, 1939.

"La doctrina matrimonial de Hugo de San Caro." *Archivo Teológico Granadino* 1 (1938): 27–56.

Abusch, Tzvi (ed.). *Riches Hidden in Secret Places: Ancient Near Eastern Studies in Memory of Thorkild Jacobsen.* Winona Lake, Indiana, 2002.

Adams, Marilyn McCord. *Some Later Medieval Theories of the Eucharist: Thomas Aquinas, Giles of Rome, Duns Scotus, and William Ockham.* Oxford, 2010.

Adnès, Pierre. *Le mariage.* Tournai, 1963.

Aertsen, Jan A. and Andreas Speer (eds.). *Was ist Philosophie in Mittelalter? Qu'est-ce que la philosophie au moyen âge? What is Philosophy in the Middle Ages? Akten des X. Internationalen Kongresses für Mittelalterliche Philosophie der Société Internationale pour l'Etude de la Philosophie Médiévale, 25. bis 30. August 1997 in Erfurt.* Miscellanea Mediaevalia 26. Berlin, 1998.

Alesandro, John A. *Gratian's Notion of Marital Consummation.* Rome, 1971.

Allen, Prudence. *The Concept of Woman: The Aristotelian Revolution 750 BC–AD 1250.* Montréal, 1985.

Althaus, Paul. *The Ethics of Martin Luther.* Trans. R. C. Schultz. Philadelphia, 1965.

d'Alverny, Marie Thérèse. "Comment les théologiens et les philosophes voient la femme." *Cahiers de civilization médiévale* 20 (1977): 105–28.

Alves Pereira, Bernard. *La Doctrine du mariage selon saint Augustin.* Paris, 1930.

Anderson, Gary. "Celibacy or Consummation in the Garden? Reflections on Early Medieval and Christian Interpretations of the Garden of Eden." *Harvard Theological Review* 82 (1989): 121–48.

Andersen, Per, Kirsi Salonen, Heller Møller Sigh, and Helle Vogt (eds.). *Law and Marriage in Medieval and Early Modern Times. Proceedings of the Eighth Carlsberg Academy Conference on Medieval Legal History 2011.* Copenhagen, 2012.

Andrée, Alexander. "Anselm of Laon Unveiled: The *Glosae super Iohannem* and the Origins of the *Glossa Ordinaria* on the Bible." *Mediaeval Studies* 73 (2011): 217–60.

   "Laon Revisited: Master Anselm and the Creation of a Theological School in the Twelfth Century." *Journal of Medieval Latin* 22 (2012): 257–81.

Andrews, Frances, Christoph Egger, and Constance M. Rousseau (eds.). *Pope, Church and City: Essays in Honour of Brenda M. Bolton.* Leiden, 2004.

Anné, Lucien. *Les rites des fiançailles et la donation pour cause de mariage sous le Bas-Empire.* Louvain, 1941.

   "La conclusion du mariage dans la tradition et le droit de l'Église latine jusqu'au VIe siècle." *Ephemerides Theologicae Lovanienses* 12 (1935): 513–50.

Antoine, Philippe. *Le mariage. Droit canonique et coutumes africaines.* Théologie historique 90. Paris, 1992.

Archibald, Elizabeth. *Incest and the Medieval Imagination.* Oxford, 2001.

Arnórsdóttir, Agnes S. *Property and Virginity: The Christianization of Marriage in Medieval Iceland 1200–1600.* Aarhus, 2010.

   "Marriage Contracts in Medieval Iceland." *THTH* 360–89.

Aubert, Jean-Marie. *La femme. Antiféminism et christianisme.* Paris, 1975.

   "Sacramentalité et réalité humaine du mariage." *Review de droit canonique* 30 (1980): 140–50.

Augustinus Magister. Congrès international augustinien (1954: Paris, France). 3 vols. Paris, 1954–1955.

Aurell, Martin (ed.). *Les stratégies matrimoniales (IXe–XIIIe siècle).* Histoires de famille. La parenté au moyen âge 14. Turnout, 2013.

L'aveu. Antiquité et Moyen Âge. Actes de la table ronde de Rome (28–30 mars 1984). Rome, 1986.

Avignon, Carole. "Marché matrimonial clandestin et officines de clandestinité à la fin du Moyen Âge: l'exemple du diocèse de Rouen." *Revue Historique* 312.3 (2010): 515–49.

Aymans, Winfried, Anna Egler, and Joseph Listl (eds.). *Fides et ius: Festschrift für Georg May zum 65. Geburtstag.* Regensburg, 1991.

Ayres, Lewis. "Measure, Number, and Weight." In Fitzgerald, *Augustine through the Ages,* 550–52.

Bachrach, Bernard S. and David Nicholas (eds.). *Law, Custom, and the Social Fabric in Medieval Europe: Essays in Honor of Bryce Lyon.* Kalamazoo, 1990.

Baciocchi, J. de. "Structure sacramentaire du mariage." *Nouvelle revue théologique* 74 (1952): 916–29.

Baer, Richard A., Jr. *Philo's use of the Categories Male and Female.* Arbeiten zur Literatur und Geschichte des hellenistischen Judentums, III. Leiden, 1970.

Bagnall, Roger S. "Church, State, and Divorce in Late Roman Egypt." In Selig and Somerville, *Florilegium Columbianum,* 41–72.

Baldwin, John W. "Five Discourses on Desire: Sexuality and Gender in Northern France around 1200." *Speculum* 66.4 (1991): 797–819.

"An edition of the Long Version of Peter the Chanter's Verbum Abbreviatum." *Journal of Ecclesiastical History* 57.1 (2006): 78–85.

"An edition of the Long Version of Peter the Chanter's Verbum Abbreviatum." *Journal of Ecclesiastical History* 57.1 (2006): 78–85.

The Language of Sex: Five Voices from Northern France around 1200. Chicago, 1994.

Masters, Princes, and Merchants: The Social Views of Peter the Chanter and His Circle. 2 vols. Princeton, 1970.

"La vie sexuelle de Philippe Auguste." In *Rouche, Mariage et sexualité au moyen âge,* 220–29.

Balsdon, John P. V. D. *Roman Women: Their History and Habits.* London, 1962.

Baltensweiler, Heinrich. *Die Ehe in Neuen Testament. Exegetische Untersuchungen über Ehe, Ehelosigkeit und Ehescheidung.* Zürich and Stuttgart, 1967.

Bandlien, Bjørn. Trans. B. van der Hoek. *Strategies of Passion: Love and Marriage in Medieval Iceland and Norway.* Turnhout, 2005.

Barnes, Patricia M. "The Anstey Case." In Barnes and Slade, *Medieval Miscellany,* 1–24.

Barnes, Patricia M. and C. F. Slade (eds.). *A Medieval Miscellany for Doris Mary Stenton.* Publications of the Pipe Roll Society, NS 36 for the year 1960. London, 1962.

Barnes, Timothy D. Review of J. J. O'Donnell, *Augustine: Confessions.* Oxford, 1992. *Classical Philology* 89 (1994): 293–99.

Barr, Jane. "The Vulgate Genesis and St Jerome's Attitude to Women." *Studia Patristica* 18 (1982): 268–73.

Barr, Helen and Anne M. Hutchinson. *Text and Commentary from Wyclif to Bale.* Turnhout, 2005.

Bartlett, Robert. *Trial by Fire and Water: The Medieval Judicial Ordeal.* Oxford, 1986.

Basdevant-Gaudemet, Brigitte. *Église et autorités: Études d'histoire de droit canonique médival.* Cahiers de l'Institut d'Anthropologie Juridique 14. Limoges, 2006.

"Le mariage d'après la correspondance d'Yves de Chartres," *Revue historique de droit français et étranger* 61 (1983): 195–215. [Also repr. in Basdevant-Gaudemet, *Église et autorités.*]

Bassett, William M. (ed.). *The Bond of Marriage: An Ecumenical and Interdisciplinary Study.* Notre Dame, 1968.

Bataillon, Louis-Jacques, N. Bériou, G. Dahan, and R. Quinto (eds.). *Étienne Langton: Prédicateur, bibliste, théologien.* Bibliothèque d'histoire culturelle du Moyen Âge. Turnhout, 2010.

Bataillon, Louis-Jacques, Gilbert Dahan, and Pierre-Marie Gy (eds.). *Hugues de Saint-Cher (1263). Bibliste et théologien.* Bibliothèque d'histoire culturelle du Moyen Âge 1. Turnhout, 2004.

Batey, Richard A. *New Testament Nuptial Imagery.* Leiden, 1971.

Baümer, Remigius (ed.). *Von Konstanz nach Trient. Beiträge zur Geschichte der Kirche von den Reformkonzilien bis zum Tridentinum. Festgabe für August Franzen.* Munich, 1972.

Beatus Innocentius PP. V (Petrus de Tarantasia O.P). Studia et documenta. Rome, 1943. [Various authors.]

Beck, Henry G. J. *Pastoral Care of Souls in South-East France during the Sixth Century.* Analecta Gregoriana 51. Rome, 1950.

Beckwith, John. *Early Medieval Art.* London, 1964.

Bellitto, Christopher M. *Renewing Christianity: A History of Church Reform from Day One to Vatican II.* New York, 2001.

Bels, Pierre. *Le mariage des protestants français jusqu'en 1685. Fondements doctrinaux et pratique iuridique.* Paris, 1968.

Beltrán de Heredia, Vicente. *Domingo de Soto. Estudio biográfico documentado*. Biblioteca de Teólogos Españoles, Dirigida por los Dominicos de las Provincias de España 20, B5. Salamanca, 1960. [Repr. Madrid, 1961.]

"Soto (Dominique de)." In *Dictionnaire de théologie catholique*, 14.2:2423–31.

Bender, Ludovicus. *Forma iuridica celebrationis matrimonii. Commentarius in canones 1094–1099*. Rome, 1960.

Berger, Adolf. *Encyclopedic Dictionary of Roman Law*. Transactions of the American Philosophical Society, NS 43.2. Philadelphia, 1953.

Bérandy, Roger. "Le mariage des chrétiens. Étude historique." *Nouvelle revue théologique* 104 (1982): 50–59.

Bériou, Nicole. "La confession dans les écrits théologiques et pastoraux du XIIIe siècle: Médication de l'âme ou démarche judiciaire?" In *L'aveu*, 261–82.

Bériou, Nicole and David L. d'Avray with P. Cole, J. Riley-Smith, and M. Tausche. *Modern Questions about Medieval Sermons: Essays on Marriage, Death, History and Sanctity*. Spoleto, 1994.

Bériou, Nicole and David L. d'Avray. "Henry of Provins, O.P.'s Comparison of the Dominican and Franciscan Orders with the 'Order' of Matrimony." In Bériou and d'Avray, *Modern Questions about Medieval Sermons*, 71–75.

"The Image of the Ideal Husband in Thirteenth-Century France." In Bériou and d'Avray, *Modern Questions about Medieval Sermons*, 31–69.

Berkhofer, Robert F. "Marriage, Lordship, and the 'Greater Unfree' in Twelfth-Century France." *Past and Present* 173 (2001): 3–27.

Berman, Harold J. *Law and Revolution: The Formation of the Western Legal Tradition*. Cambridge, MA, 1983.

Law and Revolution II: The Impact of the Protestant Reformations on the Western Legal Tradition. Cambridge, MA, 2003.

Berman, Harold J. and John Witte, Jr. "The Transformation of Western Legal Philosophy in Lutheran Germany." *Southern California Law Review* 62 (1989): 1573–1660.

Bernards, Matthäus. *Speculum Virginum: Geistigkeit und Seelenleben der Frau im Hochmittelalter*. Forschungen zur Volkskunde, Bd. 36/38. Cologne, 1955. [2nd edition: Cologne, 1982. Beihefte zum Archiv für Kulturgeschichte, Hft. 16.]

Bernau, Anke, Ruth Evans, and Sarah Salih (eds.). *Medieval Virginities*. Toronto, 2003.

Bernhard, Jean. "Augustin et l'indissolubilité du mariage. Évolution de sa pensée." *Recherches Augustiniennes* 5 (1968): 139–55.

"Le décret *Tametsi* du Concile de Trente: Triomphe du consensualisme matrimonial ou institution de la forme solennelle du mariage?" *RDC* 30 (1980): 209–34.

"Évolution du sens de la forme de célébration du mariage dans l'Église d'occident." *RDC* 30 (1980): 187–205.

"Le mariage sacrement au Concile de Trente." *Revue de droit canonique* 42 (1992): 269–85.

"Théologie et droit matrimonial." *RDC* 39 (1989): 69–92.

Bernhard, Jean, Charles Lefebvre, and Francis Rapp. *L'Époque de la réforme et du concile de Trente*. = Histoire du Droit et des Institutions de l'Église en Occident, 14. Paris, 1989.

Berrouard, Marie-François. "L'enseignement de saint Augustin sur le mariage dans le Tract. 9, 2 in *Iohannis Evangelium*." *Augustinus* 1 (1967): 83–96.

Besnier, Robert. "Le mariage en Normandie des origines au XIIIe siècle." *Normannia* 7 (1934): 69–110.

Bethune, Brian Francis. *The Text of the Christian Rite of Marriage in Medieval Spain*. Doctoral dissertation, Toronto, 1987.

Bevilacqua, A. J. "The History of the Indissolubility of Marriage." *Proceedings of the Catholic Theological Society of America* 22 (1967): 253–308.

Bieniak, Magdalena. "The Sentences Commentary of Hugh of St.-Cher." In Rosemann, *Mediaeval Commentaries on the Sentences of Peter Lombard*, 2:111–148.

Biller, Peter. *The Measure of Multitude: Population in Medieval Thought.* Oxford, 2000.

———. "Birth-Control in the West in the Thirteenth and Early Fourteenth Centuries." *Past and Present* 94 (1982): 3–26.

Biller, Peter and Alastair J. Minnis (eds.). *Handling Sin: Confession in the Middle Ages.* York Studies in Medieval Theology 2. York, 1998.

——— (eds). *Medieval Theology and the Natural Body.* York Studies in Medieval Theology 1. York, 1997.

Bishop, Jane. "Bishops as Marital Advisors in the Ninth Century." In Kirshner and Wemple, *Women of the Medieval World*, 53–84.

Bitel, Lisa M. and Felice Lifshitz (eds.). *Gender and Christianity in Medieval Europe: New Perspectives.* Philadelphia, 2008.

Bittremieux, Joseph. "De instanti collationis Adamo justitiae originalis et gratiae: Doctrina S. Bonaventurae." *Ephemerides theologicae Lovanienses* 1 (1924): 168–73.

———. "La distinction entre la justice originelle et la grâce sanctifiante d'après saint Thomas d'Aquin." *Revue Thomiste* 6 (1921): 121–50.

Blažek, Pavel. *Die mittelalterliche Rezeption der aristotelischen Philosophie der Ehe. Von Robert Grosseteste bis Bartholomäus von Brügge (1246/1247–1309).* Studies in Medieval and Reformation Traditions 117. Leiden, 2007.

———. "Divorce. Greek and Latin Patristics, and Orthodox Churches." *Encyclopedia of the Bible and Its Reception*, 6:1006–08. Berlin, 2013.

Bliemetzrieder, Franz P. *Anselms von Laon systematische Sentenzen.* BGPhMA 18.2–3. Münster, 1919.

———. "Autour de l'oeuvre théologique d'Anselme de Laon." *RThAM* 1 (1929): 435–83.

———. "Gratian und die Schule Anselms von Laon." *Archiv für katholisches Kirchenrecht* 112 (1932): 37–63.

———. "L'oeuvre d'Anselme de Laon et la littérature théologique contemporaine." *RThAM* 5 (1933): 275–91; 6 (1934): 261–83; 7 (1935): 28–51.

———. "Paul Fournier und das literarische Werk Ivos von Chartres." *Archiv für katholisches Kirchenrechte* 115 (1935): 53–91.

———. "Théologie et théologiens de l'école épiscopale de Paris avant Pierre Lombard." *RThAM* 3 (1931): 273–91.

———. "Trente-trois pièces inédités de l'oeuvre théologique d'Anselm de Laon." *RThAM* 2 (1930): 54–75.

———. *Zu den Schriften Ivos von Chartres (d. 1116). Ein literargeschichtlicher Beitrag.* Sitzungsberichte der kaiserl. Akademie der Wissenschaften zu Wien, Philos.-hist. Klasse, 182 Bd. 6. Abh. Vienna, 1917.

Blumenthal, Uta-Renate. "Pope Gregory VII and the Prohibition of Nicolaitism." In Frassetto, *Medieval Purity and Piety*, 239–67.

Blumenthal, Uta-Renate, Anders Winroth, and Peter Landau (eds.). *Canon Law, Religion, and Politics: Liber Amicorum Robert Somerville.* Washington, D.C., 2012.

Bocarius, Antonina S. "The Marriage of Unfree Persons: Twelfth-Century Decretals and Letters." *Studia Gratiana* 27 (Rome, 1996): 483–506.

Boccafola, Kenneth E. *The Requirement of Perpetuity for the Impediment on Impotence.* Analecta Gregoriana 200. Series Facultatis Iuris Canonici, sectio B, num. 35. Rome, 1975.

Bodéüs, Richard. *The Political Dimensions of Aristotle's Ethics.* Trans. Jan E. Garrett. Albany, N.Y., 1993.

Boissard, E. "Les fins du mariage dans la théologie scolastique." *Revue thomiste* 49 (1948): 289–309.

Bonfield, Lloyd (ed.). *Marriage, Property, and Succession.* Comparative Studies in Continental and Anglo-American Legal History 10. Berlin, 1992.

Bonfield, Lloyd, Richard M. Smith, and Keith Wrightson (eds.). *The World We Have Gained: Histories of Population and Social Stucture.* Oxford, 1986.

Bonnefoy, Jean-François. "La question hypothétique *Utrum si homo non peccasset?* au XIIIe siècle." *Revista española de teología* 14 (1954): 326–68.

Boone, Marc. "State Power and Illicit Sexuality: The Persecution of Sodomy in Late Medieval Bruges." *Journal of Medieval History* 22.2 (1996): 135–53.

Borgolte, Michael (ed.). *Das europäische Mittelater im Spannungsbogen des Vergleichs: Zwanzig internationale Beiträge zu Praxis, Problemen und Perspektiven der historischen Komparatistik.* Berlin, 2001.

Bouchard, Constance B. *Those of My Blood: Creating Noble Families in Medieval Francia.* Philadelphia, 2001.

"Consanguinity and Noble Marriages in the Tenth and Eleventh Centuries." *Speculum* 56.2 (1981): 268–87.

Bornstein, Daniel and Roberto Rusconi (eds.). *Women and Religion in Medieval and Renaissance Italy.* Trans. M. J. Schneider. Chicago, 1996.

Bossy, John. *Christianity in the West 1400–1700.* Oxford, 1985.

Bougard, François, Laurent Feller, and Régine Le Jan (eds.). *Dots et douaires dans le haut moyen âge.* Collection de l'École Française de Rome 295. Rome, 2002.

Bougerol, Jacques-Guy. *Introduction to the Works of Bonaventure.* Trans. José de Vinck. Paterson, New Jersey, 1964.

Boureau, Alain. "Hugues de Saint-Cher commentateur des Sentences. Le cas du sacrement du mariage." In Bataillon et al., *Hugues de Saint-Cher,* 427–64.

Bovini, Giuseppe. "Le scene della *dextrarum iunctio* nell'arte cristiana." *Bullettino della commissione archeologica communale di Roma* 72 (1946–1948): 103–17.

Bowerstock, Glen W., Peter Brown, and Oleg Grabar (eds.). *Late Antiquity: A Guide to the Postclassical World.* Cambridge, MA., 1999.

Bowlin, John. *Contingency and Fortune in Aquinas's Ethics.* Cambridge Studies in Religion and Critical Thought series. Cambridge, 1999.

Boxer, Marilyn J. and Jean H. Quataert (eds.). *Connecting Spheres: Women in the Western World, 1500 to the Present.* Oxford, 1987.

Boyle, Leonard E. "St Thomas Aquinas and the Third Millennium." In Duggan et al., *Omnia Disce,* 294–307.

Božitković, Georgio. *S. Bonaventura doctrina de gratia et libero arbitrio.* Marienbad, 1919.

Brady, Ignatius. "The Distinctions of Lombard's *Book of Sentences* and Alexander of Hales." *Franciscan Studies* 25 (1965): 90–116.

Prolegomena: See Peter Lombard, *Sententiae in IV libris distinctae.*

"The Rubrics of Peter Lombard's *Sentences.*" *Pier Lombardo* 6 (1962): 5–25.

Brand, Paul A. "New Light on the Anstey Case." *Essex Archaeology and History* 15 (1983): 68–83.

Brandileone, Francesco. "Die *Subarrhatio cum anulo.* Ein Beitrag zur Geschichte des mittelalterlichen Eheschliessungsrechtes." *Deutsche Zeitschrift für Kirchenrecht* 10 (1901): 311–40.

Brantley, Jessica. *Reading in the Wilderness: Private Devotion and Public Performance in Late Medieval England.* Chicago, 2007.

Braunisch, Reinhard. "Johannes Gropper (1503–1559)." In Cüppers, *Kölner Theologen*, 172–99.
"Die 'Artikell' der 'Warhafftigen Antwort' (1545) des Johannes Gropper. Zur Verfasserfrage des Worms-Regensburger Buches (1540/41). In Baümer, *Von Konstanz nach Trient*, 519–45.
Brecht, Martin. *Die frühe Theologie des Johannes Brenz*. Tübingen, 1966.
Martin Luther: His Road to Reformation 1483–1521. Trans. J. L. Schaaf. Minneapolis, 1985.
Martin Luther: Shaping and Refining the Reformation 1521–1532. Trans. J. L. Schaaf. Minneapolis, 1990.
Bressan, Luigi. *Il canone tridentino sul divorzio per adulterio e l'interpretazione degli autori*. Analecta Gregoriana, 194. Rome, 1973.
Brett, Martin and Kathleen G. Cushing (eds.). *Readers, Texts and Compilers in the Earlier Middle Ages*. Farnham, 2009.
Breuer, Christine. *Reliefs und Epigramme griechischer Privatgrabmäler. Zeugnisse bürgerlichen Selbstverständnisses vom 4. bis 2. Jahrhundert v. Chr.* Cologne and Vienna, 1995.
Brooke, Christopher N. L. "Gregorian Reform in Action: Clerical Marriage in England, 1050–1200." *Cambridge Historical Journal* 12.1 (1956): 1–21.
Marriage in Christian History: An Inaugural Lecture. Cambridge, 1978.
The Medieval Idea of Marriage. Oxford, 1989.
"Marriage and Society in the Central Middle Ages." In Outhwaite, *Marriage and Society*, 17–34.
Brooke, Christopher N. L., David Luscombe, Geoffrey Martin, and Dorothy Owen (eds.). *Church and Government in the Middle Ages: Essays Presented to C. R. Cheney on his 70th Birthday*. Cambridge, 1976.
Broudéhoux, Jean-Paul. *Mariage et famille chez Clément d'Alexandrie*. Paris, 1970.
Brower, Jeffrey. "Medieval Theories of Relations." *Stanford Encyclopedia of Philosophy* (Winter 2010 Edition), URL: http://plato.stanford.edu/archives/win2010/entries/relations-medieval/.
Brown, Peter. *The Body and Society: Men, Women and Renunciation in Early Christianity*. London, 1989.
Brundage, James A. *Law, Sex, and Christian Society in Medieval Europe*. Chicago and London, 1987.
Brundage, James A. *Sex, Law and Marriage in the Middle Ages*. Variorum Reprints. Aldershot, 1993.
"Concubinage and Marriage in Medieval Canon Law." *Journal of Medieval History* 1 (1975): 1–17.
"Implied Consent to Intercourse." In Laiou, *Consent and Coercion*, 245–56.
"Intermarriage between Christians and Jews in Medieval Canon Law." *Jewish History* 3.1 (1988): 25–40.
"Judicial Space: Female Witnesses in Medieval Canon Law." *Dumbarton Oaks Papers* 52 (1998): 147–56.
"Marriage and Sexuality in the Decretals of Pope Alexander III." In Liotta, *Miscellanea Rolando Bandinelli, Papa Alessandro II*, 59–83.
Medieval Canon Law. London, 1995.
The Medieval Origins of the Legal Profession: Canonists, Civilians, and Courts. Chicago, 2008.
"The Medieval Battle of the Faculties: Theologians v. Canonists." In Blumenthal, Winroth, and Landau, *Canon Law, Religion, and Politics*, 272–83.
"Prostitution, Miscegenation and Sexual Purity in the First Crusade." In Edbury, *Crusade and Settlement*, 57–65.
"Rape and Marriage in Medieval Canon Law." *RDC* 28 (1978): 62–75. [Repr. in Brundage, *Law and Marriage in the Middle Ages*.]

"Sexuality and Society in the Fifth Century A.D.: Augustine and Julian of Eclanum." In Gabba, *Tria Corda*, 49–70.

"Sin, Crime, and the Pleasures of the Flesh: The Medieval Church Judges Sexual Offenses." In Linehan and Nelson, *The Medieval World*, 294–307.

Bryan, Lindsay. "Marriage and Morals in the Fourteenth Century: The Evidence of Bishop Hamo's Register." *English Historical Review* 121 (2006): 467–86.

Buitendag, Johan. "Marriage in the Theology of Martin Luther." *HTS Teologiese Studies/ Theological Studies* 63.2 (2007): 445–61.

Bullough, D. A. "Age of Consent: A Historical Overview." *Journal of Psychology and Human Sexuality* 16 (2006): 25–42.

"Medieval Medical and Scientific Views of Women." *Viator* 4 (1973): 485–501.

"Early Medieval Social Groupings: The Terminology of Kinship." *Past and Present* 45 (1969): 3–18.

Bullough, Vern L. and James Brundage (eds.). *Handbook of Medieval Sexuality*. New York, 1996.

Sexual Practices and the Medieval Church. Buffalo, 1982.

Burns, J. Patout. "Marital Fidelity as a Remedium Concupiscentiae: An Augustinian Proposal." *Augustinian Studies* 44.1 (2013): 1–35.

Burns, James H. (ed.). *Cambridge History of Medieval Political Thought c. 350–c. 1450*. Cambridge, 1988.

Burr, David. "Olivi on Marriage: The Conservative as Prophet." *Journal of Medieval and Renaissance Studies* 2 (1972): 183–204.

The Sprirtual Franciscans: From Protest to Persecution in the Century after Saint Francis. Pennsylvania, 2001.

The Persecution of Peter Olivi. Transactions of the American Philosophical Society. New Series 66.5. Philadelphia, 1976.

Butler, Sara M. "'I will never consent to be wedded with you!' Coerced Marriage in the Courts of Medieval England." *Canadian Journal of History* 39.2 (2004): 247–70.

Cadden, Joan. *Meanings of Sex Differences in the Middle Ages: Medicine, Science, and Culture*. Cambridge, 1993.

"'Nothing Natural is Shameful': Vestiges of a Debate about Sex and Science in a Group of Late-Medieval Manuscripts." *Speculum* 76.1 (2001): 66–89.

Caffarra, Carlo. "Création et redemption." In *Problèmes doctrinaux du mariage chrétien*, 218–310.

Cahill, Lisa Sowle and Dietmar Mieth (eds.). *The Family. = Concilium* 1995/4. London, 1995.

Cairns, John W. and Paul J. du Plessis (eds.). *The Creation of the Ius Commune: From Casus to Regula*. Edinburgh Studies in Law 7. Edinburgh, 2010.

Campbell, Gerard J. "St Jerome's Attitude towards Marriage and Woman." *American Ecclesiastical Review* 143 (1960): 310–20 and 384–94.

Campbell, Ken M. (ed.). *Marriage and Family in the Biblical World*. Downers Grove, Illinois, 2003.

Cantarella, Eva. "Homicides of Honor: The Development of Italian Adultery Law over Two Millennia." In Kertzer and Saller, *The Family in Italy*, 229–44.

Caravale, Giorgio. *Sulle tracce dell'eresia. Ambrogio Catarino Politi (1484–1553)*. Florence, 2007.

Cardman, Francine. "The Medieval Question of Women and Orders." *Thomist* 42 (1978): 582–99.

Carlier, Myriam and Tim Soens (eds.). *The Household in Late Medieval Cities, Italy and Northwestern Europe Compared: Proceedings of the International Conference Ghent, 21st–22nd January 2000*. Studies in Urban Social, Economic and Political History of the Medieval and Early Modern Low Countries 12. Leuven-Apeldoorn, 2001.

Carozzi, Claude. "Le fondements de la tripartition sociale chez adalbéron de Laon." *Annales, économies, sociétés, civilisations* 33.4 (1978): 683–702.

Carrodeguas, Celestino. *La sacramentalidad del matrimonio. Doctrina de Tomás Sánchez, S. J.* Madrid, 2003.

Carroll, Christopher. "The Last Great Carolingian Church Council: The Tribur Synod of 895." *Annuarium Historiae Conciliorum* 33 (2001): 9–25.

Castan Lacoma, Laureano. "El origen del capitulo 'Tametsi' del concilio de Trento contra los matrmonios clandestinos." *Revista Española de Derecho Canónico* 14 (1959): 613–66.

Castello, Carlo. "Lo strumento dotale come prova del matrimonio." *Studia et documenta historiae et iuris* 4 (1938): 208–44.

Catazzo, Eutimio. *De iustitia et peccato originali juxta S. Bonaventuram*. Theses ad lauream 18. Convento S. Lucia, Vicenza, 1942.

Catholic Encyclopedia. 15 vols. New York, 1907–1914.

Cavallar, Osvaldo and Julius Kirschner. "Making and Breaking Betrothal Contracts ('Sponsalia') in Late Trecento Florence." In Condorelli, *Panta rei*, 1:395–452.

Cavallo, Adolpho Salvatore. *Medieval Tapestries in the Metropolitan Museum of Art*. New York 1993.

"Seven Scenes from the Story of the Seven Sacraments and Their Prefigurations in the Old Testament." In Cavallo, *Medieval Tapestries*, 156–73 (= ch. 5).

Cereti, Giovanni. *Divorzio, nuove nozze et penitenza nella Chiesa primitiva*. Studi e recerche 26. Bologna, 1977.

"The Reconciliation of Remarried Divorcees according to Canon 8 of the Council of Nicea." In Provost and Walf, *Ius Sequitur Vitam*, 193–207.

Chadwick, Henry. *The Sentences of Sextus*. Cambridge, 1959.

Chadwick, Owen. *Catholicism and History: The Opening of the Vatican Archives*. Cambridge, 1978.

Chantraine, Georges. "Le mustérion paulinien selon les Annotations d'Erasme." *Recherches de science religieuse* 58 (1970): 351–82.

"Mysterium et sacramentum dans le Dulce bellum inexpertis." In *Colloquium Erasmianum*, 33–45.

Chapman, David M. "Marriage and Family in Second Temple Judaism." In Campbell, *Marriage and Family*, 183–239.

Chiffoleau, Jacques. "Dire l'indicible. Remarques sur le catégorie de *nefandum* du XIIe au XVe siècle." *Annales. Economies, sociétés, civilisations* 45.2 (1990): 289–324.

"'*Ecclesia de occultis non judicat*'? L'Église, le secret et l'occulte du XIIe au XVe siècle." *Micrologus: Nature, Sciences and Medieval Societies* 14, *The Secret* (2006): 359–81.

Clanchy, Michael T. *Abelard: A Medieval Life*. Oxford, 1999.

Clanchy, Michael T. and Lesley Smith. "Abelard's Description of the School of Laon: What Might It Tell Us about Early Scholastic Teaching?" *Nottingham Medieval Studies* 54 (2010): 1–34.

Clark, Elizabeth A. "Adam's only companion: Augustine and the early Christian debate on marriage." In Edwards and Spector, *The Olde Daunce*, 15–31 (with notes on 240–54).

Ascetic Piety and Women's Faith: Essays on Late Antique Christianity. Studies in Women and Religion 20. Lewiston, N.Y., 1986.

Clark, Elizabeth A. "Heresy, Asceticism, Adam and Eve: Interpretations of Genesis 1–3 in the Later Latin Fathers." In E. A. Clark, *Ascetic Piety and Women's Faith*, 353–85.

"Vitiated Seeds and Holy Vessels: Augustine's Manichean Past." In Clark, *Ascetic Piety and Women's Faith*, 291–349.

Clark, R. Scott. "*Iustitia imputata Christi*: Alien or Proper to Luther's Doctrine of Justification?" *Concordia Theological Quarterly* 70 (2006): 269–310.

Classen, Alrecht (ed.). *Sexuality in the Middle Ages and Early Modern Times: New Approaches to a Fundamental Cultural-Historical and Literary-Anthropological Theme.* Fundamentals of Medieval and Early Modern Culture 3. Berlin, 2008.

Clemoes, Peter and Kathleen Hughes. *England before the Conquest: Studies in Primary Sources Presented to Dorothy Whitelock*. Cambridge, 1971.

Cloke, Gillian. *"This Female Man of God." Women and Spiritual Power in the Patristic Age, AD 350–450*. London and New York, 1995.

Cochelin, Isabelle and Karen E. Smyth (eds.). *Medieval Life Cycles: Continuity and Change.* International Medieval Research 18. Turnhout, 2013.

Cochini, Christian. *Apostolic Origins of Priestly Celibacy*. Trans. Nelly Marans. San Francisco, 1990. [Translation of *Origines apostoliques du célibat sacerdotale*, 1981.]

Cohen, David. "The Augustan Law on Adultery: The Social and Cultural Context." In Kertzer and Saller, *The Family in Italy*, 109–26.

Cohen, Boaz. *Jewish and Roman Law: A Comparative Study*. 2 vols. New York, 1966.

"On the Theme of Betrothal in Jewish and Roman Law." *Proceedings of the American Academy for Jewish Research* 18 (1948–1949): 67–135.

Cohen, Jeffrey J. and Bonnie Wheeler. *Becoming Male in the Middle Ages*. New York and London, 1999.

Cohen, Jeremy. *"Be Fertile and Increase, Fill the Earth and Master it." The Ancient and Medieval Career of a Biblical Text*. Ithaca, 1989.

Cohick, Lynn H. *Women in the World of the Earliest Christians: Illuminating Ancient Ways of Life*. Grand Rapids, 2009.

Coleman, David. *Creating Christian Granada: Society and Religious Culture in an Old-World Frontier City, 1492–1600*. Ithaca, 2003.

Colish, Marcia L. "Another Look at the School of Laon." *AHDLMA* 53 (1986): 7–22.

"From the Sentence Collection to the Sentence Commentary and the Summa: Parisian Scholastic Theology, 1130–1215." In Hamesse, *Manuels, programmes de cours et techniques d'enseignement*, 9–29.

Collins, Raymond F. *Divorce in the New Testament*. Collegeville, Minnesota, 1992.

Colloquium Erasmianum. Actes du Colloque International réuni à Mons du 26 au 29 oct. 1967 à l'occasion du cinquième centenaire de la naissance d'Érasme. Mons, 1968.

Combs, William W. "Erasmus and the *Textus Receptus*." *Detroit Baptist Seminary Journal* 1 (1996): 35–53.

Condorelli, Orazio (ed.). *"Panta rei": Studi dedicati a Manlio Bellomo*. 4 vols. Rome, 2004.

Conklin, George. "Ingeborg of Denmark, Queen of France, 1193–1223." In Duggan, *Queens and Queenship*, 39–52

Connell, William T. (ed.). *Society and the Individual in Renaissance Florence*. Berkeley, 2002.

Conner, Randy. "Les Molles et les Chausses: Mapping the Isle of Hermaphrodites in Premodern France." In Livia and Hall, *Queerly Phrased*, 127–46.

Connolly, Patrick. "Contrasts in the Western and Eastern Approaches to Marriage." *Studia Canonica* 35 (2001): 357–402.

Constable, Giles. *Three Studies in Medieval Religious and Social Thought: The Interpretation of Martha and Mary. The Ideal of the Imitation of Christ. The Orders of Society.* Cambridge, 1995.

Cooper, Kate and Jeremy Gregory (eds.). *Discipline and Diversity: Papers Read at the 2005 Summer Meeting and the 2006 Winter Meeting of the Ecclesiastical History Society.* Studies in Church History 43. Rochester, N.Y., 2007.

Corbet, Patrick. *Autour de Burchard de Worms. L'Église allemande et les interdits de parenté (IXème–XIIème siècle).* Frankfurt am Main, 2001.

Corbet, Patrick. "Le douaire dans le droit canonique jusqu'à Gratien." In Bougard et al., *Dots et douaires,* 43–55.

Corbett, Percy E. *The Roman Law of Marriage.* Oxford, 1930.

Coriden, James A. *The Indissolubility Added to Christian Marriage by Consummation: An Historical Study of the Period from the End of the Patristic Age to the Death of Pope Innocent III.* Rome, 1961.

Combs, William W. "Erasmus and the Textus Receptus." *Detroit Baptist Journal* 1 (1996): 35–53.

Constable, Giles. *Three Studies of Medieval Religious Thought.* Cambridge, 1998.

Corecco, Eugenio, Niklaus Herzog, and Angela Scola (eds.). *Le droits fondamentaux du chrétien dans l'Église et dans la société. Actes du IVe Congrès international de droit canonique, Fribourg (Suisse) 6-11.X.1980.* Fribourg (Suisse), 1981.

Cosgrove, Art (ed.). *Marriage in Ireland.* Dublin, 1985.

——— "Consent, Consummation and Indissolubility: Some Evidence from Medieval Ecclesiastical Courts." *Downside Review* 109 (1991): 94–104.

——— "Marriage in Medieval Ireland." In Cosgrove, *Marriage in Ireland,* 25–50.

——— "Marrying and Marriage Litigation in Medieval Ireland." *THTH* 332–59.

Corbet, Patrick. "Le douaire dans le droit canonique jusqu'à Gratien." In Bougard, *Dots et Douaires,* 43–55.

Cottiaux, Jean. *La sacralisation du mariage de la Genèse aux incises matthéennes: Contribution à une théologie de développement dogmatique, à l'histoire de la discipline de moeurs, et aux problèmes posés par l'abolue indissolubilité du mariage chrétien.* Paris, 1982.

Courtney, William J. "The King and the Leaden Coin: The Economic Background of 'Sine qua non' causality." *Traditio* 28 (1972): 185–209.

Cousin, Victor. *Ouvrages inédits d'Abélard.* Paris, 1836.

Cowdrey, H. E. J. "Pope Gregory VII and the Chastity of the Clergy." In Frassetto, *Medieval Purity and Piety,* 269–302.

Coxe, H. O. *Laudian Manuscripts. Bodleian Library Quarto Catalogues II.* With corrections by Richard W. Hunt. Oxford, 1973.

Crook, John. "Patria potestas." *Classical Quarterly* n.s. 17.1 (1967): 113–22.

Crouzel, Henri. *L'Église primitive face au divorce du premier au cinquième siècle.* Paris, 1970.

——— *Virginité et mariage selon Origène.* Paris, 1963.

——— "Divorce et remariage dans l'Église primitive. Quelques réflexions de méthodologie historique." *Nouvelle revue théologique* 98 (1976): 891–917.

——— "La concupiscence charnelle dans le mariage selon saint Augustin." *Bulletin de littérature ecclesiastique* 1987: 287–308.

——— "Le remariage après séparation pour adultère selon les Pères latins." *Bulletin de Littérature Ecclesiastique* 75 (1974): 189–204.

——— "Les Pères de l'Église ont-ils permis le remariage après séparation?" *Bulletin de Littérature Ecclésiastique* 70 (1969): 3–43.

"Remarriage after Divorce in the Primitive Church: À propos of a Recent Book." *Irish Theological Quarterly* 38 (1971): 21–41.

"Séparation ou remariage selon les pères anciens." *Gregorianum* 47 (1966): 472–94.

Cullum, Patricia H., and Katherine J. Lewis (eds.). *Holiness and Masculinity in the Middle Ages*. Religion and Culture in the Middle Ages series. Cardiff, 2004.

Religious Men and Masculine Identity in the Middle Ages. Gender in the Middle Ages 9. Rochester, N.Y., 2013.

Cunningham, Terence P. "The Bond of Marriage." In McDonagh, *The Meaning of Christian Marriage*, 92–113.

Cüppers, Hubert (ed.). *Kölner Theologen. Von Rupert von Deutz bis Wilhelm Nyssen*. Cologne, 2004.

Cushing, Kathleen G. *Reform and the Papacy in the Eleventh Century: Spirituality and Social Change*. Manchester, 2005.

D'Avray, David L. *Medieval Marriage Sermons: Mass Communication in a Culture without Print*. Oxford, 2001.

Medieval Marriage: Symbolism and Society. Oxford, 2005.

"Comparative History of the Medieval Church's Marriage System." In Borgolte, *Das europäische Mittelater im Spannungsbogen des Vergleichs*, 209–21.

"The Gospel of the Marriage Feast of Cana and Marriage Preaching in France." In Bériou and d'Avray, *Modern Questions*, 135–53.

"Marriage Ceremonies and the Church in Italy after 1215." In Dean and Lowe, *Marriage in Italy*, 107–15.

"Peter Damian, Consanguinity and Church Property." In Smith and Ward, *Intellectual Life in the Middle Ages*, 71–81.

"Some Franciscan Ideas about the Body." In Bériou and d'Avray, *Modern questions*, 3–29.

"Symbolism in Medieval Religious Thought." In Linehan and Nelson, *The Medieval World*, 267–78.

D'Avray, David L. and M. Tausche. "Marriage Sermons in *Ad status* Collections of the Central Middle Ages." *Archives d'histoire doctrinale et littéraire de moyen âge* 40 (1980): 71–119. [Repr. In Bériou and d'Avray, *Modern Questions*, 77–134.]

D'Elia, Anthony F. *The Renaissance of Marriage in Fifteenth-Century Italy*. Cambridge, MA., 2004.

D'Entrèves, Alessandro P. *The Medieval Contribution to Political Thought: Thomas Aquinas, Marsilius of Padua, Richard Hooker*. New York, 1959.

Dachowski, Elizabeth. "Tertius est optimus: Marriage, Continence and Virginity in the Politics of Late Tenth- and Early Eleventh-Century Francia." In Frassetto, *Medieval Purity and Piety*, 117–29.

Daube, David. *Collected Works of David Daube*. Ed. Calum M. Carmichael. Vol. 1: *Talmudic Law*. University of California at Berkeley, 1992.

"Historical Aspects of Informal Marriage." In *Collected Works of David Daube*, 1:153–63.

"Origen and the Punishment of Adultery in Jewish Law." In *Collected Works of David Daube*, 1:167–71.

Daudet, Pierre. *L'établissement de la compétence le l'église en matière de divorce et de consanguinité (France Xème–XIIème siècles)*. Études sur l'histoire de la jurisdiction matrimoniale. Paris, 1941.

Les origines carolingiennes de la compétence exclusive de l'église. Études sur l'histoire de la jurisdiction matrimoniale. Paris, 1933.

Dauvillier, Jean. *Le mariage dans le droit classique de l'église depuis le Décret de Gratien (1140) jusqu'á mort de Clément V (1314)*. Paris, 1933.

Davidson, Nicholas. "Theology, Nature and the Law: Sexual Sin and Sexual Crime in Italy from the Fourteenth to the Seventeenth Century." In Dean and Lowe, *Crime, Society and the Law in Renaissance Italy*, 74–78.

Davies, Glenys. "The Significance of the Handshake Motif in Classical Funerary Art." *American Journal of Archaeology* 89 (1985): 627–40.

Dawes, Gregory W. *The Body in Question: Metaphor and Meaning in the Interpretation of Ephesians 5:21–33*. Leiden, 1998.

Dean, Trevor and Kate J. P. Lowe (eds.). *Crime, Society and the Law in Renaissance Italy*. Cambridge, 1994.

(eds). *Marriage in Italy, 1300–1650*. Cambridge, 1998.

Decker, Raymond. "Institutional Authority versus Personal Responsibility in the Marriage Sections of Gratian's *A Concordance of Discordant Canons*." *The Jurist* 32 (1972): 51–65.

Delhaye, Philippe. "The Development of the Medieval Church's Teaching on Marriage." *Concilium* 55 (1970): 83–88. "Fixation dogmatique de la théologie médiévale du mariage (*sacramentum, vinculum, ratum et consummatum*)." *Concilium* 55 (1970): 77–81.

"Le dossier anti-matrimonial de l'*Adversus Jovinianum* et son influence sur quelques écrits latins su XIIᵉ siècle." *Mediaeval Studies* 13 (1951): 65–86

Dépinay, J. *Le régime dotal. Étude historique, critique et pratique*. Droit français, étranger et international privé. Paris, 1902.

Depreux, Philippe. "La dotation de l'épouse en Aquitaine septentrionale du IXe au XIIe siècle." In Bougard et al., *Dots et douaires*, 219–44.

Desjardins, R. "Le Christ *sponsus* et l'Église *sponsa* chez saint Augustin." *Bulletin de littérature ecclésiastique* 67 (1966): 241–56.

Devisse, Jean. *Hincmar, archevêque de Reims, 845–882*. 3 vols. Geneva, 1975–1976.

Dhanis, Édouard. "Quelques anciennes formules septénaires des sacrements." *Revue d'histoire ecclésiastique* 26 (1930): 574–608, 916–50; 27 (1931): 5–26.

di Ciano, Marco. Le *arrhae sponsaliciae* in diritto romano e comparato. Tesi di Dottorato, Università degli studi di Ferrara, 2009.

di Mattia, Giuseppe. "Il decreto *Tametsi* e le sue radici nel Concilio di Bologna." *Apollinaris* 53 (1980): 476–500.

Dib, P. "Affinité." *DDC* 1:264–285.

Dictionary of the Middle Ages. Ed. Joseph Strayer. 13 vols + supplement. New York, 1982–1989. Supplement, ed. William C. Jordan, New York, 2003.

Dictionnaire de droit canonique. Ed. R. Naz. 7 vols. Paris, 1907–1953. [DDC]

Dictionnaire de théologie catholique. Ed. Alfred Vacant et al. 15 vols. in 30. Paris, 1903–1972.

Die Handschriftliche Überlieferung der Werke des heiligen Augustinus. Vienna, 1969–.

Diefendorf, Barbara B. *Paris City Councillors in the Sixteenth Century: The Politics of Patrimony*. Princeton, 1983.

DiTommaso, Lorenzo and L. Turescu (eds.). *The Reception and Interpretation of the Bible in Late Antiquity: Proceedings of the Montréal Colloquium in Honour of Charles Kannengiesser, 11–13 October 2006*. Leiden, 2008.

Donahue, Charles, Jr. "Bassianus, That Is to Say, Bazianus? Bazianus and Johannes Bassianus on Marriage." *Revista internazionale di diritto comune* 14 (2005): 41–82.

"The Canon Law on the Formation of Marriage and Social Practice in the Later Middle Ages." *Journal of Family History* 8 (1983): 144–58.

"The Case of the Man who Fell into the Tiber: The Roman Law of Marriage at the Time of the Glossators." *American Journal of Legal History* 22 (1978): 1–53.

"The Dating of Alexander the Third's Marriage Decretals: Dauvillier Revisited after Fifty Years." *Zeitschrift der Savigny-Stiftung für Rechtsgeschichte* 99 (Kanonistische Abteilung 68) (1982): 70–124.

"English and French Marriage Cases: Might the Differences Be Explained by Differences in the Property Systems?" In *Bonfield, Marriage, Property, and Succession,* 339–66.

Johannes Faventinus on Marriage (With an Appendix Revisiting the Question of the Dating of Alexander III's Marriage Decretals." In Müller and Sommar, *Medieval Church Law and the Origins of the Western Legal Tradition,* 179–97.

Law, Marriage, and Society in the Later Middle Ages. Cambridge, 2007.

"The Policy of Alexander the Third's Consent Theory of Marriage." Monumenta Iuris Canonici, series C: Subsidia, vol. 5 (Vatican City, 1976), = *Proceedings of the Fourth International Congress of Canon Law,* ed. Stephan Kuttner, 251–81.

"Was there a Change in Marriage Law in the Late Middle Ages?" *Rivista internazionale di diritto comune* 6 (1995): 49–80.

Doran, John. "Innocent III and the Uses of Spiritual Marriage." In Andrews et al., *Pope, Church and City,* 101–14.

Dove, Mary. "Sex, Allegory and Censorship: A Reconsideration of Medieval Commentaries on the Song of Songs." *Literature and Theology* 10.4 (1996): 317–28.

Doyle, Eric. "The Question of Women Priests and the Argument *in persona Christi.*" *Irish Theological Quarterly* 50 (1983–1984): 212–221.

Doyle, Thomas P. (*ed.*). *Marriage Studies: Reflections in Canon Law and Theology.* Vol. III. Washington, D.C., 1985.

Drachman, Bernard. "Betrothal." *Jewish Encyclopedia,* vol. 3 (1903), 125–28.

Drew, Katherine F. *Law and Society in Early Medieval Europe.* Variorum Reprints. London: 1988.

Driver, Godfrey R. and John C. Miles. The Babylonian Laws, *vol.* 1: Legal Commentary. Oxford, 1952.

Duby, Georges. *Le chevalier, la femme et le prêtre. Le mariage dans la France féodale.* Paris, 1981.
The Knight, the Lady and the Priest: The Making of Modern Marriage in Medieval France. Trans. Barbara Bray. Chicago, 1983.
Medieval Marriage: Two Models from Twelfth-Century France. Trans. Elborg Forster. Baltimore, 1978.

Dufour, Jean. "Louis VI, Roi de France (1108–1137), à la lumière des actes royaux des sources narratives." *Académie des inscriptions et Belles-Lettres. Comptes rendus des séances, April–June 1990,* 134.2 (Paris, 1990): 456–82.

Duggan, Anne (ed.). "The Nature of Alexander III's Contribution to Marriage Law, with Special Reference to Licet preter solitum." In Andersen, Salonen, Sigh, and Vogt, *Law and Marriage in Medieval and Early Modern Times,* 43–63.
Queens and Queenship in Medieval Europe. Woodbridge, 1997.

Duggan, Anne, Joan Greatrex, and Brenda Bolton (eds.). *Omnia disce: Medieval Studies in Memory of Leonard Boyle, O.P.* Aldershot, 2005.

Duggan, Charles. "Equity and Compassion in Papal Marriage Decretals to England." In van Hoecke and Welkenhuysen, *Love and Marriage in the Twelfth Century,* 59–87.

Dulles, Avery. "Symbol, Myth, and the Biblical Revelation." *Theological Studies* 27.1 (1966): 1–26.

Dunbabin, Jean. *A Hound of God: Pierre de la Palud and the Fourteenth-Century Church.* Oxford, 1991.

Dupont, Anthony, Wim François, Paul van Geest, and Mathijs Lamberigts. "Sex." In *Oxford Guide to the Historical Reception of Augustine* 3:1726–37.

Duval, André. "Contrat et sacrement de mariage au concile de Trente." *La Maison-Dieu* 127 (1976): 34–63.

"La formule *Ego vos in matrimonium conjungo* ... au concile de Trente." *La Maison-Dieu* 99 (1969): 144–53.

"Le concile de Trente et la distinction entre le contrat et le sacrement de marriage." *Revues des sciences philosophiques et théologiques* 65 (1981): 286–94.

Dzon, Mary. *The Image of the Wanton Christ Child in the Apocryphal Infancy Legends of Late Medieval England*. Doctoral dissertation, Toronto, 2004.

"Wanton Boys in Middle English Texts and the Christ Child in Minneapolis, University of Minnesota, MS Z822 N81." In Cochelin and Smyth, *Medieval Lifecycles*, 81–145.

Edbury, Peter W. (ed.). *Crusade and Settlement*. Cardiff, 1985.

Edwards, Robert R. and S. Spector (eds.). *The Olde Daunce: Love, Friendship and Marriage in the Medieval World*. New York, 1991.

Eells, H. "The Origin of the Regensburg Book." *Princeton Theological Review* 26 (1928): 355–72.

Ehrle, Franz. "Zur Vorgeschichte des Concils von Vienne." In Ehrle and Denifle, *Archiv für Literatur- und Kirchengeschichte des Mittelalters*, vol. 2 (Berlin, 1886), 353–416, and vol. 3 (Berlin, 1887), 1–195.

Ehrle, Franz and Heinrich Denifle (eds.). *Archiv für Literatur- und Kirchengeschichte des Mittelalters*. 7 vols. Freiburg im Breisgau, etc., 1885–1900.

Eisenach, Emlyn. *Husbands, Wives, and Concubines: Marriage, Family, and Social Order in Sixteenth-Century Verona*. Sixteenth Century Essays and Studies 69. Kirksville, Missouri, 2004.

Elliott, Dyan. *Fallen Bodies: Pollution, Sexuality, and Demonology in the Middle Ages*. Philadelphia, 1999.

"The Physiology of Rapture and Female Spirituality." In Biller and Minnis, *Medieval Theology and the Natural Body*, 141–74.

"The Priest's Wife: Female Erasure in the Gregorian Reform." In Elliott, *Fallen Bodies*, 81–106.

Spiritual Marriage: Sexual Abstinence in Medieval Wedlock. Princeton, 1993.

"Sex in Holy Places: An Exploration of a Medieval Anxiety." *Journal of Women's History* 6.3 (1994): 6–34.

Encyclopedia of Christianity. Ed. Erwin Fahlbusch et al. 5 vols. Grand Rapids and Leiden, 2008.

Encyclopedia of the Bible and Its Reception. Berlin, 2013.

Engh, Line C. *Gendered Identities in Bernard of Clairvaux's "Sermons on the Song of Songs": Performing the Bride*. Brepols, 2014.

Ennen, Edith. *Frauen im Mittelalter*. 2nd edition. Munich, 1985.

The Medieval Woman. Trans. E. Jephcott. Oxford, 1989. [Translation of Ennen, *Frauen im Mittelalter*.]

Emmen, Aquilino. "Verginità e matrimonio nella valutazione dell'Olivi." *Studi Francescani* 64 (1967): 11–57.

Esmein, Adhémar. *Le mariage en droit canonique*. 2nd edition, ed. R. Génestal and J. Dauvillier. 2 vols. Paris, 1929, 1935. [First edition published Paris, 1891.] [Abbr. Esmein-Genestal]

Etienne, J. "Ruard Tapper (1487–1559)." *Louvain Studies* 5 (1975): 284–86.

Études d'histoire du droit canonique dédiées à Gabriel Le Bras. 2 vols. Paris, 1965.

Evans, Gillian R. (ed.). *A History of Pastoral Care*. London, 2000.

Evans Grubbs, Judith. *Law and Family in Late Antiquity: The Emperor Constantine's Marriage Legislation*. Oxford, 1995.

    Women and the Law in the Roman Empire: A Sourcebook on Marriage, Divorce and Widowhood. Abingdon, U.K., 2002.

    "Abduction Marriage in Antiquity: A Law of Constantine (CTh ix. 24. 1) and Its Social Context." *Journal of Roman Studies* 79 (1989): 59–83.

    "Marriage Contracts in the Roman Empire." In Lovén and Stömberg, Ancient Marriage, 78–101.

    "'Marriage More Shameful than Adultery'. Slave-Mistress Relationships, 'Mixed Marriages', and Late Roman Law." *Phoenix* 47.2 (1993): 125–54.

    "Marrying and Its Documentation in Later Roman law." *THTH* 43–94.

    "'Pagan' and 'Christian' Marriage: The State of the Question." *Journal of Early Christian Studies* 2.4 (1994): 361–412.

Evdokimov, Paul. *Sacrament de l'amour. Le mystère coniugale à la lumière de la tradition orthodoxe*. Paris, 1962.

Fanning, John Edward. *Sacramentality in the Marriage Doctrine of Hincmar of Rheims: A Doctrinal-Juridical Analysis of the Letter De nuptiis Stephani*. Doctoral dissertation, Gregorian University, Rome, 1992.

Farmer, Sharon. *Surviving Poverty in Medieval Paris*. Ithaca, N.Y., 2002.

    "Persuasive Voices: Clerical Images of Medieval Wives." *Speculum* 61 (1986): 517–43.

Farnedi, Giustino (ed.). *La celebrazione cristiana del matrimonio: simboli e testi: atti del II Congresso internazionale di liturgia, Roma, 27-31 maggio 1985*, = Studia Anselmiana 93, = Analecta liturgica 11. Rome, 1986.

Fayer, Carla. *La familia romana: aspetti giuridici ed antiquari. Parte seconda: Sponsalia, matrimonio, dote*. Problemi e Ricerche di Storia Antica 21. Rome, 2005.

Feller, Laurent. "Morgengabe, dot, tertia: rapport introductif." In Bougard et al., *Dots et douaire*, 1–25,

Fellhauer, David E. "*Consortium omnis vitae* as a juridical element of marriage." *Studia Canonica* 13 (1979): 3–171.

Féret, H.-M. "*Sacramentum, res*, dans la langue théologique de s. Augustin." *Revue des Sciences philosophiques et théologiques* 29 (1940): 218–43.

Filser, Hubert. *Ekklesiologie und Sakramentenlehre des Kardinals Johannes Gropper. Eine Glaubenslehre zwischen Irenik und Kontroverstheologie im Zeitalter der Reformation*. Studien zur systematischen Theologie und Ethik, Bd. 6. Münster, 1995.

Finch, A. J. "Parental Authority and the Problem of Clandestine Marriage in the Later Middle Ages." *Law and History Review* 8.2 (1990): 189–204.

Finnis, John. "The Truth in Legal Positivism." In George, *Autonomy of Law*, 195–214. [Repr. in J. Finnis, *Philosophy of Law: Collected Essays*, vol. 4 (Oxford, 2011), 174–88.]

Fitzgerald, Allan D. (ed.). *Augustine through the Ages: An Encyclopedia*. Grand Rapids, 1999.

Flanagan, Donal. "The Sacrament of Marriage." In McDonagh, *The Meaning of Christian Marriage*, 36–61.

Flandrin, Jean-Louis. *Families in Former Times: Kinship, Household and Sexuality*. Trans. R. Southern. New York, 1979.

    Un temps pour embrasser: aux origines de la morale sexuelle occidentale (VIe–XIe siècle). Paris, 1983.

Flint, Valerie I. J. "The 'School of Laon': A Reconsideration." *RThAM* 43 (1976): 89–110.

Folliet, Georges. "Les trois catégories de chrétiens. A partir de Luc (17, 34–36), Matthieu (24, 40–41) et Ézéchiel (14, 14)." In *Augustinus Magister*, communications, vol. 2 (Paris, 1954–1955), 631–44.

"Les trois catégories de chrétiens. Survie d'un thème augustinien." *L'année théologique augustinienne* 14 (1954): 82–96.

Fontaine, Jacques, et al. *Grégoire le Grand: Chantilly, Centre Culturel Les Fontaines, 15–19 septembre 1982*. Paris, 1986.

Forster, Marc. *The Counter-Reformation in the Villages: Religion and Reform in the Bishopric of Speyer, 1560–1720*. Ithaca, 1992.

Fournier, Paul. *Les officialités au Moyen Âge. Étude sur l'organisation, la compétence et la procédure des tribunaux ecclésiastiques ordinaires en France, de 1180 à 1328*. Paris, 1880.

Frank, Roberta. "Marriage in Twelfth- and Thirteenth-Century Iceland." *Viator* 4 (1973): 473–84.

Frankenberry, Nancy K. (ed.). *Radical Interpretation in Religion*. Cambridge, 2002.

"Religion as a 'Mobile Army of Metaphors'." In Frankenberry, *Radical Interpretation in Religion*, 171–87.

Fransen, Gérard. Review of H. J. F. Reinhardt, *Die Ehelehre der Schule des Anselms von Laon*. *Revue théologique de Louvain* 9 (1978): 202–04.

"La formation du lien matrimoniale au moyen âge." *RDC* 21 (1971): 106–26. [Also published in Metz and Schlick, *Le lien matrimonial*, 106–26.]

"Le lettre de Hincmar de Reims au sujet deu mariage d'Étienne: Une relecture." In Lievens, Van Mingroot, and Verbeke, *Pascua Mediaevalia*, 133–46.

"Varia ex manuscriptis." *Traditio* 21 (1965): 515–20.

Frakes, Robert M. *Contra Potentium Iniurias: The Defensor Civitatis and Late Roman Justice*. Münchener Beiträge zur Papyrusforschung und antiken Rechtsgeschichte 90. Munich, 2001.

Frassetto, Michael (ed.). *Medieval Purity and Piety: Essays on Medieval Clerical Celibacy and Religious Reform*. New York and London, 1998.

Freedman, Paul. *Images of the Medieval Peasant*. Stanford, 1999.

Freisen, Joseph. *Geschichte des kanonischen Eherechts bis sum Verfall der Glossenliteratur*. Paderborn, 1893. [Repr. Aalen, 1963.]

Friedman, Mordechai A. *Jewish Marriage in Palestine: A Cairo Genizah Study*. 2 vols. Tel-Aviv and New York, 1980–1981.

Frier, Bruce W. "Natural Fertility and Family Limitation in Roman Marriage." *Classical Philology* 89.4 (1994): 318–33.

Frier, Bruce W. and Thomas A. J. McGinn. *A Casebook on Roman Family Law*. Oxford, 2004.

Fuhrmann, Horst. "Ökumenische Konzil und seine historische Grundlagen." *Geschichte in Wissenschaft und Unterricht* 12 (1961): 672–95.

"The Pseudo-Isidorian Forgeries." In Jasper and Fuhrmann, *Papal Letters in the Early Middle Ages*, 137–95.

Furry, Timothy J. *Allegorizing History: The Venerable Bede, Figural Exegesis, and Historical Theology*. Eugene, OR, 2013.

Fussenegger, Geroldus. "*Littera septem sigillorum* contra doctrinam Petri Ionnis Olivi edita." *Archivum Franciscanum Historicum* 47 (1954): 45–53.

Gabba, Emilio (ed.). *Tria Corda: Scritti in onore di Arnaldo Momigliano*. Como, 1983.

Gagnér, Sten. *Studien zur Ideengeschichte der Gesetzgebung*. Acta Universitatis Upsaliensis. Studia Iuridica Upsaliensia 1. Stockholm, 1960.

Ganshof, François-Louis. "L'"épreuve de la croix' dans le droit de la monarchie franque." In *Studi in onore di Alberto Pincherle*, 217–31.

"Le statut de la femme dans la monarchie franque." *Société Jean Bodin, Receuils* 12 (1962): 5–58.

"Note sur deux textes de droit canonique dans le *Liber Floridus*." In *Études d'histoire du droit canonique*, 1:99–115.

Gardner, Jane F. *Women in Roman Law and Society*. London, 1976.

Garnsey, Paul. *Ideas of Slavery from Aristotle to Augustine*. W. B. Stanford Memorial Lectures. Cambridge, 1996.

Garrison, Marsha. "Marriage: The Status of Contract. An Essay on Weitzman's *The Marriage Contract*." *University of Pennsylvania Law Review* 131.4 (1983): 1039–62.

Gastaldelli, Ferruccio. "La *Summa Sententiarum* di Ottone da Lucca: Conclusione di un dibattito secolare." *Salesianum* 42 (1980): 537–46.

Gaudemet, Jean. *Le bréviaire d'Alaric et les Epitome*. Ius Romanum Medii Aevi 1, 2 b aa b. Milan, 1965.

Droit de l'Église et vie sociale au Moyen Âge. Variorum Reprints. Northampton, 1989.

L'Église dans l'Empire romain (IVe–Ve siècles). = Histoire du droit et des insitutions de l'Église en occident 3. Paris, 1958.

Église et cité: Histoire du droit canonique. Paris, 1994.

Le mariage en occident. Le moeurs et le droit. Paris, 1987.

Sociétés et mariage. Strasbourg: CERDIC, 1980. [Collected articles.]

"Indissolubilité et consommation du mariage. L'apport d'Hincmar de Reims." *RDC* 30 (1980): 28–40.

"L'apport d'Augustin à la doctrine mediévale du mariage." *Augustinianum* 27 (1987): 559–570.

"L'évolution de la notion de *sacramentum* en matière de mariage." *RDC* 41 (1991): 71–79.

"Le lien matrimonial: les incertitudes du haut moyen-âge." *RDC* 21 (1971): 81–105.

"Le mariage, un contrat?" *Revue des sciences morales et politiques* 150.2 (1995): 161–73.

"Les origines historiques de la faculté de rompre le mariage non consommé." In Gaudemet, *Sociétés et mariage* (Strasbourg, 1980), 210–29.

"Les sources du Décret de Gratien." *RDC* 48.2 (1998): 247–61.

"Marriage et procréation: Les aspects historiques." *RDC* 45 (1995): 245–56.

"Recherche sur les origines historiques de la faculté de rompre le mariage non consommé." In *Proceedings of the Fifth International Congress of Medieval Canon Law*, ed. S. Kuttner and K. Pennington, = *Monumenta Iuris Canonici*, series C, subsidia, vol. 6 (Vatican City, 1980), 309–32.

Review of Joseph Huber, Der Ehekonsens im Römischen Recht (q.v.). Revue d'histoire de droit, = Tijdschrift voor Rechtsgeschiedenis 47 (1979): 171–73.

Gellinek, C. "Marriage by Consent in Literary Sources of Medieval Germany." *Studia Gratiana* 12 (1967): 557–79.

Gelting, Michael H. "Marriage, Peace and the Canonical Incest Prohibitions: Making Sense of an Absurdity?" In Korpiola, *Nordic Perspectives on Medieval Canon Law*, 93–124.

Gennep, Arnold van. *Les rites de passage*. Paris, 1909.

The Rites of Passage. Trans. M. B. Vizedon and G. L. Caffee. Chicago, 1960. [Translation of *Les rites de passage*.]

George, Robert P. (ed.). *The Autonomy of Law: Essays on Legal Positivism*. Oxford, 1996.

Gereste, Régis-Claude. "Quand les chrétiens ne se mariaient pas à l'Église. Histoire des cinq premiers siècles." *Lumière et Vie* 82 (1967): 24–27.

Geyer, Bernhard. *Die Sententiae divinitatis: Ein Sentenzenbuch der Gilbertschen Schule.* BGPhM 7.2–3. Münster, 1909.

Ghellinck, Joseph de. "Un chapitre dans l'histoire de la définition des sacrements au XIIe siècle." In *Mélanges Mandonnet*, 2:79–96.

"Magister Vacarius. Un juriste théologien peu amiable pour les canonistes." *Revue d'histoire ecclesiastique* 44 (1949): 173–78.

"The Sentences of Anselm of Laon and their Place in the Codification of Theology during the XIIth Century." *Irish Theological Quarterly* 6 (1911): 427–441.

Gibson, Margaret T. and Janel L. Nelson (eds.). *Charles the Bald: Court and Kingdom.* Oxford, 1981.

Gies, Frances and Joseph Gies. *Marriage and the Family in the Middle Ages.* New York, 1987.

Ginther, James R. and Carl N. Still (eds.). *Essays in Mediaeval Philosophy and Theology in Memory of Walter Principe, CSB: Fortresses and Launching Pads.* Aldershot, 2005.

Girard, René. "Marriage in Avignon in the Second Half of the Fifteenth Century." *Speculum* 28.3 (1953): 485–98.

Giraud, Cédric. *Per verba magistri. Anselme de Laon et son école au XIIe siècle.* Turnhout, 2010.

"Le recueil de sentences de l'école de Laon Principium et causa: Un cas de pluri-attribution." In M. Goullet, *Parva pro magnis munera*, 245–69.

Giraud, Cédric and Constant J. Mews. "Le Liber pancrisis, un florilège des Pères et des maîtres modernes du XIIe siècle." *Bulletin du Cange* 64 (2006): 145–91.

Gladd, Benjamin. Revealing the *Mysterion:* The Use of Mystery in Daniel and Second Temple Judaism with Its Bearing on First Corinthians. Beihefte zur Zeitschrift für die neutestamentliche Wissenschaft, 160. Berlin and New York, 2008.

Glorieux, Palémon. *Répertoire des maîtres en théologie de Paris au XIIIe siècle.* 2 vols. Études de philosophie médiévale 17–18. Paris, 1933, 1934.

Goetz, Hans-Werner. *Leben im Mittelalter vom 7. bis zum 13. Jahrhundert.* Munich, 1986.

Gold, Penny S. "The marriage of Mary and Joseph in the twelfth-Century Ideology of Marriage." In Bullough and Brundage, *Sexual Practices and the Medieval Church*, 102–117.

Goldberg, P. J. P. "Gender and Matrimonial Litigation in the Church Courts in the Later Middle Ages: The Evidence of the Court of York." *Gender and History* 19.1 (2007): 43–59.

Goody, Jack. *The Development of the Family and Marriage in Europe.* Cambridge, 1983.

The Oriental, the Ancient and the Primitive: Systems of Marrriage and the Family in the Pre-Industrial Societies of Eurasia. Cambridge, 1990.

Goullet, Monique (ed.). *Parva pro magnis munera. Études de littérature tardo-antique et médiévale offertes à François Dolbeau par ses élèves.* Turnhout, 2009.

Gordley, James. "*Ardor quaerens intellectum*: Sex within Marriage According to the Canon Lawyers and Theologians of the 12th and 13th centuries." *Zeitschrift der Savigny-Stiftung für Rechtsgeschichte. Kanonistiche Abteilung* 114 (1997): 305–32.

Gouron, André. "Sur les sources civilistes et la datation des Sommes de Rufin et d'Etienne de Tournai." *BMCL* 16 (1986): 55–70.

Grabka, Gregory. "Cardinal Hosius and the Council of Trent." *Theological Studies* 7 (1946): 558–76.

Grant, Michael and Rachel Kitzinger (eds.). *Civilization of the Ancient Mediterranean: Greece and Rome.* 3 vols. New York, 1988.

Gray, Douglas. "London, British Library, Additional MS 37049 – A Spiritual Encyclopedia." In Barr and Hutchinson, *Text and Commentary from Wyclif to Bale*, 99–116.

Greene, Robert A. "Instinct of Nature: Natural Law, Synderesis, and the Moral Sense." *Journal of the History of Ideas* 58.2 (1997): 173–98.

Greengus, Samuel. "The Old Babylonian Marriage Contract." *Journal of the American Oriental Society* 89 (1969): 505–32.

"Redefining 'Inchoate Marriage' in Old Babylonian Contexts." In Abusch, *Riches Hidden in Secret Places*, 123–39.

Gregory, Donald J. *The Pauline Privilege: An Historical Synopsis and Commentary.* Washington, D.C., 1931.

Gottlieb, Beatrice. "The Meaning of Clandestine Marriage." In Wheaton and Hareven, *Family and Sexuality*, 49–83.

Grant, Michael and R. Kitzinger (eds.). *Civilization of the Ancient Mediterranean: Greece and Rome.* 3 vols. New York, 1988.

Guareschi, Massimiliano. "Fra *canones* e *leges*: Magister Vacarius e il matrimonio." *Mélanges de l'École française de Rome: Moyen-Âge – Temps modernes* 111.1 (1999): 105–39.

Gudeman, Stephen. "The *Compadrazgo* as a Reflection of the Natural and Spiritual Person." *Proceedings of the Royal Anthropological Institute of Great Britain and Ireland* 1971: 45–71.

"Spiritual Relationships and Selecting a Godparent." *Man*, n.s. 10 (1975): 221–37.

Guibert, Joseph de. "Le texte de Guillaume de Paris sur l'essence du sacrement de mariage." *Recherches de science religieuse* 4 (1914): 422–27.

Gunten, F. von. "La doctrine de Cajétan sur l'indissolubilité de mariage." *Angelicum* 43 (1966): 62–72.

Gy, Pierre-Marie. "Le nouveau rituel romain du mariage." *La Maison-Dieu* 98 (1969): 124–43.

Hacke, Daniela. *Women, Sex, and Marriage in Early Modern Venice.* Aldershot, 2004.

Hagen, Kenneth. "Was Luther a 'Monk'?" *Lutheran Quarterly* 24.2: 183–85.

Hall, Edwin. *The Arnolfini Betrothal: Medieval Marriage and the Enigma of Van Eyck's Double Portrait.* Berkeley, 1994.

Hall, John A. *The Sacraments in the Compilatio questionum theologie of Magister Martinus: Critical Edition with Commentary.* Doctoral dissertation, University of Notre Dame, Indiana, 2010.

Halley, Janet. "Behind the Law of Marriage (I): From Status/Contract to Marriage System." *Unbound* 6.1 (2010): 1–58.

Hamesse, Jacqueline. *Les Auctoritates Aristotelis. Un florilège médiéval. Étude historique et édition critique.* Philosophes Médiévaux 17. Louvain and Paris, 1974.

(ed.). *Les prologues médiévaux. Actes du colloque international.* Turnhout, 2000.

(ed.). *Manuels, programmes de cours et techniques d'enseignement dans les universites medievales.* Louvain-la-Neuve, 1994.

"Johannes de Fonte, compilateur des Parvi Flores, le témoignage de plusieurs manuscrits de la bibliothèque vaticane." *Archivum Franciscanum Historicum* 88 (1995): 515–31.

Hanawalt, Barbara A. *The Ties That Bound. Peasant Families in Medieval England.* Oxford and New York, 1986.

Hanawalt, Barbara A. and David Wallace (eds.). *Bodies and Disciplines: Intersections of Literature and History in Fifteenth-Century England.* Minneapolis, 1996.

Hanley, Philip L. "*Ex opere operantis*." *New Catholic Encyclopedia.*

Hanley, Sarah. "Engendering the State: Family Formation and State Building in Early Modern France." *French Historical Studies* 16.1 (1989): 4–27.

"Family and State in Early Modern France: The Marriage Pact." In Boxer and Quataert, *Connecting Spheres*, 53–63.

"'The Jurisprudence of the Arrêts': Marital Union, Civil Society, and State Formation in France, 1550–1650." *Law and History Review* 21.1 (2003): 1–40.

Hansen, Lars Ivar (ed.). *Family, Marriage and Property Devolution in the Middle Ages.* Tromsø, 2000.

Haring, Nicholas M. "The Interaction Between Canon Law and Sacramental Theology in the Twelfth Century." *Monumenta Iuris Canonici*, series C: Subsidia, vol. 5, = *Proceedings of the Fourth International Congress of Medieval Canon Law* (Città del Vaticano, 1976), 483–93.

"St. Augustine's Use of the Word 'Character'." *Mediaeval Studies* 14 (1952): 79–97.

"The *Sententiae Magistri A* (Vat. *Ms. lat.* 4361) and the School of Laon." *Mediaeval Studies* 17 (1955): 1–45.

Harlow, Mary and Ray Laurence. "Betrothal, Mid-Late Childhood and the Life Course." In Lovén and Strömberg, *Ancient Marriage*, 56–77.

Harrington, Joel F. *Reordering Marriage and Society in Reformation Germany.* Cambridge, 1995.

"*Hausvater* and *Landesvater*: Paternalism and Marriage Reform in Sixteenth-Century Germany." *Central European History* 25.1 (1992): 52–75.

Harrison, Carol. "Measure, Number, and Weight in Saint Augustine's Aesthetics." *Augustinianum* 28 (1998): 591–602.

Hartmann, Wilfried and Gerhard Schmitz (eds.). *Fortschritt durch Fälschungen? Ursprung, Gestalt und Wirkungen der pseudoisidorischen Fälschungen.* Hannover, 2001.

Hartmann, Wilfried and Kenneth Pennington (eds.). *The History of Medieval Canon Law in the Classical Period, 1140–1234: From Gratian to the Decretals of Pope Gregory IX.* Washington, D.C., 2008.

Haskell, Ann S. "The Paston Women on Marriage in Fifteenth-Century England." *Viator* 4 (1973): 459–71.

Head, Thomas. "The Marriages of Christina of Markyate." *Viator* 21 (1990): 75–101.

Heaney, Seamus P. *The Development of the Sacramentality of Marriage from Anselm of Laon to Thomas Aquinas.* Dissertation, Catholic University of America. Washington, D.C, 1963.

Heckel, Johannes. *Lex Charitatis: A Juristic Disquisition on Law in the Theology of Martin Luther.* Trans. and ed. by G. G. Krodel et al. Grand Rapids, 2010.

Heidecker, Karl. Trans. Tanis M. Guest. *The Divorce of Lothar II: Christian Marriage and Political Power in the Carolingian World.* Ithaca, 2010.

Heimann, Adelheid. "Die Hochzeit von Adam und Eva im Paradies nebst einigen andern Hochzeitsbildern." *Wallraf-Richartz Jahrbuch* 37 (1975): 11–40.

Heinzmann, Richard. *Die Unsterblichkeit der Seele und die Auferstehung des Leibes.* Münster, 1965.

Helmholz, R. H. *Marriage Litigation in Medieval England.* Cambridge, 1974.

The Spirit of the Classical Canon Law. Athens, GA: Univ. of Georgia Press, 1996.

Hen, Yitzhak. *Culture and Religion in Merovingian Gaul, AD 481–751.* Leiden, 1995.

Hendrix, Scott. "Luther on Marriage." *Lutheran Quarterly* 14 (2000): 335–50. [Repr. in Wengert, *Harvesting Martin Luther's Reflections*, 169–84.]

Henninger, Mark G. *Relations: Medieval Theories 1250–1325.* Oxford, 1989.

Henquinet, F. M. "Les écrits de Frère Guerric de Saint-Quentin. RThAM 6 (1934): 184–214, 284–312, 394–410.

Herlihy, David. "The Family and Religious Ideologies in Medieval Europe." *Journal of Family History* 12 (1987): 3–17. [Repr. in Herlihy, *Women, Family, and Society*, 154–73.]

"Making Sense of Incest: Woman and the Marriage Rules of the Early Middle Ages." In Bachrach and Nicholas, *Law, Custom, and the Social Fabric in Medieval Europe*, 96–109. [Repr. in Herlihy, *Women, Family, and Society*, 1–16.]

"The Medieval Marriage Market," in D. B. J. Randall, *Medieval and Renaissance Studies* no. 6, 3–21. [Repr. in Herlihy, *Social History of Italy and Western Europe*.] *Medieval Households*. Cambridge, MA, 1985.

The Social History of Italy and Western Europe, 700–1500: *Collected Studies*. Variorum Reprints. London, 1978.

Women, Family and Society in Medieval Europe: Historical Essays, 1978–1991. Providence, 1995.

Herlihy, David and Christiane Klapisch-Zuber. *Tuscans and their Families: A Study of the Florentine Catasto of 1427*. New Haven, 1985. [Translation of *Les Toscans et leurs familles. Une étude du Catasto florentin de 1427*. Paris, 1978.]

Herreros González, Carmen and Maria Carmen Santapau Pastor. *Pedro Guerrero: Vida y obra de un ilustre riojano del siglo XVI*. Ciencias históricas (Instituto de Estudios Riojanos) 23. Logroño, 2012.

Hersch, Karen K. *The Roman Wedding: Ritual and Meaning in Antiquity*. Cambridge, 2010.

Heyer, René. "Aspects temporels dans la formation du lien matrimonial chez Gratien." *RDC* 48.2 (1998): 349–61.

Hilaire, Jean. *Le régime des biens entre époux dans la région de Montpellier du début du XIIIe siècle à la fin du XVIe siècle*. Montpellier, 1957.

Hill, Rosalind. "Marriage in Seventh-Century England." In King and Stevens, *Saints, Scholars, and Heroes*, vol. 1: *The Anglo-Saxon Heritage*, 67–73.

Histoire des conciles oecuméniques, t. 10: See La Brosse et al.

Histoire des conciles oecuméniques, t. 11: See Lecler et al.

Histoire du christianisme des origines à nos jours, tome V: Apogée de la papauté et expansion de la Chrétienté (1054–1274). Ed. André Vauchez et al. Paris, 1993.

Hocedez, Edgar. *Richard de Middleton: Sa vie, ses oeuvres, sa doctrine*. Spicilegium Sacrum Lovaniense, Études et Documents 7. Louvain, 1925.

Hocutt, Max. "Aristotle's Four Becauses." *Philosophy* 49 (1974): 385–99.

Hoecke, Willy van and Andries Welkenhuysen (eds.). *Love and Marriage in the Twelfth Century*. Mediaevalia Lovaniensia, series I, studia VIII. Leuven, 1981.

Hogg, James. An Illustrated Yorkshire Carthusian Religious Miscellany British Library London Additional MS. 37049. *Vol. 3: The Illustrations*. Analecta Cartusiana 95. Salzburg, 1981.

Horowitz, M. C. "The Image of God in Man: Is Woman Included (Gen. 1:27)?" *Harvard Theological Review* 72 (1979): 175–206.

Huber, Joseph. *Der Ehekonsens im römischen Recht. = Analecta Gregoriana* 204. Rome, 1977.

Hughes, Diane Owen. "From Brideprice to Dowry in Mediterranean Europe." *Journal of Family History* 3 (1978): 262–96.

Hunter, David G. "Augustine and the Making of Marriage in Roman North Africa." *Journal of Early Christian Studies* 11.1 (2003): 63–85.

"Augustine, Sermon 354A: Its Place in His Thought on Marriage and Sexuality," *Augustinian Studies* 32 (2002): 39–60.

"Augustinian Pessimism? A New Look at Augustine's Teaching on Sex, Marriage, and Celibacy." *Augustinian Studies* 25 (1994): 153–77.

"Bono viduitatis, De." In Fitzgerald, *Augustine through the Ages*, 111–12.

"The Date and Purpose of Augustine's De continentia." Augustinian Studies 26.2 (1995): 7–24.

"Helvidius, Jovinian, and the Virginity of Mary in Late Fourth-Century Rome." *Journal of Early Christian Studies* 1 (1993): 47–71.

"Between Jovinian and Jerome: Augustine and the Interpretation of 1 Corinthians 7." *Studia Patristica* 43 (2006): 131–36.

Marriage in the Early Church. Minneapolis, 1992.

Marriage, Celibacy, and Heresy in Ancient Christianity: The Jovinianist Controversy. Oxford Early Christian Studies. Oxford, 2007

"Marrying and the Tabulae Nuptiales in Roman North Africa." In Reynolds and Witte, *To Have and to Hold*, 95–113.

"The Reception and Interpretation of Paul in Late Antiquity: 1 Corinthians 7 and the Ascetic Debates." in DiTommaso and Turescu, *The Reception and Interpretation of the Bible in Late Antiquity*, 281–303.

"Rereading the Jovinianist Controversy: Asceticism and Clerical Authority in Late Ancient Christianity." *Journal of Medieval and Early Modern Studies* 33.3 (2003): 453–70.

"Resistance to the Virginal Ideal in Late-Fourth-Century Rome: The Case of Jovinian." *Theological Studies* 48 (1987): 45–64.

"On the Sin of Adam and Eve: A Little-Known Defense of Marriage and Childbearing by Ambrosiaster." *Harvard Theological Review* 82 (1989): 283–99.

Iung, H. "Cognatio spiritualis." *DDC* 3, 952–70.

d'Izarny, Raymond. "Mariage et consécration virginale au VIe siècle." *La vie spirituelle*, supp. 6 (1953): 92–118.

Jacquart, Danielle and Claude Thomasset. "Albert le Grand et les problèmes de sexualité." *History and Philosophy of the Life Sciences* 3 (1981): 73–93.

Sexuality and Medicine in the Middle Ages. Trans. M. Adamson. Cambridge, 1988. [Translation of *Sexualité et savoir médical au moyen Âge*, Paris, 1985.]

Jaski, Bart. "Marriage Laws in Ireland and on the Continent in the Early Middle Ages." In Meeks and Simms, *The Fragility of Her Sex*, 14–42.

Jasper, Detlev and Horst Fuhrmann. *Papal Letters in the Early Middle Ages*. History of Medieval Canon Law series. Washington, D.C., 2001.

Jedin, Hubert. *History of the Council of Trent*. Trans. E. Graf. 2 vols. London, 1957–1961. [Uncompleted translation of *Geschichte des Konzils von Trient*.]

Geschichte des Konzils von Trient. 4 vols. in 5. Freiburg, 1949–1975.

Jenkins, Alan K. and Patrick Preston. *Biblical Scholarship and the Church: A Sixteenth-Century Crisis of Authority*. Aldershot, 2007.

Jeschke, Thomas, F. Retucci, G. Guldentops, and A. Speer. "Durandus von St. Pourçain und sein Sentenzenkommentar. Eine kritische Edition der A- und B-Redaktion." *Bulletin de Philosophie Médiévale* 51 (2009): 113–43.

Jewish Encyclopedia. Isidore Singer, general editor. 12 vols. New York, 1901–1906.

Jochens, Jenny M. "The Church and Sexuality in Medieval Iceland." *Journal of Medieval History* 6 (1980): 377–92.

"'Með Jákvæði Hennar Sjálfar': Consent as a Signifier in the Old Norse World." In Laiou, *Consent and Coercion*, 271–289.

Johnson, Brandy Schnautz. "The Making of Marriage in Thirteenth Century England: Verb Tense, Popular Legalism, and the Alexandrine Law of Marriage." *Texas Journal of Women and the Law* 15 (2005–2006): 271–303.

Jolowicz, Herbert F. and B. Nicholas, *Historical Introduction to Roman Law*. Cambridge, 1972.

Joyce, George H. *Christian Marriage: An Historical and Doctrinal Study*. 2nd edition. London, 1948. [First edition published London and New York, 1933.]

Kaiser, Wolfgang. *Die Epitome Iuliani: Beiträge zum römischen Recht im frühen Mittelalter und zum byzantinischen Rechtsunterricht*. Frankfurt, 2004.

Kalb, Herbert. *Studien zur Summa Stephans von Tournai. Ein Beitrag zur kanonistischen Wissenschaftsgeschichte des späten 12. Jahrhunderts.* Innsbruck, 1983.

Kalifa, Simon. "Singularités matrimoniales chez les anciens Germains. Le rapt et le droit de la femme à disposer d'elle-même." *Revue historique de droit français et étranger*, 4th series, 48 (1970): 199–225.

Kamas, Juraj. *The Separation of the Spouses with the Bond Remaining: Historical and Canonical Study with Pastoral Applications.* Tesi Gregoriana, Serie Diritto Canonico 20. Rome, 1997.

Kamen, Henry. *The Phoenix and the Flame: Catalonia and the Counter Reformation.* New Haven, 1993.

Kaplan, Marion A. (ed.). *The Marriage Bargain: Women and Dowries in European History.* New York, 1985.

Karras, Ruth Mazo. *From Boys to Men: Formations of Masculinity in Late Medieval Europe.* Philadelphia, 2003.

    Common Women: Prostitution and Sexuality in Medieval England. New York, 1996.

    "The History of Marriage and the Myth of Friedelehe." *Early Medieval Europe* 14.2 (2006): 119–51.

    "Prostitution in Medieval Europe," in Bullough and Brundage, *Handbook of Medieval Sexuality*, 243–60.

    "The Regulation of Sexuality in the Late Middle Ages," *Speculum* 86 (2011): 1010–1039.

    "Thomas Aquinas's Chastity Belt: Clerical Masculinity in Medieval Europe." In Bitel and Lifshitz, *Gender and Christianity in Medieval Europe*, 52–67.

    "Sexuality in the Middle Ages." In Linehan and Nelson, *The Medieval World*, 279–93.

    "Sharing Wine, Women, and Song: Masculine Identity Formation in Medieval European Universities." In Cohen and Wheeler, *Becoming Male in the Middle Ages*, 187–202.

    Sexuality in Medieval Europe: Doing unto Others. New York, 2005.

    "Two Models, Two Standards: Moral Teaching and Sexual Mores." In Hanawalt and Wallace, *Bodies and Disciplines*, 123–38.

    Unmarriages: Women, Men, and Sexual Unions in the Middle Ages. Philadelphia, 2012.

    "Gendered Sin and Misogyny in John of Bromyard's Summa predicantium." *Traditio* 47 (1992): 233–57.

Kelly, John N. D. *Jerome.* London, 1975.

Kelly David F. "Sexuality and Concupiscence in Augustine." *Annual of the Society of Christian Ethics* 1983: 81–116.

Kelly, William. *Pope Gregory II on Divorce and Remarriage: A Canonical-Historical Investigation of the Letter "Desiderabilem mihi" with Special Reference to the Response Quod proposuisti.* Analecta Gregoriana 203, Ser. Fac. Iuris Can. sectio B, 37. Rome, 1976.

Kéry, Lotte. *Canonical Collections of the Early Middle Ages (ca. 400–1140): A Bibliographical Guide to the Manuscripts and Literature.* Washington, D.C., 1999.

    "Non enim homines de occultis, sed de manifestis iudicant. La culpabilité dans le droit pénal de l'Église à lépoque classique." *RDC* 53.2 (2003): 311–36.

Kertzer, David I. and Richard P. Saller (eds.). *The Family in Italy from Antiquity to the Present.* New Haven, 1991.

Kilmartin, E. J. "Ex opere operato." *New Catholic Encyclopedia*.

King, Margaret L. "Caldiera and the Barbaros on Marriage and the Family: Humanist Reflections of Venetian Realities." *Journal of Medieval and Renaissance Studies* 6 (1976): 19–50. [Repr. in King, *Humanism, Venice, and Women*.]

    Humanism, Venice, and Women: Essays on the Italian Renaissance. Variorum Collected Studies. Aldershot, 2005.

"Personal, Domestic, and Republican Values in the Moral Philosophy of Giovanni Caldiera." *Renaissance Quarterly* 28.4 (1975): 535–74. [Repr. in King, *Humanism, Venice, and Women*.]

King, Margot H. and Wesley M. Stevens (eds.). *Saints, Scholars and Heroes: Studies in Medieval Culture in Honor of Charles W. Jones*. 2 vols. Collegeville, 1979.

King, P. D. "The Barbarian Kingdoms." In Burns, *Cambridge History of Medieval Political Thought*, 123–53.

    Law and Society in the Visigothic Kingdom. Cambridge Studies in Medieval Life and Thought, Third Series, vol. 5. Cambridge, 1972.

Kirshner, Julius F. and S. F. Wemple (eds.). *Women of the Medieval World: Essays in Honor of John H. Mundy*. Oxford, 1985.

Klapisch-Zuber, Christiane (ed.). *A History of Women: Silence of the Middle Ages*. Cambridge, MA., 1992.

Klosko, George (ed.). *The Oxford Handbook of the History of Political Philosophy*. Oxford, 2011.

Knibbs, Eric. "The Interpolated *Hispana* and the Origins of Pseudo-Isidore." *Zeitschrift der Savigny-Stiftung für Rechtsgeschichte: Kanonistische Abteilung* 99.1 (2013): 1–71.

Knuuttila, Simo. *Emotions in Ancient and Medieval Philosophy*. Oxford, 2004.

Kochuthara, Shaki G. *The Concept of Sexual Pleasure in the Catholic Moral Tradition*. Rome, 2007.

Kolb, Robert. "Two-Kingdoms Doctrine." In *Encyclopedia of Christianity*, 8:569–75.

Kondratuk, Laurent. "Un témoignage á l'heure de Tametsi: Les Institutiones iuris canonici de Lancelotti (1563)." *RDC* 53.1 (2003): 27–40.

Korpiola, Mia. "An Act or a Process? Competing Views on Marriage Formation and Legitimacy Medieval Europe," in Hansen, *Family, Marriage and Property Devolution*, 31–54.

    Between Betrothal and Bedding: Marriage Formation in Sweden 1200–1600. Leiden, 2009.

    (ed.). *Nordic Perspectives on Medieval Canon Law*. Publications of the Matthias Calonius Society 2. Helsinki, 1999.

    (ed.). *Regional Variations in Matrimonial Law and Custom in Europe*, 1150–1600. Leiden, 2011.

    "Rethinking Incest and Heinous Sexual Crime: Changing Boundaries of Secular and Ecclesiastical Jurisdiction in Late Medieval Sweden." In Musson, *Boundaries of the Law*, 102–17.

    "The Two Husbands of Helleka Horn: Interpreting the Canon Law of Marriage in Late Medieval Sweden." In Condorelli, *Panta rei*, 3:153–81.

Kors, Jean-Baptiste. *La justice primitive et le péché originel d'après s. Thomas. Les sources, la doctrine*. Paris, 1922.

Köstler, Rudolf. "Ringwechsel und Trauung." *Zeitschrift der Savigny-Stiftung für Rechtsgeschichte. Kanonistiche Abteilung* 22 (1933): 1–33.

    "Raub-, Kauf- und Friedelehe bei den Germanen." *Zeitschrift der Savigny-Stiftung für Rechtsgeschichte, germanistische Abteilung* 63 (1943): 92–136.

Krahmer, Shawn M. "The Virile Bride of Bernard of Clairvaux." *Church History* 69.2 (2000): 304–27.

Kraye, Jill and Risto Saarinen (eds.). *Moral Philosophy on the Threshold of Modernity*. The New Synthese Historical Library 57. Dordrecht, 2005.

Kress, Berthold. "Noah, Daniel and Job – The Three Righteous Men of Ezekiel 14.14 in Medieval Art." *Journal of the Warburg and Courthauld Institutes* 67 (2004): 259–67.

Kuefler, Mathew. *The Manly Eunuch: Masculinity, Gender Ambituity, and Christian Ideology in Late Antiquity*. Chicago, 2001.

    "The Marriage Revolution in Late Antiquity: The Theodosian Code and Later Roman Marriage Law." *Journal of Family History* 32.4 (2007): 343–70.

Kuiters, R. "Saint Augustin et l'indissolubilité du mariage." *Augustiniana* 9 (1959): 5–11.

Kümper, Hiram. "Did Medieval Canon Marriage Law Invent our Modern Notion of Rape? Revisiting the Idea of Consent before and after 1200." In Andersen, Salonen, Sigh, and Vogt, *Law and Marriage in Medieval and Early Modern Times*, 111–25.

Kuttner, Stephan. "Ecclesia de occultis non iudicat." In *Acta Congressus Iuridici Internationalis, Romae 1934* (Rome 1935), 3:225–46.

    History of Ideas and Doctrines of Canon Law in the Middle Ages. Variorum Reprints. Collected Studies series 113. London, 1980. [2nd edition. 1992.]

    (ed.) *Proceedings of the Third International Congress of Medieval Canon Law, Strasbourg, 3–6 September 1968*. Monumenta Iuris Canonici, Series C, Subsidia 4. Vatican City, 1971.

    "Sur les origines du term 'droit positif." *Revue historique de droit français et étranger*, 4ᵉ série, 15 (1936): 728–40. [Repr. in Kuttner, *History of Ideas and Doctrines*.]

La Bonnardière, Anne-Marie. "La date du *De continentia* de saint Augustin." *Revue des études augustiniennes* 5 (1959): 121–27.

La Brosse, Olivier de, Jospeph Lecler, Henri Holstein, and Charles Lefebvre. *Latran V et Trente, 1512–1517 et 1545–1548*. Histoire des conciles oecuméniques 10. Paris, 1975.

Laberge, Damasus. "Fr. Petri Ioannis Olivi O.F.M., tria scripta sui ipsius apologetica annorum 1283 et 1285." *Archivum Franciscanum Historicum* 28 (1935): 115–55, 374–407 and 29 (1936): 98–141, 365–95.

Laeuchli, Samuel. *Power and Sexuality: The Emergence of Canon Law at the Synod of Elvira*. Philadelphia, 1972.

Lagarde, André. *The Latin Church in the Middle Ages*. Trans. Archibald Alexander. New York, 1915.

Lähteenmäki, Olavi. *Sexus und Ehe bei Luther*. Schriften der Luther-Agricola-Gesellschaft 10. Turku, 1955.

Laiou, Angeliki E. (ed.). *Consent and Coercion to Sex and Marriage in Ancient and Medieval Societies*. Washington, D.C., 1993.

    "*Consensus Facit Nuptias — et Non*: Pope Nicholas I's *Responsa* to the Bulgarians as a Source for Byzantine Marriage Customs." *Rechtshistorisches Journal* 4 (1985): 189–201.

    "Sex, Consent, and Coercion in Byzantium." In Laiou, *Consent and Coercion*, 109–221.

Landau, Peter. "Gratian und die Sententiae Magistri A." In Mordek, *Aus Archiven und Bibliotheken*, 311–26.

    "Hadrians IV. Decretale *Dignum est* (X 4.9.1) und die Eheschließung Unfreier in der Diskussion von Kanonisten und Theologen des 12. und 13. Jahrhunderts." *Studia Gratiana* 12 (1967) (= *Collectanea S. Kuttner*, vol. 2): 511–53.

    "The Origins of Legal Science in England in the Twelfth Century: Lincoln, Oxford and the Career of Vacarius." Brett and Cushing, *Readers, Texts and Compilers*, 165–82.

Landau, Peter and Martin Petzolt (eds.). *De iure canonico Medii Aevi: Festschrift für Rudolf Weigand.* = *Studia Gratiana* 27. Rome, 1996.

Landgraf, Artur M. *Introduction à l'histoire de la littérature théologique de la scolastique naissante*. Trans. Louis-B. Geiger. Ed. Albert-M. Landry. Publications de l'Institut d'Études Médiévales, Université de Montréal, 22. Montréal and Paris, 1973.

Larrainzar, Carlos. "La distinction entre *fides pactionis* y *fides consensus* en el Corpus Iuris Canonici." *Ius canonicum* 21 (1981): 31–100.

Larson, Atria A. "Early Stages of Gratian's Decretum and the Second Lateran Council: A Reconsideration." *Bulletin of Medieval Canon Law* 27 (2007): 21–56.

Larsson Lovén, Lena and Agneta Strömberg (eds.). *Ancient Marriage in Myth and Reality*. Newcastle upon Tyne, 2010.

Larsson Lovén, Lena. "Coniugal Concordia: Marriage and Marital Ideals on Roman Funerary Monuments." In Larsson Lovén and Strömberg, *Ancient Marriage in Myth and Reality*, 204–20.

Laurent, Marie-Hyacinthe. *Le bienheureux Innocent V (Pierre de Tarentaise) et son temps*. Vatican City, 1947.

Le Bras, Gabriel. "Le mariage dans le théologie et le droit de l'Eglise du XIe au XIIIe siècle." *Cahiers de civilization médiévale* 11 (1968): 191–202.

——— "Mariage. La doctrine du mariage chez les théologiens et les canonistes depuis l'an mille." *DDC* 9.2:2123–2317.

Le Jan, Régine. "Aux origines de douaire médiévale (VIe–Xe siècle)." In Le Jan, *Femmes, pouvoir et société*, 53–67.

——— *Femmes, pouvoir et société dans le haut Moyen Âge*. Médiévistes français 1. Paris, 2001.

Lechner, Josef. *Die Sacramentenlehre des Richard von Mediavilla*. Müncher Studien zur historischen Theologie 5. Munich, 1925.

Lecler, Joseph, Henri Holstein, Pierre Adnès, and Charles Lefebvre. *Le concile de Trente 1551–1563*. Histoire des conciles oecuméniques 11. Paris, 1981.

Leclercq, Jean. *Le mariage vu par les moines au XIIe siècle*. Paris, 1983.

——— "L'amour et le mariage vus par des clercs et des religieux, spécialement au XIIe siècle." In van Hoecke and Welkenhuysen, *Love and Marriage in the Twelfth Century*, 102–115.

——— *Monks and Love in Twelfth Century France*. Oxford, 1979.

——— *Monks on Marriage: A Twelfth Century View*. New York, 1982.

——— *Recueil d'études sur saint Bernard et ses écrits*. 5 vols. Rome, 1962–1992.

Leeming, Bernard. *Principles of Sacramental Theology*. 2nd edition. London and Westminster, MD, 1960.

Lefebvre-Teillard, Anne. *Les officialialités à la veille du Concile de Trente*. Paris, 1973.

——— "A propos d'une lettre à Guillaume: La filiation légitime dans l'oeuvre d'Ives de Chartres." *Studia Gratiana* 27 (Rome, 1996): 287–309.

——— "Régle et réalité dans le droit matrimonial a la fin du moyen-âge." *RDC* 30 (1980): 42–53.

Lefèvre, Georges. *Anselmi Laudunensis et Radulfi fratris eius Sententias excerptas*. Mediolanum Aulercorum [Évreux], 1895.

——— *De Anselmo Laudunensi Scholastico (1050–1117)*. Dissertation, Faculté des lettres de Paris. Mediolanum Aulercorum [Évreux], 1895.

——— *Les variations de Guillaume de Champeaux*. = *Travaux et mémoires de l'Univeresité de Lille*, tome 6, mémoire 20. Lille, 1898.

Legg, John Wickham. *Ecclesiological Essays*. The Library of Liturgiology and Ecclesiology for English Readers, vol. 7, ed. Vernon Staley. London, 1905.

——— "Notes on the Marriage Service in the Book of Common Prayer of 1549." In Legg, *Ecclesiological Essays*, 181–218.

Lievens, R., Erik van Mingroot, and Werner Verbeke (eds.). *Pascua Mediaevalia. Studies voor Prof. Dr. J. M. de Smet*. Mediaevalia Lovaniensia 1.10. Louvain, 1983.

Lemaire, André. "La dotatio de l'épouse de l'époque mérovingienne au XIIIe siècle." *Revue historique de droit français et étranger*, 4th series, 8 (1929): 569–80.

——— "Origine de la règle Nullum sine dote fiat coniugium." In *Mélanges Paul Fournier*, 415–24.

Lenherr, T. "Der Begriff 'executio' in der *Summa Decretorum* des Huguccio." *Archiv für katholisches Kirchenrecht* 150 (1981): 5–44.

Lettmann, Reinhard. *Die Diskussion über die klandestinen Ehen und die Einführung einer zur Gültigkeit verpflichtenden Eheschließungsform auf dem Konzil von Trient*. Münsterische Beiträge zur Theologie, Heft 31. Münster, 1966.

Levin, Eve. *Sex and Society in the World of the Orthodox Slavs, 900–1700.* Ithaca, 1989.

Le lien matrimoniale. Colloque du CERDIC. Ed. R. Metz and J. Schlick. Strasbourg, 1970.

Lievens, Robrecht, Erik Van Mingroot, and Werner Verbeke (eds.). *Pascua Mediaevalia: Studies voor Prof. Dr. J.M. de Smet.* Leuven, 1983.

Linder, Klaus M. "Courtship and the Courts: Marriage and Law in Southern Germany, 1350–1550." ThD dissertation, Harvard University, 1988.

Linehan, Peter and Janet L. Nelson (eds.). *The Medieval World.* London, 2001.

Liotta, Filippo. *La continenza dei chierici nel pensiero canonistico classico, da Gratziano a Gregorio IX.* Milan, 1979.

Liotta, Filippo (ed.). *Miscellanea Rolando Bandinelli, Papa Alessandro III.* Siena, 1986.

Lipgens, Walter. *Kardinal Johannes Gropper, 1503–1559, und die Anfänge der katholischen Reform in Deutschland.* Münster, Westf., 1951.

Lipton, Emma. *Affections of the Mind: The Politics of Sacramental Marriage in Late Medieval English Literature.* Notre Dame, Indiana, 2007.

Livia, Anna and Kira Hall (eds.). *Queerly Phrased: Language, Gender, and Sexuality.* Oxford, 1997.

Loader, William. *Sexuality in the Jesus Tradition.* Grand Rapids, 2005.

The New Testament on Sexuality. Grand Rapids, 2012.

Lombardi, Daniela. "Intervention by Church and State in Marriage Disputes in Sixteenth- and Seventeenth- Century Florence." In Dean and Lowe, *Crime, Society and the Law in Renaissance Italy,* 142–56.

Matrimoni de antico regime. Annali dell'Istituto storico italo-germanico in Trento, Monografie 34. Bologna, 2001.

Longeaux, Jacques de. *Amour, marriage et séxualité d'après la Bible.* Cahiers de l'École cathédrale 22. Paris, 1996.

Looper-Friedman, Susan E. "The Decline of Manus-Marriage in Rome." *Tijdschrift voor Rechtsgeschiedenis* 55 (1987): 281–96.

López Martín, Juan. *Don Pedro Guerrero: epistolario y documentación.* Publicaciones del Instituto Español de Historia Eclesiástica: Subsidia, no. 13. Rome, 1974.

"El voto de Don Pedro Guerrero sobre el sacramento del matrimonio en el Concilio de Trento." *Archivo Teológico Granadino* 44 (1981): 147–219.

La imagen del obispo en el pensamiento teológico-pastoral de don Pedro Guerrero en Trento. Publicaciones del Instituto Español de Historia Eclesiástica: Monografías num. 16. Rome, 1971.

Lottin, Odon. *Psychologie et morale au XIIe et XIIIe siècles,* Tome V: *Problèmes d'histoire littéraire. L'école d'Anselme de Laon et de Guillaume de Chapeaux.* Gembloux (Belgique), 1959. [Cited as Lottin, PsM V]

"A propos de la date de deux florilèges concernant Anselme de Laon." *RThAM* 26 (1959): 307–14.

"Les *Sententiae Atrebatenses.*" *RThAM* 10 (1938): 205–224, 344–57.

"Nouveaux fragments théologiques de l'école d'Anselme de Laon." *RThAM* 11 (1939): 242–59 [NF 1–15], 305–23 [NF 16–21]; 12 (1940): 49–77 [NF 52–120]; 13 (1946): 202–21 [NF 259–329], 261–81 [NF 330–97]; 14 (1947): 5–31 [NF 398–491], 157–85 [NF 492–580].

"Pour une édition critique du *Liber Pancrisis.*" *RThAM* 13 (1946): 185–201 [NF 121–258].

"Un nouveau témoin du *Liber Pancrisis.*" *RThAM* 23 (1956): 114–18.

"Une tradition spéciale du texte des *Sententiae divinae paginae.*" In *Studia Mediaevalia in honorem admodum Reverendi Patris Raymundi Josephi Martin,* 147–69.

Lössl, Josef. "De nuptiis et concupiscentia." In *Oxford Guide to the Historical Reception of Augustine* 1:353–58.

Luscombe, David E. *The School of Peter Abelard.* Cambridge, 1969.

Lynch, Joseph H. *Godparents and Kinship in Early Medieval Europe*. Princeton, 1986.

Lynch, Kilian F. "The Theory of Alexander of Hales on the Efficacy of the Sacrament of Matrimony." *Franciscan Studies* 11 (1951): 69–139.

"Texts Illustrating the Causality of the Sacraments from William of Melitona, *Assisi Bibl. Comm. 182*, and *Brussels Bibl. Royale 1542*." *Franciscan Studies* 17 (1957): 238–72.

"A *Terminus ante quem* for the *Commentary* of Alexander of Hales." *Franciscan Studies* 10 (1950): 46–68.

Maas, Pauline H. J. T. *The Liber sententiarum Magistri A: Its Place admidst the Sentences Collections of the First Half of the 12th Century*. Middeleeuwse Studies 11. Nijmegen, 1995.

Macfarlane, Alan. *Marriage and Love in England: Modes of Reproduction 1300–1840*. Oxford, 1986.

Mackin, Theodore. *Divorce and Remarriage*. Marriage in the Catholic Church series. New York, 1984.

"Ephesians 5:21–33 and Radical Indissolubility." In Doyle, *Marriage Studies* III 1–45.

The Marital Sacrament. Marriage in the Catholic Church series. New York, 1989.

"The Primitive Christian Understanding of Marriage." In Scott and Warren, *Perspectives on Marriage*, 24–29.

What is Marriage? Marriage in the Catholic Church series. New York, 1982.

Macy, Gary. *The Hidden History of Women's Ordination: Female Clergy in the Medieval West*. Oxford, 2007.

Marthaler, Berard L. *Original Justice and Sanctifying Grace in the Writings of Saint Bonaventure*. Miscellanea francescana. Rome, 1965.

Meyvaert, Paul. "Bede's Text of the Libellus Responsionum of Gregory the Great to Augustine of Canterbury." In Clemoes and Hughes, *England before the Conquest*, 15–33.

"Le Libellus Responsionum à Augustin de Cantorbéry: Une oeuvre authentique de saint Grégoire le Grand." In Fontaine et al., *Grégoire le Grand*, 543–50.

Maier, Anneliese. "Per la storia del processo contro l'Olivi." *Rivista di storia della chiesa in Italia* 5 (1951): 326–39.

Maitland, Frederic W. "Magistri Vacarii *Summa de matrimonio*. Introduction." *Law Quarterly Review* 13 (1887): 133–43. "Vacarius on Marriage (Text)," ibid., 270–87.

"Vacarius on Marriage (Text)." *Law Quarterly Review* 13 (1887): 270–87.

Makowski, Elizabeth M. "The Coniugal Debt in Medieval Canon Law." *Journal of Medieval History* 3 (1977): 99–114 and 167.

Malerbe, Louis. *Le mariage au début du XIIIème siècle d'après la Summa du cardinal Robert de Courson*. Thèse de doctorat, Faculté de droit canonique, Institut catholique de Paris, 1924.

Manenti, C. *Dell'inapponibilità di condizioni al negozi giuridici e in specie delle condizioni apposte al matrimonio*. Siena, 1889.

Manetti, Giovanni. *Theories of the Sign in Classical Antiquity*. Advances in Semiotics series. Trans. Christine Richardson. Bloomington, 1993. [Translation of Manetti, *Le teorie del segno nell'antichità classica*, Milan, 1987.]

Manselli, Raoul. "Il monaco Enrico e la sua Eresia." *Bulletino dell Instituto Storico Italiano* 65 (1953): 1–63.

Manzanares, Julio. "El 'munus regendi' según Pedro Guerrero y Juan de Fonseca." In Corecco, *Les droits fondamentaux*, 773–86.

Marchetto, Giuliano. *Il divorzio imperfetto. I giuristi medievali e la separazione dei coniugi*. Annali dell'Instituto storico italo-germanico in Trento, Monografie 48. Bologna, 2008.

Marius, Richard. *Martin Luther: The Christian between God and Death*. Cambridge, MA, 1999.

"Henry VIII, Thomas More, and the Bishop of Rome." In *Albion* 10 (1978), = *Quincentennial Essays on St. Thomas More*: Selected Papers from the Thomas More College Conference, 89–107.

Thomas More: A Biography. Cambridge, MA, 1984.

Martin, Francis. "Marriage in the New Testament Period." In Olsen, *Christian Marriage*, 50–100.

"Marriage in the Old Testament and Intertestamental Periods." In Glenn W. Olsen, *Christian Marriage*, 1–49.

Martin, Jochen. "Zur Anthropologie von Heiratsregeln und Besitzübertragung. 10 Jahre nach den Goody-Thesen," *Historische Anthropologie* 1 (1993): 149–62.

Martindale, Jane. "Charles the Bald and the Government of the Kingdom of Aquitaine." In Gibson and Nelson, *Charles the Bald*, 115–38.

Matecki, Berndt. *Der Traktat In primis hominibus*. Adnotationes in ius canonicum 20. Frankfurt am Main, 2001.

Mathisen, Ralph W. (ed.). *Law, Society, and Authority in Late Antiquity*. Oxford, 2001.

Mathon, Gérard. *Le mariage des chrétiens. Tome I: Des origines au concile de Trente; Tome II: Du concile de Trente à nos jours*. Bibliothèque d'Histoire du Christianisme 31, 34. Paris, 1993, 1994.

Il matrimonio nella società altomedievale. Settimane di studio del Centro italiano di studi sull'alto medioevo 24. 2 vols. Spoleto, 1977.

Mattei, P. "Le divorce chez Tertullian. Examen de la question à la lumière des développments que le *De monogamia* consacre à ce sujet." *Revue des sciences religieuses* 60 (1986): 207–34.

Matter, E. Ann. *The Voice of my Beloved: The Song of Songs in Western Medieval Christianity*. Philadelphia, 1990.

Mattheeuws, Alain. *Les "Dons" du marriage. Recherche de théologie morale et sacramentelle*. Ouvertures 19. Bruxelles, 1996.

Matthews, John E. "Interpreting the Interpretationes of the Breviarium." In Mathisen, *Law, Society, and Authority*, 11–32.

Laying Down the Law: A Study of the Theodosian Code. New Haven, 2000.

Mattia, G. di. "Il decreto *Tametsi* e le sue radici nel concilio di Bologna." *Apollinaris* 53 (1980): 476–500.

Mattox, Mickey L. "Luther on Eve, Women, and the Church." In Wengert, *The Pastoral Luther*, 251–70.

McAuley, Finbarr. "Canon Law and the End of the Ordeal." *Oxford Journal of Legal Studies* 26.3 (2006): 473–513.

McCain, Paul T. "Receiving the Gifts of God in His Two Kingdoms." *Logia* 8.3 (1999): 29–40.

McDonagh, Enda (ed.). *The Meaning of Christian Marriage*. New York, 1963.

McDougall, Sarah. *Bigamy and Christian Identity in Late Medieval Champagne*. Philadelphia, 2012.

"The Making of Marriage in Medieval France." *Journal of Family History* 38.2 (2013): 103–21.

"The Prosecution of Sex in Late Medieval Troyes." In Classen, *Sexuality in the Middle Ages and Early Modern Times*, 691–713.

McEvoy, James. "Grosseteste's Reflections on Aristotelian Friendship: A 'New' Commentary on Nicomachean Ethics VIII." In McEvoy, *Robert Grosseteste: New Perspectives*, 149–68.

Robert Grosseteste: New Perspectives on His Thought and Scholarship. Instrumenta Patristica et Mediaevalia 27. Turnhout, 1995.

McGovan, R. J. "Augustine's Spiritual Equality: The Allegory of Man and Woman with regard to *imago Dei*." *Revue des études augustiniennes* 33 (1987): 255–64.

McKeon, Peter R. "The Carolingian Councils of Savonnièrres (859) and Tusey (860) and Their Background." *Revue Bénédictine* 84 (1974): 75–100.

McLaughlin, Eleanor. "Equality of Souls, Inequality of Sexes: Women in Medieval Theology." In Ruether, *Religion and Sexism*, 213–66.

McLaughlin, Megan. "The Bishop as Bridegroom: Marital Imagery and Clerical Celibacy in the Eleventh and Early Twelfth Centuries." In Frassetto, *Medieval Purity and Piety*, 209–37.

"The Church as Bride in Late Anglo-Saxon and Norman England." In Aurell, *Les strategies matrimoniales*, 257–66.

Sex, Gender, and Episcopal Authority in an Age of Reform, 1000–1122. Cambridge, 2010.

McLaughlin, Terence P. "The Formation of the Marriage Bond According to the *Summa Parisiensis*." *Mediaeval Studies* 15 (1953): 208–12.

McNamara, Jo-Ann and Suzanne F. Wemple. "Marriage and divorce in the Frankish Kingdom." In Stuard, *Women in Medieval Society*, 95–124.

"The Power of Women through the Family in Medieval Europe: 500–1100." *Feminist Studies* 1.3–4 (1973): 126–41.

McSheffrey, Shannon. "'I Will Never Have None against My father's Will': Consent and the Making of Marriage in the Late Medieval Diocese of London." In Rousseau and Rosenthal *Women, Marriage, and Family*, 153–74.

Marriage, Sex, and Civic Culture in Late Medieval London. Philadelphia, 2006.

"Place, Space, and Situation: Public and Private in the Making of Marriage in Late-Medieval London." *Speculum* 79.4 (2004): 960–90.

Medieval Commentaries on the Sentences of Peter Lombard. Vol. 1, ed. G. R. Evans; Vol. 2, ed. P. W. Rosemann. Leiden, 2002, 2009.

Meeks, Christine and Katharine Simms (eds.). *"The Fragility of Her Sex"? Medieval Irishwomen in Their European Context*. Dublin, 1996.

Meigne, Maurice. "Concile ou collection d'Elvire?" *Revue d'histoire ecclésiastique* 70 (1975): 361–87.

Mélanges Joseph de Ghellinck, S. J. 2 vols. Museum Lessianum, Section historique, no. 13. Gembloux, 1951.

Mélanges Mandonnet. Études d'histoire littéraire et doctrinale du moyen âge. 2 vols. Bibliothèque thomiste 13–14. Paris, 1930.

Mélanges Paul Fournier. Publiées sous les auspices de la Société d'histoire du droit. Paris: Sirey, 1929.

Mellick, H. "In Defence of a Fifteenth-Century Manuscript." *Parergon* 8 (1974): 20–24.

Merêa, Paulo. "Le mariage *sine consensu parentum* dans le droit romain vulgaire occidental." *Mélanges Fernand Visscher IV = Revue internationale des droits le l'antiquité* 5 (1950): 203–17.

Métral, Marie-Odile. *Le mariage. Les hésitations de l'Occident*. Paris, 1977.

Metz, René. *La consécretation des vierges dans l'Église romaine. Étude d'histoire de la liturgie*. Paris, 1954.

"Le statut de la femme en droit canonique médiévale." Société Jean Bodin, *Recueils* 12 (1962): 59–113.

"Recherches sur la condition de la femme selon Gratien." *Studia Gratiana* 12 (1967): 379–96.

Mews, Constant J. *Abelard and His Legacy*. Variorum Collected Studies Series. Aldershot, 2001.

"Orality, Literacy and Authority in the Twelfth-Century Schools." *Exemplaria* 2 (1990): 475–500. [Repr. in Mews, *Reason and Belief in the Age of Roscelin and Abelard*.]

Reason and Belief in the Age of Roscelin Abelard. Variorum Collected Studies Series. Aldershot, 2002.

"The Sententie of Peter Abelard." *RThAM* 53 (1986): 130–84. [Repr. in Mews, *Abelard and His Legacy*.]

Meyendorff, John. *Marriage: An Orthodox Perspective*. New York, 1970.

"Christian Marriage in Byzantium: The Canonical and Liturgical Tradition." *Dumbarton Oaks Papers* 44 (1990): 99–107.

Meyer, Herbert. "Friedelehe und Mutterrecht." *Zeitschrift der Savigny-Stiftung für Rechtsgeschichte*, germanistiche Abteilung 47 (1927): 198–286.

Mezger, F. "Did the Institution of Marriage by Purchase Exist in the Old Germanic Law?" *Speculum* 18.3 (1943): 369–71.

Michaélidès, Dimitri. *Sacramentum chez Tertullian*. Paris, 1970.

Milhaven, John Giles. "Aquinas on Sexual Pleasure." *Journal of Religious Ethics* 5 (1977): 157–81.

Miller, Geoffrey David. *Marriage in the Book of Tobit*. Berlin and New York, 2011.

Miller, Jeremy. "A Note on Aquinas and the Ordination of Women." *New Blackfriars* 61 (1980): 185–90.

Miller, Maureen C. "Clerical Identity and Reform: Notarial Descriptions of the Secular Clergy in the Po Valley, 750–1200." In Frassetto, *Medieval Purity and Piety*, 305–35.

"Masculinity, Reform, and Clerical Culture: Narratives of Episcopal Holiness in the Gregorian Era." *Church History* 72.1 (2003): 25–52.

"Why the Bishop of Florence Had to Get Married." *Speculum* 81.4 (2006): 1055–91.

Minnich, Nelson M. "The Voice of Theologians in General Councils from Pisa to Trent." *Theological Studies* 59.3 (1998): 420–41.

Minnis, Alastair. "De impedimento sexus: Women's Bodies and Medieval Impediments to Female Ordination." In Biller and Minnis, Medieval Theology and the Natural Body, 109–39.

Mirkovic, Miroslava. *The Later Roman Colonate and Freedom*. Transactions of the American Philosophical Society 87.2. Philadelphia, 1997.

Mitterauer, Michael. "Christianity and Endogamy." *Continuity and Change* 6.3 (1991): 293–333.

Molin, Jean-Baptiste. "Symboles, rites et textes du mariage au moyen âge latin." In Farnedi, *La celebrazione cristiana del matrimonio*, = *Studia Anselmiana* 93, = *Analecta liturgica* 11 (Rome, 1986): 107–27.

Molin, Jean-Baptiste and Protais Mutembe. *Le rituel du mariage en France du XIIe au XVIe siècle*. Théologie historique 26. Paris, 1974.

Moore, Philip S. *The Works of Peter of Poitiers, Master in Theology and Chancellor of Paris (1193–1205)*. Publications in Mediaeval Studies 1. Notre Dame, Ind., 1936.

Moore, R. I. "Property, Marriage, and the Eleventh-Century Revolution: A Context for Early Medieval Communism." In Frassetto, *Medieval Purity and Piety*, 189–208.

Morelle, Laurent. "Marriage and Diplomatics: Five Dower Charters from the Regions of Laons and Soissons, 1163–1181." THTH 165–214.

"Marriage et diplomatique: Autour de cinq chartes de douaire dans le Laonnois-Soissonnais 1163–1181." *Bibliothèque de l'École des chartes* 146 (1988): 225–71.

"Une charte nuptiale laonnoise de 1158 conservée en original." *Bibliothèque de l'École des chartes* 168 (2010): 209–24.

Mordek, Hubert (ed.). *Aus Archiven und Bibliotheken. Festschrift für Raymund Kottje zum 65. Geburtstag*. Freiburger Beiträge zur Mittelalterlichen Geschichte, Studien und Texte, Bd 3. Frankfurt am Main, 1992.

Morenzoni, Franco. *Des écoles aux paroisses. Thomas de Chobham et la promotion de la prédication au début du XIIIe siècle*. EAMA 30. Paris, 1995.

Morenzoni, Franco and Jean-Yves Tilliette (eds.). *Autour de Guillaime d'Auvergne († 1249)*. Turnhout, 2005.

Morris, Colin. *The Papal Monarchy: The Western Church from 1050 to 1250*. Oxford, 1989.

Mortensen, Beth M. *The Relation of the Juridical and Sacramental according to Thomas Aquinas*. Dissertation, Universität Freiburg. Freiburg, Schweiz, 2012.

Moule, Carolyn Janet. *Entry into Marriage in the Late Eleventh and Twelfth Centuries (c. 1090–1181)* Doctoral dissertation, University of Cambridge, 1983.

Mousourakis, George. *The Historical and Institutional Context of Roman Law*. Aldershot, U.K., 2003.

Mullenders, J. B. *Le mariage presumé*. Analecta Gregoriana 181. Rome, 1971.

Müller, Michael. *Die Lehre des hl. Augustinus von der Paradiesehe und ihre Auswirkung in der Sexualethik des 12. und 13. Jahrhunderts bis Thomas von Aquin*. Regensburg, 1954.

Müller, Wolfgang P. and Mary E. Sommar (eds.). *Medieval Church Law and the Origins of the Western Legal Tradition: A Tribute to Kenneth Pennington*. Washington, D.C., 2006.

Munier, Charles. "Divorce, remariage et pénitence dans L'Église primitive." *Revue des sciences religieuses* 52 (1978): 97–117.

    Mariage et virginité dans l'Église ancienne Ier–IIIe siècles. Traditio Christiana 6. Berne and New York, 1987.

Munk, Connie M. *A Study of Pope Innocent III's Treatise, De quadripartita specie nuptiarum*. Dissertation, University of Kansas, 1975.

Murphy, Sean E. "Concern about Judaizing in Academic Treatises on the Law, c. 1130–c. 1230." *Speculum* 82.3 (2007): 560–94.

Murray, Jacqueline (ed.). *Conflicted Identities and Multiple Masculinities: Men in the Medieval West*. New York, 1999.

    "Gendered Souls in Sexed Bodies: The Male Construction of Sexuality in Some Medieval Confessors' Manuals." In Biller and Minnis, *Handling Sin*, 79–93.

    "Individualism and Consensual Marriage: Some Evidence from Medieval England." In Rousseau and Rosenthal, *Women, Marriage, and the Family*, 121–51.

    "Masculinizing Religious Life: Sexual Prowess, the Battle for Chastity, and Monastic Identity." In Cullum and Lewis, *Holiness and Masculinity in the Middle Ages*, 24–42.

Murray, Jacqueline and Konrad Eisenbichler (eds.). *Sex and Sexuality in the Premodern West*. Toronto, 1996.

Murray, Robert. *Symbols of Church and Kingdom: A Study in Early Syriac Tradition*. London and New York, 1975.

Musson, Anthony (ed.). *Boundaries of the Law: Geography, Gender and Jurisprudence in Medieval and Early Modern Europe*. Aldershot, 2005.

Nautin, Pierre. "Divorce et remariage dans la tradition de l'église latine. Quelques reflexions de méthodologie historique." *Recherches de science religieuse* 62 (1974): 7–54.

    "Divorce et remarriage chez saint Épiphane." *Vigiliae Christianae* 37 (1983): 157–73.

Nelson, Janet L. *Charles the Bald*. London, 1992.

    Politics and Ritual in Early Medieval Europe. London and Ronceverte, 1986.

    "Queens as Jezebels: The Careers of Brunhild and Balthild in Merovingian History." In Nelson, *Politics and Ritual*, 1–48.

New Catholic Encyclopedia. 18 vols. New York and Washington, D.C., 1967–1988.

Newman, William A. *Jus Divinum and the Sacrament of Penance in Two Tridentine Theologians: Melchior Cano and Ruard Tapper*. Dissertation, Catholic University of America. Washington, D.C., 1969.

Nicholas, Barry. *An Introduction to Roman Law*. Oxford, 1962.

Nichols, Ann Eljenholm. *Seeable Signs: The Iconography of the Seven Sacraments, 1350–1544*. Woodbridge, U.K., and Rochester, New York, 1994.

Nickson, Margaret A. E. "The 'Pseudo-Reinerius' Treatise: The Final Stage of a Thirteenth-Century Work on Heresy from the Diocese of Passau." *AHDLMA* 34 (1967): 255–314.

Nolan, Michael. "Aquinas and the Act of Love." In *New Blackfriars* 77 (1996): 115–130.

Nold, Patrick. *Marriage Advice for a Pope: John XXII and the Power to Dissolve*. Leiden, 2009.

Noonan, John T., Jr. *Canons and Canonists in Context*. Goldbach, 1997. [Collected essays.]

  Contraception: A History of Its Treatment by the Catholic Theologians and Canonists. Cambridge, 1965.

  "Marital affection in the canonists." *Studia Gratiana* 12 (1967), = *Collectanea Stephan Kuttner II* (Bologna, 1967), 479–509.

  "Novel 22." In Bassett, *The Bond of Marriage*, 41–90.

  Power to Dissolve: Lawyers and Marriages in the Courts of the Roman Curia. Cambridge, Mass.: Belknap, Harvard Univ. Press, 1972.

  "Power to choose." *Viator* 4 (1973): 419–34.

  "Who Was Rolandus?" In Pennington and Somerville, *Law, Church and Society*, 21–48.

Norris, T. "Why the Marriage of Christians Is One of the Seven Sacraments." *Irish Theological Quarterly* 51 (1985): 37–51.

North, William L., Jay Rubenstein, and John D. Cotts. "The Experience of Reform: Three Perspectives." In Stephen Murillo (ed.), *Haskins Society Journal* 10 (Woodbridge, 2002), 113–61.

Nörr, Dieter. "The Matrimonial Legislation of Augustus: An Early Instance of Social Engineering." *Irish Jurist* 16 (1981): 350–64.

Ó Corráin, Donnchadh. "Marriage in Early Ireland." In Cosgrove, *Marriage in Ireland*, 5–24.

O'Malley, John W. *Trent: What Happened at the Council*. Cambridge, MA, 2013.

O'Meara, John J. and Ludwig Bieler (eds.). *The Mind of Eriugena*. Dublin, 1973.

Oberman, Heiko. A. *Luther: Man Between God and the Devil*. Trans. E. Walliser-Schwarzbart. New Haven, 1989.

Oesterlé, G. "Consanguinité." *DDC* 4:232–48.

  "Privilège Paulin." *DDC* 7:229–80.

Olsen, Viggo N. *New Testament Logia on Divorce: A Study of Their Interpretation from Erasmus to Milton*. Tübingen, 1971.

Osborne Kenan B. (ed.). "Alexander of Hales." In Osborne, *History of Franciscan Theology*, 1–38.

  The History of Franciscan Theology. St Bonaventure, New York, 1994.

Osuna, Belén M.; and Carmen O. García. "*Pretium pudicitiae* y donación nupcial." *Revista de estudios histórico-jurídicos* 26 (2004): 61–84.

Ott, Ludwig. *Untersuchungen zur theologischen Briefliteratur der Frühscholastik unter besonderer berücksichtigung des Viktorinerkreises*. BGPhThMA 34. Münster, 1937.

  "Walter von Mortagne und Petrus Lombardus in ihrem Verhältnis zueinander." In *Mélanges Joseph de Ghellinck*, 2:647–97.

Otten, Willemien. "Augustine on Marriage, Monasticism, and the Community of the Church." *Theological Studies* 59 (1998): 385–405.

Outhwaite, R. B. *Clandestine marriage in England, 1500–1850*. London, 1995.

  (ed.). *Marriage and Society: Studies in the Social History of Marriage*. New York, 1981.

Ozment, Steven. *The Age of Reform 1250–1550: An Intellectual and Religious History of Late Medieval and Reformation Europe*. New Haven, 1980.

When Fathers Ruled: Family Life in Reformation Europe. Cambridge, MA, 1983.

Oxford Classical Dictionary. Ed. Simon Hornblower, Anthony Spawforth, and Esther Eidinow. 4th edition. Oxford, 2012.

Oxford Guide to the Historical Reception of Augustine. Ed. Karla Pollmann, Willemien Otten, et al. 3 vols. Oxford, 2013.

Pabel, Hilmar M. "Exegesis and Marriage in Erasmus' Paraphrases on the New Testament." In Pabel and Vessey, *Holy Scripture Speaks,* 175–209.

Pabel, Hilmar M. and Mark Vessey (eds.). *Holy Scripture Speaks: The Production and Reception of Erasmus' Paraphrases on the New Testament.* Toronto, 2002.

Pagden, Anthony. "The School of Salamanca." In Klosko, *Oxford Handbook of the History of Political Philosophy,* 246–57.

Parish, Helen L. *Clerical Celibacy in the West, c.1100–1700.* Farnham, Surrey, 2009.

Parisse, Michel. "Préambules de chartes." In Hamesse, *Prologues,* 141–69.

Veuves et veuvage dans le haut moyen âge. Table ronde organisée à Göttingen par la Mission Historique Française en Allemagne. Paris, 1993.

Payer, Pierre J.. *The Bridling of Desire. Views of Sex in the Later Middle Ages.* Toronto, 1993.

"Early Medieval Regulations Concerning Marital Sexual Regulations." *Journal of Medieval History* 6 (1980): 353–76.

"Foucault on Penance and the Shaping of Sexuality." *Studies in Religion/Sciences Religieuses* 14.3 (1985): 313–20.

Sex and the Penitentials. Toronto, 1984.

Payne, John B. *Erasmus: His Theology of the Sacraments* (Richmond, Virginia, 1971).

Pedersen, Frederik. "Did the Medieval Laity Know the Canon Law Rules on Marriage? Some Evidence from Fourteenth-Century York Cause Papers." *Mediaeval Studies* 56 (1994): 89–109.

Marriage Disputes in Medieval England. London, 2000.

"Marriage Contracts and the Church Courts of Fourteenth-Century England." *THTH* 287–331.

Pennington, Kenneth. "The Decretalists 1190 to 1234." In Hartmann and Pennington, *History of Medieval Canon Law,* 211–45.

The Prince and the Law, 1200–1600: Sovereignty and Rights in the Western Legal Tradition. Berkeley, 1993.

Popes, Canonists, and Texts, 1150–1550. Variorum Reprints. Aldershot, 1993.

"Pope Innocent III's Views on Church and State: A Gloss to Per Venerabilem. In Pennington and Somerville, *Law, Church and Society,* 49–67. [Repr. with corrections in Pennington, *Popes, Canonists, and Texts.*

Pennington, Kenneth and Robert Somerville (eds.). *Law, Church and Society: Essays in Honor of Stephan Kuttner.* Philadelphia, 1977.

Pennington, Kenneth and W. P. Müller. "The Decretists: The Italian School." In Hartmann and Pennington, *The History of Medieval Canon Law,* 121–73.

Peper, Bradley M. "On the Mark: Augustine's Baptismal Analogy of the *nota militaris.*" *Augustinian Studies* 38.2 (2007): 353–63.

Perdue, Leo G., Joseph Blenkinsopp, John C. Collins, and Carol Meyers. *Families in Ancient Israel.* The Family, Religion, and Culture series. Louisville, 1997.

Peters, Christine. "Gender, Sacrament and Ritual: The Making and Meaning of Marriage in Late Medieval and Early Modern England." *Past and Present* 169 (2000): 63–96.

Petit, François. "Gauthier de Mortagne." *Analecta Praemonstratensia* 50 (1974): 158–70.

Philippe, M.-D. "*Analogon* and *Analogia* in the Philosophy of Aristotle." *The Thomist* 33 (1969): 1–74.

Pierce, Joanne. "A Note on the *Ego vos conjungo* in Medieval French Marriage Liturgy." *Ephemerides Liturgicae* 99 (1985): 290–99.

Pilsner, Joseph. *The Specification of Human Actions in St. Thomas Aquinas*. Oxford Theological Monographs series. Oxford, 2006.

Pinckaers, Servais. "Ce que le moyen âge pensait du mariage." *La vie spirituelle*, supp. 20 (1967): 413–30.

Pinto de Oliveira, Carlos-Josaphat (ed.). *Ordo Sapientiae et Amoris. Image et message de saint Thomas d'Aquin à travers les récentes études historiques, herméneutiques et doctrinales. Hommage au professeur Jean-Pierre Torrell à l'occasion de son 65ᵉ anniversaire*. Studia Friburgensia. Fribourg, 1993.

Plumpe, Joseph. *Mater Ecclesia: An Inquiry into the Concept of the Church as Mother in Early Christianity*. Catholic University of America Studies in Christian Antiquity 5. Washington, D.C., 1943.

Pohle, Joseph. *The Sacraments: A Dogmatic Treatise*. Trans. Arthur Preuss. 4 vols. St. Louis, 1915–1917. [Translation of *Die allgemeine und spezielle Sakramentenlehre*, 5th edition.]

Poirel, Dominique. "Love of God, Human Love: Hugh of St. Victor and the Sacrament of Marriage." *Communio* 24 (1997): 99–109.

Pollock, Frederic and Frederic W. Maitland. *The History of English Law before the Time of Edward I*. 2 vols. 2nd edition. Cambridge, 1898.

Posthumous-Meyjes, G. H. M. "Exponents of Sovereignty: Canonists as Seen by Theologians in the Late Middle Ages." In Wood, *The Church and Sovereignty*, 299–312.

Pourrat, Pierre. *Theology of the Sacraments: A Study in Positive Theology*. Authorized Translation of the Third Edition. St. Louis, Mo., 1910.

Power, Kim. "Concubine/Concubinage." In Fitzgerald, *Augustine through the Ages*, 222–23.

Powicke and Cheney, *Councils & Synods*: See bibliography of primary sources.

Preston, Patrick. "Catherinus versus Luther, 1521." *History* 88.3 (2003): 364–78.

Principe, Walter H. "Guerric of Saint-Quentin, O.P., on the question: *Utrum Filius Dei esset incarnatus si homo non peccasset?*" In Pinto de Oliveira, *Ordo Sapientiae et Amoris*, 509–37.

"Preternatural." *New Catholic Encyclopedia* 11:763–64.

Quaestiones concerning Christ from the First Half of the Thirteenth Century." *Mediaeval Studies* 39 (1977): 1–59; 42 (1980): 1–40; 43 (1981): 1–57; 44 (1982): 1–82; 50 (1988): 1–45.

Problèmes doctrinaux du mariage chrétien. Commission théologique internationale. Louvain-la-Neuve, 1979.

Provost, James H. and Knut Walf (eds.). *Ius Sequitur Vitam: Studies in Canon Law Presented to P. J. M. Huizing*. Louvain, 1991.

Quinn, John F. "Bonaventure." *Dictionary of the Middle Ages*, 2:313–19.

"Chronology of St. Bonaventure (1217–1274)." *Franciscan Studies* 32 (1972): 168–86.

"St Bonaventure and the Sacrament of Matrimony." *Franciscan Studies* 34 (1974): 101–43.

Quinto, Riccardo. "La constitution du texte des Quaestiones theologiae." In Bataillon et al., *Étienne Langton*, 525–62.

Rabinowitz, Jacob J. "On the Definition of Marriage as *consortium omnis vitae*." *Harvard Theological Revue* 57 (1964): 55–56.

Raditsa, Leo F. "Augustus' Legislation concerning Marriage, Procreation, Love Affairs, and Adultery." *Aufstieg und Niedergang der römischen Welt* 2.13 (1980): 278–339.

Randall, Dale B. J. (ed.). *Medieval and Renaissance Studies, no. 6: Proceedings of the Southeastern Institute of Medieval and Renaissance Studies, Summer, 1974* Durham, N.C., 1976.

Rawlings, Helen. *Church, Religion and Society in Early Modern Spain*. Houndmills, Basingstoke, U.K., 2002.

Rawson, Beryl (ed.). *Marriage, Divorce, and Children in Ancient Rome.* Oxford, 1991.

(ed.). *The Family in Ancient Rome: New Perspectives.* Ithaca, New York, 1986.

"Children in the Roman Familia." In Rawson, *The Family in Ancient Rome,* 170–200

Reinhardt, Heinrich J. F. *Die Ehelehre der Schule des Anselm von Laon. Eine theologie- und kirchenrechtsgeschichtlliche Untersuchung zu den Ehetexten der frühen Pariser Schule des 12. Jahrhunderts.* BGPhThMA, neue Folge, Bd. 14. Münster, 1974.

Reekmans, Louis. "La *dextrarum iunctio* dans l'iconographie romaine et paléochrétienne." *Bulletin de l'Institut Historique Belge de Rome* 31 (1958): 29–95.

Rees Jones, Sarah. "The Household and English Urban Government in the Later Middle Ages." In Carlier and Soens, *The Household in Late Medieval Cities,* 71–87.

Renwart, Léon. "L'intention du ministre des sacraments, problème male posé? Un peu d'histoire." *Nouvelle revue théologique* 81 (1959): 469–88.

Resnick, Irven M. "Marriage in Mediaeval Culture: Consent Theory and the Case of Mary and Joseph." *Church History* 69.2 (2000): 350–71.

Reuter, Amandus. *Sancti Aurelii Augustini doctrina de bonis matrimonii.* Analecta Gregoriana, vol. 27, Series Theologica, Sectio B (num. 12). Rome, 1942.

Reynolds, Philip L. "Analogy of Names in Bonaventure," *Mediaeval Studies* 65 (2003): 117–62.

Articles in the Oxford Guide to the Historical Reception of Augustine: "De adulterinis coniugiis," 1:226–29; "*De bono coniugali*," 1:243–46; "*De bono viduitatis*," 1:246–50; "Marriage," 3:1369–75.

"Bonaventure on Gender and Godlikeness." *Downside Review* 106 (1988): 171–94.

"Bonaventure's Theory of Resemblance." *Traditio* 58 (2003): 219–55.

"Efficient Causality and Instrumentality in Thomas Aquinas's Theology of the Sacraments." In Ginther and Steel, Essays in *Medieval Philosophy and Theology,* 67–84.

Food and the Body: Some Peculiar Questions in High Medieval Theology. Leiden, 1999.

Marriage in the Western Church. *The Christianization of Marriage during the Patristic and Early Medieval Periods.* Supplements to Vigiliae Christianae 24. Leiden, 1994. [Abbr. MWCh]

"Marriage, Sacramental and Indissoluble: Sources of the Catholic doctrine." *Downside Review* 109 (1991): 105–50.

"Marrying and Its Documentation in Pre-Modern Europe: Consent, Celebration, and Property," *THTH* 1–42.

"Properties, Causality and Epistemological Optimism in Thomas Aquinas." *Recherches de théologie et philosophie médiévales* 68 (2001): 270–305.

"Scholastic Theology and the Case against Women's Ordination." *Heythrop Journal* 36 (1995): 249–85.

"The Regional Origins of Theories about Marital Consent and Consummation during the Twelfth Century." In Korpiola, Regional Variations, 43–75.

"When Medieval Theologians Talked about Marriage, What Were They Really Talking about?" In Andersen, Salonen, Sigh, and Vogt, *Law and Marriage in Medieval and Early Modern Times,* 11–42.

Reynolds, Philip L. and John Witte, Jr. (eds.). *To Have and to Hold: Marrying and Its Documentation in Western Europe,* 400–1600. Cambridge, 2007. [Abbr. THTH]

Ruether, Rosemary Radford (ed.). *Religion and Sexism: Images of Women in the Jewish and Christian Traditions.* New York, 1974.

Ribordy, Geneviève. "*Faire les nopces*": Le mariage de la noblesse française (1375–1475). Toronto, 2004.

"The Two Paths to Marriage: The Preliminaries of Noble Marriage in Late Medieval France." *Journal of Family History* 26.3 (2001): 323–36.

Richardot, Hubert. *Les pactes de séparation amiable des époux*. Paris, 1930.

Riddle, John M. *Contraception and Abortion from the Ancient World to the Renaissance*. Cambridge, MA, 1992.

Rider, Catherine. *Magic and Impotence in the Middle Ages*. Oxford, 2006.

Riisøy, Anne I. *Sexuality, Law and Legal Practice and the Reformation in Norway*. The Northern World 44. Leiden, 2009.

Rincón, Tomás. *El matrimonio, misterio y signo: Siglos IX–XIII*. Pamplona, 1971. [Second volume in the series, *El matrimonio, misterio y signo*.]

Rio, Alice. "Self-Sale and Voluntary Entry into Unfreedom, 300–1100." *Journal of Social History* 45.3 (2012): 661–85.

Ritzer, Korbinian. *Formen, Riten und religiöses Brauchtum der Eheschließung in den christlichen Kirchen des ersten Jahrtausands*. 2nd edition. Münster, 1981. [1st edition published 1962.]

    Le mariage dans les églises chrétiennes du Ier au XIe siècle. Paris, 1970. [Translation of 1st edition of Ritzer, *Formen, Riten, und religiöses Brauchtum*.]

Roberts, James B. *The Banns of Marriage: An Historical Synopsis and Commentary*. J.C.D. Dissertation. Catholic University of America Canon Law Studies, 64. Washington, D.C., 1931.

Robinson, Adam P. *The Career of Cardinal Giovanni Morone (1509–1580): Between Council and Inquisition*. Farnham, 2012.

Roche, W. J. "Measure, Number, and Weight in Saint Augustine." *The New Scholasticism* 15.4 (1941): 350–76.

Rocke, Michael J. *Forbidden Friendships: Homosexuality and Male Culture in Renaissance Florence*. New York, 1996.

    "Il controllo dell'omosessualità a Firenze nel XV secolo: Gli Ufficiali de Notte." *Quaderni Storici* 66 (1987): 701–23.

Rolker, Christof. *Canon Law and the Letters of Ivo of Chartres*. Cambridge Studies in Medieval Life and Thought, Fourth Series. Cambridge, 2009.

    "Kings, Bishops and Incest: Extension and Subversion of the Ecclesiastical Marriage Jurisdiction around 1100." In Cooper and Gregory, *Discipline and Diversity*, 159–68.

    "Two Models of Incest: Conflict and Confusion in High Medieval Discourse on Kinship and Marriage." In Andersen et al., *Law and Marriage in Medieval and Early Modern Times*, 139–59.

Roman, J. "Summa d'Huguccio sur le décret de Gratien d'après le manuscrit 3891 de la Bibliothèque Nationale, *Causa XXVII, Quaestio II* (Théories sur la formation du mariage)." *Revue historique de droit français et étranger*, 2nd series 27 (1903): 715–805.

Romano, Dennis. *Housecraft and Statecraft: Domestic Service in Renaissance Venice, 1400–1600*. Baltimore, 1996.

Rondet, Henri. *Introduction à l'étude de la théologie du mariage*. Paris, 1960.

Roper, Lyndal. *Oedipus and the Devil: Witchcraft, Religion and Sexuality in Early Modern Europe*. London, 1994.

    "Sexual Utopianism in the German Reformation." *Journal of Ecclesiastical History* 42.3 (1991): 394–418. [Repr. in Roper, *Oedipus and the Devil*, 80–105.]

Rorem, Paul. "The Early Latin Dionysius: Eriugena and Hugh of St. Victor." *Modern Theology* 24.4 (2008): 601–14. [Repr. as an appendix in Rorem, *Hugh of Saint Victor*, 167–76.]

    Hugh of Saint Victor. Great Medieval Thinkers series. Oxford, 2009.

Rosemann, Philipp W. (ed.). *Medieval Commentaries on the Sentences of Peter Lombard*, vol. 2. Leiden, 2009.

Peter Lombard. Great Medieval Thinkers series. Oxford, 2004.

The Story of a Great Medieval Book: Peter Lombard's Sentences. Peterborough, Ontario, 2007.

Rosier-Catach, Irène. *La parole efficace. Signe, rituel, sacré*. Paris, 2004.

"Signes sacramentels et signes magiques: Guillaume d'Auvergne et la théorie de pacte." In Morenzoni and Tilliette, *Autour de Guillaume d'Auvergne*, 93–144.

Rousseau, Constance M. "The Spousal Relationship: Marital Society and Sexuality in the Letters of Pope Innocent III." *Mediaeval Studies* 56 (1994): 89–109.

Rousseau, Constance M. and Joel T. Rosenthal (eds.). *Women, Marriage, and Family in Medieval Christendom: Essays in Memory of Michael M. Sheehan, C.S.B.* Kalamazoo, 1998.

Rouche, Michel (ed.). *Mariage et sexualité au Moyen Age. Accord ou cris?* Paris, 2000.

Ruggiero, Guido. *The Boundaries of Eros: Sex Crime and Sexuality in Renaissance Venice.* Oxford, 1985.

Rummel, Erika. *Erasmus and His Catholic Critics.* 2 vols. Bibliotheca Humanistica et Reformatorica. Nieuwkoop, 1989.

Rushforth, G. McN. "Seven Sacraments Compositions in English Medieval Art." *Antiquaries Journal* 9.2 (1929): 83–100.

Ryan, J. Joseph. "Saint Peter Damiani and the Sermons of Nicholas of Clairvaux: A Clarification." *Mediaeval Studies* 9 (1947): 151–61.

Ryan, Liam. "The Indissolubility of Marriage in Natural Law: A Disputed Point in the Teaching of St. Thomas Aquinas." *Irish Theological Quarterly* 30 (1963): 293–310, and 31 (1964): 62–77.

Saarinen, Risto. "Ethics in Luther's Theology: The Three Orders." In Kraye and Saarinen, *Moral Philosophy on the Threshold of Modernity*, 195–215.

Sacré, Dirk and Gilbert Tournoy (eds.). *Myricae: Essays on Neo-Latin Literature in Memory of Jozef Ijsewijn.* Supplementa Humanistica Lovaniensia 16. Leuven, 2000.

Sahaydachny Bocarius, Antonina. "The Marriage of Unfree Persons: Twelfth-Century Decretals and Letters." In Landau and Petzolt, *De iure canonico Medii Aevi*, 483–506.

Salisbury, Eve (ed.). *The Trials and Joys of Marriage.* TEAMS Middle English Texts series. Kalamazoo, 2002.

Saller, Richard P. "Men's Age at Marriage and Its Consequences in the Roman Family." *Classical Philology* 82 (1987): 21–34.

Patriarchy, Property and Death in the Roman Family. Cambridge Studies in Population, Economy and Society in Past Time. Cambridge, 1994.

"*Patria potestas* and the Stereotype of the Roman Family." *Continuity and Change* 1 (1986): 7–22.

Sampley, J. Paul. *"And the Two Shall Become One Flesh": A Study of Traditions in Ephesians 5:21–33.* Society for New Testament Studies Monograph Series 16. Cambridge, 1971.

Sandler, Lucy F. "The Handclasp in the *Arnolfini Wedding*: A Manuscript Precedent." *The Art Bulletin* 66.3 (1984): 488–91.

Santinelli, Emmanuelle. *Des femmes éplorées? Les veuves dans la société aristocratique du haut Moyen Âge.* Paris, 2003.

Satlow, Michael L. *Jewish Marriage in Antiquity.* Princeton, 2001.

Saunders, Corinne J. *Rape and Ravishment in the Literature of Medieval England.* Cambridge, 2001.

Sayers, Jane E. *Papal Judges Delegate in the Province of Canterbury, 1198–1254: A Study in Ecclesiastical Jurisdiction and Administration.* Oxford, 1971.

Scalco, Eugenio. "*Sacramentum conniubii* et institution nuptiale." *Ephemerides Theologicae Lovanienses* 69 (1993): 27–47.

Scarisbrick, J. J. *Henry VIII*. Berkeley, 1968.

Schahl, Claude. *La doctrine des fins du mariage dans la théologie scholastique*. Paris, 1948.

Schaus, Margaret (ed.). *Women and Gender in Medieval Europe: An Encyclopedia*. New York, 2006.

Scheidel, Walter. "Roman Funerary Commemoration and the Age at First Marriage." *Classical Philology* 102.4 (2007): 389–402.

Schillebeeckx, Édouard. *Marriage: Secular Reality and Saving Mystery*. Trans. N. D. Smith. 2 vols. London and Melbourne: Sheed and Ward, 1965. [One-volume edition: London, 1976.]

Schlatter, Frederic W. "The Author of the *Opus imperfectum in Matthaeum*." *Vigiliae Christianae* 42 (1988): 364–75.

Schmitt, Emile. *Le mariage chrétien dans l'oeuvre de saint Augustin. Une théologie baptismale de la vie conjugale*. Paris, 1983.

Schmitt, J. "Tradition et relectures au premier siècle chrétien." *RDC* 30 (1980): 55–68.

Schmugge, Ludwig. *Marriage on Trial: Late Medieval German Couples at the Papal Court*. Trans. Atria A. Larson. Washington, D.C., 2012. [Originally published as *Ehen vor Gericht: Paare der Renaissance vor dem Papst*. Berlin, 2008.]

Schnell, Rüdiger. "The Discourse on Marriage in the Middle Ages." *Speculum* 73 (1998): 771–86.

Schoovaerts, M. Gustaf, "L'amour et le mariage selon les lettres d'Yves de Chartres." *Studia Canonica* 22 (1988): 305–25.

Schott, Clausdieter. "Der stand der Leges-Forchung." *Frümittelalterliche Studien* 13 (1979): 29–55.

Schulte, Johann Friedrich von. *Die Geschichte der Quellen und Literatur des canonischen Rechts von Gratian bis auf die Gegenwart*. 3 vols in 4. Stuttgart, 1875–1880. [Repr. Graz, 1956.]

Schumpp, Meinrad M. *Das Buch Tobias*. Münster in Westfalen, 1933.

Scott, Kieran and Michael Warren (eds.). *Perspectives on Marriage: A Reader*. New York, 1993.

Searle, Mark and Kenneth W. Stevenson. *Documents of the Marriage Liturgy*. Collegeville, Minnesota, 1992.

Sears, Elizabeth and Thelma K. Thomas (eds.). *Reading Medieval Images: The Art Historian and the Object*. Ann Arbor, 2002.

Seed, Patricia. "The Church and the Patriarchal Family: Marriage Conflicts in Sixteenth- and Seventeenth-Century New Spain." *Journal of Family History* 10.3 (1985): 284–93.

To Love, Honor, and Obey in Colonial Mexico: Conflicts over Marriage Choice, 1574–1821. Stanford, California, 1988.

Selderhuis, Herman J. *Marriage and Divorce in the Thought of Martin Bucer*. Trans. J. Vriend and L. D. Bierma. Sixteenth Century Studies 48. Kirksville, MS, 1999.

Selig, Karl-Ludwig and Robert Somerville (eds.). *Florilegium Columbianum: Essays in Honor of Paul Oskar Kristeller*. New York, 1987.

Shanzer, Danuta. "*Avulsa a latere meo*: Augustine's Spare Rib — *Confessions* 6.15.21." *Journal of Roman Studies* 92 (2002): 157–76.

Shaw, Brent D. "The Age of Roman Girls at Marriage: Some Reconsiderations." *Journal of Roman Studies* 77 (1987): 30–46.

Sheehan, Michael M. *Marriage, Family, and Law in Medieval Europe: Collected Studies*. Ed. James K. Farge. Toronto, 1996.

"The Bishop of Rome to a Barbarian King on the Rituals of Marriage." In Sheehan and Farge, *Marriage, Family, and Law*, 278–291.

"Choice of Marriage Partner in the Middle Ages: Development and Mode of Application of a Theory of Marriage." *Studies in Medieval and Renaissance History*, NS 1 (1978): 3–33. [Repr. in *Marriage, Family, and Law in Medieval Europe*, 87–117.]

"Family and Marriage, Western European." *Dictionary of the Middle Ages* 14:608–12.

"Maritalis affectio Revisited." In Sheehan and Farge, *Marriage, Family, and Law*, 262–277.

"Marriage and Family in English Conciliar and Synodal Legislation." In Sheehan and Farge, *Marriage, Family, and Law*, 77–86.

"Marriage Theory and Practice in the Conciliar Legislation and Diocesan Statutes of Medieval England." *Mediaeval Studies* 40 (1978): 408–60. [Repr. in *Marriage, Family, and Law*, 118–76.]

"Sexuality, Marriage, Celibacy, and the Family in Central and Northern Italy: Christian Legal and Moral Guides in the Early Middle Ages. " In Sheehan and Farge, *Marriage, Family, and Law*, 292–310.

"The European Family and the Cannon Law." In Sheehan and Farge, *Marriage, Family, and Law*, 247–261.

"The Formation and Stability of Marriage in 14th Century England: Evidence of an Ely Register." Mediaeval Studies 33 (1971): 228–63. [Repr. in Sheehan and Farge, *Marriage, Family, and Law*, 38–76.]

"Theory and Practice: Marriage of the Unfree and the Poor in Medieval Society." *Mediaeval Studies* 50 (1988): 457–87. [Repr. in Sheehan and Farge, *Marriage, Family, and Law*, 211–46.]

Shirt, David J. "*Cligés* – A Twelfth-Century Matrimonial Case Book?" *Forum for Modern Language Studies* 18 (1982): 75–89.

Shogimen, Takashi. "The Relationship between Theology and Canon Law: Another Context of Political Thought in the Early Fourteenth Century." *Journal of the History of Ideas* 60.3 (1999): 417–31.

Silvain, René. "La tradition des Sentences d'Anselme de Laon." AHDLMA 16 (1948): 1–52.

Sirks, Adriaan J. B. "The *episcopalis audientia* in Late Antiquity." *Droit et cultures* 65 (2013): 79–88.

Sim, David C. *The Gospel of Matthew and Christian Judaism: The History and Social Setting of the Matthean Community*. Edinburgh, 1998.

Simonin, Henri-Dominique. "Le écrits de Pierre de Tarentaise." In *Beatus Innocentius*, 163–335.

Simonin, Henri-Dominique and G. Meersseman. *De sacramentorum efficientia apud theologos ord. praed. Fasc. I: 1229–1276*. Rome, 1936.

Smith, Lesley. *The Glossa Ordinaria: The Making of Medieval Bible Commentary*. Leiden, 2009.
"William of Auvergne and Confession." In Biller and Minnis, *Handling Sin*, 95–107.

Smith, Lesley and Benedicta Ward (eds.). *Intellectual Life in the Middle Ages: Essays Presented to Margaret Gibson*. London, 1992.

Smith, Charles E. *Papal Enforcement of Some Medieval Marriage Laws*. Louisiana, 1940.

Somerville, Robert. Review of Maas, *The Liber Sententiarum Magistri A.* (1995). *Speculum* 74 (1999): 207–09.

Sommar, Mary E. *The Correctores Romani: Gratia's Decretum and the Counter-Reformation Humanists*. Pluralisierung & Autorität, Bd. 19. Berlin, 2009.
"Twelfth-Century Scholarly Exchanges." In Müller and Sommar, *Medieval Church Law*, 123–33.

Southern, Richard W. *Scholastic Humanism and the Unification of Europe. Vol. 1: Foundations; Vol. 2: The Heroic Age*. Oxford, 1995, 2001.

Sperling, Jutta. "Marriage at the Time of the Council of Trent (1560–70): Clandestine Marriages, Kinship Prohibitions, and Dowry Exchange in European Comparison." *Journal of Early Modern History* 8.1–2 (2004): 67–108.

Stahl, Harvey. "Eve's Reach: A Note on the Dramatic Elements in the Hildesheim Doors." In Sears and Thomas, *Reading Medieval Images*, 163–75.

Ste. Croix, Geoffrey E. M. de. *Christian Persecution, Martyrdom, and Orthodoxy*. Edited by M. Whitby and J. Streeter. Oxford, 2006.

Stegmüller, Friedrich. "*Sententie Berolinenses*: Eine neugefundene Sentenzensammlung aus der Schule des Anselm von Laon." *RThAM* 11 (1939): 33–61

Stein, Peter. "Vacarius and the Civil Law." In Brooke et al., *Church and Government in the Middle Ages*, 119–38.

Stephenson, John R. "The Two Governments and the Two Kingdoms in Luther's Thought," *Scottish Journal of Theology* 34.4 (1981): 321–37.

Stevenson, Kenneth W. *The Nuptial Blessing: A Study of Christian Marriage Rites*. London, 1982. [Repr. New York, 1983.]

"The Origins of the Nuptial Blessing." *Heythrop Journal* 21 (1980): 412–416.

Stinnisen, Wilfried. *Aristoteles over de Vriendschap: Boeken VIII en IX van de Nicomachische Ethiek med de commentaren van Aspasius en Michaël in de Latijnse vertaling van Grosseteste*. Brussels, 1963.

Stock, Brian. *The Implications of Literacy: Written Language and Models of Interpretation in the Eleventh and Twelfth Centuries*. Princeton, 1983.

Stone, Lawrence. "Passionate Attachments in the West in Historical Perspective." In Scott and Warren, *Perspectives on Marriage*, 171–79.

Stone, Rachel. "'Bound from Either Side': The Limits of Power in Carolingian Marriage Disputes." *Gender and History* 19.3 (2007): 467–82.

Strasser, Ulrike. *State of Virginity: Gender, Religion, and Politics in an Early Modern Catholic State*. Ann Arbor, 2004.

Strocchia, Sharon T. "Naming a Nun: Spiritual Exemplars and Corporate Identity in Florentine Convents, 1450–1530." In Connell, *Society and the Individual in Renaissance Florence*, 215–240.

"When the Bishop Married the Abbess: Masculinity and Power in Florentine Episcopal Entry Rites, 1300–1600." *Gender and History* 19 (2007): 346–68.

Stuard, Susan Mosher (ed.). *Women in Medieval Society*. Philadelphia, 1976.

Stubbings, Frank. "The Art of Good Living (STC 791)." *Transactions of the Cambridge Bibliographical Society* 10.4 (1994): 535–38.

Studer, Basile. "'Sacramentum et exemplum' chez saint Augustin." *Recherches augusti-niennes* 10 (1975): 87–141.

Studi in onore di Alberto Pincherle. Studi et materiali di storia delle religioni 38. Rome, 1967.

Studia Mediaevalia in honorem admodum Reverendi Patris Raymundi Josephi Martin. Bruges, [1948].

Sutton, Kenneth M. *The Papacy and the Levant (1204–1571)*. 4 vols. Memoirs of the American Philosophical Society 114, 127, 161, 162. Philadelphia, 1976–1984.

Taliadoros, Jason. *Law and Theology in Twelfth-Century England: The Works of Master Vacarius (c. 1115/1120-c. 1200)*. Disputatio 10. Turnhout, 2006.

"Synthesizing the Legal and Theological Thought of Master Vacarius." *Zeitschrift der Savigny-Stiftung für Rechtsgeschichte. Kanonistische Abteilung* 95 (2009): 48–77.

Tallon, Alain. *La France et le Concile de Trent (1518–1563)*. Bibliothèque des Écoles françaises d'Athènes et de Rome, no. 295. Rome, 1997.

Tanner, Norman. "Pastoral Care: The Fourth Lateran Council of 1215." In Evans, *History of Pastoral Care*, 112–25.

Tejero, Eloy. *El matrimonio, misterio y signo: Siglos XIV ad XVI*. Pamplona, 1971. [Third volume in the series, *El matrimonio, misterio y signo*.]

Telle, Emile V. *Érasme de Rotterdam et le septième sacrament*. Geneva, 1954.

Teske, Roland J. "The Good Samaritan (Lk 10:29–37) in Augustine's Exegesis." In Van Fleteren and Schnaubelt, *Augustine: Biblical Exegete*, 347–57.

"William of Auvergne on Philosophy as divinalis and sapientialis." In Aertsen and Speer, *Was ist Philosophie in Mittelalter?* 475–81.

Thibodeaux, Jennifer D. "The Defense of Clerical Marriage: Religious Identity and Masculinity in the Writings of Anglo-Norman Clerics." In Cullum and Lewis, *Religious Men and Masculine Identity in the Middle Ages*, 46–63.

Thomas, Joseph A. C. *Textbook of Roman Law*. New York, 1976.

Thompson, Bard. *Humanists and Reformers: A History of the Renaissance and Reformation*. Grand Rapids, 2007.

Thompson, Steven. "Was Ancient Rome a Dead Wives Society? What Did the Roman Paterfamilias Get Away With?" *Journal of Family History* 31.1 (2006): 3–27.

Thomson, Kenneth John. "A Comparison of the Consultations of Marsilius of Padua and William of Ockham Relating to the Tyrolese Marriage of 1341–1342." *Archivum Franciscan Historicum* 63 (1970): 3–43.

Thurston, Herbert. "Marriage, Ritual of." *Catholic Encyclopedia* 9:703–09.

Torrell, Jean-Pierre. *Saint Thomas Aquinas, vol 1: The Person and His Work*. Trans. Robert Royal. Washington, D.C., 1996. Revised edition, 2005.

Torrell, Jean-Pierre. "Christology in the Quodlibets of Guerric of Saint-Quentin: A Precursor of Thomas Aquinas?" In Ginther and Still, *Essays in Medieval Philosophy and Theology*, 53–66.

Toubert, Pierre. "La théorie de mariage chez les moralistes carolingiens." In *Il matrimonio nella società altomedievale*, 1:233–82 (followed by discussion, 283–85).

"L'institution du mariage chrétien, de l'antiquité tardive à l'an mil." In *Morfologie sociali e culturali in Europa fra tarda antichità e alto medioevo*, vol. 1 (Spoleto, 1998), 503–49.

Tranvik, Mark D. "Luther on Baptism." *Lutheran Quarterly* 13 (1999): 75–90. [Repr. in Wengert, *Harvesting Martin Luther's Reflections*, 23–37.]

Treggiari, Susan. "Consent to Roman Marriage: Some Aspects of Law and Reality." *Classical Views/Echos du monde classique*, n.s. 26 (1982): 34–44.

"Digna condicio: Betrothals in the Roman Upper Class." *Echos du monde classique/Classical Views* 27, n.s. 3 (1984): 419–51.

"Divorce Roman Style: How Easy and How Frequent Was It?" In Rawson, *Marriage, Divorce and Children in Ancient Rome*, 31–46.

"Marriage and Family in Roman Society." In Campbell, *Marriage and Family*, 132–82.

"Putting the Bride to Bed." *Echos du monde classique/Classic Views* 38 (1994): 311–31.

"Roman Marriage." In Grant and Kitzinger, *Civilization of the Ancient Mediterranean*, 3:1343–54.

Roman Marriage: Iusti coniuges from the Time of Cicero to the Time of Ulpian. Oxford, 1991.

Trevett, Christine. *Montanism: Gender, Authority and the New Prophecy*. Cambridge, 1996.

Trigg, Jonathan D. *Baptism in the Theology of Martin Luther*. Leiden, 1994.

Turner, Denys. *Eros and Allegory: Medieval Exegesis of the Song of Songs*. Kalamazoo, 1995.

Ullmann, Walter. *The Growth of Papal Government in the Middle Ages: A Study in the Ideological Relation of Clerical to Lay Power*. 3rd edition. London, 1970.

Urbanik, Jakub. "A Broken Marriage Promise and Justinian as a Lover of Chastity. On Novela 74 and P. Cair. Masp. I 67092 (553)." *Journal of Juristic Papyrology* 41 (2011): 123–51.

Valois, Noël. *Guillaume d'Auvergne, Évêque de Paris (1228–1249) sa vie et ses ouvrages* Paris, 1880.

Van Caenegem, Rooul C. *English Lawsuits from William I to Richard I.* 2 vols. Selden Society Publications 106–107. London, 1990, 1991.

Van den Eynde, Damien. *Les définitions des sacrements pendant la première période de la théologie scolastique (1050–1240).* Rome and Louvain, 1950.

"Stephen Langton and Hugh of St. Cher on the Causality of the Sacraments." *Franciscan Studies* 11.3–4 (1951): 141–55.

"The Theory of the Composition of the Sacraments in Early Scholasticism (1125–1240)." *Franciscan Studies* 11.1 (1951): 1–20, 117–44; 12.1 (1952): 1–26.

Van der Poel, Mark. *Cornelius Agrippa: The Humanist Theologian and His Declamations.* Leiden, 1997.

"Erasmus, Rhetoric and Theology: The Encomium matrimonii." In Sacré and Tournoy, *Myricae*, 207–27.

Van Fleteren, Frederick and Joseph C. Schnaubelt (eds.). *Augustine: Biblical Exegete.* New York, 2001.

Van Roo, William A. *Grace and Original Justice according to St. Thomas.* Analecta Gregoriana cura Pontificiae Universitatis Gregorianae 75. Series Facultatis Theologicae, A.13. Rome, 1955.

VanDrunen, David. N. *Natural Law and the Two Kingdoms: A Study in the Development of Reformed Social Thought.* Emory University Studies in Law and Religion. Grand Rapids, 2010.

Verbraken, Pierre-Patrick. "Les fragments conservés de sermons perdus de saint Augustin." *Revue Bénédictine* 84.3–4 (1974): 245–70,

Vereecke, L. "Mariage et sexualité au déclin du moyen âge." *La vie spirituelle*, supp. 57 (1961): 199–225.

Verlinden, Charles. "Le 'mariage' des esclaves." In *Il matrimonio nella società altomedievale*, 2:569–93.

Veyne, Paul. "La famille et l'amour sous le haut-empire Romain." *Annales* 33 (1978): 35–63.

Villers, Robert. *Rome et le droit privé.* Paris, 1977.

Viscuso, Patrick Demetrios. *A Byzantine Theology of Marriage: The Syntagma kata stoicheion of Matthew Blastares.* Doctoral dissertation, Catholic University of America. Washington, D.C., 1989.

Vleeschouwers-Van Melkebeek, Monique. "Classical Canon Law on Marriage. The Making and Breaking of Households." In Carlier and Soens, *The Household in Late Medieval Cities*, 15–23.

Vliet, A. H. van and C. G. Breed. *Marriage and Canon Law: A Concise and Complete Account.* London, 1964.

Vogel, Cyrille. "Le rôle du liturge dans la formation du lien conjugal." *RDC* 30 (1980): 7–27.

"Les rites de la célébration du mariage. Leur signification dans la formation du lien durant le haut moyen âge." In *Il matrimonio nella società altomedievale*, 1:397–465 (followed by discussion, 467–72).

Vogt, Helle. *The Function of Kinship in Medieval Nordic Legislation.* Leiden, 2010.

Volterra, Edoardo. *La conception du mariage d'après les juristes romains.* Padua, 1940.

"Iniustum matrimonium." In *Studi in onore di Gaetano Scherillo* (Milan: Cisalpino-La Goliardica, 1972, 3 vols), vol. 2, 441–70.

Von Hörmann, Walther. *Quasiaffinität. Rechtshistorische Untersuchungen zu den Affinitätswirkungen der Verlöbnisses nach westlichem und kirchlichem Rechte.* 2 vols. Innsbruch, 1906.

Wack, Mary Francis. "The Measure of Pleasure: Peter of Spain on Men, Women, and Lovesickness." *Viator* 17 (1986): 174–96.

Waelkens, Laurent L. J. M. "Medieval Family and Marriage Law: From Actions of Status to Legal Doctrine." In Cairns and Plessis, *The Creation of the Ius Commune*, 103–25.

Wahl, Francis X. *The Matrimonial Impediments of Consanguinity and Affinity: An Historical Synopsis and Commentary*. Dissertation. Catholic University of America Canon Law Studies 90. Washington, D.C., 1934.

Walther-Holtzmann-Kartei: Regesta decretalium saeculi XII. Stephan Kuttner Institute of Medieval Canon Law. URL: www.kuttner-institute.jura.uni-muenchen.de/holtzmann_formular.htm (accessed November 14, 2013).

Watson, Alan. *The Law of Persons in the Later Roman Republic*. Oxford, 1967.

———. "The Evolution of Law: The Roman System of Contracts." *Law and History Review* 2 (1984): 1–20.

———. *Legal Origins and Legal Change*. London, 1991.

———. *Rome of the XII Tables: Persons and Property*. Princeton, 1975.

———. "*Usu, farre(o), coemptione*." *Studia et Documenta Historiae et Iuris* 29 (1963): 337–38. [Repr. in Watson, *Legal Origins and Legal Change*, 9–10.]

Watt, J. A. "Spiritual and Temporal Powers." In Burns, *Cambridge History of Medieval Political Thought*, 367–423.

Weaver, F. Ellen and Jean Laporte. "Augustine and Women: Relationships and Teachings." *Augustinian Studies* 12 (1981): 115–31.

Weber, Hubert P. "The *Glossa in IV libros Sententiarum* by Alexander of Hales." In Rosemann, *Medieval Commentaries on the Sentences of Peter Lombard*, 2:79–110.

Wei, John C. "Gratian and the School of Laon." *Traditio* 64 (2009): 279–322.

———. "The Sentence Collection *Deus non habet initium vel terminum* and Its Reworking, *Deus itaque summe atque ineffabiliter bonus*." *Mediaeval Studies* 73 (2011): 1–118.

Weigand, Rudolf. *Die Glossen zum Dekret Gratians: Studien zu den frühen Glossen und Glossenkompositionen*. 2 vols. Studia Gratiana 25–26. Rome, 1991.

———. *Liebe und Ehe im Mittelalter*. Goldbach, 1993.

———. *Die Naturrechtslehre des Legisten und Dekretisten von Irnerius bis Accursius und Gratian bis Johannes Teutonicus*. Münchener theologische Studien III: Kanonistische Abteilung, Bd. 26. München, 1967.

———. "Die Dekretabbreviatio 'Quonium egestas' under ihre Glossen." In Aymans et al., *Fides et ius*, 249–65.

———. "Die Glossen des Cardinalis (Magister Hucbald?) zum Dekret Gratians, besonders zu C.27 q.2." *BMCL* 3 (1973): 73–95.

———. "Kanonistische Ehetraktate aus dem 12. Jahrhundert." In Kuttner, *Proceedings of the Third International Congress of Medieval Canon Law*, 59–79. [Repr. in Weigand, *Liebe und Ehe im Mittelalte*, 37*–57*.]

———. "The Transmontane Decretists." In Hartmann and Pennington, *History of Medieval Canon Law*, 174–210.

Weisheipl, James A. (ed.). *Albertus Magnus and the Sciences*. Studies and Texts, Pontifical Institute of Mediaeval Studies. Toronto, 1980.

———. "The Life and Works of St. Albert the Great." In Weisheipl, *Albertus Magnus and the Sciences*, 13–51.

Weisweiler, Henri. *Maître Simon et son groupe De sacramentis. Textes inédits*. Spicilegium Sacrum Lovaniense, Études et Documents, 17. Louvain, 1937.

———. *Das Schrifttum der Schule Anselms von Laon und Wilhelms von Champeaux in deutschen Bibliotheken*. BGPhMA 33.1–2. Münster, 1936.

"L'École d'Anselme de Laon de de Guillaume de Champeaux. Noveaux Documents." *RThAM* 4 (1932): 237–69, 371–91.

"La *Summa sententiarum*, source de Pierre Lombard." *RThAM* 6 (1934): 143–83.

"Le recueil des sentences 'Deus de cuius principio et fine tacetur' et son remaniement." *RThAM* 5 (1933): 245–74.

Weitzman, Lenore J. *The Marriage Contract: Spouses, Lovers, and the Law.* New York, 1981.

Wemple, Suzanne F. *Women in Frankish Society: Marriage and the Cloister, 500–900.* Philadelphia, 1981.

"Consent and Dissent to Sexual Intercourse in Germanic Societies from the Fifth to the Tenth Century." In Laiou, *Consent and Coercion,* 227–243.

Wengert, Timothy J. (ed.). *Harvesting Martin Luther's Reflections on Theology, Ethics, and the Church.* Grand Rapids, 2004.

The Pastoral Luther: Essays on Martin Luther's Practical Theology. Grand Rapids, 2009.

Werckmeister, Jean. "L'apparition de la doctrine due mariage contrat dans le droit canonique due 12ᵉ siècle." *RDC* 53.1 (2003): 5–25.

"Le deux version du De matrimonio de Gratien." *RDC* 48.2 (1988): 301–16.

Westbrook, Raymond. *Old Babylonian Marriage Law.* Archiv für Orientforschung 23. Horn, Austria, 1988.

Wheaton, Robert and Tamara K. Hareven. *Family and Sexuality in French History.* Philadelphia, 1980.

Whittaker, C. W. and Oleg Grabar. "Slavery." In Bowerstock et al., *Late Antiquity,* pp. 698–700.

Williams, George H. *The Radical Reformation.* 3rd edition. Kirksville, Missouri, 1992.

Williams, John R. "The Cathedral School of Reims in the Time of Master Alberic, 1118–1136." *Traditio* 20 (1964): 93–114.

Williams, Thomas (ed.). *The Cambridge Companion to Duns Scotus.* Cambridge, 2003.

"Introduction: The Life and Works of John Duns the Scot." In Williams, *Cambridge Companion to Duns Scotus,* 1–14.

Willsch, Alois. *Das Verständnis der Ehe im Enchiridion des Johannes Gropper. Ein Beitrag Zum Eheverständnis der vortridentinischen katholischen Kontroverstheologie des 16. Jahrhunderts.* St. Ottilien, 1990.

Wilmart, A. "Une rédaction française des Sentences dites d'Anselme de Laon." *RThAM* 11 (1939): 119–44.

Wilson, Water T. *The Sentences of Sextus.* Atlanta, 2012.

Wilson, Adrian and Joyce Lancaster Wilson. *A Medieval Mirror: Speculum humanae salvationis, 1324–1500.* Berkeley, 1984.

Wilson, Katherina M. and Elizabeth M. Makowski. *Wykked Wyves and the Woes of Marriage: Misogamous Literature from Juvenal to Chaucer.* Albany, 1990.

Winn, Mary Beth. *Anthoine Vérar: Parisian Publisher, 1485–1512: Prologues, Poems and Presentations.* Travaux d'Humanisme et Renaissance, no. 313. Geneva, 1997.

Winroth, Anders. *The Making of Gratian's Decretum.* Cambridge, 2000.

"Marital Consent in Gratian's Decretum." In Brett and Cushing (eds.), *Readers, Texts and Compilers,* 111–21.

"Neither Slave nor Free: Theology and Law in Gratian's Thoughts on the Definition of Marriage and Unfree Persons." In Müller and Sommar, *Medieval Church Law and the Origins of the Western Legal Tradition,* 97–109.

Witte, John, Jr. *God's Joust, God's Justice: Law and Religion in the Western Tradition.* Grand Rapids, 2006.

Law and Protestantism: The Legal Teachings of the Lutheran Reformation. Cambridge, 2002.

"The Goods and Goals of Marriage." In *Notre Dame Law Review* 76.3 (2001): 1019–1071.

"The Reformation of Marriage Law in Martin Luther's Germany: Its Significance Then and Now." *Journal of Law and Religion* 4.2 (1986): 293–351.

From Sacrament to Contract: Marriage, Religion, and Law in the Western Tradition. Louisville, 1997.

Wolff, Hans J. *Written and Unwritten Marriages in Hellenistic and Postclassical Law.* Haverford, Pennsylvania, 1939.

"Doctrinal Trends in Postclassical Roman Marriage Law." *Zeitschrift der Savigny-Stiftung für Rechtsgeschichte, romanistiche Abteilung* 67 (1950): 261–319.

Wood, Diana (ed.). *The Church and Sovereignty, c.590–1918: Essays in Honour of Michael Wilks.* Ecclesiastical History Society, Studies in Church History, Subsidia 9. Oxford, 1991

Worby, Sam. *Law and Kinship in Thirteenth-Century England.* Woodbridge, 2010.

Zaccaria, Raffaella. "Delfini, Giovanni Antonio." In *Dizionario Biografico degli Italiani*, vol. 30 (Rome, 1988), 546–50.

Zechiel-Eckes, Klaus. "Auf Pseudoisidors Spur, oder: Versuch einen dichten Schleier zu lüften." In Hartmann and Schmitz, *Fortschritt durch Fälschungen?* 1–28.

Zeimentz, Hans. *Ehe nach der Lehre der Frühscholastik.* Düsseldorf, 1973.

Zimmerman, Reinhard. *The Law of Obligations: Roman Foundations of the Civilian Tradition.* Oxford, 1996.

"*Stipulatio* (stipulation)." *Oxford Classical Dictionary.* 4th edition, 2012.

Index

1042 *Index*

574, 578, 588–89, 610–11, 613, 619, 629, 644,
695–96, 706, 729, 736, 738–39, 744, 756,
761–62, 764, 766, 774, 791–92, 812, 813, 884,
964
Avicenna (Ibn Sina), 496, 509n192, 543n113, 698

Bandinus, 275n151, 441–42
Barbaro, Franceso, 774
"bed undefiled" (*thorus immaculatus*, Heb 13:4),
12, 19, 731, 733, 757, 800, 812–13, 820, 824, 835,
836, 925
Bede, 13–15, 239, 294, 297, 417–18, 421–22
Bellarmine, Robert, 32, 597n145
Benedictus Levita (pseudo-), 44, 241n155, 447n197,
919n86
Bernard of Clairvaux, 82–83, 297, 363, 905, 922
Bernard of Pavia, 793
bestiality, 35, 508, 776
betrothal, 15, 18, 34, 43, 47–48, 60–61, 63, 65, 73,
76, 84, 87, 90, 92, 157–208, 209–10, 211n13,
212–14, 223–24, 231–87, 296, 306, 310, 323, 362,
364, 378, 382, 389, 390, 407, 414–16, 426–28,
440–41, 449, 455–57, 561, 563, 585, 597,
651–52, 715, 734, 735, 764, 768, 784–85, 786,
789, 792–93, 796, 802, 873, 894. See also
Consent to marriage, spousal; *Desponsatio*;
Sponsalia; *Sponsiones*; Spousals.
betrothal distinction, 199–208, 246, 249, 252, 256,
276, 297, 305, 306, 310, 362, 389, 390, 414, 416,
426, 428, 563
blessing, nuptial, 12, 16–17, 28, 34, 38, 44–45, 48,
50–51, 90–91, 95–96, 98, 120, 180, 183, 187,
198, 211, 226, 239–40, 258, 281, 305, 323,
330–31, 364, 374, 399, 404, 414, 428, 343–45,
466, 468, 472, 474, 487, 578, 579, 582, 586–87,
590, 593, 595, 598–99, 602–9, 614, 618, 635,
644, 647–48, 651–57, 665, 675–76, 679, 716,
721, 723–24, 734, 744, 753, 770–71, 777,
785–86, 789, 796–98, 799, 803, 812, 823–24,
826, 829, 831–32, 837–38, 847, 851–52, 863,
869–70, 871–73, 887, 907, 917, 920, 926–27,
941, 947, 959, 979, 981
as a sacramental, 50, 98, 399, 468, 598, 651, 655,
721
blessing, original (Gen 1:28), 20, 104–5, 126, 132,
136, 296, 331, 343–45, 434, 382, 392, 411, 416,
425, 439, 454, 579, 581–82, 584–86, 598, 758,
812, 819, 835–37, 873
blessing, post-diluvial, 126, 417, 429, 439, 454, 523,
581, 587, 826
Bonaventure, 8, 24n59, 50, 71, 84, 451, 464–65, 468,
477–78, 483, 485, 489–90, 493–94, 499,
533–34, 543–45, 548, 580n76, 581–83, 585, 591,
602–3, 608, 629–30, 633n36, 634n42, 636n50,

637–38, 649, 651–57, 658, 662, 675, 678–79,
794–95, 852, 934
Book of Common Prayer, 753n125
Brenz (Brentius), Iohannes, 754, 826, 872, 888,
891n200, 909
Breviarium Alaricanum: See *Lex Romana
Visigothorum.*
Burchard of Worms, 48, 448n204, 449
Bucer, Martin, 754, 781, 826, 909

Cajetan, Thomas de Vio, 558n3, 722–23, 724, 817,
823, 827, 937, 958, 981
Cana, wedding at (John 2:1–11), 13, 17, 19–20,
58–59, 61, 138, 152, 321–32, 343, 389, 418, 548,
627, 645, 662, 739, 758, 793, 832
Cano, Melchor, 507, 721, 723–24, 788, 797, 801,
821, 838, 858, 917, 958, 981
Castellani, Alberto, 97, 787–88, 838, 917, 946
Cardinalis, 257n53, 264, 266–67, 285, 627n22
Castagna, Giovanni Battista (archbishop of
Rossano), 900, 923n104, 935, 942, 950–51,
974–75
Catherine of Aragon, 732
Catharinus, Ambrosius (Lancellotto Politi), 77, 79,
80, 82, 84, 813–14, 817–32, 857–58, 861–62,
866–67, 870, 874n117, 876, 882, 886–93, 895,
931
celibacy, 4, 9, 11, 14, 25, 29–31, 52, 67, 102–3,
107–9, 114, 117–18, 121–22, 125–29, 132, 134–36,
139, 146, 149, 152, 168, 179n130, 186, 196, 198,
215, 225, 229, 298, 319, 324, 331, 336–37,
341–43, 346, 360–61, 366, 377–79, 382,
386–87, 394–95, 398, 400, 408–10, 424–25,
429, 465, 493, 510, 514, 522, 529, 562, 608–9,
614, 620, 695–96, 714, 727, 730–31, 738,
742–44, 748–49, 752–53. See also Continence;
Virginity.
certa verba, 157, 205, 470, 482, 720, 721, 724, 852
Cervini, Marcello, 805, 808
Chaucer, Geoffrey, 20, 68, 82
Ciocchi del Monte, Giovanni Maria (Pope Julius
III), 805, 817, 866, 868
clandestine marriage, 35, 49–50, 60–61, 80–81,
89n215, 97–98, 207, 259, 280, 323, 398–99, 410,
428, 434–36, 472–74, 487–88, 562, 599–605,
715, 730, 740–42, 751, 753–54, 761–62, 765,
767–87, 789, 797–800, 802–3, 804, 809–12,
815–18, 826, 832–34, 838–40, 843, 847, 848–982
Codex Theodosianus, 174, 176–77
Collectio decem partium, 217, 218, 231
Collectio Tripartita, 189, 234, 235n116, 236,
237n127, 238n136, 447
common good (*bonum commune*): See Public
good.

CPSIA information can be obtained
at www.ICGtesting.com
Printed in the USA
LVOW04*0019170117

521187LV00025B/773/P